Law, Medicine and Ethics

PATRICIA A. KING
Carmack Waterhouse Professor of Law,
Medicine, Ethics and Public Policy
Georgetown University

JUDITH AREEN
Paul Regis Dean Professor of Law
Georgetown University

LAWRENCE O. GOSTIN
Associate Dean for Research and Academic Programs
Professor of Law, Georgetown University
Director, Center for Law and the Public's Health

FOUNDATION PRESS
NEW YORK, NEW YORK
2006

Foundation Press, of Thomson/West, has created this publication to provide you with accurate and authoritative information concerning the subject matter covered. However, this publication was not necessarily prepared by persons licensed to practice law in a particular jurisdiction. Foundation Press is not engaged in rendering legal or other professional advice, and this publication is not a substitute for the advice of an attorney. If you require legal or other expert advice, you should seek the services of a competent attorney or other professional.

© 2006 By FOUNDATION PRESS

       395 Hudson Street
       New York, NY 10014
       Phone Toll Free 1–877–888–1330
       Fax (212) 367–6799
       fdpress.com
Printed in the United States of America
ISBN–13: 978–1–58778–912–0
ISBN–10: 1–58778–912–4

 TEXT IS PRINTED ON 10% POST CONSUMER RECYCLED PAPER

P.A.K.

To Roger, Elizabeth and in memory of Grayce.

J.A.

To Rich and Jonathan.

L.O.G.

To Jean, Bryn and Kieran.

*

PREFACE

This Reader is drawn from the third edition of Law, Science and Medicine, an influential text that has been widely used in both law schools and undergraduate courses since the first edition appeared in 1984.

The materials in this Reader can serve not only as the primary text in courses on bioethics or on law, medicine and ethics, but as a useful supplement for courses in health policy. Too often students, whether in undergraduate or graduate programs, discuss legal and medical issues without access to the actual judicial decisions, statutes, and other technical materials that are essential for meaningful analysis.

There are daily reminders of the currency and importance of the issues addressed in this Reader from gene therapy to cloning; from the funding of basic medical research to the use of human subjects in drug trials. Although such issues arise with increasing frequency—in courtrooms, legislative chambers, and executive agencies as well as in the popular and professional press—our society often seems perplexed about how to deal with them.

A major source of this problem is the lack of exposure that many people have to the values, methods, and assumptions of the legal, medical and scientific communities. This has led to a gulf of misunderstanding between scientists and nonscientists. This gulf may widen as more complex issues are presented by the growing sophistication and powers of the life sciences (from their theoretical underpinnings to their applications at the bedside) and as well-publicized incidents make the public apprehensive about progress in medicine.

To be able to work across traditional boundaries, students of law, medicine and ethics need exposure to core materials not only from legal and scientific disciplines, but from philosophy and ethics. They need them to be presented within a structure that enables the students to unravel the issues, analyze their content, and construct a framework for their own future roles as informed citizens in a society seeking new relationships at the interface of law , medicine and ethics. These are the objectives we attempt to fulfill in this Reader.

The overarching issue in this Reader is how society ought to learn about and respond to law, medicine and ethics. Five themes are explored:

- The use and misuse of medical expertise in making public policy. What factors determine when an expert's views are invaluable and when they are irrelevant, and what weight should such views be given by the public and its representatives?

- Who decides: the need to find appropriate institutions to promote, to direct, and even to curtail medical progress. What are the strengths and weaknesses of agencies, legislatures, courts, the executive, private groups, individual scientists, and lay people when the question is who should control medical science at the various stages of its development and use?

- The application of risk assessment or cost-benefit analysis to medical issues. How, if at all, should these techniques guide those making public policy in the face of scientific uncertainty?

- The contrasting value systems of law, medicine and ethics. How can one reconcile medicine's ethic of scientific progress with the law's focus on individual rights and interests and its obligation to provide an orderly process of dispute resolution even when information is imperfect?

- The ethical and religious implications of developments in law and medicine. When medical science arguably alters the very nature of humanity, what are the consequences from an ethical or religious viewpoint?

Chapter One of this text demonstrates the potential of genetics to produce vast benefits as well as harms and inequities to human beings. The Chapter ranges from the scientific history of Mendel and the social history of eugenics to modern genomics and proteomics. Chapter Two addresses private control of medical professionals and examines the strengths as well as the weaknesses of individual and collective decision making about medical care. Chapter Three examines the law's view of the human body, exploring property rights in the body, transplantation of body parts, and the use of human subjects in medical research. Chapter Four explores the legal and ethical issues surrounding death and dying, including controversies over abating life-saving treatment, regulating competency, and physician-assisted dying. The final chapter, Chapter Five, examines the issues raised by reproductive technologies, including preimplantation genetic diagnosis which combines in vitro fertilization with the advances in genomics presented in Chapter One.

We are grateful to the many students at Georgetown and elsewhere whose hard work and ideas have helped to shape this text. We are especially thankful for the efforts of the following fellows, students, and administrators who helped to research and edit this book: Auburn Daily, Joleen Okun, Katrina Pagonis, David Plattner, Lesley Stone, Amber Murray, Swati Kabaria, Megan Lewis and James Weir. We would like to offer a special thanks to Lance Gable, who coordinated the research for the book, and Steven Barbour, who handled the often voluminous administrative responsibilities. Finally, we would like to again thank our families for their support during this process.

PATRICIA KING
JUDITH AREEN
LAWRENCE O. GOSTIN

Washington, D.C.
September 2005

NOTE ON EDITING

Deletions from materials are indicated by ellipses except when the omitted material consists only of citations or footnotes. All footnotes in the excerpted sections are numbered according to the original source except when noted. All footnotes added by the authors are indicated with ascending lower-case letters.

ACKNOWLEDGMENTS

Law, Medicine & Ethics

Adrienne Asch, REPRODUCTIVE TECHNOLOGY AND DISABILITY IN REPRODUCTIVE LAWS FOR THE 1990's (Sherrill Cohen & Nadine Taub eds., 1989).

Advisory Committee on Human Radiation Experiments, Final Report 342-48 (1995).

ALEXANDER I. SOLZHENITSYN, THE CANCER WARD. (1968).

Allen Buchanan et al., *Two Models for Genetic Intervention in* FROM CHANCE TO CHOICE (2000).

Allen D. Roses, *Pharmacogenetics and the Practice of Medicine* 405 NATURE 857 (2000).

American Medical Association, *Principles of Medical Ethics.* (2004).

Anita L. Allen, *Genetic Privacy: Emerging Concepts and Values in Genetic Secrets* IN PROTECTING PRIVACY AND CONFIDENTIALITY IN THE GENETIC ERA: 33-34 (Mark A. Rothstein ed., 1997).

Bartha Maria Knoppers et al., *Commercialization of Genetic Research and Public Policy* 286 SCI. 2277–2278 (1999).

Bonnie Steinbock & Ron McClamrock, *When Is Birth Unfair to the Child?* 24 HASTINGS CTR. REP. 15 (1994).

C.R. Austin, *Human Embryos: The Debate on Assisted Reproduction* (1989).

Curtis A. Kin, *Coming Soon to the "Genetic Supermarket" Near You* 48 STAN. L. REV. 1573 (1996).

Decision-Making Dilemmas Concerning Testing and Management 55 OBSTRETRICAL & GYNECOLOGICAL SURVEY 373–384 (2000).

Elizabeth Pennisi, *Human Genome: Reaching Their Goal Early*, Sequencing Labs Celebrate. 300 SCIENCE 409 (2003).

Eric Cassel, *The Nature of Suffering and the Goals of Medicine.* 306 NEW ENG. J. MED. 639 (1982).

Francis S. Collins et al., *New Goals for the U.S. Human Genome Project*: 1998–2003: 282 SCIENCE 682 (1998).

Franz J. Ingelfinger, *Informed (But Uneducated) Consent.* 287 New Eng. J. MED. 465, 465-66 (1972)

Fred Rosner, *Human Experimentation in Judaism.* BIOMEDICAL ETHICS AND JEWISH LAW 408, 410 (2001).

Gilbert Meilaender, *Gifts of the Body: Human Experimentation.* BIOETHICS: A PRIMER FOR CHRISTIANS: 106-113 (1996).

H. Tristram Engelhardt, Jr., *Medicine and the Concept of the Person in* CONTEMPORARY ISSUES IN BIOETHICS 94, 94-99 (Tom Beauchamp and LeRoy Walters eds., 1982).

Hans Jonas, *Philosophical Reflections on Experimenting With Human Subjects*. EXPERIMENTATION WITH HUMAN SUBJECTS: 1-4, 9-14 (1970).

Harold Edgar and David J. Rothman, *The Institutional Review Board and Beyond*: *Future Challenges to the Ethics of Human Experimentation* 73 MILBANK QUARTERLY 489, 489–491 (1995).

Henry Beecher, *Ethics and Clinical Research* 274 N.ENG.J.MED. 1354 (1966).

International Ethical Guidelines for Biomedical Research Involving Human Subjects. Council for International Organizations of Medical Sciences (CIOMS) in Collaboration with the World Health Organization (2002).

J.D. Watson & F.H.C. Crick, *A Structure for Deoxyribose Nucleic Acid.* 171 NATURE 737 (1953)

James Rachels, Active and Passive Euthanasia. 292 NEW.ENG. J. MED. 78, 78–80 (1975).

Jimmy Carter, Solar Energy. President's Message to Congress, 15 WEEKLY COMP. OF PRES. DOC. 1098 (1979).

Jocelyn Kaiser, *Public-Private Group Maps Out Initiatives.* 96 SCIENCE 827 (2002).

Jon W. Gordon, *Genetic Enhancement in Humans* 283 SCI. 2023–2024 (1999).

Jonathan D. Moreno, *Convenient and Captive Populations.* BEYOND CONSENT: 111-116 (1998).

Karen Grandstrand Gervais, *Advancing the Definition of Death*: *A Philosophical Essay.* 3 MED. HUMANITIES REV. 7 (1989).

Kennedy Institute of Ethics, *Genetic Testing and Genetic Screening.* KIEJ (Updated 2004).

Kennedy Institute of Ethics, *Scope Note 24*: *Human Gene Therapy.* KIEJ. (Updated 2004).

Kenneth Offit et al., The "Duty to Warn" a Patient's Family Members About Hereditary Disease Risks. 292 JAMA 1469 (2004)

Laurie Goldberg Strongin, *The Promise of Preimplantation Genetic Diagnosis*. GENETICS & PUB. POL'Y CTR. (2004), available at http://www.dnapolicy.org/pdfs/Strongin_PGD_7.03.pdf (last visited July 15, 2004).

Leon R. Kass, *Thinking About the Body*. TOWARD A MORE NATURAL SCIENCE 276, 276–96, 298 (1985).

Lewis Thomas, *Dying as Failure.* 447 ANNALS 1, 2–4 (Renée Fox, Spec. Ed. 1980).

Linus Pauling, *Reflections on the New Biology.* 15 UCLA L. REV. 267 (1968).

Lori Andrews & Dorothy Nelkin, BODY BAZAAR: THE MARKET FOR HUMAN TISSUE IN THE BIOTECHNOLOGY AGE: 60–62 (2001).

Mark A. Rothstein & Phyllis Griffin Epps, *Ethical and Legal Implications of Pharmacogenomics* 2 NATURE REVIEWS GENETICS: 228-231 (2001).

Michael J. Green & Jeffrey R. Botkin, *Genetic Exceptionalism in Medicine: Clarifying the Differences between Genetic and Nongenetic Tests* 138 ANNALS INTERNAL MED 571 (2003).

Patricia A. King, *The Dangers of Difference, Revisited*. THE STORY OF BIOETHICS: FROM SEMINAL WORKS TO CONTEMPORARY EXPLORATIONS (2003).

Paul M. McNeill, *International Trends in Research Regulations: Science as Negotiation*. RESEARCH ON HUMAN SUBJECTS ETHICS, LAW, AND SOCIAL POLICY (1998).

Report on the Ethical, Medical, and Legal Issues in Treatment Decisions: 197–203 (March 1983).

Richard S. Cooper et al., *Race and Genomics* 348 NEW ENG. J. MED. 1166 (2003).

Robert S. Morison, *Bioethics After Two Decades*. 11 HASTINGS CENTER RPT. 8 (April 1981).

Robert Steinbrook, *Protecting Research Subjects—The Crisis at Johns Hopkins*. 346 NEW ENG. J. MED. 716 (2002).

Stuart Mill, *On Liberty* (excerpts) (1859).

The President's Council on Bioethics, Human Cloning and Human Dignity: An Ethical Inquiry 1, xxvi-xxix, 60-61 (2002).

The President's Council on Bioethics, *Screening and Selection for Genetic Conditions and Traits in* REPRODUCTION AND RESPONSIBILITY: THE REGULATION OF NEW BIOTECHNOLOGIES (2004).

Tom Clarke, *DNA's Family Tree*. 422 NATURE 791 (2003).

Tom L. Beauchamp and James F. Childress, *Principles of Biomedical Ethics* (excerpts) (2001).

Vicki Brower, *Proteomics: Biology in the Post-Genomic Era*. 2 EMBO REPORTS 558-9 (2001).

Xavier Bosch, *Researchers Try to Unlock Human Genome Potential*. 360 THE LANCET 1481 (2002).

Xunwu Chen, A CONFUCIAN JUSTIFICATION OF EXPERIMENTING WITH HUMAN SUBJECTS CONFUCIAN BIOETHICS (1999).

*

SUMMARY OF CONTENTS

DETAILED TABLE OF CONTENTS

TABLE OF CASES

Principal cases are in bold type. Non-principal cases are in roman type. References are to Pages.

LAW, MEDICINE AND ETHICS

*

CHAPTER 1

THE HUMAN GENOME: PATHWAYS TO HEALTH

Law, Medicine and Ethics is about pathways to health. How do scientific pursuits evolve from the laboratory to the physician's office and hospital through to interventions to safeguard the public's health? Law can facilitate that process by, for example, incentivizing scientific innovation and efficient delivery of vaccines and pharmaceuticals to the market. Science and medicine pose deeply complex ethical and social issues, and policy makers often turn to law as a means to regulate research, the professions, and private activities. There is no subject that better illustrates the difficult problems that inhere in law, medicine and ethics than the human genome.

I. SCIENTIFIC DISCOVERY AND ADVANCEMENT

A. MENDEL AND HOW GENETICS BEGAN

Gregor Mendel is considered the father of genetics, although he did not enjoy such recognition during his lifetime. Modern genetics had its humble beginning in Mendel's garden, where he examined and quantified the physical traits in pea plants to predict future generations' traits and explain familial resemblances. Charting seven traits (plant height, flower color and position, seed color and shape, and pod color and shape), Mendel concluded that certain particles or "factors" were being transmitted inter-generationally and that these factors were directly responsible for physical traits.

Hereditary traits, he concluded, are determined by cellular elements, now called genes, which exist in pairs, and are responsible for all heritable characteristics. Mendel's law of segregation found that each genetic trait is produced by a pair of alleles that separate (segregate) during reproduction and persist unchanged through successive generations of hereditary trans-mission. Under his law of independent assortment, genes are distributed randomly and independently of genes for other characteristics. When different alleles for a certain characteristic are inherited, only the dominant trait will be expressed; they do not blend, as previously thought. *See* Daniel L. Hartl & Orel Vitezslav, *What did Gregor Mendel Think he Discovered?*, 131 GENETICS 245 (1992).

After initial rejection at peer review, Mendel's paper, "Experiments on Plant Hybridization" was published in 1865. Initially, his paper received little attention, and it was rarely cited by botanists or biologists over the next 35 years. The rationale for Mendel's lack of recognition has been thought to exemplify everything from the failure of traditional modes of scientific communication to the phenomenon of "premature scientific discovery." *See* Vannevar Bush, *As We May Think*, in FROM MEMEX TO HYPERTEXT: VANNEVAR BUSH AND THE MIND'S MACHINE (James M. Nyce et al., eds. 1991); GUNTHER S. STENT, *Prematurity and Uniqueness in Scientific Discovery*, *in* PARADOXES OF PROGRESS 94–114 (1978). Despite inaccurate interpretations of what Mendel had shown, he gained recognition in 1900 when several European botanists verified his work.

In the decade that followed, Mendel's paper and the contemporary description of his findings stimulated an enormous amount of work in the newly formed field of genetics, particularly in England and the United States. For the generation of scientists who came to think of themselves as "Mendelians," the paper of 1865, and its author, became an inspirational symbol of the revolutionary findings that awaited biologists in the study of heredity. In 1900, shortly after the "rediscovery," the geneticist William Bateson began an article in the *Journal of the Royal Horticultural Society* with the claim that, "An exact determination of the laws of heredity will probably work more change in man's outlook on the world, and in his power over nature, than any other advance in natural knowledge that can be clearly foreseen." WILLIAM BATESON, Mendel's Principles of Heredity (1913).

With this recognition of genetics' importance, scientists began to associate inheritance with chromosomes and to find models—in fruit flies, predominantly—that would help build upon that initial foundation. Two decades later, researchers determined DNA, rather than protein, was the carrier of inheritance. In addition, DNA polymerase was discovered and biochemical regulating units of inheritance were identified, laying the foundation for the future biotechnology revolution. Scientists knew that the DNA molecule was made of a few relatively simple chemicals. However, no one was sure how these simple chemicals combined to carry the huge amount of information required to recreate a living thing. A young American geneticist named James Watson was one of the few researchers who realized that the only way to determine whether nucleic acids carried genes was to understand their structure.

B.   MORE THAN 50 YEARS AFTER WATSON AND CRICK

James Watson and Francis Crick provided the foundation for modern genetic research by proposing that the structure of DNA was a double-stranded helix of complementary nucleic acids.[1] On the death of Francis Crick in July 2004, *The Times of London* wrote:

> The beauty of the double helix was that it immediately suggested a way in which the genetic instructions of the cell could be passed on when it divided, to produce a perfect copy. One helix unfurled from the other and

---

1. The breakthrough by Watson and Crick led to lasting bitterness over their use of X-ray photographs taken by Rosalind Franklin at Kings College London, whose crucial role they never fully acknowledged. *See* Brenda Maddox, *The Double Helix and the "Wronged Heroine"*, 421 NATURE 407 (2003).

then built its own matching helix before curling up again.... It also suggested that the order of the base pairs along the helix was a kind of code, containing the instructions used by genes to make proteins. Crick played a major role in working out this code—the key to life itself, shared by every living organism on Earth.

Nigel Hawkes, *Crick: He Revealed the Beauty and Code of Biology*, THE TIMES (London), July 30, 2004, at 2.

Watson and Crick received the Nobel Prize for Medicine in 1962 "for their discoveries concerning the molecular structure of nucleic acids and its significance for information transfer in living material."

J.D. Watson & F.H.C. Crick, *A Structure for Deoxyribose Nucleic Acid*

171 NATURE 737 (1953).

We wish to put forward a radically different structure for the salt of deoxyribose nucleic acid. This structure has two helical chains each coiled round the same axis. We have made the usual chemical assumptions, namely, that each chain consists of phosphate diester groups joining ï-D-deoxyribofuranose residues with 3',5' linkages. The two chains (but not their bases) are related by a dyad perpendicular to the fibre axis. Both chains follow right-handed helices, but owing to the dyad the sequences of the atoms in the two chains run in opposite directions.

The structure is an open one, and its water content is rather high. At lower water contents we would expect the bases to tilt so that the structure could become more compact.

The novel feature of the structure is the manner in which the two chains are held together by the purine and pyrimidine bases. The planes of the bases are perpendicular to the fibre axis. They are joined together in pairs, a single base from the other chain, so that the two lie side by side with identical z-co-ordinates. One of the pair must be a purine and the other a pyrimidine for bonding to occur. The hydrogen bonds are made as follows: purine position 1 to pyrimidine position 1; purine position 6 to pyrimidine position 6.

If it is assumed that the bases only occur in the structure in the most plausible tautomeric forms (that is, with the keto rather than the enol configurations) it is found that only specific pairs of bases can bond together. These pairs are: adenine (purine) with thymine (pyrimidine), and guanine (purine) with cytosine (pyrimidine).

In other words, if an adenine forms one member of a pair, on either chain, then on these assumptions the other member must be thymine; similarly for guanine and cytosine. The sequence of bases on a single chain does not appear to be restricted in any way. However, if only specific pairs of bases can be formed, it follows that if the sequence of bases on one chain is given, then the sequence on the other chain is automatically determined.

———

More than fifty years later, the legacy of Watson and Crick's findings continues to flourish, as they provided the impetus to scrutinize DNA, the genetic material of life, more fully. The structure defined by Watson and Crick gave scientists a critical tool for revealing how DNA encodes the genetic information that is passed from adults to offspring. Now, the DNA of any organism can be represented as a letter code, loaded into a computer database, and shared internationally among scientists. DNA technology has become essential to understanding the fundamental processes of life and the causes of health and disease.

Tom Clarke, *DNA's Family Tree*

422 NATURE 791 (2003).

The structure made it obvious that the molecule encodes information. Almost as important, however, "it explained how all that information could be compacted into a cell," says Robert Olby, a science historian at the University of Pittsburgh in Pennsylvania. DNA's tight spiral showed how genetic information can be packed into chromosomes.

. . .

Through the 1950s, researchers put flesh on the bones of Watson and Crick's structure. In 1955, geneticist Seymour Benzer of Purdue University, Indiana, showed that genes in bacteria consist of long stretches of DNA letters, and that just one error could render them useless.

And once researchers discovered how cells boss their genetic information about, they could really start making use of DNA. In 1956, biochemist Arthur Kornberg found the enzyme used to copy DNA, a finding that earned him a Nobel Prize. In 1957 Crick cracked the genetic code, showing how genetic information is translated into the protein molecules that do the work in cells.

In the late 1950s and '60s, researchers discovered enzymes that could split the two strands of DNA apart, stick them back together again, and even bite into DNA strands at the sites of specific sequences. These molecular tools made it possible to cut out lengths of DNA from one organism and paste them into another—genetic engineering was born.

The other major step was figuring out how to read genetic sentences. DNA sequencing, as it became known, was pioneered by the British biochemist Frederick Sanger.

Sanger developed a way of marking the bases of DNA with radioactive tags that could be read using X-rays. Using this technique, he produced the first complete list of the DNA letters needed to code for the structure of a complete protein, insulin, a feat that netted him his second Nobel Prize in 1980.

Sanger's invention gave birth to the science of genomics. With it, we gained the power to compare genes—allowing us to analyze patterns of disease, the evolution of species, and the history of human groups and individuals.

C. DECODING THE STRUCTURE OF LIFE: MAPPING THE HUMAN GENOME

1. TIMELINE AND ACCOMPLISHMENTS

Building upon the seminal work of Mendel and Watson and Crick, researchers involved in the Human Genome Project sequenced the human genome, providing the order of base pairs (adenine, thymine, guanine, and cytosine) in human DNA. Prior to the completion of this 15–year project, the largest genome, or complete set of an organism's DNA, to be sequenced belonged to the fruit fly.[2] Scientists' ability to replicate these findings with the human genome, which is 25 times as large and infinitely more complex, shows the recent rapid advancements in genetic research. The Human Genome Project, which originated when Congress funded the National Institutes of Health's (NIH) and Department of Energy's (DOE) efforts to sequence DNA, has given scientists a more systematic understanding of the human genome.

Francis S. Collins et al., *New Goals for the U.S. Human Genome Project: 1998–2003*

282 SCI. 682 (1998).

The Human Genome Project (HGP) is fulfilling its promise as the single most important project in biology and the biomedical sciences—one that will permanently change biology and medicine. With the recent completion of the genome sequences of several microorganisms.... the door has opened wide on the era of whole genome science. The ability to analyze entire genomes is accelerating gene discovery and revolutionizing the breadth and depth of biological questions that can be addressed in model organisms. These exciting successes confirm the view that acquisition of a comprehensive, high-quality human genome sequence will have unprecedented impact and long-lasting value for basic biology, biomedical research, biotechnology, and health care. The transition to sequence-based biology will spur continued progress in understanding gene-environment interactions and in development of highly accurate DNA-based medical diagnostics and therapeutics.

Human DNA sequencing, the flagship endeavor of the HGP, is entering its decisive phase. It will be the project's central focus during the next 5 years. While partial subsets of the DNA sequence ... have proven enormously valuable, experience with simpler organisms confirms that there can be no substitute for the complete genome sequence....

Availability of the human genome sequence presents unique scientific opportunities, chief among them the study of natural genetic variation in humans. Genetic or DNA sequence variation is the fundamental raw material for evolution. Importantly, it is also the basis for variations in risk among individuals for numerous medically important, genetically complex human diseases. An understanding of the relationship between genetic variation and disease risk promises to change significantly the future

---

2. The fruit fly genome was not completed until March 2000.

prevention and treatment of illness. The new focus on genetic variation, as well as other applications of the human genome sequence, raises additional ethical, legal, and social issues that need to be anticipated, considered, and resolved.

NOTES AND QUESTIONS

The ultimate goal of the Human Genome Project was to develop effective approaches for disease prevention, diagnosis, and treatment through a better understanding of the contribution of genes to the development and functioning of the human body. It was designed to expand our knowledge and grasp of the interactions among genes and between genes and environmental influences. Researchers' specific goals—many of which are still ongoing—were to: locate and map all human genes; discover the entire DNA sequence of the human genome; store this information in databases accessible to researchers and the public; create resources for data analysis; map and sequence the genomes of other living organisms; and study the impact that genetic information and technologies may have on society, including ethical and legal ramifications.

The culmination of these efforts was the publication of the draft sequence in 2001, which provided insight into 90% of the human genome's three billion base pairs. International Human Genome Sequencing Consortium, *Initial Sequencing and Analysis of the Human Genome*, 409 NATURE 860–921 (2001). In April 2003, the International Human Genome Sequencing Consortium announced its task was complete and published a final product in which nearly all bases were identified in the correct order.

Elizabeth Pennisi, *Human Genome: Reaching Their Goal Early, Sequencing Labs Celebrate*

300 SCI. 409 (2003).

It may sound like science by press release, as no formal report has been published, but the news is spectacular all the same: The International Human Genome Sequencing Consortium announced on 14 April that it has completed its work. In a note of rare unanimity, the leaders of the United States, Britain, China, France, Germany, and Japan issued a joint proclamation honoring their scientists who worked on the project.

Twice before—in 2000 and 2001—researchers celebrated draft sequences of the human genome. But the new product is much more complete and of higher quality: 99% of what can be done with current technology is now done, sequencers say. And virtually all the bases are now identified in their proper order, which was not true of the draft versions.

. . .

Completing this labor-intensive phase will come as a big relief for many involved. They were spurred to a faster pace in 1998, when sequencer J. Craig Venter boasted that his new company, Celera Genomics in Rockville, Maryland, would sequence the human genome first. The consortium scrambled to prevent that from happening. Both Celera and the public groups completed drafts in June 2000 and published reports on them simultaneously in February 2001.

Once that milestone had been reached, [questions remained as to whether the public project would finish first]. But the public consortium hunkered down and delivered on the promise 2 years ahead of schedule, says Francis Collins, director of the National Human Genome Research Institute (NHGRI). The U.S. share amounted to about 53% of the 2.9 billion bases, costing $2.7 billion over the project's 15–year duration.

The consortium set out to meet a standard of one error in 10,000 bases; the just-finished version is 10 times better than that. Now only the most difficult regions remain to be done, including about 400 stretches of repetitive DNA and centromeres, which divide the chromosomes. "This is a reference sequence," says Collins, one that will be used by biologists for many years to come.

Even so, sequencers have not yet determined the number of human genes. Three years ago they were so confident that they would have the answer by now that many made bets on their predictions, planning to declare the winner this spring. That's not going to happen, says Collins; there is no clear answer from computer programs that are trained to identify genes. Two years ago, the two drafts indicated there were 35,000 to 45,000 genes. Now the rough estimate "stands a little under 30,000," says Collins.

As the genome community inches toward an accurate gene count, it's also endorsing new, even grander research schemes. . . .

If sequencing the genome was akin to landing a human on the moon, then this new vision calls for landing more humans on the moon, says Edward Rubin, director of the Department of Energy (DOE) Joint Genome Institute. DOE intends to focus on sequencing nonmammalian genomes, including microbes important as potential energy sources. But NHGRI's [broad agenda, unveiled last week,] has many elements, such as extending the haplotype map, a five-nation effort to describe individual and group DNA variations. A project called ENCODE will determine the functions of the genes. And Collins hopes to launch a resource to enable researchers to screen new proteins for interactions with any of about a million small molecules, potentially to find drug candidates. . . .

Nevertheless, the completed genome is already making biologists' work easier, Pollard says—not just by identifying genes but also by revealing what regulates gene expression. He predicts that biology will continue to reap broad benefits: For that reason, it's the right time for Collins and his collaborators "to set off a few fireworks."

NOTES AND QUESTIONS

The sequencing of the human genome is a scientific milestone, opening the door to breathtaking possibilities in medicine and public health. As we will see, the human genome project offers the possibility of developing better prevention and treatment, not only for genetic diseases, but also for complex chronic diseases, such as cancers and cardiovascular disease, that affect large populations.

Despite the undoubted prospective benefits, the potential for harm is apparent. Genetic information can deeply affect personal privacy, stigmatize individuals and groups, and even result in discrimination in employment and insurance. To address these issues, Congress devoted 5% of human genome funding to the exploration of the ethical, legal, and social issues (ELSI). *See* Robert Cook–Deegan, *The Human Genome Project: The Formation of Federal Policies in the United States, 1986–1990,* in BIOMEDICAL POLITICS 99–175 (Kathi E. Hanna ed., 1991). The ELSI program placed science and ethics on a parallel track—both forms of exploration could go ahead simultaneously. Was this a reasoned method to ensure safe and ethical practice in science and medicine? Could some of the legal and ethical issues have been foreseen, thereby providing boundaries for the scientific enterprise? Is it possible that the science will progress so quickly that sober ethical reflection may be too late? For further discussion of the ELSI project, *see* Sec. V, *infra.*

2. THE HAPMAP PROJECT

A primary goal of the Public Consortium was to make a complete sequence of the human genome widely available for scientists and research-ers to stimulate research that would improve human health and serve the greatest public good. In furtherance of this objective, scientists and funding groups from six countries launched a three-year project called the Interna-tional Haplotype Map (HapMap) Project in 2002. The HapMap will make the knowledge gained about the human genome easier to use by describing the human genome in terms of haplotypes. The HapMap project is based on the premise that genes tend to be inherited in blocks of closely associated genes. In these genes, single nucleotide polymorphisms (SNPs) are the points where individuals differ in their genetic sequences. On a given block, the pattern of SNPs is known as a haplotype. The value of the HapMap project lies in allowing scientists to examine the approximately 500,000 tag SNPs from the haplotype blocks instead of the 10 million SNPs in the human genome.

Xavier Bosch, *Researchers Try to Unlock Human Genome Potential*

360 THE LANCET 1481 (2002).

An international consortium of researchers has launched a US$100 million, 3–year project to create a new map of the human genome, which aims to understand how common patterns of variation among genes are related to disease. The International Haplotype Map (HapMap) Project is a collaborative effort between the US National Institutes of Health, Canada, Japan, China, the SNP consortium, and the Wellcome Trust Sanger Insti-tute in the UK.

This project is "indeed groundbreaking and exciting", Francis Collins, director of the National Human Genome Research Institute, Bethesda, USA, told *The Lancet.* The HapMap will be a "powerful tool to help us take the next quantum leap toward understanding the fundamental contribution that genes make to common illnesses like cancer, diabetes, and mental illness." The theory behind the project is that the variation in genetic code from person to person may not be a disordered, random scattering of single base variation but probably exists as ordered blocks of sequence variation or haplotypes.

"The benefit of being able to address gene mapping from the perspective of blocks or haplotypes, rather than single SNPs, is greatly diminished cost and time required to identify genes involved in common genetic diseases", says Peter Doris, Center for Human Genetics, University of Texas Health Science Center. But he notes that "such economies derive from facts that are not yet in evidence."

Furthermore, "while the common disease/common variant hypothesis is reasonable and supported by some existing knowledge, whether it is correct or not is presently unknowable." If it is not correct, he argues, the investment of money, talent, and time may be a costly error. Collins says, "I suspect it [the hypothesis] will not be correct for all disease genes ... but if it is even correct for a modest fraction it will be fantastically useful."

To create the HapMap, DNA will be taken from blood samples from 200 to 400 people in widely distributed geographic regions. Samples will be collected from people in Nigeria, Japan, China and US residents with ancestry from northern and western Europe. The sampling strategy has been designed to ensure that participants can give full, informed consent without giving away any identifying medical or personal information.

The samples will be processed and stored at the Coriell Institute for Medical Research, Camden, NJ. Then researchers from academic centres, non-profit research groups, and private companies in Japan, UK, Canada, China, and USA will analyse the samples to generate the HapMap, the results of which will be freely available on the internet.

NOTES AND QUESTIONS

1. *What do HapMap Data Reveal About the Human Experience?* The entire human population shares 99.9% of their DNA sequences. What do these data tell us about the sameness or differences among groups of different race and origin? The remaining 0.1% of DNA sequences contains the genetic variants that influence how people differ in their risk of disease and in their response to environmental stressors or pharmaceuticals. Because common haplotypes occur with varying frequency among different populations, data for the HapMap will be gathered from four native populations and the SNP and haplotype frequencies for each population will be calculated. Could the comparisons among these groups and the wider population result in stigmatization or discrimination of persons within the group? If a variant associated with a certain disease has a higher frequency among one population and the risks associated with that variant are over generalized to members of that population, what are the likely social implications? Could the HapMap project's categorization of an individuals' genetic data on the basis of a population's ancestral geography result in labels such as "race," which is largely socially constructed, being incorrectly viewed as a precise and highly meaningful biological construct? Greater understanding of the genetic basis of race could lead to health improvements or new kinds of stereotypes. *See* Robin Marantz Henig, *The Genome in Black and White (and Gray)*, N.Y. Times Mag., Oct. 10, 2004, p. 46. What might scientists or policy makers do to prevent the misuse of genomic information for the purposes of stigma or discrimination? *See* further, Sec. V, *infra*.

2. *Indigenous Groups and Genetics Research.* Should scientists be concerned about their choice of vulnerable native populations? Some geneticists have attempted to gather genetic information from indigenous groups facing extinction. Is genetic research on vulnerable populations appropriate?

Indigenous peoples' organizations now question the purpose behind research that is done on indigenous population groups. In certain parts of the world, indigenous peoples are facing cultural extinction. Where there is mass logging of tropical rain forests, for example, indigenous people who live there are depleted of food and water resources, and driven from their homes. They eventually join the ranks of waged laborers in logging camps and cash crop plantations. As their social fabric breaks up, they are in danger of losing their identity and culture. The struggle to survive as a people is a pressing concern of many groups. In this context, the call for researchers to collect genetic materials from indigenous populations, before they disappear as distinctive genetic groups, may appear to some as grossly insensitive and callous.

Chee Heng Leng et al., International Bioethics Committee, Bioethics and Human Population Genetics Research 16, United Nations Educational, Scientific and Cultural Organization, CIP/BIO/95/CONF.002/5 (Nov. 15, 1995).

3. *Is Public Access Consistent with Private Innovation?* The HapMap policy of openness has led to concerns about what Francis Collins called "parasitic intellectual property claims." Carina Dennis, *The Rough Guide to the Genome*, 425 NATURE 758 (2003). Scientists could combine public data with their own, and then patent the findings in a way that restricts others' ability to work freely with the HapMap data. Is it likely that scientists will use freely available information from the HapMap for personal gain? For a more complete discussion of intellectual property issues in genetics, *see* Marco Segre & Edna Sadayo Miazato Iwamura, *Bioethics, Intellectual Property, and Genomics*, 56 REV. HOSP. CLIN. FAC. MED. S. PAULO 97 (2001). *See also* Sec. IV, *infra*.

D.   FROM GENOMICS TO PROTEOMICS

Upon completion of the Human Genome Project, the proteomics era began. To researchers' surprise, the Human Genome Project showed that humans possess only 10,000–20,000 more genes than the fruit fly or the roundworm. It became clear that proteins, rather than genes, are responsible for an organism's complexity. Therefore, the key to understanding health and disease within an organism is to understand how its proteins function.

Vicki Brower, *Proteomics: Biology in the Post–Genomic Era*

2 EMBO REPORTS 558–9 (2001).

In June 2001, when the Human Genome Project and Celera completed the first maps of the human genome, Francis Collins, head of the government-sponsored HGP, warned that only then would the real race begin. This was a prophetic insight indeed. No sooner was the human genome decoded than we found ourselves in the "post-genomic era"—where the name of the game is proteomics. Proteomics is not only the systematic separation, cataloguing and study of all of the proteins produced in an organism, it is also the study of how proteins change structure, interact with other proteins, and ultimately give rise to disease or health in an organism. Since its application in drug discovery promises huge economic returns, it comes as no surprise that biotechnology, computer and software companies around the world are rushing to pour capital and resources into this new research field.

Proteomics is more complex by several orders of magnitude than genomics, with no one company, laboratory or consortium remotely able to run the race alone. Moreover, no one technology will be able to fulfill proteomics' numerous tasks, and new developments are sorely needed.

With the publication of the draft of the human genome in the February 16, 2001 issues of *Science* and *Nature* came what many had already suspected: instead of the earlier estimate of about 100,000 human genes, the actual count reduced this figure by 75%. If humans have only 10,000–20,000 more genes than the fruitfly and the roundworm, then the big question is how do we manage to be so complex? The answer: proteins—not genes—are responsible for an organism's complexity. The interaction of proteins in a complex network adds up to how an organism functions. The key to understanding health and disease within an organism is, therefore, to understand how its proteins function. In a multicellular organism, one needs to be able to look at the entire system in an integrated way. Proteomics is the study of where each protein is located in a cell, when the protein is present and for how long, and with which other proteins it is interacting. Proteomics means looking at many events at the same time and connecting them. New tools are necessary to enable the study of this web of events—to create a movie, rather than a static snapshot of the activities taking place.

A further dimension was added to this complex picture when scientists from the University of Pennsylvania School of Medicine reported this May in *Nature* that proteins are more active and dynamic than they had imagined. The interior of a protein is much more liquid-like than scientists originally anticipated. Everything is moving, and it's moving all the time, very fast.... [Proteins] move so much that it dramatically influences how they work. This is the beginning of a long new story that will have a lot to do with understanding protein function. The concept of proteins as dynamic entities may ultimately help scientists target more accessible sites for drug development.

Currently, drug developers are working with only about 400–500 targets, many of which are receptors. With the shift from genomics to proteomics and the concomitant evolution of technology, many scientists expect the number of potential "druggable" targets to expand many hundred-fold to between 10,000 and 20,000. With such numbers, it will become necessary to winnow through targets rapidly and accurately to determine which should be pursued. The marriage of business and science within the proteomics field indeed promises to achieve this.

A formidable task for proteomics is to develop new tools that can help scientists analyze cellular function with speed and accuracy. Proteins are too numerous, diverse and interactive to be studied by a single method. Proteomics, therefore, is comprised of a number of interrelated, overlapping disciplines: functional and structural genomics, functional and structural proteomics, and bioinformatics—a convergence of "wet" and "dry" laboratories.

Jocelyn Kaiser, *Public–Private Group Maps Out Initiatives*

296 SCI. 827 (2002).

A new group hoping to spur a global effort to determine the structure and function of all proteins made by the human body kicked into gear last week. The Human Proteome Organization (HUPO), an international alliance of industry, academic, and government members, laid out its first set of initiatives and has begun knocking on industry doors for funding.

HUPO was formed about a year ago by a group of scientists who wanted to make sure that companies don't lock up basic proteomics data under trade secrecy. The founders also wanted to include more countries than participated in the Human Genome Project. . . .

[HUPO's initial list of projects] is a mix of technology, tools, and research. For example, HUPO's bioinformatics plan would develop community-wide standards for presenting mass spectrometry and protein-protein interaction data. Another initiative would create a collection of antibodies for the primary proteins made by the 30,000 or more human genes. HUPO also wants to identify thousands of new proteins present in small amounts in blood, which would be very valuable to companies developing diagnostic tests. All the data would be freely available through public databases. . . .

. . .

While HUPO is forging ahead with its first projects, the U.S. National Institutes of Health (NIH) is still mapping out its own proteomics strategy. At a meeting last week in Bethesda, Maryland, proteomics experts went back and forth over possible recommendations on the best way for NIH to encourage the field's development. . . .

NOTES AND QUESTIONS

Proteomics is the study of where each protein is located in a cell, when and for how long the protein is present, and with which other proteins it interacts. Unlike the genome, which is relatively static, the proteome changes constantly in response to tens of thousands of intra-and extra-cellular environmental signals. The proteome varies with health or disease, the nature of each tissue, the stages of cell development, and effects of drug treatments. As such, the proteome is defined as the proteins present in a sample (a tissue, organism, or cell culture) at a certain point in time. Because proteins are too numerous, diverse, and interactive to be studied through a single method, proteomics is comprised of numerous interrelated disciplines including functional and structural genomics, functional and structural proteomics, and bioinformatics. These disciplines require the simultaneous monitoring of different cellular activity so researchers can comprehend the connection between these activities. Technology currently lags behind these demands, and a primary task of these growing disciplines is to develop new tools that can help scientists analyze cellular function quickly and accurately.

The promise that proteomics holds for drug discovery has peaked the interest of biotechnology and computer and software companies which are pouring capital and resources into this growing field. Most pharmaceuticals are directed against proteins and the more that is known about them, the more effective drugs may be. This source of funding is crucial to a field that demands large-scale, costly projects.

However, important questions remain. Will the biotechnology industry make sufficient investments in the program and will their investments be targeted toward the most important health problems? Will the private sector insist on exercising control of the direction of research and hold the results as proprietary information? Will the role of the private sector, therefore, impede certain important discoveries? Some researchers have suggested that a dedicated funding pool and collaborative effort similar to that established for the Human Genome Project are needed to ensure that proteomics attains its projected status as "a watershed in biology and medicine." Mike Tyers & Matthias Mann, *From Genomics to Proteomics*, 422 NATURE 196 (2003). Do you agree and, if so, how much public funding should be devoted to such efforts?

As with genomics, proteomics raises the crucial questions of the nature and scope of private investment, the interaction between private and public access to information, and the best ways to regulate the emerging field. The goal is to spur innovation, pool scarce resources, make advances publicly accessible, and do all of this in an ethically acceptable manner. Needless to say, these are not easy goals to achieve and, in many cases, the objectives are in tension with one another.

II. THE ROLE OF GENOMICS IN UNDERSTANDING HEALTH AND DISEASE

Some scholars use the terms genetics and genomics interchangeable, but there is a difference. Genetics is the study of "single genes and their effects," while genomics is the study of the "functions and interactions of all the genes in the genome." *See* Alan E. Guttmacher & Francis S. Collins, *Genomic Medicine: A Primer*, 347 NEW ENG. J. MED. 1512 (2002). Muin Khoury reflects on the meaning and importance of genomics:

> This definition implies a quantitative difference between the two fields (the study of multiple genes vs. one gene, which could make genetics part of genomics). In addition, there is a qualitative shift between genetics and genomics in medical and public health applications, ranging from the concept of disease in genetics to the concept of information in genomics. Perhaps more accurately, this shift may be best viewed as a continuum with no clear breakpoint, from single gene disorders with high penetrance to genetic information obtained from multiple loci in somatic cells.
>
> The practice of medical genetics has traditionally focused on those conditions that are known to be due to mutations in single genes (e.g., Huntington disease), whole chromosomes (e.g., trisomy 21 in Down syndrome[3]), or associated with birth defects and developmental disabilities. For these conditions, a traditional genetic services model applies with its accompanying medical processes (genetic counseling/testing/management) and public health processes (assuring delivery of genetic services and newborn screening). On the other hand, the practice of genomics in medicine and public health will center on information resulting from variation at one or multiple loci and strong interactions with environmental factors (broadly defined to include diet, drugs, infectious agents, chemicals, physical agents, and behavioral factors). As will be illustrated, genetic information can come from inherited variation in germ cells or acquired variation in somatic

---

3. Down syndrome is caused by trisomy 21—the inheritance of an extra copy of chro-   mosome 21.

cells[4] (such as in cancer) or could be associated with gene products and expression. Such information can be used in diagnosis, treatment, prediction, and prevention of all diseases, not only genetic disorders. For traditional single-gene disorders, when genetic information is obtained on patients and their relatives, it is used for diagnosing or predicting a genetic disease state. For most human diseases, however, genetic information at one locus is modified by information from many other loci and their interaction with nongenetic risk factors, so much so, that the sum of such genetic information cannot be thought of as disease state but more as biological markers or disease risk factors.

Muin J. Khoury, *Genetics and Genomics in Practice: The Continuum from Genetic Disease to Genetic Information in Health and Disease*, 5 GENETICS IN MED. 261 (2003).

The following section explores the role of genomics in health and health care. The discussion ranges from current applications of genetic knowledge to future uses. We begin with the most frequently used genetic methods—testing and screening. The section goes on to "imagine the future." There are multiple potential applications of genetic knowledge including pharmacogenomics, gene therapy, and genetic enhancement that may revolutionize (for good or bad) health care and public health.

A.   GENETIC TESTING AND SCREENING

Kennedy Institute of Ethics, *Genetic Testing and Genetic Screening*

KIEJ (Updated 2004).

The completion of the mapping of the human genome ... shifts the spotlight of ethical inquiry from general questions about genetic research to specific issues with such topics as genetic screening. Ethical dilemmas with genetic testing and screening were foreseen over three decades ago by bioethicists who asked whether questionable applications could stop "legitimate pursuits" and whether genetic disease might come to be viewed as "transmissible" in the sense of being contagious.

     . . .

In 1983, the report of the U.S. President's Commission for the Study of Ethical Problems in Medicine and Biomedical and Behavioral Research predicted that before the end of the century genetic screening and counseling would become major components of both public health and individual medical care. Following the identification of a gene linked to breast cancer, *BRCA1*, Dr. Francis Sellers Collins, director of the National Center for Human Genome Research, said that "it is not inconceivable that every woman in America may want to be screened for this gene. The economic, ethical, and counseling issues will be very daunting." While genetic testing for *BRCA* mutations has been available commercially since 1996, the results of an evaluation done by the Centers for Disease Control and

---

4. Germ cells are sperm, ovum, and their developmental precursors; somatic cells are all cells other than germ cells.

Prevention (CDC) indicated that population-based screening "... is not recommended because of the complexity of test interpretation and limited data on clinical validity and utility." Educational materials about gene tests and international directories of clinics and laboratories providing genetic testing services can be found on the Web.

As a greater proportion of the U.S. population lives beyond 85 years of age, interest in genetic testing for end-of-life conditions such as Alzheimer Disease (AD) continues to grow. Stephen G. Post observes that the "too-hopeful" general public has assigned a degree of scientific certainty to the as yet preliminary genetic findings for AD, and that teaching critical thinking skills about genetic testing to the general public is of the highest priority.

The [US Congress' Office of Technology Assessment (OTA)] defines genetic testing as "the use of specific assays to determine the genetic status of individuals already suspected to be at high risk for a particular inherited condition. The terms genetic test, genetic assay, and genetic analysis are used interchangeably to mean the actual laboratory examination of samples." In contrast, genetic screening usually uses the same assays employed for genetic testing but is distinguished from genetic testing by its target population. The National Academy of Sciences (NAS) defines screening as the systematic search of populations for persons with latent, early, or asymptomatic disease.

Philip Boyle points out that the language used to describe genetic variation is important and asks what words should be used: "*Defects, flaws, deleterious genes, disorders*, or the more neutral *conditions*? Using words such as *normal*—and its corollary, *abnormal*—is likely to foster stigmatization and discrimination."

Areas of focus in genetic testing include: prenatal diagnosis, newborn screening, carrier screening, forensic screening, and susceptibility screening.

Prenatal diagnosis discerns whether a fetus is at risk for various identifiable genetic diseases or traits. Prenatal diagnosis is made using amniotic fluid, fetal cells, and fetal or maternal blood cells obtained during amniocentesis testing; alpha fetoprotein assays or chorionic villus sampling; or ultrasound tomography, which creates fetal images on a screen. Another method, known as fetoscopy, uses a camera on a needle inserted in the uterus to view the fetus. Since prenatal screening began in 1966, the number of metabolic defects and genetic disorders that can be diagnosed prenatally has expanded greatly. There is also discussion of requiring testing for parents who are participating in an in vitro fertilization program and are at genetic risk. Preimplantation testing of embryos might ensure that only embryos free of genetic disease or problem traits would be placed in the uterus.[5]

Newborn screening involves the analysis of blood or tissue samples taken in early infancy in order to detect genetic diseases for which early intervention can avert serious health problems or death. Newborn screen-

5. [Eds.—Prenatal screening will be discussed further in terms of genetic en-   hancement, *infra*. See also discussion of prenatal screening Chapter 5, Sec. II, *infra*.]

ing first came into use in the early 1960s with the ability to test newborns for a rare metabolic disease, phenylketonuria (PKU), which causes mental retardation and can be prevented by following a special diet. Two other examples of newborn screening, in place since the 1970s, are the testing of African–American infants for sickle cell anemia and Ashkenazic Jews for Tay–Sachs disease.

Carrier screening identifies individuals with a gene or a chromosome abnormality that may cause problems either for offspring or the person screened. The testing of blood or tissue samples can indicate the existence of a particular genetic trait, changes in chromosomes, or changes in DNA that are associated with inherited diseases in asymptomatic individuals. Groups tested include persons at risk or a cross-section of the general public for occurrence statistics. Examples of carrier screening include the previously mentioned tests for sickle cell anemia and for Tay–Sachs disease. In the last few years, screening tests have also been developed for cystic fibrosis, Duchenne muscular dystrophy, hemophilia, Huntington's disease, and neurofibromatosis. Recently it also has become possible to identify certain cancer prone individuals through genetic testing.

Forensic testing, which is the newest area to use information obtained from genetic testing, seeks to discover a genetic linkage between suspects and evidence discovered in criminal investigations. Test results have been presented as proof of innocence or guilt in court cases, and jury verdicts have been based on this type of genetic evidence. Critics note that forensic laboratories often test just once, unlike research laboratories, which test many times, and that mistakes can be made. Concern is expressed, too, about the confidentiality of DNA profiles obtained from criminal investigations and stored in national police databanks. Debate now centers on standards and quality control, but it is accepted that the technologies accurately detect genetic differences between humans and are "new, powerful tools to clear the innocent and convict the guilty." Since DNA is unique, many people are reluctant to see such information become part of any national database, which might include information not only about identity but also about proclivity toward disease or behavior.

Finally, **susceptibility screening** is used to identify workers who may be susceptible to toxic substances that are found in their workplace and may cause future disabilities. In 1986, Morton Hunt wrote in the *New York Times Magazine* that 390,000 workers become disabled by occupational illness each year; he thinks these illnesses are precipitated by genetic hypersusceptibility since co-workers are unaffected.

In an early classic work, the National Academy of Sciences says screening can be used for medical intervention and research; for reproductive information; for enumeration, monitoring, and surveillance; and for registries of genetic disease and disability. Many factors affect the use of any routine screening: customs of care (including both professional guidelines and possible malpractice); education of the public about the results and limitations of genetic testing; availability, training, and education of personnel to perform testing; financing of such screening (particularly third-party payor responsibilities); stigmatization and discrimination issues; quality assurance of laboratories and DNA test kits; and costs and cost effectiveness.

. . .

Not everyone thinks that the growing field of genetic testing and screening is beneficial. The potential problems raised both by those who favor testing and screening and those who oppose it are similar, but one faction thinks that regulatory or legislative solutions to the problems can be found while concerned opponents find the knowledge itself less valuable and the problems unsolvable. Opponents of widespread genetic testing and screening regard the acceptance of eugenic theories and scientists' inability to control outcomes of their genetic research as dangerous. They foresee a need to outlaw technologies that threaten privacy or civil rights and a need to protect against genetic discrimination. "We need to engage in active debates about the practical consequences of genetic forecasts for our self-image, our health, our work lives, our social relationships, and our privacy." Disability advocates and feminists have criticized genetic screening because they think it fosters intolerance for less than perfect people.

Another possible negative effect is the pressure that might be placed on individuals, as a result of cost-benefit analysis, to test or to be tested. Individuals might thereby be forced to know their genetic predispositions, to tell others, or to act to save society long-term costs resulting in a "new eugenics based, not on undesirable characteristics, but rather on cost-saving." Now that British insurers have government approval to use the results of screening for Huntington's disease to assess insurance premiums, consumer groups say that individuals will be reluctant to have such tests and risk denial of coverage. On the other hand, Lowe points out that genetic testing will not create more illness than presently exists, and it could lead to a reduction in costs due to early treatment.[3] Lippman suggests that control over genetics would create an elite who could control the general populace, particularly if mandatory testing or intervention were viewed as a community good.[4] Other potential adverse effects of such screening include the development of prejudice against those tested and found at risk and the feeling of tested persons that they are predetermined victims of fate or are being branded as "abnormal."

. . .

Issues of confidentiality loom large in discussions of genetic testing and screening. According to the Privacy Commission of Canada, genetic privacy has two dimensions: protection from the intrusions of others and protection from one's own secrets....

The President's Commission, in a 1983 study, concluded that genetic information "should not be given to unrelated third parties, such as insurers or employers, without the explicit and informed consent of the person screened or a surrogate for that person." The Commission recom-

3. Robert Lowe, *Genetic Testing and Insurance: Apocalypse Now?* 40 DRAKE LAW REVIEW 507–532 (1991).

4. Abby Lippman, *Mother Matters: A Fresh Look at Prenatal Genetic Testing*, 5 ISSUES IN REPRODUCTIVE AND GENETIC ENGINEERING 141–154 (1992).

mended that information stored in computers should be coded and that compulsory genetic screening cannot be justified to create a health gene pool or to reduce health costs. More recently, the NIH/DOE Working Group on the Ethical, Legal and Social Implications of Human Genome Research recommended that health insurers should consider a moratorium on the use of genetic tests in underwriting.

In the area of data protection and professional secrecy, genetic information for health care, the diagnosis or prevention of disease, and for research should be stored separately from other personal records. In addition, those handling the information should be bound by professional rules of confidentiality and legislative rules, and any unexpected findings should be given only to the person tested.

The literature on genetic discrimination suggests several areas of sensitivity: the workplace, where employers may choose to test job applicants, or those already employed, for susceptibility to toxic substances or for genetic variations that could lead to future disabilities, thereby raising health or workmen's compensation costs; the insurers (either life or health insurance companies) who might use genetic information or tests as criteria for denying coverage or require reproductive testing to be done for cost containment purposes; and law enforcement officials, who may test and/or use information without informed consent. Thomas H. Murray thinks that "genetic testing in the workplace was a putative public health measure in its old form and now is used as a means of saving money or promoting health." He opines that access to genetic testing involves considerations of justice since genetic testing competes with other scarce resources and it may emphasize racial and ethnic differences.

. . .

As early as the 1970s, the National Academy of Sciences looked at legal principles and raised questions about the extent of disclosure of test results to the person screened, the extent of disclosure to others without the consent of the person screened, the constitutional barriers to mandatory screening by states, and the constitutional difficulties encountered if screening is done by racial or ethnic group. In a 1992 report, OTA offers six areas for possible action by Congress: genetics education for the public; genetics training and education of health care professionals; discrimination (access to health care coverage); laboratory and other regulation; means of automating diagnostics; and facilitating use of genetic assays in clinical practice.

In an article aimed at family physicians, Howard Stein writes of the physician-patient relationship and reminds his fellow physicians that "[g]enetic knowledge does not occur in a social vacuum. The scientific account is neither the only story, nor the entire story. Decisions to know or not to know, to have children or not to have children, to label as diseased or not, are part of wider life histories, language, and group fantasies." Legal challenges, government regulation, extensive education, and collective bargaining will all be part of the ongoing process needed to solve the complex dilemmas that result from widespread genetic testing and genetic screening.

NOTES AND QUESTIONS

1. *The Future of Genetic Testing.* There are currently some 1,000 genetic tests, 90% of which are related to single-gene disorders. Gene tests (also called DNA-based tests) are the newest and most sophisticated techniques to test for genetic disorders and involve direct examination of the DNA molecule itself. Other genetic tests include biochemical tests for gene products such as enzymes and other proteins and for microscopic examination of stained or fluorescent chromosomes. Currently, testing can cost hundreds or thousands of dollars, depending on the number of mutations tested. However, with advancing technology, scientists are confident that genetic testing will become far less expensive and therefore more accessible to the larger population. In the near future it may be possible for a physician to order a battery of genetic tests from a single drop of blood at a reasonable cost. This may dramatically improve lives by clarifying diagnoses and directing physicians toward appropriate interventions. Interventions can include genetic therapy, changes in diet or environmental exposures, or reproductive counseling. Despite the benefits, widespread availability of genetic tests raises difficult social, ethical, and legal questions.

2. *Would Widespread Use of Genetic Testing Lead to Breaches of Privacy, Stigmatization, and Discrimination?* Much of the early literature on genetics focused on the potential for invasion of privacy, stigma, and discrimination. Advocacy groups feared that genetic information was deeply private, revealing something quite intimate about individual lives. If this information were disclosed to family and friends it could cause stigmatization; if it were disclosed to employers it could cause discrimination in the workplace; and if it were disclosed to insurers it could result in exclusion from coverage. As a result, much legislative activity has been devoted toward genetic privacy and anti-discrimination at the federal and state level. *See* Lawrence O. Gostin et al., GENETICS POLICY AND LAW: A REPORT FOR POLICYMAKERS (National Conference of State Legislatures, 2001); discussion Sec. IV, *infra*. Some fear that genetic discrimination may extend beyond the health care system. What if genetic tests revealed a likelihood of adverse personality traits such as anti-social behavior or dangerousness? Could this information be used by, say, immigration, criminal justice, or homeland security officials?

3. *What Benefits Does Genetic Testing Offer for Patients and Populations?* Almost everyone supports genetic testing that is reliable and which leads to cost effective interventions. The health care system can improve lives by accurately identifying those with genetic disorders and providing beneficial counseling or treatment. For example, all newborns in the United States are screened for phenylketonuria (PKU) and changes in diet for those found positive have proved highly effective in preventing the mental retardation that PKU can cause. Consider briefly the capacity of genetic testing and screening to move health care from a palliative endeavor to a more preventative undertaking:

> It is likely that the major genetic factors involved in susceptibility to common diseases like diabetes, heart disease, Alzheimer's disease, cancer and mental illness will be uncovered in the course of the next 5 to 7 years. For many of these conditions, altering diet, lifestyle, or medical surveillance could be beneficial for high-risk individuals. That will open the door to wider availability of genetic tests to identify individual predispositions to future illness, potentially for virtually anyone. If applied properly, this could usher in a new era of individualized preventive medicine that could have considerable health benefits.

Francis S. Collins, A Brief Primer on Genetic Testing, Address at the World Economic Forum (January 24, 2003).

4. *Should Genetic Testing be Encouraged if it has Insufficient Predictive Value or if There are no Effective Interventions?* Genetic testing becomes far more controversial if it is insufficiently reliable and there are no clear medical interventions. This is true for predictive genetic tests such as for breast cancer or Huntington's disease. Patients may have unrealistic expectations for these kinds of tests, believing that they are highly scientific. In fact, there is a great deal of variability in genetic conditions. A positive test result does not mean that a person will necessarily develop clinical disease, but rather provides a *range* of probability. Even if an individual does develop clinical disease, the test cannot predict when symptoms will appear or how serious they will be. Just as important, a positive test may not yield unequivocal benefits. Certainly, the individual may choose to use the information for life planning (e.g., Huntington's disease) or attempt extreme forms of prophylaxis (radical mastectomy for a positive *BRCA* test). Beyond these measures, medicine can offer very little in terms of interventions. Consider this sobering assessment of genetic determinism:

> People tend to see genetic information as more definitive and predictive than other types of data, in the sense that "you cannot change your genes" and that "genes tell all about your future." This notion of genetic determinism, however, includes an unwarranted sense of inevitability, because it reflects a fundamental failure to understand the nature of biologic systems. The DNA sequence is not the Book of Life. Human characteristics are the product of complex interactions over time between genes—both a person's own and those of other organisms—and the environment. Both germ-line and somatic cells undergo mutations, the latter being a primary way in which cancer develops. Moreover, a pathogenic mutation does not doom one to ill health; many diseases can be treated. As is true for so many conditions in medicine, clinicians have a variable but usually limited ability to predict when, how severely, and even whether a person with a genetic predisposition to a certain illness is going to become ill.

Ellen Wright Clayton, *Ethical, Legal, and Social Implications of Genomic Medicine*, 349 NEW ENG. J. MED. 562–569 (2003).

5. *Is Reproductive Counseling following Genetic Testing Socially Acceptable?* Sometimes the only clear intervention is counseling to allow couples to reproductively plan. Women may choose to avoid or terminate pregnancies armed with the information that their children have a probability of a genetic impairment such as Down Syndrome, Cystic Fibrosis, or Tay Sachs disease. Needless to say, reproductive counseling is highly controversial, partly because of the infamous history of eugenics and partly because of contemporary political battles over abortion. There is also the voice of the disability movement arguing that a decision not to have a child because it will be less-than-perfect sends precisely the wrong message. Those who believe that a woman has the right to terminate a pregnancy for *any* reason may still pause if the reason given is that the infant will not live up to certain expectations for health, intelligence, and/or attractiveness. *See* Adrienne Asche, et al., *Respecting Persons with Disabilities and Preventing Disability: Is There a Conflict?, in* THE HUMAN RIGHTS OF PERSONS WITH INTELLECTUAL DISABILITIES: DIFFERENT BUT EQUAL (Stanley S. Herr et al. eds., 2003); discussion of eugenics and genetics, *infra* Sec. V.

Sozos J. Fasouliotis & Joseph G. Schenker, *BRCA1 and BRCA2 Gene Mutations: Decision–Making Dilemmas Concerning Testing and Management*

55 OBSTETRICAL & GYNECOLOGICAL SURVEY 373–384 (2000).

Familial clustering of breast and ovarian cancer cases has drawn the attention of scientists for years, but it was not until 1971 that the breast-ovarian cancer syndrome was defined. Since then, several population-based epidemiologic studies also suggested that heredity contributes to the development of some breast and ovarian cancers.

At the same time, other groups initiated studies that sought to elucidate the genetic basis of this form of cancer, culminating in the discovery that many cases of early-onset familial breast and ovarian cancer were caused by a gene on the long arm of chromosome 17. An intense gene-hunting effort resulted in the identification of the *BRCA1* gene in the fall of 1994; and, in 1995, a second gene, named *BRCA2*, was also detected. These two genes are probably responsible for the vast majority of inherited breast and ovarian cancers (75–90 percent), and their discovery ushered in the era of genetic susceptibility testing for cancer.

The identification ... of genes resulting in an inherited predisposition for breast and ovarian cancer offers potential for novel therapeutic intervention. The opportunity to answer questions about the population genetics of cancers that previously had been confounded by epidemiological complexities. The genetic epidemiology of breast and ovarian cancer attributable to *BRCA* gene mutations has become increasingly well characterized. These technological advances encompass an equally significant body of scientific, ethical, legal, and psychological questions and issues pertaining to the most appropriate and effective use of this technology. Although most published consensus opinions have generally urged caution to one degree or another in the widespread implementation of genetic screening for cancer predisposition, it is evident that tests for mutations recently have become commercially available and that commercial availability will become more widespread in the very near future

. . .

BRCA1 and *BRCA2* Testing: Ethical and Social Implications

Genetic testing, as a means of identifying members of families who encompass a high risk of developing cancer, has been considered as one of the most important medical advances. However, uncontrolled access to genetic testing raised a dilemma, especially when preliminary reports indicated that there was a strong interest both in the general population and in high-risk families for performing the test. The complexities and, for the time being, also uncertainties of giving or receiving genetic counseling about the results of such tests in addition to complex medical, scientific, and technical matters such as the reliability of genetic screening tests, the interpretability and predictive value of positive test results, and the clinical ability to prevent cancers in presymptomatic individuals who test positive, prompted medical and scientific organizations to develop criteria for appropriate population testing.

The vast majority of persons who currently seek genetic screening and counseling are usually women with a family history of breast and/or ovarian cancer. The detection of a *BRCA* mutation in a woman may initiate a search for that particular mutation in other female members of that family. In addition, male family members are also encouraged to consider testing because *BRCA1* mutations are found to be associated with an increased risk of colon and prostate cancer and *BRCA2* mutations with an increased risk of breast cancer.

However, from experience to date, serious concerns are raised about our ability to identify appropriate patients for genetic testing when considering the relationship between family history and mutation status in families with breast and/or ovarian cancer patients. Patients from high-penetrance families can be identified easily, but testing only these patients will miss many mutation carriers. On the other hand, testing all women from families with suggestive family histories will produce a very low yield of positive results and will still miss those mutation carriers with negative family histories

. . .

Despite the biologic uncertainties and the potential discrimination and other social and personal problems, biotechnology companies have developed and marketed tests for the detection of *BRCA* gene mutations. The risk of a possible financial and psychological exploitation of the public are obvious. Test providers explain the commercialization of such tests as a result of the increasing public demand and that the incompleteness of our knowledge and the problems involved in the incorporation of testing into clinical practice do not provide sufficient grounds for withholding information. The well-known principle in cancer diagnosis and treatment that states that "prevention is better than treatment, and that early diagnosis is better than late diagnosis" is often used as an argument by these companies that propose that genetic predisposition testing will aid in both prevention and testing. They conclude that insisting on additional research before recommending widespread screening or suggesting that it should not be a decision for the patient alone is seen as unduly cautious or paternalistic.

Although the patient's right to information is one that should greatly be respected, several other issues, mainly those related to the ethical, legal, and psychosocial implications of test results, should in no way be ignored. Misuse of genetic information potentially could have disastrous implications for the psychological well being, family relationships, future marital status, employment, and life or health insurance issues.

Because the fear of genetic discrimination exists, the issues of disclosure of information and confidentiality prove to be essential. Healthcare professionals should actively advocate that genetic testing for *BRCA1* and *BRCA2* and other mutations be used constructively to modify rather than to stigmatize individuals or deprive them of appropriate care

. . .

Although genetic testing on the children of *BRCA* carriers may be of interest, currently there is a debate as to whether parents have the authority to verify the gene status of their child for such genetic diseases as hereditary breast-ovarian cancer or Huntington disease or for any other late-onset gene that does not manifest until adulthood without that child's consent. Because the results of such a study may "stigmatize" an otherwise "normal" child for the rest of his life, a limit on parental authority may be justified. On the other hand, the serious health implications of these genetic mutations suggests that intervention, including the early application of preventive measures or even gene correction, may make it desirable to know the individual's genetic status at a young age. However, because interventional strategies are currently limited, the ethical opinion widely accepted is that parents should not be free to have their children screened for late-onset genetic diseases until the children are able to give their consents

. . .

Conclusion

Physicians need to recognize the limitations and complexities of the new information, and the implementations that this might have on their patients, including the risks to patients of being stigmatized as susceptible by insurers or employers, and the psychological and social risks that may revolve with the application of this new technology. Nevertheless, genetic testing for inherited cancer susceptibility is a reality, and thus physicians are called to prepare and help their patients to face these new and challenging opportunities. Despite the current recognized difficulties and uncertainties, in the future, the ultimate goal should be the development of new and more effective management strategies so that in cases of identification of *BRCA1* and *BRCA2* or other cancer-susceptibility genes, physicians cannot only predict future risks, but also reduce those risks or prevent the disease entirely before it can occur.

NOTES AND QUESTIONS

1. *The Psychological Impact of Genetic Testing.* Fasouliotis and Schenker note the psychological stress associated with genetic testing. After all, a woman informed that she is at high risk of breast or ovarian cancer is deeply affected. How should the potential for psychological harm impact the availability and use of genetic testing in general? If there are few, if any, effective medical interventions for a disease, should the potential for psychological harm militate against genetic testing?

2. *Would Patients be Placed under too Much Pressure to use Genetic Technologies?* Despite the limited utility, patients may be under considerable pressure to use available testing technology. Businesses may aggressively market the tests (e.g., direct-to-consumer advertisements); managed care companies and physicians may feel obliged to make them available due to patient demand or liability concerns; and family members may be keenly interested in the results. This might lead to difficult ethical dilemmas such as whether individuals would seek tests for the benefit of family members. Would patients have an expectation of confidentiality or would they feel obliged to disclose the test result to interested family members? *See* further, Sec. IV, *infra*.

3. *What Forms of Regulation, if any, are Necessary for Genetic Testing?* Some scholars and practitioners have expressed concern because few regulations exist to evaluate the accuracy and reliability of genetic testing. Most tests are categorized as services, which the Food and Drug Administration (FDA) does not regulate, and only a few states have established regulatory guidelines. Given that a handful of companies have started marketing test kits directly to the public, is this lack of government oversight troubling or will existing market forces adequately protect users' well being? Some of these companies make dubious claims about how the kits not only test for disease but also serve as tools for customizing medicine, vitamins, and foods to each individual's genetic makeup. Is it likely that individuals who purchase such kits will seek out genetic counseling to help them interpret results and make the best possible decisions regarding their personal welfare?

Katskee v. Blue Cross/Blue Shield

Supreme Court of Nebraska, 1994.
245 Neb. 808, 515 N.W.2d 645.

■ WHITE, J.

In January 1990, upon the recommendation of her gynecologist, Dr. Larry E. Roffman, appellant consulted with Dr. Henry T. Lynch regarding her family's history of breast and ovarian cancer, and particularly her health in relation to such a history. After examining appellant and investigating her family's medical history, Dr. Lynch diagnosed her as suffering from a genetic condition known as breast-ovarian carcinoma syndrome. Dr. Lynch then recommended that appellant have a total abdominal hysterectomy and bilateral salpingo-oophorectomy, which involves the removal of the uterus, the ovaries, and the fallopian tubes. Dr. Roffman concurred in Dr. Lynch's diagnosis and agreed that the recommended surgery was the most medically appropriate treatment available.

After considering the diagnosis and recommended treatment, appellant decided to have the surgery. In preparation for the surgery, appellant filed a claim with Blue Cross/Blue Shield. Both Drs. Lynch and Roffman wrote to Blue Cross/Blue Shield and explained the diagnosis and their basis for recommending the surgery. Initially, Blue Cross/Blue Shield sent a letter to appellant and indicated that it might pay for the surgery. Two weeks before the surgery, Dr. Roger Mason, the chief medical officer for Blue Cross/Blue Shield, wrote to appellant and stated that Blue Cross/Blue Shield would not cover the cost of the surgery. Nonetheless, appellant had the surgery in November 1990.

Appellant filed this action for breach of contract, seeking to recover $6,022.57 in costs associated with the surgery.... [The District Court granted a motion for summary judgment filed by Blue Cross/Blue Shield].

. . .

Blue Cross/Blue Shield contends that appellant's costs are not covered by the insurance policy. The policy provides coverage for services which are medically necessary. The policy defines "medically necessary" as follows:

> The services, procedures, drugs, supplies or Durable Medical Equipment provided by the Physician, Hospital or other health care provider, in the diagnosis or *treatment of the Covered Person's Illness,* Injury, or Pregnancy, which are:

> *Appropriate for the symptoms and diagnosis of the patient's Illness,* Injury *or* Pregnancy

. . .

> We shall determine whether services provided are Medically Necessary.
> Services will not automatically be considered Medically Necessary because
> they have been ordered or provided by a Physician.

(Emphasis supplied.) Blue Cross/Blue Shield denied coverage because it
concluded that appellant's condition does not constitute an illness, and thus
the treatment she received was not medically necessary....

An insurance policy is to be construed as any other contract to give
effect to the parties' intentions at the time the contract was made. When
the terms of the contract are clear, a court may not resort to rules of
construction, and the terms are to be accorded their plain and ordinary
meaning as the ordinary or reasonable person would understand them. In
such a case, a court shall seek to ascertain the intention of the parties from
the plain language of the policy.

When interpreting the plain meaning of the terms of an insurance
policy, we have stated that the "natural and obvious meaning of the
provisions in a policy is to be adopted in preference to a fanciful, curious, or
hidden meaning." ...

Applying these principles, our interpretation of the language of the
terms employed in the policy is guided by definitions found in dictionaries,
and additionally by judicial opinions rendered by other courts which have
considered the meaning of these terms....

[Dorland's Illustrated Medical Dictionary (27th ed. 1988) defines disease as:]

> [A]ny deviation from or interruption of the normal structure or function of
> any part, organ, or system ... of the body that is manifested by a
> characteristic set of symptoms and signs and whose etiology [theory of
> origin or cause], pathology [origin or cause], and prognosis may be known
> or unknown....

The Iowa Supreme Court considered the meaning of the terms "disease" and "illness" as these terms are used in insurance policies. In
Witcraft v. Sundstrand Health & Dis. Gr., 420 N.W.2d 785 (Iowa 1988), the
Iowa Supreme Court stated that the terms "illness," "sickness," and
"disease" are ordinarily synonymous in the context of an insurance policy
and that these terms are defined as a " 'morbid condition of the body, a
deviation from the healthy or normal condition of any of the functions or
tissues of the body.' " *Id.* at 788 (quoting 45 C.J.S. *Insurance* § 893
(1946))....

. . .

We find that the language used in the policy at issue in the present
case is not reasonably susceptible of differing interpretations and thus not
ambiguous. The plain and ordinary meaning of the terms "bodily disorder"
and "disease," as they are used in the policy to define illness, encompasses
any abnormal condition of the body or its components of such a degree that
in its natural progression would be expected to be problematic; a deviation
from the healthy or normal state affecting the functions or tissues of the
body; an inherent defect of the body; or a morbid physical or mental state
which deviates from or interrupts the normal structure or function of any

part, organ, or system of the body and which is manifested by a characteristic set of symptoms and signs.

The issue then becomes whether appellant's condition—breast-ovarian carcinoma syndrome—constitutes an illness.

Blue Cross/Blue Shield argues that appellant did not suffer from an illness because she did not have cancer. Blue Cross/Blue Shield characterizes appellant's condition only as a "predisposition to an illness (cancer)" and fails to address whether the condition itself constitutes an illness. Brief for appellee at 13. This failure is traceable to Dr. Mason's denial of appellant's claim. Despite acknowledging his inexperience and lack of knowledge about this specialized area of cancer research, Dr. Mason denied appellant's claim without consulting any medical literature or research regarding breast-ovarian carcinoma syndrome. Moreover, Dr. Mason made the decision without submitting appellant's claim for consideration to a claim review committee. . . .

Appellant's condition was diagnosed as breast-ovarian carcinoma syndrome. To adequately determine whether the syndrome constitutes an illness, we must first understand the nature of the syndrome.

.   .   .

According to Dr. Lynch, some forms of cancer occur on a hereditary basis. Breast and ovarian cancer are such forms of cancer which may occur on a hereditary basis. It is our understanding that the hereditary occurrence of this form of cancer is related to the genetic makeup of the woman. In this regard, the genetic deviation has conferred changes which are manifest in the individual's body and at some time become capable of being diagnosed.

.   .   .

Women diagnosed with the syndrome have at least a 50–percent chance of developing breast and/or ovarian cancer, whereas unaffected women have only a 1.4–percent risk of developing breast or ovarian cancer. In addition to the genetic deviation, the family history, and the significant risks associated with this condition, the diagnosis also may encompass symptoms of anxiety and stress, which some women experience because of their knowledge of the substantial likelihood of developing cancer.

The procedures for detecting the onset of ovarian cancer are ineffective. Generally, by the time ovarian cancer is capable of being detected, it has already developed to a very advanced stage, making treatment relatively unsuccessful. Drs. Lynch and Roffman agreed that the standard of care for treating women with breast carcinoma syndrome ordinarily involves surveillance methods. However, for women at an inordinately high risk for ovarian cancer, such as appellant, the standard of care may require radical surgery which involves the removal of the uterus, ovaries, and fallopian tubes.

Dr. Lynch explained that the surgery is labeled "prophylactic" and that the surgery is prophylactic as to the prevention of the onset of cancer. Dr. Lynch also stated that appellant's condition itself is the result of a genetic deviation from the normal, healthy state and that the recommended surgery treats that condition by eliminating or significantly reducing the presence of the condition and its likely development.

. . .

In light of the plain and ordinary meaning of the terms "illness," "bodily disorder," and "disease," we find that appellant's condition constitutes an illness within the meaning of the policy. . . .

Although appellant's condition was not detectable by physical evidence or a physical examination, it does not necessarily follow that appellant does not suffer from an illness. The record establishes that a woman who suffers from breast-ovarian carcinoma syndrome does have a physical state which significantly deviates from the physical state of a normal, healthy woman. Specifically, appellant suffered from a different or abnormal genetic constitution which, when combined with a particular family history of hereditary cancer, significantly increases the risk of a devastating outcome.

We are mindful that not every condition which itself constitutes a predisposition to another illness is necessarily an illness within the meaning of an insurance policy. . . .

. . .

In the present case, the medical evidence regarding the nature of breast-ovarian carcinoma syndrome persuades us that appellant suffered from a bodily disorder or disease and, thus, suffered from an illness as defined by the insurance policy. Blue Cross/Blue Shield, therefore, is not entitled to judgment as a matter of law. Moreover, we find that appellant's condition did constitute an illness within the meaning of the policy. We reverse the decision of the district court and remand the cause for further proceedings.

NOTES AND QUESTIONS

1. In *Katskee*, the court found that a genetic makeup entailing a fifty percent likelihood of contracting ovarian cancer, which is difficult to detect and progresses swiftly toward a terminal stage, constitutes a disease. What about a 25 percent disposition to ovarian cancer? What about a 50 percent disposition to a treatable illness? Should a patient be financially forced by her insurance company to run the risk of contracting a treatable illness and enduring the associated pain and suffering when effective prophylactic treatment is available?

2. *Who Should Pay for the Costs of Prophylactic Treatment?* The opinion of the Supreme Court of Nebraska in *Katskee* is important not only for defining the terms "illness," "sickness," and "disease," but for considering the extent to which health insurance contracts cover prophylactic medical procedures. As genetic screening enables modern medicine to predict future disease, patients increasingly may seek prophylactic interventions. Who should decide whether such preventive treatments are medically necessary: the treating physician, the patient, or the third party payer? To what extent should cost effectiveness be determinative and, in the cost benefit calculation, what weight should be given to the anxiety of patients and their families?

B.   PHARMACOGENOMICS

Due to the complexity and needed research, another application of genetic knowledge, pharmacogenomics, has only been used to a limited extent. Pharmacogenomics, literally the intersection of pharmaceuticals and genetics, is the study of how an individual's genetic inheritance affects the body's response to drugs. It holds the promise that drugs might one day be tailor-made for individuals and adapted to each person's genetic make-up. Environment, diet, age, lifestyle, and state-of-health all can influence a person's response to medicines, but understanding an individual's genetic makeup is thought to be the key to creating personalized drugs with greater efficacy and safety.

Allen D. Roses, *Pharmacogenetics and the Practice of Medicine*

405 NATURE 857 (2000).

"If it were not for the great variability among individuals medicine might as well be a science and not an art." The thoughts of Sir William Osler in 1892 reflect the view of medicine over the past 100 years. The role of physicians in making the necessary judgments about the medicines that they prescribe is often referred to as an art, reflecting the lack of objective data available to make decisions that are tailored to individual patients. Just over a hundred years later we are on the verge of being able to identify inherited differences between individuals which can predict each patient's response to a medicine. This ability will have far-reaching benefits in the discovery, development and delivery of medicines. Sir William Osler, if he were alive today, would be re-considering his view of medicine as an art not a science.

Every individual is a product of the interaction of their genes and the environment. Pharmacogenetics is the study of how genetic differences influence the variability in patients' responses to drugs. Through the use of pharmacogenetics, we will soon be able to profile variations between individuals' DNA to predict responses to a particular medicine. The medical significance and economic value of a simple, predictive medicine response profile, which will provide information on the likelihood of efficacy and safety of a drug for an individual patient, will change the practice and economics of medicine. The ability to rapidly profile patients who are likely to benefit from a particular medicine will also streamline drug development and provide opportunities to develop discrete medicines concurrently for different patients with similar disease phenotypes. Other than relatively rare and highly penetrant diseases related to mutations of a single gene inherited in families, science has never before had the tools to characterize the nuances of inherited metabolic variations that interact over time and lead to common diseases. Powerful pharmacogenetic research tools are now becoming available to classify the heterogeneity of disease as well as individual responses to medicines.

An ongoing ethical debate concerning potential genetic applications and the impact on individuals and families accompanies scientific advances.

Clearly defined terminology should form the basis for informative discussions so that the word "genetics" is not demonized. For example, tests that are specific to disease genes can help diagnose disease, determine the carrier status of an individual or predict the occurrence of disease. These are quite distinct from profiles that, for example, are specific for genes involved in drug metabolism, which provide information on how a medicine will be metabolized in an individual. In the near future (1–3 years) there will be non-disease-and non-gene-specific pharmacogenetic profiles developed to determine whether an individual is likely to respond to a medicine and/or to not experience serious side effects. Language needs to be more precise so that there can be clarity, especially for public policy debates. Pharmacogenetics is not gene therapy, not genetically modified foods, not genetic engineering, and not cloning of humans or their organs. Ethical, legal and social implications for "genetic tests" of single-gene mutational diseases should not automatically be assumed for other non-disease-specific applications simply because they are labeled imprecisely as "genetic tests." Use of inaccurate terminology may hinder and delay the significant health-care benefits that will accrue from pharmacogenetics.

It is important to discuss how the benefits of pharmacogenetics can be applied to drug development and the provision of better health care today— 3–5 years before the widespread application of pharmacogenetics. This will enable the maximum benefits for patients to be obtained as rapidly as possible.

Mark A. Rothstein & Phyllis Griffin Epps, *Ethical and Legal Implications of Pharmacogenomics*

2 Nature Reviews Genetics 228–231 (2001).

A new model of clinical trials

Pharmacogenomics promises to reduce the time and money required to develop a drug. The ability to predict drug efficacy by genotyping participants during the early stages of clinical trials for a drug would enable researchers to recruit for later trials only those patients who, according to their genotype, are likely to benefit from the drug. As a result, clinical trials could become smaller, cheaper and faster to run.

. . .

As in other areas of genetic research that involve human subjects, the likely effect of pharmacogenomics on clinical trials raises important questions regarding informed consent, which might include considerations of privacy and confidentiality. Current ideas regarding patient autonomy and informed consent require that patients agree to enter into research on the basis of adequate information regarding the risks and consequences of participation. Genotyping that is appropriate to pharmacogenomic research might not produce information regarding susceptibility to disease or early death, but it might reveal evidence of genetic variation that could lead to individuals being classified as "difficult to treat", "less profitable to treat", or "more expensive to treat." The fear of being so classified could act as a barrier to the recruitment of research participants.

Fear of stigmatization might prove to be a significant barrier to participation in clinical trials among members of population subgroups. Genetic variations of pharmacological significance are known to occur in varying frequency in groups categorized by their ethnicity. For example, isoniazid is an anti-tuberculosis drug that is inactivated by acetylation; its impaired metabolism by slow acetylation causes it to accumulate to toxic levels. Variation in the *N*-acetyl transferase 2 (*NAT2*) gene accounts for whether individuals are rapid or slow acetylators of isoniazid, as well as of other therapeutic and carcinogenic compounds. About 50% of individuals in many Caucasian populations are genotypically slow acetylators of isoniazid, but more than 80% of individuals in certain Middle Eastern populations and fewer than 20% in the Japanese population have the slow acetylator phenotype.

The significance of data that imply a role for ethnicity in research has been a source of considerable debate among the research ethics community. One issue is how to advise potential research participants about the possibility of social harms from group-based findings even where the research is conducted without using the names of participants. Another matter of considerable debate in the literature is whether it is necessary or feasible to engage in community consultation when genetic research focuses on socially or politically distinct population subgroups.

Cost as a barrier to access

Pharmacogenomic drugs will be expensive, cheaper clinical trials notwithstanding. Collectively, the pharmaceutical industry is investing huge amounts of time and money in the development of new technologies that will yield drugs that are more effective than those already available. Without the opportunity to recoup their investment, drug companies will not continue their efforts. At the same time, insurance systems and consumers are struggling to absorb the rising costs of pharmaceutical products.

. . .

Those groups characterized by less-profitable genotypes are at risk of becoming therapeutic "orphans." At present, pharmaceuticals for rare diseases are termed "orphan drugs." The United States and Japan have enacted legislation to stimulate research and the development of orphan drugs through market mechanisms, such as tax-based cost incentives and time-limited monopolies, with varying degrees of governmental intervention. Canada, Sweden, France, the United Kingdom and other countries rely on broader national drug policies based on more substantial governmental intervention. As clinical trials increasingly consist of genetically non-diverse groups, policy makers will need to consider whether to expand the concepts underlying orphan drug policies to stimulate research into and the development of drugs for populations who, by virtue of their genetic make-up, face inequities in drug development efforts.

Cost might act as a barrier to access to pharmacogenomics in that the cost of participating in clinical trials or of the resulting drug therapy might be excluded from insurance coverage. Particularly in the United States, where managed care systems attempt to contain costs by rationing medical services, public and private third-party payers have refused or been reluctant to pay for treatments that they deem "experimental" or not "medically necessary." If consumers must absorb rising pharmaceutical costs, pharmacogenomics will not introduce new questions so much as it will intensify existing ones about equitable access to medical care.

Professional standards of care

. . .

As pharmacogenomic-based drugs increase in prevalence over the next several years, the use of genotyping or genetic testing as a diagnostic tool and the prescription of medications based on genotypic information will become the standard of care for physicians. Pharmacogenomics might provide greater information about the likelihood of a drug being effective or causing adverse reactions in persons possessing a particular genetic characteristic, and will certainly yield drugs that are more likely to be suitable for smaller, specific groups of individuals. By increasing the information available for consideration in drug therapy and the importance of matching the right drug to the right person, pharmacogenomics will raise the standard of care applicable to all involved in the safe prescription and distribution of pharmaceuticals.

As information regarding the genotype of an individual becomes increasingly important to safe prescription and dosage, pharmacists might be charged with greater knowledge of their customers' genetic information than they now require. The increased amount of genetic information in pharmacies raises privacy and confidentiality concerns, especially where pharmacists belong to large pharmacy chains or corporations with widely accessible, centralized records. For physicians and pharmacists, the issue of continuing professional education and record maintenance will become more important, not only for improving competence but also for preventing liability.

Pharmacogenomics is likely to increase the burden shared by the pharmaceutical industry to provide adequate warnings of the limitations and dangers of their products. In the United States, for example, pharmaceutical manufacturers have a duty to warn physicians about any known or knowable risks, or dangers, of the use of a manufactured drug. Many states in the US will impose strict liability on a drug company for harm caused by the failure to adequately warn against the dangerous propensities of a drug that it has manufactured.

. . .

In June 2000, four individuals filed a class action lawsuit against SmithKline Beecham, alleging that the manufacturer of a vaccine for Lyme disease knew that some individuals would be susceptible to arthritis on exposure to the vaccine because of their genotype, but failed to warn about this by labelling. Similar cases involve malpractice actions by the patient against the prescribing physician, who in turn seeks to recover against the manufacturer for failure to provide adequate information. Put simply, pharmacogenomics will raise the legal stakes for all involved whenever a patient suffers adverse reactions from the use of a drug that might have been contraindicated based on his or her genotype.

Conclusion

By lessening the uncertainty associated with the selection of drug targets and the design of human clinical studies in the development of new drugs, pharmacogenomics will result in the production of safer, more effective drugs for use in therapeutic medicine. The integration of pharmacogenomic technology into the drug development process and the practice of medicine will require consideration of ethical, social and legal questions. Answers to these questions might well determine the level of social acceptance and realization of the benefits of pharmacogenomic technology.

NOTES AND QUESTIONS

There are an estimated 100,000 deaths and 2 million hospitalizations that occur each year in the United States as a result of adverse drug response. Pharmacogenomics could materially reduce this high burden of morbidity and premature mortality, thus providing powerful benefits to society. Certainly, pharmacogenetics is not as socially and politically charged as gene therapy, genetic engineering, or cloning. Yet, as Mark Rothstein explains, there are important legal and ethical questions that remain unanswered. These questions apply at each stage of the research, development, and marketing processes. Would the requirements of informed consent and confidentiality change for human subjects and patients? How would the FDA approval procedures accommodate designer drugs and what could the agency do to ensure that physicians and patients receive full information about appropriate clinical uses? Would drug companies selectively develop and market drugs to more profitable sectors, thereby excluding certain races or classes from full access to the technology? Would the new medications be affordable to the population, particularly the poor or uninsured? Would pharmacogenomics fuel even higher drug costs with all the repercussions for employers, insurers, and government programs such as Medicaid and Medicare? Alternatively, might pharmacogenomics reduce costs by better tailoring drugs to patients' individual needs? If a pharmaceutical that is currently marketed to a large cross-section of the population is shown to be effective only in a small sub-group of that population, what disincentives might this create for industry to engage in expensive research and development? Finally, would individuals and groups be subjected to stigma due a label of "hard to treat?" These issues require society to formulate a careful response. Could the market ensure full and equitable access to the technology in a socially acceptable way? If not, what legal, regulatory, or liability reforms might be necessary? The choices are not easy.

C.   GENE THERAPY: GERMLINE V. SOMATIC CELL INTERVENTIONS

Kennedy Institute of Ethics, *Scope Note 24: Human Gene Therapy*

KIEJ (Updated 2004).

On September 14, 1990 researchers at the U.S. National Institutes of Health performed the first (approved) gene therapy procedure on four-year old Ashanti DeSilva. Born with a rare genetic disease called severe combined immune deficiency (SCID), she lacked a healthy immune system, and was vulnerable to every passing germ. Children with this illness usually develop overwhelming infections and rarely survive to adulthood; a common childhood illness like chickenpox is life-threatening. Ashanti led a cloistered existence—avoiding contact with people outside her family, remaining in the sterile environment of her home, and battling frequent illnesses with massive amounts of antibiotics.

In Ashanti's gene therapy procedure, doctors removed white blood cells from the child's body, let the cells grow in the lab, inserted the missing gene into the cells, and then infused the genetically modified blood cells back into the patient's bloodstream. Laboratory tests have shown that the therapy strengthened Ashanti's immune system; she no longer has recurrent colds, she has been allowed to attend school, and she was immunized against whooping cough. This procedure was not a cure; the white blood cells treated genetically only work for a few months, and the process must be repeated every few months.

Although this simplified explanation of a gene therapy procedure sounds like a happy ending, it is little more than an optimistic first chapter in a long story; the road to the first approved gene therapy procedure was rocky and fraught with controversy. The biology of human gene therapy is very complex, and there are many techniques that still need to be developed and diseases that need to be understood more fully before gene therapy can be used appropriately. The public policy debate surrounding the possible use of genetically engineered material in human subjects has been equally complex. Major participants in the debate have come from the fields of biology, government, law, medicine, philosophy, politics, and religion, each bringing different views to the discussion.

In studying the ethics of gene therapy, one should make a distinction between therapy on the somatic (non reproductive) cells and the germ (reproductive) cells of an individual. Only the germ cells carry the genes that will be passed on to the next generation. Some commentators on gene therapy have objected to any form of genetic manipulation, no matter how well-intentioned. Many others approve of the use of somatic cell therapy, but hesitate to allow the use of germ-line gene therapy that could have an unforeseeable effect on future generations. Still others have argued that with proper regulation and safeguards, germ-line gene therapy is a logical extension of the progress made to date, and an ethically acceptable procedure.

Techniques

The first somatic cell gene therapy procedure inserted a normal gene into the DNA of cells in order to compensate for the nonfunctioning defective gene. This technique involves obtaining blood cells from a person afflicted with a genetic disease and then introducing a normal gene into the defective cell. [This can be done by directly introducing the new DNA into the cells or by using domesticated viruses. It is important that the DNA be inserted in the correct cell and at the correct place in the cell's genome.]

. . .

Germ-line gene therapy is technically more difficult, and as noted, raises more ethical challenges. The two main methods of performing germ-line gene therapy would be: 1) to treat a pre-embryo that carries a serious genetic defect before implantation in the mother (this necessitates the use of in vitro fertilization techniques); or 2) to treat the germ cells (sperm or egg cells) of afflicted adults so that their genetic defects would not be passed on to their offspring. This approach requires the technical expertise to delete the defective gene and insert a properly functioning replacement.

Candidate Diseases for Gene Therapy

Gene therapy is likely to have the greatest success with diseases that are cause by single gene defects. By the end of 1993, gene therapy had been approved for use on such diseases as severe combined immune deficiency, familial hypercholesterolemia, cystic fibrosis, and Gaucher's disease. Most protocols to date are aimed toward the treatment of cancer; a few are also targeted toward AIDS. Numerous disorders are discussed as candidates for gene therapy: Parkinson's and Alzheimer's diseases, arthritis, and heart disease. The Human Genome Project, an ongoing effort to identify the location of all the genes in the human genome, continues to identify genetic diseases.

Eve Nichols describes the criteria for selection of disease candidates for human gene therapy: 1) the disease is an incurable, life-threatening disease; 2) organ, tissue and cell types affected by the disease have been identified; 3) the normal counterpart of the defective gene has been isolated and cloned; 4) the normal gene can be introduced into a substantial sub-fraction of the cells from the affected tissue; or that introduction of the gene into the available target tissue, such as bone marrow, will somehow alter the disease process in the tissue affected by the disease; 5) the gene can be expressed adequately (it will direct the production of enough normal protein to make a difference); and 6) techniques are available to verify the safety of the procedure.

Brief History of Gene Therapy in the United States

The first attempt at human gene therapy was performed under questionable circumstances by University of California at Los Angeles (UCLA) researcher, Dr. Martin Cline. Without the approval of his UCLA IRB, Cline performed a recombinant DNA transfer into cells of the bone marrow of two patients with hereditary blood disorders in Italy and Israel. At the time, Italy did not have IRBs, and Dr. Cline did not disclose fully to the Israeli IRB the exact nature of the gene transfers he proposed. In October 1980, the *Los Angeles Times* published details of Dr. Cline's activities. Dr. Cline suffered grave consequences for his over exuberance. He was forced to resign his department chairmanship at UCLA, he lost some grants, and for a period of three years, all of his applications for grant support were accompanied by a report of the investigations into his activities in 1979–1980.

In light of Dr. Cline's experiment, and at the prompting of the National Council of Churches, the Synagogue Council of America and the United States Catholic Conference, the President's Commission for the

Study of Ethical Problems in Medicine and Biomedical and Behavioral Research became involved with the issue of gene therapy and released a landmark study called *Splicing Life* in 1982. The President's Commission vigorously defended the continuation of [gene therapy] research. *Splicing Life* responded to the concern that scientists were playing God, concluding that we can distinguish between acceptable and unacceptable consequences of gene therapy research. The Commission suggested the [Recombinant DNA Advisory Committee (RAC)] broaden the scope of its review to include the ethical and social implications of gene therapy.

In 1984 the RAC created a new group, called the Human Gene Therapy Working Group (later called the Human Gene Therapy Subcommittee (HGTS)) specifically to review gene therapy protocols. The first task of the Working Group was to produce the "Points to Consider for Protocols for the Transfer of Recombinant DNA into the Genome of Human Subjects" document as a guide for those applying for RAC approval of gene therapy protocols.

Another outcome of the hearing was the 1984 U.S. Office of Technology Assessment (OTA) background paper *Human Gene Therapy*, which stressed the difference between somatic and germ-line gene therapy. The OTA also issued an important survey on public opinion regarding genetic technologies

. . .

In October 1999, the death of Jesse Gelsinger, the first fatality in a gene therapy experiment, was reported in *Nature*. Subsequent investigations revealed that the deaths of six gene therapy patients had not received the usual public disclosure that has characterized gene therapy research. Gelsinger's death also raised questions about researcher entrepreneurial activities and conflict-of-interest, and about government oversight procedures. The United States Senate held hearings on this topic on February 2, 2000, and the heightened scrutiny has resulted in increased reporting of adverse effects and renewed oversight by both NIH and FDA.

The success of a multi-center trial for treating children with SCID held from 2000 and 2002 was questioned when two of the ten children treated at the trial's Paris center developed a leukemia-like condition. Clinical trials were halted temporarily, but resumed after regulatory review of the protocol in the United States, the United Kingdom, France, Italy, and Germany.

Arguments in Favor of Gene Therapy

The central argument in favor of gene therapy is that it can be used to treat desperately ill patients, or to prevent the onset of horrible illnesses. Conventional treatment has failed for the candidate diseases for gene therapy, and for these patients, gene therapy is the only hope for a future. Many commentators liken somatic cell gene therapy to other new medical technologies, and argue that we have an obligation to treat patients if we can. . . .

Eric Juengst summarized the arguments in favor of and against human germ-line gene therapy in 1991:[22] 1) germ-line gene therapy offers a true cure, and not simply palliative or symptomatic treatment; 2) germ-line gene therapy may be the only effective way of addressing some genetic diseases; 3) by preventing the transmission of disease genes, the expense and risk of somatic cell therapy for multiple generations is avoided; 4) medicine should respond to the reproductive health needs of prospective parents at risk for transmitting serious genetic diseases; and 5) the scientific community has a right to free inquiry, within the bounds of acceptable human research.

While the development of germ-line gene therapy techniques will undoubtedly place some embryos at risk in the laboratory, once the successful techniques are developed, the therapy could help parents and researchers avoid the moral dilemma of disposing of "defective" embryos in the lab if the embryos could be repaired.

Arguments Against Gene Therapy

Many persons who voice concerns about somatic cell gene therapy use a "slippery slope" argument against it. They wonder whether it is possible to distinguish between "good" and "bad" uses of the gene modification techniques, and whether the potential for harmful abuse of the technology should keep us from developing more techniques. Other commentators have pointed to the difficulty of following up with patients in long-term clinical research. Gene therapy patients would need to be under surveillance for decades to monitor long-term effects of the therapy on future generations. Some are troubled that many gene therapy candidates are children too young to understand the ramifications of gene therapy treatment.

Others have pointed to potential conflict of interest problems pitting an individual's reproductive liberties and privacy interests against the interests of insurance companies, or society not to bear the financial burden of caring for a child with serious genetic defects. Issues of justice and resource allocation have also been raised: in a time of strain on our health care system, can we afford such expensive therapy? Who should receive gene therapy? If it is made available only to those who can afford it, "the distribution of desirable biological traits among different socioeconomic and ethnic groups would become badly skewed."

Arguments specifically against the development of germ-line gene therapy techniques include: 1) germ-line gene therapy experiments would involve too much scientific uncertainty and clinical risks, and the long term effects of such therapy are unknown; 2) such gene therapy would open the door to attempts at altering human traits not associated with disease, which could exacerbate problems of social discrimination; 3) as germ-line gene therapy involves research on early embryos and effects their offspring, such research essentially creates generations of unconsenting research subjects; 4) gene therapy is very expensive, and will never be cost effective enough to merit high social priority; 5) germ-line gene therapy would

22. Eric T. Juengst, *Human Germline Engineering*, 16 J. MED. & PHIL. 587–694 (1991).

violate the rights of subsequent generations to inherit a genetic endowment that has not been intentionally modified.

NOTES AND QUESTIONS

1. *Government Oversight of Gene Therapy.* A very limited number of patients now receive gene therapy through clinical trials, but the Food and Drug Administration (FDA) has not approved any form of gene therapy for use in the general population. Clinical trials involving gene therapy have a unique oversight process that is conducted by the National Institutes of Health (NIH) and FDA. The NIH oversight process is undertaken through the Recombinant DNA Advisory Committee (RAC) and is informed by the NIH Guidelines for Research Involving Recombinant DNA Molecules. The FDA operates through regulation including scientific review, research, testing, and compliance activities. FDA regulations apply to all clinical gene therapy research, while NIH governs gene therapy research that is either supported with NIH funds or conducted at or sponsored by institutions that receive funding for recombinant DNA research. Currently, the majority of somatic cell gene therapy research is subject to the NIH Guidelines. The RAC, however, will not currently consider or approve research protocols using germline gene therapy. National Human Genome Research Institute, National Institutes of Health, *Germline Gene Transfer, at* http://www.genome.gov/10004764.

2. In Utero *Genetic Therapy.* Due to heightened concern after Jesse Gelsinger's death, NIH added the following statement to its guidelines:

> The RAC continues to explore the issues raised by the potential of *in utero* gene transfer clinical research. However, the RAC concludes that, at present, it is premature to undertake any *in utero* gene transfer clinical trial. Significant additional preclinical and clinical studies addressing vector transduction efficacy, biodistribution, and toxicity are required before a human in utero gene transfer protocol can proceed. In addition, a more thorough understanding of the development of human organ systems, such as the immune and nervous systems, is needed to better define the potential efficacy and risks of human *in utero* gene transfer. Prerequisites for considering any specific human *in utero* gene transfer procedure include an understanding of the pathophysiology of the candidate disease and a demonstrable advantage to the *in utero* approach. Once the above criteria are met, the RAC would be willing to consider well rationalized human *in utero* gene transfer clinical trials.

Notice of Action Under the NIH Guidelines for Research Involving Recombinant DNA Molecules 66 Fed. Reg. 1146–47 (Jan. 5, 2001).

3. *Gene Therapy on Somatic Cells.* Given the high risks of somatic gene therapy and the (as yet) unproven value, should this research continue? Are the oversight arrangements instituted by the federal government sufficient to prevent harms or abuses? If research is warranted, should children or other incompetent persons be allowed to participate? What about institutionalized populations such as prisoners or mental patients? Gene therapy is a promising treatment that can help seriously ill patients or prevent the onset of horrible illnesses, but research risks are considerable. Does this suggest that market freedoms should be curtailed by state regulation?

4. *Germline Gene Therapy.* Germline therapy is more scientifically and ethically complex than somatic cell gene therapy and, therefore, more controversial. Could germline therapy have unintended consequences on future generations, and should it therefore be viewed with extreme caution? Germline therapy may serve to "repair" defective embryos rather than leave parents with the hard choice of terminating a pregnancy or having a child with a severe genetic condition.

5. *Liberty, Privacy, and Distributive Justice.* Gene therapy, both somatic and germline, raises additional questions. There are conflict of interest problems that might pit an individual's reproductive liberties and privacy interests against the interests of insurance companies or society not to bear the financial burden of caring for a child with serious genetic defects. Consider also the problems of distributive justice. Who should receive gene therapy? If it is made available only to those who can afford it, desirable biological traits may be distributed unevenly among different socioeconomic and ethnic groups.

D.   GENETIC ENHANCEMENT: SELECTION OF DESIRED TRAITS

Underlying many people's concerns regarding genetic testing and gene therapy are concerns over genetic enhancement. The application of genetic technology in the reproductive setting allows parents to exercise greater choice in determining various characteristics of their offspring. Genetic technology allows parents to screen embryos and select for embryos on the basis of their genetic makeup. In addition, gene transfer technology would allow even greater parental control as parents could insert genes of interest, rather than simply screening for a certain genotype.

The President's Council on Bioethics, *Screening and Selection for Genetic Conditions and Traits*

in REPRODUCTION AND RESPONSIBILITY: THE REGULATION OF NEW BIOTECHNOLOGIES 89, 89–93 (2004).

The ability to screen developing human life for chromosomal abnormalities and genetic disorders has been ours for some time. Individuals and doctors have for many years been able to test fetuses in utero, either through the genetic analysis of cells obtained from amniotic fluid by amniocentesis (in the second trimester) or through genetic analysis of chorionic villus samples obtained from the placenta by biopsy (in the first trimester). The "selection" that follows such testing is achieved by means of abortion; it amounts to "selecting against" a developing fetus with a diagnosed genetic disease or other unwanted trait (for example, maleness or femaleness).

More recently, however, innovations in assisted reproduction and molecular genetics have yielded new ways to test early-stage embryos in vitro for genetic markers and characteristics. After such testing only those embryos with the desired genetic characteristics are transferred to initiate a pregnancy. By comparison with the older form of screening, this approach is more "positively" selective; it amounts more to "choosing in" rather than merely "weeding out." Methods to test or screen eggs and sperm before fertilization are also being developed, and at least one type of sperm sorting—sorting by the presence of X or Y chromosomes—is already in use in several clinical trials. These two new techniques for testing early-stage embryos—preimplantation genetic diagnosis (PGD) and sperm sorting—are the subjects of the following discussion.

.   .   .

A. Preimplantation Genetic Diagnosis of Embryos

PGD is a technique that permits clinicians to analyze embryos in vitro for certain genetic (or chromosomal) traits or markers and to select accordingly for purposes of transfer. The early embryo (six to eight cells) is biopsied by removal of one or two cells, and the sample cell(s) is then examined for the presence or absence of the markers of interest. PGD is practiced in approximately fifty clinics worldwide, the majority of them located in the United States. PGD was first used in 1989 as an adjunct to in vitro fertilization (IVF) for treating infertility. Official statistics do not tell us how many children have been conceived following PGD. Estimates vary widely; one recent report suggested that "more than 1,000 babies have been born worldwide."

PGD was initially used for sex identification to avoid transfer of embryos with X-linked genetic diseases, such as Lesch Nyhan syndrome, hemophilia, and X-linked mental retardation. PGD is now most commonly used to detect aneuploidies (that is, an abnormal number of chromosomes). Some aneuploidies prevent the embryo from implanting, whereas others are associated with disorders such as Down syndrome and Turner syndrome. PGD is used also to detect monogenic diseases such as cystic fibrosis and Tay Sachs disease. More recently PGD has been used to select embryos that would be compatible tissue donors for older siblings in need of transplants. In still other cases PGD has been used for elective (non-medical) sex selection. Today at least one-third of individuals who use PGD are otherwise fertile, and this number may increase as the potential uses of PGD expand.

At present, PGD can identify genetic markers that correlate with (or suggest a predisposition for) more than one hundred diseases, including illnesses that become manifest much later in life, such as early-onset Alzheimer disease. As genomic knowledge increases and more genes that correlate with diseases are identified, the applications for PGD will likely increase. In principle any known gene and its variants can be tested for, and with improved methods for amplifying genetic screening on small samples, it may some day be possible to test the single cell removed from the embryo for hundreds of genetic markers. Dr. Francis Collins, director of the National Human Genome Research Institute, recently speculated that within five to seven years the major contributing genes for diabetes, heart disease, cancer, mental illness, Parkinson disease, stroke, and asthma will be identified. Many couples with family histories of these diseases may be drawn to PGD, even in the absence of infertility. Moreover, if genetic associations with other, non-medical conditions are identified, PGD might one day be used to screen for positive traits and characteristics such as height, leanness, or temperament.

PGD is a multi-step process requiring considerable technical skill and expertise in the fields of genetics and reproductive medicine. Because the testing is performed on early embryos in vitro, individuals electing to use PGD must undergo in vitro fertilization. Typically, embryo biopsy is performed three days after fertilization when the embryo is at the six-to eight-cell stage. The researcher makes a small hole in the zona pellucida (using a sharp pipette, acidic solution, or laser), and then inserts a suction pipette into the opening and removes one or two cells ("blastomeres"). Some researchers wait until the embryo reaches the blastocyst stage (approximately five to six days after fertilization, when the given embryo has grown to approximately one hundred cells) to undertake this biopsy. The procedure is technically less demanding at this stage and more cells can be removed and analyzed.

Once collected, the blastomeres or trophectoderm cells can be analyzed by a variety of means depending on the purpose of the test. PGD for detection of monogenic diseases is performed using a technique called "polymerase chain reaction" (PCR). Sex identity and chromosomal abnormalities are detected using a technique called fluorescence in situ hybridization (FISH). PCR allows clinicians to amplify sections of the DNA sequence, providing them with enough DNA to detect specific gene mutations. In FISH, labeled markers bind to chromosomes, permitting the researcher to observe and enumerate such chromosomes.

In all these procedures, timing is critical. The clinician must complete the analysis before the embryo develops beyond the stage at which it can be successfully transferred. If the biopsy is performed on Day 3, the practitioner has approximately forty-eight hours in which to complete the analysis, verify results, and discuss options with the patient or patients.

The error rate for PGD has been estimated between 1 and 10 percent, depending on the assay used. Several technical difficulties may compromise accuracy. Working with so few cells—in many cases only one or two—leaves little room for technical error. PCR can be problematic. In some instances, for example, one allele fails to amplify to a detectable level. This phenomenon, called "allele dropout," can lead to misdiagnosis. Contamination of the PGD sample can also lead to misdiagnosis. Technical difficulties associated with FISH may also affect accuracy of diagnosis. Following the transfer of the selected embryos and the initiation of pregnancy, clinicians routinely follow up with chorionic villus sampling and amniocentesis to confirm the results of PGD.

B.   Genetic Analysis of Gametes

As well as testing early embryos, researchers are also trying to test and screen gametes (ova and sperm) before fertilization.

1.   Preimplantation Genetic Diagnosis of Ova.

As an alternative to embryonic PGD, clinicians can now perform a similar analysis on the developing oocyte, by testing DNA from the polar bodies—nucleus-containing protrusions that are ultimately shed from the maturing oocyte. As with cells obtained from embryo biopsy, PCR or FISH can be used to test for, respectively, monogenic diseases or chromosomal abnormalities (most aneuploidies are maternally derived). The utility of polar body analysis is limited, however, in that it reveals only the maternal contribution to the child's genotype.

2.   Sperm Selection.

Another form of gamete screening is sperm sorting. A number of techniques are now under study, all of them aimed at controlling the sexes of the children ultimately conceived from these gametes. Most techniques to sort sperm have proven unreliable. These have included albumin gradients, percoll gradients, sephadex columns, and modified swim-up techniques. One technique currently in clinical trials—commercially called Microsort—has proven more successful. It exploits the difference in total DNA content between X-chromosome (female-producing) sperm and Y-chromosome (male-producing) sperm. The researcher collects the sperm sample and stains it with a fluorescent dye, bisbenzimide, which binds to the DNA in each sperm. A female-producing sperm shines brighter because it has 2.8 percent more DNA than the androgenic sperm, owing to the larger size of the X-chromosome. Using fluorescence-based separating equipment, the researcher sorts the sperm into X-bearing and Y-bearing preparations. The appropriate preparation is selected according to the couple's preference and used to inseminate the woman. The latest statistics report a 90 percent success rate for conceiving female children and 72 percent success for conceiving male children.

Jon W. Gordon, *Genetic Enhancement in Humans*

283 Sci. 2023–2024 (1999).

Dramatic advances in gene transfer technology since the early 1980s have prompted consideration of its use in humans to enhance phenotypic traits. The notion that genetic modification could confer special advantages on an individual has generated excitement. Controversial issues surround this prospect, however. A practical concern is determining how to ensure equal access to such advanced medical technologies. There has also been speculation that genetic enhancement might affect human evolution, and philosophical objections have been raised, based on the belief that to intervene in such fundamental biological processes is to "play God." Although such philosophical questions cannot be resolved through data analysis, we nevertheless have the tools in hand to objectively assess our state of progress.

. . .

Defining genetic enhancement

Some experts have argued that "enhancement" can have different meanings depending on the circumstances. For example, when a disease is common, the risk for developing the disorder may be considered the norm, and genetic alleviation of that risk might be regarded as a form of enhancement. This kind of semantic gamesmanship is misleading. The obvious public concern does not relate to improvement of traits for alleviation of deficiencies or reduction of disease risk, but to augmentation of functions that without intervention would be considered entirely normal. To raise the athletic capabilities of a schoolyard basketball player to those of a professional or to confer the talents of Chopin on a typical college music professor is the sort of genetic enhancement that many find troublesome. The experts in the gene transfer field should acknowledge the distinction in order to avoid causing public distrust and undermining the deliberative process.

Another important distinction is that between genetic changes that are heritable and those that cannot be genetically transmitted. At the present time, gene transfer approaches that involve the early embryo are far more effective than somatic cell gene therapy methodologies. Embryo gene transfer affords the opportunity to transform most or all cells of the organism and thus overcomes the inefficient transformation that plagues somatic cell gene transfer protocols. Moreover, the commonly used approaches to embryo gene insertion—pronuclear microinjection and transfection of embryonic stem cells—are associated with stable, high expression of donor DNA. Typically, however, genetic changes introduced into the embryo extend to the gametes and are heritable.

Scenarios can be constructed wherein introduced genes could be deleted from germ cells or early embryos derived from the treated individual.... Germline gene transfer has already succeeded in several animal species. Because of this and the general belief that voluntary abstention from germline modification in humans is unlikely, a candid discussion of genetic enhancement must include the possibility that changes introduced will be transmitted to offspring.

The state of the art

Animal experiments thus far have attempted to improve what are intuitively regarded as "simple" traits such as growth rate or muscle mass. Efforts to genetically improve the growth of swine have involved insertion of transgenes encoding growth hormone. Nevertheless, despite the fact that growth hormone transgenes are expressed well in swine, increased growth does not occur. Although the transgenic animals fortuitously have less body fat, these unexpected benefits cannot be extrapolated to human clinical protocols. Before a human embryo is treated with recombinant DNA, we must know exactly what we are doing.

Another spectacular failed attempt at enhancement resulted from efforts to increase muscle mass in cattle.... When gene transfer was accomplished, the transgenic calf initially exhibited muscle hypertrophy, but muscle degeneration and wasting soon followed. Unable to stand, the debilitated animal was killed.

. . .

Given the inherent limitations of the gene transfer approach to enhancement, discussion of extending such procedures to humans is scientifically unjustified. We clearly do not yet understand how to accomplish controlled genetic modification of even simple phenotypes.

... The genome only provides a blueprint for formation of the brain; the finer details of assembly and intellectual development are beyond direct genetic control and must perforce be subject to innumerable stochastic and environmental influences.

Genetic engineering and human evolution

Some have suggested that genetic enhancement and related reproductive technologies now give us the power to control human evolution. This solemn pronouncement is totally without scientific foundation. The evolution of the human species may be understood as a nonrandom change in allelic frequencies resulting from selective pressure. The change progresses over generations because individuals with specific patterns of alleles are favored reproductively. If new alleles were introduced by gene transfer, the impact on the species would be negligible. Every month worldwide approximately 11 million babies are born. The addition of one genetically modified individual could not significantly affect gene frequencies. Moreover, if the "enhanced" individual had his or her first child at the age of 20, then 2,640,000,000 unengineered children would be born during the interval between the birth and procreation of the gene recipient. Even if 1,000 successful gene transfers were performed per year, a number not likely to be achieved in the foreseeable future, those newborns would constitute only 1/132,000 of all live births. Thus, any effort to enhance the human species experimentally would be swamped by the random attempts of Mother Nature.

Finally, there is no certainty that genetically enhanced individuals would have greater biological fitness, as measured by reproductive success. A genius or great athlete who has no children has no biological fitness as defined in evolutionary theory. For these reasons, neither gene transfer nor any of the other emerging reproductive technologies will ever have a significant impact on human evolution.

Developing policy

If we accept the notion that genetic enhancement is not practicable in the near future, what policies should we develop concerning the use of such technology? The decision to undertake any form of invasive medical intervention immediately renders the treatment subject a patient who has a right to informed consent as well as to protection from unjustifiably dangerous medical manipulation. Our inability to predict the consequences of an attempt at genetic enhancement makes informed consent impossible, and current knowledge from animal experiments tells us that embryo gene transfer is unsafe ... The risks are so high and the documented efficacy is so low for gene transfer that it could not compare favorably to straightforward prenatal diagnosis even when a compelling need for therapy exists, as in cases of genetic disease. The use of gene transfer for elective purposes such as enhancement would stray far beyond the limits of acceptable medical intervention.

To attempt genetic enhancement with extant methods would clearly be medically unacceptable, but attempts to ban gene transfer legally could be a cumbersome approach to limiting its clinical use. Verification of compliance would be difficult. The diverse resources required for gene transfer necessitate that the procedure be carried out in facilities equipped for in vitro fertilization. Direct inspection would be required to uncover gene transfer procedures in such facilities. This would impose on the privacy of patients undergoing accepted assisted reproduction procedures such as sperm injection. Moreover, gene transfer can be easily concealed; in the case of pronuclear microinjection, only a few seconds are needed to complete the process. Legal restrictions can also be easily avoided by performing the procedure outside the area of jurisdiction.

. . .

Fear of genetic manipulation may encourage proposals to limit basic investigations that might ultimately lead to effective human gene transfer. History has shown that effort is far better spent in preparing society to cope with scientific advances than in attempting to restrict basic research. Gene transfer studies may never lead to successful genetic enhancement, but they are certain to provide new treatment and prevention strategies for a variety of devastating diseases. No less significant is the potential for this research to improve our understanding of the most complex and compelling phenomenon ever observed—the life process. We cannot be expected to deny ourselves this knowledge.

NOTES AND QUESTIONS

1. *Is Genetic Enhancement Unethical?* For many years, in utero genetic testing has allowed parents to select against a developing fetus that has been diagnosed with a genetic disease or found to possess unwanted traits. Couples who undergo in vitro fertilization may now have their embryos screened for genetic disease before they are even implanted. Innovations in assisted reproduction and molecular genetics have resulted in new ways to test early-stage embryos in vitro for genetic markers and characteristics. In thinking about the ethics of selection, does it matter what the parent is selecting for? Would it matter, for example, if the selection were for simple sex preference or to choose an infant who would be a desirable organ donor for a sibling? Many people probably would approve selection against a discrete genetic disease such as Tay Sachs or Down syndrome. What if the selection were for one or more late onset chronic conditions such as diabetes, schizophrenia, or Alzheimer's disease? Recent advancements in genetic knowledge may someday allow parents to positively select certain traits rather than merely weed them out. If a parent chooses a positive trait such as beauty, strength, intelligence, or the ability to function on less sleep, is that morally wrong? *See* Leroy Walters, et al., THE ETHICS OF HUMAN GENE THERAPY (1996).

2. *How Can Ethical Arguments for or Against Genetic Enhancement be Appropriately Formulated?* If ethical questions do arise with genetic enhancement, how would they be articulated? Some people might object because they define an embryo or fetus as human life. Once this definition is accepted, any destruction of a life form becomes ethically troublesome. Others have an aversion to too much manipulation of natural biological processes. How valid is the argument that fetal selection is "unnatural," perhaps even bordering on eugenics? Is the fact that a scientific method is "aberrant" or against "God's plan" ethically relevant? (Putting it more starkly, does the "yuck factor" have any moral relevance?). Still others might be troubled by the diminution of the child's autonomy if he or she were "bred" to be, say, an athlete, musician, or scientist. Is genetic enhancement inconsistent with the child's interest in autonomy? If so, why? Couldn't children choose to ignore their inherited traits and follow their own path (e.g., foreswearing sports or music in favor of some other pursuit)?

3. *How Important are Considerations of Distributive Justice in Genetic Enhancement?* Some may claim that a parent seeking a healthy and vigorous child is a social good and highly consistent with the conventional parental role. After all, parents may marry based, in part, on their mate's perceived virtues such as beauty or intelligence. However, what if the higher socioeconomic classes began to aggressively pursue positive traits for their offspring and the same goal was out-of-reach for poorer communities? Would this be fair? Would it increase socioeconomic and health disparities among difference races and classes? Does it matter if disparities are widened and, if so, why?

4. *Does it Matter if Enhancement is for a Single Generation only or for Future Generations?* People may choose to enhance physical or mental attributes for themselves or their children. However, does it matter if those enhancements will carry on indefinitely to future generations? After all, if an attribute is truly positive, why object to carrying it forward to future generations? Does this somehow adversely affect the evolutionary process? Does it pose unnecessary and irremediable risks? Does it exacerbate the problems of distributive justice?

III. MORAL PRINCIPLES AND ETHICAL THEORIES

Tom L. Beauchamp and James F. Childress, PRINCIPLES OF BIOMEDICAL ETHICS

12–13, 57–58, 63–64, 113–115, 165–167, 226–228, 337, 340–341, 348–350, 352, 355–357, 362–364, 369–371 (2001).

A Framework of Moral Principles

The common morality contains a set of moral norms that includes principles that are basic for biomedical ethics. . . . Most classical ethical theories include these principles in some form, and traditional medical codes presuppose at least some of them.

. . . [W]e defend four clusters of moral principles that serve this function. The four clusters are (1) *respect for autonomy* (a norm of respecting the decision-making capacities of autonomous persons), (2) *nonmaleficence* (a norm of avoiding the causation of harm), (3) *beneficence* (a group of norms for providing benefits and balancing benefits against risks and costs), and (4) *justice* (a group of norms for distributing benefits, risks, and costs fairly).

Nonmaleficence and beneficence have played a central historical role in medical ethics, whereas respect for autonomy and justice were neglected in traditional medical ethics but came into prominence because of recent developments. To illustrate this traditional neglect, consider the work of British physician Thomas Percival. In 1803, he published *Medical Ethics*, which was the first well formed account of medical ethics in the long history of the subject. This book served as the prototype for the American Medical Association's (AMA) first code of ethics in 1847. Easily the dominant influence in both British and American medical ethics of the period, Percival argued (using somewhat different language) that maleficence and beneficence fix the physician's primary obligations and triumph over the patient's preferences and decision-making rights in circumstances of serious conflict. Percival failed to appreciate the power of principles of respect for autonomy and distributive justice, but, in fairness to him, we must acknowledge that these considerations are now ubiquitous in discussions of biomedical ethics in a way they were not when he wrote at the turn of the nineteenth century.

That four clusters of moral "principles" are central to biomedical ethics is a conclusion the authors of this work have reached by examining *considered moral judgments* and the way *moral beliefs cohere*....

The Nature of Autonomy

The word *autonomy,* derived from the Greek *autos* ("self") and *nomos* ("rule," "governance," or "law"), originally referred to the self-rule or self-governance of independent city-states. *Autonomy* has since been extended to individuals and has acquired meanings as diverse as self-governance, liberty rights, privacy, individual choice, freedom of the will, causing one's own behavior, and being one's own person. Clearly autonomy is not a univocal concept in either ordinary English or contemporary philosophy and needs to be refined in light of particular objectives....

Personal autonomy is, at a minimum self-rule that is free from both controlling interference by others and from limitations, such as inadequate understanding, that prevent meaningful choice. The autonomous individual acts freely in accordance with a self-chosen plan, analogous to the way an independent government manages its territories and sets its policies. A person of diminished autonomy, by contrast, is in some respect controlled by others or incapable of deliberating or acting on the basis of his or her desires and plans. For example, prisoners and mentally retarded individuals often have diminished autonomy. Mental incapacitation limits the autonomy of retarded persons, whereas coercive institutionalization constrains the autonomy of prisoners.

Virtually all theories of autonomy agree that two conditions are essential: (1) *liberty* (independence from controlling influences) and (2) *agency* (capacity for intentional action)....

. . .

To respect an autonomous agent is, at a minimum, to acknowledge that person's right to hold views, to make choices, and to take actions based on personal values and beliefs. Such respect involves respectful *action,* not merely a respectful *attitude.* It also requires more than noninterference in others' personal affairs. It includes, at least in some contexts, obligations to build up or maintain others' capacities for autonomous choice while helping to allay fears and other conditions that destroy or disrupt their autonomous actions. Respect, on this account, involves acknowledging decision-making rights and enabling persons to act autonomously, whereas disrespect for autonomy involves attitudes and actions that ignore, insult, or demean others' rights of autonomy.

Why is such respect owed to persons? [T]wo philosophers ... have influenced contemporary interpretations of respect for autonomy ... : Immanuel Kant and John Stuart Mill. Kant argued that respect for autonomy flows from the recognition that all persons have unconditional worth, each having the capacity to determine his or her own moral destiny. To violate a person's autonomy is to treat that person merely as a means, that is, in accordance with others' goals without regard to that person's own goals. Mill was primarily concerned about the "individuality" of autonomous agents. He argued that society should permit individuals to develop according to their convictions, as long as they do not interfere with a like expression of freedom by others; but he also insisted that we sometimes are obligated to seek to persuade others when they have false or ill-considered views. Mill's position requires both not interfering with and actively strengthening autonomous expression, whereas Kant's entails a moral imperative of respectful treatment of persons as ends in themselves. In their different ways, these two philosophies both support the principle of respect for autonomy.

This principle can be stated as a negative obligation and as a positive obligation. As a *negative* obligation: *Autonomous actions should not be subjected to controlling constraints by others.* The principle asserts a broad, abstract obligation that is free of exceptive clauses, such as "We must respect individuals' views and rights *so long as their thoughts and actions do not seriously harm other persons.*" This principle of respect for autonomy needs specification in particular contexts to become a practical guide to conduct and appropriate specification will, in due course, incorporate valid exceptions. . . .

As a *positive* obligation, this principle requires respectful treatment in disclosing information and fostering autonomous decision-making. In some cases, we are obligated to increase the options available to persons. Many autonomous actions could not occur without others' material cooperation in making options available. Respect for autonomy obligates professionals in health care and research involving human subjects to disclose information, to probe for and ensure understanding and voluntariness, and to foster adequate decision-making. As some contemporary Kantians declare, the demand that we treat others as ends requires that we assist persons in achieving their ends and foster their capacities as agents, not merely that we avoid treating them solely as means to our ends.

Temptations sometimes arise in health care for physicians and other professionals to foster or perpetuate patients' dependency, rather than to promote their autonomy. But discharging the obligation to respect patients' autonomy requires equipping them to overcome their sense of dependence and achieve as much control as possible and as they desire. These positive obligations of respect for autonomy derive, in part, from the special fiduciary obligations that health care professionals have to their patients and researchers to their subjects.

. . .

Nonmaleficence

The principle of nonmaleficence asserts an obligation not to inflict harm on others. In medical ethics, it has been closely associated with the maxim *Primum non nocere*: "Above all [or first] do no harm." Health care professionals frequently invoke this maxim, yet its origins are obscure and its implications unclear. Often proclaimed the fundamental principle in the Hippocratic tradition of medical ethics, it does not appear in the Hippocratic corpus, and a venerable statement sometimes confused with it—"at least, do no harm"—is a strained translation of a single Hippocratic passage.

Nonetheless, the Hippocratic oath clearly expresses an obligation of non-maleficence and an obligation of beneficence: "I will use treatment to help the sick according to my ability and judgment, but I will never use it to injure or wrong them."

. . .

The Distinction between Nonmaleficence and Beneficence

Many types of ethical theory, including both utilitarian and nonutilitarian theories, recognize a principle of nonmaleficence. Some philosophers combine nonmaleficence with beneficence in a single principle.

. . .

[W]e group the principles of nonmaleficence and beneficence conceptually in an arrangements of four norms:

Nonmaleficence

1. One ought not to inflict evil or harm.

Beneficence

2. One ought to prevent evil or harm.
3. One ought to remove evil or harm.
4. One ought to do or promote good.

Each of the three forms of beneficence requires taking action by helping—preventing harm, removing harm, and promoting good, whereas nonmaleficence only requires *intentionally refraining* from actions that cause harm. Rules of nonmaleficence therefore take the form "Do not do X."

. . .

Rules Supported by the Principle of Nonmaleficence

The principle of nonmaleficence supports many more specific moral rules (though principles other than nonmaleficence help justify these rules in some instances). Typical examples include:

1. Do not kill.
2. Do not cause pain or suffering.
3. Do not incapacitate.
4. Do not cause offense.
5. Do not deprive others of the goods of life.

Beneficence

. . . [P]rinciples of beneficence potentially demand more than the principle of nonmaleficence because agents must take positive steps to help others, not merely refrain from harmful acts. . . .

In ordinary English the term *beneficence* connotes acts of mercy, kindness, and charity. Forms of beneficence also typically include altruism, love, and humanity. We will understand beneficent action even more broadly, so that it includes all forms of action intended to benefit other persons. *Beneficence* refers to an *action* done for the benefit of others;

benevolence refers to the *character trait* or virtue of being disposed to act for the benefit of others; and *principle of beneficence* refers to a moral obligation to act for the benefit of others. Many acts of beneficence are not obligatory, but a principle of beneficence, in our usage, asserts an obligation to help others further their important and legitimate interests.

Beneficence and benevolence have played central roles in some ethical theories. Utilitarianism, for example, is systematically arranged on a principle of beneficence (the principle of utility), and, during the Scottish Enlightenment, major figures, such as Francis Hutcheson and David Hume, made benevolence the centerpiece of the common-morality theories. In all these theories, benefiting others is conceived as an aspect of human nature that motivates us to act in the interests of others. These theories closely associate this goal with the goal of morality itself.

. . .

Critics often charge that the principle of utility (sometimes called "proportionality") allows society's interest to override individual interests and rights. In biomedical research, for example, the principle of utility suggests that dangerous research on human subjects can be undertaken, and ought to be undertaken, if its likely benefit to society outweighs the danger to individual subject. Yet this charge can only be leveled at an *unconstrained* principle of utilitarian balancing. As advantage of our account is that the principle of utility that we defend can be legitimately constrained by the other principles we advance.

. . .

The Concept of Justice

. . .

The terms *fairness, desert* (what is deserved), and *entitlement* have been used by various philosophers in attempts to explicate *justice*. These accounts interpret justice as fair, equitable, and appropriate treatment in light of what is due or owed to persons. Standards of justice are needed whenever persons are due benefits or burdens because of their particular properties or circumstances, such as being productive or having been harmed by another person's acts. One who has a valid claim based in justice has a right, and therefore is due something. An injustice thus involves a wrongful act or omission that denies people benefits to which they have a right or distributes burdens unfairly.

The term *distributive justice* refers to fair, equitable, and appropriate distribution in society determined by justified norms that structure the terms of social cooperation. Its scope includes policies that allot diverse benefits and burdens such as property, resources, taxation, privileges, and opportunities. *Distributive justice* refers broadly to the distribution of all rights and responsibilities in society, including, for example, civil and political rights. It is to be distinguished from other types of justice, including *criminal* justice, which refers to the just infliction of punishment, and *rectificatory* justice, which refers to just compensation for transactional problems such as breaches of contracts and malpractice.

Problems of distributive justice arise under conditions of scarcity and competition to obtain goods or to avoid burdens. If ample fresh water existed for industrial disposal of waste materials, and no subsequent harm to human beings or other forms of life occurred from this disposal, it would not be necessary to restrict use. Many contemporary discussions of just benefits in prepaid health maintenance programs, just programs of care for the mentally retarded, and appropriate sources of funds for national health insurance similarly involve such trade-offs that have been fashioned under these conditions of scarcity and competition.

.   .   .

Common to all theories of justice is a minimal formal requirement traditionally attributed to Aristotle. Equals must be treated equally, and unequals must be treated unequally. This principle of formal justice ... is "formal" because it identifies no particular respects in which equals ought to be treated equally and provide no criteria for determining whether two or more individuals are in fact equals.

.   .   .

Philosophers and others have proposed each of the following principles as a valid material principle of distributive justice:

1. To each person an equal share
2. To each person according to need
3. To each person according to effort
4. To each person according to contribution
5. To each person according to merit
6. To each person according to free-market exchanges

No obvious barrier prevents acceptance of more than one of these principles, and some theories of justice accept all six as valid. A plausible moral thesis is that each of these material principles identifies a prima facie obligation whose weight cannot be assessed independently of particular contexts or spheres in which they are especially applicable.

.   .   .

Most societies invoke several of these material principles in framing public policies, appealing to different principles in different spheres and contexts. For example, unemployment subsidies, welfare payments, and many health care programs are distributed on the basis of need (and to some extent on other criteria such as previous length of employment); jobs and promotions in many sectors are awarded on the basis of demonstrated achievement and merit; the higher incomes of some professionals are allowed and often encouraged on grounds of free-market wage scales, superior effort, merit, or potential social contribution; and, at least theoretically, the opportunity for elementary and secondary education is distributed all citizens.

Moral Theories

[This section] treats five types of moral theory: utilitarianism, Kantianism, liberal individualism, communitarianism, and the ethics of care. Some knowledge of these general perspectives is indispensable for reflective study of biomedical ethics because much of the field's literature draws on their methods and conclusions.

. . .

Utilitarianism: Consequence–Based Theory

Consequentialism is a label affixed to theories holding that actions are right or wrong according to the balance of their good and bad consequences. The right act in any circumstance is the one that produces the best overall result, as determined from an impersonal perspective that gives equal weight to the interests of each affected party. The most prominent consequence-based theory, utilitarianism, accepts one and only one basic principle of ethics: the principle of utility. This principle asserts that we ought always to produce the maximal balance of positive value over disvalue (or the least possible disvalue, if only undesirable results can be achieved). The classical origins of this theory are found in the writings of Jeremy Bentham (1748–1832) and John Stuart Mill (1806–1873).

At first sight, utilitarianism seems entirely compelling. Who would deny that evil should be minimized and positive value increased? Moreover, utilitarians offer many examples from everyday life to show that the theory is practicable and that we all engage in a utilitarian method of calculating what should be done by balancing goals and resources and considering the needs of everyone affected. Examples include designing a family budget and creating a new public park in a wilderness region. Utilitarians maintain that their theory renders explicit and systematic what is already implicit in everyday deliberation and justification.

The Concept of Utility

Although utilitarians share the conviction that we should morally assess human actions in terms of their production of maximal value, they disagree concerning which values should be maximized. Many utilitarians maintain that we ought to produce *agent-neutral or intrinsic* goods; that is, goods such as happiness, freedom and health that every rational person values. These goods are valuable in themselves, without reference to their further consequences or to the particular values held by individuals.

Bentham and Mill are *hedonistic* utilitarians because they conceive utility entirely in terms of happiness or pleasure, two broad terms they treat as synonymous. They appreciate that many human actions do not appear to be performed for the sake of happiness. For example, when highly motivated professionals, such as research scientists, work themselves to the point of exhaustion in search of new knowledge, they often do not appear to be seeking pleasure or personal happiness. Yet Mill proposes that such persons are initially motivated by success or money, both of which promise happiness. Along the way, either the pursuit of knowledge provides pleasure, or such persons never stop associating their hard work with the success or money they hope to gain.

However, many recent utilitarian philosophers have argued that values other than happiness have intrinsic worth. Some list friendship, knowledge, health, and beauty among these intrinsic values, whereas others list personal autonomy, achievement and success, understanding, enjoyment, and deep personal relationships. Even when their lists differ, these utilitarians concur that the greatest good should be assessed in terms of the total intrinsic value produced by an action. . . .

. . .

Kantianism: Obligation–Based Theory

A second type of theory denies much that utilitarian theories affirm. Often called *deontological* (i.e. a theory that some features of actions other than or in addition to consequences make actions right or wrong), this type is now increasingly called *Kantian,* because the ethical thought of Immanuel Kant (1724–1804), has shaped many of its formulations.

. . .

Obligation From Categorical Rules

. . . Kant argued that morality is grounded in pure reason, not in tradition, intuition, conscience, emotion, or attitudes such as sympathy. Kant saw human beings as creatures with rational powers to resist desire and with the freedom to do so.

One of Kant's most important claims is that the moral worth of an individual's action depends exclusively on the moral acceptability of the rule (or "maxim") on which the person acts. As Kant puts it, moral obligation depends on the rule that determines the individual's will, where the rule is understood as a morally valid reason that justifies the action. For Kant, one must act not only *in accordance with* but *for the sake of* obligation.

. . . [I]magine a man who desperately needs money and knows that he will not be able to borrow it unless he promises repayment in a definite time, but who also knows that he will not be able to repay it within this period. He decides to make a promise that he knows he will break. Kant asks us to examine the man's reason, that is, his maxim. "When I think myself in want of money, I will borrow money and promise to pay it back, although I know that I cannot do so." This maxim, Kant says, cannot pass a test that he calls the *categorical imperative.* This imperative tells us what must be done irrespective of our desires. In its major formulation, Kant states the categorical imperative as follows: "I ought never to act except in such a way that I can also will that my maxim become a universal law." Kant says that this one principle justifies all particular imperatives of obligation (all "ought" statements that morally obligate).

. . .

Kant appears to have more than one categorical imperative, because his several formulations are very differently worded. His second formulation is at least as influential as the first: "One must act to treat every person as an end and never as a means only." It has often been said that this principle categorically requires that we should never treat another as a means to our ends, but this interpretation misrepresents Kant's views. He argues only that we must not treat another *merely* or *exclusively* as a means to our ends. When human research subjects volunteer to test new drugs, they are treated as a means to others' ends, but they have a choice in the matter and retain control over their lives. Kant does not prohibit theses uses of consenting persons. He insists only that they be treated with the respect and moral dignity to which every person is entitled.

. . .

Contemporary Kantian Ethics

Several writers in contemporary ethical theory have accepted and developed a Kantian account, broadly construed.

. . .

[John] Rawls has challenged utilitarian theories while attempting to develop Kantian themes of reason, autonomy, and equality. For example, he argues that vital moral considerations, such as individual rights and the just distribution of goods among individuals, depend less on social factors, such as individual happiness and majority interests, than on Kantian conceptions of individual worth, self-respect, and autonomy. For Rawls, any philosophy in which the right to individual autonomy legitimately out-weighs the dictates of rational moral principles is unacceptable. Even courageous and conscientious actions do not merit respect unless they accord with moral principles derived from reason.

In his recent writings, Rawls has stressed that his work presents a political conception of justice, rather than a comprehensive moral theory. That is, his account is "a moral conception worked out for a specific subject, namely, the basic structure of a constitutional democratic regime." As such, it does not presuppose a comprehensive moral doctrine such as Kant's, and Rawls maintains that his theory is Kantian by "analogy not identity." The upshot seems to be that Rawls expresses Kantian themes without commitment to a general Kantian moral theory.

Liberal Individualism: Rights–Based Theory

Thus far we have concentrated on terms such as the following from moral discourse: *obligation, permissible action, virtue,* and *justification.* The language of *rights* is no less important. Statements of rights provide vital protection s of life, liberty, expression and property. They protect against oppression, unequal treatment, intolerance, arbitrary invasion of privacy, and the like. Some philosophers and framers of political declarations even regard rights as the basic language for expressing the moral point of view.

. . .

We analyze rights theory . . . as liberal individualism, the conception that a democratic society must carve out a certain space within which the individual may pursue personal projects. Liberal individualism has, in recent years, challenged the reigning utilitarianism and Kantian moral theories. H.L.A. Hart has described this challenge as a switch from an "old faith that some form of utilitarianism . . . *must* capture the essence of political morality" to a new faith in "a doctrine of basic human rights, protecting specific basic liberties and interests of individuals."

This faith may be new, but liberal individualism is not a new development in moral and political theory. At least since Thomas Hobbes, liberal individualists have employed the language of rights to buttress moral and political arguments, and the Anglo–American legal tradition has heavily relied upon this language. . . .

The legitimate role of civil, political, and legal rights in protecting the individual from societal intrusions is now beyond serious dispute, but the idea that individual rights provide the fountainhead for moral and political theory has been strongly resisted—for example, by many utilitarians and Marxists. They note that individual interests are often at odds with communitarian and institutional interests.

Communitarianism: Community–Based Theory

Several approaches in contemporary philosophy and political theory have little sympathy with liberal individualism. In these theories, everything fundamental in ethics derives from communal values: the common good, social goals, traditional practices, and cooperative virtues. Communitarism is such a theory. Conventions, traditions, loyalties and the social nature of life and institutions figure . . . prominently in communitarianism.

. . .

Contemporary communitarians repudiate liberal *theory* and challenge current societies established on liberal premises, including many contemporary Western political states. According to communitarians, these societies lack a commitment to the general welfare, to common purposes, and to education in citizenship, while expecting and even encouraging social and geographic mobility, distanced personal relationships, welfare dependencies, breakdowns in family life and marital fidelity, political fragmentation, and the like. The number of abandoned children and elderly parents, social and family disintegration, the disappearance of meaningful democracy, and the lack of effective communal programs are, according to the communitarians, the disastrous products of liberalism. Charles Taylor [for example] argues the type of autonomy valued by liberals cannot be developed in the absence of family and other community structures. However, liberalism's emphasis on individual rights makes no provision for the development and maintenance of the necessary communities and instead views individuals as isolated atoms existing independently of one another.

. . .

Ethics of Care: Relationship–Based Accounts

The *ethics of care* . . . shares some premises with communitarian ethics, including . . . an emphasis on traits valued in intimate personal relationships, such as sympathy, compassions, fidelity, discernment, and love. *Caring* in these accounts refers to care for emotional commitment to, and willingness to act on behalf of persons with whom one has a significant relationship. Noticeably downplayed are Kantian universal rules, impartial utilitarian calculations, and individual rights.

. . .

The ethics of care originated primarily in feminist writings. . . . The hypothesis that "women speak in a different voice"—a voice that traditional ethical theory has drowned out-arose in Carol Gilligan's book, *In a Different Voice*. . . . In her studies, female subjects typically view morality in terms of responsibilities of care deriving from attachments to others, whereas male subjects typically see morality in terms of rights and justice. Men look to and are formed by freely accepted relationships and agreements: women look to and are formed by contextually given relationships, such as those of the family.

. . .

Annette Baier . . . hears in contemporary female philosophers, despite their diversity, the same difference voice that Gilligan heard in her studies, but one made "reflective and philosophical." She deplores the near-exclusive emphasis in modern moral philosophy on universal rules and principles, and she . . . rejects Kantian contractarian models with their emphasis on justice, rights, law, and particularly autonomous choices by free and equal agents. The conditions of social cooperation, especially in families and in communal decision-making, are, Baier observes, typically unchosen and intimate, and they involve unequals in a relational network. She argues that traditional ethical theories . . . capture only a piece of the larger moral world.

NOTES AND QUESTIONS

The National Commission for the Protection of Human Subjects of Biomedical and Behavioral Research was the first public national body established to shape bioethics policy in the United States. It was created by Congress in 1974 through Pub. L. 93–348. One of the charges to the Commission was to identify the basic ethical principles that should underlie the conduct of biomedical and behavioral research involving human subjects and to develop guidelines which should be followed to assure that such research is conducted in accordance with those principles. In 1979, the Commission issued *The Belmont Report: Ethical Principles and Guidelines For Protection of Human Subjects of Biomedical and Behavioral Research.* The Report was the outgrowth of an intensive four-day period of discussions held at the Smithsonian's Institution's Belmont Conference Center supplemented by the monthly deliberations of the Commission that were held over a period of nearly four years. The Report identified three basic principles as "particularly relevant to the ethics of research involving human subjects: the principles of respect of persons, beneficence, and justice."

The Report further explained:

1. *Respect for Persons.* Respect for persons incorporates at least two ethical convictions: first, that individuals should be treated as autonomous agents, and second, that persons with diminished autonomy are entitled to protection. The principle of respect for persons thus divides into two separate moral requirements:

the requirement to acknowledge autonomy and the requirement to protect those
with diminished autonomy.

.   .   .

2. *Beneficence.* Persons are treated in an ethical manner not only be respecting
their decisions and protecting them from harm, but also by making efforts to secure
their well-being. Such treatment falls under the principle of beneficence.

.   .   .

3. *Justice.* Who ought to receive the benefits of research and bear its burdens?
This is a question of justice, in the sense of "fairness in distribution" or "what is
deserved."

.   .   .

[T]he selection of research subjects needs to be scrutinized in order to
determine whether some classes (e.g. welfare patients, particular racial and
ethnic minorities, or persons confined to institutions are being systematically
selected simply because of their easy availability, their compromised position, or
their manipulability, rather than for reasons directly related to the problem
being studied. Finally, whenever research supported by public funds leads to
the development of therapeutic devices and procedures, justice demands both
that these not provide advantages only to those who can afford them and that
such research should not unduly involve persons from groups unlikely to be
among the beneficiaries of subsequent applications of the research.

The first National Commission was succeeded in 1978 by the President's
Commission for the Study of Ethical Problems in Medicine and Biomedical and
Behavioral Research, in 1988 by the Biomedical Ethics Advisory Committee, in 1996
by the National Bioethics Advisory Commission, and in 2001 by the President's
Council on Bioethics. A more detailed list of these and other ethical commissions
and their reports can be found at www.bioethics.gov/reports/past_commissions.

IV.   SCIENCE POLICY AND REGULATION: COMPETITION OR CONTROL?

The rapid progress that characterized the end of the Human Genome
Project resulted largely from the competition that existed between private
and public researchers. Once J. Craig Venter announced that his company,
Celera, would complete the sequence first, his public counterparts were
spurred to action. As a result, both initiatives finished at the same time,
and completed the project ahead of schedule. Does this vignette suggest
that competition may spur innovation and efficiency in genomic research?

Competition in science can be a powerful driver; for over a decade,
genetic research has been consistently financed by more private than public
monies. *See* John Burris et al., *The Human Genome Project After a Decade:
Policy Issues*, 20 NATURE GENETICS 333–335 (1998). Genetic information is
being used, in many cases, as an investment that will generate revenue for
private companies. Although market activity could provide a significant
incentive for innovation, will it skew priorities and impede rapid public
dissemination of discoveries? For example, some experts worry that patent
filings are beginning to replace journal articles as the primary outlet for
public disclosure. Sharing information in this way, they contend, has
reduced the body of literature available on genomics. Could this shift

threaten the shared knowledge that is so crucial to rapid progress? Additionally, entrepreneurs pursue profits in the most lucrative markets, but do not always focus on social goals or the needs of the poor. Is public financing and regulation warranted to help ensure a balance between private innovation and public goods? Furthermore, when public funds are used in genetic research, should the pricing of the resulting product be regulated to reflect the taxpayer contribution to the product's development? How would such a policy impact the pace of research and the ability of the government to encourage research in the public interest?

Lori Andrews & Dorothy Nelkin, Body Bazaar: The Market for Human Tissue in the Biotechnology Age
60–62 (2001).

People increasingly feel they are paying twice for research—once to the government to fund the research, and then again to the biotech companies who sell them products developed from taxpayer-funded research. In the pharmaceutical field, patents are generally thought to be necessary in order to encourage the discovery of drugs, and to fund the testing of these drugs in animals and humans. But genetic discoveries are very different from drug development. The public pays for the research that yields discoveries of genetic associations with disease. Genetic testing can be applied to humans as soon as the gene is accurately identified, without costly clinical trials. Financial compensation is thus less warranted.

The high costs of genetic tests and treatments seems ludicrous, given that taxpayers have provided much of the funding for their discovery. The NIH paid $4.6 million toward discovery of gene predisposing women to breast cancer.

This situation—in which private companies such as Myriad, which holds the patent on *BRCA1* gene predisposing to cancer and charges $2,400 per screening, get a boost from taxpayer-funded research—occurs daily. Sixty-three percent of gene patents are based on research funded with federal money. The same thing occurs with funding for drug research. A Boston Globe investigative report revealed "a billion-dollar taxpayers' subsidy for pharmaceutical companies already awash in profits." Of the 50 top-selling drugs, 48 benefited from federal research money in their development or testing phases. A kidney cancer drug, Proleukin, benefited from $46 million in research funds. Patients nevertheless pay up to $20,000 per treatment.

A. The Problem of Patenting: Who Owns DNA?

Over three million genome-related patent applications were filed by 2004. Patent priority is determined on the "first to invent" principle: whoever can demonstrate that he or she made the invention first receives property rights for 20 years and has a one-year grace period after publishing the discovery. Inventors must (1) identify novel genetic sequences; (2) specify the sequence's product; (3) specify how the product functions in nature or is used; and (4) enable one skilled in the field to use the sequence for its stated purpose. Guidelines enacted in January 2001 require that patent applicants demonstrate "specific and substantial utility that is credible" before their genetic discoveries are patentable.[6]

However, some argue that these requirements are too lenient. This rubric permits multiple patents on different parts of gene sequence—for instance, the gene *and* the protein—which creates an undue monetary burden on researchers working with that sequence. In addition to these extra costs, it also allows patents for gene fragments, or expressed sequence tags (ESTs) that represent less than 5% of a single gene, to play a gate-keeping role that may stultify the speed and production of the commercial fruits of more comprehensive genomic research. The degree to which products are substantially different is determined by the courts. In *Festo Corp. v. Shoketsu Kinzoku Kogyo Kabushiki Co.*, the Supreme Court entered the controversy, seeking to protect patent holders while affording researchers some flexibility when working with previously patented technology. As you read *Festo*, consider its application to genome-related patents.

Festo Corp. v. Shoketsu Kinzoku Kogyo Kabushiki Co.

Supreme Court of the United States, 2002.
535 U.S. 722, 122 S.Ct. 1831, 152 L.Ed.2d 944.

■ JUSTICE KENNEDY delivered the opinion of the Court.

This case requires us to address once again the relation between two patent law concepts, the doctrine of equivalents and the rule of prosecution history estoppel. The Court considered the same concepts in *Warner-Jenkinson Co. v. Hilton Davis Chemical Co.*, 520 U.S. 17 (1997), and reaffirmed that a patent protects its holder against efforts of copyists to evade liability for infringement by making only insubstantial changes to a patented invention. At the same time, we appreciated that by extending protection beyond the literal terms in a patent the doctrine of equivalents can create substantial uncertainty about where the patent monopoly ends. *Id.*, at 29. If the range of equivalents is unclear, competitors may be unable to determine what is a permitted alternative to a patented invention and what is an infringing equivalent.

To reduce the uncertainty, *Warner-Jenkinson* acknowledged that competitors may rely on the prosecution history, the public record of the patent proceedings. In some cases the Patent and Trademark Office (PTO) may have rejected an earlier version of the patent application on the ground that a claim does not meet a statutory requirement for patentability. 35 U.S.C. § 132 (1994 ed., Supp. V). When the patentee responds to the rejection by narrowing his claims, this prosecution history estops him from

---

6. In *Diamond v. Chakrabarty*, genetically engineered (modified) bacteria could be patented because they did not occur naturally in nature. 447 U.S. 303, 100 S.Ct. 2204, 65 L.Ed.2d 144 (1980). In this case, Chakrabarty had modified a bacteria to create an oil-dissolving bioengineered microbe. The patent examiner rejected the claim because the microorganisms were living things that could not be patented under 35 U.S.C. § 101. The Court ruled that Chakrabarty had produced a new bacterium that was not naturally occurring and was thus patentable under § 101.

later arguing that the subject matter covered by the original, broader claim was nothing more than an equivalent. Competitors may rely on the estoppel to ensure that their own devices will not be found to infringe by equivalence.

In the decision now under review the Court of Appeals for the Federal Circuit held that by narrowing a claim to obtain a patent, the patentee surrenders all equivalents to the amended claim element. Petitioner asserts this holding departs from past precedent in two respects. First, it applies estoppel to every amendment made to satisfy the requirements of the Patent Act and not just to amendments made to avoid pre-emption by an earlier invention, *i.e.*, the prior art. Second, it holds that when estoppel arises, it bars suit against every equivalent to the amended claim element. The Court of Appeals acknowledged that this holding departed from its own cases, which applied a flexible bar when considering what claims of equivalence were estopped by the prosecution history. Petitioner argues that by replacing the flexible bar with a complete bar the Court of Appeals cast doubt on many existing patents that were amended during the application process when the law, as it then stood, did not apply so rigorous a standard.

We granted certiorari to consider these questions.

. . .

Petitioner Festo Corporation owns two patents for an improved magnetic rodless cylinder, a piston-driven device that relies on magnets to move objects in a conveying system. The device has many industrial uses and has been employed in machinery as diverse as sewing equipment and the Thunder Mountain ride at Disney World. Petitioner's patent applications, as often occurs, were amended during the prosecution proceedings. The application for the first patent, the Stoll Patent (U.S. Patent No. 4,354,-125), was amended after the patent examiner rejected the initial application because the exact method of operation was unclear and some claims were made in an impermissible way. (They were multiply dependent.) 35 U.S.C. § 112 (1994 ed.). The inventor, Dr. Stoll, submitted a new application designed to meet the examiner's objections and also added certain references to prior art. 37 CFR § 1.56 (2000). The second patent, the Carroll Patent (U.S. Patent No. 3,779,401), was also amended during a reexamination proceeding. The prior art references were added to this amended application as well. Both amended patents added a new limitation—that the inventions contain a pair of sealing rings, each having a lip on one side, which would prevent impurities from getting on the piston assembly. The amended Stoll Patent added the further limitation that the outer shell of the device, the sleeve, be made of a magnetizable material.

After Festo began selling its rodless cylinder, respondents (whom we refer to as SMC) entered the market with a device similar, but not identical, to the ones disclosed by Festo's patents. SMC's cylinder, rather than using two one-way sealing rings, employs a single sealing ring with a two-way lip. Furthermore, SMC's sleeve is made of a nonmagnetizable alloy. SMC's device does not fall within the literal claims of either patent, but petitioner contends that it is so similar that it infringes under the doctrine of equivalents.

SMC contends that Festo is estopped from making this argument because of the prosecution history of its patents. The sealing rings and the magnetized alloy in the Festo product were both disclosed for the first time in the amended applications. In SMC's view, these amendments narrowed the earlier applications, surrendering alternatives that are the very points of difference in the competing devices—the sealing rings and the type of alloy used to make the sleeve. As Festo narrowed its claims in these ways in order to obtain the patents, says SMC, Festo is now estopped from saying that these features are immaterial and that SMC's device is an equivalent of its own.

. . .

The patentee, as the author of the claim language, may be expected to draft claims encompassing readily known equivalents. A patentee's decision to narrow his claims through amendment may be presumed to be a general disclaimer of the territory between the original claim and the amended claim. *Exhibit Supply*, 315 U.S., at 136–137 ("By the amendment [the patentee] recognized and emphasized the difference between the two phrases and proclaimed his abandonment of all that is embraced in that difference"). There are some cases, however, where the amendment cannot reasonably be viewed as surrendering a particular equivalent. The equivalent may have been unforeseeable at the time of the application; the rationale underlying the amendment may bear no more than a tangential relation to the equivalent in question; or there may be some other reason suggesting that the patentee could not reasonably be expected to have described the insubstantial substitute in question. In those cases the patentee can overcome the presumption that prosecution history estoppel bars a finding of equivalence.

. . .

On the record before us, we cannot say petitioner has rebutted the presumptions that estoppel applies and that the equivalents at issue have been surrendered. Petitioner concedes that the limitations at issue—the sealing rings and the composition of the sleeve—were made in response to a rejection for reasons under § 112, if not also because of the prior art references. As the amendments were made for a reason relating to patentability, the question is not whether estoppel applies but what territory the amendments surrendered. While estoppel does not effect a complete bar, the question remains whether petitioner can demonstrate that the narrowing amendments did not surrender the particular equivalents at issue. On these questions, SMC may well prevail, for the sealing rings and the composition of the sleeve both were noted expressly in the prosecution history. These matters, however, should be determined in the first instance by further proceedings in the Court of Appeals or the District Court.

The judgment of the Federal Circuit is vacated, and the case is remanded for further proceedings consistent with this opinion.

NOTES AND QUESTIONS

1. *Intellectual Property Protections: Incentives or Barriers to Future Research?* Did the Supreme Court strike the right balance in *Festo*? There are strong arguments both for and against patenting genes and creating private databases. Protection of intellectual property provides industry with strong incentives to pursue new discoveries essential to progress in medicine and science. *See* John Burris et al., *The Human Genome Project After a Decade: Policy Issues*, 20 NATURE GENETICS 333–335 (1998). One study even suggested that without the incentives that patents and privatization offer, 60% of pharmaceutical products would not have been able to reach the market. *See* Simone Ayme, *Bridging the Gap Between Molecular Genetics and Metabolic Medicine: Access to Genetic Information*, 159 EUR. J. PEDIATRICS 183–185 (2000). With patenting, researchers are rewarded for their findings and may use revenue gained from patenting to further their research. Efforts are not wastefully duplicated and all researchers are assured access to new inventions.

Despite the undoubted stimulus to innovation, some commentators oppose strong intellectual property protection. They claim that biotechnology patents are inappropriately awarded at the easiest step of research and should be reserved for those who determine biological function or application. Because patents remain secret until they are granted, companies may develop a product only to discover that they have infringed on another's newly granted patent. Could patent stacking, the awarding of separate patents for an EST, a gene, and its protein, discourage product development due to the high royalty costs that all patent holders in the sequence would collect? Even if patents are not stacked, critics argue that the costs associated with patented research data will impede the development of serviceable diagnostics and therapeutics. Of those that are developed, private companies who own certain patents will enjoy a monopoly over certain genetic markets. More fundamentally, some opponents argue that patent holders are being permitted to inappropriately own part of a basic constituent of life. Is this a valid critique? In a 5–4 holding in *Diamond v. Chakrabarty*, 447 U.S. 303, 100 S.Ct. 2204, 65 L.Ed.2d 144 (1980), the Supreme Court allowed patenting on life forms for the first time when it ruled that a human-made, genetically engineered bacterium capable of breaking down components of crude oil constituted a new and useful "manufacture" or "composition of matter" that could be patented under 35 U.S.C. § 101. The Universal Declaration on the Human Genome and Human Rights states that the human genome "is the heritage of humanity." *See* Sec. IV, *infra*. Does this militate against "ownership" of genetic discoveries?

2. *Public Access to Mapping Data.* There is a conflict between intellectual property protection and open dissemination of mapping data to the public. *See* Paul L. Pearson, *Genome Mapping Databases: Data Acquisition, Storage and Access*, 1 CURRENT SCI. 119 (1991). Ready access to genetic information through programs such as the Human Genome Organization (HUGO) and HapMap currently allow anyone with internet access to obtain information on genetic diseases, genes and their locations, and mutations that have been found on cloned genes. Merck Research Laboratories has solidified these efforts by sponsoring a university-based effort to place comparable information to that found in private databases in the public domain. *See* Robert Cook–Deegan et al., *Intellectual Property: Patents, Secrecy and DNA.* 293 SCI. 217 (2001). Is this endeavor by Merck and other companies motivated by a public spirit or self-interest? Further research must be done before genetic information is commercially viable. By making current findings readily available to scientists, can these companies expedite the process of moving innovation from the bench to the market? Is a desire to expedite the process the only incentive for companies to sponsor such efforts?

3. *Patenting and the Public Interest.* Should policy makers reduce intellectual property protection for the public good? Congress has prohibited patents in a few cases, such as patenting nuclear weapons, where it believed the issuance of a patent was contrary to the public interest. The American Medical Association has made a similar request for Congress to prohibit patenting of medical and surgical procedures. With regard to human gene patenting, Rep. Lynn Rivers introduced two bills (H.R. 3967 and H.R. 3966) to the 107th Congress to address some of the problems surrounding gene patenting, but no action was taken.

B.   THE PROBLEM OF COMMERCIALIZATION: MINING AND HARVESTING DNA

Some commentators lament that we have entered an age of *"homo economicus"* in which human genetic material is increasingly becoming an object of trade: tissues, cell lines, and DNA will become commodities in a way that "violates body integrity, exploits powerless people, intrudes on human values, distorts research agendas, and weakens public trust in scientists and clinicians." Dorothy Nelkin et al., *Homo Economicus: Commercialization of Body Tissue in the Age of Biotechnology*, 28 HASTINGS CENT. REP. 30, 31 (Sept./Oct. 1998). A legislative approach to these issues could control unbridled commercialization by defining genetic materials as personal attributes rather than property, but no such standard currently exists. Instead, administrative guidelines include a plethora of conflicting DNA "banking" standards with little or no guidance regarding commercialization. Meanwhile, tissue can be extracted from people during routine care or research trials, stored indefinitely, and plumbed for information that could reveal information about entire groups of people. Furthermore, the individuals potentially subject to these measures need not be notified of possible commercial uses or allowed the opportunity to reject such applications. *See* National Bioethics Advisory Committee, RESEARCH INVOLVING HUMAN BIOLOGICAL MATERIALS: ETHICAL ISSUES AND POLICY GUIDANCE (1999). The NBAC report does not recommend any action regarding commercialization, but states that the topic deserves further consideration. Is government inactivity in this area a form of benign neglect or a purposeful laissez-faire approach allowing the market to drive genetic commercialization?

Consider the following statement:

> It is hypocritical to pretend that a free market in genetic information can exist when the very individuals whose privacy rights are being violated are not empowered to participate in that market. Far from promoting a free market in genetic information, the lack of government regulation merely sanctions a forced expropriation of information from those individuals least capable of protecting their own interests.

Richard S. Fedder, *To Know or Not to Know*, 21 J. LEG. MED. 557 (2000).

Bartha Maria Knoppers et al., *Commercialization of Genetic Research and Public Policy*

286 SCI. 2277–2278 (1999).

We are in the age of *"Homo economicus."* Human genetic material is increasingly an object of commerce. For organs at least, there is some international consensus against commercial trade. However, an overview of the issues raised by human genetics reveals confusion and concern among policy-makers and the general public about the appropriateness of commercialization. For society to deal with these new technologies, it is crucial to evaluate four emerging approaches to policy-making and to look at possible strategies in dealing with specific issues.

Human Rights Approach

Through the filter of human rights codes, constitutions, and international conventions, this approach relies on the courts. It circumscribes the applications of new technologies that otherwise might encourage discriminatory or stigmatizing practices. Policy-oriented decisions of high-ranking courts are strengthened by the fact that public interest groups can obtain standing to participate and help case law reflect public values. Such cases clarify issues and set far-reaching precedents in the interpretation of, for example, the right to privacy, or discrimination resulting from application of new technologies in the areas of employment or insurance. Yet, on the whole, they are ad hoc in nature and achieved after the technology has already been integrated into research and health care. Furthermore, like all litigation, the process is a costly and lengthy one. Finally, if the court is timorous and refuses to go beyond the facts or issues, it is a limited recourse.

Statutory Approach

In this method, specific legislation crafted in response to new technologies addresses the implications of scientific advances through prohibitions, constraints, or moratoria. This method has the advantage of immediate certainty, clarification, and precision, as well as being an expression of political consensus. Furthermore, such legislation can also prospectively foreclose avenues of research by prohibiting techniques such as the creation of human chimeras. The danger of this approach is that such legislation is limited to the current issues and tends to close the public debate. Moreover, if such statutes are adopted in rapid succession, there is a risk of contradictory positions and of inadequate definitions. The latter is particularly true when terms such as "embryo" or "cloning" are defined, for example, only to find that new knowledge or different techniques escape the statutory definition. Finally, if hastily adopted because of public outcry, they will be lacking a proper foundation based on scientific risk assessment.

Administrative Approach

A third possibility is an administrative approach through governmental or professional bodies. Such an approach allows for the gradual development of self-regulatory professional codes of conduct and, where necessary, licensing, monitoring, and quality assurance. Professionally and procedurally oriented, it ensures a "buy-in" by those involved, resulting in greater effectiveness and integration into practice. These professional codes, ethical guidelines, and standards of practice, however, can be seen as self-serving and as a way to avoid either lawsuits or restrictive legislation. Furthermore, the public does not participate in the drafting of these codes. Another drawback of this incremental approach is that it "administers" technologies through codes or standards and usually fails to explicitly enunciate the value-choices underlying their acceptance or to explain why certain constraints have been instituted.

Market–Driven Approach

Finally, a liberal, market-driven approach maintains that proper, professional practices will ultimately "win-out" in an unfettered marketplace. This approach seems to be the most flexible and supportive of scientific research. Technological development is dependent on investment and support, either public or private. The market, however, is also subject to lobbying by special interest groups, including those who stand to gain financially from public investment or lack of public control, and those who, for a variety of reasons, see certain technologies as potentially harmful or in conflict with their particular values. The difficulty these advocacy groups have in compromising inhibits the consensus necessary for successful, albeit limited, government-initiated oversight. This leaves the development of any given technology to the vagaries of the market, the chilling effect of litigation, and consumer choice. This is evident in the proliferation of private, unregulated infertility clinics and of mail-order genetic tests.

Particular Issues and Recommendations

Status of genetic material as it relates to commercialization. The current commercialization of the genomics revolution has led to concern that turning tissue, cell lines, and DNA into commodities "violates body integrity, exploits powerless people, intrudes on human values, distorts research agendas, and weakens public trust in scientists and clinicians." Respect for genetic material as part of the person and of humanity is consistent with the domestic positions of most countries. For example, in UNESCO's 1997 *Universal Declaration on the Human Genome and Human Rights*, the genome is considered to be the common heritage of humanity. The Declaration takes no position on the issue of the status of individual human genetic material except to maintain that "in its natural state [it] should not give rise to financial gains." Likewise regional instruments such as the European *Directive on the Legal Protection of Biotechnological Inventions* and the *Convention on Human Rights and Biomedicine* adopt this broad approach and consider human genetic material as part of the person and not as property.

. . .

Policy-makers should be sensitive to specific social, legal, and policy implications. Government inactivity could be perceived as endorsing a laissez-faire and market-driven approach. This would violate important societal values in most countries. Yet, in the face of the current trend toward commercialization of genetic research, extensive legislative interference could dry up the largely private sponsorship of genetic research.

Furthermore, the increasingly multicentered and international nature of human genetic research and pharmacogenomics suggests that the time is ripe for international harmonization. Although the Human Genome Organization (HUGO) has begun this effort, regional and international bodies such as the Council of Europe and the World Health Organization (WHO) would do well to develop a model professional code of DNA banking practices. The continued absence of common international, professional standards on the basic choices to be offered research participants will result in the continuation of contradictory approaches and undermine the possibility of procuring fundamental population data necessary to good science and so, good ethics.

Patents. Two approaches have appeared with regard to the issue of the patentability of human genetic material. The first, largely confined to Europe, and exemplified by the 1998 European Directive maintains that the human body or the simple discovery of some component (including gene sequences or partial sequences) are not patentable inventions [article 5(a)]. The second is market driven and leads to a situation of fragmentary and overlapping patents. This occurs whether the patent rights granted are broad or limited to partial sequences. According to HUGO, this has resulted in problems because, whether broad or narrow, these rights, preclude patenting of innovative disease gene discoveries, act as obstacles to investment, and are deterrents to deposition of information into databases

. . .

In the long run, it remains for national patent offices to take leadership in a way that inhibits a totally market-driven approach from impeding international, scientific collaboration. Failure to do so will eventually lead to costly litigation and loss of potential therapeutic advances.

Conflicts of interest. During the past 15 years, universities and health-care institutions have looked increasingly at private sources to pay expenses associated with research. Academic health-care centers conduct some kinds of research that may generate special concerns. Principal among these is the development or evaluation of products intended for clinical application that could have great commercial value. Concern grows as the boundary is increasingly blurred between the basic research conducted in the academic health center laboratories and the derivative product development that is often in the commercial sector.

Commercial partnerships represent unfamiliar terrain for many university and health research institutions. They increase institutional obligations to minimize or even eliminate the potential for conflicts of interest that arise when private financial gain becomes part of the research equation. Universities and health-care institutions require strong and clear policies to deal with conflicts of interest, as well as effective ethics review bodies to evaluate human subjects research. Because research institutions themselves face potential conflicts of interest, policy-making is best handled by legislative action that would establish standards and require local institutions, both public and private, to adopt appropriate policies and review mechanisms. It should also ensure that those responsible for conflict of interest and research ethics review have adequate funding as well as sufficient autonomy.

Conclusion

Each approach has advantages and disadvantages. The choice between them, or a mix thereof, depends on the degree of public trust in their credibility and effectiveness and on the state of the particular debate. Policy-makers should frame their decisions according to the values and needs of the persons and populations who contributed to genetic research and have legitimate expectations of participating in the benefits thereof.

C.   REGULATING SCIENCE AND MEDICINE

1.   INTERNATIONAL GUIDELINES

Due to the cooperative and international nature of genetic development, is it appropriate for guidelines to be adopted across nations to ensure that countries do not create multilayered barriers to advancement and application? The Human Genome Organization (HUGO) has begun this effort, and the Hereditary Diseases Program of the WHO has proposed guidelines, but no formal adoption has resulted. The only firm outline of international guidelines was created by the General Conference of the United Nations Educational, Scientific and Cultural Organization (UNESCO) in 1997.

UNESCO, which is comprised of 190 member states, adopted the Universal Declaration on the Human Genome and Human Rights to address the unresolved ethical issues of the rapid advancements in science and technology. UNESCO Gen. Conf. Res. 29 C/Res.16, *reprinted in* Records of the General Conference, UNESCO, 29th Sess., 29 C/Resolution 19, at 41 (1997) (adopted by the UN General Assembly, G.A. res. 152, U.N. GAOR, 53rd Sess., U.N. Doc. A/RES/53/152 (1999)) (1997). This document, which identified the genome as the common heritage of humanity, obliges member states to "take appropriate measures to promote the principles set out in the Declaration and encourage their implementation." Namely, it is an effort to place the dignity and privacy of individuals above the push for genetic knowledge and advancement. With regard to commercialization, it takes no specific position, but identifies human genetic material as a part of people rather than property and states that "in its natural state [the human genome] should not give rise to financial gains" (Article 4).

Universal Declaration on the Human Genome and Human Rights

UNESCO Gen. Conf. Res. 29 C/Res.16, *reprinted in* Records of the General Conference, UNESCO, 29th Sess., 29 C/Resolution 19, at 41 (1997) (adopted by the UN General Assembly, G.A. res. 152, U.N. GAOR, 53rd Sess., U.N. Doc. A/RES/53/152 (1999)) (1997).

Introduction

The Universal Declaration on the Human Genome and Human Rights, which was adopted unanimously and by acclamation by the General Conference of UNESCO at its 29th session on 11 November 1997, is the first universal instrument in the field of biology. The uncontested merit of this text resides in the balance it strikes between safeguarding respect for human rights and fundamental freedoms and the need to ensure freedom of research.

Together with the Declaration, UNESCO's General Conference adopted a resolution for its implementation, which commits States to taking appropriate measures to promote the principles set out in the Declaration and encourage their implementation.

The moral commitment entered into by States in adopting the Universal Declaration on the Human Genome and Human Rights is a starting point, the beginning of international awareness of the need for ethical issues to be addressed in science and technology. It is now up to States, through the measures they decide to adopt, to put the Declaration into practice and thus ensure its continued existence.

A.   *Human dignity and the human genome*

Article 1

The human genome underlies the fundamental unity of all members of the human family, as well as the recognition of their inherent dignity and diversity. In a symbolic sense, it is the heritage of humanity.

Article 2

(a) Everyone has a right to respect for their dignity and for their rights regardless of their genetic characteristics.

(b) That dignity makes it imperative not to reduce individuals to their genetic characteristics and to respect their uniqueness and diversity.

Article 3

The human genome, which by its nature evolves, is subject to mutations. It contains potentialities that are expressed differently according to each individual's natural and social environment including the individual's state of health, living conditions, nutrition and education.

Article 4

The human genome in its natural state shall not give rise to financial gains.

B.   *Rights of the persons concerned*

Article 5

(a) Research, treatment or diagnosis affecting an individual's genome shall be undertaken only after rigorous and prior assessment of the potential risks and benefits pertaining thereto and in accordance with any other requirement of national law.

(b) In all cases, the prior, free and informed consent of the person concerned shall be obtained. If the latter is not in a position to consent, consent or authorization shall be obtained in the manner prescribed by law, guided by the person's best interest.

(c) The right of each individual to decide whether or not to be informed of the results of genetic examination and the resulting consequences should be respected.

(d) In the case of research, protocols shall, in addition, be submitted for prior review in accordance with relevant national and international research standards or guidelines.

(e) If according to the law a person does not have the capacity to consent, research affecting his or her genome may only be carried out for his or her direct health benefit, subject to the authorization and the protective conditions prescribed by law. Research which does not have an expected direct health benefit may only be undertaken by way of exception, with the utmost restraint, exposing the person only to a minimal risk and minimal burden and if the research is intended to contribute to the health benefit of other persons in the same age category or with the same genetic condition, subject to the conditions prescribed by law, and provided such research is compatible with the protection of the individual's human rights.

Article 6

No one shall be subjected to discrimination based on genetic characteristics that is intended to infringe or has the effect of infringing human rights, fundamental freedoms and human dignity.

Article 7

Genetic data associated with an identifiable person and stored or processed for the purposes of research or any other purpose must be held confidential in the conditions set by law.

Article 8

Every individual shall have the right, according to international and national law, to just reparation for any damage sustained as a direct and determining result of an intervention affecting his or her genome.

Article 9

In order to protect human rights and fundamental freedoms, limitations to the principles of consent and confidentiality may only be prescribed by law, for compelling reasons within the bounds of public international law and the international law of human rights.

C.   Research on the human genome

Article 10

No research or research applications concerning the human genome, in particular in the fields of biology, genetics and medicine, should prevail over respect for the human rights, fundamental freedoms and human dignity of individuals or, where applicable, of groups of people.

Article 11

Practices which are contrary to human dignity, such as reproductive cloning of human beings, shall not be permitted. States and competent international organizations are invited to co-operate in identifying such practices and in taking, at national or international level, the measures necessary to ensure that the principles set out in this Declaration are respected.

Article 12

(a) Benefits from advances in biology, genetics and medicine, concerning the human genome, shall be made available to all, with due regard for the dignity and human rights of each individual.

(b) Freedom of research, which is necessary for the progress of knowledge, is part of freedom of thought. The applications of research, including applications in biology, genetics and medicine, concerning the human genome, shall seek to offer relief from suffering and improve the health of individuals and humankind as a whole.

D.   Conditions for the exercise of scientific activity

Article 13

The responsibilities inherent in the activities of researchers, including meticulousness, caution, intellectual honesty and integrity in carrying out their research as well as in the presentation and utilization of their findings, should be the subject of particular attention in the framework of research on the human genome, because of its ethical and social implications. Public and private science policy-makers also have particular responsibilities in this respect.

Article 14

States should take appropriate measures to foster the intellectual and material conditions favourable to freedom in the conduct of research on the human genome and to consider the ethical, legal, social and economic implications of such research, on the basis of the principles set out in this Declaration.

Article 15

States should take appropriate steps to provide the framework for the free exercise of research on the human genome with due regard for the principles set out in this Declaration, in order to safeguard respect for human rights, fundamental freedoms and human dignity and to protect public health. They should seek to ensure that research results are not used for non-peaceful purposes.

Article 16

States should recognize the value of promoting, at various levels, as appropriate, the establishment of independent, multidisciplinary and pluralist ethics committees to assess the ethical, legal and social issues raised by research on the human genome and its application.

E.   Solidarity and international co-operation

Article 17

States should respect and promote the practice of solidarity towards individuals, families and population groups who are particularly vulnerable to or affected by disease or disability of a genetic character. They should foster, *inter alia,* research on the identification, prevention and treatment of genetically-based and genetically-influenced diseases, in particular rare as well as endemic diseases which affect large numbers of the world's population.

Article 18

States should make every effort, with due and appropriate regard for the principles set out in this Declaration, to continue fostering the international dissemination of scientific knowledge concerning the human genome, human diversity and genetic research and, in that regard, to foster scientific and cultural co-operation, particularly between industrialized and developing countries.

Article 19

(a) In the framework of international co-operation with developing countries, States should seek to encourage measures enabling:

(i) assessment of the risks and benefits pertaining to research on the human genome to be carried out and abuse to be prevented;

(ii) genetics, taking into consideration their specific problems, to be developed and strengthened;

(iii) developing countries to benefit from the achievements of scientific and technological research so that their use in favour of economic and social progress can be to the benefit of all;

(iv) the free exchange of scientific knowledge and information in the areas of biology, genetics and medicine to be promoted.

(b) Relevant international organizations should support and promote the initiatives taken by States for the above-mentioned purposes.

F.   Promotion of the principles set out in the Declaration

Article 20

States should take appropriate measures to promote the principles set out in the Declaration, through education and relevant means, *inter alia* through the conduct of research and training in interdisciplinary fields and through the promotion of education in bioethics, at all levels, in particular for those responsible for science policies.

Article 21

States should take appropriate measures to encourage other forms of research, training and information dissemination conducive to raising the awareness of society and all of its members of their responsibilities regarding the fundamental issues relating to the defense of human dignity which may be raised by research in biology, in genetics and in medicine, and its applications. They should also undertake to facilitate on this subject an open international discussion, ensuring the free expression of various socio-cultural, religious and philosophical opinions.

NOTES AND QUESTIONS

The Declaration takes a human rights approach to regulating genetic research, contextualizing rights and duties of researchers, practitioners, and individuals in terms of international human rights norms. Note, however, the Declaration's relatively weak expression of states' obligations under Articles 20 and 21. These provisions focus on the state's role as educator rather than as regulator. If a state does no more than educate, and declines to regulate, is it implicitly endorsing a market-driven approach?

2.   REGULATORY INITIATIVES IN THE UNITED STATES

Inaction at the international level has been mirrored by lack of progress on the national stage as well. With the completion of the Human Genome Project and the first wave of genetic tests for chronic diseases entering the commercial marketplace, there is intense interest in informed public policy to manage genetic commercialization. Legislators have expressed interest in genetic privacy and anti-discrimination, the appropriate use of genetic services and technologies, and the integration of genetics in health, environmental, and social policy. While nearly twelve bills were read and referred to Congressional committees between 2002 and 2004, no federal legislative action has been taken.

In February 2000, President Clinton signed an executive order that prohibits federal departments and agencies from using genetic information in any hiring or promotion action. As a result of this action, federal employers cannot request or require employees to undergo genetic tests in order to evaluate an employee's ability to perform his or her job; use protected genetic information to classify employees in a manner that deprives them of advancement opportunities; or obtain or disclose genetic information about employees or potential employees, except when it is necessary to provide medical treatment to employees, ensure workplace health and safety, or provide occupational and health researchers access to data. *See* EXEC. ORDER 13145, 65 FED. REG. 6,877 (Feb. 10, 2000).

In 1999, the Secretary's Advisory Committee on Genetic Testing (SACGT) was established to advise the Department of Health and Human Services on the medical, scientific, ethical, legal, and social issues raised by genetic testing. SACGT, *About SACGT*, at http://www4.od.nih.gov /oba/sacgt.htm. Muin Khoury and colleagues described SACGT's recommendations:

> There was an overwhelming concern on the part of the public regarding discrimination in employment and insurance. The advisory committee recommended the support of legislation preventing discrimination on the basis of genetic information and increased oversight of genetic testing. The Food and Drug Administration was charged as the lead agency and was urged to take an innovative approach and consult experts outside the agency. The goal is to generate specific language for the labeling of genetic tests, much as drugs are described in the *Physicians' Desk Reference*. Such labeling would provide persons considering, and health professionals recommending, genetic tests with information about the clinical validity and value of the test—what information the test will provide, what choices will be available to people after they know their test results, and the limits of the test.

Muin J. Khoury et al., *Population Screening in the Age of Genomic Medicine*, 348 NEW ENG. J. MED. 50, 56 (2003). In July 2004, the SACGT was allowed to expire and the Secretary's Advisory Committee on Genetics, Health, and Society (SACGHS) was formed to replace it. Secretary's Advisory Committee on Genetics, Health, and Society, *at* http://www4.od.nih.gov/oba/SACGHS.htm (last visited Oct. 12, 2004).

Secretary's Advisory Committee on Genetic Testing, ENHANCING THE OVERSIGHT OF GENETIC TESTS: RECOMMENDATIONS OF THE SACGT

8–14 (2000).

CURRENT SYSTEM OF OVERSIGHT OF GENETIC TESTS

As part of its charge, SACGT reviewed the provisions for oversight of genetic tests already in place. Currently, government agencies accord genetic and nongenetic tests the same level of oversight. Genetic tests are regulated at the federal level through three mechanisms:

1) the Clinical Laboratory Improvement Amendments (CLIA) (42 CFR 493);

2) the Federal Food, Drug, and Cosmetic Act (21 USC 301 et seq.); and

3) during investigational phases, the Federal Policy for the Protection of Human Subjects (45 CFR 46, 21 CFR 50, and 21 CFR 56).

Four Department of Health and Human Services (DHHS) organizations have roles in the oversight of genetic tests: the Centers for Disease Control and Prevention (CDC), the Food and Drug Administration (FDA), the Health Care Financing Administration (HCFA), and the Office for Human Research Protection (OHRP). Although they do not have regulatory functions, NIH, the Health Resources and Services Administration (HRSA), and the Agency for Healthcare Research and Quality (AHRQ) support research activities and demonstration projects that generate knowledge about and experience with genetics and genetic testing. In addition, some states regulate genetic tests, and some professional organizations have issued relevant guidelines for professional practice.

The Roles of CDC and HCFA

All laboratory tests performed for the purpose of providing information about the health of an individual must be conducted in laboratories certified under CLIA. The CLIA program provides oversight of laboratories through on-site inspections conducted every two years by HCFA, using its own scientific surveyors or surveyors of deemed organizations or state-operated CLIA programs approved for this purpose. This oversight includes a comprehensive evaluation of the laboratory's operating environment, personnel, proficiency testing, quality control, and quality assurance. Although laboratories under CLIA are responsible for all aspects of the testing process (from specimen collection through analysis and reporting of the results), CLIA oversight has emphasized intra-laboratory processes as opposed to the clinical uses of test results. HCFA and CDC are taking steps to develop more specific laboratory requirements for genetic testing under CLIA, including provisions for the pre-and post-analytical phases of the testing process, and CDC issued a Notice of Intent in the *Federal Register* to gather public comment on the proposed changes. Currently, CLIA does not address additional aspects of oversight that are critical to the appropriate use of genetic tests, such as clinical validity including clinical sensitivity and clinical specificity, clinical utility, and issues related to informed consent and genetic counseling.

Through its Office of Genetics and Disease Prevention, CDC also has a role in addressing the public health impact of advances in genetic research; furthering the collection, analysis, dissemination, and use of peer-reviewed epidemiologic information on human genes; and coordinating the translation of genetic information into public health research, policy, and practice. CDC is also leading an interagency effort to explore how voluntary, public/private partnerships might help encourage and facilitate the gathering, review, and dissemination of data on the clinical validity of genetic tests. Two pilot data collection efforts, one for cystic fibrosis and one for hereditary hemochromatosis, are in the preliminary stages.

The Role of FDA

All laboratory tests and their components are subject to FDA oversight under the Federal Food, Drug, and Cosmetic Act. Under this law, laboratory tests are considered to be diagnostic devices, and tests that are packaged and sold as kits to multiple laboratories require pre-market approval or clearance by FDA. This pre-market review involves an analysis of the device's accuracy as well as its analytical sensitivity and analytical specificity. Pre-market review is performed based on data submitted by sponsors to scientific reviewers in the Division of Clinical Laboratory Devices in FDA's Office of Device Evaluation. . . .

Most new genetic tests are being developed by laboratories and are being provided as clinical laboratory services. These tests are referred to as in-house tests or "home brews." FDA has stated that it has authority, by law, to regulate such tests, but the agency has elected as a matter of enforcement discretion to not exercise that authority, in part because the number of such tests is estimated to exceed the agency's current review capacity.

However, FDA has taken steps to establish a measure of regulation of home brew tests by instituting controls over the active ingredients (analyte-specific reagents) used by laboratories to perform genetic tests. This regulation subjects reagent manufacturers to certain general controls, such as good manufacturing practices.

With few exceptions, however, the current regulatory process does not require a pre-market review of the reagents. (The exceptions involve certain reagents that are used to ensure the safety of the blood supply and to test for high-risk public health problems such as HIV and tuberculosis.) The regulation restricts the sale of reagents to laboratories performing high-complexity tests and requires that certain information accompany both the reagents and the test results. The labels for the reagents must, among other things, state that "analytical and performance characteristics are not established." Also, the test results must identify the laboratory that developed the test and its performance characteristics and must include a statement that the test "has not been cleared or approved by the U.S. FDA." In addition, the regulation prohibits direct marketing of most home brew tests to consumers. In 1999, FDA established the Molecular and Clinical Genetics Panel of the Medical Devices Advisory Committee to serve as a source of independent advice in the area of DNA-based diagnostics.

The Role of Regulations Protecting Human Subjects

Additional oversight is provided during the research phase of genetic testing if the research involves human subjects or identifiable samples of their DNA. OHRP and FDA administer regulations governing the protection of human research subjects. OHRP oversees the protection of human research subjects in DHHS-funded research. FDA oversees the protection of human research subjects in trials of investigational (not yet approved) devices, drugs, or biologics being developed for eventual commercial use.

Fundamental requirements of these regulations are that experimental protocols involving human subjects must be reviewed by an organization's Institutional Review Board (IRB) to assure the safety of the subjects, to review and approve the informed consent process, and to evaluate whether risks outweigh potential benefits. The regulations apply if the trial is funded in whole or in part by a DHHS agency or if the trial is conducted with the intent to develop a test for commercial use. However, FDA regulations do not apply to laboratories developing home brew genetic tests.

. . .

The Role of the States

State health agencies, particularly state public health laboratories, have an oversight role in genetic testing, including the licensure of personnel and facilities that perform genetic tests. State public health laboratories and state-operated laboratory licensure programs, which have been deemed equivalent to the federal CLIA program, are responsible for quality assurance activities. A few states, such as New York and California, have promulgated regulations that go beyond the requirements of CLIA. States also administer newborn screening programs and provide other genetic services through maternal and child health programs.

The state newborn screening laboratories must meet the requirements of CLIA's quality control and proficiency testing programs, but in general there is little federal oversight of their programs. State newborn screening laboratories and many commercial laboratories that perform testing for state newborn screening programs have used the National Newborn Screening Quality Assurance Program for verifying test accuracy and for meeting CLIA quality assurance requirements. This is particularly important because of the absence of HCFA-approved proficiency testing programs for newborn screening.

CONCLUSIONS AND RECOMMENDATIONS

Genetic tests offer great promise and provide hope for many people who wish to improve the health of their families and themselves. At the same time, if introduced prematurely or applied inappropriately, the outcomes of genetic testing could place some individuals and groups at risk. Thus, an important balance must be struck between the need to encourage the development and dissemination of new tests and the need to ensure that their introduction yields more benefit than harm.

SACGT is aware of the risks of genetic tests and the unique ability of these risks to extend beyond the individual being tested to the family and population. Although many citizens believe that the risks and potential benefits of genetic tests are no different than those posed by any other type of medical test, there is a widespread perception that these tests *are* different and that people experience genetic testing in a way that is dissimilar to the experience of other forms of medical testing. In light of public concerns as well as the potential revolutionary and widespread impact of genetic tests and other genetic technologies on the practice of medicine and health care, society should be assured that genetic tests meet the highest standards available and that information obtained through genetic testing is protected from abuse.

. . .

Current oversight does not specifically address whether genetic education and qualified counseling should be made available for all genetic tests. Genetic test results may be difficult to interpret and present in an understandable manner, raise important questions related to disclosure of test results to family members, and sometimes involve difficult treatment decisions. Because of these intricate issues, some have suggested that those who offer genetic tests should be encouraged or required to make genetic education or counseling available to those considering genetic testing and their family members.

Even after a test has been accepted into clinical practice, some observers have suggested that because of the predictive power of some genetic tests and the impact that test results may have on individuals and their families, tests should not be administered unless the individual has been fully informed of the test's risks and benefits and documentation of written informed consent has been obtained. There is currently no requirement for such an informed consent.

NOTES AND QUESTIONS

What are the implications of the relative paucity of regulation in the development and use of genetic technology? In such an environment, can the public be assured that genetic testing will not be "introduced prematurely or applied inappropriately?" Some argue that genetic tests are not materially different from other kinds of clinical tests and, therefore, should not be subject to more intense regulation. Are predictive genetic tests sufficiently different to warrant more rigorous governmental oversight? Suppose the FDA were to require genetic tests to be "safe and effective" before being approved for use. What would it take to prove that a genetic test is "effective?" Would it only require that the test be sufficiently sensitive and specific? Alternatively, would manufacturers have to prove that there were clinically useful interventions to prevent or ameliorate the disease in question?

Finally, should the federal government or the states require that genetic counseling be made available to patients who undergo testing?

Curtis A. Kin, *Coming Soon to the "Genetic Supermarket" Near You*

48 STAN. L. REV. 1573 (1996).

In general, the federal government has not enacted any blanket prohibitions on experimentation with or applications of biotechnology and gene therapy for human subjects. Researchers need only meet the regulatory guidelines and agency policies of the Coordinated Framework on Biotechnology. A federal inter-agency working group proposed the Coordinated Framework in 1984 to address health and environmental concerns triggered by emerging biotechnology and genetic experiments. The Coordinated Framework, however, does not explicitly address the cosmetic enhancement or alteration capabilities of biotechnology and gene therapy because, at the time of its conception, such applications were just coming to fruition. To this day, the Coordinated Framework and other regulatory policies for biotechnology and gene therapy have not properly addressed those capabilities, despite the dawning reality of effective genetic manipulation technologies.

. . .

The old fears and criticisms of eugenics do not apply to the new eugenics movement, which is neither state-sponsored nor an experiment imposed on unwilling participants. Rather, the new eugenics respects individual autonomy in what Robert Nozick has termed the "genetic supermarket," where individuals freely shop and choose the features and traits they desire for themselves and their children. Supporters of the new eugenics argue that the "genetic supermarket" poses no significant problems because there exists no centralized control over the future of human development.

Although the "genetic supermarket" may preserve autonomy by permitting individuals to choose or to refuse biotech and genetic enhancement, unregulated and unrestricted enhancement applications may nevertheless lead to disastrous results. Eugenics should be scrutinized in terms of its consequences, not simply in terms of the motives of its actors. Even if individual actors do not intend their choices to cause larger population effects, the collective results of individual actions may create devastating societal consequences. Thus, in order to protect society from the net effects of individual choices, the government must regulate enhancement applications of emerging genetics. The threat "isn't that the government will get involved in reproductive [and genetic] choices, but that it won't."

. . .

In a market economy in which individuals seek to gain competitive advantage over one another, it seems inevitable that the availability of new enhancement applications would trigger a "race to perfection" among individual actors.

V. Genetics and Society: Ethical, Legal, and Social Implications

As mentioned earlier, Congress devoted 5% of human genome funding to the ethical, legal, and social issues (ELSI). Congress thus recognized the powerful effects of genetics on individuals and communities as well as the need to consider ethics and law as guideposts for scientific progress. This section discusses important social issues such as privacy, discrimination, and distributive justice. An overarching question is whether genetic data are fundamentally the same as, or different from, other health data. Put another way, should genetics policies be specially designed to take account of the important and unique attributes of the human genome?

A. Genetics Exceptionalism

Thus far, this chapter has demonstrated the vast potential for genetic information to transform our understanding of health and disease. Some scholars see genetic information as so scientifically crucial and so personally intimate that it should attain an "exceptional" status. Exceptionalists view genetic information as distinct from, and more sensitive than, other personal health information. This perspective maintains that genetic information is so closely associated with personal, family, and group identity that its misuse could severely affect people's life opportunities. Policies based on exceptionalism give genetic information special status and protection especially in privacy and anti-discrimination laws. This heightened status is analogous to the decision by many states to treat HIV/AIDS status differently than information about other sexually transmitted diseases such as syphilis, gonorrhea, and hepatitis B.

Michael J. Green & Jeffrey R. Botkin, *Genetic Exceptionalism in Medicine: Clarifying the Differences between Genetic and Nongenetic Tests*

138 Annals Internal Med. 571–575 (2003).

The identification of disease-conferring genes and the development of tests to confirm or predict genetic predisposition to disease have been greeted with enthusiasm by the scientific community, but numerous ethical problems related to testing have been identified. Some suggest that genetic testing for susceptibility to diseases such as breast cancer is like any other evaluation of asymptomatic persons and should be handled no differently from cholesterol testing. This point of view is not widely held, however. Others have recommended treating genetic tests as "special" by requiring rules to protect privacy, by providing elaborate pretest education and psychological counseling, and by obtaining meaningful informed consent before genetic testing is performed. Some have argued that certain genetic tests should be offered only in experimental protocols. Legislators have passed laws to limit or prohibit discriminatory uses of genetic information, and an advisory committee to the U.S. Surgeon General has recommended that governmental agencies oversee all genetic testing.

. . .

In this paper, we discuss predictive genetic testing, that is, testing of asymptomatic persons for future health problems. Sometimes known as *susceptibility testing,* this practice often raises particularly troubling ethical concerns. In predictive genetic testing, genetic material is analyzed to identify particular mutations or polymorphisms that increase the probability of disease development. Predictive testing differs from diagnostic testing in that the former is generally used to identify risks in those without symptoms, whereas the latter is used to confirm diagnoses in those who are ill.

Common Factors among Genetic and Nongenetic Predictive Tests

Predictive genetic tests have at least three features in common with nongenetic predictive tests. First, each has a similar main purpose: to identify those at increased risk for developing a health-related disorder later in life (for example, *BRCA1/BRCA2* testing to identify risk for breast cancer or cholesterol evaluation to identify risk for heart attack or stoke). Second, the clinical process for obtaining genetic and nongenetic predictive information is often similar. A patient and physician address health maintenance or discuss a health concern, and a history and physical examination are conducted. Ideally, the physician determines whether additional information is needed, mentions the availability of a test to the patient, and discusses the risks and benefits of testing. If the patient decides to be tested, there is little physical risk other than that involved in a simple blood draw or cheek swab. Third, storage and retrieval of results of genetic and nongenetic tests are the same, in the written or computerized medical record. All of the advantages and disadvantages of medical record keeping, including lapses of privacy, apply equally to genetic and nongenetic information. Thus, genetic and nongenetic tests have several features in common. To understand the rationale for approaching genetic information with special care, it is necessary to examine arguments about the purportedly unique features of this information.

Do Genetic Tests Warrant Exceptional Treatment?

The claim that genetic information is unique and deserves special consideration is known as "genetic exceptionalism." There are several reasons why one might be tempted to treat genetic information, particularly that gathered through predictive genetic tests, as exceptional: 1) It can help predict a person's medical future, 2) it divulges information about family members, 3) it has been used to discriminate and stigmatize, and 4) it may result in serious psychological harm. Such reasons have not been universally persuasive, however and a more detailed evaluation shows that there are few, if any, morally relevant differences between genetic and nongenetic tests. We examine each of the preceding four claims in turn.

Claim 1:   Genetic Information Can Predict a Person's Medical Future

One defining characteristic of genetic testing is that it uses molecular information to draw conclusions about a person's past, present, and future health. Susan Vance, whose mother, aunt, two cousins, and two sisters had breast cancer, learned, just before surgery to remove both breasts, that she did not carry the mutated gene that ran in her family. Knowledge of her genetic makeup led to cancellation of surgery, a life-altering event. However, the ability to alter lives by predicting future health is not unique to genetic testing. A positive result on an HIV test portends the development of AIDS, a positive result on a tuberculin skin test may foretell the development of active tuberculosis, and high blood pressure or cholesterol measurements may indicate an increased risk for heart disease. Each of these revelations can be life altering. As such, the mere fact that genetic information is predictive does not distinguish it from nongenetic information.

There are, however, two important differences between the predictive capabilities of genetic and nongenetic tests. First, although both can identify risk factors for future illness, detection of highly penetrant genetic mutations may indicate a substantially higher risk than abnormalities discovered by nongenetic tests. For instance, persons with genetic mutations for Huntington disease or familial adenomatous polyposis are nearly certain to develop Huntington disease or colon cancer. So, while the type of information delivered by both genetic and nongenetic tests may be similar, for some positive genetic test results the risks detected are greater and disease is inevitable.

The second difference is one of perception. Our society views genetic information as somehow more central to our core being than other types of biological information. Right or wrong, genetic information is believed to reveal who we "really" are, so information from genetic testing is often seen as more consequential than that from other sources.

Claim 2: Genetic Test Results Divulge Information about Family Members

Another feature of predictive genetic testing is that results can affect a patient's family. If a woman inherits a mutation in a *BRCA1/BRCA2* gene, her risk for breast or ovarian cancer is markedly increased, as is that of her female siblings and children. Likewise, a gene mutation for susceptibility to colon cancer has implications for relatives: Should they be tested? Is there an obligation to disclose test results to relatives who may be affected?

. . .

What is different between genetic and nongenetic predictive tests is that genetic tests identify predispositions that are exclusively transmitted vertically (from parent to child), while nongenetic tests identify predispositions transmitted in a variety of ways (exposure to common environmental risk factors or person-to-person contact). Thus, through genetic information, a definitive diagnosis can sometimes be made even in a patient who declines to be tested. For example, if a grandparent and grandchild carry the relevant mutation for Huntington's disease, the parent between these generations also carries the faulty gene and will almost certainly develop the disease.

Claim 3:   Genetic Information Can Be Used To Discriminate against and Stigmatize Individuals

Historically, genetic information has been used to discriminate against individuals and groups, particularly Jewish persons and other minorities. In the early 1900s, bolstered by a popular eugenics movement supported by prominent intellectuals, politicians, and scientists, such discriminatory practices were common in the United States. There is considerable concern that the proliferation of new genetic tests could once more lead to unfair or restrictive practices. Several studies have documented discrimination by insurers and employers, although a recent review concluded that actual discrimination by health insurers is rare. Despite state and federal legislation to limit or prohibit genetic discrimination in the United States, recent rulings in the United Kingdom permit insurers to consider genetic test results when issuing policies, and fear of genetic discrimination in the United States has been cited as one of the greatest barriers to the integration of genetic tests into clinical practice.

However disturbing such reports of discrimination may be, genetic information is not the only medical information used for stigmatization or discrimination. Insurance underwriters routinely rely on such information as HIV status, serum cholesterol levels, alcohol or narcotic addiction, and even blood pressure to determine eligibility and rates for life or disability insurance. For years, patients with AIDS and leprosy have been stigmatized. In addition, as Susan Sontag ably illustrated by citing tuberculosis and cancer as examples, people often use vilifying metaphors to describe patients who are ill, particularly if their disease is poorly understood. If it is wrong to use genetic information to discriminate, stigmatize, or limit access to employment or insurance, it is no less wrong to employ nongenetic information for the same purposes.

Claim 4:   Genetic Testing Can Cause Serious Psychological Harm

A final argument for genetic exceptionalism is that the results of genetic tests may have substantial psychological consequences, such as depression, anxiety, and persistent fear. However, psychological risks to patients are not unique to those who undergo predictive genetic testing, nor are the risks more severe. Patients who learn they may have diseases ranging from HIV infection to hypertension also experience distress, and research on "labeling" shows that simply telling a person he or she has any type of medical disorder can adversely affect that person's life.

.   .   .

Discussion

The introduction of genetic tests into medical practice raises numerous ethical and policy issues. These tests can help predict the future, have implications for kin, may be used to stigmatize, and often lead to psychological distress. Because of these concerns, some people claim that predictive genetic testing requires special handling. However, as we have shown, little about genetic tests themselves is exceptional, since such problems also occur with nongenetic tests.

We suggest that genetic information is simply one of several types of medical data that have the potential to help or to harm people. Like nongenetic information, genetic data can be used to help guide decisions about lifestyle choices, reproductive behavior, and medical interventions. Like nongenetic information, genetic data can, when misused, cause damage. If genetic information is not exceptional, then, which if any predictive tests of asymptomatic persons should be handled with special care and caution? One way to answer this question is to consider a test's effect on the patient in relation to four domains: 1) the degree to which information learned from the test can be stigmatizing, 2) the effect of the test results on others, 3) the availability of effective interventions to alter the natural course predicted by the information, and 4) the complexity involved in interpreting test results.

. . .

Tests for conditions that are less stigmatizing, have few serious implications for others, can be effectively treated, and yield results clinicians are trained to interpret require no additional consent and privacy precautions beyond standard, accepted procedures. Examples include glucose or cholesterol testing, tests of thyroid-stimulating hormone for hypothyroidism, and perhaps testing for suspected hereditary hemochromatosis. In effect, the justification for applying extra scrutiny to a test has little to do with the biological underpinnings of the disease or the method by which the information is obtained. Rather, the way a test is treated should depend on the consequences of its use in clinical practice. Whether the test is "genetic" is only marginally relevant.

In conclusion, the introduction of predictive genetic testing into medical practice does not fundamentally alter the obligations of physicians to their patients, nor does it introduce novel ethical dilemmas. Physicians must remain committed to avoiding unnecessary harm. However, because both genetic and nongenetic information can result in net benefit or harm, practitioners and patients must consider the consequences of any predictive testing *before* an asymptomatic person learns what he or she might not want to know. If a test could identify a risk for a stigmatizing disease, negatively affect others, identify a disease with no acceptable and effective treatment, and yield complex results difficult for practicing clinicians to interpret, the need for that test (whether genetic or nongenetic) should be carefully assessed.

NOTES AND QUESTIONS

Does genetic information deserve a special status in health policy formulation? If so, what kinds of data should be afforded this status? Is genetic information so integral to health that it cannot realistically be separated from other health information? A growing body of research shows that nearly all health conditions may have a genetic basis. If this is the case, then would segregating genetic information from other health information be practical and effectual? Likewise, because diseases result from the interaction between genes and environment, genetic advances will likely extend and expand current medical practices rather than supplant such efforts. Besides the entanglement problems, would limiting the free use of genetic information hinder the development of beneficial genetic services and technologies? *See generally*, Lawrence O. Gostin & James G. Hodge, Jr., *Genetics Privacy and the Law: An End to Genetics Exceptionalism*, 40 JURIMETRICS J. 21 (1999).

Should persons with genetic disorders receive greater legal protection than those with equally serious diseases that are attributable to other causes? Might genetics exceptionalism inadvertently stigmatize individuals with genetic diseases? Which would be the preferable approach to problems of discrimination: a generic antidiscrimination statute that applies to a broad range of diseases and disabilities such as the Americans with Disabilities Act or a genetic-specific antidiscrimination law?

B.   GENETIC PRIVACY AND THE DISCLOSURE OF GENETIC INFORMATION

The rapid increase in genetic testing and the use of family history data have resulted in the substantial collection and use of genetic data in the health care and public health systems. These genetic data reveal important information about an individual's current and future health, as well as the health of family members. Profound ethical questions are posed by the collection and use of genetic data.

1.   GENETIC PRIVACY

Anita L. Allen, *Genetic Privacy: Emerging Concepts and Values in Genetic Secrets*

in PROTECTING PRIVACY AND CONFIDENTIALITY IN THE GENETIC ERA 33–34 (Mark A. Rothstein ed., 1997).

The Four Dimensions of Genetic Privacy

The word *privacy* has a wide range of meanings. It is used ambiguously in law and morals to describe and prescribe, denote and connote, praise and blame. "Genetic privacy" is no less rich in ambiguity than "privacy." Although the expression "genetic privacy" is a product of recent developments in science, it does not stand for a wholly new concept. "Genetic privacy" signifies applications of the familiar concept of privacy to genetic-related phenomena.

When used to label issues that arise in contemporary bioethics and public policy, "privacy" generally refers to one of four categories of concern. They are: (1) informational privacy concerns about access to personal information; (2) physical privacy concerns about access to persons and personal spaces; (3) decisional privacy concerns about governmental and other third-party interference with personal choices; and (4) proprietary privacy concerns about the appropriation and ownership of interests in human personality. "Genetic privacy" typically refers to one of these same four general categories.

"Genetic privacy" often denotes informational privacy, including the confidentiality, anonymity, or secrecy of the data that result from genetic testing and screening. Substantial limits on third-party access to confidential, anonymous, or secret genetic information are requirements of respect for informational privacy. However, family members may possess moral rights to undisclosed genetic data that patients and the professionals who serve them legitimately withhold from other third parties.

George Annas had informational privacy in mind when he warned that "control of and access to the information contained in an individual's genome gives others potential power over the personal life of the individual by providing a basis not only for counseling, but also for stigmatizing and discrimination." Likewise, Alan Westin was thinking of informational privacy when he defined "genetic privacy" by reference to what he called the "core concept of privacy"—namely, "the claim of an individual to determine what information about himself or herself should by known by others." Westin's definition captures well much of the informational dimension of genetic privacy and its connection to ideals of self-determination. Although it is adequate for purposes of a discussion of informational privacy, Westin's definition leaves important physical, decisional, and proprietary dimensions of genetic privacy in the shadows.

The genetic privacy concerns heard today range far beyond informational privacy to concerns about physical, decisional, and proprietary privacy. Briefly, issues of physical privacy underlie concerns about genetic testing, screening, or treatment without voluntary and informed consent. In the absence of consent, these practices constitute unwanted physical contact, compromising interests in bodily integrity and security. Decisional privacy concerns are heard in calls for autonomous decision making by individuals, couples, or families who use genetic services. A degree of choice with regard to genetic counseling, testing, and abortion are requirements of respect for decisional privacy. The fourth category of privacy concern, proprietary privacy, encompasses issues relating to the appropriation of individuals' possessory and economic interest in their genes and other putative bodily repositories of personality.

. . .

The human genome contains many mysteries that await scientific discovery. The air of mystery that shrouds gene science often shrouds discourse about genetic privacy, too. Yet genetic privacy is only an expansive concept, not an unfathomable one.

NOTES AND QUESTIONS

Informational privacy may be defined as the right of an individual to control access to personal genetic information. Scholars such as Anita Allen have explained why society should respect a patient's interest in informational privacy. There is the normative claim that patients' autonomy demands a certain control over personal information. There is also the pragmatic claim that protection of privacy will encourage patients to come forward for testing and treatment. It is for these reasons that policy makers and the public often assert that genetic data should be kept private, and released only with the patient's informed consent.

This assertion raises a number of questions: Should patients have a more robust right to control access to genetic information than they have to control access to other kinds of health information—a form of genetics exceptionalism? What are the implications of a strong, perhaps near-absolute, right to control personal genetic information? Should society grant such control to individuals in the face of competing demands for use of genetic information for the common good? A certain tension exists between individual privacy and collective interests in research, health care, and public health. When faced with a choice between maintaining patient privacy and furthering important societal goals, which should prevail and why?

The same kinds of conflicts arise with some of the other dimensions of genetic privacy offered by Allen. Consider the dimension of proprietary privacy. If individuals have unfettered possessory and economic interests in their genes, would this impede genetic research and scientific innovation?

2.   THE "DUTY TO WARN" AND THE "RIGHT TO KNOW"

Kenneth Offit et al., *The "Duty to Warn" a Patient's Family Members About Hereditary Disease Risks*
292 JAMA 1469 (2004).

Genetic tests for specific adult-onset disorders (eg, breast and colon cancer) are now commercially available, and results of research studies for genetic polymorphisms that predict drug effects, for example, response to statin therapy, have recently been published. The failure to warn family members about their hereditary disease risks has resulted in malpractice suits against physicians in the United States. [Pate v. Threlkel, 661 So.2d 278 (Fla. 1995); Safer v. Estate of Pack, 677 A.2d 1188 (N.J. App. 1996), appeal denied, 683 A.2d 1163 (N.J. 1996); Molloy v. Meier, 679 N.W.2d 711 (Minn. 2004) reproduced in Sec. IV, *infra*.] This past year, the obligation, if any, to warn family members of identification of a cancer gene mutation was the topic of discussion among professional societies and advocacy groups. Concerns have been raised regarding the conflict between the physician's ethical obligations to respect the privacy of genetic information vs the potential legal liabilities resulting from the physician's failure to notify at-risk relatives. In many cases, state and federal statutes that bear on the issue of "duty to warn" of inherited health risk are also in conflict. This article discusses these issues and suggests that health care professionals have a responsibility to encourage but not to coerce the sharing of genetic information in families, while respecting the boundaries imposed by the law and by the ethical practice of medicine.

CASE EXAMPLE

A 40–year-old woman presents for a follow-up consultation. She has a family history of breast cancer, heart disease, and Alzheimer disease. At her first visit, the physician had counseled her and provided genetic testing and now tells the patient that she was found to have an inherited BRCA2 mutation that markedly increases her risk for developing breast cancer and/or ovarian cancer. The testing laboratory has also suggested a "genomic profile" that will predict risk for Alzheimer disease as well as sensitivity to a variety of drugs. The patient's sister, who is sitting in the waiting room, has a 50% chance of inheriting this same BRCA2 mutation. Although the physician had discussed the importance of familial risk notification before testing, the patient declines the strong recommendation that she share the results of her genetic tests with her sister and asks that this information be kept completely confidential.

Does this physician have an obligation to tell the patient's sister that she, too, may have inherited these genetic predispositions? If this sister later develops advanced breast cancer, or has a "preventive surgery" unnecessarily, can she take legal action, claiming that the physician had an obligation to contact her about her genetic risk?

ETHICAL AND LEGAL BACKDROP: THE PRACTITIONER'S DUTY TO WARN OF GENETIC RISK

Respect for patients' autonomous choice lies at the heart of bioethical theory. When a physician's notion of "beneficence" (an act done for the benefit of others) and the patient's autonomy come into conflict, an ethical imperative may compel the physician to override the patient's autonomy. A key assumption underlying the ethical justification for a "duty to warn" is the availability of medical interventions to reduce the risk of developing a disease or to lessen the ensuing harm. For some hereditary disorders, such as Huntington disease and Alzheimer disease, effective medical interventions are either minimal or just emerging. For other inherited diseases, there are proven means of prevention, as is the case for dietary modification to prevent the development of mental retardation from phenylketonuria. Presymptomatic interventions can significantly reduce the future harm caused by some common malignancies. For example, surgical removal of the ovaries and fallopian tubes after childbearing in women with BRCA mutations reduces the subsequent risk of developing breast or ovarian cancer by 75%. Other studies have demonstrated the efficacy of screening and prevention in hereditary breast, colon, thyroid, and other cancers. However, for some cancer syndromes, genetic risks may be incompletely defined and interventions may be ineffective, and the impact of failing to warn relatives of their hereditary risk for cancer is less clear. Fewer than 1% of clinicians surveyed believed that a breach of patient confidentiality would be warranted to warn at-risk relatives about a disease for which no medical interventions exist.

CASE LAW IN STATE APPELLATE COURTS

The precedent-setting test of the "duty to warn" in a medical setting stems from a 1976 decision, Tarasoff v. the Regents of the University of California, [551 P.2d 334 (Cal. 1976),] which dealt with a psychotherapist's failure to warn the plaintiffs' deceased daughter of his patient's stated intention to kill her. The California Supreme Court ruled that a physician is required to breach patient confidentiality and take reasonable actions to warn an identifiable third party in instances where the patient poses a serious and imminent threat to that party. Three subsequent lawsuits against physicians have focused attention on the specific question of the duty to warn relatives regarding their hereditary risk for cancer. In Pate v. Threlkel, [661 So. 2d 278 (Fla. 1995),] appellant Heidi Pate filed suit against her mother's physician because he failed to warn her of the risks of hereditary thyroid cancer. In this syndrome, medullary thyroid cancer, and possibly pheochromocytoma and parathyroid hyperplasia, are inherited in an autosomal dominant fashion. Recognition of this syndrome can enable prophylactic removal of the thyroid gland before cancers are clinically detected, followed by thyroid hormone administration. Three years after her mother's diagnosis, Ms Pate was found to have advanced stage thyroid cancer. She claimed that if she had been warned earlier, her cancer could have been detected at a curable stage.

The Supreme Court of Florida agreed with Ms Pate's claim that Dr Threlkel was obliged by accepted medical practice to warn her mother of the need to share the cancer risks with her children. The court concluded that because the standard of care was developed with the specific purpose of benefiting the patient's children, the issue of privity was irrelevant. The court did recognize the logistical challenges posed by having to contact at-risk relatives but noted that, "in any circumstances in which the physician has a duty to warn of a genetically transferable disease, that duty will be satisfied by warning the patient." [Id. at 282.]

In Safer v. Estate of Pack, [677 A.2d 1188,] the court espoused a much more expansive "duty to warn." In this case, Donna Safer sued the estate of the late Dr George Pack, claiming that more than 30 years earlier, when Dr Pack treated her father for multiple polyposis, Dr Pack failed to fulfill his professional duty to warn those at risk for the hereditary disease. In familial adenomatous polyposis, the presence of hundreds or thousands of polyps in childhood leads inevitably to colon cancer by 40 years of age. Prophylactic colectomy in the late teen years remains the intervention of choice for these patients, although recent studies have shown that anti-inflammatory drugs, such as sulindac or celecoxib, may also play a role in management. Thirty years after her father's diagnosis, Donna Safer presented with both polyposis and advanced colorectal cancer. Ms Safer contended that, if she had been told of her elevated risk as a child, she could have benefited from early detection and avoided metastatic colorectal cancer.

Contrary to the Pate ruling, the New Jersey court asserted that a physician's duty to warn at-risk relatives is not, in all cases, met by simply informing the patient of the hereditary nature of the disease. The New Jersey ruling proffered that physicians must take "reasonable steps" to guarantee that immediate family members are warned. The jury in this case ultimately decided in favor of Dr Pack, based on evidence that Safer had indeed undergone rectal screening at the age of 10 years, indicating that she (through her mother) had been sufficiently warned of her elevated risk. However, this favorable decision for the defendant did not obviate the appellate court ruling defining a duty to warn family members of hereditary disease risk in a manner that is comprehensive in scope and may not be feasible for most practitioners.

In May 2004, in Molloy v. Meier, [679 N.W.2d 711,] the Minnesota Supreme Court allowed a parent to proceed with a lawsuit against the physicians who had treated her daughter more than 10 years earlier. In this case, Kimberly Molloy claimed that the physicians failed to inform her and her second husband about future risks due to a hereditary form of mental retardation, fragile X syndrome, present in her first daughter. The court held that "a physician's duty regarding genetic testing and diagnosis extends beyond the patient to biological parents who foreseeably may be harmed by a breach of that duty." In this case, which stems more from an alleged failure to perform a diagnostic test than from a failure to breach confidentiality to warn of a genetic disease, the mother and her second husband stated they would not have conceived another child if they had known of the diagnosis of fragile X syndrome in the mother's first child.

FEDERAL STATUTES AND OTHER CASE LAW

The Pack case notwithstanding, disclosures without patient consent are regulated by a stringent health information privacy rule known as the Standards for Privacy of Individually Identifiable Health Information (Privacy Rule), promulgated under the Health Insurance Portability and Accountability Act of 1996 (HIPAA). Noncompliance with the Privacy Rule may result in civil or criminal penalties.

Included in these regulations are certain "public interest" exceptions to the strict nondisclosure policy that otherwise protects "individually identifiable health information" (including genetic information). These exceptions comprise instances in which the public interest is at risk, ie, there is a "serious and imminent threat to the health or safety of a person or the public"; the threat constitutes an imminent, serious threat to an identifiable third party and the physician has the capacity to avert significant harm. Examples of circumstances requiring a breach of patient confidentiality include the apprehension of an individual by law enforcement and to curtail certain infectious disease.

It is questionable whether the uncertain probability of a future genetic disease constitutes an imminent harm or a threat to the public interest. It has been argued that infectious diseases meet such a criterion. In Tenuto v Lederle Laboratories, [90 N.Y.2d 606 (N.Y. 1997),] the New York Court of Appeals extended a physician's duty to third parties "when the service performed on behalf of the patient necessarily implicated protection of . . . other identified persons forseeably at risk because of the relationship with the patient, whom the doctor knows or should know may suffer harm by relying on prudent performance of the medical service." The court found that the pediatrician had a duty to warn his patient's father, who had not been vaccinated against polio, about the risk of contracting polio from his son after the child was vaccinated.

. . .

THE POSITION OF PROFESSIONAL SOCIETIES

A Presidential Commission and subsequent reports have defined conditions under which it would be ethically acceptable for physicians to breach confidentiality and disclose information to relatives. These conditions include (1) the high likelihood of harm if the relative were not warned, (2) the identifiability of the relative, and (3) the notion that the harm resulting from failure to disclose would outweigh the harm resulting from disclosure. In the absence of a federally defined general legal "duty to rescue," which exists in certain parts of Canada, the health care professional's duty to warn is generally viewed as discretionary and not compulsory, ie, legally excusable and not legally mandated.

. . .

COMMENT

Against this background of ethical and legal "directives that are in conflict," some lawyers have concluded that considering the legal liabilities, "physicians might understandably conclude that warning relatives is the least risk[y] option." These scholars claim that none of the contested legal constraints and salient social policies serve as legitimate barriers to the requirement to warn of genetic risk for disease. Such an argument would be supported by the Safer malpractice case, as well as the Molloy case in progress in Minnesota. Questioning the notion of genetic information as "property" in the legal sense and casting doubt on the claim of an undue burden on physicians, health care professionals could be held liable for a failure to warn relatives at increased risk of an inheritable genetic disease.

How then is a physician to resolve the competing ethical mandates of autonomy (respect for genetic privacy) and beneficence (duty to warn) while under threat of litigation following either course of action? ...

The cornerstone of the patient-physician relationship is the assurance of confidentiality. This assurance is especially relevant to genetic information. A universal "duty to warn" would make the patient-physician relationship subservient to a more diffuse public health obligation, benefiting an unspecified number of nonpatient relatives. In the pretesting "negotiation" represented by the "genetic Miranda warning," patients who decline to share their genetic information with relatives could be subject to the coercive, threatened withdrawal of their physicians' care. Consumer and advocacy groups have expressed concern about such scenarios. . . . Indeed, it seems reasonable to question the propriety of coercive threats, whether before genetic testing or afterward. The pretest discussion of duty to warn obligations could be represented in the form of a "contract" between the patient and the physician. Such an a priori understanding of the patient's responsibility regarding notification of family members may provide the physician with some measure of legal protection, but does not address the ultimate liability should the patient later opt to withdraw from the "contract."

In considering the "duty to warn" of genetic risk, a clinical distinction must be made between high penetrance (100% risk) cancer susceptibility syndromes with proven means of intervention, syndromes of variable penetrance with less well-established interventions (such as Alzheimer disease), and low penetrance syndromes in which risk for outcome or toxicity may be only mildly elevated. In each of these circumstances, the potential implications of a failure to warn will be very different.

From a practical standpoint, physicians are in no position to undertake the primary responsibility for identifying and communicating with an untold number of their patients' relatives who might be at some unspecified risk from genetic predispositions. Even if all the patient's affected relatives could be reached, each would require counseling and education that would impose completely unrealistic burdens on the physician. The imposition of such burdens (and the attendant threat of liability should those burdens be unassumed) would discourage physician involvement in the emerging subspecialty of genetic medicine.

. . .

Moreover, the arguments for institutionalizing a "duty to warn" are contrary to the regulations that govern medical records privacy under HIPAA. In addition, certain states have enacted statutes that prohibit the disclosure of genetic information without the prior written consent of the individual tested (eg, New York civil rights law and public health law amendments).

Thus, in considering whether to breach patient confidentiality to warn of risks of a genetic disease, clinicians need to balance the actual risk of that disease, the efficacy of potential preventive interventions, as well as emerging legal considerations and potential liabilities. Overriding patient confidentiality and genetic privacy might very well mean violation of HIPAA and certain state regulations, with attendant civil or criminal liability. At the same time, in one state appellate court decision that has not been overturned, the estate of a physician was held liable for his failure to warn relatives of hereditary disease risk. . . .

An expanded national discussion of the ethical and legal implications of genetic risk notification is required to guide practitioners of "molecular medicine." Fear of loss of privacy among susceptible populations could discourage families from seeking access to potentially life-saving genetic testing. In the genomic era, clinical testing will be offered to predict disease occurrence, as well as sensitivities to drugs or environmental exposures. Because the laws of Mendel will continue to apply to these new markers of genetic risk, the issues surrounding familial notification will loom even larger. The increasing availability of DNA testing will require greater emphasis on informed consent as a process of communication and education, so as to better facilitate the translation of genomic medicine to clinical practice.

NOTES AND QUESTIONS

1. *A Physician's Duty?* Offit and colleagues focus on the obligations of a medical practitioner when confronted with a patient who has a genetic predisposition to a disease that might be shared by close relatives. Physicians owe a duty principally to the patient who surely is entitled to receive any relevant health information. Should the physician's duty extend beyond the patient to biological family members who may be harmed by the failure to disclose genetic information?

2. *A Patient's Duty?* What about the duty of patients who have learned that their genetic makeup predisposes them to an illness? What are the patient's duties, if any, to warn his or her siblings, children, and other relatives? Should a patient ever have a duty to disclose this information? Hook and colleagues discuss varying perspectives on the obligations of patients with regard to genetic testing:

> One of the fundamental principles of the ELSI project is the idea of the right not to know—that patients should be able to remain in ignorance, particularly about late-onset disorders, if they so desire. The right not to know may appear to make sense if there is no remedy for a disease associated with a specific genotype. However, what if the lack of information could prove detrimental to

other family members, especially the children of the affected individual? Both sides of the issue have been discussed; some experts have taken a more extreme position: "Knowingly, capriciously, or negligently transmitting a defective gene that causes pain and suffering and an agonizing death to an offspring is certainly a moral wrong if not a legal harm." Taking this claim to its full conclusion, it is further argued that parental obligations are paramount, and if reproduction is contemplated, there is an ethical obligation to prevent harm to the offspring, requiring that one's genotype should be determined so that appropriate steps can be taken to avert disease in future generations.

However, the aforementioned extreme view disregards the potential harm of both psychological stress and societal repercussions to the would-be parent. Because the chance of passing along the defect is often a statistical risk, rather than an absolute certainty, the following question is important: What calculus should be performed to clearly establish when the risk is sufficient to demand that procreation not be pursued? Furthermore, on practical grounds, each and every one of us has the potential to pass on genetic liabilities, which in turn may cause suffering and pain to our offspring. How much pain and suffering are required to necessitate pursuit of adoption or gene therapy (if and when available)?

C. Christopher Hook et al., *Primer on Medical Genomics Part XIII: Ethical and Regulatory Issues*, 79 MAYO CLIN. PROC. 645, 646 (2004). Hook, like Offit, concludes that educating and counseling patients is preferred over the imposition of a duty to warn. When, if ever, is more direct action by a doctor required? When, if ever, should a patient be compelled to divulge genetic information to family members?

3. *Public interest exceptions to privacy and genetics exceptionalism.* Offit and colleagues mention the "public interest" exceptions to medical privacy laws and its application in the context of infectious diseases. Is reluctance amongst the medical community to apply the "public interest" exception to genetic information an example of genetics exceptionalism? Is it appropriate? Note that in some cases, the status of patients with TB who fail to comply with their drug regimen can be reported to the public health officials to protect the public interest, and the patient might be confined as a result. Is it more or less intrusive to inform a patient's close family relatives of the results of a patient's genetic test and counsel them as to their potential risks?

Molloy v. Meier

Supreme Court of Minnesota, 2004.
679 N.W.2d 711.

■ MEYER, J.

This case arises out of the medical treatment of S.F., the daughter of Kimberly Molloy and her ex-husband, Robert Flomer. As a young girl, S.F. was treated by appellant Dr. Diane M. Meier ... When S.F. was three years old, Dr. Meier noted during a check-up that S.F. was developmentally delayed.

In her notes from the May 18 visit, Dr. Meier wrote "? chromosomes + fragile X," which meant she intended to order chromosomal testing and testing for Fragile X syndrome. In May of 1992, a Fragile X chromosomal test capable of diagnosing the disorder with 70 to 80 percent accuracy was in widespread use. Dr. Meier conceded that "it was appropriate to test

[S.F.] for Fragile X in keeping with accepted standards of pediatric practice on May 18, 1992" . . .

. . . Dr. Meier received the [chromosome] test results, telephoned the Flomers and informed them that the test results were negative; i.e., normal. However, Dr. Meier failed to mention that Fragile X testing had not been performed. The Flomers then informed Molloy that the test results were "normal." Based on the fact that Dr. Meier had mentioned Fragile X in her discussion of chromosomal testing, Molloy assumed that the negative test results included a negative result for Fragile X.

Meanwhile, on June 23, 1992, S.F. was referred . . . [to] Dr. Reno Backus . . . Molloy inquired about her chances of conceiving another child with S.F.'s defect. According to Molloy, Dr. Backus responded that S.F.'s problems were not genetic in origin and the risk that Molloy might give birth to another child like S.F. was extremely remote, especially with a father other than Robert Flomer. Dr. Backus was aware that chromosomal testing had been done but he made his assessment before the test results were known.

Several years later S.F. was referred to Dr. Kathryn Green. . . . There were no Fragile X testing results in the chart because the testing had never been done.

In the meantime, Molloy remarried and gave birth to M.M. on June 30, 1998. M.M. showed signs of the same developmental difficulties as S.F., so his pediatrician, Dr. David Tilstra, ordered Fragile X testing for him. The Fragile X test results were positive; i.e., M.M. carried the Fragile X genetic disorder. When Dr. Tilstra received the positive results, he counseled Kimberly and Glenn Molloy about Fragile X syndrome and recommended that they and other potentially affected family members receive testing. Based on Dr. Tilstra's recommendation, S.F. and Kimberly Molloy were tested for Fragile X, and it was discovered that they both carried the genetic disorder.

Molloy commenced this lawsuit on August 23, 2001, alleging that Drs. Meier, Backus, and Green and their employers were negligent in the care and treatment rendered to S.F., Kimberly Molloy, and Glenn Molloy by failing to order Fragile X testing on S.F., failing to properly read those lab tests that were performed, mistakenly reporting that S.F. had been tested for Fragile X, and failing to provide counseling to Kimberly and Glenn Molloy regarding the risk of passing an inheritable genetic abnormality to future children. Molloy claimed she would not have conceived M.M. if Drs. Meier, Backus, and Green had correctly diagnosed S.F. with Fragile X and informed Molloy of the diagnosis.

. . . Molloy presented expert testimony of a pediatrician and a pediatric neurologist who described the prevailing standard of care in the medical community with respect to testing and counseling for genetic disorders. The experts indicated that a patient who exhibits the symptoms of this disorder with a family history of mental retardation should be tested for Fragile X. Further, a physician who identifies the possibility of Fragile X has a responsibility to follow up to confirm that the tests are performed.

Finally, the physician of a child with Fragile X has an obligation to provide genetic counseling to the child's family.

. . .

Molloy advances two legal theories. She first argues that a physician-patient relationship existed between her and the appellants that gave rise to a legal duty to warn her about the risks of becoming pregnant as a carrier of Fragile X. Additionally, Molloy urges this court to hold that even if a physician-patient relationship cannot be established, a physician's duty to warn others of a patient's genetic disorder arises from the foreseeability of injury.

The appellants argue that their duty is owed only to S.F., the person with whom they had a physician-patient relationship. The appellants claim that they met with S.F. solely for S.F.'s own benefit and not for the benefit of her family. If any duty extended beyond the minor patient, the appellants argue that it should reach only those parties who have a contractual relationship with the physician, in this case the Flomers, S.F.'s custodial parents.

. . .

Our decision today is informed by the practical reality of the field of genetic testing and counseling; genetic testing and diagnosis does not affect only the patient. Both the patient and her family can benefit from accurate testing and diagnosis. And conversely, both the patient and her family can be harmed by negligent testing and diagnosis. Molloy's experts indicate that a physician would have a duty to inform the parents of a child diagnosed with Fragile X disorder. The appellants admit that their practice is to inform parents in such a case. The standard of care thus acknowledges that families rely on physicians to communicate a diagnosis of the genetic disorder to the patient's family. It is foreseeable that a negligent diagnosis of Fragile X will cause harm not only to the patient, but to the family of the patient as well. This is particularly true regarding parents who have consulted the physicians concerning the patient's condition and have been advised of the need for genetic testing.

We therefore hold that a physician's duty regarding genetic testing and diagnosis extends beyond the patient to biological parents who foreseeably may be harmed by a breach of that duty. In this case, the patient suffered from a serious disorder that had a high probability of being genetically transmitted and for which a reliable and accepted test was widely available. The appellants should have foreseen that parents of childbearing years might conceive another child in the absence of knowledge of the genetic disorder. The appellants owed a duty of care regarding genetic testing and diagnosis, and the resulting medical advice, not only to S.F. but also to her parents. In recognizing this duty, we . . . conclude that the duty arises where it is reasonably foreseeable that the parents would be injured if the advice is negligently given.

Appellants suggest that recognizing a duty to Molloy would extend a physician's duty to an unreasonable extent, requiring the physician to seek out and inform distant relatives. . . . [W]e need not, and do not, address whether the duty recognized here extends beyond biological parents who foreseeably will rely on genetic testing and diagnosis and therefore foreseeably may be injured by negligence in discharging the duty of care.

NOTES AND QUESTIONS

1. Ellen Wright Clayton uses the case of a man who died of colon cancer in the 1960s to illustrate the complexities of the so-called "right to know" genetic information:

> When the same disease developed in his daughter approximately 25 years later, she obtained her father's pathology slides, discovered that he had had diffuse adenomatous polyposis coli, and sued the estate of her father's surgeon, alleging that the physician should have warned her about her 50 percent risk of having the disorder. An intermediate appellate court in New Jersey ruled that the physician had a duty to warn the daughter directly (she would have been a child at the time of her father's death), perhaps even over her father's objections.

> This is only one court's view in one case, but given how much attention it received, it is important to ask whether this was a good result. Two central tenets of Western medicine are that physicians should focus on the interests of their patients and that they should protect the confidentiality of their patients' medical information. Yet the tools of genomic medicine often reveal information about health risks faced not only by patients but also by their relatives. What should clinicians do? It seems clear that they should tell their patients about the risks faced by family members. The harder questions are whether physicians are ethically permitted to contact the relatives themselves, in contravention of traditional patient-centered norms, and whether they should be legally required to do so.

> This issue must be viewed in the light of the fact that the duty to protect confidentiality is not absolute. Physicians are required to report numerous infectious diseases, and they have been held liable for failing to warn people whom their patients have specifically threatened with violence. The question then becomes more complex: are genetic risks sufficiently similar to these existing exceptions to the requirement of confidentiality that they warrant an exception as well? Over the years, numerous prominent advisory bodies have said no, opining that physicians should be permitted to breach confidentiality in order to warn third parties of genetic risks only as a last resort to avert serious harm.

> These learned opinions, however, are not the end of the matter, in part because they lack the force of law. In fact, as the case above illustrates, relatives have sued the primary patients' physicians for failing to warn them of their own genetic risks—and won limited victories, although none have been awarded monetary damages. The decisions in the colon-cancer case and a similar one in Florida have been criticized for both their legal reasoning and their deviation from ethical guidelines, but they have not been overturned and, in the tradition of the common law, may be persuasive to other courts. Physicians who breach their patients' confidentiality and warn family members are not likely to incur substantial liability, even under HIPAA. As a result, physicians might understandably conclude that warning relatives is the least risky option.

> The existing directives are thus in conflict: "expert consensus," ethical analysis, and the HIPAA regulations argue for honoring confidentiality, whereas at least one legal opinion holds that physicians fail to warn a patient's relatives at

their peril. Given the press of other business, legislators are not likely to resolve this conflict soon. In this setting, clinicians should inform their patients about the risks their relatives face, discuss the appropriateness of sharing this information and offer assistance, trust—usually realistically—that patients will in turn tell their relatives who are at risk, and hope that the courts will get it right in the future.

Ellen Wright Clayton, *Ethical, Legal, and Social Implications of Genomic Medicine*, 349 New Eng. J. Med. 562, 566–567 (2003).

2. Patients may be keenly interested in genetic information for the purposes of treatment, reproductive decisionmaking, or life planning. If no beneficial intervention exists, patients are faced with the hard choice about whether they want to know their future health status such as the probability of developing Huntington's or Alzheimer's disease. This is an agonizing decision. How can society ensure that patients receive sound genetic counseling to assist them in such a momentous decision?

3.   HUMAN GENETIC RESEARCH DATABASES: THE PROMISE OF TRANS–NATIONAL BIOBANKS

Before the advent of the Human Genome Project and ensuing research, scientists could collect genetic data from a relatively small number of people and address rare, single-gene diseases. More common diseases are now viewed through a genomic lens. To understand complex diseases such as cancer, diabetes or schizophrenia, it is necessary to collect genetic information from a broader group of people. Human Genetic Research Databases (HGRDs) have amassed thousands of people's genetic material so that it may be stored for research purposes. HGRDs involve the collection, storage, and analysis of genetic samples in the form of blood or tissue. The genetic information is linked with clinical, genealogical, and/or lifestyle information from a specific population, and the data are stored in searchable databases for the use of researchers. *See* Bartha Maria Knoppers, *International Lessons: Biobanks, in* Institute of Medicine, Genomics and the Public's Health in the 21st Century: Workshop Report (Forthcoming 2005); Melissa A. Austin, et al., *Monitoring Ethical, legal, and Social Issues in Developing Population Genetic Databases*, 5 Genetics in Med. 451 (2003). HGRDs are sometimes referred to as biobanks, cohorts, gene banks, population studies, or genome databases. HGRDs offer great promise for understanding gene/gene and gene/environment interactions in human diseases. At the same time they hold the potential to embarrass or harm individuals or groups. Can these important social experiments be conducted in an ethically acceptable manner?

To date, a number of HGRDs have been established or proposed, including Iceland DeCode Biobank; United Kingdom Biobank; Estonian Genome Project; CARTaGENE in Québec, Canada; UmanGenomics in Vasterbotten, Sweden; Genome Institute of Singapore; and Personalized Medicine Research Project (PMRP) in Wisconsin. *See* Melissa A. Austin, et al., *Genebanks: A Comparison of Eight Proposed International Genetic Databases*, 6 Community Genetics 37–45 (2003). Perhaps the most publicly discussed HGRD is the Iceland DeCode Biobank:

> Modern information technology ... offers the possibility of mining large
> data sets for knowledge, without a priori hypotheses, by systematically

juxtaposing various data in the search for the best fit. This kind of pure combinatorial analysis may be particularly powerful in the case of the common diseases, most of which are complex and have remained beyond the reach of the classic hypothesis-driven approach to biomedical research. However, to take full advantage of the new techniques, it is important to have access to large amounts of primary data in one place. This calls for large data bases on health care that can be mined for knowledge, either alone or in combination with other data on disease and health, such as variations in the human genome.

. . .

According to the law, the data in the IHD [Icelandic Healthcare Database] will be collected under the assumption of "presumed consent." Presumed consent is a nebulous concept, but in the context of this project, we regard it as the consent of society to the use of health care information according to the norms of society. These norms may vary from one society to another and may change with time. It is important that the data in the IHD will be only data from medical records that are produced in the process of delivering health care. Some argue that presumed consent is inconsistent with the right of individuals to decide for themselves and actually amounts to no consent at all. However, presumed consent is the standard used for research on health care data that is produced in the process of delivering medical services. It is not certain that we would have health care as we know it today if explicit consent had been a prerequisite for the use of medical data.

. . .

The majority of the international bioethics community has supported the use of broad consent. . . . Some members of this community, however, remain skeptical of the wisdom of broad consent because of the difficulties in making certain that consent is informed. Informed consent was devised to protect the autonomy of individual subjects against overzealous scientists. Nobody should participate in biomedical research unless he or she makes an informed decision to do so, and nobody should be coerced or tricked into making such a decision. The goal is to protect the autonomy of the individual; the tool is informed consent.

. . .

Why should Icelanders trust a private company to protect their personal health care information? It is probably better for a private company to hold this information than for the state to do so, since governments can violate the privacy of individuals to advance the interests of society as a whole. Moreover, if a health care data base managed by a private company violates privacy, the company can be closed down. According to the Icelandic law, deCODE will lose the license to develop and use the data base if the conditions of the license, including the stipulations regarding the protection of privacy, are not met. Violations of the data-base law are also punishable by monetary fines and imprisonment.

. . .

Since the data that are entered into the IHD are simply copies of data that will remain within health care institutions, it is not easy to see how the data base could restrict the freedom of science. There is, however, some concern that the commercial mission of private enterprise will influence the way research on the data base is performed and how the results are distributed and used.

It is important to ensure that research based on the IHD meets international ethical standards. Therefore, the IHD will be subject to the oversight of four government regulatory bodies: the Data Protection Commission of Iceland (appointed by the ministry of justice), an interdisciplinary bioethics committee, the National Bioethics Committee, and an operational oversight committee (the last three appointed by the minister of health).

Jeffrey R. Gulcher & Kári Stefánsson, *The Icelandic Healthcare Database and Informed Consent*, 342 NEW ENG. J. MED. 1827, 1827–1830 (2000).

NOTES AND QUESTIONS

1. *Informed Consent for Participation in HGRDs.* The establishment of genetic databases raises formidable ethical issues. Will each individual be permitted to give or withhold consent before collection of tissue is permitted? If so, would this undermine the scientific integrity of the data by introducing a sampling bias? Do traditional notions of informed consent, when applied to the vast scale of biobanks, unduly inhibit progress? What further consent may be necessary to authorize future or secondary uses of the data? Are notions such as "presumed consent," "broad consent," "generalized consent," "community consent," or "community consultation" helpful or do they distort the true meaning of informed consent?

2. *Protection of Privacy.* How will personal genetic information stored in HGRDs be kept private? Persons whose data are stored on HGRDs express concern about the privacy of their genetic information. Large scale databases may not be able to provide the degree of privacy traditionally expected in the health care system. If personally identifiable data are disclosed to family members, employers or insurers, patients may be embarrassed or harmed. How can researchers protect against stigma and discrimination? These are important questions that have thus far thwarted the development of systematic genetic databases in the United States. Many scholars believe that privacy rules should attach to personally identifiable data, but not anonymous or aggregate data. Given that genetic information is, by definition, associated with a specific individual, does it make sense to think of genetic data as unidentifiable? Would it be reasonable to think of genetic data as anonymous if it would be extraordinarily difficult to identify the source of a single individual in a large database? Other scholars suggest that privacy rules could be relaxed if the data are "linkable" or "double-coded." Linkable data systems make it very difficult for the researchers themselves to identify individuals from their databases because linking data with individuals requires a "key" that is held by a third (neutral) party. Provided that the researcher cannot gain access to the "key," should these data be regarded as effectively anonymous?

3. *Personal Feedback: The "Right to Know."* If data are identifiable or linkable, should individuals have a right to know if their genetic material reveals something important for their health and life? Suppose the data reveal that an individual has a predisposition to a disease that could be prevented or ameliorated? Should the holders of the data have a duty to inform the individual? What about feedback of data that are not wholly reliable or clinically useful to the individual? How practical would it be to assure personal feedback with very large data systems?

4. *Privately Operated Biobanks.* While some biobanks are state-run or non-profit, others are privately organized commercial ventures that will sell their findings to drug companies. Does private data banking pose special ethical concerns? Is it likely that private companies would sufficiently respect patient interests? Would private ventures aggressively and adequately pursue the public interest?

5. *Global Aspects of Biobanks*. As mentioned above, biobanks have been established in many parts of the world. However, they are subject to different national laws[7] and policies,[8] and have highly disparate forms of organization. Is there a case for harmonization of data sets held by biobanks to make them more interchangeable and useful to researchers around the globe? At present, there is a lack of internationally agreed upon rules and common taxonomy, making databases incompatible. There is also a proliferation of international guidelines relating to biobanks.[9]

7. *The Governance of Biobanks*. Biobanks raise important questions about the commercial exchange of human tissue, financial incentives for participation in research, fairness to donors, public access to research materials, and incentives for scientific innovation. Given the novel and large-scale implications of biobanks, there has been a great deal of discussion regarding how they should be governed. Neither government nor private control has provided a comprehensive model for addressing the complexities and potential risks that biobanks involve. David and Richard Winickoff have proposed an innovative solution to this quandary:

> The consent forms that private biobanks use often include clauses that waive donors' rights to their blood and tissue samples. These clauses result from the increasing private investment in research and recent claims by tissue donors for a share of the profits derived from their samples. These clauses are legally and ethically problematic. First, hospital consent forms that transfer property rights to institutional biobanks may be legally unenforceable as contractual promises owing to "power asymmetry" and "undue influence." Second, the legal transfer of property might signal to the donors that they have given up any control of the samples, which would undermine their right to withdrawal. Soliciting and obtaining gifts of tissue by informed consent overextends its traditional role and threatens the trust between the donor and the institution. Despite some debate about private-sector collaborations with medical institutions, private biobanks are amassing millions of samples, and health centers seem ready to supply them. More creative thinking is needed to solve the problems in the governance of biobanks.
>
> When a person agrees to donate tissue, the recipient has a responsibility to serve as a trustee, or steward, of the tissue in order to ensure protection of the contribution. The National Research Council has suggested that for a worldwide collection of DNA, "a more sophisticated and complicated approach would be to form an international organization to serve as a trustee and fund-holder for all the sampled populations." The charitable trust is a promising legal structure for handling such a set of obligations, for promoting donor partic-

7. *See, e.g.*, Human Gene Research Act, Dec. 13, 2000 (Est.); Biobanks [Health Care] Act, May 23, 2002 (Swed.); Act on Biobanks, May 13, 2000 (Ice.); Act on Biobanks, Feb. 21, 2003 (Nor.).

8. *See, e.g.*, Canadian Biotechnology Advisory Committee, Genetic Research and Privacy (2004); German National Ethics Council, Biobanks for Research (2004); France: CCNE Opinion 77, Ethical Issues Raised by Collections of Biological Material and Associated Information Data: "Biobanks" (2003); Australia law Reform Commission, Essentially Yours, Part E: Human Genetic Databases (2003).

9. *See, e.g.*, Human Genome Organization (HUGO), Statement on Human Genomic Databases (Dec. 2002); World Health Organization, Genetic Databases: Assessing the Benefits and the Impact on Human Rights and Patient Rights (2003); UNESCO, International Declaration on Human Genetic Data (2003). *See also*, Melissa A. Austin, et al., *Applying International Guidelines on Ethical, Legal and Social Issues to New International Genebanks*, JURIMETRICS (Forthcoming 2005).

ipation in research governance, and for stimulating research that will benefit the public.

Under a trust agreement, the tissue donor, or settlor, formally expresses a wish to transfer his or her property interest in the tissue to the trust. The permission form could be used for this purpose. The settlor appoints a trustee of the property, who has legal fiduciary duties to keep or use the property for the benefit of a specified party, the beneficiary. In a charitable trust, the general public acts as the beneficiary.

A charitable trust is an elegant and flexible legal model that has a number of advantages over private biobanks. First, charitable trusts accord well with the altruism that characterizes gifts of tissue. If altruistic donations are solicited by hospitals for research, then the hospitals should act as stewards rather than as brokers. Second, the architect of the trust can provide the donor group with an advisory role in the governance of the trust. We believe that the patient population of a medical center, with appropriate leadership from the institution, would have the necessary sense of community to make the advisory role meaningful. Finally, private biobanks may be forced to sell off their inventory in the event of bankruptcy, but charitable trusts have the advantage of longevity. This feature is important not only for donors but also for researchers who perform longitudinal studies.

The Charitable Trust as a Model for Genomic Biobanks, 349 NEW ENG. J. MED. 1180–1184 (2003).

C.   STRATIFICATION, JUSTICE, AND OPPORTUNITY

The field of genetics is deeply complex, not only because of the science but also, as we have seen, because of the difficult ethical, legal, and social problems which inhere in the field. Genetics research, almost by definition, stratifies the population according to the genetic predisposition for sickness and premature death. It is only by singling out individuals and groups at high genetic risk that it is possible to offer counseling, preventive strategies, or treatment. In this sense, genetic stratification offers great opportunity. If researchers did not, for example, identify people at risk of genetic disease (e.g., sickle cell among African Americans or Tay Sachs among Ashkenazi Jews), they could not offer beneficial services. Indeed, questions of fairness would arise if minorities were excluded from research or needed services. Thus, stratification is essential for fulfilling the promise of genetics to individuals and groups of all religions, races, and cultures.

Stratification, of course, is also the *sine qua non* of stigma and discrimination. Unfair treatment is based on difference and genetics can underscore the differences (as well as the similarities) among people. Just as singling out individuals or groups for genetic risk can bring benefits, so too can it bring harm. People who are labeled as genetically different can suffer embarrassment, stigma, and discrimination. Still worse, these individuals can suffer the humiliation of policies designed to limit their reproductive opportunities. There are shameful historical precedents for just these kinds of harm, which helps explain the public's distrust of overly ambitious projects in the field of genetics. Stratification affects groups as well as individuals. A finding that certain ethnic, religious, or racial groups have adverse genetic traits can be hurtful.

Stratification raises squarely the problem of distributive justice. The benefits and burdens of genetic discovery should be distributed fairly.

Those in need should have fair opportunities of receiving services irrespective of race, social class, or other status. Those who are vulnerable should not have to bear disproportionate hardships in research, practice, or policies. Most people would agree that genetic fairness is a worthy goal. Where people disagree, however, is how to determine fair allocations of benefits and burdens.

1. THE HISTORICAL LESSONS OF EUGENICS

The core notion of eugenics, that people's lives will probably go better if they have genes conducive to health and other advantageous traits, has lost little of its appeal. Eugenics, in this very limited sense, shines a beacon even as it casts a shadow. Granted, when our society last undertook to improve our genes, the result was mayhem. The task for humanity now is to accomplish what eluded the eugenicists entirely, to square the pursuit of genetic health and enhancement with the requirements of justice

Allen Buchanan et al., From Chance to Choice: Genetics and Justice 56–57 (2000)

The modern-day genetics movement must overcome the sad legacy of eugenics. No matter how noble the intentions of geneticists today, their efforts to improve public health through genetic intervention are likely to elicit haunting memories of a less well-intentioned era. In the first half of the past century, eugenics—the study of hereditary improvement of the human race by controlled selective breeding—became a popular field of inquiry, particularly in Germany. Long before the emergence of Adolf Hitler, Germans were interested in eugenics. Dr. Alfred Ploetz founded the Archives of Race–Theory and Social Biology in 1904 and the German Society of Racial Hygiene in 1905. Under Hitler, the lurking danger of eugenic thought was unleashed in the form of the Holocaust, in which millions who were deemed unfit for life perished at the hands of the Nazis.

The eugenics movement was not limited to Germany. In the United States, as recently as the 1930s, state laws authorized the sterilization of "undesirable" citizens; sterilization statutes remained on the books in many states until the 1960s. Justice Oliver Wendell Holmes approved eugenic policy when, in 1927, he authorized the sterilization of a young woman with mental retardation, commenting, "Three generations of imbeciles are enough." Buck v. Bell, 274 U.S. 200, 207, 47 S.Ct. 584, 71 L.Ed. 1000 (1927).

While modern genetics rejects the policies of eugenics and seeks health improvement, there is still, as the following reading suggests, pause for concern.

Allen Buchanan et al., *Two Models for Genetic Intervention*

in From Chance to Choice 11–14, 55–60 (2000).

THE PUBLIC HEALTH MODEL

Our "ethical autopsy" on eugenics identifies two quite different perspectives from which genetic intervention may be viewed. The first is what we call the public health model; the second is the personal choice model.

The public health model stresses the production of benefits and the avoidance of harms for groups. It uncritically assumes that the appropriate mode of evaluating options is some form of cost-benefit (or cost-effectiveness) calculation. To the extent that the public health model even recognizes an ethical dimension to decisions about the application of scientific knowledge or technology, it tends to assume that sound ethical reasoning is exclusively consequentialist (or utilitarian) in nature. In other words, it assumes that whether a policy or an action is deemed to be right is thought to depend solely on whether it produces the greatest balance of good over bad outcomes.

More important, consequentialist ethical reasoning—like cost-benefit and cost-effectiveness calculations—assumes that it is not only possible but permissible and even mandatory to aggregate goods and bads (costs and benefits) across individuals. Harms to some can be offset by gains to others; what matters is the sum. Critics of such simple and unqualified consequentialist reasoning, including ourselves, are quick to point out its fundamental flaws: Such reasoning is distributationally insensitive because it fails to take seriously the separateness and inviolability of persons.

. . .

THE PERSONAL SERVICE MODEL

Today eugenics is almost universally condemned. Partly in reaction to the tendency of the most extreme eugenicists to discount individual freedom and welfare from the supposed good of society, medical geneticists and genetic counselors since World War II have adopted an almost absolute commitment to "nondirectiveness" in their relations with those seeking genetic services. Recoiling from the public health model that dominated the eugenics movement, and especially from the vertical disease metaphor, they publicly endorse the view that genetic tests and interventions are simply services offered to individuals—goods for private consumption—to be accepted or refused as individuals see fit.

This way of conceiving of genetic interventions takes them out of the public domain, relegating them to the sphere of private choices. Advocates of the personal service model proclaim that the fundamental value on which it rests is individual autonomy. Whether a couple at risk for conceiving a child with a genetic disease takes a genetic test and how they use the knowledge thus obtained is their business, not society's, even if the decision to vaccinate a child for common childhood infectious diseases is a matter of public health and as such justifies restricting parental choice.

The personal service model serves as a formidable bulwark against the excesses of the crude consequentialist ethical reasoning that tainted the application of the public health model in the era of eugenics. But it does so at a prohibitive price: It ignores the obligation to prevent harm as well as some of the most basic requirements of justice. By elevating autonomy to the exclusion of all other values, the personal service model offers a myopic view of the moral landscape.

. . .

In addition, if genetic services are treated as goods for private consumption, the cumulative effects of many individual choices in the "genetic marketplace" may limit the autonomy of many people, and perhaps of all people. Economic pressures, including requirements for insurability and employment, as well as social stigma directed toward those who produce children with "defects" that could have been avoided, may narrow rather than expand meaningful choice. Finally, treating genetic interventions as personal services may exacerbate inequalities in opportunities if the prevention of genetic diseases or genetic enhancements are available only to the rich. It would be more accurate to say, then, that the personal service model gives free reign to some dimensions of the autonomy of some people, often at the expense of others.

NOTES AND QUESTIONS

1. *The Personal Service Model and Eugenics.* Buchanan and colleagues seem to imply that the use of the personal service model ensures that genetic interventions will not amount to eugenics. Other authors, however, claim that there is a new eugenics movement based on the personal service model. Recall Curtis A. Kin's description of the new eugenics movement:

> The old fears and criticisms of eugenics do not apply to the new eugenics movement, which is neither state-sponsored nor an experiment imposed on unwilling participants. Rather, the new eugenics respects individual autonomy in what Robert Nozick has termed the "genetic supermarket," where individuals freely shop and choose the features and traits they desire for themselves and their children. Supporters of the new eugenics argue that the "genetic supermarket" poses no significant problems because there exists no centralized control over the future of human development.

Curtis A. Kin, *Coming Soon to the "Genetic Supermarket" Near You*, 48 STAN. L. REV. 1573 (1996), *reproduced in* Sec. III, *supra*. Does the lack of state action make the personal service model any less threatening? The International Bioethics Committee talks about eugenics in terms of attitudes, rather than state action:

> [T]here is an underlying assumption [amongst eugenicists] that genetic differences between individuals constitute a rational basis for labels of "superior" and "inferior." The point is that eugenics is built upon an *attitude* that seeks its justification in science.... These are habits of mind and ways of thinking philosophically that are hostile to the key notion of the inherent dignity of the human individual and the inviolable and inalienable human rights that arise from the international consensus about the value of human beings.

Chee Heng Leng et al., Bioethics and Human Population Genetics Research 16, United Nations Educational, Scientific and Cultural Organization, CIP/ BIO/95/CONF.002/5 (Nov. 15, 1995). Under this conception of eugenics, the actor is less relevant. Can eugenics be carried about by individual consumers of genetic interventions? If so, what are the state's obligations in upholding human rights and the inherent dignity of human beings? To what extent should the "genetic supermarket" be regulated?

2. *The Public Health Model of Genetic Intervention.* While the public health model of genetic intervention has been largely supplanted by the personal service model, the "crude consequentialist ethical reasoning that tainted the application of the public health model in the era of eugenics" is not solely a thing of the past. The International Bioethics Committee gives the example of the Singapore Government, whose populations policies are "guided by eugenics—women who graduate from universities are encouraged to bear more children in the belief that their children have higher 'intelligence', while less-educated women are offered disincentives to have more than two children." Chee Heng Leng et al., Bioethics and Human Population Genetics Research 16, United Nations Educational, Scientific and Cultural Organization, CIP/BIO/95/CONF.002/5 (Nov. 15, 1995).

2.   GENETIC STRATIFICATION BASED ON RACE AND ETHNICITY

Recent genetic studies have been interpreted in significantly different ways, with some observers arguing that new genetic information is undermining traditional notions of race by proving that race is nothing more than a social construct and is not biologically based. Other observers reach very different conclusions, arguing that genetic studies confirm that race is biologically rooted. This controversy may have far-reaching effects on public policy.

Richard S. Cooper et al., *Race and Genomics*
348 NEW ENG. J. MED. 1166 (2003).

Race is a thoroughly contentious topic, as one might expect of an idea that intrudes on the everyday life of so many people. The modern concept of race grew out of the experience of Europeans in naming and organizing the populations encountered in the rapid expansion of their empires. As a way to categorize humans, race has since come to take on a wide range of meanings, mixing social and biologic ingredients in varied proportions. This plasticity has made it a tool that fits equally well in the hands of demagogues who want to justify genocide and eugenics and of health scientists who want to improve surveillance for disease. It is not surprising, therefore, that diametrically opposing views have been voiced about its scientific and social value. Indeed, few other concepts used in the conduct of ordinary science are the subject of a passionate debate about whether they actually exist.

Into this storm of controversy rides genomics. With the acknowledgment that race is the product of a marriage of social and biologic influences, it has been proposed that genomics now at least offers the opportunity to put its biologic claims to an objective test. If those claims are validated, race will become a way to choose drug therapy for patients, categorize persons for genetic research, and understand the causes of disease. Genomics, with its technological innovations and authority as "big science," might thereby solve the conundrum of race and bring peace to the warring factions.

Promotion of a drug for a race-specific "niche market" could distract physicians from therapies for which unequivocal evidence of benefit already exists. Race-specific therapy draws its rationale from the presumption that the frequencies of genetic variants influencing the efficacy of the drug are substantially different among races. This result is hard to demonstrate for any class of drugs, including those used to treat heart failure. Although a study of polymorphisms in drug-metabolizing enzymes did, in fact, show statistically significant variation in allele frequencies according to race, neither racial categories nor genetic clusters were sufficiently precise to make them clinically useful in guiding the choice of drugs. What is lost in these arguments is the difficulty of translating differences among groups into a test that has adequate predictive value to help with clinical decisions. Race can help to target screening for a disease-associated mutation that is present at a high frequency in one population and is virtually absent in another, but it is impossible for race as we recognize it clinically to provide both perfect sensitivity and specificity for the presence of a DNA-sequence variant. For this reason, race has never been shown to be an adequate proxy for use in choosing a drug; if you really need to know whether a patient has a particular genotype, you will have to do the test to find out.

The availability of high-throughput genotyping creates the opportunity for increasingly sophisticated analyses of the extent to which continental populations vary genetically. Analysis of a large set of multiallelic microsatellite loci has shown that it is possible to cluster persons into population groups with high statistical accuracy. Although clustering persons according to geographic origin has been accomplished most effectively with the use of highly informative, rapidly mutating, microsatellite loci, the use of single-nucleotide polymorphisms (SNPs) or their corresponding haplotypes also results in some degree of classification according to continent.

However, the public health relevance of these data remains controversial. One view holds that the ability to categorize persons according to continental "race" validates the clinical and epidemiologic use of self-reported racial ancestry in terms of the categories of white, black, Asian, Pacific Islander, and Native American used by the U.S. Census. We disagree. The success of microsatellite loci in classifying persons according to continental group depends in part on the cumulative effect of minor differences in the frequencies of common alleles and in part on the effect of population-specific alleles. In neither case is it apparent that such differences have relevance for traits that are important to health. Most population-specific microsatellite alleles are unlikely to be functional; rather, like a last name, they merely help to verify the geographic origin of a person's ancestry. Accumulated small differences in common alleles will yield differences in population risk only if a disease is caused primarily by interactions among multiple loci, and this is both mathematically and biologically implausible

The real effect of the biologic concept of race has always been its implications for common quantitative traits. Marked differences in the rates of cardiovascular diseases, for example, have been held up as examples of how race matters. Reframed in genomic terms, it is argued that if "biological is defined by susceptibility to, and natural history of, a chronic disease, then … numerous studies … have documented biological differences among the races." However, there is no body of evidence to support these broad claims about chronic diseases. Although it is obvious that many genetic diseases vary markedly among populations, those conditions are generally rare. Tay Sachs disease, cystic fibrosis, and hemoglobinopathies, for example, are absent in many populations but present in others. But for these conditions, continental populations are not the categories of interest:

persons of Jewish descent, not "whites," share a risk of Tay Sachs disease; the frequency of cystic fibrosis varies widely within Europe; and thalassemia occurs in a variety of populations distributed from Italy to Thailand.

Many single-gene disorders have now been defined at the molecular level, and the emerging challenge faced by geneticists is to "make the genome relevant to public health." Defining the molecular underpinnings of common chronic diseases has therefore become the central focus of genetic epidemiology. By extension, some investigators have turned with renewed enthusiasm to race as a tool for categorizing population risk. This approach draws on the practice, of long standing in the public health field in the United States, of granting priority to race or ethnic background as a demographic category—a surveillance practice, it is worth noting, that is virtually unique in the world. At the present time, however, very little is known about the genetic component of diseases of complex causation. Few, if any, well-characterized susceptibility genes have been identified for any of the degenerative conditions that kill at least 5 percent of the population, and we do not even know whether the individual variants are common or rare or whether they affect a protein's structure or its level of expression.

Since we do not know about the genetic variants that predispose persons to common chronic diseases, one might assume that arguments for the existence of genetic predispositions would be made for all population groups equally. The reality is very different. Minority groups, particularly blacks in the United States, are assumed to be genetically predisposed to virtually all common chronic diseases. Genes are regularly proposed as the cause when no genetic data have been obtained, and the social and biologic factors remain hopelessly confounded. Even when molecular data are collected, causal arguments are based on nonsignificant findings or genetic variation that does not have an established association with the disease being studied. Coincidence is not a plausible explanation of the widespread occurrence of this practice over time and across subdisciplines. The correlation between the use of unsupported genetic inferences and the social standing of a group is glaring evidence of bias and demonstrates how race is used both to categorize and to rank order subpopulations.

Not only are the relevant genetic data absent, but the distribution of polygenic phenotypes does not suggest that race is a useful category. Consider as an example height, a continuous trait that is highly heritable in all populations. Does continental race tell us something useful about average height? People who attain both the tallest stature (the Masai) and the shortest (the Biaka) are found in sub-Saharan Africa; Swedish people have traditionally been much taller than Sicilians; and although Japanese people used to be short, the current generation of children in Japan cannot fit in the desks in schools. The concept of race does not summarize this information effectively. If that complexity is multiplied by thousands of traits, which are randomly distributed among groups within continents, one gets an idea of the limitations of race as a classification scheme.

Although the rapid pace of change in genomics makes today's conclusions obsolete tomorrow, some predictions are in order. We can expect genomics increasingly to negate the old-fashioned concept that differences in genetic susceptibility to common diseases are racially distributed. In any common disease, many genes are likely to be involved, and each gene will have many variants. All the current data indicate that susceptibility alleles tend to be old, have moderate-to-small effects, and are shared among many populations. The *APOE 4* allele, a well-studied example that contributes to a small extent to individual and potential risk for traits such as heart disease and dementia, is found in virtually all populations, albeit at varying rates.

Recent genomic surveys have also shown that as few as three to five common haplotypes capture the bulk of segregating variation at any specific locus throughout the genome, and those haplotypes are generally represented in the populations of all continents. Therefore, if susceptibility alleles for chronic diseases are located on common haplotypes, those alleles must be shared by members of all populations. Measuring the net effect of these genetic influences in a given population will require summing the frequencies of these susceptibility alleles in all genomic regions, while taking into account the environmental factors that are either difficult to measure or wholly unknown. Given these daunting epidemiologic challenges, it will be very difficult to calculate the "genetic susceptibility score" for any particular racial category.

This point requires further attention. There is no doubt that there are some important biologic differences among populations, and molecular techniques can help to define what those differences are. Some traits, such as skin color, vary in a strikingly systematic pattern. The inference does not follow, however, that genetic variation among human populations falls into racial categories or that race, as we currently define it, provides an effective system for summarizing that variation. The confused nature of this debate is apparent when we recognize that although everyone, from geneticists to laypersons, tends to use "race" as if it were a scientific category; with rare exceptions, no one offers a quantifiable definition of what a race is in genetic terms. The free-floating debate that results, while entertaining, has little chance of advancing this field.

What is at stake is a more practical question—namely, has genomics provided evidence that race can act as a surrogate for genetic constitution in medicine or public health? Our answer is no. Race, at the continental level, has not been shown to provide a useful categorization of genetic information about the response to drugs, diagnosis, or causes of disease.

But in the United States, there is substantial variation in health status among major population subgroups. This self-evident truth has been the driving force behind the use of racial or ethnic categories in surveillance for disease. Among persons who are less convinced by the genetic data, variation in environmental exposure is seen as the cause of this phenomenon, and it follows that differences in health occur because privilege and power are unequal in racially stratified societies. The globalization of complex chronic diseases seems to confirm the view that all populations are susceptible and that variation in rates can be understood as the result of differential exposure to environmental causes.

Although we acknowledge the salience of these arguments, the value of continental race as a classification scheme must be questioned in this context much as it was in the context of genetics. For example, persons who could be classified as having "African ancestry" have wide variation in rates of hypertension and diabetes, as do all large continental populations. Without the context provided by such variables as the level of education, occupation, type of diet, and place of residence, race as a social category is not a useful predictor of health outcomes. Just as most genetic heterogeneity occurs within populations, there is enormous variation in the patterns of culture-derived behavioral and risk factors. An unintended result of categorizing people according to race can be to foreclose the question of why they have ill health, leaving us blind to the meaning of the more relevant local and individual context.

Race, in the metaphor introduced above, is the product of an arranged marriage between the social and biologic worlds. Although it often seems to travel back and forth between these parallel universes, it maintains a home in both. From the social sphere, race has inherited certain attributes that cannot be alienated from its meaning, no matter how hard we might try. The concept of race has currency in everyday discourse and is an epistemological category independent of the action of geneticists. From the beginning, it has been used not just to organize populations, but to create a classification scheme that explains the meaning inherent in the social order, according to which some groups dominate others. There is a tendency for scientists to ignore the messy social implications of what they do. At the extreme, the argument is made that "we just tell the truth about nature," and its negative consequences are political problems that do not concern us. Whether or not such a position is defensible from an ethical point of view, the debate over race cannot be sidestepped so easily. Race already has a meaning. To invoke the authority of genomic science in the debate over the value of race as a category of nature is to accept the social meaning as well.

In the 20th century, physics promised us knowledge of how the universe works, space travel, and the ability to harness the atom as an infinite source of energy. Although vast amounts of knowledge did flow from research in those areas, the consequences in practice were not always benign. The accumulated record of peaceful and nonpeaceful atomic energy subsequently led many physicists to understand more fully that science is a part of society. In this century, biology—especially genomics—has emerged as the beacon of science leading us into the future, where data on the genetic sequence will unlock the secret of life. For genomics to fall in lock step with the socially defined use of race is not a propitious beginning to that journey. The ability to catalogue molecular variants in persons and populations has thrust genetics into a new relationship with society. Interpreting that catalogue within the existing framework of race, as was done in the case of eugenics, violates the principles that give science its unique status as a force outside the social hierarchy, one that does not take sides in factional contests. Racial affiliation draws on deep emotions about group identity and the importance of belonging. The discovery that races exist is not an advance of genomic science into uncharted territory; it is an extension of the atavistic belief that human populations are not just organized, but ordered.

NOTES AND QUESTIONS

1. *The Methodological Problem of Using Race in Genetic Studies.* Many research-ers use self-identified race in genetic studies. However, self-identification may be methodologically flawed because people do not accurately report their biological race to researchers. The reason may be that race is, in substantial part, socially constructed and individuals feel a cultural attachment to certain groups.

2. *The Responsibility of Researchers in Interpreting Biological Differences in Race.* What are the responsibilities of geneticists, ethicists, and policy makers when interpreting studies on genetics and race? Some geneticists will interpret findings to reinforce a biological basis for race, while others will interpret findings to disprove any biological basis. The International Bioethics Committee suggests that it may not be wise to leave the responsibility of fighting racism to scientific debate. "[W]hat science finds is what science finds, and these findings should be put in support of fundamental human rights which derive from the universal belief in the inherent dignity of the human individual. Such values cannot be 'proved' by science, and neither can they be 'disproved' by science." Chee Heng Leng et al., Bioethics and Human Population Genetics Research 16, United Nations Educational, Scientific and Cultural Organization, CIP/BIO/95/CONF.002/5 (Nov. 15, 1995).

3. *The Future of Race in Genetics Research.* Will research on genetic variation enable people to be grouped in new, positive ways to better tailor prevention and treatment or reinforce existing patterns of racial, ethnic or socioeconomic stratification?

4. *Genomics and Distributive Justice.* The poor are over-represented among low-literacy patients, making it less likely that they would be sufficiently informed to seek genetic benefits. They are also more likely to be served in settings with less skilled personnel and lower quality of care. Finally, the poor have less access to health services due to their lack of health insurance coverage. Does all this mean that the genomics revolution will increase, rather than decrease, socioeconomic and health disparities?

3. THE RISKS OF STRATIFICATION: GENETIC DISCRIMINATION

Recall Articles 1 & 2 Universal Declaration on the Human Genome and Human Rights:

> The human genome underlies the fundamental unity of all members of the human family as well as the recognition of their inherent dignity and diversity. In a symbolic sense, it is the heritage of humanity. Everyone has a right of respect for his or her dignity and his or her human rights regardless of their genetic characteristics. That dignity makes it imperative not to reduce individuals to their genetic characteristics and to respect their uniqueness and diversity.

Second Workshop on International Cooperation for the Human Genome Project: Ethics, *Valencia Declaration on Ethics and the Human Genome Project*, 2 J. INT. BIOETHIQUE 94–95 (1991).

Despite these promising sentiments, the public continues to express concern about genetic discrimination in employment, health or life insurance, education, and even loans. There are no systematic studies on the frequency of genetic discrimination but data suggest that it does occur. *See* Lawrence Low, et al., *Genetic Discrimination in Life Insurance: Empirical Evidence from a Cross Sectional Survey of Genetic Support Groups in the*

United Kingdom, 317 BMJ 1632–1635 (1998) (13% of surveyed population had experienced genetic discrimination). As Ellen Wright Clayton notes, the problem of genetic discrimination is more complex than it first appears:

> The question of whether genetic information should ever be used to affect one's access to health and other forms of insurance has been a dominant issue of public concern in the past decade. People cite fear of losing insurance as a major reason to avoid genetic testing. Others argue that discrimination by insurance companies is not a problem, often pointing out that few of these cases, which are difficult for employees to win, have been filed. Insurers assert that they do not perform tests to obtain genetic information but argue that they should be free to use such information if it is available, citing the need to avoid "moral hazard"—the risk that people who know they will become ill or die soon will try to obtain insurance at regular rates. In response to consumer pressure, many states have passed laws in this area.

Ellen Wright Clayton, *Ethical, Legal, and Social Implications of Genomic Medicine*, 349 NEW ENG. J. MED. 562, 563 (2003).

> [Clayton goes on to illustrate the complexity of genetic discrimination by examining a case involving Burlington Northern Santa Fe Railroad (BNSF):]

> ... Allegedly relying on the advice of its company physician, who in turn had apparently relied on the representations of a diagnostic company, BNSF began obtaining blood for DNA testing from employees who were seeking disability compensation as a result of carpal tunnel syndrome that occurred on the job. The employees were reportedly not told the purpose of the tests, which was to detect a mutation associated with hereditary neuropathy with liability to pressure palsies. The company's motive for pursuing testing was never made clear, but it seems reasonable to suspect that BNSF would have tried to deny disability benefits to any employee who had such a mutation, arguing that the mutation, and not the job, caused the carpal tunnel syndrome. When the company's practice came to light, it was almost immediately stopped by the federal Equal Employment Opportunity Commission, and shortly thereafter, the company settled claims brought by its employees for an undisclosed amount of money.

> What lessons can be learned here? One is that the company's effort to find mutations for hereditary neuropathy with liability to pressure palsies made little sense. This disorder is very rare, affecting about 3 to 10 persons per 100,000, and more important, although carpal tunnel syndrome can be a part of hereditary neuropathy with liability to pressure palsies, it has not been reported as the sole symptom. The injuries these employees sustained were not the result of an epidemic of hereditary neuropathy with liability to pressure palsies. Getting the biologic process correct is a critical step in making decisions about genetic testing.

> Another important lesson is that identifying a genetic predisposition to carpal tunnel syndrome would not have been the end of the discussion in the eyes of the law. The company got in trouble because its practice violated numerous laws forbidding discrimination in the workplace. In particular, the Americans with Disabilities Act permits employers to require a medical evaluation only under clearly specified circumstances. Testing employees after they were disabled without their informed consent clearly fell outside the bounds of this and other antidiscrimination laws.

The actions of BNSF led to widespread criticism and, not surprisingly, to calls to ban genetic discrimination in the workplace. Although some states have enacted laws, the need for federal action has grown as the Supreme Court has progressively narrowed the protection provided under the Americans with Disabilities Act. The answer, however, is not simply to forbid employers to use genetic information or to require genetic testing.

Id., at 563–64.

Clayton goes on to consider the most appropriate response to discrimination, beginning with how genetic information fits within the broader framework of antidiscrimination laws, which "were passed to create a certain kind of society, one in which people must be included regardless of race, sex, or disability, even at some cost to employers":

> ... Biology alone does not determine the social outcome. To use an analogy, an employer cannot exclude women from the workplace, even if he or she believes, with some justification, that women are more likely than men to take time off to care for family members. At the same time, employers are not required to bear unlimited costs to promote these social goals—the employee, male or female, who misses months of work at a time to care for sick relatives can still be fired.
>
> A similar debate about social goals and the limits of our pursuit of them must occur with regard to genetic discrimination. The Equal Employment Opportunity Commission recently awarded damages to Terri Sergeant, who was fired from her job as an office manager for an insurance broker because she required extremely expensive medication to treat her at-worst mildly symptomatic alpha$_1$-antitrypsin deficiency. A person's need for expensive health care is not sufficient reason to fire that person or to refuse to hire him or her in the first place. The fact that the costs may cause the employer to go under or to decide not to provide health insurance simply underlines the inherent weakness of employment-based health insurance.
>
> At the same time, one can imagine a genetic condition that might affect a person's ability to perform a job in ways that could not be accommodated with reasonable efforts. Suppose a person with a recurrent and untreatable cardiac arrhythmia that leads to loss of consciousness, owing to an inherited ion-channel defect, is seeking employment as a long-distance truck driver. Because of the risk to third parties, such a person would not even be able to get a driver's license in many jurisdictions. The more difficult question—and the one posed particularly with respect to genetics—would arise if an asymptomatic person had a predisposing, but incompletely penetrant, mutation for the same disorder. Deciding what to do about such predispositions will require close attention both to the true, as opposed to the feared, likelihood that symptoms will develop and to the complex weighing of the interests of the individual, the employer, and society.
>
> A similar calculus must be applied to every question regarding who can obtain and use genetic information to distinguish, or discriminate, among people in ways that affect their ability to obtain social goods, such as health insurance and education. If, as is likely, some uses are deemed to be appropriate, the challenge for clinicians will be to discuss with their patients the potential adverse social consequences of testing so that the patients can make informed choices about whether or not to proceed with testing.

Id., at 565–66.

NOTES AND QUESTIONS

1. *Genetic Antidiscrimination Statutes.* In order to safeguard against discriminatory practices, over 75% of states had, by 2004, enacted genetic discrimination legislation pertaining to employment, health insurance, or both. However, these measures contain loopholes, define genetic information in varying ways, and offer disparate degrees of protection. Definitions vary from state to state, such that one state may protect only DNA and RNA while another may extend protection to family history data and other medical information that could offer genetic information. State laws are also hampered by federal preemption under ERISA, which prevents states from regulating employer risk retention plans. *See* James M. Jeffords & Tom Daschle, *Political Issues in the Genome Era*, 291 SCI. 1249–1251 (2001).

At the federal level, the Health Insurance Portability and Accountability Act of 1996 (HIPAA) does not allow group health plans or those who insure group health plans to use genetic information as a basis for implementing rules for eligibility for the plan. However, HIPAA does not protect people who buy insurance as individuals, nor limit insurers' ability to collect or disclose people's genetic information. Title I of the Americans with Disabilities Act (ADA), enforced by the Equal Employment Opportunity Commission (EEOC), and similar disability-based antidiscrimination laws such as the Rehabilitation Act of 1973 also fail to offer complete employment protection. The ADA protects against discrimination based on a clinically manifest genetic disease amounting to a disability, but, as of yet, no federal court has ruled that pre-symptomatic testing for a predisposition to a disease is protected under the ADA. Jennifer Chorpening, *Genetic Disability: A Modest Proposal to Modify the ADA to Protect Against Some Forms of Genetic Discrimination*, 82 N.C.L. Rev. 1441, 1452 (2004).

2. *What are the Values Underlying Genetic Antidiscrimination Legislation?* There is, of course, the deep intuition that people should not be adversely treated because of a genetic condition over which they have no control. In addition to the issue of justice, does discrimination legislation have an instrumental value? Would people be more likely to come forward for testing, counseling, and treatment if they did not fear discrimination? Does genetic discrimination, therefore, warrant a definitive legislative solution?

3. *The Complexity of Genetic Discrimination.* "Discrimination" literally means treating people differently. However, treating people differently is not always wrong. Is it possible that in some cases there are ethically appropriate reasons for genetic discrimination? Suppose that an employer uses genetic information to exclude a person from a job based on that individual's hyper-susceptibility to a workplace toxin. Would that be unethical? What if the employer used genetic information to fire a person whose genes show that he or she is not (either currently or in the future) able to perform the functions of the job? Finally, what if an employer fired an individual at high risk of a chronic costly disease? Should the employer be compelled to provide health insurance for a person likely to develop an expensive health condition? What if an individual knew she was *BRCA1* positive, placing her for high risk for breast or ovarian cancer? Should she be permitted to hide this information from her employer or insurer? Would this be a form of moral hazard?

4. *Discrimination and Genetics Exceptionalism.* Do persons with genetic disease have a better case for protection against discrimination than those with diseases of non-genetic origin? Consider two women with breast cancer—one with a positive *BRCA* test and the other with a negative test. Both are fired from their job or excluded from health insurance based on their illness. What is the appropriate policy response?

VI.   CONCLUSION

The human genome project demonstrates the capacity for remarkable scientific innovation. If science is nurtured and incentivized, it can lead to a future of better health for individuals and populations. At the same time, the human genome raises novel questions of ethics and law. Must scientific progress inevitably pose a cost to society, or can ethical problems be effectively addressed by timely, thoughtful foresight? As the science, and its implications for the medical and public health communities, become increasingly clear, the law must be prepared to untangle the questions that enhanced diagnosis and treatment will evoke. While science will give physicians and public health officials the tools to improve human life, the legal system must provide boundaries that maximize the beneficial implications while curtailing discrimination and invasions of privacy. Above all, there is the question of social justice, which demands that the benefits and burdens of genomics be distributed fairly, irrespective of race or socioeconomic status.

CHAPTER 2

PRIVATE CONTROL OF SCIENCE AND MEDICINE

I. PROFESSIONALS AND THEIR ORGANIZATIONS AND INSTITUTIONS

A. WHAT IS A PROFESSION?

Newmark v. Gimbel's, Inc.

Supreme Court of New Jersey, 1969.
54 N.J. 585, 258 A.2d 697.

■ FRANCIS, J.

This appeal involves the liability of a beauty parlor operator for injury to a patron's hair and scalp allegedly resulting from a product used in the giving of a permanent wave. The action was predicated upon charges of negligence and breach of express and implied warranty. Trial was had before the county district court and a jury. At the close of the proof, the court ruled as a matter of law that the warranty theory of liability was not maintainable because in giving a permanent wave a beauty parlor is engaged in rendering a service and not a sale.... The Appellate Division reversed holding that a fact issue existed requiring jury decision as to whether there was an implied warranty of fitness of the lotion applied to Mrs. Newmark's hair and scalp for the purpose of producing the permanent wave....

. . .

... For about a year and a half prior to the incident in question, Mrs. Newmark had been a patron of one of defendants' shops where she had a standing appointment every week to have her hair washed and set. She was usually attended by the same operator, one William Valante. During that period ... she had purchased permanent waves there, at least one having been given by Valante, and she had not experienced any untoward results.

On November 16, 1963, pursuant to an appointment, Mrs. Newmark went to the beauty parlor where she inquired of Valante about a permanent wave that was on special sale. He told her that her fine hair was not right for the special permanent and that she needed a "good" permanent wave. She agreed to accept the wave suggested by him. Valante conceded that the wave she received was given at his suggestion and that in accepting it she relied on his judgment as to what was good for her hair. Both Valante and Mrs. Newmark testified there was nothing wrong with her hair or scalp before the wave was given.

Valante proceeded to cut and wash her hair after which he put her head under a dryer for about 10 minutes. The hair was then sectioned off, a permanent wave solution marketed under the name "Helene Curtis Candle Wave" was applied with cotton and the hair was rolled section by section. Following this, more of the waving solution was put on by an applicator-bottle. Then a cream was placed along the hairline and covered with cotton. About three to five minutes after the last of the waving solution had been applied Mrs. Newmark experienced a burning sensation on the front part of her head. She complained to Valante who added more cream along the hairline. This gave some relief but after a few minutes she told him that it was burning again. The burning sensation continued but was alleviated when Valante brought her to a basin and rinsed her hair in lukewarm water. The curlers were then removed, a neutralizing solution was applied and allowed to remain for about seven minutes, and her hair was again rinsed. After this Valante set her hair and again put her under the dryer where she remained for about 25 minutes. The burning sensation returned and she promptly informed Valante who reduced the heat of the dryer thereby giving her partial relief. When the dryer operation was completed her hair was combed, and she left the parlor.

That evening her head reddened, and during the following day her entire forehead was red and blistered. A large amount of hair fell out when it was combed. . . .

. . .

It seems to us that the policy reasons for imposing warranty liability in the case of ordinary sales are equally applicable to a commercial transaction such as that existing in this case between a beauty parlor operator and a patron. Although the policy reasons which generate the responsibility are essentially the same, practical administration suggests that the principle of liability be expressed in terms of strict liability in tort thus enabling it to be applied in practice unconfined by the narrow conceptualism associated with the technical niceties of sales and implied warranties. . . . One, who in the regular course of a business sells or applies a product (in the sense of the sales-service hybrid transaction involved in the present case) which is in such a dangerously defective condition as to cause physical harm to the consumer-patron, is liable for the harm. Consumption in this connection includes all ultimate uses for which the product is intended. 2 Restatement, Torts 2d, § 402A, p. 347 (1965) adopts this view. Obviously the ultimate use of the Helene Curtis permanent wave solution intended by both manufacturer and beauty parlor operator was its application to the hair of a patron. And as Comment 1 to the Restatement section says, "the customer in a beauty shop to whose hair a permanent wave solution is applied by the shop is a consumer." 2 Restatement, *supra*, at p. 354.

Defendants claim that to hold them to strict liability would be contrary to *Magrine v. Krasnica*, 94 N.J.Super. 228, 227 A.2d 539 (Cty.Ct.1967), *aff'd sub nom.* Magrine v. Spector, 100 N.J.Super. 223, 241 A.2d 637 (App.Div.1968), *aff'd* 250 A.2d 129 (1969). We cannot agree. Magrine, a patient of the defendant-dentist, was injured when a hypodermic needle being used, concededly with due care, to administer a local anesthetic broke off in his gum or jaw. The parties agreed that the break resulted from a latent defect in the needle. It was held that the strict liability in tort doctrine was not applicable to the professional man, such as a dentist, because the essence of the relationship with his patient was the furnishing of professional skill and services. We accepted the view that a dentist's bill for services should be considered as representing pay for that alone. The use of instruments, or the administration of medicines or the providing of medicines for the patient's home consumption cannot give the ministrations the cast of a commercial transaction. Accordingly the liability of the dentist in cases involving the ordinary relationship of doctor and patient must be tested by principles of negligence, i.e., lack of due care and not by application of the doctrine of strict liability in tort.

Defendants suggest that there is no doctrinal basis for distinguishing the services rendered by a beauty parlor operator from those rendered by a dentist or a doctor, and that consequently the liability of all three should be tested by the same principles. On the contrary there is a vast difference in the relationships. The beautician is engaged in a commercial enterprise; the dentist and doctor in a profession. The former caters publicly not to a need but to a form of aesthetic convenience or luxury, involving the rendition of non-professional services and the application of products for which a charge is made. The dentist or doctor does not and cannot advertise for patients; the demand for his services stems from a felt necessity of the patient. In response to such a call the doctor, and to a somewhat lesser degree the dentist, exercises his best judgment in diagnosing the patient's ailment or disability, prescribing and sometimes furnishing medicines or other methods of treatment which he believes, and in some measure hopes, will relieve or cure the condition. His performance is not mechanical or routine because each patient requires individual study and formulation of an informed judgment as to the physical or mental disability or condition presented, and the course of treatment needed. Neither medicine nor dentistry is an exact science; there is no implied warranty of cure or relief. There is no representation of infallibility and such professional men should not be held to such a degree of perfection. There is no guaranty that the diagnosis is correct. Such men are not producers or sellers of property in any reasonably acceptable sense of the term. In a primary sense they furnish services in the form of an opinion of the patient's condition based upon their experienced analysis of the objective and subjective complaints, and in the form of recommended and, at times, personally administered medicines and treatment. Practitioners of such callings, licensed by the State to practice after years of study and preparation, must be deemed to have a special and essential role in our society, that of studying our physical and mental ills and ways to alleviate or cure them, and that of applying their knowledge, empirical judgment and skill in an effort to diagnose and then to relieve or to cure the ailment of a particular patient. Thus their paramount function—the essence of their function—ought to be regarded as the furnishing of opinions and services. Their unique status and the rendition of these sui generis services bear such a necessary and intimate relationship to public health and welfare that their obligation ought to be grounded and expressed in a duty to exercise reasonable competence and care toward their patients. In our judgment, the nature of the services, the utility of and the need for them, involving as they do, the health and even survival of many people, are so important to the general welfare as to outweigh in the policy scale any need for the imposition on dentists and doctors of the rules of strict liability in tort.

. . .

Accordingly, a factual issue was presented at trial for jury determination as to (1) whether the permanent wave solution was defective, and (2) whether it was the proximate cause of the [plaintiff's injury]. An affirmative answer by the jury would warrant a verdict for the plaintiffs.

The judgment of the Appellate Division is affirmed for the reasons stated, and the cause is remanded for a new trial.

NOTES AND QUESTIONS

1. Do you find the rationale of the *Newmark* court persuasive? Should dentists and physicians be held to a different standard of professional conduct in their dealings with the public than hair stylists? Are they?

Consider John H. McArthur & Francis D. Moore, *Commerce and Professionalism in Medial Care*, 277 JAMA 941, 985 (1997):

> The current trend towards the invasion of commerce into medical care, an arena formerly under the exclusive purview of physicians, is seen . . . as an epic clash of cultures between the commercial and professional traditions in the United States. Both have contributed to U.S. society for centuries; both have much to offer in strengthening medical care and reducing costs. At the same time, this invasion by commercialism of an area formerly governed by professionalism poses severe hazards to the care of the sick and the welfare of communities: the health of the public and the public health. . . .
>
> . . .
>
> In a commercial environment seeking to maximize revenue from each clinical encounter, both volume and quality of such clinical services are inevitably threatened. . . .
>
> Such compromises and distortions of clinical care place physicians in a severe ethical dilemma: shall they follow the dictates of conscience and known good practice in giving every consideration to the aid and comfort of the patient, or shall they save money for their employers? Such dilemmas are among the most severe ethical challenges in the practice of physicians and surgeons today.

2. Do you agree with the distinction that the *Newmark* Court draws between the professional, who fulfills a socially necessary service, and a non-professional, who merely engages in commercial activities that do not relate to a social need?

Consider the discussion of the concept of autonomy by David Blumenthal, *The Vital Role of Professionalism in the Context of Autonomy and Self-Control*, HEALTH AFF. 252 (1994):

> . . . Many doctors equate professionalism with autonomy—to be left alone to do what they want, not only medically but financially. Autonomy, however, is not a divine right of medical or other professionals. Rather . . . it is a legal, institutional, and moral privilege that is granted by society and that must be earned by health care providers through observing certain standards of behavior, including at least the following. (1) *Altruism.* Professionals are expected to resolve conflicts between their interests and their patients' interests in favor of the patients. (2) *A commitment to self-improvement.* Professionals are expected

to master new knowledge about their trade and to incorporate it continually into their practice. They are expected to contribute individually to the knowledge base that informs their discipline. (3) *Peer Review:* Because of their specialized knowledge, professionals are uniquely positioned to supervise that work of their peers, to protect consumers against the failures of professionalism.

3. Is the definition of "professional" found in *Newmark* consistent with the Eleventh Circuit's definition in *Dybach v. State of Florida Department of Corrections*, in which the court stated: "[t]he term 'professional' is not restricted to the traditional professions of law, medicine and theology. It includes those professions which have a recognized status and which are based on the acquirement of professional knowledge through prolonged study. It also includes the artistic professions, such as acting or music." Dybach v. State of Florida Department of Corrections, 942 F.2d 1562, 1564 (11th Cir. 1991).

4. Consider William J. Goode's discussion of what constitutes a profession. William J. Goode, *Encroachment, Charlatanism, and the Emerging Profession: Psychology, Medicine, and Sociology*, XXV AM. SOC. REV. 902–914 (1960):

> ... [The] two core characteristics [of professions] are "a prolonged specialized training in a body of abstract knowledge, and a collectivity or service orientation." Among the "derived characteristics," which are presumably "caused" by the core characteristics, are five which refer to autonomy: "(1) The profession determines its own standards of education and training. ... (3) Professional practice is often legally recognized by some form of licensure. (4) Licensing and admission boards are manned by members of the profession. (5) Most legislation concerned with the profession is shaped by that profession.... (7) The practitioner is relatively free of lay evaluation and control."

5. Compare Robert W. Hamilton, *Professional Partnerships in the United States*, J. CORP. L. 1045, 1045–46 (2001):

What is a "Professional Occupation"?

> What is meant by a "professional" occupation in the United States? Undoubtedly the phrase (at least in the United States) brings to mind traditional occupations such as physicians, dentists, lawyers, accountants, architects, and the like. However, the issue of definition is more complicated than it first appears.

> American states have a long tradition of creating licensure boards for persons desiring to go into certain trades or occupations. The licensing authority is typically a board created by state statute that is given authority to require a written examination, a review of background and experience, a period of association and training under the supervision of a licensed person, and often a hands-on demonstration of skill and competence in the particular occupation. If this is the test of whether a person is a "professional," the category is broad indeed. In Texas, for example, the following is a partial list of the occupations that require a license: Architects; Attorneys at law; Airplane pilots; Barbers; Certified public accountants; Chiropractors; Clinical social workers; Dentists; Dieticians; Persons fitting and dispensing hearing aids; Land surveyors; Licensed marriage counselors; Licensed family counselors; Life insurance agents; Local recording agents; Morticians; Nurses; Nursing home administrators; Optometrists; Osteopaths; Physicians with a wide variety of specialties; Physical therapists; Plumbers; Podiatrists; Polygraph examiners; Private investigators; Private security agency administrators; Professional counselors; Professional engineers; Psychologists; Public accountants; Public surveyors; Real

estate brokers; Surgeons; Structural pest controllers; Tax professionals; Veterinarians; Vocational nurses.

6. Hamilton's list of Texas occupations requiring a license includes "Barber." If the *Newmark* case had been decided in Texas, would the result have been different?

7. Compare Edmund Pellegrino, *What Is a Profession?*, 12 J. Allied Health 168, 174–75 (1983):

> A profession ... is not something a university or a licensing or accrediting body confers. *Having* credentials is incidental to *being* a professional. To be a professional is to make a promise to help, to keep that promise, and to do so in the best interests of the patient. It is to accept the trust the patient must place in us as a moral imperative, one that the ethos of the marketplace or competition does not expect us in our society to honor. The special nature of the helping and healing professions is rooted in the fact that people become ill and need to trust others to help them restore health.

> You may object that I have described an ideal state, that many professionals are in fact insensitive to the vulnerability of those who seek their help, and that many physicians, lawyers, and even ministers have been and are motivated by self-interest.... Sadly, such abuses are undeniable. They are not, fortunately, perpetrated by the majority of professionals. But even if they were, that fact would not change the philosophical foundations of the relationship. To define a profession by the way professionals behave is to accept what *is* for what *ought* to be.

> Another objection may be that lawyers, physicians, and ministers are ordinary people. Why should we expect them to behave more nobly than their fellows?

> ...

> There can be only one response. Violations of morality do not establish immorality as a guide for human behavior. The nature of the relationships we have described are grounded in the human condition. They impose moral obligations that must transcend standards of moral behavior in society at large. A true professional is, in sum, an ordinary person called to extraordinary duties by the nature of the activities in which he or she has chosen to engage.

B. Establishing Norms and Standards of Conduct

Fineman v. New Jersey Department of Human Services

Supreme Court of New Jersey, Appellate Division, 1994.
272 N.J.Super. 606, 640 A.2d 1161.

■ Landau, J.A.D.

In this appeal by the defendants, New Jersey Department of Human Services (DHS) and the New Jersey Memorial Home for Disabled Soldiers, Sailors, Marines and their Wives and Widows (Home), ... we focus upon N.J.S.A. 34:19–3c(1) and (3), portions of the Conscientious Employee Protection Act (CEPA), N.J.S.A. 34:19–1 to 19–8. No less than its common law precursors, CEPA requires judicial resolution of threshold legal issues respecting existence of a statutory, regulatory or other clear mandate of public policy before the trier of fact determines whether an employee has been retaliated against for acting upon an objectively reasonable belief of the existence of such clear mandate by objecting to or refusing to perform acts in violation of the mandate....

Procedural Setting

Following termination of his at-will employment, plaintiff filed a CEPA complaint in the Law Division against DHS; the Home; Joseph Cagno, its Chief Executive Officer; and Robert J. Brezo, the Assistant Chief Executive Officer. He demanded a jury trial, asserting that his termination constituted unlawful retaliatory action under N.J.S.A. 34:19–3c(1) and 3c(3).[1] . . .

Essentially, the jury was asked to determine whether plaintiff was terminated for a refusal to see or treat certain patients in excess of his originally assigned work load or for objecting thereto; and whether such refusal or objection was based upon reasonable belief that the temporary assignment evidenced a general policy or practice of patient care which violated a law or regulation (N.J.S.A. 34:19–3c(1)) or was incompatible with a clear mandate of public policy (N.J.S.A. 34:19–3c(3)), inclusive of applicable Department of Health regulations, the Hippocratic Oath, and the American Medical Association Principles of Medical Ethics.

On motion at the conclusion of plaintiff's case and again after all evidence was presented, the trial judge considered the threshold legal determinations required by *Pierce v. Ortho Pharmaceutical Corp.,* 84 N.J. 58, 417 A.2d 505 (1980), which predated and furnished the underlay for legislative adoption of CEPA, as well as our opinion in *Warthen v. Toms River Comm. Mem. Hosp.,* 199 N.J.Super. 18, 488 A.2d 229 (App.Div.) *certif. denied,* 501 A.2d 926 (1985). The judge concluded, as a matter of law, that the physicians' Hippocratic Oath and American Medical Association Code of Ethics, read in conjunction with N.J.A.C. 8:39–23.1, *et seq.* (mandatory medical services standards for long-term nursing care facilities) could be found to constitute, for CEPA purposes, a regulation (N.J.S.A. 34:19–3c(1)) or "clear mandate of public policy" (N.J.S.A. 34:19–3c(3)) which plaintiff could reasonably have believed would be violated were he to provide temporary medical coverage in excess of the one hundred resident caseload to which he was specifically assigned. He then submitted these questions to the jury:

> 1. Did plaintiff Milton Fineman reasonably believe that the Memorial Home's activity, policy or practice respecting a physician's patient responsibilities was: (A) In violation of a law, rule or regulation promulgated pursuant to law? (B) Incompatible with a clear mandate of public policy governing the public health, safety or welfare?

If you have answered "yes" to either #1A or #1B, or both, go to Question #2.

---

1. N.J.S.A. 34:19–3 provides in pertinent part:

An employer shall not take any retaliatory action against an employee because the employee does any of the following:

* * *

c. Objects to, or refuses to participate in any activity, policy or practice which the employee reasonably believes:

(1) is in violation of a law, or a rule or regulation promulgated pursuant to law;

(2) is fraudulent or criminal; or

(3) is incompatible with a clear mandate of public policy concerning the public health, safety or welfare or protection of the environment.

If you have answered "no" to both #1A and #1B, return to the courtroom.

2. Did the plaintiff Milton Fineman object, either in writing or orally, to the Memorial Home's activity policy or practice, or did the Plaintiff Milton Fineman refuse to participate in the defendant's policy or practice respecting patient care?

3. Was a determinative factor in the defendant's decision to discharge the plaintiff the result of the action taken by the plaintiff, as described in Question #2 above, and thus, in retaliation for the action taken by the plaintiff as found in Question #2?

If the answer to Question #3 is "yes," you have rendered a verdict in favor of the plaintiff and you shall return to the courtroom.

If the answer to Question #3 is "no," you have rendered a verdict in favor of the defendant and you shall return to the courtroom.

The jury answered "yes" to each question. The trial judge then entered judgment ordering plaintiff's reinstatement, a $1,000 fine for violation of N.J.S.A. 34:19–5g payable by the Home; and damages in the amount of $273,546 together with pre-judgment interest in the amount of $36,389.

Facts

The Home is a long-term care facility (nursing home) for disabled or elderly soldiers, sailors, marines, and their wives and widows. It is not a hospital. It receives federal subsidies as a state veteran's facility which is supervised by DHS, but is also inspected by the Veteran's Administration and the New Jersey Department of Health.

On May 1, 1987, plaintiff was hired as a physician specialist at the Home. The medical director, Dr. Zubeda Rajput, provided plaintiff with information outlining his duties and responsibilities, which included covering for other staff physicians when they were absent or on vacation. Plaintiff was assigned as primary care physician for Units One–A and One–B, containing one hundred residents. He was also to provide on-call duties during certain evenings and weekends. Plaintiff's duties and responsibilities were described in the following fashion at time of hire:

Subject: *Duties and/or Responsibilities are as follows but are not limited to:*

Assigned to Units 1A and 1B. Responsible for total medical care in that unit. Workdays are 8:30 A.M. to 4:30 P.M.

Share *on duty* calls with other staff physicians. Presently will be every 3rd week.

To make rounds daily on your assigned unit.

To visit all nursing stations on weekends and/or holidays, when on call.

Responsible to complete all patient's medical records in the assigned unit and provide coverage for the facility.

To accept the responsibilities and duties of other staff physicians when they are on vacation, etc.

Directly responsible to the Medical Director and Assistant Chief Executive Officer.

. . .

[(emphasis in original)].

When plaintiff was hired, Dr. Alan Kulick was assigned as primary care physician in Unit Two and Dr. Rajput was to be the primary care physician for Unit Three. The Home had a total of approximately three hundred residents, divided equally among the three units.

Plaintiff testified that he read a prior memo from Cagno stating that there should always be two physicians attending the institution. He also said he received similar information from Dr. Rajput. The record makes clear that when "on-call", or when on the rotating weekend/holiday duty, a staff physician would ordinarily have temporary responsibility for all three hundred residents, subject to back-up provided by local hospitals and physicians.

. . .

After plaintiff was hired, Dr. Kulick took a vacation from May 26 to June 3. Dr. Rajput was granted sick leave from June 2 to June 21, so that for part of June 2 and all day June 3, plaintiff was the only full-time physician present. The Home also regularly utilized local physicians and hospitals as necessary.

Shortly after Dr. Rajput returned on June 21, she was granted a six-month leave of absence, leaving two full-time physicians at the Home, but no formal vacancy in the three-physician complement. Cagno promised to try to get another physician on a full-time or part-time basis, but left for reserve military service in early July without completing that effort.

Plaintiff points out, and we note, that in the course of seeking to achieve a higher level of compensation for staff physicians to facilitate the attraction of candidates such as plaintiff, defendants had previously called to the attention of superiors in DHS the serious condition presented by having only two full-time physicians. We find nothing in the record to suggest that any defendant attempted to prevent plaintiff from seeking additional medical coverage or indeed the additional compensation he repeatedly requested for his higher-than-expected work load. To the contrary, although plaintiff was evidently dissatisfied with the vigor and competence of their efforts, the uncontroverted record suggests that defendants were actively engaged in trying to achieve the same goals as plaintiff.

In early July, plaintiff and Dr. Kulick met with Cagno and Assistant CEO Brezo to discuss securing an additional physician, and additional compensation because of their added work load. Their concerns were brought to the attention of the Department's chief medical officer, Dr. Epstein. In fact, both Kulick and plaintiff were encouraged to contact Dr. Epstein directly to discuss additional compensation, as well as possible alternatives to the two-doctor situation. Additionally, it was agreed that plaintiff's complaints of negligence would be investigated and an administrative review conducted. In the meantime, Cagno was meeting with some success in arranging for part-time physician coverage, although plaintiff may not have been aware of this. Plaintiff was instructed to provide coverage for the residents.

Dr. Kulick had asked for a vacation week. He was told that he could go only if plaintiff would give written assurance that he would cover for him. Plaintiff declined to do so because that would leave him as the only staff physician for the three hundred residents. Nonetheless, Dr. Kulick simply departed for a one-week vacation on July 30 without authorization, and plaintiff was involuntarily faced with being the only full-time physician at the Home for the week. On July 30, plaintiff wrote to Cagno detailing the increase in his medical responsibilities. He concluded by stating:

> As a month has now gone by without adequate indication that some adjustment of conditions or rewards are to accrue I wish to advise you that starting Monday, August 3, 1987, I will resume my contract obligations ONLY as outlined above. (Referring to the duties initially outlined.)

At a meeting on July 31, plaintiff told Cagno, Brezo, and Executive Assistant Pikolicky that additional physician coverage should be provided. On August 4, he advised Director of Nurses Barbara Davis that he would not be available for coverage of Units Two and Three except for emergent or life threatening situations. Commencing on August 3, Marva Tiller, a nurse, reported that plaintiff refused to treat anyone outside of Unit One. On August 5, Director of Nurses Davis notified Brezo of plaintiff's refusal to see three residents in need of immediate medical attention. On August 6, she listed eleven other residents who plaintiff declined to see, even though they required medical attention. Patients in distress were referred to nearby hospitals or seen by "physicians who agreed to be on-call."

Plaintiff had also written that he would be away "without beeper" for the weekend of August 7–9.

By August 4, Cagno was able to secure physicians to serve on-call for the evenings and weekends. Cagno then recommended that plaintiff be terminated for failure to treat patients at the Home. Other people were consulted, including Brezo, Pikolicky, Division Director Leon Cheesman, and individuals in the Department of Personnel, who concluded plaintiff should be fired. Cagno contacted Dr. Epstein, Medical Consultant for the Department, who agreed with the recommendation, and passed it on to the Department's Office of Employee Relations. On August 10, Cagno told plaintiff he was fired effective August 7. He received a letter of termination signed by Cagno dated August 7.

Plaintiff testified that caring for three hundred patients was a violation of his ethical responsibilities based on the Hippocratic Oath, the American Medical Association ("AMA") Principles of Medical Ethics, and regulations governing nursing homes. Plaintiff did not know and could not say what specific regulation or statute would be violated.

. . .

Discussion

. . .

CEPA is an important expression of legislative policy designed, as its title suggests, to afford protection to conscientious employees. We view the legislation as harmonious with the common law mandate provided in [*Pierce v. Ortho Pharmaceutical Corp.*, 417 A.2d 505 (1980)]. In particular, the necessity for judicial evaluation on a case by case basis of the existence of a "clear mandate", after balancing conflicting interests, remains critical in CEPA cases. Our attention to this requirement makes consideration of the litigant's arguments somewhat more complex than the briefs suggest.

The discrete analysis required by law must, in this case, involve separate consideration of the clear mandate of public policy question in connection with: a) plaintiff's objections to his temporary assignment and to the alleged consequences of inadequate staffing policy at the Home, and b) plaintiff's refusal to participate in the policy, expressed by his openly declining to see any patients other than those to whom he was primarily assigned.

When a professional employee merely raises an objection, the consequences, and therefore the necessary weighing of competing interests, are apt to differ materially from those produced when the objection is expressed by overt acts such as refusal to give medical assistance. In the present case, Dr. Kulick's unauthorized one week vacation and Dr. Rajput's six month leave of absence undoubtedly resulted in a large increase in plaintiff's medical workload. Nonetheless, undisputed proofs showed that a number of patients for whom plaintiff was the alternate physician were refused treatment by him. We cannot determine whether all or none of these were emergent, life-threatening situations, although it appears that in at least several cases residents were in severe medical distress. Given the advanced age of most residents, it can reasonably be assumed that plaintiff's refusal to see or treat residents whose needs were brought to his attention by the nursing staff, could itself raise competing questions of medical ethics and responsibility.

In making their decision to terminate, plaintiff's refusal to see or treat Unit Two and Three patients was appropriately considered by the defendants in light of his assignment "to accept the responsibilities and duties of other staff physicians when they are on vacation, etc." and his professional obligation as the designated alternate physician. Thus, on the issue of retaliation for plaintiff's refusal to perform professional duties, the judge's balance should have taken into account not merely a single dimension of the public policy mandate asserted by plaintiff, but the existence of other applicable policies bearing upon clarity of the mandate, and whether it is beneficial to the public.

In our view, a balancing of interests test could not here support an objectively reasonable determination that there was a clear ethical and legal mandate of public policy requiring a physician to refuse to treat patients in distress. It was plain error requiring our attention in the interest of justice, for the judge to have submitted to the jury questions respecting the reasonableness of plaintiff's belief that the Home's policies were incompatible with a clear policy mandate in connection with his refusal (as distinct from his mere objection) and respecting "retaliation" for such refusal.

Members of professions, whether employees or self-employed, are often required to push the limits of endurance in order to fulfill professional responsibilities. School classes may be oversized; crime areas under-patrolled; social care centers overworked; needs of disabled persons inadequately addressed; to name only a few instances where legitimate professional frustration may be engendered because of inadequate commitment of public resources or for other reasons. We think it would be a rare case indeed where the intention of the Legislature in enacting N.J.S.A. 34:19–3c could be read by a court to find that one aspect of public policy was so clear as to override a physician's professional obligation to render medical treatment to the best of one's ability in difficult circumstances. When applied to plaintiff's *refusal to see patients* in Units Two and Three, this consideration alone was sufficient to render unclear the presence of any mandate of public policy. As to the refusal prong, the issue should have been resolved by granting defendants' motion.

In this limited context, we partially resolve the issue reserved in *Abbamont v. Piscataway Tp.*, 269 N.J.Super. 11, 23 n.5, 634 A.2d 538 (App.Div.1993) respecting scope of the "reasonable belief" language when there is no actual violation. A terminated physician who seeks relief under this statute from consequences of refusing to treat patients, must be right about existence of a statutory, regulatory or clear mandate violation. An extreme example might be refusal of an order to transfuse a patient with blood discovered to have been secured from a known hepatitis-or AIDS-infected donor, while safe alternative sources were readily available.

We turn briefly to a problem created by literal use of the disjunctive statutory language in submitting questions to the jury in this case. N.J.S.A. 34:19–3c prohibits retaliation because an employee "objects to, or refuses to participate in any activity, policy or practice which the employee reasonably believes ... etc." No distinction is drawn between a mere objection (including complaints) and the possible consequences of a refusal to participate (e.g., a refusal to carry out a professional responsibility). In ruling on the motions, the trial judge's denial was hinged only upon the reasonableness of a belief of violation of a law or regulation, or incompatibility with clear mandate of public policy, sufficient to render unlawful retaliation for *making objection* to the activity, policy or practice. Nonetheless, the form of the questions presented to the jury technically followed the statutory language but did not permit the jury to distinguish between a mere objection and a refusal to render professional services to more than a given number of patients.

Given the evidence, it is quite possible, indeed we find it probable, that the jury found plaintiff was terminated because he refused his assignment to see patients outside of Unit One, and not because of his objections. We held above that termination of an at-will physician employee for refusing to treat would not constitute a violation of N.J.S.A. 34:19–3c(1) or (3) on these facts. However, the effect of jury question number three, *supra,* was to enable the jury to so find. Because jury question two asked whether plaintiff objected to *or* refused to participate in defendant's practice of patient care, either could evoke a *yes* answer to question number three. If the jury found that the termination was occasioned by plaintiff's *refusal to treat* Unit Two and Three patients, the judgment clearly requires reversal.

To the extent the jury might have found that it was plaintiff's *objections* which triggered termination, however, we must decide whether a remand on this issue is appropriate.[7] This requires us to consider: (1) the "objects to" aspect of N.J.S.A. 34:19–3c and sufficiency of basis for a reasonable objective belief of a legal or clear policy mandate violation; and, (2) whether the evidence was sufficient to support a jury verdict that plaintiff was terminated in retaliation for making objection, as distinct from refusing to treat.

We recognize that where an employee harbors an objectively reasonable professional belief that legally and medically requisite levels of physician staffing have been violated, the legislature probably would have wished to protect an employee's right to make objection, without fear of reprisal, even if it were later found by a court that there was no actual violation. It is likely that recognition of such probable legislative intent motivated the trial judge's rulings here.

Upon review of the regulations and ethical obligations relied upon by plaintiff, in light of this record, we conclude that the regulations do not establish minimum physician staffing levels keyed to the number of residents in long term facilities. As to the impact of the codes of medical ethics upon nursing homes medical staffing, these require highly subjective evaluations, which must vary widely with the nature of each facility, the type of disorders being treated, degrees of exigency, and countless other medical factors. In this case, only plaintiff's opinion was submitted in support of his ethical evaluation. Thus, the existence of a clear mandate, even by application of the lesser balancing measure we would apply to the "objection" prong of the statute, is anything but clear to us.

Nonetheless, we note that a conscientious physician might reasonably and objectively conclude that the Home required more staff physician assistance, not only during vacation periods, but throughout the year. Indeed, defendants themselves sought to avoid continued reliance upon a two-physician staff which they believed might result in future "problems" with supervisory agencies such as the Department of Health and Veterans' Administration. The record makes clear defendants' efforts in this regard, including the hiring of plaintiff in May as a third physician. When Dr. Rajput took an extended six-month leave, physician staffing problems were rekindled.

In our view, it was not error to hold that plaintiff could reasonably and objectively believe that legal and ethical duties to provide competent medical care to residents of the Home were being inadequately served, and so make this view known. Retaliation against a physician-employee solely for making such objections known would be redressable under CEPA.

We turn, then, to our second inquiry on the "objects to" prong— sufficiency of evidence. Defendants' motions for judgment N.O.V. and for new trial were denied below.

Upon careful review of the record, we conclude that the jury could not reasonably have determined that defendants terminated plaintiff solely

---

7. As we earlier noted, the jury questions were not phrased in terms of plaintiff's *objectively* reasonable belief. Were our analysis otherwise to sustain the basis for a jury finding for plaintiff respecting the refusal to treat or the making of objection, this formulation would have constituted plain error requiring reversal.

because he objected orally and in writing, either to his temporary workload or to the general problem created by inadequate physician staffing. The evidence, much of it plaintiff's, overwhelmingly suggests that defendants were in agreement with plaintiff's complaints, were endeavoring to improve conditions, and actively encouraged his efforts to bring about both greater medical staffing and greater "rewards" for the medical staff. We find little but speculation to support a jury finding that the termination was not, as defendants have consistently stated, attributable to plaintiff's refusal to render service to the Unit Two and Three residents during the crisis created by Dr. Kulick's unauthorized vacation.

Conclusion

We have found that no statute, regulation or clear mandate of public policy supported an objectively reasonable belief that plaintiff's refusal to treat patients was warranted. Termination for that refusal did not offend N.J.S.A. 34:19–3c(1) or (3). Although application of a balancing of interests tests to the plaintiff's medical objections to defendants' practices might have supported a reasonable objective belief that a clear policy mandate was violated, there was insufficient evidence to support a jury verdict that plaintiff's termination was attributable to retaliation for such objections. It is therefore unnecessary to remand.

These conclusions render moot other issues posed on appeal and cross appeal. The judgment for plaintiff is reversed. Judgment dismissing the complaint on the merits is awarded to defendants.

NOTES AND QUESTIONS

1. In 1997, New Jersey amended the Conscientious Employee Protection Act (CEPA) to cover certified Health care professionals and violations of professional codes of ethics. N.J.S.A. 34:19 now explicitly forbids retaliatory action against a licensed or certified health care professional because the employee discloses or threatens to disclose any activity, policy or practice of the employer that the employee reasonably believes constitutes "improper quality of patient care." As used in the act, "improper quality of patient care" is defined as, "any practice, procedure, action or failure to act of an employer that is a health care provider which violates any law or any rule, regulation or declaratory ruling adopted pursuant to law, or any professional code of ethics." Actions such as testifying against the employer to a public body or refusing to participate in any activity, policy or practice that constitutes improper quality of patient care are also covered under the 1997 amendments. N.J. Stat. Ann. § 34:19 (Supp. 1999).

2. Absent a statutory provision, courts have refused to be guided by a medical code of ethics in their decisions. In Missouri v. Johnson, 968 S.W.2d 123 (Mo. 1998), the defendant contended that a mistrial should be declared because the prosecution's psychologist violated the American Medical Association's Code of Ethics by testifying. The Supreme Court of Missouri disagreed, asserting "it is not the role of this court to enforce the ethics of the AMA nor to police its membership."

The Hippocratic Oath

I swear by Apollo Physician and Asclepius and Hygieia and Panaceia and all the gods and goddesses, making them my witnesses, that I will fulfill according to my ability and judgment this oath and this covenant:

To hold him who has taught me this art as equal to my parents and to live my life in partnership with him, and if he is in need of money to give him a share of mine, and to regard his offspring as equal to my brothers in male lineage and to teach them this art—if they desire to learn it—without fee and covenant; to give a share of precepts and oral instruction and all the other learning to my sons and to the sons of him who has instructed me and to pupils who have signed the covenant and have taken an oath according to the medical law, but to no one else.

I will apply dietetic measures for the benefit of the sick according to my ability and judgment; I will keep them from harm and injustice.

I will neither give a deadly drug to anybody if asked for it, nor will I make a suggestion to this effect. Similarly I will not give to a woman an abortive remedy. In purity and holiness I will guard my life and my art.

I will not use the knife, not even on sufferers from stone, but will withdraw in favor of such men as are engaged in this work.

Whatever houses I may visit, I will come for the benefit of the sick, remaining free of all intentional injustice, of all mischief and in particular of sexual relations with both female and male persons, be they free or slaves.

What I may see or hear in the course of the treatment or even outside of the treatment in regard to the life of men, which on no account one must spread abroad, I will keep to myself holding such things shameful to be spoken about.

If I fulfill this oath and do not violate it, may it be granted to me to enjoy life and art, being honored with fame among all men for all time to come; if I transgress it and swear falsely, may the opposite of all this be my lot.

NOTES AND QUESTIONS

1. Consider ROBERT M. VEATCH, A THEORY OF MEDICAL ETHICS, 21–25 (1981):

THE HIPPOCRATIC TRADITION

While some specific, often archaic, features of the Oath were abandoned, many of its essential elements remained as the Oath began to find its place in Western culture. Specific views on surgery, the tripartite division of medicine, and the swearing by Apollo disappeared, but among the significant features retained throughout the history of the Hippocratic tradition is the view that the practice of the physician's art is a calling, something having a quasi-religious overtone. This concept carries with it a sense of loyalty to one's teachers that, by the late Middle Ages, came to mean loyalty to one's professional group.

Even more central to this common tradition is a moral perspective that dominates the Oath. At two points, a fundamental moral principle—what I shall call the Hippocratic principle—is stated. It comes first in the section related to dietetics, but many modern interpreters have generalized it so that it applies to all treatments. The taker of the Oath says, "I will apply ... measures for the benefit of the sick according to my ability and judgment; I will keep them from harm and injustice." Later, when the Oath refers to visiting the sick, the same theme is repeated: "Whatever houses I may visit, I will come for the benefit of the sick, remaining free of all intentional injustice...."[12]

This I take to be the core of professional physician ethics, the core of the Hippocratic tradition. Those who have stood in that tradition are committed to producing good for their patient and to protecting that patient from harm. (To be sure, this consequentialism was originally given a very peculiar turn in the Hippocratic cult; medicine was viewed as "the art," and special cultic values like purity and holiness heavily influenced the interpretation of what would count as benefit.) Love of the art was a central value. Modern proponents of the tradition loosely related to the Oath still retain, in varying degrees, this special vision of the good. The principle in its core has thus remained, although sometimes there are variants. Avoiding harm may be given priority over benefiting the patient, for example. This version has been given the dignity of latinization into the formula primum non nocere, "first do no harm," but this is not Hippocratic. "The Epidemics," the Hippocratic work to which this formula is sometimes attributed, does not really give a priority to avoiding harm. "As to diseases," the author of "The Epidemics" wrote, "make a habit of two things—to help, or at least to do no harm."[13]

Sometimes, especially in contemporary physician "folk" ethics, the formula is converted into the principle of preventing harm by preserving life. That is a variant without classical roots,[14] and it has received only minority support even in the decades of heroic medical interventionism in the mid-twentieth century. Only one important twentieth-century code commits the physician to the preservation of life, the World Medical Association's International Code of Medical Ethics, and that seems highly qualified with exceptions and seems targeted at the abortion issue rather than at contemporary problems in the care of the terminally ill.

. . .

From its position as a minority document for an isolated group of physicians, the Oath, together with related ethical documents from the Hippocratic corpus, gradually emerged as the dominant summary of the physician's own understanding of his ethical responsibility. The works were known to Plato, and many were commented upon by Galen (although apparently not the Oath specifically or the other deontological writings).

. . .

. . . [I]nterest in the Hippocratic tradition continued and flourished into the modern period of medical practice. In Elizabethan England, for example, we find four versions of the Hippocratic Oath, all containing variants of what I have identified as the core of the Hippocratic ethic.[23] The major Anglo–American event signaling the emergence of the Hippocratic tradition in the modern period, however, came at the end of the eighteenth century, when a

12. [Edelstein, Ancient Medicine], p. 6. The term for injustice is a general term sometimes translated as simply "harm" or "wrongdoing."

13. "The Epidemics," bk. 1, chap. 11, in Hippocrates, p. 165.

14. Darrel W. Amundsen, *The Physician's Obligation to Prolong Life: A Medical Duty without Classical Roots*, 8 HASTINGS CENTER REP. 23–30 (1978).

23. Sanford v. Larkey, *The Hippocratic Oath in Elizabethan England*, in LEGACIES IN ETHICS AND MEDICINE 218–36 (Chester Burn ed., 1977).

feud broke out at the Manchester Infirmary.[24] In 1789, an epidemic of typhoid or typhus struck, taxing the infirmary staff. At the time, medical practitioners were divided into three groups: physicians, surgeons, and apothecaries. Tensions among these groups were exacerbated when staff changes were made to respond to the epidemic. Some of the staff resigned, taking the changes to be a negative reflection on their efforts. In order to keep the peace, the trustees of the infirmary approached Thomas Percival, a physician who had been on the infirmary staff but had resigned years earlier because of physical disabilities. He had maintained close relationships with the infirmary and its staff and was asked to draw up a "scheme of professional conduct relative to hospitals and other medical charities."[25] The result was Percival's famous "Medical Ethics; or, a Code of Institutes and Precepts Adapted to the Professional Conduct of Physicians and Surgeons...." Out of these meager beginnings, in a local dispute over intraprofessional division of labor, was to emerge the foundation of Anglo–American medical ethics.[26]

American medical ethics took its lead from Percival. In 1847, at the founding meeting of the American Medical Association in Philadelphia, a code of ethics, which drew heavily upon Percival's pragmatic, problem-solving approach to professional squabbles, was approved. Like its predecessor, it reflected the core of the Hippocratic ethic, pledging physicians to "minister to the sick with due impressions of the importance of their office; reflecting that the ease, the health, and the lives of those committed to their charge, depend on their skill, attention and fidelity."[27]

That code has been revised from time to time over the past century, most significantly in 1957 and 1980. The 1957 revision replaced the detailed compilation of rules and interpretations of the earlier versions with a set of ten principles stating in more general terms the ethical mandate of the physician, and the 1980 update introduced for the first time a rights perspective into professional physician ethics. Only in these very recent versions, as we shall see in due course, did the Hippocratic commitment to benefit exclusively the patient, according to the physician's judgment, begin to give way to other ethical commitments—those that take into account the interests of the rest of society; those that take into account physicians' rights and duties as well as benefits and harms; and those that take into account the judgment of the patients and others beyond the physician.

2. Should medical students take the Hippocratic Oath upon graduation? Are the moral covenants at the heart of the oath appropriate, i.e., the promise to refrain from abortion and euthanasia, to act primarily for the benefit of the patient, to refrain from having sexual relations with patients and to lead a life in purity and holiness? Consider Edmund Pellegrino, *Ethics*, 275 JAMA 1777, 1807 (1996): "the ethical precepts of the Hippocratic Oath have an independent grounding in the nature of the patient-physician relationship." Defenders of the oath hold that medical ethics is not alterable by political, social, or economic exigency or public referendum. In their view, any ethic subject to change by social, economic, or legal fiat is no longer a viable ethic.

A recent study determined that the practice of administering a professional oath to medical students has increased significantly during this century. In 1928,

24. Thomas Percival, PERCIVAL'S MEDICAL ETHICS 29–32 (Chauncey D. Leake ed., 1927); Ivan Waddington, *The Development of Medical Ethics—A Sociological Analysis*, 19 MED. HIST. 36–51 (1975).

25. Waddington, "Development of Medical Ethics," p. 31.

26. *Ibid.*

27. AMERICAN MEDICAL ASSOCIATION, CODE OF MEDICAL ETHICS (1848).

only 19 of 79 medical schools in the United States and Canada administered the oath (24 percent). By 1958, this number had climbed to 72 percent, and to 90 percent by 1977. By 1989, 100 percent of the responding United States medical schools administered the oath at graduation. *See* Robert D. Orr et al., *Use of the Hippocratic Oath: A review of Twentieth Century Practice and a Content Analysis of Oaths Administered in Medical Schools in the U.S. and Canada in 1993*, 8 J. CLINICAL ETHICS 321, 377 (1997).

American Medical Association, Principles of Medical Ethics

(2001).

Preamble:

   The medical profession has long subscribed to a body of ethical statements developed primarily for the benefit of the patient. As a member of this profession, a physician must recognize responsibility to patients first and foremost, as well as to society, to other health professionals, and to self. The following Principles adopted by the American Medical Association are not laws, but standards of conduct which define the essentials of honorable behavior for the physician.

I.   A physician shall be dedicated to providing competent medical care, with compassion and respect for human dignity and rights.

II.   A physician shall uphold the standards of professionalism, be honest in all professional interactions, and strive to report physicians deficient in character or competence, or engaging in fraud or deception, to appropriate entities.

III.   A physician shall respect the law and also recognize a responsibility to seek changes in those requirements which are contrary to the best interests of the patient.

IV.   A physician shall respect the rights of patients, colleagues, and other health professionals, and shall safeguard patient confidences and privacy within the constraints of the law.

V.   A physician shall continue to study, apply, and advance scientific knowledge, maintain a commitment to medical education, make relevant information available to patients, colleagues, and the public, obtain consultation, and use the talents of other health professionals when indicated.

VI.   A physician shall, in the provision of appropriate patient care, except in emergencies, be free to choose whom to serve, with whom to associate, and the environment in which to provide medical care.

VII.   A physician shall recognize a responsibility to participate in activities contributing to the improvement of the community and the betterment of public health.

VIII.   A physician shall, while caring for a patient, regard responsibility to the patient as paramount.

IX.   A physician shall support access to medical care for all people.

NOTE

Should there be a code of ethics of scientists? Consider Gina Maranto, *Gene Therapy: Legal, Financial and Ethical Issues*, 4 B.U. J. SCI. & TECH. L. 3, 35–36 (1998).

> Science is "a-ethical." By this, I do not mean that scientists are unethical. Scientists operate under a system of professional ethics. Contraventions of the codes against fudging or massaging data, or fabricating results, cause great consternation within the scientific community and, in recent years, have received a good deal of attention by the media. But as an epistemological method, science does not intersect with ethics. Nowhere in the outlining of its basic precepts of how to observe the material universe, of how to test the veracity of facts, of how to construct deductions and inductions; nowhere in the methodological ponderings of Bacon, Locke, Descartes, or Buckley do ethical axioms figure.
>
> This means that if we want an ethical science, we as a society must impose values on it from the outside. Science takes as its right the pursuit of knowledge for knowledge's sake, wherever it leads. But society, not necessarily granting the same absolute permission to scientists as scientists grant themselves, may feel less convinced of the probity of certain types of investigations, especially when knowledge is translated into technology.

II.   PATIENTS, SUBJECTS AND CITIZENS

A.   WHAT CONTROL CAN INDIVIDUALS EXERCISE?

1.   THE ROLE OF ASSENT OR REFUSAL

Schloendorff v. Society of New York Hospital

Court of Appeals of New York, 1914.
211 N.Y. 125, 105 N.E. 92.

■ CARDOZO, J.

In the year 1771, by royal charter of George III, the Society of the New York Hospital was organized for the care and healing of the sick. During the century and more which has since passed, it has devoted itself to that high task. It has no capital stock; it does not distribute profits; and its physicians and surgeons, both the visiting and the resident staff, serve it without pay. . . .

To this hospital the plaintiff came in January, 1908. She was suffering from some disorder of the stomach. She asked the superintendent or one of his assistants what the charge would be, and was told that it would be $7 a week. She became an inmate of the hospital, and after some weeks of treatment, the house physician, Dr. Bartlett, discovered a lump, which proved to be a fibroid tumor. He consulted the visiting physician, Dr. Stimson, who advised an operation. The plaintiff's testimony is that the character of the lump could not, so the physicians informed her, be determined without an ether examination. She consented to such an examination, but notified Dr. Bartlett, as she says, that there must be no operation. She was taken at night from the medical to the surgical ward and prepared for an operation by a nurse. On the following day ether was administered, and, while she was unconscious, a tumor was removed. Her testimony is that this was done without her consent or knowledge. She is contradicted both by Dr. Stimson and by Dr. Bartlett, as well as by many of the attendant nurses. For the purpose of this appeal, however, since a verdict was directed in favor of the defendant, her narrative, even if improbable, must be taken as true. Following the operation, and, according to the testimony of her witnesses, because of it, gangrene developed in her left arm, some of her fingers had to be amputated, and her sufferings were intense. She now seeks to charge the hospital with liability for the wrong.

Certain principles of law governing the rights and duties of hospitals, when maintained as charitable institutions have, after much discussion, become no longer doubtful. It is the settled rule that such a hospital is not liable for the negligence of its physicians and nurses in the treatment of patients. . . .

. . .

. . . In the case at hand, the wrong complained of is not merely negligence. It is trespass. Every human being of adult years and sound mind has a right to determine what shall be done with his own body; and a surgeon who performs an operation without his patient's consent commits an assault, for which he is liable in damages. This is true, except in cases of emergency where the patient is unconscious, and where it is necessary to operate before consent can be obtained. The fact that the wrong complained of here is trespass, rather than negligence, distinguishes this case from most of the cases that have preceded it. In such circumstances the hospital's exemption from liability can hardly rest upon implied waiver. Relatively to this transaction, the plaintiff was a stranger. She had never consented to become a patient for any purpose other than an examination under ether. She had never waived the right to recover damages for any wrong resulting from this operation, for she had forbidden the operation. In this situation, the true ground for the defendant's exemption from liability is that the relation between a hospital and its physicians is not that of master and servant. The hospital does not undertake to act through them, but merely to procure them to act upon their own responsibility. . . .

. . .

The conclusion, therefore, follows that the trial judge did not err in his direction of a verdict. A ruling would, indeed, be an unfortunate one that might constrain charitable institutions, as a measure of self-protection, to limit their activities. A hospital opens its doors without discrimination to all who seek its aid. It gathers in its wards a company of skilled physicians and trained nurses, and places their services at the call of the afflicted, without scrutiny of the character or the worth of those who appeal to it, looking at nothing and caring for nothing beyond the fact of their affliction. In this beneficent work, it does not subject itself to liability for damages, though the ministers of healing whom it has selected have proved unfaithful to their trust.

The judgment should be affirmed, with costs.

NOTES AND QUESTIONS

1. From its Latin origin, the word "consent" means "to feel together," in other words, to agree or accord with another. The term has moral as well as legal implications. See, for example, the chapter on "Consent as a Canon of Loyalty with Special Reference to Children in Medical Investigations" in Professor Paul Ramsey's *The Patient as Person* 1–58 (1970), in which he urges partnership as a better term than contract to describe the consensual relation of patient and physician. The term "assent" is sometimes used to distinguish the agreement of a person (such as a child) who lacks the legal capacity to give a binding consent. Likewise, the term "permission" is sometimes used to differentiate consent (what a person may do autonomously on his or her own behalf) from what one, such as a parent, does in deciding on behalf of another. *See* NATIONAL COMMISSION FOR THE PROTECTION OF HUMAN SUBJECTS OF BIOMEDICAL AND BEHAVIORAL RESEARCH, REPORT AND RECOMMENDATIONS ON RESEARCH INVOLVING CHILDREN 13 (1977).

Consent may be either express or implied. Health caregivers often have patients sign a form, which is then referred to as "the consent." In fact, it is no such thing. Consent is the agreement between the persons involved; a "consent form" is merely a fairly formal means of documenting express consent and, if the consent itself is valid, the form serves to memorialize that fact. Implied consent occurs routinely in health care, when patients by their conduct, in cooperating with caregivers, provide the necessary authorization for caregivers' actions. *See, e.g.,* O'Brien v. Cunard Steamship Co., 154 Mass. 272, 28 N.E. 266 (1891) (passenger gave implied consent to vaccination by joining line of people receiving injections on ship). It is sometimes said that implied consent also exists for emergency treatment of patients who are incapable of consenting because of age or condition, but this is a misnomer; the exception to the usual rule is better described as presumed consent, which results from the operation of the law (in attributing to the patient the wish of a reasonable person to receive emergency treatment) rather than being implied by the patient's conduct.

2. In legal literature, the relationship of patient and physician is often spoken of as a contract. Not all these contracts are enforceable, however. For example, a release from liability for future negligence imposed as a condition for admission to a charitable research hospital has been held invalid as a matter of public policy. Tunkl v. Regents of Univ. of Cal., 60 Cal.2d 92, 32 Cal.Rptr. 33, 383 P.2d 441 (1963).

3. Judge Cardozo's ringing (and oft-quoted) declaration of a patient's right of self-determination (in an opinion that actually upholds the verdict for defendant hospital) is, if anything, less sweeping than one opinion he cited, that of Justice Brown of the Illinois Court of Appeals in *Pratt v. Davis,* in which the patient's rights in the private relationship with the physician are explicitly linked to the civil rights of citizenship. The plaintiff had admitted herself to defendant's hospital, and the defendant had removed her uterus without her prior knowledge or consent. In affirming a judgment for the plaintiff, the court stated:

> [U]nder a free government at least, the free citizen's first and greatest right, which underlies all others—the right to the inviolability of his person, in other words, his right to himself—is the subject of universal acquiescence, and this right necessarily forbids a physician or surgeon, however skillful or eminent, who has been asked to examine, diagnose, advise, and prescribe (which are at least necessary first steps in treatment and care), to violate without permission the bodily integrity of his patient by a major or capital operation, placing him under an anaesthetic for that purpose, and operating on him without his consent or knowledge. . . .

Pratt v. Davis, 118 Ill.App. 161, 166 (1905), *aff'd* 224 Ill. 300, 79 N.E. 562 (1906). The invocation of "a citizen's first and greatest right" places the issue of unconsented treatment in a different light: May the state command treatment when a physician could not, or does the common law right to personal inviolability have constitutional dimensions too?

John Stuart Mill, *On Liberty*

9, 73–75, 101 (1859).

The object of this essay is to assert one very simple principle, as entitled to govern absolutely the dealings of society with the individual in the way of compulsion and control, whether the means used be physical force in the form of legal penalties or the moral coercion of public opinion. That principle is that the sole end for which mankind are warranted, individually or collectively, in interfering with the liberty of action of any of their number is self-protection. That the only purpose for which power can be rightfully exercised over any member of a civilized community, against his will, is to prevent harm to others. His own good, either physical or moral, is not a sufficient warrant. He cannot rightfully be compelled to do or forbear because it will be better for him to do so, because it will make him happier, because, in the opinions of others, to do so would be wise or even right. These are good reasons for remonstrating with him, or reasoning with him or persuading him, or entreating him, but not for compelling him or visiting him with any evil in case he do otherwise. To justify that, the conduct from which it is desired to deter him must be calculated to produce evil to someone else. The only part of the conduct of anyone for which he is amenable to society is that which concerns others. In the part which merely concerns himself, his independence is, of right, absolute. Over himself, over his own body and mind, the individual is sovereign.

It is, perhaps, hardly necessary to say that this doctrine is meant to apply only to human beings in the maturity of their faculties. We are not speaking of children or of young persons below the age which the law may fix as that of manhood or womanhood. Those who are still in a state to require being taken care of by others must be protected against their own actions as well as against external injury....

. . .

What, then, is the rightful limit to the sovereignty of the individual over himself? Where does the authority of society begin? How much of human life should be assigned to individuality, and how much to society?

Each will receive its proper share if each has that which more particularly concerns it. To individuality should belong the part of life in which it is chiefly the individual that is interested; to society, the part which chiefly interests society.

Though society is not founded on a contract, and though no good purpose is answered by inventing a contract in order to deduce social obligations from it, everyone who receives the protection of society owes a return for the benefit, and the fact of living in society renders it indispensable that each should be bound to observe a certain line of conduct toward the rest. This conduct consists, first, in not injuring the interests of one another, or rather certain interests which, either by express legal provision or by tacit understanding, ought to be considered as rights; and secondly, in each person's bearing his share (to be fixed on some equitable principle) of the labors and sacrifices incurred for defending the society or its members from injury and molestation. These conditions society is justified in enforcing at all costs to those who endeavor to withhold fulfillment....

It would be a great misunderstanding of this doctrine to suppose that it is one of selfish indifference which pretends that human beings have no business with each other's conduct in life, and that they should not concern themselves about the well-doing or well-being of one another, unless their own interest is involved. Instead of any diminution, there is need of a great increase of disinterested exertion to promote the good of others. But disinterested benevolence can find other instruments to persuade people to their good than whips and scourges, either of the literal or the metaphorical sort. I am the last person to undervalue the self-regarding virtues; they are only second in importance, if even second, to the social. It is equally the business of education to cultivate both. But even education works by conviction and persuasion as well as by compulsion, and it is by the former only that, when the period of education is passed, the self-regarding virtues should be inculcated. Human beings owe to each other help to distinguish the better from the worse, and encouragement to choose the former and avoid the latter. They should be forever stimulating each other to increased exercise of their higher faculties and increased direction of their feelings and aims toward wise instead of foolish, elevating instead of degrading, objects and contemplations. But neither one person, nor any number of persons, is warranted in saying to another human creature of ripe years that he shall not do with his life for his own benefit what he chooses to do with it. He is the person most interested in his own well-being: the interest which any other person, except in cases of strong personal attachment, can have in it is trifling compared with that which he himself has; the interest which society has in him individually (except as to his conduct to others) is fractional and altogether indirect, while with respect to his own feelings and circumstances the most ordinary man or woman has means of knowledge immeasurably surpassing those that can be possessed by anyone else. The interference of society to overrule his judgment and purposes in what only regards himself must be grounded on general presumptions which may be altogether wrong and, even if right, are as likely as not to be misapplied to individual cases, by persons no better acquainted with the circumstances of such cases than those are who look at them merely from without. In this department, therefore, of human affairs, individuality has its proper field of action. In the conduct of human beings toward one another it is necessary that general rules should for the most part be observed in order that people may know what they have to expect; but in each person's own concerns his individual spontaneity is entitled to free exercise. Considerations to aid his judgment, exhortations to strengthen his will may be offered to him, even obtruded on him, by others; but he himself is the final judge. All errors which he is likely to commit against advice and warning are far outweighed by the evil of allowing others to constrain him to what they deem his good. . . .

. . .

It was pointed out in an early part of this essay that the liberty of the individual, in things wherein the individual is alone concerned, implies a corresponding liberty in any number of individuals to regulate by mutual agreement such things as regard them jointly, and regard no persons but themselves. This question presents no difficulty so long as the will of all the persons implicated remains unaltered; but since that will may change it is often necessary, even in things in which they alone are concerned, that they should enter into engagements with one another; and when they do, it is fit, as a general rule, that those engagements should be kept. Yet, in the laws, probably, of every country, this general rule has some exceptions. Not only persons are not held to engagements which violate the rights of third parties, but it is sometimes considered a sufficient reason for releasing them from an engagement that it is injurious to themselves. In this and most other civilized countries, for example, an engagement by which a person should sell himself, or allow himself to be sold, as a slave would be null and void, neither enforced by law nor by opinion. The ground for thus limiting his power of voluntarily disposing of his own lot in life is apparent, and is very clearly seen in this extreme case. The reason for not interfering, unless for the sake of others, with a person's voluntary acts is consideration for his liberty. His voluntary choice is evidence that what he so chooses is desirable, or at least endurable, to him, and his good is on the whole best provided for by allowing him to take his own means of pursuing it. But by selling himself for a slave, he abdicates his liberty; he foregoes any future use of it beyond that single act. He therefore defeats, in his own case, the very purpose which is the justification of allowing him to dispose of himself. He is no longer free, but is thenceforth in a position which has no longer the presumption in its favor that would be afforded by his voluntarily remaining in it. The principle of freedom cannot require that he should be free not to be free. It is not freedom to be allowed to alienate his freedom. . . .

NOTES AND QUESTIONS

1. Mill's essay, certainly among the most familiar in political philosophy, seems to have several purposes. First, it explores implications of the utilitarian philosophy Mill inherited from Jeremy Bentham (1748–1832) and from his own father James Mill (1773–1836). In utilitarianism, the measurement of the good (the Greatest Happiness Principle) depends upon a calculation of what gives a person pleasure; in *On Liberty,* Mill argues that the purpose of government is to ensure that each person is free to come to his or her own definition of happiness and to pursue it, so long as he or she does not cause harm to another in the process—comparable to the ancient maxim of property law, *sic utere tuo ut alienum non laedas* (use your own property in such a manner as not to injure that of another).

Second, Mill sees the need to reinterpret aspects of utilitarianism in light of the tensions emerging in mid–19th-century Britain between democracy (the great cause of Bentham and Mill *père*) and minority rights. Like the Jeffersonians in America, the Benthamites were democrats, believing firmly in social equality and majority rule, in place of a society governed by inherited rank and privilege. With the growth of popular democracy, Mill realized something the earlier utilitarians had not: the need to protect individuals from the pressures toward conformity exerted by the masses, often poorly educated and intolerant. *See* Elizabeth Rapaport, *Editor's Introduction, in* ON LIBERTY vii-xv (1978).

2. Physicians (and practitioners of other learned professions such as law) enjoy a protection not accorded to most people when they are accused of having negligently injured another; compliance with the customs of at least a reputable segment of one's professional peers is a complete defense against liability. Although not immune from criticism, this rule has long enjoyed academic as well as judicial approval as "probably the only workable test available," and one unlikely to comfort the quack or truly incompetent. Clarence Morris, *Custom and Negligence*, 42 COLUM.L.REV. 1147, 1164–65 (1942). The control of medical standards is thus largely in the hands of individual members of the professions and the various bodies through which they operate collectively to educate, test, and discipline themselves (as is detailed in Sec. A, *supra*).

Yet in a very real sense, the levers of control are in the hands of lay people, for it is they (and their lawyers) who identify which particular conduct by professionals will be challenged in court as negligent. Even when a good defense exists, physicians may be wary of doing (or not doing) things that increase the risk of litigation and liability. Although this fear may be overblown, some physicians are influenced enough to engage in "defensive medicine," conduct dictated by the desire to avoid malpractice liability, not by their professional judgment.

It is difficult to separate a desire to avoid liability from other motives to utilize (or overutilize) diagnostic techniques. For instance, physicians are told they can make a large profit by installing expensive diagnostic equipment in their offices; in an advertisement for a urinalysis machine, Akers Medical Technologies estimated a potential profit from fifty tests a day to be $83,540.80 a year, meaning that the $1,500 to $2,500 investment could be repaid in as little as five days. Glenn Kramon, *Good Medicine, Better Business*, N.Y. TIMES, May 15, 1988, Pt. III at 6, col. 1.

2.   THE ROLE OF DISCLOSURE

Canterbury v. Spence

United States Court of Appeals for the District of Columbia Circuit, 1972.
464 F.2d 772, cert. denied, 409 U.S. 1064, 93 S.Ct. 560, 34 L.Ed.2d 518.

■ SPOTTSWOOD W. ROBINSON, III, CIRCUIT JUDGE.

. . .

I.

. . .

At the time of the events which gave rise to this litigation, appellant was nineteen years of age, a clerk-typist employed by the Federal Bureau of Investigation. In December, 1958, he began to experience severe pain between his shoulder blades. He consulted two general practitioners, but the medications they prescribed failed to eliminate the pain. Thereafter, appellant secured an appointment with Dr. Spence, who is a neurosurgeon.

... Dr. Spence ... recommended that appellant undergo a myelogram—a procedure in which dye is injected into the spinal column and traced to find evidence of disease or other disorder—at the Washington Hospital Center.

... The myelogram revealed a "filling defect" in the region of the fourth thoracic vertebra. Since a myelogram often does no more than pinpoint the location of an aberration, surgery may be necessary to discover the cause. Dr. Spence told appellant that he would have to undergo a laminectomy—the excision of the posterior arch of the vertebra—to correct what he suspected was a ruptured disc. Appellant did not raise any objection to the proposed operation nor did he probe into its exact nature.

Appellant explained to Dr. Spence that his mother was a widow of slender financial means living in Cyclone, West Virginia, and that she could be reached through a neighbor's telephone. Appellant called his mother the day after the myelogram was performed and, failing to contact her, left Dr. Spence's telephone number with the neighbor. When Mrs. Canterbury returned the call, Dr. Spence told her that the surgery was occasioned by a suspected ruptured disc. Mrs. Canterbury then asked if the recommended operation was serious and Dr. Spence replied "not anymore than any other operation." He added that he knew Mrs. Canterbury was not well off and that her presence in Washington would not be necessary. The testimony is contradictory as to whether during the course of the conversation Mrs. Canterbury expressed her consent to the operation. Appellant himself apparently did not converse again with Dr. Spence prior to the operation.

Dr. Spence performed the laminectomy on February 11 at the Washington Hospital Center. Mrs. Canterbury traveled to Washington, arriving on that date but after the operation was over, and signed a consent form at the hospital. The laminectomy revealed several anomalies: a spinal cord that was swollen and unable to pulsate, an accumulation of large tortuous and dilated veins, and a complete absence of epidural fat which normally surrounds the spine. A thin hypodermic needle was inserted into the spinal cord to aspirate any cysts which might have been present, but no fluid emerged. In suturing the wound, Dr. Spence attempted to relieve the pressure on the spinal cord by enlarging the dura—the outer protective wall of the spinal cord—at the area of swelling.

For approximately the first day after the operation appellant recuperated normally, but then suffered a fall and an almost immediate setback. Since there is some conflict as to precisely when or why appellant fell, we reconstruct the events from the evidence most favorable to him. Dr. Spence left orders that appellant was to remain in bed during the process of voiding. These orders were changed to direct that voiding be done out of bed, and the jury could find that the change was made by hospital personnel. Just prior to the fall, appellant summoned a nurse and was given a receptacle for use in voiding, but was then left unattended. Appellant testified that during the course of the endeavor he slipped off the side of the bed, and that there was no one to assist him, or side rail to prevent the fall.

Several hours later, appellant began to complain that he could not move his legs and that he was having trouble breathing; paralysis seems to have been virtually total from the waist down. Dr. Spence was notified on the night of February 12, and he rushed to the hospital. Mrs. Canterbury signed another consent form and appellant was again taken into the operating room. The surgical wound was reopened and Dr. Spence created a gusset to allow the spinal cord greater room in which to pulsate.

Appellant's control over his muscles improved somewhat after the second operation but he was unable to void properly.... For several years after his discharge he was under the care of several specialists, and at all times was under the care of a urologist. At the time of the trial in April, 1968, appellant required crutches to walk, still suffered from urinal incontinence and paralysis of the bowels, and wore a penile clamp.

In November, 1959 on Dr. Spence's recommendation, appellant was transferred by the F.B.I. to Miami where he could get more swimming and exercise. Appellant worked three years for the F.B.I. in Miami, Los Angeles and Houston, resigning finally in June, 1962. From then until the time of the trial, he held a number of jobs, but had constant trouble finding work because he needed to remain seated and close to a bathroom. The damages appellant claims include extensive pain and suffering, medical expenses, and loss of earnings.

II.

Appellant filed suit in the District Court on March 7, 1963, four years after the laminectomy and approximately two years after he attained his majority. The complaint ... alleged, among other things, negligence in the performance of the laminectomy and failure to inform him beforehand of the risk involved....

. . .

At the close of appellant's case in chief, each defendant moved for a directed verdict and the trial judge granted both motions....

. . .

III.

Suits charging failure by a physician adequately to disclose the risks and alternatives of proposed treatment are not innovations in American law. They date back a good half-century,[7] and in the last decade they have multiplied rapidly. There is, nonetheless, disagreement among the courts and the commentators on many major questions, and there is no precedent of our own directly in point. For the tools enabling resolution of the issues on this appeal, we are forced to begin at first principles.

The root premise is the concept, fundamental in American jurisprudence, that "[e]very human being of adult years and sound mind has a right to determine what shall be done with his own body...." True consent to what happens to one's self is the informed exercise of a choice, and that entails an opportunity to evaluate knowledgeably the options available and the risks attendant upon each. The average patient has little or no understanding of the medical arts, and ordinarily has only his

---

7. *See, e.g.,* Theodore v. Ellis, 141 La. 709, 75 So. 655, 660 (1917); Wojciechowski v. Coryell, 217 S.W. 638, 644 (Mo.App.1920); Hunter v. Burroughs, 123 Va. 113, 96 S.E. 360, 366–368 (1918).

physician to whom he can look for enlightenment with which to reach an intelligent decision. From these almost axiomatic considerations springs the need, and in turn the requirement, of a reasonable divulgence by physician to patient to make such a decision possible.[15]

A physician is under a duty to treat his patient skillfully but proficiency in diagnosis and therapy is not the full measure of his responsibility. The cases demonstrate that the physician is under an obligation to communicate specific information to the patient when the exigencies of reasonable care call for it. Due care may require a physician perceiving symptoms of bodily abnormality to alert the patient to the condition. It may call upon the physician confronting an ailment which does not respond to his ministrations to inform the patient thereof. It may command the physician to instruct the patient as to any limitations to be presently observed for his own welfare, and as to any precautionary therapy he should seek in the future. It may oblige the physician to advise the patient of the need for or desirability of any alternative treatment promising greater benefit than that being pursued. Just as plainly, due care normally demands that the physician warn the patient of any risks to his well-being which contemplated therapy may involve.

The context in which the duty of risk-disclosure arises is invariably the occasion for decision as to whether a particular treatment procedure is to be undertaken. To the physician, whose training enables a self-satisfying evaluation, the answer may seem clear, but it is the prerogative of the patient, not the physician, to determine for himself the direction in which his interests seem to lie. To enable the patient to chart his course understandably, some familiarity with the therapeutic alternatives and their hazards becomes essential.

---

15. The doctrine that a consent effective as authority to form [sic] therapy can arise only from the patient's understanding of alternatives to and risks of the therapy is commonly denominated "informed consent." *See, e.g.,* Waltz & Scheuneman, *Informed Consent to Therapy,* 64 Nw.U.L.Rev. 628, 629 (1970). The same appellation is frequently assigned to the doctrine requiring physicians, as a matter of duty to patients, to communicate information as to such alternatives and risks. *See, e.g.,* Comment, *Informed Consent in Medical Malpractice,* 55 Calif.L.Rev. 1396 (1967). While we recognize the general utility of shorthand phrases in literary expositions, we caution that uncritical use of the "informed consent" label can be misleading. *See, e.g.,* Plante, *An Analysis of "Informed Consent,"* 36 Ford.L.Rev. 639, 671–72 (1968).

In duty-to-disclose cases, the focus of attention is more properly upon the nature and content of the physician's divulgence than the patient's understanding or consent. Adequate disclosure and informed consent are, of course, two sides of the same coin—the former a *sine qua non* of the latter. But the vital inquiry on duty to disclose relates to the physician's performance of an obligation, while one of the difficulties with analysis in terms of "informed consent" is its tendency to imply that what is decisive is the degree of the patient's comprehension. As we later emphasize, the physician discharges the duty when he makes a reasonable effort to convey sufficient information although the patient, without fault of the physician, may not fully grasp it. Even though the factfinder may have occasion to draw an inference on the state of the patient's enlightenment, the fact-finding process on performance of the duty ultimately reaches back to what the physician actually said or failed to say. And while the factual conclusion on adequacy of the revelation will vary as between patients—as, for example, between a lay patient and a physician-patient—the fluctuations are attributable to the kind of divulgence which may be reasonable under the circumstances.

A reasonable revelation in these respects is not only a necessity but, as we see it, is as much a matter of the physician's duty. It is a duty to warn of the dangers lurking in the proposed treatment, and that is surely a facet of due care. It is, too, a duty to impart information which the patient has every right to expect.[27] The patient's reliance upon the physician is a trust of the kind which traditionally has exacted obligations beyond those associated with arms-length transactions. His dependence upon the physician for information affecting his well-being, in terms of contemplated treatment, is well-nigh abject.... [W]e have found "in the fiducial qualities of [the physician-patient] relationship the physician's duty to reveal to the patient that which in his best interests it is important that he should know." We now find, as a part of the physician's overall obligation to the patient, a similar duty of reasonable disclosure of the choices with respect to proposed therapy and the dangers inherently and potentially involved.

This disclosure requirement, on analysis, reflects much more of a change in doctrinal emphasis than a substantive addition to malpractice law. It is well established that the physician must seek and secure his patient's consent before commencing an operation or other course of treatment. It is also clear that the consent, to be efficacious, must be free from imposition upon the patient. It is the settled rule that therapy not authorized by the patient may amount to a tort—a common law battery—by the physician. And it is evident that it is normally impossible to obtain a consent worthy of the name unless the physician first elucidates the options and the perils for the patient's edification. Thus the physician has long borne a duty, on pain of liability for unauthorized treatment, to make adequate disclosure to the patient.[36] The evolution of the obligation to communicate for the patient's benefit as well as the physician's protection has hardly involved an extraordinary restructuring of the law.

27. Some doubt has been expressed as to ability of physicians to suitably communicate their evaluations of risks and the advantages of optional treatment, and as to the lay patient's ability to understand what the physician tells him. Karchmer, *Informed Consent: A Plaintiff's Medical Malpractice "Wonder Drug,"* 31 Mo.L.Rev. 29, 41 (1966). We do not share these apprehensions. The discussion need not be a disquisition, and surely the physician is not compelled to give his patient a short medical education; the disclosure rule summons the physician only to a reasonable explanation. That means generally informing the patient in nontechnical terms as to what is at stake: the therapy alternatives open to him, the goals expectably to be achieved, and the risks that may ensue from particular treatment and no treatment. So informing the patient hardly taxes the physician, and it must be the exceptional patient who cannot comprehend such an explanation at least in a rough way.

36. We discard the thought that the patient should ask for information before the physician is required to disclose. Caveat emptor is not the norm for the consumer of medical services. Duty to disclose is more than a call to speak merely on the patient's request, or merely to answer the patient's questions: it is a duty to volunteer, if necessary, the information the patient needs for intelligent decision. The patient may be ignorant, confused, overawed by the physician or frightened by the hospital, or even ashamed to inquire. See generally Note, Restructuring Informed Consent: Legal Therapy for the Doctor–Patient Relationship, 79 YALE L.J. 1533, 1545–51 (1970). Perhaps relatively few patients could in any event identify the relevant questions in the absence of prior explanation by the physician. Physicians and hospitals have patients of widely divergent socioeconomic backgrounds, and a rule which presumes a degree of sophistication which many members of society lack is likely to breed gross inequities. See Note, Informed Consent as a Theory of Medical Liability, 1970 WIS. L.Rev. 879, 891–97.

IV.

Duty to disclose has gained recognition in a large number of American jurisdictions, but more largely on a different rationale. The majority of courts dealing with the problem have made the duty depend on whether it was the custom of physicians practicing in the community to make the particular disclosure to the patient.

. . .

There are, in our view, formidable obstacles to acceptance of the notion that the physician's obligation to disclose is either germinated or limited by medical practice. To begin with, the reality of any discernible custom reflecting a professional consensus on communication of option and risk information to patients is open to serious doubt. We sense the danger that what in fact is no custom at all may be taken as an affirmative custom to maintain silence, and that physician-witnesses to the so-called custom may state merely their personal opinions as to what they or others would do under given conditions. We cannot gloss over the inconsistency between reliance on a general practice respecting divulgence and, on the other hand, realization that the myriad of variables among patients makes each case so different that its omission can rationally be justified only by the effect of its individual circumstances. Nor can we ignore the fact that to bind the disclosure obligation to medical usage is to arrogate the decision on revelation to the physician alone. Respect for the patient's right of self-determination on particular therapy demands a standard set by law for physicians rather than one which physicians may or may not impose upon themselves.

More fundamentally, the majority rule overlooks the graduation of reasonable-care demands in Anglo–American jurisprudence and the position of professional custom in the hierarchy. The caliber of the performance exacted by the reasonable-care standard varies between the professional and non-professional worlds, and so also the role of professional custom. "With but few exceptions," we recently declared, "society demands that everyone under a duty to use care observe minimally a general standard." ... "Beyond this," however, we emphasized, "the law requires those engaging in activities requiring unique knowledge and ability to give a performance commensurate with the undertaking." Thus physicians treating the sick must perform at higher levels than non-physicians in order to meet the reasonable care standard in its special application to physicians—"that degree of care and skill ordinarily exercised by the profession in [the physician's] own or similar localities." And practices adopted by the profession have indispensable value as evidence tending to establish just what that degree of care and skill is.

We have admonished, however, that "[t]he special medical standards are but adaptions of the general standard to a group who are required to act as reasonable men possessing their medical talents presumably would." There is, by the same token, no basis for operation of the special medical standard where the physician's activity does not bring his medical knowledge and skills peculiarly into play. And where the challenge to the physician's conduct is not to be gauged by the special standard, it follows that medical custom cannot furnish the test of its propriety, whatever its relevance under the proper test may be. The decision to unveil the patient's condition and the chances as to remediation, as we shall see, is ofttimes a non-medical judgment and, if so, is a decision outside the ambit of the special standard. Where that is the situation, professional custom hardly furnishes the legal criterion for measuring the physician's responsibility to reasonably inform his patient of the options and the hazards as to treatment.

The majority rule, moreover, is at war with our prior holdings that a showing of medical practice, however probative, does not fix the standard governing recovery for medical malpractice. Prevailing medical practice, we have maintained, has evidentiary value in determinations as to what the specific criteria measuring challenged professional conduct are and whether they have been met, but does not itself define the standard. . . .

. . . In sum, the physician's duty to disclose is governed by the same legal principles applicable to others in comparable situations, with modifications only to the extent that medical judgment enters the picture. We hold that the standard measuring performance of that duty by physicians, as by others, is conduct which is reasonable under the circumstances.

V.

Once the circumstances give rise to a duty on the physician's part to inform his patient, the next inquiry is the scope of the disclosure the physician is legally obliged to make. The courts have frequently confronted this problem but no uniform standard defining the adequacy of the divulgence emerges from the decisions. Some have said "full" disclosure, a norm we are unwilling to adopt literally. It seems obviously prohibitive and unrealistic to expect physicians to discuss with their patients every risk of proposed treatment—no matter how small or remote—and generally unnecessary from the patient's viewpoint as well. . . .

The larger number of courts, as might be expected, have applied tests framed with reference to prevailing fashion within the medical profession. Some have measured the disclosure by "good medical practice," others by what a reasonable practitioner would have bared under the circumstances, and still others by what medical custom in the community would demand. We have explored this rather considerable body of law but are unprepared to follow it. The duty to disclose, we have reasoned, arises from phenomena apart from medical custom and practice. The latter, we think, should no more establish the scope of the duty than its existence. . . .

In our view, the patient's right of self-decision shapes the boundaries of the duty to reveal. That right can be effectively exercised only if the patient possesses enough information to enable an intelligent choice. The scope of the physician's communications to the patient, then, must be measured by the patient's need, and that need is the information material to the decision. Thus the test for determining whether a particular peril must be divulged is its materiality to the patient's decision: all risks potentially affecting the decision must be unmasked. And to safeguard the patient's interest in achieving his own determination on treatment, the law must itself set the standard for adequate disclosure.

Optimally for the patient, exposure of a risk would be mandatory whenever the patient would deem it significant to his decision, either singly or in combination with other risks. Such a requirement, however, would summon the physician to second-guess the patient, whose ideas on materiality could hardly be known to the physician. That would make an undue demand upon medical practitioners, whose conduct, like that of others, is to be measured in terms of reasonableness. Consonantly with orthodox negligence doctrine, the physician's liability for nondisclosure is to be determined on the basis of foresight, not hindsight; no less than any other aspect of negligence, the issue on nondisclosure must be approached from the viewpoint of the reasonableness of the physician's divulgence in terms of what he knows or should know to be the patient's informational needs....

Of necessity, the content of the disclosure rests in the first instance with the physician. Ordinarily it is only he who is in position to identify particular dangers; always he must make a judgment, in terms of materiality, as to whether and to what extent revelation to the patient is called for. He cannot know with complete exactitude what the patient would consider important to his decision, but on the basis of his medical training and experience he can sense how the average, reasonable patient expectably would react. Indeed, with knowledge of, or ability to learn, his patient's background and current condition, he is in a position superior to that of most others—attorneys, for example—who are called upon to make judgments on pain of liability in damages for unreasonable miscalculation.

From these considerations we derive the breadth of the disclosure of risks legally to be required. The scope of the standard is not subjective as to either the physician or the patient; it remains objective with due regard for the patient's informational needs and with suitable leeway for the physician's situation. In broad outline, ... "[a] risk is thus material when a reasonable person, in what the physician knows or should know to be the patient's position, would be likely to attach significance to the risk or cluster of risks in deciding whether or not to forego the proposed therapy."

The topics importantly demanding a communication of information are the inherent and potential hazards of the proposed treatment, the alternatives to that treatment, if any, and the results likely if the patient remains untreated. The factors contributing significance to the dangerousness of a medical technique are, of course, the incidence of injury and the degree of the harm threatened. A very small chance of death or serious disablement may well be significant; a potential disability which dramatically outweighs the potential benefit of the therapy or the detriments of the existing malady may summon discussion with the patient.[86]

---

86. *See* Bowers v. Talmage, [159 So.2d 888 (Fla.App.1963)] (3% chance of death, paralysis or other injury, disclosure required); Scott v. Wilson, 396 S.W.2d 532 (Tex.Civ. App.1965), *aff'd*, 412 S.W.2d 299 (Tex.1967) (1% chance of loss of hearing, disclosure required). Compare, where the physician was held not liable. Stottlemire v. Cawood, [213 F.Supp. 897 (D.D.C.), new trial denied, 215 F.Supp. 266 (1963)] (1/800,000 chance of aplastic anemia); Yeates v. Harms, [193 Kan. 320, 393 P.2d 982 (1964), on rehearing, 194 Kan. 675, 401 P.2d 659 (1965)] (1.5% chance of loss of eye); Starnes v. Taylor, 272 N.C. 386, 158 S.E.2d 339, 344 (1968) (1/250 to 1/500 chance of perforation of esophagus).

There is no bright line separating the significant from the insignificant; the answer in any case must abide a rule of reason. Some dangers—infection, for example—are inherent in any operation; there is no obligation to communicate those of which persons of average sophistication are aware. Even more clearly, the physician bears no responsibility for discussion of hazards the patient has already discovered, or those having no apparent materiality to patients' decision on therapy.[89] The disclosure doctrine, like others marking lines between permissible and impermissible behavior in medical practice, is in essence a requirement of conduct prudent under the circumstances. Whenever nondisclosure of particular risk information is open to debate by reasonable-minded men, the issue is for the finder of the facts.

VI.

Two exceptions to the general rule of disclosure have been noted by the courts.... The first comes into play when the patient is unconscious or otherwise incapable of consenting, and harm from a failure to treat is imminent and outweighs any harm threatened by the proposed treatment....

The second exception obtains when risk-disclosure poses such a threat of detriment to the patient as to become unfeasible or contraindicated from a medical point of view. It is recognized that patients occasionally become so ill or emotionally distraught on disclosure as to foreclose a rational decision, or complicate or hinder the treatment, or perhaps even pose psychological damage to the patient. Where that is so, the cases have generally held that the physician is armed with a privilege to keep the information from the patient, and we think it clear that portents of that type may justify the physician in action he deems medically warranted. The critical inquiry is whether the physician responded to a sound medical judgment that communication of the risk information would present a threat to the patient's well-being.

The physician's privilege to withhold information for therapeutic reasons must be carefully circumscribed, however, for otherwise it might devour the disclosure rule itself. The privilege does not accept the paternalistic notion that the physician may remain silent simply because divulgence might prompt the patient to forego therapy the physician feels the patient really needs. That attitude presumes instability or perversity for even the normal patient, and runs counter to the foundation principle that the patient should and ordinarily can make the choice for himself. Nor does the privilege contemplate operation save where the patient's reaction to risk information, as reasonably foreseen by the physician, is menacing. And even in a situation of that kind, disclosure to a close relative with a view to

---

89. [W]e do not subscribe to the view that only risks which would cause the patient to forego the treatment must be divulged, *see* Johnson, *Medical Malpractice—Doctrines of Res Ipsa Loquitur and Informed Consent*, 37 U.COLO.L.REV. 182, 185–91 (1965); Comment, *Informed Consent in Medical Malpractice*, 55 CALIF.L.REV. 1396, 1407 n.68 (1967); Note, 75 HARV.L.REV. 1445, 1446–47 (1962), for such a principle ignores the possibility that while a single risk might not have that effect, two or more might do so. *Accord* Waltz & Scheuneman, *Informed Consent to Therapy*, 64 Nw. U.L.REV. 628, 635–41 (1970).

securing consent to the proposed treatment may be the only alternative open to the physician.

VII.

No more than breach of any other legal duty does nonfulfillment of the physician's obligation to disclose alone establish liability to the patient. An unrevealed risk that should have been made known must materialize, for otherwise the omission, however unpardonable, is legally without consequence. Occurrence of the risk must be harmful to the patient, for negligence unrelated to injury is nonactionable. And, as in malpractice actions generally, there must be a causal relationship between the physician's failure to adequately divulge and damage to the patient.

A causal connection exists when, but only when, disclosure of significant risks incidental to treatment would have resulted in a decision against it. The patient obviously has no complaint if he would have submitted to the therapy notwithstanding awareness that the risk was one of its perils. On the other hand, the very purpose of the disclosure rule is to protect the patient against consequences which, if known, he would have avoided by foregoing the treatment. The more difficult question is whether the factual issue on causality calls for an objective or a subjective determination.

It has been assumed that the issue is to be resolved according to whether the factfinder believes the patient's testimony that he would not have agreed to the treatment if he had known of the danger which later ripened into injury. We think a technique which ties the factual conclusion on causation simply to the assessment of the patient's credibility is unsatisfactory. To be sure, the objective of risk-disclosure is preservation of the patient's interest in intelligent self-choice on proposed treatment, a matter the patient is free to decide for any reason that appeals to him. When, prior to commencement of therapy, the patient is sufficiently informed on risks and he exercises his choice, it may truly be said that he did exactly what he wanted to do. But when causality is explored at a post-injury trial with a professedly uninformed patient, the question whether he actually would have turned the treatment down if he had known the risks is purely hypothetical: "Viewed from the point at which he had to decide, would the patient have decided differently had he known something he did not know?" And the answer which the patient supplies hardly represents more than a guess, perhaps tinged by the circumstance that the uncommunicated hazard has in fact materialized.

In our view, this method of dealing with the issue on causation comes in second-best. It places the physician in jeopardy of the patient's hindsight and bitterness. It places the factfinder in the position of deciding whether a speculative answer to a hypothetical question is to be credited. It calls for a subjective determination solely on testimony of a patient-witness shadowed by the occurrence of the undisclosed risk.

Better it is, we believe, to resolve the causality issue on an objective basis: in terms of what a prudent person in the patient's position would have decided if suitably informed of all perils bearing significance. If adequate disclosure could reasonably be expected to have caused that person to decline the treatment because of the revelation of the kind of risk or danger that resulted in harm, causation is shown, but otherwise not. The patient's testimony is relevant on that score of course but it would not threaten to dominate the findings. And since that testimony would proba- bly be appraised congruently with the factfinder's belief in its reasonable- ness, the case for a wholly objective standard for passing on causation is strengthened. Such a standard would in any event ease the factfinding process and better assure the truth as its product.

VIII.

In the context of trial of a suit claiming inadequate disclosure of risk information by a physician, the patient has the burden of going forward with evidence tending to establish prima facie the essential elements of the cause of action, and ultimately the burden of proof—the risk of nonpersua- sion—on those elements. These are normal impositions upon moving liti- gants, and no reason why they should not attach in nondisclosure cases is apparent. The burden of going forward with evidence pertaining to a privilege not to disclose, however, rests properly upon the physician. This is not only because the patient has made out a prima facie case before an issue on privilege is reached, but also because any evidence bearing on the privilege is usually in the hands of the physician alone. . . .

. . . .

There are obviously important roles for medical testimony in such cases, and some roles which only medical evidence can fill. Experts are ordinarily indispensible to identify and elucidate for the factfinder the risks of therapy and the consequences of leaving existing maladies untreated. They are normally needed on issues as to the cause of any injury or disability suffered by the patient and, where privileges are asserted, as to the existence of any emergency claimed and the nature and seriousness of any impact upon the patient from risk-disclosure. Save for relative infre- quent instances where questions of this type are resolvable wholly within the realm of ordinary human knowledge and experience, the need for the expert is clear.

The guiding consideration our decisions distill, however, is that medi- cal facts are for medical experts and other facts are for any witnesses— expert or not—having sufficient knowledge and capacity to testify to them.[121] It is evident that many of the issues typically involved in nondis- closure cases do not reside peculiarly within the medical domain. Lay

---

121. Lucy Webb Hayes Nat. Training School v. Perotti, [136 U.S.App.D.C. 122, 127–29, 419 F.2d 704, 709–11 (1969)], (per- mitting patient to wander from closed to open section of psychiatric ward); Monk v. Doctors Hosp., 131 U.S.App.D.C. [174,] 177, 403 F.2d [580,] 583 (operation of electro- surgical machine); Washington Hosp. Center v. Butler, 127 U.S.App.D.C. 379, 384 F.2d 331 (1967) (fall by unattended x-ray patient); Young v. Fishback, 104 U.S.App.D.C. 372, 373, 262 F.2d 469, 470 (1958) (bit of gauze left at operative site); Garfield Memorial Hosp. v. Marshall, 92 U.S.App.D.C. [234,] 240, 204 F.2d [721,] 726 (newborn baby's head striking operating table); Goodwin v. Hertzberg, 91 U.S.App.D.C. 385, 386, 201 F.2d 204, 205 (1952) (perforation of urethra); Byrom v. Eastern Dispensary & Cas. Hosp., 78 U.S.App.D.C. [42,] 43, 136 F.2d [278,] 279 (failure to further diagnose and treat after unsuccessful therapy); Grubb v. Groover, 62 App.D.C. 305, 306, 67 F.2d 511, 512 (1933), cert. denied, 291 U.S. 660, 54 S.Ct. 377, 78 L.Ed. 1052 (1934) (burn while unattended during x-ray treatment).

witness testimony can competently establish a physician's failure to disclose particular risk information, the patient's lack of knowledge of the risk, and the adverse consequences following the treatment. Experts are unnecessary to a showing of the materiality of a risk to a patient's decision on treatment, or to the reasonably, expectable effect of risk disclosure on the decision. These conspicuous examples of permissible uses of nonexpert testimony illustrate the relative freedom of broad areas of the legal problem of risk nondisclosure from the demands for expert testimony that shackle plaintiffs' other types of medical malpractice litigation.

. . .

X.

. . . [T]he evidence was clearly sufficient to raise an issue as to whether Dr. Spence's obligation to disclose information on risks was reasonably met or was excused by the surrounding circumstances. Appellant testified that Dr. Spence revealed to him nothing suggesting a hazard associated with the laminectomy. His mother testified that, in response to her specific inquiry, Dr. Spence informed her that the laminectomy was no more serious than any other operation. When, at trial, it developed from Dr. Spence's testimony that paralysis can be expected in one percent of laminectomies, it became the jury's responsibility to decide whether that peril was of sufficient magnitude to bring the disclosure duty into play. There was no emergency to frustrate an opportunity to disclose, and Dr. Spence's expressed opinion that disclosure would have been unwise did not foreclose a contrary conclusion by the jury. There was no evidence that appellant's emotional makeup was such that concealment of the risk of paralysis was medically sound. Even if disclosure to appellant himself might have bred ill consequences, no reason appears for the omission to communicate the information to his mother, particularly in view of his minority. The jury, not Dr. Spence, was the final arbiter of whether nondisclosure was reasonable under the circumstances.

. . .

Reversed and remanded for a new trial.

NOTES AND QUESTIONS

1. PRESIDENT'S COMMISSION, MAKING HEALTH CARE DECISIONS 23–29 (1982):

The distinctive role and function of the courts in American society have been major influences in shaping informed consent. . . .

Only by understanding this process and the practical difficulties in carrying it out can the development of the legal doctrine of informed consent be appreciated.

First, the medical malpractice cases that find their way to court invariably involve medical interventions that did not go well. Not only has the patient been physically injured by the intervention, but the patient is sufficiently displeased by the outcome so as to initiate legal action, with its well-known costs and tribulations, which may include the destruction of any positive relationship between patient and professional. When there was a strong preexisting bond between patient and professional, and when the patient was prepared for the possibility of an adverse outcome, litigation is less likely. Thus, the courts' perspective is necessarily shaped by their near-exclusive experience with injured, unhappy patients. The far more numerous instances in which care is provided without serious misadventure do not come before them. . . .

Second, and more specific to informed consent, courts see only those cases in which particular allegedly undisclosed risks associated with medical procedures have led to actual injuries. . . . [S]ignificantly, in such cases attention tends to focus almost automatically on the particular procedure employed and on the risk that resulted in injury . . . rather than whether the overall course of care, and the extended process of disclosure, discussion, and decisionmaking regarding care, were properly respectful of the patient's right of self-determination. . . .

Third, courts must grapple with difficulties posed by the impact of hindsight on the litigation process. Such problems arise in a number of contexts, and if not resolved satisfactorily may endanger the integrity of the courts' truth-seeking function.

Two closely related instances of such difficulties involve the centrally important determinations of whether information that was not disclosed was "material" to the patient . . . and whether the provider's failure to disclose this information "caused" the patient to undertake the course of action that resulted in injury. In both instances, the patient's own testimony about what would have been important to know and how that information would have affected his or her decision may be colored by hindsight, as well as by the patient's recognition that different reconstructions of hypothetical past decisions may help determine whether the case is won or lost. Thus, . . . the courts have understandably tried to limit the impact of possibly speculative and potentially self-serving testimony.

.   .   .

The fourth influence of the litigation process on the evolution of informed consent law is that courts must determine whether required disclosures were in fact made. . . . As in many other legal contexts, written documentation of disclosure and consent can provide useful evidence—hence, the ubiquitous "informed consent form." Unfortunately, all too often such forms can become a substitute for, rather than merely a record of a continual process of disclosure, discussion, and consent. If providers come to believe (probably incorrectly) that their obligation to obtain the patient's informed consent can be satisfied by securing a signature—even if a patient is drowsy, drugged, or confused or the form is abstruse, jargon-ridden, or largely unintelligible—the law's inclination to rely on written documentation may pervert its central purpose in requiring informed consent.

Finally, the structure of lawsuits requires the naming of particular defendants who will bear financial responsibility in the event of an adverse judgment. . . . [C]laims are typically directed against parties with "deep pockets," usually institutions and individual physicians. This pattern does not necessarily reflect the activities of other members of the health care team, particularly nurses, with regard to informing patients and securing their consent.

Thus, the litigation process has shaped the legal doctrine of informed consent. . . . Taken together, these [factors] have brought the current law to an uneasy compromise among ethical aspirations, the realities of medical practice, and the exigencies of the litigation process.

2. As *Canterbury* makes clear, even when a plaintiff has shown that a physician-defendant breached the duty of disclosure, there is no liability unless "causation" and "materialized risk" are also shown. The barrier for plaintiffs presented by the causation requirement is demonstrated by the *Canterbury* case itself: on retrial, the plaintiff lost after the defense brought out that he had submitted to another laminectomy (between the time of the first and second trials), which made it difficult—albeit not logically impossible, in light of his changed circumstances—for the plaintiff to maintain that had he known the risks he would not have undergone the first operation. Compare *Ashe v. Radiation Oncology Associates*, 9 S.W.3d 119 (Tenn. 1999), in which the plaintiff was faced with a similar causation problem. In Ashe, the plaintiff sustained radiation myelitis and was rendered paraplegic after receiving radiation treatment for a tumor found in her lung. During the jury trial contradictory testimony provided by the plaintiff made it uncertain whether the plaintiff would have proceeded with the radiation treatment had she known of the one to two percent chance of suffering radiation myelitis. As a result, the district court entered a directed verdict in favor of the defendant physician. The Court of Appeals and the Tennessee Supreme Court reversed the District Court's judgment, asserting that the testimony of the plaintiff as to whether or not she would undergo the procedure did not preclude her from bringing her informed consent claim. In reaching its decision, the Tennessee Supreme Court adopted the objective standard of causation found in *Canterbury* and asserted that "the dispositive issue is not whether [the plaintiff] would herself have chosen a different course of treatment. The issue is whether a reasonable patient in [the plaintiff's] position would have chosen a different course of treatment." *Id*. at 124. The case was remanded to allow the jury to determine causation, despite the contradictory testimony of the plaintiff.

3. Some states still adhere to the original "physician-centered" standard, which requires that the physician merely provide the information that a reasonable physician would provide to a patient in similar circumstances. This standard tends to insulate the physician, as professional customs and accepted practices serve as a reasonable defense for omitting certain alternatives. As a result, it has been criticized as being excessively paternalistic. After *Canterbury* a growing number of states moved away from using a professional standard of disclosure. By 1994, twenty-five states followed a professional standard and twenty-two a "reasonable person" or "subjective patient" standard. A majority of the population and doctors now reside in jurisdictions that have rejected the professional standard of disclosure. Of the sixteen states that have legislation on disclosure, fourteen use a professional standard. Of the states without legislation, twenty have adopted a patient based standard while only eleven have adopted a professional standard. Anthony Szczygiel, *Beyond Informed Consent*, 21 OHIO N. U. L. REV. 171 (1994).

The patient-centered standard has been refined further, taking on two distinct forms. Most jurisdictions employ an objective test, which simply asks what information would be necessary for a reasonable patient to make an informed decision. A minority of jurisdictions, however, have rejected this approach as it invites patient passivity. Instead, these jurisdictions have adopted a subjective test, which grants more autonomy to the individual patient. Suzanne K. Ketler, *The Rebirth of Informed Consent: A Cultural Analysis of the Consent Doctrine After* Schreiber v. Physicians Insurance Co. of Wisconsin, 95 NW. U. L. REV. 1029 (Spring 2001). The approach requires that the fact finder rely on the testimony of the patient in order to determine what that specific patient would have done if given additional information. The subjective approach has also been attacked by critics, as being too abstract as it "not only poses a purely hypothetical question, but seeks to answer the hypothetical question." Ashe v. Radiation Oncology Associates, 9 S.W.3d 119, 122 (Tenn. 1999).

4. Although most states have declined to go as far as *Canterbury* in imposing obligations on physicians beyond those customary among medical professionals, it can be argued that the jurisdictions following the *Canterbury* view do not go far enough because disclosure and causation are to be measured by the standard of the reasonably prudent person not the particular patient. In reaching his conclusions, Judge Robinson relied heavily on the influential article by Jon R. Waltz and Thomas W. Schueneman, *Informed Consent to Therapy*, 64 NW.U.L.REV. 628, 640–46 (1970), which suggested that it would be too burdensome on physicians and too uncertain for jurors to adopt a "subjective" standard. Yet in place of the preferences of the physician, does the reasonable prudence standard not simply substitute the views of the jurors? What about patients with idiosyncratic notions or unusual preferences or phobias? Since even physicians sometimes disagree about the "right" treatment, why cannot patients? Are patients under a duty to anyone to make reasonable decisions? *See* Alexander Capron, *Informed Consent in Catastrophic Disease Research and Treatment*, 124 U.PA.L.REV. 340, 407–09 (1974).

5. What should patients be told? Are people's answers to this question likely to vary depending on whether they are patients (ranging from those deciding about elective procedures to those offered previously untested treatments for a desperate illness), medical educators, physicians, physicians' or hospitals' lawyers (counseling their clients versus defending them once suit has been brought), judges, or jurors?

Consider the form proposed by Dr. Preston J. Burnham:

CONSENT FORM FOR HERNIA PATIENTS:

I, _____, being about to be subjected to a surgical operation said to be for repair of what my doctor thinks is a hernia (rupture or loss of belly stuff—intestines—out of the belly through a hole in the muscles), do hereby give said doctor permission to cut into me and do duly swear that I am giving my informed consent, based upon the following information:

Operative procedure is as follows: The doctor first cuts through the skin by a four-inch gash in the lower abdomen. He then slashes through the other things—fascia (a tough layer over the muscles) and layers of muscle—until he sees cord (tube that brings the sperm from testicle to outside) with all its arteries and veins. The doctor then tears the hernia (thin sac of bowels and things) from the cord and ties off the sac with a string. He then pushes the testicle back into the scrotum and sews everything together, trying not to sew up the big arteries and veins that nourish the leg.

Possible complications are as follows:

1. Large artery may be cut and I may bleed to death.

2. Large vein may be cut and I may bleed to death.

3. Tube from testicle may be cut. I will then be sterile on that side.

4. Artery or veins to testicles may be cut—same result.

5. Opening around cord in muscles may be made too tight.

6. Clot may develop in these veins which will loosen when I get out of bed and hit my lungs, killing me.

7. Clot may develop in one or both legs which may cripple me, lead to loss of one or both legs, go to my lungs, or make my veins no good for life.

8. I may develop a horrible infection that may kill me.

9. The hernia may come back again after it has been operated on.

10. I may die from general anesthesia.

11. I may be paralyzed if spinal anesthesia is used.

12. If either is used, it could explode inside me.

13. I may slip in the hospital bathroom.

14. I may be run over going to the hospital.

15. The hospital may burn down.

I understand: the anatomy of the body, the pathology of the development of hernia, the surgical technique that will be used to repair the hernia, the physiology of wound healing, the dietetic chemistry of the foods that I must eat to cause healing, the chemistry of body repair, and the course which my physician will take in treating any of the complications that can occur as a sequel of repairing an otherwise simple hernia.

_____

Patient

_____

Lawyer for Patient

_____

Lawyer for Doctor

_____

Lawyer for Hospital

_____

Lawyer for Anesthesiologist

_____

Mother-in-Law

_____

Notary Public

Burnham, *Medical Experimentation on Humans*, 152 SCI. 448–50 (1966).

In a more serious (albeit somewhat startling) vein, William Bennett describes what he calls "An Arm and a Leg" game he played with his medical school classmates. Imagine that having found a tiny blemish on the fourth toe of your right foot, your physician tells you the choice is between removing the toe (in which case you will be totally cured), and dying (swiftly and relatively painlessly) of a rare and otherwise untreatable cancer. Bennett assumes that all but the very vain would have the toe removed and be "grateful for the opportunity to strike such a favorable bargain with fate." He then changes the rules of the game: What if the blemish were on your thigh (loss of leg), internally in the pelvis (lower half of body must be removed), and so forth, to the futuristic point when all that can be saved is your brain, alive in a bath of fluid. Bennett, *The Science Watch*, HARV. MAG. 6 (Jan./Feb. 1982). Noting that people draw the line for themselves in varying places, "according to principles I have not divined," Dr. Bennett concludes that decisions in the world about trading longevity for comfort, convenience, bodily integrity, or physical pleasure are even more complex than in his game because in real life physicians cannot make any flat guarantees. He illustrates the tradeoffs involved through the results of research conducted by Barbara J. McNeil, Ralph Weichselbaum, and Stephen G. Pauker, physicians associated with Howard and Tufts medical schools.

To clarify the way their subjects (normal volunteers) feel about the value of life now, as opposed to a few years from now, the investigators invited each volunteer to gamble with the remaining years of his life. First, each player was told that he could flip a coin. If it came up heads, he would be granted 25 more years of expected life; if tails, death would come [in] a few months. In effect, anyone who was about to flip the coin had a life expectancy of twelve and a half years (but would only be able to collect zero or 25 years). But before the flip, the experimenters gave each player a way out: Instead of flipping the coin, he would take a flat guarantee—say, ten more years of life. In this deal, the subject paid for certainty by bargaining away some of his life expectancy (two and a half years, in this example). If a player accepted the ten-year warranty, he was then asked about a shorter period, and so on down to the minimum guarantee of life that he would accept to avoid the gamble.

What McNeil, Weichselbaum, and Pauker found was that subjects varied considerably in their willingness to gamble on the jackpot of 25 years. Many would settle for a short-term sure thing rather than risk the flip. Others were inclined to go for the extra years.

. . .

. . . What McNeil and her colleagues have demonstrated is that . . . people don't all have the same values. Thus, a physician who bases his choice of therapy on his own values, or even those of some imaginary average, may rob his patients of what they want most.

William Bennett, *The Science Watch*, HARV.MAG. 6 (Jan./Feb. 1992).

See also Barbara McNeil, Stephen G. Pauker, Harold C. Sox & Amos Tversky, *On the Elicitation of Preferences for Alternative Therapies*, 306 NEW ENG.J.MED. 1259 (1982) which suggests that the quality of medical decisionmaking would be improved if physicians (and patients) were aware of the way variations in presenting information affect decisions (such as viewing surgery for lung cancer as more attractive, relative to radiation therapy, when the same data are framed in terms of the probability of living rather than the probability of dying).

6. Compare the approaches of three state legislatures:

Iowa Written Informed Consent Law

Iowa Code Ann. § 147.137 (2004).

A consent in writing to any medical or surgical procedure or course of procedures in patient care which meets the requirements of this section shall create a presumption that informed consent was given. A consent in writing meets the requirements of this section if it:

1. Sets forth in general terms the nature and purpose of the procedure or procedures, together with the known risks, if any, of death, brain damage, quadriplegia, paraplegia, the loss or loss of function of any organ or limb, or disfiguring scars associated with such procedure or procedures, with the probability of each such risk if reasonably determinable.

2. Acknowledges that the disclosure of that information has been made and that all questions asked about the procedure or procedures have been answered in a satisfactory manner.

3. Is signed by the patient for whom the procedure is to be performed, or if the patient for any reason lacks legal capacity to consent, is signed by a person who has legal authority to consent on behalf of that patient in those circumstances.

New York Informed Consent Law

N.Y.Pub.Health Code § 2805–d (2004).

1. Lack of informed consent means the failure of the person providing the professional treatment or diagnosis to disclose to the patient such alternatives thereto and the reasonably foreseeable risks and benefits involved as a reasonable medical practitioner under similar circumstances would have disclosed, in a manner permitting the patient to make a knowledgeable evaluation.

2. The right of action to recover from medical dental or podiatric malpractice based on a lack of informed consent is limited to those cases involving either (a) non-emergency treatment, procedure or surgery, or (b) a diagnostic procedure which involved invasion or disruption of the integrity of the body.

3. For a cause of action therefor it must also be established that a reasonably prudent person in the patient's position would not have undergone the treatment or diagnosis if he had been fully informed and that the lack of informed consent is a proximate cause of the injury or condition for which recovery is sought.

4. It shall be a defense to any action for medical dental or podiatric malpractice based upon an alleged failure to obtain such an informed consent that:

(a) the risk not disclosed is too commonly known to warrant disclosure; or

(b) the patient assured the medical practitioner he would undergo the treatment, procedure or diagnosis regardless of the risk involved, or the patient assured the medical practitioner that he did not want to be informed of the matters to which he would be entitled to be informed; or

(c) consent by or on behalf of the patient was not reasonably possible; or

(d) the medical dental or podiatric practitioner after considering all of the attendant facts and circumstances, used reasonable discretion as to the manner and extent to which such alternatives or risks were disclosed to the patient because he reasonably believed that the manner and extent of such disclosure could reasonably be expected to adversely and substantially affect the patient's condition.

Georgia Medical Disclosure Law

Ga.Code Ann. § 31–9–6.1 (2004).

(a) Except as otherwise provided in this Code section, any person who undergoes any surgical procedure under general anesthesia, spinal anesthesia, or major regional anesthesia or any person who undergoes an amniocentesis diagnostic procedure or a diagnostic procedure which involves the intravenous or intraductal injection of a contrast material must consent to such procedure and shall be informed in general terms of the following:

(1) A diagnosis of the patient's condition requiring such proposed surgical or diagnostic procedure;

(2) The nature and purpose of such proposed surgical or diagnostic procedure;

(3) The material risks generally recognized and accepted by reasonably prudent physicians of infection, allergic reaction, severe loss of blood, loss or loss of function of any limb or organ, paralysis or partial paralysis, paraplegia or quadriplegia, disfiguring scar, brain damage, cardiac arrest, or death involved in such proposed surgical or diagnostic procedure which, if disclosed to a reasonably prudent person in the patient's position, could reasonably be expected to cause such prudent person to decline such proposed surgical or diagnostic procedure on the basis of the material risk of injury that could result from such proposed surgical or diagnostic procedure;

(4) The likelihood of success of such proposed surgical or diagnostic procedure;

(5) The practical alternatives to such proposed surgical or diagnostic procedure which are generally recognized and accepted by reasonably prudent physicians; and

(6) The prognosis of the patient's condition if such proposed surgical or diagnostic procedure is rejected.

(b)(1) If a consent to a surgical or diagnostic procedure is required to be obtained under this Code section and such consent is not obtained in writing in accordance with the requirements of this Code section, then no presumption shall arise as to the validity of such consent.

(2) If a consent to a diagnostic or surgical procedure is required to be obtained under this Code section and such consent discloses in general terms the information required in subsection (a) of this Code section, is duly evidenced in writing, and is signed by the patient or other person or persons authorized to consent pursuant to the terms of this chapter, then such consent shall be rebuttably presumed to be a valid consent.

(c) In situations where a consent to a surgical or diagnostic procedure is required under this Code section, it shall be the responsibility of the responsible physician to ensure that the information required by subsection (a) of this Code section is disclosed and that the consent provided for in this Code section is obtained. The information provided for in this Code section may be disclosed through the use of video tapes, audio tapes, pamphlets, booklets, or other means of communication or through conversations with nurses, physician's assistants, trained counselors, patient educators, or other similar persons known by the responsible physician to be knowledgeable and capable of communicating such information; provided, however, that for the purposes of this Code section only, if any employee of a hospital or ambulatory surgical treatment center participates in any such conversations at the request of the responsible physician, such employee shall be considered for such purposes to be solely the agent of the responsible physician.

(d) A failure to comply with the requirements of this Code section shall not constitute a separate cause of action but may give rise to an action for medical malpractice as defined in Code Section 9–3–70 and as governed by other provisions of this Code relating to such actions; and any such action shall be brought against the responsible physician or any hospital, ambulatory surgical treatment center, professional corporation, or partnership of which the responsible physician is an employee or partner and which is responsible for such physician's acts, or both, upon a showing:

(1) That the patient suffered an injury which was proximately caused by the surgical or diagnostic procedure;

(2) That information concerning the injury suffered was not disclosed as required by this Code section; and

(3) That a reasonably prudent patient would have refused the surgical or diagnostic procedure or would have chosen a practical alternative to such proposed surgical or diagnostic procedure if such information had been disclosed;

provided, however, that, as to an allegation of negligence for failure to comply with the requirements of this Code section, the expert's affidavit required by Code Section 9–11–9.1 shall set forth that the patient suffered an injury which was proximately caused by the surgical or diagnostic procedure and that such injury was a material risk required to be disclosed under this Code section.

(e) The disclosure of information and the consent provided for in this Code section shall not be required if:

(1) An emergency exists as defined in Code Section 31–9–3;

(2) The surgical or diagnostic procedure is generally recognized by reasonably prudent physicians to be a procedure which does not involve a material risk to the patient involved;

(3) If a patient or other person or persons authorized to give consent pursuant to this chapter make a request in writing that the information provided for in this Code section not be disclosed;

(4) A prior consent, within 30 days of the surgical or diagnostic procedure, complying with the requirements of this Code section to the surgical or diagnostic procedure has been obtained as a part of a course of treatment for the patient's condition; provided, however, that if such consent is obtained in conjunction with the admission of the patient to a hospital for the performance of such procedure, the consent shall be valid for a period of 30 days from the date of admission or for the period of time the person is confined in the hospital for that purpose, whichever is greater; or

(5) The surgical or diagnostic procedure was unforeseen or was not known to be needed at the time consent was obtained, and the patient has consented to allow the responsible physician to make the decision concerning such procedure.

(f) A prior consent to surgical or diagnostic procedures obtained pursuant to the provisions of this Code section shall be deemed to be valid consent for the responsible physician and all medical personnel under the direct supervision and control of the responsible physician in the performance of such surgical or diagnostic procedure and for all other medical personnel otherwise involved in the course of treatment of the patient's condition.

(g) The Composite State Board of Medical Examiners shall be required to adopt and have the authority to promulgate rules and regulations governing and establishing the standards necessary to implement this chapter specifically including but not limited to the disciplining of a physician who fails to comply with this Code section.

(h) As used in this Code section, the term "responsible physician" means the physician who performs the procedure or the physician under whose direct orders the procedure is performed by a nonphysician.

7. As detailed as they are, the statutes on informed consent fail to illuminate many issues. For example, could a patient knowingly consent to a "local" standard of care by a physician in a rural area (that is, one lower than that prevailing "nationally," meaning in the major medical centers where physicians are trained and whence expert witnesses are typically recruited), perhaps because the patient values other aspects of the physician's treatment or simply wishes to avoid having to travel to the city for treatment? And what of the costs of treatment? The President's Commission found that 70% of the public thought physicians should initiate discussion of this subject, but only 38% of the physicians report doing so. MAKING HEALTH CARE DECISIONS 79 (1982). Furthermore, may a physician withhold information about a treatment alternative that is not worth its costs in the physician's view, or one that is not covered by the patient's health insurance plan? Indeed, are those who sell health insurance or memberships in prepaid group health plans obligated by the law of informed consent to make sure potential buyers receive a comprehensible explanation of the scope of their coverage including all limitations on treatment for all potential illnesses?

B. WHAT LIMITATIONS SHOULD BE PLACED ON INDIVIDUAL CHOICE?

1. BASED ON CONCERN FOR OTHERS

Jacobson v. Massachusetts

Supreme Court of the United States, 1905.
197 U.S. 11, 25 S.Ct. 358, 49 L.Ed. 643.

■ JUSTICE HARLAN delivered the opinion of the court.

This case involves the validity, under the Constitution of the United States, of certain provisions in the statutes of Massachusetts relating to vaccination.

The Revised Laws of that commonwealth provide that "the board of health of a city or town, if, in its opinion, it is necessary for the public health or safety, shall require and enforce the vaccination and revaccination of all the inhabitants thereof, and shall provide them with the means of free vaccination. Whoever, being over twenty-one years of age and not under guardianship, refuses or neglects to comply with such requirement shall forfeit $5."

An exception is made in favor of "children who present a certificate, signed by a registered physician, that they are unfit subjects for vaccination."

Proceeding under the above statutes, the board of health of the city of Cambridge, Massachusetts, on the 27th day of February, 1902, adopted the following regulation: "Whereas, smallpox has been prevalent to some extent in the city of Cambridge, and still continues to increase; and whereas, it is necessary for the speedy extermination of the disease that all persons not protected by vaccination should be vaccinated; and whereas, in the opinion of the board, the public health and safety require the vaccination or revaccination of all the inhabitants of Cambridge; be it ordered, that all the inhabitants habitants of the city who have not been successfully vaccinated since March 1st, 1897, be vaccinated or revaccinated."

. . .

The above regulations being in force, the plaintiff in error, Jacobson, was proceeded against by a criminal complaint in one of the inferior courts of Massachusetts. The complaint charged that ... the defendant, being over twenty-one years of age and not under guardianship, refused and neglected to comply with [Massachusetts vaccination requirements].

. . .

We pass without extended discussion the suggestion that the particular section of the statute of Massachusetts now in question (§ 137, chap. 75) is in derogation of rights secured by the preamble of the Constitution of the United States. Although that preamble indicates the general purposes for which the people ordained and established the Constitution, it has never been regarded as the source of any substantive power conferred on the government of the United States, or on any of its departments. Such powers embrace only those expressly granted in the body of the Constitution, and such as may be implied from those so granted. Although, therefore, one of the declared objects of the Constitution was to secure the blessings of liberty to all under the sovereign jurisdiction and authority of the United States, no power can be exerted to that end by the United States, unless, apart from the preamble, it be found in some express delegation of power, or in some power to be properly implied therefrom.

We also pass without discussion the suggestion that the above section of the statute is opposed to the spirit of the Constitution. Undoubtedly, as observed by Chief Justice Marshall, speaking for the court in Sturges v.

Crowninshield, 4 Wheat. 122, 202, "the spirit of an instrument, especially of a constitution, is to be respected not less than its letter; yet the spirit is to be collected chiefly from its words." We have no need in this case to go beyond the plain, obvious meaning of the words in those provisions of the Constitution which, it is contended, must control our decision.

. . .

The authority of the state to enact this statute is to be referred to what is commonly called the police power,—a power which the state did not surrender when becoming a member of the Union under the Constitution. Although this court has refrained frained from any attempt to define the limits of that power, yet it has distinctly recognized the authority of a state to enact quarantine laws and "health laws of every description;" indeed, all laws that relate to matters completely within its territory and which do not by their necessary operation affect the people of other states. According to settled principles, the police power of a state must be held to embrace, at least, such reasonable regulations established directly by legislative enactment as will protect the public health and the public safety. It is equally true that the state may invest local bodies called into existence for purposes of local administration with authority in some appropriate way to safeguard the public health and the public safety. The mode or manner in which those results are to be accomplished is within the discretion of the state, subject, of course, so far as Federal power is concerned, only to the condition that no rule prescribed by a state, nor any regulation adopted by a local governmental agency acting under the sanction of state legislation, shall contravene the Constitution of the United States, nor infringe any right granted or secured by that instrument. A local enactment or regulation, even if based on the acknowledged police powers of a state, must always yield in case of conflict with the exercise by the general government of any power it possesses under the Constitution, or with any right which that instrument gives or secures.

We come, then, to inquire whether any right given or secured by the Constitution is invaded by the statute as interpreted by the state court. The defendant insists that his liberty is invaded when the state subjects him to fine or imprisonment for neglecting or refusing to submit to vaccination; that a compulsory vaccination law is unreasonable, arbitrary, and oppressive, and, therefore, hostile to the inherent right of every freeman to care for his own body and health in such way as to him seems best; and that the execution of such a law against one who objects to vaccination, no matter for what reason, is nothing short of an assault upon his person. But the liberty secured by the Constitution of the United States to every person within its jurisdiction does not import an absolute right in each person to be, at all times and in all circumstances, wholly freed from restraint. There are manifold restraints to which every person is necessarily subject for the common good. On any other basis organized society could not exist with safety to its members. Society based on the rule that each one is a law unto himself would soon be confronted with disorder and anarchy. Real liberty for all could not exist under the operation of a principle which recognizes the right of each individual person to use his own, whether in respect of his person or his property, regardless of the injury that may be done to others. This court has more than once recognized it as a fundamental principle that "persons and property are subjected to all kinds of restraints and burdens in order to secure the general comfort, health, and prosperity of the state; of the perfect right of the legislature to do which no question ever was, or upon acknowledged general principles ever can be, made, so far as natural persons are concerned." In Crowley v. Christensen, 137 U. S. 86, 89, we said: "The possession and enjoyment of all rights are subject to such reasonable conditions as may be deemed by the governing authority of the country essential to the safety, health, peace, good order, and morals of the community. Even liberty itself, the greatest of all rights, is not unrestricted license to act according to one's own will. It is only freedom from restraint under conditions essential to the equal enjoyment of the same right by others. It is, then, liberty regulated by law." In the Constitution of Massachusetts adopted in 1780 it was laid down as a fundamental principle of the social compact that the whole people covenants with each citizen, and each citizen with the whole people, that all shall be governed by certain laws for "the common good," and that government is instituted "for the common good, for the protection, safety, prosperity, and happiness of the people, and not for the profit, honor, or private interests of any one man, family, or class of men." The good and welfare of the commonwealth, of which the legislature is primarily the judge, is the basis on which the police power rests in Massachusetts.

Applying these principles to the present case, it is to be observed that the legislature of Massachusetts required the inhabitants of a city or town to be vaccinated only when, in the opinion of the board of health, that was necessary for the public health or the public safety. The authority to determine for all what ought to be done in such an emergency must have been lodged somewhere or in some body; and surely it was appropriate for the legislature to refer that question, in the first instance, to a board of health composed of persons residing in the locality affected, and appointed, presumably, because of their fitness to determine such questions. To invest such a body with authority over such matters was not an unusual, nor an unreasonable or arbitrary, requirement. Upon the principle of self-defense, of paramount necessity, a community has the right to protect itself against an epidemic of disease which threatens the safety of its members. It is to be observed that when the regulation in question was adopted smallpox, according to the recitals in the regulation adopted by the board of health, was prevalent to some extent in the city of Cambridge, and the disease was increasing. If such was the situation,—and nothing is asserted or appears in the record to the contrary,—if we are to attach, any value whatever to the knowledge which, it is safe to affirm, in common to all civilized peoples touching smallpox and the methods most usually employed to eradicate that disease, it cannot be adjudged that the present regulation of the board of health was not necessary in order to protect the public health and secure the public safety. Smallpox being prevalent and increasing at Cambridge, the court would usurp the functions of another branch of government if it adjudged, as matter of law, that the mode adopted under the sanction of the state, to protect the people at large was arbitrary, and not justified by the necessities of the case. We say necessities of the case, because it might be that an acknowledged power of a local community to protect itself against an epidemic threatening the safety of all might be exercised in particular circumstances and in reference to particular persons in such an arbitrary, unreasonable manner, or might go so far beyond what was reasonably required for the safety of the public, as to authorize or compel the courts to interfere for the protection of such persons. Wisconsin, M. & P. R. Co. v. Jacobson, 179 U. S. 287; 1 Dill. Mun. Corp. 4th ed. §§ 319–325, and authorities in notes; Freurid, Police Power, §§ 63 et seq. In Hannibal & St. J. R. Co. v. Husen, 95 U. S. 465, 471–473, this court recognized the right of a state to pass sanitary laws, laws for the protection of life, liberty, health, or property within its limits, laws to prevent persons and animals suffering under contagious or infectious diseases, or convicts, from coming within its borders. But, as the laws there involved went beyond the necessity of the case, and, under the guise of exerting a police power, invaded the domain of Federal authority, and violated rights secured by the Constitution, this court deemed it to be its duty to hold such laws invalid. If the mode adopted by the commonwealth of Massachusetts for the protection of its local communities against smallpox proved to be distressing, inconvenient, or objectionable to some,—if nothing more could be reasonably affirmed of the statute in question,—the answer is that it was the duty of the constituted authorities primarily to keep in view the welfare, comfort, and safety of the many, and not permit the interests of the many to be subordinated to the wishes or convenience of the few. There is, of course, a sphere within which the individual may assert the supremacy of his own will, and rightfully dispute the authority of any human government,—especially of any free government existing under a written constitution, to interfere with the exercise of that will. But it is equally true that in every well-ordered society charged with the duty of conserving the safety of its members the rights of the individual in respect of his liberty may at times, under the pressure of great dangers, be subjected to such restraint, to be enforced by reasonable regulations, as the safety of the general public may demand. An American citizen arriving at an American port on a vessel in which, during the voyage, there had been cases of yellow fever or Asiatic cholera, he, although apparently free from disease himself, may yet, in some circumstances, be held in quarantine against his will on board of such vessel or in a quarantine station, until it be ascertained by inspection, conducted with due diligence, that the danger of the spread of the disease among the community at large has disappeared. The liberty secured by the 14th Amendment, this court has said, consists, in part, in the right of a person "to live and work where he will"; and yet he may be compelled, by force if need be, against his will and without regard to his personal wishes or his pecuniary interests, or even his religious or political convictions, to take his place in the ranks of the army of his country, and risk the chance of being shot down in its defense. It is not, therefore, true that the power of the public to guard itself against imminent danger depends in every case involving the control of one's body upon his willingness to submit to reasonable regulations established by the constituted authorities, under the sanction of the state, for the purpose of protecting the public collectively against such danger.

It is said, however, that the statute, as interpreted by the state court, although making an exception in favor of children certified by a registered physician to be unfit subjects for vaccination, makes no exception in case of adults in like condition. But this cannot be deemed a denial of the equal protection of the laws to adults; for the statute is applicable equally to all in like condition, and there are obviously reasons why regulations may be appropriate for adults which could not be safely applied to persons of tender years.

Looking at the propositions embodied in the defendant's rejected offers of proof, it is clear that they are more formidable by their number than by their inherent value. Those offers in the main seem to have had no purpose except to state the general theory of those of the medical profession who attach little or no value to vaccination as a means of preventing the spread of smallpox, or who think that vaccination causes other diseases of the body. What everybody knows the court must know, and therefore the state court judicially knew, as this court knows, that an opposite theory accords with the common belief, and is maintained by high medical authority. We must assume that, when the statute in question was passed, the legislature of Massachusetts was not unaware of these opposing theories, and was compelled, of necessity, to choose between them. It was not compelled to commit a matter involving the public health and safety to the final decision of a court or jury. It is no part of the function of a court or a jury to determine which one of two modes was likely to be the most effective for the protection of the public against disease. That was for the legislative department to determine in the light of all the information it had or could obtain. It could not properly abdicate its function to guard the public health and safety. The state legislature proceeded upon the theory which recognized vaccination as at least an effective, if not the best-known, way in which to meet and suppress the evils of a smallpox epidemic that imperiled an entire population. Upon what sound principles as to the relations existing between the different departments of government can the court review this action of the legislature? If there is any such power in the judiciary to review legislative action in respect of a matter affecting the general welfare, it can only be when that which the legislature has done comes within the rule that, if a statute purporting to have been enacted to protect the public health, the public morals, or the public safety, has no real or substantial relation to those objects, or is, beyond all question, a plain, palpable invasion of rights secured by the fundamental law, it is the duty of the courts to so adjudge, and thereby give effect to the Constitution.

Whatever may be thought of the expediency of this statute, it cannot be affirmed to be, beyond question, in palpable conflict with the Constitution. Nor, in view of the methods employed to stamp out the disease of smallpox, can anyone confidently assert that the means prescribed by the state to that end has no real or substantial relation to the protection of the public health and the public safety. Such an assertion would not be consistent with the experience of this and other countries whose authorities have dealt with the disease of smallpox. And the principle of vaccination as a means to prevent the spread of smallpox has been enforced in many states by statutes making the vaccination of children a condition of their right to enter or remain in public schools.

The latest case upon the subject of which we are aware is Viemester v. White, decided very recently by the court of appeals of New York. That case involved the validity of a statute excluding from the public schools all children who had not been vaccinated [sic]. One contention was that the statute and the regulation adopted in exercise of its provisions was inconsistent with the rights, privileges, and liberties of the citizen. The contention was overruled, the court saying, among other things:

> Smallpox is known to be a dangerous and contagious disease. If vaccination strongly tends to prevent the transmission or spread of this disease, it logically follows that children may be refused admission to the public schools until they have been vaccinated. The appellant claims that vaccination does not tend to prevent smallpox, but tends to bring about other diseases, and that it does much harm, with no good. It must be conceded that some laymen, both learned and unlearned, and some physicians of great skill and repute, do not believe that vaccination is a preventive of smallpox. The common belief, however, is that it has a decided tendency to prevent the spread of this fearful disease, and to render it less dangerous to those who contract it. While not accepted by all, it is accepted by the mass of the people, as well as by most members of the medical profession. It has been general in our state, and in most civilized nations for generations. It is generally accepted in theory, and generally applied in practice, both by the voluntary action of the people, and in obedience to the command of law. Nearly every state in the Union has statutes to encourage, or directly or indirectly to require, vaccination; and this is true of most nations of Europe.... A common belief, like common knowledge, does not require evidence to establish its existence, but may be acted upon without proof by the legislature and the courts.... The fact that the belief is not universal is not controlling, for there is scarcely any belief that is accepted by everyone. The possibility that the belief may be wrong, and that science may yet show it to be wrong, is not conclusive; for the legislature has the right to pass laws which, according to the common belief of the people, are adapted to prevent the spread of contagious diseases. In a free country, where the government is by the people, through their chosen representatives, practical legislation admits of no other standard of action, for what the people believe is for the common welfare must be accepted as tending to promote the common welfare, whether it does in fact or not. Any other basis would conflict with the spirit of the Constitution, and would sanction measures opposed to a Republican form of government. While we do not decide, and cannot decide, that vaccination is a preventive of smallpox, we take judicial notice of the fact that this is the common belief of the people of the state, and, with this fact as a foundation, we hold that the statute in question is a health law, enacted in a reasonable and proper exercise of the police power.

Since, then, vaccination, as a means of protecting a community against smallpox, finds strong support in the experience of this and other countries, no court, much less a jury, is justified in disregarding the action of the legislature simply because in its or their opinion that particular method was—perhaps, or possibly—not the best either for children or adults.

. . .

The defendant offered to prove [that vaccination did not prevent the spread of smallpox;] that vaccination "quite often" caused serious and permanent injury to the health of the person vaccinated; that the operation "occasionally" resulted in death; that it was "impossible" to tell "in any particular case" what the results of vaccination would be, or whether it would injure the health or result in death; . . . that vaccine matter is "quite often" impure and dangerous to be used, but whether impure or not cannot be ascertained by any known practical test; that the defendant refused to submit to vaccination for the reason that he had, "when a child," been caused great and extreme suffering for a long period by a disease produced by vaccination; and that he had witnessed a similar result of vaccination, not only in the case of his son, but in the cases of others.

These offers [of proof by the defendant], in effect, invited the court and jury to go over the whole ground gone over by the legislature when it enacted the statute in question. The legislature assumed that some children, by reason of their condition at the time, might not be fit subjects of vaccination; and it is suggested—and we will not say without reason—that such is the case with some adults. But the defendant did not offer to prove that, by reason of his then condition, he was in fact not a fit subject of vaccination. . . . Could he reasonably claim . . . an exemption because "quite often," or "occasionally," injury had resulted from vaccination, or because it was impossible, in the opinion of some, by any practical test, to determine with absolute certainty whether a particular person could be safely vaccinated?

It seems to the court that an affirmative answer to these questions would practically strip the legislative department of its function to care for the public health and the public safety when endangered by epidemics of disease. Such an answer would mean that compulsory vaccination could not, in any conceivable case, be legally enforced in a community, even at the command of the legislature, however widespread the epidemic of smallpox, and however deep and universal was the belief of the community and of its medical advisers that a system of general vaccination was vital to the safety of all.

We are not prepared to hold that a minority, residing or remaining in any city or town where smallpox is prevalent, and enjoying the general protection afforded by an organized local government, may thus defy the will of its constituted authorities, acting in good faith for all, under the legislative sanction of the state. If such be the privilege of a minority, then a like privilege would belong to each individual of the community, and the spectacle would be presented of the welfare and safety of an entire population being subordinated to the notions of a single individual who chooses to remain a part of that population. We are unwilling to hold it to be an element in the liberty secured by the Constitution of the United States that one person, or a minority of persons, residing in any community and enjoying the benefits of its local government, should have the power thus to dominate the majority when supported in their action by the authority of the state. While this court should guard with firmness every right appertaining to life, liberty, or property as secured to the individual by the supreme law of the land, it is of the last importance that it should not invade the domain of local authority except when it is plainly necessary to do so in order to enforce that law. The safety and the health of the people of Massachusetts are, in the first instance, for that commonwealth to guard and protect. They are matters that do not ordinarily concern the national government. So far as they can be reached by any government, they depend, primarily, upon such action as the state, in its wisdom, may take; and we do not perceive that this legislation has invaded any right secured by the Federal Constitution.

Before closing this opinion we deem it appropriate, in order to prevent misapprehension as to our views, to observe—perhaps to repeat a thought already sufficiently expressed, namely—that the police power of a state, whether exercised directly by the legislature, or by a local body acting under its authority, may be exerted in such circumstances, or by regulations so arbitrary and oppressive in particular cases, as to justify the interference of the courts to prevent wrong and oppression. Extreme cases can be readily suggested. Ordinarily such cases are not safe guides in the administration of the law. It is easy, for instance, to suppose the case of an adult who is embraced by the mere words of the act, but yet to subject whom to vaccination in a particular condition of his health or body would be cruel and inhuman in the last degree. We are not to be understood as holding that the statute was intended to be applied to such a case, or, if it was so intended, that the judiciary would not be competent to interfere and protect the health and life of the individual concerned. "All laws," this court has said, "should receive a sensible construction. General terms should be so limited in their application as not to lead to injustice, oppression, or an absurd consequence. It will always, therefore, be presumed that the legislature intended exceptions to its language which would avoid results of this character. The reason of the law in such cases should prevail over its letter." Until otherwise informed by the highest court of Massachusetts, we are not inclined to hold that the statute establishes the absolute rule that an adult must be vaccinated if it be apparent or can be shown with reasonable certainty that he is not at the time a fit subject of vaccination, or that vaccination, by reason of his then condition, would seriously impair his health, or probably cause his death. No such case is here presented. It is the cause of an adult who, for aught that appears, was himself in perfect health and a fit subject of vaccination, and yet, while remaining in the community, refused to obey the statute and the regulation adopted in execution of its provisions for the protection of the public health and the public safety, confessedly endangered by the presence of a dangerous disease.

We now decide only that the statute covers the present case, and that nothing clearly appears that would justify this court in holding it to be unconstitutional and inoperative in its application to the plaintiff in error.

The judgment of the court below must be affirmed.

It is so ordered.

Bradshaw v. Daniel

Supreme Court of Tennessee, 1993.
854 S.W.2d 865.

■ ANDERSON, JUSTICE.

On July 19, 1986, Elmer Johns went to the emergency room at Methodist Hospital South in Memphis, Tennessee, complaining of headaches, muscle aches, fever, and chills. He was admitted to the hospital under the care and treatment of the defendant, Dr. Chalmers B. Daniel, Jr. Dr. Daniel first saw Johns on July 22, 1986, at which time he ordered the drug Chloramphenicol, which is the drug of choice for a person in the latter stages of Rocky Mountain Spotted Fever. Johns' condition rapidly deteriorated, and he died the next day, July 23, 1986. An autopsy was performed, and the Center for Disease Control in Atlanta conclusively confirmed, in late September 1986, that the cause of death was Rocky Mountain Spotted fever. Although Dr. Daniel communicated with Elmer Johns' wife, Genevieve, during Johns' treatment, he never advised her of the risks of exposure to Rocky Mountain Spotted Fever, or that the disease could have been the cause of Johns' death.

A week after her husband's death, on August 1, 1986, Genevieve Johns came to the emergency room of Baptist Memorial Hospital in Memphis, Tennessee, with similar symptoms of chills, fever, mental disorientation, nausea, lung congestion, myalgia, and swelling of the hands. She was admitted to the hospital and treated for Rocky Mountain Spotted Fever, but she died three days later, on August 4, 1986, of that disease. It is undisputed that no patient-physician relationship existed between Genevieve Johns and Dr. Daniel.

The plaintiff, William Jerome Bradshaw, is Genevieve Johns' son. He filed this suit alleging that the defendant's negligence in failing to advise Genevieve Johns that her husband died of Rocky Mountain Spotted Fever, and in failing to warn her of the risk of exposure, proximately caused her death.

. . .

The defendant physician argues that he owed his patient's wife no legal duty because first, there was no physician-patient relationship, and second, Rocky Mountain Spotted Fever is not a contagious disease and, therefore, there is no duty to warn of the risk of exposure.

We begin our analysis by examining how we determine when a legal duty may be imposed upon one for the benefit of another. While duty was not part of the early English common law jurisprudence of tort liability, it has since become an essential element in negligence cases. No claim for negligence can succeed in the absence of any one of the following elements: (1) a duty of care owed by the defendant to the plaintiff; (2) conduct falling below the applicable standard of care amounting to a breach of that duty; (3) an injury or loss; (4) causation in fact; and (5) proximate, or legal cause. The existence or non-existence of a duty owed to the plaintiff by the defendant is entirely a question of law for the court.

. . .

[T]he imposition of a legal duty reflects society's contemporary policies and social requirements concerning the right of individuals and the general public to be protected from another's act or conduct. Indeed, it has been stated that " 'duty' is not sacrosanct in itself, but is only an expression of the sum total of those considerations of policy which lead the law to say that the plaintiff is entitled to protection." Prosser, § 53 at 358....

The defendant contends that the absence of a physician-patient relationship negates the existence of a duty in this case. While it is true that a physician-patient relationship is necessary to the maintenance of a medical malpractice action, it is not necessary for the maintenance of an action based on negligence, and this Court has specifically recognized that a physician may owe a duty to a non-patient third party for injuries caused by the physician's negligence, if the injuries suffered and the manner in which they occurred were reasonably foreseeable.

Here, we are asked to determine whether a physician has an affirmative duty to warn a patient's family member about the symptoms and risks of exposure to Rocky Mountain Spotted Fever, a non-contagious disease. Insofar as we are able to determine, there is no reported decision from this or any other jurisdiction involving circumstances exactly similar to those presented in this case.

We begin by observing that all persons have a duty to use reasonable care to refrain from conduct that will foreseeably cause injury to others.

In determining the existence of a duty, courts have distinguished between action and inaction. Professor Prosser has commented that "the reason for the distinction may be said to lie in the fact that by 'misfeasance' the defendant has created a new risk of harm to the plaintiff, while by 'nonfeasance' he has at least made his situation no worse, and has merely failed to benefit him by interfering in his affairs."

Because of this reluctance to countenance nonfeasance as a basis of liability, as a general rule, under the common law, one person owed no affirmative duty to warn those endangered by the conduct of another.

To mitigate the harshness of this rule, courts have carved out exceptions for cases in which the defendant stands in some special relationship to either the person who is the source of the danger, or to the person who is foreseeably at risk from the danger. *Lindsey*, 689 S.W.2d at 859; *Tarasoff*, 551 P.2d at 343; Restatement (Second) of Torts § 315 (1964). Accordingly,

> while an actor is always bound to prevent his acts from creating an unreasonable risk to others, he is under the affirmative duty to act to prevent another from sustaining harm only when certain socially recognized relations exist which constitute the basis for such legal duty.

Harper & Kime, *The Duty to Control the Conduct of Another*, 43 YALE L.J. 886, 887 (1934).

One of the most widely known cases applying that principle is *Tarasoff, supra,* in which the California Supreme Court held that when a psychotherapist determines or, pursuant to the standards of his profession, should determine that his patient presents a serious danger of violence to another, the therapist has an affirmative duty to use reasonable care to protect the intended victim against such danger, and the duty may require the physician to warn the intended victim of the danger. 551 P.2d at 340. The special relationship of the patient to his psychotherapist supported imposition of the affirmative duty to act for the benefit of third persons. 551 P.2d at 343–44.

Decisions of other jurisdictions have employed the same analysis and held that the relationship of a physician to his patient is sufficient to support the duty to exercise reasonable care to protect third persons against foreseeable risks emanating from a patient's physical illness. Specifically, other courts have recognized that physicians may be liable to persons infected by a patient, if the physician negligently fails to diagnose a contagious disease, or having diagnosed the illness, fails to warn family members or others who are foreseeably at risk of exposure to the disease.

For example, in *Hofmann,* an action was brought against a physician by a child who had contracted tuberculosis as a result of the physician's negligent failure to diagnose the disease in his patient, the child's father. Reversing a summary judgment for the physician, the Florida District Court of Appeals held

> that a physician owes a duty to a minor child who is a member of the immediate family and living with a patient suffering from a contagious disease to inform those charged with the minor's well being of the nature of the contagious disease and the precautionary steps to be taken to prevent the child from contracting such disease and that the duty is not negated by the physician negligently failing to become aware of the presence of such a contagious disease.

241 So.2d at 753.

Likewise, in *Shepard,* a wrongful death action was filed by the mother of a child who was infected and died of spinal meningitis after the physician failed to diagnose the disease in his patient, the mother. Again, reversing a summary judgment in favor of the defendant on the issue of legal duty, the Michigan Court of Appeals stated that the

> defendant had a physician-patient relationship with plaintiff. This was a special relationship with the one who allegedly infected Eric, leading to his death.... Because defendant had a special relationship with plaintiff we conclude that defendant owed a duty of reasonable care to Eric. As plaintiff's son and a member of her household, Eric was a foreseeable potential victim of defendant's conduct.

390 N.W.2d at 241.

Finally in *Wojcik,* an action was brought by a woman who was infected with tuberculosis against the physician who discovered her husband had the disease, but did not inform her. The New York court held that the physician owed a duty to warn his patient's wife of the risks associated with contracting the disease and stated that

> one who by reason of his professional relations is placed in a position where it becomes his duty to exercise ordinary care to protect others from injury or danger is liable in damages to those injured by reason of his failure to do so.

183 N.Y.S.2d at 358.

Returning to the facts of this case, first, it is undisputed that there was a physician-patient relationship between Dr. Daniel and Elmer Johns. Second, here, as in the contagious disease context, it is also undisputed that Elmer Johns' wife, who was residing with him, was at risk of contracting the disease. This is so even though the disease is not contagious in the narrow sense that it can be transmitted from one person to another. Both Dr. Daniel and Dr. Prater, the plaintiff's expert, testified that family members of patients suffering from Rocky Mountain Spotted Fever are at risk of contracting the disease due to a phenomenon called clustering, which is related to the activity of infected ticks who transmit the disease to humans. Dr. Prater also testified that Dr. Daniel negligently failed to diagnose the disease and negligently failed to warn his patient's wife, Genevieve Johns, of her risk of exposure to the source of disease. Dr. Daniel's expert disputed these conclusions, but Dr. Daniel conceded there is a medical duty to inform the family when there is a diagnosis of the disease. Thus, this case is analogous to the *Tarasoff* line of cases adopting a duty to warn of danger and the contagious disease cases adopting a comparable duty to warn. Here, as in those cases, there was a foreseeable risk of harm to an identifiable third party, and the reasons supporting the recognition of the duty to warn are equally compelling here.

We, therefore, conclude that the existence of the physician-patient relationship is sufficient to impose upon a physician an affirmative duty to warn identifiable third persons in the patient's immediate family against foreseeable risks emanating from a patient's illness. Accordingly, we hold that under the factual circumstances of this case, viewing the evidence in a light most favorable to the plaintiff, the defendant physician had a duty to warn his patient's wife of the risk to her of contracting Rocky Mountain Spotted Fever, when he knew, or in the exercise of reasonable care, should have known, that his patient was suffering from the disease. Our holding here is necessarily limited to the conclusion that the defendant physician owed Genevieve Johns a legal duty. We express no opinion on the other elements which would be required to establish a cause of action for common-law negligence in this case.

NOTES AND QUESTIONS

1. Should the reasoning of *Bradshaw* extend to genetically transferable diseases? Should a physician have an affirmative duty to warn the children of a patient that their father has a disease that could be passed down genetically? If so, should that duty stop at the children, or extend further down the genetic line? How long should that duty be imposed on the doctor?

In Pate v. Threlkel, 661 So.2d 278 (Fla. 1995), the Supreme Court of Florida found that a duty exists if the children of the patient establish that a reasonably prudent physician would give such a warning pursuant to the prevailing standard of care. Because a physician is prohibited from disclosing a patient's medical condition to others in most instances, warning the patient will satisfy this duty.

In Safer v. Pack, 291 N.J.Super. 619, 677 A.2d 1188 (1996), the court recognized a duty to warn, but declined to hold that simply warning the patient would satisfy this duty. The court felt that it might be necessary for the physician to resolve a conflict between his broader duty to warn and his fidelity to an expressed preference of the patient that nothing be said to family members about the details of the disease.

2. A physician who wrongly discloses a patient's medical records faces potential liability under several headings, including breach of fiduciary duty, invasion of privacy, and other torts, as well as revocation of license for unprofessional conduct. In Berthiaume's Estate v. Pratt, 365 A.2d 792 (Me. 1976), the court found that a physician could be liable for an invasion of privacy for taking photographs of a patient without permission, even though the photos were never intended to be published. The photographs were compiled to study the progression of the patient's disease, and even though the court acknowledged the need for medical research, the rights of the individual were considered overriding.

2.   BASED ON CONCERN FOR THE INDIVIDUAL

United States v. Cannabis Cultivator's Club

United States District Court, N.D. California, 1999.
1999 WL 111893.

■ BREYER, DISTRICT J.

Now before the Court is plaintiff's motion to dismiss the complaint-in-intervention in its entirety. After carefully considering the papers submitted by the parties, and having had the benefit of oral argument on February 5, 1999, the motion to dismiss is GRANTED.

BACKGROUND

In early 1998, plaintiff filed separate lawsuits against six medical cannabis cooperatives and several individuals associated with those cooperatives, alleging that the defendants' distribution of marijuana violated the Controlled Substances Act, 21 U.S.C. § 841(a)(1), and that their illegal conduct should be enjoined pursuant to 21 U.S.C. § 882(a). In May 1998, the Court granted a preliminary injunction enjoining all defendants from engaging in the distribution of marijuana in violation of 21 U.S.C. § 841(a)(1).

Several months later, the Court granted the motion of four individuals, Edward Neil Brundridge, Ima Carter, Rebecca Nikkel, and Lucia Y. Vier ("Intervenors"), to intervene as defendants in the government's action pursuant to Federal Rule of Civil Procedure 24(b). The Intervenors are members of the defendant Oakland, Marin or Ukiah medical cannabis cooperatives. They seek a judicial declaration that they have a fundamental right "to be free from governmental interdiction of their personal, self-funded medical choice, in consultation with their personal physician, to alleviate suffering through the only effective treatment available for them." They also seek an order enjoining the United States from interfering with the Intervenors' exercise of this fundamental right, and in particular, they seek to enjoin the United States from prohibiting the cooperatives from distributing marijuana to the Intervenors.

Plaintiff subsequently moved to dismiss the Intervenors' complaint in its entirety.

DISCUSSION

Plaintiff contends that under the Ninth Circuit's decision in *Carnohan v. United States*, 616 F.2d 1120 (9th Cir.1980), the Intervenors' complaint fails as a matter of law. In *Carnohan*, the plaintiff brought a declaratory proceeding to secure the right to obtain and use laetrile in a nutritional program for the prevention of cancer. The court held that since the Food and Drug Administration ("FDA") had determined that laetrile was a new drug, and laetrile did not meet the standards for distribution of a new drug, the plaintiff had to bring an Administrative Procedure Act ("APA") action to challenge the FDA's decision. The plaintiff argued further that the FDA's regulatory scheme is so burdensome as applied to individuals that it infringes upon constitutional rights. The Ninth Circuit responded:

> We need not decide whether Carnohan has a constitutional right to treat himself with home remedies of his own confection. *Constitutional rights of privacy and personal liberty do not give individuals the right to obtain laetrile free of the lawful exercise of government police power.*

Id. at 1121 (emphasis added).

Carnohan disposes of the Intervenors' claims. Regardless of whether the Intervenors have a right to treat themselves with marijuana which they themselves grow (a remedy of their own confection), the Ninth Circuit has held that they do not have a constitutional right to *obtain* marijuana from the medical cannabis cooperatives free of government police power. To hold otherwise would directly contradict the *Carnohan* holding.

The Intervenors attempt to distinguish Carnohan and the other cases cited by plaintiff on the grounds that the Intervenors (1) do not seek to compel government action and are not asserting that they have a fundamental constitutional right to obtain a particular medication, and (2) seek to use cannabis upon the recommendation of their personal physicians to alleviate their suffering through the only effective treatment available for them. Neither of these alleged distinctions persuades the Court than *Carnohan* is not controlling here.

First, the Intervenors' characterization of their complaint as not seeking a declaration of a right to obtain a particular medication is belied by the plain language of their complaint and their arguments in support of their motion to intervene. If the issue before the Court were whether the Intervenors have a right to use marijuana which they have grown themselves, the Court would not have granted them leave to intervene since such a claim is not related to the claims raised by the United States' lawsuits. By their complaint, however, the Intervenors seek an order enjoining the United States from enforcing the Controlled Substances Act against the medical cannabis cooperatives in which they are members. Complaint in Intervention at ¶¶ 19–21. Indeed, in their motion to intervene, they emphasized that their complaint alleges that they have a "protectable interest in *obtaining* cannabis." Motion to Intervene at 11 (emphasis added); *see also id.* at 5 ("If the cooperatives are prevented from distributing cannabis, the [Intervenors] will not be able to legally obtain cannabis that is safe and effective."). Thus, the Intervenors' complaint seeks an order that they have a fundamental right to obtain to a particular medication, marijuana, from a particular source, the medical cannabis cooperatives. *Carnohan*, however, holds that there is no constitutional right to obtain medication free from the lawful exercise of the government's police powers.

The fact that California law does not prohibit the distribution of medical marijuana under certain circumstances is not relevant as to whether the Intervenors have a fundamental right. If that were the case, whether one had a fundamental right to treat oneself with marijuana would depend on whether the state in which one lived prohibited such conduct.

Second, that the Intervenors' personal physicians recommended marijuana is not a material distinction. If one does not have a right to obtain medication free from government regulation, there is no reason one would have that right upon a physician's recommendation. In *Kulsar v. Ambach*, 598 F.Supp. 1124 (W.D.N.Y.1984), for example, medical patients alleged that New York laws that prohibited *their personal physician* from administering a particular treatment for their hypoglycemic disorders were unconstitutional. The court dismissed their constitutional claim on the ground that the "constitutional right of privacy does not give individuals the right to obtain a particular medical treatment 'free of the lawful exercise of government police power.' " *Id.* at 1126 (citing Carnohan, 616 F.2d 1120).

The Intervenors' argument that marijuana is the only effective treatment for their symptoms is also not persuasive. In *Rutherford v. United States*, 616 F.2d 455 (10th Cir.1980), a case relied upon by the *Carnohan* court, terminally ill cancer patients brought suit to enjoin the United States from interfering with interstate shipments of the sale of laetrile. The trial court had held that the cancer patients had a right "to be let alone," or "a constitutional right of privacy to permit them, as terminally ill cancer patients, to take whatever treatment they wished regardless of whether the FDA regarded the medication as 'effective' or 'safe.' " *Id.* at 456. The Tenth Circuit reversed:

> It is apparent in the context with which we are here concerned that the decision by the patient whether to have a treatment or not is a protected right, but his selection of a particular treatment, or at least a medication, is within the area of governmental interest in protecting public health. The premarketing requirement of the Federal Food, Drug and Cosmetic Act, 21 U.S.C. § 355, is an exercise of Congressional authority to limit the patient's choice of medication.

Id. at 457. The Rutherford plaintiffs had no other treatment alternative. They believed that without the laetrile they would die. The Tenth Circuit nonetheless held that the *Rutherford* plaintiffs did not have a constitutional right to obtain laetrile. *See also* Smith v. Shalala, 954 F.Supp. 1, 3 (D.D.C.1996) ("While there are decisions recognizing that competent adults have a fundamental right to refuse medical treatment, *Cruzan v. Director, Missouri Dept. of Health*, 497 U.S. 261 (1990), and to determine the time and manner of their death, free from governmental interference, ... nothing in those decisions suggests that the government has an affirmative obligation to set aside its regulations in order to provide dying patients access to experimental medical treatments").

Here, the plaintiffs similarly believe, and on a motion to dismiss the Court must assume they could prove, that marijuana is the only effective treatment for their symptoms. Congress and the FDA disagree. If the Intervenors believe the FDA and Congress are wrong, they should challenge the legal prohibition on the distribution of marijuana through an APA or similar action. *Carnohan* and *Rutherford* hold, however, that there is no fundamental right to obtain the medication of choice. Accordingly, the Intervenors' claim that they do have such a right, and that the United States should be enjoined from interfering with that right, will be dismissed without leave to amend.

As is set forth above, the Court does not interpret the Intervenors' complaint as alleging a fundamental right to treat themselves with cannabis which they themselves have grown. The Intervenors' motion to intervene was based on their assertion that if the cooperatives are closed, they will not be able to treat their symptoms with cannabis. Nonetheless, to the extent the complaint does make such claim, such claim does not raise a question of fact or law in common with the claims or defenses in these related lawsuits. *See* Fed.R.Civ.P. 24(b)(2). Accordingly, to the extent the complaint-in-intervention makes such a claim, it shall be dismissed without prejudice.

CONCLUSION

For the foregoing reasons, plaintiff's motion to dismiss is GRANTED. Intervenors' claims for a declaration that they have a fundamental right to obtain marijuana for their personal, medical use without interference from the United States, and their claims seeking to enjoin the United States' efforts to close the cooperatives, are DISMISSED without leave to amend. Intervenors' claims seeking an order that they have a fundamental right to treat themselves with marijuana which they themselves have grown, to the extent the Intervenors' complaint makes such claims, are DISMISSED without prejudice.

IT IS SO ORDERED.

NOTES AND QUESTIONS

1. The California court took note of the FDA litigation in the *Rutherford* case. In *United States v. Rutherford*, 442 U.S. 544, 99 S.Ct. 2470, 61 L.Ed.2d 68 (1979), the United States Supreme Court reversed the Tenth Circuit. The Court found no basis in the 1938 Food, Drug, and Cosmetic Act or in the 1962 Amendments, which added the requirements of safety and efficacy, to exempt from premarket approval drugs used to treat terminally ill patients. Recognition of such an exemption should be left to "legislative judgment, not judicial inference."

> Only when a literal construction of a statute yields results so manifestly unreasonable that they could not fairly be attributed to congressional design will an exception to statutory language be judicially implied. Here, however, we have no license to depart from the plain language of the Act, for Congress could reasonably have intended to shield terminal patients from ineffectual or unsafe drugs.

Id. at 555.

On remand, the court of appeals upheld the district court's finding that the exemption under the 1938 grandfather provisions, 21 U.S.C. § 321(p)(1), was inapplicable, but reversed the lower court's ruling that Laetrile was entitled to an exemption under the 1962 grandfather provision. Rutherford v. United States, 616 F.2d 455 (10th Cir.1980). The court concluded that it is acceptable for the state, through congressional enactment and FDA enforcement, to limit patients' access to medications: "The decision by the patient whether to have a treatment or not is a protected right, but his selection of a particular treatment, or at least a medication, is within the area of governmental interest in protecting public health." *Id.* at 457.

While the litigation over the FDA's refusal to approve Laetrile was wending its way through the courts, two other developments were occurring. On the one hand, the legislatures in over half the states passed bills legalizing Laetrile therapy within their borders. On the other hand, the National Cancer Institute sponsored a multi-institution clinical trial of Laetrile. That study found that, even when combined with the "metabolic" therapy (vitamins, enzymes, and a special diet) recommended by therapists who oppose conventional cancer treatment, Laetrile provided no substantive benefits in terms of cure, improvement or stabilization of cancer, improvement of symptoms, or extension of life span; several patients did, however, manifest symptoms of, or dangerous blood levels of, cyanide poisoning. Charles G. Moertel et al., *A Clinical Trial of Amygdalin (Laetrile) in the Treatment of Human Cancer*, 306 NEW ENGL.J.MED. 201 (1982).

2. The FDA Commissioner expressed concern that a "substantial group of persons afflicted with cancer is avoiding effective therapy altogether and using Laetrile instead." If the latter failing can be outlawed, what about the former? Suppose a patient, diagnosed as suffering from a cancer that will be fatal if not treated, chooses no treatment or only palliative treatment (whether provided by a licensed physician or by, say, the local liquor store). Should the Laetrile cases be read to recognize state authority to keep citizens from making unwise medical choices or merely to regulate the practice of health care and, specifically, behavior that is potentially fraudulent?

3. Both those judges who approved of the ban on Laetrile and those who did not apparently accept governmental regulation of addictive drugs (including prohibition when appropriate). Why is that? Stripped of their association with criminal activity, why are such drugs beyond the realm of individual choice? Is it for the reason that Mill excluded slavery from those things the state must leave alone—that is, one cannot claim the freedom to alienate one's freedom? Or simply for paternalistic reasons, that the drugs in question are deleterious to health?

4. New York has allowed recovery against an alternative medicine practitioner for failing to obtain informed consent from a patient. Charell v. Gonzalez, 251 A.D.2d 72, 673 N.Y.S.2d 685 (1998).

5. The United States Supreme Court has held that medical necessity is no defense to prosecution for distributing marijuana. U.S. v. Oakland Cannabis Buyers' Cooperative, 532 U.S. 483, 121 S.Ct. 1711, 149 L.Ed.2d 722 (2001). The opinion is set forth on pages 995–998, infra.

3.   BASED ON CONCERN FOR THOSE WHO CANNOT DECIDE FOR THEMSELVES

Rains v. Belshe

Court of Appeals, First District, 1995.
32 Cal.App.4th 157, 38 Cal.Rptr.2d 185.

■ PETERSON, PRESIDING JUSTICE.

The Legislature enacted in 1992, and amended in 1994, Health and Safety Code section 1418.8. That amended statute generally allows certain incompetent patients residing in skilled nursing facilities or intermediate care facilities to receive medical treatment, after a physician has determined a patient's incapacity to give informed consent to such treatment and an interdisciplinary review team has determined the treatment is medically appropriate. We find this statute as amended to be constitutional, and reverse the trial court's contrary ruling.

I. *FACTS AND PROCEDURAL HISTORY*

This appeal presents solely legal issues concerning the facial constitutionality of Health and Safety Code section 1418.8 as last amended. . . .

The challenged statute provides . . . as follows:

"§ 1418.8. Medical intervention requiring informed consent; resident lacking decision-making capacity; interdisciplinary team review

"(e) Where a resident of a skilled nursing facility or intermediate care facility has been prescribed a medical intervention by a physician and surgeon that requires informed consent and the physician has determined that the resident lacks capacity to make health care decisions and there is no person with legal authority to make those decisions on behalf of the resident, the facility shall, except as provided in subdivision *(h)*, conduct an interdisciplinary team review of the prescribed medical intervention prior to the administration of the medical intervention. The interdisciplinary team shall oversee the care of the resident utilizing a team approach to assessment and care planning and shall include the resident's attending physician, a registered professional nurse with responsibility for the resident, other appropriate staff in disciplines as determined by the resident's needs, and, where practicable, a patient representative, in accordance with applicable federal and state requirements. The review shall include all of the following:

"(1) A review of the physician's assessment of the resident's condition.

"(2) The reason for the proposed use of the medical intervention.

"(3) A discussion of the desires of the patient, where known. To determine the desires of the resident, the interdisciplinary team shall interview the patient, review the patient's medical records and consult with family members or friends, if any have been identified.

"(4) The type of medical intervention to be used in the resident's care, including its probable frequency and duration.

"(5) The probable impact on the resident's condition, with and without the use of the medical intervention.

"(6) Reasonable alternative medical interventions considered or utilized and reasons for their discontinuance or inappropriateness.

"(f) A patient representative may include a family member or friend of the resident who is unable to take full responsibility for the health care decisions of the resident, but has agreed to serve on the interdisciplinary team, or other person authorized by state or federal law.

"(g) The interdisciplinary team shall periodically evaluate the use of the prescribed medical intervention at least quarterly or upon a significant change in the resident's medical condition.

"(h) In case of an emergency, after obtaining a physician and surgeon's order as necessary, a skilled nursing or intermediate care facility may administer a medical intervention which requires informed consent prior to the facility convening an interdisciplinary team review."

. . .

II.   *DISCUSSION*

. . .

The Legislature was required to deal here with a very difficult and perplexing problem: how to provide nonemergency but necessary and appropriate medical treatment, frequently of an ongoing nature, to nursing home patients who lack capacity to consent thereto because of incompetence, and who have no surrogate or substitute decision maker with legal authority to consent for them. This was a legal conundrum of long standing; and although it has been held that the consent of the patient will be implied for emergency care, the question of the proper means of securing the consent of such incompetent patient for ongoing, medically necessary care, not rising to the level of an emergency, is one which is not fully addressed or satisfactorily answered by existing case law. This problem required an effective legislative solution which would allow timely medical treatment of incompetent nursing home patients on an ongoing basis, without the delay of two to six months frequently necessary to secure a ruling on a petition authorizing treatment under Probate Code section 3201. It is highly significant that section 1418.8, subdivision (e) requires a patient representative to be a member of the interdisciplinary team overseeing the patient's care, to consider the need for medical intervention from the patient's point of view. While there may be exigent circumstances in which the participation of such a representative is not practicable, due to temporary unavailability, illness, or similar causes, the Legislature clearly required the routine and ongoing participation of a patient representative in such medical care decisions to insure that nothing is overlooked from the patient's perspective.

. . .

A.   *Section 1418.8 Does Not Violate the Privacy Provisions of the California Constitution*

   1.   Recent Relevant Precedents

. . .

In *Hill v. National Collegiate Athletic Assn.* [865 P.2d 633 (1994)], our high court found no violation of the constitutional right of privacy from a nonconsensual drug testing program, including observation of urination, the medical testing of urine, and the exchange of confidential medical information attendant upon the administration of the drug testing, for persons participating in college athletic programs. The court advanced an analytical framework for deciding questions arising under this constitutional right of privacy, and found that a violation of the constitutional right of privacy is only established where three conditions are shown: "(1) a legally protected privacy interest; (2) a reasonable expectation of privacy in the circumstances; and (3) conduct by defendant constituting a serious invasion of privacy."

Further, the high court observed: "No community could function if every intrusion into the realm of private action, no matter how slight or trivial, gave rise to a cause of action for invasion of privacy.... Actionable invasions of privacy must be sufficiently serious in their nature, scope, and actual or potential impact to constitute *an egregious breach of the social norms underlying the privacy right.*"

. . .

In *Heller v. Norcal Mutual Ins. Co.* [876 P.2d 999 (1994)], our high court also found no violation of the constitutional right of privacy where the plaintiff's treating physician shared private medical information with an insurer, after the plaintiff-patient filed a medical malpractice action, even though the plaintiff-patient did not consent to the disclosure. Applying the *Hill* analysis, the court found the patient did not have a reasonable expectation of privacy under these circumstances, because information about her medical history would inevitably have to be disclosed in her malpractice action: . . .

In light of the *Hill* and *Heller* cases, decided after the trial court ruled in the case at bench, the scope of the state constitutional right of privacy has been considerably clarified. . . .

2. Privacy Rights

We apply the analytical framework stated in *Hill, supra,* to the claim that section 1418.8 is unconstitutional under the California Constitution's right of privacy. The *Hill* analysis requires us to assess section 1418.8 in terms of whether it will have an unconstitutional result because the following circumstances are present: "(1) a legally protected privacy interest; (2) a reasonable expectation of privacy in the circumstances; and (3) conduct . . . constituting a serious invasion of privacy."

a. Legally Protected Privacy Interest

As to the first of the three prongs of the *Hill* test, we conclude patients in nursing homes, like all other persons, certainly have a legally protected privacy interest in their own personal bodily autonomy and medical treatment, under the rubric of " 'autonomy privacy.' " "Autonomy privacy is also a concern of the Privacy Initiative [which added privacy as an enumerated right under article I, section 1 of the California Constitution]. The ballot arguments refer to the federal constitutional tradition of safeguarding certain intimate and personal decisions from government interference in the form of penal and regulatory laws. [Citation.] But they do not purport to create any unbridled right of personal freedom of action that may be vindicated in lawsuits against either government agencies or private persons or entities. [&] Whether established social norms . . . protect a specific personal decision from public or private intervention is to be determined from the usual sources of positive law governing the right to privacy—common law development, constitutional development, statutory enactment, and the ballot arguments accompanying the Privacy Initiative.''

We must stress in this context that we deal here with the privacy rights of persons who are initially determined by their physicians to be incompetent to make medical decisions or provide effective informed consent, and who are in need of medical intervention, according to the medical judgment of their treating physicians, yet have no surrogate who can provide a proxy for consent. Nothing said herein affects the rights of other persons who are competent to provide or withhold their consent, or who seek judicial intervention to uphold those rights.

Nor do any of the "usual sources of positive law" identified in *Hill, supra,* impose an absolute and inflexible right to refuse treatment for persons determined *not* to be competent, for obvious reasons; such a rule would lead to unacceptable neglect of the medical needs of incompetent persons. Neither the development of the common law, nor the statutory enactment in issue here, nor the ballot arguments in support of the adoption of the privacy right, purport to prevent medical professionals from administering necessary treatment in these circumstances. Thus, while the patients in issue here have a legally protected privacy interest, this interest is considerably attenuated by the fact they are determined by their physicians to be in need of medical care, yet incompetent to provide the necessary consent for that care. Under these circumstances, patients may also have an important interest in securing treatment, even though unable to provide consent, so as to avoid constant pain, injury, malnutrition, or physical decline. In sum, while there is certainly a legally protected privacy interest here, it is not an "unbridled right" which may be applied in isolation, regardless of the specific circumstances and pressing medical needs of these patients.

b. Reasonable Expectation of Privacy

Next, under the *Hill* analysis we must determine whether section 1418.8 would unconstitutionally interfere with the "reasonable expectation of privacy" of these particular nursing home patients. "Even when a legally cognizable privacy interest is present, other factors may affect a person's reasonable expectation of privacy." "In addition, customs, practices, and physical settings surrounding particular activities may create or inhibit reasonable expectations of privacy." "A 'reasonable' expectation of privacy is an objective entitlement founded on broadly based and widely accepted community norms."

In *Heller, supra,* our Supreme Court expanded on this point in the context of an alleged privacy violation resulting from the nonconsensual disclosure of the plaintiff's medical condition and other private information, after she brought a medical malpractice action. The high court found the plaintiff could not have had a reasonable expectation of privacy sufficient to establish a privacy violation, because the circumstances were such that her medical history would inevitably have been exposed during the litigation: "By placing her physical condition in issue in the ... litigation, plaintiff's expectation of privacy regarding that condition was substantially lowered by the very nature of the action." "Because the information would most likely have been discovered during the ordinary course of litigation, defendants' conduct in revealing information about plaintiff's treatment and physical condition does not violate the state constitutional guarantee against invasion of privacy as a matter of law.''

Here, as in *Heller,* the patient's reasonable expectation of privacy over private medical facts is considerably lessened by the circumstances in which this case arises. It is questionable if a person in need of medical care who is incompetent may ever have a *reasonable* expectation of privacy which would prevent timely medical intervention and treatment. Certainly it is inevitable that such persons residing in nursing homes, who are required to be under the care of a treating physician as a condition of admission. The patient's expectation of privacy is, accordingly, greatly lessened. Indeed, since the providing of necessary medical care to patients residing in nursing homes is the obvious and legitimate purpose of this care in general, it would be surprising to find that a statute passed by the Legislature in furtherance of this purpose was unconstitutional as a privacy violation. . . .

The social norms affecting persons residing in nursing homes are primarily concerned with providing sustenance, shelter, and necessary medical care in a residential setting. While persons residing in nursing homes obviously have a reasonable expectation of privacy relating to aspects of their lives which are not connected to the medical purposes of the facility, it can hardly be doubted that the reasonable expectation of privacy as it relates to medical care must be diminished. Just as persons in need of medical care must sometimes disrobe for an examination, or expose their bodies to observation by medical personnel during needed surgery, certain particular social norms apply to the provision of medical care to patients of nursing homes who are incompetent, in the professional opinion of their physicians. Our currently prevailing social norms obviously find acceptable, in the context of needed medical treatment, much which would otherwise be clearly unacceptable. Here the Legislature, as a reflection of those social norms, enacted section 1418.8 in order to insure provision of prompt ongoing medical care to incompetent persons in need of that care. This clearly accords with the reasonable expectation of patients: that if they became incompetent they will continue to receive their necessary medical care on a timely basis. The particular nature of this setting, in which nursing homes must continue to provide necessary care to incompetent resident patients on an ongoing and timely basis, indicates section 1418.8 would not unconstitutionally violate reasonable expectations of privacy.

c. Seriousness of the Invasion of Privacy

The third factor specified by the *Hill* court was the seriousness of the invasion of privacy rights which would result from the challenged conduct. Once again, consideration of this factor does not support a finding of violation of the constitutional privacy right.

Considered in the abstract, a serious invasion of privacy would seem to result from the provision of medical treatment on a nonconsensual basis. However, as in *Heller, supra,* the focus cannot be placed in isolation on the fact that medical care is in issue; medical care inevitably implicates the autonomy of the body and concomitant privacy questions. Indeed, as in

Hill, supra, we cannot focus solely on the fact that medical information or personal autonomy is at issue, without also relating this fact to the circumstances in which the case arises in order to decide the seriousness of the privacy invasion in question. Rather, in deciding the question of the seriousness of the invasion on the authority of *Hill,* we must also focus on the fact that we deal here with persons who, based upon expert medical judgment, are incompetent to provide or withhold consent, and in need of medical care which would ordinarily require such consent. It is inevitable that the medical condition and private medical facts of such patients will be in issue, whether the decision to treat or not to treat these persons is made by a conservator of the person, by a court under Probate Code section 3201, or by a medical interdisciplinary team under section 1418.8. It is very hard to see how the invasion of privacy is more serious when the issue is decided by a medical team, as opposed to a conservator, the holder (frequently a layman) of a patient's durable power of attorney, or a court relying on expert medical reports or testimony, since a decision by some outside person, even if only by default, will "inevitably" be made under the circumstances.

In sum, consideration of the three factors specified by the analysis in *Hill, supra,* does not support the claim that the right of privacy attaches here so as to invalidate section 1418.8. . . .

B. *Section 1418.8 Does Not Violate the Due Process Provisions of the California Constitution or the Federal Constitution.*

Petitioner next contends that section 1418.8 denies due process of law to patients of nursing homes who lack capacity to make decisions regarding their health care where there is no person with legal authority to make such decisions for them.

Petitioner's rationale is based on two interrelated contentions that the procedures established by the Legislature in such circumstances deny procedural due process to the resident patients of such nursing homes. They are:

First, that section 1418.8 permits an initial *nonjudicial* determination of the patient's incompetence by a physician or surgeon, preceding the subsequent medical intervention decision.

Second, that section 1418.8 unconstitutionally authorizes medical intervention in the case of such a patient without notice, hearing before an independent decision maker, testimony, cross-examination, a written statement by the fact finder, and a surrogate for the patient "whose only allegiances are to the desires or best interests of the patient, rather than to the provider."

. . .

1.   Determination of Incompetency by Physician

The amended statute sets forth a clear test for determination by the physician of a resident patient's capacity to make decisions concerning health care: A patient lacks that capacity if "unable to understand the nature and consequences of the proposed medical intervention, including its risks and benefits, or . . . unable to express a preference regarding the intervention.'' In making this capacity determination, the resident patient's physician must: (1) interview the patient, (2) review the patient's medical records, (3) consult with nursing home staff as appropriate, (4) consult with family members and friends of the patient if such have been identified.

It is common knowledge that the determinate evidentiary factor in court hearings, both civil and criminal, by which the mental capacity of human beings is decided, is the expressed expert views of the medical profession. Petitioner ... argues that a hypothetical possibility exists, which this record does not support, that a physician may misrepresent the mental capacity of a nursing home patient to consent to medical intervention in order to impose that treatment for the financial gain of the physician or an associated institution.

Petitioner then urges that due process, allegedly lacking under her hypothetical proposition, requires that adversarial hearings must always be held after a physician concludes, following the protocol the Legislature has painfully and carefully constructed, a patient with no surrogate lacks capacity to consent to medical intervention.

Capacity determination, which must be decided under section 1418.8 *before* required medical intervention is activated thereunder on potentially thousands of elderly nursing home patients in this state, would thereby be delayed, as would such treatment. No case cited to us, or disclosed by our independent research, has suggested that procedural due process requires postponement of medical intervention for a nursing home patient who is found by a physician to lack capacity to consent thereto until, in each case, the medical capacity issue is separately decided in some adversarial hearing.

To so rule would not only be cumbersome to thousands of these patients and to the courts, it would presume the bias if not dishonesty of physicians opining as to the patient's capacity. We emphatically decline to adopt that presumption. Prompt and effective medical treatment of these unfortunate citizens would be seriously jeopardized.

We believe our elected Legislature is, more than any other single institution, better able to reflect a proper balance of social values at stake in this significant and difficult problem, and that it has done so in enacting section 1418.8. We reject adoption of petitioner's suggestion on the rationale proposed. To do otherwise would negate the Legislature's reforming work on a speculative basis, one absolutely contrary to the ethical standards of the medical profession. Nursing home patients are not denied due process because their incapacity to give consent to medical intervention is initially determined by a physician and surgeon, rather than by a judicial or quasi-judicial hearing.

This is particularly true here in view of the provisions of section 1418.8, subdivision (j), *ante.* As we observe in part II.B.2. and footnote 7, *post,* of this opinion, due process is assured because there is also the right to secure judicial review of a physician's determination of the patient's *incapacity* to give informed consent to that medical intervention, which is the predicate condition for the application of section 1418.8.

2. Patient Representative

Petitioner also theorizes that section 1418.8 is unconstitutional because, although the statute requires that a patient representative serve on the interdisciplinary review team which provides the surrogate consent for any medical procedure, there may be some person in a nursing home who lacks any patient representative to serve on the interdisciplinary review team. However, the statutory definition of a patient representative in section 1418.8 is so broad that it is hard to see how this could be true. Even if a patient lacks a spouse and has no surviving next of kin, and even if there is no conservator or person holding a power of attorney, and no public agency such as the ombudsman or public guardian willing to serve in this capacity, the statute still allows any "friend" of the patient to serve in this capacity and represent the patient's interests. This would include patient advocates, legal counsel, and all other persons having an interest in the welfare of the patient. It appears almost impossible to conceive of a patient who could not have a patient representative, under this standard. Certainly petitioner has not presented any convincing proof to the contrary. Moreover, as our Supreme Court observed in *County of Nevada v. MacMillen* (1974) 522 P.2d 1345, " 'We cannot, and need not in this proceeding, pass upon all hypothetical situations and tenuous circumstances which may be presented by counsel. While we recognize that a valid statute may be unconstitutionally applied, the precise limitations to be placed on the words in question can best be specified when actual cases requiring such interpretation are presented. [Citation.]' " (*Quoting* from *Stein v. Howlett* (1972) 289 N.E.2d 409, 415.)

Moreover, due process does not require that medical decisions be made in the first instance by lawyers and judges. As the federal Supreme Court observed in *Parham, supra,* 442 U.S. at pp. 607–608, "[D]ue process is not violated by use of informal, traditional medical investigative techniques.... The mode and procedure of medical diagnostic procedures is not the business of judges." As it also observed, the interposition of judicial norms would be of questionable value where the decision being made is, at bottom, simply a medical diagnosis concerning competency and the need for treatment: "[W]e do not accept the notion that the shortcomings of specialists can always be avoided by shifting the decision from a trained specialist using the traditional tools of medical science to an untrained judge or administrative hearing officer after a judicial-type hearing. Even after a hearing, the nonspecialist decisionmaker must make a medical-psychiatric decision. Common human experience and scholarly opinions suggest that the supposed protections of an adversary proceeding to determine the appropriateness of medical decisions ... may well be more illusory than real."

More critically, any due process argument fails because it does not take into account the provision of subdivision (j) of section 1418.8, which provides: "Nothing in this section shall in any way affect the right of a resident of a skilled nursing facility or intermediate care facility for whom medical intervention has been prescribed, ordered, or administered pursuant to this section to seek appropriate judicial relief to review the decision to provide the medical intervention." Thus, affected persons or their representatives, such as a friend, public guardian, or other concerned person or entity, are afforded an avenue by which they may obtain "appropriate judicial relief," including a temporary restraining order and other injunctive relief prior to treatment, thereby satisfying due process principles.

Here we do not deal with involuntary commitment to a mental hospital, with all the attendant consequences of such a commitment, which would naturally trigger a need for rather extensive due process protections. Instead, we deal with a statutory procedure by which the equivalent of informed consent may be provided, by a patient representative if practicable, and in exigent circumstances by health professionals, so as to allow necessary medical treatment to be afforded to already admitted patients of nursing homes on a routine, ongoing basis. This is consistent with due process, which does not require a judicial officer to make first-line determinations regarding medical treatments.

The opportunity to seek a decision by a neutral decision maker as to any particular medical intervention also nullifies petitioner's objection that section 1418.8 violates due process. Even though the statute allows the patient's physician to determine *initially* whether the patient lacks the capacity to make medical decisions, and the interdisciplinary team assessing the reasons for the treatment under section 1418.8 would also often include the physician who had initially prescribed the treatment under review, this initial decision is not final. Parties seeking to object to such a decision, including the patient, the patient's representative, or a public agency which supervises or investigates the care provided by nursing homes, still retain full access to a neutral determination by a court under subdivision (j) of section 1418.8. This comports with due process principles.

Section 1418.8 in its subdivision (f) further contemplates compliance with applicable federal and state requirements designed to protect nursing home patients, such as the standards set and regulations promulgated under 42 United States Code section 1395i–3 and 42 Code of Federal Regulations, section 483.1 *et seq.*, which both limit and supplement the interdisciplinary team decisionmaking approach by granting certain rights and safeguards to affected residents. In addition, section 1418.8 by its own terms applies only to the relatively nonintrusive and routine, ongoing medical intervention which may be afforded by physicians in nursing homes; it does not purport to grant blanket authority for more severe medical interventions such as medically necessary, one-time procedures which would be carried out at a hospital or other acute care facility, as to which compliance with Probate Code section 3200 *et seq.* would still be required, except in emergency situations. Finally, the protections of state law which apply to any particular medical intervention or procedure would continue to apply. Consideration of these numerous statutory safeguards undermines the claim that section 1418.8 violates due process standards.

"In light of the foregoing discussion the due process challenge is without merit." Considering section 1418.8 in its totality, including the right to seek judicial relief and the other safeguards granted not only by section 1418.8 itself but also in the other state and federal regulatory standards referenced therein, we find the statute affords due process under both the state and federal Constitutions.

.   .   .

III. *DISPOSITION*

The judgment is reversed, and the matter is remanded to the trial court with directions to enter a new order denying the petition. Each party shall bear its own costs.

■ KING and HANING, JJ., concur.

NOTE

The California Health and Safety Code was amended in 1996 to provide closer review of treatments involving physical or chemical restraints. The Code now provides: "If the emergency results in the application of physical or chemical restraints, the interdisciplinary team shall meet within one week of the emergency for an evaluation of the medical intervention." CALIFORNIA HEALTH & SAFETY CODE § 1418.8 (West 2004).

In re Seiferth

Court of Appeals of New York, 1955.
309 N.Y. 80, 127 N.E.2d 820.

■ VAN VOORHIS, J.

This is a case involving a fourteen-year-old boy with cleft palate and harelip, whose father holds strong convictions with which the boy has become imbued against medicine and surgery. This proceeding has been instituted by the deputy commissioner of the Erie County Health Department on petition to the Children's Court to have Martin declared a neglected child, and to have his custody transferred from his parents to the Commissioner of Social Welfare of Erie County for the purpose of consenting to such medical, surgical and dental services as may be necessary to rectify his condition. The medical testimony is to the effect that such cases are almost always given surgical treatment at an earlier age, and the older the patient is the less favorable are likely to be the results according to experience. The surgery recommended by the plastic surgeon called for petitioner consists of three operations: (1) repair of the harelip by bringing the split together; (2) closing the cleft or split in the rear of the palate, the boy being already too late in life to have the front part mended by surgery; and (3) repairing the front part of the palate by dental appliances. The only risk of mortality is the negligible one due to the use of anesthesia. These operations would be spaced a few months apart and six months would be expected to complete the work, two years at the outside in case of difficulty. Petitioner's plastic surgeon declined to be precise about how detrimental it would be to the prognosis to defer this work for several years. He said: "I do not think it is emergent, that is has to be done this month or next month, but every year that goes is important to this child, yes." A year and a half has already elapsed since this testimony was taken in December, 1953.

Even after the operation, Martin will not be able to talk normally, at least not without going to a school for an extended period for concentrated speech therapy. There are certain phases of a child's life when the importance of these defects becomes of greater significance. The first is past, when children enter grade school, the next is the period of adolescence, particularly toward the close of adolescence when social interests arise in secondary school. Concerning this last, petitioner's plastic surgeon stated: "That is an extremely important period of time. That child is approaching that age where it is very important that correction, that it is very significant that correction made at this time could probably put him in a great deal better position to enter that period of life than would otherwise. Another thing which is difficult is that we have very excellent speech facilities at the Buffalo Public Schools through grade level. At secondary school level and in higher age groups speech training facilities are less satisfactory, so that it is important that it be done at this age. However, the most important thing of all is this gradually progressive [sic] with time. The earlier done, the better results. Normally the lip is repaired in early infancy, one to three years of age. Speech training would begin at school or earlier. Every year lost has been that much more lost to the boy. Each year lost continues to be lost. The time to repair is not too early." He testified that in twenty years of plastic surgery he had never encountered a child with this boy's defects who had not been operated upon at his age. Nevertheless, he testified that such an operation can be performed "from the time the child is born until he dies." In this doctor's view, the consideration bulked larger than the quality of postoperative results, that the boys increasing social contacts required that he be made to look and to speak normally as he approached adolescence.

Everyone testified that the boy is likeable, he has a newspaper route, and his marks in school were all over 90 during the last year. However, his father did testify that recently the boy had withdrawn a little more from his fellows, although he said that "As soon as anyone contacts Martin, he is so likeable nobody is tempted to ridicule him. . . . Through his pleasantness he overcomes it."

The father testified that "If the child decides on an operation, I shall not be opposed", and that "I want to say in a few years the child should decide for himself ... whether to have the operation or not." The father believes in mental healing by letting "the forces of the universe work on the body", although he denied that this is an established religion of any kind stating that it is purely his own philosophy and that "it is not classified as religion." There is no doubt, however, that the father is strong minded about this, and has inculcated a distrust and dread of surgery in the boy since childhood.

The Erie County Children's Court Judge caused the various surgical procedures to be explained to Martin by competent and qualified practitioners in the field of plastic surgery and orthodontia. Photographs of other children who had undergone similar remedial surgery were exhibited to him showing their condition both before and after treatment. He was also taken to the speech correction school where he heard the reproduction of his own voice and speech, as well as records depicting various stages of progress of other children. He met other children of his own age, talked to them and attended class in speech correction. Both the boy and the father were given opportunity to ask questions, which they did freely not only of the professional staff but of the different children.

On February 11, 1954, Martin, his father and attorney met after these demonstrations in Judge Wylegala's chambers. Judge Wylegala wrote in his opinion that Martin "was very much pleased with what was shown him, but had come to the conclusion that he should try for some time longer to close the cleft palate and the split lip himself through 'natural forces.'" After stating that an order for surgery would have been granted without hesitation if this proceeding had been instituted before this child acquired convictions of his own, Judge Wylegala summed up his conclusions as follows: "After duly deliberating upon the psychological effect of surgery upon this mature, intelligent boy, schooled as he has been for all of his young years in the existence of 'forces of nature' and his fear of surgery upon the human body, I have come to the conclusion that no order should be made at this time compelling the child to submit to surgery. His condition is not emergent and there is no serious threat to his health or life. He has time until he becomes 21 years of age to apply for financial assistance under County and State aid to physically handicapped children to have the corrections made. This has also been explained to him after he made known his decision to me." The petition accordingly was dismissed.

The Appellate Division, Fourth Department, reversed by a divided court, and granted the petition requiring Martin Seiferth to submit to surgery.

As everyone agrees, there are important considerations both ways. The Children's Court has power in drastic situations to direct the operation over the objection of parents. Nevertheless, there is no present emergency, time is less of the essence than it was a few years ago insofar as concerns the physical prognosis, and we are impressed by the circumstance that in order to benefit from the operation upon the cleft palate, it will almost certainly be necessary to enlist Martin's co-operation in developing normal speech patterns through a lengthy course in concentrated speech therapy. It will be almost impossible to secure his co-operation if he continues to believe, as he does now, that it will be necessary "to remedy the surgeon's distortion first and then go back to the primary task of healing the body." This is an aspect of the problem with which petitioner's plastic surgeon did not especially concern himself, for he did not attempt to view the case from the psychological view point of this misguided youth. Upon the other hand, the Children's Court Judge, who saw and heard the witnesses, and arranged the conferences for the boy and his father which have been mentioned, appears to have been keenly aware of this aspect of the situation, and to have concluded that less would be lost by permitting the lapse of several more years, when the boy may make his own decision to submit to plastic surgery, than might be sacrificed if he were compelled to undergo it now against his sincere and frightened antagonism. One cannot be certain of being right under these circumstances, but this appears to be a situation where the discretion of the trier of the facts should be preferred to that of the Appellate Division. Harrington v. Harrington, 48 N.E.2d 290.

The order of the Appellate Division should be reversed and that of the Children's Court reinstated dismissing the petition, without prejudice to renew the application if circumstances warrant.

■ FULD, J., dissenting.

Every child has a right, so far as is possible, to lead a normal life and, if his parents, through viciousness or ignorance, act in such a way as to endanger that right, the courts should, as the legislature has provided, act on his behalf. Such is the case before us.

The boy Martin, twelve years old when this proceeding was begun, fourteen now, has been neglected in the most egregious way. He is afflicted with a massive harelip and cleft palate which not only grievously detract from his appearance but seriously impede his chances for a useful and productive life. Although medical opinion is agreed that the condition can be remedied by surgery, that it should be performed as soon as possible and that the risk involved is negligible, the father has refused to consent to the essential operation. His reason—which is, as the Appellate Division found, entirely unsubstantial—was that he relies on "forces in the universe" which will enable the child to cure himself of his own accord. He might consent to the operation, he said, if the boy "in a few years" should favor one.

It is quite true that the child's physical life is not at peril—as would be the situation if he had an infected appendix or a growth on the brain—but it may not be questioned, to quote from the opinion below, "What is in danger is his chance for a normal, useful life." Judge Van Voorhis does not, I am sure, take issue with that, but he feels that the boy will benefit, to a greater extent, from the operation if he enters the hospital with a mind favorably disposed to surgery. Therefore he counsels delay, on the *chance*— and that is all it is—on the *chance* that at some future time the boy may make his own decision to submit to plastic surgery.

It would, of course, be preferable if the boy were to accede to the operation, and I am willing to assume that, if he acquiesces, he will the more easily and quickly react to the postoperative speech therapy. However, there is no assurance that he will, either next year, in five years or six, give his consent. Quite obviously, he is greatly influenced by his father, quite plainly a victim of the latter's unfortunate delusions. And, beyond that, it must be borne in mind that there is little if any risk involved in the surgery and that, as time goes on, the operation becomes more difficult.

Be that as it may, though, it is the court which has a duty to perform, Children's Court Act, § 24, and it should not seek to avoid that duty by foisting upon the boy the ultimate decision to be made. Neither by statute nor decision is the child's consent necessary or material, and we should not permit his refusal to agree, his failure to co-operate, to ruin his life and any chance for a normal, happy existence; normalcy and happiness, difficult of attainment under the most propitious conditions, will unquestionably be impossible if the disfigurement is not corrected.

Moreover, it is the fact, and a vital one, that this is a proceeding brought to determine whether the parents are neglecting the child by refusing and failing to provide him with necessary surgical, medical and dental service, Children's Court Act, § 2, subd. 4, cl. (e). Whether the child condones the neglect, whether he is willing to let his parents do as they choose, surely cannot be operative on the question as to whether or not they are guilty of neglect. They are not interested or concerned with whether he does nor does not want the essential operation. They have arbitrarily taken the position that there is to be no surgery. What these parents are doing, by their failure to provide for an operation, however well-intentioned, is far worse than beating the child or denying him food or clothing. To the boy, and his future, it makes no difference that it may be ignorance rather than viciousness that will perpetuate his unfortunate condition. If parents are actually mistreating or neglecting a child, the circumstance that he may not mind it cannot alter the fact that they are guilty of neglect and it cannot render their conduct permissible.

The welfare and interests of a child are at stake. A court should not place upon his shoulders one of the most momentous and far-reaching decisions of his life. The court should make the decision, as the statute contemplates, and leave to the good sense and sound judgment of the public authorities the job of preparing the boy for the operation and of getting him as adjusted to it as possible. We should not put off decision in the hope and on the chance that the child may change his mind and submit at some future time to the operation.

The order of the Appellate Division should be affirmed.

Sell v. United States

The Supreme Court of the United States, 2003.
539 U.S. 166, 123 S.Ct. 2174, 156 L.Ed.2d 197.

■ JUSTICE BREYER delivered the opinion of the Court.

The question presented is whether the Constitution permits the Government to administer antipsychotic drugs involuntarily to a mentally ill criminal defendant—in order to render that defendant competent to stand trial for serious, but nonviolent, crimes.

I.

A.

Petitioner Charles Sell, once a practicing dentist, has a long and unfortunate history of mental illness. In September 1982, after telling doctors that the gold he used for fillings had been contaminated by communists, Sell was hospitalized, treated with antipsychotic medication, and subsequently discharged. In June 1984, Sell called the police to say that a leopard was outside his office boarding a bus, and he then asked the police to shoot him. Sell was again hospitalized and subsequently released. On various occasions, he complained that public officials, for example, a State Governor and a police chief, were trying to kill him. In April 1997, he told law enforcement personnel that he "spoke to God last night," and that "God told me every [Federal Bureau of Investigation] person I kill, a soul will be saved."

In May 1997, the Government charged Sell with submitting fictitious insurance claims for payment. *See* 18 U.S.C. § 1035(a)(2). A Federal Magistrate Judge (Magistrate), after ordering a psychiatric examination, found Sell "currently competent," but noted that Sell might experience "a psychotic episode" in the future. The judge released Sell on bail. A grand jury later produced a superseding indictment charging Sell and his wife with 56 counts of mail fraud, 6 counts of Medicaid fraud, and 1 count of money laundering.

In early 1998, the Government claimed that Sell had sought to intimidate a witness. The Magistrate held a bail revocation hearing. Sell's behavior at his initial appearance was, in the judge's words, " 'totally out of control,' " involving "screaming and shouting," the use of "personal insults" and "racial epithets," and spitting "in the judge's face." A psychiatrist reported that Sell could not sleep because he expected the FBI to " 'come busting through the door,' " and concluded that Sell's condition had worsened. After considering that report and other testimony, the Magistrate revoked Sell's bail.

In April 1998, the grand jury issued a new indictment charging Sell with attempting to murder the FBI agent who had arrested him and a former employee who planned to testify against him in the fraud case. The attempted murder and fraud cases were joined for trial.

In early 1999, Sell asked the Magistrate to reconsider his competence to stand trial. The Magistrate sent Sell to the United States Medical Center for Federal Prisoners at Springfield, Missouri, for examination. Subsequently the Magistrate found that Sell was "mentally incompetent to stand trial." He ordered Sell to "be hospitalized for treatment" at the Medical Center for up to four months, "to determine whether there was a substantial probability that [Sell] would attain the capacity to allow his trial to proceed."

Two months later, Medical Center staff recommended that Sell take antipsychotic medication. Sell refused to do so. The staff sought permission to administer the medication against Sell's will. That effort is the subject of the present proceedings.

B.

We here review the last of five hierarchically ordered lower court and Medical Center determinations. First, in June 1999, Medical Center staff sought permission from institutional authorities to administer antipsychotic drugs to Sell involuntarily. A reviewing psychiatrist held a hearing and considered Sell's prior history; Sell's current persecutional beliefs (for example, that Government officials were trying to suppress his knowledge about events in Waco, Texas, and had sent him to Alaska to silence him); staff medical opinions (for example, that "Sell's symptoms point to a diagnosis of Delusional Disorder but ... there well may be an underlying Schizophrenic Process"); staff medical concerns (for example, about "the persistence of Dr. Sell's belief that the Courts, FBI, and federal government in general are against him"); an outside medical expert's opinion (that Sell suffered only from delusional disorder, which, in that expert's view, "medication rarely helps"); and Sell's own views, as well as those of other laypersons who know him (to the effect that he did not suffer from a serious mental illness).

The reviewing psychiatrist then authorized involuntary administration of the drugs, both (1) because Sell was "mentally ill and dangerous, and medication is necessary to treat the mental illness," and (2) so that Sell would "become competent for trial." The reviewing psychiatrist added that he considered Sell "dangerous based on threats and delusions if outside, but not necessarily in[side] prison" and that Sell was "[a]ble to function" in prison in the "open population."

Second, the Medical Center administratively reviewed the determination of its reviewing psychiatrist. A Bureau of Prisons official considered the evidence that had been presented at the initial hearing, referred to Sell's delusions, noted differences of professional opinion as to proper classification and treatment, and concluded that antipsychotic medication represents the medical intervention "most likely" to "ameliorate" Sell's symptoms; that other "less restrictive interventions" are "unlikely" to work; and that Sell's "pervasive belief" that he was "being targeted for nefarious actions by various governmental . . . parties," along with the "current charges of conspiracy to commit murder," made Sell "a potential risk to the safety of one or more others in the community." The reviewing official "upheld" the "hearing officer's decision that [Sell] would benefit from the utilization of anti-psychotic medication."

Third, in July 1999, Sell filed a court motion contesting the Medical Center's right involuntarily to administer antipsychotic drugs. In September 1999, the Federal Magistrate who had ordered Sell sent to the Medical Center held a hearing. The evidence introduced at the hearing for the most part replicated the evidence introduced at the administrative hearing, with two exceptions. First, the witnesses explored the question of the medication's effectiveness more thoroughly. Second, Medical Center doctors testified about an incident that took place at the Medical Center *after* the administrative proceedings were completed. In July 1999, Sell had approached one of the Medical Center's nurses, suggested that he was in love with her, criticized her for having nothing to do with him, and, when told that his behavior was inappropriate, added " 'I can't help it.' " He subsequently made remarks or acted in ways indicating that this kind of conduct would continue. The Medical Center doctors testified that, given Sell's prior behavior, diagnosis, and current beliefs, boundary-breaching incidents of this sort were not harmless and, when coupled with Sell's inability or unwillingness to desist, indicated that he was a safety risk even within the institution. They added that he had been moved to a locked cell.

In August 2000, the Magistrate found that "the government has made a substantial and very strong showing that Dr. Sell is a danger to himself and others at the institution in which he is currently incarcerated"; that "the government has shown that anti-psychotic medication is the only way to render him less dangerous"; that newer drugs and/or changing drugs will "ameliorat[e]" any "serious side effects"; that "the benefits to Dr. Sell . . . far outweigh any risks"; and that "there is a substantial probability that" the drugs will "retur[n]" Sell "to competency." The Magistrate concluded that "the government has shown in as strong a manner as possible, that anti-psychotic medications are the only way to render the defendant not dangerous and competent to stand trial." The Magistrate issued an order authorizing the involuntary administration of antipsychotic drugs to Sell . . . but stayed that order to allow Sell to appeal the matter to the Federal District Court. . . .

Fourth, the District Court reviewed the record and, in April 2001, issued an opinion. The court addressed the Magistrate's finding "that defendant presents a danger to himself or others sufficient" to warrant involuntary administration of antipsychotic drugs. After noting that Sell subsequently had "been returned to an open ward," the District Court held the Magistrate's "dangerousness" finding "clearly erroneous." The court limited its determination to Sell's "dangerousness *at this time* to himself and to those around him *in his institutional context.*"

Nonetheless, the District Court *affirmed* the Magistrate's order permitting Sell's involuntary medication. The court wrote that "anti-psychotic drugs are medically appropriate," that "they represent the only viable hope of rendering defendant competent to stand trial," and that "administration of such drugs appears necessary to serve the government's compelling interest in obtaining an adjudication of defendant's guilt or innocence of numerous and serious charges" (including fraud and attempted murder). The court added that it was "premature" to consider whether "the effects of medication might prejudice [Sell's] defense at trial." The Government and Sell both appealed.

Fifth, in March 2002, a divided panel of the Court of Appeals affirmed the District Court's judgment. 282 F.3d 560 (CA8 2002). The majority affirmed the District Court's determination that Sell was not dangerous. The majority noted that, according to the District Court, Sell's behavior at the Medical Center "amounted at most to an 'inappropriate familiarity and even infatuation' with a nurse." The Court of Appeals agreed, "[u]pon review," that "the evidence does not support a finding that Sell posed a danger to himself or others at the Medical Center."

The Court of Appeals also affirmed the District Court's order requiring medication in order to render Sell competent to stand trial. Focusing solely on the serious fraud charges, the panel majority concluded that the "government has an essential interest in bringing a defendant to trial." It added that the District Court "correctly concluded that there were no less intrusive means." After reviewing the conflicting views of the experts . . . the panel majority found antipsychotic drug treatment "medically appropriate" for Sell. . . . It added that the "medical evidence presented indicated a reasonable probability that Sell will fairly be able to participate in his trial." One member of the panel dissented primarily on the ground that the fraud and money laundering charges were "not serious enough to warrant the forced medication of the defendant."

. . .

III.

We turn now to the basic question presented: Does forced administration of antipsychotic drugs to render Sell competent to stand trial unconstitutionally deprive him of his "liberty" to reject medical treatment? U.S. Const., Amdt. 5 (Federal Government may not "depriv[e]" any person of "liberty ... without due process of law"). Two prior precedents, *Washington v. Harper*, 494 U.S. 210 (1990), and *Riggins v. Nevada*, 504 U.S. 127 (1992), set forth the framework for determining the legal answer.

In *Harper*, this Court recognized that an individual has a "significant" constitutionally protected "liberty interest" in "avoiding the unwanted administration of antipsychotic drugs." The Court considered a state law authorizing forced administration of those drugs "to inmates who are ... gravely disabled or represent a significant danger to themselves or others." The State had established "by a medical finding" that Harper, a mentally ill prison inmate, had "a mental disorder ... which is likely to cause harm if not treated." The treatment decision had been made "by a psychiatrist," it had been approved by "a reviewing psychiatrist," and it "ordered" medication only because that was "in the prisoner's medical interests, given the legitimate needs of his institutional confinement."

The Court found that the State's interest in administering medication was "legitima[te]" and "importan[t]," ... and it held that "the Due Process Clause permits the State to treat a prison inmate who has a serious mental illness with antipsychotic drugs against his will, if the inmate is dangerous to himself or others and the treatment is in the inmate's medical interest." The Court concluded that, in the circumstances, the state law authorizing involuntary treatment amounted to a constitutionally permissible "accommodation between an inmate's liberty interest in avoiding the forced administration of antipsychotic drugs and the State's interests in providing appropriate medical treatment to reduce the danger that an inmate suffering from a serious mental disorder represents to himself or others."

In *Riggins*, the Court repeated that an individual has a constitutionally protected liberty "interest in avoiding involuntary administration of antipsychotic drugs"—an interest that only an "essential" or "overriding" state interest might overcome. The Court suggested that, in principle, forced medication in order to render a defendant competent to stand trial for murder was constitutionally permissible. The Court, citing *Harper*, noted that the State "would have satisfied due process if the prosecution had demonstrated ... that treatment with antipsychotic medication was medically appropriate and, considering less intrusive alternatives, essential for the sake of Riggins' *own safety or the safety of others*." 504 U.S., at 135 (emphasis added). And it said that the State "*[s]imilarly* ... might have been able to justify medically appropriate, involuntary treatment with the drug by establishing that it could not obtain an adjudication of Riggins' guilt or innocence" of the murder charge "by using less intrusive means." *Ibid.* (emphasis added). Because the trial court had permitted forced medication of Riggins without taking account of his "liberty interest," with a consequent possibility of trial prejudice, the Court reversed Riggins' conviction and remanded for further proceedings. Justice KENNEDY, concurring in the judgment, emphasized that antipsychotic drugs might have side effects that would interfere with the defendant's ability to receive a fair trial. *Id.*, at 145 (finding forced medication likely justified only where State shows drugs would not significantly affect defendant's "behavior and demeanor").

These two cases, *Harper* and *Riggins*, indicate that the Constitution permits the Government involuntarily to administer antipsychotic drugs to a mentally ill defendant facing serious criminal charges in order to render that defendant competent to stand trial, but only if the treatment is medically appropriate, is substantially unlikely to have side effects that may undermine the fairness of the trial, and, taking account of less intrusive alternatives, is necessary significantly to further important governmental trial-related interests.

This standard will permit involuntary administration of drugs solely for trial competence purposes in certain instances. But those instances may be rare. That is because the standard says or fairly implies the following:

First, a court must find that *important* governmental interests are at stake. The Government's interest in bringing to trial an individual accused of a serious crime is important. That is so whether the offense is a serious crime against the person or a serious crime against property. In both instances the Government seeks to protect through application of the criminal law the basic human need for security. *See Riggins, supra,* at 135–136 (" '[P]ower to bring an accused to trial is fundamental to a scheme of 'ordered liberty' and prerequisite to social justice and peace' " (*quoting* Illinois v. Allen, 397 U.S. 337, 347 (1970) (Brennan, J., concurring)).

Courts, however, must consider the facts of the individual case in evaluating the Government's interest in prosecution. Special circumstances may lessen the importance of that interest. The defendant's failure to take drugs voluntarily, for example, may mean lengthy confinement in an institution for the mentally ill—and that would diminish the risks that ordinarily attach to freeing without punishment one who has committed a serious crime. We do not mean to suggest that civil commitment is a substitute for a criminal trial. The Government has a substantial interest in timely prosecution. And it may be difficult or impossible to try a defendant who regains competence after years of commitment during which memories may fade and evidence may be lost. The potential for future confinement affects, but does not totally undermine, the strength of the need for prosecution. The same is true of the possibility that the defendant has already been confined for a significant amount of time (for which he would receive credit toward any sentence ultimately imposed, *see* 18 U.S.C. § 3585(b)). Moreover, the Government has a concomitant, constitutionally essential interest in assuring that the defendant's trial is a fair one.

Second, the court must conclude that involuntary medication will *significantly further* those concomitant state interests. It must find that administration of the drugs is substantially likely to render the defendant competent to stand trial. At the same time, it must find that administration of the drugs is substantially unlikely to have side effects that will interfere significantly with the defendant's ability to assist counsel in conducting a trial defense, thereby rendering the trial unfair. *See Riggins, supra,* at 142–145 (Kennedy, J., concurring in judgment).

Third, the court must conclude that involuntary medication is *necessary* to further those interests. The court must find that any alternative, less intrusive treatments are unlikely to achieve substantially the same results. *Cf.* Brief for American Psychological Association as *Amicus Curiae* 10–14 (nondrug therapies may be effective in restoring psychotic defendants to competence); *but cf.* Brief for American Psychiatric Association et al. as *Amici Curiae* 13–22 (alternative treatments for psychosis commonly not as effective as medication). And the court must consider less intrusive means for administering the drugs, *e.g.*, a court order to the defendant backed by the contempt power, before considering more intrusive methods.

Fourth, as we have said, the court must conclude that administration of the drugs is *medically appropriate*, *i.e.*, in the patient's best medical interest in light of his medical condition. The specific kinds of drugs at issue may matter here as elsewhere. Different kinds of antipsychotic drugs may produce different side effects and enjoy different levels of success.

We emphasize that the court applying these standards is seeking to determine whether involuntary administration of drugs is necessary significantly to further a particular governmental interest, namely, the interest in rendering the defendant *competent to stand trial*. A court need not consider whether to allow forced medication for that kind of purpose, if forced medication is warranted for a *different* purpose, such as the purposes set out in *Harper* related to the individual's dangerousness, or purposes related to the individual's own interests where refusal to take drugs puts his health gravely at risk. 494 U.S., at 225–226. There are often strong reasons for a court to determine whether forced administration of drugs can be justified on these alternative grounds *before* turning to the trial competence question.

For one thing, the inquiry into whether medication is permissible, say, to render an individual nondangerous is usually more "objective and manageable" than the inquiry into whether medication is permissible to render a defendant competent. *Riggins*, 504 U.S., at 140 (KENNEDY, J., concurring in judgment). The medical experts may find it easier to provide an informed opinion about whether, given the risk of side effects, particular drugs are medically appropriate and necessary to control a patient's potentially dangerous behavior (or to avoid serious harm to the patient himself) than to try to balance harms and benefits related to the more quintessentially legal questions of trial fairness and competence.

For another thing, courts typically address involuntary medical treatment as a civil matter, and justify it on these alternative, *Harper*-type grounds. Every State provides avenues through which, for example, a doctor or institution can seek appointment of a guardian with the power to make a decision authorizing medication—when in the best interests of a patient who lacks the mental competence to make such a decision. And courts, in civil proceedings, may authorize involuntary medication where the patient's failure to accept treatment threatens injury to the patient or others.

If a court authorizes medication on these alternative grounds, the need to consider authorization on trial competence grounds will likely disappear. Even if a court decides medication cannot be authorized on the alternative grounds, the findings underlying such a decision will help to inform expert opinion and judicial decisionmaking in respect to a request to administer drugs for trial competence purposes. At the least, they will facilitate direct medical and legal focus upon such questions as: Why is it medically appropriate forcibly to administer antipsychotic drugs to an individual who (1) is *not* dangerous *and* (2) is competent to make up his own mind about treatment? Can bringing such an individual to trial *alone* justify in whole (or at least in significant part) administration of a drug that may have adverse side effects, including side effects that may to some extent impair a defense at trial? We consequently believe that a court, asked to approve forced administration of drugs for purposes of rendering a defendant competent to stand trial, should ordinarily determine whether the Government seeks, or has first sought, permission for forced administration of drugs on these other *Harper*-type grounds; and, if not, why not.

When a court must nonetheless reach the trial competence question, the factors discussed above ... should help it make the ultimate constitutionally required judgment. Has the Government, in light of the efficacy, the side effects, the possible alternatives, and the medical appropriateness of a particular course of antipsychotic drug treatment, shown a need for that treatment sufficiently important to overcome the individual's protected interest in refusing it?

The Medical Center and the Magistrate in this case, applying standards roughly comparable to those set forth here and in *Harper*, approved forced medication substantially, if not primarily, upon grounds of Sell's dangerousness to others. But the District Court and the Eighth Circuit took a different approach. The District Court found "clearly erroneous" the Magistrate's conclusion regarding dangerousness, and the Court of Appeals agreed. Both courts approved forced medication solely in order to render Sell competent to stand trial.

We shall assume that the Court of Appeals' conclusion about Sell's dangerousness was correct. But we make that assumption *only* because the Government did not contest, and the parties have not argued, that particular matter. If anything, the record before us, described in Part I, suggests the contrary.

The Court of Appeals apparently agreed with the District Court that "Sell's inappropriate behavior ... amounted at most to an 'inappropriate familiarity and even infatuation' with a nurse." 282 F.3d, at 565. That being so, it also agreed that "the evidence does not support a finding that Sell posed a danger to himself or others at the Medical Center." *Ibid*. The Court of Appeals, however, did not discuss the potential differences (described by a psychiatrist testifying before the Magistrate) between ordinary "over-familiarity" and the same conduct engaged in persistently by a patient with Sell's behavioral history and mental illness. Nor did it explain why those differences should be minimized in light of the fact that the testifying psychiatrists concluded that Sell was dangerous, while Sell's own expert denied, not Sell's dangerousness, but the efficacy of the drugs proposed for treatment.

The District Court's opinion, while more thorough, places weight upon the Medical Center's decision, taken after the Magistrate's hearing, to return Sell to the general prison population. It does not explain whether that return reflected an improvement in Sell's condition or whether the Medical Center saw it as permanent rather than temporary. *Cf. Harper*, 494 U.S., at 227, and n. 10, (indicating that physical restraints and seclusion often not acceptable substitutes for medication).

Regardless, as we have said, we must assume that Sell was not dangerous. And on that hypothetical assumption, we find that the Court of Appeals was wrong to approve forced medication solely to render Sell competent to stand trial. For one thing, the Magistrate's opinion makes clear that he did *not* find forced medication legally justified on trial competence grounds alone. Rather, the Magistrate concluded that Sell *was* dangerous, and he wrote that forced medication was "the only way to render the defendant *not dangerous and* competent to stand trial." App. 335 (emphasis added).

Moreover, the record of the hearing before the Magistrate shows that the experts themselves focused mainly upon the dangerousness issue. Consequently the experts did not pose important questions—questions, for example, about trial-related side effects and risks—the answers to which could have helped determine whether forced medication was warranted on trial competence grounds alone. Rather, the Medical Center's experts conceded that their proposed medications had "significant" side effects and that "there has to be a cost benefit analysis." And in making their "cost-benefit" judgments, they primarily took into account Sell's dangerousness, not the need to bring him to trial.

The failure to focus upon trial competence could well have mattered. Whether a particular drug will tend to sedate a defendant, interfere with communication with counsel, prevent rapid reaction to trial developments, or diminish the ability to express emotions are matters important in determining the permissibility of medication to restore competence … but not necessarily relevant when dangerousness is primarily at issue. We cannot tell whether the side effects of antipsychotic medication were likely to undermine the fairness of a trial in Sell's case.

Finally, the lower courts did not consider that Sell has already been confined at the Medical Center for a long period of time, and that his refusal to take antipsychotic drugs might result in further lengthy confinement. Those factors, the first because a defendant ordinarily receives credit toward a sentence for time served, 18 U.S.C. § 3585(b), and the second because it reduces the likelihood of the defendant's committing future crimes, moderate—though they do not eliminate—the importance of the governmental interest in prosecution.

V.

For these reasons, we believe that the present orders authorizing forced administration of antipsychotic drugs cannot stand. The Government may pursue its request for forced medication on the grounds discussed in this opinion, including grounds related to the danger Sell poses to himself or others. Since Sell's medical condition may have changed over time, the Government should do so on the basis of current circumstances.

The judgment of the Eighth Circuit is vacated, and the case is remanded for further proceedings consistent with this opinion.

It is so ordered.

NOTES AND QUESTIONS

1.   The President's Commission, Making Health Care Decisions 177–78 (1982) states:

> [T]wo different standards ... have traditionally guided decisionmaking for the incapacitated: "substituted judgment" and "best interests." Although these standards are now used in health care situations, they have their origins in a different context—namely, the resolution of family disputes and decisions about the control of the property of legal incompetents. When people become seriously disabled and unable to manage their property, they may be judged incompetent and a guardian appointed to make financial and property decisions. These doctrines were developed to instruct guardians about the boundaries of their powers without issuing detailed and specific guidelines and to provide a standard for guidance of courts that must review decisions proposed by a guardian.
>
> Simply stated, under the substituted judgment standard, the decisions made for an incapacitated person should attempt to arrive at the same choice the person would make if competent to do so (but within boundaries of "reasonableness" intended to protect the incompetent). Under the best interests standard, decisions are acceptable if they would promote the welfare of the hypothetical "average person" in the position of the incompetent, which may not be the same choice the individual would make (but which may still have some aspects of subjectivity to it).
>
> Despite the long legal history of both these standards, they provide only hazy guidance for decisionmaking even in their original contexts, not to mention in the often far more complex, urgent, and personal setting of health care. Although a number of recent cases involving decisions about health care for incapacitated patients have given courts the opportunity to clarify these often vague guidelines, increased confusion may have accompanied some of the attempts to add precision to these doctrines.

In your view, did the courts in the cases above use the appropriate standards?

2.   Consider Professor John Rawls's justification for use of the "substituted judgment" standard:

> In the original position the parties assume that in society they are rational and able to manage their own affairs. Therefore they do not acknowledge any duties to self, since this is unnecessary to further their good. But once the ideal conception is chosen, they will want to insure themselves against the possibility that their powers are undeveloped and they cannot rationally advance their interests, as in the case of children; or that through some misfortune or accident they are unable to make decisions for their good, as in the case of those seriously injured or mentally disturbed. It is also rational for them to protect themselves against their own irrational inclinations by consenting to a scheme of penalties that may give them a sufficient motive to avoid foolish actions and by accepting certain impositions designed to undo the unfortunate consequences of their imprudent behavior. For these cases the parties adopt principles stipulating when others are authorized to act in their behalf and to

override their present wishes if necessary; and this they do recognizing that sometimes their capacity to act rationally for their good may fail, or be lacking altogether.

Thus the principles of paternalism are those that the parties would acknowledge in the original position to protect themselves against the weakness and infirmities of their reason and will in society. Others are authorized and sometimes required to act on our behalf and to do what we would do for ourselves if we were rational, this authorization coming into effect only when we cannot look after our own good. Paternalistic decisions are to be guided by the individual's own settled preferences and interests insofar as they are not irrational, or failing a knowledge of these, by the theory of primary goods. As we know less and less about a person, we act for him as we would act for ourselves from the standpoint of the original position. We try to get for him the things he presumably wants whatever else he wants. We must be able to argue that with the development or the recovery of his rational powers the individual in question will accept our decision on his behalf and agree with us that we did the best thing for him.

The requirement that the other person in due course accepts his condition is not, however, by any means sufficient, even if this condition is not open to rational criticism. Thus imagine two persons in full possession of their reason and will who affirm different religious or philosophical beliefs; and suppose that there is some psychological process that will convert each to the other's view, despite the fact that the process is imposed on them against their wishes. In due course, let us suppose, both will come to accept conscientiously their new beliefs. We are still not permitted to submit them to this treatment.

JOHN RAWLS, A THEORY OF JUSTICE 248–250 (1971).

C. WHAT MATTERS REQUIRE COLLECTIVE ACTION—AND HOW?

Harold Edgar and David J. Rothman, *The Institutional Review Board and Beyond: Future Challenges to the Ethics of Human Experimentation*
73 MILBANK QUARTERLY 489, 489–491 (1995).

As a political and governance institution, nothing in the regulatory domain resembles the institutional review board (IRB). To invert the classic story about God delegating authority to a committee to perfect His creations and getting a giraffe in return, the IRB is the giraffe, so odd is it when compared to other creatures in the jungle.

Despite its many idiosyncrasies, over the past two decades IRBs have transformed the conduct of research projects involving human subjects. Unquestionably, their very existence has tempered the inevitable propensity of researchers to pursue investigations without dispassionately weighing the risks they are asking others to assume or fully informing their subjects of them. Indeed, IRBs have been so successful as to set an international standard for monitoring clinical research.

Nevertheless, in the American context, the very proliferation of these committees, to the point where they are to be found in every type of institution conducting research, raises critical questions about uniform standards and performance. Is it truly the case that a "one size fits all" approach works well? Are the same general procedures for appointing members and defining their obligations appropriate for reviewing research conducted not only at the Central Intelligence Agency (CIA), the Bureau of Prisons, and the National Institutes of Health (NIH), but also at for-profit hospitals, local community hospitals, and university-affiliated, tertiary-care centers? Does it make sense to give the leadership of an institution, which by its very nature cannot survive without the funds and fame brought in by clinical research, the responsibility for appointing the membership of a monitoring committee? ... IRBs can take credit for remarkable accomplishments, but it may be time to revise the framework governing human experimentation.

THE IRB STRUCTURE

The IRB system rests on two sets of federal regulations.* The first commits various agencies of the U.S. government to securing IRB approval before research is conducted on human subjects, either in house or through the grants they fund for outside projects. Government-supported biomedical research is the paradigm case. Before any federal money can be expended on research involving human subjects, the regulations require that a protocol must be approved by this institutionally based committee, with a membership of no less than five persons, at least one of whom must not be affiliated with the institution. The IRB's central charges are, first, to review whether the benefits of the proposed research outweigh the risks, and second, to make certain that the investigators have explained all the relevant issues so as to secure the subject's informed consent. Although the federal regulations that establish the IRB system apply only to federal activities and federally funded grants, many states require IRB review for all research performed within their jurisdiction, no matter how it is funded. Moreover, the vast majority of academic institutions choose to review all their research protocols through an IRB, rather than reviewing some, but not others, on the basis of who is providing the funding.

Contrary to what many people presume, IRB regulations do not require the review of all innovations in medical practice, let alone all instances of physicians following their preferred treatment strategies without ascertaining whether their approach works better than someone else's. The IRB focuses exclusively on activities intended to gain generalizable knowledge, and to the extent that someone, a surgeon for example, forswears an interest in general knowledge and presumes that the best way to treat Parkinson's disease is to burn the brain's pallidum—to take an illustration from the *Wall Street Journal*'s headline story of February 22, 1995—that surgeon need not bring his new technique before an IRB.

Independent of federal funding regulations, the Food and Drug Administration (FDA) requires that protocols involving human subjects and new drugs or medical devices must be approved by IRBs. For example, were a surgeon to use a new commercial medical device in order to accomplish a proposed intervention, FDA procedures would be triggered. Insofar as testing new drugs on human subjects is concerned, FDA regulations are in important respects the same as those imposed by the Department of Health and Human Services (DHHS) on research institutions seeking grants. Yet

* [Eds.—The relevant regulations are set forth in Chapter 3 *infra*.]

FDA oversight differs in several important respects. FDA reviewers themselves examine the merits of the protocol and do not leave all decision-making to the IRB. Thus, in ways that overlap or supersede an IRB finding, FDA reviewers may reject research that they consider too risky or may compel investigators to carry out more animal studies before beginning clinical trials. At the same time, the FDA may impose strict regulations on the manufacture of drugs and biologics before they are tested, again going well beyond the IRB's usual safety concerns.

. . .

Thus, the power to approve or disapprove research on ethical grounds is granted to a local institutional committee, composed of members of the same institution (with the one necessary exception) that is seeking the funding. Moreover, by all reports, the members who dominate the IRB discussions are these insiders, not the outsiders (who are everywhere a distinct minority). So, in effect, the key decision-makers on the IRB are colleagues who must live with any disappointed applicants whose protocols they have rejected. Furthermore, most IRB committee members are themselves researchers and the standards they set for others will come back to bite them too.

To be sure, the IRB is uniquely well protected from formal institutional domination. Unlike most committees, which are structured to exercise power delegated by a parent and are ultimately responsible to that parent, an IRB decision to disapprove research may not legally be overturned by the institution. For example, if it believes it has grounds to do so, an IRB can effectively terminate a researcher's career at a particular institution by rejecting his protocols or by insisting on such close supervision that it becomes impossible for him to carry out investigations. . . .

Nevertheless, the IRB's autonomy and isolation are largely theoretical, in that no federal controls or regulations exist on how the institution decides who gets appointed to the committee, how long those persons stay, or on what grounds a member may be dismissed or not reappointed. . . . Similarly, there are no formal controls on the selection of the outside and unaffiliated members, whose professional qualifications thus may not always be clear. While many of these outsiders may understand and appreciate the scientific or ethical dimensions of research, there is no way to ensure that they are anything other than a friend of a trustee, looking for an opportunity to participate in an institutional activity.

. . .

In effect, then, the regulations governing the IRB are, to say the least, a permeable shield, with no strong framework to ensure that subjects' interests take precedence over institutional ones. The judgments that will be made on this basis need not be so flagrant as to eventually provoke a scandal. Balancing research risks against benefits is complicated, and a committee that consistently makes the calculus in favor of the research will hardly ever be identified. On occasion, a glaring miscalculation will command headlines; the decision of the UCLA IRB to allow investigators to withdraw medication from schizophrenic patients in the course of a trial may be one such instance. But the overriding point is not how typical the

UCLA actions are, but how the IRB system provides so few bulwarks against this tilt in decision making.

To put the case bluntly, if one were to look at the IRB exclusively in terms of formal structure and organizing principles, it would seem to be a paper tiger. An individual serving on the body and an institution organizing it may fulfill the highest ethical standards; any one participant may claim, with full justice, that his or her IRB is exemplary in its functioning. Nevertheless, there are very few provisions in the regulations that protect against bodies that might be sloppy, venal, or subservient to the institution. Put another way, the quality of an IRB's work depends to an inordinate degree on the conscience and commitment of its volunteer members.

NOTES AND QUESTIONS

1.   The Federal Government has recognized the need for nonscientific and unaffiliated members on IRBs. Should the federal regulations, however, require more than one lay member on each IRB? More than one member unaffiliated with the institution? How likely is a lay member to make an extensive contribution to IRB deliberations? Should lay members be expected to focus primarily on the adequacy of informed consent forms? Are lay members likely to perform effectively where deliberations concern complex scientific and technical data?

2.   Consider the system in Denmark which, until recently, required that each IRB or Research Ethical Committee (REC) be composed of three lay members and three medical/scientific members, reflecting "an awareness that lay members can be overawed on a committee with a majority of medical members." In 1992, the Danish Parliament passed a law that altered the composition of their RECs. Although the Committees can now have between six and ten members, there must always be one lay member more than the number of professional members. The system appears to work well. Jesse A. Goldner, *An Overview of Legal Controls on Human Experimentation and the Regulatory Implications of Taking Professor Katz Seriously*, 38 ST. LOUIS L.J. 63, 107 (1993).

3.   The composition and actions of some IRBs have been criticized. The Office for Protection from Research Risks (OPRR), a small office at the National Institute of Health, oversees patient safety at more than 500 institutions. In May of 1999, the OPRR suspended all medical research involving human subjects at Duke University Medical Center after finding several deficiencies in Duke's IRB. The IRB often approved studies without significant information, wrongly allowed patients to waive informed consent, and failed to monitor patient safety as studies progressed. They also found that the objectivity of the IRB was compromised because two members of the board (the director and assistant director of the Office of Grants and Contracts) were responsible for bringing in federal research money. It was in their best interest to approve all study proposals.

Duke responded quickly to the charges made by the OPRR. The Dean of the Medical School and the Chancellor of Health Affairs met with federal investigators in Washington and agreed to make the necessary changes to assure patient protection. The two members of the IRB with conflicts of interest were barred from voting and members for a second review board have been recruited. Duke's immediate response allowed them to resume research in a matter of days.

For more discussion of the weaknesses and strengths of IRBs, *see* Chapter 3, Sec. II.

In re Brooklyn Navy Yard Asbestos Litigation

United States Court of Appeals, Second Circuit, 1992.
971 F.2d 831.

■ OAKES, CHIEF JUDGE:

BACKGROUND

From the 1930's through 1966, thousands of workers at the New York Naval Shipyard, commonly known as the Brooklyn Navy Yard (BNY), breathed air laden with carcinogenic asbestos fibers. Manufacturers of the asbestos-containing products used at BNY did not warn users of the hazards posed by asbestos dust. Nor did the Navy warn its workers of those hazards, despite its own knowledge of the danger of asbestos. Decades after exposure, many of these workers found themselves with asbestos-related injuries—lung cancer, colon cancer, mesothelioma, laryngeal cancer, pleural disease, asbestosis.

New York amended its statute of limitations in 1986 to start the running of the statute from discovery of the disease. The legislation explicitly revived previously barred asbestos actions. Prior to 1986, the New York statute of limitations ran from the date of exposure. New York's state and federal courts were soon inundated with previously barred asbestos suits. Of several thousand jointly managed asbestos actions filed in the Eastern District of New York, the Southern District of New York, and the Supreme Court of the State of New York, roughly six hundred involved workers exposed to asbestos at BNY. The BNY cases were consolidated by a joint federal-state order. Through the efforts of Referee and Settlement Master Kenneth R. Feinberg, and under the supervision of Judge Jack B. Weinstein and Justice Helen E. Freedman, most of the BNY plaintiffs settled most of their claims.

The BNY cases heading for trial were divided into three categories: Phase I for cases in which over 90% of plaintiffs' asbestos exposure occurred at BNY; Phase II for cases in which 50% to 90% of exposure occurred there; and Phase III for the remainder. The sixty-four Phase I cases were tried jointly in federal court before Judge Weinstein. Later, the fifteen Phase II and Phase III cases went to consolidated trial, before the same judge and jury. The trials were handled with utmost care to ensure that the jurors could assimilate the vast amounts of information necessary to assess the claims. In Phase I, after four months of trial and four weeks of deliberation, the jury rendered fifty-two verdicts in favor of plaintiffs, with damages in excess of thirty million dollars, and twelve verdicts for the defense. In Phases II and III, the jury returned twelve plaintiffs' verdicts, with damages over seven million dollars, and three defense verdicts. The jury awarded no punitive damages, but found every company that shipped asbestos-containing products to BNY liable to at least some plaintiff for failure to warn workers of asbestos's health hazards.

Judge Weinstein then embarked upon the tortuous course charted by New York statutes for molding those jury verdicts into judgments. These computations determined how the judgments would be affected by settlements and bankruptcies, as well as the assessment of prejudgment interest.

Defendants now appeal, arguing that plaintiffs' evidence of causation was insufficient as a matter of law and that the court failed adequately to instruct the jury regarding the doctrine of superseding cause, and challenging a number of the court's interpretations and applications of New York's verdict-molding statutes. Plaintiffs cross-appeal, challenging among other things the court's decision to exclude their design defect claim, and, like defendants, criticizing various of the district court's verdict-molding decisions. In addition, two individual plaintiffs raise issues in addition to those raised by the plaintiffs as a group. Plaintiff Feldman urges that the jury's finding that her husband did not die from asbestos-related illness was against the weight of the evidence, warranting a new trial; plaintiffs Barone attack their pain and suffering award as shockingly low.

DISCUSSION

. . .

I.   Trial Issues

A.   Causation

. . .

In considering a contention that the evidence was insufficient to support plaintiffs' claim, we view the evidence in the light most favorable to the plaintiffs. Viewed in that light, the evidence at trial established that asbestos-containing products made by the defendants were used interchangeably throughout the shipyard, and that the environment was extremely dusty with asbestos fibers. The plaintiffs proved that they or their decedents spent time at BNY and were exposed to asbestos there, that defendants' asbestos-containing products were used in the shipyard and contributed to the asbestos fibers in the air, and that they developed diseases medically linked to asbestos exposure. Because the events happened years ago, and many of those exposed to the asbestos are deceased, to require precision of proof would impose an insurmountable burden. As we see no reason to overrule [earlier decisions] in favor of a stricter standard of causation, we find plaintiffs' proof sufficient to support the jury's finding that plaintiffs' injuries were caused by exposure to asbestos from defendants' products.

B.   Navy's Intervening Failure to Warn

The evidence at trial showed that the United States Navy knew of the dangers of asbestos exposure but, with single-minded focus on building warships expeditiously, failed to warn its workers or take available precautions, such as ventilating work areas, wetting down the insulation, or requiring that workers wear respirators. Plaintiffs, as naval employees, were barred under the workers' compensation statute from pursuing a tort remedy against the United States. *See* N.Y.Work.Comp.Law § 11 (McKinney 1992). Defendants, however, advance two arguments premised on the Navy's culpability. First, they contend that the sophistication of the Navy as an intermediary relieved manufacturers of their duty to warn the naval employees. Second, they argue that even if the defendants had a duty to warn, the Navy's failure was a superseding cause of plaintiffs' injuries, relieving defendants of liability.

We find no merit in defendants' contention that they justifiably relied on the Navy to communicate potential hazards to those who would ultimately work with defendants' asbestos-containing products. The jury found—unsurprisingly—that defendants had a duty to warn users of the dangers associated with their products. Given that the record supports neither a finding that defendants actually relied on the Navy to warn its workers, nor a finding that any such reliance would have been justifiable, the presence of the Navy as an alleged "sophisticated intermediary" or "knowledgeable user" does not call into question the jury's finding of defendants' duty to warn. *See* Restatement (Second) of Torts § 388, cmt. n (1965). The sophisticated intermediary doctrine protects a manufacturer from liability only if the chain of distribution is such that the duty to warn ultimate users should fall on an intermediary in that chain, rather than on the manufacturer. *See, e.g.*, Wolfgruber v. Upjohn Co., 72 A.D.2d 59, 62–63, 423 N.Y.S.2d 95, 97–98 (1979) (applying responsible intermediary theory to relieve drug manufacturer of liability where the prescribing physician should have warned the user of the product's dangers), *aff'd*, 52 N.Y.2d 768, 417 N.E.2d 1002 (1980); Rivers v. AT & T Technologies, Inc., 147 Misc.2d 366, 372, 554 N.Y.S.2d 401, 405 (Sup.Ct.1990) (relieving bulk chemical manufacturer of liability to ultimate user where user was "too remote in the chain of distribution" and manufacturer "provided extensive warnings to its immediate distributees and each of the parties in the chain of distribution was a responsible intermediary").

Unlike the sophisticated intermediary theory, defendants' superseding cause argument assumes a duty to warn but suggests that an intervening cause broke the causal chain connecting plaintiffs' injuries to defendants' breach of that duty. Defendants assert that the district court failed adequately to instruct the jury regarding superseding cause. In *McLaughlin v. Mine Safety Appliances Co.*, 11 N.Y.2d 62, 71–72, 181 N.E.2d 430 (1962), the New York Court of Appeals held that the trial court should have charged that a firefighter's failure to warn a nurse of the hazard of unwrapped heat blocks could have superseded the defendant manufacturer's negligence in failing to print an adequately visible warning on the heat blocks' packaging. More recently, the New York Supreme Court, Appellate Division, reversed a plaintiff's verdict where the trial judge refused to instruct the jury that if the decedent's employer had actual knowledge of the hazards of trichloroethylene vapors, its negligence in failing to warn its employee or to provide him with breathing apparatus may have constituted a superseding cause, relieving the chemical manufacturer and distributor of liability for their own failure to warn. Billsborrow v. Dow Chem., U.S.A., 177 A.D.2d 7, 17–19, 579 N.Y.S.2d 728, 734–35 (1992).

In the present case, however, Judge Weinstein's charge was adequate. Judge Weinstein reminded the jury that defendants introduced evidence concerning the Navy's knowledge of asbestos hazards and failure to warn its employees, and instructed the jury that proximate cause would be lacking if, because of a breach of duty by the Navy, "a warning by defendants would have had no appreciable effect in protecting the workers." While the charge was neither as thorough nor as clear on the question of superseding cause as it might have been, it sufficed to alert the jury to the possibility of finding that the Navy's conduct interrupted the causal chain between defendants' failure to warn and plaintiffs' injuries. If the jury had concluded that the Navy was fully responsible for plaintiffs' injuries, it would have known from the district court's charge to absolve the defendants.

In any event, the absence of a precise, emphatic instruction on superseding cause was at most harmless error. To supersede a defendant's negligence, an intervening cause must be neither normal nor foreseeable. Woodling v. Garrett Corp., 813 F.2d 543, 555 (2d Cir.1987); Lynch v. Bay Ridge Obstetrical & Gynecological Assocs., 72 N.Y.2d 632, 636, 532 N.E.2d 1239, 1241 (1988); Restatement (Second) of Torts § 442 (1965). An intervening act breaks the causal nexus only if it is "extraordinary under the circumstances, not foreseeable in the normal course of events." Derdiarian v. Felix Contracting Corp., 51 N.Y.2d 308, 315, 414 N.E.2d 666, 670 (1980). The Navy's conduct in failing to protect its workers from the hazards of asbestos exposure, while reprehensible, was anything but unforeseeable. The record shows that the Navy's use of asbestos-containing products at BNY, and the constantly dusty conditions there, were unhidden and widely known. The district court charged the jury that, to find a defendant liable, it must determine that the defendant "actually was or should have been aware that its products, *when used as the manufacturer would reasonably foresee it would be used in the Navy Yard,* could cause injury to those exposed to the dust from the product." (Emphasis added.) Thus, the jury necessarily found that defendants knew or should have known that the Navy did not maintain a safe workplace and did not adequately warn its workers. The Navy's intervening failure to warn was entirely foreseeable; there is nothing unjust in holding defendants liable for their own negligence, notwithstanding the Navy's additional lapse. *See Woodling,* 813 F.2d at 556 ("[T]he fact that the intervening actor, such as an employer who controls defective machinery, knows of the dangers and merely fails to warn or otherwise protect the plaintiff does not of itself relieve the original actor from liability.").

.   .   .

III.   *Individual Appeals*

A.   Feldman

Plaintiff Goldie Feldman appeals from a judgment in favor of defendants and the denial of her motion for a new trial. The jury found that the disease and death of Feldman's husband were not related to asbestos exposure.

Hyman Feldman worked as a pipe fitter at BNY from 1942 until 1945 or 1946. The medical evidence regarding Mr. Feldman, while suggesting that he may have died from asbestos-related mesothelioma, does not rule out a finding that he died from adenocarcinoma caused by his thirty to thirty-five years of pack-a-day cigarette smoking. The evidence of the asbestos-relatedness of Mr. Feldman's death—particularly given the brevity of his asbestos exposure and the endurance of his smoking habit—is not so overwhelming as to warrant setting aside the jury verdict.

> When a jury's determination is based on an interpretation of facts within their sphere, New York law does not permit a reviewing court to set aside the verdict unless the evidence so preponderates in favor of the party against whom the verdict was rendered that it is clear that the jury did not reach its conclusion on a fair interpretation of the evidence, or if a contrary conclusion is the only reasonable inference that can be made from the proven facts. The federal standard in this circuit is virtually identical.

Billiar v. Minnesota Mining & Mfg. Co., 623 F.2d 240, 247–48 (2d Cir.1980) (citations omitted).

In affirming the judgment against Feldman, we are mindful of the dangers of a streamlined trial process in which testimony must be curtailed and jurors must assimilate vast amounts of information. The systemic urge to aggregate litigation must not be allowed to trump our dedication to individual justice, and we must take care that each individual plaintiff's— and defendant's—cause not be lost in the shadow of a towering mass litigation. *See generally* Peterson & Selvin, *supra*, Law & Contemp. Probs., Summer 1991, at 228 (Mass tort cases "have produced results that sometimes seem capricious" and resulted in "differential treatment of plaintiffs with similar injuries"); Judith Resnik, *From "Cases" to "Litigation"*, Law & Contemp. Probs., Summer 1991, at 5 (tracing the growth of aggregate mass tort litigation and the weakening link between individuals and lawsuits).

Every indication, however, is that the jury in this asbestos litigation considered each claim with utmost care and individualized attention. The jurors spent four weeks deliberating. They asked for the full file on each case, and gave each case hours or days of attention. Judge Weinstein called it "one of the best juries I've ever had," and noted the "remarkable" consistency in its work. Transcript of Motions, *In re New York City Asbestos Litigation*, No. TS 90–9999 (E.D.N.Y. May 7, 1991), at 12–13. We conclude that while the evidence would have supported a verdict in favor of Feldman, it also supported a reasonable inference that Mr. Feldman's death was caused by cigarettes rather than asbestos, and it was the jury's prerogative to make that inference.

B. Barone

Roberta and Perrell Barone appeal from a damage award of $25,000 for their decedent's pain and suffering prior to death. Anthony Barone— Roberta's husband and Perrell's father—died of asbestos-related adenocarcinoma in 1959, at the age of 41, after a year of bodily deterioration. Mr. Barone's widow and daughter testified about the intense pain he endured and his humiliating loss of bladder and bowel control. Plaintiffs contend that, based on the evidence of Mr. Barone's condition, and viewed in comparison to awards in similar cases, the $25,000 award for pain and suffering was so low as to shock the conscience.

Pinning dollar amounts to suffering is inherently subjective, and peculiarly within the province of the jury. Nevertheless, we will reject a damage award if it is "so grossly and palpably inadequate as to shock the court's conscience." *Korek*, 734 F.2d at 929. Given the record here, replete with undisputed testimony of lengthy and intense suffering, we find that the award shocks the conscience and therefore remand the Barone case for a new trial confined to the issue of pain and suffering.

Accordingly, the judgment of the district court is affirmed in part, reversed in part, and remanded for further proceedings in accordance with this opinion.

. . .

NOTE

During bankruptcy proceedings in 1986, a trust was established to pay future asbestos injury claims against Johns–Manville Corporation, a manufacturer of asbestos. Later it was determined that the trust was insufficient to meet all present and future claims. In In re Joint E. & S. Dist. Asbestos Litigation, 878 F.Supp. 473 (E.D.N.Y.1995), Judge Weinstein "end[ed] the incredibly convoluted and complex Manville asbestos litigation" by approving a settlement that allowed for pro rata distribution of the trusts remaining assets to claimants.

Asbestos litigation continues today, still defying judicial resolution. The focus of the problem is the class action lawsuit. Proponents of class actions argue that because of the size of the these mass tort actions, the cases are unmanageable outside of the class context. "Usually high litigation costs, unusually long delays, and limitations upon the total amount of resources available for payment, together mean that most potential plaintiffs may not have a realistic alternative." Ortiz v. Fibreboard, 527 U.S. 815, 119 S.Ct. 2295, 2325 (1999) (Breyer, J., Dissenting). Critics claim that class certification creates problems. Specifically, class certification encourages plaintiffs with weaker claims to join the suit, hoping to gain from even a small settlement. With larger numbers of litigants, the risk of an adverse judgment is increased, as well as settlement pressure on the defendant. Barry F. McNeil & Beth L. Fancsal, *Mass Torts and Class Actions: Facing Increased Scrutiny*, 167 F.R.D. 483 (5th Cir. 1996).

As of August 2004, the Unite States Senate was still struggling with the question of whether to establish a national administrative claims resolution process to compensate victims of asbestos exposure. Under the pending legislation, a trust fund would be established, and paid for by businesses and their insurers. The trust fund could be as large as $145 billion. *See* NATIONAL JOURNAL CONGRESS DAILY, August 3, 2004.

Robert S. Morison, *Bioethics After Two Decades*

11 Hastings Center Rpt. 8, 8–9, 12 (April 1981).

Like Sigmund Freud I was brought up as a biologist and have never overcome it. Also like the great man, and long before I read *Civilization and its Discontents,* I had been impressed by the tension between the two sides of human biological nature-one's needs as an individual and one's dependence on a society. . . .

A biologist who influenced me more directly than Freud . . . was the geneticist C.H. Waddington. Particularly memorable in his essays on the relationship between biology and ethics was his elaboration of the concept of "stochastic morality." Conventional ethics and morals, he said, deal largely with one-to-one situations; the ethics of the future must take into account actions at a distance of varying probability. Paradigmatically, the Ten Commandments tell particular individuals to honor particular fathers and mothers and to avoid stealing identifiable maid-servants from identifiable neighbors. Waddington was among the first to formulate explicitly a new kind of crime, the victims of which could be identified only as statistics. . . .

It was not crime in the conventional legal sense nor the interest in ethical problems involving probable damage to unidentifiable persons that primarily attracted attention to the new field of bioethics. Advances in biology and medicine were creating new problems about conduct of the traditional person-to-person sort. Even more frequently, old ethical concerns were brought forth in new dress, more strikingly colored and more precisely cut. . . .

The greatest achievement so far may be methodological. Current biomedical ethics has shown the academy that interdisciplinary scholarship really is possible. Perhaps, success was in part due to the active participation of physicians, clergy, and lawyers with practical experience in decision making involving several different interests. It may also be significant that much of the early activity originated in partially or completely independent institutes or societies unencumbered with traditional academic rules and prejudices. Two recent developments may work against this interdisciplinary approach. The first is the growing tendency to professionalize the field. . . .

Equally ominous is the tendency to turn ethical principles into legal regulations. . . . Further contributing to the regulatory edicts was the rapid decline in respect for all authority figures that has characterized the last two decades of American life. On the whole, doctors have fared better in the polls than most others; even so, they are too suspect to be allowed to follow their traditional ways unrestrained except by conscience. Finally, the growing interest in stochastic morality led naturally to a search for ways to protect unidentifiable people from the acts of corporations and other faceless entities.

[M]edical ethics was designed to help doctors to make the right choices in the moral problems that confronted them and their patients. In this primitive view one readily acknowledged that doctors carried a particular kind of power and authority. This in turn placed upon them the obligation to use this power with wisdom and due respect for the dignity of those in their care. This would now be regarded as an elitist conception, and as such it is suspect in our egalitarian society.

Whether one likes it or not, however, in any society some individuals are more equal than others. In the case of doctors the primary sources of authority and power are the possession of special knowledge and the inheritance of a particular tradition. There is also an awareness that doctors are acquainted with death and have made many decisions involving the life and death of others.

This special position of those in authority has not made them immune from social control, nor should it. Two broad approaches are commonly employed. The first seeks to control the individual from the inside by making him or her a better person. The second tries to achieve the same end by means of laws, constitutions, licensing arrangements, and the like. . . .

One looked to the resurgence of bioethics primarily for an enrichment of the understanding and a quickening of the sense of responsibility in individual physicians. It rapidly became obvious that the same movement could help lay people to know more about the potential effects of advances in biology and medicine so that they could share in the decisions affecting themselves and their loved ones. . . .

Perhaps the most serious difficulty with the general principles underlying such matters as abortion, euthanasia, suicide, or genetic engineering is the lack of general agreement about them. . . . Our pluralistic society was founded on the proposition that differences of opinion of this kind are in fact irresolvable by argument or political compromise. Well aware of the melancholy history of European efforts to use the temporal power to enforce religious consistency, the Founding Fathers of the United States wisely declared religious differences beyond the reach of government action. Why have we not followed their example and been willing to leave these currently urgent bioethical questions involving individuals to the individual conscience? Perhaps their apparent novelty and the technical trappings with which they are surrounded have deluded us into thinking that they are primarily technical questions subject to a "technological fix". . . .

[S]everal areas of biomedical ethics do transcend the purview of the individual conscience and may properly be dealt with on a national, as well as an individual, basis. Particularly appropriate are areas of stochastic morality, as suggested above. Some formal regulation of the use of human subjects and animals in medical experimentation is already in force and seems in principle to be appropriate, although it is doubtful if it can ever take the place of an acute ethical sense on the part of the researcher. Many issues involved in the equitable distribution of medical care require a societal rather than an individual frame of reference. Particularly worthy of a broader analysis are the social consequences of the "medicalization" of human problems. . . .

There is certainly enough to do at every level without reaching down to regulate matters better left to the individual conscience, quickened and deepened by philosophical discussion but unconfined by the metaphysical conviction of a vocal minority or even a moral majority.

NOTE

Robert Morrison identifies those areas in bioethics that he believes should be regulated on a public basis rather than being left to lay control (or to the conscience of the professional). Are there other areas, in your view, in which private control is inadequate? Consider the shortcomings of tort litigation revealed in *In re Brooklyn Navy Yard Asbestos Litigation*. Consider also the proper role for the criminal law in protecting individuals from wrongdoing. *See, e.g.*, People v. Phillips, 64 Cal.2d 574, 51 Cal.Rptr. 225, 414 P.2d 353 (1966) (Overturning murder conviction of chiropractor who had represented to parents of eight year old victim that he could cure the victim's eye cancer without the surgery recommended by physicians at UCLA).

CHAPTER 3

THE HUMAN BODY

I. OWNERSHIP OF THE BODY

A. WHO OWNS THE BODY AND ITS PARTS?

Moore v. Regents of the University of California

Supreme Court of California, en banc, 1990.
51 Cal.3d 120, 271 Cal.Rptr. 146, 793 P.2d 479.

■ PANELLI, J.

I. INTRODUCTION

We granted review in this case to determine whether plaintiff has stated a cause of action against his physician and other defendants for using his cells in potentially lucrative medical research without his permission. Plaintiff alleges that his physician failed to disclose preexisting research and economic interests in the cells before obtaining consent to the medical procedures by which they were extracted. The superior court sustained all defendants' demurrers to the third amended complaint, and the Court of Appeal reversed. We hold that the complaint states a cause of action for breach of the physician's disclosure obligations, but not for conversion.

II. FACTS

Our only task in reviewing a ruling on a demurrer is to determine whether the complaint states a cause of action. Accordingly, we assume that the complaint's properly pleaded material allegations are true and give the complaint a reasonable interpretation by reading it as a whole and all its parts in their context. . . .

The plaintiff is John Moore (Moore), who underwent treatment for hairy-cell leukemia at the Medical Center of the University of California at Los Angeles (UCLA Medical Center). The five defendants are: (1) Dr. David W. Golde (Golde), a physician who attended Moore at UCLA Medical Center; (2) the Regents of the University of California (Regents), who own and operate the university; (3) Shirley G. Quan, a researcher employed by the Regents; (4) Genetics Institute, Inc. (Genetics Institute); and (5) Sandoz Pharmaceuticals Corporation and related entities (collectively Sandoz).

Moore first visited UCLA Medical Center on October 5, 1976, shortly after he learned that he had hairy-cell leukemia. After hospitalizing Moore and "withdr[awing] extensive amounts of blood, bone marrow aspirate, and other bodily substances," Golde confirmed that diagnosis. At this time all defendants, including Golde, were aware that "certain blood products and blood components were of great value in a number of commercial and scientific efforts" and that access to a patient whose blood contained these substances would provide "competitive, commercial, and scientific advantages."

On October 8, 1976, Golde recommended that Moore's spleen be removed. Golde informed Moore "that he had reason to fear for his life, and that the proposed splenectomy operation ... was necessary to slow down the progress of his disease." Based upon Golde's representations, Moore signed a written consent form authorizing the splenectomy.

Before the operation, Golde and Quan "formed the intent and made arrangements to obtain portions of [Moore's] spleen following its removal" and to take them to a separate research unit.... These research activities "were not intended to have ... any relation to [Moore's] medical ... care." However, neither Golde nor Quan informed Moore of their plans to conduct this research or requested his permission....

Moore returned to the UCLA Medical Center several times between November 1976 and September 1983. He did so at Golde's direction and based upon representations "that such visits were necessary and required for his health and well-being, and based upon the trust inherent in and by virtue of the physician-patient relationship...." On each of these visits Golde withdrew additional samples of "blood, blood serum, skin, bone marrow aspirate, and sperm." On each occasion Moore travelled to the UCLA Medical Center from his home in Seattle because he had been told that the procedures were to be performed only there and only under Golde's direction.

"In fact, [however,] throughout the period of time that [Moore] was under [Golde's] care and treatment, ... the defendants were actively involved in a number of activities which they concealed from [Moore] ..." Specifically, defendants were conducting research on Moore's cells and planned to "benefit financially and competitively ... [by exploiting the cells] and [their] exclusive access to [the cells] by virtue of [Golde's] ongoing physician-patient relationship ..."

Sometime before August 1979, Golde established a cell line from Moore's T-lymphocytes.[2] On January 30, 1981, the Regents applied for a patent on the cell line, listing Golde and Quan as inventors. "[B]y virtue of an established policy ..., [the] Regents, Golde, and Quan would share in any royalties or profits ... arising out of [the] patent." The patent issued on March 20, 1984, naming Golde and Quan as the inventors of the cell line and the Regents as the assignee of the patent.

. . .

2. A T-lymphocyte is a type of white blood cell. T-lymphocytes produce lymphokines, or proteins that regulate the immune system. Some lymphokines have potential therapeutic value. If the genetic material responsible for producing a particular lymphokine can be identified, it can sometimes be used to manufacture large quantities of the lymphokine through the techniques of recombinant DNA. (*See* U.S. Congress, Office of Technology Assessment, New Developments in Biotechnology: Ownership of Human Tissues and Cells (1987) at pp. 31–46 (hereafter OTA Report)).

With the Regents' assistance, Golde negotiated agreements for commercial development of the cell line and products to be derived from it. Under an agreement with Genetics Institute, Golde "became a paid consultant" and "acquired the rights to 75,000 shares of common stock." Genetics Institute also agreed to pay Golde and the Regents "at least $330,000 over three years, including a pro-rata share of [Golde's] salary and fringe benefits, in exchange for . . . exclusive access to the materials and research performed" on the cell line and products derived from it. . . .

Based upon these allegations, Moore attempted to state 13 causes of action. Each defendant demurred to each purported cause of action. The superior court, however, expressly considered the validity of only the first cause of action, conversion. Reasoning that the remaining causes of action incorporated the earlier, defective allegations, the superior court sustained a general demurrer to the entire complaint with leave to amend. . . .

With one justice dissenting, the Court of Appeal reversed, holding that the complaint did state a cause of action for conversion. The Court of Appeal agreed with the superior court that the allegations against Genetics Institute and Sandoz were insufficient, but directed the superior court to give Moore leave to amend. The Court of Appeal also directed the superior court to decide "the remaining causes of action, which [had] never been expressly ruled upon."

III. DISCUSSION

A. Breach of Fiduciary Duty and Lack of Informed Consent

Moore repeatedly alleges that Golde failed to disclose the extent of his research and economic interests in Moore's cells before obtaining consent to the medical procedures by which the cells were extracted.[6] These allegations, in our view, state a cause of action against Golde for invading a legally protected interest of his patient. This cause of action can properly be characterized either as the breach of a fiduciary duty to disclose facts material to the patient's consent or, alternatively, as the performance of medical procedures without first having obtained the patient's informed consent.

Our analysis begins with three well-established principles. First, "a person of adult years and in sound mind has the right, in the exercise of control over his own body, to determine whether or not to submit to lawful medical treatment." (Cobbs v. Grant (1972) 8 Cal.3d 229, 242; *cf.* Schloendorff v. Society of New York Hospital (1914) 211 N.Y. 125.) Second, "the patient's consent to treatment, to be effective, must be an informed consent." Third, in soliciting the patient's consent, a physician has a fiduciary duty to disclose all information material to the patient's decision.

These principles lead to the following conclusions: (1) a physician must disclose personal interests unrelated to the patient's health, whether research or economic, that may affect the physician's professional judgment; and (2) a physician's failure to disclose such interests may give rise to a

---

6. In this opinion we use the inclusive term "cells" to describe all of the cells taken from Moore's body, including blood cells, bone marrow, spleen, etc.

cause of action for performing medical procedures without informed consent or breach of fiduciary duty.

. . .

Indeed, the law already recognizes that a reasonable patient would want to know whether a physician has an economic interest that might affect the physician's professional judgment. As the Court of Appeal has said, "[c]ertainly a sick patient deserves to be free of any reasonable suspicion that his doctor's judgment is influenced by a profit motive." (*Magan Medical Clinic v. Cal. State Bd. of Medical Examiners* (1967) 249 Cal.App.2d 124.). . . .

. . .

. . . [A] physician who treats a patient in whom he also has a research interest has potentially conflicting loyalties. This is because medical treatment decisions are made on the basis of proportionality—weighing the benefits *to the patient* against the risks *to the patient*. As another court has said, "the determination as to whether the burdens of treatment are worth enduring for any individual patient depends upon the facts unique in each case," and "the patient's interests and desires are the key ingredients of the decision-making process." (Barber v. Superior Court (1983) 147 Cal. App.3d 1006, 1018–1019.) A physician who adds his own research interests to this balance may be tempted to order a scientifically useful procedure or test that offers marginal, or no, benefits to the patient. The possibility that an interest extraneous to the patient's health has affected the physician's judgment is something that a reasonable patient would want to know in deciding whether to consent to a proposed course of treatment. It is material to the patient's decision and, thus, a prerequisite to informed consent.

. . .

We acknowledge that there is a competing consideration. To require disclosure of research and economic interests may corrupt the patient's own judgment by distracting him from the requirements of his health. But California law does not grant physicians unlimited discretion to decide what to disclose. Instead, "it is the prerogative of the patient, not the physician, to determine for himself the direction in which he believes his interests lie." (Cobbs v. Grant, *supra*, 502 P.2d 1.) . . .

Accordingly, we hold that a physician who is seeking a patient's consent for a medical procedure must, in order to satisfy his fiduciary duty and to obtain the patient's informed consent, disclose personal interests unrelated to the patient's health, whether research or economic, that may affect his medical judgment.

We turn now to the allegations of Moore's . . . complaint to determine whether he has stated . . . a cause of action. . . .

Moore alleges that, prior to the surgical removal of his spleen, Golde "formed the intent and made arrangements to obtain portions of his spleen following its removal from [Moore] in connection with [his] desire to have regular and continuous access to, and possession of, [Moore's] unique and rare Blood and Bodily Substances." Moore was never informed prior to the splenectomy of Golde's "prior formed intent" to obtain a portion of his spleen. In our view, these allegations adequately show that Golde had an undisclosed research interest in Moore's cells at the time he sought Moore's consent to the splenectomy. Accordingly, Moore has stated a cause of action for breach of fiduciary duty, or lack of informed consent, based upon the disclosures accompanying that medical procedure.

We next discuss the adequacy of Golde's alleged disclosures regarding the postoperative takings of blood and other samples. In this context, Moore alleges that Golde "expressly, affirmatively and impliedly represent-ed ... that these withdrawals of his Blood and Bodily Substances were necessary and required for his health and well-being." However, Moore also alleges that Golde actively concealed his economic interest in Moore's cells during this time period. "[D]uring each of these visits ..., and even when [Moore] inquired as to whether there was any possible or potential com-mercial or financial value or significance of his Blood and Bodily Sub-stances, or whether the defendants had discovered anything ... which was or might be ... related to any scientific activity resulting in commercial or financial benefits ..., the defendants repeatedly and affirmatively repre-sented to [Moore] that there was no commercial or financial value to his Blood and Bodily Substances ... and in fact actively discouraged such inquiries."

Moore admits in his complaint that defendants disclosed they "were engaged in strictly academic and purely scientific medical research...." However, Golde's representation that he had no financial interest in this research became false, based upon the allegations, at least by May 1979, when he "began to investigate and initiate the procedures ... for [obtain-ing] a patent" on the cell line developed from Moore's cells.

In these allegations, Moore plainly asserts that Golde concealed an economic interest in the postoperative procedures. Therefore, applying the principles already discussed, the allegations state a cause of action for breach of fiduciary duty or lack of informed consent.

. . .

B. *Conversion*

Moore also attempts to characterize the invasion of his rights as a conversion: a tort that protects against interference with possessory and ownership interests in personal property. He theorizes that he continued to own his cells following their removal from his body, at least for the purpose of directing their use, and that he never consented to their use in potential-ly lucrative medical research. Thus, to complete Moore's argument, defen-dants' unauthorized use of his cells constitutes a conversion. As a result of the alleged conversion, Moore claims a proprietary interest in each of the products that any of the defendants might ever create from his cells or the patented cell line.

No court, however, has ever in a reported decision imposed conversion liability for the use of human cells in medical research.[15] While that fact

---

15. The absence of such authority can-not simply be attributed to recent develop-ments in technology. The first human tumor cell line, which still is widely used in re-search, was isolated in 1951.

does not end our inquiry, it raises a flag of caution. In effect, what Moore is asking us to do is to impose a tort duty on scientists to investigate the consensual pedigree of each human cell sample used in research. To impose such a duty, which would affect medical research of importance to all of society, implicates policy concerns far removed from the traditional, two-party ownership disputes in which the law of conversion arose. Invoking a tort theory originally used to determine whether the loser or the finder of a horse had the better title, Moore claims ownership of the results of socially important medical research, including the genetic code for chemicals that regulate the functions of every human being's immune system.

We have recognized that, when the proposed application of a very general theory of liability in a new context raises important policy concerns, it is especially important to face those concerns and address them openly. Moreover, we should be hesitant to "impose [new tort duties] when to do so would involve complex policy decisions" especially when such decisions are more appropriately the subject of legislative deliberation and resolution....

Accordingly, we first consider whether the tort of conversion clearly gives Moore a cause of action under existing law....

1. Moore's Claim Under Existing Law

"To establish a conversion, plaintiff must establish an actual interference with his *ownership* or *right of possession*.... Where plaintiff neither has title to the property alleged to have been converted, nor possession thereof, he cannot maintain an action for conversion."

Since Moore clearly did not expect to retain possession of his cells following their removal, to sue for their conversion he must have retained an ownership interest in them. But there are several reasons to doubt that he did retain any such interest. First, no reported judicial decision supports Moore's claim, either directly or by close analogy. Second, California statutory law drastically limits any continuing interest of a patient in excised cells. Third, the subject matters of the Regents' patent—the patented cell line and the products derived from it, it cannot be Moore's property.

Neither the Court of Appeal's opinion, the parties' briefs, nor our research discloses a case holding that a person retains a sufficient interest in excised cells to support a cause of action for conversion. We do not find this surprising, since the laws governing such things as human tissues, transplantable organs, blood, fetuses, pituitary glands, corneal tissue, and dead bodies deal with human biological materials as objects sui generis, regulating their disposition to achieve policy goals rather than abandoning them to the general law of personal property. It is these specialized statutes, not the law of conversion, to which courts ordinarily should and do look for guidance on the disposition of human biological materials.

Lacking direct authority for importing the law of conversion into this context, Moore relies, as did the Court of Appeal, primarily on decisions addressing privacy rights. One line of cases involves unwanted publicity. (Lugosi v. Universal Pictures, 603 P.2d 425 (1979); Motschenbacher v. R.J. Reynolds Tobacco Company, 498 F.2d 821 (9th Cir.1974) [interpreting Cal. law].) These opinions hold that every person has a proprietary interest in his own likeness and that unauthorized, business use of a likeness is redressible as a tort. But in neither opinion did the authoring court expressly base its holding on property law. . . .

Not only are the wrongful-publicity cases irrelevant to the issue of conversion, but the analogy to them seriously misconceives the nature of the genetic materials and research involved in this case. Moore, adopting the analogy originally advanced by the Court of Appeal, argues that "[i]f the courts have found a sufficient proprietary interest in one's persona, how could one not have a right in one's own genetic material, something far more profoundly the essence of one's human uniqueness than a name or a face?" However, as the defendants' patent makes clear—and the complaint, too, if read with an understanding of the scientific terms which it has borrowed from the patent—the goal and result of defendants' efforts has been to manufacture lymphokines. Lymphokines, unlike a name or a face, have the same molecular structure in every human being and the same, important functions in every human being's immune system. Moreover, the particular genetic material which is responsible for the natural production of lymphokines, and which defendants use to manufacture lymphokines in the laboratory, is also the same in every person; it is no more unique to Moore than the number of vertebrae in the spine or the chemical formula of hemoglobin.

. . .

The next consideration that makes Moore's claim of ownership problematic is California statutory law, which drastically limits a patient's control over excised cells. Pursuant to Health and Safety Code section 7054.4, "[n]otwithstanding any other provision of law, recognizable anatomical parts, human tissues, anatomical human remains, or infectious waste following conclusion of scientific use shall be disposed of by interment, incineration, or any other method determined by the state department [of health services] to protect the public health and safety." Clearly the Legislature did not specifically intend this statute to resolve the question of whether a patient is entitled to compensation for the nonconsensual use of excised cells. A primary object of the statute is to ensure the safe handling of potentially hazardous biological waste materials. Yet one cannot escape the conclusion that the statute's practical effect is to limit, drastically, a patient's control over excised cells. By restricting how excised cells may be used and requiring their eventual destruction, the statute eliminates so many of the rights ordinarily attached to property that one cannot simply assume that what is left amounts to "property" or "ownership" for purposes of conversion law.

It may be that some limited right to control the use of excised cells does survive the operation of this statute. There is, for example, no need to read the statute to permit "scientific use" contrary to the patient's expressed wish. A fully informed patient may always withhold consent to treatment by a physician whose research plans the patient does not approve. That right, however, as already discussed, is protected by the fiduciary-duty and informed-consent theories.

Finally, the subject matter of the Regents' patent: the patented cell line and the products derived from it cannot be Moore's property. This is because the patented cell line is both factually and legally distinct from the cells taken from Moore's body. Federal law permits the patenting of organisms that represent the product of "human ingenuity," but not naturally occurring organisms. (Diamond v. Chakrabarty (1980) 447 U.S. 303, 309–310.) Human cell lines are patentable because "[l]ong-term adaptation and growth of human tissues and cells in culture is difficult, often considered an art ...," and the probability of success is low. It is this *inventive effort* that patent law rewards, not the discovery of naturally occurring raw materials. Thus, Moore's allegations that he owns the cell line and the products derived from it are inconsistent with the patent, which constitutes an authoritative determination that the cell line is the product of invention....

2.   Should Conversion Liability Be Extended?

. . .

There are three reasons why it is inappropriate to impose liability for conversion based upon the allegations of Moore's complaint. First, a fair balancing of the relevant policy considerations counsels against extending the tort. Second, problems in this area are better suited to legislative resolution. Third, the tort of conversion is not necessary to protect patients' rights. For these reasons, we conclude that the use of excised human cells in medical research does not amount to a conversion.

Of the relevant policy considerations, two are of overriding importance. The first is protection of a competent patient's right to make autonomous medical decisions.... The second important policy consideration is that we not threaten with disabling civil liability innocent parties who are engaged in socially useful activities, such as researchers who have no reason to believe that their use of a particular cell sample is, or may be, against a donor's wishes.

To reach an appropriate balance of these policy considerations is extremely important. In its report to Congress, the Office of Technology Assessment emphasized that "[u]ncertainty about how courts will resolve disputes between specimen sources and specimen users could be detrimental to both academic researchers and the infant biotechnology industry, particularly when the rights are asserted long after the specimen was obtained. The assertion of rights by sources would affect not only the researcher who obtained the original specimen, but perhaps other researchers as well."

. . .

Research on human cells plays a critical role in medical research. This is so because researchers are increasingly able to isolate naturally occurring, medically useful biological substances and to produce useful quantities of such substances through genetic engineering. These efforts are beginning to bear fruit. Products developed through biotechnology that have already been approved for marketing in this country include treatments and tests for leukemia, cancer, diabetes, dwarfism, hepatitis-B, kidney transplant rejection, emphysema, osteoporosis, ulcers, anemia, infertility, and gynecological tumors, to name but a few.

The extension of conversion law into this area will hinder research by restricting access to the necessary raw materials. Thousands of human cell lines already exist in tissue repositories.... At present, human cell lines are routinely copied and distributed to other researchers for experimental purposes, usually free of charge. This exchange of scientific materials, which still is relatively free and efficient, will surely be compromised if each cell sample becomes the potential subject matter of a lawsuit.

To expand liability by extending conversion law into this area would have a broad impact. The House Committee on Science and Technology of the United States Congress found that "49 percent of the researchers at medical institutions surveyed used human tissues or cells in their research." Many receive grants from the National Institutes of Health for this work. In addition, "there are nearly 350 commercial biotechnology firms in the United States actively engaged in biotechnology research and commercial product development and approximately 25 to 30 percent appear to be engaged in research to develop a human therapeutic or diagnostic reagent.... Most, but not all, of the human therapeutic products are derived from human tissues and cells, or human cell lines or cloned genes."

In deciding whether to create new tort duties we have in the past considered the impact that expanded liability would have on activities that are important to society, such as research. For example, in *Brown v. Superior Court*, 751 P.2d 470, the fear that strict product liability would frustrate pharmaceutical research led us to hold that a drug manufacturer's liability should not be measured by those standards. We wrote that, "[i]f drug manufacturers were subject to strict liability, they might be reluctant to undertake research programs to develop some pharmaceuticals that would prove beneficial or to distribute others that are available to be marketed, because of the fear of large adverse monetary judgments."

As in *Brown*, the theory of liability that Moore urges us to endorse threatens to destroy the economic incentive to conduct important medical research. If the use of cells in research is a conversion, then with every cell sample a researcher purchases a ticket in a litigation lottery. Because liability for conversion is predicated on a continuing ownership interest, "companies are unlikely to invest heavily in developing, manufacturing, or marketing a product when uncertainty about clear title exists." In our view, borrowing again from *Brown,* "[i]t is not unreasonable to conclude in these circumstances that the imposition of a harsher test for liability would not further the public interest in the development and availability of these important products." (Brown v. Superior Court, 751 P.2d 470.)

. . .

If the scientific users of human cells are to be held liable for failing to investigate the consensual pedigree of their raw materials, we believe the

Legislature should make that decision. Complex policy choices affecting all society are involved, and "[l]egislatures, in making such policy decisions, have the ability to gather empirical evidence, solicit the advice of experts, and hold hearings at which all interested parties present evidence and express their views...."

Finally, there is no pressing need to impose a judicially created rule of strict liability, since enforcement of physicians' disclosure obligations will protect patients against the very type of harm with which Moore was threatened. So long as a physician discloses research and economic interests that may affect his judgment, the patient is protected from conflicts of interest. Aware of any conflicts, the patient can make an informed decision to consent to treatment, or to withhold consent and look elsewhere for medical assistance. As already discussed, enforcement of physicians' disclosure obligations protects patients directly, without hindering the socially useful activities of innocent researchers.

For these reasons, we hold that the allegations of Moore's third amended complaint state a cause of action for breach of fiduciary duty or lack of informed consent, but not conversion.

IV. DISPOSITION

The decision of the Court of Appeal is affirmed in part and reversed in part....

■ Mosk, J, dissenting.

The majority first take the position that Moore has no cause of action for conversion under existing law because he retained no "ownership interest" in his cells after they were removed from his body....

The majority's first reason is that "no reported judicial decision supports Moore's claim, either directly or by close analogy." Neither, however, is there any reported decision rejecting such a claim. The issue is as new as its source: the recent explosive growth in the commercialization of biotechnology.

· · ·

The majority's ... last reason for their conclusion that Moore has no cause of action for conversion under existing law is that "the subject matter of the Regents' patent: the patented cell line and the products derived from it cannot be Moore's property."

· · ·

... The majority's point wholly fails to meet Moore's claim that he is entitled to compensation for defendants' unauthorized use of his bodily tissues *before* defendants patented the Mo cell line: defendants undertook such use immediately after the splenectomy on October 20, 1976, and continued to extract and use Moore's cells and tissue at least until September 20, 1983; the patent, however, did not issue until March 20, 1984, more than seven years after the unauthorized use began. Whatever the legal consequences of that event, it did not operate retroactively to immunize defendants from accountability for conduct occurring long before the patent was granted.

Nor did the issuance of the patent in 1984 necessarily have the drastic effect that the majority contend. To be sure, the patent granted defendants the exclusive right to make, use, or sell the invention for a period of 17 years. (35 U.S.C. § 154.) But Moore does not assert any such right for himself. Rather, he seeks to show that he is entitled, in fairness and equity, to some share in the profits that defendants have made and will make from their commercial exploitation of the Mo cell line. I do not question that the cell line is primarily the product of defendants' inventive effort. Yet likewise no one can question Moore's crucial contribution to the invention—an invention named, ironically, after him: but for the cells of Moore's body taken by defendants, *there would have been no Mo cell line.*

Nevertheless the majority conclude that the patent somehow cut off all Moore's rights: past, present, and future to share in the proceeds of defendants' commercial exploitation of the cell line derived from his own body tissue. The majority cite no authority for this unfair result, and I cannot believe it is compelled by the general law of patents: a patent is not a license to defraud. Perhaps the answer lies in an analogy to the concept of "joint inventor.".... "The joint invention provision guarantees that all who contribute in a substantial way to a product's development benefit from the reward that the product brings.... *A patient's claim to share in the profits flowing from a patent would be analogous to that of an inventor whose collaboration was essential to the success of a resulting product. The patient was not a coequal, but was a necessary contributor to the cell line.*" (Danforth, *Cells, Sales, & Royalties: The Patient's Right to a Portion of the Profits* (1988) 6 YALE L. & POL'Y REV. 179, 197, fns. omitted, italics added.)

Under this reasoning, which I find persuasive, the law of patents would not be a bar to Moore's assertion of an ownership interest in his cells and their products sufficient to warrant his sharing in the proceeds of their commercial exploitation.

Having concluded mistakenly, in my view, that Moore has no cause of action for conversion under existing law, the majority next consider whether to "extend" the conversion cause of action to this context....

. . .

.... [W]hatever merit the majority's single policy consideration may have is outweighed by two contrary considerations, i.e., policies that are promoted by recognizing that every individual has a legally protectible property interest in his own body and its products. First, our society acknowledges a profound ethical imperative to respect the human body as the physical and temporal expression of the unique human persona. One manifestation of that respect is our prohibition against direct abuse of the body by torture or other forms of cruel or unusual punishment. Another is our prohibition against indirect abuse of the body by its economic exploitation for the sole benefit of another person. The most abhorrent form of such exploitation, of course, was the institution of slavery. Lesser forms, such as indentured servitude or even debtor's prison, have also disappeared. Yet their specter haunts the laboratories and boardrooms of today's biotechnological research-industrial complex. It arises wherever scientists or industrialists claim, as defendants claim here, the right to appropriate and exploit a patient's tissue for their sole economic benefit; the right, in other words, to freely mine or harvest valuable physical properties of the patient's body: "Research with human cells that results in significant economic gain for the researcher and no gain for the patient offends the traditional mores of our society in a manner impossible to quantify. Such research tends to treat the human body as a commodity, a means to a profitable end. The dignity and sanctity with which we regard the human whole, body as well as mind and soul, are absent when we allow researchers to further their own interests without the patient's participation by using a patient's cells as the basis for a marketable product." (Danforth, *supra,* 6 YALE L. & POL'Y REV. at p. 190, fn. omitted.)

A second policy consideration adds notions of equity to those of ethics. Our society values fundamental fairness in dealings between its members, and condemns the unjust enrichment of any member at the expense of another. This is particularly true when, as here, the parties are not in equal bargaining positions. We are repeatedly told that the commercial products of the biotechnological revolution "hold the promise of tremendous profit." (*Toward the Right of Commerciality, supra,* 34 UCLA L.REV. at p. 211.) . . .

There is, however, a third party to the biotechnology enterprise: the patient who is the source of the blood or tissue from which all these profits are derived. While he may be a silent partner, his contribution to the venture is absolutely crucial: . . . . Yet defendants deny that Moore is entitled to any share whatever in the proceeds of this cell line. This is both inequitable and immoral. As Dr. Thomas H. Murray, a respected professor of ethics and public policy, testified before Congress, "the person [who furnishes the tissue] should be justly compensated. . . . If biotechnologists fail to make provision for a just sharing of profits with the person whose gift made it possible, the public's sense of justice will be offended and no one will be the winner." (Murray, *Who Owns The Body? On the Ethics of Using Human Tissue for Commercial Purposes* (Jan.–Feb. 1986) IRB: A REVIEW OF HUMAN SUBJECTS RESEARCH, at p. 5.)

. . . . In short, as the Court of Appeal succinctly put it, "If this science has become science for profit, then we fail to see any justification for excluding the patient from participation in those profits."

NOTES AND QUESTIONS

1. John Moore subsequently settled the nondisclosure claim with "significantly diminished economic expectations." Telephone Interview with Christopher E. Angelo, counsel for John Moore, appellant (Sept. 27, 1993). California law mandates a $250,000 ceiling for non-economic damages in medical malpractice actions. WEST'S ANN. CAL. CIV. CODE 3333.2 (2004).

As part of his contract with Genetics Institute, Inc. and Sandoz Pharmaceuticals Corp., Dr. Golde purchased 75,000 shares of Genetics Institute stock for a nominal fee. At the time the California Supreme Court heard the case, Dr. Golde's stock was estimated to be worth $2.4 million. J.E. Ferrell, *Do Your Organs Belong to You?*, S.F. CHRON., Feb. 4, 1990, at 13.

2.   Consider the following case summary:

> In *United States v. Arora*, the personal animosity between two scientists employed by the National Institute of Health reached its peak when one of them maliciously destroyed cultured human cells produced by the other. The United States brought a civil action for conversion against the delinquent researcher. The court, using a pure property analysis, held that the cell, though a product of a living body, was property capable of conversion.

Remigius N. Nwabueze, *Biotechnology and the New Property Regime in Human Bodies and Body Parts*, 24 LOY. L.A. INT'L & COMP. L. REV. 19, 43 (2002).

Can this ruling be reconciled with the holding of Moore? Should scientists retain property rights over excised cells when the individual from which the cells were taken cannot?

3.   In the years since the California Supreme Court's ruling in *Moore* the issue of ownership over human tissue has not gone away quietly. Instead, groups continue to initiate actions in order to obtain compensation. Consider Donna M. Gitter, *Ownership of Human Tissue: A Proposal for Federal Recognition of Human Research Participants' Property Rights in Their Biological Material*, 61 WASH. & LEE L. REV. 257, 259–261 (2004):

> In the past, one would have expected families afflicted by a degenerative and fatal disease to rejoice at medical researchers' development of reliable carrier and prenatal screening to detect the genetic mutation causing the condition. However, a recent legal action, initiated by families suffering from a rare genetic disorder known as Canavan disease against the researchers who isolated the gene associated with this condition, illustrates the complexities inherent in the relationships among human research participants and medical researchers in our current era of genomic exploration and commercialization. In that case, Greenberg v. Miami Children's Hospital Research Institute, Inc., the plaintiffs included a group of parents who gave birth to children afflicted with Canavan disease and also three nonprofit community groups dedicated to assisting those affected by this condition. All plaintiffs supplied some combination of tissue, autopsy, blood, urine, and other pathology samples, personal data, funding, and other resources in order to advance medical research of Canavan disease. The plaintiffs alleged that the defendants, a scientific researcher and a hospital, breached both their duty of informed consent and their fiduciary duty when they failed to disclose to the plaintiffs their intention to patent the gene and diagnostic test for Canavan disease. In addition, the plaintiffs asserted that the defendants wrongfully converted the plaintiffs' property by using the plaintiffs' contributions to reap personal economic benefit rather than to promote widely affordable and accessible carrier and prenatal testing for Canavan disease in accordance with the plaintiffs' goals. According to the plaintiffs, had they known of the defendants' intention to patent the gene associated with Canavan disease, they either would have imposed restrictions on the researchers' use of their genetic material in order to avoid commercialization of the Canavan disease gene or, instead, would have chosen to donate their samples to researchers who pursued objectives compatible with their own. Based upon these same facts, the plaintiffs also asserted claims of unjust enrichment, fraudulent concealment, and misappropriation of trade secrets. On May 29, 2003, Judge Federico A. Moreno of the United States District Court for the Southern District of Florida dismissed five of the plaintiffs' six claims pursuant to Federal Rule of Civil Procedure 12(b)(6) for failure to state a claim upon which relief may be granted. He did, however, hold that only the plaintiffs' unjust enrichment cause of action survived the motion.

Among the myriad ethical and legal issues raised, but not resolved, by the Greenberg action is the optimal means of distribution among biomedical researchers and their research participants of any rights in commercial products and revenues derived from human tissue. . . .

Additionally, Gitter believes that extending ownership rights over human tissue in biomedical research is essential in order to insure continued progress in the field. The conclusion she reaches directly contradicts the *Moore* court's belief that extending such rights would impose crippling transaction costs on the biomedical research industry.

[Extending property rights over human tissue for research purposes] promises to stimulate biomedical research in many ways. First, the promise of compensation encourages research participation by individuals who might otherwise decline to behave altruistically while others profit, and, what is more, who face the inconvenience, medical risks, loss of privacy, and possibility of genetic discrimination inherent in such participation. Second, the promise of profits also fosters self-checking by individuals who will initiate significant research by informing biomedical researchers of the value and uniqueness of their tissue. Third, the possibility of a liability action creates even greater incentive for researchers to provide informed consent, especially because the monetary damages will prove great enough to serve a deterrent effect. Fourth, this model's recognition of research participants' right to bargain with researchers will help to ensure that the tissue ends up in the hands of the highest bidder, who, it is hoped, will put the tissue to its most valuable use. Fifth, and just as important, notions of equity militate that research participants, who supply useful scientific raw materials, and encounter risks through their participation, are entitled to compensation, in light of researchers' own pecuniary gain. Any other approach threatens to lead to a decrease in public support of such research, lest the public perceive that researchers obtain scientific inputs from them for free and then charge them for the commercial outputs.

4. Following the *Greenberg* court's ruling on the defendant's motion to dismiss, but before a trial could be conducted on the merits of the plaintiff's unjust enrichment claim, the parties settled their dispute through mediation. Telephone Interview with Karen L. Stetson, counsel for Miami Children's Hospital, defendant (June 15, 2004).

5. Since *Moore*, patient groups have been searching for a way to maintain property rights in the tissue they provide to researchers. PXE International, a patient group founded by Sharon and Patrick Terry may have found a way. PXE International is a group that is composed of thousands of families that have been affected by the genetic disorder Pseudoxanthoma Elasticum (PXE). The Terry's founded the organization in 1996 after learning that they had passed the disorder to their two children. Since its formation the group has established a blood and tissue bank which serves as a repository for research materials provided by its membership. This allows PXE International to act as a "firewall between patients and researcher to ensure maximum research participation."

PXE International has used its position as the premier patient group for those afflicted with PXE to make tremendous strides in PXE research. Sharon Terry was a full partner in the discovery of the PXE gene and was named as a co-inventor on the patent application as a result. Terry was then able to negotiate for the remaining intellectual property rights from the other co-inventors. She then transferred the property interest to PXE International. As a result, all members of the organization—those families that supplied tissue samples and contributed to the organizations success—are now part owners of the patent through their affiliation with PXE International.

Today PXE International is turning the *Moore* decision on its head. Through the operation of its tissue bank, PXE International routinely contracts with researchers and provides funding and the necessary research materials in exchange for licensing rights to any patents or other results from the research. As a result, those who supplied the research materials have essentially been able to maintain a property interest in their bodily material, and have used those interests to extract concessions from researchers. These contracts have yet to be challenged and it will be interesting to see how a court will approach this practice in light of the *Moore* decision. Interview with Patrick Terry, July 27, 2004.

B.   THE BODY AS COMMODITY: WHEN BODY PARTS ARE TO BE TRANSPLANTED

Newman v. Sathyavaglswaran

United States Court of Appeals for the Ninth Circuit, 2002.
287 F.3d 786.

■ FISHER, J.

Parents, whose deceased children's corneas were removed by the Los Angeles County Coroner's office without notice or consent, brought this 42 U.S.C. § 1983 action alleging a taking of their property without due process of law. The complaint was dismissed by the district court for a failure to state a claim upon which relief could be granted. We must decide whether the longstanding recognition in the law of California, paralleled by our national common law, that next of kin have the exclusive right to possess the bodies of their deceased family members creates a property interest, the deprivation of which must be accorded due process of law under the Fourteenth Amendment of the United States Constitution. . . .

I.   FACTUAL AND PROCEDURAL BACKGROUND

In reviewing the district court's dismissal . . . "we must 'take as true all allegations of material fact stated in the complaint and construe them in the light most favorable to the nonmoving party.'" . . . Robert Newman and Barbara Obarski (the parents) each had children, Richard Newman and Kenneth Obarski respectively, who died in Los Angeles County in October 1997. Following their deaths, the Office of the Coroner for the County of Los Angeles (the coroner) obtained possession of the bodies of the children and, under procedures adopted pursuant to California Government Code § 27491.47 as it then existed, removed the corneas from those bodies without the knowledge of the parents and without an attempt to notify them and request consent. The parents became aware of the coroner's actions in September 1999 and subsequently filed this § 1983 action alleging a deprivation of their property without due process of law in violation of the Fourteenth Amendment.

The coroner filed a Rule 12(b)(6) motion to dismiss, arguing that the parents could not have a property interest in their deceased children's corneas. . . .

II.   PROPERTY INTERESTS IN DEAD BODIES

The Fourteenth Amendment prohibits states from "depriv[ing] any person of life, liberty, or property, without due process of law." U.S. Const.

amend. XIV, § 1. At the threshold, a claim under § 1983 for an unconstitutional deprivation of property must show (1) a deprivation (2) of property (3) under color of state law.... If these elements are met, the question becomes whether the state afforded constitutionally adequate process for the deprivation.... Here, it is uncontested that the coroner's action was a deprivation under color of state law. The coroner argues, however, that the dismissal of the parents' complaint was proper because they could not have a property interest in their children's corneas.

... [T]he Supreme Court repeatedly has affirmed that [possession and control of one's own person] ... rank[s] as one of the fundamental liberties protected by the "substantive" component of the Due Process Clause.... The Court has not had occasion to address whether the rights of possession and control of one's own body, the most "sacred" and "carefully guarded" of all rights in the common law ... are property interests protected by the Due Process Clause. Nor has it addressed what Due Process protections are applicable to the rights of next of kin to possess and control the bodies of their deceased relatives.

... [T]he first step of our analysis is to analyze the history of rules and understandings of our nation with respect to the possession and protection of the bodies of the dead.

A.   History of Common Law Interests in Dead Bodies

Duties to protect the dignity of the human body after its death are deeply rooted in our nation's history. In a valuable history of the subject, the Supreme Court of Rhode Island recounted:

> By the civil law of ancient Rome, the charge of burial was first upon the person to whom it was delegated by the deceased; second, upon the *scripti haeredes* (to whom the property was given), and if none, then upon the *haeredes legitimi* or *cognati* in order.... The heirs might be compelled to comply with the provisions of the will in regard to burial. And the Pontifical College had the power of providing for the burial of those who had no place of burial in their own right.

Pierce v. Proprietors of Swan Point Cemetery, 10 R.I. 227, 235–36, 1872 WL 3575 (1872) (citations omitted).

In 17th century England, and in much of Europe, duties to bury the dead and protect the dignified disposition of the body ... were borne primarily by churches, which had a duty to bury the bodies of those residing in their parishes.... These duties, and the explanation of their genesis in the rights of the dead, carried over into New England colonial practice....

The Roman practice of including duties to protect the body of the dead in civil law had no parallel in the early English common law because burials were matters of ecclesiastical cognizance.... Thus, [no formal property right was established]....

A change in the common law in England can be traced to the 1840 case of *Rex v. Stewart,* 12 AD. & E. 773 (1840). In that case, the socially recognized right of the dead to a dignified disposition, previously enforced only through ecclesiastical courts, was interpreted as creating enforceable common law duties. The question before the court was whether the hospital in which "a pauper" died or the parish in which she was to be buried was under a duty to carry the body to the grave. *Id.* at 774. The court expressed "extreme difficulty in placing . . . any legal foundation" for either rule, but stated it was unwilling to discharge the case "considering how long the practice had prevailed, and been sanctioned, of burying such persons at the expense of the parish, and the general consequences of holding that such practice ha[d] no warrant in law." *Id.* at 776–77. It stated the premises that, under long-standing tradition, "[e]very person . . . has a right to Christian burial . . . that implies the right to be carried from the place where his body lies to the parish cemetery" and "bodies . . . carried in a state of naked exposure to the grave [ ] would be a real offence to the living, as well as an apparent indignity to the dead." *Id.* at 777–78. From these traditional understandings, the court concluded that "[t]he feelings and interests of the living require" that "the common law cast [ ] on some one the duty of carrying to the grave, decently covered, the dead body of any person dying in such a state of indigence as to leave no funds for that purpose." *Id.* at 778. That duty, it held, was imposed on "the individual under whose roof a poor person dies. . . ."

Many early American courts adopted Blackstone's description of the common law, holding that "a dead body is not the subject of property right." *Bessemer Land*, 18 So. at 567. The duty to protect the body by providing a burial was often described as flowing from the "universal . . . right of sepulture," rather than from a concept of property law. Wynkoop v. Wynkoop, 42 Pa. 293, 300–01, 1861 WL 5846 (1862). As cases involving unauthorized mutilation and disposition of bodies increased toward the end of the 19th century, paralleling the rise in demand for human cadavers in medical science and use of cremation as an alternative to burial . . . courts began to recognize an exclusive right of the next of kin to possess and control the disposition of the bodies of their dead relatives, the violation of which was actionable at law.

. . .

C.   The Right to Transfer Body Parts

The first successful transplantation of a kidney in 1954 led to an expansion of the rights of next of kin to the bodies of the dead. In 1968, the National Conference of Commissioners on Uniform State Laws approved the Uniform Anatomical Gift Act (UAGA), adopted by California the same year, which grants next of kin the right to transfer the parts of bodies in their possession to others for medical or research purposes. Cal. Health & Safety Code § 7150 et seq. The right to transfer is limited. The California UAGA prohibits any person from "knowingly, for valuable consideration, purchas[ing] or sell[ing] a part for transplantation, therapy, or reconditioning, if removal of the part is intended to occur after the death of the decedent," Cal. Health & Safety Code § 7155, as does federal law, 42 U.S.C. § 274e (prohibiting the "transfer [of] any human organ for valuable consideration"); *cf.* Finley v. Atl. Transport Co., 115 N.E. 715, 717 (1917) ("[T]here is no right of property in a dead body . . . as understood in the commercial sense."); Larson v. Chase, 50 N.W. 238, 239 (1891) ("[A] dead body is not property in the common commercial sense of that term[.]").

In the 1970s and 1980s, medical science improvements and the related demand for transplant organs prompted governments to search for new ways to increase the supply of organs for donation. . . . Many perceived as a hindrance to the supply of needed organs the rule implicit in the UAGA that donations could be effected only if consent was received from the decedent or next of kin. . . . In response, some states passed "presumed consent" laws that allow the taking and transfer of body parts by a coroner without the consent of next of kin as long as no objection to the removal is known. California Government Code § 27491.47, enacted in 1983, was such a law.

III.   DUE PROCESS ANALYSIS

"[T]o provide California non-profit eye banks with an adequate supply of corneal tissue," S. Com. Rep. SB 21 (Cal.1983), § 27491.47(a) authorized the coroner to "remove and release or authorize the removal and release of corneal eye tissue from a body within the coroner's custody" without any effort to notify and obtain the consent of next of kin "if . . . [t]he coroner has no knowledge of objection to the removal." The law also provided that the coroner or any person acting upon his or her request "shall [not] incur civil liability for such removal in an action brought by any person who did not object prior to the removal . . . nor be subject to criminal prosecution." § 27491.47(b).

. . .

In two decisions the Sixth Circuit, the only federal circuit to address the issue until now, held that the interests of next of kin in dead bodies recognized in Michigan and Ohio allowed next of kin to bring § 1983 actions challenging implementation of cornea removal statutes similar to California's. Whaley v. County of Tuscola, 58 F.3d 1111 (6th Cir.1995) (Michigan); Brotherton v. Cleveland, 923 F.2d 477 (6th Cir.1991) (Ohio). The Sixth Circuit noted that courts in each state had recognized a right of next of kin to possess the body for burial and a claim by next of kin against others who disturb the body. *Whaley*, 58 F.3d at 1116; *Brotherton*, 923 F.2d at 482. Those common law rights, combined with the statutory right to control the disposition of the body recognized in each state's adoption of the UAGA, was held to be sufficient to create in next of kin a property interest in the corneas of their deceased relatives that could not be taken without due process of law. *Whaley*, 58 F.3d at 1117; *Brotherton*, 923 F.2d at 482.

The supreme courts of Florida and Georgia, however, have held that similar legal interests of next of kin in the possession of the body of a deceased family member, recognized as "quasi property" rights in each state, are "not . . . of constitutional dimension." Georgia Lions Eye Bank, Inc. v. Lavant, 335 S.E.2d 127, 128 (1985); State v. Powell, 497 So.2d 1188, 1191 (Fla.1986) (commenting that "[a]ll authorities generally agree that the next of kin have no property right in the remains of a decedent"). The Florida Supreme Court recently rejected the broad implications of the reasoning in *Powell*, distinguishing that decision as turning on a balance between the public health interest in cornea donation and the " 'infinitesimally small intrusion' " of their removal. Crocker v. Pleasant, 778 So.2d 978, 985, 988 (Fla.2001)....

We agree with the reasoning of the Sixth Circuit and believe that reasoning is applicable here. Under traditional common law principles, serving a duty to protect the dignity of the human body in its final disposition that is deeply rooted in our legal history and social traditions, the parents had exclusive and legitimate claims of entitlement to possess, control, dispose and prevent the violation of the corneas and other parts of the bodies of their deceased children. With California's adoption of the UAGA, Cal. Health and Safety Code § 7151.5, it statutorily recognized other important rights of the parents in relation to the bodies of their deceased children—the right to transfer body parts and refuse to allow their transfer. These are all important components of the group of rights by which property is defined, each of which carried with it the power to exclude others from its exercise.... Thus, we hold that the parents had property interests in the corneas of their deceased children protected by the Due Process Clause of the Fourteenth Amendment.

. . .

Because the property interests of next of kin to dead bodies are firmly entrenched in the "background principles of property law," based on values and understandings contained in our legal history dating from the Roman Empire, California may not be free to alter them with exceptions that lack "a firm basis in traditional property principles." *Phillips*, 524 U.S. at 165–68.

The effect of § 27491.47 was to remove a procedure—notice and request for consent prior to the deprivation—and a remedy—the opportunity to seek redress for the deprivation in California's courts. A state may not evade due process analysis by defining " '[p]roperty' . . . by the procedures provided for its deprivation." Cleveland Bd. of Educ. v. Loudermill, 470 U.S. 532, 541 (1985). "While the legislature may elect not to confer a property interest . . . it may not constitutionally authorize the deprivation of such an interest, once conferred, without appropriate procedural safeguards." *Id.* (citations omitted). With § 27491.47, California eliminated procedural safeguards but retained the interest.

When the coroner removed the corneas from the bodies of the parents' deceased children and transferred them to others, the parents could no longer possess, control, dispose or prevent the violation of those parts of their children's bodies....

At bottom, "[p]roperty rights serve human values. They are recognized to that end, and are limited by it." State v. Shack, 277 A.2d 369, 372 (1971). The property rights that California affords to next of kin to the body of their deceased relatives serve the premium value our society has historically placed on protecting the dignity of the human body in its final disposition. California infringed the dignity of the bodies of the children when it extracted the corneas from those bodies without the consent of the parents. The process of law was due the parents for this deprivation of their rights.

. . .

The dismissal of the parents' § 1983 claim is REVERSED and RE-MANDED for further proceedings.

NOTES AND QUESTIONS

1. Does recognizing an "entitlement" in a decedent's remains clarify or confuse the legal status of the body? Generally, entitlements have been found in contexts other than the body. *See*, e.g., Connell v. Higginbotham, 403 U.S. 207, 208, 91 S.Ct. 1772 (1971) (recognizing a property interest in public employment that proscribes dismissal without due process safeguards); Goldberg v. Kelly, 397 U.S. 254, 90 S.Ct. 1011 (1970) (finding that welfare benefits granted under statutory and administrative eligibility standards are entitled to constitutional protection). Consider the troubling case of Arnaud v. Odom, 870 F.2d 304 (5th Cir.1989), *cert. denied*, 493 U.S. 855, 110 S.Ct. 159 (1989). There, a state coroner conducted unauthorized medical experiments upon the corpses of two infant children. In denying the plaintiff parents' claim for deprivation of property and liberty interests, the court held:

> We decline to create from the substantive parameters of the due process clause a liberty interest in next of kin to be free from state-occasioned mutilation of the body of a deceased relative and to possess the body for burial in the same condition in which death left the body.

Id. at 305.

2. *Compare* Remigius N. Nwabueze, *Biotechnology and the New Property Regime in Human Body Parts*, 24 Loy. L.A. Int'l & Comp. L. Rev. 19, 31–34 (2002):

> Because of such difficulties with tort claims, plaintiffs and U.S. courts often resort to the concept of quasi-property in a corpse. Many times, the intent is to avoid the requirements of proving willful or wanton conduct by the defendant or the similar problem of proving accompanying physical or pecuniary loss.
>
> The concept of quasi-property is an ingenious invention by U.S. courts to help a deserving plaintiff. It is a legal fiction because it has no relationship with property in the legal sense. It merely embodies the next-of-kin's sepulchral rights, which are not based in property, such as the right to possession and custody of the corpse for burial. It also gives a right to determine the time, place and manner of burial and to have the deceased delivered to the next-of-kin in the same way as it was when life left it.
>
> In contrast, application of the concept of quasi-property has been used in both a jurisdictional and remedial sense. It has proven to be a handy jurisdictional device to grant standing to a plaintiff. A strict application of the British no-property rule denies standing where a plaintiff does not suffer any detriment by the desecration of property he has no right to. In *Ritter v. Couch*, the U.S. quasi-property concept recognizes that a plaintiff has an analogous property interest in a dead body that, if desecrated, would give him or her standing.
>
> In *Ritter*, the plaintiffs objected to the defendant's acquisition of an old cemetery containing their relatives' burial sites. Since the plaintiffs did not pay for the burial plots and merely had a license to bury their relatives there, the defendant contended the plaintiffs had no standing. The court, using the quasi-property concept, held that the plaintiffs had standing. According to the court,

"while a dead body is not property in the strict sense of the common law, it is a quasi-property, over which the relatives of the deceased have rights which our courts of equity will protect."

The use of the quasi-property concept occurs more in the remedial context. This concept is usually a last resort when a plaintiff's tort claim fails for the reasons already given. Thus, in *Blanchard v. Brawley*, the court held that Louisiana law did not allow recovery of damages on account of a third party's injury and instead, resorted to the general rule of quasi-property to find for the plaintiffs. The remedial or substantive use of the concept was also evident in most of the cases cited.

. . .

While some U.S. courts have shown the greatest accommodation to a plaintiff, using the quasi-property concept, others have refused to resort to this concept when the plaintiff is required to show pure ownership or a right to possession, as in actions for conversion or detinue. In such cases, the quasi-property concept is stripped of its fictional property characteristics.

For instance, in *Crocker v. Pleasant*, the plaintiffs asserted an infringement of their due process right under the Fourteenth Amendment of the U.S. Constitution and failed. Similarly, in *Keyes v. Konkel*, the plaintiff's possessory claim of a relative's dead body, allegedly detained by an undertaker, also failed. The court in *Keyes* observed that "no return of the property can be ordered in case of the replevin of a dead body" and that the concept of quasi-property did not apply to "damage to the corpse as property, but rather damage to the next of kin by infringement of his right to have the body delivered to him for burial." Also, in *Culpepper v. Pearl St. Bldg. Inc.*, the plaintiffs used the concept to argue conversion of their son's corpse due to mistaken cremation by the defendant. The court rejected "the fictional theory that a property right exists in a dead body which would support an action for conversion."

. . .

In conclusion, most U.S. court decisions are revolutionary in their use of the quasi-property concept as a significant basis for U.S. law on dead bodies even though this concept does not offer comprehensive protection to a plaintiff. The continuing debate on this subject and its potential solutions, tend to obviate the defects currently used in tort-based causes of action. As such, the suggested solution found in the American Restatement of Law 2d, Torts, 274, becomes relevant.

Are quasi-property interests in dead bodies sufficient to insure the proper disposition of the body and to prevent mutilation? Should the law go further and extend full property rights to dead bodies or should society be more concerned with increasing the supply of donor organs?

McFall v. Shimp

Court of Allegheny County, Pennsylvania, 1978.
10 Pa. D. & C.3d 90.

■ FLAHERTY, J.

Plaintiff, Robert McFall, suffers from a rare bone marrow disease and the prognosis for his survival is very dim, unless he receives a bone marrow transplant from a compatible donor. Finding a compatible donor is a very difficult task and limited to a selection among close relatives. After a search and certain tests, it has been determined that only defendant is suitable as a donor. Defendant refuses to submit to the necessary transplant, and before the court is a request for a preliminary injunction which seeks to compel defendant to submit to further tests, and, eventually, the bone marrow transplant.

Although a diligent search has produced no authority, plaintiff cites the ancient statute of King Edward I, 81 Westminster 2, 13 Ed. I, c. 24, pointing out, as is the case, that this court is a successor to the English courts of Chancery and derives power from this statute, almost 700 years old. The question posed by plaintiff is that, in order to save the life of one of its members by the only means available, may society infringe upon one's absolute right to his "bodily security"?

The common law has consistently held to a rule which provides that one human being is under no legal compulsion to give aid or to take action to save another human being or to rescue. A great deal has been written regarding this rule which, on the surface, appears to be revolting in a moral sense. Introspection, however, will demonstrate that the rule is founded upon the very essence of our free society. It is noteworthy that counsel for plaintiff has cited authority which has developed in other societies in support of plaintiff's request in this instance. Our society, contrary to many others, has, as its first principle, the respect for the individual, and that society and government exist to protect the individual from being invaded and hurt by another. Many societies adopt a contrary view which has the individual existing to serve the society as a whole. In preserving such a society as we have, it is bound to happen that great moral conflicts will arise and will appear harsh in a given instance. In this case, the chancellor is being asked to force one member of society to undergo a medical procedure which would provide that part of that individual's body would be removed from him and given to another so that the other could live. Morally, this decision rests with defendant, and, in the view of the court, the refusal of defendant is morally indefensible. For our law to *compel* defendant to submit to an intrusion of his body would change every concept and principle upon which our society is founded. To do so would defeat the sanctity of the individual, and would impose a rule which would know no limits, and one could not imagine where the line would be drawn.

This request is not to be compared with an action at law for damages, but rather is an action in equity before a chancellor, which, in the ultimate, if granted, would require the forceable submission to the medical procedure. For a society which respects the rights of *one* individual, to sink its teeth into the jugular vein or neck of one of its members and suck from it sustenance for *another* member, is revolting to our hard-wrought concepts of jurisprudence. Forceable extraction of living body tissue causes revulsion to the judicial mind. Such would raise the spectre of the swastika and the Inquisition, reminiscent of the horrors this portends.

This court makes no comment on the law regarding plaintiff's rights in an action at law for damages, but has no alternative but to deny the requested equitable relief. An order will be entered denying the request for a preliminary injunction.

ORDER

And now, July 26, 1978, upon consideration of the request for a preliminary injunction, hearing thereon, arguments and briefs submitted, it is ordered, adjudged, and decreed that the request for a preliminary injunction is herewith denied.

NOTES AND QUESTIONS

1. Robert McFall died in Pittsburgh on August 10, 1978, at the age of 39, three weeks after unsuccessfully suing his cousin. *Transition*, NEWSWEEK, Aug. 21, 1978, at 79. News of his predicament increased bone marrow registries; more than a thousand people offered to donate their bone marrow to him. Albin Krebs, *Notes on People*, N.Y. TIMES, July 29, 1978, at 42.

2. The right of an adult to choose whether or not to donate an organ has never been questioned by courts. Heavy debate, however, revolves around the issue of the rights of minors and the mentally incompetent concerning consent to organ donation. Should a parent be allowed to consent to an organ transplant from one child in order to save the life of another? Consider Robert W. Griner, *Live Organ Donations Between Siblings and the Best Interest Standard: Time for Stricter Judicial Intervention*, 10 GA. ST. U. L. REV. 589, 592–93 (1994):

> The seminal reported case involving a transplant between siblings is *Strunk v. Strunk*. The prospective donor was a twenty-seven-year-old with a mental age of approximately six years. The prospective recipient was his twenty-eight-year-old mentally competent brother, suffering from end-stage kidney failure. Tissue compatibility testing of the family, including several collateral relatives, revealed that the sibling was the only acceptable donor. The parents sought permission from the court to authorize the procedure.... [T]he court held that it had the authority to allow the operation and, based on the expert testimony of a psychiatrist, found that the survival of his brother was psychologically in the incompetent's best interest.

> A different result was reached in *In re Richardson*. The parents of a seventeen-year-old incompetent sought the court's authorization to allow the transplantation of a kidney to his thirty-two-year-old sister. The court denied permission based on property law. Because Louisiana state law provides unqualified protection from intrusion into a property right, "it is inconceivable ... that it affords less protection to a minor's right to be free in his person from bodily intrusion to the extent of loss of an organ unless such loss be in the best interest of the minor." The court found the asserted psychological benefit to be gained by the donor to be highly speculative and, in this case, unlikely. The court concluded "that neither the parents nor the courts can authorize surgical intrusion ... for the purpose of donating one of his kidneys...."

Griner concludes that courts should intervene on the behalf of children and mental incompetents as parents and guardians are incapable of making decisions that are solely in the best interests of their wards. *Supra*, 613.

Compare Michael Morley, *Proxy Consent to Organ Donation by Incompetents*, 111 YALE L.J. 1215 (2002):

> Where grave interests are not at stake, or reasonable people can disagree over the proper resolution, the judgment of the parent-guardian should be respected. As a Missouri court noted, where "there is a difference of medical opinion as to the efficacy of a proposed treatment, or where medical opinion differs as to which of two or more suggested remedies should be followed,

requiring the exercise of a sound discretion, the opinion of the parent should not be lightly overridden.''

Moreover, courts have explicitly recognized that organ donation to family members is a moral, albeit not legal, obligation. In the words of one judge, ''Morally, this decision rests with defendant [a potential donor] and, in the view of the court, the refusal of defendant is morally indefensible.'' For the state to preclude parent-guardians from consenting on behalf of their wards to do the right thing is to strip children and the mentally impaired of their dignity by exempting them from the moral obligations incumbent upon members of families.

3. What if the parents of a sick child in need of a transplant conceive for the purposes of finding a suitable donor? What are the ethical implications of such an act, and should parents be allowed such control over their children? Consider Robert W. Griner, *Live Organ Donations Between Siblings and the Best Interest Standard: Time for Judicial Intervention*, 10 Ga. St. U. L. Rev. 589, 604–05 (1994):

While conceiving to produce a potential donor does not necessarily preclude a family from loving a child, it does present problems with respect to rationalizing consent for a procedure that confers no physiologic value on the donor. The issue arises whether simply being born into a family immediately confers a fully developed familial relationship or whether the relationship requires time to develop and mature. An infant, especially a newborn, is arguably a stranger to the family and community. At a minimum, however, the basic time sequence with respect to decision-making seems reversed. Earlier cases depended upon an established relationship, usually sibling, to confer the benefit that justifies the decision to donate. Under the circumstances of parity for donation, the decision to donate precedes establishment of the relationship upon which the conferring benefit is premised. Even under the best interest standard, the reasoning seems skewed and attenuated. Because events do not conform to the standard, the best interest test should be inapplicable under these circumstances.

Compare Michael T. Morley, *Proxy Consent to Organ Donation by Incompetents*, 111 Yale L.J. 1215, 1247–48 (2002):

Even from an ethical standpoint, it is unclear that the practice should be subject to condemnation. Opponents might claim that children could somehow be psychologically harmed by the knowledge that they were conceived primarily for their organs. Far from being a decisive argument against conception, however, this claim gives rise to what in philosophical circles is referred to as the ''future person'' problem. It is difficult to claim that being born for a particular reason (or through a particular type of advanced reproductive technology) is against a child's best interests, or inflicts a net harm on that child. But for that parental motive or advanced technology, the child would not exist. Put another way, one cannot easily say that a child whose conception was primarily motivated by the need for a kidney or bone marrow is wronged, because the alternative for that child is never to have been born at all.

Furthermore, conceiving a child to save a life is hardly a motive that warrants moral condemnation, even from the perspective of the child herself. After all, the child ''might well prefer that to the idea that one was an 'accident,' . . . [conceived] because contraception or abortion were not available, conceived to cement a failing marriage, to continue a family line, to qualify for welfare aid, to sex-balance a family, or as an experiment in child-rearing.'' People conceive and give birth to children for a wide range of reasons, and often for mixed reasons or even no reason at all. In light of some of the commonly accepted purposes for giving birth, doing so to save a life can hardly be a ground for moral reproach. For these reasons, the possibility of parents giving birth to children to act as organ donors does not constitute a compelling argument against recognizing the right of parent-guardians to tender proxy consent.

Brown v. Delaware Valley Transplant Program

Superior Court of Pennsylvania, 1992.
420 Pa.Super. 84, 615 A.2d 1379.

■ McEwen, J.

Lawrence Brown was brought to the emergency room of Brandywine Hospital at 5:20 p.m. on October 30, 1984, suffering from a gunshot wound of the left supra orbital region and, within the hour, was determined by a neurosurgeon, James P. Argires, M.D., to be suffering from a terminal head injury. As a result of his diagnosis, Dr. Argires advised the Delaware Valley Transplant Program (DVTP) that Mr. Brown, who was placed on life support systems, was a potential donor of organs for transplantation and, at approximately 7:15 p.m. that evening a tissue typing biopsy was performed. Cerebral death was documented at 10:35 p.m. on October 30, 1984, and the kidneys and heart of the decedent were removed for transplantation during the early morning hours of November 1, 1984. The first relative of the decedent to be located as a result of the search undertaken by state police was the decedent's sister, Virginia Brown, who was located at her office at 10:15 on the morning of November 1, 1984.

This action was subsequently commenced by appellants: Virginia Brown, the sister of the decedent, in her capacity as an individual as well as administratrix of the estate of Lawrence Brown; Thomas Brown, the father of the decedent; and Joan Spina and Johnnie Lee Brown, the sister and brother of the decedent. Appellants named as defendants in the action the Delaware Valley Transplant Program (hereinafter DVTP); Arthur Harrell, coordinator for DVTP; Brandywine Hospital; the president of Brandywine Hospital, Norman Ledwin; the administrator of the Brandywine Hospital, Phillippe Oullette; James Argires, the aforementioned neurosurgeon; the executive director of DVTP, Howard Nathan; the attorney for the Hospital, Samuel Heed; and Charles Wagner, M.D., the surgeon who removed the organs for transplantation.[1]

Appellants sought money damages from appellees based upon appellees' participation in the harvesting of Lawrence Brown's heart and kidneys. The complaint filed by appellants sets forth causes of action for:

(1) mutilation of a corpse,

(2) intentional infliction of emotional distress,

(3) civil conspiracy, and

(4) assault and battery.

---

1. Attorney Samuel Heed and Charles Wagner, M.D., are no longer parties to the action. This Court affirmed the dismissal of all counts against Attorney Heed in *Brown v. Delaware Valley Transplant Program,* 539 A.2d 1372. (1988), and counsel for appellants stated during the presentation of oral argument that Dr. Wagner had been dismissed as a result of appellants' determination that he had acted in "good faith."

[handwritten margin note: Did Dr's act in good faith]

Following the close of the pleadings, all appellees moved for summary judgment on the basis of the qualified immunity afforded by Section 8607(c) of the Anatomical Gift Act, 20 Pa.C.S. § 8607(c). The trial court granted the motion for summary judgment on the basis of the qualified immunity, and this timely appeal was taken from the judgment entered in favor of all appellees.

Appellants contend that there exist material issues of fact as to whether appellees acted in good faith or whether appellees sought to avoid the provisions of the Act so as to obtain the decedent's organs without the consent of any of the individuals authorized by Section 8602(b) of the Act to give such consent. Essentially the allegations of appellants' complaint are based upon appellants' belief that appellees purposefully circumvented the provisions of the Pennsylvania Anatomical Gift Act, thus precluding application of the good faith defense provided by Section 8607(c) of the Act. We find that there is no dispute as to any *material* fact, that the undisputed evidence of record establishes the good faith of appellees, and that appellees are, as a matter of law, entitled to the qualified immunity provided by the Act. We, therefore, affirm the judgment entered in favor of appellees.

[handwritten margin note: PA has stat.]

The Uniform Anatomical Gift Act has been adopted, with minor variations, in all fifty states and the District of Columbia. Section 8602(b) of the Pennsylvania Act, which is identical to the Uniform Act, establishes a descending order of priority for those persons with authority to make an anatomical gift:

> b) Any of the following persons, in order of priority stated, *when persons in prior classes are not available at the time of death,* and in the absence of actual notice of contrary indications by the decedent or actual notice of opposition by a member of the same or a prior class, may give all or any part of the decedent's body for any purpose specified in Section 8603 of this code:
>
> (1) the spouse;
>
> (2) an adult son or daughter;
>
> (3) either parent;
>
> (4) an adult brother or sister;
>
> (5) a guardian of the person of the decedent at the time of his death; and
>
> (6) *any other person authorized or under obligation to dispose of the body.*

[handwritten margin note: ambiguous. P – It doesn't have it]

> * * *
>
> c) The persons authorized by subsection (b) of this section may make the gift after or immediately before death.

20 Pa.C.S. § 8602.

> Section 8607(c) of the Act provides that any person who acts in good faith in accord with the terms of this chapter or with the anatomical gift laws of another state or a foreign country is not liable for damages in any civil action or subject to prosecution in any criminal proceeding for his act.

20 Pa.C.S. § 8607(c).

The argument of appellants that appellees were guilty of a purposeful failure to act as well as purposeful non-disclosure is based upon the following facts as recited in appellants' brief:

"Between 6:00 p.m. and midnight on October 30, 1984, the Pennsylvania state police had obtained a voter registration card, an unemployment card, an address, a post office box, a Social Security number, and a witness' statement that the person he had seen shot was named 'Larry' and determined that such information was a sufficiently accurate and positive identification to formulate the basis for a sworn affidavit that the victim of the shooting was Larry Brown." At this same point in the chronology of events, the Delaware Valley Transplant Program had also obtained information indicating that the shooting victim had been identified as Lawrence Brown by an "apparent girlfriend." It is further undisputed that by 9:15 a.m. the following morning the individual in the hospital had been positively identified by the shooter as Larry Brown, a resident of Frank's Folly Campground. Notwithstanding the foregoing, the [appellees] maintain even today, more than five years later, that *no one* in the hospital or the Transplant Program knew the identity of Larry Brown at this same point in time. Finally, it is absolutely clear, both from deposition testimony as well as the defendants' summary judgment motion, that at no time on October 30, 1984, did anyone from Brandywine Hospital or the Transplant Program make any attempt of any kind to locate the next of kin of Larry Brown.

Essentially, counsel for appellants argues that three facts preclude the entry of summary judgment in favor of appellees:

(1) that the state police rather than any of the appellees were the only individuals actively searching for Larry Brown's next of kin;

(2) that the appellees, aware of the decedent's tentative identification as Larry Brown, caused all references to the decedent in the petition as originally filed to be to "John Doe" instead of "Larry Brown"; and

(3) that counsel for appellees represented to the trial court that there was no authority directly on point which would authorize the trial court to enter an order granting permission to the DVTP to harvest decedent's heart and kidneys.

We conclude, for reasons hereinafter set forth, that these facts, accepted as true for purposes of ruling upon the entry of summary judgment, do not provide any basis upon which to disturb the ruling of the distinguished Judge Charles B. Smith that appellees were entitled to the good faith immunity provided by the Act.

Appellants contend that the appellees' reliance upon the efforts of the state police to locate the decedent's next of kin is evidence of their lack of good faith and their indifference to the requirement that consent be obtained, if possible, from a close relative pursuant to the classifications established by Section 8602(b). We disagree. The qualified immunity provided by Section 8607(c) of the Act requires a "good faith" attempt to comply with all of the statutory requirements for organ donation. The statute does *not* require any particular type of search for members of higher classes in order to establish the unavailability of members of that class. Section 8607(c) of the Pennsylvania statute was adopted verbatim from Section 7(c) of the Uniform Anatomical Gift Act, and was designed to simplify, facilitate, and encourage organ donation. As noted in the Comment to Section 7 of the Uniform Act:

> the entire Section 7 merits genuinely liberal interpretation to effectuate the purpose and intent of the Uniform Act, that is to encourage and facilitate the important and ever increasing need for human tissue and organs for medical research, education and therapy, including transplantation.

The difficulty encountered by the State Police in their attempt to expeditiously locate Larry Brown's relatives was occasioned not by any failure on the part of appellees but rather by reason of the estrangement between Larry Brown and his family. The state police came into possession of decedent's voter registration card and a Social Security card, but neither document contained a photograph or identified members of his family. The state police quickly located Pamela Batson, the decedent's paramour with whom he had resided for the nine months immediately preceding his death, but Ms. Batson indicated that she believed the decedent's parents were dead and that the decedent's two sisters and one brother, whose names she did not know, did not reside in Pennsylvania. Moreover, the personal effects of the decedent, which were located at the home he shared with Ms. Batson, did not include any documents or correspondence containing the names or addresses of any family member.

The deposition testimony of the troopers involved in the search for Larry Brown's relatives firmly established a good faith effort on their part which culminated in the notification of Virginia Brown, less than forty-eight hours after the decedent was brought to the emergency room, at 10:15 a.m. on the morning of November 1, 1984. The testimony of appellants themselves established that the difficulty encountered by the state police was the result of family estrangement and not lack of diligent police effort:

> Appellant Virginia Brown, the sister of the decedent and administratrix of his estate, testified that she had not spoken with her brother in four or five years and did not know where he was living at the time of his death.
>
> Appellant Thomas Brown, the father of the decedent testified that he had not seen his son for at least one year and did not know where he was living at the time of his death.
>
> Appellant Joan Brown Spina, another sister of decedent, testified that she had not spoken with the decedent for approximately three years prior to his death and appellee Johnnie Lee Brown testified that he had last seen his brother approximately four years before his death.

Thus, the record establishes that at the time of the decedent's death on the evening of October 30, 1984, none of the individuals authorized by Section 8602(b)(1) through (b)(5) to make a decision concerning organ donation were available, and demonstrates as well that the State Police, acting at the request of the appellees, conducted a diligent, good faith effort to locate the members of the decedent's family. Nor was there any suggestion, from any source, that the decedent or any of the individuals enumerated in sub-sections (b)(1) through (b)(5) were opposed to organ donation.[3]

---

3. Each of the appellants has candidly testified that they are not morally or ethically opposed to organ donation and do not know what their response would have been to a

The Act authorizes, in the absence of the individuals specified by Section 8602(b)(1) through (b)(5), "any other person authorized or under obligation to dispose of the body," to make the decision regarding organ donation. As a result, appellees, pursuant to Section (b)(6) of the Act, proceeded to obtain a court order authorizing the hospital to make the decision regarding organ donation. Appellees unquestionably proceeded in accordance with the intent of the Pennsylvania Uniform Anatomical Gift Act, since the priority scheme established by section 8602(b) was drafted "taking into account the very limited time available following death for the successful removal of such critical tissues as the kidney, the liver and the heart." *8A Uniform Laws Annotated* at p. 35 (1983).

As a result, we conclude that the undisputed facts of record establish, as a matter of law, the good faith of appellees in attempting to locate those individuals specified in subsections (b)(1) through (b)(6) of Section 8602 of the Act. . . .

Appellants also contend that two specific facts related to the court proceedings create a genuine issue of material fact precluding summary judgment:

> First, that the emergency petition submitted to the Court of Common Pleas of Chester County identified the decedent as "John Doe" when the hospital and the state police were by then reasonably certain that the decedent's name was Larry Brown; and

> Second, that counsel for the Hospital, Attorney Heed, in response to an inquiry from the Court as to the existence of a specific statute authorizing the court to direct the harvesting of the decedent's organs for transplantation, responded that he was not aware of "specific authority that will allow you to do that, but I would certainly think you would have the general power to do that".

There is no merit to either contention, for neither the designation of the decedent as "John Doe" on the petition, nor the statement that counsel was unaware of *specific* authority for the entry of the requested order creates an issue of fact as to whether appellees made a good faith attempt to comply with the provisions of the Pennsylvania Uniform Anatomical Gift Act.

Counsel for the Hospital stated to the court that he had caused the petition to be drafted identifying the decedent as "John Doe, Caucasian male, age 28" as a result of *counsel's* lack of knowledge that the decedent had, by that time, been tentatively identified as Lawrence Brown. Appellee Norman Ledwin, who was present for the hearing, advised the court that the police had identified the decedent as Larry Brown, that his girlfriend had been located, that no relatives had been found yet, and that the hospital sought to secure the permission of the court since the decedent's girlfriend was not an individual who could make a decision regarding organ donation.

timely request for organ donation which all hospitals are required to make "on or before the occurrence of death in an acute care general hospital" pursuant to Section 8608(a) of the Act, 20 Pa.C.S. § 8608(a).

The court, as a result of the exchange with Attorney Heed and Appellee Ledwin, amended the petition and order to reflect the decedent's name as Lawrence Brown. Appellants have not produced any evidence from any source that appellees had purposely sought to conceal the decedent's name from the court. Nor can such an inference be drawn under the circumstances of this case since no positive identification of the decedent had yet been made, no photographic identification had been recovered, and no medical or dental records of the decedent had been obtained. Thus, while the state police and hospital personnel believed that the decedent was Lawrence Brown, their identification remained tentative.

Nor may a court draw the inference desired by appellants from counsel's statement to the court that he was unaware of "specific authority" authorizing the court to order the harvesting and transplantation of the decedent's organs due to the exigency of the situation and the inability of the state police to locate any relatives. We simply find unacceptable the argument of appellants that counsel's failure to cite, in response to the court's inquiry, the Pennsylvania Uniform Anatomical Gift Act, 42 Pa.C.S. § 8602, is evidence of bad faith.

The Act, in fact, does *not* specifically authorize a court to enter an order granting the hospital the right to donate an individual's organs where none of the relatives designated in Section 8602(b) can be located at the time of death. Moreover, our research does not disclose that any appellate forum, in any of the jurisdictions which have adopted the Uniform Act, has addressed the use of a court order in lieu of consent by any of the individuals designated in the Act. While counsel could certainly have persuasively argued that a court order authorizing the hospital to harvest the decedent's organs was impliedly authorized by Section 8602(b)(6), counsel's failure to so assert cannot, under any stretch of the imagination, be considered evidence of bad faith. As the learned trial court observed, appellees "complied with the requirements of the Act, and in fact, went beyond that which was required of them by seeking a court order granting its consent."

We agree and even observe that it was not the actions of appellees which inspired, during our study of this appeal, a sense of a diminished presence of good faith. In any event, we conclude that the trial court properly granted the motions of appellees for summary judgment.

Order affirmed.

■ JOHNSON, J., dissenting:

. . .

The Majority concludes that the hospital was qualified, under the Act, to donate Larry Brown's organs for transplant purposes under 20 Pa.C.S. § 8602(b)(6). The Majority also finds that the appellees are immune from civil liability, under 20 Pa.C.S. § 8607(c), because they acted in good faith. I reject both of these conclusions.

First, appellees have not proven, as a matter of law, that the hospital qualified as a person who may execute an anatomical gift, under 20 Pa.C.S. § 8602(b)(6). The Majority accepts the trial court's determination that the hospital was an authorized donor under § 8602(b)(6), stating that there was compliance "with the intent" of the Act. The trial court determined that the appellees were authorized donors through reference to the definitions contained in 20 Pa.C.S. § 8601. This section states in pertinent part:

> "Person." Means an individual, corporation, government or governmental subdivision or agency, business trust, estate, trust, partnership or association, or any other legal entity.

While the trial court correctly concluded that the hospital, in the present case, is included in the definition of "person" under the Act, it does not automatically follow that the hospital was "authorized or under obligation to dispose of the body" of Larry Brown. Neither the appellees nor the Majority cite to authority which permits the hospital to qualify, as a matter of law, as a donor under 20 Pa.C.S. § 8602(b)(6).

At oral argument, council for the hospital directed us to 35 Pa.S. § 1092 to support the allegation that the hospital was authorized to dispose of the body of the decedent, as required for donors under 20 Pa.S. § 8602(b)(6). This statute provides only that various entities and organizations, including hospitals, are required to report any bodies which must be buried at public expense, to the Anatomical Board of the State of Pennsylvania. 35 Pa.S. § 1092. Nowhere does the statute state that hospitals are authorized or under an obligation to dispose of dead bodies. Moreover, under a related statute, 35 Pa.S. § 1114, any body which remains unclaimed thirty-six hours after death, falls under the jurisdiction of the Anatomical Board of the State of Pennsylvania. If the Anatomical Board declines jurisdiction over the body, 35 Pa.S. § 1092 directs that the body will be commended to the county commissioners or county executive officers for burial at county expense. Nowhere in this Act, entitled Disposition of Dead Human Bodies, are hospitals given authority or placed under an obligation to dispose of dead bodies. *See* 35 Pa.S. § 1091–1123.

. . .

However, even if I were to conclude that the hospital was authorized to dispose of the body of the decedent, the disposition of this case through the grant of a motion for summary judgment would remain improper, as the question of whether the appellees have acted in good faith, so as to be immune from liability under 20 Pa.C.S. § 8607(c), is one of material fact which must be submitted to the jury.

NOTES AND QUESTIONS

1. In 1988, a man in California was found unconscious on a sidewalk. Six hours after he died, his heart was transplanted into Norton Humphreys, a 58–year-old former staff physician at the hospital where the transplant was performed. The police had searched in vain for the man's relatives for twenty-four hours. *Man's Heart Transplanted Without Prior Consent*, N.Y. TIMES, Apr. 24, 1988, at 22. The law defines a "reasonable" search as one that "has been underway for at least 12 hours." CAL.HEALTH & SAFETY CODE § 7151.5 (West 2004). Do you think the California law is ethical?

Other states have adopted similar statutes. In the wake of the first heart transplant, the Commonwealth of Virginia authorized the Chief Medical Examiner or his or her deputies to harvest suitable organs from bodies under jurisdiction (such as deaths by violence) when an "immediate need" exists for such organs for transplantation, "insufficient time [exists] to contact the next of kin ... and no known objection by the next of kin is foreseen," and organ removal would not interfere with an autopsy or investigation. 1968 Va. Acts 305. Subsequently, the Virginia legislature cut back the Medical Examiner's authority. Va. Code Ann. § 32.1–287 (2004). Maryland authorizes the chief medical examiner or his or her deputy to retrieve organs following a "reasonable, unsuccessful search" for the next-of-kin. Md. Code Ann., Est. & Trusts § 4–509 (2004). For a recent survey of organ donation legislation, case law, and state medical examiner practices, *see* Teresa Shafer et al., *Impact of Medical Examiner/Coroner Practices on Organ Recovery in the United States*, 272 JAMA 1607 (1994).

2. In the United States the waiting list for organs is constantly growing. According to the United Network for Organ Sharing (UNOS), in June of 2004 there were a total of 85,606 candidates waiting for organ transplants. This list was composed of 58,666 individuals awaiting a kidney; 17,471 individuals awaiting a new liver; 1,613 individuals awaiting a pancreas; 3,514 individuals awaiting a heart; and 3,934 individuals awaiting a lung. Organ Procurement and Transplantation Network, Organ by Waiting Time: Current U.S. Waiting List (June 29, 2004), *available at* http://www.optn.org/latestData/rptData.asp.

Meeting this demand in 2003 were 13,276 donors, from whom a total of 25,454 transplants were completed. Organ Procurement and Transplantation Network, Donors Recovered in the U.S. by Donor Type (June 29, 2004) *available at* http://www.optn.org/latestData/rptData.asp; Organ Procurement and Transplantation Network, Transplants in the U.S. by Recipient Age (June 29, 2004) *available at* http://www.optn.org/latestData/rptData.asp. Due to the meager supply of organs flowing to those in need, over 50% of individuals on the waiting list must wait between 6 months to 3 years for a new organ. Organ Procurement and Transplantation Network (June 29, 2004), *available at* http://www.optn.org/latestData/rptData.asp.

Looking at these numbers, there appears to be a severe gap between available organs and those in need. Some commentators such as economist David Kaserman, however, believe that these numbers are misleading. A more telling number of the current situation is the net additions to the waiting list, which is simply the number of candidates per year that exceed the supply of organs for that year. Under this measure, in 2002 the list grew by 2,053 candidates over the 2001 level. Compared to the 85,606 individuals currently on the list, this number appears to be much more manageable when thinking about how to bridge the gap between supply and demand. *See* David Kaserman, *Markets for Organs: Myths and Misconceptions*, 18 J. Contemp. Health L. & Pol'y 567 (2002).

Consider also the analysis of David E. Jefferies:

> An estimated 20,000 usable cadavers are buried each year without having had any of their organs harvested. These cadavers could provide 40,000 kidneys and 20,000 hearts, livers, and lung pairs. Unfortunately, most people die without donating their organs. Current data from the Center for Disease Control suggests that only fifteen percent of people actually become organ donors.

David E. Jefferies, *The Body as Commodity: The Use of Markets to Cure the Organ Deficit*, 5 Ind. J. Global Legal Stud. 621 (1998).

3. To overcome the persistent deficit in organs, should society abandon the requirement of consent that lies at the core of the Uniform Anatomical Gift Act (UAGA)? 8A U.L.A. 15 (1983) (amended 1987). Drafted in 1968, some form of the UAGA had been adopted by all fifty states and the District of Columbia by 1973.

The UAGA authorizes any competent adult to permit or forbid the posthumous use of his or her organs for transplantation, research, or teaching. A preference to donate can be embodied in a will or a non-testamentary document, such as a donor card. If the prospective donor has not indicated a preference, the next-of-kin may donate.

The original UAGA was celebrated because it "encourage[d] socially desirable virtues such as altruism and benevolence without running the risk of abusing individual rights." Arthur L. Caplan, *Organ Transplants: The Cost of Success*, THE HASTINGS REPORT 23 (1983).

In 1987 the UAGA was amended to incorporate two important changes. First, the amended UAGA expressly condemns the sale of human organs stating that "[a] person may not knowingly, for valuable consideration, purchase or sell a part for transplantation or therapy, if removal the part is intended to occur after the death of the decedent." Uniform Anatomical Gift Act 10(a). Secondly, the amended UAGA includes a provision for routine inquiry. "Under routine inquiry, a physician is required to notify the hospital of a potential organ donor. A member of the hospital's staff will then follow up by informing the family of its options concerning donation of the deceased's organs." David E. Jefferies, *The Body as Commodity: The Use of Markets to Cure the Organ Deficit*, 5 IND. J. GLOBAL LEGAL STUD. 630 (1998).

The system of organ procurement used in the United States has been termed an "opt-in" system because individuals are not presumed to wish to donate their organs posthumously. Instead, an individual must take affirmative steps to indicate a wish to donate. This system has not produced enough organs for those in need as the data reprinted above demonstrates.

Many European countries, by contrast have adopted an "opt-out" or "presumed consent" approach. In such systems it is assumed that all citizens have consented to having their organs harvested after death. Only if a decedent has recorded his or her objects to such a harvest are physicians prohibited from harvesting the decedent's organs. In theory the European approach should yield more organs. In practice, however, it has been only modestly more successful than the opt-in system used in the United States.

For a review of proposals to overcome organ donor scarcity—including voluntary giving, mandatory choice, presumed consent, and free market approaches—see Judith Areen, *A Scarcity of Organs*, 38 J. LEGAL EDUC. 555 (1988); Phyllis Coleman, *"Brother, Can You Spare A Liver?" Five Ways to Increase Organ Donation*, 31 VAL. U. L. REV. 1 (1996); Andrew C. MacDonald, *Organ Donation: The Time Has Come to Refocus the Ethical Spotlight*, 8 STAN. L. & POL'Y REV. 177 (1997); Shelby E. Robinson, *Organs for Sale? An Analysis of Proposed Systems for Compensating Organ Providers*, 70 U. COL. L. REV. 1019 (1999).

4. In 1983, H. Barry Jacobs, a physician, created a company to broker human kidneys. Following a 1977 conviction for mail fraud involving Medicare billing, the Virginia state medical board revoked Dr. Jacobs' license to practice medicine. Dr. Jacobs intended to solicit healthy individuals, including those from developing countries, to sell one of their kidneys at their chosen price. Dr. Jacobs estimated that donors would charge up to $10,000 per kidney; he planned to charge an additional service fee of $2000 to $5000. Margaret Engel, *Va. Doctor Plans Company to Arrange Sale of Human Kidneys*, WASH. POST, Sept. 19, 1983, at A9.

In 1984, Congress enacted the National Organ Transplant Act (amended 1988), which provides in pertinent part:

(a) Prohibition. It shall be unlawful for any person to knowingly acquire, receive, or otherwise transfer any human organ for valuable consideration for use in human transplantation if the transfer affects interstate commerce.

(b) Penalties. Any person who violates subsection (a) shall be fined not more than $50,000 or imprisoned not more than five years, or both.

(c) Definitions. For purposes of subsection (a):

(1) The term "human organ" means the human (including fetal) kidney, liver, heart, lung, pancreas, bone marrow, cornea, eye, bone, and skin or any subpart thereof and any other human organ (or any subpart thereof, including that derived from a fetus) specified by the Secretary of Health and Human Services by regulation.

(2) The term "valuable consideration" does not include the reasonable payments associated with the removal, transplantation, implantation, processing, preservation, quality control, and storage of a human organ or the expenses of travel, housing, and lost wages incurred by the donor of a human organ in connection with the donation of the organ.

(3) The term "interstate commerce" has the meaning prescribed for it by section 201(b) of the Federal Food, Drug and Cosmetic Act.

42 U.S.C. § 274e (2004).

5. Is a ban on organ sales appropriate? Proponents of commercialization argue that the concern about exploitation of organ sellers is unfounded: Assuming that a clear, informative explanation of the risks can be given the parent donating to a child, what is it that makes the same clear, informative explanation of risks invalid if the incentive is money rather than love? Would you feel [that donating is better than selling] if you were poor and if the $100,000 you got for one kidney, invested at interest rates of 10 percent, would double your family's income, or send your child to medical school, or pay for surgery for your sick husband? *See* Buc & Bernstein, *Buying and Selling Human Organs Is Worth a Harder Look,* HEALTHSCAN, Oct. 1984, at 3, 4; *see also* Gregory S. Crespi, *Overcoming the Legal Obstacles to the Creation of a Futures Market in Bodily Organs,* 55 OHIO ST.L.J. 1 (1994); Lloyd R. Cohen, *Increasing the Supply of Transplant Organs: The Virtues of a Futures Market,* 58 GEO.WASH.L.REV. 1 (1989).

6. Because of the shortage of transplantable organs, physicians and scientists have attempted to find alternative methods for providing patients in need with viable organs. One such method is xenotransplantation. "Xenotransplantation is a medical advance that would allow physicians to use animal organs to replace failing human organs for transplantation purposes." This development has been accompanied by several problems, such as "increased graft rejection, possible cross-species disease transfer, and moral objection by some groups." S. Gregory Boyd, *Considering a Market in Human Organs,* 4 N.C. J.L. & TECH. 417, 428–29 (2003).

Some states have attempted to increase the rate of organ donation through legislation that does not violate either the UAGA or NOTA by providing "valuable consideration" in exchange for an organ.

In 1994, Pennsylvania passed Act 102, which created the Governor Robert P. Casey Memorial Organ and Tissue Donation Awareness Trust Fund. This fund is supported through one-dollar voluntary donations on driver's licenses and vehicle registrations. The fund provides up to $3,000 per donor to help with the cost of "reasonable hospital and other medical expenses, funeral expenses and incidental expenses incurred by the donor or donor's family in connection with making a vital organ donation." The money is paid directly to the hospital, funeral home, hotel, or other organization responsible for providing the service the donor requires for the transplant. No part of the money goes directly to the "donor's family, next of kin or estate," and it is all for donation-related expenditures.

Even though the Act became law in 1994, an actual program that paid expense benefits did not result until January 2002. The trust fund has more than one million dollars, and three million Pennsylvanians have signed up to be organ donors. Even by the end of 2000, when the fund was not yet paying expense benefits, 37.4% of Pennsylvania drivers had signed up to be organ donors. The current version of the program only distributes a $300 benefit. In spite of the reduction from the $3,000 authorized to the $300 current payment, nineteen donors or donor families applied for the benefit in the first six months of operation between January and May. Eighteen of the nineteen donor applicants were living, and one donor applicant was deceased.

In the coming years, this pilot program will help answer many questions about compensated organ donation. The program is an implicit recognition of property rights in body parts and an example of the state yielding to individual choice and compensation. One could view the fund as a type of limited organ market. In this market, the state is compensating donors with a fixed price for donation. If successful, the program could pave the way for other organ market permutations.

S. Gregory Boyd, *Considering a Market in Human Organs*, 4 N.C. J. L. & TECH. 417, 459 (2003).

Attempts to increase the supply of viable organs have resulted in serious international human rights abuses:

Another method of procuring organs for transplant, albeit one seldom used, is the nationalization of cadavers. In the few countries that have adopted this method, very substantial human rights violations have occurred. The most common of these human rights violations occur when the state removes the organs of criminals by methods of state execution. An example of this sort of state-sponsored crime comes from Bosnia, where a Bush administration study reports that a Serbian internment camp doctor is alleged to have killed prisoners of war to remove their organs.

China provides an example of state-sponsored execution for organs. China has officially allowed the harvest of organs from executed prisoners since 1984. By Chinese law, harvest is allowed in one of three circumstances: (1) if the prisoner's body is not claimed; (2) if the prisoner has consented; or (3) if the prisoner's family has consented.

China, however, has not always adhered to its own laws. Executions of condemned prisoners appear to be scheduled around transplant needs and, in some instances, even deliberately botched so the prisoners will still be alive when their organs are removed. The carrying out of state-sponsored executions without public notice or witnesses facilitates China's ability to execute prisoners for the purpose of obtaining their organs.

Although many of the China stories sound incredible, they are not without support. Numerous reports of these practices have been confirmed not only by doctors and judges witnessing the executions, but by members of the Chinese Communist Party as well. A Chinese government document explains the procedures to be used in this practice which harvests 2,000 to 3,000 organs per year.

"The use of the corpses or organs of executed criminals must be kept strictly secret, and attention must be paid to avoiding negative repercussions. [The removal of organs] should normally be carried out within the utilizing unit. Where it is genuinely necessary, then with the permission of the people's court that is carrying out the death sentence, a surgical vehicle from the health department may be permitted to drive onto the execution grounds to remove the organs, but it is not permitted to use a vehicle bearing health department insignia or to wear white clothing. Guards must remain around the execution grounds while the operation for organ removal is going on."

David E. Jefferies, *The Body as Commodity: The Use of Markets to Cure the Organ Deficit*, 5 IND. J. GLOBAL LEGAL STUD. 621, 642–644 (1998).

C.   THE RELATIONSHIP BETWEEN BODY AND HUMAN BEING

Leon R. Kass, *Thinking About the Body*

TOWARD A MORE NATURAL SCIENCE 276, 276–96, 298 (1985).

· · ·

What is the relation between a human being and his body? Never a simple question, it is today even more puzzling, thanks, in part, to new surgical and technological developments that also give it great practical importance. On one side, we have a living body apparently devoid of all human activity in the permanently unconscious young woman who still manages to breathe spontaneously on her own for several years. On the other side, we have a human being alienated from his living body in the man who believes he is really a woman trapped inside a man's body and who undergoes surgery for "gender reassignment." In between, an increasing number of people walk around bearing other people's blood, corneas, kidneys, hearts, and livers; successful transplantation even of brain cells is currently proceeding in animals. . . . Implantable and attachable mechanical organs add to our possible confusion, as do the more prevalent but less spectacular phenomena of wigs, tattoos, silicone injections, and various forms of body-building and remodeling.

If practice turns to theory for clarification and assistance, it finds there nearly equal disorder. . . . On one side are the corporealists, for whom there is nothing but body and who aspire to explain all activities of life, including thought and feeling, in terms of the motions of inorganic particles. On the other side, say especially in ethics, are the theorists of personhood, consciousness, and autonomy, who treat the essential human being as pure will and reason, as if bodily life counted for nothing, or did not even exist. The former seeks to capture man for dumb and mindless nature; the latter treats man in isolation, even from his own nature. At the bottom of the trouble, I suspect, is the hegemony of modern natural science, to whose view of nature even the partisans of personhood and subjectivity adhere, given that their attempt to locate human dignity in consciousness and mind presupposes that the subconscious living body, not to speak of nature in general, is utterly without dignity or meaning of its own. These prejudices of theory do not accord well with our experience.

· · ·

There are, of course, obstacles to thinking about the body. First of all, the body or, to avoid begging the question, most of it is mute. True enough, each of us has experience of his or her own body, but that experience is entirely subrational (i.e., inarticulate and speechless) and probably even largely unconscious. The materials for thought are available, but the handles are not ready made. In fact a second obstacle it seems that there may be no *naturally* or universally appropriate way to think about the body and no universally valid "plain truths" about the body, since different cultures vary widely in their assessments of the nature and worth of what we call "the body." Questions about the body are tied to questions about life, death, and soul; the whole cosmic picture is soon at issue, and about such matters, we are well aware, cultures differ....

Men's customs regarding dead bodies, like customs in general, are both powerful and powerfully different. But not all-powerful or altogether different.... First, everybody ... dies. Everybody, sooner or later, becomes a body. Second, everybody does *something* with the dead bodies of the deceased ancestors. Human beings everywhere recognize human mortality; human beings everywhere feel a sense of responsibility to the deceased, elicited by ties of kinship. These samenesses seem to me at least as significant as the differences in funeral practice. Beneath and beyond the different ways human beings think or feel or act, there do seem to be at least a few universal truths about the body and its human meaning....

. . .

Looking Up to the Body

. . .

Perhaps the first thing that strikes us in looking at the body any living body is that it *is* a whole, a unity, a one. It has a boundary, a surface, that clearly delimits it from everything that it is not. It is solid but shapely, corporeal but articulated, enmattered but most definitely formed. The forms are distinctive each one, though individuated, is always one of a *kind,* with a distinctive shape, attitude, look, and way of moving. When the living body moves, it moves as a whole; if we are able to observe it growing, we see that it grows as a whole. It is capable, when injured, of making itself whole, through remarkable powers of self-healing, and it generates other wholes formed like itself. And, in the higher animals, the form and patterns of the body acquire a plasticity useful for communicating to other wholes of the same species, expressing in look or in gesture something of the state of the life within.

In his study of *Animal Forms and Patterns,*[5] Adolf Portmann explores the meaning of bodily form and demonstrates its revelatory character. He observes, for example, that with ascent up the mammalian line comes a marked accentuation of two poles of the animal body, one the center of awareness and expression, the other the center of reproductive activity. At the head pole, the head is progressively demarcated off from the rest of the body, and a marked and mobile face is eventually formed in the higher mammals, receiving and communicating meaningful looks; the genital pole is also progressively distinguished, by the descent of the testes, special patterns of hair or coloration, and other ornamentation.... These developments reach a certain peak in man, though the head and tail poles are no

5. Adolf Portmann, Animal Forms and   Faber and Faber, 1964).
Patterns, trans. by Hella Czech, (London:

longer poles, due to the fact that man has acquired an upright posture, which places his head high above his groin....

Nearly all of what I have to say about the upright posture comes from an essay, "The Upright Posture,"[6] by the late German–American neurologist-psychologist, Erwin Straus, an essay one can hardly praise too highly and whose riches I barely begin to tap. Straus seeks to articulate a biologically oriented psychology that interprets human experience not as a train of percepts, thoughts, or volitions occurring in a sequestered mind or consciousness, but as a manifestation of man's position in the world, directed toward it, acting and suffering. He shows the close correspondence between human physique and certain basic traits of human experience and behavior that ultimately connects our rationality with our bodily uprightness....

Though upright posture characterizes the human species, each of us must struggle to attain it.... Moreover, automatic regulation does not suffice; staying up takes continuous attention and activity. Awakeness is necessary for uprightness; uprightness is necessary for survival. Yet our standing in the world is always precarious; we are always in danger of falling. Our natural stance is, therefore, one of "resistance," or "withstanding," of becoming constant, stable.

This instituted and oppositional but precarious posture introduces an ambivalence into all human behavior. "Upright posture removes us from the ground, keeps us away from things, and holds us aloof from our fellowman. All of these three distances can be experienced either as gain or as loss."[9] We enjoy the freedom of motion that comes with getting up, but we miss and often sink back to enjoy the voluptuous pleasures of reclining and relaxing. We miss the immediate commerce with things given to animals and crawling infants, but enjoy instead the pleasures of confronting a true and distant horizon, as interested seeing becomes detached beholding. As upright, we enjoy our dignity and bearing and the opportunity to encounter one another "face-to-face," yet this very rectitude makes us distant and aloof—verticals that never meet. To meet, we must bend or incline toward one another, or express our intentions to one another in some departure from strict verticality.

In upright posture, the upper extremities, no longer needed to support and carry the body, are free to acquire new tasks. Much has been made of the significance of the opposable thumb and the prehensile hand. But this is a small part of the story. The free swinging of the arms is crucial to the psychological experience of what Straus calls "action space," not the neutral homogeneous space of objective Cartesian science, but lived space, my space, a sphere of *my* action, which somehow both belongs to and gives rise to my sense of myself and to which I am related through body, limbs, and hands. In relation to action space, the hands develop into a true sense organ—a tool of "gnostic touching," ranking with the eye and ear in powers of discrimination. The hand also functions, in cooperation with eye

---

6. Erwin Straus, "The Upright Posture," in his *Phenomenological Psychology,* New York: Basic Books, 1966, pp. 137–165.

9. Ibid., p. 143.

and ear and mind, to form new kinds of world-relations. Among its many new functions is pointing:

> In pointing, also, man's reach exceeds his grasp. Upright posture enables us to see things in their distance without any intention of incorporating them. In the totality of this panorama that unfolds in front of us, the pointing finger singles out one detail.... Pointing is a social gesture I do not point for myself; I indicate something to someone else. To distant things, within the visible horizon, we are related by common experience. As observers, we are directed, although through different perspectives, to one and the same thing, to one and the same world. Distance creates new forms of communication.[10]

. . .

The dumb human body, rightly attended to, shows all the marks of, and creates all the conditions for, our rationality and our special way of being-in-the-world. Our bodies demonstrate, albeit silently, that we are more than just a complex version of our animal ancestors, and, conversely, that we are also more than an enlarged brain, a consciousness somehow grafted onto or trapped within a blind mechanism that knows only survival. The body-form *as a whole* impresses on us its inner powers of thought and action. Mind and hand, gait and gaze, breath and tongue, foot and mouth— all are part of a single package, suffused with the presence of intelligence. We are *rational* (i.e., *thinking*) animals, down to and up from the very tips of our toes. No wonder, then, that even a corpse still shows the marks of our humanity.

Looking Down on the Body

We can, it seems, be justly proud of our upright posture and the other bodily marks of the rational existence for which we are natured. But pride goeth before a fall. Our bodies are not only organized and self-organizing wholes, independent centers of awareness, thought and desire, and sources of purposive motions; we are not only self-maintaining and self-healing beings, individuated, well-defined, and discrete; not only upright, well-proportioned, and dignified in carriage; not only clever and dextrous, separate but in face-to-face communication with our fellows, through pointings, gestures, and articulate speech. Our bodies are also isolated, finally unshareable eyes, even in sexual union and privatizing; vulnerable and weak; often mute and opaque; and frequently concealing rather than revealing of the soul within. Though highly touted as compliant tools, they all too often are an impediment and obstacle to our wills that refuse to do what we want them to have you, too, perhaps, recently tried to slide into second base? And our bodies are sometimes ugly and misshapen, and very frequently ridiculous: in short, a positive embarrassment to anyone with pride. Such is the ancient discovery of our race when, its pride newly aroused, it first began to think about the body, which seems to have occurred when it first began to think at all. The body, after all, first comes to light as naked.

. . .

10. Ibid., pp. 154–155.

What is the meaning of nakedness? Why is the awareness of one's nakedness shameful? To be naked means, of course, to be defenseless, unguarded, exposed a sign of our vulnerability before the elements and the beasts.... In looking, as it were, for the first time upon our bodies as sexual beings, we discover how far we are from anything divine. As a sexual being, none of us is complete or whole, either within or without. We have need for and are dependent on a complementary other, even to realize our own bodily nature. We are halves, not wholes, and we do not command the missing complementary half. Moreover, we are not internally whole, but divided. We are possessed by an unruly or rebellious "autonomous" sexual nature within one that does not heed our commands ... we, too, face within an ungovernable and disobedient element, which embarrasses our claim to self-command. (The punishment fits the crime: The rebel is given rebellion.) We are compelled to submit to the mastering desire within and to the wiles of its objects without; and in surrender, we lay down our pretense of upright lordliness, as we lie down with necessity. On further reflection, we note that the genitalia are also a sign of our perishability, in that they provide for those who will replace us. Finally, all this noticing is itself problematic. For in turning our attention to our own insufficiency, dependence, perishability, and lack of self-command, we manifest a further difficulty, the difficulty of self-consciousness itself. For a doubleness is now present in the soul, through which we scrutinize ourselves, seeing ourselves as others see us, no longer assured of the spontaneous, immediate, unself-conscious participation in life no longer enjoying what Rousseau longingly referred to as "the sentiment of existence," experienced with a whole heart and soul undivided against itself. Self-scrutiny, self-absorption, attention to ourselves being seen by others, vanity, and that perhaps greatest evil which is self-loathing all these possible ills of thinking are coincident with self-consciousness; and self-consciousness is coincident with learning of our nakedness our incompleteness, insufficiency, dependence, mortality, and the lack of self-command. Reason's first and painful discovery was of its own poor carcass. Rational we may be, but abidingly animal.

What are we to think of this doubleness imprinted on our bodies and essential to our being: on the one hand, our uprightness, our dignity, our capacity though we are only a part, here and now, to stand up before and to the world, to contemplate the whole and to think the eternal; and, on the other hand, our being weighted down, self-divided, naked, needy, and alone? We have, as it were, been demonstrating a possible and proper answer. Necessity may be a mark of our lowliness, but recognizing and owning up to our relation to necessity is not itself lowly. On the contrary, it is a mark of our dignity.... The rise of man may be ambiguous, but it is nonetheless a rise.

The animals, too, are naked, but they know no shame. They, too, experience necessity, but they neither *know* it nor know it *as necessary*. Thinking about the body may sober the thinker, and dispel his delusions of autonomy, but it does not cripple him. For one thing, the discovery of nakedness, however humbling, is a genuine discovery; our eyes are indeed opened. The so-called fall of man is identical to his mental awakening.... Aroused from dormant potentiality, human ingenuity and manual dexterity give birth to the arts, at first glance, to cover our shame, but in truth to

elevate and humanize the otherwise degradingly necessary. For in awareness of our need, we are capable not only of succumbing to it, but of
meeting it in a knowing and dignified way.... And, finally, in and *only* in
the discovery of our own lack of divinity comes the first real openness to
the divine. *Immediately* after making themselves girdles, reports the bibli-
cal author, "they heard the Lord God walking in the Garden," the first
explicit mention that man attended to or even noticed the divine presence.

The significance of this stage of anthropological self-development has
been marvelously summarized by Kant, in his "Conjectural Beginning of
Human History," which is, in effect, largely a commentary on the Garden
of Eden story:

> In the case of animals, sexual attraction is merely a matter of transient,
> mostly periodic impulse. But man soon discovered that for him this
> attraction can be prolonged and even increased by means of the imagina-
> tion.... The fig leaf (3:7), then, was a far greater manifestation of reason
> than that shown in the earlier stage of development. For the one [i.e.,
> desiring the forbidden fruit] shows merely a power to choose the extent to
> which to serve impulse; but the other rendering—an inclination more
> inward and constant by removing its object from the senses—already
> reflects consciousness of a certain degree of mastery of reason over im-
> pulse. *Refusal* was the feat which brought about the passage from merely
> sensual to spiritual attractions, from merely animal desire gradually to
> love, and along with this from the feeling of the merely agreeable to a taste
> for beauty, at first only for beauty in man but at length for beauty in
> nature as well. In addition, there came a first hint at the development of
> man as a moral creature. This came from the sense of decency, which is an
> inclination to inspire others to respect by proper manners, i.e., by conceal-
> ing all that which might arouse low esteem. Here, incidentally, lies the real
> basis of true sociability.

> This may be a small beginning. But if it gives a wholly new direction to
> thought, such a beginning is epoch-making. It is then more important than
> the whole immeasurable series of expansions of culture which subsequently
> spring from it.[15]

Crucial to the development of genuine sociability and culture is the
perception of one's place in the line of generations. Those who aspire to
autonomy and self-sufficiency are prone to forget, indeed eager to forget,
that the world did not and does not begin with them. Civilization is
altogether a monument to ancestors biological and cultural, to those who
came before, in whose debt one always lives, like it or not. We can pay this
debt, if at all, only by our transmission of life and teachings to those who
come after. Mind, freely wandering, in speculation or fantasy, can forget
time and relation, but a mind that thinks on the body will be less likely to
do so. In the navel are one's forebears, in the genitalia our descendants.
These reminders of perishability are also reminders of perpetuation; if we
understand their meaning, we are even able to transform the necessary and
shameful into the free and noble.... Embodiment is a curse only for those
who believe they deserve to be gods.

15. Immanuel Kant, "Conjectural Beginning of Human History," trans. by Emil
Fackenheim, in *Kant on History*, Lewis White
Beck, ed., Indianapolis: Bobbs–Merrill, 1963,
p. 57.

Where do we now stand regarding the body? What has our thinking about the body thus far revealed? The body bears throughout the marks both of human dignity and human abjection. It points us beyond itself, even to the heavenly and divine, and permits us to see and think and scheme; but it reminds us, too, of our debt and our duties to those who have gone before, that we are not our own source, neither in body nor in mind. Our dignity consists not in denying but in thoughtfully acknowledging and elevating the necessity of our embodiment, rightly regarding it as a gift to be cherished and respected. Through ceremonious treatment of mortal remains and through respectful attention to our living body and its inherent worth, we stand rightly when we stand reverently before the body, both living and dead.

But thinking about the body is revealing not only about body; on reflection, it sheds light also on thought and its puzzling relation to the being that thinks. . . .

The living body of the thinker has extension length, breadth, width and place; his thoughts have neither. He is here and now; they can be anywhere and of any time in the best case timeless and enduring. Necessarily embodied, the thinking man is mortal, yet his thought as such may live on, especially as it is revivified in other and later minds. However much our minding depends on the proper organization and function of our bodily parts, we cannot but suspect that thought and mind are not corporeal. And, in any case, the thinker and his body are not simply of one mind. The body, even in upright posture, has its own subrational needs and aspirations not to speak of pains and disorders that get in the way of thinking: an empty stomach or a full bladder make thinking difficult; the aphrodisiac pleasure makes it impossible. Can we equate the human being *as thinker* with his body, even with his living, breathing, and moving body? How exactly can organic body think or feel or desire or wonder or know? Thinking about the body of thinkers returns us to that mystery of mysteries which is its own ground: the being of an embodied mind or a thoughtful body. This is not a problem to be solved, but a question and perplexity to be faced, I suspect, permanently. We can here do little more than acknowledge it.

Thinking about the body is both exhilarating and sobering for the thinker: exhilarating because it shows the possibility of a more integrated account of his own psychosomatic being against the prejudices of corporealists, subjectivists, and dualists by showing the way in which his body prepares him (or, shall I say, itself) for the active life of thought and communication; sobering because it teaches him his vulnerability, dependence, and connectedness, exploding his illusions of and pretensions to autonomy. Thinking about the body is also constraining and liberating for the thinker: constraining because it shows him the limits on the power of thought to free him from embodiment, setting limits on thought understood as a tool for mastery; liberating because it therefore frees him to wonder about the irreducibly mysterious union and concretion of mind and body that we both are and live.

NOTES AND QUESTIONS

1. For a comprehensive review of secular and religious thought on the moral significance of the body, see Thomas H. Murray, *On the Human Body as Property:*

The Meaning of Embodiment, Markets, and the Meaning of Strangers, 20 J.L.RE-
FORM 1055, 1062–74 (1987); OFFICE OF TECHNOLOGY ASSESSMENT, U.S. CONGRESS, NEW
DEVELOPMENTS IN BIOTECHNOLOGY: OWNERSHIP OF HUMAN TISSUES AND CELLS-SPECIAL
REPORT, 129, 137–39, 141–43 (1989). *See also* Courtney S. Campbell, *Religion and
the Body in Medical Research*, 8 KENNEDY INST. ETHICS J. 275 (1998).

2. For an interesting examination of philosophical and religious traditions and the
property paradigm, see Courtney S. Campbell, *Body, Self, and the Property Paradigm*, HASTINGS CENTER REP. 34 (1992).

3. For a thoughtful discussion of scientific and social views of the body, *see* Lori
Andrews and Dorothy Nelkin, *Whose Body Is It Anyway? Disputes Over body Tissue
in a Biotechnology Age*, 351 LANCET 53 (1998).

Bonnichsen v. United States

United States Court of Appeals for the Ninth Circuit, 2004.
367 F.3d 864.

■ GOULD, J.

This is a case about the ancient human remains of a man who hunted
and lived, or at least journeyed, in the Columbia Plateau an estimated 8340
to 9200 years ago, a time predating all recorded history from any place in
the world, a time before the oldest cities of our world had been founded, a
time so ancient that the pristine and untouched land and the primitive
cultures that may have lived on it are not deeply understood by even the
most well-informed men and women of our age. Seeking the opportunity of
study, a group of scientists as Plaintiffs[1] in this case brought an action
against, *inter alia*, the United States Department of the Interior, challenging various Indian tribes'[2] claim to one of the most important American
anthropological and archaeological discoveries of the late twentieth century, and challenging the Interior Department's decision honoring the tribes'
claim. The discovery that launched this contest was that of a human
skeleton, estimated by carbon dating to be 8340 to 9200 years old, known
popularly and commonly as "Kennewick Man," but known as "the Ancient
One" to some American Indians who now inhabit regions in Washington,
Idaho, and Oregon, roughly proximate to the site on the Columbia River at
Kennewick, Washington, where the bones were found. From the perspective of the scientists-Plaintiffs, this skeleton is an irreplaceable source of
information about early New World populations that warrants careful
scientific inquiry to advance knowledge of distant times. Yet, from the
perspective of the intervenor-Indian tribes the skeleton is that of an

1. Plaintiffs are experts in their respective fields. Plaintiff Bonnichsen is Director of
the Center for the Study of the First Americans at Oregon State University. Plaintiff
Brace is Curator of Biological Anthropology
at the University of Michigan Museum of
Anthropology. Plaintiffs Gill, Haynes, Jantz,
and Steele are anthropology professors.
Plaintiff Owsley is division head for physical
anthropology at the Smithsonian Institution's National Museum of Natural History.

Plaintiff Stanford is Director of the Smithsonian's Paleo Indian Program.

2. The Tribal Claimants—present in
this appeal as intervenors—are the Confederated Tribes & Bands of the Yakama Indian
Nation, the Nez Perce Tribe of Idaho, the
Confederated Tribes of the Umatilla Indian
Reservation, and the Confederated Tribes of
the Colville Reservation.

ancestor who, according to the tribes' religious and social traditions, should be buried immediately without further testing.

Plaintiffs filed this lawsuit seeking to stop the transfer of the skeleton by the government to the tribes for burial, and the district court held in favor of the scientists-Plaintiffs. The Secretary of the Interior and the intervenor-Indian tribes appeal. We have jurisdiction under 28 U.S.C. § 1291 and affirm the judgment of the district court barring the transfer of the skeleton for immediate burial and instead permitting scientific study of the skeleton.

I.

In July 1996, teenagers going to a boat race discovered a human skull and bones near the shore of the Columbia River just outside Kennewick, Washington. The remains were found on federal property under the management of the United States Army Corps of Engineers ("Corps") and, at the request of the county coroner, were removed for analysis by an anthropologist, Dr. James Chatters, pursuant to an Archaeological Resources Protection Act of 1979 ("ARPA"), 16 U.S.C. §§ 470aa–470mm,

The skeleton attracted attention because some of its physical features, such as the shape of the face and skull, differed from those of modern American Indians. Many scientists believed the discovery might shed light on the origins of humanity in the Americas. On August 31, 1996, Dr. Douglas Owsley, Division Head for Physical Anthropology at the Smithsonian Institution in Washington, D.C., made arrangements for Dr. Chatters to bring this important find to the Smithsonian's National Museum of Natural History for further study.

Indian tribes from the area of the Columbia River opposed scientific study of the remains on religious and social grounds.[8] Four Indian groups (the "Tribal Claimants") demanded that the remains be turned over to them for immediate burial. The Tribal Claimants based their demand on the Native American Graves Protection and Repatriation Act ("NAGPRA"), 25 U.S.C. § 3001 et seq. The Corps agreed with the Tribal Claimants and, citing NAGPRA, seized the remains on September 10, 1996, shortly before they could be transported to the Smithsonian. The Corps also ordered an immediate halt to DNA testing, which was being done using the remainder of the bone sample that had been submitted earlier for radiocarbon dating. After investigation, the Corps decided to give the remains to the Tribal Claimants for burial. As required by NAGPRA, the Corps published a "Notice of Intent to Repatriate Human Remains" in a local newspaper on September 17, 1996, and September 24, 1996.

The scientists and others, including the Smithsonian Institution, objected to the Corps' decision, arguing that the remains were a rare discovery of national and international significance. In late September and

---

8. For example, the Tribal Claimants urged that "when a body goes into the ground, it is meant to stay there until the end of time. When remains are disturbed and remain above the ground, their spirits are at unrest.... To put these spirits at ease, the remains must be returned to the ground as soon as possible." ... the evidence, "did not fully consider or resolve certain difficult legal questions," and "assumed facts that proved to be erroneous."

early October 1996, several scientists asked Major General Ernest J. Herrell, Commander of the Corps' North Pacific Division, to allow qualified scientists to study the remains.

. . .

On March 24, 1998, the Corps and the Secretary of the Interior entered into an agreement that effectively assigned to the Secretary responsibility to decide whether the remains were "Native American" under NAGPRA, and to determine their proper disposition. The Department of the Interior then assumed the role of lead agency on this case.

Almost two years after this matter was remanded, the Secretary's experts began to examine the remains in detail. The experts estimated that Kennewick Man was 5′9″ to 5′10″ tall, 45 to 50 years of age when he died, and 15 to 20 years old when the projectile point became embedded in his hip. The experts could not determine, from non-destructive examination of the skeleton alone, when Kennewick Man lived. However, analysis of sediment layers where the skeleton was found supported the hypothesis that the remains dated back not less than 7600 years ago and Kennewick Man could have lived more than 9000 years ago (the date indicated by the initial radiocarbon dating of the skeleton). Further study of the sediment was recommended, but the Corps' decision to bury the discovery site in April 1998 prevented completion of those studies.

The experts compared the physical characteristics of the remains—e.g., measurements of the skull, teeth, and bones—with corresponding measurements from other skeletons. They concluded that Kennewick Man's remains were unlike those of any known present-day population, American Indian or otherwise.

The Secretary's experts cautioned, however, that an apparent lack of physical resemblance between the Kennewick Man's remains and present-day American Indians did not completely rule out the possibility that the remains might be biologically ancestral to modern American Indians. Moreover, although Kennewick Man's morphological traits did not closely resemble those of modern American Indian populations, the Secretary's experts noted that Kennewick Man's physical attributes are generally consistent with the very small number of human remains from this period that have been found in North America.

Relying solely on the age of the remains and the fact that the remains were found within the United States, on January 13, 2000, the Secretary pronounced Kennewick Man's remains "Native American" within NAGPRA's meaning. And on September 25, 2000, the Secretary determined that a preponderance of the evidence supported the conclusion that the Kennewick remains were culturally affiliated with present-day Indian tribes. For this reason, the Secretary announced his final decision to award Kennewick Man's remains to a coalition of the Tribal Claimants. The Corps and the Secretary also denied Plaintiffs' request to study the remains.

Plaintiffs filed an amended complaint in the district court challenging the Secretary's decisions. The district court again ruled in Plaintiffs' favor. As pertinent to this appeal, the district court vacated the Secretary's decisions as contrary to the Administrative Procedure Act, 5 U.S.C.

§ 706(2)(A) ("APA"), on the ground that the Secretary improperly concluded that NAGPRA applies.

. . .

III.

Our review of the Secretary's decision to transfer Kennewick Man to
the Tribal Claimants is governed by the APA, which instructs courts to
"hold unlawful and set aside agency action, findings, and conclusions found
to be … arbitrary, capricious, an abuse of discretion, or otherwise not in
accordance with law." 5 U.S.C. § 706(2)(A).

NAGPRA vests "ownership or control" of newly discovered Native
American human remains in the decedent's lineal descendants or, if lineal
descendants cannot be ascertained, in a tribe "affiliated" with the remains.
25 U.S.C. § 3002(a). NAGPRA mandates a two-part analysis. The first
inquiry is whether human remains are Native American within the statute's meaning. If the remains are not Native American, then NAGPRA
does not apply. However, if the remains are Native American, then NAG-
PRA applies, triggering the second inquiry of determining which persons or
tribes are most closely affiliated with the remains.

The parties dispute whether the remains of Kennewick Man constitute
Native American remains within NAGPRA's meaning. HN13Go to the
description of this Headnote. NAGPRA defines human remains as "Native
American" if the remains are "of, or relating to, a tribe, people, or culture
that is indigenous to the United States." 25 U.S.C. § 3001(9). The text of
the relevant statutory clause is written in the present tense ("of, or
relating to, a tribe, people, or culture that is indigenous"). Thus the statute
unambiguously requires that human remains bear some relationship to a
presently existing tribe, people, or culture to be considered Native American.

It is axiomatic that, in construing a statute, courts generally give
words not defined in a statute their "ordinary or natural meaning." United
States v. Alvarez–Sanchez, 511 U.S. 350, 357 (1994); *see also* Williams v.
Taylor, 529 U.S. 420, 431 (2000) (holding that courts "give the words of a
statute their ordinary, contemporary, common meaning, absent an indication Congress intended them to bear some different import") (internal
quotation marks omitted).

In the context of NAGPRA, we conclude that Congress's use of the
present tense is significant. The present tense "in general represents
present time." R. Pence and D. Emery, A Grammar of Present–Day English
262 (2d ed. 1963). Congress, by using the phrase "is indigenous" in the
present tense, referred to presently existing tribes, peoples, or cultures. We
must presume that Congress gave the phrase "is indigenous" its ordinary
or natural meaning. Alvarez–Sanchez, 511 U.S. at 357. We conclude that
Congress was referring to presently existing Indian tribes when it referred
to "a tribe, people, or culture that is indigenous to the United States." 25
U.S.C. § 3001(9) (emphasis added).

NAGPRA also protects graves of persons not shown to be of current
tribes in that it protects disjunctively remains "of, or relating to" current

indigenous tribes. Thus, NAGPRA extends to all remains that relate to a tribe, people, or culture that is indigenous to the United States, see 25 U.S.C. § 3001(9) (defining human remains as Native American if they are "of, or relating to, a tribe, people, or culture that is indigenous to the United States") (emphasis added).

Our conclusion that NAGPRA's language requires that human remains, to be considered Native American, bear some relationship to a presently existing tribe, people, or culture accords with NAGPRA's purposes. As regards newly discovered human remains, NAGPRA was enacted with two main goals: to respect the burial traditions of modern-day American Indians and to protect the dignity of the human body after death. NAGPRA was intended to benefit modern American Indians by sparing them the indignity and resentment that would be aroused by the despoiling of their ancestors' graves and the study or the display of their ancestors' remains. See H.R. Rep. No. 101–877, at 4369 (1990)....

Congress's purposes would not be served by requiring the transfer to modern American Indian of human remains that bear no relationship to them. Yet, that would be the result under the Secretary's construction of the statute, which would give Native American status to any remains found within the United States regardless of age and regardless of lack of connection to existing indigenous tribes. The exhumation, study, and display of ancient human remains that are unrelated to modern American Indians was not a target of Congress's aim, nor was it precluded by NAGPRA.

NAGPRA was also intended to protect the dignity of the human body after death by ensuring that Native American graves and remains be treated with respect. See S. Rep. No. 101–473, at 6 (1990) ("The Committee believes that human remains must at all times be treated with dignity and respect."); H.R. Rep. No. 101–877, at 4372 (1990) ("Some Indian representatives testified that the spirits of their ancestors would not rest until they are returned to their homeland....") (emphasis added). Congress's purpose is served by requiring the return to modern-day American Indians of human remains that bear some significant relationship to them.

Despite the statute's language and legislative history, the Secretary argues that the district court's interpretation "improperly collapses" NAGPRA's first inquiry (asking whether human remains are Native American) into NAG–PRA's second inquiry (asking which American Indians or Indian tribe bears the closest relationship to Native American remains). The Secretary is mistaken. Though NAGPRA's two inquiries have some commonality in that both focus on the relationship between human remains and present-day Indians, the two inquiries differ significantly. The first inquiry requires only a general finding that remains have a significant relationship to a presently existing "tribe, people, or culture," a relationship that goes beyond features common to all humanity. The second inquiry requires a more specific finding that remains are most closely affiliated to specific lineal descendants or to a specific Indian tribe. The district court's interpretation of NAGPRA preserves the statute's two distinct inquiries. Because the record shows no relationship of Kennewick

Man to the Tribal Claimants, the district court was correct in holding that NAGPRA has no application.

The Secretary finally argues that, under *Chevron U.S.A. v. Natural Res. Def. Council*, 467 U.S. 837 (1984), we must defer to the Secretary's interpretation of "Native American." The Secretary by regulation has defined "Native American" to mean "of, or relating to, a tribe, people, or culture indigenous to the United States." 43 C.F.R. § 10.2(d). The Secretary's regulation, enacted through notice and comment rulemaking, defines Native American exactly as NAGPRA defines it, with one critical exception: the regulation omits the present-tense phrase "that is." Compare 25 U.S.C. § 3001(9) ("a culture that is indigenous to the United States") (emphasis added) with 43 C.F.R. § 10.2(d) ("a culture indigenous to the United States") (emphasis added). We hold, for the reasons discussed above, that NAGPRA's requirement that Native American remains bear some relationship to a presently existing tribe, people, or culture is unambiguous, and that the Secretary's contrary interpretation therefore is not owed Chevron deference. *See Chevron*, 467 U.S. at 842–43 ("If the intent of Congress is clear, that is the end of the matter; for the court, as well as the agency, must give effect to the unambiguously expressed intent of Congress.") . . . . We hold that . . . NAGPRA requires that human remains bear a significant relationship to a presently existing tribe, people, or culture to be considered Native American. The district court did not err in reaching that conclusion.

The requirement that we must give effect, if possible, to every word Congress used supports our holding that human remains must be related to a currently existing tribe to come within NAGPRA's protection. Under the Secretary's view of NAGPRA, all graves and remains of persons, predating European settlers, that are found in the United States would be "Native American," in the sense that they presumptively would be viewed as remains of a deceased from a tribe "indigenous" to the United States, even if the tribe had ceased to exist thousands of years before the remains were found, and even if there was no showing of any relationship of the remains to some existing tribe indigenous to the United States. Such an extreme interpretation, as was urged by the Secretary here, *see supra* note 17, would render superfluous NAGPRA's alternative "relating to" method for establishing remains as "Native American" (i.e., if remains are "of, or relating to, a tribe that is indigenous to the United States"). If accepted, the Secretary's interpretation would mean that the finding of any remains in the United States in and of itself would automatically render these remains "Native American." This interpretation would leave no meaning for the "relating to" clause, unless we were to interpret the clause to cover remains found outside the United States. But we cannot conclude that Congress intended an absurd result, for Congress could not be considered to have jurisdiction over disposition of human remains found in some other country. By reading NAGPRA's definition of "Native American" literally, meaning is given to each of its terms. Some remains may be covered because they are remains of a tribe, people, or culture that is indigenous, while other remains may be covered because they are "related to" a currently existing indigenous tribe, people, or culture.

. . .

Our conclusion that NAGPRA requires human remains to bear some relationship to a presently existing tribe, people, or culture to be considered "Native American" is also reinforced by how NAGPRA defines "sacred objects." NAGPRA defines "sacred objects" as "specific ceremonial objects which are needed by traditional Native American religious leaders for the practice of traditional Native American religions by their present day adherents." 25 U.S.C. § 3001(3)(C) (emphasis added). A literal reading of this definition reveals that any artifact to be deemed a "sacred object" must be connected to the practice of an American Indian religion by present-day peoples. This reading is consistent with our reading of "Native American"; that is, just as there must be a relationship between an artifact and a presently existing peoples for the artifact to be a "sacred object" under NAGPRA, there must be a relationship between a set of remains and a presently existing tribe, people, or culture for those remains to be "Native American" under NAGPRA.

Although NAGPRA does not specify precisely what kind of a relationship or precisely how strong a relationship ancient human remains must bear to modern Indian groups to qualify as Native American, NAGPRA's legislative history provides some guidance on what type of relationship may suffice. The House Committee on Interior and Insular Affairs emphasized in its report on NAGPRA that the statute was being enacted with modern-day American Indians' identifiable ancestors in mind. *See, e.g.,* H.R. Rep. No. 101–877, at 4372 (1990) ("Indian representatives testified that the spirits of their ancestors would not rest until they are returned to their homeland...." (emphasis added)); id. at 4369 ("For many years, Indian tribes have attempted to have the remains and funerary objects of their ancestors returned to them." (emphasis added)). Human remains that are 8340 to 9200 years old and that bear only incidental genetic resemblance to modern-day American Indians, along with incidental genetic resemblance to other peoples, cannot be said to be the Indians' "ancestors" within Congress's meaning. Congress enacted NAGPRA to give American Indians control over the remains of their genetic and cultural forbearers, not over the remains of people bearing no special and significant genetic or cultural relationship to some presently existing indigenous tribe, people, or culture.

The age of Kennewick Man's remains, given the limited studies to date, makes it almost impossible to establish any relationship between the remains and presently existing American Indians. At least no significant relationship has yet been shown. We cannot give credence to an interpretation of NAGPRA advanced by the government and the Tribal Claimants that would apply its provisions to remains that have at most a tenuous, unknown, and unproven connection, asserted solely because of the geographical location of the find.

IV.

Finally, we address the Secretary's determination that Kennewick Man's remains are Native American, as defined by NAGPRA. We must set aside the Secretary's decision if it was "arbitrary" or "capricious" because the decision was based on inadequate factual support. *See* 5 U.S.C. § 706(2)(A). We review the full agency record to determine whether substantial evidence supports the agency's decision that Kennewick Man is "Native American" within NAG–PRA's meaning. Here, after reviewing the record, we conclude that the record does not contain substantial evidence that Kennewick Man's remains are Native American within NAGPRA's meaning.

The administrative record contains no evidence—let alone substantial evidence—that Kennewick Man's remains are connected by some special or significant genetic or cultural relationship to any presently existing indigenous tribe, people, or culture. An examination of the record demonstrates the absence of evidence that Kennewick Man and modern tribes share significant genetic or cultural features.

No cognizable link exists between Kennewick Man and modern Columbia Plateau Indians. When Kennewick Man's remains were discovered, local coroners initially believed the remains were those of a European, not a Native American, because of their appearance. Later testing by scientists demonstrated that the cranial measurements and features of Kennewick Man most closely resemble those of Polynesians and southern Asians, and that Kennewick Man's measurements and features differ significantly from those of any modern Indian group living in North America.

Scant or no evidence of cultural similarities between Kennewick Man and modern Indians exists. One of the Secretary's experts, Dr. Kenneth Ames, reported that "the empirical gaps in the record preclude establishing cultural continuities or discontinuities, particularly before about 5000 B.C." Dr. Ames noted that, although there was overwhelming evidence that many aspects of the "Plateau Pattern" were present between 1000 B.C. and A.D. 1, "the empirical record precludes establishing cultural continuities or discontinuities across increasingly remote periods." He noted that the available evidence is insufficient either to prove or disprove cultural or group continuity dating back earlier than 5000 B.C., which is the case with regard to the Kennewick Man's remains, and that there is evidence that substantial changes occurred in settlement, housing, diet, trade, subsistence patterns, technology, projectile point styles, raw materials, and mortuary rituals at various times between the estimated date when Kennewick Man lived and the beginning of the "Plateau Culture" some 2000 to 3000 years ago.

Dr. Ames' conclusions about the impossibility of establishing cultural continuity between Kennewick Man and modern Indians is confirmed by other evidence that the Secretary credited. For example, the Secretary acknowledges that the record shows that there were no villages or permanent settlements in the Columbia Plateau region 9000 years ago and that human populations then were small and nomadic, traveling long distances in search of food and raw materials. The Secretary's experts determined, and the Secretary acknowledged, that it was not until 2000 to 3000 years ago that populations began to settle into the villages and bands that may have been the antecedents of modern Indian tribes something like those encountered by European settlers and colonists. As the Secretary summarized, "cultural discontinuities are suggested by evidence that the cultural group existing 8500–9500 years ago was likely small in size and highly mobile while the Plateau culture consisted of larger, more sedentary groups.''

The Secretary also acknowledges that ''there is very little evidence of burial patterns during the 9500–8500 period and significant temporal gaps exist in the mortuary record for other periods.'' So, even if we assume that Kennewick Man was part of a stable social group living in the area, it still would be impossible to say whether his group's burial practices were related to modern tribes' burial practices. The Secretary also noted that ''the linguistic analysis was unable to provide reliable evidence for the 8500–9500 period.''

The Secretary's only evidence, perhaps, of a possible cultural relationship between Kennewick Man and modern-day American Indians comes in the form of oral histories. One of the Secretary's experts, Dr. Daniel Boxberger, concluded that modern day Plateau tribes' oral histories—some of which can be interpreted to refer to ancient floods, volcanic eruptions, and the like—are ''highly suggestive of long-term establishment of the present-day tribes.'' Stated another way, Dr. Boxberger noted that oral traditions showed no necessary tale of a superseding migration with newer peoples displacing older ones. But evidence in the record demonstrates that oral histories change relatively quickly, that oral histories may be based on later observation of geological features and deduction (rather than on the first teller's witnessing ancient events), and that these oral histories might be from a culture or group other than the one to which Kennewick Man belonged. . . .

Considered as a whole, the administrative record might permit the Secretary to conclude reasonably that the Tribal Claimants' ancestors have lived in the region for a very long time. However, because Kennewick Man's remains are so old and the information about his era is so limited, the record does not permit the Secretary to conclude reasonably that Kennewick Man shares special and significant genetic or cultural features with presently existing indigenous tribes, people, or cultures. We thus hold that Kennewick Man's remains are not Native American human remains within the meaning of NAGPRA and that NAGPRA does not apply to them. Studies of the Kennewick Man's remains by Plaintiffs-scientists may proceed pursuant to ARPA.

We remand to the district court for further proceedings consistent with this opinion.

AFFIRMED.

NOTE

In July of 2004 both the Northwest tribes and the Justice Department decided not to appeal the decision of the Ninth Circuit. The tribes involved in the suit decided, instead, to seek a legislative solution. The tribes will work together in an attempt to persuade Congress to amend the Native American Graves Protection and Repatriation Act. According to the leaders of the tribes' efforts, the act must be strengthened so that it fulfills Congress' original intent. Richard L. Hill, *U.S. Justice Agency Won't Appeal Kennewick Man Case*, THE OREGONIAN, July 21, 2004, at B10.

Since the Native American Graves Protection and Repatriation Act was enacted in 1990, over 10,000 human remains have been returned from the more than 100,000 skeletons stored in museums. The largest single repatriation of Native American remains to date consists of skeletons of nearly 2,000 Pueblo Indians, which were returned by Harvard's Peabody Museum to the tribe's ancestors in the Pecos Valley site in New Mexico. Harvard had stored and studied the bones for over 70 years. Carey Goldberg, *Pueblo Awaits Its Past in Bones From Harvard*, N.Y. Times, May 20, 1999, at A18.

For a thoughtful exposition of this complex issue from a curator's perspective, see Peter H. Welsh, *Repatriation and Cultural Preservation: Potent Objects, Potent Pasts*, 25 U.Mich.J.L.Ref. 837 (1992). For an overview of federal and state law, see John B. Winski, *There Are Skeletons in the Closet: The Repatriation of Native American Human Remains and Burial Objects*, 34 Ariz.L.Rev. 187 (1992). For a proposed solution regarding disposition of unidentified or unaffiliated remains, see David J. Harris, *Respect for the Living and Respect for the Dead: Return of Indian and Other Native American Burial Remains*, 39 Wash.U.J.Urb. & Contemp.L. 195 (1991).

II. Humans as Research Subjects

A. Overview

Hans Jonas, *Philosophical Reflections on Experimenting With Human Subjects*

Experimentation with Human Subjects
1–4, 9–14 (1970).

Experimenting with human subjects is going on in many fields of scientific and technological progress. It is designed to replace the over-all instruction by natural, occasional experience with the selective information from artificial, systematic experiment which physical science has found so effective in dealing with inanimate nature. Of the new experimentation with man, medical is surely the most legitimate; psychological, the most dubious, biological (still to come), the most dangerous. I have chosen here to deal with the first only, where the case *for* it is strongest and the task of adjudicating conflicting claims hardest....

The Peculiarity of Human Experimentation

Experimentation was originally sanctioned by natural science. There it is performed on inanimate objects, and this raises no moral problems. But as soon as animate, feeling beings become the subjects of experiment, as they do in the life sciences and especially in medical research, this innocence of the search for knowledge is lost and questions of conscience arise. The depth to which moral and religious sensibilities can become aroused over these questions is shown by the vivisection issue. Human experimentation must sharpen the issue as it involves ultimate questions of personal dignity and sacrosanctity. One profound difference between the human experiment and the physical (beside that between animate and inanimate, feeling and unfeeling nature) is this: The physical experiment employs small-scale, artificially devised substitutes for that about which knowledge is to be obtained, and the experimenter extrapolates from these models and simulated conditions to nature at large. Something deputizes for the "real thing"—balls rolling down an inclined plane for sun and planets, electric discharges from a condenser for real lightning, and so on. For the most part, no such substitution is possible in the biological sphere. We must operate on the original itself, the real thing in the fullest sense, and perhaps affect it irreversibly. No simulacrum can take its place. Especially in the human sphere, experimentation loses entirely the advantage of the clear division between vicarious model and true object. Up to a point, animals may fulfill the proxy role of the classical physical experiment. But in the end man himself must furnish knowledge about himself, and the comfortable separation of noncommittal experiment and definitive action vanishes.... Human experimentation for whatever purpose is always *also* a responsible, nonexperimental, definitive dealing with the subject himself. And not even the noblest purpose abrogates the obligations this involves.

. . .

Before going any further, we should give some more articulate voice to the resistance we feel against a merely utilitarian view of the matter. It has to do with a peculiarity of human experimentation quite independent of the question of possible injury to the subject. What is wrong with making a person an experimental subject is not so much that we make him thereby a means (which happens in social contexts of all kinds), as that we make him a thing—a passive thing merely to be acted on, and passive not even for real action, but for token action whose token object he is. His being is reduced to that of a mere token or "sample." This is different from even the most exploitative situations of social life: there the business is real, not fictitious. The subject, however much abused, remains an agent and thus a "subject" in the other sense of the word. The soldier's case is instructive: Subject to most unilateral discipline, forced to risk mutilation and death, conscripted without, perhaps against, his will—he is still conscripted with his capacities to act, to hold his own or fail in situations, to meet real challenges for real stakes. Though a mere "number" to the High Command, he is not a token and not a thing. (Imagine what he would say if it turned out that the war was a game staged to sample observations on his endurance, courage, or cowardice.)

These compensations of personhood are denied to the subject of experimentation, who is acted upon for an extraneous end without being engaged in a real relation where he would be the counterpoint to the other or to circumstance. Mere "consent" (mostly amounting to no more than permission) does not right this reification. Only genuine authenticity of volunteering can possibly redeem the condition of "thinghood" to which the subject submits.... Let us now look at the nature of the conflict, and especially at the nature of the claims countering in this matter those on behalf of personal sacrosanctity.

The setting for the conflict most consistently invoked in the literature is the polarity of individual versus society—the possible tension between the individual good and the common good, between private and public welfare....

... We do not normally—that is, in nonemergency conditions—give the state the right to conscript labor, while we do give it the right to "conscript" money, for money is detachable from the person as labor is not. Even less than forced labor do we countenance forced risk, injury, and indignity.

But in time of war our society itself supersedes the nice balance of the social contract with an almost absolute precedence of public necessities over individual rights. In this and similar emergencies, the sacrosanctity of the individual is abrogated, and what for all practical purposes amounts to a near-totalitarian, quasi-communist state of affairs is *temporarily* permitted to prevail. In such situations, the community is conceded the right to make calls on its members, or certain of its members, entirely different in magnitude and kind from the calls normally allowed. It is deemed right that a part of the population bears a disproportionate burden of risk of a disproportionate gravity; and it is deemed right that the rest of the community accepts this sacrifice, whether voluntary or enforced, and reaps its benefits—difficult as we find it to justify this acceptance and this benefit by any normal ethical categories. We justify it transethically, as it were, by the supreme collective emergency, formalized, for example, by the declaration of a state of war.

Medical experimentation on human subjects falls somewhere between this overpowering case and the normal transactions of the social contract. On the one hand, no comparable extreme issue of social survival is (by and large) at stake. And no comparable extreme sacrifice or foreseeable risk is (by and large) asked. On the other hand, what is asked goes decidedly beyond, even runs counter to, what it is otherwise deemed fair to let the individual sign over of his person to the benefit of the "common good." Indeed, our sensitivity to the kind of intrusion and use involved is such that only an end of transcendent value or overriding urgency can make it arguable and possibly acceptable in our eyes.

Health as a Public Good

The cause invoked is health and, in its more critical aspect, life itself— clearly superlative goods that the physician serves directly by curing and the researcher indirectly by the knowledge gained through his experiments. There is no question about the good served nor about the evil fought— disease and premature death. But a good to whom and an evil to whom? Here the issue tends to become somewhat clouded. In the attempt to give experimentation the proper dignity (on the problematic view that a value becomes greater by being "social" instead of merely individual), the health in question or the disease in question is somehow predicated on the social whole, as if it were society that, in the persons of its members, enjoyed the one and suffered the other.

In trying to resolve some of the complexities and ambiguities lurking in these conceptualizations, I have pondered a particular statement, made in the form of a question, which I found in the *Proceedings* of the earlier *Daedalus* conference: "Can society afford to discard the tissues and organs of the hopelessly unconscious patient when they could be used to restore the otherwise hopelessly ill, but still salvageable individual?" And somewhat later: "A strong case can be made that society can ill afford to discard the tissues and organs of the hopelessly unconscious patient; they are greatly needed for study and experimental trial to help those who can be salvaged."[7].... Let me, for a moment, take the question literally. "Discarding" implies proprietary rights—nobody can discard what does not belong to him in the first place. Does society then own my body? "Salvaging" implies the same and, moreover, a use-value to the owner. Is the life-extension of certain individuals then a public interest? "Affording" implies a critically vital level of such an interest—that is, of the loss or gain involved. And "society" itself—what is it? When does a need, an aim, an obligation become social? Let us reflect on some of these terms.

What Society Can Afford

"Can Society afford ...?" Afford what? ... The specific question seems to be whether society can afford to let some people die whose death might be deferred by particular means if these were authorized by society. Again, if it is merely a question of what society can or cannot afford, rather than of what it ought or ought not to do, the answer must be: Of course, it can. If cancer, heart disease, and other organic, noncontagious ills, especially those tending to strike the old more than the young, continue to exact their toll at the normal rate of incidence (including the toll of private anguish and misery), society can go on flourishing in every way.

Here, by contrast, are some examples of what, in sober truth, society cannot afford. It cannot afford to let an epidemic rage unchecked; a persistent excess of deaths over births, but neither—we must add—too great an excess of births over deaths; too low an average life expectancy even if demographically balanced by fertility, but neither too great a longevity with the necessitated correlative dearth of youth in the social body; a debilitating state of general health; and things of this kind. These are plain cases where the whole condition of society is critically affected, and the public interest can make its imperative claims. The Black Death of the Middle Ages was a *public* calamity of the acute kind; the life-sapping ravages of endemic malaria or sleeping sickness in certain areas are a public calamity of the chronic kind. Such situations a society as a whole can truly not "afford," and they may call for extraordinary remedies, including, perhaps, the invasion of private sacrosanctities.

. . .

Society and the Cause of Progress

Much weaker is the case where it is a matter not of saving but of improving society. Much of medical research falls into this category. As stated before, a permanent death rate from heart failure or cancer does not threaten society. So long as certain statistical ratios are maintained, the incidence of disease and of disease-induced mortality is not (in the strict sense) a "social" misfortune. I hasten to add that it is not therefore less of a human misfortune, and the call for relief issuing with silent eloquence from each victim and all potential victims is of no lesser dignity. But it is

---

7. Proceedings of the Conference on the Ethical Aspects of Experimentation on Human Subjects, November 3–4, 1967 (Boston, Massachusetts).

misleading to equate the fundamentally human response to it with what is owed to society: it is owed by man to man—and it is thereby owed by society to the individuals as soon as the adequate ministering to these concerns outgrows (as it progressively does) the scope of private spontaneity and is made a public mandate. It is thus that society assumes responsibility for medical care, research, old age, and innumerable other things not originally of the public realm (in the original "social contract"), and they become duties toward "society" (rather than directly toward one's fellow man) by the fact that they are socially operated.

. . . . As eager beneficiaries of its gains, we now owe to "society," as its chief agent, our individual contributions toward its *continued pursuit.* I emphasize "continued pursuit." Maintaining the existing level requires no more than the orthodox means of taxation and enforcement of professional standards that raise no problems. The more optional goal of pushing forward is also more exacting. We have this syndrome: Progress is by our choosing an acknowledged interest of society, in which we have a stake in various degrees; science is a necessary instrument of progress; research is a necessary instrument of science; and in medical science experimentation on human subjects is a necessary instrument of research. Therefore, human experimentation has come to be a societal interest.

The destination of research is essentially melioristic. It does not serve the preservation of the existing good from which I profit myself and to which I am obligated. Unless the present state is intolerable, the melioristic goal is in a sense gratuitous, and this not only from the vantage point of the present. Our descendants have a right to be left an unplundered planet; they do not have a right to new miracle cures. . . .

The Melioristic Goal, Medical Research, and Individual Duty

Nowhere is the melioristic goal more inherent than in medicine. . . .

. . .

[W]e must look outside the sphere of the social contract, outside the whole realm of public rights and duties, for the motivations and norms by which we can expect ever again the upwelling of a will to give what nobody—neither society, nor fellow man, nor posterity—is entitled to. There are such dimensions in man with trans-social wellsprings of conduct, and I have already pointed to the paradox, or mystery, that society cannot prosper without them, that it must draw on them, but cannot command them.

Fred Rosner, *Human Experimentation in Judaism*
Biomedical Ethics and Jewish Law 408, 410 (2001).

Human life is sacrosanct, and of supreme and infinite worth. Any chance to save life, however remote, must be pursued at all costs. The obligation to save a person from any hazard to his life or health devolves on anyone able to do so. Every life is equally valuable and inviolable, including that of criminals, prisoners, and defectives. One must not sacrifice one life to save another, or even any number of others. No one has the right to volunteer his life. No one has the right to injure his own or anyone else's life. No one has the right to injure his own or anyone else's body, except for therapeutic purposes. No one has the right to refuse medical treatment deemed necessary by competent opinion. Measures involving some immediate risks of life may be taken in attempts to prevent certain death later. There is no restriction on animal experiments for medical purposes.[4]

. . .

Human experimentation may involve healthy volunteers and/or sick patients. In Judaism, healthy people may altruistically volunteer for a research study that involves little or no risk (e.g., blood drawing). A seriously ill patient is required to accept standard medical therapy which is known to be efficacious even if side effects may occur. If standard therapy has failed or is not available, a patient is allowed but not obligated to accept experimental therapy even if the risks are significant. Experimentation on human patients must have therapeutic intent. Experimental medications or surgical procedures may not be undertaken solely to determine toxicity or possible benefit to others. They must at least have the potential to benefit the patient at hand. The decision to assume the risk of high mortality or severe morbidity with hope of benefit from the experimental treatment must, if possible, be made by the patient.

Xunwu Chen, *A Confucian Justification of Experimenting with Human Subjects*

CONFUCIAN BIOETHICS 217–218 (1999).

[A] Confucian justification of a therapeutic experiment consists in the argument that an experiment is justified when it is a wise thing to do based on the scientific evidence and, in addition, a right thing to do because it confirms the spirit of righteousness in line with humanity, care, and propriety. Accordingly, an experiment should be rejected if it is either not scientifically wise or it will do wrong to the patient, or both. Good reason here thus consists not only in scientific evidence, but also in the idea of righteousness.

. . .

A non-therapeutic medical or biological experiment with human subjects is justified when its performance under the circumstances would be vouched for by the possibility that the knowledge it yields could have a significant contribution to the welfare of a community in particular or the welfare of humankind in general, a contribution that no one could reasonably reject or deny, and in addition, when its performance would not be disallowed by the principle of righteousness in line with humanity. . . . The idea of "not being disallowed by the principle of righteousness in line with humanity" is meant not only to rule out inhumane experiments, but also to exclude experiments under inhumane circumstances. Inhumane experi-

---

4. Jakobovits, I. Medical experimentation on humans in Jewish Law. *Proc. Assn Orthodox Jewish Scientists*, New York, Vol. 1, 1966. Reprinted in *Jewish Bioethics* (F. Rosner and J.D. Bleich, Eds.), New York, Sanhedrin Press, 1979, pp. 377–383.

ments refer to those experiments that are not meant to serve but to destroy humanity. An example of this kind of experiment is that which is meant to produce bio-chemical weapons, bacteria weapons, etc. Experiments that are performed under inhumane conditions include those that coerce specific groups to become subjects of the experiment, those that do not make necessary preparation to reduce the burden and suffering of the human individuals (the subjects) in the experiments, those that are not based on solid scientific knowledge and evidence but are performed because of the availability of subjects in specific circumstances (e.g., there are plenty of subjects if one were to use war prisoners or prisoned criminal, etc.) or due to political expedience, those that are both deceitful and exploitative, etc.

Gilbert Meilaender, *Gifts of the Body: Human Experimentation*

BIOETHICS: A PRIMER FOR CHRISTIANS 106–113 (1996).

It would be hard to deny that we have reaped enormous benefits from modern medicine, based as it is upon scientific experimentation. We need only recall a disease such as polio, so feared only forty years ago and now so rare in this country, to remind ourselves what medical research has done for our lives. Aimed not primarily at the care of particular patients but at the acquisition of generalizable knowledge that may help future sufferers, research has radically altered the landscape of medicine.

. . .

Any serious Christian evaluation of the place of medical research must reckon with the human tendency toward idolatry. We can make—and probably have made—an idol of medical advance.... Although we grant that death is inevitable, we do not admit that any medical cause of death cannot be overcome. The paradox is likely to incline us feverishly in the direction of experimentation and research.... Our evaluation of the place of medical research in human life ought also to reflect our understanding of the meaning of suffering. It is a great evil from which Jesus himself shrank back, and we ought to do what we can—including engaging in medical research—to relieve it. But the march of progress within human history is not itself redemptive, and God ultimately deals with suffering in His own mysterious way. God bears it into death—demonstrating thereby that no other gods of our own making, however powerful they may seem, can deal sufficiently with the suffering that marks our lives. Christians therefore have no good reason to renounce the cause of medical research, but our commitment to it ought to be a chastened one, liberated from the fear that makes an idol of our hopes.

. . .

If Christians are to love any neighbor who is in need, this may be reason enough to consider participating in research when an appropriate occasion arises.... Scientific medicine has made it possible for us to put nature to the test, and we have gradually come to believe that such testing is imperative—that because we *can* gain knowledge that will help future sufferers, we *must* do so. The requirement of consent was developed both to make research possible and to limit it: to make it possible by authorizing us to enlist those who truly volunteer; to limit it by guarding against out tendency to use some, without their full consent, for the good of others. Because the consent requirement sets limits to the advance of research, we will always be tempted to find ways around it.

B. A HISTORY OF EXPERIMENTAL ABUSES
1. THE NAZI WAR CRIMES TRIALS[a]

a. *United States v. Karl Brandt*

This case is often referred to as the "Medical Case" because 20 of the 23 defendants were doctors, including Karl Brandt, personal physician to Adolph Hitler. The case was tried at the Palace of Justice in Nuremberg from December 1946 to July 1947 before a tribunal consisting of Walter Beals, the Chief Justice of the Supreme Court of the State of Washington; Harold Sebring, an Associate Justice of the Supreme Court of Florida; and Johnson Crawford, former Judge of a District Court of Oklahoma.

The authority of the tribunal derived from a series of agreements among the Allied Powers reached in the aftermath of World War II. In May of 1945, President Truman authorized Robert Jackson, an Associate Justice of the Supreme Court of the United States, to represent the United States "in preparing or prosecuting charges of atrocities and war crimes against such of the leaders of the European Axis powers and their principal agents and accessories as the United States may agree with any of the United Nations to bring to trial before an international military tribunal." Exec.Order No. 9547, 3 C.F.R. 703 (1945).

On August 8, 1945, the London Agreement was signed by Jackson for the United States. U.S. EAS 472, 59 Stat. 1544, 82 UNTS 279. The Agreement, made with France, Great Britain and the U.S.S.R., established an International Military Tribunal to try war crimes. It also affirmed the right of the participants to establish their own courts to try war criminals in their zone of occupation.

On December 20, 1945, representatives of the same four nations signed Control Council Law No. 10, which was designed to implement the London Agreement. The Law established uniform definitions of certain war crimes and procedures for each nation to follow when prosecuting suspected war criminals in its zone of occupation.

Opening Statement by Telford Taylor, Brigadier General, for the Prosecution

TRIALS OF WAR CRIMINALS BEFORE THE NUREMBERG MILITARY TRIBUNALS UNDER CONTROL COUNCIL LAW No. 10 (1949).

· · ·

a. All the materials relating to the Nuremberg Trials are from Trials of War Criminals Before the Nuremberg Military Tribunals Under Control Council Law No. 10 (1949), unless otherwise noted.

I turn now to the main part of the indictment and will outline at this point the prosecution's case relating to those crimes alleged to have been committed in the name of medical or scientific research.... What I will cover now comprehends all the experiments charged as war crimes[b] in paragraph 6 and as crimes against humanity[c] in paragraph 11 of the indictment, and the murders committed for so-called anthropological purposes which are charged as war crimes in paragraph 7 and as crimes against humanity in paragraph 12 of the indictment.

Before taking up these experiments one by one, let us look at them as a whole. Are they a heterogeneous list of horrors, or is there a common denominator for the whole group?

A sort of rough pattern is apparent on the face of the indictment. Experiments concerning high altitude, the effect of cold, and the potability of processed sea water have an obvious relation to aeronautical and naval combat and rescue problems. The mustard gas and phosphorous burn experiments, as well as those relating to the healing value of sulfanilamide for wounds, can be related to air-raid and battlefield medical problems. It is well known that malaria, epidemic jaundice, and typhus were among the principal diseases which had to be combated by the German Armed Forces and by German authorities in occupied territories.

To some degree, the therapeutic pattern outlined above is undoubtedly a valid one, and explains why the Wehrmacht, and especially the German Air Force, participated in these experiments. Fanatically bent upon conquest, utterly ruthless as to the means or instruments to be used in achieving victory, and callous to the sufferings of people whom they regarded as inferior, the German militarists were willing to gather whatever scientific fruit these experiments might yield.

But our proof will show that a quite different and even more sinister objective runs like a red thread through these hideous researches. We will show that in some instances the true object of these experiments was not how to rescue or to cure, but how to destroy and kill. The sterilization experiments were, it is clear, purely destructive in purpose. The prisoners at Buchenwald who were shot with poisoned bullets were not guinea pigs to test an antidote for the poison; their murderers really wanted to know how quickly the poison would kill. This destructive objective is not superficially

---

b. [Eds.—Defined by Control Council Law 10, Art. II § 1(b) as:

Atrocities or offences against persons or property constituting violations of the laws or customs of war, including but not limited to, murder, ill treatment or deportation to slave labour or for any other purpose, of civilian population from occupied territory, murder or ill treatment of prisoners of war or persons on the seas, killing of hostages, plunder of public or private property, wanton destruction of cities, towns, or devastation not justified by military necessity.]

c. [Eds.—Defined by Control Council Law 10, Art. II § 1(c) as:

Atrocities and offences, including but not limited to murder, extermination, enslavement, deportation, imprisonment, torture, rape or other inhumane acts committed against any civilian population, or persecutions on political, racial or religious grounds whether or not in violation of the domestic laws of the country where perpetrated.]

as apparent in the other experiments, but we will show that it was often there.

Mankind has not heretofore felt the need of a word to denominate the science of how to kill prisoners more rapidly and subjugate people in large numbers. This case and these defendants have created this gruesome question for the lexicographer. For the moment we will christen this macabre science "thanatology," the science of producing death. The thanatological knowledge, derived in part from these experiments, supplied the techniques for genocide, a policy of the Third Reich, exemplified in the "euthanasia" program and in the widespread slaughter of Jews, gypsies, Poles, and Russians. This policy of mass extermination could not have been so effectively carried out without the active participation of German medical scientists.

I will now take up the experiments themselves. . . .

. . .

C.   Malaria Experiments

Another series of experiments carried out at the Dachau concentration camp concerned immunization for and treatment of malaria. Over 1,200 inmates of practically every nationality were experimented upon. The malaria experiments were carried out under the general supervision of a Dr. Schilling, with whom the defendant Sievers and others in the box collaborated. The evidence will show that healthy persons were infected by mosquitoes or by injections from the glands of mosquitoes. Catholic priests were among the subjects. The defendant Gebhardt kept Himmler informed of the progress of these experiments. Rose furnished Schilling with fly eggs for them, and others of the defendants participated in various ways which the evidence will demonstrate.

After the victims had been infected, they were variously treated with quinine, neosalvarsan, pyramidon, antipyrin, and several combinations of these drugs. Many deaths occurred from excessive doses of neosalvarsan and pyramidon. According to the findings of the Dachau court, malaria was the direct cause of 30 deaths and 300 to 400 others died as a result of subsequent complications.

. . .

I.   Sterilization Experiments

In the sterilization experiments conducted by the defendants at Auschwitz, Ravensbrueck, and other concentration camps, the destructive nature of the Nazi medical program comes out most forcibly. The Nazis were searching for methods of extermination, both by murder and sterilization, of large population groups, by the most scientific and least conspicuous means. They were developing a new branch of medical science which would give them the scientific tools for the planning and practice of genocide. The primary purpose was to discover an inexpensive, unobtrusive, and rapid method of sterilization which could be used to wipe out Russians, Poles, Jews, and other people. Surgical sterilization was thought to be too slow and expensive to be used on a mass scale. A method to bring about an unnoticed sterilization was thought desirable.

Medicinal sterilizations were therefore carried out. A Dr. Madaus had stated that caladium seguinum, a drug obtained from a North American plant, if taken orally or by injection, would bring about sterilization. In 1941 the defendant Pokorny called this to Himmler's attention, and suggested that it should be developed and used against Russian prisoners of war. I quote one paragraph from Pokorny's letter written at that time:

> If, on the basis of this research, it were possible to produce a drug which after a relatively short time, effects an imperceptible sterilization on human beings, then we would have a powerful new weapon at our disposal. The thought alone that the 3 million Bolsheviks, who are at present German prisoners, could be sterilized so that they could be used as laborers but be prevented from reproduction, opens the most far-reaching perspectives.

As a result of Pokorny's suggestion, experiments were conducted on concentration camp inmates to test the effectiveness of the drug. At the same time efforts were made to grow the plant on a large scale in hothouses.

At the Auschwitz concentration camp sterilization experiments were also conducted on a large scale by a Dr. Karl Clauberg, who had developed a method of sterilizing women, based on the injection of an irritating solution. Several thousand Jewesses and gypsies were sterilized at Auschwitz by this method.

Conversely, surgical operations were performed on sexually abnormal inmates at Buchenwald in order to determine whether their virility could be increased by the transplantation of glands. Out of 14 subjects of these experiments, at least 2 died.

The defendant Gebhardt also personally conducted sterilizations at Ravensbrueck by surgical operation. The defendant Viktor Brack, in March 1941, submitted to Himmler a report on the progress and state of X-ray sterilization experiments. Brack explained that it had been determined that sterilization with powerful X-rays could be accomplished and that castration would then result. The danger of this X-ray method lay in the fact that other parts of the body, if they were not protected with lead, were also seriously affected. In order to prevent the victims from realizing that they were being castrated, Brack made the following fantastic suggestion in his letter written in 1941 to Himmler, from which I quote:

> One way to carry out these experiments in practice would be to have those people who are to be treated line up before a counter. There they would be questioned and a form would be given them to be filled out, the whole process taking 2 or 3 minutes. The official attendant who sits behind the counter can operate the apparatus in such a manner that he works a switch which will start both tubes together (as the rays have to come from both sides). With one such installation with two tubes about 150 to 200 persons could be sterilized daily, while 20 installations would take care of 3,000 to 4,000 persons daily. In my opinion the number of daily deportations will not exceed this figure.

. . .

*b.   The Judgment of the Court and the Establishment of the
Nuremberg Code*

The Proof as to War Crimes and Crimes Against Humanity

TRIALS OF WAR CRIMINALS BEFORE THE NUREMBERG MILITARY TRIBUNALS UNDER CONTROL COUNCIL LAW
No. 10 (1949).

Judged by any standard of proof the record clearly shows the commission of war crimes and crimes against humanity substantially as alleged in counts two and three of the indictment. Beginning with the outbreak of World War II criminal medical experiments on non-German nationals, both prisoners of war and civilians, including Jews and "asocial" persons, were carried out on a large scale in Germany and the occupied countries. These experiments were not the isolated and casual acts of individual doctors and scientists working solely on their own responsibility, but were the product of coordinated policy-making and planning at high governmental, military, and Nazi Party levels, conducted as an integral part of the total war effort. They were ordered, sanctioned, permitted, or approved by persons in positions of authority who under all principles of law were under the duty to know about these things and to take steps to terminate or prevent them.

PERMISSIBLE MEDICAL EXPERIMENTS

The great weight of the evidence before us is to the effect that certain types of medical experiments on human beings, when kept within reasonably well-defined bounds, conform to the ethics of the medical profession generally. The protagonists of the practice of human experimentation justify their views on the basis that such experiments yield results for the good of society that are unprocurable by other methods or means of study. All agree, however, that certain basic principles must be observed in order to satisfy moral, ethical and legal concepts:

1.   The voluntary consent of the human subject is absolutely essential.

This means that the person involved should have legal capacity to give consent; should be so situated as to be able to exercise free power of choice, without the intervention of any element of force, fraud, deceit, duress, overreaching, or other ulterior form of constraint or coercion; and should have sufficient knowledge and comprehension of the elements of the subject matter involved as to enable him to make an understanding and enlightened decision. This latter element requires that before the acceptance of an affirmative decision by the experimental subject there should be made known to him the nature, duration, and purpose of the experiment; the method and means by which it is to be conducted; all inconveniences and hazards reasonably to be expected; and the effects upon his health or person which may possibly come from his participation in the experiment.

The duty and responsibility for ascertaining the quality of the consent rests upon each individual who initiates, directs or engages in the experiment. It is a personal duty and responsibility which may not be delegated to another with impunity.

2.   The experiment should be such as to yield fruitful results for the good of society, unprocurable by other methods or means of study, and not random and unnecessary in nature.

3.   The experiment should be so designed and based on the results of animal experimentation and a knowledge of the natural history of the disease or other problem under study that the anticipated results will justify the performance of the experiment.

4.   The experiment should be so conducted as to avoid all unnecessary physical and mental suffering and injury.

5.   No experiment should be conducted where there is an *a priori* reason to believe that death or disabling injury will occur; except, perhaps, in those experiments where the experimental physicians also serve as subjects.

6.   The degree of risk to be taken should never exceed that determined by the humanitarian importance of the problem to be solved by the experiment.

7.   Proper preparations should be made and adequate facilities provided to protect the experimental subject against even remote possibilities of injury, disability, or death.

8.   The experiment should be conducted only by scientifically qualified persons. The highest degree of skill and care should be required through all stages of the experiment of those who conduct or engage in the experiment.

9.   During the course of the experiment the human subject should be at liberty to bring the experiment to an end if he has reached the physical or mental state where continuation of the experiment seems to him to be impossible.

10.   During the course of the experiment the scientist in charge must be prepared to terminate the experiment at any stage, if he has probable cause to believe, in the exercise of the good faith, superior skill and careful judgment required of him that a continuation of the experiment is likely to result in injury, disability, or death to the experimental subject.

Of the ten principles which have been enumerated our judicial concern, of course, is with those requirements which are purely legal in nature—or which at least are so clearly related to matters legal that they assist us in determining criminal culpability and punishment. To go beyond that point would lead us into a field that would be beyond our sphere of competence. However, the point need not be labored. We find from the evidence that in the medical experiments which have been proved, these ten principles were much more frequently honored in their breach than in their observance. Many of the concentration camp inmates who were the victims of these atrocities were citizens of countries other than the German Reich. They were non-German nationals, including Jews and "asocial persons", both prisoners of war and civilians, who had been imprisoned and forced to submit to these tortures and barbarities without so much as a semblance of trial. In every single instance appearing in the record, subjects were used who did not consent to the experiments; indeed, as to some of the experiments, it is not even contended by the defendants that the subjects occupied the status of volunteers. In no case was the experimental subject at liberty of his own free choice to withdraw from any experiment. In many cases experiments were performed by unqualified persons; were conducted at random for no adequate scientific reason, and under revolting physical conditions. All of the experiments were conducted with unnecessary suffering and injury and but very little, if any, precautions were taken to protect or safeguard the human subjects from the possibilities of injury, disability, or death. In every one of the experiments the subjects experienced extreme pain or torture, and in most of them they suffered permanent injury, mutilation, or death, either as a result of the experiments or because of lack of adequate follow-up care.

Obviously all of these experiments involving brutalities, tortures, disabling injury, and death were performed in complete disregard of international conventions, the laws and customs of war, the general principles of criminal law as derived from the criminal laws of all civilized nations, and Control Council Law No. 10. Manifestly human experiments under such conditions are contrary to "the principles of the law of nations as they result from the usages established among civilized peoples, from the laws of humanity, and from the dictates of public conscience."

[*Signed*] Walter B. Beals
Presiding Judge

Harold L. Sebring
Judge

Johnson T. Crawford
Judge

NOTES AND QUESTIONS

1. For a compelling account of the Nuremberg Trials, *see* TELFORD TAYLOR, THE ANATOMY OF THE NUREMBERG TRIALS: A PERSONAL MEMOIR (1992).

2. The judgment at Nuremberg establishes, at the very least, that physicians conducting medical experiments on human beings cannot escape legal responsibility for their participation by pointing to the state's involvement. What then should be the state's responsibility for experiments on human subjects which it (a) orders to be performed; (b) requires to be performed as a condition for regulatory approval (e.g., drugs); (c) funds; or (d) permits to be performed on persons within its custody (e.g., prisoners)? *Cf.* Nevin v. United States, 696 F.2d 1229 (9th Cir.1983) (finding governmental immunity from Federal Tort Claims Act wrongful death action where chief chemical officer's decision to use a particular strain of bacterium for study simulating biological warfare attack on San Francisco in 1950 constituted discretionary function), *cert. denied*, 464 U.S. 815, 104 S.Ct. 70, 78 L.Ed.2d 84 (1983).

3. In 1981, American journalists first reported abuses involving experiments conducted on human beings during World War II by Unit 731 of the Japanese Imperial Army, headquartered in Manchuria. Designed to develop treatments for the medical problems faced by the Japanese Army, the studies included frostbite and pressure chamber experiments, vivisections, and biological warfare simulations. The United States, in exchange for the data, granted immunity from war crimes prosecution to the Japanese who conducted the experiments. *See* SHELDON H. HARRIS, FACTORIES OF DEATH (1994); Nicholas D. Kristof, *Unmasking Horror—A*

Special Report: Japan Confronting Gruesome War Atrocity, N.Y. TIMES, Mar. 17, 1995, at A1. When, if ever, is it acceptable to profit from information derived from unethically conducted research?

4. Operation Paperclip was a secret U.S. intelligence operation whose purpose was to bring Nazi doctors to the United States in order to benefit from their scientific knowledge, some of which had been gained through unethical human experimentation. Their scientific knowledge made possible the development of technology to protect astronauts from violent acceleration, lack of oxygen, unnatural temperature, and weightlessness, all part of space travel. It has been argued that without the information gleaned from the Nazi experiments, the United States would not have achieved space travel. Is this sufficient justification for using the information? For a complete description of Operation Paperclip, *see* TOM BOWER, THE PAPERCLIP CONSPIRACY (1987) and LINDA HUNT, SECRET AGENDA: THE UNITED STATES GOVERNMENT, NAZI SCIENTISTS AND PROJECT PAPERCLIP (1991).

5. In its Final Report issued in 1995, the Advisory Committee on Human Radiation Experiments (ACHRE) established by President Clinton reported on the reactions of American medical researchers to the Nuremberg Medical Trial:

> The Nuremberg Medical Trial received coverage in the American popular press, but it would almost certainly be an exaggeration to refer to this attention as exhaustive. Historian David Rothman has provided the following summary of the trial's coverage in the *New York Times:*

> Over 1945 and 1946 fewer than a dozen articles appeared in the *New York Times* on the Nazi [medical] research; the indictment of forty-two doctors in the fall of 1946 was a page-five story and the opening of the trial, a page-nine story. (The announcement of the guilty verdict in August 1947 was a front-page story, but the execution of seven of the defendants a year later was again relegated to the back pages.)

The Advisory Committee's Ethics Oral History Project suggests that American medical researchers, perhaps like the American public generally, were not carefully following the daily developments in Nuremberg. Even among American medical researchers who might have been aware of events at Nuremberg, it seems that many did not perceive specific personal implications in the Medical Trial. Rothman has enunciated this historical view most fully. He asserts that "the prevailing view was that [the Nuremberg medical defendants] were Nazis first and last; by definition nothing they did, and no code drawn up in response to them, was relevant to the United States." Jay Katz has offered a similar summation of the immediate response of the medical community to the Nuremberg Code: "It was a good code for barbarians but an unnecessary code for ordinary physicians."

Several participants in the Ethics Oral History Project affirmed the interpretations of Rothman and Katz, using similar language. Said one physician: "There was a disconnect [between the Nuremberg Code and its application to American researchers].... The interpretation of these codes [by American physicians] was that they were necessary for barbarians, but [not for] fine upstanding people."

6. Some argue that ACHRE downplayed the effect of the Nuremberg Code in the United States in order to claim that American medical researchers conducting human experiments had no idea that they were bound by an ethical code. This served to justify ACHRE's conclusion that only some of the human subjects of radiation experiments deserved individual apologies from the United States government, while other human subjects should receive no notification or medical follow-up. For a comprehensive critique of ACHRE's recommendations, *see* David Egliman et al., *Ethical Aerobics: ACHRE's Flight from Responsibility*, 6 ACCOUNTABILITY IN RES. 15 (1998).

2.   EXPERIMENTAL ABUSES IN THE UNITED STATES

a.   A Physician Blows the Whistle

Henry Beecher,[d] *Ethics and Clinical Research*
274 NEW ENG.J.MED. 1354 (1966).

Human experimentation since World War II has created some difficult problems with the increasing employment of patients as experimental subjects when it must be apparent that they would not have been available if they had been truly aware of the uses that would be made of them. Evidence is at hand that many of the patients in the examples to follow never had the risk satisfactorily explained to them, and it seems obvious that further hundreds have not known that they were the subjects of an experiment although grave consequences have been suffered as a direct result of experiments described here. There is a belief prevalent in some sophisticated circles that attention to these matters would "block progress." But, according to Pope Pius XII, "... science is not the highest value to which all other orders of values ... should be subordinated."

I am aware that these are troubling charges. They have grown out of troubling practices. They can be documented as I propose to do, by examples from leading medical schools, university hospitals, private hospitals, governmental military departments (the Army, the Navy and the Air Force), governmental institutes (the National Institutes of Health), Veterans Administration hospitals and industry. The basis for the charges is broad.

I should like to affirm that American medicine is sound, and most progress in it soundly attained. There is, however, a reason for concern in certain areas, and I believe the type of activities to be mentioned will do great harm to medicine unless soon corrected. It will certainly be charged that any mention of these matters does a disservice to medicine, but not one so great, I believe, as a continuation of the practices to be cited.

Experimentation in man takes place in several areas: in self-experimentation; in patient volunteers and normal subjects; in therapy; and in the different areas of experimentation on a patient not for his benefit but for that, at least in theory, of patients in general. The present study is limited to this last category.

.   .   .

Frequency of Unethical or Questionably Ethical Procedures

Nearly everyone agrees that ethical violations do occur. The practical question is, how often? A preliminary examination of the matter was based on 17 examples, which were easily increased to 50. These 50 studies contained references to 186 further likely examples, on the average 3.7 leads per study; they at times overlapped from paper to paper, but this

d. [Eds.—Dr. Beecher was the Henry   thesia at Harvard University.]
Isaiah Dorr Professor of Research in Anes-

figure indicates how conveniently one can proceed in a search for such material. The data are suggestive of widespread problems but there is need for another kind of information, which was obtained by examination of 100 consecutive human studies published in 1964, in an excellent journal; 12 of these seemed to be unethical. If only one quarter of them is truly unethical, this still indicates the existence of a serious situation. . . .

The Problem of Consent

All so-called codes are based on the bland assumption that meaningful or informed consent is readily available for the asking. As pointed out elsewhere, this is very often not the case. Consent in any fully informed sense may not be obtainable. Nevertheless, except, possibly, in the most trivial situations, it remains a goal toward which one must strive for sociologic, ethical, and clear-cut legal reasons. There is no choice in the matter.

If suitably approached, patients will accede, on the basis of trust, to about any request their physician may make. At the same time, every experienced clinician investigator knows that patients will often submit to inconvenience and some discomfort, if they do not last very long, but the usual patient will never agree to jeopardize seriously his health or his life for the sake of "science."

In only 2 of the 50 examples originally compiled for this study was consent mentioned. Actually, it should be emphasized in all cases for obvious moral and legal reasons, but it would be unrealistic to place much dependence on it. In any precise sense statements regarding consent are meaningless unless one knows how fully the patient was informed of all risks, and if these are not known, the fact should also be made clear. A far more dependable safeguard than consent is the presence of a truly *responsible* investigator.

Examples of Unethical or Questionably Ethical Studies

. . . . During ten years of study of these matters it has become apparent that thoughtlessness and carelessness, not a willful disregard of the patient's rights, account for most of the cases encountered. Nonetheless, it is evident that in many of the examples presented, the investigators have risked the health or the life of their subjects. No attempt has been made to present the "worst" possible examples; rather, the aim has been to show the variety of problems encountered.

References to the examples presented are not given, for there is no intention of pointing to individuals, but rather, a wish to call attention to widespread practices. All, however, are documented to the satisfaction of the editors of the *Journal*.

Known Effective Treatment Withheld

Example 1. It is known that rheumatic fever can usually be prevented by adequate treatment of streptococcal respiratory infections by the parenteral administration of penicillin. Nevertheless, definitive treatment was withheld, and placebos were given to a group of 109 men in service, while benzathine penicillin G was given to others.

The therapy that each patient received was determined automatically by his military serial number arranged so that more men received penicillin than received placebo. In the small group of patients studied 2 cases of acute rheumatic fever and 1 of acute nephritis developed in the control patients, whereas these complications did not occur among those who received the benzathine penicillin G.

.   .   .

Example 3. This involved a study of the relapse rate in typhoid fever treated in two ways. In an earlier study by the present investigators chloramphenicol had been recognized as an effective treatment for typhoid fever, being attended by half the mortality that was experienced when this agent was not used. Others had made the same observations, indicating that to withhold this effective remedy can be a life-or-death decision. The present study was carried out to determine the relapse rate under the two methods of treatment; of 408 charity patients 251 were treated with chloramphenicol, of whom 20, or 7.97 percent died. Symptomatic treatment was given, but chloramphenicol was withheld in 157, of whom 36 or 22.9 percent died. According to the data presented, 23 patients died in the course of this study who would not have been expected to succumb if they had received specific therapy.

.   .   .

Physiologic Studies

Example 5. In this controlled, double-blind study of the hematologic toxicity of chloramphenicol, it was recognized that chloramphenicol is "well known as a cause of aplastic anemia" and that there is a "prolonged morbidity and high mortality of aplastic anemia" and that "chloramphenicol-induced aplastic anemia can be related to dose...." The aim of the study was "further definition of the toxicology of the drug...."

Forty-one randomly chosen patients were given either 2 or 6 gm. of chloramphenicol per day; 12 control patients were used. "Toxic bone-marrow depression, predominantly affecting erythropoiesis, developed in 2 of 20 patients given 2.0 gm. and in 18 of 21 given 6 gm. of chloramphenicol daily." The smaller dose is recommended for routine use.

.   .   .

Example 16. This study was directed toward determining the period of infectivity of infectious hepatitis. Artificial induction of hepatitis was carried out in an institution for mentally defective children in which a mild form of hepatitis was endemic. The parents gave consent for the intramuscular injection or oral administration of the virus, but nothing is said regarding what was told them concerning the appreciable hazards involved.

A resolution adopted by the World Medical Association states explicitly: "Under no circumstances is a doctor permitted to do anything which would weaken the physical or mental resistance of a human being except from strictly therapeutic or prophylactic indications imposed in the interest of the patient." There is no right to risk an injury to 1 person for the benefit of others.

Example 17. Live cancer cells were injected into 22 human subjects as part of a study of immunity to cancer. According to a recent review, the subjects (hospitalized patients) were "merely told they would be receiving 'some cells' "—"... the word cancer was entirely omitted...."

Example 18. Melanoma was transplanted from a daughter to her volunteering and informed mother, "in the hope of gaining a little better understanding of cancer immunity and in the hope that the production of tumor antibodies might be helpful in the treatment of the cancer patient." Since the daughter died on the day after the transplantation of the tumor into her mother, the hope expressed seems to have been more theoretical than practical, and the daughter's condition was described as "terminal" at the time the mother volunteered to be a recipient. The primary implant was widely excised on the twenty-fourth day after it had been placed in the mother. She died from metastatic melanoma on the four hundred and fifty-first day after transplantation. The evidence that this patient died of diffuse melanoma that metastasized from a small piece of transplanted tumor was considered conclusive.

.   .   .

Publication

In the view of the British Medical Research Council it is not enough to ensure that all investigation is carried out in an ethical manner: it must be made unmistakably clear in the publications that the proprieties have been observed. This implies editorial responsibility in addition to the investigator's. The question rises, then, about valuable data that have been improperly obtained. It is my view that such material should not be published. There is a practical aspect to the matter: failure to obtain publication would discourage unethical experimentation. How many would carry out such experimentation if they *knew* its results would never be published? Even though suppression of such data (by not publishing it) would constitute a loss to medicine, in a specific localized sense, this loss, it seems, would be less important than the far-reaching moral loss to medicine if the data thus obtained were to be published. Admittedly, there is room for debate. Others believe that such data, because of their intrinsic value, obtained at a cost of great risk or damage to the subjects, should not be wasted but should be published with stern editorial comment. This would have to be done with exceptional skill, to avoid an odor of hypocrisy.

NOTES AND QUESTIONS

1. Do you agree that medical and scientific journals should regulate the ethical aspects of research the reports of which are submitted for publication? If so, how should such regulation be carried out? If not, should journals simply disregard blatant violations of ethical norms? Consider the observations of Jay Katz:

> [A policy of publishing only ethical reports] would impose an inordinate amount of work on the editors of journals, for publication of articles would now indicate that the investigators have complied with "ethical standards," at least to the satisfaction of the editors. In the light of complex "ethical" problems raised by contemporary research practices—problems which have as yet hardly been subjected to careful and relentless analysis—this is quite an extraordinary and staggering assignment.

Editorial Rewritten, 22 CLIN.RES. 10, 11 (1974).

2. A survey of 102 biomedical research journals found that 48 (47%) require institutional review board (IRB) approval as a prerequisite for publication of studies involving human subjects, 25 (24%) do not present or refer the author to any information on human research ethics, 15 (15%) referred authors to the Uniform Requirements for Manuscripts Submitted to Biomedical Journals, 3 (3%) referred authors to the Declaration of Helsinki, and 10 (10%) indicated only that informed consent should be obtained. *See* Robert J. Amdur & Chuck Biddle, *Institutional Review Board Approval and Publication of Human Research Results*, 277 JAMA 909 (1997).

3. What if a proffered report presents an important discovery that was obtained in an unethical manner? What of the argument that the harm has been done? What of the risk that without disseminating the results, the research may be repeated by another investigator, causing additional subjects to be exposed to unnecessary risk? *See* Terra Ziporyn, *What the Nazis Called "Medical Research" Haunts the Scientific Community to This Day*, 263 JAMA 791 (1990).

4. The debate over use of Nazi data has evoked strong responses from Holocaust survivors. Consider the view of one survivor of Mengele's infamous twin experiments:

> [T]he emotional scars are so deep that only now, more than 40 years later, are we attempting to face our past and come to terms with it. I know that it will always hurt to remember that we were reduced to the lowest form of existence. We were treated like animals—we were his guinea pigs. But it hurts 10 times more today to realize that some American scientists and doctors want to use this data regardless of the unethical manner in which it was obtained; regardless of the pain and suffering paid by the victims. The advocates for the use of the data claim they want to save human lives. It is obnoxious to me that some of the advocates are so magnanimous with other peoples' lives and suffering.
>
> The data ... should be shredded and placed in a transparent monument, as evidence that they exist, but cannot be used. It should be a lesson to the world that human dignity and human life are more important than any advance in science or medicine.

Eva Mozes Kor, *Nazi Experiments as Viewed by a Survivor of Mengele's Experiments*, in WHEN MEDICINE WENT MAD: BIOETHICS AND THE HOLOCAUST, 3–4, 7 (Arthur L. Caplan, ed., 1992). Should survivors be allowed to determine the fate of the Nazi medical data?

b.   The Tuskegee Syphilis Study

At almost the same time that the abuses at Dauchau and Auschwitz began, the United States Public Health Service was recruiting participants for a long term study of syphilis. Almost 400 black males were the unwitting subjects of this experiment, which was to continue for more than 40 years.

Testimony of Fred Gray, *Hearings Before the Subcommittee on Health of the Senate Committee on Labor and Public Welfare*

93d Cong., 1st Sess., 1033–39 (1973).

MR. GRAY. Mr. Chairman and members of the committee, as has been indicated I am Fred Gray, a member of the Alabama Legislature, representing Barbour, Bullock, and Macon Counties. Tuskegee is the county seat of Macon County. I am also an attorney and as such I represent about 40 of the living participants in the Tuskegee Study. It is in that capacity that I appear before this committee today.

We also represent heirs of approximately 15 families of the deceased participants. . . .

.   .   .

This is the first time that any governmental agency has permitted them to present their side of the story. I have brought with me two of the participants, Mr. Pollard and Mr. Scott.

According to the participants, this is how they became involved in the Tuskegee Study. In 1932, notices were issued by Dr. Smith and Nurse Rivers, announcing a new health program in Macon County.

These notices were circulated throughout the county by mail and at churches and schools. The new program consisted of taking blood tests. Only blacks were given notices and only black males subsequently participated in the program. They were uneducated, poor, and lived in rural areas. No whites were selected to participate in the study.

After the blood tests were taken the men were told various things by those in charge. Some were told they had bad blood. However, they did not know what bad blood meant at that time.

Others were told nothing of what they had. None were ever told they had syphilis. Most knew nothing about syphilis. They were not told they were involved in a study.

The participants never signed any written consent nor were they asked to sign one. Some were told they would receive money but some never did. Many, however, received $25 and a 25–year certificate of appreciation in 1958.

.   .   .

Sometime in the late 40's or early 50's, there was a massive effort to get all persons in Macon County treated who had syphilis. Most of the whites and many blacks were sent to Birmingham to receive such treatment.

However, those who participated in the Tuskegee Study were not permitted to receive such treatment. It was not until the summer of 1972 that the participants learned through the news media that they were part of the Tuskegee Study and many of those persons even today still do not know that they have syphilis or that they are part of a study.

.   .   .

Senator Kennedy. . . . Let's start with you, Mr. Pollard. Would you tell us a little bit about how you heard about this study, how you became involved?

Mr. Pollard. Back in 1932, I was going to school back then and they came around and said they wanted to have a clinic blood testing up there.

SENATOR KENNEDY. How old were you then?

MR. POLLARD. How old was I? Well, I was born in 1906. I had been married—no, I hadn't been married. Anyhow, they came around and give us the blood tests. After they give us the blood tests, all up there in the community, they said we had bad blood. After then they started giving us the shots and give us the shots for a good long time. I don't remember how long it was. But after they got through giving us those shots, they give me a spinal tap. That was along in 1933. They taken me over to John Henry Hospital.

SENATOR KENNEDY. That is rather unpleasant, isn't it, a spinal tap?

MR. POLLARD. It was pretty bad with me.

SENATOR KENNEDY. I have had a spinal tap myself. They stick that big, long needle into your spine.

MR. POLLARD. That is right, at John Andrew Hospital. After that, we went over early that morning, a couple of loads of us, and they taken us upstairs after giving us the spinal shot. They sit me down in the chair and the nurse and the doctor got behind and give me the shot. Then they take us upstairs in the elevators, our heels up and head down. They kept us there until five o'clock that evening, and then the nurse brought us back home.

After then, I stayed in the bed. I had taken down a day or two after I got through with the spinal tap. I stayed in bed 10 days or two weeks and the nurse came out there and give me some pills. I don't think she give me any of the medicine at that time, but just gave me some of the pills. Anyhow, she made several trips out there and I finally got in pretty good shape afterwards. It looked like my head was going back.

So after then they went to seen us once a year. They sent out notices for us to meet at Shiloh School. Sometimes they would just take the blood sample and give us some medicine right there at the school, under the oak tree where we met at Shiloh.

. . .

SENATOR KENNEDY. What did they do, ask you to come back once in a while or every couple of weeks?

MR. POLLARD. That is it. They would give us the date to come back and take those shots.

SENATOR KENNEDY. What were the shots for, to cure the bad blood?

MR. POLLARD. Bad blood, as far as I know of.

SENATOR KENNEDY. Did you think they were curing bad blood?

MR. POLLARD. I didn't know. I just attended the clinic.

SENATOR KENNEDY. They told you to keep coming back and you did?

MR. POLLARD. When they got through giving the shots, yes. Then they give us that spinal puncture.

SENATOR KENNEDY. Did they tell you why they were giving a spinal puncture?

MR. POLLARD. No.

SENATOR KENNEDY. Did you think it was because they were trying to help you?

MR. POLLARD. To help me, yes.

SENATOR KENNEDY. You wanted some help?

MR. POLLARD. That is right. They said I had bad blood and they was working on it.

SENATOR KENNEDY. How long did they keep working on it?

MR. POLLARD. After that shot, that spinal shot.

SENATOR KENNEDY. When was that?

MR. POLLARD. That was in 1933.

SENATOR KENNEDY. 1933?

MR. POLLARD. That is right. I don't remember what month it was in, but I know it was in 1933.

SENATOR KENNEDY. Did they treat you after that? Did they treat you after 1933?

MR. POLLARD. Yes. They treat me every year. They would come down and see us every year. Of course, during that time, after I taken that spinal puncture, I wore a rubber belt around my stomach. It had a long strand around it and I would run it around, come back in front and tie it in a bow knot. They used a little ointment or salve that I rubbed on my stomach. I reckon I wore it a year or six months, something like that. After then they would see us once a year up to 25 years.

SENATOR KENNEDY. During this time, did they indicate to you what kind of treatment they were giving you, or that you were involved in any kind of test or experiment?

MR. POLLARD. No, they never did say what it was.

SENATOR KENNEDY. What did you think they were doing, just trying to cure the bad blood?

MR. POLLARD. That is all I knew of.

SENATOR KENNEDY. Did they ever take any more blood and examine it and tell you the blood was getting better?

MR. POLLARD. They would take out blood, though.

SENATOR KENNEDY. What did they tell you after they would take the blood?

MR. POLLARD. They would just give us the pills and sometimes they would give us a little tablet to put under our tongue for sore throats. Then they would give us the green medicine for a tonic to take after meals.

SENATOR KENNEDY. You thought they were treating the bad blood?

MR. POLLARD. That is right.

SENATOR KENNEDY. During this time did they ever give you any compensation or any money?

MR. POLLARD. After that 25 years they gave me $25, a $20 and a $5 bill.

SENATOR KENNEDY. After 25 years?

MR. POLLARD. That is it. They give me a certificate.

SENATOR KENNEDY. They gave you a what?

MR. POLLARD. They gave me a certificate and a picture with six of us on there.

. . .

SENATOR KENNEDY. It is a certificate of merit, is it?

"U.S. Public Health Service. This certificate is awarded in grateful recognition of 25 years of participation in the Tuskegee Medical Research Study."

MR. POLLARD. I have one of these and then I have one with a picture of five more on it.

SENATOR KENNEDY. Were you glad to get it? Were you glad to get that certificate?

MR. POLLARD. Yes.

NOTES AND QUESTIONS

1. Fred Gray later filed a $1.8 billion damage suit against the federal government on behalf of all the study participants. Pollard v. United States, 384 F.Supp. 304 (M.D.Ala.1974). Upon settlement, the government agreed to pay each survivor $37,500 and the estate of each deceased syphilitic subject $15,000. *See $37,500 Is Awarded for Each Survivor of Syphilis Project*, N.Y. TIMES, Feb. 6, 1975, at 35. Was the award adequate? If not, what amount would have been? How should one determine adequacy in such a case?

2. Did the Tuskegee Study researchers, and the United States Public Health Service and Department of Health, Education and Welfare officials comply with the Nuremberg Code? Did they commit a crime against humanity?

3. President Clinton issued an official apology to the surviving subjects of the Tuskegee study and their families on May 16, 1997. Clinton also announced a $200,000 grant to Tuskegee University to launch a Center for Bioethics in Research and Health Care, as well as the creation of fellowships for post-graduate studies in bioethics, with emphasis on recruiting minority students. *See* Alison Mitchell, *Clinton Regrets "Clearly Racist" U.S. Study*, N.Y. TIMES, May 17, 1997, at 10.

PATRICIA A. KING, *THE DANGERS OF DIFFERENCE, REVISITED*

THE STORY OF BIOETHICS: FROM SEMINAL WORKS TO CONTEMPORARY EXPLORATIONS 197–198, 200–204, 207–210 (2003).

The Tuskegee Syphilis Study was not an aberration, as African Americans were extensively used as the subjects of medical experimentation during the nineteenth century. Rather, the study can be seen as one chapter in the long history of still-extant racial ideologies and practices in U.S. science and medicine. The Tuskegee Syphilis Study has, however, attained a special status. As Susan Reverby points out in the introduction to her influential book *Tuskegee's Truths*, "[t]he Tuskegee Study is America's metaphor for racism in medical research." As Reverby makes clear, there are many dimensions to the study, each emphasizing different aspects of the multifaceted interactions between researchers and their subjects and even between science itself and the culture in which it flourishes. Interestingly, even though much has been written about the Tuskegee Syphilis Study, bioethicists have largely failed to explore the impact of racism in research beyond its implications for informed consent.

. . .

Addressing Underrepresentation in Clinical Research

Calls for post-*Belmont Report* inclusion of African Americans into study populations first surfaced in the mid–1980s. In 1984, the U.S. Department of Health and Human Services (DHHS) established the Task Force on Black and Minority Health to examine health issues of blacks and other minorities, and the task force issued its report in 1985. The report called attention to the significant gaps that existed in scientific knowledge on the health status of African Americans and other minorities and noted the need for greater inclusion of racial and ethnic minorities in medical research. The report was largely ignored.

It was primarily the emergence of HIV/AIDS in the early 1980s that fostered the changing attitudes on the value of studying minority groups. HIV/AIDS grabbed public attention as a deadly syndrome that science was powerless to cure or control, and HIV/AIDS initially seemed to affect only one group in the United States—gay men, a group that was well-organized on health care issues. . . . As the AIDS epidemic spread to other groups, including racial and ethnic minorities and other disadvantaged persons, the members of the newly affected subgroups also began to insist on access to research protocols. The formerly persuasive arguments for protecting minority groups from unethical treatment by excluding their members from research populations were suddenly outweighed by the interest in giving such persons their best hope for survival by granting access to the promising therapies available only in research trials.

In addition to the emerging view that members of minority groups combating particular illnesses should be allowed to participate in clinical trials of possible remedies, there grew a wider concern that women and minority health issues had been generally ignored. Some were concerned that too little attention had been paid to diseases and conditions that disproportionately affected minorities and women. In addition, some researchers questioned whether research results produced from trial groups that were overwhelmingly male and white were equally applicable to other groups.

The largely scientific question of whether research results obtained from populations that were overwhelmingly white and male were applicable to other population groups was not the only problem. This "one-size-fits-all" approach to research also implicitly established "white and male" as being equivalent to "normal." Such a practice labeled those other than white males as "different"—and, by implication, possibly inferior. Such assumptions were not only inappropriate in scientific protocols, they were also likely to reinforce culturally negative stereotypes of minority groups.

. . .

Laws and policies that seek to include underrepresented groups in research pools are supported by the ethical principles of beneficence and justice as developed in *The Belmont Report*. However, a necessary side effect of such inclusion policies is that, in striving to account for and protect the interests of specific subgroups, researchers must focus great attention on the physical differences of the groups studied. This focus might be beneficial—as, for example, when uncovering disparities in health. Lurking within this style of research, however, is also the possibility that research data collected from different racially representative research pools might identify significant genetic differences among the subgroups studied. These possibilities raise a dilemma.

On the one hand, if real biological differences are identified between minority research groups and the white male "norm," then it is reasonable to assume that past research strategies may have benefited the health status of white males to the detriment of other groups and that affirmative efforts to rectify the knowledge gap are warranted. Furthermore, if specific health problems are discovered to be linked to specific minority subgroups, difficult issues of research priorities are implicated. Fair distribution of research burdens and benefits would seem to require examination of potentially discriminatory policies and practices well beyond those that could be solved by the mere increase of representation in clinical trials. Therefore, racial and ethnic minorities potentially benefit from research that targets the diseases and conditions that disproportionately affect them.

On the other hand, the prospect of identifying significant health disparities or biological differences in minority racial or ethnic groups carries with it the possibility of feeding existing negative stereotypes, biases, and racist ideologies. The possible existence of non-sex-trait genetic differences between men and women is relatively uncontroversial; but the possibility of discovering significant genetic differences between racial and ethnic minorities on one side and whites on the other is another matter entirely. In the past, belief in such differences supported practices that were harmful.

. . .

Tuskegee's Lessons

. . .

The Tuskegee study demonstrates the many ways in which individuals and groups can be put at risk by participation in medical research. . . . [T]he Tuskegee study is useful in understanding why the members of easily accessible groups are at risk for coercion and exploitation in research. The study was conducted in the rural, poor, and segregated Deep South. The subjects' lack of economic resources limited their access to health care and made them vulnerable to the promise of free medical care.

The African American males who were chosen as subjects of the Tuskegee Syphilis Study were isolated geographically and psychologically from both whites and middle-class African Americans, and as the study began in the midst of the Depression, the subjects were politically powerless in a profound way. The prevailing culture of their time devalued them as human beings, and the reason for their easy accessibility simply cannot be understood without acknowledging the racism that dominated the culture in which they lived. Later, when penicillin, though available, was not provided to the subjects, a factor that surely contributed to that decision was the perception that the lives of the subjects (and the lives of their spouses and children) were not valuable.

In contemporary society, where so many minorities lack health insurance and so many others receive health coverage or care from public programs, minority communities continue to be fertile grounds for recruiting subjects. The possibility of receiving an individual benefit in a free clinical trial might be more alluring to minorities than whites, and minorities are accordingly disproportionately vulnerable to the associated risk of physical harms and to the risk of being taken advantage of as a group.

. . . [M]edicine is rightly interested in exploring human differences at the molecular level that may lead to more effective interventions, and the frequency of genes that might play a role in predisposition to disease or to drug response does vary among population groups. The critical question, however, is whether any identified genetic variation for disease incidence or drug response is coextensive with *socially* defined categories of race and ethnicity. It is entirely possible that a person labeled "white" might be more genetically similar to someone labeled "Native American" than to another white. Can (and should) important differences among humans be identified by reliance on socially constructed categories of race and ethnicity?

. . .

What policies should be adopted to "move beyond race" or guide a transition? Tuskegee's lessons have application here. A critical first step would be to devise a research program that would explore many plausible explanations for the differences that have been detected. Differences between blacks and whites in disease susceptibilities and responses to clinical interventions may be the result of genetic differences, environmental factors (including shared cultural and dietary differences), or fundamental differences in the pathogenesis of diseases. All of the possible contributors—not just genetics—should be examined.

. . .

There are, of course, no easy answers to the question of how medicine should make the transition away from using race-based research to identify genetic and other causes of disease. The Tuskegee Syphilis Study warns that including minorities in clinical research might improve the well-being of individuals and groups but only if there is attention to the context in which the research takes place. Research that produces ambiguous or ill-defined correlations between race and disease risks rekindling debates over the relative roles of heredity versus environment, and the negative impact of renewing arguments over genetically superior versus genetically inferior groups of humans might overwhelm any potential positive impact on minority health status.

Some practices can be modified relatively quickly. Researchers should take pains to accurately describe their results when they submit their articles for publication. They might, for example, be required by journals in which they publish to describe their study populations with relevant scientific terms rather than simply using categories such as "black" or "African American" and "white"—terms that perpetuate misperceptions while contributing little. Indeed, the development of a "standard lexicon" of accurate, neutral, and nonstigmatizing language should be a priority of funding agencies.

. . . I believe that the Tuskegee Syphilis Study offers lessons that we should heed when considering this matter, as it demonstrates the many ways in which minorities can be put at risk in medical research. Only when we fully recognize the potential pitfalls of race-based research can we design policies and protocols that can benefit minority groups without harming them.

c. The Human Radiation Experiments

In re Cincinnati Radiation Litigation

United States District Court for the Southern District of Ohio, 1995.
874 F.Supp. 796.

■ BECKWITH, DISTRICT JUDGE.

The Complaint in this much-publicized matter alleges that the Defendants engaged in the design and implementation of experiments from 1960 to 1972 to study the effects of massive doses of radiation on human beings in preparation for a possible nuclear war. The experiments utilized terminal cancer patients who were not informed of the consequences of their participation nor, indeed, informed of the existence or purpose of the experiments. The Complaint alleges that most of the patients selected were African American and, in the vernacular of the time, charity patients. The Complaint further alleges that the various Defendants actively concealed the nature, purpose and consequences of the experiments. The allegations of the Complaint make out an outrageous tale of government perfidy in dealing with some of its most vulnerable citizens. The allegations are inflammatory and compelling, creating a milieu in which it is difficult to objectively examine the allegations for legal sufficiency or to apply a view of constitutional rights unilluminated by the legal evolution that has taken place since 1972 when the experiments at issue ended. . . .

. . .

The Plaintiffs' substantive due process claim in this case is grounded upon the premise that individuals have a liberty interest in their bodily integrity that is protected by the Due Process Clause of the Fourteenth Amendment, and particularly upon the premise that nonconsensual experiments involving extremely high doses of radiation, designed and supervised by military doctors and carried out by City hospital physicians violate that right.

The right to be free of state-sponsored invasion of a person's bodily integrity is protected by the Fourteenth Amendment guarantee of due process. In *Albright v. Oliver*, 114 S.Ct. 807 (1994), Chief Justice Rehnquist, writing for the Court, specifically noted that "the protections of substantive due process have for the most part been accorded to matters relating to marriage, family, procreation, *and the right to bodily integrity.*" The allegations set forth in Plaintiffs' Second Amended Complaint are sufficient to bring the Plaintiffs' claims within the purview of that right.

. . .

Many of the cases recognizing constitutional causes of action for nonconsensual medical treatment involve plaintiffs who were either prisoners or were involuntarily committed to psychiatric institutions. In their various memoranda and at oral argument, the Defendants argue that Plaintiffs were voluntarily present at Cincinnati General Hospital when the Human Radiation Experiments were performed. The Defendants argue that all of the Plaintiffs came to the hospital of their own volition and could have left the hospital at any time they chose. Since the liberty interest at issue has only been extended to prison inmates and patients involuntarily confined in psychiatric institutions, the Defendants argue that Plaintiffs cannot base their cause of action on this liberty interest. In support of this contention, the Defendants point specifically to *Rogers v. Okin*, 478 F.Supp. 1342 (D.Mass.1979), *aff'd. in part, rev'd. in part*, 634 F.2d 650 (1st Cir.1980), *vacated and remanded sub nom. Mills v. Rogers*, 457 U.S. 291 (1982).

. . .

This argument fails at this stage of the litigation. . . . [I]t is not at all clear that Plaintiffs were voluntary patients at Cincinnati General Hospital. The Plaintiffs in this case are all alleged to have been poor. Discovery may demonstrate that the only hospital in the city to treat indigent patients was Cincinnati General Hospital. If this is so, the Court would be reluctant to hold that a person with only one hospital from which to choose voluntarily enters that hospital when he becomes ill. Regardless of that factual uncertainty, Defendants argument still fails for the following reasons.

The Plaintiffs allege that they were purposefully misled in several respects. First, Plaintiffs allege that they were specifically not informed that the radiation they were receiving was for a military experiment rather than treatment of their cancer. Further, Plaintiffs allege that they were never informed that the amount of radiation they were to receive would cause burns, vomiting, nausea, bone marrow failure, severe shortening of life expectancy, or even death. When a person is purposefully misled about such crucial facts as these, he can no longer be said to exercise that degree of free will that is essential to the notion of voluntariness.

> To manipulate men, to propel them toward goals which we see but they
> may not, is to deny their human essence, to treat them as objects without

wills of their own, and therefore to degrade them. This is why to lie to men, or to deceive them, that is, to use them as means for our not their own, independently conceived ends, even if it is to their own benefit, is, in effect to treat them as sub-human, to behave as if their ends are less ultimate and sacred than our own.... For if the essence of men is that they are autonomous beings—authors of values, of ends in themselves ... —then nothing is worse than to treat them as if they were not autonomous but natural objects whose choices can be manipulated.[11]

. . .

In 1990, the Supreme Court unequivocally held that the "forcible injection of medication into a nonconsenting person's body represents a substantial interference with that person's liberty." *Washington v. Harper,* 494 U.S. 210, 229 (1990). Still, other cases support the recognition of a general liberty interest in refusing medical treatment. *Riggens v. Nevada,* 504 U.S. 127 (1992) (forced administration of antipsychotic medication during trial violated Fourteenth Amendment); *Youngberg v. Romeo,* 457 U.S. 307, 315 (government has duty to protect involuntarily committed mental patients from physical assault). *See also Cruzan v. Director, Missouri Department of Health,* 497 U.S. 261 (1989) (Fourteenth Amendment has been held to include medical decision-making, reflecting the "principle that a competent person has a constitutionally protected liberty interest in refusing unwanted medical treatment.")

Determining that a person has a "liberty interest" under the Due Process Clause does not end the inquiry; whether a person's constitutional rights have been violated must be determined by balancing his liberty interest against the relevant state interests. Indeed, compulsory vaccinations, compelled blood tests and extractions of contraband material from the rectal cavity have sometimes been upheld on a showing of clear necessity, procedural regularity, and minimal pain. However, each of these cases has acknowledged that an aspect of fundamental liberty was at stake and that the government's burden was to provide more than minimal justification for its action. ... These several cases indicate that in order to maintain an action under the Fifth Amendment, it is sufficient that a plaintiff demonstrate that an invasion of bodily integrity was deficient in procedural regularity, or that it was needlessly severe.

When an individual's bodily integrity is at stake, a determination that the state has accorded adequate procedural protection should not be made lightly. Since bodily invasions often cannot be readily remedied after the fact through damage awards in the way that most deprivations of property can, *Parratt v. Taylor,* 451 U.S. 527 (1981) (state remedy provides due process where no immunity bars tort suit for prison mail clerk's negligent loss of prisoner's mail-order hobby kit), the state must precede any deliberate invasion with formalized procedures. This is precisely what the Supreme Court held in *Washington v. Harper,* 494 U.S. at 210. In *Washington,* the Supreme Court held that the extent of a prisoner's right under the Due Process Clause to avoid the unwanted administration of an antipsychotic drug had to be defined within the context of the inmate's confine-

---

11. Isaiah Berlin, FOUR ESSAYS ON LIBERTY 136–37 (1969).

ment. *Id.* at 215. At issue was a policy that required the state to establish by medical finding a mental disorder that was likely to cause harm to the prisoner or inmate community if it was not treated by antipsychotic medication. *Id.* at 211. Upholding the policy, and thus the nonconsensual administration of the drug, the Court emphasized that the policy at issue required both a prescription by a physician and a review by an objective outside physician to ensure that the treatment would be ordered only if it was in the prisoner's medical interest, given the legitimate needs of his confinement. *Id.* at 216. It was the procedural structure surrounding the nonconsensual administration of the medication that kept the state-sponsored invasion of bodily integrity within the boundaries of due process.

. . .

The allegations in the Complaint indicate that procedural regularity was absent and that the invasion of bodily integrity was severe. In essence, the allegations in the Complaint amount to a claim that the individual Defendants blatantly lied to the Plaintiffs. Unlike in *Washington v. Harper,* a decision was not made by the treating physician that Plaintiffs' medical condition required drastic doses of radiation. Rather, the allegations give rise to the question of whether Plaintiffs were receiving medical treatment at all. This absence of procedural safeguards alone is sufficient to trigger the protections of the Due Process Clause. However, the allegations contained even more.

The allegations also indicate that the Plaintiffs received needlessly severe invasions of their bodily integrity. Unlike in *Schmerber,* where the invasion was minimal and had no lasting side effects, the invasion Plaintiffs allege in this case was total and partial body radiation, which caused burns, vomiting, diarrhea and bone marrow failure, and resulted in death or severe shortening of life. These allegations are more than sufficient to trigger Fifth Amendment protection.

Thus, . . . the Court is compelled to hold that the individual and *Bivens* Defendants may not assert the defense of qualified immunity. The qualified immunity defense is reserved to those officials who are sued for their exercise of discretionary responsibilities delegated to them by the government. There can be no doubt that the . . . Defendants' alleged instigation of and participation in the Human Radiation Experiments were acts far beyond the scope of their delegated powers. The individual and *Bivens* Defendants, many of whom were physicians, were not acting as physicians when they conducted experiments on unwitting subjects at Cincinnati General Hospital. Rather, the Defendants were acting as scientists interested in nothing more than assembling cold data for use by the Department of Defense. While many government officials are authorized to conduct research, the individual and *Bivens* Defendants were hired by the City to care for the sick and injured. The Constitution never authorizes government officials, regardless of their specific responsibilities, to arbitrarily deprive ordinary citizens of liberty and life.

Nevertheless, the Court will consider both prongs of the qualified immunity defense. First, the preceding analysis accepts, for purposes of this motion, the facts in the Complaint detailing state-sponsored experiments involving procedural due process irregularity, severe pain and death, and purposeful deception. These allegations are more than adequate to state a cause of action under the Due Process Clause of the Fourteenth Amendment.

. . .

The Court must next determine whether the conduct alleged by Plaintiffs was clearly unconstitutional when the Human Radiation Experiments were performed. . . . [T]he right that Plaintiffs assert must have been sufficiently clear during the period between 1960 and 1972 that a reasonable official would have understood that his actions violated that right. . . .

The conduct attributed to the individual and *Bivens* Defendants—all representatives of government—strikes at the very core of the Constitution. Even absent the abundant case law that has developed on this point since the passage of the Bill of Rights, the Court would not hesitate to declare that a reasonable government official must have known that by instigating and participating in the experimental administration of high doses of radiation on unwitting subjects, he would have been acting in violation of those rights. Simply put, the legal tradition of this country and the plain language of the Constitution must lead a reasonable person to the conclusion that government officials may not arbitrarily deprive unwitting citizens of their liberty and their lives.

If the Constitution were held to permit the acts alleged in this case, the document would be revealed to contain a gaping hole. This is so in part because the alleged conduct is so outrageous in and of itself, and also because a constitution inadequate to deal with such outrageous conduct would be too feeble in method and doctrine to deal with a very great amount of equally outrageous activity. Indeed, virtually all of the rights that we as a nation hold sacred would be subject to the arbitrary whim of government.

. . .

. . . [T]he contours of the right to be free from unwanted bodily intrusions has been developed over a long line of cases. As early as 1884, the Supreme Court recognized that the liberty right of the Fourteenth Amendment protected the integrity of one's body. *See Hurtado v. People of California*, 110 U.S. 516 (1884). In 1891, the Supreme Court explicitly stated that "no right is more sacred, or is more carefully guarded, by the common law, than the right of every individual to the possession and control of his own person, free from all restraint or interference of others unless by clear and unquestionable authority of law." *Union Pacific Railroad Co. v. Botsford*, 141 U.S. 250, 251 (1891). . . .

In *Skinner v. Oklahoma*, 316 U.S. 535 (1942), the Supreme Court struck down a statute that mandated the sterilization of habitual criminals convicted of crimes of moral turpitude. Although the Supreme Court's analysis was couched in equal protection terms, the Court nevertheless observed that the invasive medical procedure of sterilization performed without the consent of the patient, "forever deprived [the individual] of a basic liberty." *Id.* at 541.

Finally, in *Rochin v. California,* 342 U.S. 165 (1952), the Supreme Court made clear that "our notions of liberty are inextricably entwined with our idea of physical freedom and self-determination." *Cruzan v. Director, Missouri Department of Health,* 497 U.S. 261, 287 (O'Connor, J. concurring). In *Rochin,* a defendant in a narcotics case swallowed a number of capsules when he was confronted by the police. After unsuccessfully attempting to retrieve the capsules by hand, the police forcibly extricated the capsules from the defendant's stomach. *Rochin,* 342 U.S. at 166.

The Supreme Court, reversing the defendant's criminal conviction, held that the government's conduct in obtaining the capsules violated the Due Process Clause. Due process was denied, according to Justice Frankfurter, who wrote for the Court, because the forced stomach pumping "offended those canons of decency and fairness which expressed the notions of justice of English-speaking peoples even toward those charged with the most heinous offenses." *Id.* at 169. In a phrase that has endured as a shorthand for the holding, Justice Frankfurter then went on to add that the government's conduct "shocked the conscience." *Id.*

.   .   .

The invasions of bodily integrity alleged in this case are *more* extreme than those at issue in either *Skinner* or *Rochin.* ... Thus, had this set of facts come before this Court in 1972, the Court would have found that Plaintiffs had stated a valid claim under the Due Process Clause of the Constitution. The right at issue and its contours were sufficiently well-defined by the Supreme Court prior to 1972 such that the individual and *Bivens* Defendants should have known that their conduct would violate the Constitution.

.   .   .

The Nuremberg Code is part of the law of humanity. It may be applied in both civil and criminal cases by the federal courts in the United States.[23] At the very least, by the time the Human Radiation Experiments were designed, the Nuremberg Code served as a tangible example of conduct that "shocked the conscience," as contemplated in *Rochin, supra. Rochin* came only five years after the Nuremberg trials. Certainly Justice Frankfurter and the other members of the Court were influenced by the state-sponsored atrocities delineated in the Medical Case. Thus, even were the Nuremberg Code not afforded precedential weight in the courts of the United States, it

---

23. *See United States v. Stanley,* 483 U.S. 669, 710, 107 S.Ct. 3054, 3066 (1987) (O'Connor, J. dissenting). In *Stanley,* the Army administered LSD to an unwitting enlisted man. Under the *Feres* doctrine, the Supreme Court held that Mr. Stanley could not obtain money damages from the military for his involvement in the experiment. Writing for a five-four Court, Justice Scalia expressed concern that permitting an enlisted man to sue the Army "would call into serious question military discipline and decision-making." In her forceful dissent, Justice O'Connor relied on the Nuremberg Code for the proposition that due process guarantees the subjects of human experiments the right to voluntary and informed consent. Because Plaintiffs in this case are not military personnel, the Court is convinced that Justice O'Connor's dissent in *Stanley* controls.

cannot be readily dismissed from its proper context in this case. The individual and *Bivens* Defendants, as physicians and other health professionals, must have been aware of the Nuremberg Code, the Hippocratic Oath, and the several pronouncements by both world and American medical organizations adopting the Nuremberg Code. It is inconceivable to the Court that the individual and *Bivens* Defendants, when allegedly planning to perform radiation experiments on unwitting subjects, were not moved to pause or rethink their procedures in light of the forceful dictates of the Nuremberg Tribunal and the several medical organizations.

The allegations in this case indicate that the government of the United States, aided by officials of the City of Cincinnati, treated at least eighty-seven (87) of its citizens as though they were laboratory animals. If the Constitution has not clearly established a right under which these Plaintiffs may attempt to prove their case, then a gaping hole in that document has been exposed. The subject of experimentation who has not volunteered is merely an object. The Plaintiffs in this case must be afforded at least the opportunity to present their case. As Justice O'Connor indicated in her dissent from *United States v. Stanley,* 483 U.S. 669 (1987),

> [t]he United States military played an instrumental role in the criminal prosecution of Nazi officials who experimented with human beings during the Second World War ... and the standards that the Nuremberg Military Tribunals developed to judge the behavior of the defendants stated that the voluntary consent of the human subject is absolutely essential ... to satisfy moral, ethical, and legal concepts.... If this principle is violated, the very least society can do is to see that the victims are compensated, as best they can be, by the perpetrators. I am prepared to say that our Constitution's promise of due process of law guarantees this much.

Id. at 710.

The doctrine of qualified immunity does not insulate the individual and *Bivens* Defendants from liability for their deliberate and calculated exposure of cancer patients to harmful medical experimentation without their informed consent. No judicially-crafted rule insulates from examination the state-sponsored involuntary and unknowing human experimentation alleged to have occurred in this case. Accordingly, the individual and *Bivens* Defendants' motion to dismiss the substantive due process claim is DENIED.

C. EVOLUTION OF PUBLIC REGULATION OF HUMAN EXPERIMENTATION

1. THE ADOPTION OF INFORMED CONSENT TO PROTECT SUBJECTS

a. The Common Law Standard

Halushka v. University of Saskatchewan

Saskatchewan Court of Appeals, 1965.
53 D.L.R.2d 436.

■ HALL, J.

The appellants Wyant and Merriman were medical practitioners employed by the appellant University of Saskatchewan. The appellant Wyant was professor of anaesthesia and chief of the department of anaesthetics at the University Hospital. The appellant Merriman was director of the cardio-pulmonary laboratory. As part of their duties in the employ of the appellant University of Saskatchewan, the appellants Wyant and Merriman conducted and carried out medical research projects, some of which involved the comparative study of anaesthetics. When anaesthetics were administered the subjects were obtained from the employment office.

The respondent, a student at the University of Saskatchewan, had attended summer school in 1961. On August 21, 1961, he went to the employment office to find a job. At the employment office he was advised that there were no jobs available but that he could earn $50 by being the subject of a test at the University Hospital. The respondent said that he was told that the test would last a couple of hours and that it was a "safe test and there was nothing to worry about".

The respondent reported to the anaesthesia department at the University Hospital and there saw the appellant Wyant. The conversation which ensued concerning the proposed test was related by the respondent as follows:

> Doctor Wyant explained to me that a new drug was to be tried out on the Wednesday following. He told me that electrodes would be put in my both arms, legs and head and that he assured me that it was a perfectly safe test [and that] it had been conducted many times before. He told me that I was not to eat anything on Wednesday morning that I was to report at approximately nine o'clock, then he said it would take about an hour to hook me up and the test itself would last approximately two hours, after the time I would be given fifty dollars, pardon me, I would be allowed to sleep first, fed and then given fifty dollars and driven home on the same day.

The appellant Wyant also told the respondent that an incision would be made in his left arm and that a catheter or tube would be inserted into his vein.

. . .

CONSENT FOR TESTS ON VOLUNTEERS

I, WALTER HALUSHKA, age 21 of 236–3rd Street Saskatoon hereby state that I have volunteered for tests upon my person for the purpose of study of

"Heart & Blood Circulation Response under General Anaesthesia"

The tests to be undertaken in connection with this study have been explained to me and I understand fully what is proposed to be done. I agree of my own free will to submit to these tests, and in consideration of the remuneration hereafter set forth, I do release the chief investigators,

Drs. G.M. Wyant and J.E. Merriman

their associates, technicians, and each thereof, other personnel involved in these studies, the University Hospital Board, and the University of Saskatchewan from all responsibility and claims whatsoever, for any untoward effects or accidents due to or arising out of said tests, either directly or indirectly.

I understand that I shall receive a remuneration of $50.00 for each test a series of One tests.

> Witness my hand and seal.
>
> "WALTER HALUSHKA" (signed)
>
> "IRIS ZAECHTOWSKI" (Witness)

Date: Aug. 22/61

The respondent described the circumstances surrounding the signing of ex. D.1, saying:

> He then gave me a consent form, I skimmed through it and picked out the word "accident" on the consent form and asked Doctor Wyant what accidents were referred to, and he gave me an example of me falling down the stairs at home after the test and they trying to sue the University Hospital as a result. Being assured that any accident that would happen to me would be at home and not in the Hospital I signed the form.

The test contemplated was known as "The Heart and Blood Circulation Response under General Anaesthesia", and was to be conducted jointly by the appellants Wyant and Merriman, using a new anaesthetic agent known commercially as "Fluoromar". This agent had not been previously used or tested by the appellants in any way.

The respondent returned to the University Hospital on August 23, 1961, to undergo the test. The procedure followed was that which had been described to the respondent and expected by him, with the exception that the catheter, after being inserted in the vein in the respondent's arm, was advanced towards his heart. When the catheter reached the vicinity of the heart, the respondent felt some discomfort. The anaesthetic agent was then administered to him. The time was then 11:32 a.m. Eventually the catheter tip was advanced through the various heart chambers out into the pulmonary artery where it was positioned.

[The level of anesthesia was increased due to some coughing by the respondent., then decreased when appellants saw changes in the respondent's cardiac rhythm. At 12:25 the respondent suffered a complete cardiac arrest. The appellants Wyant and Merriman and their assistants took immediate steps to resuscitate the respondent's heart, which began functioning again after one minute and thirty seconds.]

The respondent was unconscious for a period of four days. He remained in the University Hospital as a patient until discharged 10 days later. On the day before he was discharged the respondent was given fifty ($50) dollars by the appellant Wyant. At that time the respondent asked the appellant Wyant if that was all he was going to get for all he went through. The appellant said that fifty dollars was all that they had bargained for but that he could give a larger sum in return for a complete release executed by the respondent's mother or elder sister.

As a result of the experiment the appellants concluded that as an anaesthetic agent "Fluoromar" had too narrow a margin of safety and it was withdrawn from clinical use in the University Hospital.

The respondent brought action against the appellants, basing his claim for damages on two grounds, namely, trespass to the person and negligence. . . .

2 claims

The medical evidence established that the use of any anaesthetic agent involves a certain amount of risk and should be accompanied by care and caution. In general medical practice the risk involved in the use of an anaesthetic agent is balanced against the threat to life presented by the ailment to be treated. It is standard procedure to obtain a medical history of the patient and in some cases to conduct a complete physical examination before administering a general anaesthetic. The medical history is for the most part obtained by interrogating the patient himself. The taking of a medical history usually involves investigation of the functioning of certain of the organic systems. Included are questions primarily related to the heart to ascertain whether the patient has had any specific heart disease, such as high blood pressure or rheumatic fever in the past.

standard

In the instant case the appellants Wyant and Merriman admit that the cardiac arrest would not have occurred if the respondent had not undergone the test, the arrest being caused by the anaesthetic agent used. Dr. Baltzan [an expert called by appellants] was of the opinion that the test itself had been well conducted. He also gave his opinion that the insertion of a catheter into the heart is not a dangerous procedure.

If a patient does not die immediately from cardiac arrest, the damage which might ensue can vary in degree from none at all to eventual death with all intermediate degrees possible. Brain damage is the usual cause of death and most of the intermediate damage occurring will be to the brain. The brain cells can be damaged either permanently or temporarily. The portion of the brain most susceptible to damage under these circumstances is that which controls the highest functions, that is, the thinking functions as contrasted to the lowest or automatic functions. Major damage is objective as the patient is totally oblivious to his surroundings. Minor degrees of damage are more subjective as they are confined to emotional and intellectual attributes and are difficult to detect clinically. Dr. Baltzan had examined the respondent prior to the trial and could find no abnormality but he stated that he knew of no equipment available today which would necessarily and unequivocally determine whether there had been minor brain damage.

risks of damag

In Dr. Baltzan's opinion a certain amount of pain would be associated with the incision necessary for the open massage of the heart and expected general discomfort at the site of the incision for a month or two. The respondent himself testified that he experienced a considerable amount of pain in the chest area and that a portion of his left arm was numb for approximately six weeks.

harm

[The respondent testified that since the cardiac arrest, he suffered from fatigue and inability to concentrate or think, which led to a decline in his grades. He failed in six or seven subjects that year, and therefore did not try to continue with his University course.]

harm

The appellants, at the close of the respondent's case, moved a nonsuit. The motion was denied by the trial Judge. The questions then put to the jury and the answers to them were as follows:

Q.   1. Did the plaintiff consent to the performance of the test made by the defendant doctors? A. No.

Q.   2. If the answer to Question 1 is no, did the defendant doctors commit a trespass in the performance of the test? A. Yes.

Q.   3. Were the defendant doctors or either of them negligent in the performance of the test? A. Yes.

Q.   4. If the answer to Question 3 is yes, in what respect was there negligence? A. (1) Lack of full explanation to the plaintiff of the test at the time of the so-called "consent". (2) Failure to acquire medical history of the plaintiff and to perform a Physical examination of the plaintiff. (3) Lack of liaison between the two defendant doctors throughout this test.

Q.   5. If the answer to Question 2 or Question 3 is yes, then at what amount do you assess the plaintiff's damage? A. $22,500.00.

From these findings and the judgment thereon the appellants appeal on the grounds:

1.   That the learned trial judge erred in refusing to withdraw the plaintiff's claim from the jury on the ground that there was no evidence upon which the jury could find liability against the defendants or either of them.

2.   That the learned trial judge misdirected the jury in respect of the consent which had been signed by the plaintiff and further erred in instructing them that this was a case of a doctor and patient relationship whereas he should have charged the jury that it was a contractual relationship.

3.   That the findings of the jury on all the questions submitted to them were perverse.

4.   That in any event damages awarded were excessive.

The main issue before the jury concerning the respondent's claim of trespass to the person was that of consent. The attachment of the electrodes, the administration of anaesthetic and the insertion of the catheter were each an intentional application of force to the person of the respondent. When taken as a whole they certainly constitute a trespass which would be actionable unless done with consent. . . . The appellants rely upon ex. D.1 and the conduct of the respondent as evidence of consent.

In ordinary medical practice the consent given by a patient to a physician or surgeon, to be effective, must be an "informed" consent freely given. It is the duty of the physician to give a fair and reasonable explanation of the proposed treatment including the probable effect and any special or unusual risks. The relationship between the physician and patient under such circumstances was described by Hodgins, J.A., in *Kenny v. Lockwood*, [1932] 1 D.L.R. 507 at pp. 519–20, [1932] O.R. 141, where he said:

> The relationship of surgeon and patient is naturally one in which trust and confidence must be placed in the surgeon. His knowledge, skill and experience are not and cannot be known to the patient, and within proper

limits it would seem to require that when an operation is contemplated or proposed a reasonable clear explanation of it and of the natural and expected outcome should be vouchsafed.

A similar view has been adopted in some of the United States of America, and has been referred to in *Wall v. Brim* (1943), 138 F.2d 478; *Mitchell v. Robinson* (1960), 334 S.W.2d 11; and *Natanson v. Kline* (1960), 350 P.2d 1093. In the latter case the position was stated at p. 1106 of the report as follows:

> In our opinion the proper rule of law to determine whether a patient has given an intelligent consent to a proposed form of treatment by a physician was stated and applied in *Salgo v. Leland Stanford, Etc. Bd. Trustees*, 1957, 154 Cal.App.2d 560, 317 P.2d 170. This rule in effect compels disclosure by the physician in order to assure that an informed consent of the patient is obtained. The duty of the physician to disclose, however, is limited to those disclosures which a reasonable medical practitioner would make under the same or similar circumstances. How the physician may best discharge his obligation to the patient in this difficult situation involves primarily a question of medical judgment. So long as the disclosure is sufficient to assure an informed consent, the physician's choice of plausible courses should not be called into question if it appears, all circumstances considered, that the physician was motivated only by the patient's best therapeutic interests and he proceeded as competent medical men would have done in a similar situation.

It was on the basis of the ordinary physician-patient relationship that the learned trial Judge charged the jury on the matter of consent. In dealing with this part of the case he said:

> In the circumstances of this case I will say that before signing such a document the plaintiff was entitled to a reasonably clear explanation of the proposed test and of the natural and expected results from it.

In my opinion the duty imposed upon those engaged in medical research, as were the appellants Wyant and Merriman, to those who offer themselves as subject for experimentation, as the respondent did here, is at least as great as, if not greater than, the duty owed by the ordinary physician or surgeon to his patient. There can be no exceptions to the ordinary requirements of disclosure in the case of research as there may well be in ordinary medical practice. The researcher does not have to balance the probable effect of lack of treatment against the risk involved in the treatment itself. The example of risks being properly hidden from a patient when it is important that he should not worry can have no application in the field of research. The subject of medical experimentation is entitled to a full and frank disclosure of all the facts, probabilities and opinions which a reasonable man might be expected to consider before giving his consent. The respondent necessarily had to rely upon the special skill, knowledge and experience of the appellants. . . .

. . .

Although the appellant Wyant informed the respondent that a "new drug" was to be tried out, he did not inform him that the new drug was in fact an anaesthetic of which he had no previous knowledge, nor that there was risk involved with the use of an anaesthetic. Inasmuch as no test had been previously conducted using the anaesthetic agent "Fluoromar" to the knowledge of the appellants, the statement made to the respondent that it was a safe test which had been conducted many times before, when considered in the light of the medical evidence describing the characteristics of anaesthetic agents generally, was incorrect and was in reality a nondisclosure.

The respondent was not informed that the catheter would be advanced to and through his heart but was admittedly given to understand that it would be merely inserted in the vein in his arm. While it may be correct to say that the advancement of the catheter to the heart was not in itself dangerous and did not cause or contribute to the cause of the cardiac arrest, it was a circumstance which, if known, might very well have prompted the respondent to withhold his consent. The undisclosed or misrepresented facts need not concern matters which directly cause the ultimate damage if they are of a nature which might influence the judgment upon which the consent is based.

. . .

In view of the foregoing, there was no misdirection on the question of consent of which the appellants can complain and there was evidence upon which the jury could find that the respondent gave no effectual consent or release to the appellants. The appellants cannot, therefore, succeed on their first three grounds of appeal in so far as they relate to the respondent's claim of trespass.

. . .

[The court next held that the damages, while "generous" were not excessive.]

Appeal dismissed.

b. *Governmental Regulations*

(1) *FIRST STAGE: EARLY ACTIONS BY CONGRESS, FDA AND NIH*

Following the disclosure of deformities caused by Thalidomide in infants born in 1961 and 1962 primarily in Western Europe, Congress directed the Food and Drug Administration (FDA) to impose stricter controls on the clinical testing of new drugs in this country.[1] The new law specifically directed FDA to issue regulations to ensure that investigators "will inform any human beings to whom [investigational] drugs, or any controls used in connection therewith, are being administered, or their representatives, that such drugs are being used in investigational purposes and will obtain the consent of the human being or their representatives except where they deem it not feasible or, in their professional judgment, contrary to the best interests of such human beings."[2]

---

[1] More than a dozen cases of Thalidomide deformities occurred in this country. Herbert L. Ley, Jr., *Federal Law and Patient Consent*, 169 ANNALS N.Y. ACAD. SCI. 523 (1970).

[2] Drug Amendments of 1962, P.L. No. 87B781, 76 Stat. 780.

Initially, FDA implemented its mandate by issuing regulations that did not elaborate on the statutory language.[3] By 1967, amid growing indications of failure to obtain subject consent in many investigations, FDA proposed stronger regulations governing consent.[4] The new regulations provided in pertinent part:

(b) This means that the consent of such humans (or the consent of their representatives) to whom investigational drugs are administered primarily for the accumulation of scientific knowledge, for such purposes as studying drug behavior, body processes, or the course of disease, must be obtained in all cases and, in all but exceptional cases, the consent of patients under treatment with investigational drugs or the consent of their representatives must be obtained.

. . .

(d) "Exceptional cases" as used in paragraph (b) of this section are those relatively rare cases in which it is not feasible to obtain the patient's consent or the consent of his representative, or in which as a matter of professional judgment exercised in the best interest of a particular patient under the investigator's care, it would be contrary to that patient's welfare to obtain his consent.

. . .

(f) "Not feasible" is limited to cases wherein the investigator is not capable of obtaining consent because of inability to communicate with the patient or his representative; for example, the patient is in a coma or is otherwise incapable of giving consent, his representative cannot be reached, and it is imperative to administer the drug without delay.

(g) "Contrary to the best interests of such human beings" applies when the communication of information to obtain consent would seriously affect the patient's well-being and the physician has exercised a professional judgment that under the particular circumstances of this patient's case, the patient's best interests would suffer if consent were sought.

(h) "Consent" means that the person involved has legal capacity to give consent, is so situated as to be able to exercise free power of choice, and is provided with a fair explanation of pertinent information concerning the investigational drug. This latter element means that before the acceptance of an affirmative decision by such person the investigator should carefully consider and make known to him (taking into consideration such person's well-being and his ability to understand) the nature, expected duration, and purpose of the administration of said investigational drug; the method and means by which it is to be administered; the hazards involved; the existence of alternative forms of therapy, if any; and the beneficial effects upon his health or person that may possibly come from the administration of the investigational drug.

When consent is necessary under the rules set forth in this section, the consent of persons receiving an investigational new drug in Phase 1 and Phase 2 investigations (or their representatives) shall be in writing. When consent is necessary under such rules in Phase 3 investigations, it is the responsibility of investigators, taking into consideration the physical and mental state of the patient, to decide when it is necessary or preferable to obtain consent in other

---

3. 21 C.F.R. §§ 130–37 (1963).

4. *See generally* William J. Curran, *Government Regulation of the Use of Human Subjects, in Medical Research: The Approach of Two Federal Agencies, in* Experimentation With Human Subjects 402 (Paul Freund ed., 1970).

than written form. When such written consent is not obtained, the investigator must obtain oral consent and record that fact in the medical record of the person receiving the drug.[5]

Thus the new regulations allowed no exceptions to the consent requirement in non-therapeutic studies. The adopted definition of informed consent combined concepts from both the Nuremberg Code and the Declaration of Helsinki.

In 1966, the Surgeon General of the United States directed that all research proposals submitted for financial support from the Public Health Service undergo prior review by an investigator's institutional associates "to assure an independent determination of the protection of the rights and welfare of the individual or individuals involved, of the appropriateness of the methods used to secure informed consent and of the risks and potential medical benefits of the investigation."[6] In 1971, the Public Health Service extended the directive into a formal Institutional Guide to DHEW [Department of Health, Education and Welfare] Policy on Protection of Human Subjects, and strengthened the requirement that the research undergo peer review at the investigator's institution by requiring that the peer committee "be composed of sufficient members with varying backgrounds to assure complete and adequate review of projects."[7] In addition, the 1971 Guide established that no "member of an institutional committee shall be involved in either the initial or continuing review of an activity in which he has a professional responsibility."[8]

In 1972, the national press reported on the Tuskegee Syphilis Study. Congress became increasingly active as well, holding hearings on Tuskegee and other controversial areas of research, including psychosurgery and fetal research. The result was the National Research Act of 1974, Pub.L. No. 93–348, 88 Stat. 342, which established the National Commission for the Protection of Human Subjects of Biomedical and Behavioral Research. The Act also imposed a moratorium on non-therapeutic research conducted or funded by HEW on any living human fetus. The moratorium was to remain in effect until the National Commission recommended whether and under what circumstances research on fetuses should be conducted. The Commission was directed by the Act to make its report on fetal research within four months after the members took office.

5. 32 Fed.Reg. 3994 (1967), codified as 21 C.F.R. §§ 136–37. The three phases of drug testing have been described by the FDA as follows:

"a. Clinical Pharmacology. This is ordinarily divided into two phases: Phase 1 starts when the new drug is first introduced into man—only animal and in vitro data are available—with the purpose of determining human toxicity, metabolism, absorption, elimination, and safe dosage range; phase 2 covers the initial trials on a limited number of patients for specific disease control or prophylaxis purposes...." [Phases 1 and 2 ordinarily are conducted in highly controlled settings.]

"b. Clinical Trial. This phase 3 provides the assessment of the drug's safety and effectiveness and optimum dosage schedules in the diagnosis, treatment or prophylaxis of groups of subjects involving a given disease or condition." FDA Form 1571 (10/82). [Phase 3 ordinarily involves the administration of the experimental drug in normal clinical settings to patients who have the illness or condition for which the drug, if approved, would be used.]

6. President's Commission, Compensating for Research Injuries 33 (1982).

7. *Id.* at 36.

8. *Id.*

The mandated report was submitted to the Secretary of HEW on July 25, 1975. It was the first of a series of reports submitted by the Commission covering such related topics as research on children and research on prisoners, all of which played a very influential role both in shaping later federal regulations and in justifying the establishment in 1978 of a second national commission, entitled the President's Commission for the Study of Ethical Problems in Medicine and Biomedical and Behavioral Research.[9]

The spurt of congressional activity in 1974 coincided with the release by HEW of its first regulations governing research involving human subjects.[10] The regulations provided that HEW would fund no research involving human subjects unless an appropriate committee of the sponsoring institution had approved the research as being in accordance with relevant federal regulations designed to ensure that informed consent would be obtained from all participants.

(II) SECOND STAGE: CURRENT REGULATIONS OF THE UNITED STATES DEPARTMENT OF HEALTH AND HUMAN SERVICES

The HHS (formerly HEW) regulations have undergone a number of changes since they were first promulgated in 1974. Most addressed additional protection for particularly vulnerable subjects, such as fetuses and pregnant women,[11] and children.[12] Regulations governing research on the institutionally mentally disabled have been proposed but never finalized.[13]

On August 8, 1978, the FDA proposed more detailed standards for the institutional review committees, now termed Institutional Review Boards (IRBs).[14] On January 26, 1981, HHS published a standard regulatory framework for IRB review of research whether conducted or funded by HHS or by the FDA.[15] The current regulations exempt from their requirements certain kinds of research that normally present little or no risk of harm to subjects, such as surveys, interviews, or observations of public behavior, and studies of data or documents.

In June 1991, protection for human research subjects increased substantially when a number of federal agencies adopted the Common Rule regulations.[16] Previously, only research conducted or funded by the FDA or HHS was subject to the regulations; now almost all research conducted or funded by a federal agency is required to comply with the regulations on human subjects protections.[17]

9. Title III, Pub.L. 95–622 (1978) as amended by Pub.L. 97–377 (1982).

10. 39 Fed.Reg. 18,914 (May 10, 1974).

11. 45 C.F.R. § 46 subpart B (1994).

12. 45 C.F.R. § 46 subpart D (1994).

13. 43 Fed.Reg. 53,956 (1978).

14. 43 Fed.Reg. 35,186 (Aug. 8, 1978).

15. 46 Fed.Reg. 8366 (Jan. 26, 1981).

16. 56 Fed.Reg. 28,003 et seq. (June 18, 1991).

17. Federal departments and agencies that conduct or fund clinical research include the Agency for International Development (AID), Department of Agriculture, Department of Energy, National Aeronautics and Space Administration, Department of Commerce, Consumer Product Safety Commission, Department of Housing and Urban Development, Department of Justice, Department of Defense, Department of Education, Department of Veterans Affairs, Environmental Protection Agency, Department of Health and Human Services, Food and Drug Administration, National Science Foundation, and Department of Transportation.

Several offices have been created to provide guidance and oversight of compliance with the regulations. The Office for Protection from Research Risks (OPRR) was created in 1972 as a part of NIH to ensure the safety of research participants. The NIH Revitalization Act of 1993[18] established the Office of Research Integrity (ORI), an independent group that reports to the Secretary of HHS on misconduct in research. In 2000, the OPRR was replaced by the Office of Human Research Protections (OHRP), which is now a part of HHS. The OHRP is intended to provided leadership for the federal agencies that conduct human subjects research under the Common Rule.

Department of Health and Human Services, *Regulations on Protection of Human Subjects*
45 C.F.R. Pt. 46 (2004).

§ 46.101   To what does this policy apply?

(a) Except as provided in paragraph (b) of this section, this policy applies to all research involving human subjects conducted, supported or otherwise subject to regulation by any federal department or agency which takes appropriate administrative action to make the policy applicable to such research. This includes research conducted by federal civilian employees or military personnel, except that each department or agency head may adopt such procedural modifications as may be appropriate from an administrative standpoint. It also includes research conducted, supported, or otherwise subject to regulation by the federal government outside the United States.

(1) Research that is conducted or supported by a federal department or agency, whether or not it is regulated as defined in § 46.102(e), must comply with all sections of this policy.

(2) Research that is neither conducted nor supported by a federal department or agency but is subject to regulation as defined in § 46.102(e) must be reviewed and approved, in compliance with § 46.101, § 46.102, and § 46.107 through § 46.117 of this policy, by an institutional review board (IRB) that operates in accordance with the pertinent requirements of this policy.

(b) Unless otherwise required by department or agency heads, research activities in which the only involvement of human subjects will be in one or more of the following categories are exempt from this policy:

(1) Research conducted in established or commonly accepted educational settings, involving normal educational practices, such as (i) research on regular and special education instructional strategies, or (ii) research on the effectiveness of or the comparison among instructional techniques, curricula, or classroom management methods.

(2) Research involving the use of educational tests (cognitive, diagnostic, aptitude, achievement), survey procedures, interview procedures or observation of public behavior, unless:

18.   Pub.L. 103–43 (1993).

(i) Information obtained is recorded in such a manner that human subjects can be identified, directly or through identifiers linked to the subjects; and (ii) any disclosure of the human subjects' responses outside the research could reasonably place the subjects at risk of criminal or civil liability or be damaging to the subjects' financial standing, employability, or reputation.

(3) Research involving the use of educational tests (cognitive, diagnostic, aptitude, achievement), survey procedures, interview procedures, or observation of public behavior that is not exempt under paragraph (b)(2) of this section, if:

(i) The human subjects are elected or appointed public officials or candidates for public office; or (ii) federal statute(s) require(s) without exception that the confidentiality of the personally identifiable information will be maintained throughout the research and thereafter.

(4) Research, involving the collection or study of existing data, documents, records, pathological specimens, or diagnostic specimens, if these sources are publicly available or if the information is recorded by the investigator in such a manner that subjects cannot be identified, directly or through identifiers linked to the subjects.

(5) Research and demonstration projects which are conducted by or subject to the approval of department or agency heads, and which are designed to study, evaluate, or otherwise examine:

(i) Public benefit or service programs; (ii) procedures for obtaining benefits or services under those programs; (iii) possible changes in or alternatives to those programs or procedures; or (iv) possible changes in methods or levels of payment for benefits or services under those programs.

(6) Taste and food quality evaluation and consumer acceptance studies, (i) if wholesome foods without additives are consumed or (ii) if a food is consumed that contains a food ingredient at or below the level and for a use found to be safe, or agricultural chemical or environmental contaminant at or below the level found to be safe, by the Food and Drug Administration or approved by the Environmental Protection Agency or the Food Safety and Inspection Service of the U.S. Department of Agriculture.

. . .

§ 46.102 Definitions.

. . .

(d) *Research* means a systematic investigation, including research development, testing and evaluation, designed to develop or contribute to generalizable knowledge. Activities which meet this definition constitute research for purposes of this policy, whether or not they are conducted or supported under a program which is considered research for other purposes. For example, some demonstration and service programs may include research activities.

(e) *Research subject to regulation,* and similar terms are intended to encompass those research activities for which a federal department or agency has specific responsibility for regulating as a research activity, (for example, Investigational New Drug requirements administered by the Food and Drug Administration). It does not include research activities which are incidentally regulated by a federal department or agency solely as part of the department's or agency's broader responsibility to regulate certain types of activities whether research or non-research in nature (for example, Wage and Hour requirements administered by the Department of Labor).

(f) *Human subject* means a living individual about whom an investigator (whether professional or student) conducting research obtains

(1) Data through intervention or interaction with the individual, or

(2) Identifiable private information. *Intervention* includes both physical procedures by which data are gathered (for example, venipuncture) and manipulations of the subject or the subject's environment that are performed for research purposes. Interaction includes communication or interpersonal contact between investigator and subject. *Private information* includes information about behavior that occurs in a context in which an individual can reasonably expect that no observation or recording is taking place, and information which has been provided for specific purposes by an individual and which the individual can reasonably expect will not be made public (for example, a medical record). Private information must be individually identifiable (i.e., the identity of the subject is or may readily be ascertained by the investigator or associated with the information) in order for obtaining the information to constitute research involving human subjects.

. . .

(i) *Minimal risk* means that the probability and magnitude of harm or discomfort anticipated in the research are not greater in and of themselves than those ordinarily encountered in daily life or during the performance of routine physical or psychological examinations or tests.

. . .

§ 46.107 IRB membership.

(a) Each IRB shall have at least five members, with varying backgrounds to promote complete and adequate review of research activities commonly conducted by the institution. The IRB shall be sufficiently qualified through the experience and expertise of its members, and the diversity of the members, including consideration of race, gender, and cultural backgrounds and sensitivity to such issues as community attitudes, to promote respect for its advice and counsel in safeguarding the rights and welfare of human subjects. In addition to possessing the professional competence necessary to review specific research activities, the IRB shall be able to ascertain the acceptability of proposed research in terms of institutional commitments and regulations, applicable law, and standards of professional conduct and practice. The IRB shall therefore include persons knowledgeable in these areas. If an IRB regularly reviews research that involves a vulnerable category of subjects, such as children, prisoners, pregnant women, or handicapped or mentally disabled persons, consideration shall be given to the inclusion of one or more individuals who are knowledgeable about and experienced in working with these subjects.

(b) Every nondiscriminatory effort will be made to ensure that no IRB consists entirely of men or entirely of women, including the institution's consideration of qualified persons of both sexes, so long as no selection is made to the IRB on the basis of gender. No IRB may consist entirely of members of one profession.

(c) Each IRB shall include at least one member whose primary concerns are in scientific areas and at least one member whose primary concerns are in nonscientific areas.

(d) Each IRB shall include at least one member who is not otherwise affiliated with the institution and who is not part of the immediate family of a person who is affiliated with the institution.

(e) No IRB may have a member participate in the IRB's initial or continuing review of any project in which the member has a conflicting interest, except to provide information requested by the IRB.

(f) An IRB may, in its discretion, invite individuals with competence in special areas to assist in the review of issues which require expertise beyond or in addition to that available on the IRB. These individuals may not vote with the IRB.

. . .

§ 46.109   IRB review of research.

(a) An IRB shall review and have authority to approve, require modifications in (to secure approval), or disapprove all research activities covered by this policy.

(b) An IRB shall require that information given to subjects as part of informed consent is in accordance with § 46.116. The IRB may require that information, in addition to that specifically mentioned in § 46.116, be given to the subjects when in the IRB's judgment the information would meaningfully add to the protection of the rights and welfare of subjects.

(c) An IRB shall require documentation of informed consent or may waive documentation in accordance with § 46.117.

(d) An IRB shall notify investigators and the institution in writing of its decision to approve or disapprove the proposed research activity, or of modifications required to secure IRB approval of the research activity. If the IRB decides to disapprove a research activity, it shall include in its written notification a statement of the reasons for its decision and give the investigator an opportunity to respond in person or in writing.

(e) An IRB shall conduct continuing review of research covered by this policy at intervals appropriate to the degree of risk, but not less than once per year, and shall have authority to observe or have a third party observe the consent process and the research.

§ 46.110   Expedited review procedures for certain kinds of research involving no more than minimal risk, and for minor changes in approved research.

(a) The Secretary, HHS, has established, and published as a Notice in the Federal Register, a list of categories of research that may be reviewed by the IRB through an expedited review procedure. The list will be amended, as appropriate after consultation with other departments and agencies, through periodic republication by the Secretary, HHS, in the Federal Register. A copy of the list is available from the Office for Protection from Research Risks, National Institutes of Health, HHS, Bethesda, Maryland 20892.

(b) An IRB may use the expedited review procedure to review either or both of the following:

(1) Some or all of the research appearing on the list and found by the reviewer(s) to involve no more than minimal risk,

(2) Minor changes in previously approved research during the period (of one year or less) for which approval is authorized.

. . .

§ 46.111   Criteria for IRB approval of research.

(a) In order to approve research covered by this policy the IRB shall determine that all of the following requirements are satisfied:

(1) Risks to subjects are minimized: (i) By using procedures which are consistent with sound research design and which do not unnecessarily expose subjects to risk, and (ii) whenever appropriate, by using procedures already being performed on the subjects for diagnostic or treatment purposes.

(2) Risks to subjects are reasonable in relation to anticipated benefits, if any, to subjects, and the importance of the knowledge that may reasonably be expected to result. In evaluating risks and benefits, the IRB should consider only those risks and benefits that may result from the research (as distinguished from risks and benefits of therapies subjects would receive even if not participating in the research). The IRB should not consider possible long-range effects of applying knowledge gained in the research (for example, the possible effects of the research on public policy) as among those research risks that fall within the purview of its responsibility.

(3) Selection of subjects is equitable. In making this assessment the IRB should take into account the purposes of the research and the setting in which the research will be conducted and should be particularly cognizant of the special problems of research involving vulnerable populations, such as children, prisoners, pregnant women, mentally disabled persons, or economically or educationally disadvantaged persons.

(4) Informed consent will be sought from each prospective subject or the subject's legally authorized representative, in accordance with, and to the extent required by § 46.116.

(5) Informed consent will be appropriately documented, in accordance with, and to the extent required by § 46.117.

(6) When appropriate, the research plan makes adequate provision for monitoring the data collected to ensure the safety of subjects.

(7) When appropriate, there are adequate provisions to protect the privacy of subjects and to maintain the confidentiality of data.

(b) When some or all of the subjects are likely to be vulnerable to coercion or undue influence, such as children, prisoners, pregnant women, mentally disabled persons, or economically or educationally disadvantaged persons, additional safeguards have been included in the study to protect the rights and welfare of these subjects.

. . .

§ 46.113   Suspension or termination of IRB approval of research.

An IRB shall have authority to suspend or terminate approval of research that is not being conducted in accordance with the IRB's requirements or that has been associated with unexpected serious harm to subjects. Any suspension or termination of approval shall include a statement of the reasons for the IRB's action and shall be reported promptly to the investigator, appropriate institutional officials, and the department or agency head.

. . .

NOTES AND QUESTIONS

1. A few states have enacted laws governing research on human subjects in general. *See* Cal. Health & Safety Code §§ 24170–24179 (West 2004); Fla. Stat. Ann. §§ 381.026(4)(e), 381.85 (West 2004); 410 Ill. Comp. Stat. 50/3.1 (2004); Md. Code Ann., Health—General §§ 13–2001–13–2004 (2004); N.H. Rev. Stat. Ann. § 151:21 (2004); N.Y. Pub.Health §§ 2440–2446 (Consol.2002); Va.Code Ann. §§ 32.1–162.16 to 32.1–162.20 (Michie 2001). Many states have provisions to protect patients in long-term care facilities and ensure that they have the right to refuse to participate in experimental treatment. *See* Conn. Gen. Stat. § 19a–550(b)(3) (2004); Del. Code Ann. tit. 16, § 1121(4) (2004); Ga. Code Ann. § 31–8–108(c) (2004); Md. Code Ann., Health—General § 19.344 (2004); Mass. Gen. Laws ch. 111, § 70E (2004); Minn. Stat. § 144.651 (2004); Mo. Rev. Stat. § 198.088(1)(6)(c) (2004); N.J. Stat. Ann. § 30:13–5 (West 2004); N.C. Gen. Stat. § 131E–117(4) (2004); Ohio Rev. Code Ann. § 3721.13(A)(12) (West 2004); Or. Rev. Stat. § 441.605(3) (2004); R.I. Gen. Laws § 23–17.5–7 (2004); S.C. Code Ann. § 44–81–40(C)(5) (Law. Co-op. 2004); Tex. Health & Safety Code Ann. § 242.501(a)(9) (Vernon 2004); Wash. Rev. Code Ann. § 74.42.040(4) (West 2004).

Other states have enacted laws protecting specific categories of subjects. *See* N.M. Stat. Ann. § 24–9A (Michie 2004) (restricting research involving pregnant women); Wyo. Stat. Ann. § 25–5–132(d)(ii) (Michie 2004) (protecting minors who are residents of training schools from being subjected to experimental medical or psychological research without valid consent). A number of states have enacted restrictions on research involving institutionalized persons with developmental disabilities or mental illness. *See* Colo. Rev. Stat. § 27–10.5–114 (2003); Del. Code Ann. tit. 16, § 1561(8)(d) (2004); D.C. Code Ann. § 6–1969 (2004); Fla. Stat. Ann. § 393.13(4)(c)(6) (West 2004); Me. Rev. Stat. Ann. tit. 34–B, § 5605(8)(G) (West 2004); Minn. Stat. §§ 144.651, 245B.04 (2004); Mo. Rev. Stat. § 630.115(1) (2004); Mont. Code Ann. §§ 53–20–147, 53–21–147 (2004); N.J. Stat. Ann. §§ 30:6D–5, 30:4–24.2 (West 2004); N.D. Cent. Code §§ 25–01.2–09, 25–03.1–40 (2004); R.I. Gen. Laws § 40.1–24.5–5(11) (2004); S.D. Codified Laws §§ 27A–12–3.20, 27B–8–41 (Michie 2004); Wis. Stat. § 51.61(1) (2004).

2. Many commentators have begun to question whether the IRB process sufficiently protects the interests of human subjects. Members of the scientific community have raised the concern that the increasing number and complexity of clinical trials is overburdening the IRB system and causing hasty, superficial reviews. *See* Donald F. Philips, *IRBs Search for Answers and Support During a Time of Institutional Change*, 283 JAMA 729 (2000). Critics have also pointed out that many IRB members have become financially involved in the research that they are asked to review, raising serious questions about their impartiality. *See* Marcia Angell, *Editorial, Is Academic Medicine for Sale?* 342 NEW ENG. J. MED. 1516 (2000); Christopher Windham, *Safety-Board Staffs Face Conflicts; Study Finds Almost Half Of Medical Faculty Were Health–Sector Consultants*, WALL ST. J., August 19, 2003, at D3.

In response these and other concerns, the Office of Human Research Protections (OHRP) commissioned a report through the Institute of Medicine (IOM) to investigate IRBs and the current system of research oversight. The report, *Responsible Research: A Systems Approach to Protecting Research Participants* (Daniel D. Federman et al., eds., 2003), provides a detailed review of the current protections in human research and calls for broad changes to the entire system, including increased federal guidance and monitoring. It also recommends that IRBs should be renamed "ERBs" (Ethics Review Boards), which should function on a regional level and should focus almost exclusively on ethical issues. *Id.* at 70. Several other commentators have offered their perspectives on what reforms should be taken. *See generally* Carl H. Coleman, *Rationalizing Risk Assessment in Human Subject Research*, 46 ARIZ. L. REV. 1 (2004); Michael A. Morse, et al., *Monitoring and Ensuring Safety During Clinical Research*, 285 JAMA 1201 (2001); and Michaele C. Christian et al., *A Central Institutional Review Board for Multi-institutional Trials*, 346 NEW ENG. J. MED. 1405 (2002) (describing the success of the National Cancer Institute's one year pilot study of a central review board system).

2.   INTERNATIONAL REGULATION

Paul M. McNeill, *International Trends in Research Regulations: Science as Negotiation*

RESEARCH ON HUMAN SUBJECTS: ETHICS, LAW, AND SOCIAL POLICY.
243–246, 251–254, 262–263 (1998).

Internationally there are changes in the way in which science and research are conceptualized and conducted. These changes reflect changing views about what counts as knowledge, acceptable ways to arrive at knowledge, and the status of that knowledge in relation to other views and other human activities. This paper explores the idea that these changing perspectives on epistemology and ontology are related to changes in the regulation of research. They have a bearing on two basic questions in the approval of research: "Who should decide on what is ethical in science and research?" and "How should scientific activity be allowed to proceed?"

. . .

BACKGROUND

Most countries rely on committees to regulate research involving human participants. The system of review by committee was developed in the United States in the 1960s and adopted by most other developed countries subsequently.[1] It has been endorsed by international convenants [*sic*], most notably by the Council for International Organizations of Medical Sciences (CIOMS).[2]

The predominant model of research regulation is that any researcher, before embarking on any research involving human participants, must seek and gain approval for that research from a committee. The committee, specially constituted to consider the ethics of research has the power to recommend modifications to the proposed research, reject the application outright, or approve of the research. Committees worldwide reject very few proposals although the application process results in modifications being made to a proportion of them.[3] The setting for the committee is different in different countries, but with few exceptions, committees are based in an institution, usually a research institute within which the research is conducted, or are established within a regional authority, such as an area health board.

. . .

SELF–REGULATION OR INDEPENDENT REVIEW

. . .

The position taken by international and national codes of ethics is that the interest of the research subject must be paramount. For example, the Declaration of Helsinki states that: "[c]oncern for the interests of the subject must always prevail over the interest of science and society".[9] If the interests of the research institute dominate on a review committee it is possible that "concern for the interests of the subject" may be over-shadowed by other needs, such as the need to meet research deadlines and to ensure a flow of research money to the institution. In these circumstances review by peers can be mere "window-dressing" which (like the ethical codes of some professions) serves the predominant role of deflecting public criticism without significantly altering the behaviour of individuals within the profession. The United Kingdom Royal College of Physicians' guidelines state that committees should "provide reassurance to the public".[11] That is a reasonable objective if the public can be assured that the

1. P.M. McNeill, *The Ethics and Politics of Human Experimentation* (Cambridge: Cambridge University Press, 1993) at 37–50.

2. Council for International Organizations of Medical Sciences (CIOMS) in collaboration with the World Health Organization (WHO), *International Ethical Guidelines for Biomedical Research Involving Human Subjects* (Geneva: CIOMS, 1993) [hereinafter *CIOMS Guidelines*].

3. In Australia, for example, 63% were approved on first consideration and only 2.7% were rejected. A further 14.7% were approved after clarification and 17.3% were approved after modification by the researcher. *See* McNeill, *supra* note 1 at 89.

9. World Medical Association, *Declaration of Helsinki: Recommendations Guiding Medical Doctors in Biomedical Research involving Human Subjects*. Adopted at the 18th World Medical Assembly in Helsinki in June 1964. Amended at the 29th World Medical Assembly in Tokyo in October 1975; at the 35th World Medical Assembly in Venice in October 1983; and at the 41st World Medical Assembly in Hong Kong in 1989, amended principle 1.5. See also Australian National Health and Medical Research Council, *Statement on Human Experimentation and Supplementary Notes* (Canberra: NHMRC, 1992), supplementary note 1.6 as reproduced in McNeill (1993), *supra* note 1 at 261.

11. See paragraph 2.1 of The Royal College of Physicians of London, *Guidelines on the Practice of Ethics Committees in Medical Research involving Human Subjects*, 2d ed.

review process is effective in protecting review participants. It is a concern however, if reassurance of the public, rather than sound review, is the *raison d'être* of a committee.

Given this concern, it is not surprising that rules governing review committees in most countries have added various people to the in-house review team. In the United States members of institutional review boards (or IRBs as they are known) were originally described as "associates" of the researcher.[12] Subsequent regulations required the addition of a non-scientist, (such as a lawyer, ethicist, or member of the clergy) and a member not otherwise affiliated with the institution (who became known as the community member). The UK College of Physicians' guidelines added a nurse and lay members to the basic peer review team.[14] The Australian National Health and Medical Research Council initially required "at least one member not associated with the institute" in addition to the "peer group" and subsequently added a minister of religion, a lawyer and two lay members.

. . .

TRENDS TOWARD STRONGER COMMUNITY REPRESENTATION

Research ethics review is an evolving field. In every country the basic peer review model adopted from the United States has been applied and developed in different ways. There are some commonalities in these developments, however. . . . What I find in a number of countries is a trend toward stronger community representation on committees. . . . This is evident in a number of ways:

(1) There is a trend toward recognizing the need for a balance of community members (or at least members from outside of the institution) and members from the research institute. Denmark has long required an equal number of "lay members" and "medical/scientific" members. New Zealand now requires that the "lay membership" should "approximate one half of the total membership."[40] In Australia a recent report to the Minister of Health notes that community members are often significantly out-numbered by institutional and medical committee members. It recommends that "not less than half the committee should consist of non-medical members from outside the institution."

(2) Recent descriptions of community members make it obvious that these members are not chosen as ordinary or typical members of the community. For example, the UK College of Physicians' guidelines state explicitly that lay members should be "persons of responsibility and standing." The recent review in Australia recommended that lay mem-

(London: College of Physicians, 1990) at 3 [hereinafter *UK College of Physicians' Guidelines*].

12. W.J. Curran, "Governmental Regulation of the Use of Human Subjects in Medical Research P: The Approach of Two Federal Agencies" (1969) 98:2 Daedalus 542 at 577. Reprinted in P.A. Freund, ed., *Experimentation with Human Subjects* (New York: George Braziller, 1970).

14. See *UK College of Physicians' Guidelines, supra* note 11 at 9–10.

40. New Zealand Department of Health, *Standard for Ethics Committees Established to Review Research and Ethical Aspects of Health Care* (Wellington: New Zealand Department of Health, 1991) at para. 3.2 [hereinafter *NZ Standard*].

bers "should be respected by the community" and they should have "the ability to represent the community (with current or recent community involvement) and to mirror community standards."[44] This is clearly not the same as choosing members for a jury. These people are chosen in a representational capacity. It is acknowledged that this is representation without the members having a specific constituency from which they are nominated and to which they report.

. . .

(5) There is an increasing recognition of the need for specific representation by particular community groups. The CIOMS guidelines, for example, offer the following recommendation:

> Committees that often review research directed at specific diseases or impairments, such as AIDS or paraplegia, should consider the advantages of including as members or consultants' patients with such diseases or impairments. Similarly, committees that review research involving such vulnerable groups as children, students, aged persons or employees should consider the advantages of including representatives of, or advocates for, such groups.[48]

> Similarly the Australian Report on Committees recommends that where a research ethics committee is in a locality which includes "ethnic" or Aboriginal population, community members may be appointed from amongst those populations especially where the committee considers research "principally carried out amongst those groups."[49] In those circumstances the Australian Social and Behavioural Research Report also suggests the inclusion of Aboriginal people or "people from non-English speaking backgrounds." The New Zealand Standard requires those forming review committees to "take account of the need for . . . knowledge and experience of . . . women's health, patient advocacy and Tikanga Maori."[51]

> These guidelines (or recommendations) for review committees all require representation of the interests of particular (potential) research participants. The Australian Report on Committees gives a rationale in terms of appointment of "local" members. However the effect is toward greater representation of people who may participate in research.

. . .

In summary therefore, there are international trends toward a stronger representation by community members. This consists of a growing trend for equal or greater numbers of community members on committees; chairpersons to be elected from the community members; the selection of people "of standing" as community members who are more capable of withstanding pressure from other committee members; and suggestions

44. *Australian Report on Committees,* *supra* note 28 at 46.

48. *CIOMS Guidelines, supra* note 2 at 40–41.

49. *Australian Report on Committees,* *supra* note 28 at 46. Further on the same page it is stated that "due regard should be paid to the ethnic backgrounds of the research subjects dealt with by the researchers". Read for "ethnic" (in common Australian parlance) "non-English speaking" immigrants to Australia or people who strongly identify with the "non-English speaking" origins.

51. *NZ Standard, supra* note 40 at para. 3.7 [alteration in original].

that community members represent research participants in general and particular groups of potential research participants (where research with those groups is likely to be considered by the committee). These trends are consistent with a rationale of representation of the interest of the research participants. The question asked at the outset was "Who should decide on what is ethical in science and research?" The answer being given internationally is: people with research expertise and an equal number of people who are independent and able to represent research participants.

. . .

CONCLUSIONS

Internationally there are many changes in the review of research: what counts as "research"; the extension of a requirement for review beyond medical research to include behavioural, social, anthropological and other fields; change in arrangements for committees themselves, their composition, and whether one committee can act in the place of many. . . .

The predominant trend . . . is toward a view of science and research as negotiated perspectives between different possible views in society. Ethical review is ultimately a weighing of values and a part of negotiation for a better life. Necessarily, this must take into account the different views of what constitutes the good life in our increasingly multi-cultural societies. The most appropriate people to weigh those different values, and reach a decision about whether a particular research program should go ahead or not, should represent those most affected. This is ethical review in the postmodern world.

International Ethical Guidelines for Biomedical Research Involving Human Subjects

Council for International Organizations of Medical Sciences (CIOMS) in Collaboration with the World Health Organization (2002).

Guideline 1: Ethical justification and scientific validity of biomedical research involving human beings

The ethical justification of biomedical research involving human subjects is the prospect of discovering new ways of benefiting people's health. Such research can be ethically justifiable only if it is carried out in ways that respect and protect, and are fair to, the subjects of that research and are morally acceptable within the communities in which the research is carried out. Moreover, because scientifically invalid research is unethical in that it exposes research subjects to risks without possible benefit, investigators and sponsors must ensure that proposed studies involving human subjects conform to generally accepted scientific principles and are based on adequate knowledge of the pertinent scientific literature.

Guideline 2: Ethical review committees

All proposals to conduct research involving human subjects must be submitted for review of their scientific merit and ethical acceptability to one or more scientific review and ethical review committees. The review committees must be independent of the research team, and any direct financial or other material benefit they may derive from the research should not be contingent on the outcome of their review. The investigator must obtain their approval or clearance before undertaking the research. The ethical review committee should conduct further reviews as necessary in the course of the research, including monitoring of its progress.

Guideline 3: Ethical review of externally sponsored research

An external sponsoring organization and individual investigators should submit the research protocol for ethical and scientific review in the country of the sponsoring organization, and the ethical standards applied should be no less stringent than they would be for research carried out in that country. The health authorities of the host country, as well as a national or local ethical review committee, should ensure that the proposed research is responsive to the health needs and priorities of the host country and meets the requisite ethical standards.

Guideline 4: Individual informed consent

For all biomedical research involving humans the investigator must obtain the voluntary informed consent of the prospective subject or, in the case of an individual who is not capable of giving informed consent, the permission of a legally authorized representative in accordance with applicable law. Waiver of informed consent is to be regarded as uncommon and exceptional, and must in all cases be approved by an ethical review committee.

Guideline 5: Obtaining informed consent: Essential information for prospective research subjects

Before requesting an individual's consent to participate in research, the investigator must provide the following information, in language or another form of communication that the individual can understand:

1) that the individual is invited to participate in research, the reasons for considering the individual suitable for the research, and that participation is voluntary;

2) that the individual is free to refuse to participate and will be free to withdraw from the research at any time without penalty or loss of benefits to which he or she would otherwise be entitled;

3) the purpose of the research, the procedures to be carried out by the investigator and the subject, and an explanation of how the research differs from routine medical care;

4) for controlled trials, an explanation of features of the research design (e.g., randomization, double-blinding), and that the subject will not be told of the assigned treatment until the study has been completed and the blind has been broken;

5) the expected duration of the individual's participation (including number and duration of visits to the research centre and the total time involved) and the possibility of early termination of the trial or of the individual's participation in it;

6) whether money or other forms of material goods will be provided in return for the individual's participation and, if so, the kind and amount;

7) that, after the completion of the study, subjects will be informed of the findings of the research in general, and individual subjects will be informed of any finding that relates to their particular health status;

8) that subjects have the right of access to their data on demand, even if these data lack immediate clinical utility (unless the ethical review committee has approved temporary or permanent non-disclosure of data, in which case the subject should be informed of, and given, the reasons for such non-disclosure);

9) any foreseeable risks, pain or discomfort, or inconvenience to the individual (or others) associated with participation in the research, including risks to the health or well-being of a subject's spouse or partner;

10) the direct benefits, if any, expected to result to subjects from participating in the research;

11) the expected benefits of the research to the community or to society at large, or contributions to scientific knowledge;

12) whether, when and how any products or interventions proven by the research to be safe and effective will be made available to subjects after they have completed their participation in the research, and whether they will be expected to pay for them;

13) any currently available alternative interventions or courses of treatment;

14) the provisions that will be made to ensure respect for the privacy of subjects and for the confidentiality of records in which subjects are identified;

15) the limits, legal or other, to the investigators' ability to safeguard confidentiality, and the possible consequences of breaches of confidentiality;

16) policy with regard to the use of results of genetic tests and familial genetic information, and the precautions in place to prevent disclosure of the results of a subject's genetic tests to immediate family relatives or to others (e.g., insurance companies or employers) without the consent of the subject;

17) the sponsors of the research, the institutional affiliation of the investigators, and the nature and sources of funding the research;

18) the possible research uses, direct or secondary, of the subject's medical records and of biological specimens taken in the course of clinical care (See also Guidelines 4 and 18 Commentaries);

19) whether it is planned that biological specimens collected in the research will be destroyed at its conclusion, and, if not, details about their storage (where, how, for how long, and final disposition) and possible future use, and that subjects have the right to decide about such future use, to refuse storage, and to have the material destroyed (See Guideline 4 Commentary);

20) whether commercial products may be developed from biological specimens, and whether the participant will receive monetary or other benefits from the development of such products;

21) whether the investigator is serving only as an investigator or as both investigator and the subject's physician;

22) the extent of the investigator's responsibility to provide medical services to the participant;

23) that treatment will be provided free of charge for specified types of research-related injury or for complications associated with the research, the nature and duration of such care, the name of the organization or individual that will provide the treatment, and whether there is any uncertainty regarding funding of such treatment;

24) in what way, and by what organization, the subject or the subject's family or dependants will be compensated for disability or death resulting from such injury (or, when indicated, that there are no plans to provide such compensation);

25) whether or not, in the country in which the prospective subject is invited to participate in research, the right to compensation is legally guaranteed;

26) that an ethical review committee has approved or cleared the research protocol.

Guideline 6: Obtaining informed consent: Obligations of sponsors and investigators

Sponsors and investigators have a duty to:

— refrain from unjustified deception, undue influence, or intimidation;

— seek consent only after ascertaining that the prospective subject has adequate understanding of the relevant facts and of the consequences of participation and has had sufficient opportunity to consider whether to participate;

— as a general rule, obtain from each prospective subject a signed form as evidence of informed consent–investigators should justify any exceptions to this general rule and obtain the approval of the ethical review committee (See Guideline 4 Commentary, *Documentation of consent*);

— renew the informed consent of each subject if there are significant changes in the conditions or procedures of the research or if new information becomes available that could affect the willingness of subjects to continue to participate; and,

— renew the informed consent of each subject in long-term studies at predetermined intervals, even if there are no changes in the design or objectives of the research.

Guideline 7: Inducement to participate in research

Subjects may be reimbursed for lost earnings, travel costs and other expenses incurred in taking part in a study; they may also receive free medical services. Subjects, particularly those who receive no direct benefit from research, may also be paid or otherwise compensated for inconvenience and time spent. The payments should not be so large, however, or the medical services so extensive as to induce prospective subjects to consent to participate in the research against their better judgment ("undue inducement"). All payments, reimbursements and medical services provided to research subjects must have been approved by an ethical review committee.

Guideline 8: Benefits and risks of study participation

For all biomedical research involving human subjects, the investigator must ensure that potential benefits and risks are reasonably balanced and risks are minimized.

— Interventions or procedures that hold out the prospect of direct diagnostic, therapeutic or preventive benefit for the individual subject must be justified by the expectation that they will be at least as advantageous to the individual subject, in the light of foreseeable risks and benefits, as any available alternative. Risks of such "beneficial" interventions or procedures must be justified in relation to expected benefits to the individual subject.

— Risks of interventions that do not hold out the prospect of direct diagnostic, therapeutic or preventive benefit for the individual must be justified in relation to the expected benefits to society (generalizable knowledge). The risks presented by such interventions must be reasonable in relation to the importance of the knowledge to be gained.

Guideline 9: Special limitations on risk when research involves individuals who are not capable of giving informed consent

When there is ethical and scientific justification to conduct research with individuals incapable of giving informed consent, the risk from research interventions that do not hold out the prospect of direct benefit for the individual subject should be no more likely and not greater than the risk attached to routine medical or psychological examination of such persons. Slight or minor increases above such risk may be permitted when there is an overriding scientific or medical rationale for such increases and when an ethical review committee has approved them.

. . .

Guideline 11: Choice of control in clinical trials

As a general rule, research subjects in the control group of a trial of a diagnostic, therapeutic, or preventive intervention should receive an established effective intervention. In some circumstances it may be ethically acceptable to use an alternative comparator, such as placebo or "no treatment."

Placebo may be used:

— when there is no established effective intervention;

— when withholding an established effective intervention would expose subjects to, at most, temporary discomfort or delay in relief of symptoms;

— when use of an established effective intervention as comparator would not yield scientifically reliable results and use of placebo would not add any risk or serious or irreversible harm to the subjects.

. . .

Guideline 13: Research involving vulnerable persons

Special justification is required for inviting vulnerable individuals to serve as research subjects, and if they are selected, the means of protecting their rights and welfare must be strictly applied.

[Guidelines 14, 15, 16, and 17 list specific considerations when research participants are children, mentally disordered individuals, women, and pregnant women, respectively.]

. . .

Guideline 19: Right of injured subjects to treatment and compensation

Investigators should ensure that research subjects who suffer injury as a result of their participation are entitled to free medical treatment for such injury and to such financial or other assistance as would compensate them equitably for any resultant impairment, disability or handicap. In the case of death as a result of their participation, their dependants are entitled to compensation. Subjects must not be asked to waive the right to compensation.

NOTES AND QUESTIONS

1.   The Council for International Organizations of Medical Sciences (CIOMS) is an international nongovernmental organization that was founded in 1949 under the auspices of the World Health Organization (WHO) and the United Nations Educational, Scientific and Cultural Organization (UNESCO). CIOMS began its work on ethics in biomedical research in the late 1970s, when it set out to prepare guidelines "to indicate how the ethical principles that should guide the conduct of biomedical research involving human subjects, as set forth in the Declaration of Helsinki, could be effectively applied, particularly in developing countries, given their socioeconomic circumstances, laws and regulations, and executive and administrative arrangements." The result was the first draft of the *Proposed International Ethical Guidelines for Biomedical Research Involving Human Subjects* in 1982. Advances in medicine and biotechnology as well as changing research practices led to the revised guidelines, *International Ethical Guidelines for Biomedical Research Involving Human Subjects* in 1993. The latest version of the guidelines was promulgated in response to growing concern in the international community about research in economically disadvantaged countries. *See* Background, Council for Int'l Org. of Med. Sciences & World Health Org., *International Ethical Guidelines for Biomedical Research Involving Human Subjects*, 7–10 (2002).

2.   There has been considerable controversy over the ethics of conducting clinical trials in developing countries where there may be little or no regulation of research with human subjects. Ethicists have argued that such research should only be allowed if it addresses an important health problem in that country, and that conducting a trial in a developing country simply because it is more convenient or efficient is never a sufficient justification. *See* Harold T. Shapiro & Eric M. Meslin, *Ethical Issues in the Design and Conduct of Clinical Trials in Developing Countries*, 345 NEW ENG. J. MED. 139, (2001). In 2001, the National Bioethics Advisory Commission issued detailed guidelines for U.S. researchers who sponsor or conduct research in developing countries. *See* Ethical and Policy Issues in International Research: Clinical Trials in Developing Countries, Bethesda, Md.: National Bioethics Advisory Commission, 2001, *available at* http://www.georgetown.edu/research/nrcbl/nbac/clinical/Vol1.pdf. The guidelines cover such issues as involvement of the community, cultural barriers to proper disclosure and informed consent requirements, post-trial benefits, and building host country capacity to review and conduct trials. In response to stories of continuing violations and exploitation, a bill entitled the Safe Overseas Human Testing Act was introduced in the House of

Representatives in 2002. H.R. 5249, 107th Cong. The bill was designed to give Congress control over "the export of drugs and other test articles intended for overseas clinical investigations involving human participants in order to foster public health and safety, prevent injury to U.S. foreign policy, and preserve the credibility of the United States as a responsible trading partner." The bill would require a license approved by the President for export of test articles, and clinical trials conducted abroad would be required to substantially meet all the ethical standards for trials based in the United States. Do you think that this bill is a practical solution? Would drug companies be able to evade enforcement of these standards?

3. Cultural differences make it difficult to promulgate a single set of international ethical guidelines. Certain cultures, including most Western cultures, emphasize personal autonomy and consent while others place more value on self sacrifice and altruism. For a comprehensive discussion of African, Asian, Eastern Mediterranean, Latin American, North American, and European perspectives on human subjects research, *see Cultural Perspectives on Ethics and Research on Human Subjects, in* ETHICS AND RESEARCH ON HUMAN SUBJECTS: INTERNATIONAL GUIDELINES 173–216 (Z. Bankowski & R.J. Levine, eds., 1992).

4. Europe has established its own ethical guidelines in addition to the international treaties. The Council of Europe, an intergovernmental organization with 45 member states, adopted the Convention on Human Rights and Biomedicine (CHRB) in 1997. Although the CHRB is not binding unless an individual member state ratifies it, many of the guidelines reflect existing law on human subjects research. *See* Council of Europe, Convention on Human Rights and Biomedicine, *reprinted in* 36 I.L.M. 817 (1997). In 2001, the Council developed a supplementary Draft Protocol on Biomedical Research to be added to the CHRB. *See* Council of Europe Steering Committee on Bioethics, Draft Additional Protocol to the Convention on Human Rights and Biomedicine, on Biomedical Research, July 18, 2001, *available at* http://www.legal.coe.int/bioethics/gb/pdf/CDBI–INF(2001)5E.pdf. Also in 2001, the Council of Ministers of the European Union adopted a Directive on Clinical Trials, which became binding on members states of the EU on May 1, 2004. Council Directive 2001/20/EC, 2001 O.J. (L 121) 33–44. The Directive was intended to simplify and harmonize the regulation of clinical trials across Europe and ensure uniformity in protections for subjects. Some nations, however, are concerned that the implementation of the Directive will actually impede and inhibit publicly funded clinical trials. In the UK, a joint project has been set up by the Department of Health and the Medical Research Council to provide advice to researchers on how to comply with the law while minimizing unnecessary burdens. *See* Kent Woods, Editorial, *Implementing the European Clinical Trials Directive*, 328 BRIT. MED. J. 240 (2004).

5. For a discussion of the differences between the U.S. and French systems of human subjects protections and how U.S. laws could be improved, *see* Ivan Berlin & David A. Gorelick, *The French Law on "Protection of Persons Undergoing Biomedical Research": Implications for the U.S.*, 31 J.L. MED. & ETHICS 434 (2003).

D. ASSESSMENT OF CURRENT REGULATIONS

1. RESEARCH OR INNOVATIVE THERAPY? THE SCOPE OF CURRENT REGULATIONS

Karp v. Cooley

United States Court of Appeals for the Fifth Circuit, 1974.
493 F.2d 408, *cert. denied* 419 U.S. 845, 95 S.Ct. 79, 42 L.Ed.2d 73.

■ BELL, J.

Medical history was made in 1969 when Dr. Denton A. Cooley, a thoracic surgeon, implanted the first totally mechanical heart in 47–year-old Haskell Karp. This threshold orthotopic cardiac prosthesis[1] also spawned this medical malpractice suit by Mr. Karp's wife, individually and as executrix of Mr. Karp's estate, and his children, for the patient's wrongful death.... [T]he district court in a carefully considered opinion directed a verdict for the defendant-appellees, Dr. Denton A. Cooley and Dr. Domingo S. Liotta. For reasons stated herein, we affirm.

. . .

FACTS

[Haskell Karp had a long and difficult ten-year history of cardiac problems. He suffered several serious heart attacks and had been hospitalized on a number of different occasions. An electronic demand pacemaker was inserted in May, 1968, which resulted in additional hospitalizations, leading Mr. Karp to seek the assistance of Dr. Cooley.]

MRS. KARP'S TESTIMONY

Mrs. Karp's testimony in relevant part was that at the time of his hospital admission March 5, Mr. Karp's physical condition was "as normal as any man in the courtroom" and that he was in no pain or discomfort. She testified Dr. Homer L. Beazley, a cardiologist, examined Mr. Karp on March 6 and on a daily basis after that. She said Dr. Cooley first saw Haskell Karp on Tuesday, March 11. She said Dr. Cooley recommended a heart transplant, but that Mr. Karp rejected this suggestion. She said Dr. Cooley next saw Mr. Karp about a week later when he began to talk about a "wedge procedure" and an aneurysm. She then testified that she next saw Dr. Cooley the day before Mr. Karp's surgery on April 3, 1969, although she admitted that Dr. Cooley had seen Mr. Karp the night before on April 2 when she was not present. Mrs. Karp testified Dr. Cooley came into the hospital room about 6:30 or 7:00 p.m. on April 3. As Mrs. Karp described this meeting:

"When Dr. Cooley came in, he said, 'I have a paper here for you to sign for Mr. Karp's surgery,'[4] and I looked at him, and said, 'Why do you want to

---

1. The mechanical heart implant was actually the second stage of a three stage procedure. On April 4, 1969, Dr. Cooley first attempted a ventriculoplasty, or as sometimes termed a wedge excision, or wedge resection. That proved unsuccessful, and it was then that the mechanical heart was implanted in Mr. Karp, where it sustained Mr. Karp for approximately sixty-four hours. A donor heart was then available, and the transplant operation was performed on the morning of April 7, 1969. Mr. Karp died at 4:10 p.m., April 8, 1969, some thirty-two hours after the transplant surgery.

4. This consent form was prepared by Dr. Cooley and Mr. Henry Reinhard, Assistant Administrator of St. Luke's Episcopal Hospital, on April 3 especially for the Karp operation. While there is a conflict in the testimony between Mrs. Karp, Dr. Cooley, and Mr. Reinhard as to *when* Mr. Karp signed the form, there is no dispute that Mr. Karp signed it, and that both Mr. and Mrs. Karp's signatures were verified consequently by Mr. Reinhard. The consent form reads as follows:

CONSENT TO OPERATION

April 3, 1969

1. I, Haskell Carp, [sic] request and authorize Dr. Denton A. Cooley and such other surgeons as he may designate to perform upon me, in St. Luke's Episcopal Hospital of Houston, Texas, cardiac surgery for ad-

operate,' you know, 'tomorrow after keeping us here so long? Can you tell me about it?'

"And he said, 'Mr. Karp has taken a sudden turn for the worse. His aneurysm is about to burst. If we wait too long, we may not be able to get into his heart to repair anything.'

"He says, 'I still don't know whether we can even wait till tomorrow.'

"I said to him, 'You once told me, Dr. Cooley, that . . . you thought he needed a transplant.' I said, 'Do you still think that's the answer.'

"And Dr. Cooley said to me, 'Mrs. Karp, there is a donor heart that will be available and that we will use if there's that need for it.' . . .

"He says, 'Will you sign this now?' And I looked at my husband, and I guess he was in tears because I was shaking. And Dr. Cooley said to me, 'don't worry about the shock element to your husband because I told him exactly what I told you now last night.'

"So then my husband said, 'Honey, he told me this last night.' He said, 'Go ahead. We'll sign the agreement.'

"And that's what happened. My husband signed it—. . . . Then he gave it to me to sign. And I says, 'I got to read it first.'

"And I started to go down it and I was glancing at the—it was all too bewildering and all of a sudden I came across some sort of a mechanical device, and I said, 'Dr. Cooley, what's this thing here that you have?'

"I said, 'what's mechanical device?'

"And he said, 'well you know, Mrs. Karp, when we operate on a heart we have to take the heart out of the body. So what we do is use what's commonly known as a heart lung machine and we attach the pipes from the machine to the different arteries that they sever to take the heart out. And this here keeps the flow of blood going through the body and the oxygen so that there will not be any damage to the body.'

"So he says the reason that he put that into the consent was because the one that they had in the operating room, I believe he said, worked for a matter of maybe two hours or something and this here one was a new model and it was proven in the laboratory, but he [sic] hasn't been used on a human being yet. But that this here should sustain him if he should die on the table. He says it would sustain him for at least thirty minutes in order to get the donor heart into my husband's body."

vanced cardiac decompensation and myocardial insufficiency as a result of numerous coronary occlusions. The risk of this surgery has been explained to me. In the event cardiac function cannot be restored by excision of destroyed heart muscle and plastic reconstruction of the ventricle and death seems imminent, I authorize Dr. Cooley and his staff to remove my diseased heart and insert a mechanical cardiac substitute. I understand that this mechanical device will not be permanent and ultimately will require replacement by a heart transplant. I realize that this device has been tested in the laboratory but has not been used to sustain a human being and that no assurance of success can be made. I expect the surgeons to exercise every effort to preserve my life through any of these means. No assurance has been made by anyone as to the results that may be obtained.

. . . .

Signature s/Haskell Karp

Haskell Karp.

WITNESSES: s/Mrs. Haskell Karp

Mrs. Haskell Karp (wife)

s/Henry C. Reinhard, Jr.

Henry D. Reinhard, Jr.

... [Mrs. Karp] also testified that Mr. Karp at the time of the April 3 meeting with Dr. Cooley was as normal as when he entered the hospital, that his physical appearance was the same and there was no appearance of pain; and that Mr. Karp was able to walk around the hospital even the morning of the operation. She said both Dr. Beazley and Dr. Cooley had said the wedge excision had a 70 per cent chance of success, and that Dr. Cooley had said that in his own personal experience he had less than a five per cent chance of failure and that it "seemed like it hardly ever failed."

DR. COOLEY'S TESTIMONY

Dr. Cooley testified that he first saw Mr. Karp on or about March 5, 1969 and that he recommended a heart transplant which Mr. Karp rejected, preferring "some alternative procedure." Dr. Cooley said tests then showed Mr. Karp had triple vessel disease where all three coronary arteries were occluded. He said electrocardiograms showed evidence of extensive scarring and damage and that his chest x-rays showed enormous cardiac enlargement. In addition, said Dr. Cooley, he had a pacemaker which was about to fail. Dr. Cooley said he estimated that Karp's chances of dying in the operating room as a result of the wedge procedure were approximately thirty per cent. He testified that as some three weeks passed, Mr. Karp grew increasingly impatient waiting for a donor's availability in the event the wedge excision failed. Dr. Cooley said it was the custom of medical doctors in the community to advise a patient of risks of surgery "within certain boundaries ... but not every contingency can be explained to a layman about the threat and the risk of open heart surgery or the type of device which we are using, many of which are being used for the first time in a patient." About a week before the operation of April 4, 1969, Dr. Cooley said he began to discuss with Mr. Karp the possibility of another alternative "which I did not think was proper when he initially came to the hospital."

"I told him we had no heart donor available, had no prospect of one ... I told him that there was a possibility that we had a device which would sustain his life in the event that he would die on the operating table. We had a device which would sustain his life, hopefully, until we could get a suitable donor. I had told him that I did not know whether it would take a matter of hours or days, weeks, or maybe not at all, but it would sustain his life and give us another possibility of salvaging him through heart transplantation."

Dr. Cooley said he did not recall who was present when these discussions began. Dr. Cooley described his discussion of this device:

"I told him that it was a heart pump similar to the one that we used in open-heart surgery; that it was a reciprocating-type pump with the membrane, in which the pumping element never became in contact with the bloodstream; that it was designed in such a manner that it would not damage the bloodstream or it would cause minimal damage to the bloodstream; that it would be placed in his body to take over the function of the dead heart and to propel blood throughout his body during this interim until we could have a heart transplant.... I told him this device had not been used in human beings; that it had been used in the laboratory; that we had been able to sustain the circulation in calves and that it had not been used in human beings.''

.   .   .

... [Dr. Cooley] stated that [during the operation] there was fibrillation and that he attempted an electrical countershock at least once. He stated that there was a sinus type or nodal rhythm at that point but that the rhythm contraction was too weak to support life due to the fact that there simply was too much scar tissue in the heart.... Mr. Karp's heart was then removed and the mechanical device was inserted. Dr. Cooley said that the mechanical heart functioned very well and Mr. Karp responded to stimulation within 15 or 20 minutes after the incision was closed. His blood pressure was well sustained according to Dr. Cooley and he showed signs of cerebral activity. Dr. Keats said that Mr. Karp was amazingly well following the operation, that the records reflect that he was responding reasonably to commands within 20 minutes postoperatively. Dr. Keats testified that the endotracheal tube was removed about 1:20 a.m., and that he saw Mr. Karp some time the next morning at which time he was responsive and could communicate.

After the mechanical heart had been inserted, Dr. Cooley said he went to Mrs. Karp and told her that the wedge procedure had been unsuccessful; that he had proceeded with the use of the mechanical device and that they were going to try to get a donor. The transplant operation was performed on the morning of April 7, 1969, approximately 64 hours after the mechanical device had been implanted in Mr. Karp. He died the next day, April 8, 1969, some 32 hours after the transplant surgery.

.   .   .

INFORMED CONSENT

Suits charging failure by a physician adequately to disclose the risks and alternatives of proposed treatment are not innovations in American law. They date back a good half-century and in the last decade have increased in number. The courts and commentators have not been in agreement on the substantive requirements or the nature of the proof required, but the Texas requirements are reasonably well-settled and stringent.

.   .   .

The Texas standard against which a physician's disclosure or lack of disclosure is tested is a medical one which must be proved by expert medical evidence of what a reasonable practitioner of the same school of practice and the same or similar locality would have advised a patient under similar circumstances.... As we understand appellants' contention, it is that Mr. Karp was not told about the number of animals tested or the results of those tests; that he was not told there was a chance of permanent injury to his body by the mechanical heart, that complete renal shutdown could result from the use of the prosthesis, that the device was "completely experimental;" and that Dr. Cooley failed to tell Mr. Karp that Dr. Beazley had said Mr. Karp was not a suitable candidate for surgery.... [T]he March 6 notation, made during the course of an initial evaluation, was in

Dr. Beazley's view not a medical opinion but a reservation about the psychological or emotional acceptance of less than a perfect result.

What is missing from the evidence presented is the requisite expert testimony as to *what* risks under these circumstances a physician should disclose.... Dr. Cooley's undisputed testimony is that he began discussing with Mr. Karp the proposed wedge excision and the alternative procedure of a mechanical heart as a stopgap to a transplant about a week before the April 4 operation. He said he next talked with Mr. Karp the evening of April 2. The consent form was prepared on April 3 and although there is a dispute as to *when* it was signed, there is no question it was signed by Mr. Karp. Thus it was against the backdrop of at least two conversations with Dr. Cooley, at which Mrs. Karp was not present, that Mr. Karp was presented and signed the consent document. The consent form is consistent with Dr. Cooley's testimony of what he told Mr. Karp. Although not necessarily conclusive, what Haskell Karp consented to and was told is best evidenced by this document.... It is of considerable import that each step of the three-stage operation, objected to due to an alleged lack of informed consent, was specifically set out in the consent document signed by the patient....

· · ·

The only expert testimony was that Mr. Karp was near death prior to the wedge excision operation. Mrs. Karp says she does not complain of the informed consent for the wedge excision. The only expert testimony was that death was also imminent after the wedge excision. There is no expert evidence that says as a reasonable medical probability the mechanical heart caused Karp's death. The expert testimony at best links the mechanical heart as only one of the "possible" but less likely causes of the secondary cause of death, renal failure.

Finally, there is no proof that Mr. Karp would *not* have consented to the operative procedures had the alleged undisclosed material risks been disclosed.

Appellants failed to produce substantial evidence establishing a medical standard as to what disclosures should have been made to Mr. Karp, any violation of that standard, or causation. Thus, the trial court properly directed a verdict for defendants on the informed consent question.

· · ·

A Texas court bound in traditional malpractice actions to expert medical testimony to determine how a reasonably careful and prudent physician would have acted under the same or similar circumstances ... would not likely vary that evidentiary requirement for an experimentation charge. This conclusion is also suggested by the few reported cases where experimentation has been recognized as a separate basis of liability.[22] The record contains no evidence that Mr. Karp's treatment was other than

---

22. *See* Salgo v. Leland Stanford Univ. Bd. of Trustees, 1957, 154 Cal.App.2d 560, 577, 317 P.2d 170; Fortner v. Koch, 1935, 272 Mich. 273, 261 N.W. 762; Owens v. McCleary, 1926, 313 Mo. 213, 223, 281 S.W. 682, 685; Carpenter v. Blake, 1872, 60 Barb. (N.Y.) 488, *rev'd on other grounds*, 50 N.Y. 696.

therapeutic and we agree that in this context an action for experimentation must be measured by traditional malpractice evidentiary standards. Whether there was informed consent is necessarily linked to the charge of experimentation, and Mr. Karp's consent was expressly to all three stages of the operation actually performed—each an alternative in the event of a preceding failure. As previously discussed, appellants have not shown an absence of Mr. Karp's informed consent. Causation and proximate cause are also requisite to an actionable claim of experimentation. Even if . . . [other testimony] were admitted and did establish a standard and a departure from that standard in using this prosthetic device, substantial evidence . . . on causation and proximate cause simply is not reflected in the record. That alone would warrant the directed verdict on this issue.

NOTES AND QUESTIONS

1. Consider the conclusions of the National Commission for the Protection of Human Subjects of Biomedical Research in its *Belmont Report* 2–4 (1978):

> It is important to distinguish between biomedical and behavioral research, on the one hand, and the practice of accepted therapy on the other, in order to know what activities ought to undergo review for the protection of human subjects of research. The distinction between research and practice is blurred partly because both often occur together (as in research designed to evaluate a therapy) and partly because notable departures from standard practice are often called "experimental" when the terms "experimental" and "research" are not carefully defined.

> For the most part, the term "practice" refers to interventions that are designed solely to enhance the well-being of an individual patient or client and that have a reasonable expectation of success. The purpose of medical or behavioral practice is to provide diagnosis, preventive treatment or therapy to particular individuals.* By contrast, the term "research" designates an activity designed to test a hypothesis, permit conclusions to be drawn, and thereby to develop or contribute to generalizable knowledge (expressed, for example, in theories, principles, and statements of relationships). Research is usually described in a formal protocol that sets forth an objective and a set of procedures designed to reach that objective.

> When a clinician departs in a significant way from standard or accepted practice, the innovation does not, in and of itself, constitute research. The fact that a procedure is "experimental," in the sense of new, untested or different, does not automatically place it in the category of research. Radically new procedures of this description should, however, be made the object of formal

---

* Although practice usually involves interventions designed solely to enhance the well-being of a particular individual, interventions are sometimes applied to one individual for the enhancement of the well-being of another (e.g., blood donation, skin grafts, organ transplants) or an intervention may have the dual purpose of enhancing the well-being of a particular individual, and, at the same time, providing some benefit to others (e.g., vaccination, which protects both the person who is vaccinated and society general-ly). The fact that some forms of practice have elements other than immediate benefit to the individual receiving an intervention, however, should not confuse the general distinction between research and practice. Even when a procedure applied in practice may benefit some other person, it remains an intervention designed to enhance the well-being of a particular individual or groups of individuals; thus, it is practice and need not be viewed as research.

research at an early stage in order to determine whether they are safe and effective. Thus, it is the responsibility of medical practice committees, for example, to insist that a major innovation be incorporated into a formal research project.

Research and practice may be carried on together when research is designed to evaluate the safety and efficacy of a therapy. This need not cause any confusion regarding whether or not the activity requires review; the general rule is that if there is any element of research in an activity, that activity should undergo review for the protection of human subjects.

2. Should a distinction be drawn between innovation in surgery and innovation in pharmacology? Consider the observations of Professor Ruth Macklin, *Ethical Implications of Surgical Experiments*, 70 Am. College of Surgeons Bull. 2, 5 (1985):

It seems true that surgery, compared with other areas of medical practice, subjects fewer innovative procedures to prior review and sustained clinical investigation. An editorial in the *New York Times* following the implantation of the ... artificial heart in William Schroeder stated: "No one would think of letting an experimental drug on the market until it had been adequately tested for safety and efficacy. Unfortunately, no agency exists to regulate novel surgical procedures, doubtless because of an assumption that surgeons can be trusted to regulate themselves." The *Times* is mistaken, since ... [HHS] is the agency that regulates biomedical research of all sorts....

However, if surgeons fail to develop research protocols for their experimental or innovative procedures, then those procedures will not receive the sort of detailed scrutiny that drugs and devices must get before being approved by the FDA. It is incumbent on surgeons working at the frontier of their specialty to develop such research protocols and adhere to the canons of clinical investigation practiced by researchers in other areas of medical science. Only then can surgical experiments and innovative practices meet the tests designed to protect patients from ethically unacceptable innovations. And only then will individual surgeons become less prone to attacks of the kind that have been directed at the individuals who implanted the Phoenix heart, the baboon heart, and maybe even the Jarvik heart.

3. Medical sociologists Renee C. Fox and Judith P. Swazey suggest that therapeutic innovation exists on a continuum, but that rigid distinctions are often drawn for economic or other reasons:

[T]herapeutic innovation, rather than being conceptualized and discussed in dichotomous and static terms as either "experiment" or "therapy," should be viewed as a dynamic process or continuum that usually moves from animal experiments to clinical trials with gravely or terminally ill patients beyond the help of conventional treatments to, if warranted, use with less and less critically ill patients. Single indicators, such as patient morbidity or mortality, the number of times a new drug, device, or procedure has been tried, or the length of time it has been used, do not determine an intervention's location on the spectrum. This is one reason physicians do not have standardized, clear-cut terms to designate the developmental stages of a new therapy and why they often use elaborate, equivocal, emotionally charged language to characterize its clinical status. As the history of organ transplantation shows clearly, this classificatory aspect of the experiment-therapy dilemma is an issue whose import goes far beyond semantic preciseness or academic hairsplitting. Evaluation of the status of a particular procedure is a primary criterion for deciding on whom and under what circumstances it may be justifiably used and—of increasing salience to patients and physicians—whether its costs will be reimbursed by health insurance.

RENEE C. FOX & JUDITH P. SWAZEY, SPARE PARTS—ORGAN REPLACEMENT IN AMERICAN SOCIETY 9 (1992); *see also* Nancy M.P. King, *Experimental Treatment: Oxymoron or Aspiration? Regulating Medical Experimentation*, 25 HASTINGS CENTER REP., July 1995, at 6 (arguing that the label "experimental" is applied to medical technology in three disparate contexts: medical malpractice, reimbursement, and research regulation).

2.   SHOULD WE RELY ON INFORMED CONSENT TO PROTECT SUBJECTS?

Franz J. Ingelfinger, *Informed (But Uneducated) Consent*

287 NEW ENG. J. MED. 465, 465–66 (1972).

The trouble with informed consent is that it is not educated consent. Let us assume that the experimental subject, whether a patient, a volunteer, or otherwise enlisted, is exposed to a completely honest array of factual detail. He is told of the medical uncertainty that exists and that must be resolved by research endeavors, of the time and discomfort involved, and of the tiny percentage of risk of some serious consequences of the test procedure. He is also reassured of his rights and given a formal, quasilegal statement to read. No exculpatory language is used. With his written signature, the subject then caps the transaction, and whether he sees himself as a heroic martyr for the sake of mankind, or as a reluctant guinea pig dragooned for the benefit of science, or whether, perhaps, he is merely bewildered, he obviously has given his "informed consent." Because established routines have been scrupulously observed, the doctor, the lawyer, and the ethicist are content.

But the chances are remote that the subject really understands what he has consented to—in the sense that the responsible medical investigator understands the goals, nature, and hazards of his study. How can the layman comprehend the importance of his perhaps not receiving, as determined by the luck of the draw, the highly touted new treatment that his roommate will get? How can he appreciate the sensation of living for days with a multi-lumen intestinal tube passing through his mouth and pharynx? How can he interpret the information that an intravascular catheter and radiopaque dye injection have a 0.01 per cent probability of leading to a dangerous thrombosis or cardiac arrhythmia? It is moreover quite unlikely that any patient-subject can see himself accurately within the broad context of the situation, to weigh the inconveniences and hazards that he will have to undergo against the improvements that the research project may bring to the management of his disease in general and to his own case in particular. The difficulty that the public has in understanding information that is both medical and stressful is exemplified by [a] report [in the New England Journal Of Medicine, August 31, 1972, page 433]—that only half the families given genetic counseling grasped its impact.

Nor can the information given to the experimental subject be in any sense totally complete. It would be impractical and probably unethical for the investigator to present the nearly endless list of all possible contingencies; in fact, he may not himself be aware of every untoward thing that might happen. Extensive detail, moreover, usually enhances the subject's confusion. Epstein and Lasagna showed that comprehension of medical information given to untutored subjects is inversely correlated with the elaborateness of the material presented.[1] The inconsiderate investigator, indeed, conceivably could exploit his authority and knowledge and extract "informed consent" by overwhelming the candidate-subject with information.

Ideally, the subject should give his consent freely, under no duress whatsoever. The facts are that some element of coercion is instrumental in any investigator-subject transaction. Volunteers for experiments will usually be influenced by hopes of obtaining better grades, earlier parole, more substantial egos, or just mundane cash. These pressures, however, are but fractional shadows of those enclosing the patient-subject. Incapacitated and hospitalized because of illness, frightened by strange and impersonal routines, and fearful for his health and perhaps life, he is far from exercising a free power of choice when the person to whom he anchors all his hopes asks, "Say, you wouldn't mind, would you, if you joined some of the other patients on this floor and helped us to carry out some very important research we are doing?" When "informed consent" is obtained, it is not the student, the destitute bum, or the prisoner to whom, by virtue of his condition, the thumb screws of coercion are most relentlessly applied; it is the most used and useful of all experimental subjects, the patient with disease.

When a man or woman agrees to act as an experimental subject, therefore, his or her consent is marked by neither adequate understanding nor total freedom of choice. The conditions of agreement are a far cry from those visualized as ideal. Jonas would have the subject identify with the investigative endeavor so that he and the researcher would be seeking a common cause: "Ultimately, the appeal for volunteers should seek ... free and generous endorsement, the appropriation of the research purpose into the person's [i.e., the subject's] own scheme of ends."[2] For Ramsey, "informed consent" should represent a "covenantal bond between consenting man and consenting man [that] makes them ... joint adventurers in medical care and progress."[3] Clearly, to achieve motivations and attitudes of this lofty type, an educated and understanding, rather than merely informed, consent is necessary.

Although it is unlikely that the goals of Jonas and of Ramsey will ever be achieved, and that human research subjects will spontaneously volunteer rather than be "conscripted," efforts to promote educated consent are in order. In view of the current emphasis on involving "the community" in such activities as regional planning, operation of clinics, and assignment of

1. Epstein, L.C., and Lasagna, L. "Obtaining informed consent: form or substance." Arch.Intern.Med. 123:682–688, 1969.

2. Jonas, H.: "Philosophical reflections on experimenting with human subjects." Daedalus 98:219–247, Spring 1969.

3. Ramsey, P.: "The ethics of a cottage industry in an age of community and research medicine." N.Engl.J.Med. 284:700–706, 1971.

priorities, the general public and its political leaders are showing an increased awareness and understanding of medical affairs. But the orientation of this public interest in medicine is chiefly socio-economic. Little has been done to give the public a basic understanding of medical research and its requirements not only for the people's money but also for their participation. The public, to be sure, is being subjected to a bombardment of sensation-mongering news stories and books that feature "breakthroughs," or that reveal real or alleged exploitations—horror stories of Nazi-type experimentation on abused human minds and bodies. Muckraking is essential to expose malpractices, but unless accompanied by efforts to promote a broader appreciation of medical research and its methods, it merely compounds the difficulties for both the investigator and the subject when "informed consent" is solicited.

The procedure currently approved in the United States for enlisting human experimental subjects has one great virtue: patient-subjects are put on notice that their management is in part at least an experiment. The deceptions of the past are no longer tolerated. Beyond this accomplishment, however, the process of obtaining "informed consent," with all its regulations and conditions, is no more than elaborate ritual, a device that, when the subject is uneducated and uncomprehending, confers no more than the semblance of propriety on human experimentation. The subject's only real protection, the public as well as the medical profession must recognize, depends on the conscience and compassion of the investigator and his peers.

NOTES AND QUESTIONS

1. What would it mean for a physician-researcher to give a patient-subject "complete" information? Is it realistic to expect a physician-researcher to give a patient-subject information upon which to base an independent decision? Will not the patient-subject generally regard the physician as a source of treatment and guidance, rather than as a source of information, and give great weight to that advice? Although it may be desirable, is it feasible to reduce the influence that a physician-researcher has over a patient? *See* Paul S. Appelbaum et al., *False Hopes and Best Data: Consent to Research and the Therapeutic Misconception*, HASTINGS CENTER REP., Apr. 1987, at 20.

2. Consider the views of Jay Katz:

[T]he rights of research subjects to self-determination cannot be safeguarded until a number of underlying problems affecting the informed consent process in decisive ways have been resolved. The underlying problems are these: (1) The obfuscation of the distinction between therapy and research and the accompanying confusion of patients and subjects; (2) the impact of the ideology of medical professionalism on the conduct of human experimentation; (3) the unclarity about the different tasks of medicine and research; and (4) the impact of the informed consent process on the mind-set of physician-investigators and the principles that govern the invitation to participation in research.

Jay Katz, *Human Experimentation and Human Rights*, 38 ST. LOUIS L.J. 7, 11–12 (1993). Studies have shown that most patients believe that enrollment in a clinical trial will be medically beneficial to them, even though often it is not. *See e.g.* Christopher Daugherty et al., *Perceptions of Cancer Patients and Their Physicians Involved in Phase I Trials*, 13 J. CLINICAL ONCOLOGY 1062, 1064 (1995) (finding that almost ninety percent of patients with advanced cancer taking part in Phase One clinical trials think they will receive medical benefit from participating, despite having been told otherwise). Is this phenomenon a problem of misinformation, or does it simply indicate that terminally ill patients are providing themselves with comfort through hope?

3. Paying volunteers to participate in clinical trials has often been cited as an ethically questionable practice, due to the concern that money creates an undue inducement to participate in high risk experiments. The pharmaceutical company Eli Lilly was criticized for paying homeless alcoholics to participate in their Phase I clinical trials, on the basis the subjects' desperation and poverty made it impossible for them to give bona fide informed consent to the study. *See* Raymond De Vries, *Businesses Are Buying the Ethics They Want*, WASH. POST, February 8, 2004, at B02. Should the government ban companies from recruiting the homeless? Is it paternalistic to think that homelessness obscures an individual's judgment of his or her best interests? A recent study examined the issues of economic coercion and risk assessment in clinical trial volunteers and determined that increased payment levels did not create undue inducement. The results indicated that increased payment did not alter participants' perception of risk, and that payment actually more strongly influenced willingness to participate among wealthier people. *See* Scott D. Halpern et al., *Empirical Assessment of Whether Moderate Payments Are Undue or Unjust Inducements for Participation in Clinical Trials*, 164 ARCHIVES OF INTERNAL MEDICINE 801 (2004).

4. Several recent events have prompted increased scrutiny of informed consent procedures and design and reporting requirements in clinical trials. In 1993, a National Institutes of Health study of an experimental hepatitis drug, fialuridine, resulted in the death of five of the study's 15 subjects. Two survivors required liver transplants. An FDA investigation found that the drug's adverse effects were not reported or analyzed so as to warn of toxicity. The FDA also found several violations of scientific procedures. Subsequent investigations, conducted by the NIH and the Institute of Medicine, however, found no significant discrepancies in the design or conduct of the study. *See* Charles Marwick, *NIH Panel Report of "No Flaws" in FIAU Trials at Variance with FDA Report*, 272 JAMA 9 (1994). The incident prompted the FDA to announce proposed changes in reporting requirements for adverse events associated with prescription drugs and biological products. *See* 59 Fed.Reg. 54046 (Oct. 27, 1994).

In 1999, the highly publicized death of 18–year old Jesse Gelsinger in a gene-therapy trial at the University of Pennsylvania heightened concern that informed consent procedures were not adequately protecting research subjects. The Department of Health and Human Services commissioned a report on the incident from the Institute of Medicine, which recommended that federal regulators should strengthen their oversight of both public and private clinical trials. The report, *Responsible Research: A Systems Approach to Protecting Research Participants* (Daniel D. Federman et al., eds., 2003), emphasized that consent forms should focus more on communicating risks of the trial, not on shielding institutions or researchers from potential liability. 123–126. It also advised that informed consent should be considered an ongoing process, in which research subjects and investigators are in constant discussion. *Id.* at 120.

5. In 1996, the FDA promulgated regulations that provide an exception to the informed consent requirements for emergency research. In order to qualify for this exception, the proposed research must meet several criteria. The human subjects must be in a life-threatening situation for which available treatments are unproven or unsatisfactory, and obtaining informed consent is not feasible because (i) their medical condition prevents subjects from giving informed consent; (ii) the investigational emergency intervention must be administered before consent from the subjects' legally authorized representatives is feasible; and (iii) there is no reasonable way to identify prospectively the individuals likely to become eligible for participation in the clinical investigation. Participation in the research must also offer the prospect of direct benefit to the subjects in light of known risks and benefits of both the standard and the experimental therapy. *See* 21 C.F.R. § 50.24 (2003).

Some critics of the FDA regulation on emergency research argue that it is a glaring relaxation of fundamental informed consent standards, and a step back toward the atrocities of Nuremberg and Tuskegee. They maintain that consent is such a fundamental principle that consent standards should be higher in research than in standard care, and that patients would want to know if they were involved in clinical trials. *See* Norman Fost, *Waived Consent for Emergency Research*, 24 AM. J.L. & MED. 163 (1998).

The first experiment conducted under the FDA emergency research regulation, which became effective on November 1, 1996, was halted in the summer of 1997 because 24 out of 52 trauma patients who received a blood substitute called HemAssist died, two more than expected considering their head injuries, and far more than the death rate of those who received routine treatment. *See* Jeremy Mainer, *Testing Without Asking: The Most Controversial Aspect About Medical Research Trials Involving a Blood Substitute Was Not the Higher than Expected Death Rate but the Fact that Patients Never Gave their Consent*, CHI. TRIB., January 17, 1999, at C1. Approximately 15 similar experiments have been approved by the FDA since the emergency exception regulation was created in 1996. The most recent study began in December 2003, which tested PolyHeme, another synthetic blood substitute, on adults who were in shock due to blood loss. The study hopes to involve 720 patients before completion, and the preliminary results are promising—death rates appear to have been reduced by more than half. *See* Rob Stein, *An Experiment in Saving Lives; Emergency Patients Unwittingly Get Artificial Blood*, WASH. POST, Mar 23, 2004, at A01.

3.   IRBs: ARE THEY WORKING?

Testimony of Ezekiel J. Emanuel M.D., Ph.D., Chief, Center for Clinical Bioethics, National Institutes of Health, Hearing Before the President's Council on Bioethics

Institutional Review Boards (IRBs): President's Council on Bioethics, Sixth Meeting, Session 2. September 12, 2002.

DR. EMANUEL: I think it's fair to say that everyone seems dissatisfied with the current system of protecting human research participants. Many of our researchers find the system onerous and more of a hurdle to get over than something that is value-added.

IRB members who serve on the oversight bodies ... find the regulations quite opaque, feel in a bind between federal oversight and what they're supposed to do for their institution. The pharmaceutical and biotechnology industry finds the process very time-consuming, very inefficient, and very resistant to innovative and novel approaches in research.

Regulators feel frustrated. They get criticized by the federal government and the public for not doing enough. They get criticized by institutions for being too intrusive.

And the public is afraid, uncertain. They believe greatly in biomedical research, but recent polls have certainly shown them to be much more concerned than they ever were. I think the cover of Time magazine over the summer that showed a human subject in a guinea pig cage attests to this concern.

I don't think it is misplaced. Since 1999, the federal government oversight body, OHRP—that is the Office for Human Research Protection—has stopped or suspended research at 13 major research institutions. This includes two of the top ten medical centers in this country, and a third of the top ten medical centers in this country had a major scandal involving the death of a patient, but was not actually closed.

. . .

I think the problems can be divided into . . . three domains: structural . . . , the IRB review process itself, and assessing the performance of both clinical research and that process.

. . .

. . . . The first structural problem is that . . . not all research, biomedical research, in this country is actually covered by the federal regulations. Research that's not funded by the NIH, research that's not seeking FDA approval . . . isn't covered by oversight. This covers some very important research.

. . .

Second, . . . there's no mechanism . . . for addressing major ethical issues in research or for assessing the social value of research. There was a national commission; there was a President's commission; there was NBAC; there is this Council; there is another group called NHRPAC, which has just been disbanded—for occasionally looking at major ethical issues in research, but these are stop-and-start events. They're not systematically organized.

. . .

The third problem: We rely on local institutional-based IRBs. When this was developed 25 years ago, that might have been reasonable when a lot of the research happened at our major academic settings like Johns Hopkins, the NIH, Harvard, UCSF, but in fact a lot of research, or maybe even today a majority of research, has now filtered out into private practices, clinics, and a lot of other organizations. There is a mismatch, many people feel, between the fact that we have institution-based IRBs, but a lot of the research isn't even occurring anymore at institutions.

. . .

Many IRBs, certainly before these recent scandals, were resource-starved. . . . [T]he scandals have gotten the attention of many institutions, especially if you can close down Johns Hopkins, and Johns Hopkins has announced or indicated that they have doubled the amount of money they devote to their IRB. But I think in general there's still a ... lack of resources ..., and, importantly, IRBs have to compete with all the other demands for medical institutions that are under increasing price pressure.

Fifth, there's a lack of attention to institutional conflicts of interest. One of the problems of having your IRB be institution-bound is that the IRB is actually regulating the research within the institution that is paying the IRB. That is an inherent conflict of interest....

Sixth, there's a very poorly defined mechanism for investigator conflict-of-interest rules and the IRB's role in enforcing those rules. An investigator in this country can be subject to as many as five different conflict-of-interest rules: one from the institution where they work; one from the NIH; one from the FDA; one maybe from their professional society, and if they work at a state institution, there's frequently state conflict-of-interest rules.

They all differ. It is very unclear how to follow them, and it is very unclear how that is matched with submitting a protocol....

Seven, there has been inadequate education of clinical investigators and IRB members. The NIH has recently mandated that for its grantees there be education and training, although there's no curricula requirement; no one knows what the content is supposed to do, and, importantly, therefore, no one knows what the sort of core material they're supposed to understand and any way of assessing whether it works or not....

Eight, the system is replete with repetitive reviews. So, for example, if I do a research study, which I once did at Harvard, involving five other cities and hospitals in all those other cities, and ultimately there were 40 different hospitals, I actually had to get that protocol reviewed at 42 different places to do the research, all of them looking at the exact same thing over and over again. Sometimes this process can take a year and involve a lot of people's attention and energy....

Those are structural problems. Now I want to shift to the IRB process problems....

Getting your research approved is a time-consuming process. It has become longer and longer.... [M]ost investigators are increasingly frustrated. Six months from submission to approval is not unusual. You often have to go through scientific review, which can take several months. Then the IRB frequently meets only monthly, and if you don't get on the schedule, the IRB frequently has corrections or modifications they want made. You then have to go back in front of the IRB. It is a very lengthy process.

Ten, there's poor quality control of the IRB reviews. One of the things we learned from the Johns Hopkins episode is that the investigator submitted information about the drug being used, but it wasn't complete or comprehensive information. The IRB relied on that information, did not proactively investigate further. This happens frequently.

. . .

Eleven, there's is excessive focus on the informed consent process at IRBs and excessive focus within that just on the document and what is, I think, derisively but not inaccurately called "wordsmithing" of the document. Now some of that wordsmithing is important to make sure that the language and the level of comprehensibility is correct ... but a large part of it is just altering words for preferences without any real focus on its importance.

. . .

Twelve, there's substantial deficiency on how IRBs monitor research and conduct ... continuing or annual reviews. It's frequently said ... that IRBs see the research protocol at the start, and then the ball rolls down the hill. They have no idea whether the research is actually being implemented as stated, and continuing review, the annual review, is a very perfunctory thing, done frequently in just a handful of minutes for very complicated studies. This is a very, very serious problem.

I think one of the most serious problems ... is we have a very inefficient and ineffective adverse event reporting system. Adverse events are those problems that arise in the course of a trial, people having reactions to drugs or complications that need to be reported.

It is now required that every IRB [be] informed. The FDA has a very strict timeline, a strict rating criteria. The NIH is a much more loose, very undefined system. More importantly, if you have a large trial with lots of centers, you have to send the same information to all the IRBs and they have to make a decision, each individually, what to do, frequently without knowing how many people have been enrolled, are these three cases a large number of cases, a small number of cases, how serious. It is a very time-consuming process, but doesn't do a lot to protect the people on research studies.

The last two problems I want to talk about ... are what I call performance assessment problems....

We have almost no data about IRB function and how well they do their function, and whether, in fact, they actually protect patients. We don't know a lot about what goes on, where they spend their time. Is there a relationship between bad continuing review and harm to patients?

Fifteen, probably more serious is no one in this country, not the Director of the NIH, no one at Pharma or at Bio, and not the commissioner of the FDA, can tell you how many research trials are going on today in the United States, how many people are enrolled in research trials, how many people experience serious toxicities, and, indeed, how many people die on research trials. We don't record that information anywhere.

NOTES AND QUESTIONS

1. ClinicalTrials.gov is a large searchable database that was developed by the FDA and the NIH, through the National Library of Medicine, which became operational in 2000. The database provides information on studies of drugs for serious or life-threatening conditions, as required by section 113 of the FDA Modernization Act of 1997. Pub. L. No. 105–115 § 113, 111 Stat. 2310 (codified as amended at 42 U.S.C.

§ 282 (1997)). The NIH and other federal agencies, universities, and other organizations sponsor most of the studies listed, yet the database includes only a small percentage of all clinical trials, and many studies that should be registered are not. The FDA Modernization Act did not provide an enforcement mechanism, and as a result, many industry-sponsored trials are not registered. *See* Robert Steinbrook, *Public Registration of Clinical Trials*, 351 NEW ENG. J. MED. 315 (2004).

2.   There have been a number of recent requests for the creation of a database that reports all ongoing clinical trials and their results. In June 2004, the AMA recommended that the Department of Health and Human Services (DHHS) "establish a comprehensive registry for all clinical trials conducted in the United States; every clinical trial should have a unique identifier; and all results from registered clinical trials should be made publicly available through either publication or an electronic data-repository." Council on Scientific Affairs, American Medical Association, *Featured CSA Report: Influence of Funding Source on Outcome, Validity, and Reliability of Pharmaceutical Research* (A–04), June 2004, *available at* http://www.ama-assn.org/ama/pub/article/print/2036–8608.html. The AMA also recommended that "Institutional Review Boards consider registration of clinical trials to an existing registry as condition of approval." *Id.* Dr. Elias A. Zerhouni, director of the NIH stated recently that there was a "very high" likelihood the government would soon require the nation's drug companies to publicly report results from all research experiments, and that drug makers would probably agree to participate if such a database were created. *See* Raja Mishra, *NIH Backs Disclosure of All Drug Research*, BOSTON GLOBE, June 25, 2004, at D1. On June 30, 2004, Pharmaceutical Research and Manufacturers of America (PhRMA), the leading industry trade group, released an updated version of its principles for the conduct of clinical trials and communication of the results. Although PhRMA did not comment directly on the AMA recommendations, the updated principles provide that "There will be timely communication of meaningful study results, regardless of the outcome of the study. The results must be reported in an objective, accurate and complete manner, with a discussion of the limitations of the study. Study sponsors will not suppress or veto publications." *See* Pharmaceutical Research and Manufacturers of America, *Updated Principles for Conduct of Clinical Trials and Communication of Clinical Trial Results*, June 30, 2004, *available at* http://www.phrma.org/mediaroom/press/releases/30.06.2004.427.cfm.

Robert Steinbrook, *Protecting Research Subjects—The Crisis at Johns Hopkins*

346 NEW ENG. J. MED. 716 (2002).

Ellen Roche, a 24–year-old technician at the Johns Hopkins Asthma and Allergy Center and a healthy volunteer in a study of asthma funded by the National Institutes of Health, died on June 2, 2001. Prompted by Roche's death, the federal Office for Human Research Protections reviewed the system at the Johns Hopkins Medical Institutions for protecting research subjects and found widespread deficiencies.

On July 19, 2001, the office suspended all federally supported research projects at Johns Hopkins and several affiliated institutions—not because of Roche's death but because of the additional problems that had been identified. Johns Hopkins quickly took corrective action, and the suspension was lifted.[2] Nonetheless, the suspension was "a gigantic shock" to an

---

2.   Carome M. Human subjects protections under Multiple Project Assurance (MPA) M–1011. Letter to Johns Hopkins. Rockville, Md.: Office for Human Research

institution that "has always prided itself on excellence in care and excellence in research," according to Dr. Edward D. Miller, dean of the Johns Hopkins University School of Medicine.

Along with the 1999 death of 18–year-old Jesse Gelsinger in a gene-transfer trial at the University of Pennsylvania and the suspension of federally supported research at other prominent institutions, the shutdown at Johns Hopkins has focused attention on the safety of medical research, particularly when the subjects are healthy volunteers or are employed at the institution where the research takes place. The shutdown has also spurred efforts to improve the effectiveness of the various groups that have a role in protecting research subjects, including investigators, institutional review boards (IRBs), sponsors, and the institutions where the research is conducted. In this report, I examine the crisis at Johns Hopkins and the ongoing response.

BACKGROUND

Federally supported research at an institution is suspended only "when there are systemic problems and when not doing so poses an immediate threat to the potential well-being of the research subject," according to Dr. Greg Koski, director of the Office for Human Research Protections. In 2001, about 50,000 persons participated as research subjects in studies at Johns Hopkins. At the time of the shutdown, there were about 2500 active protocols. Between fiscal years 1995 and 2000, the total value of the research and training grants that the Johns Hopkins University School of Medicine received from the National Institutes of Health increased from $185 million to $305 million; the medical school is consistently at or near the top in rankings of institutions according to total federal research support.[3]

When people are enrolled in a study, there is an inherent trade-off between the potential importance of the information that may be gained and the potential risk to the subject. "At a certain point some patient is going to die in clinical trials," Miller said. "There is no question about it." The challenge is to do everything possible to ensure the safety of research subjects and to make the risk as small as possible. The alternative, according to Miller, "is not to do any clinical investigation, the status quo, and still have children on ventilators after polio."

Research involving healthy people is a particular focus of concern because it often has no direct therapeutic potential. Many argue that such research requires a higher standard for minimizing risks than research involving people who are sick and who may die from their underlying disease. "Research on normal subjects and research on people who are motivated by sickness are very different issues," said Karen H. Rothenberg, dean of the University of Maryland School of Law.

Protections, Department of Health and Human Services, July 22, 2001.

   3. NIH support to U.S. medical schools, FY's 1970–2000: Johns Hopkins University School of Medicine. Bethesda, Md.: National Institutes of Health, March 14, 2001. Accessed February 7, 2002, at http://silk.nih.gov/pub lic/cbz2zoz.@www.med.rank.dsncc.)

In large research institutions, employees often participate in studies. The reason for their participation may be an altruistic desire to help the sick, the opportunity to make extra money and get time off from work, or even subtle or explicit coercion. Like other institutions, Johns Hopkins has rules against directly soliciting staff members for research or recruiting employees who report to a researcher or who work in the same group. Many staff members participated in studies at the Asthma and Allergy Center, where Roche worked, and signs were posted soliciting volunteers. Roche was listed in a registry of normal volunteers and had been in a number of previous studies.

THE ASTHMA STUDY

Asthma is a potentially fatal disease. Its prevalence has increased in recent years, particularly in urban areas. The purpose of the study for which Roche volunteered, which was entitled "Mechanisms of Deep Inspiration–Induced Airway Relaxation," was to gain a better understanding of the pathophysiology of asthma. . . .

Hexamethonium was chosen because it blocks neurotransmission by nonadrenergic, noncholinergic nerves, which were thought to be the nerves that were involved. The substance was once used to treat hypertension but was removed from the U.S. market in 1972 after the Food and Drug Administration (FDA) found that it was ineffective. The hexamethonium bromide used in the study was obtained from a chemical company and was labeled, "For laboratory use only, not for drug, household, or other uses." It was prepared for administration in a laboratory at the Asthma and Allergy Center at Johns Hopkins.

THE DEATH OF ELLEN ROCHE

The events leading to and following Roche's death in June 2001 are summarized in Table 2. If Roche had completed the study, she would have received up to $365—$25 for each of the first-phase visits and $60 for each of the second-phase visits.[6]

In the consent form, hexamethonium was described as "a medication that has been used during surgery, as a part of anesthesia; this is capable of stopping some nerves in your airways from functioning for a short period." The section on risks stated that hexamethonium "may reduce your blood pressure and may make you feel dizzy especially when you stand up." Pulmonary or other potential toxic effects were not mentioned. The consent document was later criticized as having "failed to indicate that inhaled hexamethonium was experimental and not approved by the FDA" and because it referred to hexamethonium as a "medication."[1]

Roche received hexamethonium on May 4; she was the third subject who received it. Mild shortness of breath and a cough had developed in the

6. Report of internal investigation into the death of a volunteer research subject. Johns Hopkins Medicine, July 16, 2001. (Accessed February 7, 2002, at http://www.hopkinsmedicine.org/press/2001/july/report_of_internal_investigation.htm.)

1. McNeilly PJ, Carome M. Human subjects protections under Multiple Project Assurance (MPA) M–1011. Letter to Johns Hopkins. Rockville, Md.: Office for Human Research Protections, Department of Health and Human Services, July 19, 2001.

first subject, resolving over a period of about eight days. The second subject, who received hexamethonium while the first subject still had symptoms, did not report any symptoms.

The day after Roche inhaled about 1 g of hexamethonium, a cough developed. She was hospitalized on May 9 and died on June 2. An autopsy showed diffuse alveolar damage but established no specific etiologic diagnosis. An internal review committee concluded that although the cause will never be certain, "the inhaled hexamethonium phase of the experiment was either solely responsible for [her] illness or played an important contributory role."

Dr. Alkis Togias, who directed the study, did not report the symptoms in the first subject to the IRB until Roche was hospitalized. The same day, he said he learned through an additional literature search that hexamethonium can have pulmonary toxic effects. Togias told the internal review committee that the adverse event in the first subject "was not an 'unexpected and serious adverse event,' because it was selflimited and required no treatment and therefore did not require immediate reporting." According to the committee's report, he thought the symptoms were related to an upper respiratory tract infection and did not seriously consider the possibility of hexamethonium toxicity until later.

THE INTERNAL INVESTIGATION

Roche's death led to four separate reviews of clinical research at Johns Hopkins. These were conducted by internal and external review committees convened by the university, by the FDA, and by the Office for Human Research Protections. After Roche died, Johns Hopkins temporarily suspended all studies involving healthy volunteers. The internal review committee, which "had full access to all the information" was established "to give us a very frank look at all aspects of the issues involved," said Miller.

The internal review committee found that the "study had solid scientific rationale and was well designed" and that the use of hexamethonium "was scientifically sound." Nonetheless, it criticized the IRB for approving the study without requiring "more safety evidence for a non-FDA approved drug no longer in clinical use, and administered by a non-standard route." Togias was criticized for not reporting the symptoms in the first subject promptly, not delaying the exposure of the next subject to hexamethonium until the symptoms in the first subject had resolved, and not searching "more comprehensively" for previous reports that hexamethonium has pulmonary toxicity. "Our internal report was very critical of the fact that when patient number one had a cough, we did not take a variety of other steps that we should have," Miller said. "It was critical that we didn't rethink the protocol and look at every part of it again."

.   .   .

A particularly contentious issue has been whether the IRB, as part of its efforts to obtain additional safety data, should have asked Togias to obtain a written opinion from the FDA on the need for an investigational new drug (IND) application for the use of inhaled hexamethonium. Such an application might have led to a more intensive review of hexamethonium, as well as the discovery of more information about its potential toxicity. The report of the internal review committee stated that the requirements were unclear. The committee acknowledged that the FDA had not responded in a timely fashion to a query from other investigators at Johns Hopkins about another substance. It concluded, however, that the IRB should have asked Togias "to obtain a written opinion from the FDA about the need for an IND [application] for inhaled hexamethonium for safety reasons."

THE FDA REVIEW

On June 28, about a month after Roche died, the FDA criticized Togias for failing "to submit an IND [application] prior to conducting [the] clinical investigation" with hexamethonium and for failing to inform potential subjects that "inhalation administration of hexamethonium was an experimental use of the drug."[8] In an interview, Dr. David Lepay, senior adviser for clinical science at the FDA, said, "They did not specifically ask [the] FDA about this study or this compound." Lepay acknowledged, however, that the FDA had to do a better job of responding to queries and providing investigators with clear information about when IND applications are required. We need a "very tight and coordinated system to answer [these sorts of] queries properly and consistently," he said.

THE SUSPENSION OF FEDERALLY SUPPORTED RESEARCH

On July 16, five staff members from the Office for Human Research Protections, three outside consultants, and a representative from the FDA began an intensive on-site evaluation of the death of Ellen Roche and the system of protection for research subjects at Johns Hopkins. On July 19, in a letter that was hand delivered to Miller, the office detailed its conclusion that there was widespread lack of compliance with federal regulations and announced the suspension of "all Federally supported research projects at the covered institutions."

The strongest criticism was the office's conclusion that the medical school's two IRBs failed to review new protocols properly and to provide a "substantive and meaningful" review of ongoing projects. "The minutes and audiotapes of IRB meetings, and our discussions with IRB members and administrators, indicate that no review takes place at convened meetings for most protocols undergoing initial review. Most protocols are neither individually presented nor discussed at a convened meeting of any IRB."

The office criticized the minutes of the IRBs for often failing "to document the basis for requiring changes in research" or discussion of "unresolved concerns following review by the IRB subcommittee." It noted that minutes "do not yet exist for 18 of the last 21 meetings dating back to October 2000." In a subsequent letter, the office said that "not preparing minutes for nearly all meetings ... for over 9 months is generally considered an unacceptable practice."

8. Shaffer JD. FDA form 483 inspectional observations. Baltimore: Food and Drug Administration, June 28, 2001. (FEI no. 3003350724.) (Accessed February 7, 2002, at http://www.fda.gov/ora/frequent/483s/johnhopkins483.html.)

On July 21, Johns Hopkins submitted a corrective plan.[11] The Office for Human Research Protections accepted it on July 22—subject to restrictions, conditions, and ongoing monitoring—and the suspension was lifted. University officials agreed to make many changes, including re-reviewing about 2600 protocols using procedures consistent with federal regulations. The net effect was that whereas some studies could continue, others remained suspended pending a re-review and approval.

The Office for Human Research Protections was particularly concerned that protocols had been extensively reviewed by subcommittees of the IRBs, but not by the full committees, a procedure that university officials defended. An IRB should have members with a broad range of expertise, including members whose primary interests are in nonscientific areas; thus, federal officials viewed the larger group as the key review body. The office noted that "the site visit team did not find the use of executive subcommittees to be objectionable in and of itself" but "unanimously found that the executive subcommittee review process, which does not represent substantive and meaningful IRB review, was used to preempt review by the IRB at convened meetings for most research projects."

. . .

JOHNS HOPKINS'S RESPONSE

Johns Hopkins initially took a combative stance toward the Office for Human Research Protections and vigorously defended its practices. "We find it difficult to understand why a relatively new agency would take these draconian measures in an institution that has cared for thousands of people in clinical trials," Miller said in a statement that was broadcast on public television in July. "We have done clinical trials for over a hundred years here at Hopkins. We have had one death in all of these years in a human, healthy volunteer."[12]

Within weeks, however, officials at the medical center were emphasizing collaboration, not confrontation,[13] and were talking about the need for a "real culture change" within the institution, according to Miller. This change is required to reject the view that "compliance inhibits creativity" and that regulations to protect research subjects "are just rules that get in our way." The specific changes included more resources; new procedures; more training for investigators and for IRB members, chairs, and staff; and the appointment of a vice dean for clinical investigation to oversee the process.

Spending on IRB personnel and activities has increased from about $1 million to about $2 million per year, according to Miller. The number of

11. Miller ED, Dang CV, Schaffer GF Human subjects protections under Multiple Project Assurance (MPA) M–1011. Letter to Michael A. Carome, Office for Human Research Protections. Baltimore: Johns Hopkins Medicine, July 21, 2001. (Accessed February 7, 2002, at http://www.hopkinsmedicine.org/press/2001/july/actionplanletter.htm.)

12. Online NewsHour: research halt. NewsHour with Jim Lehrer. July 20, 2001 (transcript). (Accessed February 7, 2002, at http://www.pbs.org/ newshour/bb/health/july-dec01/hopkins_7–20.html.)

13. Bor J. Hopkins admits flaws, adjusts to new rules; med school swallows bitter pill of criticism. Baltimore Sun. September 27, 2001:1A.

review boards has increased to six: two at Bayview and four at the medical center's main campus. An independent board, the Western Institutional Review Board of Olympia, Washington, has also been retained to review selected new protocols, particularly multicenter studies of pharmaceuticals. The university is strengthening and standardizing its procedures for literature reviews and for the reporting of adverse events to the review boards. It now requires that investigators obtain a written response from the FDA with regard to the use of an unapproved substance in clinical research. The research pharmacy at Johns Hopkins has greater involvement in preparing such substances for clinical use and in quality control. In an addendum to its report, the external review committee said it was "very pleased and gratified" by these initiatives.

An unsettled issue is the use of employees and students as healthy volunteers in research. Although he acknowledged the criticisms of the external review committee, Miller pointed out, "People work at these institutions oftentimes not just as a job, but because they really want to be involved and they want to contribute [to research]." The university has established a committee chaired by Ruth Faden, executive director of the Johns Hopkins Bioethics Institute, to make recommendations.

. . .

THE FUTURE

The protection of research subjects is a shared responsibility of many individual people and groups. The safety of subjects is particularly dependent on the investigators who conduct the study and on their prompt recognition of potential adverse events. Investigators, however, conduct clinical research as part of a broader framework. Johns Hopkins has now committed itself "to do the best job we can and to be responsive," said Dr. Michael J. Klag, the new vice dean for clinical investigation.

Johns Hopkins continues to be monitored by the Office for Human Research Protections. "They indicated they have work to do," said Koski, the director of the office. "They seem to be making a very concerted and diligent effort. They have stated their goal they want to be a leader and model in the area [of protecting research subjects]. I think that is exactly where they should be."

Table 2. Events Leading Up to and Following the Death of Ellen Roche.	
Date	Event
September 18, 2001	The Institutional Review Board (IRB) at the Johns Hopkins Bayview Medical Center approves a study, "Mechanisms of Deep Inspiration–Induced Airway Relaxation." The study is part of the research plan funded by a grant from the National Institutes of Health, "Lung Inflation in Airways Hyper–Responsiveness."
April 16, 2001	Ellen Roche, a 24–year old healthy volunteer and a technician at the Johns Hopkins Asthma and Allergy Center, provides consent to participate in the study and begins the protocol.
April 23, 2001	Subject 1 [another healthy volunteer] receives about 1 g of hexamethonium by inhalation. The baseline values for forced expiratory volume in one second (FEV_1) and

Date	Event
	forced vital capacity (FVC) are 2.68 and 3.23, respectively.
April 25, 2001	Subject 1 reports mild shortness of breath and a nonproductive cough. The values for FEV_1 and FVC are reduced to 2.33 and 2.74, respectively.
May 3, 2001	Subject 1 reports complete resolution of symptoms. The values for FEV_1 and FVC are 2.41 and 2.91, respectively—somewhat reduced, as compared with the values on April 23 but similar to those obtained when the subject entered the study.
May 4, 2001	Roche (Subject 3 in the study) receives about 1 g of hexamethonium by inhalation.
May 5, 2001	A dry cough develops in Roche.
May 9, 2001	Roche is hospitalized at Bayview Medical Center with a fever, hypoxemia, and abnormalities on a chest film. The IRB is notified of adverse events in Subject 1 and Roche; the study is placed on hold.
May 12, 2001	Progressive dyspnea develops in Roche, and she is transferred to the intensive care unit.
June 2, 2001	Roche dies as a result of progressive hypotension and multiorgan failure.
July 16, 2001	An internal review committee at Johns Hopkins reports that Roche's death "was most likely the result of participation in the hexamethonium phase of the experiment."
October 11, 2001	Johns Hopkins announces a financial settlement with the Roche family.

NOTES AND QUESTIONS

1. Johns Hopkins quickly reached a settlement of an undisclosed amount with the family of Ellen Roche. It also plans to erect a memorial in her name. *See Family of Fatality in Study Settles with Johns Hopkins*, N.Y. TIMES, Oct. 12, 2001, at A20. Complete reports and statements by Johns Hopkins on the death of Ellen Roche are available on the Johns Hopkins website at http://www.hopkinsmedicine.org/ researchvolunteerdeath.html.

2. The deaths of Ellen Roche and Jesse Gelsinger focused the public's attention on the inadequacies of IRBs and human subjects protections in general. The state of Maryland amended its laws on humans research to allow for greater transparency of the IRB process and stricter controls on privately funded research. *See* MD. CODE ANN., HEALTH–GENERAL § 13–2001 (2004). On the federal level, a Senate hearing in April 2002 examined the current safeguards and called for legislation that will increase protection of research subjects while still facilitating critical medical research. *See* Protecting Human Subjects in Research: Are Current Safeguards Enough?: *Hearing before the Subcommittee on Public Health of the Committee on Health, Education, Labor, and Pensions*, United States Senate, 107th Cong. (2002). Two similar bills were introduced in the House and the Senate that called for increased federal oversight of research, modification of IRB functions, promulgation of rules regarding financial conflicts of interest, the ability to seek injunctive relief for research that has been deemed harmful, and substantial fines for violation of research regulations. *See* S. 3060, 107th Cong. (2002), H.R. 4697, 107th Cong. (2002). Do you think that these measures will be effective in protecting human subjects? For a comprehensive proposal for reforming the entire IRB system, *see* Ann Wood, et al., *The Crisis in Human Participants Research: Identifying the Problems and Proposing Solutions*, (September 2002) (unpublished paper presented to the President's Council on Bioethics, *available at* http://www.bioethics.gov/background/emanuelpaper.html).

3. Should volunteers who have been injured as a result of the research be given financial compensation? Although federal regulations require that consent forms explain whether medical care or compensation will be provided [45 C.F.R. § 46.116 (2001)], there is currently no requirement that researchers provide such care or compensation. If the research institution does not offer these services, then the only remaining option for an injured participant is to pursue compensation through legal action. Many national commissions have examined these issues over the past three decades and have recommended the establishment of a national compensation program. *See* Tuskegee Syphilis Study Ad Hoc Advisory Panel 1973; President's Commission for the Study of Ethical Problems in Medicine and Biomedical and Behavioral Research, *Compensating for Research Injuries: The Ethical and Legal Implications of Programs to Redress Injured Subjects*, (1982); Advisory Committee on Human Radiation Experiments, Final Report, (1995); National Bioethics Advisory Commission, *Ethical and Policy Issues In Research Involving Human Participants*, (2001). For a summary of the issues and existing limited compensation programs *see* Larry D. Scott, *Research-Related Injury: Problems and Solutions*, 31 J.L. MED. & ETHICS 419 (2003).

E.   PROTECTING THE MOST VULNERABLE SUBJECTS

Hans Jonas, *Philosophical Reflections on Experimenting With Human Subjects*

EXPERIMENTATION WITH HUMAN SUBJECTS 18–21, 24–26 (1970).

"Identification" as the Principle of Recruitment in General

.... [O]ne should look for ... subjects where a maximum of identification, understanding, and spontaneity can be expected—that is, among the most highly motivated, the most highly educated, and the least "captive" members of the community. From this naturally scarce resource, a descending order of permissibility leads to greater abundance and ease of supply, whose use should become proportionately more hesitant as the exculpating criteria are relaxed. An inversion of normal "market" behavior is demanded here—namely, to accept the lowest quotation last (and excused only by the greatest pressure of need); to pay the highest price first.

The ruling principle in our considerations is that the "wrong" of reification can only be made "right" by such *authentic identification with the cause* that it is the subject's as well as the researcher's cause—whereby his role in its service is not just permitted by him, but *willed*. That sovereign will of his which embraces the end as his own restores his personhood to the otherwise depersonalizing context. To be valid it must be autonomous and informed. The latter condition can, outside the research community, only be fulfilled by degrees; but the higher the degree of the understanding regarding the purpose and the technique, the more valid becomes the endorsement of the will. A margin of mere trust inevitably remains. Ultimately, the appeal for volunteers should seek this free and generous endorsement, the appropriation of the research purpose into the person's own scheme of ends.

.   .   .

The Rule of the "Descending Order" and Its Counter–Utility Sense

We have laid down what must seem to be a forbidding rule to the number-hungry research industry. Having faith in the transcendent potential of man, I do not fear that the "source" will ever fail a society that does not destroy it—and only such a one is worthy of the blessings of progress. But "elitistic" the rule is (as is the enterprise of progress itself), and elites are by nature small. The combined attribute of motivation and information, plus the absence of external pressures, tends to be socially so circumscribed that strict adherence to the rule might numerically starve the research process. This is why I spoke of a descending order of permissibility, which is itself permissive, but where the realization that it is a *descending* order is not without pragmatic import. Departing from the august norm, the appeal must shift from idealism to docility, from high-mindedness to compliance, from judgment to trust. Consent spreads over the whole spectrum. I will not go into the casuistics of this penumbral area. I merely indicate the principle of the order of preference: The poorer in knowledge, motivation, and freedom of decision (and that, alas, means the more readily available in terms of numbers and possible manipulation), the more sparingly and indeed reluctantly should the reservoir be used, and the more compelling must therefore become the countervailing justification.

Let us note that this is the opposite of a social utility standard, the reverse of the order by "availability and expendability": The most valuable and scarcest, the least expendable elements of the social organism, are to be the first candidates for risk and sacrifice. It is the standard of *noblesse oblige;* and with all its counter-utility and seeming "wastefulness," we feel a rightness about it and perhaps even a higher "utility," for the soul of the community lives by this spirit. It is also the opposite of what the day-to-day interests of research clamor for, and for the scientific community to honor it will mean that it will have to fight a strong temptation to go by routine to the readiest sources of supply—the suggestible, the ignorant, the dependent, the "captive" in various senses.[12] I do not believe that heightened resistance here must cripple research, which cannot be permitted; but it may indeed slow it down by the smaller numbers fed into experimentation in consequence. This price—a possibly slower rate of progress—may have to be paid for the preservation of the most precious capital of higher communal life.

Experimentation on Patients

So far we have been speaking on the tacit assumption that the subjects of experimentation are recruited from among the healthy. To the question "Who is conscriptable?" the spontaneous answer is: Least and last of all the sick—the most available of all as they are under treatment and observation anyway. That the afflicted should not be called upon to bear additional burden and risk, that they are society's special trust and the

12. This refers to captives of circumstance, not of justice. Prison inmates are, with respect to our problem, in a special class. If we hold to some idea of guilt, and to the supposition that our judicial system is not entirely at fault, they may be held to stand in a special debt to society, and their offer to serve—from whatever motive—may be accepted with a minimum of qualms as a means of reparation.

physician's trust in particular—these are elementary responses of our moral sense. Yet the very destination of medical research, the conquest of disease, requires at the crucial stage trial and verification on precisely the sufferers from the disease, and their total exemption would defeat the purpose itself. In acknowledging this inescapable necessity, we enter the most sensitive area of the whole complex, the one most keenly felt and most searchingly discussed by the practitioners themselves. No wonder, it touches the heart of the doctor-patient relation, putting its most solemn obligations to the test.

. . .

No Experiments on Patients Unrelated to Their Own Disease

Although my ponderings have, on the whole, yielded points of view rather than definite prescriptions, premises rather than conclusions, they have led me to a few unequivocal yeses and noes. The first is the emphatic rule that patients should be experimented upon, if at all, *only* with reference to *their disease*. Never should there be added to the gratuitousness of the experiment as such the gratuitousness of service to an unrelated cause. This follows simply from what we have found to be the *only* excuse for infracting the special exemption of the sick at all—namely, that the scientific war on disease cannot accomplish its goal without drawing the sufferers from disease into the investigative process. If under this excuse they become subjects of experiment, they do so *because,* and only because, of *their* disease.

This is the fundamental and self-sufficient consideration. That the patient cannot possibly benefit from the unrelated experiment therapeutically, while he might from experiment related to his condition, is also true, but lies beyond the problem area of pure experiment. I am in any case discussing nontherapeutic experimentation only, where *ex hypothesi* the patient does not benefit. Experiment as part of therapy—that is, directed toward helping the subject himself—is a different matter altogether and raises its own problems, but hardly philosophical ones. As long as a doctor can say, even if only in his own thought: "There is no known cure for your condition (or: You have responded to none); but there is promise in a new treatment still under investigation, not quite tested yet as to effectiveness and safety; you will be taking a chance, but all things considered, I judge it in your best interest to let me try it on you"—as long as he can speak thus, he speaks as the patient's physician and may err, but does not transform the patient into a subject of experimentation. Introduction of an untried therapy into the treatment where the tried ones have failed is not "experimentation on the patient."

Generally, and almost needless to say, with all the rules of the book, there is something "experimental" (because tentative) about every individual treatment, beginning with the diagnosis itself; and he would be a poor doctor who would not learn from every case for the benefit of future cases, and a poor member of the profession who would not make any new insights gained from his treatments available to the profession at large. Thus, knowledge may be advanced in the treatment of any patient, and the interest of the medical art and all sufferers from the same affliction as well as the patient himself may be served if something happens to be learned from his case. But this gain to knowledge and future therapy is incidental to the *bona fide* service to the present patient. He has the right to expect that the doctor does nothing to him just in order to learn.

In that case, the doctor's imaginary speech would run, for instance, like this: "There is nothing more I can do for you. But you can do something for me. Speaking no longer as your physician but on behalf of medical science, we could learn a great deal about future cases of this kind if you would permit me to perform certain experiments on you. It is understood that you yourself would not benefit from any knowledge we might gain; but future patients would." This statement would express the purely experimental situation, assumedly here with the subject's concurrence and with all cards on the table. In Alexander Bickel's words: "It is a different situation when the doctor is no longer trying to make [the patient] well, but is trying to find out how to make others well in the future."[13]

But even in the second case, that of the nontherapeutic experiment where the patient does not benefit, at least the patient's own disease is enlisted in the cause of fighting that disease, even if only in others. It is yet another thing to say or think: "Since you are here—in the hospital with its facilities—anyway, under our care and observation anyway, away from your job (or, perhaps, doomed) anyway, we wish to profit from your being available for some other research of great interest we are presently engaged in." From the standpoint of merely medical ethics, which has only to consider risk, consent, and the worth of the objective, there may be no cardinal difference between this case and the last one. I hope that the medical reader will not think I am making too fine a point when I say that from the standpoint of the subject and his dignity there is a cardinal difference that crosses the line between the permissible and the impermissible, and this by the same principle of "identification" I have been invoking all along. Whatever the rights and wrongs of any experimentation on any patient—in the one case, at least that residue of identification is left him that it is his own affliction by which he can contribute to the conquest of that affliction, his own kind of suffering which he helps to alleviate in others; and so in a sense it is his own cause. It is totally indefensible to rob

13.   ... To spell out the difference between the two cases: In the first case, the patient himself is meant to be the beneficiary of the experiment, and directly so; the "subject" of the experiment is at the same time its object, its end. It is performed not for gaining knowledge, but for helping him—and helping him in the *act* of performing it, even if by its results it also contributes to a broader testing process currently under way. It is in fact part of the treatment itself and an "experiment" only in the loose sense of being untried and highly tentative. But whatever the degree of uncertainty, the motivating anticipation (the wager if you like) is for success, and success here means the subject's own good. To a pure experiment, by contrast, undertaken to gain knowledge, the difference of success and failure is not germane, only that of conclusiveness and inconclusiveness. The "negative" result has as much to teach as the "positive." Also, the true experiment is an act distinct from the uses later made of the findings. And, most important, the subject experimented on is distinct from the eventual beneficiaries of those findings: He lets himself be used as a means toward an end external to himself (even if he should at some later time happen to be among the beneficiaries himself). With respect to his own present needs and his own good, the act is gratuitous.

the unfortunate of this intimacy with the purpose and make his misfortune a convenience for the furtherance of alien concerns. The observance of this rule is essential, I think, to at least attenuate the wrong that nontherapeutic experimenting on patients commits in any case.

ALEXANDER I. SOLZHENITSYN, THE CANCER WARD

164 (1968).

How he craved to be healed!—despite those harrowing months and years of by now hopeless treatments, he would suddenly recover completely. His back would heal and he would stand up straight and walk with a firm step, feeling like a new man. Greetings, Dr. Lyudmila Afanasyevna! I'm well—see?

How they all craved to hear of such a wonder-working doctor, of a medicine unknown to the doctors here! These people might have admitted or denied that they believed in such a thing, but all of them, to a man, felt, deep in their hearts, that there really was such a doctor, such a dispenser of herbs or such an old village woman living somewhere, and that they only had to learn where, take that medicine, and they would be saved.

It was impossible that their lives were already doomed!

Laugh as we may at miracles as long as we are strong, healthy and flourishing, let life become hopelessly wedged and crushed so that only a miracle can save us—and we shall believe in that one and only and altogether extraordinary miracle.

NOTES AND QUESTIONS

1. On December 2, 1982, at the University of Utah Medical Center in Salt Lake City, Dr. Barney J. Clark, a 61 year old retired dentist, became the first recipient of a permanent artificial heart. N.Y. TIMES, Dec. 3, 1982, at A1, col. 2.

Dr. Clark appeared to have been near death with an inoperable heart condition known as cardiomyopathy. Until June 1982, a patient with such a condition would not, according to FDA requirements, have been eligible for this particular procedure. The FDA had determined that implant surgery should be performed only on a patient who was already receiving conventional open heart surgery and who was not functioning sufficiently well to remain alive. In June 1982, the FDA approved an amendment to enable patients with inoperable cardiomyopathy to be able to take advantage of artificial heart implantation.

Dr. Clark was chosen by a six member selection committee, which carefully scrutinized his emotional and physical health and reached the conclusion that he was both sufficiently stable to withstand the surgery and its aftermath and sufficiently motivated by a desire to contribute to the advancement of science.

The University's Institutional Review Board (IRB), a panel of doctors, nurses, lawyers and philosophers, drafted the consent form that Dr. Clark signed for the 7 ½ hour operation.

On March 23, the 112th day after surgery, Dr. Clark died. His death was a result of the total collapse and failure of his circulatory system and other organs of his body. The polyurethane heart, which had beat 13 million times, was finally turned off with a key by members of the medical team. N.Y. Times, Mar. 25, 1983 at A1, col. 5.

The period of time during which Dr. Clark had lived with the artificial heart had been riddled with medical problems. On December 4, surgery had been performed to correct leaks in a malfunctioning lung; on December 11, Dr. Clark had suffered seizures; on December 14, the surgeons had replaced the left side of the heart after a crack had developed; and on March 3, the patient began to deteriorate seriously, developing aspiration pneumonia, kidney failure, and infection of the bowel. Note that the doctors felt compelled by medical ethics to conduct the artificial heart experiment on someone who was in poor health from the start. N.Y. Times, Mar. 25, 1983, at A20, col. 3. Do you agree?

2.   Even today, there are few options for patients with end-stage heart failure. Heart transplants are risky, and donors are in short supply. Clinical trials have begun on a radical new treatment—bypass surgery combined with the process of cutting open the heart to reshape it and getting rid of some scar tissue to help it pump more efficiently. The experiment, sponsored by the National Heart, Lung, and Blood Institute, is to take place at 90 centers around the world and will include 2,800 patients who will be followed for seven years. The study will compare those who receive the experimental surgery to other patients who receive medicine alone, or medicine and bypass surgery. Initial results have been promising. *See* Denise Grady, *Putting a Weakened Heart in Experimental Hands*, N.Y. Times, July 19, 2004, at A1.

3.   Consider David J. Rothman, Strangers at the Bedside 252 (1991):

> [T]he central issue now . . . is not how to protect the human subject from the investigator but how to ensure that all those who wish to be human subjects have a fair opportunity to enter a protocol. The nightmare image has shifted from an unscrupulous researcher taking advantage of a helpless inmate to a dying patient desperate to join a drug trial and have a chance at life.

4.   The use of placebos in clinical trials has generated considerable debate in the medical community. The placebo-controlled trial is considered an important method in establishing safety and efficacy of a new treatment. The American Medical Association (AMA) advocates the continued use of placebos even in some cases where effective treatments have already been established. Am. Med. Ass'n Council on Ethical & Judicial Affairs, Opinion No. E-2.075, *The Use of Placebo Controls in Clinical Trials* (1996), *available at* http://www.ama-assn.org/apps/pf_new/pf_on-line?f_n=browse & doc= policyfiles/HnE/E-2.075.HTM. The FDA also relies heavily on data from placebo-controlled trials when reviewing applications for new drugs. *See* Kenneth J. Rothman & Karin B. Michels, *The Continuing Unethical Use Of Placebo Controls (Sounding Board)*, 331 New Eng. J. Med. 394 (1994). Opponents of the use of placebos, however, denounce the practice as unethical when there is a known treatment option, and the World Medical Association (WMA) amended the Declaration of Helsinki in 2000 to include tighter controls on placebos, stating that unless the condition is minor, control-group participants must receive the "best current" treatment. World Med. Ass'n, Declaration of Helsinki: Ethical Principles for Medical Research Involving Human Subjects (amended 2000), *available at* http://www.wma.net/e/policy/b3.htm.

The issue of placebos is especially contentious in the context of research in third world countries, such as HIV/AIDS research in Africa. Scientists argue that costs of research will be prohibitively high if best current treatment must be given to control groups, while ethicists maintain that economic reasons should not justify lower standards of research practice in poor countries. The European Group on Ethics in Science and New Technologies, an ethics body that issues guidelines for the European Union, announced its departure from the stringent guidelines of the

Declaration of Helsinki when it stated that placebo-controlled trials can sometimes be justified in developing countries, even when proven treatments are available in wealthy countries. This decision has been criticized by the WMA as putting the interest of society ahead of the interest of individuals involved in clinical trials, a premise that was rejected in the Declaration of Helsinki. *See* Gretchen Vogel, *Ethics Group Gives Qualified Nod to Placebos*, 299 Sci. 295 (2003).

5. Should the government regulate the use of unorthodox devices, drugs, and methods to treat terminally ill patients? *See* United States v. Rutherford, 442 U.S. 544, 99 S.Ct. 2470, 61 L.Ed.2d 68 (1979).

6. On June 2, 1993, Congress enacted the National Institutes of Health Revitalization Act of 1993, Pub.L. No. 103–43, amending Part G of title IV of the Public Health Services Act to "ensure" that women and minorities are included as subjects in clinical trials supported or conducted by the National Institutes of Health. *See* 107 Stat. 133, 42 U.S.C. § 289a–2.

This act codified the creation of the National Institutes of Health Office of Research on Women's Health (established in 1990 to address gender inequity in clinical trials) and defined its mandate as promoting research on women's health. 42 U.S.C. § 287 (West 1991), amended by 42 U.S.C.A. § 287(d)(2) (West Supp. 1999); *see NIH Starts Women's Health Office*, N.Y. TIMES, Sept. 11, 1990, at C9.

NIH guidelines for intramural and extramural research now require that women and minority groups be included in NIH-sponsored clinical trials, unless doing so would be inappropriate. 42 U.S.C. § 289a–2; *see also* Food & Drug Administration, Guideline for the Study and Evaluation of Gender Differences in the Clinical Evaluation of Drugs, Notice, 58 Fed.Reg. 39406 (1993) (stating that subjects in a clinical study should mirror the target population).

When a pregnant woman is to be the subject of research supported by the U.S. Department of Health and Human Services, an Institutional Review Board cannot approve the study unless appropriate studies have been performed on animals and nonpregnant individuals, 45 C.F.R. § 46.206(a)(2) (1993), and "(1) [t]he purpose of the activity is to meet the health needs of the mother and the fetus will be placed at risk only to the minimum extent necessary to meet such needs, or (2) the risk to the fetus is minimal." 45 C.F.R. § 46.207(a) (1993). In addition, the "mother and father" must be legally competent and, after being fully informed of the study's potential effect on the fetus, grant their informed consent. In limited circumstances, the father's informed consent is not required: (i) the reason for the activity is to meet the mother's health needs, (ii) the father's identity or whereabouts cannot be reasonably ascertained, (iii) the father is not reasonably available, or (iv) the pregnancy resulted from rape. 45 C.F.R. § 46.207(b) (1993). For a thoughtful discussion of this issue, *see* 1 Institute of Medicine, Women and Health Research: Ethical and Legal Issues of Including Women in Clinical Studies 110–14 (Anna C. Mastroianni et al. eds., 1994).

For a comprehensive account of the ethical and social issues raised by the exclusion of women in clinical research, *see* Karen H. Rothenberg, *Gender Matters: Implications for Clinical Research and Women's Health Care*, 32 HOUS. L. REV. 1201 (1996). For a discussion of the DES experiments and tort liability, and the implications for current clinical trials on HIV and AIDS, *see* Anna C. Mastroianni, *HIV, Women, and Access to Clinical Trials: Tort Liability and Lessons from DES*, 5 DUKE J. GENDER L. & POL'Y 167 (1998).

Mink v. University of Chicago

United States District Court for the Northern District of Illinois, 1978.
460 F.Supp. 713.

■ GRADY, J.

Plaintiffs have brought this action on behalf of themselves and some 1,000 women who were given diethylstilbestrol ("DES") as part of a medical experiment conducted by the defendants, University of Chicago and Eli Lilly & Company, between September 29, 1950, and November 20, 1952. The drug was administered to the plaintiffs during their prenatal care at the University's Lying–In Hospital as part of a double blind study to determine the value of DES in preventing miscarriages. The women were not told they were part of an experiment, nor were they told that the pills administered to them were DES. Plaintiffs claim that as a result of their taking DES, their daughters have developed abnormal cervical cellular formations and are exposed to an increased risk of vaginal or cervical cancer. Plaintiffs also allege that they and their sons have suffered reproductive tract and other abnormalities and have incurred an increased risk of cancer.

The complaint further alleges that the relationship between DES and cancer was known to the medical community as early as 1971, but that the defendants made no effort to notify the plaintiffs of their participation in the DES experiment until late 1975 or 1976 when the University sent letters to the women in the experiment informing them of the possible relationship between the use of DES in pregnant women and abnormal conditions in the genital tracts of their offspring. The letter asked for information to enable the University to contact the sons and daughters of the plaintiffs for medical examination.

The complaint seeks recovery on three causes of action. The first alleges that the defendants committed a series of batteries on the plaintiffs by conducting a medical experiment on them without their knowledge or consent. The administration of DES to the plaintiffs without their consent is alleged to be an "offensive invasion of their persons" which has caused them "severe mental anxiety and emotional distress due to the increased risk to their children of contracting cancer and other abnormalities." The second count is grounded in products liability and seeks to recover damages from defendant Lilly premised on its manufacture of DES as a defective and unreasonably dangerous drug. Finally, the plaintiffs allege that the defendants breached their duty to notify plaintiffs that they had been given DES while pregnant and that children born from that pregnancy should consult a medical specialist. Throughout the complaint plaintiffs claim the defendants intentionally concealed the fact of the experiment and information concerning the relationship between DES and cancer from the plaintiffs.

Both defendants have moved to dismiss the complaint for failure to state a claim. We will deny the motions as to the first cause of action, and grant the motions as to the second and third causes of action.

Battery

We must determine whether the administration of a drug, DES, to the plaintiffs without their knowledge or consent constitutes a battery under Illinois law. The defendants argue that the plaintiffs' first count is really a "lack of informed consent" case premised on negligence. Because the named plaintiffs have not alleged specific physical injury to themselves, the defendants contend they have failed to state a claim for negligence and the count should be dismissed. However, if we find the action to be based on a battery theory, it may stand notwithstanding the lack of an allegation of personal physical injury.

. . .

Illinois courts have adopted the modern approach to true informed consent cases, and have treated them as negligence actions. However, they have not overruled earlier cases which recognize a cause of action in battery for surgery performed without a patient's consent. Pratt v. Davis, 224 Ill. 300, 79 N.E. 562 (1906). Thus, it appears the two separate theories continue to exist in Illinois, and battery may be the proper cause of action in certain situations, for example, where there is a total lack of consent by the patient.

The question thus becomes whether the instant case is more akin to the performance of an unauthorized operation than to the failure to disclose the potential ramifications of an agreed to treatment. We think the situation is closer to the former. The plaintiffs did not consent to DES treatment; they were not even aware that the drug was being administered to them. They were the subjects of an experiment whereby non-emergency treatment was performed upon them without their consent or knowledge.

. . .

Battery is defined as the unauthorized touching of the person of another. To be liable for battery, the defendant must have done some affirmative act, intended to cause an unpermitted contact.

. . .

The administration of DES to the plaintiffs was clearly intentional. It was part of a planned experiment conducted by the defendants. The requisite element of intent is therefore met, since the plaintiffs need show only an intent to bring about the contact; an intent to do harm is not essential to the action.

The act of administering the drug supplies the contact with the plaintiffs' persons. . . . Had the drug been administered by means of a hypodermic needle, the element of physical contact would clearly be sufficient. We believe that causing the patient to physically ingest a pill is indistinguishable in principle.

Finally, there is the question of consent.

. . .

The defendants argue that the plaintiffs consented to treatment when they admitted themselves to the University's Lying–In Hospital for prenatal care. The scope of the plaintiffs' consent is crucial to their ultimate recovery in a battery action. The defendants' privilege is limited at least to acts substantially similar to those to which the plaintiffs consented. If the defendants went beyond the consent given, to perform substantially different acts, they may be liable. The time, place and circumstances will affect the nature of the consent given. . . . These questions, however, are questions of fact which are to be determined by the jury, not by this court on a motion to dismiss. The plaintiffs have alleged sufficient lack of consent to the treatment involved to state a claim for battery against both defendants.

Strict Liability

In their second cause of action, plaintiffs allege that the DES ingested by them was "defective and unreasonably dangerous at the time it was manufactured, and Lilly is therefore strictly liable to the plaintiffs for their damages."

. . .

Clearly, one of the essential elements in a claim for strict liability is physical injury to the plaintiff. The closest the complaint comes to alleging physical injury is the allegation of a "risk" of cancer. . . .

. . .

The plaintiffs argue that they have alleged personal physical injury in paragraph 1, which states that DES "has or may cause reproductive tract and other abnormalities in themselves." There is no indication that any of the named plaintiffs have suffered any of these "abnormalities." Without more concrete allegations of injury to the named plaintiffs, the second count must be dismissed for failure to state a claim.

Failure to Notify

In their third cause of action, plaintiffs assert that the defendants breached their duty to inform plaintiffs and their children of the experiment and of the precautions which the children should take to minimize the risk of contracting cancer. This duty allegedly arose in 1971 when the defendants learned of the relationship between DES and cancer. Plaintiffs claim that defendant Lilly had made no attempt to contact the plaintiff class, and that the notice given by the University in 1975 and 1976 was insufficient to fulfill the obligation because of the delay, and because it failed to advise of the precautions which should be taken by DES children.[14] This failure to notify has allegedly "injured some plaintiffs, increasing the risk of cancer to their children by depriving them of the ability to take the medically recommended precautions, including frequent check-ups."

We agree that both defendants had a duty to notify the plaintiff patients of the risks inherent in DES treatment when they became aware, or should have become aware, of the relationship between DES and cancer. . . . The University's duty to notify is simply an extension of the duty of physicians to warn their patients of the risks inherent in treatment. Canterbury v. Spence, 464 F.2d 772 (1972), cert. denied, 409 U.S. 1064 (1972). The fact the knowledge of the risk was obtained after the patient

14. The plaintiffs also take issue with the University's failure to inform patients that they did not consent to taking DES and therefore might have a legal claim against the defendants. There is no duty in these circumstances to inform potential litigants of possible legal claims. Moreover, each patient should know whether or not she consented to DES treatment.

was treated does not alter the obligation. If the defendant fails to notify the patient when the risk becomes known, he has breached this duty.

Defendant Lilly has a continuing obligation as a manufacturer of drugs to warn of risks inherent in its drugs.... [T]o state a claim against either defendant, the plaintiffs must allege injury to themselves attributable to the breach of the duty to notify. The required injury differs from that in the previous counts in that this injury must be caused by the delay in notice, or failure to notify the plaintiffs in 1971—for example, aggravation of a prior injury, or increase in damage caused by the failure to seek treatment. However, the only injury alleged by the plaintiffs in this count is the increased risk of cancer to their children. Due to the lack of any allegations of physical injury to the named plaintiffs caused by the defendants' breach of their duty to notify, the third cause of action must be dismissed for failure to state a claim.

[The court rejected defendants' contentions that the actions were barred as a matter of law by the statute of limitations and by the doctrine of charitable immunity. The plaintiffs were permitted to amend the second and third counts of their complaint. The court dismissed the amended complaint, however, ruling that plaintiffs could not recover damages based on their new allegations that many of the women in the experiment were physically injured or have died as a result of ingesting DES, because class representatives must show that they personally, and not merely unidentified members of their class, have suffered an injury.]

NOTE

On February 26, 1982, the district court approved a settlement between the parties in which the defendants, without admitting any wrongdoing, paid plaintiffs a lump sum of $225,000 and agreed to provide treatment without charge to any child of a subject in the Chicago DES experiment who develops cancer. The defendants also agreed to keep open for five years the free DES clinics they had been operating. *University of Chicago to Pay $225,000 to 3 Over DES*, N.Y. TIMES, Feb. 27, 1982, at 6. For a thorough legal analysis of this case, *see* Marjorie Maguire Shultz, *From Informed Consent to Patient Choice: A New Protected Interest*, 95 YALE L. J. 219 (1985).

Jonathan D. Moreno, *Convenient and Captive Populations*

BEYOND CONSENT 111–116 (1998).

Clinical research is a complex, expensive and valued social activity. One of the conditions that makes clinical research possible is a subject population that is convenient, both in terms of availability for recruitment and for monitoring through the course of a study. Examples of such populations are prisoners, institutionalized persons, military personnel, and those in "status relationship" (those of lesser power) such as students and research staff.

Some of these populations are convenient in the sense that they are readily available, such as students. Others are not only readily available but also captive, that is, constrained in their movements and choices by virtue of explicit conditions formally imposed on them by societal decision. The paradigm case of a captive population is those who are imprisoned. Other populations seem to occupy a middle ground between short-term hospitalized patients and long-term prisoners, including students, institutionalized persons, and military personnel. Among the ways that these populations differ from others are their degree of availability, the greater likelihood that those who are captive can be coerced or manipulated into participation by virtue of their dependent status, and that captive populations are more likely than others to be readily available for research activities for extended periods, enhancing their attractiveness to the research enterprise.

. . .

Because these groups are not convenient or captive—or even vulnerable—in the same ways, crafting a just, efficacious, and reasonable public policy in the use of these populations in biomedical and behavioral research is not easy. For instance, a rough notion of justice may find it acceptable to impose greater burdens on prisoners because of their debt to society. Similarly, it might be argued that those who are institutionalized may need to be used to serve some important research goal, especially if no other population so readily presents itself for study. Nevertheless, historically these attitudes have sometimes had baleful consequences. Further, our intuitions about justice in research may yield inconsistent results. For example, turning soldiers into "guinea pigs" may either be offensive to patriotic sensibilities or seem reasonable in light of soldierly duties; while students and laboratory workers could be viewed either as too easily coerced into research or as the most appropriate candidates due to their ability to understand an experiment's purposes.

. . .

Prisoners

There is none more fully captive than the long-term prisoner. Among the apocrypha of medical history are tales of the use of living criminals as subjects in various medical studies in the ancient world, including poison experiments and vivisection. In the eighteenth century, European physicians exposed prisoners to venereal disease, cancers, typhoid, and scarlet fever. An influential study of pellagra in 1914 used Mississippi convicts and presaged greater use of this population. During World War II in the United States, many prisoners agreed to participate in studies of conditions such as malaria and sexually transmitted diseases, partly as an expression of patriotism and partly in response to other motivations such as opportunities for payment and early parole.

. . .

Over the next decade several drug manufactures made substantial investments in prison research, and in some cases even erected buildings with state-of the-art laboratory facilities at penitentiaries. By 1960, as many as 20,000 federal prisoners were participants in medical experiments.[6] In 1973, the Pharmaceutical Manufacturers Association estimated that about 70% of Phase I drug tests were carried out of prisoners, or about 3600 individuals.[7] American prisoners and prison-based facilities were also being used to test drugs for researchers abroad.

Some prison experiments were sponsored by the federal government. One involved the irradiation of the testicle of 131 prisoners in state penitentiaries in Oregon and Washington State between 1963 and 1973 and was funded by the Atomic Energy Commission (AEC). There were clear rules in place within the AEC that should have applied to these studies, including a requirement for written consent from subjects. However, in 1995, the President's ACHRE found that these rules were not fully observed in the testicular irradiation research. Among other things, ACHRE was critical of the failure to use to word cancer in listing possible risks, especially with these healthy, "volunteer" subjects.

. . .

The premise that prison research is acceptable if prisoners are free to decline to participate is, admittedly, question-begging. . . . Yet, there may be validity in the claim that research participation can forge a sense of connection to society among those who otherwise have little opportunity to feel part of any community beyond the institution. As the National Commission heard from one inmate, "It makes a prisoner feel good to volunteer. It makes him feel like he's doing something productive." But, the National Commission also heard that the primary reason for volunteering was financial, because opportunities in prison to earn money for oneself or loved ones on the outside are few.[13]

During the early 1990s, prison research was allowable under federal regulation for only four highly restricted kinds of research: minimal risk research on incarceration and criminal behavior, studies of prison as institutions or prisoners as incarcerated person, research on conditions that particularly affect prisoners as a class, and studies of therapies likely to benefit the prisoner.[14] Under the last two conditions prison studies have been conducted on HIV/AIDS and on multiple drug-resistant tuberculosis, a disease that can occur in prisons due to the combination of the density of living conditions and a high prevalence of HIV.

There has, therefore, been a shift from well-established use of prisoners for research purposes to a protectionist regulatory framework. To find a proposed research project ethically sound, this protectionist philosophy requires a narrow construal of potential benefits to prisoners as a group or as individuals. There is considerable irony about the formation of the current public policy concerning prison research. In the most thorough

6.   Renee Fox, cited in H.M. Pappworth, *Human Guinea Pigs: Experimentation on Man* (Boston: Beacon Press, 1967).

7.   "Prison Research: Ethics Behind Bars," Nature 242:153; 1973.

13.   Victor E. Cohn, "Prison Test Ban Opposed," Washington Post, March 14, 1976, at A7.

14.   "Additional DHHS Protections Pertaining to Biomedical and Behavioral Research Involving Prisoners as Subjects." 45 *Code of Federal Regulations* 46, subpart C, 1993.

scholarly analysis of the policy shift that took place in the late 1970s on the use of prisoners as subjects, historian Jon Harkness concludes that there was no contemporary social consensus on the matter. Instead, Harkness contends, retrospective consensus formed in opposition to prison research only after it had been banned by the DHEW for administrative reasons.[16]

. . .

According to the Belmont principles, prison research would create ethical difficulties *even if conducted in a manner consistent with respect for person and beneficence*, because it singles out a specific population for research participation which will then be disproportionate to that of other groups. Thus even if the problem of coercion was resolved to our complete satisfaction, and even if we knew that participation advances the rehabilitation process, there would still be a fatal flaw. Because prisoners have in fact played a disproportionate role in research whenever and wherever such research has been permitted, their use would normally be unethical no matter how ethically satisfactory the research was in other respects.

NOTES AND QUESTIONS

1. For a detailed description of the type and extent of experiments conducted on prisoners, see Allen M. Hornblum, Acres of Skin: Human Experiments at Holmesburg Prison (1998).

2. Despite concerns about coercion and abuse of prisoners in clinical trials, many prisoners' rights advocates and prisoners themselves have fought for the right to gain access to clinical trials, especially those studying new drugs for HIV/AIDS. In 1981 a lawsuit initiated by prisoners of the Michigan State Penitentiary at Jackson, *Fante v. Department of Health and Human Services*, Civil Action No. 80–72778, (E.D. Mich. filed July 29, 1980), cited in 46 Fed. Reg. 35085 (1981), prompted FDA to stay the effective date of its regulations of inmate involvement in clinical trials. *See* Eileen Kelly, *Expanding Prisoners' Access to AIDS–Related Clinical Trials: An Ethical and Clinical Imperative*, 75 The Prison Journal 48, 57 (1995). Many states have lifted bans or eased restrictions on clinical trials in prisons because of lawsuits or political pressure from groups advocating for equal rights for prisoners. *See* Daniel Golden, *Experimental Medications Returning to Mass. Prisons*, Boston Globe, Oct. 11, 1993, at 1. The Department of Health and Human Services Office for Human Research Protections has issued a new guidance document on the implementation of the federal regulations on research with prisoners, 45 C.F.R. 46, Subpart C, detailing the responsibilities of IRBs and institutions. See OHRP Guidance on the Involvement of Prisoners in Research (May 23, 2003), *available at* http://www.hhs.gov/ohrp/humansubjects/guidance/prisoner.htm.

Advisory Committee on Human Radiation Experiments, Final Report
342–48 (1995).

THE STUDIES AT THE FERNALD SCHOOL

Researchers from the Massachusetts Institute of Technology, working in cooperation with senior members of the Fernald staff, carried out

16. John E. Harkness, op. cit., 1996.

nontherapeutic nutritional studies with radioisotopes at the state school in the late 1940s and early 1950s. The subjects of these nutritional research studies were young male residents of Fernald, who were members of the school's "science club." In 1946, one study exposed seventeen subjects to radioactive iron. The second study, which involved a series of seventeen related subexperiments, exposed fifty-seven subjects to radioactive calcium between 1950 and 1953. It is clear that the doses involved were low and that it is extremely unlikely that any of the children who were used as subjects were harmed as a consequence. These studies remain morally troubling, however, for several reasons. First, although parents or guardians were asked for their permission to have their children involved in the research, the available evidence suggests that the information provided was, at best, incomplete. Second, there is the question of the fairness of selecting institutionalized children at all, children whose life circumstances were by any standard already heavily burdened.

Parental Authorization

The Massachusetts Task Force found two letters sent to parents describing the nutrition studies and seeking their permission. The first letter, a form letter signed by the superintendent of the school, is dated November 1949. The letter refers to a project in which children at the school will receive a special diet "rich" in various cereals, iron, and vitamins and for which "it will be necessary to make some blood tests at stated intervals, similar to those to which our patients are already accustomed, and which will cause no discomfort or change in their physical condition other than possibly improvement." The letter makes no mention of any risks or the use of a radioisotope. Parents or guardians are asked to indicate that they have no objection to their son's participation in the project by signing an enclosed form.

The second letter, dated May 1953, we quote in its entirety:

Dear Parent:

In previous years we have done some examinations in connection with the nutritional department of the Massachusetts Institute of Technology, with the purposes of helping to improve the nutrition of our children and to help them in general more efficiently than before.

For the checking up of the children, we occasionally need to take some blood samples, which are then analyzed. The blood samples are taken after one test meal which consists of a special breakfast meal containing a certain amount of calcium. We have asked for volunteers to give a sample of blood once a month for three months, and your son has agreed to volunteer because the boys who belong to the Science Club have many additional privileges. They get a quart of milk daily during that time, and are taken to a baseball game, to the beach and to some outside dinners and they enjoy it greatly.

I hope that you have no objection that your son is voluntarily participating in this study. The first study will start on Monday, June 8th, and if you have not expressed any objections we will assume that your son may participate.

Sincerely yours,

Clemens E. Benda, M.D.

[Fernald] Clinical Director

Approved: ———

Malcom J. Farrell, M.D.

[Fernald] Superintendent

Again, there is no mention of any risks or the use of a radioisotope. It was believed then that the risks were minimal, as indeed they appear to have been, and as a consequence, school administrators and the investigators may have thought it unnecessary to raise the issue of risks with the parents. There was *no basis,* however, for the implication in both letters that the project was intended for the children's benefit or improvement. This was simply not true.

The conclusion of the Massachusetts Task Force was that these experiments were conducted in violation of the fundamental human rights of the subjects. This conclusion is based in part on the task force's assessment of these letters. Specifically, the task force found that

> [t]he researchers failed to satisfactorily inform the subjects and their families that the nutritional research studies were non-therapeutic; that is, that the research studies were never intended to benefit the human subjects as individuals but were intended to enhance the body of scientific knowledge concerning nutrition.

> The letter in which consent from family members was requested, which was drafted by the former Fernald superintendent, failed to provide information that was reasonably necessary for an informed decision to be made.

Fairness and the Use of Institutionalized Children

The Fernald experiments also raise quite starkly the particular ethical difficulties associated with conducting research on members of institutionalized populations—especially where some of the residents have mental impairments. Living conditions in most of these institutions (including Fernald and Wrentham) have improved considerably in recent years, and sensitivity toward people with cognitive impairments has likewise increased. As Fred Boyce, a subject in one of these experiments has put it, "Fernald is a much better place today, and in no way does it operate like it did then. That's very important to know that."

The Massachusetts Task Force describes conditions in state-operated facilities like Fernald, particularly as they bear on human experimentation, as follows:

> Until the 1970s, the buildings were dirty and in disrepair, staff shortages were constant, brutality was often accepted, and programs were inadequate or nonexistent. There were no human rights committees or institutional review boards. If the Superintendent (in those days required to be a medical doctor) "cooperated" in an experiment and allowed residents to be subjects, few knew and no one protested. If nothing concerning the experiments appeared in the residents' medical records, if "request for consent" letters were less than forthright, or if no consent was obtained there was no one in a position of authority to halt or challenge such procedures.

Although public attitudes toward people who are institutionalized are admittedly different today than they were fifty years ago, it is likely that this state of affairs would have been troubling to most Americans even then. Historian Susan Lederer has revealed several episodes of experimentation with institutionalized children in America that caused considerable public outcry even before 1940, presaging the concern generated by Willowbrook when this research became a public issue in the 1960s.

The LMRI staff reported in the early 1960s that the pediatric researchers whom they had gathered agreed in principle that the convenience of conducting research on institutionalized children did not outweigh the moral problems associated with this practice:

> Several investigators spoke about the practical advantages of using institutionalized children who are already assembled in one location and living within a standard, controlled environment. But the conferees agreed that there should be no differential recruitment of ward patients rather than private patients, of institutionalized children rather than children living in private homes, or of handicapped rather than healthy children.

A particularly poignant dimension of the unfairness of using institutionalized children as subjects of research is that it permits investigators to secure cooperation by offering as special treats what other, noninstitutionalized children would find far less exceptional. The extra attention of a "science club," a quart of milk, and an occasional outing were for the boys at Fernald extraordinary opportunities. As Mr. Boyce put it:

> I won't tell you now about the severe physical and mental abuse, but I can assure you, it was no Boys' Town. The idea of getting consent for experiments under these conditions was not only cruel but hypocritical. They bribed us by offering us special privileges, knowing that we had so little that we would do practically anything for attention; and to say, I quote, "This is their debt to society," end quote, as if we were worth no more than laboratory mice, is unforgivable.

Even when a child was able to resist the offers of special attention and refused to participate in the experiment, the investigators seem to have been unwilling to respect the child's decision. One MIT researcher, Robert S. Harris, explicitly noted that "it seemed to [him] that the three subjects who objected to being included in the study [could] be induced to change their minds." Harris believed that the recalcitrant children could be "induced" to join in the study by emphasizing "the Fernald Science Club angle of our work."

From the perspective of the science, it was considered important to conduct the research in an environment in which the diet of the children-subjects could be easily controlled. From this standpoint, the institutional setting of Fernald was ideal. The institutional settings of the boarding schools in the Boston area, however, would have offered much the same opportunity. Although the risks were small, the "children of the elite" were rarely if ever selected for such research. It is not likely that these children would have been willing to submit to blood tests for extra milk or the chance to go to the beach.

The question of what is ethical in the context of unfair background conditions is always difficult. Perhaps the investigators, who were not responsible for the poor conditions at Fernald, believed that the opportunities provided to the members of the Science Club brightened the lives of these children, if only briefly. Reasoning of this sort, however, can all too easily lead to unjustifiable disregard of the equal worth of all people and to unfair treatment.

Today, fifty years after the Fernald experiments, there are still no federal regulations protecting institutionalized children from unfair treatment in research involving human subjects. The Committee strongly urges the federal government to fill this policy void by providing additional protections for institutionalized children.

CONCLUSION

If an ethical evaluation of human experiments depended solely upon an assessment of the risks to subjects as they could reasonably be anticipated at the time, the radiation experiments conducted on children reviewed in this chapter would be relatively unproblematic. During this time, the association between radiation exposure and the subsequent development of cancer was not well understood, and in particular, little was known about iodine 131 and the risk of thyroid cancer. Both researchers and policymakers appear to have been alert to considerations of harm and concerned about exposing children to an unacceptable level of risk.

At the same time, however, the scientific community's experience with radionuclides in humans was limited, and this approach to medical investigation was new. Although the available data about human risk were encouraging and the biological susceptibility of children to the effects of radiation was not appreciated, we are left with the lingering question of whether investigators and agency officials were *sufficiently* cautious as they began their work with children. This is a difficult judgment to make at any point in the development of a field of human research; it is particularly difficult to make at forty or fifty years' remove. Investigators and officials had to make decisions under conditions of considerable uncertainty; this is commonplace in science and in medicine. Although the biological susceptibility of children was not then known, investigators and officials held the view that children should be accorded extra protection in the conduct of human research, and they made what they thought were appropriate adjustments when using children as subjects. If human research never proceeded in the face of uncertainty, there would be no such experiments. How little uncertainty is acceptable in research involving children is a question that remains unresolved. Today, we continue to debate what constitutes minimal risk to children, in radiation and in other areas of research. The regulations governing research on children offer little in the way of guidance, either with respect to conditions of uncertainty about risk or when risks are known.

As best as we can determine, in eleven of the twenty-one experiments we reviewed, the risks were in a range that would today likely be considered as more than minimal, and thus as unacceptable in nontherapeutic research with children according to current federal regulations. It is possible, however, that four of the eleven might be considered acceptable by the "minor increase over minimal risk" standard. In these four experiments, the average risk estimates were between one and two per thousand, the studies were directed at the subjects' medical conditions, and they may well have had the potential to obtain information of "vital importance."

Physical risk to subjects is not the only ethically relevant consideration in evaluating human experiments. With the exception of the studies at Fernald, we know almost nothing about whether or how parental authorization for the remaining nineteen experiments we reviewed was obtained. And with the exception of the Fernald studies and the experiment at Wrentham, we know very little about the children who were selected to be the subjects of this research. Therefore, we cannot comment on the general ethics of these other experiments.

The experiments at Fernald and at the Wrentham School unfairly burdened children who were already disadvantaged, children whose interests were less well protected than those children living with their parents or children who were socially privileged. At the Fernald School, where more is known, there was some attempt to solicit the permission of parents, but the information provided was incomplete and misleading. The investigators successfully secured the cooperation of the children with offers of extra milk and an occasional outing—incentives that would not likely have induced children who were less starved for attention to willingly submit to repeated blood tests.

Part II

One researcher speaking almost thirty-five years ago set out the fundamental moral issue with particular frankness and clarity:

> ... we are talking here about first and second class citizens. This is a concept none of our consciences will allow us to live with.... The thing we must all avoid is two types of citizenry.

It might have been common for researchers to take advantage of the convenience of experimenting on institutionalized children, but the Committee does not believe that convenience offsets the moral problems associated with employing these vulnerable children as research subjects—now or decades ago.

NOTES AND QUESTIONS

Patients who are institutionalized in mental health facilities comprise another population that may be selected to participate in research despite diminished capacity to grant informed consent. A New York court ordered the state Office of Mental Health (OMH) to halt its estimated $52 million worth of experiments on children and mentally ill patients whose surrogates (e.g., relatives or friends) had granted consent as permitted under OMH regulations. T.D. v. New York State Office of Mental Health, 165 Misc.2d 62, 626 N.Y.S.2d 1015 (1995). Each of the six plaintiffs, patients involuntarily hospitalized in state psychiatric facilities, had been found by a court to be mentally incapable of giving or withholding informed consent. *Id.* at 1017. Despite their objections, all had been judicially ordered to submit to non-FDA-approved medication, or FDA-approved medication administered for non-approved uses. *Id.* The court found that the Commissioner of OMH had exceeded his statutory authority in promulgating the regulations, and declared them—and the research conducted under them—invalid. *Id.* at 1022–23; *see also*

Philip J. Hilts, *Judge Tells Health Department to Stop Experiments on Patients*, N.Y. TIMES, Mar. 26, 1995, at 52. The ruling was upheld on appeal. *See* T.D. v. New York State Office of Mental Health, 228 A.D.2d 95, 650 N.Y.S.2d 173 (1996). The court held that the state's rules governing psychiatric experiments on children and the mentally ill are unconstitutional under the due process provisions of the state and Federal constitutions.

Current federal regulations do not require special protections for mental patients who participate in human research studies by consent. Psychiatric researchers at the National Institutes of Mental Health, UCLA, and the University of Maryland have changed their procedures for obtaining informed consent, however. *See* Dolores Kong, *Debatable Forms of Consent*, BOSTON GLOBE, November 16, 1998, at A1. The National Bioethics Advisory Commission (NBAC) issued a report on mental health patients, recommending that IRBs require an assessment of the research subject's decision-making capability before any research is conducted, as well as increased patient representation on local review boards. *See* National Bioethics Advisory Commission, *Research Involving Persons with Mental Disorders That May Affect Decisionmaking Capacity* (1998). Several states have passed laws regulating or restricting research on mentally ill or institutionalized persons. *See* part C, section 3(1)(b)(iii), *supra*. The National Institutes of Mental Health has also published a booklet that details guidelines and recommendations for people with mental illness who want to participate in a clinical trial. *See* National Institute of Mental Health, *A Participant's Guide to Mental Health Clinical Research* (2000), *available at* http://www.nimh.nih.gov/publicat/NIMHclinres.pdf. For more discussion of NBAC's role in creating federal guidelines for mental health research, *see* Robert Michels, *Are Research Ethics Bad for Our Mental Health?*, 340 NEW ENG. J. MED. 1427 (1999).

A recent psychiatric experiment involving minority children was investigated by federal officials at the former Office of Protection from Research Risks. The experiment was conducted by the New York State Psychiatric Institute, which is affiliated with Columbia University and Mount Sinai School of Medicine. Until 1995, researchers at the institute gave 36 children, all of whom were 6–to 10–year-old black and Hispanic boys and younger brothers of juvenile delinquents, intravenous doses of fenfluramine, a component of the banned diet drug Fen–Phen, to study their hypothesis that violent or criminal behavior may be predicted by levels of certain brain chemicals. Critics raise the fact that fenfluramine has never been approved for use by minors, and that the institution's IRB deemed the study posed a "more than minimal" research risk and provided no therapeutic benefits, but approved it anyway. *See* Rick Weiss, *Volunteers at Risk in Medical Studies: Complex Research Projects Strain System of Safeguards*, WASH. POST, August 1, 1998, at A1. The year long OPRR investigation found no violations by the New York State Psychiatric Institute, however, two similar experiments by Mount Sinai and City Univerity of New York involving injecting fenfluramine in hyperactive children were faulted for failure to comply with federal regulations on research with children. Neither institution was fined, but both Mount Sinai and CUNY were required to submit to tighter Federal oversight on their research with human subjects until they completed corrections in their research process. *See* Nina Bernstein, *2 Institutions Faulted for Tests on Children*, N.Y. TIMES, June 12, 1999, at B5.

For a thoughtful analysis of the policy issues and some recommendations for revising federal regulations and informed consent processes, *see* Rebecca Dresser, *Mentally Disabled Research Subjects: The Enduring Policy Issues*, 276 JAMA 67 (1996); and Norman G. Poythress, *Obtaining Informed Consent for Research: A Model for Use With Participants Who Are Mentally Ill*, 30 J. LAW, MED. & ETHICS 367 (2002).

Department of Health and Human Services, *Additional Protections for Children Involved as Subjects in Research*

45 C.F.R. § 46 (2004).

§ 46.401   To what do these regulations apply?

(a) This subpart applies to all research involving children as subjects, conducted or supported by the Department of Health and Human Services.

. . .

§ 46.404   Research not involving greater than minimal risk.

HHS will conduct or fund research in which the IRB finds that no greater than minimal risk to children is presented, only if the IRB finds that adequate provisions are made for soliciting the assent of the children and the permission of their parents or guardians, as set forth in § 46.408.

§ 46.405   Research involving greater than minimal risk but presenting the prospect of direct benefit to the individual subjects.

HHS will conduct or fund research in which the IRB finds that more than minimal risk to children is presented by an intervention or procedure that holds out the prospect of direct benefit for the individual subject, or by a monitoring procedure that is likely to contribute to the subject's well-being, only if the IRB finds that:

(a) The risk is justified by the anticipated benefit to the subjects;

(b) The relation of the anticipated benefit to the risk is at least as favorable to the subjects as that presented by available alternative approaches; and

(c) Adequate provisions are made for soliciting the assent of the children and permission of their parents or guardians, as set forth in § 46.408.

§ 46.406   Research involving greater than minimal risk and no prospect of direct benefit to individual subjects, but likely to yield generalizable knowledge about the subject's disorder or condition.

HHS will conduct or fund research in which the IRB finds that more than minimal risk to children is presented by an intervention or procedure that does not hold out the prospect of direct benefit for the individual subject, or by a monitoring procedure which is not likely to contribute to the well-being of the subject, only if the IRB finds that:

(a) The risk represents a minor increase over minimal risk;

(b) The intervention or procedure presents experiences to subjects that are reasonably commensurate with those inherent in their actual or expected medical, dental, psychological, social, or educational situations;

(c) The intervention or procedure is likely to yield generalizable knowledge about the subjects' disorder or condition which is of vital importance for the understanding or amelioration of the subjects' disorder or condition; and

(d) Adequate provisions are made for soliciting assent of the children and permission of their parents or guardians, as set forth in § 46.408.

§ 46.407   Research not otherwise approvable which presents an opportunity to understand, prevent, or alleviate a serious problem affecting the health or welfare of children.

HHS will conduct or fund research that the IRB does not believe meets the requirements of § 46.404, § 46.405, or § 46.406 only if:

(a) The IRB finds that the research presents a reasonable opportunity to further the understanding, prevention, or alleviation of a serious problem affecting the health or welfare of children; and

(b) The Secretary, after consultation with a panel of experts in pertinent disciplines (for example: science, medicine, education, ethics, law) and following opportunity for public review and comment, has determined either:

(1) That the research in fact satisfies the conditions of § 46.404, § 46.405, or § 46.406, as applicable, or

(2) The following:

(i) The research presents a reasonable opportunity to further the understanding, prevention, or alleviation of a serious problem affecting the health or welfare of children;

(ii) The research will be conducted in accordance with sound ethical principles;

(iii) Adequate provisions are made for soliciting the assent of children and the permission of their parents or guardians, as set forth in § 46.408.

§ 46.408   Requirements for permission by parents or guardians and for assent by children.

(a) In addition to the determinations required under other applicable sections of this subpart, the IRB shall determine that adequate provisions are made for soliciting the assent of the children, when in the judgment of the IRB the children are capable of providing assent. In determining whether children are capable of assenting, the IRB shall take into account the ages, maturity, and psychological state of the children involved. This judgment may be made for all children to be involved in research under a particular protocol, or for each child, as the IRB deems appropriate. If the IRB determines that the capability of some or all of the children is so limited that they cannot reasonably be consulted or that the intervention or procedure involved in the research holds out a prospect of direct benefit that is important to the health or well-being of the children and is available only in the context of the research, the assent of the children is not a necessary condition for proceeding with the research. Even where the IRB determines that the subjects are capable of assenting, the IRB may still waive the assent requirement under circumstances in which consent may be waived in accord with § 46.116 of Subpart A.

(b) In addition to the determinations required under other applicable sections of this subpart, the IRB shall determine, in accordance with and to the extent that consent is required by § 46.116 of Subpart A, that adequate provisions are made for soliciting the permission of each child's parents or guardian. Where parental permission is to be obtained, the IRB may find that the permission of one parent is sufficient for research to be conducted under § 46.404 or § 46.405. Where research is covered by §§ 46.406 and 46.407 and permission is to be obtained from parents, both parents must give their permission unless one parent is deceased, unknown, incompetent, or not reasonably available, or when only one parent has legal responsibility for the care and custody of the child.

(c) In addition to the provisions for waiver contained in § 46.116 of Subpart A, if the IRB determines that a research protocol is designed for conditions or for a subject population for which parental or guardian permission is not a reasonable requirement to protect the subjects (for example, neglected or abused children), it may waive the consent requirements in Subpart A of this part and paragraph (b) of this section, provided an appropriate mechanism for protecting the children who will participate as subjects in the research is substituted, and provided further that the waiver is not inconsistent with Federal, state or local law. The choice of an appropriate mechanism would depend upon the nature and purpose of the activities described in the protocol, the risk and anticipated benefit to the research subjects, and their age, maturity, status, and condition.

NOTES AND QUESTIONS

1. On December 3, 2003 President Bush signed the Pediatric Research Equity Act, which now gives the FDA the legal authority to require that drug companies conduct pediatric clinical trials on medications used by children. Pediatric Research Equity Act of 2003, Pub. L. 108–155, § 1, 117 Stat. 1936, (codified as amended at 21 U.S.C.A § 355c (2003)). Politicians have hailed the law as a way to increase the number of adult medicines that are safe for children, however, there is lingering concern in the scientific community about the ethics of research on children. *See* Melissa Healy, *When Kids Take the Risks: Children Enrolled in Clinical Trials Usually Do Not Directly Benefit and May Suffer Health Consequences*, L.A. TIMES, Jan 19, 2004, at F1. A study examining the IRB process in pediatric research concluded that IRBs lacked consistent application of federal risk-benefit categories and that the decisions often contradicted available risk data or even the federal regulations themselves. Seema Shah et al., *How Do Institutional Review Boards Apply Federal Risk and Benefit Standards for Pediatric Research?* 291 JAMA 476 (2004). The Institute of Medicine, an independent scientific agency that advises the FDA and DHHS, recently released a report that addresses concerns about the adequacy of the current system for protecting children research participants. *See* Institute of Medicine, *Ethical Conduct of Clinical Research Involving Children*, March 26, 2004, *available at* http://www.iom.edu/report.asp?id=19422. For a comprehensive discussion about the role of IRBs in determining the ethics of risk in research on children, *see* Benjamin Freedman, et al., *In Loco Parentis: Minimal*

Risk as an Ethical Threshold for Research Upon Children, Hastings Center Rep., March–April 1993, at 13.

2. Non-therapeutic research on children poses very difficult questions. Some professionals argue that no one can give consent for a child in such a situation. *See, e.g.* Paul Ramsey, The Patient as Person 17 (1970). Needless to say, this approach would make it impossible to test many drugs for use by children. Compare the position of the Judicial Council of the American Medical Association:

> Consent [may be] given by a legally authorized representative of the subject under circumstances in which an informed and prudent adult would reasonably be expected to volunteer himself or his child as a subject.

Ramsey's position has been challenged by Richard McCormick in *Proxy Consent in the Experimentation Situation*, 18 Persp. Biology & Med. 2, 13–14 (1974):

> To share in the general effort and burden of health maintenance and disease control is part of our flourishing and growth as humans. To the extent that it is a good for all of us to share this burden, we all *ought* to do so and to the extent that we *ought* to do so, it is reasonable construction or presumption of our wishes to say that we would do so. The reasonableness of this presumption validates vicarious consent.... Concretely, when a particular experiment would involve no discernable risks, no notable pain, no notable inconvenience, and yet holds promise of considerable benefit, should not the child be constructed to wish this in the same way we presume he chooses his own life, because he *ought* to. I believe so.

The way Ramsey and McCormick evaluate particular nontherapeutic actions is not necessarily as far apart as their philosophic explanations might suggest. McCormick, for example, defines "no discernible risk" quite strictly and concludes that parental consent for a kidney transplant from one 3–year-old to another is without moral justification.

For a discussion arguing that children can morally participate in nontherapeutic research and that children should be included in the decision-making process, *see* Lainie Friedman Ross, *Children As Research Subjects: A Proposal to Revise the Current Federal Regulations Using a Moral Framework*, 8 Stan. L. & Pol'y Rev. 159 (1997). For recommendations for protecting subject populations with special needs and vulnerabilities, including children, women, minorities, and cognitively impaired subjects, *see* Jonathan Moreno et al., *Consent, and the Members of the Project on Informed Ethics Group*, 280 JAMA 1951 (1998).

Some critics maintain that IRB review is unlikely to compensate for the lack of federal regulations governing cognitively impaired subjects. *See* Jonathan D. Moreno, *Regulation of Research on the Decisionally Impaired: History and Gaps in the Current Regulatory System*, 1 J. Health Care L. & Pol'y 105 (1998). For suggestions to increase the effectiveness of IRB review of cognitively impaired research subjects, *see* Richard J. Bonnie, *Research with Cognitively Impaired Subjects: Unfinished Business in the Regulation of Human Research*, 54 Arch. Gen. Psychiatry 105 (1997); Alison Wichman, *Protecting Vulnerable Research Subjects: Practical Realities of Institutional Review Board Review and Approval* 1 J. Health Care L. & Pol'y 88 (1998).

3. On the authority of parents to make decisions for their children generally, *see* Judith Areen, Cases and Materials on Family Law 1124–1238 (4th ed. 1999).

Testimony of Frank C. Conahan, Assistant Comptroller General, National Security and International Affairs Division, *Hearing Before the Legislation and National Security Subcommittee of the Committee on Government Operations*

Cold War Era Experiments on Humans: Statement to U.S. House of Representatives, 103d Cong., September 28, 1994.

Mr. Conahan: Mr. Chairman and Members of the Subcommittee:

We are pleased to be here today to discuss the use of humans in tests and experiments conducted for national security purposes by the Department of Defense (DOD) and other agencies between 1940 and 1974.

. . .

The programs included tests and experiments conducted or sponsored by the Departments of the Army, the Navy, and the Air Force; the Defense Nuclear Agency; the Central Intelligence Agency (CIA); the Department of Energy; and the Department of Health and Human Services. The tests and experiments involved radiological, chemical, and biological research and were conducted to support weapon development programs, identify methods to protect the health of military personnel against a variety of diseases and combat conditions, and analyze U.S. defense vulnerabilities.

. . .

Although military regulations in effect as early as 1953 generally required that volunteers be informed of the nature and foreseeable risks of the studies in which they participated, this did not always occur. Some participants have testified that they were not informed about the test risks. Government testing and experimentation with human subjects continues today because of its importance to national security agencies. For example, the Army's Medical Research Institute for Infectious Disease uses volunteers in its tests of new vaccines for malaria, hepatitis, and other exotic diseases. Since 1974, federal regulations have become more protective of research subjects and, in general, require (1) the formation of institutional review boards and procedures and (2) researchers to obtain informed consent from human subjects and ensure that their participation is voluntary and based on knowledge of the potential risks and benefits. We are in the process of reviewing the effectiveness of these measures. A National Institutes of Health official has stated that no mechanism exists to ensure implementation of the key federal policies in this area.

. . .

Chemical Tests and Experiments

. . .

During World War II, the Army conducted tests of protective clothing and equipment in which thousands of people were exposed to mustard gas and lewisite agents. In addition, the Army developed and tested offensive chemical weapons and evaluated the effectiveness and persistency of mustard agents in different environments. In February 1993, we reported that the Army's records of its mustard test activities were not kept in a manner that readily identifies the participants.[15] However, the available records show that 1,002 soldiers were commended for their participation in tests in which they subjected themselves to pain, discomfort, and possible permanent injury for the advancement of research in protection of the armed services.

Similar to the Army's tests, the Navy conducted tests of clothing and equipment that exposed thousands to the effects of mustard gas and lewisite agents. These experiments involved (1) gas chamber tests, in which service members were completely exposed to mustard and lewisite agents while wearing protective clothing, and (2) skin tests, in which amounts of mustard agent and antivesicant ointments were applied to service members' forearms. The Navy has a list of the names of approximately 3,200 sailors who participated in mustard and lewisite agent tests performed by the Naval Research Laboratory. Additionally, Navy officials told us that between 15,000 and 60,000 Navy recruits had participated in skin tests conducted by a contractor but that the Navy had no record of the recruits' names.

From 1952 to 1975, the Army conducted a classified medical research program to develop incapacitating agents. The program involved testing nerve agents, nerve agent antidotes, psychochemicals, and irritants. The chemicals were given to volunteer service members at the Edgewood Arsenal, Maryland, and four other locations. Army documents identify a total of 7,120 Army and Air Force personnel who participated in these tests, about half of whom were exposed to chemicals....

> During the same period, the Army Chemical Corps contracted with various universities, state hospitals, and medical foundations to research the disruptive influences that psychochemical agents could have on combat troops. The Air Force also conducted experiments on the effects of LSD through contracts at five universities. According to Air Force officials and records, approximately 100 people received LSD in these experiments....

. . .

Biological Tests and Experiments

The Army conducted a series of biological warfare experiments and tests between 1949 and 1974. The purpose of these tests was to determine U.S. vulnerabilities to biological warfare. For example, between 1949 and 1969, the Army conducted several hundred biological warfare tests in which unaware populations were sprayed with bacterial tracers or stimulants that the Army thought were harmless at that time. Some of the tests involved spraying large areas, such as the cities of St. Louis and San Francisco, and others involved spraying more focused areas, such as the New York City subway system and Washington National Airport.

. . .

15. Veterans Disability: Information From Military May Help VA Assess Claims   Related to Secret Tests (GAO/NSIAD–93–89, Feb. 18, 1993).

GOVERNMENT EFFORTS TO STRENGTHEN THE PROTECTION OF HUMAN PARTICIPANTS

. . .

The 1947 Nuremberg Code of Ethics established the fundamental principles for scientists and physicians involved in using people as subjects in experiments and tests. In the Nuremberg Code, the respect for the human rights of patients, including their voluntary consent and their safety from undue physical or psychological harm, was of paramount consideration. A 1953 memorandum from the Secretary of Defense to the secretaries of the military services directed them, in essence, to adopt the Nuremberg Code as a guide for human experimentation. However, according to defense officials, some of the rules, including those related to the quality of informed consent and the capability of the subjects to withdraw without prejudice, were not followed in the 1950s and 1960s.

NOTES AND QUESTIONS

1. In 1958 Army sergeant James Stanley volunteered to participate in a program designed to test the effectiveness of protective clothing discovered. During the month that followed, the Army secretly administered LSD to Stanley on four separate occasions. As a result of the LSD exposure, Stanley suffered from hallucinations, periods of incoherence and memory loss, impaired military performance, and occasional outbursts of violence towards his wife and children. This behavior led to his discharge from the Army in 1969 and the dissolution of his marriage one year later. In 1975, Stanley learned for the first time that he had unwittingly been a part of the military's LSD tests when the Army sent him a letter soliciting his cooperation in studying the long-term effects of LSD. After the Army denied his administrative claim for compensation, he filed suit under the Federal Tort Claims Act in a case that made it to the Supreme Court in 1987. United States v. Stanley, 483 U.S. 669, 107 S.Ct. 3054, 97 L.Ed.2d 550 (1987). The Supreme Court dismissed the claim, holding that all suits were barred for injuries to servicemen that are "incident to service," and that courts should not second-guess the "unique disciplinary structure of the military establishment." Id. at 683–684.

2. Prior to the Persian Gulf War in 1990 the Department of Defense [DOD] became concerned that U.S. troops involved in Operation Desert Storm would be exposed to chemical and biological weapons. In response to a DOD request, the FDA issued an interim rule that granted waivers from its informed consent requirements for the use of two unapproved drugs in the Persian Gulf War: pyridostigmine bromide and botulinum toxoid vaccine. See 55 Fed. Reg. 52813 (December 21, 1990). On January 11, 1991, Public Citizen Health Research Group filed suit against the Department of Health and Human Services in the United States District Court on behalf of an unnamed serviceman stationed in Saudi Arabia, his wife, and all others similarly situated. The complaint alleged that the rule was outside of the FDA's statutory authority and that the Government's use of drugs on unconsenting persons was a deprivation of liberty in violation of the Fifth Amendment. The district court dismissed the suit holding that the complaint questioned "a military decision that is not subject to judicial review." Doe v. Sullivan, 756 F.Supp. 12, 14 (D.D.C. 1991). The decision was upheld on appeal. Doe v. Sullivan, 938 F.2d 1370 (1991). An estimated 250,000 to 300,000 soldiers were ordered to take pyridostigmine bromide tablets daily for as long as they were in the combat region. Since the war, over 100,000 veterans have complained of chronic illness, dubbed Gulf War Syndrome, and a report underwritten by the Pentagon has concluded that the drug pyridostigmine bromide may be responsible. *See* Steven Lee Myers, *Drug May Be Cause of Veterans' Illnesses*, N.Y. TIMES, October 19, 1999, at A18.

3.   Due to the concerns raised in the Gulf War, Congress held several hearings on the use of investigational new drugs on members of the military, and the FDA's interim rule on military waiver of informed consent went through several notice and comment hearings. 55 Fed. Reg. 52817, Dec. 21, 1990; 64 Fed. Reg. 399, Jan. 5, 1999; 64 Fed. Reg. 26657, May 17, 1999; 64 Fed. Reg. 54188, Oct. 5, 1999. In 1998 Congress signed into law 10 U.S.C. § 1107, which prohibits the administration of investigational or unapproved drugs to service members without their informed consent. The consent requirement may be waived only by the President. In 1999, the President signed Executive Order 13139, requiring that the Department of Defense must obtain informed consent from each individual member of the armed forces before administering investigational drugs, and that waivers of informed consent will be granted only "when absolutely necessary." The FDA'a interim rule was codified in its final form on October 5, 1999 at 21 C.F.R. § 50.23. The regulation states in part that

> Under 10 U.S.C. 1107(f) the President may waive the prior consent require-ment for the administration of an investigational new drug to a member of the armed forces in connection with the member's participation in a particular military operation. The statute specifies that only the President may waive informed consent in this connection and the President may grant such a waiver only if the President determines in writing that obtaining consent: Is not feasible; is contrary to the best interests of the military member; or is not in the interests of national security.

21 C.F.R. § 50.23(d)(1) (2003).

4.   In 1998, the Department of Defense (DOD) began a mass inoculation program using an anthrax vaccine (AVA) as a preventative measure against inhalation anthrax for service members and civilian employees. The program was administered without informed consent or a presidential waiver. Members of the armed forces and civilian employees of DOD filed suit for a preliminary injunction, claiming that AVA was an investigational new drug and that potential side effects from the drug could cause irreparable harm. Doe v. Rumsfeld, 297 F.Supp.2d 119 (D.D.C. 2003). The court agreed and issued an injunction barring DOD from continuing to inoculate people without their consent. The court stated that if the inoculation program was indeed necessary to the smooth functioning of the military and a matter of national security, DOD was free to seek a Presidential waiver. *Id.* at 134. The DOD's website claimed that under Saddam Hussein, Iraq had the ability to wage biological warfare, as "thousands of pounds of anthrax agent were loaded into missiles, aerial bombs and spray tanks." However, neither military personnel, nor special teams of inspectors searching in Iraq have found any stocks of anthrax or other biological agents. *See* Robert Pear, *Judge Halts Military's Required Anthrax Shots*, N.Y. TIMES, Dec. 23, 2003, at A23.

CHAPTER 4

DEATH AND DYING

I. DEFINING DEATH

State v. Guess

Supreme Court of Connecticut, 1998.
244 Conn. 761, 715 A.2d 643.

■ KATZ, J.

The sole issue on appeal is whether the term "death," as used in the Penal Code, may be construed to embrace a determination, made according to accepted medical standards, that a person has suffered an irreversible cessation of all brain functions.

The defendant, Barry Guess, was charged with murder.... [H]e was found guilty.... [H]e appealed raising ... the issue of whether, because the victim's life support systems had been disconnected after he had been shot by the defendant, the evidence presented was insufficient to support a finding of probable cause for the crime of murder. The Appellate Court ... conclud[ed] that the proximate cause of the victim's death was the bullet wound he had sustained, and the act of disconnecting the life support systems after the victim had been declared brain dead was a medically reasonable act that neither caused the victim's death nor constituted a sufficient intervening cause so as to negate the defendant's acts as the cause of death.

... [W]e granted the defendant's petition for certification as to the following issue: "Did the Appellate Court properly uphold the defendant's conviction of murder when Connecticut has not adopted the Uniform Determination of Death Act?" ... We conclude as a matter of common law that death as used in the Penal Code includes an irreversible cessation of the functioning of the brain and, accordingly, we affirm the judgment of the Appellate Court.

[Eds.—The court here sets forth the pertinent facts of the defendant's shooting of the victim.]

... Joseph Piepmeier, the neurosurgeon at Yale New Haven Hospital who had treated the victim the morning of the shooting ... testified that the victim arrived at the hospital at 1:59 a.m. in a coma with a heart rate of forty and no respiratory function. There was no evidence of brain stem function. According to Piepmeier, "[b]rain stem activity or brain stem function deals with the very basic functions of survival such as integration of movement, swallowing, breathing, controlling heart rate and blood vessels, controlling lung function, controlling how your gut works...."

[T]he very basic things that physiologically make us work [are] in the brain stem."

[]After the victim was intubated and put on a ventilator and respirator, his heart rate and blood pressure rose. He could not breathe on his own. After a while, there were discussions with the victim's family regarding disconnecting the ventilator or respirator. At about 9:30 a.m., a test was performed to determine if the victim could breathe on his own, and it was determined that he could not. His heart could not beat on its own without life support systems. According to Piepmeier, the victim was brain dead because there was no evidence of any brain activity. He went on to testify that "any death, any death, regardless of mechanism, involves a cessation of brain activity. Death, in my estimation can only occur one way, one final common pathway, and that is the cessation of brain activity, regardless of what the heart's doing or the kidneys are doing, the lungs are doing, it's immaterial. Death is defined as an event in the brain." After a question regarding the maintenance of body functions through mechanical means, Piepmeier responded, "You can be dead and through machines and medication have a beating heart and the machine blowing oxygen into your lungs and taking carbon dioxide away.... [I]t is possible for someone to be dead in a medical definition and to have machines and medications make their heart and lungs perform activities." He also testified that a doctor could issue a notice of death for a person while life support systems continue in place, although the general practice is to wait until the machines have been disconnected. The victim's parents authorized that the machines be disconnected and the victim was pronounced dead.[]

On appeal ... the defendant argued that, because the legislature had not adopted the Uniform Determination of Death Act,[4] and because the legislature did not define death in the Penal Code to include brain death, the court, in determining who or what caused the victim's death, must use a common-law definition of death, which does not include brain death, but rather depends solely upon the cessation of circulatory and respiratory functions of the body....

    . . .

The state argues in response that the legislature adopted a uniform definition of death to achieve uniformity in responding to the advances in medical technology and that the prefatory language should not be exaggerated in a way that undermines that intent. Based upon that assumption, the state contends, it is illogical to suppose that the legislature intended that the term "death" have different meanings in different contexts....

    . . .

Because the legislature did not provide a definition of death in the Penal Code, we interpret the term in accordance with its commonly approved usage.... [W]e can, as a matter of common-law adjudication,

---

4. The Uniform Determination of Death Act (1980) § 1, provides: "An individual who has sustained either (1) irreversible cessation of circulatory and respiratory functions, or (2) irreversible cessation of all func- tions of the entire brain, including the brain stem, is dead. A determination of death must be made in accordance with accepted medical standards."

define that term in tandem with medical science and technology as they have evolved in recent years.

We begin with the defendant's claim that this court has accepted a common-law definition of death that is limited to the cessation of the respiratory and circulatory systems, and that the legislature, in drafting the Penal Code without providing a statutory definition of death, intended that the common-law definition then in existence apply. In other words, according to the defendant, by failing to define the term in the Penal Code, the legislature contemplated reliance on a common-law definition frozen in time.

Although death has typically been discussed in terms of cessation of the heart and respiratory systems, the defendant has pointed to no case, and we have found none, in which this court has *expressly* defined death in such terms. Perhaps the fact that death has not been legally defined merely reflects the fact that, until now, no reason existed for this traditional medical definition to engender legal controversy. Indeed, only recently have medical science and technology evolved to the point where a person's heartbeat and respiration may be sustained mechanically even in the face of an irreversible loss of all brain functions, and where machines that artificially maintain cardiorespiratory functions have come into widespread use.

"Traditionally, in criminal prosecutions for homicide, when the fact or time of death was at issue, the common law defined death as 'the cessation of life' and set a medical standard of the stoppage of the circulatory and respiratory systems." According to pre–1960 medical standards, the cessation of life was determined by the stoppage of the circulatory and respiratory systems. The criteria of the stoppage of the circulatory and respiratory systems were cast into flux as the medical community gained a better appreciation of human physiology. See Report of President's Commission for Study of Ethical Problems in Medicine and Biomedical and Behavioral Research on Defining Death, Medical, Legal and Ethical Issues in Determination of Death (1981). "These traditional legal rules on death became troubling during the 1960's, following medical advances in three areas: (1) improved organ transplant technology, creating a need for "fresh" organs, (2) the ability of external respiratory and circulatory machines to maintain these bodily functions artificially for longer and longer periods, and (3) the enhanced ability to detect and monitor brain activity." As a result, a new medical definition of "death" centering on brain activity was developed.

The criteria by which the medical community determines brain death, first established in 1968 by the Ad Hoc Committee of the Harvard Medical School to Examine the Definition of Brain Death (Harvard Committee), include: (1) a total lack of responsivity to externally applied stimuli; (2) no spontaneous muscular movements or respiration; and (3) no reflexes, as measured by fixed, dilated pupils and lack of ocular, pharyngeal and muscle-tendon reflexes. Additionally, the Harvard Committee emphasized that these tests could be confirmed by a flat or isoelectric electroencephalogram reading, that the tests should be conducted twenty-four hours apart, and that hypothermia or the use of central nervous system depressants should be excluded as causative factors. Harvard Committee, "A Definition of Irreversible Coma," 205 JAMA 337 (1968); M. Victor, "Brain Death: An Overview," 27 Med. Trial Tech. Q. 37, 56–58 (1980).

This evolution in medicine has spawned concomitant developments in the law.... [I]n 1980, the National Conference of Commissioners on Uniform State Laws, in concert with the American Medical Association and the American Bar Association, drafted the Uniform Determination of Death Act, which created alternative standards for determining death: either the traditional irreversible cessation of circulatory and respiratory functions, or the irreversible cessation of all functions of the entire brain including the brain stem, "a determination to be made in accordance with accepted medical standards." ... Black's Law Dictionary also responded to the advances in medical science in 1979 when it included for the first time a definition of "brain death" that provides in pertinent part: "Characteristics of brain death consist of: (1) unreceptivity and unresponsiveness to externally applied stimuli and internal needs; (2) no spontaneous movements or breathing; (3) no reflex activity; and (4) a flat electroencephalograph reading after 24 hour period of observation...." Black's Law Dictionary (5th Ed. 1979)....

. . .

The question of when death has occurred carries significant legal ramifications including, but not limited to, issues of: inheritance; criminal and civil liability; termination of mechanical support; liability under insurance contracts; and exposure of physicians to medical malpractice claims. Although we are examining this issue in the context of a homicide, the defendant's position that we are wedded to a definition of death from the time the Penal Code was adopted juxtaposes uncomfortably with the medical community's capacity to sustain heartbeat and respiration through artificial means. The defendant acknowledges that brain death became the medically accepted standard for determining death some time ago.... Furthermore, there is little disagreement with respect to the criteria by which the medical community determines brain death....

. . .

We conclude that our recognition of brain-based criteria for determining death is not unfaithful to any prior judicial determinations. "Death remains the single phenomenon identified at common law; the supplemental criteria are merely adapted to account for the 'changed conditions' that a dead body may be attached to a machine so as to exhibit demonstrably false indicia of life. It reflects an improved understanding that in the complete and irreversible absence of a functioning brain, the traditional loci of life—the heart and the lungs—function only as a result of stimuli originating from outside of the body and will never again function as part of an integrated organism." Because the trial court at the hearing in probable cause reasonably found that the defendant's act of shooting the victim caused extensive brain damage, leaving the victim with no evidence of brain function, the court properly found that the state had established probable cause to charge the defendant with the crime of murder.

The judgment of the Appellate Court is affirmed.

NOTES AND QUESTIONS

1. As the *Guess* court makes clear, until the 1960s, defining death was uncomplicated. A person was considered dead when the heart ceased to beat and the lungs stopped breathing. It was not always so easy, however, to detect when these events had occurred. During the eighteenth century, macabre tales of "corpses" spontaneously reviving during funerals or after being buried were fairly common. There was widespread fear of being buried alive. With the development of the stethoscope in the mid-nineteenth century, sensitive detection of a heartbeat and thus reliable diagnosis of death using cardiopulmonary criteria became possible and eliminated fear of erroneous determinations. PRESIDENT'S COMMISSION, DEFINING DEATH 13–16 (1981); *see* Martin S. Pernick, *Back from the Grave: Recurring Controversies over Defining and Diagnosing Death in History, in* DEATH: BEYOND WHOLE-BRAIN CRITERIA 17 (Richard M. Zaner ed., 1988). In recent decades, as *Guess* also notes, the development of sophisticated support systems capable of artificially maintaining the heart and lungs has resulted in the creation of new problems in determining when death has occurred. These problems were studied by the President's Commission, which worked closely with the American Bar Association, the American Medical Association and the National Conference of Commissioners on Uniform State Laws to draft model legislation. As a result of their efforts, these organizations agreed to endorse the Uniform Definition of Death Act (UDDA) adopted by the court in *Guess*. Today all fifty states and the District of Columbia have recognized whole brain death as the governing definition of death.

The UDDA adopts a whole-brain definition of death to the exclusion of several alternative definitions. The President's Commission rejected non-brain formulations of death, such as "death as the loss of the soul," because it eschewed any involvement in what it viewed as theological matters. The President's Commission did try, however, to make its proposals as consistent as possible with religious and other practices prevalent in society. It also rejected "higher brain" definitions of death for two reasons. First, at a theoretical level, higher brain definitions resort to contested metaphysical notions, and are therefore less useful as a basis for the establishment of public policy. Is this justification compelling? Is a whole brain definition of death independent of "contested metaphysical notions?" Second, on a practical level, it was at best uncertain whether higher brain function was measurable. Moreover, acceptance of a higher brain formulation would represent a radical departure from traditional standards.

2. Do we need a definition of death for public policy purposes? Consider the view of Professor Roger Dworkin:

> The effort devoted to defining death is wasted at best, counterproductive at worst. The modern writers on death have failed to ask the most basic question about the death definition problem: What difference does it make whether somebody is dead? That question places the issue of death into the only posture in which it can be of relevance to the law—the posture of context or consequences. Whatever may be the needs of the philosopher or the ethicist, the lawyer needs only to know what consequences follow upon a given determination. Only if we are persuaded that one definition of death will always lead to a correct resolution of legal problems do we need to search for such a definition.

Roger Dworkin, *Death in Context*, 48 IND. L. J. 623, 628 (1973). Even if a unitary definition of death is not needed for public policy purposes, is such a definition desirable? Professor Dworkin's views have been criticized. *See* Alexander M. Capron, *The Purpose of Death: A Reply to Professor Dworkin*, 48 IND. L. J. 640 (1973); PRESIDENT'S COMMISSION, DEFINING DEATH 60 (1981). Are Professor Dworkin's views of greater relevance to the issue of defining when life begins? *See* Chapter 5, Sec. I., *infra*.

3. The issue of brain death has long raised causation issues in the context of homicide cases. Specifically, defendants have often argued that by removing a victim from life support at the time he is taken to a hospital, thus causing the stoppage of his circulatory and respiratory functions, it is the doctors—and not the defendants—who have "caused" the victim's death; indeed, such victims could conceivably be kept "alive" indefinitely via mechanical means. To date, however, this argument has yet to prove successful. Indeed, in a case immediately following the ruling in *Guess*, a Connecticut appellate court rejected just such a defense. *See State v. Burke*, 51 Conn.App. 798, 725 A.2d 370, 375 (1999).

4. There have been some criticisms of the UDDA. James Bernat, Charles Culver, and Bernard Gert believe that the statute is too ambiguous because it treats the irreversible cessation of cardiopulmonary functioning as a standard of death as opposed to a test to see if death has occurred. They propose a different formulation.

> An individual who has sustained irreversible cessation of all functions of the entire brain, including the brainstem, is dead
>
> > (a) In the absence of artificial means of cardiopulmonary support, death (the irreversible cessation of all brain functions) may be determined by the prolonged absence of spontaneous circulatory and respiratory functions.
> >
> > (b) In the absence of artificial means of cardiopulmonary support, death (the irreversible cessation of all brain functions) must be determined by tests of brain function.

What advantages, if any, does this formulation have over UDDA? In both situations, the determination of death must be made in accordance with accepted medical standards. J. Bernat, et al., *Defining Death in Theory and Practice*, 12 HASTINGS CTR. REP. 5 (1982).

Karen Grandstrand Gervais, *Advancing the Definition of Death: A Philosophical Essay*

3 MED. HUMANITIES REV. 7, 7–17 (1989).

In 1968, the most important *clinical document* in the history of the definition-of-death debate appeared.... This document, the report of the Ad Hoc Committee of the Harvard Medical School to Examine the Definition of Brain Death, recommended that a whole-brain-death criterion be used to determine death in respirator-dependent patients, thus creating an exception to the use of the traditional heart-and-lung criteria for determining death in a specific category of patients....

However, ... the Harvard Committee left critical *theoretical* questions out of its discussion, and people have been debating them ever since. Essentially, they all boil down to the issue of why it is all right to declare a human being dead because he or she is brain dead. Thus, the theoretical disputes concerning the definition of death have arisen because of a concern to *justify* the use of the brain-death criterion. The most important theoretical issues being debated are: What sorts of considerations *justify* the creation of the whole-brain-death exception to the use of the traditional criteria for determining death? *and,* Do those same (or possibly other) considerations *justify* the creation of any further exceptions to the use of the traditional criteria?

Although some individuals retain the traditional understanding that the human being is not dead until the body permanently ceases functioning, there are essentially two party lines in the theoretical debate: whole-brain theory and higher-brain theory. Proponents of the traditional theory have for the most part dropped out of the theoretical debate, but they are certainly a factor to reckon with in the construction of an adequate public policy in a pluralistic society such as ours. In theory, the whole-brain position requires the permanent cessation of the central functions of the entire brain; that is, the functions of consciousness and social interaction associated with the higher brain, and the vegetative functions associated with the lower brain and brainstem. Higher-brain theorists consider that an adequate theoretical defense exists for regarding the permanent cessation of higher-brain functions as the death of the human being.

The most significant U.S. *public policy document* on the determination of death, the President's Commission report entitled *Defining Death,* was published in 1981. It stands as a benediction of sorts to much of the theorizing, as well as the practice, that developed on the basis of the Harvard Committee's recommendation thirteen years earlier. Disclaiming the importance of theoretical precision, probably to divert attention from the theoretical morass it constructed in its report, the Commission adopted a whole-brain theory, opposed a higher-brain theory, and recommended that death be determined by the use of either the traditional or the brain-death criteria in its Uniform Determination of Death Act. Then, despite the fact that an individual's concept of death is ultimately a religious or philosophical matter, the Commission rejected the inclusion of a conscience clause that would allow individuals to be declared dead on the basis of a criterion consistent with their personal concept of death. At this time, the policy issues in the definition-of-death debate concern the importance of constructing a coherent theoretical foundation concerning human death for public policy ...; the articulation of an adequate theoretical position ...; the justifiability of a public policy enabling discretion through the inclusion of a conscience clause; and (if such a conscience clause is justified) the actual design of the overall policy and its conscience clause.

. . .

The Theoretical Dimension of the Definition-of-Death Debate

By now, almost everyone engaged in the definitional debate knows that it is a multi-level debate. These levels include the philosophical question concerning the *concept or definition* of human death, the medical question surrounding the *criteria* for determining death, and the medical-diagnostic problem of devising specific clinical and laboratory *tests* to determine whether a criterion is met.

. . .

Normally, we proceed from a concept to the specification of a criterion, and then on to a determination of a way of testing or measuring. In the case of the determination of death, however, these matters got out of order with the adoption of the brain-death criterion. In a theoretically blind maneuver, we adopted a criterion for determining death, along with the tests for determining that the criterion was fulfilled, without clarifying the underlying concept of death.

. . .

Since we already had in place the traditional heart-and-lung criteria for determining death, along with whatever concept of death their use presupposed (a matter on which there is no agreement), the adoption of the brain-death criterion might have been unproblematic if the underlying concept(s) of death were clear and no one was concerned that the brain-death criterion might represent a change in our definition of human death. However, the adoption of the brain-death criterion occurred in a theoretical or conceptual vacuum of sorts, a vacuum many of us have been trying to fill ever since. . . .

The UDDA itself does not convey the *concept* of death that provides the philosophical footing for the two *criteria* it specifies. Supporting arguments in other portions of the policy document make it clear that the President's Commission espouses a whole-brain theory of death. A careful examination of these arguments shows that the Commission understands this concept of death as the permanent cessation of brain-generated integrated bodily functioning, and that the role of the brain in consciousness is not included in the Commission's notion of integrated bodily functioning. . . .

In this, the post-President's Commission era, several theoretical questions linger. Is the whole-brain theory defensible? . . . In light of the fact that we use the traditional heart-lung as well as the brain-death criterion for determining death, can we come to any agreement on the conceptions or definitions underlying this practice?

. . .

In particular, what do we say about the Uniform Determination of Death Act and the justification of this policy document proffered by the President's Commission? Certainly its assertion of the unimportance of conceptual clarity where the definition of death is concerned is one way of setting these issues aside. But be that as it may, we are left with these questions on the theoretical level: Is there a strong defense that can be constructed for the whole-brain formulation of death? And then, is the higher-brain theory defensible, in spite of the objections typically raised against it? Since it is indisputable that the use of a higher-brain criterion departs from whatever understanding of death underlies the traditional criteria, what sort of argument is required to vindicate this change in the way we regard the human: namely, the change from regarding the human as an organism to regarding the human as a personal being so far as deciding what constitutes its death? These theoretical issues appear to me to be central in the definitional debate at this time. . . .

The Whole–Brain–Theory Dispute

. . . Certainly David Lamb's work stands out as the best effort to articulate a sound theoretical argument in favor of the whole-brain formulation of death. . . .

Lamb writes:

If the "loss of that which is essentially significant" is to have any meaning as a concept of death, then it must be framed so that it involves an irreversible state where the organism as a whole cannot function. Only a concept which specifies the irreversible loss of specified functions (due to the destruction of their anatomical substratum) can avoid the anomalous situation where a patient is said to be alive according to one concept but dead according to another. The only wholly satisfactory concept of death is that which trumps other concepts of death in so far as it yields a diagnosis of death which is beyond dispute. It follows that any criterion which, when fulfilled, leaves it possible for someone to say that the patient is still alive, is unsatisfactory. For this reason concepts relating specifically to psychological functions or moral qualities are wholly inadequate. In fact any criterion which, when fulfilled, leaves it possible for the organism as a whole to continue to function is inadequate.[1]

The obvious question then is this: What constitutes the continued function of the organism as a whole? Lamb does not think the changes in technology and the adoption of the brain-death criterion necessitate a new concept of death: death is still, biologically speaking, the same thing it always was: "the irreversible loss of function of the organism as a whole," which, he explains, involves the permanent loss of the capacity for consciousness as well as for breathing. In spite of the fact that he claims that "the concept of death involves a philosophical judgment that a significant change has taken place," Lamb treats the definition of death as "primarily a biological phenomenon." Given what he takes to be a non-normative (biological) definition of life, Lamb views the clarification of the concept of death to be a factual, biological pursuit. Given "that there cannot be any sense in which *there can be alternative or new ways of being dead*, ... brain death does not represent a new concept of death, but rather a situation demanding that different criteria be fulfilled." "*Brain death is a radical reformulation of traditional concepts of death rather than a new concept, since there is no new way of being dead....*" In the end, Lamb seems committed to the same reductivistic (Robert Veatch's term) justification of the brain (stem) death criterion when he writes, "the death of the organism as a whole does not occur ... until the brain, the critical system, is no longer capable of integrating the vital subsystems."

There are many challenges to whole-brain theory.... Essentially, these critiques focus on the failure of existing whole-brain theories to attend to the two central functions of the human brain: the integrative functions of the lower brain, *and* the cognitive functions of the higher brain. The argument against whole-brain theory resolves down to the objection that whole-brain theorists appeal to only the brain's integrative role, and not to its role in consciousness, in their arguments supporting the use of the brain-death criterion. In effect, then, a lower-brain concept of death, and not a whole-brain concept, is being employed.

. . .

The Higher–Brain–Theory Dispute

... [S]everal theorists have attempted to justify a concept of human death that centers on the permanent loss of the functions associated with

---

1. DAVID LAMB, DEATH, BRAIN DEATH AND ETHICS 13 (1985).

the higher brain, and thus to support the use of a neocortical criterion for the determination of death. . . .

Higher-brain theorists seem united on the point that our decision about what constitutes the death of the human being must reflect what is essentially significant to human nature, and that the permanent cessation of (embodied) consciousness qualifies, since it is a necessary condition for any of the uniquely human capacities individuals possess in differing measure. Although the human is one species among many living things, and has much in common with other species, higher-brain theorists hold either that it is an ontological error or a moral disservice to us, given our ontological distinctiveness, to determine death solely on the basis of the organismic functions humans share with other living things. Hence, the argument goes, whatever criteria we use to determine that a person has died must refer to the permanent cessation of higher-brain functions; and they need not refer to the integrative functions of the lower brain. . . .

The theoretical arguments supporting a higher-brain concept of death are divided on the nature of the arguments required to make the case. Robert Veatch, for example, maintains that the reasoning required need focus solely on the question of when death behaviors become appropriate. This suggests that a moral argument is all that is needed. In response, I think an ontological argument is required as well, and that the moral considerations Veatch provides presuppose a particular ontological view. Our conclusions about the appropriateness of death behaviors are based on an assignment of significance to the characteristics of the individual. Hence, a full justification of a concept of death requires that we cite the characteristics of the individual we now think it appropriate to treat as dead, and justify the claim that those characteristics should be considered determinative that a human being has died. And I think one can provide this by appealing to the sine qua non of personal existence, consciousness. I do not think we need a fully developed theory of personhood or personal identity. But my point is that the task of fully justifying a higher-brain concept of human death, or any concept of human death for that matter, requires both ontological and moral argumentation.

. . .

The Public Policy Dispute

. . .

Given that there is theoretical disagreement among us concerning the concept of human death, and that the use of criteria to determine death presupposes a concept of death, it is difficult to see how theoretical imprecision, and the lack of a clear defense of the underlying understanding of what death is, can be justified in a public policy document. The Uniform Determination of Death Act is guilty of both. The question that must be addressed, then, is this: What concept of death ought to be written into public policy as the default concept of death? Is the default concept to be chosen on the basis of the quality of the theoretical arguments supporting it, societal consensus, or on some other basis? Regardless of the basis upon which it is chosen, is there a workable conscience clause that can be

designed to honor our commitment to the values of pluralism and tolera-
tion? The permutations of possible answers to these questions appearing in
the literature are many, and the discussion of these issues, I believe, is only
beginning.

NOTES AND QUESTIONS

1. Gervais describes two basic approaches to defining death at the conceptual
level. Biological approaches to defining death employ arguments based upon biology
and seek to define death purely in biological terms. These arguments are typically
cast in terms of a general biological theory of the necessary conditions for life to
exist. Alternatively, they may be cast in descriptive neurophysiological terms unique
to humans. *See* DAVID LAMB, DEATH, BRAIN DEATH AND ETHICS (1985). For criticisms of
the biological approach, see KAREN G. GERVAIS, REDEFINING DEATH 45–74 (1986).

By contrast, philosophical approaches are concerned with defining death in
terms of the death of persons rather than organisms. For example, an ontological
approach, which is concerned with the existence or non-existence of entities called
"persons," defines death according to changes in the metaphysical status of these
persons. On this view, the relevant question in defining death is when (or if) a
"person" has ceased to exist. If the person no longer exists, death has occurred. *See*
Michael B. Green & Daniel Wikler, *Brain Death and Personal Identity*, 9 PHIL. &
PUB. AFF. 105–29 (1980). Alternatively, a moral approach seeks to define the death
of a person by focusing on "good" and "bad" behaviors and what differentiates
them from one another. On this view, the relevant question in defining death is
when certain behaviors, for example, the removal of vital organs, are morally
appropriate. *See* BARUCH A. BRODY, ETHICAL DECISIONS IN MEDICINE (1981); ROBERT M.
VEATCH, DEATH, DYING, AND THE BIOLOGICAL REVOLUTION (1989).

In view of Gervais' description of the approaches to defining death at the
conceptual level, how realistic is it to expect that consensus on these matters in a
pluralistic society is possible? Is consensus at the conceptual level necessary for
adequate public policy? What, if any, implications does Gervais' discussion have for
resolving the question of when life begins? *See* Chapter 5, Sec. I., *infra*.

2. Defining death in terms of the death of "persons" raises perplexing issues that
have plagued philosophers and theologians for centuries. For example, if persons
and humans are distinct, what is the relation between them? *See, e.g.*, Mario
Moussa & Thomas S. Shannon, *The Search for the New Pineal Gland: Brain Life
and Personhood*, 22 HASTINGS CTR. REP. 30 (1992). Exactly what is a person? A
mental substance as Descartes believed? A bundle of properties? A string of
memories? A continuous consciousness? For a readable rendering of the philosophy
of persons, see DEREK PARFIT, REASONS AND PERSONS 199–245 (1984). Are there any
other entities (e.g., porpoises and higher primates) that could be persons? Could a
computer ever become so sophisticated that it becomes a person? What must be lost
in order for a human to cease to be a person? *See, e.g.*, Steven Goldberg, *The
Changing Face of Death: Computers, Consciousness, and Nancy Cruzan*, 43 STAN. L.
REV. 659 (1991).

3. In view of the lack of consensus on a conceptual definition of death, defining
death may involve a trade-off between individual autonomy and governmental
interests in uniformity and efficiency. The President's Commission, while "sympathetic to the concerns and values" represented by proposals for conscience clauses,
concluded that a uniform standard was required in order to avoid "unfortunate and
mischievous results." PRESIDENT'S COMMISSION, DEFINING DEATH 80 (1981).

Two states have created "conscience clauses" that allow the patient or the next of kin to determine whether the patient would prefer to have her death defined in terms of the traditional standard. The state of New Jersey has enacted legislation which provides in pertinent part:

> The death of an individual shall not be declared upon the basis of neurological criteria ... when the licensed physician authorized to declare death, has reason to believe, on the basis of information in the individual's available medical records, or information provided by a member of the individual's family or any other person knowledgeable about the individual's personal religious beliefs that such a declaration would violate the personal religious beliefs of the individual. In these cases, death shall be declared, and the time of death fixed, solely upon the basis of cardio-respiratory criteria....

N.J. STAT. ANN. § 26:6AB1 et seq. (1987 & Supp. 1994). New York's policy is found in its State Department of Health regulation governing the determination of death. It provides:

> Each hospital shall establish and implement a written policy ... [that] shall include ... [a] procedure for the reasonable accommodation of the individual's religious or moral objection to the determination [based on whole-brain criteria]....

N.Y. COMP. CODES R. & REGS. tit. 10, § 400.16(e) (1992). For additional commentary on this issue, see Robert S. Olick, *Brain Death, Religious Freedom, and Public Policy: New Jersey's Landmark Legislative Initiative*, 1 KENNEDY INST. ETHICS J. 275 (1991); KAREN G. GERVAIS, REDEFINING DEATH 198–216 (1986). Should other states enact "conscience clauses"?

4. Are there any circumstances that justify departure from whole-brain definitions of death? This issue is posed when parents of newborns born with anencephaly wish to donate organs to other children. Infants with anencephaly are born with a functioning brain stem, but their "upper brain" or cerebral hemispheres are either wholly absent or extremely rudimentary. These infants are potential sources of organs for neonates and young children. A conservative estimate is that three out of every 10,000 total births (including aborted fetuses) are anencephalic. *See, e.g.*, D. Alan Shewmon et al., *The Use of Anencephalic Infants as Organ Sources: A Critique*, 261 JAMA 1773 (1989). Newborns with anencephaly are not dead by any currently accepted definitions of death. *See In re T.A.C.P.*, 609 So.2d 588 (Fla. 1992) (holding that current definitions of death do not include anencephaly). By the time these infants satisfy current legal standards for death (a prerequisite for organ donation known as the "dead donor rule"), many of their organs are no longer suitable for transplantation. Unless these newborns are placed on a respirator, their organs begin to deteriorate from the moment of birth due to hypoxia (lack of oxygen due to impaired respiration or circulation).

This situation has spawned numerous proposals to allow the use of organs of children suffering with anencephaly. Two of these approaches involve modification of existing standards for defining death. First, some commentators argue that the UDDA should be expanded to include anencephaly as a variant of brain death. Such a modification was proposed in the California Senate in 1986. The Florida Supreme Court refused to modify the state determination of death statute, which differs from the UDDA, because no "public necessity" justified such a modification. *In re T.A.C.P.*, 609 So.2d 588 (Fla. 1992).

Second, other commentators have proposed that anencephalic infants should be categorized as brain-absent and that brain presence should be considered as a necessary condition for personhood or humanity. On this view, anencephalic newborns are totally outside the scope of beings that brain death statutes were designed to protect. The Florida Supreme Court did not consider this possibility. Proponents argue that the brain absence criterion should be strictly limited to anencephalic newborns. Do such proposals have merit? *See* Michael R. Harrison, *The Anencephalic Newborn as Organ Donor*, 16 HASTINGS CTR. REP. 21 (1986); Wolfgang Holzgreve et al., *Kidney Transplantation from Anencephalic Donors*, 316 NEW ENG. J. MED. 1069 (1987). Should death more properly be viewed as the absence of life (however defined), or as a positive condition over and above the mere absence of life? *See* Robert D. Truog & John C. Fletcher, *Anencephalic Newborns: Can Organs Be Transplanted Before Brain Death?*, 321 NEW ENG. J. MED. 388 (1989). Critics argue that the creation of a new category would be tantamount to adopting a higher or upper brain definition of death. If this were to happen, patients in a persistent vegetative state (PVS) might also be viewed as potential organ donors. Is there a danger of a slippery slope? *See* KAREN G. GERVAIS, REDEFINING DEATH (1986); John D. Arras & Shlomo Shinnar, *Anencephalic Newborns as Organ Donors: A Critique*, 259 JAMA 2284 (1984); Alexander A. Capron, *Anencephalic Donors: Separate the Dead from the Dying*, 17 HASTINGS CTR. REP. 5 (1987); Michael B. Green & Daniel Wikler, *Brain Death and Personal Identity*, 9 PHIL. & PUB. AFF. 105 (1980).

5.   Even though there is consensus at the policy level concerning the use of whole brain standards and neurological criteria to define death, uncertainties concerning their application persist in clinical practice. The confusion in part results from the fact that whole-brain dead persons, like living patients, can be maintained for a period of time on life-support systems. This confusion raises several interrelated questions.

What conduct is ethically permissible toward humans in this condition? For example, pregnant women diagnosed as brain dead have had their biological functions artificially maintained in order to prolong the period that the fetus can be sustained in the womb. Is this appropriate treatment of a corpse or does it degrade the woman's status to "a child-bearing machine"? Does the answer depend on the stage of fetal development at the time of the mother's death? Should the body be maintained over the previously expressed objections of the pregnant woman? See Chapter 5, Sec. II., *infra*. Who should decide whether the body should be artificially maintained? Would it be ethically permissible to conduct research on the respiring body?

Second, when does death actually occur? Does death occur when legally recognized criteria are met, or when a physician pronounces death, or when a death certificate is issued? Consider *Strachan v. John F. Kennedy Memorial Hosp.*, 109 N.J. 523, 538 A.2d 346 (1988) (patient's death legally occurred, and hospital's duty to exercise reasonable care in releasing dead body to patient's next-of-kin arose when medical evidence indicated patient brain dead, rather than three days later when patient officially pronounced dead and removed from life support). For a more complete exploration of the *Strachan* case, *see* George J. Annas, *Brain Death and Organ Donation: You Can Have One Without the Other*, 18 HASTINGS CTR. REP. 28 (1988).

Third, how is the determination of death distinguished from decisions to terminate treatment? In an influential article, *A Statutory Definition of the Standards for Determining Human Death: An Appraisal and a Proposal*, 121 U. PA. L. REV. 87 (1972), Alexander M. Capron & Leon R. Kass warn against confusing the many issues that can arise in terminating life-support technology:

> [I]t is crucial to distinguish this question of "when to allow to die?" from the question ... "when to declare death?" Since very different issues are involved in these questions, confusing the one with the other clouds the analysis of both.... Although the same set of social and medical conditions may give rise

to both problems, they must be kept separate if they are to be clearly understood.

Distinguishing the question "is he dead?" from the question "should he be allowed to die?" also assists in preserving continuity with tradition, a second important principle....

Third, this incremental approach is useful for the additional and perhaps most central reason that any new means for judging death should be seen as just that and nothing more—a change in method ... but not an alteration of the meaning of "life" and "death."

Id. at 105–06. In order to avoid confusion that might be created by legislation such as the Michigan statute, Capron & Kass argue that the question of the pronouncement of death should not be enacted into legislation but rather should be left to institutional policy.

6. The continued demand for organs has rekindled interest in using non-heart-beating donors (NHBDs) for transplantation. NHBDs typically fall into one of these categories: patients on life support who can be withdrawn with proper consent or patients who unexpectedly suffer cardiac arrest and cannot be resuscitated. *See* Institute of Medicine, Non-Heart Beating Organ Transplantation: Medical and Ethical Issues in Procurement 1 (1997) [hereinafter Non-Heart Beating Organ Transplantation I]. These patients are called controlled and uncontrolled NHBDs respectively–controlled because death and organ removal can be planned following the withdrawal of life support; uncontrolled because the occurrence of cardiac arrest as well as the timing and other aspects of organ removal are not planned; and non-heart-beating because death is determined by cessation of heart and respiratory function, rather than whole brain function. *Id.*

A key question for controlled NHBDs is whether they are dead by governing legal standards. Controversy generated by the University of Pittsburgh Medical Center (UMPC) policy which was approved in May 1992 illustrates the issue. The UPMC's policy, known as the "Pittsburgh Protocol," emphasizes that consideration of organ donation under the policy may occur only after the patient, her surrogate, or her family has decided to assign her to "comfort measures only" status. *See* Institute of Medicine, Non-Heart-Beating Organ Transplantation: Practice and Protocols 134 (2000) [hereinafter Non-Heart-Beating Organ Transplantation II]. "Comfort measures only" is the UPMC's status for patients who have decided (themselves, or through surrogates) to limit or forego life-sustaining treatment—the functional equivalent of a "do not resuscitate" order. Procurement of organs may not begin until the patient meets the cardiopulmonary criteria for death—that is, the irreversible cessation of cardiopulmonary function. *See* Non-Heart-Beating Organ Transplantation II, at 138. Once the supervising operating room physician has declared death, the transplant team is summoned and immediately harvests the organs.

Clearly, the use of non-heart-beating cadavers as organ donors does not, by itself, pose any ethical problems beyond those normally associated with organ transplantation. *See* Michael A. DeVita et al., *History of Organ Donation by Patients with Cardiac Death*, 3 Kennedy Inst. Ethics J. 113, 126 (1993). Rather, ethical difficulties inherent in the Pittsburgh Protocol derive from the means it employs to minimize "warm ischemia time"—that is the time in which organs must be harvested before they become unsuitable for transplant.

First, all current statutory and judicial definitions of death specify that the loss of vital functions must be irreversible. David Cole argues that patients declared dead according to the Pittsburgh Protocol can be regarded as having irreversibly lost their vital functions only by means of an implausible and impermissibly loose construction of the word "irreversible". What the Protocol calls "irreversible" loss of cardiac function is actually a "low probability" of auto-resuscitation that precludes the possibility of medical interventions that might restart the heart. Cole concludes that the Pittsburgh Protocol is logically inconsistent with the statutory requirement that loss of vital functions be irreversible. *See* David Cole, *Statutory Definitions of Death and the Management of Terminally Ill Patients Who May Become Organ Donors after Death*, 3 KENNEDY INST. ETHICS J. 145, 153 (1993). *See also* Joanne Lynn, *Are the Patients Who Become Organ Donors Under the Pittsburgh Protocol for "Non–Heart–Beating Donors" Really Dead?*, 3 KENNEDY INST. ETHICS J. 167, 169–70, 177 (1993). Defenders of the Protocol counter Cole's argument by pointing out that patients declared dead according to the Protocol have decided against medical intervention. The fact that they might be resuscitated by the application of life-sustaining procedures is irrelevant to the issue of irreversibility; such intervention is no longer an option. *See* Tom Tomlinson, *The Irreversibility of Death: Reply to Cole*, 3 KENNEDY INST. ETHICS J. 157, 162 (1993).

Second, and perhaps more troubling, is the fact that the Protocol relies solely on cardiopulmonary criteria for its declaration of death, ignoring brain death criteria entirely. See Cole, *supra*, at 152–53; Tomlinson, *supra*, at 163–54; Lynn, *supra*, at 175–76. In so doing, the Protocol exploits a structural weakness in the UDDA that allows the Protocol to remain consistent with the language of the statute while at the same time contravening the spirit and intention of the UDDA.

Supporters of the whole-brain criteria have always maintained that it did not entail a conception of death inconsistent with the old heart-centered definition. Whole-brain criteria merely provided a different and more accurate way of measuring the same phenomenon that heart-based criteria had attempted to diagnose: irreversible loss of the brain's integrative functions. *See* PRESIDENT'S COMMISSION, DEFINING DEATH 5, 33–34 (1981). *See also* Alexander M. Capron, *Anencephalic Donors: Separate the Dead from the Dying*, 17 HASTINGS CTR. REP. 5 (1987).

Yet, the Pittsburgh Protocol compromises the primacy of whole-brain criteria by relying on cardiopulmonary criteria in declaring its potential donors dead. Technically, the Protocol is consistent with the UDDA. Its patients are pronounced dead according to cardiopulmonary criteria, which the statute allows. The problem, however, is that there are no clear empirical data proving that a patient who meets the Protocol's cardiopulmonary criteria for death—two minutes of pulselessness—is also dead according to neurological criteria—irreversible loss of whole-brain function. *See* Robert M. Arnold & Stuart J. Younger, *Back to the Future: Obtaining Organs From Non–Heart–Beating Cadavers*, 3 KENNEDY INST. ETHICS J. 103, 107 (1993). It seems plausible, then, that a patient could be declared dead and her organs harvested under the Pittsburgh Protocol long before she has irreversibly lost all her brain functions. And if irreversible loss of brain functions is a necessary condition of death—as those who framed the UDDA assumed—then patients declared dead according to the criteria of the Pittsburgh Protocol are not really dead at all. Consequently, harvesting their organs violates the dead donor rule.

The Institute of Medicine (IOM) has issued two reports, cited above, on the use of NHBDs, finding generally that "the recovery of organs from NHBDs is an important, medically effective, and ethically acceptable approach to reducing the gap that exists now and will exist in the future between the demand for and the available supply of organs for transplantation." *See* NON-HEART-BEATING ORGAN TRANSPLANTATION I, at 1. The IOM has emphasized, however, the importance of resolving variations among non-heart-beating practices and protocols in order to address the above mentioned ethical concerns and maintain public trust in organ donation. *See* NON-HEART-BEATING ORGAN TRANSPLANTATION II, at 3; NON-HEART-BEATING ORGAN TRANSPLANTATION I, at 4. Additionally, both reports recommend that not less than a five minute interval be required to determine donor death in controlled NHBDs. *See* NON-HEART-BEATING ORGAN TRANSPLANTATION II, at 2; NON-HEART-BEATING ORGAN TRANSPLANTATION I, at 5.

II.   DYING WITH DIGNITY

A.   DYING IN THE TWENTY-FIRST CENTURY

Lewis Thomas, Dying as Failure
447 ANNALS 1, 2–4.
(Renée Fox, Spec. Ed. 1980).

It is true, as everyone says these days, that doctors do not know what to do about death. Patients who are known to be dying are segregated as much as possible from all the others, and as the clinically unmistakable process of dying gets under way the doctors spend as little time in attendance as they can manage.

What is not so generally recognized is that doctors, especially young doctors, are as frightened and bewildered by the act of death as everyone else. When they avert their eyes it is not that they have lost interest, or find their attendance burdensome because wasteful of their talents; it is surely not because of occupational callousness. Although they are familiar with the business, seeing more of it at first hand than anyone else in our kind of society, they never become used to it. Death is shocking, dismaying, even terrifying.

A dying patient is a kind of freak. It is the most unacceptable of all abnormalities, an offense against nature itself.

Why is this? You'd think that this event, the most universal and inevitable of all aspects of human life, would be taken in professional stride. Was it always like this?

I think not, although I cannot be sure. My own recollection of medicine at the time when I was a medical student, in the mid–1930s, is hazy enough from this distance, but the thing I remember most clearly from the wards of the old Boston City Hospital is death as an everyday, everynight event, occurring up and down the open wards. The white curtains around each bed were usually kept drawn to one side, but when a death was about to occur the head nurse would make the rounds of the ward, moving fast, pulling each curtain across the foot of every bed. I remember the zinging sound of those curtains being yanked across on their metal rings, bed after bed. It was a commonplace ceremony, part of the working day. The sound was the sound of dying, and all the other patients, the day's survivors, knew what it signified.

The difference from a modern hospital, apart from the change from open wards to mostly private rooms, was in the age of the patients who died. Dying could occur, and did, at any age. It was not an event reserved for the very old, or for the middle-aged patients who had reached the end of their long battles with cancer or heart disease or strokes. Many of the patients who died on the open wards of the City Hospital were young people, overwhelmed by an infectious disease—lobar pneumonia, meningitis, septicemia, tuberculosis—for which there was no effective treatment of any kind.

The inevitability of death was plainer to see in those days. For a great many of the ordinary illnesses that brought patients into the hospital, dying was the expected outcome, beyond the control of any doctor. Death was more normal.

This was only forty-odd years ago. There is a difference, and it is reflected in the emotional impact of death on everyone, doctors included. But it is nothing like the difference between this century in the western world and all previous periods of human existence. Sebastian Bach had 7 brothers and sisters, of whom only 3 survived into adult life; of Bach's own 20 offspring, 11 died in childhood. I do not know what destroyed so many 18th-century children, for the records of medicine are imprecise; most likely, it was the tubercle bacillus, the streptococcus and any number of other bacterial pathogens. It is only within the last 150 years that human beings have discovered that this kind of dying can be prevented—by sanitation, less crowding, plumbing, better housing, better nutrition, public health quarantine measures and the like.

In Bach's time, death was a perfectly normal event, part of the environment, expected, even looked forward to. He lived to be 65, and was called "Old Bach" by Frederick the Great when he improvised "The Musical Offering" three years earlier. Most of his immediate family, his friends, the residents of the various prosperous towns where he lived, people in general, died young. Everyone knew about death at first hand; there was nothing unfamiliar or even queer about the phenomenon. People seem to have known a lot more about the process itself than is the case today. The "deathbed" was a real place, and the dying person usually knew where he was and when it was time to assemble the family and call for the priest.

It was easier, indeed necessary, to accept the idea of an afterlife, and the power of religion was amplified by the high visibility of dying, especially by the deaths of so many young people. Bach's cantatas are filled with reassurances about this matter, celebrations of the transitory nature of human life, the welcoming of death because of the reward to come.

Today, the average span of human life in our society stands at around 73 years, the longest run at living yet achieved. Obviously, most of the dying is done by old people. It makes a different sort of problem for the human mind. Dying is not so often the tragic striking-down that it was; it is more like the end of a slow process of running-down, more like a slow collapse. We know about its inevitability, but we do not have the same apprehension that it is there, waiting just around the corner, ready to leap.

And so we have come, just in the past 40 years, to view death as a sort of failure, just as we now look at the process of aging itself as failure. We have lost, in this changed view, the old feeling of respect for dying, and all the awe.

I do not know what we are doing to the first-hand experience of dying itself with our technology, but I suspect we may often be interfering with an important process. The awareness of dying can be an extraordinary sensation, described from time to time as a feeling of exaltation. In the days when tuberculosis was the commonest disease, causing death after a prolonged, exhausting illness, doctors could tell when death was near by a remarkable change in the patient's attitude. It was called *"spes phthisica"*, the hope of the tuberculous, and it was marked by a sense of tranquility and great peace, and something like pleasure.

Dying *is* a process, I believe. I'm not sure of it, but I think so. The organism seems to come apart in orderly stages. Sometimes patients know when the process has begun and they recognize the manifestations before the doctor is aware of them. I've seen this happen a few times. Once, on rounds, I stood at the bedside of a middle-aged man who had just been brought to the hospital with a coronary. He was lying in bed, propped up comfortably by pillows, and his chest pain had been relieved completely. The intern was describing the details of his condition, concluding that he seemed in stable condition, that all vital signs were good, when the patient interrupted in a tone of mild, rather gentle protest: "But Doctor," he said quietly but with absolute certainty, "I am dying; I'm going." And so he did, within two hours.

Most of the time, it is not a bad feeling. Sir William Osler wrote about it, pointing out that the popular notion of death agony was a fiction; people died, at the moment of the dying, in tranquility.

The act of dying was, at one time, a rather splendid event to behold, a great family occasion. Children grew up knowing all about it, observing the event, over and over again in the normal process of growing into maturity. It took place at the end of a struggle, often a short fight, against infection. When it was the result of lobar pneumonia it would usually occur after 10 days or so of violent illness, with shaking chills at the outset, then incessant coughing, chest pain, a high fever, and, finally, collapse into unconsciousness. But it was known that this disease could be recovered from, and when recovery took place it did so all at once, in a spectacular episode called the "crisis." This might happen, if the patient was lucky, on any day from the seventh on; suddenly, within a matter of a few hours, the temperature would cascade from 105E down to normal, accompanied by profuse sweating, and the patient would, just as suddenly, be well again, ready to resume normal living. The crisis, we now know, was caused by the sudden appearance in the patient's blood of antibodies against the capsular polysaccharide of the pneumococcus, and as soon as this happened the bacteria were destroyed all at once. It was one of the triumphs of human biology, no longer observable in hospitals because of penicillin's capacity to kill off the bacteria at the onset. But before antibiotics, back in the days when medicine possessed no real technology for treating infection, recovery from lobar pneumonia was the body's own accomplishment, and whether the patient lost out or survived it was a spectacular display of combat.

The time may come when medicine will have found out enough about disease mechanisms to think its way around all of today's other lethal human diseases, as effectively as by the techniques for treating infection. We may be left then with no way of dying except by wearing out in old age, barring trauma. It will be the kind of event we now call natural death, ending the lives of very old people in their sleep.

Meanwhile, we are part way along. We have not lost our fear of dying, nor our sense of its ultimate inevitability. But I am afraid that we have lost something else—our respect for it. In a sense quite new to our culture we have become ashamed of death, and we try to hide it, or hide ourselves away from it. It is, to our way of thinking, failure.

NOTES AND QUESTIONS

1. Thomas observes that societal and professional attitudes toward death have changed dramatically in recent years. His observations are pertinent to the twenty-first century as well. What social, medical, and demographic trends might be responsible for these changes?

2. Scientific and medical advances offer the promise of making living easier, but they also raise fears that dying will be prolonged, undignified, painful, and ruinously expensive. This fear has in turn led to judicial decisions and legislation recognizing patient preferences concerning refusal or termination of life-prolonging interventions and produced an energized euthanasia movement. Increasingly, there is recognition that overtreatment should not be the only concern. An Institute of Medicine report notes: "while an overtreated dying is feared, the opposite response—abandonment—is likewise frightening." INSTITUTE OF MEDICINE, APPROACHING DEATH: IMPROVING CARE AT THE END OF LIFE 15 (1997). This important report documents deficiencies in care at the end of life and makes recommendations that begin to address them.

3. Since 1980 when Thomas wrote his article, there has been a marked shift in the setting of death. By 1998 Americans were more likely to die in a nursing home or at home (45%) than die in hospitals (41%) yet "[m]oving outside the hospital setting does not ensure a good death . . . one should conclude not that end-of-life care has necessarily improved but rather that the quality of care in places other than hospitals is becoming more important." James Flory, et al., *Place of Death: U.S. Trends Since 1980*, 23 HEALTH AFFAIRS 194, 200 (2004).

4. As has been noted by a number of commentators, race can have a serious impact on end-of-life decisions. A survey of clinical patients at the University of Miami found that more blacks than whites wanted their doctors to use life-prolonging therapy regardless of their condition as well as aggressive intervention like cardiopulmonary resuscitation if they were either in a persistent vegetative state or diagnosed with a terminal illness. Dorothy E. Roberts, *The Nature of Blacks' Skepticism About Genetic Testing*, 27 SETON HALL L. REV. 971, 977 (1997) (citing P.V. Caralis et al., *The Influence of Ethnicity and Race on Attitudes toward Advance Directives, Life–Prolonging Treatments, and Euthanasia*, 4 J. CLINICAL ETHICS 155, 165 (1993)). Blacks were the least likely, on the other hand, to want physician assistance in dying. *Id.* Several reasons have been advanced to account for such differences. First, it has been suggested that some blacks may continue to be influenced by racism. Specifically, such individuals fear their doctor may attempt to terminate life support prematurely because of their race. *Id.* (citing Jill Klessig, *The Effect of Values and Culture on Life–Support Decisions*, 1157 W. J. MED. 316, 316 (1992)). These suspicions are based in part on blacks' past exploitation by the medical community, exemplified most notably by the Tuskegee Syphilis Study. *See* Patricia A. King and Leslie E. Wolf, *Empowering and Protecting Patients: Lessons for Physician–Assisted Suicide from the African–American Experience*, 82 MINN. L. REV. 1015, 1026–30 (1998). Second, "some traditional Christian religious views regarding death held among many African Americans depict pain and suffering as not to be avoided by rather to be endured as part of a spiritual commitment." LaVera Crawley et al., *Palliative and End-of-Life Care in the African American Community*, 284 JAMA 2518, 2518 (2000).

In addition to end-of-life decisions, black and Hispanic patient populations have also experienced greater deficiencies in palliative care than whites. Rima J. Oken, *Note, Curing Healthcare Providers' Failure to Administer Opioids in the Treatment of Severe Pain*, 23 CARDOZO L. REV. 1917, 1992 n.83 (2002) (citing Vence L. Bonham, *Race, Ethnicity, and Pain Treatment: Striving to Understand the Causes and Solutions to the Disparities in Pain Treatment*, 29 J. L. MED. & ETHICS 52, 63 (2001)). This is due in part to patients' ethnicity, language barriers, physician-patient communication failings, socioeconomic status, and racism. *Id.* Race also plays a key role in the availability of opioids. Indeed, a survey of New York City pharmacies revealed that those in minority neighborhoods were far less likely to have opioids in stock than those in predominately white neighborhoods. *Id.* (citing R. Sean Morrison et al., *"We Don't Carry That"—Failure of Pharmacies in Predominately Nonwhite Neighborhoods to Stock Opioid Analgesics*, 342 NEW. ENG. J. MED. 1023, 1024–25 (2000)).

United States v. Oakland Cannabis Buyers' Cooperative

Supreme Court of the United States, 2001.
532 U.S. 483, 121 S.Ct. 1711, 149 L.Ed.2d 722.

■ JUSTICE THOMAS delivered the opinion of the Court.

The Controlled Substances Act, 84 Stat. 1242, 21 U.S.C. § 801 *et seq.*, prohibits the manufacture and distribution of various drugs, including marijuana. In this case, we must decide whether there is a medical necessity exception to these prohibitions. We hold that there is not.

I.

In November 1996, California voters enacted an initiative measure entitled the Compassionate Use Act of 1996. Attempting "[t]o ensure that seriously ill Californians have the right to obtain and use marijuana for medical purposes," Cal. Health & Safety Code Ann. § 11362.5 (West Supp.2001), the statute creates an exception to California laws prohibiting the possession and cultivation of marijuana. These prohibitions no longer apply to a patient or his primary caregiver who possesses or cultivates marijuana for the patient's medical purposes upon the recommendation or approval of a physician. In the wake of this voter initiative, several groups organized "medical cannabis dispensaries" to meet the needs of qualified patients.... Respondent Oakland Cannabis Buyers' Cooperative is one of these groups.

The Cooperative is a not-for-profit organization that operates in downtown Oakland. A physician serves as medical director, and registered nurses staff the Cooperative during business hours. To become a member, a patient must provide a written statement from a treating physician assenting to marijuana therapy and must submit to a screening interview. If accepted as a member, the patient receives an identification card entitling him to obtain marijuana from the Cooperative.

In January 1998, the United States sued the Cooperative and its executive director, respondent Jeffrey Jones (together, the Cooperative), in the United States District Court for the Northern District of California. Seeking to enjoin the Cooperative from distributing and manufacturing marijuana, the United States argued that, whether or not the Cooperative's activities are legal under California law, they violate federal law. Specifically, the Government argued that the Cooperative violated the Controlled Substances Act's prohibitions on distributing, manufacturing, and possessing with the intent to distribute or manufacture a controlled substance. 21 U.S.C. § 841(a). Concluding that the Government had established a probability of success on the merits, the District Court granted a preliminary injunction.

The Cooperative did not appeal the injunction but instead openly violated it by distributing marijuana to numerous persons.... To terminate these violations, the Government initiated contempt proceedings. In defense, the Cooperative contended that any distributions were medically necessary. Marijuana is the only drug, according to the Cooperative, that can alleviate the severe pain and other debilitating symptoms of the Cooperative's patients. The District Court rejected this defense, however, after determining there was insufficient evidence that each recipient of marijuana was in actual danger of imminent harm without the drug. The District Court found the Cooperative in contempt and, at the Government's request, modified the preliminary injunction to empower the United States Marshal to seize the Cooperative's premises. Although recognizing that "human suffering" could result, the District Court reasoned that a court's "equitable powers [do] not permit it to ignore federal law." Three days later, the District Court summarily rejected a motion by the Cooperative to modify the injunction to permit distributions that are medically necessary.

The Cooperative appealed both the contempt order and the denial of the Cooperative's motion to modify. Before the Court of Appeals for the Ninth Circuit decided the case, however, the Cooperative voluntarily purged its contempt by promising the District Court that it would comply with the initial preliminary injunction. Consequently, the Court of Appeals determined that the appeal of the contempt order was moot....

The denial of the Cooperative's motion to modify the injunction, however, presented a live controversy that was appealable.... Reaching the merits of this issue, the Court of Appeals reversed and remanded. According to the Court of Appeals, the medical necessity defense was a "legally cognizable defense" that likely would apply in the circumstances. Moreover, the Court of Appeals reasoned, the District Court erroneously "believed that it had no discretion to issue an injunction that was more limited in scope than the Controlled Substances Act itself." Because, according to the Court of Appeals, district courts retain "broad equitable discretion" to fashion injunctive relief, the District Court could have, and should have, weighed the "public interest" and considered factors such as the serious harm in depriving patients of marijuana. Remanding the case, the Court of Appeals instructed the District Court to consider "the criteria for a medical necessity exemption, and, should it modify the injunction, to set forth those criteria in the modification order." *Id.*, at 1115. Following these instructions, the District Court granted the Cooperative's motion to modify the injunction to incorporate a medical necessity defense.[2]

The United States petitioned for certiorari to review the Court of Appeals' decision that medical necessity is a legally cognizable defense to violations of the Controlled Substances Act. Because the decision raises significant questions as to the ability of the United States to enforce the Nation's drug laws, we granted certiorari.

II

The Controlled Substances Act provides that, "[e]xcept as authorized by this subchapter, it shall be unlawful for any person knowingly or intentionally ... to manufacture, distribute, or dispense, or possess with intent to manufacture, distribute, or dispense, a controlled substance." 21 U.S.C. § 841(a)(1). The subchapter, in turn, establishes exceptions. For marijuana (and other drugs that have been classified as "schedule I" controlled substances), there is but one express exception, and it is available only for Government-approved research projects, § 823(f). Not conducting such a project, the Cooperative cannot, and indeed does not, claim this statutory exemption.

The Cooperative contends, however, that notwithstanding the apparently absolute language of § 841(a), the statute is subject to additional, implied exceptions, one of which is medical necessity. According to the Cooperative, because necessity was a defense at common law, medical necessity should be read into the Controlled Substances Act. We disagree.

. . .

We need not decide ... whether necessity can ever be a defense when the federal statute does not expressly provide for it. In this case, to resolve the question presented, we need only recognize that a medical necessity exception for marijuana is at odds with the terms of the Controlled Substances Act. The statute, to be sure, does not explicitly abrogate the defense. But its provisions leave no doubt that the defense is unavailable.

Under any conception of legal necessity, one principle is clear: The defense cannot succeed when the legislature itself has made a "determination of values." In the case of the Controlled Substances Act, the statute

---

2. The amended preliminary injunction reaffirmed that the Cooperative is generally enjoined from manufacturing, distributing, and possessing with the intent to manufacture or distribute marijuana, but it carved out an exception for cases of medical necessity. Specifically, the District Court ordered that "[t]he foregoing injunction does not apply to the distribution of cannabis by [the Cooperative] to patient-members who (1) suffer from a serious medical condition, (2) will suffer imminent harm if the patient-member does not have access to cannabis, (3) need cannabis for the treatment of the patient-member's medical condition, or need cannabis to alleviate the medical condition or symptoms associated with the medical condition, and (4) have no reasonable legal alternative to cannabis for the effective treatment or alleviation of the patient-member's medical condition or symptoms associated with the medical condition because the patient-member has tried all other legal alternatives to cannabis and the alternatives have been ineffective in treating or alleviating the patient-member's medical condition or symptoms associated with the medical condition, or the alternatives result in side effects which the patient-member cannot reasonably tolerate." App. to Pet. for Cert. 16a–17a.

. . .

reflects a determination that marijuana has no medical benefits worthy of an exception (outside the confines of a Government-approved research project). Whereas some other drugs can be dispensed and prescribed for medical use, see 21 U.S.C. § 829, the same is not true for marijuana. Indeed, for purposes of the Controlled Substances Act, marijuana has "no currently accepted medical use" at all. § 812.

The structure of the Act supports this conclusion. The statute divides drugs into five schedules, depending in part on whether the particular drug has a currently accepted medical use. The Act then imposes restrictions on the manufacture and distribution of the substance according to the schedule in which it has been placed. Schedule I is the most restrictive schedule. The Attorney General can include a drug in schedule I only if the drug "has no currently accepted medical use in treatment in the United States," "has a high potential for abuse," and has "a lack of accepted safety for use ... under medical supervision." §§ 812(b)(1)(A)–(C). Under the statute, the Attorney General could not put marijuana into schedule I if marijuana had any accepted medical use.

. . .

The Cooperative ... argues that use of schedule I drugs generally—whether placed in schedule I by Congress or the Attorney General—can be medically necessary, notwithstanding that they have "no currently accepted medical use." According to the Cooperative, a drug may not yet have achieved general acceptance as a medical treatment but may nonetheless have medical benefits to a particular patient or class of patients. We decline to parse the statute in this manner....

Finally, the Cooperative contends that we should construe the Controlled Substances Act to include a medical necessity defense in order to avoid what it considers to be difficult constitutional questions. In particular, the Cooperative asserts that, shorn of a medical necessity defense, the statute exceeds Congress' Commerce Clause powers, violates the substantive due process rights of patients, and offends the fundamental liberties of the people under the Fifth, Ninth, and Tenth Amendments. As the Cooperative acknowledges, however, the canon of constitutional avoidance has no application in the absence of statutory ambiguity. Because we have no doubt that the Controlled Substances Act cannot bear a medical necessity defense to distributions of marijuana, we do not find guidance in this avoidance principle. Nor do we consider the underlying constitutional issues today. Because the Court of Appeals did not address these claims, we decline to do so in the first instance.

For these reasons, we hold that medical necessity is not a defense to manufacturing and distributing marijuana....[7]

. . .

7. Lest there be any confusion, we clarify that nothing in our analysis, or the statute, suggests that a distinction should be drawn between the prohibitions on manufacturing and distributing and the other prohibitions in the Controlled Substances Act. Furthermore, the very point of our holding is that there is no medical necessity exception to the prohibitions at issue, even when the

NOTES AND QUESTIONS

1. In the past decade, federal efforts to prevent use of marijuana for medical purposes have resulted in litigation in several jurisdictions, especially California. In 1996, Arizona and California voters passed initiatives decriminalizing the use of marijuana for medical purposes. Today seven states in addition to Arizona and California-Alaska, Colorado, Hawaii, Maine, Nevada, Oregon and Washington-have statutes that permit medical use of marijuana in some circumstances.

On December 30, 1996, the federal government in response to these initiatives in Arizona and California issued a policy, "The Administration's Response to the Passage of California Proposition 215 and Arizona Proposition 200," declaring that a doctor's "action of recommending or prescribing Schedule I controlled substances is not consistent with the 'public interest' (as that phrase is used in the federal Controlled Substances Act)." Thus, physicians who provided patients with oral or written statements in order to help their patients obtain marijuana violated federal law.

In litigation that proceeded contemporaneously with *Oakland Cannabis Buyer's Coop., supra*, sick patients and physicians in California filed in early 1997 to enjoin enforcement of the policy. *Conant v. McCaffrey*, 2000 WL 1281174 (N.D. Cal. 2000). The policy was enjoined by the District Court and the order was appealed. In *Conant v. Walters*, 309 F.3d 629 (9th Cir. 2002), *cert. denied*, 540 U.S. 946, 124 S.Ct. 387, 157 L.Ed.2d 276 (2003), the court, relying on First Amendment grounds, affirmed the lower court's order enjoining the government from: (i) revoking any physician class member's DEA registration merely because the doctor makes a recommendation for the use of medical marijuana based on a sincere medical judgment and (ii) from initiating any investigation solely on that ground. *Id*. at 634.

Following the decision in *Oakland Cannabis Buyers' Coop., supra*, seriously ill users of marijuana for medical purposes on the recommendation of their physicians and two caregivers who assisted one of the patients to grow her marijuana sought injunctive and declarative relief against the United States government, alleging the unconstitutionality of the Controlled Substances Act. They argued that the Commerce Clause did not support the exercise of federal authority over their activities, the question expressly reserved in *Oakland Cannabis Buyers' Coop., supra*. The District Court denied the preliminary injunction. *Raich v. Ashcroft*, 248 F.Supp.2d 918 (N.D. Cal. 2003). That ruling was reversed on appeal. *Raich v. Ashcroft*, 352 F.3d 1222 (9th Cir. 2003), *cert. granted*, ___ U.S. ___, 124 S.Ct. 2909, 159 L.Ed.2d 811 (2004).

The Ninth Circuit with one judge dissenting concluded "that the CSA [Controlled Substances Act], as applied to the appellants, is likely unconstitutional," because appellants' class of activities—the intrastate, noncommercial cultivation, possession and use of marijuana for personal medical purposes on the advice of a physician and in accordance with state law—was different from drug trafficking and did not involve sale, exchange, or distribution, and this separate class of activities did not substantially affect interstate commerce. In addition, "this conclusion coupled with the public interests considerations and the burden faced by the appellants if . . . they are denied access to medical marijuana, warrants the entry of a preliminary injunction."

Constitutional and statutory questions to one side, what arguments support or oppose legalization of medical marijuana?

2. Despite the widespread problem of pain in American society, it has been widely acknowledged that pain of all types, including pain among patients with chronic

patient is "seriously ill" and lacks alternative
avenues for relief. . . .

conditions and those who are critically ill or near death, is undertreated in our society. This is largely due to the fact that opioids, usually the only treatment option that provides patients any kind of significant pain relief, are carefully regulated by the Drug Enforcement Administration (DEA) and other state agencies given their potential for abuse. Physicians, wary of discipline from such authorities for overprescription, are thus typically reluctant to prescribe such drugs for purposes of relieving their patients' pain. *See* Beth Packman Weinman, *Freedom From Pain*, 24 J. LEGAL MED. 495, 509 (2003). Compounding the problem, patients themselves, mistaking addiction for "legitimate pain relief seeking behavior," are equally reluctant to take such medications. *Id.* at 515–16. Also, see the discussion of the impact of the Supreme Court decisions in *Washington v. Glucksberg*, 521 U.S. 702, 117 S.Ct. 2258, 138 L.Ed.2d 772 (1997) and *Vacco v. Quill*, 521 U.S. 793, 117 S.Ct. 2293, 138 L.Ed.2d 834 (1997) on pain relief for dying patients, Sec. II. C. 2., *infra*.

Both Congress and the medical community have taken steps to make pain medication generally more available to patients. In 2001, Congress passed and President Clinton signed into law a resolution declaring this the "Decade of Pain Control and Research." H.R. Con. Res. 3244, 106th Cong. (2001) (enacted). The resolution was intended to bring attention to the subject of pain in both the public and private sectors via research and education efforts. In 2001, the DEA joined twenty-one health organizations, including the American Medical Association (AMA), in calling for balanced policy with regard to prescription pain medications. As noted in the joint statement, it is their position that "[b]oth health care professionals and law enforcement and regulatory personnel share a responsibility for ensuring that prescription pain medications are available to patients who need them, and for preventing these drugs from becoming a source of abuse or harm." *See e.g., Promoting Pain Relief and Preventing Abuse of Pain Medications: A Critical Balancing Act*, (2001), at http://www.ama-assn.org/amal/pub/up-load/mm/455/jointstatement.pdf, last visited May 30. 2004. Additionally, the AMA has itself stated that physicians who appropriately prescribe and/or administer controlled substances to relieve intractable pain should not be subject to excessive regulatory scrutiny, disciplinary action or criminal prosecution. American Medical Association, *About the AMA Position on Pain Management Using Opioid Analgesics*, (2003), at http://www.ama-assn.org/ama/pub/category/11541.html, last visited May 30, 2004. To this end, at its annual policy-making meeting in the summer of 2003, the AMA House of Delegates adopted recommendations "stating their opposition to the harassment of physicians by DEA agents in response to the appropriate prescribing of controlled substances for pain management, as well as to the inappropriate use of [21 C.F.R. § 1306.4] or any other rationale that would involve placement of licensure restrictions on physicians who use opioid analgesics ... appropriately to treat patients with pain." *Id*. Finally, the Federation of State Medical Boards' "Model Guidelines for the Use of Controlled Substances for the Treatment of Pain" similarly encourages doctors to employ adequate pain management techniques, including the prescription of opioids, and attempts to address physician concerns regarding disciplinary actions by medical boards. *Id*.

Interestingly, Attorney General John Ashcroft sent a letter to Richard Corlin, President of the AMA at the same time he issued the "Ashcroft Directive" (discussed in *Oregon v. Ashcroft*, Sec. II. C. 3., *infra*), stating:

> I want the nation's doctors to know that under this decision today they will have no reason to fear that prescription of controlled substances to control pain will lead to increased scrutiny by the DEA even when high doses of painkilling drugs are necessary and even when dosages that are needed to control pain may increase the risk of death.

Letter to Richard Corlin dated November 6, 2001.

B.   IS THERE A CONSTITUTIONAL RIGHT TO DIE?

Cruzan v. Director, Missouri Department of Health

Supreme Court of the United States, 1990.
497 U.S. 261, 110 S.Ct. 2841, 111 L.Ed.2d 224.

■ CHIEF JUSTICE REHNQUIST delivered the opinion of the Court.

. . .

On the night of January 11, 1983, Nancy Cruzan lost control of her car as she traveled down Elm Road in Jasper County, Missouri. The vehicle overturned, and Cruzan was discovered lying face down in a ditch without detectable respiratory or cardiac function. Paramedics were able to restore her breathing and heartbeat at the accident site, and she was transported to a hospital in an unconscious state. An attending neurosurgeon diagnosed her as having sustained probable cerebral contusions compounded by significant anoxia (lack of oxygen). The Missouri trial court in this case found that permanent brain damage generally results after 6 minutes in an anoxic state; it was estimated that Cruzan was deprived of oxygen from 12 to 14 minutes. She remained in a coma for approximately three weeks and then progressed to an unconscious state in which she was able to orally ingest some nutrition. In order to ease feeding and further the recovery, surgeons implanted a gastrostomy feeding and hydration tube in Cruzan with the consent of her then husband. Subsequent rehabilitative efforts proved unavailing. She now lies in a Missouri state hospital in what is commonly referred to as a persistent vegetative state: generally, a condition in which a person exhibits motor reflexes but evinces no indications of significant cognitive function. The State of Missouri is bearing the cost of her care.

After it had become apparent that Nancy Cruzan had virtually no chance of regaining her mental faculties, her parents asked hospital employees to terminate the artificial nutrition and hydration procedures. All agree that such a removal would cause her death. The employees refused to honor the request without court approval. The parents then sought and received authorization from the state trial court for termination. . . .

The Supreme Court of Missouri reversed by a divided vote. . . .

We granted certiorari to consider the question whether Cruzan has a right under the United States Constitution which would require the hospital to withdraw life-sustaining treatment from her under these circumstances.

. . .

. . . This is the first case in which we have been squarely presented with the issue whether the United States Constitution grants what is in common parlance referred to as a "right to die." We follow the judicious counsel of our decision in *Twin City Bank v. Nebeker*, 167 U.S. 196, 202 (1897), where we said that in deciding "a question of such magnitude and importance ... it is the [better] part of wisdom not to attempt, by any general statement, to cover every possible phase of the subject."

The Fourteenth Amendment provides that no State shall "deprive any person of life, liberty, or property, without due process of law." The principle that a competent person has a constitutionally protected liberty interest in refusing unwanted medical treatment may be inferred from our prior decisions. . . .

. . .

But determining that a person has a "liberty interest" under the Due Process Clause does not end the inquiry; "whether respondent's constitutional rights have been violated must be determined by balancing his liberty interests against the relevant state interests." *Youngberg v. Romeo*, 457 U.S. 307, 321 (1982).

Petitioners insist that under the general holdings of our cases, the forced administration of life-sustaining medical treatment, and even of artificially delivered food and water essential to life, would implicate a competent person's liberty interest. Although we think the logic of the cases discussed above would embrace such a liberty interest, the dramatic consequences involved in refusal of such treatment would inform the inquiry as to whether the deprivation of that interest is constitutionally permissible. But for purposes of this case, we assume that the United States Constitution would grant a competent person a constitutionally protected right to refuse lifesaving hydration and nutrition.

Petitioners go on to assert that an incompetent person should possess the same right in this respect as is possessed by a competent person. . . .

The difficulty with petitioners' claim is that in a sense it begs the question: An incompetent person is not able to make an informed and voluntary choice to exercise a hypothetical right to refuse treatment or any other right. Such a "right" must be exercised for her, if at all, by some sort of surrogate. Here, Missouri has in effect recognized that under certain circumstances a surrogate may act for the patient in electing to have hydration and nutrition withdrawn in such a way as to cause death, but it has established a procedural safeguard to assure that the action of the surrogate conforms as best it may to the wishes expressed by the patient while competent. Missouri requires that evidence of the incompetent's wishes as to the withdrawal of treatment be proved by clear and convincing evidence. The question, then, is whether the United States Constitution forbids the establishment of this procedural requirement by the State. We hold that it does not.

Whether or not Missouri's clear and convincing evidence requirement comports with the United States Constitution depends in part on what interests the State may properly seek to protect in this situation. Missouri relies on its interest in the protection and preservation of human life, and there can be no gainsaying this interest. As a general matter, the States—indeed, all civilized nations—demonstrate their commitment to life by treating homicide as a serious crime. Moreover, the majority of States in this country have laws imposing criminal penalties on one who assists another to commit suicide. We do not think a State is required to remain neutral in the face of an informed and voluntary decision by a physically-able adult to starve to death.

But in the context presented here, a State has more particular interests at stake. The choice between life and death is a deeply personal decision of obvious and overwhelming finality. We believe Missouri may legitimately seek to safeguard the personal element of this choice through the imposition of heightened evidentiary requirements. It cannot be disputed that the Due Process Clause protects an interest in life as well as an interest in refusing life-sustaining medical treatment. Not all incompetent patients will have loved ones available to serve as surrogate decisionmakers. And even where family members are present, "[t]here will, of course, be some unfortunate situations in which family members will not act to protect a patient." *In re Jobes*, 529 A.2d 434, 447 (N.J. 1987). A State is entitled to guard against potential abuses in such situations. Similarly, a State is entitled to consider that a judicial proceeding to make a determination regarding an incompetent's wishes may very well not be an adversarial one, with the added guarantee of accurate factfinding that the adversary process brings with it. Finally, we think a State may properly decline to make judgments about the "quality" of life that a particular individual may enjoy, and simply assert an unqualified interest in the preservation of human life to be weighed against the constitutionally protected interests of the individual.

In our view, Missouri has permissibly sought to advance these interests through the adoption of a "clear and convincing" standard of proof to govern such proceedings. . . .

. . .

The Supreme Court of Missouri held that in this case the testimony adduced at trial did not amount to clear and convincing proof of the patient's desire to have hydration and nutrition withdrawn. In so doing, it reversed a decision of the Missouri trial court which had found that the evidence "suggest[ed]" Nancy Cruzan would not have desired to continue such measures, but which had not adopted the standard of "clear and convincing evidence" enunciated by the Supreme Court. The testimony adduced at trial consisted primarily of Nancy Cruzan's statements made to a housemate about a year before her accident that she would not want to live should she face life as a "vegetable," and other observations to the same effect. The observations did not deal in terms with withdrawal of medical treatment or of hydration and nutrition. We cannot say that the Supreme Court of Missouri committed constitutional error in reaching the conclusion that it did.

Petitioners alternatively contend that Missouri must accept the "substituted judgment" of close family members even in the absence of substantial proof that their views reflect the views of the patient. . . .

No doubt is engendered by anything in this record but that Nancy Cruzan's mother and father are loving and caring parents. If the State were required by the United States Constitution to repose a right of "substituted judgment" with anyone, the Cruzans would surely qualify. But we do not think the Due Process Clause requires the State to repose judgment on these matters with anyone but the patient herself. Close family members may have a strong feeling—a feeling not at all ignoble or unworthy, but not entirely disinterested, either—that they do not wish to witness the continuation of the life of a loved one which they regard as hopeless, meaningless, and even degrading. But there is no automatic assurance that the view of close family members will necessarily be the same as the patient's would have been had she been confronted with the prospect of her situation while competent. All of the reasons previously discussed for allowing Missouri to require clear and convincing evidence of the patient's wishes lead us to conclude that the State may choose to defer only to those wishes, rather than confide the decision to close family members.

The judgment of the Supreme Court of Missouri is Affirmed.

■ JUSTICE O'CONNOR, concurring.

I agree that a protected liberty interest in refusing unwanted medical treatment may be inferred from our prior decisions, and that the refusal of artificially delivered food and water is encompassed within that liberty interest. I write separately to clarify why I believe this to be so.

As the Court notes, the liberty interest in refusing medical treatment flows from decisions involving the State's invasions into the body. Because our notions of liberty are inextricably entwined with our idea of physical freedom and self-determination, the Court has often deemed state incursions into the body repugnant to the interests protected by the Due Process Clause. The State's imposition of medical treatment on an unwilling competent adult necessarily involves some form of restraint and intrusion. A seriously ill or dying patient whose wishes are not honored may feel a captive of the machinery required for life-sustaining measures or other medical interventions. Such forced treatment may burden that individual's liberty interests as much as any state coercion.

The State's artificial provision of nutrition and hydration implicates identical concerns. Artificial feeding cannot readily be distinguished from other forms of medical treatment.... Requiring a competent adult to endure such procedures against her will burdens the patient's liberty, dignity, and freedom to determine the course of her own treatment. Accordingly, the liberty guaranteed by the Due Process Clause must protect, if it protects anything, an individual's deeply personal decision to reject medical treatment, including the artificial delivery of food and water.

I also write separately to emphasize that the Court does not today decide the issue whether a State must also give effect to the decisions of a surrogate decisionmaker. In my view, such a duty may well be constitutionally required to protect the patient's liberty interest in refusing medical treatment. Few individuals provide explicit oral or written instructions regarding their intent to refuse medical treatment should they become incompetent. States which decline to consider any evidence other than such instructions may frequently fail to honor a patient's intent. Such failures might be avoided if the State considered an equally probative source of evidence: the patient's appointment of a proxy to make health care decisions on her behalf....

Today's decision, holding only that the Constitution permits a State to require clear and convincing evidence of Nancy Cruzan's desire to have artificial hydration and nutrition withdrawn, does not preclude a future determination that the Constitution requires the States to implement the decisions of a patient's duly appointed surrogate. Nor does it prevent States from developing other approaches for protecting an incompetent individual's liberty interest in refusing medical treatment.... [N]o national consensus has yet emerged on the best solution for this difficult and sensitive problem. Today we decide only that one State's practice does not violate the Constitution; the more challenging task of crafting appropriate procedures for safeguarding incompetents' liberty interests is entrusted to the "laboratory" of the States, *New State Ice Co. v. Liebmann*, 285 U.S. 262, 311 (1932) (Brandeis, J., dissenting), in the first instance.

■ JUSTICE SCALIA, concurring.

The various opinions in this case portray quite clearly the difficult, indeed agonizing, questions that are presented by the constantly increasing power of science to keep the human body alive for longer than any reasonable person would want to inhabit it. The States have begun to grapple with these problems through legislation. I am concerned, from the tenor of today's opinions, that we are poised to confuse that enterprise as successfully as we have confused the enterprise of legislating concerning abortion—requiring it to be conducted against a background of federal constitutional imperatives that are unknown because they are being newly crafted from Term to Term. That would be a great misfortune.

While I agree with the Court's analysis today, and therefore join in its opinion, I would have preferred that we announce, clearly and promptly, that the federal courts have no business in this field; that American law has always accorded the State the power to prevent, by force if necessary, suicide—including suicide by refusing to take appropriate measures necessary to preserve one's life; that the point at which life becomes "worthless," and the point at which the means necessary to preserve it become "extraordinary" or "inappropriate," are neither set forth in the Constitution nor known to the nine Justices of this Court any better than they are known to nine people picked at random from the Kansas City telephone directory; and hence, that even when it is demonstrated by clear and convincing evidence that a patient no longer wishes certain measures to be taken to preserve his or her life, it is up to the citizens of Missouri to decide, through their elected representatives, whether that wish will be honored. It is quite impossible (because the Constitution says nothing about the matter) that those citizens will decide upon a line less lawful than the one we would choose; and it is unlikely (because we know no more about "life and death" than they do) that they will decide upon a line less reasonable.

. . .

. . . Case law at the time of the adoption of the Fourteenth Amendment generally held that assisting suicide was a criminal offense.... And most States that did not explicitly prohibit assisted suicide in 1868 recognized, when the issue arose in the 50 years following the Fourteenth Amendment's ratification, that assisted and (in some cases) attempted suicide were unlawful. Thus, "there is no significant support for the claim that a right to suicide is so rooted in our tradition that it may be deemed 'fundamental' or 'implicit in the concept of ordered liberty.'" (quoting *Palko v. Connecticut*, 302 U.S. 319, 325 (1937)).

Petitioners rely on three distinctions to separate Nancy Cruzan's case from ordinary suicide: (1) that she is permanently incapacitated and in pain; (2) that she would bring on her death not by any affirmative act but by merely declining treatment that provides nourishment; and (3) that preventing her from effectuating her presumed wish to die requires violation of her bodily integrity. None of these suffices. Suicide was not excused even when committed "to avoid those ills which [persons] had not the fortitude to endure." 4 Blackstone, supra, at 189. . . .

[handwritten margin note: Calls this assisted suicide]

The second asserted distinction . . . relies on the dichotomy between action and inaction. Suicide, it is said, consists of an affirmative act to end one's life; refusing treatment is not an affirmative act "causing" death, but merely a passive acceptance of the natural process of dying. I readily acknowledge that the distinction between action and inaction has some bearing upon the legislative judgment of what ought to be prevented as suicide—though even there it would seem to me unreasonable to draw the line precisely between action and inaction, rather than between various forms of inaction. . . .

But . . . [s]tarving oneself to death is no different from putting a gun to one's temple as far as the common-law definition of suicide is concerned; the cause of death in both cases is the suicide's conscious decision to "pu[t] an end to his own existence." 4 Blackstone, supra, at 189. . . .

. . .

The third asserted basis of distinction—that frustrating Nancy Cruzan's wish to die in the present case requires interference with her bodily integrity—is likewise inadequate, because such interference is impermissible only if one begs the question whether her refusal to undergo the treatment on her own is suicide. It has always been lawful not only for the State, but even for private citizens, to interfere with bodily integrity to prevent a felony. . . .

. . .

What I have said above is not meant to suggest that I would think it desirable, if we were sure that Nancy Cruzan wanted to die, to keep her alive by the means at issue here. I assert only that the Constitution has nothing to say about the subject. To raise up a constitutional right here we would have to create out of nothing (for it exists neither in text nor tradition) some constitutional principle whereby, although the State may insist that an individual come in out of the cold and eat food, it may not insist that he take medicine; and although it may pump his stomach empty of poison he has ingested, it may not fill his stomach with food he has failed to ingest. Are there, then, no reasonable and humane limits that ought not to be exceeded in requiring an individual to preserve his own life? There obviously are, but they are not set forth in the Due Process Clause. What

[handwritten margin note: she is dead + what does it mean to be human?]

assures us that those limits will not be exceeded is the same constitutional guarantee that is the source of most of our protection—what protects us, for example, from being assessed a tax of 100% of our income above the subsistence level, from being forbidden to drive cars, or from being required to send our children to school for 10 hours a day, none of which horribles are categorically prohibited by the Constitution. Our salvation is the Equal Protection Clause, which requires the democratic majority to accept for themselves and their loved ones what they impose on you and me. This Court need not, and has no authority to, inject itself into every field of human activity where irrationality and oppression may theoretically occur, and if it tries to do so it will destroy itself.

■ JUSTICE BRENNAN, dissenting:

"Medical technology has effectively created a twilight zone of suspended animation where death commences while life, in some form, continues. Some patients, however, want no part of a life sustained only by medical technology. Instead, they prefer a plan of medical treatment that allows nature to take its course and permits them to die with dignity."[1]

. . .

A grown woman at the time of the accident, Nancy had previously expressed her wish to forgo continuing medical care under circumstances such as these. Her family and her friends are convinced that this is what she would want. A guardian ad litem appointed by the trial court is also convinced that this is what Nancy would want. Yet the Missouri Supreme Court, alone among state courts deciding such a question, has determined that an irreversibly vegetative patient will remain a passive prisoner of medical technology—for Nancy, perhaps for the next 30 years.

Today the Court, while tentatively accepting that there is some degree of constitutionally protected liberty interest in avoiding unwanted medical treatment, including life-sustaining medical treatment such as artificial nutrition and hydration, affirms the decision of the Missouri Supreme Court. The majority opinion, as I read it, would affirm that decision on the ground that a State may require "clear and convincing" evidence of Nancy Cruzan's prior decision to forgo life-sustaining treatment under circumstances such as hers in order to ensure that her actual wishes are honored. Because I believe that Nancy Cruzan has a fundamental right to be free of unwanted artificial nutrition and hydration, which right is not outweighed by any interests of the State, and because I find that the improperly biased procedural obstacles imposed by the Missouri Supreme Court impermissibly burden that right, I respectfully dissent. Nancy Cruzan is entitled to choose to die with dignity.

. . .

Although the right to be free of unwanted medical intervention, like other constitutionally protected interests, may not be absolute, no state interest could outweigh the rights of an individual in Nancy Cruzan's position. Whatever a State's possible interests in mandating life-support

---

1. Rasmussen v. Fleming, 154 Ariz. 207, 211, 741 P.2d 674, 678 (1987) (en banc).

treatment under other circumstances, there is no good to be obtained here by Missouri's insistence that Nancy Cruzan remain on life-support systems if it is indeed her wish not to do so. Missouri does not claim, nor could it, that society as a whole will be benefited by Nancy's receiving medical treatment. No third party's situation will be improved and no harm to others will be averted.

The only state interest asserted here is a general interest in the preservation of life. But the State has no legitimate general interest in someone's life, completely abstracted from the interest of the person living that life, that could outweigh the person's choice to avoid medical treatment. "[T]he regulation of constitutionally protected decisions . . . must be predicated on legitimate state concerns other than disagreement with the choice the individual has made. . . . Otherwise, the interest in liberty protected by the Due Process Clause would be a nullity." Hodgson v. Minnesota, 497 U.S. 417, 435 (1990) (opinion of Stevens, J.) (emphasis added). Thus, the State's general interest in life must accede to Nancy Cruzan's particularized and intense interest in self-determination in her choice of medical treatment. There is simply nothing legitimately within the State's purview to be gained by superseding her decision.

. . .

This is not to say that the State has no legitimate interests to assert here. As the majority recognizes, Missouri has a parens patriae interest in providing Nancy Cruzan, now incompetent, with as accurate as possible a determination of how she would exercise her rights under these circumstances. Second, if and when it is determined that Nancy Cruzan would want to continue treatment, the State may legitimately assert an interest in providing that treatment. But until Nancy's wishes have been determined, the only state interest that may be asserted is an interest in safeguarding the accuracy of that determination.

Accuracy, therefore, must be our touchstone. Missouri may constitutionally impose only those procedural requirements that serve to enhance the accuracy of a determination of Nancy Cruzan's wishes or are at least consistent with an accurate determination. The Missouri "safeguard" that the Court upholds today does not meet that standard. The determination needed in this context is whether the incompetent person would choose to live in a persistent vegetative state on life support or to avoid this medical treatment. Missouri's rule of decision imposes a markedly asymmetrical evidentiary burden. Only evidence of specific statements of treatment choice made by the patient when competent is admissible to support a finding that the patient, now in a persistent vegetative state, would wish to avoid further medical treatment. Moreover, this evidence must be clear and convincing. No proof is required to support a finding that the incompetent person would wish to continue treatment.

. . .

The majority . . . argues that where, as here, important individual rights are at stake, a clear and convincing evidence standard has long been held to be an appropriate means of enhancing accuracy, citing decisions concerning what process an individual is due before he can be deprived of a liberty interest. In those cases, however, this Court imposed a clear and convincing standard as a constitutional minimum on the basis of its evaluation that one side's interests clearly outweighed the second side's interests and therefore the second side should bear the risk of error. Moreover, we have always recognized that shifting the risk of error reduces the likelihood of errors in one direction at the cost of increasing the likelihood of errors in the other. In the cases cited by the majority, the imbalance imposed by a heightened evidentiary standard was not only acceptable but required because the standard was deployed to protect an individual's exercise of a fundamental right.... In contrast, the Missouri court imposed a clear and convincing evidence standard as an obstacle to the exercise of a fundamental right.

> stand obstacle to FR.

The majority claims that the allocation of the risk of error is justified because it is more important not to terminate life support for someone who would wish it continued than to honor the wishes of someone who would not. An erroneous decision to terminate life support is irrevocable, says the majority, while an erroneous decision not to terminate "results in a maintenance of the status quo." But, from the point of view of the patient, an erroneous decision in either direction is irrevocable. An erroneous decision to terminate artificial nutrition and hydration, to be sure, will lead to failure of that last remnant of physiological life, the brain stem, and result in complete brain death. An erroneous decision not to terminate life support, however, robs a patient of the very qualities protected by the right to avoid unwanted medical treatment. His own degraded existence is perpetuated; his family's suffering is protracted; the memory he leaves behind becomes more and more distorted.

Even a later decision to grant him his wish cannot undo the intervening harm. But a later decision is unlikely in any event. "[T]he discovery of new evidence," to which the majority refers, is more hypothetical than plausible. The majority also misconceives the relevance of the possibility of "advancements in medical science," by treating it as a reason to force someone to continue medical treatment against his will. The possibility of a medical miracle is indeed part of the calculus, but it is a part of the patient's calculus. If current research suggests that some hope for cure or even moderate improvement is possible within the life span projected, this is a factor that should be and would be accorded significant weight in assessing what the patient himself would choose.

Even more than its heightened evidentiary standard, the Missouri court's categorical exclusion of relevant evidence dispenses with any semblance of accurate factfinding. The court adverted to no evidence supporting its decision, but held that no clear and convincing, inherently reliable evidence had been presented to show that Nancy would want to avoid further treatment. In doing so, the court failed to consider statements Nancy had made to family members and a close friend. The court also failed to consider testimony from Nancy's mother and sister that they were certain that Nancy would want to discontinue artificial nutrition and hydration, even after the court found that Nancy's family was loving and without malignant motive. *See* 760 S.W.2d, at 412. The court also failed to consider the conclusions of the guardian ad litem, appointed by the trial

Good enough we don't need a testimony not [handwritten marginalia]

court, that there was clear and convincing evidence that Nancy would want to discontinue medical treatment and that this was in her best interests. *Id.*, at 444 (Higgins, J., dissenting from denial of rehearing); Brief for Respondent Guardian Ad Litem 2–3. The court did not specifically define what kind of evidence it would consider clear and convincing, but its general discussion suggests that only a living will or equivalently formal directive from the patient when competent would meet this standard. *See* 760 S.W.2d, at 424–425.

Too few people execute living wills or equivalently formal directives for such an evidentiary rule to ensure adequately that the wishes of incompetent persons will be honored. While it might be a wise social policy to encourage people to furnish such instructions, no general conclusion about a patient's choice can be drawn from the absence of formalities. The probability of becoming irreversibly vegetative is so low that many people may not feel an urgency to marshal formal evidence of their preferences. Some may not wish to dwell on their own physical deterioration and mortality. Even someone with a resolute determination to avoid life support under circumstances such as Nancy's would still need to know that such things as living wills exist and how to execute one. Often legal help would be necessary, especially given the majority's apparent willingness to permit States to insist that a person's wishes are not truly known unless the particular medical treatment is specified.

As a California appellate court observed: "The lack of generalized public awareness of the statutory scheme and the typically human characteristics of procrastination and reluctance to contemplate the need for such arrangements however makes this a tool which will all too often go unused by those who might desire it." *Barber v. Superior Court*, 195 Cal. Rptr. 484, 489 (Cal. Ct. App. 1983). When a person tells family or close friends that she does not want her life sustained artificially, she is "express[ing] her wishes in the only terms familiar to her, and ... as clearly as a lay person should be asked to express them. To require more is unrealistic, and for all practical purposes, it precludes the rights of patients to forego life-sustaining treatment." *In re O'Connor*, 531 N.E.2d 607, 626 (N.Y. 1988) (Simons, J., dissenting). When Missouri enacted a living will statute, it specifically provided that the absence of a living will does not warrant a presumption that a patient wishes continued medical treatment. Thus, apparently not even Missouri's own legislature believes that a person who does not execute a living will fails to do so because he wishes continuous medical treatment under all circumstances.

The testimony of close friends and family members, on the other hand, may often be the best evidence available of what the patient's choice would be. It is they with whom the patient most likely will have discussed such questions and they who know the patient best. "Family members have a unique knowledge of the patient which is vital to any decision on his or her behalf." Newman, Treatment Refusals for the Critically and Terminally Ill: Proposed Rules for the Family, the Physician, and the State, 3 N.Y.L.S. Human Rights Annual 35, 46 (1985). The Missouri court's decision to ignore this whole category of testimony is also at odds with the practices of other States. *See, e.g., In re Peter*, 529 A.2d 419 (N.J. 1987); *Brophy v. New*

England Sinai Hospital, Inc., 497 N.E.2d 626 (Mass. 1986); *In re Severns*, 425 A.2d 156 (Del. Ch. 1980).

The Missouri court's disdain for Nancy's statements in serious conversations not long before her accident, for the opinions of Nancy's family and friends as to her values, beliefs and certain choice, and even for the opinion of an outside objective factfinder appointed by the State evinces a disdain for Nancy Cruzan's own right to choose. The rules by which an incompetent person's wishes are determined must represent every effort to determine those wishes. The rule that the Missouri court adopted and that this Court upholds, however, skews the result away from a determination that as accurately as possible reflects the individual's own preferences and beliefs. It is a rule that transforms human beings into passive subjects of medical technology. . . .

I do not suggest that States must sit by helplessly if the choices of incompetent patients are in danger of being ignored. Even if the Court had ruled that Missouri's rule of decision is unconstitutional, as I believe it should have, States would nevertheless remain free to fashion procedural protections to safeguard the interests of incompetents under these circumstances. The Constitution provides merely a framework here: Protections must be genuinely aimed at ensuring decisions commensurate with the will of the patient, and must be reliable as instruments to that end. Of the many States which have instituted such protections, Missouri is virtually the only one to have fashioned a rule that lessens the likelihood of accurate determinations. In contrast, nothing in the Constitution prevents States from reviewing the advisability of a family decision, by requiring a court proceeding or by appointing an impartial guardian ad litem.

. . .

. . . Missouri and this Court have displaced Nancy's own assessment of the processes associated with dying. They have discarded evidence of her will, ignored her values, and deprived her of the right to a decision as closely approximating her own choice as humanly possible. They have done so disingenuously in her name and openly in Missouri's own. That Missouri and this Court may truly be motivated only by concern for incompetent patients makes no matter. As one of our most prominent jurists warned us decades ago: "Experience should teach us to be most on our guard to protect liberty when the government's purposes are beneficent. . . . The greatest dangers to liberty lurk in insidious encroachment by men of zeal, well meaning but without understanding." *Olmstead v. United States*, 277 U.S. 438, 479 (1928) (Brandeis, J., dissenting).

I respectfully dissent.

■ Justice Stevens, dissenting:

Our Constitution is born of the proposition that all legitimate governments must secure the equal right of every person to "Life, Liberty, and the pursuit of Happiness." In the ordinary case we quite naturally assume that these three ends are compatible, mutually enhancing, and perhaps even coincident.

The Court would make an exception here. It permits the State's abstract, undifferentiated interest in the preservation of life to overwhelm the best interests of Nancy Beth Cruzan, interests which would, according to an undisputed finding, be served by allowing her guardians to exercise her constitutional right to discontinue medical treatment. Ironically, the Court reaches this conclusion despite endorsing three significant propositions which should save it from any such dilemma. First, a competent individual's decision to refuse life-sustaining medical procedures is an aspect of liberty protected by the Due Process Clause of the Fourteenth Amendment. Second, upon a proper evidentiary showing, a qualified guardian may make that decision on behalf of an incompetent ward. Third, in answering the important question presented by this tragic case, it is wise " 'not to attempt, by any general statement, to cover every possible phase of the subject.' " Together, these considerations suggest that Nancy Cruzan's liberty to be free from medical treatment must be understood in light of the facts and circumstances particular to her.

I would so hold: In my view, the Constitution requires the State to care for Nancy Cruzan's life in a way that gives appropriate respect to her own best interests.

.   .   .

. . . Choices about death touch the core of liberty. Our duty, and the concomitant freedom, to come to terms with the conditions of our own mortality are undoubtedly "so rooted in the traditions and conscience of our people as to be ranked as fundamental," *Snyder v. Massachusetts,* 291 U.S. 97, 105 (1934), and indeed are essential incidents of the unalienable rights to life and liberty endowed us by our Creator.

The more precise constitutional significance of death is difficult to describe; not much may be said with confidence about death unless it is said from faith, and that alone is reason enough to protect the freedom to conform choices about death to individual conscience. We may also, however, justly assume that death is not life's simple opposite, or its necessary terminus, but rather its completion. Our ethical tradition has long regarded an appreciation of mortality as essential to understanding life's significance. It may, in fact, be impossible to live for anything without being prepared to die for something. . . .

These considerations cast into stark relief the injustice, and unconstitutionality, of Missouri's treatment of Nancy Beth Cruzan. Nancy Cruzan's death, when it comes, cannot be an historic act of heroism; it will inevitably be the consequence of her tragic accident. But Nancy Cruzan's interest in life, no less than that of any other person, includes an interest in how she will be thought of after her death by those whose opinions mattered to her. There can be no doubt that her life made her dear to her family and to others. How she dies will affect how that life is remembered. The trial court's order authorizing Nancy's parents to cease their daughter's treatment would have permitted the family that cares for Nancy to bring to a close her tragedy and her death. Missouri's objection to that order subordinates Nancy's body, her family, and the lasting significance of her life to the State's own interests. The decision we review thereby interferes with constitutional interests of the highest order.

To be constitutionally permissible, Missouri's intrusion upon these fundamental liberties must, at a minimum, bear a reasonable relationship to a legitimate state end. Missouri asserts that its policy is related to a state interest in the protection of life. In my view, however, it is an effort to define life, rather than to protect it, that is the heart of Missouri's policy. Missouri insists, without regard to Nancy Cruzan's own interests, upon equating her life with the biological persistence of her bodily functions. Nancy Cruzan, it must be remembered, is not now simply incompetent. She is in a persistent vegetative state and has been so for seven years. The trial court found, and no party contested, that Nancy has no possibility of recovery and no consciousness.

It seems to me that the Court errs insofar as it characterizes this case as involving "judgments about the 'quality' of life that a particular individual may enjoy," ... Nancy Cruzan is obviously *"alive"* in a physiological sense. But for patients like Nancy Cruzan, who have no consciousness and no chance of recovery, there is a serious question as to whether the mere persistence of their bodies is *"life"* as that word is commonly understood, or as it is used in both the Constitution and the Declaration of Independence. The State's unflagging determination to perpetuate Nancy Cruzan's physical existence is comprehensible only as an effort to define life's meaning, not as an attempt to preserve its sanctity.

This much should be clear from the oddity of Missouri's definition alone. Life, particularly human life, is not commonly thought of as a merely physiological condition or function. Its sanctity is often thought to derive from the impossibility of any such reduction. When people speak of life, they often mean to describe the experiences that comprise a person's history, as when it is said that somebody "led a good life." They may also mean to refer to the practical manifestation of the human spirit, a meaning captured by the familiar observation that somebody "added life" to an assembly. If there is a shared thread among the various opinions on this subject, it may be that life is an activity which is at once the matrix for, and an integration of, a person's interests. In any event, absent some theological abstraction, the idea of life is not conceived separately from the idea of a living person. Yet, it is by precisely such a separation that Missouri asserts an interest in Nancy Cruzan's life in opposition to Nancy Cruzan's own interests. The resulting definition is uncommon indeed.

. . .

... [T]here is no reasonable ground for believing that Nancy Beth Cruzan has any *personal* interest in the perpetuation of what the State has decided is her life. As I have already suggested, it would be possible to hypothesize such an interest on the basis of theological or philosophical conjecture. But even to posit such a basis for the State's action is to condemn it. It is not within the province of secular government to circumscribe the liberties of the people by regulations designed wholly for the purpose of establishing a sectarian definition of life.

My disagreement with the Court is thus unrelated to its endorsement of the clear and convincing standard of proof for cases of this kind. Indeed, I agree that the controlling facts must be established with unmistakable clarity. The critical question, however, is not how to prove the controlling facts but rather what proven facts should be controlling. In my view, the constitutional answer is clear: The best interests of the individual, especially when buttressed by the interests of all related third parties, must prevail over any general state policy that simply ignores those interests. Indeed, the only apparent *secular* basis for the State's interest in life is the policy's persuasive impact upon people other than Nancy and her family. Yet, "[a]lthough the State may properly perform a teaching function," and although that teaching may foster respect for the sanctity of life, the State may not pursue its project by infringing constitutionally protected interests for *"symbolic* effect." *Carey v. Population Services International,* 431 U.S. 678, 715 (1977). . . .

Only because Missouri has arrogated to itself the power to define life, and only because the Court permits this usurpation, are Nancy Cruzan's life and liberty put into disquieting conflict. If Nancy Cruzan's life were defined by reference to her own interests, so that her life expired when her biological existence ceased serving *any* of her own interests, then her constitutionally protected interest in freedom from unwanted treatment would not come into conflict with her constitutionally protected interest in life. Conversely, if there were *any* evidence that Nancy Cruzan herself defined life to encompass every form of biological persistence by a human being, so that the continuation of treatment would serve Nancy's own liberty, then once again there would be no conflict between life and liberty. The opposition of life and liberty in this case are thus not the result of Nancy Cruzan's tragic accident, but are instead the artificial consequence of Missouri's effort, and this Court's willingness, to abstract Nancy Cruzan's life from Nancy Cruzan's person.

.　.　.

The Cruzan family's continuing concern provides a concrete reminder that Nancy Cruzan's interests did not disappear with her vitality or her consciousness. However commendable may be the State's interest in human life, it cannot pursue that interest by appropriating Nancy Cruzan's life as a symbol for its own purposes. Lives do not exist in abstraction from persons, and to pretend otherwise is not to honor but to desecrate the State's responsibility for protecting life. A State that seeks to demonstrate its commitment to life may do so by aiding those who are actively struggling for life and health. In this endeavor, unfortunately, no State can lack for opportunities: There can be no need to make an example of tragic cases like that of Nancy Cruzan.

I respectfully dissent.

NOTES AND QUESTIONS

1. After the Supreme Court affirmed the decision of the Missouri Supreme Court denying the Cruzans permission to remove their daughter's feeding tube, the Cruzans sought a new hearing on the basis that new evidence had been discovered.

The judge granted the rehearing. The state did not participate in this hearing at Missouri Attorney General William Webster's request. Thus, there was no opposition to the Cruzans' request. Three of Nancy's co-workers testified that she had once declared that she would prefer death to life as "a vegetable." Nancy's doctor, who initially opposed the removal of the feeding tube, agreed that Nancy should be allowed to die because her life was a "living hell." Nancy's court-appointed guardian agreed that death was in Nancy's best interests. On December 14, 1990, Judge Teel again granted the Cruzans permission to remove their daughter's feeding tube. Nancy Cruzan died at 2:55 am on December 26, 1990, in the presence of her parents and sister. Paul Hendrickson, *The Mourning After*, WASH. POST, Dec. 28, 1990, at B1.

2. Is there a constitutional right to die?

3. In 1991, the American Academy of Neurology, Child Neurology Society, American Neurological Association, American Association of Neurological Surgeons, and American Academy of Pediatrics formed the Multi–Society Task Force (MSTF) on Persistent Vegetative State for the purpose of creating a document summarizing existing medical knowledge regarding the persistent vegetative state. In 1994, the task force published their findings in a two-article consensus statement in the New England Journal of Medicine entitled *Medical Aspects of the Persistent Vegetative State*.

First, the MSTF defines the vegetative state as "a clinical condition of complete unawareness of the self and the environment, accompanied by sleep-wake cycle." The Multi–Society Task Force on PVS, *Medical Aspects of the Persistent Vegetative State*, 330 NEW ENG. J. MED. 1499 (1994). Patients in this state "show no evidence sustained, reproducible, purposeful, or voluntary behavioral responses to visual, auditory, tactile, or noxious stimuli; show no evidence of language comprehension or expression; have bowel and bladder incontinence; and have variable preserved cranial-nerve and spinal reflexes." *Id*. The MSTF goes on to define persistent vegetative state as a "vegetative state present one month after acute traumatic or nontraumatic brain injury or lasting for at least one month in patients with degenerative or metabolic disorders or developmental malformations." *Id*.

PVS differs from coma, in which the patient is not awake, and brain death, in which the patient has no brainstem function and is legally dead. *See* Ronald E. Cranford, *The Persistent Vegetative State: The Medical Reality (Getting the Facts Straight)*, 18 HASTINGS CTR. REP. 27 (1988); Ronald E. Cranford & Harmon L. Smith, *Some Critical Distinctions Between Brain Death and the Persistent Vegetative State*, 6 ETHICS SCI. & MED. 199 (1979). PVS also differs from "locked-in syndrome," a situation in which a fully conscious patient is fully paralyzed and unable to communicate.

Recovery of consciousness from a posttraumatic persistent vegetative state is unlikely after twelve months in adults and children. The Multi–Society Task Force on PVS, *supra* at 1572. Recovery from a nontraumatic persistent vegetative state after three months is exceedingly rare in both adults and children. *Id*. The life span of adults and children in such a state ranges from two to five years; survival beyond ten years is unusual. *Id*.

According to the MSTF, while several reports in the popular media have described dramatic recovery from a persistent vegetative state, unusual cases generally have been documented poorly. *Id*. Specifically, the nature of the patients' neurologic condition was unclear, or the timing of the entry into the vegetative state was atypical. *Id*. Moreover, the total number of such patients was extremely small considering the estimated prevalence of the persistent vegetative state and all were apparently left with severe disability. *Id*.

One recurring aspect of the debate over the status of PVS patients is whether these patients are capable of experiencing pain. The position of the MSTF is that "patients in a persistent vegetative state are unaware and insensate and therefore lack of cerebral cortical capacity to be conscious of pain. Almost all such patients have some degree of motor activity and eye movement that would be capable of signaling conscious perception of pain or suffering if such existed." *Id.*

In spite of this overwhelming medical consensus, the public frequently believes that a PVS patient who is not receiving nutrition and hydration is in great pain.

4. Are PVS patients persons in the philosophical sense? *See* Chapter 5, Sec. I., *infra*. Advocates for classifying PVS patients as dead use a person-based definition of death which they claim the PVS patient satisfies. Since most PVS patients can breathe without the aid of a respirator, treating PVS patients as dead raises the specter of a "respiring cadaver." Alternatively, it is possible to consider PVS patients as being alive, but not persons. *See* Ronald E. Cranford & David R. Smith, *Consciousness: The Most Critical Moral (Constitutional) Standard for Human Personhood*, 13 AM. J. L. & MED. 233 (1987–1988); Baruch A. Brody, *Special Ethical Issues in the Management of PVS Patients*, 20 L. MED. & HEALTH CARE 104 (1992). Would this view allow treatment decisions for PVS patients to be different than those for other incompetent patients?

Even if PVS patients like Nancy Cruzan are not dead, does it make sense to speak of a PVS patient who cannot have any conscious experiences as having interests that can be asserted or should be protected? Is consciousness a necessary condition for the existence of interests or do a person's best interests exist in the abstract?

5. The Cruzans' desire to terminate Nancy's treatment was opposed by medical professionals and state authorities. It is often the case, however, that a patient's family wishes to continue treatment that health care professionals considered futile. *See, e.g.*, Robert D. Truog et al., *The Problem with Futility*, 326 NEW ENG. J. MED. 1560 (1992); John J. Paris et al., *Physician's Refusal of Requested Treatment: The Case of Baby L*, 322 NEW ENG. J. MED. 1012 (1990). For example, studies have found that families of PVS patients typically prefer aggressive treatment, including transfer to acute care hospitals if necessary, for palliative treatment. *See* Donald D. Tresch et al., *Patients in a Persistent Vegetative State: Attitudes and Reactions of Family Members*, 39 J. AM. GERIATRICS SOC'Y 17 (1991); Judith W. Ross, *The Puzzle of the Permanently Unconscious*, 22 HASTINGS CTR. REP. 2 (1992). These cases pose difficult dilemmas that differ from those encountered in "right to die" cases. Under what circumstances should medical treatments be considered futile? Who should make that decision?

The difficulties posed by such questions were recently highlighted by the case of Terri Schiavo. Schiavo, in a persistent vegetative state since 1990, remains the subject of a heated legal battle between her husband Michael who sought the Florida courts' permission to remove the feeding tube keeping her alive and her parents who vehemently opposed such actions. While Mr. Schiavo maintained his wife told him she would never want to be kept alive artificially, Ms. Schiavo's parents made and released videos of her in which she appeared to smile, grunt, and moan in response to her mother's voice as well as follow a balloon with her eyes, arguing that removal of the tube would constitute murder. Abby Goodnough, *Florida Judge Authorizes Removal of Feeding Tube*, N.Y. TIMES, May 7, 2004, at A20. Mr. Schiavo ultimately won the court's permission to remove the tube following years of appeals. *In re Guardianship of Schiavo*, 851 So.2d 182 (Fla. 2d Dist. Ct. App. 2003). On October 15, 2003, within days, Governor Jeb Bush, in an extraordinary move, intervened on the parents' behalf, pushing through a bill known as "Terri's Law" which authorized him to issue a one-time stay to prevent the tube's removal. Fl. Laws. Ch. 2003–418 (2003). The law was subsequently struck down by Sixth Circuit Court Judge Douglas Baird who wrote that it "unjustifiably authorizes the governor to summarily deprive Florida citizens of their constitutional right to privacy" and illegally delegated powers to the governor reserved to the legislature, granting him "unfettered discretion" over Ms. Schiavo's fate. *Schiavo v. Bush*, 2004 WL 980028 (Fla. Cir. Ct. 2004). At the time of this writing Terri Schiavo is still alive and the case is still in the courts.

Should the principle of autonomy that undergirds the right to refuse treatment require that a competent patient's demand for treatment be respected? From a societal perspective, given the scarcity of health care resources, providing treatment to one patient may force another patient to forgo that treatment, even though the treatment may be substantially more beneficial for the patient who is unable to receive it. If, however, society is unwilling to allow patients to demand access to treatment (assuming they can pay for it), would that suggest that the real basis for respecting patients' wishes to refuse treatment has little to do with autonomy? Perhaps quality-of-life considerations are the primary motivating concerns. *See* J. MED. & PHIL. (Apr. 1995) (entire issue devoted to discussion of moral and conceptual disputes surrounding "futile" medical treatment).

C. COMPETENT PATIENTS

1. IN GENERAL

McKay v. Bergstedt

Supreme Court of Nevada, 1990.
106 Nev. 808, 801 P.2d 617.

■ STEFFEN, J.

Kenneth Bergstedt was a thirty-one-year-old mentally competent quadriplegic who sought to vindicate on appeal the lower court's decision confirming his right to die. Convinced that Kenneth's position has merit, we affirm.[1]

. . .

At the tender age of ten, Kenneth suffered the fate of a quadriplegic as the result of a swimming accident. Twenty-one years later, faced with what appeared to be the imminent death of his ill father, Kenneth decided that he wanted to be released from a life of paralysis held intact by the life-sustaining properties of a respirator. Although Kenneth was able to read, watch television, orally operate a computer, and occasionally receive limited enjoyment from wheelchair ambulation, he despaired over the prospect of life without the attentive care, companionship and love of his devoted father.

---

1. Despite this court's efforts to expedite the disposition of this appeal, Kenneth did not survive the process. As a result, we have revised certain aspects of this opinion to reflect changes necessitated by what we consider to be the tragic and untimely demise of a young man who had managed to create a modicum of quality in a life devastated by quadriplegia and total dependence on artificial respiration and the care of others. We also note that Kenneth's fear of being left at the mercy of strangers would now present an added challenge to the struggle for quality in his life if he had survived, as his father passed away within a matter of days after Kenneth's death.

The limited record before us reflects substantial evidence of facts relevant to the proceedings below and material to the framework upon which the resolution of this appeal is constructed. First, a board-certified neurosurgeon determined that Kenneth's quadriplegia was irreversible. Second, a psychiatrist examined Kenneth and found him to be competent and able to understand the nature and consequences of his decision. Third, Kenneth arrived at his decision after substantial deliberation. Fourth, Kenneth's trusted and devoted father understood the basis for his son's decision and reluctantly approved. Fifth, although Kenneth's quadriplegia was irreversible, his affliction was non-terminal so long as he received artificial respiration.

Kenneth thus petitioned the district court as a non-terminal, competent, adult quadriplegic for an order permitting the removal of his respirator by one who could also administer a sedative and thereby relieve the pain that would otherwise precede his demise. Kenneth also sought an order of immunity from civil or criminal liability for anyone providing the requested assistance. Additionally, he petitioned the court for a declaration absolving him of suicide in the removal of his life-support system.

In ruling, the district court determined that Kenneth was a mentally competent adult fully capable of deciding to forego continued life connected to a respirator. The court also found that he understood that the removal of his life support system would shortly prove fatal.

In concluding that Kenneth had a constitutional privacy right to discontinue further medical treatment, the court also ruled that given Kenneth's condition, judicial recognition of the primacy of his individual rights posed no threat to the State's interest in preserving life, adversely affected no third parties, and presented no threat to the integrity of the medical profession. The district court thus concluded that Kenneth was entitled to the relief sought.

I

. . .

Because many individuals find themselves facing a terminal condition susceptible to indefinite suspension by medical intervention, the question arises with increasing frequency and fervor concerning the extent to which persons have the right to refuse an artificial extension of life. Courts considering the question have basically agreed that the answer is to be found in the balancing of interests between the person in extremis and the State. On the one hand is the interest of the individual in determining the extent to which he or she is willing to have a devastated life continued artificially or by radical medical treatment. On the other hand, courts agree that the State has several interests of significance that must be weighed in determining whether the rights of the individual should prevail. Those interests have generally been defined as: (1) the interest of the State in preserving the sanctity of all life, including that of the particular patient involved in a given action; (2) the interest of the State in preventing suicide; (3) the interest of the State in protecting innocent third persons who may be adversely affected by the death of the party seeking relief; and

(4) the State's interest in preserving the integrity of the medical profession. We add to the list of State interests, a fifth concern which is the interest of the State in encouraging the charitable and humane care of those whose lives may be artificially extended under conditions which have the prospect of providing at least a modicum of quality living.

Under the common law, "[n]o right is held more sacred, or is more carefully guarded ... than the right of every individual to the possession and control of his own person, free from all restraint or interference of others, unless by clear and unquestionable authority of law." *Cruzan v. Director, Missouri Department of Health,* 497 U.S. 261 (1990) (quoting *Union Pacific R. Co. v. Botsford,* 141 U.S. 250, 251 (1891))…. We nevertheless agree with other courts which have held that the right to refuse medical treatment is not absolute….

We do not perceive a privacy right in either our state or federal constitution as a basis for refusing or withdrawing medical treatment and support. However, we do agree with the United States Supreme Court in *Cruzan* that a person's liberty interest is the fundamental constitutional value implicated in "right to die" cases…. Article 1, section 8 of the Constitution of the State of Nevada tracks the Fourteenth Amendment of the United States Constitution in protecting its citizens against deprivation of their right to liberty without due process of law. We conclude that Kenneth's liberty interest under both the federal and Nevada constitutions was implicated in his request to be relieved of his respirator….

… [U]nder both the common law right to refuse treatment and an individual's constitutionally protected liberty interest, such rights are not absolute and are subject to a balancing of relevant State interests.

II.

Turning, as we must, to the legitimate interests of the State, we now balance those interests against Kenneth's constitutional liberty interest and common law right of self-determination, and we do so for decisional purposes despite Kenneth's death.

1. *The interest of the State in preserving life.* The State's interest in preserving life is both fundamental and compelling. Indeed, it constitutes a basic purpose for which governments are formed. Nevertheless, the State's interest in the preservation of life is not absolute. For example, state-sponsored executions may constitute an exception to the duty to preserve life for a complex of reasons ranging from an emphasis on the value of the lives of innocent victims to the necessity of maintaining an orderly society where the quality of life is of preeminent concern. Moreover, as the quality of life diminishes because of physical deterioration, the State's interest in preserving life may correspondingly decrease. However, the State's attenuated interest does not evince a lesser appreciation for the value of life as the physical being deteriorates, but rather a recognition of the fact that all human life must eventually succumb to the aging process or to intervening events or conditions impacting the health of an individual. Moreover, an interest in the preservation of life "at all costs" is demeaning to death as a natural concomitant of life. Despite its frightening aspects, death has important values of its own. It may come as welcome relief to prolonged

suffering. It may end the indignities associated with life bereft of self-determination and cognitive activity. In the mind of some, it may satisfy longings for loved ones preceding them in death. In short, death is a natural aspect of life that is not without value and dignity.

Courts have recognized that persons may reach a condition in life where the individual preference for a natural death may have greater primacy than the State's interest in preserving life through artificial support systems. . . .

. . .

. . . [W]e . . . believe that at some point in the life of a competent adult patient, the present or prospective quality of life may be so dismal that the right of the individual to refuse treatment or elect a discontinuance of artificial life support must prevail over the interest of the State in preserving life. In instances where the prospects for a life of quality are smothered by physical pain and suffering, only the sufferer can determine the value of continuing mortality. We therefore conclude that in situations involving adults who are: (1) competent; (2) irreversibly sustained or subject to being sustained by artificial life support systems or some form of heroic, radical medical treatment; and (3) enduring physical and mental pain and suffering, the individual's right to decide will generally outweigh the State's interest in preserving life.

On the assumption that Kenneth would survive the issuance of this opinion, we reviewed his record carefully in an effort to sensitively analyze the circumstances under which he lived and the reasons that prompted him to seek a judicial imprimatur of his decision to disconnect his respirator. It appeared that Kenneth's suffering resulted more from his fear of the unknown than any source of physical pain. After more than two decades of life as a quadriplegic under the loving care of parents, Kenneth understandably feared for the quality of his life after the death of his father, who was his only surviving parent. Although Kenneth completed elementary and high school through private tutoring, study and telephone communication with his teachers, and wrote poetry and otherwise lived a useful and productive life, his physical condition was dire. His quadriplegia left him not only ventilator-dependent, but entirely reliant on others for his bodily functions and needs. His limited sources of entertainment, including reading, watching television and writing poetry through the oral operation of a computer, also required the attentive accommodations of others. Since the death of his mother in 1978, all of these services were provided by his father and attending nurses occasionally called to the home.

It thus appears, and the record so reflects, that Kenneth was preoccupied with fear over the quality of his life after the death of his father. He feared that some mishap would occur to his ventilator without anyone being present to correct it, and that he would suffer an agonizing death as a result. In contemplating his future under the care of strangers, Kenneth stated that he had no encouraging expectations from life, did not enjoy life, and was tired of suffering. Fear of the unknown is a common travail even among those of us who are not imprisoned by paralysis and a total dependency upon others. There is no doubt that Kenneth was plagued by a sense of foreboding concerning the quality of his life without his father.

Someone has suggested that there are few greater sources of fear in life than fear itself. In Kenneth's situation it is not difficult to understand why fear had such an overriding grasp on his view of the quality of his future life. Given the circumstances under which he labored to survive, we could not substitute our own judgment for Kenneth's when assessing the quality of his life. We therefore conclude that Kenneth's liberty interest in controlling the extent to which medical measures were used to continue to sustain his life and forestall his death outweighed the State's interest in preserving his life. As a competent adult beset by conditions noted above, Kenneth also enjoyed a preeminent right under the common law to withdraw his consent to a continued medical regimen involving his attachment to a respirator. In so ruling, we attach great significance to the quality of Kenneth's life as he perceived it under the particular circumstances that were afflicting him.

Notwithstanding our ruling on this issue, we note that if Kenneth had survived, our concerns under the fifth State interest discussed hereafter, would have had to be satisfied prior to Kenneth's withdrawal of his life support system.

2. *The interest of the State in preventing suicide.* Controversy continues to rage over this semantics-laden issue. Opponents of Kenneth's position describe it in terms of a state-sponsored suicide. Our research reveals no court declaring it so. We nevertheless recognize the controversy as a healthy concern for the value of an individual life.

The dictionary definition of suicide is "the act or an instance of taking one's own life voluntarily and intentionally; the deliberate and intentional destruction of his own life by a person of years of discretion and of sound mind; one that commits or attempts self-murder." Webster's Third New International Dictionary (1968). As we will attempt to show, Kenneth harbored no intent to take his own life, voluntarily or otherwise. He did not seek his own destruction and he most certainly eschewed self-murder, a fact made evident by his petition to the district court for an order declaring that the exercise of his right to decide would not amount to an act of suicide.

It is beyond cavil in one sense, that Kenneth was taking affirmative measures to hasten his own death. It is equally clear that if Kenneth had enjoyed sound physical health, but had viewed life as unbearably miserable because of his mental state, his liberty interest would provide no basis for asserting a right to terminate his life with or without the assistance of other persons. Our societal regard for the value of an individual life, as reflected in our Federal and State constitutions, would never countenance an assertion of liberty over life under such circumstances.

It must nevertheless be conceded, as noted above, that death is a natural end of living. There are times when its beckoning is sweet and benevolent. Most would consider it unthinkable to force one who is wracked [sic] with advanced, terminal, painful cancer to require a therapy regimen that would merely prolong the agony of dying for a brief season. In allowing such a patient to refuse therapy could it seriously be argued that he or she is committing an act of suicide?

The informed consent doctrine presupposes that persons faced with difficult medical decisions that will, at best, substantially alter the quality of their future lives, may elect to refuse treatment and let the processes of nature take their course. Few would conclude that exercising the right to refuse treatment would be tantamount to suicide. Such persons have not sought to contract the disease or condition that threatens both the quality and duration of their lives. Rather, they have evaluated their circumstances and determined that a future sustained by radical medical treatment or artificial means and entailing a drastic decrease in the quality of their lives, is not a valued alternative despite its effectiveness in extending life or delaying death. Moreover, we see no difference between the patient who refuses treatment and the one who accepts treatment and later refuses its continuance because of a resulting loss in the quality of life.

The primary factors that distinguish Kenneth's type of case from that of a person desiring suicide are attitude, physical condition and prognosis. Unlike a person bent on suicide, Kenneth sought no affirmative measures to terminate his life; he desired only to eliminate the artificial barriers standing between him and the natural processes of life and death that would otherwise ensue with someone in his physical condition. Kenneth survived artificially within a paralytic prison from which there was no hope of release other than death. But he asked no one to shorten the term of his natural life free of the respirator. He sought no fatal potions to end life or hurry death. In other words, Kenneth desired the right to die a natural death unimpeded by scientific contrivances.

Justice Scalia's concurring opinion in *Cruzan* suggests that "insofar as balancing the relative interests of the State and the individual is concerned, there is nothing distinctive about accepting death through the refusal of 'medical treatment,' as opposed to accepting it through the refusal of food, or through the failure to shut off the engine and get out of the car after parking in one's garage after work." *Cruzan*, 110 S. Ct. at 2862. We respectfully disagree with the learned justice. The distinction between refusing medical treatment and the other scenarios presented by Justice Scalia is the difference between choosing a natural death summoned by an uninvited illness or calamity and deliberately seeking to terminate one's life by resorting to death-inducing measures unrelated to the natural process of dying.

. . .

There is a significant distinction between an individual faced with artificial survival resulting from heroic medical intervention and an individual, otherwise healthy or capable of sustaining life without artificial support who simply desires to end his or her life. The former adult, if competent, exercises a judgment based upon an assessment of the quality of an artificially maintained life vis-à-vis the quality of a natural death. Conversely, the latter acts from a potentially reversible pessimism or mental attitude concerning only the quality of life.

We are not deciding competing interests between a nonexistent right to choose suicide and the interest of the State in preserving life. The State's interest in the preservation of life relates to meaningful life. Insofar as this State's interest is concerned, the State has no overriding interest in interfering with the natural processes of dying among citizens whose lives are irreparably devastated by injury or illness to the point where life may be sustained only by contrivance or radical intervention. In situations such as Kenneth's, only the competent adult patient can determine the extent to which his or her artificially extended life has meaning and value in excess of the death value.

. . .

As medical science continues to develop methods of prolonging life, it is not inconceivable that a person could be faced with any number of alternatives that would delay death and consign him or her to a living hell in which there is hopelessness, total dependence, a complete lack of dignity, and an ongoing cost that would impoverish loved ones. The State's interest in preserving life and preventing what some may erroneously refer to as suicide does not extend so far.

Kenneth did not wish to commit suicide. He desired only to live for as long as the state of his health would permit without artificial augmentation and support. Society had no right to force upon him the obligation to remain alive under conditions that he considered to be anathema. To rule otherwise would place an unwarranted premium on survival at the expense of human dignity, quality of life, and the value that comes from allowing death a natural and timely entrance.

. . .

3. *The interest of the State in protecting innocent third persons.* Kenneth never married and had no children. No third persons were dependent upon him financially or for comfort, support and counsel. It is true that Kenneth's father still lived at the time of Kenneth's petition, but it was realistically anticipated that the father would not survive for any extended period of time. Moreover, Robert Bergstedt acquiesced in his son's decision given the circumstances Kenneth was facing. This State interest was simply not implicated in Kenneth's request.

4. *The State's interest in preserving the integrity of the medical profession*.... The State has an unquestioned duty to see that the integrity of the medical profession is preserved and that it is never allowed to become an instrument for the selective destruction of lives deemed to have little utility.

Despite the medical profession's healing objectives, there are increasing numbers of people who fall in the category of those who may never be healed but whose lives may be extended by heroic measures. Unfortunately, there are times when such efforts will do little or nothing more than delay death in a bodily environment essentially bereft of quality. Under such conditions or the reasonably likely prospect thereof, the medical profession is not threatened by a competent adult's refusal of life-extending treatment. The President's Commission, established by Congress in 1978, and consisting of doctors, ethicists, lawyers, theologians and others, concluded:

> The voluntary choice of a competent and informed patient should determine whether or not life-sustaining therapy will be undertaken, just as such choices provide the basis for other decisions about medical treatment. Health care institutions and professionals should try to enhance patients' abilities to make decisions on their own behalf and to promote understanding of the available treatment options.... Health care professionals serve patients best by maintaining a presumption in favor of sustaining life, while recognizing that competent patients are entitled to choose to forego any treatments, including those that sustain life.

President's Commission for the Study of Ethical Problems in Medicine and Biomedical and Behavioral Research, Deciding to Forego Life–Sustaining Treatment, p. 3 (U.S. Gov.'t Printing Office 1983); *see* 42 U.S.C. § 300v (1982).

We are of the opinion that Kenneth's request to be relieved of his connection to a respirator did not present an ethical threat to the medical profession. Because a competent adult would have enjoyed a qualified constitutional and common law right to refuse a life-sustaining attachment to a respirator in the first instance, there is no reason why such an adult could not assert the same rights to reject a continuation of respirator-dependency that has proven too burdensome to endure.

5. *The State's interest in encouraging the charitable and humane care of afflicted persons.* There is a clear national and State public policy to encourage charitable contributions for the humane care and treatment of citizens stricken with various maladies and disabilities. The policy is reflected nationally by allowing deductions from the federal income tax for charitable contributions. It is also reflected throughout our society by committing scarce public assets to the funding of special legislation designed to create opportunities and facilities for physically handicapped persons. Both the purpose and effect of such legislation is to enhance the quality of life among those who are disabled in one form or another. Moreover, national and State efforts to improve the circumstances of disabled citizens are indicative of the highest social character—a society attuned to the worth of an individual irrespective of physical or mental handicap.

Kenneth's condition and predicament directly implicated the State interest here considered. Kenneth was not without a meaningful life. His ability to give expression to his intellect by means of an orally operated computer, to learn, to enjoy reading and watching videos and television all reflected the possibility of a life imbued with a potential for significant quality and accomplishment. He nevertheless feared life in the care of strangers after the demise of an attentive and caring father. It appeared to us that Kenneth needed some type of assurance that society would not cast him adrift in a sea of indifference after his father's passing. Perhaps available governmental, private and charitable support systems would not have been adequate to provide Kenneth the assurance he needed to alleviate his fears. We nevertheless conclude that absent Kenneth's intervening death, it would have been necessary to fully inform him of the care alternatives that would have been available to him after his father's death or incapacity.

III.

We elected to review this matter despite Kenneth's death and the basic lack of a controversy in order to provide guidance to others who may find themselves in similar predicaments. In so doing, we are keenly mindful of the cost and delay Kenneth suffered in order to obtain a final ruling through the court system. We agree with other courts that have concluded that persons in Kenneth's situation should not be subjected to such a burdensome process in attempting to exercise their constitutional and common law right of choice. As evidenced by the instant case and those reported in other jurisdictions, if the process involved in validating a patient's election to refuse or terminate medical treatment is unduly protracted, the patient's rights become hollow and meaningless, if not entirely ineffectual.

After studying the procedural methodology employed or discussed by the courts in the cited opinions we felt somewhat like the dinner guest who enjoyed the meal but left with an unsatiated appetite. As noted previously, other courts have agreed that a patient's right to refuse medical treatment must be weighed against the State interests we have heretofore enumerated. Unfortunately, none of the courts has provided guidance as to how and by whom the weighing process is to be accomplished.... The procedural lacuna common to these opinions may reflect a judicial timidity resulting from a tacit recognition of the legislative hue court-supplied procedures would assume. It seems clear that the specification of measures involved in properly weighing the interests of the individual and the State is more suited to a statutory resolution by the Legislature.

Given the fact that our ruling has confirmed the rights of the individual and the interests of the State, and the need to weigh both in the decisional process, we feel constrained to suggest a procedural matrix by which the weighing and decisional process may be satisfied pending statutory treatment by the Legislature. We therefore stress that the following procedure is designed to fill a temporary void which we trust will be supplanted by timely legislative action. We also emphasize that until such time as the Legislature enacts superseding legislation, the procedure established here will suffice in the determination of a competent adult patient's right to refuse or discontinue medical treatment, including the use or discontinuance of life support systems.

Guided in part by the decisions of courts in other jurisdictions ... we conclude that hereafter competent adult patients desiring to refuse or discontinue medical treatment need only conform to the following procedure: (1) Two non-attending physicians must examine the adult to determine and certify in writing, without liability except for fraud, that (a) the patient is mentally competent to understand his or her prognosis and was properly informed thereof, and that the patient was apprised of treatment alternatives and the consequences that will or are likely to result from refusing medical treatment or electing to withdraw medical therapy, including life support systems then in use; (b) the patient's condition is irreversible or the extent to which the condition may be improved through medical intervention; (c) the patient is or reasonably appears to be free of coercion or pressure in making his or her decision; (d) if the patient is non-terminal, i.e., has an estimated life expectancy of six months or more either with or without artificial life support systems, that he or she was apprised of the care options available to the patient through governmental, charitable and private sources with due regard for the value of life, and certify in writing without liability except for fraud, that the aforesaid explanation of care alternatives was given and the patient's response thereto; (2) After the preceding steps have been satisfied, if the patient chooses to refuse medical treatment or to withdraw existing medical therapy, including life support systems, one of the following alternatives will apply: (a) if the patient is terminally ill or injured, i.e., has an estimated remaining natural life expectancy (with or without artificial life support systems) of less than six months and the two non-attending physicians so certify in writing (again, without liability except for fraud), the patient's constitutional and common law rights of self-determination shall be deemed to prevail over the previously enumerated State interests, and the patient may refuse treatment or elect to have existing therapy, including any life support systems, terminated and any physician or health care provider who assists the patient in the implementation of his or her decision, including the administration of any sedative or pain medication to ease the patient's pre-death anxieties or pain, will not be subject to civil or criminal liability; (b) if the patient is non-terminal, either by virtue of artificial life support systems or a prognosis for a natural survival period in excess of six months, then the patient's decision to refuse treatment or to withdraw existing medical therapy, including life-support systems, must be weighed against the aforesaid State interests; the weighing process, pending legislative action, shall be performed by any district court judge, whose decision, with due regard for the patient's rights and the certifications of the physicians described above, will be final and not subject to appeal unless the district court judge shall determine that the interests of the State outweigh the patient's rights to refuse or terminate medical treatment. In the latter event, the patient shall enjoy a right of an expedited appeal in the event he or she elects to pursue it.

In all cases decided by a district court in favor of the patient, the court's order shall specify that any physician or health care provider who assists the patient in receiving the benefits of his or her decision with minimal pain, shall not be subject to civil or criminal liability....

In those cases classified above as terminal, the written certifications provided by the two non-attending physicians shall have the same force and effect as the order of a district court. The original of the written certifications by the physicians shall be provided to the patient as an authoritative basis for enlisting necessary assistance in accommodating [sic] the patient's decision. Any physician or health care provider who assists the patient and administers medication to minimize pain, shall enjoy the same immunity from civil or criminal liability as any such person who acted pursuant to an order of the district court. The non-attending physicians providing the certificates should retain a copy thereof in their own files.

We have burdened this opinion with the procedures set forth above in an attempt to eliminate uncertainty and minimize cost in these types of cases. We trust that our ruling will also provide a reasonably simple and expeditious method for facilitating a competent patient's decisions, while at the same time emphasizing the value of a human life and the seriousness with which these difficult and sensitive matters should be approached.

IV.

If Kenneth had survived the date of the issuance of this opinion, we would have confirmed his right to discontinue his artificial life support systems subject only to a prior consultation with a responsible health care provider or representative of the Nevada Department of Human Resources who would have informed him of the care alternatives available to him after his father's death. The value of Kenneth's life demanded nothing less.

In view of Kenneth's death, we leave him with an official ruling that his petition to be humanely relieved of the artificial contrivance to which he was attached did not constitute a prelude to suicide. As a competent adult, Kenneth sought to exercise, through lawful means, his valued constitutional and common law right to allow the natural consequences of his condition to occur—unimpeded by artificial barriers. His memory is deserving of no taint or inference relating to an act of suicide.

For the reasons set forth above, the judgment of the district court is affirmed.

. . .

■ Springer, J., dissenting:

. . .

II.

State–Assisted Suicide: Our "Clouded Ability to Assess the Suicidal Basis of Mr. Bergstedt's Request to Die"

[V]alue judgments . . . about the worth of Mr. Bergstedt's life have clouded [the] ability to properly assess the suicidal basis for Mr. Bergstedt's request to die. . . .

. . . Added to the "one-sidedness" of this case are other "clouding" factors that I think may well have affected its outcome: the extremely dramatic and sympathetic nature of Mr. Bergstedt's plea for mercy; faulty reliance on "right-to-die" cases which deal with the comatose and the terminally ill and have no application here; and, cloudiest of all, the flawed impression that persons whose lives depend on life-sustaining devices may kill themselves at will, merely by calling removal of essential-to-life machines a refusal to accept unwanted "medical treatment" or by calling their users' immediate and directly resultant demise a "natural death."

I see Kenneth Bergstedt's breathing device as being more than "medicine." It is true that the machine was introduced during a medical emergency by medical personnel. It is true also that medical and mechanical monitoring of the device must be continued and that medical personnel or paramedical personnel are required to fulfill the daily needs of persons in this kind of condition. Notwithstanding all of this, I cannot escape the conclusion that, after twenty-three years of living and breathing in this machine-aided manner, the whole process becomes something quite more than mere medical *treatment*. The mechanical breather becomes a new way of life for its user, and life cannot go on without it. Mr. Bergstedt lived at home. The "treatment" in any real sense is over; and just as heart pacemakers, artificial venous or arterial shunts, a variety of prosthetic devices and other such medically sponsored and introduced artifacts may *begin* as a medical treatment modality, the ventilator begins as a form of medical treatment but ends up as an integral part of its dependent user. Even if it is insisted that these things continue indefinitely to be considered as "treatment," they indeed become far, far more than just treatment after years and years of dependency on them.

When Kenneth Bergstedt asked the court to give legal sanction to the death-inducing act of disconnecting his breathing apparatus, he was not to my mind merely exercising his "right to be let alone," and his right to refuse unwanted medical treatment. Withdrawal of medicine or so-called "life support" may be a humane way of letting nature take its course in the lives of the near-dead or irreversibly comatose, but it is a different matter when withdrawal of these items is admitted to be the immediate and proximate cause of the death of a person who concededly is seeking to take his own life.

Use of the term "natural death" in this case is only a natural and understandable way of averting the excruciating truth. Bergstedt's explicit and express desire and intention was that of putting an immediate end to his own life. That is not what one would call a "natural death." There was nothing natural about Mr. Bergstedt's death; he killed himself. Masking this unpleasant but inescapable fact has the unfortunate result of masking the really hard question presented by this case, and that is this: If, when and how should a person in Kenneth Bergstedt's condition (or perhaps other comparable conditions) be given legal permission to have outside assistance in taking his own life, without the incurrence of civil or criminal liability by anyone involved in the process? By avoiding the question, we avoid the answer; and by avoiding the answer, we invite future agonies suffered by persons like Mr. Bergstedt, who, in my view, was not given an acceptable solution to his plight. Mr. Bergstedt is dead now, and this may let us look at these cases in a more dispassionate way and address the problems presented by this case in a proper and rational manner.

· · ·

Kenneth Bergstedt did not want to die a "natural" death; he wanted to die an immediate death. He sought an immediate death by means of disconnecting the "extension of his person" that had enabled him to live and breath for the preceding twenty-three years. Construing the ventilator in this case as a "form of extraordinary support" that can be removed at will is a terrible and terrifying rationalization and, as well, a prejudicial treatment of Mr. Bergstedt because his assisted suicide was sanctioned and facilitated only because of his disabled condition.

· · ·

I register now my strong disapproval of our courts' putting their "judicial stamp of approval" on allowing "the state to assist an individual to die only because he ... has a disability." What other conditions, physical or mental, I ask myself, will be brought to the courts as grounds for judicially approved and assisted self-destruction? We now have a growing population of people who are alive but throughout history would have been dead. Some live under conditions under which many if not most of us would probably not want to survive; yet there are those who do survive and who continue to survive under the most trying of circumstances. The distinguishing aspect of the described persons is that, unlike most of us, they do not have, because of their paralytic condition, the power to bring their lives to an end, however intolerable their lives might become. They are trapped. Life is thrust upon them—forced upon them. If a person like Mr. Bergstedt comes to the courts saying, "I have come to the end of my rope; I cannot stand it any more; you must give me the means to end my own life in peace and in dignity"; it is difficult indeed to say "no." Unfortunately it does not belong to the judicial realm to say "yes." The judicial department of government is not the proper agency to address the novel and perplexing question presented here, namely, the question of under what, if any, circumstances should a right to state-assisted suicide be granted.

. . .

IV.

Conclusion

. . .

I want to be sure that the reader of this dissent does not get this case mixed up with the "right-to-die" cases in which there is present either imminent death or permanent unconsciousness. We are not dealing here with "overtreatment" or unwanted prolongation of the dying process. Kenneth Bergstedt was severely paralyzed and ventilator-dependent and suffered from what neurologists self-descriptively call the "locked-in syndrome"; but his consciousness was intact, and he had a life-expectancy of indefinite duration. It is unclear, however, whether his decision to take his own life was completely rational or possibly a product of some kind of clinically identifiable depression.

. . .

I have agonized over this case. At one moment I am haunted by the picture of a hopeless, wretched and tortured person who has no desire except to end his suffering by ending his life. As we know, however, he did not have it within his capacity to end his life, so that he must live on, "locked" into a condition which at the time of his death Mr. Bergstedt probably saw as one of intolerable and unrelenting misery. How can any one who can help him possibly turn down his plaint? But, then, we are not even sure of the exact nature of his mental and emotional condition, or that his depression was not a temporary one.... In this case we will never know the truth because we heard only one side of the case, namely, Mr. Bergstedt's unopposed claim to the "right" to put an abrupt end to his life. Even if we assume, however, that Mr. Bergstedt's death wish was not generated by a one-sided support system and depression, my views of this case would remain the same.

. . .

I know in our jurisprudence of no right to commit suicide or to be mercifully put away by the medics, "as quick[ly] and painless[ly] as possible." There is no natural, constitutional, statutory or court-created right that would permit a person to have the assistance of another person in deliberately taking his own life. I am sure that no one would contend that Mr. Bergstedt had a right to suicidal assistance if he had not been incapable of doing the deed himself. So this brings us to the point, discussed above, that Mr. Bergstedt has been given the court-decreed right to assisted suicide only because he was disabled to the extent described. Such a decree should not have been entered.

. . .

NOTES AND QUESTIONS

1. Kenneth Bergstedt was paralyzed at the age of ten when a girl jumped on him while he was swimming in a pool and broke his neck. He suffocated when the respirator tube through which he received oxygen was removed. Kenneth's father, Richard, initially told police that on the night of October 3, 1990, he refused his son's request to unplug his life support systems. Richard claimed that he discovered Kenneth's body when he got up later that same night to check on Kenneth, and that he believed that Kenneth had unhooked himself from the respirator. Shortly thereafter, Richard told a Las Vegas newspaper that he had loosened the tracheostomy tube and had given Kenneth a sedative to alleviate any pain Kenneth might feel as he suffocated. Toxicology reports on Kenneth supported the latter version of Richard's story. *See Quadriplegic Dies Before Supreme Court Rules on His Right-to-Die*, UPI DOMESTIC NEWS RELEASE, Oct. 4, 1990. The case was initially investigated as a homicide, but no charges were brought against Richard Bergstedt, who died of lung cancer a week after his son's death. *See Man Dies After Son Fulfilled Wish to End Life Before Him*, L.A. TIMES, Oct. 12, 1990, at A29.

2. The court lists "encouraging the charitable and humane care of afflicted persons" as one of the state interests at stake in cases involving the right to refuse life-sustaining medical treatment (LSMT). Does humane care require the recognition of a handicapped individual's right to refuse/terminate LSMT? Or is the recognition of such a right merely a means by which to legitimize the state's failure to provide adequate services to such individuals? In a similar case, *Georgia v. McAfee*, 259 Ga. 579, 385 S.E.2d 651 (1989), Larry McAfee sought permission to have his respirator removed and to be injected with a sedative to alleviate the pain which would accompany his death. McAfee, like Bergstedt, was a respirator-dependent quadriplegic who could not independently perform any bodily functions. McAfee was an avid outdoorsman until May 5, 1985, when his motorcycle, which he had affectionately nicknamed "Big Red," slid off an isolated mountain road in North Georgia. Two of McAfee's vertebrae were crushed, and he would have certainly died had it not been for the efforts of a nurse who happened to be picnicking nearby. McAfee was flown to Atlanta for treatment. After a year of rehabilitation at Shepherd Spinal Center, McAfee was able to move into a small apartment outside Atlanta, where he worked as a computer consultant using a special computer.

In November 1987, McAfee's insurance settlement ran out, and he was forced to consider moving to either a hospital or a nursing home. None of the nursing homes in Georgia would admit McAfee because the care that he required cost more than the reimbursement provided by Georgia. After shopping around in different states, McAfee had himself admitted to Aristocrat Berea Skilled Nursing Facility in Ohio. McAfee complained incessantly about receiving poor care. In January 1989, he was loaded onto an ambulance plane, without his consent, and shipped to a large public hospital in Atlanta. McAfee was kept in the ICU; he maintains this was the lowest point of his experience.

After three months in the ICU with no privacy, no entertainment, and little opportunity for quiet rest, McAfee called lawyer Randall Davis to help him obtain permission to die. On August 14, 1989, McAfee petitioned the Fulton Superior Court for permission to die. Two days later, as a result of the publicity his case received, McAfee was admitted to Briarcliff Nursing Home in Alabama. On September 6, the court ruled in McAfee's favor, and on November 21, the Georgia State Supreme Court upheld the lower court decision. However, when McAfee became aware that he had options for independent living, he decided not to exercise his newly-recognized right to end his life. McAfee openly admits that he sought permission to end his life because Georgia lacked any facilities which could offer him hope of an independent lifestyle. Larry McAfee, *Invisible Man*, U.S. News & World Rep., Feb. 19, 1990, at 59. In November 1990, McAfee was forced to move back to an Atlanta hospital due to a nursing staff shortage caused by the Persian Gulf crisis. McAfee says that he once again thought about exercising his right to die. McAfee has since been moved to a special nursing home designed to promote independent living. He works as a computer consultant and acts as an advocate for the rights of the disabled. *Life's "Terrific" for McAfee at Special Nursing Home*, Atlanta J. & Const., Dec. 29, 1991, at C2.

3. In view of the fact that the options facing the disabled are often unattractive due to government inaction or inattention, is the granting of a right to die to disabled persons who are not terminally ill really a subtle form of discrimination? Should the availability of options for independent living more properly be thought of as a civil rights issue, as opposed to a medical one? *See Disabled People Say Home Care Is Needed to Use New Rights*, N.Y. Times, Oct. 14, 1990, at A22. The Supreme Court in *Olmstead v. L.C. ex rel. Zimring*, 527 U.S. 581, 119 S.Ct. 2176, 144 L.Ed.2d 540 (1999) found that unjustified institutional isolation of people with disabilities is a violation of the Americans with Disabilities Act of 1990 (ADA). This decision's interpretation of the ADA has a direct impact on Medicaid, the national program providing health and long-term services to people with disabilities.

4. A frequently cited reason for governmental refusals to provide individualized treatment for the physically disabled in order to maximize their independence is that such programs would not be cost-effective. McAfee has repeatedly charged that Georgia does not provide for individualized treatment simply because it wishes to keep the disabled "corralled" in order to keep costs of care to a minimum. Given the scarcity of public resources, and the money to pay for them, is Georgia's treatment of disabled persons justified?

5. A frequently ignored fact is that the disabled may be revenue producers themselves if adequately provided for. What impact, if any, should this fact have on any cost-benefit analysis? A January 2003 Kaiser Family Foundation poll found the following:

> Many non-elderly adults with disabilities report going without needed health care in the past year. Nearly half (46%) say they have gone without getting medical equipment they needed because of the cost; nearly four in ten say they have postponed seeking care (37%), skipped doses or didn't fill a prescription

(36%); and nearly three in ten (28%) say they went without personal assistance services in the past year because of the cost. More than a third (36%) say that in the last year, they or someone in their household has spent less on food, heat, or other basic needs in order to pay for health care.

More than half of non-elderly people with disabilities say they are very or somewhat worried that they will lose the benefits that help them get by (55%) and that they might have difficulty paying for basic needs (54%). Somewhat fewer say they are very or somewhat worried that they will become a burden on their families (44%) and that they will have to go into a nursing home or other facility (23%). Among non-elderly people with disabilities who are unemployed, more than a third (36%) say they are very or somewhat worried that getting a job would mean losing their health insurance.

Kaiser Family Foundation, *Americans' Views of Disability*, (2004), at http://www.kff.org/healthpollreport/CurrentEdition/feature/index.cfm, last visited Aug. 5, 2004.

6. One of the reasons cited by Kenneth Bergstedt and Larry McAfee for their desires to die was that their prospective quality of life was insufficient to justify further living. Adoption of the "quality of life" approach to treatment decisionmaking appears to give a criterion for deciding when a person should be allowed to refuse LSMT, but adoption of the quality-based approach creates several problems. What type of standard should be used to measure the relevant quality of life? *See* Nancy Zweibel et al., *Measuring Quality of Life Near the End of Life*, 260 JAMA 839 (1988). Should an objective or subjective standard be used? Is a subjective standard effective, since the decision to die boils down to the patient's decision that life is too difficult to live, just as in a case of suicide? Moreover, who should make the decision by applying the standard to competent patients? Note that when faced with virtually identical quality of life, Kenneth Bergstedt decided to die while Larry McAfee decided to live. Is this variability desirable, or should predictability be more important? What are the implications for the treatment of incompetent patients? What of the possibility that any such assessment may be mistaken? Should a doctor be allowed to second-guess the expressed wishes of a competent patient in the hope that the patient will change his or her mind later? *See* James F. Childress & Courtney C. Campbell, *Who Is a Doctor to Decide Whether a Person Lives or Dies?, Reflections on Dax's Case, in* DAX'S CASE: ESSAYS IN MEDICAL ETHICS AND HUMAN MEANING 23 (Lonnie D. Kliever ed., 1989).

7. Those opposed to quality of life assessments hold the "sanctity of life" position and attribute much greater weight to the state's interest in preserving life. They believe that the state's interest is absolute and argue that because all life is sacred, it should always be preserved. A sanctity of life position is certainly easier to apply, but if a person repeatedly demands to be left alone to die, is it not disrespectful and contrary to the basic premise of that position to insist on involuntary treatment? Which value is more fundamental, patient autonomy or preservation of life? For a discussion of the historical tension between these two approaches, see Albin Eser, *"Sanctity" and "Quality" of Life in a Historical–Comparative View, in* SUICIDE AND EUTHANASIA: THE RIGHTS OF PERSONHOOD (Samuel E. Wallace & Albin Eser eds., 1981).

Eric Cassel, *The Nature of Suffering and the Goals of Medicine*

306 NEW ENG. J. MED. 639 (1982).

The obligation of physicians to relieve human suffering stretches back into antiquity. Despite this fact, little attention is explicitly given to the problem of suffering in medical education, research, or practice. I will begin by focusing on a modern paradox: Even in the best settings and with the best physicians, it is not uncommon for suffering to occur not only during the course of a disease but also as a result of its treatment. To understand this paradox and its resolution requires an understanding of what suffering is and how it relates to medical care.

Consider this case: A 35–year-old sculptor with metastatic disease of the breast was treated by competent physicians employing advanced knowledge and technology and acting out of kindness and true concern. At every stage, the treatment as well as the disease was a source of suffering to her. She was uncertain and frightened about her future, but she could get little information from her physicians, and what she was told was not always the truth. She had been unaware, for example, that the irradiated breast would be so disfigured. After an oophorectomy and a regimen of medications, she became hirsute, obese, and devoid of libido. With tumor in the supraclavicular fossa, she lost strength in the hand that she had used in sculpturing, and she became profoundly depressed. She had a pathologic fracture of the femur, and treatment was delayed while her physicians openly disagreed about pinning her hip.

Each time her disease responded to therapy and her hope was rekindled, a new manifestation would appear. Thus, when a new course of chemotherapy was started, she was torn between a desire to live and the fear that allowing hope to emerge again would merely expose her to misery if the treatment failed. The nausea and vomiting from the chemotherapy were distressing, but no more so than the anticipation of hair loss. She feared the future. Each tomorrow was seen as heralding increased sickness, pain, or disability, never as the beginning of better times. She felt isolated because she was no longer like other people and could not do what other people did. She feared that her friends would stop visiting her. She was sure that she would die.

. . .

What can this case tell us about the ends of medicine and the relief of suffering? Three facts stand out: The first is that this woman's suffering was not confined to her physical symptoms. The second is that she suffered not only from her disease but also from its treatment. The third is that one could not anticipate what she would describe as a source of suffering; like other patients, she had to be asked. Some features of her condition she would call painful, upsetting, uncomfortable, and distressing, but not a source of suffering. In these characteristics her case was ordinary.

In discussing the matter of suffering with laypersons, I learned that they were shocked to discover that the problem of suffering was not directly addressed in medical education. My colleagues of a contemplative nature were surprised at how little they knew of the problem and how little thought they had given it, whereas medical students tended to be unsure of the relevance of the issue to their work.

The relief of suffering, it would appear, is considered one of the primary ends of medicine by patients and laypersons, but not by the medical profession. As in the care of the dying, patients and their friends and families do not make a distinction between physical and nonphysical sources of suffering in the same way that doctors do.

A search of the medical and social-science literature did not help me in understanding what suffering is; the word "suffering" was most often coupled with the word "pain," as in "pain and suffering."

This phenomenon reflects a historically constrained and currently inadequate view of the ends of medicine. Medicine's traditional concern primarily for the body and for physical disease is well known, as are the widespread effects of the mind-body dichotomy on medical theory and practice. I believe that this dichotomy itself is a source of the paradoxical situation in which doctors cause suffering in their care of the sick. Today, as ideas about the separation of mind and body are called into question, physicians are concerning themselves with new aspects of the human condition. The profession of medicine is being pushed and pulled into new areas, both by its technology and by the demands of its patients. Attempting to understand what suffering is and how physicians might truly be devoted to its relief will require that medicine and its critics overcome the dichotomy between mind and body and the associated dichotomies between subjective and objective and between person and object.

... [I] am going to make three points. The first is that suffering is experienced by persons. In the separation between mind and body, the concept of the person, or personhood, has been associated with that of mind, spirit, and the subjective. However, as I will show, a person is not merely mind, merely spiritual, or only subjectively knowable. Personhood has many facets, and it is ignorance of them that actively contributes to patients' suffering. The understanding of the place of the person in human illness requires a rejection of the historical dualism of mind and body.

The second point derives from my interpretation of clinical observations: Suffering occurs when an impending destruction of the person is perceived; it continues until the threat of disintegration has passed or until the integrity of the person can be restored in some other manner. It follows then, that although suffering often occurs in the presence of acute pain, shortness of breath, or other bodily symptoms, suffering extends beyond the physical. Most generally, suffering can be defined as the state of severe distress associated with events that threaten the intactness of the person.

The third point is that suffering can occur in relation to any aspect of the person, whether it is in the realm of social roles, group identification, the relation with self, body, or family, or the relation with a transpersonal, transcendent source of meaning. . . .

. . .

NOTES AND QUESTIONS

1. No general agreement has been reached as to the appropriate legal standards for ascertaining competence to provide (or refuse) informed consent to life-sustaining medical treatment. "Several tests have been proposed: the patient's ability (1) to make and express a decision; (2) to actually understand the information disclosed about the treatment and alternatives to treatment; (3) to engage in decision making in a rational manner—to rationally manipulate the available information and appreciate the implications of alternative choices; and (4) to make a decision about treatment that is reasonable in itself." Bruce J. Winick, *Competency to Consent to Treatment: The Distinction Between Assent and Objection*, 28 Hous. L. Rev. 15, 24 (1991). Which test seems to most accurately measure competence?

Often "interested parties" will question a patient's competence because they disagree with the patient's choices regarding treatment. Doctors frequently exhibit this type of behavior. The doctor has a professional code of ethics and a daily practice which emphasize treatment. Very often when a patient refuses treatment that a doctor wishes to administer, the doctor will take this refusal as evidence of incompetence. *See* William J. Winslade, *Taken to the Limits: Pain, Identity, and Self–Transformation, in* Dax's Case: Essays in Medical Ethics and Human Meaning 115 (Lonnie D. Kliever ed., 1989). Should the test for competence be the same for both the granting and refusing of consent? *See* Winick, *supra* (arguing that granting of consent should be subject to less stringent review than refusal of consent).

The current approach to evaluating competence is to presume that a patient is competent unless and until the party challenging the patient's competence proves otherwise. Given the fact that patients are by definition incapacitated in some manner and may be under medication which affects their cognitive abilities, is this presumption justified? For a general discussion of assessing incapacity, see President's Commission, Making Health Care Decisions 57–60, 169–188 (1982); Loren Both, et al., *Tests of Competency to Consent to Treatment*, 134 Am. J. Psychiatry 279 (1977).

2. Who should make treatment decisions for adolescent patients? Traditionally, adolescents were treated in a manner similar to infants and a "best interests" standard was used to make treatment decisions concerning adolescent patients. James M. Morrissey et al., Consent and Confidentiality in Health Care of Children and Adolescents: A Legal Guide 2–6 (1986). This position was based largely upon three assumptions: as a class, minors lacked the cognitive capacity to make the necessary decisions; parents have a natural right to make decisions about treatment for their children; and the parental duty to support their children gives the parent an independent interest in treatment decisions. *Id.* at ix-x. However, deference to parental decisions concerning the best interests of the adolescent patient may not always be appropriate.

The modern trend has been to allow adolescents a limited amount of autonomy to make certain types of medical decisions. Adolescents are frequently allowed to make decisions concerning treatment of substance abuse, sexually transmitted diseases, pregnancy, and abortion. *Id.* at 61–82. The Illinois Supreme Court held that a "mature minor" had the right to refuse life-saving medical treatment in *In re E.G., a Minor*, 133 Ill.2d 98, 139 Ill.Dec. 810, 549 N.E.2d 322 (1989). E.G. was a 17–year-old girl who was diagnosed with non-lymphatic leukemia. Both the girl and her mother objected to life-saving blood transfusions on religious grounds. The court held that if a court determines a minor to be mature, she has the right to refuse medical treatment.

2.   PHYSICIAN–ASSISTED SUICIDE

Washington v. Glucksberg

Supreme Court of the United States, 1997.
521 U.S. 702, 117 S.Ct. 2258, 138 L.Ed.2d 772.

■ Chief Justice Rehnquist delivered the opinion of the court.

. . . .

Petitioners in this case are the State of Washington and its Attorney General. Respondents Harold Glucksberg, M.D., Abigail Halperin, M.D.,

Thomas A. Preston, M.D., and Peter Shalit, M.D., are physicians who practice in Washington. These doctors occasionally treat terminally ill, suffering patients, and declare that they would assist these patients in ending their lives if not for Washington's assisted-suicide ban. In January 1994, respondents, along with three gravely ill, pseudonymous plaintiffs who have since died and Compassion in Dying, a nonprofit organization that counsels people considering physician-assisted suicide, sued in the United States District Court, seeking a declaration that Wash. Rev. Code § 9A.36.060(1) (1994) is, on its face, unconstitutional. *Compassion in Dying v. Washington,* 850 F. Supp. 1454, 1459 (W.D. Wash. 1994).

The plaintiffs asserted "the existence of a liberty interest protected by the Fourteenth Amendment which extends to a personal choice by a mentally competent, terminally ill adult to commit physician-assisted suicide." *Id.* at 1459. Relying primarily on *Planned Parenthood v. Casey,* 505 U.S. 833 (1992), and *Cruzan v. Dir., Missouri Dep't of Health,* 497 U.S. 261 (1990), the District Court agreed, and concluded that Washington's assisted-suicide ban is unconstitutional because it "places an undue burden on the exercise of [that] constitutionally protected liberty interest." . . .

A panel of the Court of Appeals for the Ninth Circuit reversed, emphasizing that "in the two hundred and five years of our existence no constitutional right to aid in killing oneself has ever been asserted and upheld by a court of final jurisdiction." *Compassion in Dying v. Washington,* 49 F.3d 586, 591 (1995). The Ninth Circuit reheard the case en banc, reversed the panel's decision, and affirmed the *District Court. Compassion in Dying v. Washington,* 79 F.3d 790, 798 (1996). Like the District Court, the en banc Court of Appeals emphasized our *Casey* and *Cruzan* decisions . . . and concluded that "the Constitution encompasses a due process liberty interest in controlling the time and manner of one's death—that there is, in short, a constitutionally-recognized 'right to die.' " After "[w]eighing and then balancing" this interest against Washington's various interests, the court held that the State's assisted-suicide ban was unconstitutional "as applied to terminally ill competent adults who wish to hasten their deaths with medication prescribed by their physicians." We . . . now reverse.

I.

We begin, as we do in all due-process cases, by examining our Nation's history, legal traditions, and practices. . . . In almost every State—indeed, in almost every western democracy—it is a crime to assist a suicide. The States' assisted-suicide bans are not innovations. Rather, they are long-standing expressions of the States' commitment to the protection and preservation of all human life. . . . Indeed, opposition to and condemnation of suicide—and, therefore, of assisting suicide—are consistent and enduring themes of our philosophical, legal, and cultural heritages. *See generally,* Marzen, O'Dowd, Crone & Balch, *Suicide: A Constitutional Right?,* 24 DUQ. L. REV. 1, 17–56 (1985) (hereinafter Marzen); NEW YORK STATE TASK FORCE ON LIFE AND THE LAW, WHEN DEATH IS SOUGHT: ASSISTED SUICIDE AND EUTHANASIA in the Medical Context 77–82 (May 1994) (hereinafter New York Task Force).

More specifically, for over 700 years, the Anglo–American common-law tradition has punished or otherwise disapproved of both suicide and assisting suicide. . . .

. . .

Though deeply rooted, the States' assisted-suicide bans have in recent years been reexamined and, generally, reaffirmed. Because of advances in medicine and technology, Americans today are increasingly likely to die in institutions, from chronic illnesses. Public concern and democratic action are therefore sharply focused on how best to protect dignity and independence at the end of life, with the result that there have been many significant changes in state laws and in the attitudes these laws reflect. Many States, for example, now permit "living wills," surrogate health-care decisionmaking, and the withdrawal or refusal of life-sustaining medical treatment. At the same time, however, voters and legislators continue for the most part to reaffirm their States' prohibitions on assisting suicide.

The Washington statute at issue in this case, Wash. Rev. Code § 9A.36.060 (1994), was enacted in 1975 as part of a revision of that State's criminal code. Four years later, Washington passed its Natural Death Act, which specifically stated that the "withholding or withdrawal of life-sustaining treatment . . . shall not, for any purpose, constitute a suicide" and that "[n]othing in this chapter shall be construed to condone, authorize, or approve mercy killing. . . ." Natural Death Act, 1979 Wash. Laws, ch. 112, §§ 8(1), p. 11 (codified at Wash. Rev. Code §§ 70.122.070(1), 70.122.100 (1994)). In 1991, Washington voters rejected a ballot initiative which, had it passed, would have permitted a form of physician-assisted suicide. Washington then added a provision to the Natural Death Act expressly excluding physician-assisted suicide. 1992 Wash. Laws, ch. 98, § 10; Wash. Rev. Code § 70.122.100 (1994).

California voters rejected an assisted-suicide initiative similar to Washington's in 1993. On the other hand, in 1994, voters in Oregon enacted, also through ballot initiative, that State's "Death With Dignity Act," which legalized physician-assisted suicide for competent, terminally ill adults. Since the Oregon vote, many proposals to legalize assisted-suicide have been and continue to be introduced in the States' legislatures, but none has been enacted. And just last year, Iowa and Rhode Island joined the overwhelming majority of States explicitly prohibiting assisted suicide. See Iowa Code Ann. §§ 707A.2, 707A.3 (Supp. 1997); R.I. Gen. Laws §§ 11–60–1, 11–60–3 (Supp. 1996). Also, on April 30, 1997, President Clinton signed the Federal Assisted Suicide Funding Restriction Act of 1997, which prohibits the use of federal funds in support of physician-assisted suicide. Pub. L. 105–12, 111 Stat. 23 (codified at 42 U.S.C. § 14401 et seq).

Thus, the States are currently engaged in serious, thoughtful examinations of physician-assisted suicide and other similar issues. For example, New York State's Task Force on Life and the Law—an ongoing, blue-ribbon commission composed of doctors, ethicists, lawyers, religious leaders, and interested laymen—was convened in 1984 and commissioned with "a broad mandate to recommend public policy on issues raised by medical advances." After studying physician-assisted suicide, ... the Task Force unanimously concluded that "[l]egalizing assisted suicide and euthanasia would pose profound risks to many individuals who are ill and vulnerable.... [T]he potential dangers of this dramatic change in public policy would outweigh any benefit that might be achieved." *Id.* at 120.

Attitudes toward suicide itself have changed, ... but our laws have consistently condemned, and continue to prohibit, assisting suicide. Despite changes in medical technology and notwithstanding an increased emphasis on the importance of end-of-life decisionmaking, we have not retreated from this prohibition. Against this backdrop of history, tradition, and practice, we now turn to respondents' constitutional claim.

II.

The Due Process Clause guarantees more than fair process, and the "liberty" it protects includes more than the absence of physical restraint.... The Clause also provides heightened protection against government interference with certain fundamental rights and liberty interests.... We have also assumed, and strongly suggested, that the Due Process Clause protects the traditional right to refuse unwanted lifesaving medical treatment. *Cruzan*, 497 U.S. at 278–79.

But we "ha[ve] always been reluctant to expand the concept of substantive due process because guideposts for responsible decisionmaking in this unchartered area are scarce and open-ended." *Collins*, 503 U.S. at 125. By extending constitutional protection to an asserted right or liberty interest, we, to a great extent, place the matter outside the arena of public debate and legislative action. We must therefore "exercise the utmost care whenever we are asked to break new ground in this field," ibid, lest the liberty protected by the Due Process Clause be subtly transformed into the policy preferences of the members of this Court, *Moore*, 431 U.S. at 502 (plurality opinion).

Our established method of substantive-due-process analysis has two primary features: First, we have regularly observed that the Due Process Clause specially protects those fundamental rights and liberties which are, objectively, "deeply rooted in this Nation's history and tradition," and "implicit in the concept of ordered liberty," such that "neither liberty nor justice would exist if they were sacrificed." Second, we have required in substantive-due-process cases a "careful description" of the asserted fundamental liberty interest....

. . .

Turning to the claim at issue here, the Court of Appeals stated that "properly analyzed, the first issue to be resolved is whether there is a liberty interest in determining the time and manner of one's death," or, in other words, "is there a right to die?" As noted above, we have a tradition of carefully formulating the interest at stake in substantive-due-process cases. For example, although *Cruzan* is often described as a "right to die" case, see 79 F.3d at 799; 521 U.S. at 809 (Stevens, J., concurring in judgment), we were, in fact, more precise: we assumed that the Constitution granted competent persons a "constitutionally protected right to refuse lifesaving hydration and nutrition." *Cruzan*, 497 U.S. at 279; *Id.* at 287 (O'Connor, J., concurring) ("[A] liberty interest in refusing unwanted medical treatment may be inferred from our prior decisions"). The Washington statute at issue in this case prohibits "aid[ing] another person to attempt suicide," Wash. Rev. Code § 9A.36.060(1) (1994), and, thus, the question before us is whether the "liberty" specially protected by the Due Process Clause includes a right to commit suicide which itself includes a right to assistance in doing so.

We now inquire whether this asserted right has any place in our Nation's traditions. Here, ... we are confronted with a consistent and almost universal tradition that has long rejected the asserted right, and continues explicitly to reject it today, even for terminally ill, mentally competent adults. To hold for respondents, we would have to reverse centuries of legal doctrine and practice, and strike down the considered policy choice of almost every State....

Respondents contend, however, that the liberty interest they assert is consistent with this Court's substantive-due-process line of cases, if not with this Nation's history and practice. Pointing to *Casey* and *Cruzan*, respondents read our jurisprudence in this area as reflecting a general tradition of "self-sovereignty," and as teaching that the "liberty" protected by the Due Process Clause includes "basic and intimate exercises of personal autonomy," see *Casey*, 505 U.S. at 847 ("It is a promise of the Constitution that there is a realm of personal liberty which the government may not enter"). According to respondents, our liberty jurisprudence, and the broad, individualistic principles it reflects, protects the "liberty of competent, terminally ill adults to make end-of-life decisions free of undue government interference." The question presented in this case, however, is whether the protections of the Due Process Clause include a right to commit suicide with another's assistance. With this "careful description" of respondents' claim in mind, we turn to *Casey* and *Cruzan*.

[Eds.—The Chief Justice discusses the *Cruzan* case.]

. . .

The right assumed in *Cruzan*, however, was not simply deduced from abstract concepts of personal autonomy. Given the common-law rule that forced medication was a battery, and the long legal tradition protecting the decision to refuse unwanted medical treatment, our assumption was entirely consistent with this Nation's history and constitutional traditions. The decision to commit suicide with the assistance of another may be just as personal and profound as the decision to refuse unwanted medical treatment, but it has never enjoyed similar legal protection. Indeed, the two acts are widely and reasonably regarded as quite distinct.

Respondents also rely on *Casey*.... [T]he opinion discussed in some detail this Court's substantive due process tradition of interpreting the Due Process Clause to protect certain fundamental rights and "personal decisions relating to marriage, procreation, contraception, family relationships, child rearing, and education," and noted that many of those rights and liberties "involve the most intimate and personal choices a person may make in a lifetime." *Id.* at 851.

. . .

... That many of the rights and liberties protected by the Due Process Clause sound in personal autonomy does not warrant the sweeping conclusion that any and all important, intimate, and personal decisions are so protected, ... and *Casey* did not suggest otherwise.

The history of the law's treatment of assisted suicide in this country has been and continues to be one of the rejection of nearly all efforts to permit it. That being the case, our decisions lead us to conclude that the asserted "right" to assistance in committing suicide is not a fundamental liberty interest protected by the Due Process Clause. The Constitution also requires, however, that Washington's assisted-suicide ban be rationally related to legitimate government interests.... Washington's assisted-suicide ban implicates a number of state interests....

First, Washington has an "unqualified interest in the preservation of human life." ... The State's prohibition on assisted suicide, like all homicide laws, both reflects and advances its commitment to this interest.... This interest is symbolic and aspirational as well as practical:

> []While suicide is no longer prohibited or penalized, the ban against assisted suicide and euthanasia shores up the notion of limits in human relationships. It reflects the gravity with which we view the decision to take one's own life or the life of another, and our reluctance to encourage or promote these decisions.[]

New York Task Force 131–32.

. . .

Relatedly, all admit that suicide is a serious public-health problem, especially among persons in otherwise vulnerable groups.... The State has an interest in preventing suicide, and in studying, identifying, and treating its causes....

Those who attempt suicide—terminally ill or not—often suffer from depression or other mental disorders. See New York Task Force 13–22, 126–28 (more than 95% of those who commit suicide had a major psychiatric illness at the time of death; among the terminally ill, uncontrolled pain is a "risk factor" because it contributes to depression); Physician–Assisted Suicide and Euthanasia in the Netherlands: A Report of Chairman Charles T. Canady to the Subcommittee on the Constitution of the House Committee on the Judiciary, 104th Cong., 2d Sess., 10–11 (Comm. Print 1996).... Research indicates, however, that many people who request physician-assisted suicide withdraw that request if their depression and pain are treated. H. Hendin, Seduced by Death: Doctors, Patients and the Dutch Cure 24–25 (1997) (suicidal, terminally ill patients "usually respond well to treatment for depressive illness and pain medication and are then grateful to be alive"); New York Task Force 177–178. The New York Task Force, however, expressed its concern that, because depression is difficult to diagnose, physicians and medical professionals often fail to respond adequately to seriously ill patients' needs. *Id.* at 175. Thus, legal physician-assisted suicide could make it more difficult for the State to protect depressed or mentally ill persons, or those who are suffering from untreated pain, from suicidal impulses.

The State also has an interest in protecting the integrity and ethics of the medical profession.... [T]he American Medical Association, like many other medical and physicians' groups, has concluded that "[p]hysician-assisted suicide is fundamentally incompatible with the physician's role as healer." American Medical Association, Code of Ethics § 2.211 (1994).... And physician-assisted suicide could, it is argued, undermine the trust that is essential to the doctor-patient relationship by blurring the time-honored line between healing and harming....

Next, the State has an interest in protecting vulnerable groups—including the poor, the elderly, and disabled persons—from abuse, neglect, and mistakes.... We have recognized, however, the real risk of subtle coercion and undue influence in end-of-life situations. *Cruzan*, 497 U.S. at 281. Similarly, the New York Task Force warned that "[l]egalizing physician-assisted suicide would pose profound risks to many individuals who are ill and vulnerable.... The risk of harm is greatest for the many individuals in our society whose autonomy and well-being are already compromised by poverty, lack of access to good medical care, advanced age, or membership in a stigmatized social group." New York Task Force 120.... If physician-assisted suicide were permitted, many might resort to it to spare their families the substantial financial burden of end-of-life health-care costs.

The State's interest here goes beyond protecting the vulnerable from coercion; it extends to protecting disabled and terminally ill people from prejudice, negative and inaccurate stereotypes, and "societal indifference." 49 F.3d at 592. The State's assisted-suicide ban reflects and reinforces its policy that the lives of terminally ill, disabled, and elderly people must be no less valued than the lives of the young and healthy, and that a seriously disabled person's suicidal impulses should be interpreted and treated the same way as anyone else's. See New York Task Force 101–102; Physician–Assisted Suicide and Euthanasia in the Netherlands: A Report of Chairman Charles T. Canady, at 9, 20 (discussing prejudice toward the disabled and the negative messages euthanasia and assisted suicide send to handicapped patients).

Finally, the State may fear that permitting assisted suicide will start it down the path to voluntary and perhaps even involuntary euthanasia.... Washington's ban on assisting suicide prevents such erosion.

This concern is further supported by evidence about the practice of euthanasia in the Netherlands....

We need not weigh exactly the relative strengths of these various interests. They are unquestionably important and legitimate, and Washington's ban on assisted suicide is at least reasonably related to their promotion and protection. We therefore hold that Wash. Rev. Code § 9A.36.060(1) (1994) does not violate the Fourteenth Amendment, either on its face or "as applied to competent, terminally ill adults who wish to hasten their deaths by obtaining medication prescribed by their doctors." 79 F.3d at 838.[24]

Throughout the Nation, Americans are engaged in an earnest and profound debate about the morality, legality, and practicality of physician-assisted suicide. Our holding permits this debate to continue, as it should in a democratic society. The decision of the en banc Court of Appeals is reversed, and the case is remanded for further proceedings consistent with this opinion.

It is so ordered.

■ JUSTICE SOUTER, concurring.

Three terminally ill individuals and four physicians who sometimes treat terminally ill patients brought this challenge to the Washington statute making it a crime "knowingly . . . [to] ai[d] another person to attempt suicide," Wash. Rev. Code § 9A.36.060 (1994), claiming on behalf of both patients and physicians that it would violate substantive due process to enforce the statute against a doctor who acceded to a dying patient's request for a drug to be taken by the patient to commit suicide. The question is whether the statute sets up one of those "arbitrary impositions" or "purposeless restraints" at odds with the Due Process Clause of the Fourteenth Amendment. *Poe v. Ullman*, 367 U.S. 497, 543 (1961) (Harlan, J., dissenting). I conclude that the statute's application to the doctors has not been shown to be unconstitutional, but I write separately to give my reasons for analyzing the substantive due process claims as I do, and for rejecting this one.

. . .

II.

When the physicians claim that the Washington law deprives them of a right falling within the scope of liberty that the Fourteenth Amendment guarantees against denial without due process of law, they are not claiming some sort of procedural defect in the process through which the statute has been enacted or is administered. Their claim, rather, is that the State has no substantively adequate justification for barring the assistance sought by the patient and sought to be offered by the physician. . . . The persistence of substantive due process in our cases points to the legitimacy of the modern justification for such judicial review found in Justice Harlan's dissent in Poe. . . .

. . .

24. . . . We emphasize that today we reject the Court of Appeals' specific holding that the statute is unconstitutional "as applied" to a particular class. . . . Justice Stevens agrees with the possibility that an individual plaintiff seeking to hasten her death, or a doctor whose assistance was sought, "could prevail in a more particularized challenge," *ibid.* Our opinion does not absolutely foreclose such a claim. However, given our holding that the Due Process Clause of the Fourteenth Amendment does not provide heightened protection to the asserted liberty interest in ending one's life with a physician's assistance, such a claim would have to be quite different from the ones advanced by respondents here.

2.

The argument supporting respondents' position . . . progresses through three steps of increasing forcefulness. First, it emphasizes the decriminalization of suicide. Reliance on this fact is sanctioned under the standard that looks not only to the tradition retained, but to society's occasional choices to reject traditions of the legal past. See *Poe v. Ullman*, 367 U.S. at 542 (Harlan, J., dissenting). While the common law prohibited both suicide and aiding a suicide, with the prohibition on aiding largely justified by the primary prohibition on self-inflicted death itself, see, e.g., American Law Institute, Model Penal Code § 210.5, Comment 1, pp. 92–93 & n.7 (1980), the State's rejection of the traditional treatment of the one leaves the criminality of the other open to questioning that previously would not have been appropriate. The second step in the argument is to emphasize that the State's own act of decriminalization gives a freedom of choice much like the individual's option in recognized instances of bodily autonomy. One of these, abortion, is a legal right to choose in spite of the interest a State may legitimately invoke in discouraging the practice, just as suicide is now subject to choice, despite a state interest in discouraging it. The third step is to emphasize that respondents claim a right to assistance not on the basis of some broad principle that would be subject to exceptions if that continuing interest of the State's in discouraging suicide were to be recognized at all. Respondents base their claim on the traditional right to medical care and counsel, subject to the limiting conditions of informed, responsible choice when death is imminent, conditions that support a strong analogy to rights of care in other situations in which medical counsel and assistance have been available as a matter of course. There can be no stronger claim to a physician's assistance than at the time when death is imminent, a moral judgment implied by the State's own recognition of the legitimacy of medical procedures necessarily hastening the moment of impending death.

In my judgment, the importance of the individual interest here, as within that class of "certain interests" demanding careful scrutiny of the State's contrary claim, see *Poe, supra*, at 543, cannot be gainsaid. Whether that interest might in some circumstances, or at some time, be seen as "fundamental" to the degree entitled to prevail is not, however, a conclusion that I need draw here, for I am satisfied that the State's interests described in the following section are sufficiently serious to defeat the present claim that its law is arbitrary or purposeless.

B.

. . .

I take it that the basic concept of judicial review with its possible displacement of legislative judgment bars any finding that a legislature has acted arbitrarily when the following conditions are met: there is a serious factual controversy over the feasibility of recognizing the claimed right without at the same time making it impossible for the State to engage in an undoubtedly legitimate exercise of power; facts necessary to resolve the controversy are not readily ascertainable through the judicial process; but they are more readily subject to discovery through legislative factfinding and experimentation. It is assumed in this case, and must be, that a State's interest in protecting those unable to make responsible decisions and those who make no decisions at all entitles the State to bar aid to any but a knowing and responsible person intending suicide, and to prohibit euthanasia. How, and how far, a State should act in that interest are judgments for the State, but the legitimacy of its action to deny a physician the option to aid any but the knowing and responsible is beyond question.

The capacity of the State to protect the others if respondents were to prevail is, however, subject to some genuine question, underscored by the responsible disagreement over the basic facts of the Dutch experience. This factual controversy is not open to a judicial resolution with any substantial degree of assurance at this time. It is not, of course, that any controversy about the factual predicate of a due process claim disqualifies a court from resolving it. Courts can recognize captiousness, and most factual issues can be settled in a trial court. At this point, however, the factual issue at the heart of this case does not appear to be one of those. The principal enquiry at the moment is into the Dutch experience, and I question whether an independent front-line investigation into the facts of a foreign country's legal administration can be soundly undertaken through American courtroom litigation. While an extensive literature on any subject can raise the hopes for judicial understanding, the literature on this subject is only nascent. Since there is little experience directly bearing on the issue, the most that can be said is that whichever way the Court might rule today, events could overtake its assumptions, as experimentation in some jurisdictions confirmed or discredited the concerns about progression from assisted suicide to euthanasia.

Legislatures, on the other hand, have superior opportunities to obtain the facts necessary for a judgment about the present controversy. Not only do they have more flexible mechanisms for factfinding than the Judiciary, but their mechanisms include the power to experiment, moving forward and pulling back as facts emerge within their own jurisdictions. There is, indeed, good reason to suppose that in the absence of a judgment for respondents here, just such experimentation will be attempted in some of the States. See, e.g., Or. Rev. Stat. Ann. §§ 127.800 et seq. (Supp. 1996); App. to Brief for State Legislators as Amici Curiae 1a (listing proposed statutes).

. . . The Court should accordingly stay its hand to allow reasonable legislative consideration. While I do not decide for all time that respondents' claim should not be recognized, I acknowledge the legislative institutional competence as the better one to deal with that claim at this time.

Vacco v. Quill

Supreme Court of the United States, 1997.
521 U.S. 793, 117 S.Ct. 2293, 138 L.Ed.2d 834.

■ CHIEF JUSTICE REHNQUIST delivered the opinion of the Court.

In New York, as in most States, it is a crime to aid another to commit or attempt suicide, but patients may refuse even lifesaving medical treatment. The question presented by this case is whether New York's prohibition on assisting suicide therefore violates the Equal Protection Clause of the Fourteenth Amendment. We hold that it does not.

. . .

The Equal Protection Clause commands that no State shall "deny to any person within its jurisdiction the equal protection of the laws." This provision creates no substantive rights.... Instead, it embodies a general rule that States must treat like cases alike but may treat unlike cases accordingly....

. . .

The Court of Appeals ... concluded that some terminally ill people—those who are on life-support systems—are treated differently from those who are not, in that the former may "hasten death" by ending treatment, but the latter may not "hasten death" through physician-assisted suicide. This conclusion depends on the submission that ending or refusing lifesaving medical treatment "is nothing more nor less than assisted suicide." Unlike the Court of Appeals, we think the distinction between assisting suicide and withdrawing life-sustaining treatment, a distinction widely recognized and endorsed in the medical profession and in our legal traditions, is both important and logical; it is certainly rational....

The distinction comports with fundamental legal principles of causation and intent. First, when a patient refuses life-sustaining medical treatment, he dies from an underlying fatal disease or pathology; but if a patient ingests lethal medication prescribed by a physician, he is killed by that medication....

Furthermore, a physician who withdraws, or honors a patient's refusal to begin, life-sustaining medical treatment purposefully intends, or may so intend, only to respect his patient's wishes and "to cease doing useless and futile or degrading things to the patient when [the patient] no longer stands to benefit from them." Assisted Suicide in the United States: Hearing Before the Subcomm. on the Constitution of the House Comm. on the Judiciary, 104th Cong., 368 (1996) (testimony of Dr. Leon R. Kass). The same is true when a doctor provides aggressive palliative care; in some cases, painkilling drugs may hasten a patient's death, but the physician's purpose and intent is, or may be, only to ease his patient's pain. A doctor who assists a suicide, however, "must, necessarily and indubitably, intend primarily that the patient be made dead." *Id.* at 367. Similarly, a patient who commits suicide with a doctor's aid necessarily has the specific intent to end his or her own life, while a patient who refuses or discontinues treatment might not....

The law has long used actors' intent or purpose to distinguish between two acts that may have the same result.... Put differently, the law distinguishes actions taken "because of" a given end from actions taken "in spite of" their unintended but foreseen consequences. *Feeney*, 442 U.S. at 279....

Given these general principles, it is not surprising that many courts, including New York courts, have carefully distinguished refusing life-sustaining treatment from suicide. . . .

. . .

Similarly, the overwhelming majority of state legislatures have drawn a clear line between assisting suicide and withdrawing or permitting the refusal of unwanted lifesaving medical treatment by prohibiting the former and permitting the latter. . . .

. . .

For all these reasons, we disagree with respondents' claim that the distinction between refusing lifesaving medical treatment and assisted suicide is "arbitrary" and "irrational."

New York's reasons for recognizing and acting on this distinction—including prohibiting intentional killing and preserving life; preventing suicide; maintaining physicians' role as their patients' healers; protecting vulnerable people from indifference, prejudice, and psychological and financial pressure to end their lives; and avoiding a possible slide toward euthanasia—are discussed in greater detail in our opinion in *Glucksberg*. These valid and important public interests easily satisfy the constitutional requirement that a legislative classification bear a rational relation to some legitimate end.

The judgment of the Court of Appeals is reversed.

It is so ordered.

Washington v. Glucksberg & Vacco v. Quill

Supreme Court of the United States, 1997.
521 U.S. 702.

■ JUSTICE O'CONNOR, concurring:

Death will be different for each of us. For many, the last days will be spent in physical pain and perhaps the despair that accompanies physical deterioration and a loss of control of basic bodily and mental functions. Some will seek medication to alleviate that pain and other symptoms.

The Court frames the issue in this case as whether the Due Process Clause of the Constitution protects a "right to commit suicide which itself includes a right to assistance in doing so," and concludes that our Nation's history, legal traditions, and practices do not support the existence of such a right. I join the Court's opinions because I agree that there is no generalized right to "commit suicide." But respondents urge us to address the narrower question whether a mentally competent person who is experiencing great suffering has a constitutionally cognizable interest in controlling the circumstances of his or her imminent death. I see no need to reach that question in the context of the facial challenges to the New York and Washington laws at issue here. . . . The parties and amici agree that in these States a patient who is suffering from a terminal illness and who is experiencing great pain has no legal barriers to obtaining medication, from qualified physicians, to alleviate that suffering, even to the point of causing unconsciousness and hastening death. In this light, even assuming that we would recognize such an interest, I agree that the State's interests in protecting those who are not truly competent or facing imminent death, or those whose decisions to hasten death would not truly be voluntary, are sufficiently weighty to justify a prohibition against physician-assisted suicide.

Every one of us at some point may be affected by our own or a family member's terminal illness. There is no reason to think the democratic process will not strike the proper balance between the interests of terminally ill, mentally competent individuals who would seek to end their suffering and the State's interests in protecting those who might seek to end life mistakenly or under pressure. As the Court recognizes, States are presently undertaking extensive and serious evaluation of physician-assisted suicide and other related issues. 521 U.S. at 716–18; *see* 521 U.S. at 785–88 (Souter, J., concurring in judgment). In such circumstances, "the . . . challenging task of crafting appropriate procedures for safeguarding . . . liberty interests is entrusted to the 'laboratory' of the States . . . in the first instance." *Cruzan v. Dir., Missouri Dep't of Health*, 497 U.S. 261, 292 (1990) (O'Connor, J., concurring) (citing *New State Ice Co. v. Liebmann*, 285 U.S. 262 (1932)).

. . .

■ JUSTICE STEVENS, concurring:

The Court ends its opinion with the important observation that our holding today is fully consistent with a continuation of the vigorous debate about the "morality, legality, and practicality of physician-assisted suicide" in a democratic society. I write separately to make it clear that there is also room for further debate about the limits that the Constitution places on the power of the States to punish the practice.

. . .

II.

In *Cruzan v. Director, Mo. Dept. of Health*, the Court assumed that the interest in liberty protected by the Fourteenth Amendment encompassed the right of a terminally ill patient to direct the withdrawal of life-sustaining treatment. As the Court correctly observes today, that assumption "was not simply deduced from abstract concepts of personal autonomy." Instead, it was supported by the common-law tradition protecting the individual's general right to refuse unwanted medical treatment. . . .

. . .

. . . I insist that the source of Nancy Cruzan's right to refuse treatment was not just a common-law rule. Rather, this right is an aspect of a far broader and more basic concept of freedom that is even older than the common law. This freedom embraces not merely a person's right to refuse a particular kind of unwanted treatment, but also her interest in dignity, and in determining the character of the memories that will survive long after her death. In recognizing that the State's interests did not outweigh

Nancy Cruzan's liberty interest in refusing medical treatment, *Cruzan* rested not simply on the common-law right to refuse medical treatment, but—at least implicitly—on the even more fundamental right to make this "deeply personal decision," 497 U.S. at 289 (O'Connor, J., concurring).

. . .

While I agree with the Court that *Cruzan* does not decide the issue presented by these cases, *Cruzan* did give recognition, not just to vague, unbridled notions of autonomy, but to the more specific interest in making decisions about how to confront an imminent death. Although there is no absolute right to physician-assisted suicide, *Cruzan* makes it clear that some individuals who no longer have the option of deciding whether to live or to die because they are already on the threshold of death have a constitutionally protected interest that may outweigh the State's interest in preserving life at all costs. The liberty interest at stake in a case like this differs from, and is stronger than, both the common-law right to refuse medical treatment and the unbridled interest in deciding whether to live or die. It is an interest in deciding how, rather than whether, a critical threshold shall be crossed.

III.

The state interests supporting a general rule banning the practice of physician-assisted suicide do not have the same force in all cases. First and foremost of these interests is the " 'unqualified interest in the preservation of human life,' " which is equated with " 'the sanctity of life.' " That interest not only justifies-it commands-maximum protection of every individual's interest in remaining alive, which in turn commands the same protection for decisions about whether to commence or to terminate life-support systems or to administer pain medication that may hasten death. Properly viewed, however, this interest is not a collective interest that should always outweigh the interests of a person who because of pain, incapacity, or sedation finds her life intolerable, but rather, an aspect of individual freedom.

. . .

There remains room for vigorous debate about the outcome of particular cases that are not necessarily resolved by the opinions announced today. How such cases may be decided will depend on their specific facts. In my judgment, however, it is clear that the so-called "unqualified interest in the preservation of human life," is not itself sufficient to outweigh the interest in liberty that may justify the only possible means of preserving a dying patient's dignity and alleviating her intolerable suffering.

■ JUSTICE GINSBURG, concurring:

I concur in the Court's judgments in these cases substantially for the reasons stated by Justice O'CONNOR in her concurring opinion.

■ JUSTICE BREYER, concurring:

I believe that Justice O'Connor's views, which I share, have greater legal significance than the Court's opinion suggests. I join her separate opinion, except insofar as it joins the majority. And I concur in the judgments. I shall briefly explain how I differ from the Court.

I agree with the Court in *Vacco v. Quill*, that the articulated state interests justify the distinction drawn between physician assisted suicide and withdrawal of life-support. I also agree with the Court that the critical question in both of the cases before us is whether "the 'liberty' specially protected by the Due Process Clause includes a right" of the sort that the respondents assert. I do not agree, however, with the Court's formulation of that claimed "liberty" interest. The Court describes it as a "right to commit suicide with another's assistance." 521 U.S. at 724. But I would not reject the respondents' claim without considering a different formulation, for which our legal tradition may provide greater support. That formulation would use words roughly like a "right to die with dignity." But irrespective of the exact words used, at its core would lie personal control over the manner of death, professional medical assistance, and the avoidance of unnecessary and severe physical suffering—combined.

. . .

I do not believe, however, that this Court need or now should decide whether a or a not such a right is "fundamental." That is because, in my view, the avoidance of severe physical pain (connected with death) would have to constitute an essential part of any successful claim and because, as Justice O'Connor points out, the laws before us do not force a dying person to undergo that kind of pain. Rather, the laws of New York and of Washington do not prohibit doctors from providing patients with drugs sufficient to control pain despite the risk that those drugs themselves will kill. . . .

Medical technology, we are repeatedly told, makes the administration of pain-relieving drugs sufficient, except for a very few individuals for whom the ineffectiveness of pain control medicines can mean not pain, but the need for sedation which can end in a coma. We are also told that there are many instances in which patients do not receive the palliative care that, in principle, is available, but that is so for institutional reasons or inadequacies or obstacles, which would seem possible to overcome, and which do not include a prohibitive set of laws. . . .

This legal circumstance means that the state laws before us do not infringe directly upon the (assumed) central interest (what I have called the core of the interest in dying with dignity). . . . Were the legal circumstances different—for example, were state law to prevent the provision of palliative care, including the administration of drugs as needed to avoid pain at the end of life—then the law's impact upon serious and otherwise unavoidable physical pain (accompanying death) would be more directly at issue. And as Justice O'Connor suggests, the Court might have to revisit its conclusions in these cases.

NOTES AND QUESTIONS

For additional commentary on the cases see PHYSICIAN-ASSISTED SUICIDE: EXPANDING THE DEBATE (Margaret P. Battin et al. eds., 1998); Robert A. Burt, *Disorder in the Court: Physician–Assisted Suicide and the Constitution*, 82 MINN. L. REV. 965 (1998); Yale Kamisar, *On the Meaning and Impact of the Physician–Assisted Suicide Cases*, 82 MINN. L. REV. 895 (1998); Kathryn L. Tucker, *The Death with Dignity Movement: Protecting the Rights and Expanding Options After Glucksberg and Quill*, 82 MINN. L. REV. 923 (1998).

For additional perspectives on physician-assisted suicide, see Andrew I. Batavia, *Disability and Physician–Assisted Suicide,* 336 NEW ENG. J. MED. 1671 (1997); Leslie Bender, *A Feminist Analysis of Physician–Assisted Dying and Active Voluntary Euthanasia*, 59 TENN. L. REV. 519 (1992); Patricia A. King & Leslie E. Wolf, *Empowering and Protecting Patients: Lessons for Physician–Assisted Suicide from the African–American Experience*, 82 MINN. L. REV. 1015 (1998); Jeremy A. Sitcoff, *Death With Dignity: AIDS and a Call for Legislation Securing the Right to Assisted Suicide*, 29 J. MARSHALL L. REV. 677 (1996); Susan Wolf, *Gender, Feminism and Death: Physician–Assisted Suicide and Euthanasia, in* FEMINISM AND BIOETHICS: BEYOND REPRODUCTION 282 (1996).

3. STATE INITIATIVES

The Oregon Death With Dignity Act

OREGON REVISED STATUTES, 2003 § 127.800–127.897.

Section 1: General Provisions

127.800   § 1.01.   Definitions.

The following words and phrases, whenever used in ORS 127.800 to 127.897, have the following meanings:

(1) "Adult" means an individual who is 18 years of age or older.

(2) "Attending physician" means the physician who has primary responsibility for the care of the patient and treatment of the patient's terminal disease.

(3) "Capable" means that in the opinion of a court or in the opinion of the patient's attending physician or consulting physician, psychiatrist or psychologist, a patient has the ability to make and communicate health care decisions to health care providers, including communication through persons familiar with the patient's manner of communicating if those persons are available.

(4) "Consulting physician" means a physician who is qualified by specialty or experience to make a professional diagnosis and prognosis regarding the patient's disease.

(5) "Counseling" means one or more consultations as necessary between a state licensed psychiatrist or psychologist and a patient for the purpose of determining that the patient is capable and not suffering from a psychiatric or psychological disorder or depression causing impaired judgment.

(6) "Health care provider" means a person licensed, certified or otherwise authorized or permitted by the law of this state to administer health care or dispense medication in the ordinary course of business or practice of a profession, and includes a health care facility.

(7) "Informed decision" means a decision by a qualified patient, to request and obtain a prescription to end his or her life in a humane and

dignified manner, that is based on an appreciation of the relevant facts and after being fully informed by the attending physician of:

(a) His or her medical diagnosis;

(b) His or her prognosis;

(c) The potential risks associated with taking the medication to be prescribed;

(d) The probable result of taking the medication to be prescribed; and

(e) The feasible alternatives, including, but not limited to, comfort care, hospice care and pain control.

(8) "Medically confirmed" means the medical opinion of the attending physician has been confirmed by a consulting physician who has examined the patient and the patient's relevant medical records.

(9) "Patient" means a person who is under the care of a physician.

(10) "Physician" means a doctor of medicine or osteopathy licensed to practice medicine by the Board of Medical Examiners for the State of Oregon.

(11) "Qualified patient" means a capable adult who is a resident of Oregon and has satisfied the requirements of ORS 127.800 to 127.897 in order to obtain a prescription for medication to end his or her life in a humane and dignified manner.

(12) "Terminal disease" means an incurable and irreversible disease that has been medically confirmed and will, within reasonable medical judgment, produce death within six months.

Section 2: Written Request for Medication to End One's Life in a Humane and Dignified Manner

127.805 § 2.01. Who May Initiate a Written Request for Medication.

(1) An adult who is capable, is a resident of Oregon, and has been determined by the attending physician and consulting physician to be suffering from a terminal disease, and who has voluntarily expressed his or her wish to die, may make a written request for medication for the purpose of ending his or her life in a humane and dignified manner in accordance with ORS 127.800 to 127.897.

(2) No person shall qualify under the provisions of ORS 127.800 to 127.897 solely because of age or disability.

127.810 § 2.02. Form of the Written Request.

(1) A valid request for medication under ORS 127.800 to 127.897 shall be in substantially the form described in ORS 127.897, signed and dated by the patient and witnessed by at least two individuals who, in the presence of the patient, attest that to the best of their knowledge and belief the patient is capable, acting voluntarily, and is not being coerced to sign the request.

(a) One of the witnesses shall be a person who is not:

(b) A relative of the patient by blood, marriage or adoption;

(c) A person who at the time the request is signed would be entitled to any portion of the estate of the qualified patient upon death under any will or by operation of law; or

(2) An owner, operator or employee of a health care facility where the qualified patient is receiving medical treatment or is a resident.

(3) The patient's attending physician at the time the request is signed shall not be a witness.

(4) If the patient is a patient in a long term care facility at the time the written request is made, one of the witnesses shall be an individual designated by the facility and having the qualifications specified by the Department of Human Services by rule.

Section 3: Safeguards

127.815 § 3.01. Attending Physician Responsibilities.

(1) The attending physician shall:

(a) Make the initial determination of whether a patient has a terminal disease, is capable, and has made the request voluntarily;

(b) Request that the patient demonstrate Oregon residency pursuant to ORS 127.860;

(c) To ensure that the patient is making an informed decision, inform the patient of:

(d) His or her medical diagnosis;

(e) His or her prognosis;

(f) The potential risks associated with taking the medication to be prescribed;

(g) The probable result of taking the medication to be prescribed; and

(h) The feasible alternatives, including, but not limited to, comfort care, hospice care and pain control;

(i) Refer the patient to a consulting physician for medical confirmation of the diagnosis, and for a determination that the patient is capable and acting voluntarily;

(j) Refer the patient for counseling if appropriate pursuant to ORS 127.825;

(k) Recommend that the patient notify next of kin;

(k) Counsel the patient about the importance of having another person present when the patient takes the medication prescribed pursuant to ORS 127.800 to 127.897 and of not taking the medication in a public place;

(m) Inform the patient that he or she has an opportunity to rescind the request at any time and in any manner, and offer the patient an opportunity to rescind at the end of the 15 day waiting period pursuant to ORS 127.840;

(n) Verify, immediately prior to writing the prescription for medication under ORS 127.800 to 127.897, that the patient is making an informed decision;

(o) Fulfill the medical record documentation requirements of ORS 127.855;

(p) Ensure that all appropriate steps are carried out in accordance with ORS 127.800 to 127.897 prior to writing a prescription for medication to enable a qualified patient to end his or her life in a humane and dignified manner; and

(q) Dispense medications directly, including ancillary medications intended to facilitate the desired effect to minimize the patient's discomfort, provided the attending physician is registered as a dispensing physician with the Board of Medical Examiners, has a current Drug Enforcement Administration certificate and complies with any applicable administrative rule; or

(r) With the patient's written consent:

(A) Contact a pharmacist and inform the pharmacist of the prescription; and

(B) Deliver the written prescription personally or by mail to the pharmacist, who will dispense the medications to either the patient, the attending physician or an expressly identified agent of the patient.

(2) Notwithstanding any other provision of law, the attending physician may sign the patient's death certificate.

127.820 § 3.02. Consulting Physician Confirmation.

Before a patient is qualified under ORS 127.800 to 127.897, a consulting physician shall examine the patient and his or her relevant medical records and confirm, in writing, the attending physician's diagnosis that the patient is suffering from a terminal disease, and verify that the patient is capable, is acting voluntarily and has made an informed decision.

127.825 § 3.03. Counseling Referral.

If in the opinion of the attending physician or the consulting physician a patient may be suffering from a psychiatric or psychological disorder or depression causing impaired judgment, either physician shall refer the patient for counseling. No medication to end a patient's life in a humane and dignified manner shall be prescribed until the person performing the counseling determines that the patient is not suffering from a psychiatric or psychological disorder or depression causing impaired judgment.

127.830 § 3.04. Informed Decision.

No person shall receive a prescription for medication to end his or her life in a humane and dignified manner unless he or she has made an informed decision as defined in ORS 127.800(7). Immediately prior to writing a prescription for medication under ORS 127.800 to 127.897, the attending physician shall verify that the patient is making an informed decision.

127.835 § 3.05. Family Notification.

The attending physician shall recommend that the patient notify the next of kin of his or her request for medication pursuant to ORS 127.800 to 127.897. A patient who declines or is unable to notify next of kin shall not have his or her request denied for that reason.

127.840 § 3.06. Written and Oral Requests.

In order to receive a prescription for medication to end his or her life in a humane and dignified manner, a qualified patient shall have made an oral request and a written request, and reiterate the oral request to his or her attending physician no less than fifteen (15) days after making the initial oral request. At the time the qualified patient makes his or her second oral request, the attending physician shall offer the patient an opportunity to rescind the request.

127.845   § 3.07.   Right to Rescind Request.

A patient may rescind his or her request at any time and in any manner without regard to his or her mental state. No prescription for medication under ORS 127.800 to 127.897 may be written without the attending physician offering the qualified patient an opportunity to rescind the request.

127.850   § 3.08.   Waiting Periods.

No less than fifteen (15) days shall elapse between the patient's initial oral request and the writing of a prescription under ORS 127.800 to 127.897. No less than 48 hours shall elapse between the patient's written request and the writing of a prescription under ORS 127.800 to 127.897.

. . .

127.880   § 3.14.   Construction of the Act.

Nothing in ORS 127.800 to 127.897 shall be construed to authorize a physician or any other person to end a patient's life by lethal injection, mercy killing or active euthanasia. Actions taken in accordance with ORS 127.800 to 127.897 shall not, for any purpose, constitute suicide, assisted suicide, mercy killing or homicide, under the law.

. . .

Section 6: Form of the Request.

127.897   § 6.01. Form of the Request

A request for a medication as authorized by ORS 127.800 to 127.897 shall be in substantially the following form:

REQUEST FOR MEDICATION

TO END MY LIFE IN A HUMANE AND DIGNIFIED MANNER

I, _____, am an adult of sound mind.

I am suffering from _____, which my attending physician has determined is a terminal disease and which has been medically confirmed by a consulting physician.

I have been fully informed of my diagnosis, prognosis, the nature of medication to be prescribed and potential associated risks, the expected result, and the feasible alternatives, including comfort care, hospice care and pain control.

I request that my attending physician prescribe medication that will end my life in a humane and dignified manner.

INITIAL ONE:

_____ I have informed my family of my decision and taken their opinions into consideration.

_____ I have decided not to inform my family of my decision.

_____ I have no family to inform of my decision.

I understand that I have the right to rescind this request at any time.

I understand the full import of this request and I expect to die when I take the medication to be prescribed. I further understand that although most deaths occur within three hours, my death may take longer and my physician has counseled me about this possibility.

I make this request voluntarily and without reservation, and I accept full moral responsibility for my actions.

[The request must be signed, dated, and witnessed]

Sixth Annual Report on Oregon's Death With Dignity Act March 10, 2004

(2004), _at_ http://www.ohd.hr.state.or.us/chs/pas/ar-smmry.cfm, last visited Aug. 11, 2004.

Summary

Physician-assisted suicide (PAS) has been legal in Oregon since November 1997, when Oregon voters approved the Death with Dignity Act (DWDA).... The Department of Human Services (DHS) is legally required to collect information regarding compliance with the Act and make the information available on a yearly basis. In this sixth annual report, we characterize the 42 Oregonians who, in 2003, ingested medications prescribed under provisions of the Act, and look at whether the numbers and characteristics of these patients differ from those who used PAS in prior years. Patients choosing PAS were identified through mandated physician and pharmacy reporting. Our information comes from these reports, physician interviews and death certificates. We also compare the demographic characteristics of patients participating during 1998–2003 with other Oregonians who died of the same underlying causes.

In 2003, 42 physicians wrote a total of 67 prescriptions for lethal doses of medication. The number of prescriptions written increased in each of the previous years: 58 prescriptions were written in 2002, 44 in 2001, 39 in 2000, 33 in 1999, and 24 in 1998. Thirty-nine of the 2003 prescription recipients died after ingesting the medication. Of the 28 persons who did not ingest the prescribed medication, 18 died from their illnesses, and 10 were alive on December 31, 2003. In addition, two patients who received prescriptions during 2002 and another who received a prescription in 2001 died in 2003 after ingesting their medication for a total of 42 PAS deaths during 2003.

There were four more patients who used PAS in 2003 than in 2002, and the number of patients ingesting lethal medication has increased over the six years since legalization. In 2003, 42 patients died from PAS, compared to 38 in 2002, 21 in 2001, 27 in 2000, 27 in 1999, and 16 in 1998. The 42 patients who ingested lethal medications in 2003 represent an estimated 14/10,000 total deaths, compared with 12.2 in 2002, 7.0 in 2001, 9.1 in 2000, 9.2 in 1999, and 5.5 in 1998. Compared to all Oregon decedents in 2003, PAS participants were more likely to have malignant neoplasms (83%), to be younger (median age 73 years), and to have more formal education (48% had at least a baccalaureate degree).

During the past six years, the 171 patients who took lethal medications differed in several ways from the 53,544 Oregonians dying from the same underlying diseases. Rates of participation in PAS decreased with age, but were higher among those who were divorced or never married, those with more years of education, and those with amyotrophic lateral sclerosis, HIV/AIDS, or malignant neoplasms.

Physicians indicated that patient requests for lethal medications stemmed from multiple concerns related to autonomy and control at the end of life. The three most commonly mentioned end-of-life concerns during 2003 were: loss of autonomy, a decreasing ability to participate in activities that made life enjoyable, and a loss of dignity.

During 2003, 37 patients (88%) used pentobarbital as their lethal medication, four patients (10%) used secobarbital, and one used secobarbital/amobarbital (Tuinal).

During 2003, complications were reported for three patients. All involved regurgitation and none involved seizures. One-half of patients became unconscious within four minutes of ingestion of the lethal medication and died within 20 minutes. The range of time from ingestion to death was five minutes to 48 hours. Emergency medical services were called by one patient's family to pronounce death; neither resuscitation nor transport was requested.

Although the number of Oregonians ingesting legally prescribed lethal medications has increased, the overall number of terminally ill patients ingesting lethal medication has remained small, with about 1/7 of one percent of Oregonians dying by physician-assisted suicide.

NOTES AND QUESTIONS

1. The passage of the Oregon Dying with Dignity Act has generated controversy. On November 6, 2001, Attorney General John Ashcroft reversed the position of his predecessor Janet Reno and issued an interpretive rule (known as the "Ashcroft Directive," 21 C.F.R. § 1306.04 (2001)) declaring that controlled substances to assist suicide in the United States cannot be dispensed consistently with the Controlled Substances Act (CSA) (discussed in *United States v. Oakland Cannabis Buyers' Cooperative*, Sec. II. A., *supra*). Specifically, the Ashcroft Directive stated that physician-assisted suicide served no "legitimate medical purpose" within the meaning of 21 C.F.R. § 1306.04, and that such conduct could result in the possible revocation or suspension of a physician's license. The Directive specifically targets practitioners in Oregon and instructs the Drug Enforcement Administration to enforce the determination even if state law authorizes or permits such conduct by health care practitioners. *Oregon v. Ashcroft*, 368 F.3d 1118, 1123 (9th Cir. 2004).

A doctor, pharmacist, several terminally ill patients, and the State of Oregon filed suit in federal district court, seeking declaratory and injunctive relief against the Ashcroft Directive which the district court granted. *See Oregon v. Ashcroft*, 192

F.Supp.2d 1077 (D. Or. 2002). Recently, the Ninth Circuit issued an opinion upholding the injunction, ruling that the Ashcroft Directive is unlawful and unenforceable for three reasons. First, the panel held that the Attorney General may not exercise control over an area of law traditionally reserved for state authority, like medical care, unless Congress' authorization is "unmistakably clear." Because Congress provided no indication it intended Ashcroft to regulate the practice of physician-assisted suicide, the Ashcroft Directive lacked congressional authority. Second, the panel held that the CSA expressly limited federal authority under the CSA to the field of drug abuse and prevention. Because the Ashcroft Directive sought to regulate medical practices outside these fields, it violated the plain language of the CSA. Finally, the panel held that to the limited extent the CSA authorizes the federal government to make decisions regarding the practice of medicine, Congress empowered the Secretary of Health and Human Services, not the Attorney General to make those decisions.

For additional information on the Oregon legislation and the issues it poses *see* Robert Steinbrook, *Physician-Assisted Suicide in Oregon: An Uncertain Future*, 346 New Eng. J. Med. 460–64 (2002); Ann Alpers & Bernard Lo, *Physician–Assisted Suicide in Oregon: A Bold Experiment*, 274 JAMA 483 (1995); Patrick M. Curran, Jr., *Regulating Death: Oregon's Death with Dignity Act and the Legalization of Physician–Assisted Suicide*, 86 Geo. L. J. 725 (1998); Herbert Hendin et al., *Physician-Assisted Suicide: Reflections on Oregon's First Case*, 14 Issues Law & Med. 243, 243–70 (1998); Melinda A. Lee et al., *Legalizing Assisted Suicide–Views of Physicians in Oregon*, 334 New Eng. J. Med. 310 (1996).

2. Legislative and judicial discussions about assisting suicide have focused on physicians providing assistance. Commentators disagree about whether physician participation is consistent with the goals of medicine. John Keown writes, "A responsible doctor would no more euthanize a patient just because the patient autonomously asked for it any more than the doctor would prescribe anti-depressant drugs for a patient just because the patient autonomously requested them." John Keown, *Euthanasia in the Netherlands: Sliding Down the Slippery Slope?*, 9 Notre Dame J. L. Ethics & Pub. Pol'y 407, 408 (1995).

Leon Kass argues that the doctor-patient relationship requires that the physician always respect human life in living bodies. Kass points out that the Hippocratic Oath states that a physician may "neither give a deadly drug to anybody if asked for it, nor will . . . make a suggestion to this effect." Finally, Kass asserts that death is never an improvement over life as he writes, "One cannot heal—or comfort—by making nil." Leon R. Kass, *Neither For Love Nor Money: Why Doctors Must Not Kill*, 94 Pub. Interest 25, 45 (1989); *see* David Orentlicher, *Physician Participation in Assisted Suicide*, 262 JAMA 1844 (1989).

Conversely, others feel that PAS fits within medicine's goals:

> Although healing is a core goal of medicine, the concept of healing cannot be stretched to cover the full scope of legitimate medical practice. . . . [I]nstead there is a plurality of goals of medicine, which includes healing, promoting health, and helping patients achieve a peaceful death.

Franklin G. Miller and Howard Brody, *Professional Integrity and Physician–Assisted Death*, 25 Hastings Ctr. Rep. 8, 12 (1995). Still others argue that PAS enhances the doctor-patient relationship instead of destroying it:

> The physician-patient relationship is arbitrarily ruptured if fears of legal repercussions prevent the presence of the assisting physician at the time of death. Furthermore, there is a risk that the suffering patient may botch the suicide, thus losing control over the process of dying and possibly suffering unwanted medical interventions.

Id. at 15; *see also* Timothy Quill, Death and Dignity: A Case of Individualized Decision Making, 324 NEW ENG. J. MED. 691 (1991).

There is further disagreement as to how physicians may participate. Some commentators believe that doctors should not be limited to merely prescribing medication. Instead, they should be able to actually administer medication or even give a lethal injection. They argue that laws which do not allow physicians to administer the killing agent discriminate against patients too weak to administer the prescription to themselves. *See* Franklin G. Miller and John C. Fletcher, *Physician-Assisted Suicide and Active Euthanasia, in* PHYSICIAN-ASSISTED DEATH 75 (James M. Humber et al. eds., 1993). *But see* R.F. Weir, *The Morality of Physician-assisted Suicide*, 20 L. MED. & HEALTH CARE 116 (1992).

What about the ethical responsibilities of health care professionals other than physicians? Should the roles of nurses, pharmacists, psychiatrists, and other allied health care professionals also be considered? *See* Courtney S. Campbell, *When Medicine Lost Its Moral Conscience: Oregon Measure 16*, 2 BIOLAW SUPP. 14 (1995).

3.   On April 1, 2002, the Netherlands became the first country in the world to legalize termination of life on request and assistance with suicide. Passage of the legislation follows almost thirty years of public debate about legalizing voluntary euthanasia.

The Termination of Life on Request and Assisted Suicide (Review Procedures) Act permits patients experiencing unbearable suffering to request euthanasia and exempts doctors who assist them from prosecution if they have complied with the requirements of the act. In order to comply, a physician first must practice the due care criteria, and second must report the cause of death to the municipal coroner.

The due care criteria require the attending physician to do the following:

a.   hold the conviction that the patient's request was voluntary and well-considered,

b.   hold the conviction that the patient's suffering was lasting and unbearable,

c.   has informed the patient about the situation he was in and about his prospects,

d.   and the patient hold the conviction that there was no other reasonable solution for the situation he was in,

e.   has consulted at least one other, independent physician who has seen the patient and has given his written opinion on the requirements of due care, referred to in a-d above, and

f.   has terminated a life or assisted in suicide with due care

The Act also establishes regional review committees that are charged with assessing whether a case of termination of life and assisted suicide on request complies with the due care requirements.

The Act also covers requests for termination of life or assistance with suicide made by minors. A physician may carry out the request; (1) If a patient aged 16 or older is no longer able to express his will, but prior to reaching this condition was viewed as having a reasonable understanding of his interests and has made a written statement containing a request; (2) if a minor patient between sixteen and eighteen years has a reasonable understanding of his interests and his parents or guardian have been involved in the decision making process, and (3) if a minor patient between twelve and sixteen years has a reasonable understanding of his interests and his parents and/or guardian agree with the termination of life or the assisted suicide.

James Rachels, Active and Passive Euthanasia

292 NEW ENG. J. MED. 78, 78–80 (1975).

The distinction between active and passive euthanasia is thought to be crucial for medical ethics. The idea is that it is permissible, at least in some cases, to withhold treatment and allow a patient to die, but it is never permissible to take any direct action designed to kill the patient. This doctrine seems to be accepted by most doctors, and it is endorsed in a statement adopted by the House of Delegates of the American Medical Association on December 4, 1973:

> The intentional termination of the life of one human being by another— mercy killing—is contrary to that for which the medical profession stands and is contrary to the policy of the American Medical Association.

> The cessation of the employment of extraordinary means to prolong the life of the body when there is irrefutable evidence that biological death is imminent is the decision of the patient and/or his immediate family. The advice and judgment of the physician should be freely available to the patient and/or his immediate family.

However, a strong case can be made against this doctrine. . . .

To begin with a familiar type of situation, a patient who is dying of incurable cancer of the throat is in terrible pain, which can no longer be satisfactorily alleviated. He is certain to die within a few days, even if present treatment is continued, but he does not want to go on living for those days since the pain is unbearable. So he asks the doctor for an end to it, and his family joins in the request.

Suppose the doctor agrees to withhold treatment, as the conventional doctrine says he may. The justification for his doing so is that the patient is in terrible agony, and since he is going to die anyway, it would be wrong to prolong his suffering needlessly. But now notice this. If one simply withholds treatment, it may take the patient longer to die, and so he may suffer more than he would if more direct action were taken and a lethal injection given. This fact provides strong reason for thinking that, once the initial decision not to prolong his agony has been made, active euthanasia is actually preferable to passive euthanasia, rather than the reverse. To say otherwise is to endorse the option that leads to more suffering rather than less, and is contrary to the humanitarian impulse that prompts the decision not to prolong his life in the first place.

. . .

My second argument is that the conventional doctrine leads to decisions concerning life and death made on irrelevant grounds.

Consider . . . the case of the infants with Down's syndrome who need operations for congenital defects unrelated to the syndrome to live. Sometimes, there is no operation, and the baby dies, but where there is no such defect the baby lives on. Now, an operation such as that to remove an intestinal obstruction is not prohibitively difficult. The reason why such operations are not performed in these cases is, clearly, that the child has Down's syndrome and the parents and doctor judge that because of that fact it is better for the child to die.

But notice that this situation is absurd, no matter what view one takes of the lives and potentials of such babies. If the life of such an infant is worth preserving, what does it matter if it needs a simple operation? Or, if one thinks it better that such a baby should not live on, what difference does it make that it happens to have an unobstructed intestinal tract? In either case, the matter of life and death is being decided on irrelevant grounds. It is the Down's syndrome, and not the intestines, that is the issue. The matter should be decided, if at all, on that basis, and not be allowed to depend on the essentially irrelevant question of whether the intestinal tract is blocked.

. . .

One reason why so many people think that there is an important moral difference between active and passive euthanasia is that they think killing someone is morally worse than letting someone die. But is it? Is killing, in itself, worse than letting die? To investigate this issue, two cases may be considered that are exactly alike except that one involves killing whereas the other involves letting someone die. Then, it can be asked whether this difference makes any difference to the moral assessments. It is important that the cases be exactly alike, except for this one difference, since otherwise one cannot be confident that it this difference and not some other that accounts for any variation in the assessments of the two cases. So, let us consider this pair of cases:

In the first, Smith stands to gain a large inheritance if anything should happen to his six-year-old cousin. One evening while the child is taking his bath, Smith sneaks into the bathroom and drowns the child, and then arranges things so that it will look like an accident.

In the second, Jones also stands to gain if anything should happen to his six-year-old cousin. Like Smith, Jones sneaks in planning to drown the child in his bath. However, just as he enters the bathroom Jones sees the child slip and hit his head, and fall face down in the water. Jones is delighted; he stands by, ready to push the child's head back under if it is necessary, but it is not necessary. With only a little thrashing about, the child drowns all by himself, "accidentally," as Jones watches and does nothing.

Now Smith killed the child, whereas Jones "merely" let the child die. That is the only difference between them. Did either man behave better, from a moral point of view? If the difference between killing and letting die were in itself a morally important matter, one should say that Jones's behavior was less reprehensible than Smith's. But does one really want to say that? I think not. In the first place, both men acted from the same motive, personal gain, and both had exactly the same end in view when they acted. It may be inferred from Smith's conduct that he is a bad man, although that judgment may be withdrawn or modified if certain further facts are learned about him—for example, that he is mentally deranged. But would not the very same thing be inferred about Jones from his conduct? And would not the same further considerations also be relevant to any modification of this judgment? Moreover, suppose Jones pleaded, in his own defense, "After all, I didn't do anything except just stand there and watch the child drown. I didn't kill him; I only let him die." Again, if letting die were in itself less bad than killing, this defense should have at least some weight. But it does not. Such a "defense" can only be regarded as a grotesque perversion of moral reasoning. Morally speaking, it is no defense at all.

. . .

Many people will find this judgment hard to accept. One reason, I think, is that it is very easy to conflate the question of whether killing is, in itself, worse than letting die, with the very different question of whether most actual cases of killing are more reprehensible than most actual cases of letting die. Most actual cases of killing are clearly terrible (think, for example, of all the murders reported in the newspapers), and one hears of such cases every day. On the other hand, one hardly ever hears of a case of letting die, except for the actions of doctors who are motivated by humanitarian reasons. So one learns to think of killing in a much worse light than of letting die. But this does not mean that there is something about killing that makes it in itself worse than letting die, for it is not the bare difference between killing and letting die that makes the difference in these cases. Rather, the other factors—the murderer's motive of personal gain, for example, contrasted with the doctor's humanitarian motivation—account for different reactions to the different cases.

I have argued that killing is not in itself any worse than letting die; if my contention is right, it follows that active euthanasia is not any worse than passive euthanasia. . . .

NOTES AND QUESTIONS

1. The active/passive distinction is one of several efforts to differentiate termination of treatment from active euthanasia. Some argue that the proper distinction to be made is that between omissions, or failures to act, and actions. Is this the same as the active/passive distinction? Are passive "acts" always equivalent to omissions? Others advocate a distinction between the intentional termination of a patient's life and the nonintentional termination thereof. *See* Bonnie Steinbock, *Introduction, in* KILLING AND LETTING DIE 1 (Bonnie Steinbock ed., 1990).

Still other writers distinguish termination of treatment from euthanasia by relying upon the concept of causation. These writers claim that actions which have the effect of allowing the terminal condition or disease to cause the patient's death are morally acceptable, while actions which have the effect of making a human agent the cause of death are morally unacceptable. On a causal approach:

> The withdrawal of medical care that does not combat actively a hopeless terminal condition but instead is required solely because of the patient's current disease-related helplessness would constitute euthanasia. Since such treatment does not affect the underlying terminal condition, its withdrawal would not simply allow the dying process to take its course.

Eric R. Herlan, *Maine's Living Will Act and the Termination of Life–Sustaining Medical Procedures*, 39 ME. L. REV. 83, 142 (1987). Is this causation-based approach more precise than the active/passive approach?

2. The Doctrine of Double Effect is another attempt to distinguish termination of Life Saving Medical Treatment (LSMT) from active euthanasia. This doctrine, primarily but not exclusively part of the Roman Catholic tradition, is often invoked to justify a course of conduct when two obligations are perceived to be in conflict. According to the Doctrine of Double Effect,

> [I]f one act has two consequences, the one good and the other evil, where both consequences are inevitable outcomes of the initial act itself, then the act is

morally acceptable (and, presumably, the bad result morally excusable) if these four conditions are met:

(1) Considered in and by itself, the act as such is not morally objectionable.

(2) The agent's intention in performing the act is directed towards the good to be achieved only and does not include the bad result as a desideratum.

(3) The bad result is merely the inevitable concomitant and not a means to the good result or a condition of it.

(4) There are grave reasons for engaging in the act itself such that failure to perform the act would result in at least as bad a state of affairs as the bad effect of the performance of the act.

EIKE-HENNER W. KLUGE, THE ETHICS OF DELIBERATE DEATH 16 (1981).

The doctrine is frequently criticized for being abstruse or internally incoherent. *See, e.g.*, Bonnie Steinbock, *Introduction, in* KILLING AND LETTING DIE 12 (Bonnie Steinbock ed., 1980). Is not the doctrine easily manipulable, so that it may be equally applied to the allowance and prevention of euthanasia? Even if you agree with the criticisms of the doctrine, does the doctrine nevertheless serve the practical purpose of providing an analytical framework by which to evaluate the actions of health care professionals and distinguish the morally acceptable termination of treatment from the morally unacceptable practice of active euthanasia?

One common situation in which the doctrine is applied is the use of narcotics for pain relief in a dying patient. Morphine given in doses large enough to relieve severe pain often has the side effect of hastening the patient's death. According to one physician who gave morphine to patients suffering from respiratory insufficiency, a terrifying drawn-out suffocation process ensues in which the patient struggles to breathe:

If you decide that the right thing to do is give enough morphine to depress the breathing—thereby relieving the suffering—then there is an almost direct correlation with an earlier death, as close to one-to-one as man gets, as close to a borderline case as I would want medicine to get to.

Struggling to Set Standards on Decisions at Life's Edge, WASH. POST, Apr. 21, 1983, at A1.

Compare the Doctrine of Double Effect to the President's Commission's position on unintended but foreseeable consequences:

The relevant distinction, then, is not really that a death is forbidden as a means to relieve suffering but that it is sometimes acceptable if it is a foreseeable consequence. Rather, the moral issue is whether or not the decision makers have considered the full range of foreseeable effects, have knowingly accepted whatever risk of death is entailed, and have found the risk to be justified in light of the paucity and undesirability of other options.

PRESIDENT'S COMMISSION, DECIDING TO FOREGO LIFE-SUSTAINING TREATMENT 82 (1983).

D.   THE INCOMPETENT PATIENT

1.   DECISION-MAKING IN ANTICIPATION OF INCAPACITY

Uniform Health–Care Decisions Act

1993.

Section 1.   Definitions. IN THIS [ACT]:

(1) "Advance health-care directive" means an individual instruction or a power of attorney for health care.

(2) "Agent" means an individual designated in a power of attorney for health care to make a health-care decision for the individual granting the power.

(3) "Capacity" means an individual's ability to understand the significant benefits, risks, and alternatives to proposed health care and to make and communicate a health-care decision.

(4) "Guardian" means a judicially appointed guardian or conservator having authority to make a health-care decision for an individual.

(5) "Health care" means any care, treatment, service, or procedure to maintain, diagnose, or otherwise affect an individual's physical or mental condition.

(6) "Health-care decision" means a decision made by an individual or the individual's agent, guardian, or surrogate, regarding the individual's health care, including:

    (i) selection and discharge of health-care providers and institutions;

    (ii) approval or disapproval of diagnostic tests, surgical procedures, programs of medication, and orders not to resuscitate; and

    (iii) directions to provide, withhold, or withdraw artificial nutrition and hydration and all other forms of health care.

(7) "Health-care institution" means an institution, facility, or agency licensed, certified, or otherwise authorized or permitted by law to provide health care in the ordinary course of business.

. . .

(9) "Individual instruction" means an individual's direction concerning a health-care decision for the individual.

. . .

(12) "Power of attorney for health care" means the designation of an agent to make health-care decisions for the individual granting the power.

(13) "Primary physician" means a physician designated by an individual or the individual's agent, guardian, or surrogate, to have primary responsibility for the individual's health care or, in the absence of a designation or if the designated physician is not reasonably available, a physician who undertakes the responsibility.

. . .

(16) "Supervising health-care provider" means the primary physician or, if there is no primary physician or the primary physician is not reasonably available, the health-care provider who has undertaken primary responsibility for an individual's health care.

(17) "Surrogate" means an individual, other than a patient's agent or guardian, authorized under this [Act] to make a health-care decision for the patient.

SECTION 2.   ADVANCE HEALTH-CARE DIRECTIVES.

(a) An adult or emancipated minor may give an individual instruction. The instruction may be oral or written. The instruction may be limited to take effect only if a specified condition arises.

(b) An adult or emancipated minor may execute a power of attorney for health care, which may authorize the agent to make any health-care decision the principal could have made while having capacity. The power must be in writing and signed by the principal. The power remains in effect notwithstanding the principal's later incapacity and may include individual instructions. Unless related to the principal by blood, marriage, or adoption, an agent may not be an owner, operator, or employee of [a residential long-term health-care institution] at which the principal is receiving care.

(c) Unless otherwise specified in a power of attorney for health care, the authority of an agent becomes effective only upon a determination that the principal lacks capacity, and ceases to be effective upon a determination that the principal has recovered capacity.

(d) Unless otherwise specified in a written advance health-care directive, a determination that an individual lacks or has recovered capacity, or that another condition exists that affects an individual instruction or the authority of an agent, must be made by the primary physician.

(e) An agent shall make a health-care decision in accordance with the principal's individual instructions, if any, and other wishes to the extent known to the agent. Otherwise, the agent shall make the decision in accordance with the agent's determination of the principal's best interest. In determining the principal's best interest, the agent shall consider the principal's personal values to the extent known to the agent.

(f) A health-care decision made by an agent for a principal is effective without judicial approval.

(g) A written advance health-care directive may include the individual's nomination of a guardian of the person.

SECTION 3.   REVOCATION OF ADVANCE HEALTH-CARE DIRECTIVE.

(a) An individual may revoke the designation of an agent only by a signed writing or by personally informing the supervising health-care provider.

(b) An individual may revoke all or part of an advance health-care directive, other than the designation of an agent, at any time and in any manner that communicates an intent to revoke.

(c) A health-care provider, agent, guardian, or surrogate who is informed of a revocation shall promptly communicate the fact of the revocation to the supervising health-care provider and to any health-care institution at which the patient is receiving care.

(d) A decree of annulment, divorce, dissolution of marriage, or legal separation revokes a previous designation of a spouse as agent unless otherwise specified in the decree or in a power of attorney for health care.

(e) An advance health-care directive that conflicts with an earlier advance health-care directive revokes the earlier directive to the extent of the conflict.

SECTION 4. OPTIONAL FORM.

The following form may, but need not, be used to create an advance health-care directive. The other sections of this [Act] govern the effect of this or any other writing used to create an advance health-care directive. An individual may complete or modify all or any part of the following form:

ADVANCE HEALTH–CARE DIRECTIVE

Explanation

You have the right to give instructions about your own health care. You also have the right to name someone else to make health-care decisions for you. This form lets you do either or both of these things. It also lets you express your wishes regarding donation of organs and the designation of your primary physician. If you use this form, you may complete or modify all or any part of it. You are free to use a different form.

Part 1 of this form is a power of attorney for health care. Part 1 lets you name another individual as agent to make health-care decisions for you if you become incapable of making your own decisions or if you want someone else to make those decisions for you now even though you are still capable. You may also name an alternate agent to act for you if your first choice is not willing, able, or reasonably available to make decisions for you. Unless related to you, your agent may not be an owner, operator, or employee of [a residential long-term health-care institution] at which you are receiving care.

Unless the form you sign limits the authority of your agent, your agent may make all health-care decisions for you. This form has a place for you to limit the authority of your agent. You need not limit the authority of your agent if you wish to rely on your agent for all health-care decisions that may have to be made. If you choose not to limit the authority of your agent, your agent will have the right to:

(a) consent or refuse consent to any care, treatment, service, or procedure to maintain, diagnose, or otherwise affect a physical or mental condition;

(b) select or discharge health-care providers and institutions;

(c) approve or disapprove diagnostic tests, surgical procedures, programs of medication, and orders not to resuscitate; and

(d) direct the provision, withholding, or withdrawal of artificial nutrition and hydration and all other forms of health care.

Part 2 of this form lets you give specific instructions about any aspect of your health care. Choices are provided for you to express your wishes regarding the provision, withholding, or withdrawal of treatment to keep you alive, including the provision of artificial nutrition and hydration, as well as the provision of pain relief. Space is also provided for you to add to the choices you have made or for you to write out any additional wishes.

Part 3 of this form lets you express an intention to donate your bodily organs and tissues following your death.

Part 4 of this form lets you designate a physician to have primary responsibility for your health care.

After completing this form, sign and date the form at the end. It is recommended but not required that you request two other individuals to sign as witnesses. Give a copy of the signed and completed form to your physician, to any other health-care providers you may have, to any health-care institution at which you are receiving care, and to any health-care agents you have named. You should talk to the person you have named as agent to make sure that he or she understands your wishes and is willing to take the responsibility.

You have the right to revoke this advance health-care directive or replace this form at any time.

PART 1—POWER OF ATTORNEY FOR HEALTH CARE

(1) DESIGNATION OF AGENT: I designate the following individual as my agent to make health-care decisions for me:

. . .

OPTIONAL: If I revoke my agent's authority or if my agent is not willing, able, or reasonably available to make a health-care decision for me, I designate as my first alternate agent:

. . .

(2) AGENT'S AUTHORITY: My agent is authorized to make all health-care decisions for me, including decisions to provide, withhold, or withdraw artificial nutrition and hydration and all other forms of health care to keep me alive, except as I state here:

. . .

(3) WHEN AGENT'S AUTHORITY BECOMES EFFECTIVE: My agent's authority becomes effective when my primary physician determines that I am unable to make my own health-care decisions unless I mark the following box. If I mark this box [ ], my agent's authority to make health-care decisions for me takes effect immediately.

(4) AGENT'S OBLIGATION: My agent shall make health-care decisions for me in accordance with this power of attorney for health care, any instructions I give in Part 2 of this form, and my other wishes to the extent known to my agent. To the extent my wishes are unknown, my agent shall make health-care decisions for me in accordance with what my agent determines to be in my best interest. In determining my best interest, my agent shall consider my personal values to the extent known to my agent.

(5) NOMINATION OF GUARDIAN: If a guardian of my person needs to be appointed for me by a court, I nominate the agent designated in this form. If that agent is not willing, able, or reasonably available to act as guardian, I nominate the alternate agents whom I have named, in the order designated.

PART 2—INSTRUCTIONS FOR HEALTH CARE

If you are satisfied to allow your agent to determine what is best for you in making end-of-life decisions, you need not fill out this part of the form. If you do fill out this part of the form, you may strike any wording you do not want.

(6) END–OF–LIFE DECISIONS: I direct that my health-care providers and others involved in my care provide, withhold, or withdraw treatment in accordance with the choice I have marked below:

[ ] (a) Choice Not To Prolong Life

I do not want my life to be prolonged if (i) I have an incurable and irreversible condition that will result in my death within a relatively short time, (ii) I become unconscious and, to a reasonable degree of medical certainty, I will not regain consciousness, or (iii) the likely risks and burdens of treatment would outweigh the expected benefits, OR

[ ] (b) Choice To Prolong Life

I want my life to be prolonged as long as possible within the limits of generally accepted health-care standards.

(7) ARTIFICIAL NUTRITION AND HYDRATION: Artificial nutrition and hydration must be provided, withheld, or withdrawn in accordance with the choice I have made in paragraph (6) unless I mark the following box. If I mark this box [ ], artificial nutrition and hydration must be provided regardless of my condition and regardless of the choice I have made in paragraph (6).

(8) RELIEF FROM PAIN: Except as I state in the following space, I direct that treatment for alleviation of pain or discomfort be provided at all times, even if it hastens my death:

.   .   .

(9) OTHER WISHES: (If you do not agree with any of the optional choices above and wish to write your own, or if you wish to add to the instructions you have given above, you may do so here.) I direct that:

.   .   .

SECTION 5. DECISIONS BY SURROGATE.

(a) A surrogate may make a health-care decision for a patient who is an adult or emancipated minor if the patient has been determined by the primary physician to lack capacity and no agent or guardian has been appointed or the agent or guardian is not reasonably available.

(b) An adult or emancipated minor may designate any individual to act as surrogate by personally informing the supervising health-care provider. In the absence of a designation, or if the designee is not reasonably available, any member of the following classes of the patient's family who is reasonably available, in descending order of priority, may act as surrogate:

(1) the spouse, unless legally separated;

(2) an adult child;

(3) a parent; or

(4) an adult brother or sister.

(c) If none of the individuals eligible to act as surrogate under subsection (b) is reasonably available, an adult who has exhibited special care and concern for the patient, who is familiar with the patient's personal values, and who is reasonably available may act as surrogate.

(d) A surrogate shall communicate his or her assumption of authority as promptly as practicable to the members of the patient's family specified in subsection (b) who can be readily contacted.

(e) If more than one member of a class assumes authority to act as surrogate, and they do not agree on a health-care decision and the supervising health-care provider is so informed, the supervising health-care provider shall comply with the decision of a majority of the members of that class who have communicated their views to the provider. If the class is evenly divided concerning the health-care decision and the supervising health-care provider is so informed, that class and all individuals having lower priority are disqualified from making the decision.

(f) A surrogate shall make a health-care decision in accordance with the patient's individual instructions, if any, and other wishes to the extent known to the surrogate. Otherwise, the surrogate shall make the decision in accordance with the surrogate's determination of the patient's best interest. In determining the patient's best interest, the surrogate shall consider the patient's personal values to the extent known to the surrogate.

(g) A health-care decision made by a surrogate for a patient is effective without judicial approval.

(h) An individual at any time may disqualify another, including a member of the individual's family, from acting as the individual's surrogate by a signed writing or by personally informing the supervising health-care provider of the disqualification.

(i) Unless related to the patient by blood, marriage, or adoption, a surrogate may not be an owner, operator, or employee of [a residential long-term health-care institution] at which the patient is receiving care.

. . .

SECTION 6. DECISIONS BY GUARDIAN.

(a) A guardian shall comply with the ward's individual instructions and may not revoke the ward's advance health-care directive unless the appointing court expressly so authorizes.

(b) Absent a court order to the contrary, a health-care decision of an agent takes precedence over that of a guardian.

(c) A health-care decision made by a guardian for the ward is effective without judicial approval.

. . .

SECTION 7. OBLIGATIONS OF HEALTH-CARE PROVIDER.

(a) Before implementing a health-care decision made for a patient, a supervising health-care provider, if possible, shall promptly communicate to the patient the decision made and the identity of the person making the decision.

(b) A supervising health-care provider who knows of the existence of an advance health-care directive, a revocation of an advance health-care directive, or a designation or disqualification of a surrogate, shall promptly record its existence in the patient's health-care record and, if it is in writing, shall request a copy and if one is furnished shall arrange for its maintenance in the health-care record.

(c) A primary physician who makes or is informed of a determination that a patient lacks or has recovered capacity, or that another condition exists which affects an individual instruction or the authority of an agent, guardian, or surrogate, shall promptly record the determination in the patient's health-care record and communicate the determination to the patient, if possible, and to any person then authorized to make health-care decisions for the patient.

(d) Except as provided in subsections (e) and (f), a health-care provider or institution providing care to a patient shall:

   (1) comply with an individual instruction of the patient and with a reasonable interpretation of that instruction made by a person then authorized to make health-care decisions for the patient; and

   (2) comply with a health-care decision for the patient made by a person then authorized to make health-care decisions for the patient to the same extent as if the decision had been made by the patient while having capacity.

(e) A health-care provider may decline to comply with an individual instruction or health-care decision for reasons of conscience. A health-care institution may decline to comply with an individual instruction or health-care decision if the instruction or decision is contrary to a policy of the institution which is expressly based on reasons of conscience and if the policy was timely communicated to the patient or to a person then authorized to make health-care decisions for the patient.

(f) A health-care provider or institution may decline to comply with an individual instruction or health-care decision that requires medically ineffective health care or health care contrary to generally accepted health-care standards applicable to the health-care provider or institution.

(g) A health-care provider or institution that declines to comply with an individual instruction or health-care decision shall:

   (1) promptly so inform the patient, if possible, and any person then authorized to make health-care decisions for the patient;

   (2) provide continuing care to the patient until a transfer can be effected; and

   (3) unless the patient or person then authorized to make health-care decisions for the patient refuses assistance, immediately make all reasonable efforts to assist in the transfer of the patient to another health-care provider or institution that is willing to comply with the instruction or decision.

(h) A health-care provider or institution may not require or prohibit the execution or revocation of an advance health-care directive as a condition for providing health care.

. . .

SECTION 14. JUDICIAL RELIEF.

On petition of a patient, the patient's agent, guardian, or surrogate, a health-care provider or institution involved with the patient's care, or an individual described in Section 5(b) or (c), the [appropriate] court may enjoin or direct a health-care decision or order other equitable relief. A proceeding under this section is governed by [here insert appropriate reference to the rules of procedure or statutory provisions governing expedited proceedings and proceedings affecting incapacitated persons].

. . .

NOTES AND QUESTIONS

1. Following the Supreme Court decision in *Cruzan v. Director, Missouri Department of Health*, 497 U.S. 261, 110 S.Ct. 2841, 111 L.Ed.2d 224 (1990) many states passed legislation on health care decision making. This legislation fell into three general categories. First, states authorized the use of living wills or individual instruction containing an individual's preferences. Second, states authorized the use of powers of attorney for health care. Finally, a majority of states have statutes allowing family members or others to make health care decisions for adults who lacked capacity. There was no uniformity. The Uniform Health–Care Decisions Act was intended to promote uniformity. It supersedes the Commissioners' Model Health Care Consent Act (1982), the Uniform Rights of the Terminally Ill Act (1985) and the Uniform Rights of the Terminally Ill Act (1989).

2. Forty-six states and the District of Columbia have enacted "instructional" advance directive statutes or living will statutes. These statutes allow an individual to execute a document, often called a "living will," specifying the types of treatment she is to receive in certain situations including the withholding or withdrawal of "life-prolonging" medical treatment in limited circumstances.

3. An indirect result of the decision in *Cruzan* was the enactment of the Patient Self–Determination Act of 1989, which passed as a part of the Omnibus Budget Reconciliation of 1990, 42 U.S.C. § 1395cc(f)(1) and 1396a(a) (Supp.1991). The Act requires dissemination of information about advance directives as a condition for participation in Medicare and Medicaid programs. The statute applies to hospitals, skilled nursing facilities, home health agencies, hospices, and prepaid health care organizations. 42 U.S.C. § 1395cc(f)(2), 1395l(r), 1395mm(c)(8), 1396a(w)(2). These organizations must "maintain written policies and procedures" that apply to "all adult individuals receiving medical care" concerning their rights under state law "to make decisions concerning [their] medical care," "to accept or refuse treatment," and "to formulate advance directives." 42 U.S.C. § 1395cc(f)(1), 1396a(w)(1). Patients must be given written information about these rights and the institutional policies at or before the time of admission. 42 U.S.C. § 1395cc(f)(1)(a)(i)–(ii), 1395cc(f)(2)(A)–(E), 1396a(w)(1)(A), 1396a(w)(2)(A)–(E). The language of the statute is ambiguous as to whether it applies to outpatients.

The Department of Health and Human Services must "develop and implement a national campaign to inform the public of the option to execute advance directives and of a patient's right to participate and direct health care decisions." 104 Stat.

1388–205 (1990). The Patient Self–Determination Act has generated a sizable body of commentary. *See, e.g.,* Michael A. Refolo, *The Patient Self–Determination Act of 1990: Health Care's Own Miranda,* 8 J. CONTEMP. HEALTH LAW & POL'Y 455 (1992); Kelly C. Mulholland, *Protecting the Right to Die: The Patient Self–Determination Act of 1990,* 28 HARV. J. LEGIS. 609 (1991); Charles P. Sabatino & Vicki Gottlich, *Seeking Self–Determination in the Patient Self–Determination Act,* 25 CLEARING-HOUSE REV. 639 (1991); Charles P. Sabatino et al., *Giving Life to Patient Self–Determination,* 23 HASTINGS CTR. REP. 12 (1993); Susan M. Wolf et al., *Sources of Concern About the Patient Self–Determination Act,* 325 NEW ENG. J. MED. 1666 (1991).

4.   Are instructional advance directive statutes a good idea? Is the execution of an instructional advance directive really an exercise of self-determination? Consider the views expressed by John Robertson:

> The problem ... is that the patient's interests when incompetent—viewed from her current perspective—are no longer informed by the interests and values she had when competent. The values and interests of the competent person no longer are relevant to someone who has lost the rational structure on which those values and interests rested. Unless we are to view competently held values and interests as extending even to situations in which, because of incompetency, they can no longer have meaning, it matters not that as a competent person the individual would not wish to be maintained in a debilitated or disabled state. If the person is no longer competent enough to appreciate the degree of divergence from her previous activity that produced the choice against treatment, the prior directive does not represent her current interests merely because a competent directive was issued. Although still the same person, the patient's interests have changed radically once she becomes incompetent. Yet the premise of the prior directive is that patient interests and values remain significantly the same, so that those interests are best served by following the directive issued when competent.
>
> . . .
>
> ... The difference between competent and incompetent interests is so great that if we are to respect incompetent persons, we should focus on their needs and interests as they now exist, and not view them as retaining interests and values which, because of their incompetency, no longer apply.
>
> . . .
>
> Once acknowledged, the possibility of conflict between competent wishes and incompetent interests will direct attention away from the question of what the incompetent patient wanted when competent, to the central issue of whether treatment or nontreatment best serves the interests of the now incompetent patient. If this question were faced squarely there would be no need to rely on the prior directive (unless in cases of conflict we want to privilege the competent person's certainty over the incompetent patient's need). The needs of the incompetent patient would be directly addressed, and treatment given or withheld on the basis of her current interests, as the appropriate proxy or other decisionmakers decide.

John A. Robertson, *Second Thoughts on Living Wills,* 21 HASTINGS CTR. REP. 6, 7–9 (1991).

Can provisions be specific enough to give health care providers meaningful guidance and still remain flexible? Can persons make informed choices when the nature of the illness or injury they will suffer is unknown? What effect should be given to oral, out-of-state or other advance directives lacking the requisite formalities? For discussion of these and related issues, see Norman L. Cantor, *My Annotated Living Will*, 18 L. MED. & HEALTH CARE 114 (1990); Joanne Lynn, *Why I Don't Have a Living Will*, 19 L. MED. & HEALTH CARE 101 (1991).

5.   A major alternative to instructional advance directive legislation is health care proxy or durable power of attorney for health care legislation. Thirty-three states and the District of Columbia have enacted durable power of attorney for health care laws which specifically address decisions regarding the termination of life-sustaining treatment.

These acts vary tremendously from one another in the amount of discretion that they provide the proxy. *Compare* ALASKA STAT. § 13.26.332 to 13.26.353 (Supp.1990) (proxy may not terminate life-sustaining procedures, but may enforce a living will) *with* IOWA CODE ANN. § 144B.1 to 144B.11 (Supp.1992) (proxy may make all decisions including termination of treatment and nutrition and hydration). Some statutes authorize consent but not refusal. *See, e.g.,* N.M. STAT. ANN. § 45–5–501 to 45–5–502 (Supp.1989); PA. STAT. ANN. tit. 20, § 5604 to 5607 (Supp.1989); WASH. REV. CODE ANN. 11.94.010 (Supp.1989).

Of the states without durable power of attorney for health care statutes, all have general durable power of attorney statutes which could be interpreted to authorize a durable power of attorney for health care or court decisions or attorney general opinions which make the state's general durable power of attorney statute apply to the termination of treatment as well.

6.   Despite general recognition of the right of a competent person to refuse future treatment through a living will or through a designated proxy, all state statutes impose limits on the right of the patient to refuse treatment. Although the exact definitions vary from state to state, a virtually universal limitation on the right to refuse treatment in an advance directive is the requirement that the patient be terminally ill, permanently comatose or in a persistent vegetative state. In addition, there are two other common limitations: the proscription of refusals of nutrition and hydration and pregnancy clauses.

Pregnancy clauses typically provide that in the event of pregnancy, a living will is suspended. Is the suspension of a pregnant woman's living will a form of discrimination on the basis of gender? What interest, if any, does the state have in preserving fetal life? In what way, if any, are Supreme Court abortion decisions relevant to your answer? *See* Chapter 5, Sec. II.

2.   SURROGATE DECISIONMAKING

Cruzan v. Director, Missouri Department of Health

Supreme Court of the United States, 1990.
497 U.S. 261, 110 S.Ct. 2841, 111 L.Ed.2d 224.

(The opinion is set forth in Sec. II. B., *supra*).

In re Conroy

Supreme Court of New Jersey, 1985.
98 N.J. 321, 486 A.2d 1209.

■ SCHREIBER, J.

Plaintiff, Thomas C. Whittemore, nephew and guardian of Claire Conroy, an incompetent, sought permission to remove a nasogastric feeding tube, the primary conduit for nutrients, from his ward, an eighty-four-year-old bedridden woman with serious and irreversible physical and mental impairments who resided in a nursing home. John J. Delaney, Jr., Conroy's guardian *ad litem,* opposed the guardian's petition. The trial court granted the guardian permission to remove the tube, and the Appellate Division reversed.

I

In 1979 Claire Conroy, who was suffering from an organic brain syndrome that manifested itself in her exhibiting periodic confusion, was adjudicated an incompetent, and plaintiff, her nephew, was appointed her guardian. The guardian had Ms. Conroy placed in the Parkview Nursing Home, a small nursing facility with thirty beds. There she came under the care of Dr. Kazemi, a family practitioner, and Catherine Rittel, a registered nurse, who was the nursing home administrator. . . .

. . .

At the time of trial, Ms. Conroy was no longer ambulatory and was confined to bed, unable to move from a semi-fetal position. She suffered from arteriosclerotic heart disease, hypertension, and diabetes mellitus; her left leg was gangrenous to her knee; she had several necrotic decubitus ulcers (bed sores) on her left foot, leg, and hip; an eye problem required irrigation; she had a urinary catheter in place and could not control her bowels; she could not speak; and her ability to swallow was very limited. On the other hand, she interacted with her environment in some limited ways: she could move her head, neck, hands, and arms to a minor extent; she was able to scratch herself, and had pulled at her bandages, tube, and catheter; she moaned occasionally when moved or fed through the tube, or when her bandages were changed; her eyes sometimes followed individuals in the room; her facial expressions were different when she was awake from when she was asleep; and she smiled on occasion when her hair was combed, or when she received a comforting rub.

Dr. Kazemi and Dr. Davidoff, a specialist in internal medicine who observed Ms. Conroy before testifying as an expert on behalf of the guardian, testified that Ms. Conroy was not brain dead, comatose, or in a chronic vegetative state. They stated, however, that her intellectual capacity was very limited, and that her mental condition probably would never improve. . . .

The medical testimony was inconclusive as to whether, or to what extent, Ms. Conroy was capable of experiencing pain. Dr. Kazemi thought that Ms. Conroy might have experienced some degree of pain from her severely contracted limbs, or that the contractures were a reaction to pain, but that she did not necessarily suffer pain from the sores on her legs. According to Dr. Davidoff, it was unclear whether Ms. Conroy's feeding tube caused her pain, and it was "an open question whether she [felt] pain" at all; however, it was possible that she was experiencing a great deal of pain. Dr. Davidoff further testified that she responded to noxious or painful stimuli by moaning. . . .

Both doctors testified that if the nasogastric tube were removed, Ms. Conroy would die of dehydration in about a week. Dr. Davidoff believed that the resulting thirst could be painful but that Ms. Conroy would become unconscious long before she died. Dr. Kazemi concurred that such a death would be painful.

. . .

IV

[D]ifficult questions arise in the context of patients who, like Claire Conroy, are incompetent to make particular treatment decisions for themselves. . . . [S]ubstitute decisionmakers must seek to respect simultaneously both aspects of the patient's right to self-determination—the right to live, and the right . . . to die of natural causes without medical intervention.

B.

. . .

Since the condition of an incompetent patient makes it impossible to ascertain definitively his present desires, a third party acting on the patient's behalf often cannot say with confidence that his treatment decision for the patient will further rather than frustrate the patient's right to control his own body. Nevertheless, the goal of decision-making for incompetent patients should be to determine and effectuate, insofar as possible, the decision that the patient would have made if competent. . . .

. . . [W]e hold that life-sustaining treatment may be withheld or withdrawn from an incompetent patient when it is clear that the particular patient would have refused the treatment under the circumstances involved. The standard we are enunciating is a subjective one, consistent with the notion that the right that we are seeking to effectuate is a very personal right to control one's own life. The question is not what a reasonable or average person would have chosen to do under the circumstances but what the particular patient would have done if able to choose for himself.

. . .

Although all evidence tending to demonstrate a person's intent with respect to medical treatment should properly be considered by surrogate decision-makers, or by a court in the event of any judicial proceedings, the probative value of such evidence may vary depending on the remoteness, consistency, and thoughtfulness of the prior statements or actions and the maturity of the person at the time of the statements or acts. . . .

. . .

We recognize that for some incompetent patients it might be impossible to be clearly satisfied as to the patient's intent either to accept or reject the life-sustaining treatment. . . .

We hesitate, however, to foreclose the possibility of humane actions, which may involve termination of life-sustaining treatment, for persons who never clearly expressed their desires about life-sustaining treatment but who are now suffering a prolonged and painful death. . . . We therefore hold that life-sustaining treatment may also be withheld or withdrawn from a patient in Claire Conroy's situation if either of two "best interests" tests—a limited-objective or a pure-objective test—is satisfied.

Under the limited-objective test, life-sustaining treatment may be withheld or withdrawn from a patient in Claire Conroy's situation when there is some trustworthy evidence that the patient would have refused the treatment, and the decision-maker is satisfied that it is clear that the burdens of the patient's continued life with the treatment outweigh the benefits of that life for him. By this we mean that the patient is suffering, and will continue to suffer throughout the expected duration of his life, unavoidable pain, and that the net burdens of his prolonged life (the pain and suffering of his life with the treatment less the amount and duration of pain that the patient would likely experience if the treatment were withdrawn) markedly outweigh any physical pleasure, emotional enjoyment, or intellectual satisfaction that the patient may still be able to derive from life. . . .

. . .

In the absence of trustworthy evidence, or indeed any evidence at all, that the patient would have declined the treatment, life-sustaining treatment may still be withheld or withdrawn from a formerly competent person like Claire Conroy if a third, pure-objective test is satisfied. Under that test, as under the limited-objective test, the net burdens of the patient's life with the treatment should clearly and markedly outweigh the benefits that the patient derives from life. Further, the recurring, unavoidable and severe pain of the patient's life with the treatment should be such that the effect of administering life-sustaining treatment would be inhumane. . . .

Although we are condoning a restricted evaluation of the nature of a patient's life in terms of pain, suffering, and possible enjoyment under the limited-objective and pure-objective tests, we expressly decline to authorize decision-making based on assessments of the personal worth or social utility of another's life, or the value of that life to others. . . .

. . .

C.

We emphasize that in making decisions whether to administer life-sustaining treatment to patients such as Claire Conroy, the primary focus should be the patient's desires and experience of pain and enjoyment—not the type of treatment involved. Thus, we reject the distinction that some have made between actively hastening death by terminating treatment and passively allowing a person to die of a disease as one of limited use in a legal analysis of such a decision-making situation.

. . .

. . . [W]e also reject any distinction between withholding and withdrawing life-sustaining treatment. . . .

. . .

We also find unpersuasive the distinction relied upon by some courts, commentators, and theologians between "ordinary" treatment, which they would always require, and "extraordinary" treatment, which they deem optional. See generally *Barber v. Superior Court*, 195 Cal. Rptr. 484, 491 (Cal. Ct. App. 1983). The terms "ordinary" and "extraordinary" have assumed too many conflicting meanings to remain useful. To draw a line on this basis for determining whether treatment should be given leads to a semantical milieu that does not advance the analysis.

. . .

Some commentators . . . have made yet a fourth distinction, between the termination of artificial feedings and the termination of other forms of life-sustaining medical treatment. . . .

. . .

[W]ithdrawal or withholding of artificial feeding, like any other medical treatment, would be permissible if there is sufficient proof to satisfy the subjective, limited-objective, or pure-objective test. A competent patient has the right to decline any medical treatment, including artificial feeding, and should retain that right when and if he becomes incompetent. In addition, in the case of an incompetent patient who has given little or no trustworthy indication of an intent to decline treatment and for whom it becomes necessary to engage in balancing under the limited-objective or pure-objective test, the pain and invasiveness of an artificial feeding device, and the pain of withdrawing that device, should be treated just like the results of administering or withholding any other medical treatment.

. . .

VI

. . . Ordinarily, court involvement will be limited to the determination of incompetency, and the appointment of a guardian unless a personal guardian has been previously appointed, *who* will determine whether the standards we have prescribed have been satisfied. The record in this case did not satisfy those standards. The evidence that Claire Conroy would have refused the treatment, although sufficient to meet the lower showing of intent required under the limited-objective test, was certainly not the "clear" showing of intent contemplated under the subjective test. . . .

Moreover, there was insufficient information concerning the benefits and burdens of Ms. Conroy's life to satisfy either the limited-objective or pure-objective test. Although the treating doctor and the guardian's expert testified as to Claire Conroy's condition, neither testified conclusively as to whether she was in pain or was capable of experiencing pain or thirst. . . .

The evidence *was also unclear with respect to* Ms. Conroy's capacity to feel pleasure, another issue as to which the information supplied by a neurologist might have been helpful. . . .

The trial transcript reveals no exploration of the discomfort and risks that attend nasogastric feedings. . . . Alternative modalities, including gastrostomies, intravenous feeding, subcutaneous or intramuscular hydration, or some combination, were not investigated. . . .

. . .

The judgment of the Appellate Division is reversed. In light of Ms. Conroy's death, we do not remand the matter for further proceedings.

■ HANDLER, J., concurring in part and dissenting in part.

. . .

In my opinion, the Court's objective tests too narrowly define the interests of people like Miss Conroy. While the basic standard purports to account for several concerns, it ultimately focuses on pain as the critical factor. The presence of significant pain in effect becomes the sole measure of such a person's best interests. "Pain" thus eclipses a whole cluster of other human values that have a proper place in the subtle weighing that will ultimately determine how life should end.

The Court's concentration on pain as the exclusive criterion in reaching *the* life-or-death decision in reality transmutes the best-interests determination into an exercise of avoidance and nullification rather than confrontation and fulfillment. . . .

The pain requirement . . . effectively negates other highly relevant considerations that should appropriately bear on the decision to maintain or to withdraw life-prolonging treatment. . . . Thus, some people abhor dependence on others as much, or more, than they fear pain. Other individuals value personal privacy and dignity, and prize independence from others when their personal needs and bodily functions are involved. Finally, the ideal of bodily integrity may become more important than simply prolonging life at its most rudimentary level. Persons, *like* Miss Conroy, "may well have wished to avoid . . . '[t]he ultimate horror [*not* of] death but the possibility of being maintained in limbo, in a sterile room, by machines controlled by strangers.' "

NOTES AND QUESTIONS

1. Is the *Conroy* pain-oriented test too restrictive as suggested by Judge Handler's concurring opinion? In a subsequent case, *In re Jobes*, 108 N.J. 394, 529 A.2d 434 (1987), the New Jersey Supreme Court managed to avoid the issue once more. Nancy Ellen Jobes was a thirty-one-year-old woman in an irreversible coma in a nursing home, whose family sought permission to terminate her artificially administered nutrition and hydration. Prior to her incompetency she had failed to clearly express her preferences with respect to such treatment.

The New Jersey court, citing *In re Peter*, 108 N.J. 365, 529 A.2d 419 (1987), a case decided on the same day as *Jobes*, distinguished cases involving patients in a persistent vegetative state from other cases and turned to *In re Quinlan*, 70 N.J. 10, 355 A.2d 647 (1976), *cert. denied* sub nom. *Garger v. New Jersey*, 429 U.S. 922, 97 S.Ct. 319, 50 L.Ed.2d 289 (1976) for guidance. In *Peter*, the court had concluded that patients in persistent vegetative states were not subject to the one year life-expectancy test or to the limited-objective and objective tests articulated in *Conroy*. They stated:

Under *Quinlan,* the life expectancy of a patient in a persistent vegetative state is not an important criterion in determining whether life-sustaining treatment may be withdrawn. For this patient, our "focal point . . . should be the prognosis as to the reasonable probability of return to cognitive and sapient life, as distinguished from the forced existence of . . . biological vegetative existence."

In re Peter, 529 A.2d at 424 (N.J.).

Interestingly, the New Jersey court did not use the *Quinlan* approach in deciding *Peter*. *Peter* involved an elderly nursing home patient in a persistent vegetative state who, prior to her incompetency, had executed a power of attorney. They reasoned that Ms. Peter had left clear and convincing evidence of her wishes. As a consequence, they applied the *Conroy* subjective test because it respects patients' medical preferences. They added "the *Conroy* subjective test is applicable in every surrogate-refusal treatment case, regardless of the patient's medical condition or life expectancy." 529 A.2d at 425 (N.J.).

2. Is the problem of potential abuse in nursing homes significant enough to require more demanding procedural protection for treatment termination? Would it be possible to avoid such a standard by merely removing a patient from the nursing home? Should procedural protection vary according to the location of the patient and the patient's prognosis?

3. The traditional standard for medical surrogate decisionmaking was the "best interests" standard. This standard resulted from application of general principles concerning the relationship between a guardian and a ward. ALAN MEISEL, THE RIGHT TO DIE 264–65 (1989 & Supp.1992).

In cases involving the refusal of LSMT, however, the best interests standard was not particularly helpful because of the conflicting interests involved. In response to this shortcoming, courts confronted with "right to die" cases involving incompetent patients began to fashion a different decisionmaking standard. Under the "substituted judgment" standard, the court attempted to ascertain the decision which would have been made by the incompetent had she been able to make the decision. The substituted judgment standard is also found in other areas of the law, such as in the administration of trusts and estates.

The substituted judgment standard received sustained attention with the decision in *Superintendent of Belchertown v. Saikewicz*, 373 Mass. 728, 370 N.E.2d 417 (1977). *Saikewicz* involved the question of whether chemotherapy should be administered to Joseph Saikewicz, a 67–year-old man who suffered from incurable leukemia. Saikewicz was mentally retarded and had never been mentally competent. In allowing Saikewicz to refuse chemotherapy, the court took a decidedly "more flexible view of the 'best interests' of the incompetent patient," stressing that the proper inquiry was not an objective one as to what a "reasonable person would do under the circumstances," but a subjective one inquiring into what the patient himself would have done if he were competent. *Id.* at 746–53, 370 N.E.2d at 429–33. *Saikewicz* created much confusion, however. Joseph Saikewicz had never been competent, so he had never been capable of making the type of decision which the court hypothesized. Joseph's views on the subject (if indeed he had any) were inherently unknowable.

In *In re Storar*, 52 N.Y.2d 363, 438 N.Y.S.2d 266, 420 N.E.2d 64 (1981), *cert. denied*, 454 U.S. 858, 102 S.Ct. 309, 70 L.Ed.2d 153 (1981), the New York Court of Appeals adopted a best interests standard due to the problems of applying a substituted judgment standard to never competent patients. John Storar was "profoundly mentally retarded with a mental age of about 18 months" and was a resident of a state mental facility. When he was diagnosed with terminal cancer of the bladder, his mother (who was guardian of his person) requested that blood transfusions which were necessary for his continued survival be discontinued. The director of the facility sought court authorization for continued transfusions. In granting authorization for continued treatment, the court analogized the transfusions to food and noted:

> ... [W]e do not have any proof of [the patient's wishes]. John Storar was never competent at any time during his life.... Thus it is unrealistic to attempt to determine whether he would want to continue potentially life prolonging treatment if he were competent.... Mentally John Storar was an infant and that is the only realistic way to assess his rights in this litigation.

Id. at 380, 438 N.Y.S.2d at 275, 420 N.E.2d at 72–73. According to the *Storar* court, although substituted judgment was to be used with formerly competent patients, an objective best interests standard was to be used with never-competent patients in order to protect the "State's interests, as parens patriae, in protecting the health and welfare of the child." *Id.* at 381, 438 N.Y.S.2d at 275, 420 N.E.2d at 73.

4. Section 5(b) of the Uniform Health–Care Decisions Act is an example of a Family Consent law. These statutes specify who (usually family members) and usually in what order relatives are authorized to make health care decisions for family members in specified circumstances. The provisions vary considerably from state to state.

One of the most common arguments in favor of looking to the patient's family is that the family will be the most familiar with the wishes of the incompetent patient. A second argument in favor of vesting decision with the family is that one aspect of being a person is participating in relationships with other persons, and that the patient's family represents the "core" of the patient's relationships. A third argument favoring families is that because the patient is incompetent, any interests which the patient has (or had) are of decreased importance, while those of the family are of increased importance. How persuasive are these arguments? Do they argue in favor of family decisionmaking, or merely decision by one's "significant other"?

In spite of these arguments, there are many problems with treating the family as the decision maker. Members of the patient's family are the most likely to benefit financially from inheritance or tort awards, and the potential for abuse in both of these situations is enormous. Jury awards in tort actions are typically much greater for seriously injured patients than for deceased patients. Thus, even if the patient wishes to be allowed to die, a family member may suffer a serious conflict of interest when forced to make a decision regarding the termination of treatment. Families also may be subject to pressures to manipulate the timing of the patient's death in order to maximize insurance proceeds and disability payments or to minimize inheritance taxes.

Another difficulty with arguments for family decisionmaking is that the assumption that the family reproduces the choices that would be made by the patient has not been empirically demonstrated. Although the data on this subject is scarce, one study shows that the decisions of family members who were asked to make hypothetical treatment decisions for elderly patients whose preferences were known to the doctors, but not to the family member, were "significantly closer" to the elderly patient's preferences when these judgments were made on a substituted judgment basis, rather than a best interests basis. The study concluded that while substituted judgment was empirically supported, there were significant limitations to the durable power of attorney. *See* Tom Tomlinson et al., *An Empirical Study of Proxy Consent for Elderly Persons*, 30 Gerontologist 54 (1990).

A similar study found that family members understood the patient's preferences 88% of the time when the hypothetical scenario involved treatment decisions involving the patient in her present state, but only 68% of the time if the hypothetical involved dementia in the patient. Allison B. Seckler et al., *Substituted Judgment: How Accurate Are Proxy Predictions?*, 115 Annals of Internal Med. 92 (1991). Other possible abuses include indecision on the part of the family member and dissension within the immediate family due to financial and emotional strain.

See, e.g., Melinda A. Lee & Karen Berry, *Abuse of Durable Power of Attorney for Health Care: Case Report*, 39 J. AM. GERIATRIC SOC'Y 806 (1991) (indecision); David W. Molloy et al., *Decision Making for the Incompetent Elderly: "The Daughter from California Syndrome,"* 39 J. AM. GERIATRIC SOC'Y 396 (1991) (dissension).

In spite of these difficulties, the family is still the most appealing candidate for decision maker. When faced with a conflict between would-be decision makers, courts and advisory bodies have almost invariably chosen the family. *See, e.g.*, NEW YORK STATE TASK FORCE ON LIFE AND THE LAW, WHEN OTHERS MUST CHOOSE: DECIDING FOR PATIENTS WITHOUT CAPACITY (1992) (suggesting families as decision makers to courts); PRESIDENT'S COMMISSION, DECIDING TO FOREGO LIFE-SUSTAINING TREATMENT 126–27 (1983).

5. Another potential decision maker is the physician. However, physicians may follow their own judgment rather than the preferences of the patient. Physicians have been soundly and routinely criticized for their heavy bias in favor of aggressive treatment and their "technocratic" outlook. *See* Nancy S. Jecker, *Knowing When to Stop: The Limits of Medicine*, 21 HASTINGS CTR. REP. 5 (1991). Moreover, even if physicians seek to abide by patient preferences, physicians are less able than family members to discern the patient's preferences. One study found that physicians were able to discern patient preference 72% of the time in a scenario involving termination of treatment while the patient was in the "current state of health" and 59% of the time in a dementia scenario. Seckler, *supra*, note 1. However, when the family is for some reason not available, the doctor is most likely to be the party in the best position to accurately assess the patient's prospects and wishes. *See In re Jones*, 107 Misc.2d 290, 433 N.Y.S.2d 984 (Sup.Ct.1980); *Kennedy v. Parrott*, 243 N.C. 355, 90 S.E.2d 754 (1956). For an efficiency-based argument that physicians should be the ultimate decision makers regarding DNRs, see J. Chris Hackler & F. Charles Hiller, *Family Consent to Orders Not to Resuscitate*, 264 JAMA 1281 (1990).

In *In re Conservatorship of Helga M. Wanglie*, No. PXB91–283 (Hennepin Co., Mn. D. Ct. Probate Div., 4th Dist.1991) (reprinted in 11 BioLaw Update § 12–6 (James F. Childress & Ruth D. Gaare eds., Aug.-Sept. 1991)), a Minnesota probate court was confronted with the issue of who should decide the course of treatment for an incompetent patient when the physicians believe the requested treatment to be futile. The court ruled that Oliver Wanglie was entitled to make treatment decisions for his wife. In so doing the court specifically rejected the notion that health care personnel should be allowed to make treatment decisions for incompetents. Should a family member whose judgment may easily be clouded by emotional strain be allowed to make these decisions? Should a health care professional, who is subject to potential conflicts of interest? For a discussion of how conflict between the health care team and the family may affect treatment, see Stephen H. Miles, *Interpersonal Issues in the Wanglie Case*, 2 KENNEDY INST. ETHICS J. 61 (1992).

6. Should a body independent of family members and physicians be created in order to deal with "hard" cases such as those involving termination of treatment decisions? Hospital ethics committees (HECs) are one such body. HECs began to appear in acute care facilities in the 1970s, and their prominence is at least in part attributable to the important role assigned to them in *In re Quinlan*, 70 N.J. 10, 355 A.2d 647 (1976), *cert. denied*, 429 U.S. 922, 97 S.Ct. 319, 50 L.Ed.2d 289 (1976). The number of HECs in both acute and long term care facilities has exploded over the past decade, and continues to increase. By the late 1980s, slightly fewer than two-thirds of acute care facilities across the country had established HECs. Fewer long term care facilities have established HECs, and those HECs which are to be found in long term care facilities frequently are less well developed and less active than those found in acute care facilities. PRESIDENT'S COMMISSION, DECIDING TO FOREGO LIFE-SUSTAINING TREATMENT 160–170 (1983); NEW YORK STATE TASK FORCE ON

Life and the Law, When Others Must Choose: Deciding for Patients Without Capacity 16–22 (1992).

HECs represent an interdisciplinary approach to the resolution of bioethical issues. Membership is diverse, drawing upon the different areas of expertise of the members:

> Suggested guidelines for membership often include physicians, nurses, social workers, clergy, [medical] ethicists . . ., attorneys, administrators, patient representatives, community representatives or others unaffiliated with the institution, and (especially for long-term care facilities) patients or residents. Diversity of membership provides a broad range of experience and promotes the fairness of the decision-making process. Such representation also tends to strengthen the credibility of the committee and its decisions. It provides a safeguard against conflicts of interest and helps avoid the dominance of any individual or group, or the uncritical acceptance of a single point of view.

New York State Task Force on Life and the Law, *supra*, at 18. Does the decisional model upon which HECs are based assume an adversarial situation? If so, is this the proper manner in which to make life and death treatment choices? Given the weight of the interests involved, should due process protections apply to ethics committee proceedings?

7. The state as *parens patriae* also has an interest in the treatment decision and the courts are another possible decision making mechanism whereby this interest might be protected. What are the advantages and disadvantages of court involvement? For discussion of the role of the courts, see *In re Coyler*, 99 Wash.2d 114, 660 P.2d 738 (1983) (en banc). Courts, however, are not "constituted or especially well-qualified" to make these decisions. *In re Drabick*, 200 Cal.App.3d 185, 245 Cal.Rptr. 840, 846 (1988). One major disadvantage to judicial resolution of these cases is the time-consuming nature of the judicial process. Nevertheless, some jurisdictions require court approval for termination of treatment for an incompetent, and the Wisconsin Supreme Court favored court appointed guardians for PVS patients in *In re L.W.*, 167 Wis.2d 53, 482 N.W.2d 60 (1992). *See, e.g., Severns v. Wilmington Medical Ctr., Inc.*, 421 A.2d 1334 (Del. 1980); *Superintendent of Belchertown State Sch. v. Saikewicz*, 373 Mass. 728, 370 N.E.2d 417 (1977) (The Massachusetts Supreme Court has attempted to clarify the procedural requirements of *Saikewicz* in In re Spring, 380 Mass. 629, 405 N.E.2d 115 (1980)); *Leach v. Akron Gen. Med. Ctr.*, 68 Ohio Misc. 1, 426 N.E.2d 809 (1980).

Wendland v. Wendland

Supreme Court of California, 2001.
26 Cal.4th 519, 110 Cal.Rptr.2d 412, 28 P.3d 151.

■ Werdegar, J.

In this case we consider whether a conservator of the person may withhold artificial nutrition and hydration from a conscious conservatee who is not terminally ill, comatose, or in a persistent vegetative state, and who has not left formal instructions for health care or appointed an agent or surrogate for health care decisions. Interpreting [the Probate Code] in light of the relevant provisions of the California Constitution, we conclude a conservator may not withhold artificial nutrition and hydration from such a person absent clear and convincing evidence the conservator's decision is in accordance with either the conservatee's own wishes or best interest.

The trial court in the case before us, applying the clear and convincing evidence standard, found the evidence on both points insufficient and, thus, denied the conservator's request for authority to withhold artificial nutrition and hydration. The Court of Appeal, which believed the trial court was required to defer to the conservator's good faith decision, reversed. We reverse the decision of the Court of Appeal.

I.   FACTS AND PROCEDURAL HISTORY

On September 29, 1993, Robert Wendland rolled his truck at high speed in a solo accident while driving under the influence of alcohol. The accident injured Robert's brain, leaving him conscious yet severely disabled, both mentally and physically, and dependent on artificial nutrition and hydration. Two years later Rose Wendland, Robert's wife and conservator, proposed to direct his physician to remove his feeding tube and allow him to die. Florence Wendland and Rebekah Vinson (respectively Robert's mother and sister) objected to the conservator's decision. This proceeding arose under the provisions of the Probate Code authorizing courts to settle such disputes.

Following the accident, Robert remained in a coma, totally unresponsive, for several months. During this period Rose visited him daily, often with their children, and authorized treatment as necessary to maintain his health.

Robert eventually regained consciousness. His subsequent medical history is described in a comprehensive medical evaluation later submitted to the court. According to the report, Rose "first noticed signs of responsiveness sometime in late 1994 or early 1995 and alerted [Robert's] physicians and nursing staff." Intensive therapy followed. Robert's "cognitive responsiveness was observed to improve over a period of several months such that by late spring of 1995 the family and most of his health care providers agreed that he was inconsistently interacting with his environment.... At his highest level of function between February and July, 1995, Robert was able to do such things as throw and catch a ball, operate an electric wheelchair with assistance, turn pages, draw circles, draw an 'R' and perform two-step commands." For example, "[h]e was able to respond appropriately to the command 'close your eyes and open them when I say the number 3.' ... He could choose a requested color block out of four color blocks. He could set the right peg in a pegboard. Augmented communication was met with inconsistent success. He remained unable to vocalize. Eye blinking was successfully used as a communication mode for a while, however no consistent method of communication was developed."

Despite improvements made in therapy, Robert remained severely disabled, both mentally and physically....

After Robert regained consciousness and while he was undergoing therapy, Rose authorized surgery three times to replace dislodged feeding tubes. When physicians sought her permission a fourth time, she declined. She discussed the decision with her daughters and with Robert's brother Michael, all of whom believed that Robert would not have approved the procedure even if necessary to sustain his life. Rose also discussed the decision with Robert's treating physician, Dr. Kass, other physicians, and the hospital's ombudsman, all of whom apparently supported her decision. Dr. Kass, however, inserted a nasogastric feeding tube to keep Robert alive pending input from the hospital's ethics committee.

Eventually, the 20–member ethics committee unanimously approved Rose's decision. In the course of their deliberations, however, the committee did not speak with Robert's mother or sister. Florence learned, apparently through an anonymous telephone call, that Dr. Kass planned to remove Robert's feeding tube. Florence and Rebekah applied for a temporary restraining order to bar him from so doing, and the court granted the motion ex parte.

Rose immediately thereafter petitioned for appointment as Robert's conservator. In the petition, she asked the court to determine that Robert lacked the capacity to give informed consent for medical treatment and to confirm her authority "to withdraw and/or withhold medical treatment and/or life-sustaining treatment, including, but not limited to, withholding nutrition and hydration." Florence and Rebekah (hereafter sometimes objectors) opposed the petition. After a hearing, the court appointed Rose as conservator but reserved judgment on her request for authority to remove Robert's feeding tube. The court ordered the conservator to continue the current plan of physical therapy for 60 days. . . .

After the 60–day period elapsed without significant improvement in Robert's condition, the conservator renewed her request for authority to remove his feeding tube. . . .

. . .

[At] trial . . . testifying physicians agreed that Robert would not likely experience further cognitive recovery. Dr. Kass, Robert's treating physician, testified that, to the highest degree of medical certainty, Robert would never be able to make medical treatment decisions, walk, talk, feed himself, eat, drink, or control his bowel and bladder functions. Robert was able, however, according to Dr. Kass, to express "certain desires. . . . Like if he's getting tired in therapy of if he wants to quit therapy, he's usually very adamant about that. He'll either strike out or he'll refuse to perform the task." Dr. Kobrin, Robert's neurologist, testified that Robert recognized certain caregivers and would allow only specific caregivers to bathe and help him. Both Dr. Kass and Dr. Kobrin had prescribed medication for Robert's behavioral problems. Dr. Sundance, who was retained by appointed counsel to evaluate Robert, described him as being in a "minimally conscious state in that he does have some cognitive function" and the ability to "respond to his environment," but not to "interact" with it "in a more proactive way."

. . .

Robert's wife, brother and daughter recounted preaccident statements Robert had made about his attitude towards life-sustaining health care. Robert's wife recounted specific statements on two occasions. The first occasion was Rose's decision whether to turn off a respirator sustaining the life of her father, who was near death from gangrene. Rose recalls Robert saying: "I would never want to live like that, and I wouldn't want my children to see me like that and look at the hurt you're going through as an adult seeing your father like that." On cross-examination, Rose acknowledged Robert said on this occasion that Rose's father "wouldn't want to live like a vegetable" and "wouldn't want to live in a comatose state."

After his father-in-law's death, Robert developed a serious drinking problem. After a particular incident, Rose asked Michael, Robert's brother, to talk to him. When Robert arrived home the next day he was angry to see Michael there, interfering in what he considered a private family matter. Rose remembers Michael telling Robert: "I'm going to get a call from Rosie one day, and you're going to be in a terrible accident." Robert replied: "If that ever happened to me, you know what my feelings are. Don't let that happen to me. Just let me go. Leave me alone." Robert's brother Michael testified about the same conversation. Michael told Robert: "you're drinking; you're going to get drunk. . . . [Y]ou're either going to go out and kill yourself or kill someone else, or you're going to end up in the hospital like a vegetable—laying in bed just like a vegetable." Michael remembers Robert saying in response, "Mike, whatever you do[,] don't let that happen. Don't let them do that to me." Robert's daughter Katie remembers him saying on this occasion that "if he could not be a provider for his family, if he could not do all the things that he enjoyed doing, just enjoying the outdoors, just basic things, feeding himself, talking, communicating, if he could not do those things, he would not want to live."

[T]he court found the conservator "ha[d] not met her duty and burden to show by clear and convincing evidence that conservatee Robert Wendland, who is not in a persistent vegetative state nor suffering from a terminal illness would, under the circumstances, want to die. Conservator has likewise not met her burden of establishing that the withdrawal of artificially delivered nutrition and hydration is commensurate with conservatee's best interests . . ." Based on these findings, the court granted the objectors' motion for judgment, thus denying the conservator's request for confirmation of her proposal to withdraw treatment. The court also found the conservator had acted in good faith and would be permitted to remain in that office. Nevertheless, the court limited her powers by ordering that she would "have no authority to direct . . . [any] health care provider to remove the conservatee's life sustaining medical treatment in the form of withholding nutrition and hydration."

The conservator appealed this decision. The Court of Appeal reversed. . . .

II. DISCUSSION

A. The Relevant Legal Principles

. . .

1. *Constitutional and common law principles*

One relatively certain principle is that a competent adult has the right to refuse medical treatment, even treatment necessary to sustain life. The Legislature has cited this principle to justify legislation governing medical care decisions (§ 4650), and courts have invoked it as a starting point for analysis, even in cases examining the rights of incompetent persons and the duties of surrogate decision makers. This case requires us to look beyond the rights of a competent person to the rights of incompetent conservatees and the duties of conservators, but the principle just mentioned is a logical place to begin.

That a competent person has the right to refuse treatment is a statement both of common law and of state constitutional law. . . .

The Courts of Appeal have found another source for the same right in the California Constitution's privacy clause. (Cal. Const., art. I, § 1.) The court in *Bartling v. Superior Court* (Cal. Ct. App. 1984) 209 Cal. Rptr. 220 held that a competent adult with serious, probably incurable illnesses was entitled to have life-support equipment disconnected over his physicians' objection even though that would hasten his death. "The right of a competent adult patient to refuse medical treatment," the court explained, "has its origins in the constitutional right of privacy. This right is specifically guaranteed by the California Constitution (art. I, § 1). . . . The constitutional right of privacy guarantees to the individual the freedom to choose to reject, or refuse to consent to, intrusions of his bodily integrity." (Id. at p. 195, 209 Cal. Rptr. 220.) To the same effect is the decision in *Bouvia v. Superior Court* (Cal. Ct. App. 1986) 225 Cal. Rptr. 297, in which the court directed injunctive relief requiring a public hospital to comply with a competent, terminally ill patient's direction to remove a nasogastric feeding tube. . . .

. . .

In view of these authorities, the competent adult's right to refuse medical treatment may be safely considered established, at least in California.

The same right survives incapacity, in a practical sense, if exercised while competent pursuant to a law giving that act lasting validity. For some time, California law has given competent adults the power to leave formal directions for health care in the event they later become incompetent; over time, the Legislature has afforded ever greater scope to that power. . . .

. . .

In contrast, decisions made by conservators typically derive their authority from a different basis—the *parens patriae* power of the state to protect incompetent persons. Unlike an agent or a surrogate for health care, who is voluntarily appointed by a competent person, a conservator is appointed by the court because the conservatee "has been adjudicated to lack the capacity to make health care decisions."

. . .

B. The Present Case

This background illuminates the parties' arguments, which reduce in essence to this: The conservator has claimed the power under [the probate code], as she interprets it, to direct the conservatee's health care providers to cease providing artificial nutrition and hydration. In opposition, the objectors have contended the statute violates the conservatee's rights to privacy and life under the facts of this case if the conservator's interpretation of the statute is correct.

. . .

1.   *The primary standard: a decision in accordance with the conservatee's wishes*

The conservator asserts she offered sufficient evidence at trial to satisfy the primary statutory standard, which contemplates a decision "in accordance with the conservatee's . . . wishes. . . ." The trial court, however, determined the evidence on this point was insufficient. The conservator did "not [meet] her duty and burden," the court expressly found, "to show by clear and convincing evidence that [the] conservatee . . ., who is not in a persistent vegetative state nor suffering from a terminal illness would, under the circumstances, want to die."

The conservator argues the Legislature understood and intended that the low preponderance of the evidence standard would apply. Certainly this was the Law Revision Commission's understanding. . . .

The objectors, in opposition, argue that [the probate code] would be unconstitutional if construed to permit a conservator to end the life of a conscious conservatee based on a finding by the low preponderance of the evidence standard that the latter would not want to live. We see no basis for holding the statute unconstitutional on its face. We do, however, find merit in the objectors' argument. We therefore construe the statute to minimize the possibility of its unconstitutional application by requiring clear and convincing evidence of a conscious conservatee's wish to refuse life-sustaining treatment when the conservator relies on that asserted wish to justify withholding life-sustaining treatment. . . . [W]e see no constitutional reason to apply the higher evidentiary standard to the majority of health care decisions made by conservators not contemplating a conscious conservatee's death. . . .

Notwithstanding the foregoing, one must acknowledge that the primary standard for decisionmaking set out in [the probate code] does articulate what will in some cases form a constitutional basis for a conservator's decision to end the life of a conscious patient: deference to the patient's own wishes. This standard also appears in the new provisions governing decisions by agents and surrogates designated by competent adults. As applied in that context, the requirement that decisions be made "in accordance with the principal's individual health care instructions . . . and other wishes" merely respects the principal-agent relationship and gives effect to the properly expressed wishes of a competent adult. Because a competent adult may refuse life-sustaining treatment, it follows that an agent properly and voluntarily designated by the principal may refuse treatment on the principal's behalf unless, of course, such authority is revoked.

The only apparent purpose of requiring conservators to make decisions in accordance with the conservatee's wishes, when those wishes are known, is to enforce the fundamental principle of personal autonomy. The same requirement, as applied to agents and surrogates freely designated by competent persons, enforces the principles of agency. A reasonable person presumably will designate for such purposes only a person in whom the former reposes the highest degree of confidence. A conservator, in contrast, is *not* an agent of the conservatee, and unlike a freely designated agent cannot be presumed to have special knowledge of the conservatee's health care wishes. A person with "sufficient capacity ... to form an intelligent preference" may nominate his or her own conservator, but the nomination is not binding because the appointment remains "solely in the discretion of the court". Furthermore, while statutory law gives preference to spouses and other persons related to the conservatee, who might know something of the conservatee's health care preferences, the law also permits the court in its sole discretion to appoint unrelated persons and even public conservators. While it may be constitutionally permissible to assume that an agent freely designated by a formerly competent person to make all health care decisions, including life-ending ones, will resolve such questions "in accordance with the principal's ... wishes", one cannot apply the same assumption to conservators and conservatees. For this reason, when the legal premise of a conservator's decision to end a conservatee's life by withholding medical care is that the conservatee would refuse such care, to apply a high standard of proof will help to ensure the reliability of the decision.

The function of a standard of proof is to instruct the fact finder concerning the degree of confidence our society deems necessary in the correctness of factual conclusions for a particular type of adjudication, to allocate the risk of error between the litigants, and to indicate the relative importance attached to the ultimate decision.... The default standard of proof in civil cases is the preponderance of the evidence. Nevertheless, courts have applied the clear and convincing evidence standard when necessary to protect important rights.

. . .

In this case, the importance of the ultimate decision and the risk of error are manifest. So too should be the degree of confidence required in the necessary findings of fact. The ultimate decision is whether a conservatee lives or dies, and the risk is that a conservator, claiming statutory authority to end a conscious conservatee's life "in accordance with the conservatee's ... wishes" by withdrawing artificial nutrition and hydration, will make a decision with which the conservatee subjectively disagrees and which subjects the conservatee to starvation, dehydration and death. This would represent the gravest possible affront to a conservatee's state constitutional right to privacy, in the sense of freedom from unwanted bodily intrusions, and to life. While the practical ability to make autonomous health care decisions does not survive incompetence, the ability to perceive unwanted intrusions may. Certainly it is possible, as the conservator here urges, that an incompetent and uncommunicative but conscious conservatee might perceive the efforts to keep him alive as unwanted intrusion and the withdrawal of those efforts as welcome release. But the decision to treat is reversible. The decision to withdraw treatment is not. The role of a high evidentiary standard in such a case is to adjust the risk of error to favor the less perilous result....

In conclusion, to interpret [the probate code] to permit a conservator to withdraw artificial nutrition and hydration from a conscious conservatee based on a finding, by a mere preponderance of the evidence, that the conservatee would refuse treatment creates a serious risk that the law will be unconstitutionally applied in some cases, with grave injury to fundamental rights. Under these circumstances, we may properly ask whether the statute may be construed in a way that mitigates the risk.... Here, where the risk to conservatees' rights is grave and the proposed construction is consistent with the language of the statute, to construe the statute to avoid the constitutional risk is an appropriate exercise of judicial power.

. . .

One amicus curiae argues that "[i]mposing so high an evidentiary burden [i.e., clear and convincing evidence] would ... frustrate many genuine treatment desires—particularly the choices of young people, who are less likely than older people to envision the need for advanced directives, or poor people, who are less likely than affluent people to have the resources to obtain formal legal documents." But the Legislature has already accommodated this concern in large part by permitting patients to nominate surrogate decision makers by orally informing a supervising physician and by giving effect to specific oral health care instructions. To go still farther, by giving conclusive effect to wishes inferred from informal, oral statements proved only by a preponderance of the evidence, may serve the interests of incompetent persons whose wishes are correctly determined, but to do so also poses an unacceptable risk of violating other incompetent patients' rights to privacy and life, as already explained. To the argument that applying a high standard of proof in such cases impermissibly burdens the right to determine one's own medical treatment, one need only repeat the United States Supreme Court's response to the same assertion: "The differences between the choice made *by* a competent person to refuse medical treatment, and the choice made *for* an incompetent person by someone else to refuse medical treatment, are so obviously different that the State is warranted in establishing rigorous procedures for the latter class of cases which do not apply to the former class." (*Cruzan, supra*, 497 U.S. 261, 287, fn. 12).

. . .

In the case before us, the trial court found that the conservator failed to show "by clear and convincing evidence that conservatee Robert Wendland, who is not in a persistent vegetative state nor suffering from a terminal illness would, under the circumstances, want to die." The conservator does not appear to challenge the trial court's finding on this point; her challenge, rather, is to the trial court's understanding of the law. For these reasons, we need not review the sufficiency of the evidence to support the finding. Nevertheless, given the exceptional circumstances of this case, we note that the finding appears to be correct.

. . .

2.   *The best interest standard*

Having rejected the conservator's argument that withdrawing artificial hydration and nutrition would have been "in accordance with the conservatee's ... wishes", we must next consider her contention that the same action would have been proper under the fallback best interest standard. Under that standard, "the conservator shall make the decision in accordance with the conservator's determination of the conservatee's best interest. In determining the conservatee's best interest, the conservator shall consider the conservatee's personal values to the extent known to the conservator." The trial court, as noted, ruled the conservator had the burden of establishing that the withdrawal of artificially delivered nutrition and hydration was in the conservatee's best interest, and had not met that burden.

Here, as before, the conservator argues that the trial court applied too high a standard of proof. This follows, she contends, from [the probate code], which gives her as conservator "the *exclusive* authority" to give consent for such medical treatment as she "in good faith based on medical advice determines to be necessary." ... Based on these statements, the conservator argues the trial court has no power other than to verify that she has made the decision for which the Probate Code expressly calls: a "good faith" decision "based on medical advice" and "consider[ing] the conservatee's personal values" whether treatment is "necessary" in the conservatee's "best interest." The trial court, as noted, rejected the conservator's assessment of the conservatee's best interest but nevertheless found by clear and convincing evidence that she had acted "in good faith, based on medical evidence and after consideration of the conservatee's best interests, including his likely wishes, based on his previous statements." This finding, the conservator concludes, should end the litigation as a matter of law in her favor.

... To be sure, the statute provides that "the conservator shall make the decision in accordance with *the conservator's determination* of the conservatee's best interest." But the conservator herself concedes the court must be able to review her decision for abuse of discretion. This much, at least, follows from the conservator's status as an officer of the court subject to judicial supervision. While the assessment of a conservatee's best interest belongs in the first instance to the conservator, this does not mean the court must invariably defer to the conservator regardless of the evidence.

In the exceptional case where a conservator proposes to end the life of a conscious but incompetent conservatee, we believe the same factor that principally justifies applying the clear and convincing evidence standard to a determination of the conservatee's wishes also justifies applying that standard to a determination of the conservatee's best interest: The decision threatens the conservatee's fundamental rights to privacy and life....

We need not in this case attempt to define the extreme factual predicates that, if proved by clear and convincing evidence, might support a conservator's decision that withdrawing life support would be in the best interest of a conscious conservatee. Here, the conservator offered no basis for such a finding other than her own subjective judgment that the conservatee did not enjoy a satisfactory quality of life and legally insufficient evidence to the effect that he would have wished to die. On this record, the trial court's decision was correct.

III.   CONCLUSION

For the reasons set out above, we conclude the superior court correctly required the conservator to prove, by clear and convincing evidence, either that the conservatee wished to refuse life-sustaining treatment or that to withhold such treatment would have been in his best interest; lacking such evidence, the superior court correctly denied the conservator's request for permission to withdraw artificial hydration and nutrition.... [O]ur decision today affects only a narrow class of persons: conscious conservatees who have not left formal directions for health care and whose conservators propose to withhold life-sustaining treatment for the purpose of causing their conservatees' deaths. Our conclusion does not affect permanently unconscious patients, including those who are comatose or in a persistent vegetative state, persons who have designated agents or other surrogates for health care, or conservatees for whom conservators have made medical decisions other than those intended to bring about the death of a conscious conservatee.

The decision of the Court of Appeal is reversed.

3.   THE SPECIAL CASE OF DISABLED NEWBORNS

Traditionally, law has authorized parents to make medical decisions for their children. It is assumed that parents will act with the best interests of their children in mind. Parental authority, however, is not unlimited and can be overridden by the state if children are abused or neglected. As a consequence, courts have intervened and ordered lifesaving medical treatment over parental objection.

Debates about the ethical and legal implications of forgoing treatment for seriously ill newborns and whether, if at all, parents are the appropriate decision makers began appearing in the literature in the early 1970s. More recently, parental authority has been challenged by physicians and institutions who would like to refuse or terminate medical treatment, over parental objection, on grounds of futility. Both sets of issues raise profound questions about who should make medical decisions for the seriously ill newborn.

Are parents best situated to make these decisions? Will parents be able to disregard considerations such as costs, concerns for family stability and impact on siblings? Should they? Will parents be able to overcome their own sense of guilt or loss that the birth of a seriously ill newborn may cause when they expected a normal child? Should parents be the deciders if they will not have day-to-day caretaking responsibilities or bear the expense of medical care that is considered to be futile? What if parents cannot agree?

If parental decisionmaking is desirable, should their decisions be subject to review and monitoring? If such review is warranted should it be undertaken at institutional, state or national levels? These are the sorts of questions raised by the materials in the section.

President's Commission, Deciding to Forego Life–Sustaining Treatment: A Report on the Ethical, Medical, and Legal Issues in Treatment Decisions
197–203 (March 1983).

Remarkable advances in neonatal care now make it possible to sustain the lives of many newborn infants who only one or two decades ago would have died in the first days or weeks after birth. Between 1970 and 1980, the death rate in the first 28 days of life (the neonatal period) was almost halved, the greatest proportional decrease in any decade since national birth statistics were first gathered in 1915. Improvement among the smallest infants—those at greatest risk of death and illness—has been especially dramatic: for newborns weighing 1000–1500 grams, the mortality rate has dropped from 50% to 20% since 1961; fully half the live-born infants weighing less than 1000 grams (2.2 pounds) now survive, compared with less than 10% just 20 years ago. And marked improvements have also been reported in the survival rate of infants with certain congenital defects.

Not all seriously ill newborns fare well, however. Some infants with low birth weight or severe defects cannot survive for long, despite the most aggressive efforts to save them; others suffer severe impairments either as a component of their conditions or as a result of treatments. Thus medicine's increased ability to forestall death in seriously ill newborns has magnified the already difficult task of physicians and parents who must attempt to assess which infants will benefit from various medical interventions, and which will not. Not only does this test the limits of medical certainty in diagnosis and prognosis, it also raises profound ethical issues.

Decisions about whether life-sustaining treatment is warranted for newborns arise most frequently in two general categories: infants of low birth weight and infants with life-threatening congenital abnormalities.

Low birth weight infants. Birth weight is a very strong predictor of illness and death in the neonatal period; in general, the lower the birth weight, the higher the mortality rate. About 230,000 infants born in the United States each year—7% of all live births—weigh 2500 grams or less, which is classified as low birth weight (LBW).... Very low birth weight infants—those who weigh less than 1500 grams—face an especially high risk of death; although they constitute only 1% of all newborns, they account for almost half of all infant deaths. LBW infants are also at increased risk for serious congenital defects and impairments.

Most LBW infants are premature, although some are small despite a normal gestation period. Within each LBW category, the prognosis improves with increased gestational age....

Infants with congenital abnormalities. About 4% of the approximately 3.3 million infants born in this country each year have one or more readily detectable congenital abnormalities. These infants are often born at term, rather than prematurely. These abnormalities have been traced to inheritance of defective genes (as in phenylketonuria or Marfan syndrome), chromosomal abnormalities (as in Down Syndrome), and environmental factors, including *in utero* viral infection or chemical exposure (one well-known instance being children born with limb abnormalities because their mothers had taken thalidomide). Although many causes of birth defects have been identified, the majority of congenital abnormalities are of unknown etiology and probably result from a complex interaction of genetic and environmental factors.

Two types of congenital abnormalities have been especially prominent in discussions of the ethics of neonatal care: neural tube defects (NTDs), and permanent handicaps combined with surgically correctable, life-threatening lesions. Defects involving the neural tube, which is the embryonic precursor of the brain and spinal cord, are among the most common serious birth defects of unknown etiology, affecting approximately two of every 1000 babies born in the United States. One type of NTD is anencephaly, a condition in which the brain is entirely or substantially absent. Anencephalic infants usually die within a few hours or days. Another type of NTD, meningomyelocele (spina bifida) involves abnormal development of the brain or spinal cord. Spina bifida causes physical and/or mental impairments that range widely in severity and frequently involve many organ systems. Vigorous surgical, medical, and rehabilitative therapies have improved the prognosis for many children with spina bifida. Some individuals with this condition have normal intelligence and can lead independent lives.

Public attention has . . . been focused on the second group of cases—infants who have both a correctable life-threatening defect and a permanent, irremediable handicap that is not life-threatening, such as mental retardation. One well-known example is Down Syndrome, which occurs once in about every 700 live births. Individuals with Down Syndrome are mentally retarded, although the precise extent of retardation cannot be determined in early infancy. Babies with this syndrome often have other congenital defects, particularly cardiac abnormalities. Most Down Syndrome infants do not require any unusual medical care at birth, but a minority have a complication that would be fatal unless surgically corrected during the first year of life. The two most common problems are gastrointestinal blockage and congenital heart defects. Children with an obstruction at the outlet of the stomach, for example, cannot be fed; untreated, they would develop a fatal pneumonia or starve to death. Surgical repair of this defect, however, is typically successful.

. . .

NOTES AND QUESTIONS

1. In April 1982, "Baby Doe," a newborn male with Down's syndrome and a blocked esophagus, was allowed to die with court approval after his parents refused treatment. *In re Infant Doe*, No. GU 8204–004A (Cir. Ct. Monroe Cty., Ind., Apr. 12, 1982), writ of mandamus dismissed sub nom. *State ex rel. Infant Doe v. Baker*, No. 482 S 140 (Indiana Supreme Court, May 27, 1982). Efforts to seek United States Supreme Court review were mooted because the child died. The records in this case are sealed so some pertinent facts are not available. For a description of the medical circumstances, see Correspondence, 309 NEW ENG. J. MED. 664 (1983).

The public outcry surrounding this incident was so intense that on April 30, 1982, President Ronald Reagan sent a memorandum to the Attorney General and the Secretary of Health and Human Services (HHS) citing the "*Baby Doe*" case and noting that federal law prohibits discrimination against the handicapped. In response, HHS issued on May 18, 1982, the "notice" to health care providers to "remind affected parties of the applicability of § 504 of the Rehabilitation Act of 1973."

2. Regulations subsequently issued by HHS were invalidated in *Bowen v. American Hosp. Ass'n*, 476 U.S. 610, 106 S.Ct. 2101, 90 L.Ed.2d 584 (1986). In its plurality opinion (Burger, C.J., concurring), the Supreme Court found that the mandatory provisions of the regulations were not authorized by § 504 of the Rehabilitation Act of 1973.

The Secretary of HHS had identified two types of violations of § 504 to support federal oversight of the care of disabled newborns: (1) a hospital's refusal to furnish aid to a disabled newborn solely because of the newborn's handicap and (2) a hospital's refusal to report cases of suspected medical neglect. *Id.* at 628–29.

As to the first alleged violation, the Court indicated that the Secretary had conceded that there was no case of nontreatment of an infant by a hospital "solely by reason of his handicap" because parental refusal for permission to treat was the major reason for withholding treatment. *Id.* at 631–32. The second type of case would be a violation only if the Government could show that nonreporting occurred in cases of possibly neglected handicapped infants and not in cases of possibly neglected nonhandicapped infants. *Id.* at 637–38. The Court continued:

> [N]othing in the statute authorizes the Secretary to dispense with the law's focus on discrimination and instead to employ federal resources to save the lives of handicapped newborns, without regard to whether they are victims of discrimination by recipients of federal funds or not.

Id. at 647.

The Court added that by commanding state agencies to enforce the reporting requirements, the Secretary improperly "conscripted [them] against their will as the foot soldiers in a federal crusade," and that section 504 does not give HHS authority to mandate to state agencies how they allocate their services and re-sources. Id. at 642. For a detailed account of these events, see Steven R. Smith, *Disabled Newborns and the Federal Child Abuse Amendments: Tenuous Protection*, 37 HASTINGS L. J. 765 (1986).

3. Congress amended the Child Abuse Prevention and Treatment Act in 1984. 42 U.S.C.A. § 5102 provides in pertinent part:

> (3) the term "withholding of medically indicated treatment" means the failure to respond to the infant's life-threatening conditions by providing treatment (including appropriate nutrition, hydration, and medication) which, in the treating physician's or physicians' reasonable medical judgment, will be most likely to be effective in ameliorating or correcting all such conditions, except that the term does not include the failure to provide treatment (other than appropriate nutrition, hydration, or medication) to an infant when, in the treating physician's or physicians' reasonable medical judgment, (A) the infant is chronically ill and irreversibly comatose; (B) the provision of such treatment would (i) merely prolong dying, (ii) not be effective in ameliorating or correcting all of the infant's life-threatening conditions, or (iii) otherwise be futile in terms of survival of the infant; or (C) the provision of such treatment would be virtually futile in terms of the survival of the infant and the treatment itself under such circumstances would be inhumane.

Is the abuse and neglect approach to resolving questions of appropriate treatment of handicapped newborns better than the discrimination approach? Would it be preferable to leave decisions to health care professionals and family? Consider the view of several doctors about the regulations at issue in *Bowen*. Are their remarks equally applicable to the definition of medical neglect contained in 42 U.S.C.A. § 5102?

> [A] major drawback of the Baby Doe rule stems from the nature of regulation itself.... [P]hrases such as "merely prolong dying," "death is imminent," and "survival of the infant" have implicit time frames that have not been speci-fied.... The rule only serves to create phantom acceptable and nonacceptable

courses of action that are not easily identifiable in the everyday dilemmas arising in delivery rooms.... The risk of giving the impression of being able to state ... courses of action, and leaving open the interpretation of these courses, is litigation.

D.K. Stevenson et al., *The "Baby Doe" Rule*, 255 JAMA 1909, 1911 (1986).

In order to comply with the Child Abuse and Prevention Act, the states must establish by October 9, 1985, programs for responding to reported cases, including those of "withholding of medically indicated treatment," of medical neglect. 42 U.S.C.A. § 5103(b)(2)(K). Grants to states are conditioned on their compliance with federal requirements. The regulations issued April 15, 1985, by HHS to implement this new law require that the states' programs be in writing, and that the procedures include mechanisms to obtain "[a]ccess to medical records" and "an independent medical examination of the infant." 45 C.F.R. § 1340.15(c)(4) (1985). "Infant" is defined as any child of less than one year. 45 C.F.R. § 1340.15(b)(3)(i) (1985).

The regulations included an appendix that HHS labeled "Interpretive Guidelines." 45 C.F.R. Pt. 1340. The stated purpose of this appendix is to give HHS's definition of key phrases that appear both in the Child Abuse Amendments of 1984 and in the subsequent regulations. HHS believed this was necessary for "effective implementation of the program established by the Child Abuse Amendments." Is the following interpretation from the appendix an accurate reading of the Act?

> [One] feature of the statutory definition [of "withholding of medically indicated treatment"] is that even when one of these three circumstances [(A)(B) and (C) within § 5102(3)] is present, and thus the failure to provide treatment is not a "withholding of medically indicated treatment," the infant must nonetheless be provided with appropriate nutrition, hydration, and medication.

HHS also issued "Model Guidelines for Health Care Providers to Establish Infant Care Review Committees." 50 Fed. Reg. 14,893 (1985). The purposes of the ICRC are "(1) To educate hospital personnel and families of disabled infants with life threatening conditions; (2) To recommend institutional policies and guidelines concerning the withholding of medically indicated treatment from disabled infants with life-threatening conditions; and (3) To offer counsel and review in cases involving disabled infants with life-threatening conditions." *Id.* at 14,894. HHS recommended that an ICRC be composed of at least one physician, nurse, hospital administrator, social worker, representative of a disability group, and a lay member and include a medical staff chairperson. *Id.* Does the utilization of committees such as the ICRCs unduly infringe on the rights of parents? Health care professionals? Alternatively, are they likely to improve the quality of decisionmaking for disabled newborns? Should such committees be involved in decisionmaking for all incompetent patients? Only those incompetent patients whose wishes are not known?

One physician commentator argues that the controversy resulting in the Baby Doe regulations was a diversion if viewed against the background of child health needs. He argues that the central issue for pediatrics is infant mortality but, as a result of the Baby Doe debate, intensive care rather than prevention will become the ethical imperative. John Lantos, *Baby Doe Five Years Later*, 317 NEW ENG. J. MED. 444 (1987).

Miller v. Hospital Corp. of America (HCA), Inc.

Supreme Court of Texas, 2003.
118 S.W.3d 758.

■ ENOCH, J.

The narrow question we must decide is whether Texas law recognizes a claim by parents for either battery or negligence because their premature infant, born alive but in distress at only twenty-three weeks of gestation, was provided resuscitative medical treatment by physicians at a hospital without parental consent. The court of appeals, with one justice dissenting, held that neither claim could be maintained as a matter of law because parents have no right to refuse urgently-needed life-sustaining medical treatment for their child unless the child's condition is "certifiably terminal" under the Natural Death Act (now the Advance Directives Act). And here it is undisputed that the Millers' new-born infant was not "certifiably terminal."

Although we agree with the court of appeals' judgment, our reasoning differs somewhat. First, there is no dispute in the evidence that the Millers' premature infant could not be fully evaluated for medical treatment until birth. As a result, any decisions concerning treatment for the Millers' child would not be fully informed decisions until birth. Second, the evidence further established that once the infant was born, the physician attending the birth was faced with emergent circumstances—*i.e.,* the child might survive with treatment but would likely die if treatment was not provided before either parental consent or a court order overriding the withholding of such consent could be obtained.

We hold that circumstances like these provide an exception to the general rule imposing liability on a physician for treating a child without consent. That exception eliminates the Millers' claim for battery. We further conclude that the Millers' negligence claim—premised not on any physician's negligence in treating the infant but on the hospital's policies, or lack thereof, permitting a physician to treat their infant without parental consent—fails as a matter of law for the same reasons. We accordingly affirm the court of appeals' judgment.

I. Facts

The unfortunate circumstances of this case began in August 1990, when approximately four months before her due date, Karla Miller was admitted to Woman's Hospital of Texas (the "Hospital") in premature labor. An ultrasound revealed that Karla's fetus weighed about 629 grams or 1 1/4 pounds and had a gestational age of approximately twenty-three weeks. Because of the fetus's prematurity, Karla's physicians began administering a drug designed to stop labor.

Karla's physicians subsequently discovered that Karla had an infection that could endanger her life and require them to induce delivery. Dr. Mark Jacobs, Karla's obstetrician, and Dr. Donald Kelley, a neonatologist at the Hospital, informed Karla and her husband, Mark Miller, that if they had to induce delivery, the infant had little chance of being born alive. The physicians also informed the Millers that if the infant was born alive, it would most probably suffer severe impairments, including cerebral palsy, brain hemorrhaging, blindness, lung disease, pulmonary infections, and mental retardation. Mark testified at trial that the physicians told him they had never had such a premature infant live and that anything they did to sustain the infant's life would be guesswork.

After their discussion, Drs. Jacobs and Kelley asked the Millers to decide whether physicians should treat the infant upon birth if they were forced to induce delivery. At approximately noon that day, the Millers informed Drs. Jacob and Kelley that they wanted no heroic measures performed on the infant and they wanted nature to take its course. Mark testified that he understood heroic measures to mean performing resuscitation, chest massage, and using life support machines. Dr. Kelley recorded the Millers' request in Karla's medical notes, and Dr. Jacobs informed the medical staff at the Hospital that no neonatologist would be needed at delivery. Mark then left the Hospital to make funeral arrangements for the infant.

In the meantime, the nursing staff informed other Hospital personnel of Dr. Jacobs' instruction that no neonatologist would be present in the delivery room when the Millers' infant was born. An afternoon of meetings involving Hospital administrators and physicians followed. Between approximately 4:00 p.m. and 4:30 p.m. that day, Anna Summerfield, the director of the Hospital's neonatal intensive care unit, and several physicians, including Dr. Jacobs, met with Mark upon his return to the Hospital to further discuss the situation. Mark testified that Ms. Summerfield announced at the meeting that the Hospital had a policy requiring resuscitation of any baby who was born weighing over 500 grams. Although Ms. Summerfield agreed that she said that, the only written Hospital policy produced described the Natural Death Act and did not mention resuscitating infants over 500 grams.

Moreover, the physicians at the meeting testified that they and Hospital administrators agreed only that a neonatologist would be present to evaluate the Millers' infant at birth and decide whether to resuscitate based on the infant's condition at that time. As Dr. Jacobs testified:

> [W]hat we finally decided that everyone wanted to do was to not make the call prior to the time we actually saw the baby. Deliver the baby, because you see there was this [question] is the baby really 23 weeks, or is the baby further along, how big is the baby, what are we dealing with. We decided to let the neonatologist make the call by looking directly at the baby at birth.

Another physician who attended the meeting agreed, testifying that to deny any attempts at resuscitation without seeing the infant's condition would be inappropriate and below the standard of care.

Although Dr. Eduardo Otero, the neonatologist present in the delivery room when Sidney was born, did not attend that meeting, he confirmed that he needed to actually see Sidney before deciding what treatment, if any, would be appropriate:

> Q. Can you . . . tell us from a worst case scenario to a best case scenario, what type of possibilities you've seen in your own personal practice?
>
> A. Well, the worst case scenario is . . . the baby comes out and it's dead, it has no heart rate. . . . Or you have babies that actually go through a rocky start then cruise through the rest and go home. And they may have small handicaps or they may have some problems but—learning disabilities or something like that, but in general, all babies are normal children or fairly normal children.

Q. And is there any way that you could have made a prediction, at the time of Sidney's birth, where she would fall in that range of different options?

A. No, sir.

Q. Is there any way that you can make that decision, as to whether the newborn infant will be viable or not in a case such as Sidney's, before the time of delivery, an assessment at the time of delivery?

A. No.

Mark testified that, after the meeting, Hospital administrators asked him to sign a consent form allowing resuscitation according to the Hospital's plan, but he refused. Mark further testified that when he asked how he could prevent resuscitation, Hospital administrators told him that he could do so by removing Karla from the Hospital, which was not a viable option given her condition. Dr. Jacobs then noted in Karla's medical charts that a plan for evaluating the infant upon her birth was discussed at that afternoon meeting.

That evening, Karla's condition worsened and her amniotic sac broke. Dr. Jacobs determined that he would have to augment labor so that the infant would be delivered before further complications to Karla's health developed. Dr. Jacobs accordingly stopped administering the drug to Karla that was designed to stop labor, substituting instead a drug designed to augment labor. At 11:30 p.m. that night, Karla delivered a premature female infant weighing 615 grams, which the Millers named Sidney. Sidney's actual gestational age was twenty-three and one-seventh weeks. And she was born alive.

Dr. Otero noted that Sidney had a heart beat, albeit at a rate below that normally found in full-term babies. He further noted that Sidney, although blue in color and limp, gasped for air, spontaneously cried, and grimaced. Dr. Otero also noted that Sidney displayed no dysmorphic features other than being premature. He immediately "bagged" and "intubated" Sidney to oxygenate her blood; he then placed her on ventilation. He explained why:

> Because this baby is alive and this is a baby that has a reasonable chance of living. And again, this is a baby that is not necessarily going to have problems later on. There are babies that survive at this gestational age that—with this birth weight, that later on go on and do well.

Neither Karla nor Mark objected at the time to the treatment provided.

Sidney initially responded well to the treatment, as reflected by her Apgar scores. An Apgar score records five different components of a newborn infant: respiratory effort, heart rate, reflex activity, color, and muscle tone. Each component gets a score of zero, one, or two, with a score of two representing the best condition. Sidney's total Apgar score improved from a three at one minute after birth to a six at five minutes after birth. But at some point during the first few days after birth, Sidney suffered a brain hemorrhage—a complication not uncommon in infants born so prematurely.

There was conflicting testimony about whether Sidney's hemorrhage occurred because of the treatment provided or in spite of it. Regardless of the cause, as predicted by Karla's physicians, the hemorrhage caused Sidney to suffer severe physical and mental impairments. At the time of trial, Sidney was seven years old and could not walk, talk, feed herself, or sit up on her own. The evidence demonstrated that Sidney was legally blind, suffered from severe mental retardation, cerebral palsy, seizures, and spastic quadriparesis in her limbs. She could not be toilet-trained and required a shunt in her brain to drain fluids that accumulate there and needed care twenty-four hours a day. The evidence further demonstrated that her circumstances will not change.

The Millers sued HCA, Inc., HCA–Hospital Corporation of America, Hospital Corporation of America, and Columbia/HCA Healthcare Corporation (collectively, "HCA"), and the Hospital, a subsidiary of HCA. They did not sue any physicians ... that actually treated Sidney....

The Millers' claims stemmed from their allegations that despite their instructions to the contrary, the Hospital not only resuscitated Sidney but performed experimental procedures and administered experimental drugs, without which, in all reasonable medical probability, Sidney would not have survived. The Millers also alleged that the Hospital's acts and/or omissions were performed with HCA's full knowledge and consent....

. . .

Though the Hospital was not a party at the trial against HCA, the trial court submitted questions to the jury about the Hospital's conduct. The jury found that the Hospital, without the consent of Karla or Mark Miller, performed resuscitative treatment on Sidney. The jury also found that the Hospital's and HCA's negligence "proximately caused the occurrence in question." The jury concluded that HCA and the Hospital were grossly negligent and that the Hospital acted with malice. The jury also determined that Dr. Otero acted as the Hospital's agent in resuscitating Sidney and that HCA was responsible for the Hospital's conduct under alter ego and single business enterprise theories. The trial court rendered judgment jointly and severally against the HCA defendants on the jury's verdict of $29,400,000 in actual damages for medical expenses, $17,503,066 in pre-judgment interest, and $13,500,000 in exemplary damages.

HCA appealed. The court of appeals, with one justice dissenting, reversed and rendered judgment that the Millers take nothing.

. . .

II. Analysis

This case requires us to determine the respective roles that parents and healthcare providers play in deciding whether to treat an infant who is born alive but in distress and is so premature that, despite advancements in neonatal intensive care, has a largely uncertain prognosis. Although the parties have cited numerous constitutional provisions, statutes, and cases, we conclude that neither the Texas Legislature nor our case law has addressed this specific situation. We accordingly begin our analysis by focusing on what the existing case law and statutes do address.

Generally speaking, the custody, care, and nurture of an infant resides in the first instance with the parents. As the United States Supreme Court has acknowledged, parents are presumed to be the appropriate decision-makers for their infants:

> Our jurisprudence historically has reflected Western civilization concepts of the family as a unit with broad parental authority over minor children. Our cases have consistently followed that course; our constitutional system long ago rejected any notion that a child is "the mere creature of the State" and, on the contrary, asserted that parents generally "have the right, coupled with the high duty, to recognize and prepare [their children] for additional obligations." ... Surely, this includes a "high duty" to recognize symptoms of illness and to seek and follow medical advice. The law's concept of the family rests on a presumption that parents possess what a child lacks in maturity, experience, and capacity for judgment required for making life's difficult decisions. More important, historically it has recognized that natural bonds of affection lead parents to act in the best interests of their children (*quoting* Parham v. J.R., 442 U.S. 584, 602).

The Texas Legislature has likewise recognized that parents are presumed to be appropriate decision-makers, giving parents the right to consent to their infant's medical care and surgical treatment. A logical corollary of that right, as the court of appeals here recognized, is that parents have the right not to consent to certain medical care for their infant, *i.e.*, parents have the right to refuse certain medical care.

Of course, this broad grant of parental decision-making authority is not without limits. The State's role as *parens patriae* permits it to intercede in parental decision-making under certain circumstances. As the United States Supreme Court has noted:

> [A]s persons unable to protect themselves, infants fall under the parens patriae power of the state. In the exercise of this authority, the state not only punishes parents whose conduct has amounted to abuse or neglect of their children but may also supervene parental decisions before they become operative to ensure that the choices made are not so detrimental to a child's interests as to amount to neglect and abuse.

But the Supreme Court has also pointed out:

> [A]s long as parents choose from professionally accepted treatment options the choice is rarely reviewed in court and even less frequently supervened. The courts have exercised their authority to appoint a guardian for a child when the parents are not capable of participating in the decisionmaking or when they have made decisions that evidence substantial lack of concern for the child's interests. *Id.*

The Texas Legislature has acknowledged the limitations on parental decision-making. For example, the Legislature has provided in the Family Code that the rights and duties of parents are subject to modification by court order. And Texas courts have recognized their authority to enter orders, under appropriate circumstances, appointing a temporary managing conservator who may consent to medical treatment refused by a child's parents.

With respect to consent, the requirement that permission be obtained before providing medical treatment is based on the patient's right to receive information adequate for him or her to exercise an informed decision to accept or refuse the treatment. Thus, the general rule in Texas is that a physician who provides treatment without consent commits a battery. But there are exceptions. . . .

In *Moss v. Rishworth*, 222 S.W. 225, 226 (1920), the court held that a physician commits a "legal wrong" by operating on a minor without parental consent when there is "an absolute necessity for a prompt operation, but not emergent in the sense that death would likely result immediately upon the failure to perform it." But the court in *Moss* expressly noted that "it [was] not contended [there] that any real danger would have resulted to the child had time been taken to consult the parent with reference to the operation." *Id. Moss* therefore implicitly acknowledges that a physician does not commit a legal wrong by operating on a minor without consent when the operation is performed under emergent circumstances—*i.e.,* when death is likely to result immediately upon the failure to perform it. *See id.*

Moss guides us here. We hold that a physician, who is confronted with emergent circumstances and provides life-sustaining treatment to a minor child, is not liable for not first obtaining consent from the parents. . . .

Providing treatment to a child under emergent circumstances does not imply consent to treatment despite actual notice of refusal to consent. Rather, it is an exception to the general rule that a physician commits a battery by providing medical treatment without consent. As such, the exception is narrowly circumscribed and arises only in emergent circumstances when there is no time to consult the parents or seek court intervention if the parents withhold consent before death is likely to result to the child. Though in situations of this character, the physician should attempt to secure parental consent if possible, the physician will not be liable under a battery or negligence theory solely for proceeding with the treatment absent consent.

We recognize that the Restatement (Second) of Torts § 892D provides that an individual is not liable for providing emergency treatment without consent if that individual has no reason to believe that the other, if he or she had the opportunity to consent, would decline. But that requirement is inapplicable here because, as we have discussed, the emergent circumstances exception does not imply consent.

Further, the emergent circumstances exception acknowledges that the harm from failing to treat outweighs any harm threatened by the proposed treatment, because the harm from failing to provide life-sustaining treatment under emergent circumstances is death. And as we acknowledged . . . albeit in the different context of a wrongful life claim, it is impossible for the courts to calculate the relative benefits of an impaired life versus no life at all.

Following these guiding principles, we now determine whether the Millers can maintain their battery and negligence claims against HCA. The jury found that the Hospital, through Dr. Otero, treated Sidney without the Millers' consent. The parties do not challenge that finding. Thus, we only address whether the Hospital was required to seek court intervention to

overturn the lack of parental consent—which it undisputedly did not do—
before Dr. Otero could treat Sidney without committing a battery.

The Millers acknowledge that numerous physicians at trial agreed
that, absent an emergency situation, the proper course of action is court
intervention when health care providers disagree with parents' refusal to
consent to a child's treatment. And the Millers contend that, as a matter of
law, no emergency existed that would excuse the Hospital's treatment of
Sidney without their consent or a court order overriding their refusal to
consent. The Millers point out that before Sidney's birth, Drs. Jacobs and
Kelley discussed with them the possibility that Sidney might suffer from
the numerous physical and mental infirmities that did, in fact, afflict her.
And some eleven hours before Sidney's birth, the Millers indicated that
they did not want any heroic measures performed on Sidney. The Millers
note that these factors prompted the dissenting justice in the court of
appeals to conclude that "[a]nytime a group of doctors and a hospital
administration ha[ve] the luxury of multiple meetings to change the
original doctors' medical opinions, without taking a more obvious course of
action, there is no medical emergency."

We agree that a physician cannot create emergent circumstances from
his or her own delay or inaction and escape liability for proceeding without
consent. But the Millers' reasoning fails to recognize that, in this case, the
evidence established that Sidney could only be properly evaluated when she
was born. Any decision the Millers made before Sidney's birth concerning
her treatment at or after her birth would necessarily be based on speculation. Therefore, we reject the Millers' argument that a decision could
adequately be made pre-birth that denying all post-birth resuscitative
treatment would be in Sidney's best interest. Such a decision could not
control whether the circumstances facing Dr. Otero were emergent because
it would not have been a fully informed one according to the evidence in
this case.

The Millers point out that physicians routinely ask parents to make
pre-birth treatment choices for their infants including whether to accept or
refuse in utero medical treatment and to continue or terminate a pregnancy. While that may be entirely true, the evidence here established that the
time for evaluating Sidney was when she was born. The evidence further
reflected that Sidney was born alive but in distress. At that time, Dr. Otero
had to make a split-second decision on whether to provide life-sustaining
treatment. While the Millers were both present in the delivery room, there
was simply no time to obtain their consent to treatment or to institute legal
proceedings to challenge their withholding of consent, had the Millers done
so, without jeopardizing Sidney's life. Thus, although HCA never requested
a jury instruction, nor challenged the absence of a jury instruction, on
whether Dr. Otero treated Sidney under emergent circumstances, the
evidence conclusively established that Dr. Otero was faced with emergent
circumstances when he treated Sidney. Those circumstances resulted from
not being able to evaluate Sidney until she was born, not because of any
delay or inaction by HCA, the Hospital, or Dr. Otero....

We acknowledge that certain physicians in this case initially asked the
Millers to decide whether Sidney should be resuscitated some eleven hours

before her birth. And certain physicians and Hospital administrators asked the Millers to consent to the subsequent plan developed to have a neonatologist present at Sidney's delivery to evaluate and possibly treat her. We agree that, whenever possible, obtaining consent in writing to evaluate a premature infant at birth and to render any warranted medical treatment is the best course of action. And physicians and hospitals should always strive to do so. But if such consent is not forthcoming, or is affirmatively denied, we decline to impose liability on a physician solely for providing life-sustaining treatment under emergent circumstances to a new-born infant without that consent.

> . . .

There was testimony that Dr. Otero's resuscitative treatment caused Sidney's mental and physical infirmities. But there was also testimony that it did not and, in fact, the oxygen provided during the first days of Sidney's life prevented her from suffering even further brain damage. Although the jury found that the HCA's and the Hospital's negligence caused the "occurrence in question," it is unclear what was meant by the "occurrence in question."

If that phrase refers to Sidney's mental and physical infirmities, the Millers never sued Dr. Otero or any other physician. And there was no allegation that they negligently treated Sidney, which caused her infirmities. Instead, the Millers' only negligence claim was that HCA and the Hospital had policies, or lacked policies, and took actions that allowed Sidney to be treated without their consent. Thus, their negligence claim is based on the lack of consent before treatment, just like their battery claim.

If the phrase refers to Dr. Otero resuscitating Sidney against the Millers' wishes, it was not HCA's or the Hospital's policies, or lack thereof, that permitted Dr. Otero to treat Sidney without consent. Rather, it was the emergent circumstances that caused that to happen. Because Dr. Otero treated Sidney under emergent circumstances, he did not commit a battery. And because Dr. Otero did not commit a battery, HCA is not liable derivatively. Nor was the Hospital negligent for allowing Dr. Otero to treat Sidney under the circumstances without the Millers' consent.

The Millers raise additional arguments that we need not address, given our holding on the emergent circumstances exception. Similarly, HCA raises several arguments about why it cannot be held liable for the Millers' battery and negligence claims. Although we do not need to address those arguments to resolve this case, we do address two matters that the court of appeals discussed.

HCA argues that the federal "Baby Doe" regulations are part of Texas law and forbid any denial of medical care based on quality-of-life considerations. While we do not disagree with HCA's assertion as a general proposition, HCA cites 42 U.S.C. § 5106a(b)(2)(B) as support for its contention that the Baby Doe regulations were "scrupulously followed in this case" and "faithful adherence to the public policy established by the regulations should not be thwarted through civil liability in damages...." But 42 U.S.C. § 5106a(b)(2)(B) provides that a federally-funded state must implement "procedures for responding to the reporting of medical neglect" which include:

> authority, under State law, for the State child protective services system to pursue any legal remedies, including the authority to initiate legal proceedings in a court of competent jurisdiction, as may be necessary to prevent the withholding of medically indicated treatment from disabled infants with life-threatening conditions.

Assuming that this provision applies here, it states that Texas must provide a mechanism by which the child protective services system can initiate legal proceedings to prevent the withholding of medical treatment from infants. And the Family Code and Texas Administrative Code contain such provisions.

But it is undisputed that neither the Hospital nor HCA initiated or requested child protective services to initiate legal proceedings to override the Millers' "withholding of medical treatment" by refusing to consent to Sidney's treatment. Thus, the federal funding regulations appear to contemplate legal proceedings to override the lack of parental consent, and they do not answer the question of whether Dr. Otero committed a battery by providing treatment without doing so. Further, we agree with the court of appeals' conclusion that the disposition of that issue "is governed by state law rather than federal funding authorities."

HCA also argues, and the court of appeals agreed, that parents can withhold "urgently-needed life-sustaining medical treatment" for their child only when the requirements of the Natural Death Act are satisfied— *i.e.,* only when the child is certifiably terminal. But the Act expressly states that it does not impair or supersede any legal right a person may have to withhold or withdraw life-sustaining treatment in a lawful manner. In any event, we need not decide this issue. The Millers asserted battery and negligence claims based on Dr. Otero treating Sidney without their consent. As we have discussed, when emergent circumstances exist, a physician cannot be held liable under either battery or negligence theories solely for providing life-sustaining medical treatment to a minor child without parental consent.

III. Conclusion

Dr. Otero provided life-sustaining treatment to Sidney under emergent circumstances as a matter of law. Those circumstances provide an exception to the general rule imposing liability on a physician for providing treatment to a minor child without first obtaining parental consent. Therefore, Dr. Otero did not commit a battery. And HCA cannot be held liable for the Millers' battery and negligence claims. We are not presented with and do not decide the question of whether the rule we have announced applies to adults. We affirm the court of appeals' judgment.

NOTES AND QUESTIONS

The "best interests" principle is the standard ordinarily used to make decisions for children. Is it possible to give substantive content to this principle as applied to newborns? The President's Commission recommends placing individual newborns into one of three categories in order to facilitate the determination of what is in a child's best interests:

Clearly beneficial therapies. The Commission's inquiries indicate that treatments are rarely withheld when there is a medical consensus that they would provide a net benefit to a child. Parents naturally want to provide necessary medical care in most circumstances, and parents who are hesitant at first about having treatment administered usually come to recognize the desirability of providing treatment after discussions with physicians, nurses, and others. Parents should be able to choose among alternative treatments with similarly beneficial results and among providers, but not to reject treatment that is reliably expected to benefit a seriously ill newborn substantially, as is usually true if life can be saved.

.   .   .

Clearly futile therapies. When there is no therapy that can benefit an infant, as in anencephaly or certain severe cardiac deformities, a decision by surrogates and providers not to try predictably futile endeavors is ethically and legally justifiable. Such therapies do not help the child, are sometimes painful for the infant (and probably distressing to the parents), and offer no reasonable probability of saving life for a substantial period. The moment of death for these infants might be delayed for a short time—perhaps as long as a few weeks—by vigorous therapy. Of course, the prolongation of life—and hope against hope—may be enough to lead some parents to want to try a therapy believed by physicians to be futile. As long as this choice does not cause substantial suffering for the child, providers should accept it, although individual health care professionals who find it personally offensive to engage in futile treatment may arrange to withdraw from the case.

Just as with older patients, even when cure or saving of life are out of reach, obligations to comfort and respect a dying person remain. Thus infants whose lives are destined to be brief are owed whatever relief from suffering and enhancement of life can be provided, including feeding, medication for pain, and sedation, as appropriate. Moreover, it may be possible for parents to hold and comfort the child once the elaborate means of life-support are withdrawn, which can be very important to all concerned in symbolic and existential as well as physical terms.

Ambiguous cases. Although for most seriously ill infants there will be either clearly a beneficial option or no beneficial therapeutic options at all, hard questions are raised by the smaller number for whom it is very difficult to assess whether the treatments available offer prospects of benefit—for example, a child with a debilitating and painful disease who might live with therapy, but only for a year or so, or a respirator-dependent premature infant whose long-term prognosis becomes bleaker with each passing day.

Much of the difficulty in these cases arises from factual uncertainty. For the many infants born prematurely, and sometimes for those with serious congenital defects, the only certainty is that without intensive care they are unlikely to survive; very little is known about how each individual will fare with treatment. Neonatology is too new a field to allow accurate predictions of which babies will survive and of the complications, handicaps, and potentials that the survivors might have.... When a child's best interests are ambiguous, a decision based upon them will require prudent and discerning judgment. Defining the category of cases in a way that appropriately protects and encourages the exercise of parental judgment will sometimes be difficult.

The President's Commission, Deciding to Forego Life-Sustaining Treatment at 217–223 (1983).

Table 1:

Treatment Options for Seriously Ill Newborns—Physician's Assessment in Relation to Parent's Preference

Physician's Assessment of Treatment Options*	Parents Prefer to Accept Treatment**	Parents Prefer to Forego Treatment**
Clearly beneficial	Provide treatment	Provide treatment during review process
Ambiguous or uncertain	Provide treatment	Forego treatment
Futile	Provide treatment unless provider declines to do so	Forego treatment

* The assessment of the value to the infant of the treatments available will initially be by the attending physician. Both when this assessment is unclear and when the joint decision between parents and physician is to forego treatment, this assessment would be reviewed by intra-institutional mechanisms and possibly thereafter by court.

** The choice made by the infant's parents or other duly authorized surrogate who has adequate decisionmaking capacity and has been adequately informed, based on their assessment of the infant's best interests.

The President's Commission, Deciding to Forego Life-Sustaining Treatment at 217–223 (1983).

Do you agree with the President's Commission that treatment should always be continued when parents request it except where the child is in great suffering? How do we know that treatment is beneficial? Consider the views of the President's Commission on the issue. Do you find their statement helpful?

> Though inevitably somewhat subjective and imprecise in actual application, the concept of "benefit" excludes honoring idiosyncratic views that might be allowed if a person were deciding about his or her own treatment. Rather, net benefit is absent only if the burdens imposed on the patient by the disability or its treatment would lead a competent decisionmaker to choose to forego the treatment. As in all surrogate decisionmaking, the surrogate is obligated to try to evaluate benefits and burdens from the infant's own perspective. The Commission believes that the handicaps of Down Syndrome, for example, are not in themselves of this magnitude and do not justify failing to provide medically proven treatment, such as surgical correction of a blocked intestinal tract.
>
> This is a very strict standard in that it excludes consideration of the negative effects of an impaired child's life on other persons, including parents, siblings, and society. Although abiding by this standard may be difficult in specific cases, it is all too easy to undervalue the lives of handicapped infants; the Commission finds it imperative to counteract this by treating them no less vigorously than their healthy peers or than older children with similar handicaps would be treated.

Id. at 218–219.

Re A (Children)

United Kingdom, Court of Appeal (Civil Division), 2000.
[2000] H. R. L. R. 721.

WARD, L. J.:

. . .

. . . Jodie and Mary are conjoined twins. They each have their own brain, heart and lungs and other vital organs and they each have arms and legs. They are joined at the lower abdomen. Whilst not underplaying the surgical complexities, they can be successfully separated. But the operation will kill the weaker twin, Mary. That is because her lungs and heart are too deficient to oxygenate and pump blood through her body. Had she been born a singleton, she would not have been viable and resuscitation would have been abandoned. She would have died shortly after her birth. She is alive only because a common artery enables her sister, who is stronger, to circulate life sustaining oxygenated blood for both of them. Separation would require the clamping and then the severing of that common artery. Within minutes of doing so Mary will die. Yet if the operation does not take place, both will die within three to six months, or perhaps a little longer, because Jodie's heart will eventually fail. The parents cannot bring themselves to consent to the operation. The twins are equal in their eyes and they cannot agree to kill one even to save the other. As devout Roman Catholics they sincerely believe that it is God's will that their children are afflicted as they are and they must be left in God's hands. The doctors are convinced they can carry out the operation so as to give Jodie a life which will be worthwhile. So the hospital sought a declaration that the operation may be lawfully carried out. Johnson J. granted it on 25 August 2000. The parents applied to us for permission to appeal against his order. We have given that permission and this is my judgment on their appeal.

. . .

8.   The Available Options and the Doctors' Views

There are three ways of treating this appalling situation.

(a) Permanent union: at the moment the twins survive virtually unaided, though Mary has to be fed by tube. The summary of the hospital view is that:

> This (permanent union) condemns a potentially normal Jodie to carry her very abnormal sister, Mary, throughout the life of both. In view of the anatomical disposition Jodie will be unable to walk or even sit up appropriately. She is liable to progressive high output heart failure, which may lead to her earlier death within weeks or months.

This was examined in the evidence led before the judge. The cardiologist said:

> At the moment the function of Jodie's heart is very good. We are happy with its functioning now. The difficulty we envisage for her is that at the moment she is pumping blood round both babies' circulations, and the analogy I give staff in the unit, so that it is easy to understand, is that it is like asking anybody's heart to pump up to a ten foot person. So if we suddenly grew about four feet overnight we are asking our heart to

suddenly adapt and manage to deal with that for the foreseeable future. So the difficulty these hearts get into is that in time it places such an extra strain on the heart that they begin to show signs of failure.

. . .

Q. Are you able to express an opinion upon when, if at all it is likely that Jodie will suffer . . . high cardiac output failure?

A. In terms of conjoined twins it is very difficult to be precise . . . but I think three to six months is a reasonable guide of the kind of time we could be looking at.

. . .

(b) Elective separation: the summary of the hospital's view on this is that:

[It] will lead to Mary's death, but will give Jodie the opportunity of a separate good quality life. There are concerns regarding the possibility of acute heart failure for Jodie at the time of separation. Jodie may have bladder and anorectal control problems and is likely to require additional operative intervention over time. She may have musculoskeletal anomalies, which may also require surgical correction. It is expected, however, that separation will give Jodie the option of a long-term good quality life. She should be able to walk unaided and relatively normally. Separation should allow Jodie to participate in normal life activities as appropriate to her age and development.

. . .

(c) Semi-urgent/urgent separation:

[This] may need to be considered in the event of an acute catastrophe such as Mary's death, the development of progressive heart failure for Jodie, or the development of a life-threatening condition. . . .

No-one in the case advances this option. The probability seems to be that Jodie would die first and Mary's death would follow immediately. So long as Mary is alive the real problems in the case remain whether it is elective surgery or surgery undertaken in response to the intervening event.

The hospital and all concerned with the treatment and care of the twins are in favour of elective separation. . . .

. . .

10. The prognosis for Jodie

If the twins remain united, then, as already set out, Jodie's heart may fail in three to six months or perhaps a little longer. But it will eventually fail. That is common ground in this case. Her prospect of a happy life is measurably and significantly shortened. . . .

. . .

If the operation to separate is carried out, there is a 5–6% chance the children might die. [Doctors at] Great Ormond Street [Children's Hospital] were more confident. They reported:

Surgery would probably be a low risk procedure for Jodie. The operation itself and the possibility of later complications would probably carry an overall risk of death of perhaps 1–2 per cent.

As to her life expectancy St. Mary's surgeon said:

From what we know at this time of Mary, there is nothing which suggests that the life expectancy should be any shorter than normal.... Jodie's problems are functional, if you like, rather than life-threatening. Against those risks must be balanced the opinion that there is a 64% chance of death if an emergency operation had to be undertaken and the 80–90% prospect of death within three to six months, or perhaps a little longer, if no surgery is undertaken at all.

. . .

11.   The prognosis for Mary

If the operation to separate the twins is carried out, Mary will be anaesthetized against all pain and death will be mercifully quick. The surgeon was frank in acknowledging there was really no benefit for Mary in the operation....

. . .

13.   The parents' views

It is a laudable feature of this case that despite holding different views about the twins' future, the parents and the hospital have throughout maintained a relationship of mutual respect. The highly commendable attitude of the parents is shown in this passage in their statement:

We have been spoken to on many occasions by all the treating doctors at St. Mary's Hospital and we were fully aware of the difficulties ... We have been treated with the utmost care and respect at St. Mary's Hospital and we have no difficulties or problems with any of the medical staff that are treating (us).

As parents of the children, their views are a very important part of this case. It is right, therefore, that I set them out as fully as possible:

We have of course had to give serious consideration to the various options as given to us by our daughters' treating doctors. We cannot begin to accept or contemplate that one of our children should die to enable the other to survive. That is not God's will. Everyone has the right to life so why should we kill one of our daughters to enable the other to survive. That is not what we want and that is what we have told the doctors treating Jodie and Mary. In addition we are also told that if Jodie survives and that is not known at all, then she is going to be left with a serious disability. The life we have ... is remote ... with very few, if any facilities would make it extremely difficult not only for us to cope with a disabled child but for that disabled child to have any sort of life at all.

. . .

These are things we have to think about all the time. We know our babies are in a very poor condition, we know the hospital doctors are trying to do their very best for each of them. We have very strong feelings that neither of our children should receive any medical treatment. We certainly do not want separation surgery to go ahead as we know and have been told very clearly that it will result in the death of our daughter, Mary. We cannot possibly agree to any surgery being undertaken that will kill one of our daughters. We have faith in God and are quite happy for God's will to decide what happens to our two young daughters.

In addition we cannot see how we can possibly cope either financially or personally with a child where we live, who will have the serious disabilities that Jodie will have if she should survive any operation. We know there is no guarantee of survival but she is the stronger of the two twins and if she should survive any surgery then we have to be realistic and look at what we as parents can offer to our daughter and what care and facilities are available to her in our homeland. They are virtually nil. . . .

This has meant that we have also had to give very careful consideration to leaving Jodie in England, should she survive, to be looked after by other people. . . . We do not want to leave our daughters behind, we want to take them home with us but we know in our heart of hearts that if Jodie survives and is seriously disabled she will have very little prospects on our island because of its remoteness and lack of facilities and she will fare better if she remains in this country. . . . So we came to England to give our babies the very best chance in life in the very best place and now things have gone badly wrong and we find ourselves in this very difficult situation. We did not want to be in this situation, we did not ask to be in it but it is God's will. We have to deal with it and we have to take into account what is in the very best interests of our two very young daughters.

We do not understand why we as parents are not able to make decisions about our children although we respect what the doctors say to us and understand that we have to be governed by the law of England. We do know that everyone has the best interests of our daughters at heart and this is a very difficult situation not only for us as their parents but also for all of the medical and nursing staff involved in Mary's and Jodie's treatment.

14. The Nature of these proceedings

. . .

There has been some public concern as to why the court is involved at all. We do not ask for work but we have a duty to decide what parties with a proper interest ask us to decide. Here sincere professionals could not allay a collective medical conscience and see children in their care die when they know one was capable of being saved. They could not proceed in the absence of parental consent. The only arbiter of that sincerely held difference of opinion is the court. Deciding disputed matters of life and death is surely and pre-eminently a matter for a court of law to judge.

15. The judgment of Johnson J. [The trial judge]

. . .

He held:

I was at first attracted by the thought prompted by one of the doctors, that Jodie was to be regarded as a life support machine and that the operation proposed was equivalent to switching off a mechanical aid. Viewed in that way previous authority would categorise the proposed operation as one of omission rather than as a positive act. However on reflection I am not persuaded that that is a proper view of what is proposed in the circumstances of this particular case. I have preferred to base my decision upon the view that what is proposed and what will cause Mary's death will be the interruption or withdrawal of the supply of blood which she receives from Jodie. Here the analogy is with the situation in which the court authorises the withholding of food and hydration. That, the case is made clear, is not a positive act and is lawful. Jodie's blood supply circulates from and returns to her own heart by her own circulation system, independent of the supply and return from Mary. So it was suggested that one could theoretically envisage a clamp being placed within Jodie's body to block the circulation to Mary, so that there would be the immediate consequence for Mary without any invasion of her own body. I emphasise that this was simply part of the arguments to see how the operation should be categorised in order to judge its lawfulness. It was simply one of a number of arguments, analogies and illustrations that were canvassed in final submissions which I have not found it possible to record more extensively in what is effectively an ex tempore judgment. Nevertheless I have concluded that the operation which is proposed will be lawful because it represents the withdrawal of Mary's blood supply. It is of course plain that the consequence for Mary is one that most certainly does not represent the primary objective of the operation.

. . .

The parents have appealed. . . .

III.   Medical Law

1.   The fundamental principle

The fundamental principle, now long established, is that every person's body is inviolate. . . .

It follows that:

It is well established that, as a general rule, the performance of a medical operation upon a person without his or her consent is unlawful, as constituting both the crime of battery and the tort of trespass to the person

. . .

. . .

4.   The power to give proxy consent for a young child to undergo treatment

The parents if they are married have this power: if they are not, it is the mother's.

It is abundantly plain that the law recognises that there is a *right and duty* of parents to determine whether or not to seek medical advice in respect of their child, and, having received advice, to give or withhold consent to medical treatment.

Lord Scarman in *Gillick v. West Norfolk A.H.A.* [1986] 1 A.C. 12, 184G.

. . .

5.   The effect of the parents' refusal

Since the parents are empowered at law, it seems to me that their decision must be respected and in my judgment the hospital would be no more entitled to disregard their refusal than they are to disregard an adult patient's refusal. To operate in the teeth of the parents' refusal would, therefore, be an unlawful assault upon the child.

There is, however, this important safeguard to ensure that a child receives proper treatment. Because the parental rights and powers exist for the performance of their duties and responsibilities to the child and must be exercised in the best interests of the child.

> ... [T]he common law has never treated such rights as sovereign or beyond review and control.

.   .   .

IV. Family Law

1. The test for overriding the parents' refusal

There is no doubt that, in the exercise of its wardship jurisdiction the first and paramount consideration is the well being, welfare, or interest ... of the human being concerned....

.   .   .

4. The main issues in this appeal

On the basis of foregoing analysis, the crucial questions which arise in this appeal are:

(1) Is it in Jodie's best interests that she be separated from Mary?

(2) Is it in Mary's best interests that she be separated from Jodie?

(3) If those interests are in conflict is the court to balance the interests of one against the other and allow one to prevail against the other and how is that to be done?

(4) If the prevailing interest is in favour of the operation being performed, can it be lawfully performed?

.   .   .

6. Jodie's welfare: where do her best interests lie?

... Johnson J was in my judgment plainly right to conclude that the operation would be in Jodie's best interest.

The salient facts are these. The operation itself carries a negligible risk of death or brain damage. On the contrary the operation is overwhelmingly likely to have the consequence that Jodie's life will be extended from the period of 3–6 months or a little more to one where she may enjoy a normal expectancy of life.... I will deal separately with the problems that will or may arise in the parents or others giving care to Jodie but in the context of the argument which has dominated this case, namely the sanctity of life and the worthwhileness of life, it seems to me impossible to say that this operation does not offer infinitely greater benefit to Jodie than is offered to her by letting her die if the operation is not performed.

7. A more difficult question—Mary's welfare: where do her best interests lie?

.   .   .

7.2. The welfare assessment

The question of Mary's best interest is one of the key and one of the difficult issues in this case....

. . .

The only gain I can see is that the operation would, if successful, give Mary the bodily integrity and dignity which is the natural order for all of us. But this is a wholly illusory goal because she will be dead before she can enjoy her independence and she will die because, when she is independent, she has no capacity for life. The operation is not capable of ensuring any other improvement to her condition or preventing any deterioration in her present state of health. In terms of her best health interests, there are none. To be fair to the hospital, they do not pretend that there are.

If one looks to the operations as a means of meeting any other needs, social, emotional, psychological or whatever, one again searches in vain. One cannot blind oneself to the fact that death for Mary is the certain consequence of the carrying out of this operation.

. . .

7.7.   Act or omission in this case?

I set out earlier how this operation would be performed. The first step is to take the scalpel and cut the skin. If it is theoretically possible to cut precisely down the mid-line separating two individual bodies, that is not surgically feasible. Then the doctors have to ascertain which of the organs belong to each child. That is impossible to do without invading Mary's body in the course of that exploration. There follow further acts of separation culminating in the clamping and then severing of the artery. Whether or not the final step is taken within Jodie's body so that Jodie's aorta and not Mary's aorta is assaulted, it seems to me to be utterly fanciful to classify this invasive treatment as an omission in contra-distinction to an act. Johnson J's valiant and wholly understandable attempt to do so cannot be supported and although Mr. Whitfield QC did his best, he recognised his difficulty. The operation has, therefore, to be seen as an act of invasion of Mary's bodily integrity and unless consent or approval is given for it, it constitutes an unlawful assault upon her.

. . .

7.9.   Conclusion as to Mary's best interests

The question is whether this proposed operation is in Mary's best interests. It cannot be. It will bring her life to an end before it has run its natural span. It denies her inherent right to life. There is no countervailing advantage for her at all. It is contrary to her best interests. Looking at her position in isolation and ignoring, therefore, the benefit to Jodie, the court should not sanction the operation on her.

. . .

9.3.   The weight to be given to these parents' wishes

... The views of the parents will strike a chord of agreement with many who reflect upon their dilemma. I cannot emphasise enough how much I sympathise with them in the cruelty of the agonising choice they had to make. I know because I agonise over the dilemma too. I fear, however, that the parents' wish does not convince me that it is in the children's best interest:

> (i) From Jodie's point of view they have taken the worst possible scenario that she would be wheelchair bound, destined for a life of difficulty. They fail to recognise her capacity sufficiently to enjoy the benefits of life that would be available to her were she free and independent.

> (ii) She may indeed need special care and attention and that may be very difficult to provide in their home country.

This is a real and practical problem for the family, the burden of which in ordinary family life should not be underestimated. It may seem unduly harsh on these desperate parents to point out that it is the child's best interests which are paramount, not the parents'. . . . They surely cannot so minimise Jodie's rights on the basis that the burden of possible disadvantage for her and the burdens of caring for such a child for them can morally be said to outweigh her claim to the human dignity of independence which only cruel fate has denied her.

· · ·

> (iv) In their natural repugnance at the idea of killing Mary they fail to recognise their conflicting duty to save Jodie and they seem to exculpate themselves from, or at least fail fully to face up to the consequence of the failure to separate the twins, namely death for Jodie. In my judgment, parents who are placed on the horns of such a terrible dilemma simply have to choose the lesser of their inevitable loss. If a family at the gates of a concentration camp were told they might free one of their children but if no choice were made both would die, compassionate parents with equal love for their twins would elect to save the stronger and see the weak one destined for death pass through the gates.

· · ·

10.   How is the balance to be struck?

The analytical problem is to determine what may, and what may not, be placed in each scale and what weight is then to be given to each of the factors in the scales.

· · ·

> (ii) The question which the court has to answer is whether or not the proposed treatment, the operation to separate, is in the best interests of the twins. That enables me to consider and place in the scales of each twin the worthwhileness of the treatment. That is a quite different exercise from the proscribed (because it offends the sanctity of life principle) consideration of the worth of one life compared with the other. When considering the worthwhileness of the treatment, it is legitimate to have regard to the actual condition of each twin and hence the actual balance sheet of advantage and disadvantage which flows from the performance or the non-performance of the proposed treatment. Here it is legitimate, as the cases show, to bear in mind the actual quality of life each child enjoys and may be' able to enjoy. In summary, the operation will give Jodie the prospects of

a normal expectation of relatively normal life. The operation will shorten Mary's life but she remains doomed for death. Mary has a full claim to the dignity of independence which is her human entitlement. In the words of the Rabbinical scholars involved in the 1977 case in Philadelphia, Mary is "designated for death" because her capacity to live her life is fatally compromised. The prospect of a full life for Jodie is counterbalanced by an acceleration of certain death for Mary. That balance is heavily in Jodie's favour.

. . .

Hence I am in no doubt at all that the scales come down heavily in Jodie's favour. The best interests of the twins is to give the chance of life to the child whose actual bodily condition is capable of accepting the chance to her advantage even if that has to be at the cost of the sacrifice of the life which is so unnaturally supported. I am wholly satisfied that the least detrimental choice, balancing the interests of Mary against Jodie and Jodie against Mary, is to permit the operation to be performed.

11. Conclusion on the Family Law aspect of this case

I would grant permission for the operation to take place provided, however, what is proposed to be done can be lawfully done. That requires a consideration of the criminal law to which I now turn.

[Lord Justice Ward then determined that the operation would not constitute murder under the criminal law.]

[Lord Justice Brooke agreed with the family law portion of Justice Ward's opinion. He expressed the opinion that the operation was justified under criminal law by the doctrine of necessity.]

[Lord Justice Walker would also dismiss the appeal.]

NOTES AND QUESTIONS

Jodie and Mary were surgically separated six weeks after the opinion of the Court of Appeal. Jodie survived the operation well, although she may require further surgery over the next five years, most of which will have to be performed in Britain. George J. Annas, *Conjoined Twins—The Limits of the Law at the Limits of Life*, 344 NEW ENG. J. MED. 1104 (2001).

In his article, Annas observed:

... The case seems to have been decided ... on an intuitive judgment that the state of being a conjoined twin is a disease and that separation is the indicated treatment for it, at least if such treatment affords one of the twins a chance to live. The judges identified strongly with the physicians and had little empathy with the parents or their religious beliefs....

... I would have liked to have had the parents agree to the separation (since giving Jodie a chance to live at the cost of cutting Mary's life short does seem the lesser of two evils), but I do not believe the case for separation is so strong that it demands that the authority to make the decision about medical care of their children be taken away from the parents.

Id. at 1106, 1108. Do you agree?

CHAPTER 5

REPRODUCTION AND THE NEW GENETICS

I. DEFINING LIFE

Davis v. Davis

Supreme Court of Tennessee, 1992.
842 S.W.2d 588, *cert. denied*, 507 U.S. 911, 113 S.Ct. 1259, 122 L.Ed.2d 657 (1993).

■ DAUGHTREY, J.

This appeal presents a question of first impression, involving the disposition of the cryogenically-preserved product of in vitro fertilization (IVF), commonly referred to in the popular press and the legal journals as "frozen embryos." The case began as a divorce action, filed by the appellee, Junior Lewis Davis, against his then wife, appellant Mary Sue Davis. The parties were able to agree upon all terms of dissolution, except one: who was to have "custody" of the seven "frozen embryos" stored in a Knoxville fertility clinic that had attempted to assist the Davises in achieving a much-wanted pregnancy during a happier period in their relationship.

Mary Sue Davis originally asked for control of the "frozen embryos" with the intent to have them transferred to her own uterus, in a post-divorce effort to become pregnant. Junior Davis objected, saying that he preferred to leave the embryos in their frozen state until he decided whether or not he wanted to become a parent outside the bounds of marriage.

Based on its determination that the embryos were "human beings" from the moment of fertilization, the trial court awarded "custody" to Mary Sue Davis and directed that she "be permitted the opportunity to bring these children to term through implantation." The Court of Appeals reversed, finding that Junior Davis has a "constitutionally protected right not to beget a child where no pregnancy has taken place" and holding that "there is no compelling state interest to justify ordering implantation against the will of either party." The Court of Appeals further held that "the parties share an interest in the seven fertilized ova" and remanded the case to the trial court for entry of an order vesting them with "joint control . . . and equal voice over their disposition."

. . . We granted review, not because we disagree with the basic legal analysis utilized by the intermediate court, but because of the obvious importance of the case in terms of the development of law regarding the new reproductive technologies, and because the decision of the Court of

Appeals does not give adequate guidance to the trial court in the event the parties cannot agree.

We note, in this latter regard, that their positions have already shifted: both have remarried and Mary Sue Davis (now Mary Sue Stowe) has moved out of state. She no longer wishes to utilize the "frozen embryos" herself, but wants authority to donate them to a childless couple. Junior Davis is adamantly opposed to such donation and would prefer to see the "frozen embryos" discarded. The result is, once again, an impasse, but the parties' current legal position does have an effect on the probable outcome of the case, as discussed below.

At the outset, it is important to note the absence of two critical factors that might otherwise influence or control the result of this litigation: When the Davises signed up for the IVF program at the Knoxville clinic, they did not execute a written agreement specifying what disposition should be made of any unused embryos that might result from the cryopreservation process. Moreover, there was at that time no Tennessee statute governing such disposition, nor has one been enacted in the meantime.

In addition, because of the uniqueness of the question before us, we have no case law to guide us to a decision in this case. Despite the fact that over 5,000 IVF babies have been born in this country and the fact that some 20,000 or more "frozen embryos" remain in storage, there are apparently very few other litigated cases involving the disputed disposition of untransferred "frozen embryos," and none is on point with the facts in this case.

. . .

. . . [W]e conclude that given the relevant principles of constitutional law, the existing public policy of Tennessee with regard to unborn life, the current state of scientific knowledge giving rise to the emerging reproductive technologies, and the ethical considerations that have developed in response to that scientific knowledge, there can be no easy answer to the question we now face. We conclude, instead, that we must weigh the interests of each party to the dispute, in terms of the facts and analysis set out below, in order to resolve that dispute in a fair and responsible manner.

Mary Sue Davis and Junior Lewis Davis met while they were both in the Army and stationed in Germany in the spring of 1979. After a period of courtship, they came home to the United States and were married on April 26, 1980. When their leave was up, they then returned to their posts in Germany as a married couple.

Within six months of returning to Germany, Mary Sue became pregnant but unfortunately suffered an extremely painful tubal pregnancy, as a result of which she had surgery to remove her right fallopian tube. This tubal pregnancy was followed by four others during the course of the marriage. After her fifth tubal pregnancy, Mary Sue chose to have her left fallopian tube ligated, thus leaving her without functional fallopian tubes by which to conceive naturally. The Davises attempted to adopt a child but, at the last minute, the child's birth-mother changed her mind about putting the child up for adoption. Other paths to adoption turned out to be prohibitively expensive. In vitro fertilization became essentially the only option for the Davises to pursue in their attempt to become parents.

As explained at trial, IVF involves the aspiration of ova from the follicles of a woman's ovaries, fertilization of these ova in a petri dish using the sperm provided by a man, and the transfer of the product of this procedure into the uterus of the woman from whom the ova were taken. Implantation may then occur, resulting in a pregnancy and, it is hoped, the birth of a child.

Beginning in 1985, the Davises went through six attempts at IVF, at a total cost of $35,000, but the hoped-for pregnancy never occurred. Despite her fear of needles, at each IVF attempt Mary Sue underwent the month of subcutaneous injections necessary to shut down her pituitary gland and the eight days of intramuscular injections necessary to stimulate her ovaries to produce ova. She was anesthetized five times for the aspiration procedure to be performed. Forty-eight to 72 hours after each aspiration, she returned for transfer back to her uterus, only to receive a negative pregnancy test result each time.

The Davises then opted to postpone another round of IVF until after the clinic with which they were working was prepared to offer them cryogenic preservation, scheduled for November 1988. Using this process, if more ova are aspirated and fertilized than needed, the conceptive product may be cryogenically preserved (frozen in nitrogen and stored at sub-zero temperatures) for later transfer if the transfer performed immediately does not result in a pregnancy. The unavailability of this procedure had not been a hindrance to previous IVF attempts by the Davises because Mary Sue had produced at most only three or four ova, despite hormonal stimulation. However, on their last attempt, on December 8, 1988, the gynecologist who performed the procedure was able to retrieve nine ova for fertilization. The resulting one-celled entities, referred to before division as zygotes, were then allowed to develop in petri dishes in the laboratory until they reached the four-to eight-cell stage.

Needless to say, the Davises were pleased at the initial success of the procedure. At the time, they had no thoughts of divorce and the abundance of ova for fertilization offered them a better chance at parenthood, because Mary Sue Davis could attempt to achieve a pregnancy without additional rounds of hormonal stimulation and aspiration. They both testified that although the process of cryogenic preservation was described to them, no one explained the ways in which it would change the nature of IVF for them. There is, for example, no indication that they ever considered the implications of storage beyond the few months it would take to transfer the remaining "frozen embryos," if necessary. There was no discussion, let alone an agreement, concerning disposition in the event of a contingency such as divorce.

After fertilization was completed, a transfer was performed as usual on December 10, 1988; the rest of the four-to eight-cell entities were cryogenically preserved. Unfortunately, a pregnancy did not result from the December 1988 transfer, and before another transfer could be attempted, Junior Davis filed for divorce—in February 1989. He testified that he had known that their marriage "was not very stable" for a year or more, but had hoped that the birth of a child would improve their relationship. Mary Sue Davis testified that she had no idea that there was a problem with their marriage. As noted earlier, the divorce proceedings were complicated only by the issue of the disposition of the "frozen embryos."

. . .

One of the fundamental issues the inquiry poses is whether the preembryos in this case should be considered "persons" or "property" in the contemplation of the law.... [T]hey cannot be considered "persons" under Tennessee law....

Nor do preembryos enjoy protection as "persons" under federal law. In *Roe v. Wade*, 410 U.S. 113 (1973), the United States Supreme Court explicitly refused to hold that the fetus possesses independent rights under law, based upon a thorough examination of the federal constitution, relevant common law principles, and the lack of scientific consensus as to when life begins. The Supreme Court concluded that "the unborn have never been recognized in the law as persons in the whole sense." *Id.* at 162....

Left undisturbed, the trial court's ruling would have afforded preembryos the legal status of "persons" and vested them with legally cognizable interests separate from those of their progenitors. Such a decision would doubtless have had the effect of outlawing IVF programs in the state of Tennessee. But in setting aside the trial court's judgment, the Court of Appeals, at least by implication, may have swung too far in the opposite direction.

. . .

To our way of thinking, the most helpful discussion on this point is found not in the minuscule number of legal opinions that have involved "frozen embryos," but in the ethical standards set by The American Fertility Society, as follows:

> Three major ethical positions have been articulated in the debate over preembryo status. At one extreme is the view of the preembryo as a human subject after fertilization, which requires that it be accorded the rights of a person. This position entails an obligation to provide an opportunity for implantation to occur and tends to ban any action before transfer that might harm the preembryo or that is not immediately therapeutic, such as freezing and some preembryo research.
>
> At the opposite extreme is the view that the preembryo has a status no different from any other human tissue. With the consent of those who have decision-making authority over the preembryo, no limits should be imposed on actions taken with preembryos.
>
> A third view—one that is most widely held—takes an intermediate position between the other two. It holds that the preembryo deserves respect greater than that accorded to human tissue but not the respect accorded to actual persons. The preembryo is due greater respect than other human tissue because of its potential to become a person and because of its symbolic meaning for many people. Yet, it should not be treated as a person, because it has not yet developed the features of personhood, is not yet established as developmentally individual, and may never realize its biologic potential.

Report of the Ethics Committee of The American Fertility Society, *supra*, at 34S–35S.

Although the report alludes to the role of "special respect" in the context of research on preembryos not intended for transfer, it is clear that the Ethics Committee's principal concern was with the treatment accorded the transferred embryo. Thus, the Ethics Committee concludes that "special respect is necessary to protect the welfare of potential offspring . . . [and] creates obligations not to hurt or injure the offspring who might be born after transfer [by research or intervention with a preembryo]." *Id.* at 35S. . . .

We conclude that preembryos are not, strictly speaking, either "persons" or "property," but occupy an interim category that entitles them to special respect because of their potential for human life. It follows that any interest that Mary Sue Davis and Junior Davis have in the preembryos in this case is not a true property interest. However, they do have an interest in the nature of ownership, to the extent that they have decision-making authority concerning disposition of the preembryos, within the scope of policy set by law.

Establishing the locus of the decision-making authority in this context is crucial to deciding whether the parties could have made a valid contingency agreement prior to undergoing the IVF procedures and whether such an agreement would now be enforceable on the question of disposition. . . . Despite our reluctance to treat a question not strictly necessary to the result in the case, we conclude that discussion is warranted in order to provide the necessary guidance to all those involved with IVF procedures in Tennessee in the future. . . .

We believe, as a starting point, that an agreement regarding disposition of any untransferred preembryos in the event of contingencies (such as the death of one or more of the parties, divorce, financial reversals, or abandonment of the program) should be presumed valid and should be enforced as between the progenitors. This conclusion is in keeping with the proposition that the progenitors, having provided the gametic material giving rise to the preembryos, retain decision-making authority as to their disposition.

At the same time, we recognize that life is not static, and that human emotions run particularly high when a married couple is attempting to overcome infertility problems. It follows that the parties' initial "informed consent" to IVF procedures will often not be truly informed because of the near impossibility of anticipating, emotionally and psychologically, all the turns that events may take as the IVF process unfolds. Providing that the initial agreements may later be modified by agreement will, we think, protect the parties against some of the risks they face in this regard. But, in the absence of such agreed modification, we conclude that their prior agreements should be considered binding.

It might be argued in this case that the parties had an implied contract to reproduce using in vitro fertilization, that Mary Sue Davis relied on that agreement in undergoing IVF procedures, and that the court should enforce an implied contract against Junior Davis, allowing Mary Sue to dispose of the preembryos in a manner calculated to result in reproduction. The problem with such an analysis is that there is no indication in the record that disposition in the event of contingencies other than Mary Sue Davis's pregnancy was ever considered by the parties, or that Junior Davis intended to pursue reproduction outside the confines of a continuing marital relationship with Mary Sue. We therefore decline to decide this case on the basis of implied contract or the reliance doctrine.

We are therefore left with this situation: there was initially no agreement between the parties concerning disposition of the preembryos under the circumstances of this case; there has been no agreement since; and there is no formula in the Court of Appeals opinion for determining the outcome if the parties cannot reach an agreement in the future.

In granting joint custody to the parties, the Court of Appeals must have anticipated that, in the absence of agreement, the preembryos would continue to be stored, as they now are, in the Knoxville fertility clinic. One problem with maintaining the status quo is that the viability of the preembryos cannot be guaranteed indefinitely. Experts in cryopreservation who testified in this case estimated the maximum length of preembryonic viability at two years. Thus, the true effect of the intermediate court's opinion is to confer on Junior Davis the inherent power to veto any transfer of the preembryos in this case and thus to insure their eventual discard or self-destruction.

. . . [T]he recognition of such a veto power, as long as it applies equally to both parties, is theoretically one of the routes available to resolution of the dispute in this case. Moreover, because of the current state of law regarding the right of procreation, such a rule would probably be upheld as constitutional. Nevertheless, for the reasons set out in . . . this opinion, we conclude that it is not the best route to take, under all the circumstances.

Although an understanding of the legal status of preembryos is necessary in order to determine the enforceability of agreements about their disposition, asking whether or not they constitute "property" is not an altogether helpful question. . . . [T]he essential dispute here is not where or how or how long to store the preembryos, but whether the parties will become parents. The Court of Appeals held in effect that they will become parents if they both agree to become parents. The Court did not say what will happen if they fail to agree. We conclude that the answer to this dilemma turns on the parties' exercise of their constitutional right to privacy.

. . .

Here, the specific individual freedom in dispute is the right to procreate. In terms of the Tennessee state constitution, we hold that the right of procreation is a vital part of an individual's right to privacy. Federal law is to the same effect.

. . .

The United States Supreme Court has never addressed the issue of procreation in the context of in vitro fertilization. Moreover, the extent to which procreational autonomy is protected by the United States Constitution is no longer entirely clear....

For the purposes of this litigation it is sufficient to note that, whatever its ultimate constitutional boundaries, the right of procreational autonomy is composed of two rights of equal significance—the right to procreate and the right to avoid procreation. Undoubtedly, both are subject to protections and limitations.

The equivalence of and inherent tension between these two interests are nowhere more evident than in the context of in vitro fertilization. None of the concerns about a woman's bodily integrity that have previously precluded men from controlling abortion decisions is applicable here. We are not unmindful of the fact that the trauma (including both emotional stress and physical discomfort) to which women are subjected in the IVF process is more severe than is the impact of the procedure on men. In this sense, it is fair to say that women contribute more to the IVF process than men. Their experience, however, must be viewed in light of the joys of parenthood that is desired or the relative anguish of a lifetime of unwanted parenthood. As they stand on the brink of potential parenthood, Mary Sue Davis and Junior Lewis Davis must be seen as entirely equivalent gamete-providers.

It is further evident that, however far the protection of procreational autonomy extends, the existence of the right itself dictates that decisional authority rests in the gamete-providers alone, at least to the extent that their decisions have an impact upon their individual reproductive status.... [N]o other person or entity has an interest sufficient to permit interference with the gamete-providers' decision to continue or terminate the IVF process, because no one else bears the consequences of these decisions in the way that the gamete-providers do.

Further, at least with respect to Tennessee's public policy and its constitutional right of privacy, the state's interest in potential human life is insufficient to justify an infringement on the gamete-providers' procreational autonomy....

Certainly, if the state's interests do not become sufficiently compelling in the abortion context until the end of the first trimester, after very significant developmental stages have passed, then surely there is no state interest in these preembryos which could suffice to overcome the interests of the gamete-providers. The abortion statute reveals that the increase in the state's interest is marked by each successive developmental stage such that, toward the end of a pregnancy, this interest is so compelling that abortion is almost strictly forbidden. This scheme supports the conclusion that the state's interest in the potential life embodied by these four-to eight-cell preembryos (which may or may not be able to achieve implantation in a uterine wall and which, if implanted, may or may not begin to develop into fetuses, subject to possible miscarriage) is at best slight. When weighed against the interests of the individuals and the burdens inherent in parenthood, the state's interest in the potential life of these preembryos is not sufficient to justify any infringement upon the freedom of these individuals to make their own decisions as to whether to allow a process to continue that may result in such a dramatic change in their lives as becoming parents.

The unique nature of this case requires us to note that the interests of these parties in parenthood are different in scope than the parental interest considered in other cases. Previously, courts have dealt with the child-bearing and child-rearing aspects of parenthood. Abortion cases have dealt with gestational parenthood. In this case, the Court must deal with the question of genetic parenthood. We conclude, moreover, that an interest in avoiding genetic parenthood can be significant enough to trigger the protections afforded to all other aspects of parenthood. The technological fact that someone unknown to these parties could gestate these preembryos does not alter the fact that these parties, the gamete-providers, would become parents in that event, at least in the genetic sense. The profound impact this would have on them supports their right to sole decisional authority as to whether the process of attempting to gestate these preembryos should continue. This brings us directly to the question of how to resolve the dispute that arises when one party wishes to continue the IVF process and the other does not.

Resolving disputes over conflicting interests of constitutional import is a task familiar to the courts. One way of resolving these disputes is to consider the positions of the parties, the significance of their interests, and the relative burdens that will be imposed by differing resolutions. In this case, the issue centers on the two aspects of procreational autonomy—the right to procreate and the right to avoid procreation. We start by considering the burdens imposed on the parties by solutions that would have the effect of disallowing the exercise of individual procreational autonomy with respect to these particular preembryos.

Beginning with the burden imposed on Junior Davis, we note that the consequences are obvious. Any disposition which results in the gestation of the preembryos would impose unwanted parenthood on him, with all of its possible financial and psychological consequences. The impact that this unwanted parenthood would have on Junior Davis can only be understood by considering his particular circumstances, as revealed in the record.

Junior Davis testified that he was the fifth youngest of six children. When he was five years old, his parents divorced, his mother had a nervous break-down, and he and three of his brothers went to live at a home for boys run by the Lutheran Church. Another brother was taken in by an aunt, and his sister stayed with their mother. From that day forward, he had monthly visits with his mother but saw his father only three more times before he died in 1976. Junior Davis testified that, as a boy, he had severe problems caused by separation from his parents. He said that it was especially hard to leave his mother after each monthly visit. He clearly feels that he has suffered because of his lack of opportunity to establish a relationship with his parents and particularly because of the absence of his father.

In light of his boyhood experiences, Junior Davis is vehemently opposed to fathering a child that would not live with both parents. Regardless of whether he or Mary Sue had custody, he feels that the child's bond with the non-custodial parent would not be satisfactory. He testified very clearly that his concern was for the psychological obstacles a child in such a situation would face, as well as the burdens it would impose on him. Likewise, he is opposed to donation because the recipient couple might divorce, leaving the child (which he definitely would consider his own) in a single-parent setting.

Balanced against Junior Davis's interest in avoiding parenthood is Mary Sue Davis's interest in donating the preembryos to another couple for implantation. Refusal to permit donation of the preembryos would impose on her the burden of knowing that the lengthy IVF procedures she underwent were futile, and that the preembryos to which she contributed genetic material would never become children. While this is not an insubstantial emotional burden, we can only conclude that Mary Sue Davis's interest in donation is not as significant as the interest Junior Davis has in avoiding parenthood. If she were allowed to donate these preembryos, he would face a lifetime of either wondering about his parental status or knowing about his parental status but having no control over it. He testified quite clearly that if these preembryos were brought to term he would fight for custody of his child or children. Donation, if a child came of it, would rob him twice—his procreational autonomy would be defeated and his relationship with his offspring would be prohibited.

The case would be closer if Mary Sue Davis were seeking to use the preembryos herself, but only if she could not achieve parenthood by any other reasonable means. We recognize the trauma that Mary Sue has already experienced and the additional discomfort to which she would be subjected if she opts to attempt IVF again. Still, she would have a reasonable opportunity, through IVF, to try once again to achieve parenthood in all its aspects—genetic, gestational, bearing, and rearing.

Further, we note that if Mary Sue Davis were unable to undergo another round of IVF, or opted not to try, she could still achieve the child-rearing aspects of parenthood through adoption. The fact that she and Junior Davis pursued adoption indicates that, at least at one time, she was willing to forego genetic parenthood and would have been satisfied by the child-rearing aspects of parenthood alone.

In summary, we hold that disputes involving the disposition of preembryos produced by in vitro fertilization should be resolved, first, by looking to the preferences of the progenitors. If their wishes cannot be ascertained, or if there is dispute, then their prior agreement concerning disposition should be carried out. If no prior agreement exists, then the relative interests of the parties in using or not using the preembryos must be weighed. Ordinarily, the party wishing to avoid procreation should prevail, assuming that the other party has a reasonable possibility of achieving parenthood by means other than use of the preembryos in question. If no other reasonable alternatives exist, then the argument in favor of using the preembryos to achieve pregnancy should be considered. However, if the party seeking control of the preembryos intends merely to donate them to another couple, the objecting party obviously has the greater interest and should prevail. . . .

. . . [T]he judgment of the Court of Appeals is affirmed, in the appellee's favor. This ruling means that the Knoxville Fertility Clinic is free to follow its normal procedure in dealing with unused preembryos, as long as that procedure is not in conflict with this opinion. . . .

NOTE

Aftermath. After this decision, both Mary Sue Davis and Junior Lewis Davis petitioned the Tennessee Supreme Court for rehearing. The court denied Mary Sue Davis's petition which urged, inter alia, that the court's opinion violated President Reagan's executive order of January 14, 1988 (Presidential Proclamation No. 5761), proclaiming "the unalienable personhood of every American, from the moment of conception until natural death." Ruling that it was not bound by a proclamation in "direct conflict with both the state and federal constitutions," the court granted Junior Davis's petition seeking guidance on disposition of the embryos. The normal procedure of the Knoxville Fertility Clinic was to donate surplus preembryos to childless couples, a disposition not authorized by the court's opinion. The court ruled that either of two options was available to the parties. Either both parties could consent to donate the preembryos for research or the embryos would be discarded. *Davis v. Davis,* 1992 WL 341632 (Tenn. Nov. 23, 1992). In June 1993, Junior Davis reportedly disposed of the preembryos. *7 Embryos in Custody Case Are Destroyed,* N.Y. TIMES, June 16, 1993, at A18, col. 2.

C.R. AUSTIN, HUMAN EMBRYOS: THE DEBATE ON ASSISTED REPRODUCTION
1, 22–31 (1989).

. . .

When Does a Person's Life Really Begin?

This is the key issue in debates on embryo experimentation. Probably most people who were asked this question would answer "at fertilization" (or "conception"). Certainly, several interesting and unusual things happen then . . . it is really the most *obvious* event to pick-but for biologists the preceding and succeeding cellular processes are *equally* important. . . . Nevertheless, "fertilization" continues to be the cry of many religious bodies and indeed also of the august World Medical Association, who, in 1949, adopted the Geneva Convention Code of Medical Ethics, which contains the clause: "I will maintain the utmost respect for human life from the time of conception". So we do need to look more closely at this choice, for a generally acceptable "beginning" for human life would be a great help in reaching ethical and legal consensus.

In the first place human *life,* as such, obviously begins before fertilization, since the egg or oocyte is alive before sperm entry, as were innumerable antecedent cells, back through the origin of species into the mists of time. A more practical starting point would be that of the life of the human *individual,* so it is individuality that we should be looking for, at least as one of the essential criteria. Now the earliest antecedents of the eggs, as of sperm, are the primordial germ cells, which can be seen as a group of distinctive little entities migrating through the tissues of the early embryo. When they first become recognizable, they number only about a dozen or two, but they multiply fast and soon achieve large numbers, reaching a peak of 7–10 million about 6 months after conception.... Then, despite continued active cell division, there is a dramatic decline in the cell population, which has tempted people to suggest that some sort of "selection of the fittest" occurs, but there is no good evidence in support of this idea; nor is there any good reason to look for individuality in that mercurial population. In due course, the primordial germ cells, while still under-going cell divisions, settle down in the tissues of the future ovary, change subtly in their characteristics, and thus become oogonia; and then, soon after birth, *cell division ceases,* the cells develop large nuclei and are now recognizable as primary oocytes.... From now on, there are steady cell losses but no further cell divisions (except for the polar body extrusions that occur just before ovulation and immediately after sperm penetration); it is the same entity that was a primary oocyte, becomes a fertilized egg, and then develops as an embryo.... The primary oocytes are very unusual cells, for they have the capacity to live for much longer than most other body cells; the *same* oocytes can be seen in the ovaries of women approaching the menopause—cells that have lived for about 40 years or longer. And it is with the emergence of the primary oocytes that we can hail the start of *individuality.* Then, in those oocytes that are about to be ovulated, the first meiotic division takes place—another important step, for the "shuffling" of genes that occurs at that point ... bestows *genetic uniqueness* on the oocyte. So both individuality and genetic uniqueness are established before sperm penetration and fertilization; these processes have distinctly different actions—providing the stimulus that initiates cleavage and contributing to biparental inheritance. Thus, the preferred choice for the start of the human individual should surely be the formation of the primary oocyte, but there is certainly no unanimity on this score.

Passing over now the popularity of fertilization, for many people it is instead the emergence of the embryonic disc and primitive streak that most appeals as the stage in which to identify the start of "personhood" (one or more persons, in view of the imminent possibility of twinning), and there is much to support this opinion. Here, for the first time, are structures that are designed to have a different destiny than *all the rest of the embryo—* they represent the primordium of the fetus, ... and the developmental patterns of embryo and fetus progressively diverge from this stage onwards. An additional point is that this new emergence is not inevitable, for in around one in two-thousand pregnancies the embryo grows, often to quite a large size, but there is no fetus; the clinical conditions are known as blighted ovum, dropsical ovum, hydatidiform mole, etc. Evidence suggests that hydatidiform mole is attributable to fertilization of a faulty egg, the embryo developing only under the influence of the sperm chromosomes.

At the time of appearance of the embryonic disc, and shortly beforehand, the process of implantation is occurring, and this is considered by many to have special significance in relation to embryonic potential—so far as we know, implantation cannot occur once the development of the embryo has passed the stage when interaction with the endometrium of the uterus normally takes place. Implantation is considered to begin on about the eighth day and to be complete on the fourteenth, or thereabouts, ...

But despite all that has been said, there are still many folk who remain unconvinced—is the being at this stage sufficiently "human" to qualify as the start of a person? After all, the disc is just a collection of similar cells, virtually undifferentiated, poorly delineated from its surroundings, about a fifth of a millimetre long, non-sentient, and without the power of movement. It is in no way a "body" and it does not bear the faintest resemblance to a human being—*and* the soul cannot enter yet, for the disc may yet divide in the process of twinning, and the soul being unique is indivisible. Also, it is argued that we should be looking for some spark of personality, and a moral philosopher has proposed that some sort of "responsiveness" is an essential feature.

One of the earliest succeeding changes in the direction of humanness could be the development of the heart primordium, and soon after that the beginnings of a circulatory system; the first contractions of the heart muscle occur possibly as early as day 21, with a simple tubular heart at that stage, and in the fourth week a functional circulation begins. With the heart beats we have the first movements initiated within the embryo (?fetus) and thus in a way the first real "sign of life." The conceptus is now about 6mm long. During the fifth and sixth weeks, nerve fibres grow out from the spinal cord and make contact with muscles, so that at this time or soon afterwards, a mechanical or electrical stimulus might elicit a muscle twitch; this is important for it would be the first indication of sentient existence—of "responsiveness." At this stage, too, the embryo could possibly feel pain. But, still, some would find cause to demur: only an expert could tell that this embryo/fetus, now 12–13 mm in length, with branchial arches (corresponding to the "gill-slits" in non-mammalian embryos), stubby limbs, and a prominent tail, is human. . . . A marginally more acceptable applicant is the fetus at 7½ weeks, when the hands and feet can be seen to have fingers and toes . . ., and thereafter physical resemblance steadily improves; also at this time, a special gene on the Y-chromosome (the "testis-determining factor" or TDF) is switched on, and the fetuses that have this chromosome, the males, proceed thenceforward to develop *as* males, distinguishable from females.

At about 12 weeks, electrical activity can be detected in the brain of the fetus, which could signal the dawn of consciousness. Here, we would seem to have a very logical stage marking the *start* of a person, for the cessation of electrical activity in the brain ('brain death') is accepted in both medical and legal circles as marking the *termination* of a person—as an indication that life no longer exists in victims of accidents or in patients with terminal illnesses. Around the fourth or fifth month of pregnancy, the mother first experiences movements of the fetus ('quickening'), which were regarded by St Thomas Aquinas as the first indication of life, for he believed that life was distinguished by two features, knowledge and movement; . . .

At about 24 weeks, the fetus reaches a state in which it can commonly survive outside the maternal body, with assistance, ... Just which stage marks the start of a person's life is a matter of personal opinion. Much of the foregoing argumentation may seem to some people difficult to comprehend, especially if they have not had formal training in biology, and to others may even seem irrelevant, in view of the firm line taken by many church authorities. But it really is important that we should try to reach a consensus on just when a person's life should be held to begin, for the decision does have important practical consequences—it directly affects the rights of other embryos, of fetuses, and of people, ...

H. Tristram Engelhardt, Jr., *Medicine and the Concept of the Person*

in CONTEMPORARY ISSUES IN BIOETHICS 94, 94–99 (Tom Beauchamp and LeRoy Walters eds., 1982).

Recent advances in medicine and the biomedical sciences have raised a number of ethical issues that medical ethics or, more broadly, bioethics have treated. Ingredient in such considerations, however, are fundamentally conceptual and ontological issues. To talk of the sanctity of life, for example, presupposes that one knows (1) what life is, and (2) what makes for its sanctity. More importantly, to talk of the rights of persons presupposes that one knows what counts as a person. In this paper I will provide an examination of the concept of person and will argue that the terms "human life" and even "human person" are complex and heterogeneous terms. I will hold that human life has more than one meaning and that there is more than one sense of human person. I will then indicate how the recognition of these multiple meanings has important implications for medicine.

KINDS OF LIFE AND SANCTITY OF LIFE

Whatever is meant by life's being sacred, it is rarely held that all life is equally sacred. Most people would find the life of bacteria, for example, to be less valuable or sacred than the life of fellow humans. . . . Moreover, distinctions are made with respect to humans. Not all human life has the same sanctity. The issue of brain-death, for example, turns on such a distinction. Brain-dead, but otherwise alive, human beings do not have the sanctity of normal adult human beings. That is, the indices of brain-death have been selected in order to measure the death of a person. . . .

The brain-oriented concept of death is more directly concerned with human personal life. It makes three presuppositions: (1) that being a person involves more than mere vegetative life, (2) that merely vegetative life may have value but it has no rights, (3) that a sensory-motor organ such as the brain is a necessary condition for the possibility of experience and action in the world, that is, for being a person living in the world. Thus in the absence of the possibility of brain-function, one has the absence of the possibility of personal life—that is, the person is dead. . . . The brain-oriented concept of death is of philosophical significance, for, among other things, it implies a distinction between human biological life and human personal life, between the life of a human organism and the life of a human person. . . .

We are brought then to a set of distinctions: first, human life must be distinguished as human personal and human biological life. Not all instances of human biological life are instances of human personal life. Brain-dead (but otherwise alive) human beings, human gametes, cells in human cell cultures, all count as instances of human biological life. Further, not only are some humans not persons, there is no reason to hold that all persons are humans, as the possibility of extraterrestrial self-conscious life suggests.

Second, the concept of the sanctity of life comes to refer in different ways to the value of biological life and the dignity of persons. Probably much that is associated with arguments concerning the sanctity of life really refers to the dignity of the life of persons. In any event, there is no unambiguous sense of being simply "pro-life" or a defender of the sanctity of life—one must decide what sort of life one wishes to defend and on what grounds. To begin with, the morally significant difference between biological and personal life lies in the fact, to use Kant's idiom, that persons are ends in themselves. Rational, self-conscious agents can make claims to treatment as ends in themselves because they can experience themselves, can know that they experience themselves, and can determine and control the circumstances of such experience. Self-conscious agents are self-determining and can claim respect as such. That is, they can claim the right to be respected as free agents. Such a claim is to the effect that self-respect and mutual respect turn on self-determination, on the fact that self-conscious beings are necessary for the existence of a moral order—a kingdom of ends, a community based on mutual self-respect, not force. Only self-conscious agents can be held accountable for their actions and thus be bound together solely in terms of mutual respect of each other's autonomy.

. . .

It is only respect for persons in this strict sense that cannot be violated without contradicting the idea of a moral order in the sense of the living with others on the basis of a mutual respect of autonomy. The point to be emphasized is a distinction between value and dignity, between biological life and personal life. These distinctions provide a basis for the differentiation between biological or merely animal life, and personal life, and turn on the rather commonsense criterion of respect being given that which can be respected—that is, blamed or praised. Moral treatment comes to depend, not implausibly, on moral agency. The importance of such distinctions for medicine is that they can be employed in treating medical ethical issues. As arguments, they are attempts to sort out everyday distinctions between moral agents, other animals, and just plain things. They provide a conceptual apparatus based on the meaning of obligations as respect due that which can have obligations.

The distinctions between human biological life and human personal life, and between the value of human biological life and the dignity of human personal life, involve a basic conceptual distinction that modern medical science presses as an issue of practical importance. Medicine after all is not merely the enterprise of preserving human life—if that were the case, medicine would confuse human cell cultures with patients who are persons. In fact, a maxim "to treat patients as persons" presupposes that we do or can indeed know who the persons are. These distinctions focus not only on the newly problematic issue of the definition of death, but on the question of abortion as well: issues that turn on when persons end and when they begin.

. . .

With regard to abortion, many have argued . . . that the fetus is not a person, though it is surely an instance of human biological life. Even if the fetus is a human organism that will probably be genetically and organically continuous with a human person, it is not yet such a person. Simply put, fetuses are not rational, self-conscious beings—that is, given a strict definition of persons, fetuses do not qualify as persons. One sees this when comparing talk about dead men with talk about fetuses. When speaking of a dead man, one knows of whom one speaks, the one who died, the person whom one knew before his death. But in speaking of the fetus, one has no such person to whom one can refer. There is not yet a person, a "who," to whom one can refer in the case of the fetus (compare: one can keep promises to dead men but not to men yet unborn). In short, a fetus in no way singles itself out as, or shows itself to be, a person. This conclusion has theoretical advantages, since many zygotes never implant and some divide into two. It offers as well a moral clarification of the practice of using intrauterine contraceptive devices and abortion. Whatever these practices involve, they do not involve the taking of the life of a person. This position in short involves recurring to a distinction forged by both Aristotle and St. Thomas—between biological life and personal life, between life that has value and life that has dignity.

. . . By the terms of the argument, infants, as well as fetuses, are not persons—thus, one finds infants as much open to infanticide as fetuses are left open to abortion. The question then is whether one can recoup something for infants or perhaps even for fetuses. One might think that a counterargument, or at least a mitigating argument, could be made on the basis of potentiality—the potentiality of infants or the potentiality of fetuses. That argument, though, fails because one must distinguish the potentialities of a person from the potentiality to become a person. If, for example, one holds that a fetus has the potentiality of a person, one begs the very question at issue—whether fetuses are persons. But, on the other hand, if one succeeds in arguing that a fetus or infant has the potentiality to become a person, one has conceded the point that the fetus or infant is not a person. One may value a dozen eggs or a handful of acorns because they can become chickens or oak trees. But a dozen eggs is not a flock of chickens, a handful of acorns is not a stand of oaks. In short, the potentiality of X's to become Y's may cause us to value X's very highly because Y's are valued very highly, but until X's are Y's they do not have the value of Y's.

. . . [T]hough we have sorted out a distinction between the value of human biological life and the dignity of human personal life, this distinction does not do all we want, or rather it may do too much. That is, it goes against an intuitive appreciation of children, even neonates, as not being open to destruction on request. We may not in the end be able to support that intuition, for it may simply be a cultural prejudice; but I will now try to give a reasonable exegesis of its significance.

TWO CONCEPTS OF PERSON

I shall argue in this section that a confusion arises out of a false presupposition that we have only one concept of person: we have at least two concepts (probably many more) of person. I will restrict myself to examining the two that are most relevant here. First, there is the sense of person that we use in identifying moral agents: individual, living bearers of rights and duties. That sense singles out entities who can participate in the language of morals, who can make claims and have those claims respected: the strict sense we have examined above. We would, for example, understand "person" in this sense to be used properly if we found another group of self-conscious agents in the universe and called them persons even if they were not human, though it is a term that usually applies to normal adult humans. This sense of person I shall term the strict sense, one which is used in reference to self-conscious, rational agents. But what of the respect accorded to infants and other examples of non-self-conscious or not-yet-self-conscious human life? How are such entities to be understood?

A plausible analysis can, I believe, be given in terms of a second concept or use of person—a social concept or social role of person that is invoked when certain instances of human biological life are treated as if they were persons strictly, even though they are not. A good example is the mother-child or parent-child relationship in which the infant is treated as a person even though it is not one strictly. That is, the infant is treated as if it had the wants and desires of a person—its cries are treated as a call for food, attention, care, etc., and the infant is socialized, placed within a social structure, the family, and becomes a child. The shift is from merely biological to social significance. The shift is made on the basis that the infant is a human and is able to engage in a minimum of social interaction. With regard to the latter point, severely anencephalic infants may not qualify for the role *person* just as brain-dead adults would fail to qualify; both lack the ability to engage in minimal social interaction. This use of person is, after all, one employed with instances of human biological life that are enmeshed in social roles as if they were persons. Further, one finds a difference between the biological mother-fetus relation and the social mother-child relation. The first relation can continue whether or not there is social recognition of the fetus, the second cannot. The mother-child relation is essentially a social practice.

This practice can be justified as a means of preserving trust in families, of nurturing important virtues of care and solicitude towards the weak, and of assuring the healthy development of children. Further, it has a special value because it is difficult to determine specifically when in human ontogeny persons strictly emerge. Socializing infants into the role *person* draws the line conservatively. Humans do not become persons strictly until some time after birth. Moreover, there is a considerable value in protecting anything that looks and acts in a reasonably human fashion, especially when it falls within an established human social role as infants do within the role *child*. This ascription of the role *person* constitutes a social practice that allows the rights of a person to be imputed to forms of human life that can engage in at least a minimum of social interaction. The interest is in guarding anything that could reasonably play the role *person* and thus to strengthen the social position of persons generally.

The social sense of person appears as well to structure the treatment of the senile, the mentally retarded, and the otherwise severely mentally infirm. Though they are not moral agents, persons strictly, they are treated as if they were persons. The social sense of person identifies their place in a social relationship with persons strictly. It is, in short, a practice that gives to instances of human biological life the status of persons. Unlike persons strictly, who are bearers of both rights and duties, persons in the social sense have rights but no duties. That is, they are not morally responsible agents, but are treated with respect (i.e., rights are imputed to them) in order to establish a practice of considerable utility to moral agents: a society where kind treatment of the infirm and weak is an established practice. The central element of the utility of this practice lies in the fact that it is often difficult to tell when an individual is a person strictly (i.e., how senile need one be in order no longer to be able to be a person strictly), and persons strictly might need to fear concerning their treatment (as well as the inadvertent mistreatment of other persons strictly) were such a practice not established. The social sense of person is a way of treating certain instances of human life in order to secure the life of persons strictly.

. . .

It should be stressed that the social sense of person is primarily a utilitarian construct. A person in this sense is not a person strictly, and hence not an unqualified object of respect. Rather, one treats certain instances of human life as persons for the good of those individuals who are persons strictly. As a consequence, exactly where one draws the line between persons in the social sense and merely human biological life is not crucial as long as the integrity of persons strictly is preserved. Thus there is a somewhat arbitrary quality about the distinction between fetuses and infants. One draws a line where the practice of treating human life as human personal life is practical and useful. Birth, including the production of a viable fetus through an abortion procedure, provides a somewhat natural line at which to begin to treat human biological life as human personal life. One might retort, Why not include fetuses as persons in a social sense? The answer is, Only if there are good reasons to do so in terms of utility. One would have to measure the utility of abortions for the convenience of women and families, for the prevention of the birth of infants with serious genetic diseases, and for the control of population growth against whatever increased goods would come from treating fetuses as persons. . . .

One is thus left with at least two concepts of person. On the one hand, persons strictly can and usually do identify themselves as such—they are self-conscious, rational agents, respect for whom is part of valuing freedom, assigning blame and praise, and understanding obligation. That is, one's duty to respect persons strictly is the core of morality itself. The social concept of person is, on the other hand, more mediate, it turns on central values but is not the same as respect for the dignity of persons strictly. It allows us to value highly certain but not all instances of human biological life, without confusing that value with the dignity of persons strictly. That is, we can maintain the distinction between human biological and human personal life. We must recognize, though, that some human biological life is treated as human personal life even though it does not involve the existence of a person in the strict sense.

NOTES AND QUESTIONS

1. According to Engelhardt, what properties must entities have to properly be called persons? In his book Humanhood: Essays in Biomedical Ethics, Fletcher describes fifteen positive characteristics and five negative characteristics that define a person. The positive characteristics include minimum intelligence, self-awareness, self-control, a sense of time, a sense of the future, a sense of the past, the ability to relate to other people, concern for others, communication, control of existence, curiosity, change and changeability, balance of rationality and feeling, idiosyncrasy, and neocortical function. The negative characteristics include the ideas that people are not non-or anti-artificial, people are not parental, people are not essentially sexual, people are not a bundle of rights, and people are not worshippers. Joseph Fletcher, Humanhood: Essays in Biomedical Ethics 12–18 (1979). In summarizing his theory, Fletcher states:

> Many of us look upon living and dying as we do upon health and medical care, as person-centered. This is not a solely or basically biological understanding of what it means to be "alive" and to be "dead." It asserts that a so-called vegetable, the brain-damaged victim of an auto accident or a microcephalic newborn or a case of massive neurologic deficit and lost cerebral capacity, who nevertheless goes on breathing and whose midbrain or brain stem continues to support spontaneous organ functions, is in such a situation no longer a human being, no longer a person, no longer really alive. It is *personal* function that counts, not biological function. Humanness is understood as primarily rational, not physiological. This "doctrine of man" puts the *homo* and *ratio* before the *vita*. It holds that being human is more valuable than being alive.

Id. at 151.

Do you agree with the approaches taken by Engelhardt and Fletcher? Is Austin's approach to defining when life begins in biological terms more satisfactory?

2. Austin notes that death is defined by the end of electrical activity in the brain. C.R. Austin, Human Embryos: The Debate on Assisted Reproduction 29 (1989). Should the same criteria be used to define when life begins and ends? Some have argued, for example, that the beginning of life should be defined consistently with the brain-oriented definition of death, Chapter 4, Sec. I., *supra*, although these analyses do not agree on when brain life begins. *See, e.g.*, John M. Goldenring, *The Brain–Life Theory: Towards a Consistent Biological Definition of Humanness*, 11 J. Med. Ethics 198 (1985) (brain life begins at eight weeks in utero); Hans–Martin Sass, *Brain Life and Brain Death*, 14 J. Med & Phil. 45 (1989) (calling for the beginning of life at seven weeks); Gary B. Gertler, Note, *Brain Birth: A Proposal for Defining When a Fetus is Entitled to Human Life Status*, 59 S. Cal. L. Rev. 1062 (1986) (for purposes of state intervention, human life "begins" when neocortical activity begins, between weeks 22 and 24).

Others argue that a "brain life" standard seeks consistency and symmetry at the expense of oversimplifying and obscuring both the scientific and ethical issues at stake at different stages of human life. *See, e.g.*, Mario Moussa & Thomas A. Shannon, *The Search for the New Pineal Gland*, 22 Hastings Ctr. Rep. 30 (1992).

3. Engelhardt is interested in distinguishing two concepts of persons in order to determine how different entities should be treated morally. Austin wants to reach a consensus on when life begins for practical reasons because the decision affects the rights of embryos, fetuses and persons. Similarly, the question of when life begins or when "personhood" is established arises in law and public policy in the context of abortion, the use of reproductive and genetic technologies, and experimentation on embryos and fetuses, as a means of deciding when rights entitled to recognition by the state attach.

Can inquiries about when life begins or "personhood" is established definitively dispose of the issue of whether or when the state should protect the life of fetuses or embryos? Are these primarily issues of scientific fact? Of morality? Of law? The Supreme Court in *Roe v. Wade, infra* Sec. II. A. 2., found that the fetus is not a "person" protected by the Fourteenth Amendment and also declined to define when life begins because of a lack of consensus on the issue. Do you agree? Even if it were settled that fetuses and embryos were persons deserving state protection, conflicts between them and other persons, such as their mothers, would have to be resolved. *See* Judith Jarvis Thompson, *A Defense of Abortion, in* THE PROBLEM OF ABORTION 21 (Joel Feinberg ed., 1973).

Should the effort to define the beginning of life and personhood be abandoned? Should policymakers focus instead on the reasons why life should be protected and whether those reasons are applicable to human entities at different stages of development? *See* Sissela Bok, *Who Shall Count as a Human Being?: A Treacherous Question in the Abortion Discussion, in* WHAT IS A PERSON? 213, 217 (Michael F. Goodman ed., 1988); *see also* RONALD DWORKIN, LIFE'S DOMINION: AN ARGUMENT ABOUT ABORTION, EUTHANASIA, AND INDIVIDUAL FREEDOM (1993).

4. A majority of states (thirty as of 2004) have enacted fetal homicide statutes. Two additional states have developed fetal homicide case law, and at least fifteen of the states' fetal homicide laws apply to the earliest stage of pregnancy, i.e. conception, fertilization, and post-fertilization. *See* National Conference of State Legislatures, *Fetal Homicide,* (2004), at http://www.ncsl.org, last visited July 12, 2004. Several states' penalties for the killing of fetuses are the same as those for homicide. *See, e.g.,* GA. CODE ANN. § 16–5–80 (2004), IND. CODE ANN. § 35–50–2–9(b)(16) (2004), MINN. STAT. § 2661 (2004). Other states treat feticide as a lesser offense, and impose a lesser penalty. *See, e.g.,* MISS. CODE ANN. § 97–3–37 (2003), NEV. REV. STAT. ANN. § 200.210 (2003). A few states have also enacted statutes recognizing that embryos or fetuses are "persons" or "human beings" in the context of regulating abortion or reproductive technologies. *See, e.g.,* LA. REV. STAT. ANN. § 9:123 (West 2004) (embryo is "juridical person;" limits use and destruction of embryos); MO. ANN. STAT. § 1.205 (West 2004) (preamble defines human life to begin at conception).

In tort law, historically courts did not allow civil recovery for the wrongful death of a fetus. However, after *Roe v. Wade*'s determination of fetal viability as the marker for state interest in potential life, Sec. II. A. 2., *infra*, several states have allowed successful wrongful death claims for the death of a fetus after viability. *See, e.g., Aka v. Jefferson Hosp. Ass'n,* 344 Ark. 627, 42 S.W.3d 508 (2001) (viable fetus is "person" for purposes of Arkansas wrongful death statute); *State v. McKnight,* 352 S.C. 635, 576 S.E.2d 168 (2003) (defendant liable for death of viable fetus); *Farley v. Sartin,* 195 W.Va. 671, 466 S.E.2d 522 (1995) (allowing wrongful death action for death of unborn child who reached viability).

In the context of decedents' estates, some states have also ruled that a fetus possesses inheritance rights, but only if the fetus is ultimately born alive. *See Parvin v. Dean,* 7 S.W.3d 264 (Tex. Ct. App. 1999) (allowing fetus to inherit from deceased parent); *State ex rel. Angela M.W. v. Kruzicki,* 209 Wis.2d 112, 561 N.W.2d 729, 738 (1997) (Property law creates means of fulfilling intentions of testators by protecting right of fetus to inherit property upon live birth).

At the federal level, in April 2004, President George W. Bush signed into law the Unborn Victims of Violence Act, which recognizes as a legal victim any "child in utero" who is injured or killed during the commission of a federal crime of violence.

The law defines "child in utero" as "a member of the species homo sapiens, at any stage of development, who is carried in the womb." 18 U.S.C.A. § 1841 (2004).

In 2002, the Centers for Medicare and Medicaid Services (CMS) amended a child health care regulation to include unborn children in the definition of "child." The regulation, issued under Title XXI of the Social Security Act (42 U.S.C.A. § 1397bb), authorizes payment of federal funds to states to provide health benefits for low-income children under the age of nineteen. The 2002 amendment clarified the definition of "child" to mean a child under the age of nineteen, including the period from conception to birth, to allow health benefits coverage for prenatal care and delivery. 42 CFR § 457.10. However, because the regulation covers only children, the mother's benefits cease upon the birth of the child. The child may continue to receive health benefits until his or her nineteenth birthday.

5. The *Davis* court, as well as the Supreme Court in *Roe* and *Casey, infra* Sec. II. A.2., found that the state has a legitimate interest in protecting "potential life." What is the nature of a state interest in "potential life"? Is it grounded on protecting an independent interest of the fetus or embryo in potential life, or on a separate state interest in protecting life generally?

Do you agree that society has an interest in protecting potential life? How strong is that interest? Should the state's interest in protecting potential life be the same for a preimplantation embryo and a fetus in utero?

II.   DECIDING WHETHER, WHEN, OR HOW TO REPRODUCE

Advances in reproductive technologies have vastly increased the ability of individuals and couples to plan, limit, interrupt, or promote conception and pregnancy. In addition, advances in genetic technologies provide information about characteristics of prospective parents, fetuses, and embryos that can be used to help procreative parents make decisions about whether, when, or how they will have children.

These developments raise many legal, ethical, and social issues. What does responsible procreation require of progenitors? Under what circumstances should responsible persons decide not to reproduce? Conversely, once the decision to have children is made, what, if any, obligations do procreative parents have to prevent harm and to promote the well being of the future child? What, if any, role should third parties play in assisting others to reproduce? Is there a role for government in establishing and enforcing these norms?

Finally, these emerging reproductive and genetic technologies pose significant challenges for the future. They offer the prospect of asexual reproduction as well as the utilization of human reproductive material for other than procreative purposes.

A.   WHO DECIDES?

1.   CONTRACEPTION

Griswold v. Connecticut

Supreme Court of the United States, 1965.
381 U.S. 479, 85 S.Ct. 1678, 14 L.Ed.2d 510.

■ JUSTICE DOUGLAS delivered the opinion of the Court.

Appellant Griswold is Executive Director of the Planned Parenthood League of Connecticut. Appellant Buxton is a licensed physician and a

II. Deciding Whether, When, or How to Reproduce

professor at the Yale Medical School who served as Medical Director for the League at its Center in New Haven—a center open and operating from November 1 to November 10, 1961, when appellants were arrested.

They gave information, instruction, and medical advice to married persons as to the means of preventing conception. . . .

The statutes whose constitutionality is involved in this appeal are §§ 53–32 and 54–196 of the General Statutes of Connecticut (1958 rev.). The former provides:

"Any person who uses any drug, medicinal article or instrument for the purpose of preventing conception shall be fined not less than fifty dollars or imprisoned not less than sixty days nor more than one year or be both fined and imprisoned."

Section 54–196 provides:

"Any person who assists, abets, counsels, causes, hires or commands another to commit any offense may be prosecuted and punished as if he were the principal offender."

. . .

Coming to the merits, we are met with a wide range of questions that implicate the Due Process Clause of the Fourteenth Amendment. . . . This law . . . operates directly on an intimate relation of husband and wife and their physician's role in one aspect of that relation.

The association of people is not mentioned in the Constitution nor in the Bill of Rights. The right to educate a child in a school of the parents' choice—whether public or private or parochial—is also not mentioned. Nor is the right to study any particular subject or any foreign language. Yet the First Amendment has been construed to include certain of those rights.

. . .

[Those] . . . cases suggest that specific guarantees in the Bill of Rights have penumbras, formed by emanations from those guarantees that help give them life and substance. *See* Poe v. Ullman, 367 U.S. 497, 516–522 (dissenting opinion). Various guarantees create zones of privacy. The right of association contained in the penumbra of the First Amendment is one, as we have seen. The Third Amendment in its prohibition against the quartering of soldiers "in any house" in time of peace without the consent of the owner is another facet of that privacy. The Fourth Amendment explicitly affirms the "right of the people to be secure in their persons, houses, papers, and effects, against unreasonable searches and seizures." The Fifth Amendment in its Self–Incrimination Clause enables the citizen to create a zone of privacy which government may not force him to surrender to his detriment. The Ninth Amendment provides: "The enumeration in the Constitution, of certain rights, shall not be construed to deny or disparage others retained by the people."

. . .

The present case ... concerns a relationship lying within the zone of privacy created by several fundamental constitutional guarantees. And it concerns a law which, in forbidding the use of contraceptives rather than regulating their manufacture or sale, seeks to achieve its goals by means having a maximum destructive impact upon that relationship. Such a law cannot stand in light of the familiar principle, so often applied by this Court, that a "governmental purpose to control or prevent activities constitutionally subject to state regulation may not be achieved by means which sweep unnecessarily broadly and thereby invade the area of protected freedoms." NAACP v. Alabama, 377 U.S. 288, 307. Would we allow the police to search the sacred precincts of marital bedrooms for telltale signs of the use of contraceptives? The very idea is repulsive to the notions of privacy surrounding the marriage relationship.

We deal with a right of privacy older than the Bill of Rights—older than our political parties, older than our school system. Marriage is a coming together for better or for worse, hopefully enduring, and intimate to the degree of being sacred. It is an association that promotes a way of life, not causes; a harmony in living, not political faiths; a bilateral loyalty, not commercial or social projects. Yet it is an association for as noble a purpose as any involved in our prior decisions.

Reversed.

NOTES AND QUESTIONS

1. After *Griswold,* the Court decided several cases that clarified and expanded the right of privacy. In *Eisenstadt v. Baird*, 405 U.S. 438, 92 S.Ct. 1029, 31 L.Ed.2d 349 (1972), the Court overturned a law banning the distribution of contraceptives to single persons.

Justice Brennan, writing for the Court, held that the statute, viewed as a prohibition on contraception per se, violated the rights of single persons under the equal protection clause of the Fourteenth Amendment. The Court stated,

> If under *Griswold* the distribution of contraceptives to married persons cannot be prohibited, a ban on the distribution [of contraceptives] to unmarried persons would be equally impermissible.... If the right to privacy means anything, it is the right of the individual, married or single, to be free from unwarranted governmental intrusion into matters so fundamentally affecting a person as the decision whether to bear ... a child.

405 U.S. at 453. The Court declined to answer the question of whether the Massachusetts law could be upheld as a flat ban on contraception, stating that "whatever the rights of the individual to access to contraceptives may be, the rights must be the same for the unmarried and married alike." *Id.* at 439.

In *Carey v. Population Serv. Int'l*, 431 U.S. 678, 97 S.Ct. 2010, 52 L.Ed.2d 675 (1977), the Supreme Court upheld a Southern District of New York decision declaring New York Education Law Section 6811(8) unconstitutional. Under the law, it is a crime:

> (1) for any person to sell or distribute any contraceptive of any kind to a minor under 16; (2) for anyone other than a licensed pharmacist to distribute contraceptives to persons 16 or over; and (3) for anyone, including licensed pharmacists, to advertise or display contraceptives.

Id. at 678.

Like *Griswold* and *Eisenstadt, Carey* concerned contraceptives. However, *Carey* was decided after *Roe v. Wade, infra* Sec. II. A. 2. and further clarifies the right to privacy defined within that case. The *Carey* opinion protects access to contraceptives rather than merely protecting the privacy of marital relations. Justice Brennan writing for a majority of the Court states that *"Griswold* may no longer be read as holding only that a State may not prohibit a married couple's use of contraceptives. Read in light of its progeny, the teaching of *Griswold* is that the Constitution protects individual decision in matters of child bearing from unjustified intrusion of the State." *Id.* at 687.

The right to privacy has been considered a "fundamental" right which cannot be abridged absent a "compelling" state interest. Consider, however, the Supreme Court abortion decision in *Planned Parenthood v. Casey, infra* Sec. II. A. 2., which while expressly reaffirming the *Griswold* and *Eisenstadt* decisions, never mentions a "right to privacy." Instead *Casey* grounds the abortion right in a "liberty interest" and allows the state to restrict abortion without a "compelling" interest. After *Casey*, do other privacy rights, including contraceptive decisions, remain "fundamental," deserving of heightened judicial scrutiny? *See, e.g.*, Anita L. Allen, *Autonomy's Magic Wand: Abortion and Constitutional Interpretation*, 72 B.U. L. Rev. 683 (1992); Mark A. Racanelli, Note, *Reversals: Privacy and the Rehnquist Court*, 81 Geo. L.J. 443 (1992).

Do the *Griswold, Eisenstadt*, and *Carey* decisions recognize a right to private sexual activity separate from interests in avoiding procreation? Consider the Court's decision in *Lawrence v. Texas*, 539 U.S. 558, 123 S.Ct. 2472, 156 L.Ed.2d 508 (2003), in which a Texas statute making it illegal for same sex partners to engage in sodomy was held to violate the constitutional right to liberty and thus overturned the Court's previous ruling in *Bowers v. Hardwick*, 478 U.S. 186, 106 S.Ct. 2841, 92 L.Ed.2d 140 (1986). For a discussion of the evolution of the right of privacy in judicial decisions and the implications of the *Lawrence* opinion on that right, see Edward Stein, *Introducing Lawrence v. Texas: Some Background and a Glimpse of the Future*, 10 Cardozo Women's L.J. 263 (2004). For a discussion of the implications of *Lawrence* on gay and lesbian sexuality and civil rights, see Katherine M. Franke, *The Domesticated Liberty of Lawrence v. Texas*, 104 Colum. L. Rev. 1399 (2004).

2. Does the right to privacy encompass an affirmative right to procreate? In his concurring opinion in *Griswold*, Justice Goldberg, joined by the Chief Justice and Justice Brennan, opined that the constitutional right to privacy protects the right of married couples to be free from compulsory birth control just as it protects their right to practice voluntary birth control. In Goldberg's view, it would clearly be unconstitutional for the government to pass a law mandating sterilization of husbands and wives after they have had two children. 381 U.S. at 496–97 (Goldberg, J., concurring).

If Justice Goldberg is correct, does the privacy right extend to non-coital reproduction through the use of reproductive technologies? *See* Sec. II.

B. Consider the view of John Robertson:

> Procreative liberty is best understood as a liberty or claim-right to decide whether or not to reproduce. As such, it has two independently justified aspects: the liberty to avoid having offspring and the liberty to have offspring. Because each aspect has an independent justification, each may be conceived as a different right, connected by their common concern with reproduction.

> The liberty to avoid having offspring involves the freedom to act to avoid the birth of biologic (genetically related) offspring, such as avoiding intercourse, using contraceptives, refusing the transfer of embryos to the uterus, discarding embryos, terminating pregnancies, and being sterilized. In contrast, the liberty

or freedom to have offspring involves the freedom to take steps or make choices that result in the birth of biologic offspring, such as having intercourse, providing gametes for artificial or in vitro conception, placing embryos in the uterus, preserving gametes or embryos for later use, and avoiding the use of contraception, abortion, or sterilization.

As with other liberties in a rights-based society, an actor is not obligated to exercise a particular liberty right. He or she may not choose to reproduce, or to use or not to use genetic or reproductive technologies in making those decisions. An actor may have no need to use a technology or lack the means to do so; or he or she may reject uses of particular technologies for a wide range of personal reasons, including moral or ethical concerns about the effect of particular techniques on children, on society, or on deeply held personal values, including values of how reproduction should occur. The technological imperative-that if something can be done, it will be done-is not nearly as powerful as often claimed. No one is obligated to reproduce or to use particular reproductive and genetic technologies in avoiding reproduction or in reproducing.

Like most moral and legal rights in liberal society, procreative liberty is primarily a negative claim-right-a right against interference by the state or others with reproductive decisions-not a positive right to have the state provide resources or other persons provide the gametes, conception, gestation, or medical services necessary to have or not have offspring.

John Robertson, *Procreative Liberty in the Era of Genomics*, 29 AM. J. L. & MED. 439, 447–48 (2003).

On the other hand, Dorothy Roberts believes that the dominant view of liberty as described by John Robertson has been too narrowly articulated. Consider her view:

> The dominant view of liberty reserves most of its protection only for the most privileged members of society. This approach superimposes liberty on an already unjust social structure, which it seeks to preserve against unwarranted governmental interference. Liberty protects all citizens' choices from the most direct and egregious abuses of governmental power but it does nothing to dismantle social arrangements that make it impossible for some people to make a choice in the first place. Liberty guards against government intrusion; it does not guarantee social justice . . .

> Liberals frame the issue of access to abortions or reproductive technologies, for example, as freedom from governmental interference with private decisions to sue them, rather than a claim to public resources to make these options truly available.

> . . .

> The negative view of liberty of reproductive decisionmaking not only disregards "private" obstacles to reproductive decisionmaking such as social prejudices, racist business practices, and the maldistribution of wealth, but it also disregards certain instances of state interference in poor people's reproductive decisions. It allows the state to exploit poor women's dependence on government funds to influence their reproductive choices. . . . Because this view sees poor women's waiver of their right to procreate as voluntary it does not require the government to justify its deliberate effort to deter these women from having children.

DOROTHY ROBERTS, KILLING THE BLACK BODY: RACE, REPRODUCTION, AND THE MEANING OF LIBERTY 294–97 (1997).

3. The development of long-term, convenient, inexpensive, safe, and effective contraceptives might reduce the need for abortion and sterilization which are far more controversial methods of preventing birth. Development and introduction of new contraceptive devices has been hampered, however, by the prolonged federal licensing process and political controversy surrounding abortion and family values. In 2004, the Institute of Medicine published a report on contraceptive research that advocated speedier Food and Drug Administration (FDA) approval for new contraceptive technologies. *See* INSTITUTE OF MEDICINE, NEW FRONTIERS IN CONTRACEPTIVE RESEARCH, Executive Summary, (2004), at http://www.iom.edu/report.asp?id=17893, last visited July 15, 2004.

Three new contraceptive options—the patch, the vaginal ring, and an 84–day cycle of oral contraceptives—have been licensed by the FDA since 2000. *See* Emily Herndon & Miriam Zieman, *New Contraceptive Options*, 69 AM. FAM. PHYSICIAN 853 (2004). All of the newly licensed contraceptives are pre-conception methods that prevent fertilization of the female ovum by the male sperm. This category includes the traditional barrier methods of male and female condoms, diaphragms, cervical caps, spermicidal jellies and foams which destroy the sperm before they reach the ovum, oral contraceptives and Depo–Provera (a long-acting progesterone injection) which prevent the release of ova, and the rhythm method which predicts a woman's fertile periods during which there is abstinence from unprotected intercourse.

More controversial are the post-coital or post-conception methods, which include intrauterine devices and oral contraceptives known as "morning after" pills. There are two available emergency contraceptives, one containing a high dose of an estrogen and progesterone combination (Preven®) and one containing a high dose of only progesterone (Plan B®). Because the exact mechanism of action of these emergency contraceptives is unknown, commentators disagree about whether they are contraceptives or abortifacients. Opponents of the morning-after pill argue that it amounts to abortion, because it prevents implantation of a fertilized egg, thereby causing an early abortion, while proponents argue that it prevents fertilization and thus is contraceptive. *See* A. Faundes et al., *Emergency Contraception—Clinical and Ethical Aspects*, 82 INT'L J. OF GYNECOLOGY & OBSTETRICS 297 (2003).

In thirty-three countries, including the United Kingdom, France, South Africa and Sweden, women are able to purchase emergency contraception without a doctor's prescription. In France, school nurses are allowed to dispense emergency contraception to students. *See* Planned Parenthood, *A Brief History of Emergency Hormonal Contraception*, (2004), at http://www.plannedparenthood.org, last visited July 1, 2004. Emergency contraception is currently not available without a prescription in the United States. In 2003, Women's Capital Corp. (WCC), the manufacturer of Plan B, applied to the FDA for permission to market Plan B over-the-counter (it was originally marketed as a prescription drug). Although the FDA rejected the application in May 2004, public and political outcry prompted the agency to allow WCC to edit the labeling and re-submit for review in November 2004.

2. ABORTION

Roe v. Wade
Supreme Court of the United States, 1973.
410 U.S. 113, 93 S.Ct. 705, 35 L.Ed.2d 147.

■ JUSTICE BLACKMUN delivered the opinion of the Court.

This Texas federal appeal presents constitutional challenges to state criminal abortion legislation. . . .

. . .

I.

The Texas statutes that concern us here are Arts. 1191–1194 and 1196 of the State's Penal Code. These make it a crime to "procure an abortion," as therein defined, or to attempt one, except with respect to "an abortion procured or attempted by medical advice for the purpose of saving the life of the mother." . . .

II.

Jane Roe, a single woman who was residing in Dallas County, Texas, instituted this federal action in March 1970 against the District Attorney of the county. She sought a declaratory judgment that the Texas criminal abortion statutes were unconstitutional on their face, and an injunction restraining the defendant from enforcing the statutes.

Roe alleged that she was unmarried and pregnant; that she wished to terminate her pregnancy by an abortion "performed by a competent, licensed physician, under safe, clinical conditions"; that she was unable to get a "legal" abortion in Texas because her life did not appear to be threatened by the continuation of her pregnancy; and that she could not afford to travel to another jurisdiction in order to secure a legal abortion under safe conditions. She claimed that the Texas statutes were unconstitutionally vague and that they abridged her right of personal privacy, protected by the First, Fourth, Fifth, Ninth, and Fourteenth Amendments. By an amendment to her complaint Roe purported to sue "on behalf of herself and all other women" similarly situated.

. . .

VIII.

The Constitution does not explicitly mention any right of privacy. In a line of decisions . . . the Court has recognized that a right of personal privacy, or a guarantee of certain areas or zones of privacy, does exist under the Constitution. . . .

This right of privacy, whether it be founded in the Fourteenth Amendment's concept of personal liberty and restrictions upon state action, as we feel it is, or, as the District Court determined, in the Ninth Amendment's reservation of rights to the people, is broad enough to encompass a woman's decision whether or not to terminate her pregnancy. The detriment that the State would impose upon the pregnant woman by denying this choice altogether is apparent. Specific and direct harm medically diagnosable even in early pregnancy may be involved. Maternity, or additional offspring, may force upon the woman a distressful life and future. Psychological harm may be imminent. Mental and physical health may be taxed by child care. There is also the distress, for all concerned, associated with the unwanted child, and there is the problem of bringing a child into a family already unable, psychologically and otherwise, to care for it. In other cases, as in this one, the additional difficulties and continuing stigma of unwed motherhood may be involved. . . .

On the basis of elements such as these, appellant and some *amici* argue that the woman's right is absolute and that she is entitled to terminate her pregnancy at whatever time, in whatever way, and for whatever reason she alone chooses. With this we do not agree. . . . In fact, it is not clear to us that the claim asserted by some *amici* that one has an unlimited right to do with one's body as one pleases bears a close relationship to the right of privacy previously articulated in the Court's decisions. The Court has refused to recognize an unlimited right of this kind in the past. *Jacobson v. Massachusetts*, 197 U.S. 11 (1905) (vaccination); *Buck v. Bell*, 274 U.S. 200 (1927) (sterilization).

We, therefore, conclude that the right of personal privacy includes the abortion decision, but that this right is not unqualified and must be considered against important state interests in regulation.

. . .

IX.

. . .

A. The appellee and certain *amici* argue that the fetus is a "person" within the language and meaning of the Fourteenth Amendment. In support of this, they outline at length and in detail the well-known facts of fetal development. If this suggestion of personhood is established, the appellant's case, of course, collapses, for the fetus' right to life would then be guaranteed specifically by the Amendment. The appellant conceded as much on reargument. On the other hand, the appellee conceded on reargument that no case could be cited that holds that a fetus is a person within the meaning of the Fourteenth Amendment.

The Constitution does not define "person" in so many words. . . . But in nearly all . . . instances, the use of the word is such that it has application only postnatally. . . .

All this, together with our observation, supra, that throughout the major portion of the 19th century prevailing legal abortion practices were far freer than they are today, persuades us that the word "person," as used in the Fourteenth Amendment, does not include the unborn. . . .

. . .

B. The pregnant woman cannot be isolated in her privacy. She carries an embryo and, later, a fetus, if one accepts the medical definitions of the developing young in the human uterus. See Dorland's Illustrated Medical Dictionary 478–479, 547 (24th ed. 1965). The situation therefore is inherently different from marital intimacy, or bedroom possession of obscene material, or marriage, or procreation, or education. . . . As we have intimated above, it is reasonable and appropriate for a State to decide that at some point in time another interest, that of health of the mother or that of potential human life, becomes significantly involved. The woman's privacy is no longer sole and any right of privacy she possesses must be measured accordingly.

Texas urges that, apart from the Fourteenth Amendment, life begins at conception and is present throughout pregnancy, and that, therefore, the State has a compelling interest in protecting that life from and after conception. We need not resolve the difficult question of when life begins. When those trained in the respective disciplines of medicine, philosophy, and theology are unable to arrive at any consensus, the judiciary, at this point in the development of man's knowledge, is not in a position to speculate as to the answer.

.   .   .

X.

In view of all this, we do not agree that, by adopting one theory of life, Texas may override the rights of the pregnant woman that are at stake. We repeat, however, that the State does have an important and legitimate interest in preserving and protecting the health of the pregnant woman, whether she be a resident of the State or a nonresident who seeks medical consultation and treatment there, and that it has still *another* important and legitimate interest in protecting the potentiality of human life. These interests are separate and distinct. Each grows in substantiality as the woman approaches term and, at a point during pregnancy, each becomes "compelling."

With respect to the State's important and legitimate interest in the health of the mother, the "compelling" point, in the light of present medical knowledge, is at approximately the end of the first trimester. This is so because of the now-established medical fact ... that until the end of the first trimester mortality in abortion may be less than mortality in normal childbirth. It follows that, from and after this point, a State may regulate the abortion procedure to the extent that the regulation reasonably relates to the preservation and protection of maternal health. Examples of permissible state regulation in this area are requirements as to the qualifications of the person who is to perform the abortion; as to the licensure of that person; as to the facility in which the procedure is to be performed, that is, whether it must be a hospital or may be a clinic or some other place of less-than-hospital status; as to the licensing of the facility; and the like.

This means, on the other hand, that, for the period of pregnancy prior to this "compelling" point, the attending physician, in consultation with his patient, is free to determine, without regulation by the State, that, in his medical judgment, the patient's pregnancy should be terminated.

.   .   .

With respect to the State's important and legitimate interest in potential life, the "compelling" point is at viability. This is so because the fetus then presumably has the capability of meaningful life outside the mother's womb. State regulation protective of fetal life after viability thus has both logical and biological justifications. If the State is interested in protecting fetal life after viability, it may go so far as to proscribe abortion during that period, except when it is necessary to preserve the life or health of the mother.

Measured against these standards, Art. 1196 of the Texas Penal Code, in restricting legal abortions to those "procured or attempted by medical advice for the purpose of saving the life of the mother," sweeps too broadly. The statute makes no distinction between abortions performed early in pregnancy and those performed later, and it limits to a single reason, "saving" the mother's life, the legal justification for the procedure. The statute, therefore, cannot survive the constitutional attack made upon it here.

Planned Parenthood of Southeastern Pennsylvania v. Casey

Supreme Court of the United States, 1992.
505 U.S. 833, 112 S.Ct. 2791, 120 L.Ed.2d 674.

■ Justice O'Connor, Justice Kennedy, and Justice Souter announced the judgment of the Court and delivered the opinion of the Court with respect to Parts I, II, III, V–A, V–C, and VI, an opinion with respect to Part V–E, in which Justice Stevens joins, and an opinion with respect to Parts IV, V–B, and V–D.

[This suit challenged five provisions of the Pennsylvania Abortion Control Act of 1982 on their face: § 3205, which requires that a woman seeking an abortion give her informed consent prior to the abortion procedure, and specifies that she be provided with certain information at least 24 hours before the abortion is performed; § 3206, which mandates the informed consent of one parent for a minor to obtain an abortion but provides for a judicial bypass option if the minor does not wish to or cannot obtain a parent's consent; § 3209, which requires that, unless certain exceptions apply, a married woman seeking an abortion must sign a statement indicating that she has notified her husband of intended abortion; § 3203, which defines a "medical emergency" that will excuse compliance with the foregoing requirements; and §§ 3207(b), 3214(a), and 3214(f), which impose certain reporting requirements on facilities that provide abortion services. The trial court held all the provisions unconstitutional. The Court of Appeals struck down the husband notification provision but upheld the others.]

I.

Liberty finds no refuge in a jurisprudence of doubt. Yet 19 years after our holding that the Constitution protects a woman's right to terminate her pregnancy in its early stages, *Roe v. Wade*, 410 U.S. 113 (1973), that definition of liberty is still questioned. Joining the respondents as amicus curiae, the United States, as it has done in five other cases in the last decade, again asks us to overrule *Roe*.

After considering the fundamental constitutional questions resolved by Roe, principles of institutional integrity, and the rule of stare decisis, we are led to conclude this: the essential holding of *Roe v. Wade* should b retained and once again reaffirmed.

It must be stated at the outset and with clarity that *Roe's* essential holding, the holding we reaffirm, has three parts. First is a recognition of the right of the woman to choose to have an abortion before viability and to obtain it without undue interference from the State. Before viability, the State's interests are not strong enough to support a prohibition of abortion or the imposition of a substantial obstacle to the woman's effective right to elect the procedure. Second is a confirmation of the State's power to restrict abortions after fetal viability, if the law contains exceptions for pregnancies which endanger a woman's life or health. And third is the principle that the State has legitimate interests from the outset of the pregnancy in protecting the health of the woman and the life of the fetus that may become a child. These principles do not contradict one another; and we adhere to each.

II.

Constitutional protection of the woman's decision to terminate her pregnancy derives from the Due Process Clause of the Fourteenth Amendment. It declares that no State shall "deprive any person of life, liberty, or property, without due process of law." The controlling word in the case before us is "liberty." . . .

. . .

Neither the Bill of Rights nor the specific practices of States at the time of the adoption of the Fourteenth Amendment marks the outer limits of the substantive sphere of liberty which the Fourteenth Amendment protects. . . .

The inescapable fact is that adjudication of substantive due process claims may call upon the Court in interpreting the Constitution to exercise that same capacity which by tradition courts always have exercised: reasoned judgment. Its boundaries are not susceptible of expression as a simple rule. That does not mean we are free to invalidate state policy choices with which we disagree; yet neither does it permit us to shrink from the duties of our office. . . .

Men and women of good conscience can disagree, and we suppose some always shall disagree, about the profound moral and spiritual implications of terminating a pregnancy, even in its earliest stage. Some of us as individuals find abortion offensive to our most basic principles of morality, but that cannot control our decision. Our obligation is to define the liberty of all, not to mandate our own moral code. . . .

. . .

Our law affords constitutional protection to personal decisions relating to marriage, procreation, contraception, family relationships, child rearing, and education. Carey v. Population Services International, 431 U.S., at 685. . . . These matters, involving the most intimate and personal choices a person may make in a lifetime, choices central to personal dignity and autonomy, are central to the liberty protected by the Fourteenth Amendment. At the heart of liberty is the right to define one's own concept of existence, of meaning, of the universe, and of the mystery of human life.

Beliefs about these matters could not define the attributes of personhood were they formed under compulsion of the State.

These considerations begin our analysis of the woman's interest in terminating her pregnancy but cannot end it, for this reason: though the abortion decision may originate within the zone of conscience and belief, it is more than a philosophic exercise. Abortion is a unique act. It is an act fraught with consequences for others: for the woman who must live with the implications of her decision; for the persons who perform and assist in the procedure; for the spouse, family, and society which must confront the knowledge that these procedures exist, procedures some deem nothing short of an act of violence against innocent human life; and, depending on one's beliefs, for the life or potential life that is aborted. Though abortion is conduct, it does not follow that the State is entitled to proscribe it in all instances. That is because the liberty of the woman is at stake in a sense unique to the human condition and so unique to the law. The mother who carries a child to full term is subject to anxieties, to physical constraints, to pain that only she must bear. That these sacrifices have from the beginning of the human race been endured by woman with a pride that ennobles her in the eyes of others and gives to the infant a bond of love cannot alone be grounds for the State to insist she make the sacrifice. Her suffering is too intimate and personal for the State to insist, without more, upon its own vision of the woman's role, however dominant that vision has been in the course of our history and our culture. The destiny of the woman must be shaped to a large extent on her own conception of her spiritual imperatives and her place in society.

It should be recognized, moreover, that in some critical respects the abortion decision is of the same character as the decision to use contraception, to which *Griswold v. Connecticut, Eisenstadt v. Baird*, and *Carey v. Population Services International*, afford constitutional protection. We have no doubt as to the correctness of those decisions. They support the reasoning in Roe relating to the woman's liberty because they involve personal decisions concerning not only the meaning of procreation but also human responsibility and respect for it. As with abortion, reasonable people will have differences of opinion about these matters. One view is based on such reverence for the wonder of creation that any pregnancy ought to be welcomed and carried to full term no matter how difficult it will be to provide for the child and ensure its well-being. Another is that the inability to provide for the nurture and care of the infant is a cruelty to the child and an anguish to the parent. These are intimate views with infinite variations, and their deep, personal character underlay our decisions in *Griswold, Eisenstadt*, and *Carey*. The same concerns are present when the woman confronts the reality that, perhaps despite her attempts to avoid it, she has become pregnant.

It was this dimension of personal liberty that *Roe* sought to protect. . . .

. . . . [T]he reservations any of us may have in reaffirming the central holding of *Roe* are outweighed by the explication of individual liberty we have given combined with the force of stare decisis.

. . .

IV.

.... We conclude that the basic decision in *Roe* was based on a constitutional analysis which we cannot now repudiate. The woman's liberty is not so unlimited, however, that from the outset the State cannot show its concern for the life of the unborn, and at a later point in fetal development the State's interest in life has sufficient force so that the right of the woman to terminate the pregnancy can be restricted.

. . .

We conclude the line should be drawn at viability, so that before that time the woman has a right to choose to terminate her pregnancy....

... [T]he concept of viability, as we noted in *Roe*, is the time at which there is a realistic possibility of maintaining and nourishing a life outside the womb, so that the independent existence of the second life can in reason and all fairness be the object of state protection that now overrides the rights of the woman. *See* Roe v. Wade, 410 U.S., at 163. Consistent with other constitutional norms, legislatures may draw lines which appear arbitrary without the necessity of offering a justification. But courts may not. We must justify the lines we draw. And there is no line other than viability which is more workable. To be sure, as we have said, there may be some medical developments that affect the precise point of viability, but this is an imprecision within tolerable limits given that the medical community and all those who must apply its discoveries will continue to explore the matter. The viability line also has, as a practical matter, an element of fairness. In some broad sense it might be said that a woman who fails to act before viability has consented to the State's intervention on behalf of the developing child.

The woman's right to terminate her pregnancy before viability is the most central principle of *Roe v. Wade*. It is a rule of law and a component of liberty we cannot renounce....

Yet it must be remembered that *Roe v. Wade* speaks with clarity in establishing not only the woman's liberty but also the State's "important and legitimate interest in potential life." *Roe, supra*, at 163. That portion of the decision in *Roe* has been given too little acknowledgement and implementation by the Court in its subsequent cases. Those cases decided that any regulation touching upon the abortion decision must survive strict scrutiny, to be sustained only if drawn in narrow terms to further a compelling state interest. Not all of the cases decided under that formulation can be reconciled with the holding in *Roe* itself that the State has legitimate interests in the health of the woman and in protecting the potential life within her....

Roe established a trimester framework to govern abortion regulations....

The trimester framework no doubt was erected to ensure that the woman's right to choose not become so subordinate to the State's interest in promoting fetal life that her choice exists in theory but not in fact. We do not agree, however, that the trimester approach is necessary to accomplish this objective. . . .

. . .

We reject the trimester framework, which we do not consider to be part of the essential holding of *Roe*. Measures aimed at ensuring that a woman's choice contemplates the consequences for the fetus do not necessarily interfere with the right recognized in *Roe*, although those measures have been found to be inconsistent with the rigid trimester framework announced in that case. A logical reading of the central holding in *Roe* itself, and a necessary reconciliation of the liberty of the woman and the interest of the State in promoting prenatal life, require, in our view, that we abandon the trimester framework as a rigid prohibition on all previability regulation aimed at the protection of fetal life. The trimester framework suffers from these basic flaws: in its formulation it misconceives the nature of the pregnant woman's interest; and in practice it undervalues the State's interest in potential life, as recognized in *Roe*.

. . .

. . . Not all governmental intrusion is of necessity unwarranted; and that brings us to the other basic flaw in the trimester framework: even in *Roe's* terms, in practice it undervalues the State's interest in the potential life within the woman.

. . . *Roe* began the contradiction by using the trimester framework to forbid any regulation of abortion designed to advance that interest before viability. Before viability, *Roe* and subsequent cases treat all governmental attempts to influence a woman's decision on behalf of the potential life within her as unwarranted. This treatment is, in our judgment, incompatible with the recognition that there is a substantial state interest in potential life throughout pregnancy.

The very notion that the State has a substantial interest in potential life leads to the conclusion that not all regulations must be deemed unwarranted. Not all burdens on the right to decide whether to terminate a pregnancy will be undue. In our view, the undue burden standard is the appropriate means of reconciling the State's interest with the woman's constitutionally protected liberty.

. . .

A finding of an undue burden is a shorthand for the conclusion that a state regulation has the purpose or effect of placing a substantial obstacle in the path of a woman seeking an abortion of a nonviable fetus. A statute with this purpose is invalid because the means chosen by the State to further the interest in potential life must be calculated to inform the woman's free choice, not hinder it. And a statute which, while furthering the interest in potential life or some other valid state interest, has the effect of placing a substantial obstacle in the path of a woman's choice cannot be considered a permissible means of serving its legitimate ends. . . .

Some guiding principles should emerge. What is at stake is the woman's right to make the ultimate decision, not a right to be insulated from all others in doing so. Regulations which do no more than create a structural mechanism by which the State, or the parent or guardian of a minor, may express profound respect for the life of the unborn are permitted, if they are not a substantial obstacle to the woman's exercise of the right to choose. Unless it has that effect on her right of choice, a state measure designed to persuade her to choose childbirth over abortion will be upheld if reasonably related to that goal. Regulations designed to foster the health of a woman seeking an abortion are valid if they do not constitute an undue burden.

Even when jurists reason from shared premises, some disagreement is inevitable. That is to be expected in the application of any legal standard which must accommodate life's complexity. We do not expect it to be otherwise with respect to the undue burden standard. We give this summary:

(a) To protect the central right recognized by *Roe v. Wade* while at the same time accommodating the State's profound interest in potential life, we will employ the undue burden analysis as explained in this opinion. An undue burden exists, and therefore a provision of law is invalid, if its purpose or effect is to place a substantial obstacle in the path of a woman seeking an abortion before the fetus attains viability.

(b) We reject the rigid trimester framework of *Roe v. Wade*. To promote the State's profound interest in potential life, throughout pregnancy the State may take measures to ensure that the woman's choice is informed, and measures designed to advance this interest will not be invalidated as long as their purpose is to persuade the woman to choose childbirth over abortion. These measures must not be an undue burden on the right.

(c) As with any medical procedure, the State may enact regulations to further the health or safety of a woman seeking an abortion. Unnecessary health regulations that have the purpose or effect of presenting a substantial obstacle to a woman seeking an abortion impose an undue burden on the right.

(d) Our adoption of the undue burden analysis does not disturb the central holding of *Roe v. Wade*, and we reaffirm that holding. Regardless of whether exceptions are made for particular circumstances, a State may not prohibit any woman from making the ultimate decision to terminate her pregnancy before viability.

(e) We also reaffirm Roe's holding that "subsequent to viability, the State in promoting its interest in the potentiality of human life may, if it chooses, regulate, and even proscribe, abortion except where it is necessary, in appropriate medical judgment, for the preservation of the life or health of the mother." Roe v. Wade, 410 U.S., at 164–165.

These principles control our assessment of the Pennsylvania statute, and we now turn to the issue of the validity of its challenged provisions.

V.

The Court of Appeals applied what it believed to be the undue burden standard and upheld each of the provisions except for the husband notification requirement. We agree generally with this conclusion, but refine the undue burden analysis in accordance with the principles articulated above. We now consider the separate statutory sections at issue.

A.

Because it is central to the operation of various other requirements, we begin with the statute's definition of medical emergency. Under the statute, a medical emergency is

> []that condition which, on the basis of the physician's good faith clinical judgment, so complicates the medical condition of a pregnant woman as to necessitate the immediate abortion of her pregnancy to avert her death or for which a delay will create serious risk of substantial and irreversible impairment of a major bodily function.[]

18 Pa. Cons. Stat. (1990). § 3203.

. . .

[T]he Court of Appeals . . . stated: "we read the medical emergency exception as intended by the Pennsylvania legislature to assure that compliance with its abortion regulations would not in any way pose a significant threat to the life or health of a woman." *Ibid* . . . . We . . . conclude that, as construed by the Court of Appeals, the medical emergency definition imposes no undue burden on a woman's abortion right.

B.

We next consider the informed consent requirement. Except in a medical emergency, the statute requires that at least 24 hours before performing an abortion a physician inform the woman of the nature of the procedure, the health risks of the abortion and of childbirth, and the "probable gestational age of the unborn child." The physician or a qualified nonphysician must inform the woman of the availability of printed materials published by the State describing the fetus and providing information about medical assistance for childbirth, information about child support from the father, and a list of agencies which provide adoption and other services as alternatives to abortion. An abortion may not be performed unless the woman certifies in writing that she has been informed of the availability of these printed materials and has been provided them if she chooses to view them.

Our prior decisions establish that as with any medical procedure, the State may require a woman to give her written informed consent to an abortion. *See* Planned Parenthood of Central Mo. v. Danforth, 428 U.S., at 67. In this respect, the statute is unexceptional. Petitioners challenge the statute's definition of informed consent because it includes the provision of specific information by the doctor and the mandatory 24–hour waiting period. . . . [T]he undue burden standard adopted in this opinion require[s] us to overrule in part some of the Court's past decisions, decisions driven by the trimester framework's prohibition of all previability regulations designed to further the State's interest in fetal life.

In *Akron I*, 462 U.S. 416 (1983), we invalidated an ordinance which required that a woman seeking an abortion be provided by her physician with specific information "designed to influence the woman's informed choice between abortion or childbirth." . . .

To the extent *Akron I* and *Thornburgh* [476 U.S. 747 (1986)] find a constitutional violation when the government requires, as it does here, the giving of truthful, nonmisleading information about the nature of the procedure, the attendant health risks and those of childbirth, and the "probable gestational age" of the fetus, those cases go too far, are inconsistent with *Roe's* acknowledgment of an important interest in potential life, and are overruled. . . . It cannot be questioned that psychological well-being is a facet of health. Nor can it be doubted that most women considering an abortion would deem the impact on the fetus relevant, if not dispositive, to the decision. In attempting to ensure that a woman apprehend the full consequences of her decision, the State furthers the legitimate purpose of reducing the risk that a woman may elect an abortion, only to discover later, with devastating psychological consequences, that her decision was not fully informed. If the information the State requires to be made available to the woman is truthful and not misleading, the requirement may be permissible.

We also see no reason why the State may not require doctors to inform a woman seeking an abortion of the availability of materials relating to the consequences to the fetus, even when those consequences have no direct relation to her health. . . . A requirement that the physician make available information similar to that mandated by the statute here was described in *Thornburgh* as "an outright attempt to wedge the Commonwealth's message discouraging abortion into the privacy of the informed-consent dialogue between the woman and her physician." 476 U.S., at 762. We conclude, however, that informed choice need not be defined in such narrow terms that all considerations of the effect on the fetus are made irrelevant. . . . [W]e depart from the holdings of *Akron I* and *Thornburgh* to the extent that we permit a State to further its legitimate goal of protecting the life of the unborn by enacting legislation aimed at ensuring a decision that is mature and informed, even when in so doing the State expresses a preference for childbirth over abortion. In short, requiring that the woman be informed of the availability of information relating to fetal development and the assistance available should she decide to carry the pregnancy to full term is a reasonable measure to insure an informed choice, one which might cause the woman to choose childbirth over abortion. This requirement cannot be considered a substantial obstacle to obtaining an abortion, and, it follows, there is no undue burden.

Our prior cases also suggest that the "straitjacket," of particular information which must be given in each case interferes with a constitutional right of privacy between a pregnant woman and her physician. As a preliminary matter, it is worth noting that the statute now before us does not require a physician to comply with the informed consent provisions "if he or she can demonstrate by a preponderance of the evidence, that he or she reasonably believed that furnishing the information would have result-ed in a severely adverse effect on the physical or mental health of the patient." 18 Pa. Cons. Stat. § 3205 (1990). In this respect, the statute does not prevent the physician from exercising his or her medical judgment.

Whatever constitutional status the doctor-patient relation may have as a general matter, in the present context it is derivative of the woman's position. . . . On its own, the doctor-patient relation here is . . . for constitu-tional purposes, no different from a requirement that a doctor give certain specific information about any medical procedure.

. . . To be sure, the physician's First Amendment rights not to speak are implicated, but only as part of the practice of medicine, subject to reasonable licensing and regulation by the State. We see no constitutional infirmity in the requirement that the physician provide the information mandated by the State here.

The Pennsylvania statute also requires us to reconsider the holding in *Akron I* that the State may not require that a physician, as opposed to a qualified assistant, provide information relevant to a woman's informed consent. 462 U.S., at 448. Since there is no evidence on this record that requiring a doctor to give the information as provided by the statute would amount in practical terms to a substantial obstacle to a woman seeking an abortion, we conclude that it is not an undue burden. . . . [W]e uphold the provision as a reasonable means to insure that the woman's consent is informed.

Our analysis of Pennsylvania's 24–hour waiting period between the provision of the information deemed necessary to informed consent and the performance of an abortion under the undue burden standard requires us to reconsider the premise behind the decision in *Akron I* invalidating a parallel requirement. . . . The idea that important decisions will be more informed and deliberate if they follow some period of reflection does not strike us as unreasonable, particularly where the statute directs that important information become part of the background of the decision. The statute, as construed by the Court of Appeals, permits avoidance of the waiting period in the event of a medical emergency and the record evidence shows that in the vast majority of cases, a 24–hour delay does not create any appreciable health risk. In theory, at least, the waiting period is a reasonable measure to implement the State's interest in protecting the life of the unborn, a measure that does not amount to an undue burden.

Whether the mandatory 24–hour waiting period is nonetheless invalid because in practice it is a substantial obstacle to a woman's choice to terminate her pregnancy is a closer question. The findings of fact by the District Court indicate that because of the distances many women must travel to reach an abortion provider, the practical effect will often be a delay of much more than a day because the waiting period requires that a woman seeking an abortion make at least two visits to the doctor. The District Court also found that in many instances this will increase the exposure of women seeking abortions to "the harassment and hostility of anti-abortion protestors demonstrating outside a clinic." As a result, the District Court found that for those women who have the fewest financial resources, those who must travel long distances, and those who have difficulty explaining their whereabouts to husbands, employers, or others, the 24–hour waiting period will be "particularly burdensome."

These findings are troubling in some respects, but they do not demonstrate that the waiting period constitutes an undue burden.... [U]nder the undue burden standard a State is permitted to enact persuasive measures which favor childbirth over abortion, even if those measures do not further a health interest. And while the waiting period does limit a physician's discretion, that is not, standing alone, a reason to invalidate it. In light of the construction given the statute's definition of medical emergency by the Court of Appeals, and the District Court's findings, we cannot say that the waiting period imposes a real health risk.

We also disagree with the District Court's conclusion that the "particularly burdensome" effects of the waiting period on some women require its invalidation. A particular burden is not of necessity a substantial obstacle. Whether a burden falls on a particular group is a distinct inquiry from whether it is a substantial obstacle even as to the women in that group.... [O]n the record before us, and in the context of this facial challenge, we are not convinced that the 24–hour waiting period constitutes an undue burden.

. . .

C.

Section 3209 of Pennsylvania's abortion law provides, except in cases of medical emergency, that no physician shall perform an abortion on a married woman without receiving a signed statement from the woman that she has notified her spouse that she is about to undergo an abortion. The woman has the option of providing an alternative signed statement certifying that her husband is not the man who impregnated her; that her husband could not be located; that the pregnancy is the result of spousal sexual assault which she has reported; or that the woman believes that notifying her husband will cause him or someone else to inflict bodily injury upon her. A physician who performs an abortion on a married woman without receiving the appropriate signed statement will have his or her license revoked, and is liable to the husband for damages.

. . .

[The district court's detailed findings on domestic violence against women are omitted.]

... "Studies suggest that from one-fifth to one-third of all women will be physically assaulted by a partner or ex-partner during their lifetime." AMA Council on Scientific Affairs, Violence Against Women 7 (1991). Thus on an average day in the United States, nearly 11,000 women are severely assaulted by their male partners. Many of these incidents involve sexual assault. In families where wife-beating takes place, moreover, child abuse is often present as well.

... Psychological abuse, particularly forced social and economic isolation of women, is also common. L. Walker, The Battered Woman Syndrome 27–28 (1984). Many victims of domestic violence remain with their abusers, perhaps because they perceive no superior alternative. Many abused women who find temporary refuge in shelters return to their husbands, in large part because they have no other source of income. Returning to one's abuser can be dangerous. Recent Federal Bureau of Investigation statistics disclose that 8.8% of all homicide victims in the United States are killed by their spouse. Thirty percent of female homicide victims are killed by their male partners. *Domestic Violence: Terrorism in the Home, Hearing before the Subcommittee on Children, Family, Drugs and Alcoholism of the Senate Committee on Labor and Human Resources,* 101st Cong., 2d Sess., 3 (1990).

The limited research that has been conducted with respect to notifying one's husband about an abortion, although involving samples too small to be representative, also supports the District Court's findings of fact. The vast majority of women notify their male partners of their decision to obtain an abortion. In many cases in which married women do not notify their husbands, the pregnancy is the result of an extramarital affair. Where the husband is the father, the primary reason women do not notify their husbands is that the husband and wife are experiencing marital difficulties, often accompanied by incidents of violence. Ryan & Plutzer, When Married Women Have Abortions: Spousal Notification and Marital Interaction, 51 J. Marriage & the Family 41, 44 (1989).

This information and the District Court's findings reinforce what common sense would suggest. In well-functioning marriages, spouses discuss important intimate decisions such as whether to bear a child. But there are millions of women in this country who are the victims of regular physical and psychological abuse at the hands of their husbands. Should these women become pregnant, they may have very good reasons for not wishing to inform their husbands of their decision to obtain an abortion. Many may have justifiable fears of physical abuse, but may be no less fearful of the consequences of reporting prior abuse to the Commonwealth of Pennsylvania. Many may have a reasonable fear that notifying their husbands will provoke further instances of child abuse; these women are not exempt from § 3209's notification requirement. Many may fear devastating forms of psychological abuse from their husbands, including verbal harassment, threats of future violence, the destruction of possessions, physical confinement to the home, the withdrawal of financial support, or the disclosure of the abortion to family and friends. These methods of psychological abuse may act as even more of a deterrent to notification than the possibility of physical violence, but women who are the victims of the abuse are not exempt from § 3209's notification requirement. And many women who are pregnant as a result of sexual assaults by their husbands will be unable to avail themselves of the exception for spousal sexual assault, § 3209(b)(3), because the exception requires that the woman have notified law enforcement authorities within 90 days of the assault, and her husband will be notified of her report once an investigation begins. § 3128(c). If anything in this field is certain, it is that victims of spousal sexual assault are extremely reluctant to report the abuse to the government; hence, a great many spousal rape victims will not be exempt from the notification requirement imposed by § 3209.

The spousal notification requirement is thus likely to prevent a significant number of women from obtaining an abortion. It does not merely make abortions a little more difficult or expensive to obtain; for many women, it will impose a substantial obstacle. We must not blind ourselves to the fact that the significant number of women who fear for their safety and the safety of their children are likely to be deterred from procuring an abortion as surely as if the Commonwealth had outlawed abortion in all cases.

Respondents attempt to avoid the conclusion that § 3209 is invalid by pointing out that it imposes almost no burden at all for the vast majority of women seeking abortions. They begin by noting that only about 20 percent of the women who obtain abortions are married. They then note that of these women about 95 percent notify their husbands of their own volition.... [S]ince some of these women will be able to notify their husbands without adverse consequences or will qualify for one of the exceptions, the statute affects fewer than one percent of women seeking abortions.

. . .

The analysis does not end with the one percent of women upon whom the statute operates; it begins there.... The proper focus of constitutional inquiry is the group for whom the law is a restriction, not the group for whom the law is irrelevant.

... The unfortunate yet persisting conditions we document above will mean that in a large fraction of the cases in which § 3209 is relevant, it will operate as a substantial obstacle to a woman's choice to undergo an abortion. It is an undue burden, and therefore invalid.

This conclusion is in no way inconsistent with our decisions upholding parental notification or consent requirements. Those enactments, and our judgment that they are constitutional, are based on the quite reasonable assumption that minors will benefit from consultation with their parents and that children will often not realize that their parents have their best interests at heart. We cannot adopt a parallel assumption about adult women.

... If this case concerned a State's ability to require the mother to notify the father before taking some action with respect to a living child raised by both ... it would be reasonable to conclude as a general matter that the father's interest in the welfare of the child and the mother's interest are equal.

Before birth, however, the issue takes on a very different cast. It is an inescapable biological fact that state regulation with respect to the child a woman is carrying will have a far greater impact on the mother's liberty than on the father's. The effect of state regulation on a woman's protected liberty is doubly deserving of scrutiny in such a case, as the State has touched not only upon the private sphere of the family but upon the very bodily integrity of the pregnant woman. *Cf.* Cruzan v. Director, Missouri Dept. of Health, 497 U.S., at 281. The Court has held that "when the wife and the husband disagree on this decision, the view of only one of the two marriage partners can prevail. Inasmuch as it is the woman who physically bears the child and who is the more directly and immediately affected by the pregnancy, as between the two, the balance weighs in her favor." *Danforth*, *supra*, at 71. This conclusion rests upon the basic nature of marriage and the nature of our Constitution: "The marital couple is not an independent entity with a mind and heart of its own, but an association of two individuals each with a separate intellectual and emotional makeup. If the right of privacy means anything, it is the right of the individual, married or single, to be free from unwarranted governmental intrusion into matters so fundamentally affecting a person as the decision whether to bear or beget a child." Eisenstadt v. Baird, 405 U.S., at 453. . . .

. . .

. . . For the great many women who are victims of abuse inflicted by their husbands, or whose children are the victims of such abuse, a spousal notice requirement enables the husband to wield an effective veto over his wife's decision. Whether the prospect of notification itself deters such women from seeking abortions, or whether the husband, through physical force or psychological pressure or economic coercion, prevents his wife from obtaining an abortion until it is too late, the notice requirement will often be tantamount to the veto found unconstitutional in *Danforth*. The women most affected by this law—those who most reasonably fear the consequences of notifying their husbands that they are pregnant—are in the gravest danger.

The husband's interest in the life of the child his wife is carrying does not permit the State to empower him with this troubling degree of authority over his wife. The contrary view leads to consequences reminiscent of the common law. A husband has no enforceable right to require a wife to advise him before she exercises her personal choices. If a husband's interest in the potential life of the child outweighs a wife's liberty, the State could require a married woman to notify her husband before she uses a postfertilization contraceptive. Perhaps next in line would be a statute requiring pregnant married women to notify their husbands before engaging in conduct causing risks to the fetus. After all, if the husband's interest in the fetus' safety is a sufficient predicate for state regulation, the State could reasonably conclude that pregnant wives should notify their husbands before drinking alcohol or smoking. Perhaps married women should notify their husbands before using contraceptives or before undergoing any type of surgery that may have complications affecting the husband's interest in his wife's reproductive organs. And if a husband's interest justifies notice in any of these cases, one might reasonably argue that it justifies exactly what the *Danforth* Court held it did not justify—a requirement of the husband's consent as well. A State may not give to a man the kind of dominion over his wife that parents exercise over their children.

Section 3209 embodies a view of marriage consonant with the common-law status of married women but repugnant to our present understanding of marriage and of the nature of the rights secured by the Constitution. Women do not lose their constitutionally protected liberty when they marry. The Constitution protects all individuals, male or female, married or unmarried, from the abuse of governmental power, even where that power is employed for the supposed benefit of a member of the individual's family. These considerations confirm our conclusion that § 3209 is invalid.

[The Court upheld the parental consent and recordkeeping and reporting requirements of the Pennsylvania statute.]

NOTES AND QUESTIONS

1. What remains of the *Roe* decision after *Casey*? *Casey's* "undue burden" test clearly allows some state abortion restrictions (e.g., waiting periods, informed consent requirements) which had been held unconstitutional in decisions following *Roe*. In *Stenberg v. Carhart*, 530 U.S. 914, 120 S.Ct. 2597, 147 L.Ed.2d 743 (2000), a Nebraska doctor challenged a state statute that outlawed partial birth abortions. The statute defined partial birth abortions as "an abortion procedure in which the person performing the abortion partially delivers vaginally a living unborn child before killing the unborn child and completing the delivery ... the term partially delivers vaginally a living unborn child before killing the unborn child means deliberately and intentionally delivering into the vagina a living unborn child, or a substantial portion thereof, for the purpose of performing a procedure that the person performing such procedure knows will kill the unborn child and does kill the unborn child." NEB. REV. STAT. ANN. § 28–326(9) (Supp.1999). The Supreme Court struck down the statute because its language was vague and could be understood to include both D & X (Dilation and Extraction) and D & E (Dilation and Evacuation) abortion methods. *Stenberg*, 530 U.S. at 930. In the D & E method of partial birth abortion, the cervix is dilated and the fetal tissue is cut into pieces and removed from the uterus. Janeen Berkowitz, *Stenberg v. Carhart: Women Retain Their Right to Choose*, 91 J. CRIM. L. & CRIMINOLOGY 337, 349 (2001). In the D & X method, the cervix is dilated, and the fetus is pulled out of the cervix in breech position up to the head. The doctor then suctions out the fetus's brain tissue and pulls the fetus out in one piece. Berkowitz at 351. The Court held that the statute created an undue burden for women because D & E, the most common method for performing pre-viability second trimester abortions, was included in the statute's definition of a partial birth abortion. Melissa Holsinger, *The Partial–Birth Abortion Ban Act of 2003: The Congressional Reaction to Stenberg v. Carhart*, 6 N.Y.U. J. LEGIS. & PUB. POL'Y 603, 604 (2002–03). By including the D & E method in the definition of partial birth abortions, the act creates an undue burden on women seeking even pre-viability abortions—thus, the act violated the undue burden standard of *Casey*. Although the state does indeed have legitimate interest in potential life, the Court ruled that that interest could not abridge a woman's constitutional right to abortion of a non-viable fetus. For further discussion on the undue burden standard with respect to abortion legislation, see Jeffrey A. Van Detta, *Constitutionalizing Roe, Casey and Carhart: A Legislative Due–Process Anti–Discrimination Principle That Gives Constitutional Content to the "Undue Burden" Standard of Review Applied to Abortion Control Legislation*, 10 S. CAL. REV. L. & WOMEN'S STUD. 211 (2001).

After *Stenberg*, President George W. Bush signed the Partial Birth Abortion Ban Act into law on November 5, 2003. *President Bush Signs Partial Birth Abortion Ban Act of 2003*, (2003), at http//:www.whitehouse.gov/news/releases/2003/11/20031105–1.html, last visited July 6, 2004; 18 U.S.C. § 1531 (West 2004). The Partial Birth Abortion Ban Act creates civil and criminal penalties for any doctors who perform partial birth abortions. *See* 18 U.S.C. § 1531 (2004). In 2004, Planned Parenthood Federation of America challenged the national partial birth abortion ban by bringing an action for an injunction against Attorney General John Ashcroft. *Planned Parenthood Federation of America v. Ashcroft*, 320 F.Supp.2d 957 (N.D. Cal. 2004). The court held the act unconstitutional and granted the injunction against the Attorney General because the statute created an undue burden for women seeking abortions, the statute was vague because it did not utilize medical terminology to define the partial birth abortion procedure, and the statute did not include a health exception. *Planned Parenthood* at 74.

2. *Casey* reaffirmed the *Roe* holding that a woman cannot be prohibited from choosing an abortion up to the point of viability. What does the term "viability" mean? Because viability cannot be fixed at a specific point in gestation for all fetuses and, as recognized by the *Casey* plurality, fetal viability generally will advance over time toward conception as medical capabilities improve, how do we determine when a particular fetus is viable? Who is to determine viability? In previous decisions, the court has stated that individual determinations of viability are left to the reasonable judgment of physicians. *Planned Parenthood of Central Mo. v. Danforth*, 428 U.S. 52, 96 S.Ct. 2831, 49 L.Ed.2d 788 (1976); *Colautti v. Franklin*, 439 U.S. 379, 99 S.Ct. 675, 58 L.Ed.2d 596 (1979). But may the state regulate how a physician is to determine viability? Consider *Webster v. Reproductive Health Services*, 492 U.S. 490, 109 S.Ct. 3040, 106 L.Ed.2d 410 (1989), where a 3–member plurality upheld a Missouri statute which, according to the Court's interpretation, required physicians to use reasonable medical care to determine viability upon fetuses believed to be at least 20 weeks, and to perform medical examinations and tests to determine fetal weight, age, and lung maturity if useful. The Court found that the statute, while regulating the discretion of the physician in determining viability of the fetus, did not violate the *Colautti* rule that the state may not identify only one scientific determinant of viability.

Is viability an appropriate marker for state abortion prohibitions? Is it superior to *Roe's* trimester system? Is there a better system? *See* Patricia A. King, *The Juridical Status of the Fetus: A Proposal for Legal Protection of the Unborn*, 77 MICH. L. REV. 1647 (1979); NAN D. HUNTER, TIME LIMITS ON ABORTION IN REPRODUCTIVE LAWS FOR THE 1990'S 129 (Sherrill Cohen & Nadine Taub eds., 1989); Katherine Lusby, *Self-Identification and the Morality of Abortion*, 24 U. TOL. L. REV. 121 (1992); Nancy K. Rhoden, *Trimesters and Technology: Revamping Roe v. Wade*, 95 YALE L.J. 639 (1986).

The Supreme Court in *Casey* reiterated its holding in *Roe* that after viability, the state may prohibit abortion "except where it is necessary, in appropriate medical judgment, for the preservation of the life or health of the mother." 505 U.S. at 879. What does the Court mean by "health?"

Finally, what does the Court in *Casey* and *Roe* mean when it uses the term "abortion?" Until recently, most discussions of abortion have assumed that induced termination of pregnancy would result in the death of the fetus for late abortion. Some fetuses, however, have survived attempts at abortions late in pregnancy. *See* Nancy K. Rhoden, *The New Neonatal Dilemma: Live Births from Late Abortion*, 72 GEO. L.J. 1451 (1984). The question therefore arises whether a woman is entitled only to removal of the fetus from her womb or whether she can expect death of the fetus as well. Should a woman's expectation determine the choice of method to be used in late abortions and the extent to which physicians should be obligated to treat live-born infants? For a discussion of parental rights involving live birth following induced labor at approximately twenty-three weeks, see Chapter 4, Sec. II. D.3., *supra*.

3. What are a father's interests in pregnancy? Do these interests deserve protection? What should happen if the father wants an abortion and the mother disagrees?

4. In *Casey*, the Supreme Court justifies upholding the informed consent and mandatory waiting period portions of the statute in their statement that a state may attempt to protect a fetus by "enacting legislation aimed at ensuring a decision that is mature and informed." *Casey*, 505 U.S. at 883.

Is specific attention to informed consent in the abortion context required? Consider the following argument:

> The medical standards applicable to the performance of abortion procedures like those of any other medical procedure are governed by (1) licensure standards of the medical profession and voluntary standards of professional medical organizations, and (2) the findings of civil juries in medical malpractice cases as to the proper standards of informed consent and reasonable care. No state legislature has persuasively established why these traditional mechanisms of regulation are insufficient in the case of abortion. Yet, abortion procedures are singled out for additional legislation.
>
> . . .
>
> The content, substance, and medium of presentation of information that health care professionals provide to patients to obtain their informed consent to medical procedures is a matter determined by the professional standards of the health care profession, subject to possible tort liability if a patient is injured by a procedure whose risks were not effectively disclosed beforehand. The state legislatures have generally left the health care industry unmolested in this sphere except to codify the basic legal principles of informed consent; and when they have legislated, the states have provided only fairly general guidelines to prevent consumer abuse.
>
> . . .
>
> The legislative animus against a woman's right to choose has been apparent in the informed consent statutes targeted at procedures to end pregnancy. These statutes require more than just information about the risks of an elective surgical procedure. They "morally Mirandize" the woman in an effort to arouse in her feelings of sin, guilt, and shame, as well as unrealistic portraiture of how much easier life as a (frequently single) mother can be. For example, they require that the woman be told the gestational age of the fetus, the availability of medical assistance for prenatal care, and the father's duty to provide child support. None of these "medical" risks to the patient are the subject of any other "informed" consent requirements.

Jeffrey A. Van Detta, *supra* note 1, at 246, 257–59.

Many states other than Pennsylvania have informed consent laws specifically relating to abortion. They vary widely in the specificity of disclosure. *Compare, e.g.,* TENN. CODE ANN. § 39–15–202(b) (2004) (woman must be informed of possibility of viability, physician's legal duty to preserve life of viable fetus, risks and benefits of the procedure, and social services available) *with* R.I. GEN. LAWS § 23–4.7–3 (2003) (woman must be informed of material risks of abortion procedure and "any other material facts" at physician's discretion). Most of these statutes prescribe more than disclosure of the medical risks associated with abortion. *See, e.g.,* WIS. STAT. ANN. § 253.10 (2003) (required disclosure shall include information on social services, including adoption and birth control). Are these additional disclosures appropriate? Is the decision whether to terminate pregnancy primarily a medical decision? A reproductive decision? A moral decision?

Casey also upheld a requirement that women wait twenty-four hours after receiving counseling before obtaining an abortion. What is the purpose of this requirement? Proponents of abortion rights claim that it is aimed at discouraging abortions by making the process inconvenient for women. Supporters of waiting periods respond that women should have time to think about their decision after receiving counseling. Is it helpful to require a waiting period? Would a similar "think-it-over" period be helpful in other contexts, such as sterilization?

After the *Casey* decision was handed down, several abortion clinics in Pennsylvania began allowing women to listen to a tape of the state-mandated counseling over the phone. Thus, the women only had to make one trip to the clinic. Fawn Vrazo, Pa. *Clinics Using Tapes to Counsel on Abortion*, PHILA. INQUIRER, Sept. 23, 1994, at A1. Some states permit the statutory counseling to be given by telephone, while others forbid tape recorded counseling or require an in-person meeting. *See, e.g.*, ARK. CODE ANN. § 20–16–903 (2003) (prohibiting tape-recorded counseling, but allowing telephone counseling by doctor or agent); KAN. STAT. ANN. § 65–6709 (2003) (requiring in-person counseling with physician prior to abortion procedure); S.D. CODIFIED LAWS § 34–32A–10.1 (2003) (allowing counseling to be given in person or by telephone, by doctor or doctor's agent).

Are there important differences between hearing legally-prescribed information in person, from a live person over the phone, and on a tape over the phone? In one clinic, women are asked a specific question to verify that they listened to the tape. Does this satisfy the purpose of the statute?

5. In three companion cases decided in 1977, the Supreme Court held that neither the Constitution nor federal law required states to fund nontherapeutic abortions for women with financial need. In *Beal v. Doe*, 432 U.S. 438, 97 S.Ct. 2366, 53 L.Ed.2d 464 (1977), the Court found that Title XIX of the Social Security Act, which established Medicaid, did not require Pennsylvania to fund "nontherapeutic" abortions as a precondition to receiving funds in a joint federal-state medical assistance program. *Maher v. Roe*, 432 U.S. 464, 97 S.Ct. 2376, 53 L.Ed.2d 484 (1977), held that Connecticut's refusal to pay for nontherapeutic abortions did not violate the equal protection clause. This was true, the Court said, even though Medicaid support was being provided to cover the expenses of childbirth. And in *Poelker v. Doe*, 432 U.S. 519, 97 S.Ct. 2391, 53 L.Ed.2d 528 (1977), the Court rejected a constitutional attack upon the decision of city-owned hospitals in St. Louis to finance services for childbirth while failing to provide corresponding services for nontherapeutic abortion.

In 1976, access to federal monies for abortions was restricted with the passage of the "Hyde Amendment," which prohibited federal payment for most medically necessary abortions under the Medicaid program. In *Harris v. McRae*, 448 U.S. 297, 100 S.Ct. 2671, 65 L.Ed.2d 784 (1980), the Court found that the amendment did not, in any of its forms, place an undue restriction on a woman's right to have an abortion because the due process clause does not require states to provide funds to enable people to avail themselves of constitutionally-protected choices. The failure to fund the full range of a woman's protected choices, the Court stated, was not constitutionally prohibited. Although "government may not place obstacles in the path of a woman's right to exercise her freedom of choice, it need not remove those not of its own creation." *Id*. at 316. Do you agree with the Supreme Court that the abortion funding cases are consistent with *Roe*? What is the effect of these decisions on a woman's ability to obtain an abortion? Dorothy Roberts argues that "[l]iberty protects all citizens' choices from the most direct and egregious abuses of governmental power, but it does nothing to dismantle social arrangements that make it impossible for some people to make a choice in the first place...." Dorothy Roberts, Chapter 5, Sec. II. A. 1., note 2. Thus, even though poor women have a constitutionally protected choice it is useless if they do not have the financial resources necessary to acquire an abortion.

Access to abortions, however, can be limited by more than financial constraints. The percentage of abortions performed in hospitals decreased from 22% in 1980 to 5% in 2000. Physicians for Reproductive Choice & Health & The Alan Guttmacher Institute, *An Overview of Abortion in the United States*, (2003), *at* http://www.agi-usa.org/sections/abortion.html, last visited July 19, 2004. Of the 5,801 hospitals in the United States in 2001, only 603 provided abortions. Stephanie Mueller & Susan Dudley, *Access to Abortions*, (2004), at http://www.prochoice.org, last visited July 19, 2004.

Several factors have contributed to declining access to abortions in the United States. First, most counties have limited numbers of clinics that provide abortions. For instance, in 2000, 87% of counties in the United States had no abortion provider, and in non-metropolitan areas 97% of counties had no abortion provider. *See* Mueller & Dudley at http://www.prochoice.org, last visited July 19, 2004. Furthermore, one out of every four women having an abortion has to travel fifty miles or more to reach a clinic. *See* Physicians for Reproductive Choice & The Alan Guttmacher Institute, *at* http://www.agi-usa.org/sections/abortion.html, last visited July 19, 2004. A second important factor is that as of 1995 only 12% of medical residency programs provided routine abortion training in contrast to 1978 when 26% of medical residency programs provided training. Rene Almeling et al., *Abortion Training in U.S. Obstetrics and Gynecology Residency Programs, 1998*, 32 FAM. PLAN. PERSP. 268, 268 (2000).

Anti-choice harassment and violence also limit access to abortion clinics. In an effort to protect abortion clinic staff members and patients, the U.S. Congress passed the Freedom of Access to Clinic Entrances Act, which makes it illegal for people to intentionally obstruct the entrances of clinics that provide reproductive health services. Freedom of Access to Clinic Entrances Act, 18 U.S.C. § 248 (2004). The act also prohibits protestors from injuring and intimidating patients and clinic staff members. *Id*. Finally, the act prohibits protestors from intentionally damaging or destroying a clinic because it provides reproductive health services. *Id*. In addition to the federal act, fourteen states and the District of Columbia have statutes that prohibit specific acts aimed at injuring and intimidating reproductive health care providers. The Alan Guttmacher Institute, *State Policies in Brief as of July 1, 2004*, (2004), *at* http://www.guttmacher.org/statecenter/spibs/spib_PAC.pdf, last visited July 19, 2004; *see, e.g.*, CAL. PENAL CODE § 423 (West 2004) (prohibiting obstruction of clinic entrances, threats to staff and patients, and property damage). In addition, Colorado and Massachusetts have statutes that create a "bubble zone" around clinics, requiring protestors to stand a specified distance away from the clinic entrance and away from patients entering the facility. *See, e.g.*, COLO. REV. STAT. ANN. § 18–9–122(3) (West 2004) (making it illegal for any person within 100 feet of a health care facility's entrance to approach a person within eight feet with the intent to distribute information or protest if that person has not given his/her consent). In 2000, abortion opponents sought an injunction to prevent the enforcement of the Colorado "bubble zone" statute and claimed that the statute violated their First Amendment rights. In 2000, the U.S. Supreme Court held the statute was constitutional because it was not over-broad or vague and it did not impose an unconstitutional prior restraint on speech. *Hill v. Colorado*, 530 U.S. 703, 730–37, 120 S.Ct. 2480, 147 L.Ed.2d 597 (2000). For a review of federal circuit court cases challenging the constitutionality of the Freedom of Access to Clinic Entrances Act, see Heather J. Blum–Redlich, Annotation, *Validity, Construction, and Application of Freedom of Access to Clinic Entrances Act (FACE) (18 U.S.C.A. § 248)*, 134 A.L.R. FED. 507 (2004).

6. What impact does the "abortion pill" have on the abortion controversy? Mifepristone, formerly known as RU–486, is a drug that blocks progesterone, a hormone necessary to sustain pregnancy. Marketed in the United States under the trade name Mifeprex®, it can be used as a chemical alternative to surgical abortion in the first seven weeks of pregnancy. The FDA approved regimen for medical abortion with mifepristone is one dose of mifepristone, followed by one dose of misoprostol, a drug that stimulates uterine contractions, 48 hours later. Because Mifeprex is not available through pharmacies, both drugs must be administered in the physician's office, and the physician must register and sign a Prescriber's Agreement with the FDA and the manufacturer in order to obtain the drug. *See* Food and Drug Administration, *Mifepristone Information* (2002), *at* http://www.fda.gov/cder/drug/infopage/mifepristone/default.htm (last visited June 28, 2004). In addition, another drug, methotrexate, also used in combination with misoprostol, has been used since 1993 for the purpose of medical abortions. However, according to a study published in 2003, the methotrexate-misoprostol regimen is only 84% effective at terminating early pregnancy whereas the mifepristone-misoprostol regimen is 95% effective at terminating early pregnancy. M. D. Creinin et al., *Mifepristone and Misoprostol and Methotrexate/Misoprostol in Clinical Practice for Abortion*, 188 Am. J. Obstetrics & Gynecology 664 (2003).

What implications does the use of these drugs have for traditional understandings of the terms "contraception" and "abortion"? *See, e.g.,* Susan Saylor, Comment, *The Legal Status of the Morning–After Pill: Abortion or Birth Control?*, 25 U.S.F. L. Rev. 401 (1991); *infra*, Sec. II. A. 1., note 3. What additional legal and ethical issues are raised by their use? *See generally*, Sarah Ricks, *The New French Abortion Pill: The Moral Property of Women*, 1 Yale J. L. & Fem. 75 (1989); Mindy J. Lees, Note, *I Want a New Drug: RU–486 and the Right to Choose*, 63 S. Cal. L. Rev. 1113 (1990); Leonard A. Cole, *The End of the Abortion Debate*, 138 U. Pa. L. Rev. 217 (1989); note 3, Sec. II. A., *infra*.

7. Under what circumstances, if any, should a minor be able to consent to an abortion? Should her parent(s) or the state be involved? If so, in what way? For a discussion of the issues, see Teresa Stanton Collett, *Seeking Solomon's Wisdom: Judicial Bypass of Parental Involvement in a Minor's Abortion Decision*, 52 Baylor L. Rev. 513 (2000); J. Shoshanna Ehrlich, *Grounded in the Reality of Their Lives: Listening to Teens Who Make the Abortion Decision without Involving Their Parents*, 18 Berkeley Women's L.J. 61 (2003); Katheryn D. Katz, *The Pregnant Child's Right to Self–Determination*, 62 Alb. L. Rev. 1119 (1999); Rachel Weissmann, Note, What *Choice do They Have?: Protecting Pregnant Minors' Reproductive Rights Using State Constitutions*, 1999 Ann. Surv. Am. L. 129 (1999).

3. STERILIZATION

Buck v. Bell

Supreme Court of the United States, 1927.
274 U.S. 200, 47 S.Ct. 584, 71 L.Ed. 1000.

■ Justice Holmes delivered the opinion of the Court.

This is a writ of error to review a judgment of the Supreme Court of Appeals of the State of Virginia, affirming a judgment of the Circuit Court of Amherst County, by which the defendant in error, the superintendent of the State Colony for Epileptics and Feeble Minded, was ordered to perform the operation of salpingectomy upon Carrie Buck, the plaintiff in error, for the purpose of making her sterile. 143 Va. 310. The case comes here upon the contention that the statute authorizing the judgment is void under the Fourteenth Amendment as denying to the plaintiff in error due process of law and the equal protection of the laws.

Carrie Buck is a feeble minded white woman who was committed to the State Colony above mentioned in due form. She is the daughter of a feeble minded mother in the same institution, and the mother of an illegitimate feeble minded child. She was eighteen years old at the time of the trial of her case in the Circuit Court, in the latter part of 1924. An Act of Virginia, approved March 20, 1924, recites that the health of the patient and the welfare of society may be promoted in certain cases by the sterilization of mental defectives, under careful safeguard, & c.: that the sterilization may be effected in males by vasectomy and in females by salpingectomy, without serious pain or substantial danger to life: that the Commonwealth is supporting in various institutions many defective persons who if now discharged would become a menace but if incapable of procreating might be discharged with safety and become self-supporting with benefit to themselves and to society; and the experience has shown that heredity plays an important part in the transmission of insanity, imbecility, & c. The statute then enacts that whenever the superintendent of certain institutions including the above named State Colony shall be of opinion that it is for the best interests of the patients and of society that an inmate under his care should be sexually sterilized, he may have the operation performed upon any patient afflicted with hereditary forms of insanity, imbecility, & c., on complying with the very careful provisions by which the act protects the patients from possible abuse.

. . .

The attack is not upon the procedure but upon the substantive law. It seems to be contended that in no circumstances could such an order be justified. It certainly is contended that the order cannot be justified upon the existing grounds. The judgment finds the facts that have been recited and that Carrie Buck "is the probable potential parent of socially inadequate offspring, likewise afflicted, that she may be sexually sterilized without detriment to her general health and that her welfare and that of society will be promoted by her sterilization," and thereupon makes the order. In view of the general declarations of the legislature and the specific findings of the Court, obviously we cannot say as matter of law that the grounds do not exist, and if they exist they justify the result. We have seen more than once that the public welfare may call upon the best citizens for their lives. It would be strange if it could not call upon those who already sap the strength of the State for these lesser sacrifices, often not felt to be such by those concerned, in order to prevent our being swamped with incompetence. It is better for all the world, if instead of waiting to execute degenerate offspring for crime, or to let them starve for their imbecility, society can prevent those who are manifestly unfit from continuing their kind. The principle that sustains compulsory vaccination is broad enough to cover cutting the Fallopian tubes. *Jacobson v. Massachusetts*, 197 U.S. 11. Three generations of imbeciles are enough.

. . .

Judgment affirmed.

NOTES AND QUESTIONS

1. There is evidence that Justice Holmes' remark that the Buck family represented "three generations of imbeciles" was incorrect. Carrie Buck was reportedly an avid reader and lived a full life. *See* Paul A. Lombardo, *Three Generations, No*

Imbeciles: New Light on Buck v. Bell, 60 N.Y.U. L. REV. 30, 61 (1985). Dr. Roy Nelson, Director of the Lynchburg Hospital where many sterilizations took place, located both Carrie Buck and her sister Doris, who also was sterilized, and reported that neither was mentally retarded by today's standards. Sandra G. Boodman & Glenn Frankel, *Over 7500 Sterilized by Virginia*, WASH. POST, Feb. 23, 1980, at A1. Carrie Buck's daughter Vivian, who died at age eight of the measles, reportedly performed well in school, at one point making the honor roll. Lombardo, *supra*.

In late 1980, a class action suit was filed on behalf of persons sterilized in Virginia. *See* Poe v. Lynchburg, 518 F.Supp. 789 (W.D. Va. 1981). The suit sparked an in-depth study of sterilization in Virginia, which found that from 1924 to 1979, approximately 7,259 persons were sterilized. The suit eventually settled, and the state agreed to locate and compensate persons sterilized. PHILLIP R. REILLY, THE SURGICAL SOLUTION: A HISTORY OF INVOLUNTARY STERILIZATION IN THE UNITED STATES 156–57 (1991). For a good account of the history of the eugenics movement, see DANIEL KEVLES, IN THE NAME OF EUGENICS: GENETICS AND THE USE OF HUMAN HEREDITY (1985).

In 2002, Virginia Governor Mark R. Warner formally apologized to Carrie Buck and the thousands of other individuals who were involuntarily sterilized. William Branigin, *Warner Apologizes to Victims of Eugenics; Woman Who Challenged Sterilizations Honored*, WASH. POST, May 3, 2002, at B01. Virginia was the first state to apologize for its eugenic history and it was soon thereafter followed by Oregon, California, North Carolina, and South Carolina. Additionally, following the apology, North Carolina's government set up a compensation program for the survivors of forced sterilization that provided them with health care and education benefits. Associated Press, *Sterilization Compensation OK'd*, RICHMOND TIMES-DISPATCH, Sept 29, 2003, at A14. For further discussion on America's history with the eugenics movement, see Paul A. Lombardo, *Taking Eugenics Seriously: Three Generations of ??? Are Enough?*, 30 FLA. ST. U. L. REV. 191 (2003).

2. In *Skinner v. Oklahoma*, 316 U.S. 535, 62 S.Ct. 1110, 86 L.Ed. 1655 (1942), decided after *Buck,* the Supreme Court invalidated on equal protection grounds a state statute allowing the sterilization of persons convicted more than once of certain offenses. Other offenses, such as embezzlement, were specifically exempted from the statute. Despite the broad language in the last paragraph of Justice Holmes's *Buck* opinion, the *Skinner* court struck down the statute. *Buck* was distinguished as follows:

> In *Buck v. Bell* ... the Virginia statute was upheld though it applied only to feeble-minded persons in institutions of the State. But it was pointed out that "so far as the operations enable those who otherwise must be kept confined to be returned to the world, and thus open the asylum to others, the equality aimed at will be more nearly reached".... Here there is no such saving feature. Embezzlers are forever free. Those who steal or take in other ways are not.

Skinner, 316 U.S. at 542. Is there any force left to the *Buck* decision after *Skinner?* *See* Paul A. Lombardo, *Medicine, Eugenics, and the Supreme Court: From Coercive Sterilization to Reproductive Freedom*, 13 J. CONTEMP. HEALTH L. & POL'Y 1 (1996); Michael G. Silver, Note, *Eugenics and Compulsory Sterilization Laws: Providing Redress for the Victims of a Shameful Era in United States History*, 72 GEO. WASH. L. REV. 862 (2004).

3. The practice of involuntary sterilization was spurred by the eugenics movement fathered by Frances Galton in the late 1800s. Galton coined the term "eugenics" as a policy for modifying and improving the human species through manipulating what were thought to be heritable traits, by either preventing births or encouraging propagation of "desirable" traits. For an excellent history of involuntary sterilization, see Phillip R. Reilly, *supra* Aftermath (1991). For a history of the German sterilization program and its reliance on the American model, see ROBERT PROCTOR, RACIAL HYGIENE: MEDICINE UNDER THE NAZIS (1988).

Involuntary sterilization projects occurred during the 20th century in several European countries in addition to Germany. In 2002, the Center for Reproductive Rights and Poradòa conducted a survey of 230 Romani women living in Slovakia. The survey revealed that at least 110 of those women had been sterilized without their consent since 1989 when communism ended and the government claimed to have stopped performing involuntary sterilization on women. CENTER FOR REPRODUCTIVE RIGHTS AND PORADÒA, BODY AND SOUL: FORCED STERILIZATION AND OTHER ASSAULTS ON ROMA REPRODUCTIVE FREEDOM IN SLOVAKIA 14 (2003). Researchers discovered that women were not told by doctors that they were going to be sterilized, they were not provided information about the sterilization procedure, and women under eighteen were sterilized without the permission of their parents. *Id.* at 15. In 1997 a Swedish newspaper reported on state-funded sterilization that occurred in Sweden between 1934 and 1974. *See* Dan Balz, *Sweden Sterilized Thousands of "Useless" Citizens for Decades*, WASH. POST, August 29, 1997, at A1. The Swedish law mandated that people who were considered mentally ill be sterilized as well as people who exhibited antisocial behavior. *Id.* at A1. Some couples were even sterilized because doctors thought that they might be bad parents. *Id.* When the program began, approximately 70% of the people sterilized were women; however, by the 1950s and 1960s, 90% of the people sterilized were women. *Id.* Sweden's sterilization program was not unique; there were similar programs during this time period in Austria, Belgium, Denmark, Germany, Norway, and Switzerland. *Id.*

4. There have also been recent sterilization abuses of non-institutionalized persons in the United States. In 1973, national controversy erupted over accusations that a physician at a federally-funded Alabama clinic was sterilizing black teenage girls including the Relf sisters without their consent. A lawsuit was filed by the Relfs and others to ban the use of federal funds for sterilization. *Relf v. Weinberger*, 372 F.Supp. 1196 (D.D.C. 1974). The District Court found that an estimated 100,000 to 150,000 poor women were sterilized annually in federally-funded programs, and that physicians sometimes coerced women to be sterilized by conditioning their provision of abortion and obstetrical services to poor women on the requirement that the women be sterilized. *Id.*; *see also* Laurie Nsiah–Jefferson, *Reproductive Laws, Women of Color, and Low Income Women*, in REPRODUCTIVE LAWS IN THE 1990'S (Sherrill Cohen and Nadine Taub eds., 1989); DOROTHY E. ROBERTS, KILLING THE BLACK BODY: RACE, REPRODUCTION, AND THE MEANING OF LIBERTY 1997, Beverly Horsburgh, *Schrdegreesodinger's Cat, Eugenics, and the Compulsory Sterilization of Welfare Mothers: Deconstructing an Old/New Rhetoric and Constructing the Reproductive Right to Natality for Low–Income Women of Color*, 17 CARDOZO L. REV. 531 (1996).

The current regulations governing federal funds for sterilization operations (see 42 C.F.R. §§ 441.250–441.259 (2004); 42 C.F.R. §§ 50.201–50.210 (2004)) prohibit the use of federal funds for the sterilization of institutionalized persons and those declared incompetent by a state or federal court. § 441.206. In addition, the regulations require the informed consent of the patient, that the patient be at least twenty-one years old, and that absent life-threatening emergency, there be at least a thirty-day waiting period (but not more than 180 days) before the physician may perform the procedure. §§ 50.203, 441.257, 441.258.

5. Do mentally disabled persons have a constitutional "right" to be sterilized? In *In re Conservatorship of Valerie N.*, 40 Cal.3d 143, 219 Cal.Rptr. 387, 707 P.2d 760 (1985), the court found unconstitutional a state statute barring all nontherapeutic sterilizations, holding that mentally incompetent persons have the same rights as others to avoid pregnancy:

> True protection of procreative choice can be accomplished only if the state permits the court-supervised substituted judgment of the conservator to be exercised on behalf of a conservatee who is unable to personally exercise this right. Limiting the exercise of that judgment by denying the right of effective contraception through sterilization to this class of conservatees denies them a right held not only by conservatees who are competent to consent, but by all other women.

Id. at 168.

What standard, substituted judgment or best interests, is preferable in such cases? Should individual and family autonomy in these decisions be respected, or should the courts become involved? For a discussion of these issues and of current restrictive sterilization laws, see Elizabeth S. Scott, *Sterilization of Mentally Retarded Persons: Reproductive Rights and Family Autonomy*, 1986 Duke L. J. 806 (1986); Roberta Cepko, *Involuntary Sterilization of Mentally Disabled Women*, 8 Berkeley Women's L. J. 122 (1993); Joe Zumpano–Canto, *Nonconsensual Sterilization of the Mentally Disabled in N.C.: An Ethics Critique of the Statutory Standard and its Judicial Interpretation*, 13 J. Contemp. Health L. & Pol'y 79 (1996).

6. What degree of mental impairment would you require before permitting nonconsensual sterilization? In *In re Romero*, the Supreme Court of Colorado reversed a district court decision which authorized the sterilization of a thirty-seven-year-old mother of two children who had suffered brain damage as the result of oxygen deprivation at the age of thirty-three. 790 P.2d 819 (Colo.1990) (en banc). Ms. Romero lived in a nursing home and was the legal ward of her mother who petitioned for the sterilization order. Evidence was presented that Ms. Romero's IQ was seventy-four falling within the category "borderline intellectual functioning" but not mentally retarded. Ms. Romero had testified that she wished to remain capable of having another child, although she had no immediate intention to become pregnant. *Id.* at 824. The majority determined that the threshold question was whether the individual was competent to give or withhold consent. They established a standard for determining competence to make a sterilization decision: "An individual should be deemed competent to grant or withhold consent if the individual understands the nature of the district court's proceedings, the relationship between sexual activity and reproduction and the consequences of the sterilization procedure." *Id.* at 822–23. Is this a workable standard?

7. Are decisions to terminate the pregnancy of a mentally disabled woman similar to or different from decisions to sterilize mentally disabled persons? Who should make these decisions? Are medical ethics committees better equipped than courts to make them? Committees can include doctors, social workers, and representatives from the disabled community.

B. Aiding Reproduction

> [Y]ou probably wonder why we haven't just given up and adopted. I am not sure I can explain it satisfactorily. Some people find it hard to give up the idea of someone to carry on the family name, the genes—the part of their ancestry that would be passed down; for others the costs of treatment may be covered while adoption is not; and for others, medical success always seems to be just around the corner with scientific advances and optimistic physicians making it difficult to give up the ideal.

Testimony of Deborah Gerrity, President of Metropolitan Washington Area Chapter of RESOLVE, Inc. [an infertility support group] Before the Human

Resources & Intergovernmental Relations Subcomm. Regarding the Federal Response to the Problem of Infertility (July 14, 1988).

> Hardly a day passes without reports of . . . instances in which common assumptions concerning human reproduction are challenged. There is no doubt that one of the most dramatic and poignant areas of change in the last decades of the twentieth century centers on this most fundamental level of human life—procreation of our future. The way we approach this future will very much depend on how we deal with the rapidly expanding array of reproductive technologies and services that are now emerging.

ROBERT H. BLANK, REGULATING REPRODUCTION (1990).

> It would on the one hand be illusory to claim that scientific research and its applications are morally neutral; on the other hand one cannot derive criteria for guidance from mere technical efficiency, from research's possible usefulness to some at the expense of others, or, worse still, from prevailing ideologies. Thus science and technology require, for their own intrinsic meaning, an unconditional respect for the fundamental criteria of the moral law. . . . [T]he gift of human life must be actualized in marriage through the specific and exclusive acts of husband and wife, in accordance with the laws inscribed in their persons and in their union.

INSTRUCTION ON RESPECT FOR HUMAN LIFE IN ITS ORIGIN AND ON THE DIGNITY OF PROCREATION: REPLIES TO CERTAIN QUESTIONS OF THE DAY, VATICAN DOCTRINAL STATEMENT (1987).

> Since reproductive technologies so intimately affect women's bodies, our pregnancies, our children and our lives, we cannot avoid being actively involved in their appraisal. But the attempt to reclaim motherhood as a female accomplishment should not mean giving the natural priority over the technological—that pregnancy is natural and good, technology unnatural and bad. It is not at all clear what a "natural" relationship to our fertility, our reproductive capacity, would look like. . . . In the feminist critique of reproductive technologies, it is not technology as an *"artificial invasion of the human body"* that is at issue—but whether we can create the political and cultural conditions in which such technologies can be employed by women to shape the experience of reproduction according to their own definitions.

Michelle Stanworth, *The Deconstruction of Motherhood, in* REPRODUCTIVE TECHNOLOGIES: GENDER, MOTHERHOOD AND MEDICINE (1987).

1.   GAMETE DONATION

People v. Sorensen

Supreme Court of California, 1968.
68 Cal.2d 280, 66 Cal.Rptr. 7, 437 P.2d 495.

■ McCOMB, JUSTICE.

Defendant appeals from a judgment convicting him of violating section 270 of the Penal Code (willful failure to provide for his minor child), a misdemeanor.

The settled statement of facts recites that seven years after defendant's marriage it was medically determined that he was sterile. His wife desired a child, either by artificial insemination or by adoption, and at first defendant refused to consent. About 15 years after the marriage defendant agreed to the artificial insemination of his wife. Husband and wife, then residents of San Joaquin County, consulted a physician in San Francisco. They signed an agreement, which is on the letterhead of the physician, requesting the physician to inseminate the wife with the sperm of a white male. The semen was to be selected by the physician, and under no circumstances were the parties to demand the name of the donor. The agreement contains a recitation that the physician does not represent that pregnancy will occur. The physician treated Mrs. Sorensen, and she became pregnant. Defendant knew at the time he signed the consent that when his wife took the treatments she could become pregnant and that if a child was born it was to be treated as their child.

A male child was born to defendant's wife in San Joaquin County on October 14, 1960. The information for the birth certificate was given by the mother, who named defendant as the father. Defendant testified that he had not provided the information on the birth certificate and did not recall seeing it before the trial.

For about four years the family had a normal family relationship, defendant having represented to friends that he was the child's father and treated the boy as his son. In 1964, Mrs. Sorensen separated from defendant.... Defendant obtained a decree of divorce....

In the summer of 1966 when Mrs. Sorensen became ill and could not work, she applied for public assistance under the Aid to Needy Children program. The County of Sonoma supplied this aid until Mrs. Sorensen was able to resume work. Defendant paid no support for the child since the separation in 1964, although demand therefor was made by the district attorney. The municipal court found defendant guilty of violating section 270 of the Penal Code and granted him probation for three years on condition that he make payments of $50 per month for support through the district attorney's office.

. . .

... [T]he only question for our determination is:

Is the husband of a woman, who with his consent was artificially inseminated with semen of a third-party donor, guilty of the crime of failing to support a child who is the product of such insemination, in violation of section 270 of the Penal Code?

. . .

The law is that defendant is the lawful father of the child born to his wife, which child was conceived by artificial insemination to which he consented, and his conduct carries with it an obligation of support within the meaning of section 270 of the Penal Code.

. . .

... [A] reasonable man who, because of his inability to procreate, actively participates and consents to his wife's artificial insemination in the hope that a child will be produced whom they will treat as their own, knows that such behavior carries with it the legal responsibilities of fatherhood and criminal responsibility for nonsupport. One who consents to the production of a child cannot create a temporary relation to be assumed and disclaimed at will, but the arrangement must be of such character as to impose an obligation of supporting those for whose existence he is directly responsible. As noted by the trial court, it is safe to assume that without defendant's active participation and consent the child would not have been procreated.

. . .

The question of the liability of the husband for support of a child created through artificial insemination is one of first impression in this state and has been raised in only a few cases outside the state, none of them involving a criminal prosecution for failure to provide. Although other courts considering the question have found some existing legal theory to hold the "father" responsible, results have varied on the question of legitimacy. . . .

. . .

The public policy of this state favors legitimation (*Estate of Lund*, 26 Cal.2d 472, 481, 490, 159 P.2d 643, 162 A.L.R. 606), and no valid public purpose is served by stigmatizing an artificially conceived child as illegitimate. . . .

In the absence of legislation prohibiting artificial insemination, the offspring of defendant's valid marriage to the child's mother was lawfully begotten and was not the product of an illicit or adulterous relationship. . . . [D]efendant is the lawful father of the child conceived through heterologous artificial insemination and born during his marriage to the child's mother.

The judgment is affirmed.

Jhordan C. v. Mary K.

California Court of Appeal, First District, 1986.
179 Cal.App.3d 386, 224 Cal.Rptr. 530.

■ KING, J.

. . .

Mary K. and Victoria T. appeal from a judgment declaring Jhordan C. to be the legal father of Mary's child, Devin. The child was conceived by artificial insemination with semen donated personally to Mary by Jhordan. We affirm the judgment.

In late 1978, Mary decided to bear a child by artificial insemination and to raise the child jointly with Victoria, a close friend who lived in a nearby town. Mary sought a semen donor by talking to friends and acquaintances. This led to three or four potential donors with whom Mary spoke directly. She and Victoria ultimately chose Jhordan after he had one personal interview with Mary and one dinner at Mary's home.

The parties' testimony was in conflict as to what agreement they had concerning the role, if any, Jhordan would play in the child's life. According to Mary, she told Jhordan she did not want a donor who desired ongoing involvement with the child, but she did agree to let him see the child to satisfy his curiosity as to how the child would look. Jhordan, in contrast, asserts they agreed he and Mary would have an ongoing friendship, he would have ongoing contact with the child, and he would care for the child as much as two or three times per week.

None of the parties sought legal advice until long after the child's birth. They were completely unaware of the existence of Civil Code section 7005. They did not attempt to draft a written agreement concerning Jhordan's status.

Jhordan provided semen to Mary on a number of occasions during a six month period commencing in late January 1979. On each occasion he came to her home, spoke briefly with her, produced the semen, and then left. The record is unclear, but Mary, who is a nurse, apparently performed the insemination by herself or with Victoria.

Contact between Mary and Jhordan continued after she became pregnant. Mary attended a Christmas party at Jhordan's home. Jhordan visited Mary several times at the health center where she worked. He took photographs of her. When he informed Mary by telephone that he had collected a crib, playpen, and high chair for the child, she told him to keep those items at his home. At one point Jhordan told Mary he had started a trust fund for the child and wanted legal guardianship in case she died; Mary vetoed the guardianship idea but did not disapprove the trust fund.

Victoria maintained a close involvement with Mary during the pregnancy. She took Mary to medical appointments, attended birthing classes, and shared information with Mary regarding pregnancy, delivery, and child rearing.

Mary gave birth to Devin on March 30, 1980. Victoria assisted in the delivery. Jhordan was listed as the father on Devin's birth certificate.[1] Mary's roommate telephoned Jhordan that day to inform him of the birth. Jhordan visited Mary and Devin the next day and took photographs of the baby.

Five days later Jhordan telephoned Mary and said he wanted to visit Devin again. Mary initially resisted, but then allowed Jhordan to visit, although she told him she was angry. During the visit Jhordan claimed a right to see Devin, and Mary agreed to monthly visits.

Through August 1980 Jhordan visited Devin approximately five times. Mary then terminated the monthly visits. Jhordan said he would consult an attorney if Mary did not let him see Devin. Mary asked Jhordan to sign a contract indicating he would not seek to be Devin's father, but Jhordan refused.

---

1.   This occurred as a result of the filing of an amended birth certificate based upon a judgment against Jhordan in Sonoma County's action for reimbursement of public assistance benefits paid for the child.

In December 1980, Jhordan filed an action against Mary to establish paternity and visitation rights. In June 1982, by stipulated judgment in a separate action by the County of Sonoma, he was ordered to reimburse the county for public assistance paid for Devin's support. The judgment ordered him to commence payment, through the district attorney's office, of $900 in arrearages as well as future child support of $50 per month. In November 1982, the court granted Jhordan weekly visitation with Devin at Victoria's home.

Victoria had been closely involved with Devin since his birth. Devin spent at least two days each week in her home. On days when they did not see each other they spoke on the telephone. Victoria and Mary discussed Devin daily either in person or by telephone. They made joint decisions regarding his daily care and development. The three took vacations together. Devin and Victoria regarded each other as parent and child. Devin developed a brother-sister relationship with Victoria's 14–year-old daughter, and came to regard Victoria's parents as his grandparents. Victoria made the necessary arrangements for Devin's visits with Jhordan.

In August 1983, Victoria moved successfully for an order joining her as a party to this litigation. Supported by Mary, she sought joint legal custody (with Mary) and requested specified visitation rights, asserting she was a de facto parent of Devin. (*See, e.g., Guardianship of Phillip B.*, (Cal. Ct. App. 1983) 188 Cal. Rptr. 781.) Jhordan subsequently requested an award of joint custody to him and Mary.

After trial the court rendered judgment declaring Jhordan to be Devin's legal father. However, the court awarded sole legal and physical custody to Mary, and denied Jhordan any input into decisions regarding Devin's schooling, medical and dental care, and day-to-day maintenance. Jhordan received substantial visitation rights as recommended by a court-appointed psychologist. The court held Victoria was not a de facto parent, but awarded her visitation rights (not to impinge upon Jhordan's visitation schedule), which were also recommended by the psychologist.

. . .

We begin with a discussion of Civil Code section 7005, which provides in pertinent part: "(a) If, under the supervision of a licensed physician and with the consent of her husband, a wife is inseminated artificially with semen donated by a man not her husband, the husband is treated in law as if he were the natural father of a child thereby conceived.... [&] (b) The donor of semen provided to a licensed physician for use in artificial insemination of a woman other than the donor's wife is treated in law as if he were not the natural father of a child thereby conceived."

Civil Code section 7005 is part of the Uniform Parentage Act (UPA), which was approved in 1973 by the National Conference of Commissioners on Uniform State Laws.... The UPA was adopted in California in 1975....

... [T]he California Legislature has afforded unmarried as well as married women a statutory vehicle for obtaining semen for artificial insemination without fear that the donor may claim paternity, and has likewise provided men with a statutory vehicle for donating semen to married and unmarried women alike without fear of liability for child support. Subdivision (b) states only one limitation on its application: the semen must be "provided to a licensed physician." Otherwise, whether impregnation occurs through artificial insemination or sexual intercourse, there can be a determination of paternity with the rights, duties and obligations such a determination entails.

Mary and Victoria first contend that despite the requirement of physician involvement stated in Civil Code section 7005, subdivision (b), the Legislature did not intend to withhold application of the donor nonpaternity provision where semen used in artificial insemination was not provided to a licensed physician. They suggest that the element of physician involvement appears in the statute merely because the Legislature assumed (erroneously) that all artificial insemination would occur under the supervision of a physician. Alternatively, they argue the requirement of physician involvement is merely directive rather than mandatory.

We cannot presume, however, that the Legislature simply assumed or wanted to recommend physician involvement, for two reasons.

First, the history of the UPA (the source of section 7005) indicates conscious adoption of the physician requirement. The initial "discussion draft" submitted to the drafters of the UPA in 1971 did not mention the involvement of a physician in artificial insemination; the draft stated no requirement as to how semen was to be obtained or how the insemination procedure was to be performed. (H. Krause, Illegitimacy: Law and Social Policy (1971) pp. 240, 243.) The eventual inclusion of the physician requirement in the final version of the UPA suggests a conscious decision to require physician involvement.

Second, there are at least two sound justifications upon which the statutory requirement of physician involvement might have been based. One relates to health: a physician can obtain a complete medical history of the donor (which may be of crucial importance to the child during his or her lifetime) and screen the donor for any hereditary or communicable diseases. Indeed, the commissioners' comment to the section of the UPA on artificial insemination cites as a "useful reference" a law review article which argues that health considerations should require the involvement of a physician in statutorily authorized artificial insemination. (9A West's U.Laws Ann. (1979) U.Par. Act, comrs. com. to § 5, p. 593, *citing* Wadlington, *Artificial Insemination: The Dangers of a Poorly Kept Secret* (1970) 64 Nw.U.L.Rev. 777, 803; *see also* Comment, *Artificial Insemination and Surrogate Motherhood—A Nursery Full of Unresolved Questions* (1981) 17 Willamette L.Rev. 912, 926.) This suggests that health considerations underlie the decision by the drafters of the UPA to include the physician requirement in the artificial insemination statute.

Another justification for physician involvement is that the presence of a professional third party such as a physician can serve to create a formal, documented structure for the donor-recipient relationship, without which, as this case illustrates, misunderstandings between the parties regarding the nature of their relationship and the donor's relationship to the child would be more likely to occur.

It is true that nothing inherent in artificial insemination requires the involvement of a physician. Artificial insemination is, as demonstrated here, a simple procedure easily performed by a woman in her own home. Also, despite the reasons outlined above in favor of physician involvement, there are countervailing considerations against requiring it. A requirement of physician involvement, as Mary argues, might offend a woman's sense of privacy and reproductive autonomy, might result in burdensome costs to some women, and might interfere with a woman's desire to conduct the procedure in a comfortable environment such as her own home or to choose the donor herself.

However, because of the way section 7005 is phrased, a woman (married or unmarried) can perform home artificial insemination or choose her donor and still obtain the benefits of the statute. Subdivision (b) does not require that a physician independently obtain the semen and perform the insemination, but requires only that the semen be "provided" to a physician. Thus, a woman who prefers home artificial insemination or who wishes to choose her donor can still obtain statutory protection from a donor's paternity claim through the relatively simple expedient of obtaining the semen, whether for home insemination or from a chosen donor (or both), through a licensed physician.

. . .

Mary and Victoria next contend that even if section 7005, subdivision (b), by its terms does not apply where semen for artificial insemination has not been provided to a licensed physician, application of the statute to the present case is required by constitutional principles of equal protection and privacy (encompassing rights to family autonomy and procreative choice).

Mary and Victoria argue the failure to apply section 7005, subdivision (b), to unmarried women who conceive artificially with semen not provided to a licensed physician denies equal protection because the operation of other paternity statutes precludes a donor assertion of paternity where a married woman undergoes artificial insemination with semen not provided to a physician.

This characterization of the effect of the paternity statutes as applied to married women is correct. In the case of the married woman her husband is the presumed father (Civ.Code, § 7004, subd. (a)(1)), and any outsider—including a semen donor, regardless of physician involvement—is precluded from maintaining a paternity action unless the mother "relinquishes for, consents to, or proposes to relinquish for or consent to, the adoption of the child." (Civ.Code, § 7006, subd. (d).) An action to establish paternity by blood test can be brought only by the husband or mother. (Evid.Code, § 621, subds. (c) & (d); *see* Vincent B. v. Joan R. (Cal. Ct. App. 1981) 179 Cal. Rptr. 9; Ferguson v. Ferguson (Cal. Ct. App. 1981) [179 Cal. Rptr. 108].)

But the statutory provision at issue here—Civil Code section 7005, subdivision (b)—treats married and unmarried women equally. Both are denied application of the statute where semen has not been provided to a licensed physician.

The true question presented is whether a completely different set of paternity statutes—affording protection to husband and wife from any claim of paternity by an outsider (Civ.Code, §§ 7004, 7006; Evid.Code § 621)—denies equal protection by failing to provide similar protection to an unmarried woman. The simple answer is that, within the context of this question, a married woman and an unmarried woman are not similarly situated for purposes of equal protection analysis. In the case of a married woman, the marital relationship invokes a long-recognized social policy of preserving the integrity of the marriage. (*See* Estate of Cornelious (Cal. 1984) 674 P.2d 245; Vincent B. v. Joan R., *supra*, 179 Cal. Rptr. 9.) No such concerns arise where there is no marriage at all.

.   .   .

Mary and Victoria contend that they and Devin compose a family unit and that the trial court's ruling constitutes an infringement upon a right they have to family autonomy, encompassed by the constitutional right to privacy. But this argument begs the question of which persons comprise the family in this case for purposes of judicial intervention. Characterization of the family unit must precede consideration of whether family autonomy has been infringed.

The semen donor here was permitted to develop a social relationship with Mary and Devin as the child's father. During Mary's pregnancy Jhordan maintained contact with her. They visited each other several times, and Mary did not object to Jhordan's collection of baby equipment or the creation of a trust fund for the child. Mary permitted Jhordan to visit Devin on the day after the child's birth and allowed monthly visits thereafter. The record demonstrates no clear understanding that Jhordan's role would be limited to provision of semen and that he would have no parental relationship with Devin; indeed, the parties' conduct indicates otherwise.

We do not purport to hold that an oral or written nonpaternity agreement between the parties would have been legally binding; that difficult question is not before us (and indeed is more appropriately addressed by the Legislature). We simply emphasize that for purposes of the family autonomy argument raised by Mary, Jhordan was not excluded as a member of Devin's family, either by anonymity, by agreement, or by the parties' conduct.

In short, the court's ruling did not infringe upon any right of Mary and Victoria to family autonomy, because under the peculiar facts of this case Jhordan was not excluded as a member of Devin's family for purposes of resolving this custody dispute.

Mary and Victoria argue that the physician requirement in Civil Code section 7005, subdivision (b), infringes a fundamental right to procreative choice, also encompassed by the constitutional right of privacy.

But the statute imposes no restriction on the right to bear a child. Unlike statutes in other jurisdictions proscribing artificial insemination other than by a physician, subdivision (b) of section 7005 does not forbid self-inseminations nor does the statute preclude personal selection of a donor or in any other way prevent women from artificially conceiving children under circumstances of their own choice. The statute simply addresses the perplexing question of the legal status of the semen donor, and provides a method of avoiding the legal consequences that might otherwise be dictated by traditional notions of paternity.

Finally, Mary and Victoria contend that even if the paternity judgment is affirmed Victoria should be declared a de facto parent, based on her day-to-day attention to Devin's needs ..., in order to guarantee her present visitation rights and ensure her parental status in any future custody or visitation proceedings. Present resolution of the de facto parenthood issue for these purposes would be premature and merely advisory. Victoria's visitation rights have been legally recognized and preserved by court order. If no further custody or visitation proceedings occur, the issue of Victoria's de facto parent status and its legal effect will never arise.

We wish to stress that our opinion in this case is not intended to express any judicial preference toward traditional notions of family structure or toward providing a father where a single woman has chosen to bear a child. Public policy in these areas is best determined by the legislative branch of government, not the judicial. Our Legislature has already spoken and has afforded to unmarried women a statutory right to bear children by artificial insemination (as well as a right of men to donate semen) without fear of a paternity claim, through provision of the semen to a licensed physician. We simply hold that because Mary omitted to invoke Civil Code section 7005, subdivision (b), by obtaining Jhordan's semen through a licensed physician, and because the parties by all other conduct preserved Jhordan's status as a member of Devin's family, the trial court properly declared Jhordan to be Devin's legal father.

The judgment is affirmed.

NOTES AND QUESTIONS

1. Sperm and ovum donation permit deliberate separation of the biological act of producing a child from the psychological process of nurturing and raising the child. How should we define "family" and "parenthood"? Should there be a difference between "genetic" and "social" parenthood? While artificial insemination (AID) is problematic because there are two "fathers" (the biological and rearing fathers), ovum donation with surrogacy, *see* Sec. II. C., *infra* raises further ethical and legal concerns since it may result potentially in three "mothers": the genetic mother (the ovum donor), the gestational mother (the ovum recipient who carries the child), and the social mother (the woman who raises the child).

The issue in *Jhordan C. v. Mary K.* was whether the California version of the 1973 Uniform Parentage Act applied in a situation in which the sperm donor did not transfer his sperm to a licensed physician as called for by the act. As of December 2000, eighteen states in addition to California had enacted versions of the 1973 Uniform Parentage Act. UNIFORM PARENTAGE ACT, 9 U.L.A. (Supp. 2004). Oklahoma has enacted a statute similar to UPA (1973) that provides that children resulting from oocyte donation are the legitimate children of the recipient husband and wife if both consent to the procedure. 10 OKL. ST. ANN. § 554 ch. 24 (1990).

Should physicians be required to perform artificial insemination? Some states expressly require that a physician perform the procedure. *See, e.g.,* GA. CODE ANN. § 43–34–42 (2003) (making performance of AI without a medical license a felony),

Ark. Code Ann. § 9–10–202 (2003) (requiring that physicians perform AI), Idaho Code § 39–5402 (2003) (requiring that physicians perform AI). What is the rationale for involving physicians in the AI procedure? Do sperm banks perform the same screening functions as physicians? For a persuasive argument against the medicalization of artificial insemination, see Daniel Wilker & Norma J. Wilker, *Turkey Baster Babies: The Demedicalization of Artificial Insemination*, 69 Milbank Q. 3 (1991).

With the development of numerous assisted reproductive techniques, the UPA was revised in 2000 to include the 1988 Uniform Status of Children of Assisted Conception Act (USCACA), and it was further amended in 2002. The 2002 amendment maintained the essence of UPA (2000), but it clarified the language of the Act so that it referred to children of both married and unmarried parents. Uniform Parentage Act, 9 U.L.A. (amended 2002) (Supp. 2004). In the UPA (2000), a donor is defined as a person who produces eggs or sperm used for assisted reproduction, but does not include a husband who provides sperm, or a wife who provides eggs for use in assisted reproduction by the wife. 9 U.L.A. § 102 (Supp. 2004). UPA (2000) also provides that "a donor is not a parent of a child conceived by means of assisted reproduction." 9 U.L.A. § 702 (Supp. 2004). As of 2004, Delaware, Texas, Washington, and Wyoming had adopted versions of UPA (2000). *Id.* For a discussion of the Uniform Parentage Act, see Paula Roberts, *Biology and Beyond: The Case for Passage of the New Uniform Parentage Act*, 35 Fam. L.Q. 41 (2001).

2. Parentage of children born of gamete donation has been a widely litigated issue. The majority of cases are in agreement with *Sorensen* that when a married couple utilizes donor insemination, the resulting child is the legal child of both spouses, as long as both consented to the procedure. *See Brown v. Brown*, 83 Ark.App. 217, 125 S.W.3d 840 (2003); *Lane v. Lane*, 121 N.M. 414, 912 P.2d 290 (App. 1996); *Jackson v. Jackson*, 137 Ohio App.3d 782, 739 N.E.2d 1203 (2000).

As is reflected in *Jhordan C.,* when a non-married couple (lesbian couples, unwed couples, transsexual couples) utilizes donor insemination, the result is more complicated. Several courts have ruled that the non-genetic parent in a homosexual relationship that includes children conceived by artificial insemination has no parental rights. *See Maria B. v. Superior Court*, 13 Cal.Rptr.3d 494 (Cal. Ct. App. 2004) (lesbian partner did not have obligation to support partner's child, even though she participated and encouraged artificial insemination), *State ex. rel. DRM*, 109 Wash.App. 182, 34 P.3d 887 (2001) (mother's former partner not child's "parent" under UPA). Other courts have allowed either custody or visitation for the non-genetic parent. *See E.N.O. v. L.M.M.*, 429 Mass. 824, 711 N.E.2d 886 (1999) (court found lesbian partner to be child's de facto parent and honored parenting agreement allowing visitation); *V.C. v. M.J.B.*, 163 N.J. 200, 748 A.2d 539 (2000) (although lesbian woman not entitled to legal custody of former partner's child, she had visitation rights); *L.S.K. v. H.A.N.*, 813 A.2d 872 (Pa. Super. Ct., 2002) (lesbian partner who participated in and encouraged artificial insemination procedure had parental support obligation to child); *Rubano v. DiCenzo*, 759 A.2d 959 (R.I. 2000) (where both parties signed agreement stating intentions joint custody of child permitted). What concerns does this raise about the family structure in these "new" families? Consider the Wisconsin Supreme Court's decision in *Sporleder v. Hermes*, where the court denied custody to the plaintiff's partner's child because of the fear that such allowance would open the door to "multiple parties claiming custody of children by virtue of their in loco parentis status" 162 Wis.2d 1002, 471 N.W.2d 202 (1991). For further discussion on this issue, see Melanie B. Jacobs, *Micah Has One Mommy and One Legal Stranger: Adjudicating Maternity for Nonbiological Lesbian Coparents*, 50 Buff. L. Rev. 341 (2002); Ryiah Lilith, *The G.I.F.T. of Two Biological and Legal Mothers*, 9 Am. U. J. Gender. So. Pol'y. & L. 207 (2001); Nancy Polikoff, *This Child Does Have Two Mothers: Redefining Parenthood to Meet the Needs of*

Children in Lesbian–Mother and Other Nontraditional Families, 78 GEO. L. J. 459, 527–545, 561–568 (1990).

Who should be the legal parents in the case of a lesbian couple where one woman donates the egg and after in vitro fertilization with sperm from an anonymous donor the embryo is implanted into the second woman's uterus? Recall the provision of UPA (2000) which provides that a donor is not the parent of the child who results from assisted reproduction. 9 U.L.A. § 702 (Supp. 2004). Does this provision of UPA (2000) really clarify the parental status of all people who decide to utilize assisted reproduction as a method of conception or does it merely complicate the situation?

The issue of paternity rights in an unwed heterosexual relationship was addressed by California courts in 2000. In *Dunkin v. Boskey*, 82 Cal.App.4th 171, 98 Cal.Rptr.2d 44 (2000), the parties who had lived together for five years entered into a written contract to create a child using donor insemination. Both parties agreed to care for and support the child as if he or she were a genetic parent. The relationship ended and the mother denied Dunkin any custody or visitation with the child. *Id.* The trial court dismissed Dunkin's paternity action on the basis that he lacked standing to sue for custody and visitation, and also dismissed his breach of contract claim. The appellate court agreed with the trial court that Dunkin could not be given paternity or custodial rights under the law, because he was not the biological father and did not adopt the child. *Id.* at 52–53. However, the court ruled that the contractual agreement was binding upon both parties because otherwise Boskey would have been unjustly enriched in having reaped the benefits of the contract without fulfilling her part of the bargain. *Id.* at 57. Thus, Dunkin could claim monetary damages for unjust enrichment against Boskey. *Id.* at 61. Is this a satisfactory result?

3. Does parenthood mean something different for men and women? Historically, motherhood has been defined by giving birth while fatherhood has been defined by the man's relationship to the mother. *See* Janet Dolgin, *Just a Gene: Judicial Assumptions About Parenthood*, 40 UCLA L. REV. 637, 644 (1993). Should a biological link, a relationship with the child's mother, or an intent to parent determine legal responsibilities to children? *See* Marjorie Maguire Shultz, *Reproductive Technologies and Intent–Based Parenthood: An Opportunity for Gender Neutrality*, 1990 WIS. L. REV. 297 (advocating recognition of intent-based parental rights); John L. Hill, *What Does It Mean to be a "Parent"? The Claims for Biology as the Basis for Parental Rights*, 66 N.Y.U. L. REV. 353 (1991) (favoring intent over biology as determinant of parental rights). As a matter of public policy, could the widespread use of AID (artificial insemination by third party donor) help perpetuate the notion sometimes common in our society that biological fatherhood does not necessarily entail responsibilities to children?

4. In ovum (also called "egg" or "oocyte") donation, a woman's egg is donated to another woman, usually for use in In Vitro Fertilization (IVF) or Gamete Intrafallopian Transfer (GIFT). *See* Sec. II. B. 2., *infra.* There are generally three potential sources for egg donors: women who are undergoing IVF, from whom "spare eggs are harvested for donation; women who are undergoing a surgical procedure where ovum can be recovered incidentally; and the most common source, women who undergo hormonal stimulation of the ovaries and ovum recovery solely for the purpose of donating eggs." *See* Martin M. Quigley *Editorial, The New Frontier of the Reproductive Age*, 268 JAMA 1320 (1992).

Couples who need ova have several options: female relatives, pooled brokerages, direct solicitation from women or assisted reproductive clinics, or oocyte sharing. PRESIDENT'S COUNCIL ON BIOETHICS, REPRODUCTION AND RESPONSIBILITY: THE REGULATION OF NEW BIOTECHNOLOGIES 148 (2004). Pooled brokerages recruit donors and create databases with information about the donors for couples to read. *Id.* The brokerages assist in matching couples and donors by providing psychological counseling, medical screening, and legal counseling for the couple and the donor. *Id.* at 149. When couples solicit individuals for egg donation, they often place advertisements in college newspapers. *Id.*; *see* Jeffrey P. Kahn, *The Ethics of Egg Donation*, 81 MINN. MED.: J. CLINICAL & HEALTH AFF. 12 (1998) (describing advertisements in Princeton University newspaper offering women as much as $35,000 for egg donations). Finally, couples can obtain ova from oocyte sharing, a program in which women receiving infertility treatments agree to share their ova with couples in exchange for discounted infertility treatments. PRESIDENT'S COUNCIL ON BIOETHICS at 149.

Healthy donor ova are a scarce resource: a woman is born with all the eggs she will ever have (while a man can continually regenerate sperm) and the process of obtaining eggs is much more complicated than that for sperm. Women who donate ova must undergo hormonal stimulation and a surgical procedure (either laparoscopy or ultrasound needle) to remove the eggs. Laparoscopy involves inserting a probe through the woman's abdomen while she is under general anesthesia. The ultrasound needle is inserted through the vagina and requires local anesthesia. Lawrence J. Kaplan & Carolyn M. Kaplan, *Natural Reproduction and Reproduction–Aiding Technologies, in* THE ETHICS OF REPRODUCTIVE TECHNOLOGY 25 (Kenneth D. Alpern ed., 1992). The procedure entails some risks: the hormones used have been associated with an increased risk of ovarian cancer. Mary Anne Rossing et al., *Ovarian Tumors in a Cohort of Infertile Women*, 331 NEW ENG. J. MED. 771, 772–74 (1994). In addition, donors might experience premenstrual syndrome-like symptoms or ovarian hyperstimulation syndrome. There is also a slight risk of infection from the surgery or of complications from the anesthesia. Andrea D. Gurmankin, *Risk Information Provided to Prospective Oocyte Donors in a Preliminary Phone Call*, 1 AM. J. BIOETHICS 3 (2001). In light of these risks, the Canadian Royal Commission on New Reproductive Technologies proposed a ban on paying women for ova donations because the members felt that it was unethical to ask healthy women to take this type of risk. *See* Gladys White, *Young Women Wanted: The Hopes and Hazards of Oocyte Donation and What Nurses Can Do*, 101 AM. J. NURSING 60 (2001). Does the fact that a woman donating eggs is placed at some degree of medical risk, while a man donating sperm is not, argue against ovum donation?

To deal with the scarcity of ova, some people have suggested the possibility of using ova from cadavers or even aborted fetuses. *Britain Fears Effects, Regulates Use of Donor Eggs*, CHI. TRIB. Aug. 7, 1994 at 11. What ethical dilemmas are raised by using ova from cadavers or fetuses to assist couples or individuals to have a child?

Ovum donation also raises the possibility that older women, who are either in menopause or unwilling to risk natural conception with their own ova, may bear children with the aid of younger, healthier, donated ova. In essence, ovum donation in these cases aims to reverse the "natural" aging process rather than to treat "medical" infertility in younger women of childbearing age. *See, e.g.*, Mark V. Sauer et al., *Pregnancy After Age 50: Application of Oocyte Donation to Women after Menopause*, 341 LANCET 321 (1993). Is there an appropriate age to be a parent? Should there be an age limit for post-menopausal women?

For a review of the ethical and legal issues surrounding oocyte donation, see Katheryn D. Katz, *Ghost Mothers: Human Egg Donation and the Legacy of the Past*, 57 ALB. L. REV. 733 (1994); National Advisory Board on Ethics in Reproduction, *Ethical Questions Raised by Oocyte Donation and Values Informing This Report, in* NEW WAYS OF MAKING BABIES: THE CASE OF EGG DONATION (Cynthia Cohen ed., 1996); PRESIDENT'S COUNCIL ON BIOETHICS 147–52 (2004).

5. Should we be concerned about the potential effect of gamete donation on children? Studies and case reports indicate that young children conceived with these technologies are not adversely affected by knowing of their origin. *See* Golombock et al. *Families With Children Conceived by Donor Insemination: A Follow–Up at Age Twelve*, 73 CHILD DEV. 952 (2002); Vanfraussen et al. *Family Functioning in Lesbian Families Created by Donor Insemination*, 73 AM. J. ORTHOPSYCHIATRY 78 (2003). In contrast to children, studies of adults show that they often feel alienated from their families and resentful toward their parents for depriving them of what they consider a fundamental part of themselves—their genetic history. *See* Turner and Coyle, *What Does it Mean to be a Donor Offspring? The Identity Experiences of Adults Conceived by Donor Insemination and the Implications for Counseling and Therapy*, 15 HUM. REPROD. 2041 (2000); Anonymous, *How it Feels to be a Child of Donor Insemination*, 324 BMJ 797 (2002). Consider the following transcript from a program that included two women in their mid-thirties who had been conceived through AID.[1] Both expressed anger over their inability to gain knowledge about their genetic backgrounds and personal identities:

> Phil Donahue: Right. [W]hy are you angry ...? Why wouldn't you think your mother's 1948 Herculean effort to become pregnant would be applauded? She certainly wanted a baby.
>
> [Guest No. 1]: Well, as I got into this and started developing and studying this research—it's not just my family that ended in divorce. There's evidence regular adoptive families are ending in divorce a lot.—the AI doesn't solve all the infertile couple's problems. It's really the beginning.
>
> Phil Donahue: O.K. But I still don't know why you're upset.
>
> [Guest No. 1]: I want to know who I am. I want to know my name. I want to know my medical history. I had two miscarriages. And when I found out on the radio that a man or his—or a woman's father might have left the sperm bad to cause the miscarriages, I want to know, is it a guilt trip on me that people put on me? What did I eat wrong that caused these babies to die? What about these fifty unknown numbers of other children my father was and maybe is still producing through AI. Are all of my half sisters also having miscarriages? ... I want to contact my father anonymously if need be and ask him, please, he's got weak sperm. I've got bad feet, bad nearsighted eyes—
>
> Phil Donahue: And you want to know—
>
> [Guest No. 1]:—what did he get out of this picture?
>
> Audience: (Laughter).
>
> Phil Donahue:—you want to know if there's any genetic information that might explain the difficulties you've sustained, huh?
>
> [Guest No. 1]: With my miscarriages, yeah.
>
> . . .
>
> Phil Donahue: Do you understand [the first guest's] anger?
>
> [Guest No. 2]: Absolutely.
>
> Phil Donahue: You feel it, too?
>
> [Guest No. 2]: Absolutely.
>
> Phil Donahue: What is it that you're angry about?
>
> [Guest No. 2]: It has to do with betrayal. It has to do with—
>
> Phil Donahue: Well, who's betrayed?

---

1. Donahue Transcript No. 08033.

[Guest No. 2]:—my parents in keeping this a secret, for a start. It has to do with the medical establishment in thinking that a person's genetic background is so unimportant that it can simply be ignored. It has to do with a falsified birth certificate which is routine in artificial insemination. This donor is not named on the birth certificate; the wife's husband is simply named.

Phil Donahue: Yeah. So this is a—

[Guest No. 2]: It's a conspiracy.

Phil Donahue:—a conspiracy by a lot of educated professional people—

[Guest No. 2]: Yes.

Phil Donahue:—with the cooperation and the contribution of your own mother and stepfather, I guess—

[Guest No. 2]: Absolutely.

Phil Donahue:—to deny you information which—

[Guest No. 2]: The truth.

Phil Donahue:—you think is essential.

[Guest No. 2]: Absolutely.

Should information about donors be available to children? Several European countries, including the Netherlands, United Kingdom, Sweden, Austria, and Germany allow donor information to be available to children born of gamete donation. Dyer C, *Fertility Watchdog Says that Donor Identity Should be Revealed*, 325 BMJ 237 (2002); Weber W, *Dutch Sperm Donors Will Remain Anonymous for Another Two Years*, 355 LANCET 1249 (2000); Guido Pennings, *The Right to Privacy and Access to Information About One's Genetic Origins*, 20 MED. & L. 1 (2001). Disclosure is not yet required in the United States. Would making donor information available to offspring adversely affect gamete donation rates? Do persons reproducing with donor gametes have interests that should be protected? What are the implications on confidentiality of medical information?

6.   Storing gametes and/or accumulating data about potential gamete donors may assist recipients in their efforts to have children with specified characteristics such as race, eye color, height, body type, IQ, and even hobbies and income. *See* American Society for Reproductive Medicine, *Guidelines for Oocyte Donation*, 77 FERTILITY & STERILITY S6 (Supp. 5 2002). For example, the California industrialist Robert Graham organized a sperm bank known as the Repository for Germinal Choice, with deposits from Nobel Prize laureates and other highly intelligent people, which selected its clientele based on intelligence. Four prize winners, including Dr. William Shockley, the scientist controversial for his views of inheritance and intelligence, made "repeated" donations. Shockley specifically endorsed the project's goal of "increasing people at the top of the population." *See Nobel Winner Says He Gave Sperm for Women to Bear Gifted Babies*, N.Y. TIMES, Mar. 1, 1981, at A6, col. 2. The sperm bank closed its doors in 1999 after Graham died. What interest might a state assert in regulating banks such as the Repository for Germinal Choice? What effect could such "characteristics" shopping have on our perception of children?

Data about individuals who are potential donors can be used for the same purpose. According to the President's Council on Bioethics, pooled oocyte brokerages solicit a pool of potential donors, create donor profiles including photographs, biographical data, medical histories and educational background, and allow potential recipients to browse their database of donors for a fee. One such brokerage, Tiny Treasures, specializes in Ivy League ovum donors, and its database includes SAT scores, grade point averages, and compensation requests. *See* THE PRESIDENT'S

Council on Bioethics, Reproduction and Responsibility: The Regulation of New Biotechnologies 148–49 (2004). What concerns do specialty brokerages such as Tiny Treasures raise? Should recipient requests for specified characteristics be honored? Should there be limits? It was reported that an infertile black woman married to a white man sought a white ovum donor so that her child would escape discrimination. *See* Eugene Robinson, *Designer Babies' Spark Criticism*, Wash. Post, Jan. 1, 1994, at A15.

Should deaf couples using artificial insemination be allowed to specify that they would like sperm from a deaf donor? Consider the case of a lesbian couple who used artificial insemination by a deaf donor to conceive two deaf children. When the couple initially approached a sperm bank in search of a deaf donor, staff members told them that donors were screened and eliminated if they had conditions such as deafness. The couple eventually received sperm from a deaf friend. *See* Liza Mundy, *A World of Their Own; In the eyes of his parents, if Gauvin Hughes McCullough turns out to be deaf, that will be just perfect*, Wash. Post Mag., March 31, 2002. Deaf parents who want deaf children defend their decision by describing deafness as a culture, i.e. a condition into which some people are normally born rather than as a disability. *See* N. Levy, *Deafness, Culture, and Choice*, 28 J. Med. Ethics 284 (2002).

7. Should frozen semen (or unused ova left in the ovaries) be available for persons desiring to reproduce after the death of the donor? If donation is permitted, who should make the decision: the donor prior to his or her death, the storage facility or family members? *See* Hecht v. Superior Court, 16 Cal.App.4th 836, 20 Cal.Rptr.2d 275 (1993) (woman allowed to inseminate herself with deceased boyfriend's sperm previously stored at sperm bank). Should children resulting from posthumous conception be entitled to support or to inherit from the decedent's estate? *See Woodward v. Commissioner of Social Security*, 435 Mass. 536, 760 N.E.2d 257 (2002) (woman who conceived twin daughters two years after husband's death permitted to claim husband's Social Security benefits on daughters' behalf).

Should the posthumous donor be considered the legal parent of the child conceived of his or her gametes? The Uniform Parentage Act of 2000 states, "if an individual who consented in a record to be a parent by assisted reproduction dies before placement of eggs, sperm, or embryos, the deceased individual is not a parent of the resulting child unless the deceased spouse consented in a record that if assisted reproduction were to occur after death, the deceased individual would be a parent of the child." 9 U.L.A § 707 (2004). Several states have adopted similar versions of this portion of the UPA governing parentage of posthumously conceived children. *See* Colo. Rev. Stat. § 19–4–106 (2004), La. Rev. Stat. Ann. § 391.1 (2004), Tex. Family Code Ann. § 160.707 (2004). In at least one state, North Dakota, a person who dies before conception using his or her sperm cannot be the legal parent of the resulting child in any circumstance. *See* N.D. Cent. Code § 14–18–04 (2004).

For a detailed discussion about posthumous sperm retrieval, see Frances Batzer et. al, *Postmortem Parenthood and the Need for a Protocol with Posthumous Sperm Procurement*, 79 Fertility & Sterility 1263 (2003). Although several European countries have enacted regulation limiting posthumous reproduction, the United States has yet to do so. Joal Hill, *Posthumous Sperm Retrieval*, 361 Lancet 1834 (2003). In 2001, New York Senator Ray Goodman introduced a New York State Bill to mandate consent for posthumous sperm retrieval, but the bill was never passed into law. 2001 NY S.B. 669 (Jan 2001).

8. What requirements, if any, should be met before gamete donors are allowed to transfer sperm and ova to third parties? Should gamete storage facilities be subject to national regulation? Little regulation of the gamete donation industry exists. Although there were between 350 and 450 sperm banks in the United States in 1998, the American Association of Tissue Banks (AATB) reports on its website that as of 2004 there were only ten AATB accredited sperm banks in the United States. John Crister, *Current Statutes of Semen Banking in USA*, HUM. REPROD. 55–67 (Supp. 2 1998) (discussing number of sperm banks in United States); American Association of Tissue Banks, *Reproductive Tissue* (2004), *at* http://www.aatb.org, last visited July 19, 2004 (listing AATB accredited sperm banks).

Is it necessary to create safety guidelines regulating gamete donation? In May 2004, the Food and Drug Administration (FDA) released its rule, *Eligibility Determination for Donors of Human Cells, Tissues and Tissue–Based Products*. *See* 21 CFR § 1271 (2004). The rule outlines the required screening of candidates for tissue donation (including gamete donation) to ensure that donors with communicable diseases are not allowed to donate tissue and requires that records be maintained for a ten years. *See id*. The rule also requires that donors be screened for HIV, Hepatitis, and other sexually transmitted diseases such as chlamydia and gonorrhea. *See id*. Finally, the rule requires that donor sperm be quarantined for six months before becoming eligible for use so that the donor can be retested for diseases. *See id*. The American Society for Reproductive Medicine has issued guidelines similar to those created by the FDA that recommend testing for donor sperm. To review the specific guidelines, see American Society for Reproductive Medicine, *Guidelines for Sperm Donation*, 77 FERTILITY & STERILITY S2 (Supp. 5 2002).

The cost of artificial insemination, although not as substantial as the cost of other assisted reproductive technologies, is high. The cost per cycle of artificial insemination is estimated to be between $400 and $700, and many women undergo as many as three cycles before achieving pregnancy. *See* Kristine S. Knaplund, *Postmortem Conception and a Father's Last Will*, 46 ARIZ. L. REV. 91 (2004). Thus, many women may be deterred from using the technology based on cost alone. Although several states have enacted legislation requiring insurance companies to cover the treatment of infertility, only two states, New Jersey and Illinois, specifically require coverage for artificial insemination—the majority of states that require infertility treatment coverage refer to in-vitro fertilization (a much more expensive procedure). *See* National Conference of State Legislatures, *50 States Summary of Legislation Related to Insurance Coverage for Infertility Therapy*, (2004), *at* http://www.ncsl.org/programs/health/50infert.html, last visited July 1, 2004.

What requirements, if any, should be met before gamete donors are allowed to transfer sperm and ova to third parties? Should payments, including discounts for fertility services, to gamete donors be prohibited? Should it depend on the circumstances of retrieval? In 2000, the average payment to men for sperm donations was between $60 and $70 per donation. PRESIDENT'S COUNCIL ON BIOETHICS, REPRODUCTION AND RESPONSIBILITY: THE REGULATION OF NEW BIOTECHNOLOGIES 147 (2004). Women who donate ova can receive between $5,000 and $15,000, and if they have unique skills, talents, or post graduate degrees they often receive more money. Egg Donation, Inc., *Compensation Issues*, (2004), *at* http://www.eggdonor.com, last visited July 21, 2004. Because of the high payment rate for ova donors the Ethics Committee of the American Society for Reproductive Medicine reports that payment of women for oocyte donation raises ethical concerns because some women might conceal serious health conditions in order to be eligible to donate ova and make money, women might underestimate the physical and psychological risks associated with ova donation because of the financial incentive, and because paying women for donating oocytes devalues human life because it implies that oocytes are property. American Society of Reproductive Medicine, *Financial Incentives in Recruitment of Oocyte Donors*, 74 FERTILITY & STERILITY 216, 217 (2000).

Acquisition of human tissue usually requires the informed consent of the donor. Are there matters pertaining to gamete donation that require special attention? For example, should donors be told how their gametes will be used? Should donors be able to specify characteristics of recipients in terms of race, ethnicity, religion, or marital status? To read a study evaluating whether ova donation programs give donors information that is sufficient enough for donors to give their informed consent to the procedure, see Andrea D. Gurmankin, *Risk Information Provided to Prospective Oocyte Donors in a Preliminary Phone Call*, 1 AM J. BIOETHICS 3 (2001).

Some organizations have issued guidelines containing the information that ova donors must receive in order to give their informed consent. For instance, the American Society for Reproductive Medicine recommends that programs give donors information about the physical, psychological, and legal implications of oocyte donation including the potential negative consequences of donating oocytes. American Society of Reproductive Medicine, *Financial Incentives in Recruitment of Oocyte Donors*, 74 FERTILITY & STERILITY 216, 217 (2000). Furthermore, the New York State Task Force on Life and the Law has created a guidebook for women who are considering donating ova. The guidebook includes information about the ova donation process, physical and psychological risks associated with ova donation, and an explanation of informed consent. *See* NEW YORK STATE TASK FORCE ON LIFE AND THE LAW, THINKING OF BECOMING AN EGG DONOR?: GET THE FACTS BEFORE YOU DECIDE! (2002).

2. IN VITRO FERTILIZATION

Davis v. Davis

Supreme Court of Tennessee, 1992.
842 S.W.2d 588, *cert. denied*, 507 U.S. 911, 113 S.Ct. 1259, 122 L.Ed.2d 657 (1993).

(The opinion is set forth in Section I, *supra*).

NOTES AND QUESTIONS

1. The basic in vitro fertilization (IVF) technique involves fertilizing an egg outside the woman's body and introducing the embryo into the uterus. Lawrence J. Kaplan & Carolyn M. Kaplan, *Natural Reproduction and Reproduction–Aiding Technologies*, in THE ETHICS OF REPRODUCTIVE TECHNOLOGY 25–26 (Kenneth D. Alpern ed., 1992). There are now several variations on the IVF method. In Gamete Intrafallopian Transfer (GIFT) the eggs are removed from the ovary, mixed with sperm, and placed back in the fallopian tube. *Id.* at 26. Since fertilization occurs in vivo, this technique may be seen as more "natural" and may be more acceptable to those who have moral objections to the creation of an embryo in a Petri dish. Ethics Committee of the American Fertility Society, *Ethical Considerations of the New Reproductive Technologies*, 53 FERTILITY & STERILITY 54S–55S (Supp. 2 1990). In Zygote Intrafallopian Transfer (ZIFT), the eggs are fertilized in the laboratory and then inserted into the fallopian tube instead of the uterus. CENTERS FOR DISEASE CONTROL AND PREVENTION, 2001 ASSISTED REPRODUCTIVE TECHNOLOGY SUCCESS RATES: NATIONAL SUMMARY AND FERTILITY CLINIC REPORTS 3 (2003). Intracytoplasmic sperm injection (ISCI) is used for couples with male factor infertility, unexplained infertility or in which fertilization failed after using the traditional IVF technique. Shehua Shen et al., *Statistical Analysis of Factors Affecting Fertilization Rates and Clinical Outcome Associated with Intracytoplasmic Sperm Injection*, 79 FERTILITY & STERILITY 355, 355–56 (2003). In ICSI, doctors pre-select one sperm and inject it into an egg. After fertilization occurs, the doctors insert the embryo into the uterus. Matthew Retzloff & Mark Hornstein, *Is Intracytoplasmic Sperm Injection Safe?*, 80 FERTILITY & STERILITY 851, 851 (2003).

IVF techniques, while providing great benefits, especially to married couples who would otherwise have been childless, have also brought ethical dilemmas. IVF procedures (except GIFT) create embryos outside of the womb and raise questions about how these embryos can be utilized. For example, the embryos may be screened for genetic diseases or abnormalities prior to implantation. Such screening would assure that only healthy embryos would be implanted.

Another ethical dilemma arises when embryos are frozen and stored for long periods. The technique of freezing the "spare" embryos has some advantages because it reduces the number of times that a woman undergoes hormonal extraction of ova. Moreover, freezing embryos eliminates the need to implant large quantities of embryos at once, thus limiting the possibility of a multiple pregnancy. American Medical Association Board of Trustees Report, *Frozen Pre–Embryos*, 263 JAMA 2484, 2484–85 (1990).

Freezing and storing embryos, however, also raises questions about whether, when, or how they should be disposed of. In 2003, there were as many as 400,000 frozen embryos in storage, and technology exists that could allow them to be frozen for up to fifty years or longer. Sharon Hoffman & Andrew Morris, *Symposium: Emerging Issues in Population Health: National and International Global Perspectives*, 31 J.L. MED. & ETHICS 721, 722 (2003). Only three states have adopted legislation dealing with the disposition of frozen embryos. *See* FLA. STAT. ANN. § 742.17 (West 2004) (written agreement between couple and doctor providing for future of embryos is required and if no agreement couple must make decisions jointly); La. REV. STAT. ANN. § 9:121–9:133 (West 2004) (standard for resolving disputes about frozen embryos is the best interest of the embryo); N.H. REV. STAT. ANN. § 168–B:13 thru 168–B:15, 168–B:18 (2003) (embryos must be frozen within 14 days of fertilization).

Other countries also have been grappling with the disposition of frozen embryos. The British Human Embryology and Fertilisation Act requires that embryos be destroyed after being stored for five years. British Human Embryology and Fertilization Act, 1990 Ch. 37. The European Society of Human Reproduction and Embryology has also recommended that European countries adopt a policy that embryos will be stored for five years with the option of one five-year renewal or that embryos be stored for three years with the option of two three-year renewals. *See* European Society of Human Reproduction and Embryology, *The Cryopreservation of Human Embryos*, 16 HUM. REPROD. 1049 (2001). Similarly, fertility clinics in Australia are required to store frozen embryos for a maximum of ten years. Fertility Society of Australia Reproductive Technology Accreditation Committee, *The Fertility Society of Australia Reproductive Technology Accreditation Committee Code of Practice for Centers Using Assisted Reproductive Technology (Revised April 2002)*, at http://www.fsa.au.com/rtac (last visited July 22, 2004). For a discussion of the legal and ethical issues surrounding the destruction of frozen embryos, see Heidi Forster, *The Legal and Ethical Debate Surrounding the Storage and Destruction of Frozen Human Embryos: A Reaction to the Mass Disposal in Britain and the Lack of Law in the United States*, 76 WASH. U. L. Q. 759 (1998).

What should couples do when they want to dispose of their frozen embryos? One option for them is to donate their "extra" embryos to other infertile couples. However, most couples choose to retain their extra embryos for use in future pregnancies. *See* Christopher Newton et al., *Embryo Donation: Attitudes Toward Donation Procedures and Factors Predicting Willingness to Donate*, 18 HUM. REPROD. 878, 878 (2003). A 1996 survey conducted by the American Society for Reproductive Medicine found that of the 108 fertility clinics surveyed, 98% froze embryos and 72% offered embryo donation. However, only 37% of the clinics had actually performed embryo donation. Sheryl Kinsberg et al., *Embryo Donation Programs and Polices in North America: Survey Results and Implications for Health and Mental Health Professionals*, 73 FERTILITY & STERILITY 215, 216 (2000).

A second option is to destroy embryos. Should couples be able to make a binding decision to destroy embryos in specified circumstances at the time the embryos are created? Recall *Davis v. Davis*, where the court determined that in a dispute about disposition of embryos, ordinarily the partner seeking to avoid parenthood should prevail but if the couple had an agreement about disposition it should control. *See* Chapter 5, Sec. I., *supra*. For a similar result, see *Kass v. Kass*, 91 N.Y.2d 554, 673 N.Y.S.2d 350, 696 N.E.2d 174 (1998) (agreement between donors regarding disposition of embryos presumed valid and binding). Other courts have reached different results. *See A.Z. v. B.Z.*, 431 Mass. 150, 725 N.E.2d 1051 (2000) (wife could not retain embryos after divorce despite infertility treatment consent form giving her control of extra embryos because husband did not want additional children); *J.B. v. M.B.*, 170 N.J. 9, 783 A.2d 707 (2001) (enforce agreement entered into at the time infertility treatment begins subject to right of either party to change his or her preferences in which case the interests of both parties will be evaluated); *In re Marriage of Witten*, 672 N.W.2d 768 (Iowa 2003) (agreement enforceable subject to right of either party to change his or her mind in which case no disposition of embryos possible without mutual agreement).

A third but controversial option is to use frozen embryos for research. Human embryo research can potentially not only increase knowledge about infertility and embryological development, but also may prove significant in the development of contraceptives and knowledge about cancer. Should research on embryos be permitted? Should the research purpose matter? In 1993, the National Institutes of Health (NIH) decided that human embryo research was acceptable and recommended that some types of human embryo research be federally funded. *See* Note on Stem Cell Research, Chapter 5, Sec. II. B. 4., *infra*. For a criticism of the premises of the NIH Report, see Daniel Callahan, *The Puzzle of Profound Respect*, 25 HASTINGS CTR. REP. 39, 39–40 (1995). The President's Council on Bioethics in its report REPRODUCTION AND RESPONSIBILITY: THE REGULATION OF NEW BIOTECHNOLOGIES identifies two types of state regulation: (1) states which regulate research on aborted fetuses and embryos and (2) states that define embryo research broadly so that it encompasses cryopreservation, preimplantation genetic diagnosis, and gene transfer. THE PRESIDENT'S COUNCIL ON BIOETHICS, REPRODUCTION AND RESPONSIBILITY: THE REGULATION OF NEW BIOTECHNOLOGIES 5 (2004). To read a transcript of a discussion about state legislation of the use of embryos for research, see Lori B. Andrews & Leon Kass, *Stem Cell Research: Current Law and Policy with Emphasis on the States* (2003), at http://www.bioethics.gov/transcripts/july03/session4.html (last visited August 13, 2004).

In order to avoid the problem of disposition, all embryos could be transferred to the woman's womb. In some cases, however, multiple transfer of embryos results in multiple pregnancies which offer the potential of more offspring than the infertile couple may desire, or present a risk of harm to the pregnant women or the fetuses. Selective termination in utero of one or more fetuses offers a possible resolution of the dilemma presented. However, fetal reduction poses potential problems because all of the fetuses could be lost or because the woman could experience adverse psychological consequences after choosing to abort some of the fetuses while saving others. *See* American Society for Reproductive Medicine, *Guidelines on Number of Embryos Transferred: Committee Report* (2004), at http://www.asrm.org/Media/Practice/practice.html (last visited July 19, 2004). For a general discussion of these matters, see Lisa Barrett Mann, *How Many is Too Many?: Risks Spur Effort to Curb Multiple Births*, WASH. POST, July 20, 2004 at F1.

In an attempt to reduce the number of multiple pregnancies that result from IVF, ASRM has issued guidelines for doctors and patients to use when deciding how many embryos to implant. ASRM uses guidelines instead of regulations like those used in the United Kingdom that mandate no more than three pre-embryos be implanted in a woman because guidelines allow doctors to provide more flexible, individualized treatment. *See* Carson Strong, *Octuplets and Ethics*, 72 Fertility & Sterility 970 (1999) (discussing British regulations); American Society for Reproductive Medicine at 1 (discussing the advantages of guidelines over regulation). The ASRM guidelines are based on the age of the woman and the likelihood of success of pregnancy occurring. For instance, the guidelines encourage doctors to implant no more than two embryos in women under thirty-five years old who have an average likelihood of success and one embryo in women with a high likelihood of success. *Id.*

2.   What is the moral and legal status of frozen embryos? Are they human beings, property, or tissue? The answers to these questions become significant when dealing with disposition of embryos, as illustrated in *Davis*. However, the classification of embryos has other consequences as well. Could liability issues arise if a frozen embryo is accidentally thawed? What if a clinic or doctor is charged with taking a frozen embryo or gametes without the consent of the couple? Should the criminal law punish this, and if so, under what theory? Kidnapping? Theft? If theft, can an embryo be assigned a monetary value? Finally, what if a child results from the "stolen" embryo?

A highly publicized scandal in 1995 brought some of these issues to the forefront. Renowned fertility expert Dr. Ricardo Asch (who developed the GIFT technique and ran a clinic associated with University of California, Irvine) was accused of taking several eggs that he had removed from one patient and using them, without the patient's consent, in IVF for a second patient. Three of the eggs were fertilized (it is not clear with whose sperm) and implanted in another woman, who later had a baby. He was also accused of falsifying records in order to make it appear as though the woman consented to donate the eggs. *Fertility Fraud*, Orange County Reg., May 19, 1995, at A1. *Prato–Morrison v. Doe*, 103 Cal.App.4th 222, 126 Cal.Rptr.2d 509 (Cal. Ct. App. 2002), a case stemming from this scandal, involved a custody battle over twin girls who were allegedly conceived with the Morrisons' stolen genetic material. The court dismissed the case because the Morrisons were unable to produce sufficient evidence of a genetic link to the twins, but stated that "had the Morrisons presented proof of a genetic link to the twins sufficient to establish their standing to pursue a parentage action, it would not have been in the best interests of the twins to have the Morrisons intrude into their lives ... [T]he twins are now almost fourteen years old ... [T]he Morrisons will not be allowed to disrupt the Does' family in order to satisfy [their] unilateral desire, however strong, to turn their genetic connection into a personal relationship." *Id.* at 516. Do you think that courts should look only to the child's best interest in deciding custody cases such as these? Consider the following proposal:

> If only one of the mothers expresses a desire to parent the child, the court should recognize that woman as the child's legal mother. If, on the other hand, both women demonstrate an intent to parent the child, the law should recognize both as the child's legal mothers and resolve their competing claims as a custody matter. Because a gestational mother takes immediate possession of the baby upon birth and will establish a significant bond with the child while a case is litigated, this Article proposes a modified best interest test to determine custody. This test would presume that it is in the child's best interests to award primary custody to the gestational mother, but would leave the door open for evidence to the contrary. Courts should then determine what level of contact with the non-custodial mother, if any, is in the child's best interests.

Alice M. Noble–Allgire, *Switched at the Fertility Clinic: Determining Maternal Rights when a Child is Born from Stolen or Misdelivered Genetic Material*, 64 MO. L. REV. 517, 594 (1999). For further discussion on parentage of children born of stolen genetic material, see Rebecca S. Snyder, *Reproductive Technology and Stolen Ova: Who is the Mother?*, 16 L. & INEQUALITY 289 (1998).

The question of liability also arises under the civil law. While a breach of contract action might be maintained against a clinic, how should damages be quantified? Should a couple be able to sue for intentional or negligent infliction of emotional distress? *See Del Zio v. Presbyterian Hospital*, 74 Civ. 3558 (mem. S.D.N.Y. Apr. 13, 1978).

The ability to freeze embryos indefinitely also allows embryos that have been fertilized and frozen at the same time to be gestated and born years later, or even years apart. For example, a woman gave birth to a child from a frozen embryo which was the third of a set of triplets. Two years before, she had given birth to the first two children of the "set," and had requested that the other embryo be frozen for future use. *Frozen Embryo Produces a Boy*, BOSTON GLOBE, July 31, 1994, at 13. Since embryos can be frozen indefinitely, isn't there the possibility of "twins" being born many years apart, or even a woman gestating her own "sister"? Should the use of these technologies to achieve pregnancy in such situations be regulated? Prohibited? What should be done with frozen embryos if the gamete providers are no longer living?

3. The world first learned of IVF with the birth of Louise Brown, the first "test tube baby," in 1978. In their book, Louise's parents make the following statement.

I don't remember Mr. Steptoe saying his method of producing babies had ever worked and I certainly didn't ask. I just assumed that hundreds of children had already been born through being conceived outside their mother's wombs.

LESLEY & JOHN BROWN WITH S. FREEMAN, OUR MIRACLE CALLED LOUISE: A PARENTS' STORY (1979).

The Browns' statement points to an ongoing aspect of the use of reproductive technologies in the United States: there is virtually no regulation or oversight of research or clinical practice involving these techniques.

Initially, the technique was considered experimental, and the Department of Health, Education, and Welfare, (currently HHS) regulations at the time prohibited federal funding of IVF research unless the grant application was reviewed by the Department's Ethics Advisory Board (EAB). Although the EAB issued a report on ethical aspects of IVF research in 1979, see 44 Fed.Reg. 35033 (1979), it ceased to exist shortly after the establishment of the President's Commission. 45 C.F.R. § 46.204(a) (1984). This effectively eliminated any type of governmental oversight in the area. The requirement that the EAB review all research applications was eliminated by Congress in the National Institutes of Health Reauthorization Law. P.L. 103–43; 107 Stat. 122 (1993), codified at 42 U.S.C. § 281 et seq.

Despite the government's lack of regulatory oversight, demand for IVF led to the establishment of fertility clinics, which perform IVF services as well as research. Except for some state regulations, these clinics operate mostly unregulated. The lack of oversight raises concern.

An early concern was fertility clinics' potentially deceptive advertisement about "pregnancy" rates. Congress passed the Fertility Clinic Success Rate and Certification Act as a response. The Act authorized the Department of Health and Human Services to design a program of state certification of fertility clinics according to certain standards, including quality control measures, recordkeeping and inspections. 42 U.S.C. § 263a–2 (2004). It also required HHS to establish a uniform standard for defining pregnancy success rates and required reporting of success

rates. 42 U.S.C. § 263a–1(b)(2) (2004). At the time that the Act was passed, Congress did not appropriate any fund for the act and thus it was not implemented until 1994. In 1995, the Centers for Disease Control began issuing the annual *Assisted Reproductive Technology Report* that provides an overview of the type, number, and outcome of ART cycles performed in U.S. clinics. The report also includes individual clinic tables that provide ART success rates and other information from each clinic that submitted and verified its data, and a list of reporting and non-reporting clinics. *See* Centers for Disease Control, *Assisted Reproductive Technology Reports*, (2001), at http://www.cdc.gov/reproductivehealth/index.html, last visited July 16, 2004.

Should fertility clinics be regulated? If so, by whom: the federal government, state governments, the profession, or all of the above? The President's Council on Bioethics, has recommended strengthening the Fertility Clinic Success Rate and Certification Act. It recommends that success rate reporting be done in terms of patients treated as opposed to cycles of treatment, because under the current guidelines, it is impossible to know the number of patients being treated annually, the success rates per cycle of treatment, and the number of women who fail to conceive entirely through ART. The Council also would require the publication of the risks and side effects of ARTs, to facilitate the protection of patients, and also information about the cost of therapy, innovative and adjunct technologies (ICSI, PGD, sperm-sorting). Finally, the Council recommends stricter enforcement of the Act and stronger penalties to enhance compliance (under the current Act, the only penalty is publication of the fertility center's name as a non-reporting center). *See* PRESIDENT'S COUNCIL ON BIOETHICS, REPRODUCTION AND RESPONSIBILITY: THE REGULATION OF NEW BIOTECHNOLOGIES 205 (2004).

Britain has passed a comprehensive statute regulating reproductive technologies and established a regulatory board, the Human Fertilisation and Embryology Authority. *See* Sec. II. B. 3., note 5, *infra*.

4. Should recipients or other entities determine the "parental fitness" of potential recipients of reproductive technologies? The British Human Fertilisation and Embryology Act of 1990 requires that as a condition for licensure, a facility not provide services to a woman "unless account has been taken of the welfare of any child who may be born as a result of the treatment (including the need of that child for a father) ..." Section 13(5). The Act's implementing code of practice requires that treatment centers screen recipients in a fashion similar to adoption screening. *See* Gillian Douglas et al., *The Right to Found a Family*, 142 NEW L. J. 488–90, 537–38 (1992).

In 1996, the Society of Assisted Reproductive Technology conducted a survey of 108 ART programs to catalog the programs' policies for selecting donors and recipients of embryos. The Society found that 64% of the programs surveyed required psychological screening of recipients for parental suitability. The survey also revealed that 61% of the programs required that the recipients meet with a mental health professional to ensure that they were giving informed consent and to confirm that they had considered the ethical and psychological issues related to conceiving using the help of reproductive technologies. Finally, of the programs surveyed 100% viewed married couples as eligible recipients, 61% viewed unmarried couples as eligible recipients, 55% viewed lesbian couples as eligible recipients, and 59% viewed single women as eligible recipients. Sheryl A. Kingsberg et al., *Embryo Donation Programs and Policies in North America: Survey Results and Implications for Health and Mental Health Professionals*, 73 FERTILITY & STERILITY 215, 218 (2000).

The American Society for Reproductive Medicine has also issued specific guidelines for recipients of artificial insemination, ova, and embryos. The Society recommends that all recipients undergo psychological counseling that includes sessions about dealing with the impact of a successful implantation, dealing with the psychological implications of receiving a donation, and dealing with the feelings that they might have about the medical conditions that prevented them from conceiving naturally. The Society also recommends that ova recipients over forty-five years old should undergo counseling to ensure that they are prepared for motherhood. *See* American Society for Reproductive Medicine, *Guidelines for Therapeutic Donor Insemination: Sperm, Guidelines for Oocyte Donation*, 70 FERTILITY & STERILITY 1S (Supp. 3 1998); *Guidelines for Embryo Donation*, 70 FERTILITY & STERILITY 7S (Supp. 3 1998); *Psychological Assessment for Oocyte Donors and Recipients*, 9S (Supp. 3 1998); *Psychological Guidelines for Embryo Donation*, 70 FERTILITY & STERILITY 10S (Supp. 3 1998).

Can these restrictions be justified regardless of technology, i.e., for natural parenting as well? For a critique of limited access to reproductive technologies, see CHRISTINE OVERALL, ETHICS AND HUMAN REPRODUCTION: A FEMINIST ANALYSIS (1987). For a proposal to license parents in general, see Roger W. MacIntire, *Parenthood Training or Mandatory Birth Control: Take Your Choice*, PSYCHOL. TODAY, Oct. 1973, at 34; *see also* Hugh LaFollette, *Licensing Parents*, 9 PHIL & PUB. AFF. 182 (1980); Claudia Mangel, *Licensing Parents: How Feasible?*, 22 FAM. L.Q. 17 (1988); Michael J. Sandmire & Michael Wald, *Licensing Parents-A Response to Claudia Mangel's Proposal*, 24 FAM. L.Q. 53 (1990).

5. IVF is costly; a single attempt costs between $7,000 and $11,000. Tarun Jain et al., *Insurance Coverage and Outcomes of In Vitro Fertilization*, 347 NEW ENG. J. MED. 661, 661 (2002). The average cost for a live birth on the first cycle is over $60,000. P.J. Neumann et al., *The Cost of a Successful Delivery with In Vitro Fertilization*, 331 NEW ENG. J. MED. 239, 241 (1994). As of 2002, Illinois, Massachusetts, New Jersey, and Rhode Island were the only states with legislation requiring complete insurance coverage of IVF. Five states including Arkansas, Hawaii, Maryland, Ohio, and West Virginia have enacted legislation that mandated partial coverage of IVF procedures. *See* Tarun Jain et al., at 661; *see, e.g.,* ARK. CODE ANN. § 23–86–118 (Michie 2003) (disability insurance cannot exclude IVF); MD. CODE ANN., INS. § 15–810 (2004) (medical insurance required to cover IVF at same level as other pregnancy related claims); TEX. INS. CODE ANN. § 1366(A) (Vernon 2004) (same). Most statutes governing insurance coverage for IVF only cover procedures for married couples. Should the public bear costs for IVF through the insurance system? Do assisted reproductive techniques impose costs to society outweighing their benefits?

3. SURROGACY

In re Baby M.

Supreme Court of New Jersey, 1988.
109 N.J. 396, 537 A.2d 1227.

■ WILENTZ, C.J.

In this matter the Court is asked to determine the validity of a contract that purports to provide a new way of bringing children into a family. For a fee of $10,000, a woman agrees to be artificially inseminated with the semen of another woman's husband; she is to conceive a child, carry it to term, and after its birth surrender it to the natural father and his wife. . . .

We invalidate the surrogacy contract because it conflicts with the law and public policy of this State. While we recognize the depth of the yearning of infertile couples to have their own children, we find the payment of money to a "surrogate" mother illegal, perhaps criminal, and potentially degrading to women. Although in this case we grant custody to the natural father, the evidence having clearly proved such custody to be in the best interests of the infant, we void both the termination of the surrogate mother's parental rights and the adoption of the child by the wife/stepparent. We thus restore the "surrogate" as the mother of the child. We remand the issue of the natural mother's visitation rights to the trial court, since that issue was not reached below and the record before us is not sufficient to permit us to decide it *de novo*.

We find no offense to our present laws where a woman voluntarily and without payment agrees to act as a "surrogate" mother, provided that she is not subject to a binding agreement to surrender her child. . . .

I.

FACTS

In February 1985, William Stern and Mary Beth Whitehead entered into a surrogacy contract. It recited that Stern's wife, Elizabeth, was infertile, that they wanted a child, and that Mrs. Whitehead was willing to provide that child as the mother with Mr. Stern as the father.

The contract provided that through artificial insemination using Mr. Stern's sperm, Mrs. Whitehead would become pregnant, carry the child to term, bear it, deliver it to the Sterns, and thereafter do whatever was necessary to terminate her maternal rights so that Mrs. Stern could thereafter adopt the child. Mrs. Whitehead's husband, Richard,[1] was also a party to the contract; Mrs. Stern was not. Mr. Whitehead promised to do all acts necessary to rebut the presumption of paternity under the Parentage Act. N.J.S.A. 9:17–13a(1),–14a. Although Mrs. Stern was not a party to the surrogacy agreement, the contract gave her sole custody of the child in the event of Mr. Stern's death. Mrs. Stern's status as a nonparty to the surrogate parenting agreement presumably was to avoid the application of the baby-selling statute to this arrangement.

Mr. Stern, on his part, agreed to attempt the artificial insemination and to pay Mrs. Whitehead $10,000 after the child's birth, on its delivery to him. In a separate contract, Mr. Stern agreed to pay $7,500 to the Infertility Center of New York ("ICNY"). The Center's advertising campaigns solicit surrogate mothers and encourage infertile couples to consider surrogacy. ICNY arranged for the surrogacy contract by bringing the parties together, explaining the process to them, furnishing the contractual form, and providing legal counsel.

The history of the parties' involvement in this arrangement suggests their good faith. William and Elizabeth Stern were married in July 1974, having met at the University of Michigan, where both were Ph.D. candidates. Due to financial considerations and Mrs. Stern's pursuit of a medical

---

1. Subsequent to the trial court proceedings, Mr. and Mrs. Whitehead were divorced, and soon thereafter Mrs. Whitehead remarried. . . .

degree and residency, they decided to defer starting a family until 1981. Before then, however, Mrs. Stern learned that she might have multiple sclerosis and that the disease in some cases renders pregnancy a serious health risk. Her anxiety appears to have exceeded the actual risk, which current medical authorities assess as minimal. Nonetheless that anxiety was evidently quite real, Mrs. Stern fearing that pregnancy might precipitate blindness, paraplegia, or other forms of debilitation. Based on the perceived risk, the Sterns decided to forego having their own children. The decision had a special significance for Mr. Stern. Most of his family had been destroyed in the Holocaust. As the family's only survivor, he very much wanted to continue his bloodline.

Initially the Sterns considered adoption, but were discouraged by the substantial delay apparently involved and by the potential problem they saw arising from their age and their differing religious backgrounds....

The paths of Mrs. Whitehead and the Sterns to surrogacy were similar. Both responded to advertising by ICNY. The Sterns' response, following their inquiries into adoption, was the result of their long-standing decision to have a child. Mrs. Whitehead's response apparently resulted from her sympathy with family members and others who could have no children (she stated that she wanted to give another couple the "gift of life"); she also wanted the $10,000 to help her family.

. . .

Mrs. Whitehead had reached her decision concerning surrogacy before the Sterns, and had actually been involved as a potential surrogate mother with another couple. After numerous unsuccessful artificial inseminations, that effort was abandoned. Thereafter, the Sterns learned of the Infertility Center, the possibilities of surrogacy, and of Mary Beth Whitehead. The two couples met to discuss the surrogacy arrangement and decided to go forward. On February 6, 1985, Mr. Stern and Mr. and Mrs. Whitehead executed the surrogate parenting agreement. After several artificial inseminations over a period of months, Mrs. Whitehead became pregnant. The pregnancy was uneventful and on March 27, 1986, Baby M was born.

... Her birth certificate indicated her name to be Sara Elizabeth Whitehead and her father to be Richard Whitehead. In accordance with Mrs. Whitehead's request, the Sterns visited the hospital unobtrusively to see the newborn child.

Mrs. Whitehead realized, almost from the moment of birth, that she could not part with this child. She had felt a bond with it even during pregnancy....

Nonetheless, Mrs. Whitehead was, for the moment, true to her word. Despite powerful inclinations to the contrary, she turned her child over to the Sterns on March 30 at the Whiteheads' home.

. . .

Later in the evening of March 30, Mrs. Whitehead became deeply disturbed, disconsolate, stricken with unbearable sadness. She had to have her child. She could not eat, sleep, or concentrate on anything other than her need for her baby. The next day she went to the Sterns' home and told them how much she was suffering.

The depth of Mrs. Whitehead's despair surprised and frightened the Sterns. She told them that she could not live without her baby, that she must have her, even if only for one week, that thereafter she would surrender her child. The Sterns, concerned that Mrs. Whitehead might indeed commit suicide, not wanting under any circumstances to risk that, and in any event believing that Mrs. Whitehead would keep her word, turned the child over to her. . . .

The struggle over Baby M began when it became apparent that Mrs. Whitehead could not return the child to Mr. Stern. Due to Mrs. Whitehead's refusal to relinquish the baby, Mr. Stern filed a complaint seeking enforcement of the surrogacy contract. He alleged, accurately, that Mrs. Whitehead had not only refused to comply with the surrogacy contract but had threatened to flee from New Jersey with the child in order to avoid even the possibility of his obtaining custody. The court papers asserted that if Mrs. Whitehead were to be given notice of the application for an order requiring her to relinquish custody, she would, prior to the hearing, leave the state with the baby. And that is precisely what she did. After the order was entered, *ex parte,* the process server, aided by the police, in the presence of the Sterns, entered Mrs. Whitehead's home to execute the order. Mr. Whitehead fled with the child, who had been handed to him through a window while those who came to enforce the order were thrown off balance by a dispute over the child's current name.

The Whiteheads immediately fled to Florida with Baby M. . . .

Eventually the Sterns discovered where the Whiteheads were staying, commenced supplementary proceedings in Florida, and obtained an order requiring the Whiteheads to turn over the child. Police in Florida enforced the order, forcibly removing the child from her grandparents' home. She was soon thereafter brought to New Jersey and turned over to the Sterns. The prior order of the court, issued *ex parte,* awarding custody of the child to the Sterns *pendente lite,* was reaffirmed by the trial court. . . . Pending final judgment, Mrs. Whitehead was awarded limited visitation with Baby M.

The Sterns' complaint, in addition to seeking possession and ultimately custody of the child, sought enforcement of the surrogacy contract. Pursuant to the contract, it asked that the child be permanently placed in their custody, that Mrs. Whitehead's parental rights be terminated, and that Mrs. Stern be allowed to adopt the child, *i.e.,* that, for all purposes, Melissa become the Sterns' child.

The trial took thirty-two days over a period of more than two months. . . . [The trial court] held that the surrogacy contract was valid; ordered that Mrs. Whitehead's parental rights be terminated and that sole custody of the child be granted to Mr. Stern; and, after hearing brief testimony from Mrs. Stern, immediately entered an order allowing the adoption of Melissa by Mrs. Stern, all in accordance with the surrogacy contract. Pending the outcome of the appeal, we granted a continuation of visitation to Mrs. Whitehead, although slightly more limited than the visitation allowed during the trial.

. . .

II.

INVALIDITY AND UNENFORCEABILITY OF SURROGACY CONTRACT

We have concluded that this surrogacy contract is invalid. Our conclusion has two bases: direct conflict with existing statutes and conflict with the public policies of this State, as expressed in its statutory and decisional law.

. . .

A. Conflict with Statutory Provisions

. . .

(I) Our law prohibits paying or accepting money in connection with any placement of a child for adoption. N.J.S.A. 9:3–54a. Violation is a high misdemeanor. N.J.S.A. 9:3–54c. Excepted are fees of an approved agency (which must be a nonprofit entity, N.J.S.A. 9:3–38a) and certain expenses in connection with childbirth. N.J.S.A. 9:3–54b.[4]

Considerable care was taken in this case to structure the surrogacy arrangement so as not to violate this prohibition. The arrangement was structured as follows: the adopting parent, Mrs. Stern, was not a party to the surrogacy contract; the money paid to Mrs. Whitehead was stated to be for her services—not for the adoption; the sole purpose of the contract was stated as being that "of giving a child to William Stern, its natural and biological father"; the money was purported to be "compensation for services and expenses and in no way . . . a fee for termination of parental rights or a payment in exchange for consent to surrender a child for adoption"; the fee to the Infertility Center ($7,500) was stated to be for legal representation, advice, administrative work, and other "services." Nevertheless, it seems clear that the money was paid and accepted in connection with an adoption. . . .

. . . The payment of the $10,000 occurs only on surrender of custody of the child and "completion of the duties and obligations" of Mrs. Whitehead, including termination of her parental rights to facilitate adoption by Mrs. Stern. As for the contention that the Sterns are paying only for services

4. N.J.S.A. 9:3–54 reads as follows:

a. No person, firm, partnership, corporation, association, or agency shall make, offer to make or assist or participate in any placement for adoption and in connection therewith

(1) Pay, give or agree to give any money or any valuable consideration, or assume or discharge any financial obligation; or

(2) Take, receive, accept or agree to accept any money or any valuable consideration.

b. The prohibition of subsection a. shall not apply to the fees or services of any approved agency in connection with a placement for adoption, nor shall such prohibition apply to the payment or reimbursement of medical, hospital or other similar expenses incurred in connection with the birth or any illness of the child, or to the acceptance of such reimbursement by a parent of the child.

c. Any person, firm, partnership, corporation, association or agency violating this section shall be guilty of a high misdemeanor.

and not for an adoption, we need note only that they would pay nothing in the event the child died before the fourth month of pregnancy, and only $1,000 if the child were stillborn, even though the "services" had been fully rendered. Additionally, one of Mrs. Whitehead's estimated costs, to be assumed by Mr. Stern, was an "Adoption Fee," presumably for Mrs. Whitehead's incidental costs in connection with the adoption.

Mr. Stern knew he was paying for the adoption of a child; Mrs. Whitehead knew she was accepting money so that a child might be adopted; the Infertility Center knew that it was being paid for assisting in the adoption of a child. The actions of all three worked to frustrate the goals of the statute. It strains credulity to claim that these arrangements, touted by those in the surrogacy business as an attractive alternative to the usual route leading to an adoption, really amount to something other than a private placement adoption for money.

. . .

(2) The termination of Mrs. Whitehead's parental rights, called for by the surrogacy contract and actually ordered by the court, fails to comply with the stringent requirements of New Jersey law. Our law, recognizing the finality of any termination of parental rights, provides for such termination only where there has been a voluntary surrender of a child to an approved agency or to the Division of Youth and Family Services ("DYFS"), accompanied by a formal document acknowledging termination of parental rights, N.J.S.A. 9:2–16,–17; N.J.S.A. 9:3–41; N.J.S.A. 30:4C–23, or where there has been a showing of parental abandonment or unfitness. A termination may ordinarily take one of three forms: an action by an approved agency, an action by DYFS, or an action in connection with a private placement adoption. The three are governed by separate statutes, but the standards for termination are substantially the same, except that whereas a written surrender is effective when made to an approved agency or to DYFS, there is no provision for it in the private placement context. See N.J.S.A. 9:2–14; N.J.S.A. 30:4C–23.

. . .

Our statutes, and the cases interpreting them, leave no doubt that where there has been no written surrender to an approved agency or to DYFS, termination of parental rights will not be granted in this state absent a very strong showing of abandonment or neglect. That showing is required in every context in which termination of parental rights is sought, be it an action by an approved agency, an action by DYFS, or a private placement adoption proceeding, even where the petitioning adoptive parent is, as here, a stepparent. . . .

In this case a termination of parental rights was obtained not by proving the statutory prerequisites but by claiming the benefit of contractual provisions. From all that has been stated above, it is clear that a contractual agreement to abandon one's parental rights, or not to contest a termination action, will not be enforced in our courts. The Legislature would not have so carefully, so consistently, and so substantially restricted termination of parental rights if it had intended to allow termination to be achieved by one short sentence in a contract. . . .

(3) The provision in the surrogacy contract stating that Mary Beth Whitehead agrees to "surrender custody . . . and terminate all parental rights" contains no clause giving her a right to rescind. It is intended to be an irrevocable consent to surrender the child for adoption—in other words, an irrevocable commitment by Mrs. Whitehead to turn Baby M over to the Sterns and thereafter to allow termination of her parental rights. . . . Such a provision, however, making irrevocable the natural mother's consent to surrender custody of her child in a private placement adoption, clearly conflicts with New Jersey law.

. . .

There is only one irrevocable consent, and that is the one explicitly provided for by statute: a consent to surrender of custody and a placement with an approved agency or with DYFS. The provision in the surrogacy contract, agreed to before conception, requiring the natural mother to surrender custody of the child without any right of revocation is one more indication of the essential nature of this transaction: the creation of a contractual system of termination and adoption designed to circumvent our statutes.

C.   Public Policy Considerations

. . .

The surrogacy contract guarantees permanent separation of the child from one of its natural parents. Our policy, however, has long been that to the extent possible, children should remain with and be brought up by both of their natural parents. . . . This is not simply some theoretical ideal that in practice has no meaning. The impact of failure to follow that policy is nowhere better shown than in the results of this surrogacy contract. A child, instead of starting off its life with as much peace and security as possible, finds itself immediately in a tug-of-war between contending mother and father.

The surrogacy contract violates the policy of this State that the rights of natural parents are equal concerning their child, the father's right no greater than the mother's. . . . The whole purpose and effect of the surrogacy contract was to give the father the exclusive right to the child by destroying the rights of the mother.

The policies expressed in our comprehensive laws governing consent to the surrender of a child, stand in stark contrast to the surrogacy contract and what it implies. Here there is no counseling, independent or otherwise, of the natural mother, no evaluation, no warning.

The only legal advice Mary Beth Whitehead received regarding the surrogacy contract was provided in connection with the contract that she previously entered into with another couple. Mrs. Whitehead's lawyer was referred to her by the Infertility Center, with which he had an agreement to act as counsel for surrogate candidates. His services consisted of spending one hour going through the contract with the Whiteheads, section by section, and answering their questions. Mrs. Whitehead received no further legal advice prior to signing the contract with the Sterns.

Mrs. Whitehead was examined and psychologically evaluated, but if it was for her benefit, the record does not disclose that fact. The Sterns regarded the evaluation as important, particularly in connection with the question of whether she would change her mind. Yet they never asked to see it, and were content with the assumption that the Infertility Center had made an evaluation and had concluded that there was no danger that the surrogate mother would change her mind. From Mrs. Whitehead's point of view, all that she learned from the evaluation was that "she had passed." It is apparent that the profit motive got the better of the Infertility Center. Although the evaluation was made, it was not put to any use, and understandably so, for the psychologist warned that Mrs. Whitehead demonstrated certain traits that might make surrender of the child difficult and that there should be further inquiry into this issue in connection with her surrogacy. To inquire further, however, might have jeopardized the Infertility Center's fee. The record indicates that neither Mrs. Whitehead nor the Sterns were ever told of this fact, a fact that might have ended their surrogacy arrangement.

Under the contract, the natural mother is irrevocably committed before she knows the strength of her bond with her child. She never makes a totally voluntary, informed decision, for quite clearly any decision prior to the baby's birth is, in the most important sense, uninformed, and any decision after that, compelled by a pre-existing contractual commitment, the threat of a lawsuit, and the inducement of a $10,000 payment, is less than totally voluntary. Her interests are of little concern to those who controlled this transaction.

. . .

Worst of all, however, is the contract's total disregard of the best interests of the child. There is not the slightest suggestion that any inquiry will be made at any time to determine the fitness of the Sterns as custodial parents, of Mrs. Stern as an adoptive parent, their superiority to Mrs. Whitehead, or the effect on the child of not living with her natural mother.

. . .

This is the sale of a child, or, at the very least, the sale of a mother's right to her child, the only mitigating factor being that one of the purchasers is the father. Almost every evil that prompted the prohibition of the payment of money in connection with adoptions exists here.

. . .

The point is made that Mrs. Whitehead *agreed* to the surrogacy arrangement, supposedly fully understanding the consequences. Putting aside the issue of how compelling her need for money may have been, and how significant her understanding of the consequences, we suggest that her consent is irrelevant. There are, in a civilized society, some things that money cannot buy. . . . There are, in short, values that society deems more important than granting to wealth whatever it can buy, be it labor, love, or life. Whether this principle recommends prohibition of surrogacy, which presumably sometimes results in great satisfaction to all of the parties, is not for us to say. We note here only that, under existing law, the fact that Mrs. Whitehead "agreed" to the arrangement is not dispositive.

The long-term effects of surrogacy contracts are not known, but feared—the impact on the child who learns her life was bought, that she is the offspring of someone who gave birth to her only to obtain money; the impact on the natural mother as the full weight of her isolation is felt along with the full reality of the sale of her body and her child; the impact on the natural father and adoptive mother once they realize the consequences of their conduct. Literature in related areas suggests these are substantial considerations, although, given the newness of surrogacy, there is little information.

The surrogacy contract creates, it is based upon, principles that are directly contrary to the objectives of our laws. It guarantees the separation of a child from its mother; it looks to adoption regardless of suitability; it totally ignores the child; it takes the child from the mother regardless of her wishes and her maternal fitness; and it does all of this, it accomplishes all of its goals, through the use of money.

Beyond that is the potential degradation of some women that may result from this arrangement. In many cases, of course, surrogacy may bring satisfaction, not only to the infertile couple, but to the surrogate mother herself. The fact, however, that many women may not perceive surrogacy negatively but rather see it as an opportunity does not diminish its potential for devastation to other women.

In sum, the harmful consequences of this surrogacy arrangement appear to us all too palpable. In New Jersey the surrogate mother's agreement to sell her child is void. Its irrevocability infects the entire contract, as does the money that purports to buy it.

. . .

III.

TERMINATION

We have already noted that under our laws termination of parental rights cannot be based on contract, but may be granted only on proof of the statutory requirements. That conclusion was one of the bases for invalidating the surrogacy contract. Although excluding the contract as a basis for parental termination, we did not explicitly deal with the question of whether the statutory bases for termination existed. We do so here.

[The court concluded that no statutory basis for termination of parental rights existed.]

. . .

V.

CUSTODY

Having decided that the surrogacy contract is illegal and unenforceable, we now must decide the custody question without regard to the provisions of the surrogacy contract that would give Mr. Stern sole and permanent custody. . . .

Our reading of the record persuades us that the trial court's decision awarding custody to the Sterns (technically to Mr. Stern) should be affirmed since "its findings ... could reasonably have been reached on sufficient credible evidence present in the record." *Beck v. Beck*, 432 A.2d 63 (N.J. 1981) (quoting *State v. Johnson*, 199 A.2d 809 (N.J. 1964)); ... More than that, on this record we find little room for any different conclusion. The trial court's treatment of this issue, 525 A.2d 1128, is both comprehensive and, in most respects, perceptive. We agree substantially with its analysis with but few exceptions that, although important, do not change our ultimate views.

. . .

VI.

VISITATION

The trial court's decision to terminate Mrs. Whitehead's parental rights precluded it from making any determination on visitation.... Our reversal of the trial court's order, however, requires delineation of Mrs. Whitehead's rights to visitation. It is apparent to us that this factually sensitive issue, which was never addressed below, should not be determined *de novo* by this Court. We therefore remand the visitation issue to the trial court for an abbreviated hearing and determination as set forth below.

. . .

We have decided that Mrs. Whitehead is entitled to visitation at some point, and that question is not open to the trial court on this remand. The trial court will determine what kind of visitation shall be granted to her, with or without conditions, and when and under what circumstances it should commence....

. . .

CONCLUSION

This case affords some insight into a new reproductive arrangement: the artificial insemination of a surrogate mother. The unfortunate events that have unfolded illustrate that its unregulated use can bring suffering to all involved. Potential victims include the surrogate mother and her family, the natural father and his wife, and most importantly, the child. Although surrogacy has apparently provided positive results for some infertile couples, it can also, as this case demonstrates, cause suffering to participants, here essentially innocent and well-intended.

We have found that our present laws do not permit the surrogacy contract used in this case. Nowhere, however, do we find any legal prohibition against surrogacy when the surrogate mother volunteers, without any payment, to act as a surrogate and is given the right to change her mind and to assert her parental rights. Moreover, the Legislature remains free to deal with this most sensitive issue as it sees fit, subject only to constitutional constraints.

. . .

The judgment is affirmed in part, reversed in part, and remanded for further proceedings consistent with this opinion....

NOTE

AFTERMATH: Mary Beth Whitehead (who has remarried and is now Mary Beth Whitehead–Gould) has visitation rights with the child, Melissa, two days per week, every other weekend, and for two weeks every summer. While the Sterns have no other children, Gould has four besides Melissa. Melissa reportedly calls Mary Beth "Mom" and Betsy Stern "Betsy." For a follow-up to the case, five years after the New Jersey Supreme Court's decision, see Susan Squire, *Whatever Happened to Baby M?*, REDBOOK, Jan. 1994, at 60.

Johnson v. Calvert

Supreme Court of California, en banc, 1993.
5 Cal.4th 84, 19 Cal.Rptr.2d 494, 851 P.2d 776, *cert. denied*, 510 U.S. 874, 114 S.Ct. 206, 126 L.Ed.2d 163.

■ PANELLI, J.

In this case we address several of the legal questions raised by recent advances in reproductive technology. When, pursuant to a surrogacy agreement, a zygote[5] formed of the gametes of a husband and wife is implanted in the uterus of another woman, who carries the resulting fetus to term and gives birth to a child not genetically related to her, who is the child's "natural mother" under California law? Does a determination that the wife is the child's natural mother work a deprivation of the gestating woman's constitutional rights? And is such an agreement barred by any public policy of this state?

We conclude that the husband and wife are the child's natural parents, and that this result does not offend the state or federal Constitution or public policy.

Mark and Crispina Calvert are a married couple who desired to have a child. Crispina was forced to undergo a hysterectomy in 1984. Her ovaries remained capable of producing eggs, however, and the couple eventually considered surrogacy. In 1989 Anna Johnson heard about Crispina's plight from a coworker and offered to serve as a surrogate for the Calverts.

On January 15, 1990, Mark, Crispina, and Anna signed a contract providing that an embryo created by the sperm of Mark and the egg of Crispina would be implanted in Anna and the child born would be taken into Mark and Crispina's home "as their child." Anna agreed she would relinquish "all parental rights" to the child in favor of Mark and Crispina. In return, Mark and Crispina would pay Anna $10,000 in a series of installments, the last to be paid six weeks after the child's birth. Mark and Crispina were also to pay for a $200,000 life insurance policy on Anna's life.

The zygote was implanted on January 19, 1990. Less than a month later, an ultrasound test confirmed Anna was pregnant.

---

5. An organism produced by the union of two gametes. (McGraw–Hill Dict. of Scien- tific and Technical Terms (4th ed. 1989) p. 783.)

Unfortunately, relations deteriorated between the two sides. Mark learned that Anna had not disclosed she had suffered several stillbirths and miscarriages. Anna felt Mark and Crispina did not do enough to obtain the required insurance policy. She also felt abandoned during an onset of premature labor in June.

In July 1990, Anna sent Mark and Crispina a letter demanding the balance of the payments due her or else she would refuse to give up the child. The following month, Mark and Crispina responded with a lawsuit, seeking a declaration they were the legal parents of the unborn child. Anna filed her own action to be declared the mother of the child, and the two cases were eventually consolidated. The parties agreed to an independent guardian ad litem for the purposes of the suit.

The child was born on September 19, 1990, and blood samples were obtained from both Anna and the child for analysis. The blood test results excluded Anna as the genetic mother. The parties agreed to a court order providing that the child would remain with Mark and Crispina on a temporary basis with visits by Anna.

At trial in October 1990, the parties stipulated that Mark and Crispina were the child's genetic parents. After hearing evidence and arguments, the trial court ruled that Mark and Crispina were the child's "genetic, biological and natural" father and mother, that Anna had no "parental" rights to the child, and that the surrogacy contract was legal and enforceable against Anna's claims. The court also terminated the order allowing visitation. Anna appealed from the trial court's judgment. The Court of Appeal for the Fourth District, Division Three, affirmed. We granted review.

Determining Maternity Under the Uniform Parentage Act

The Uniform Parentage Act . . . [and] Civil Code sections 7001 and 7002 replace the distinction between legitimate and illegitimate children with the concept of the "parent and child relationship." The "parent and child relationship" means "the legal relationship existing between a child and his natural or adoptive parents incident to which the law confers or imposes rights, privileges, duties, and obligations. It includes the mother and child relationship and the father and child relationship." (Civ. Code, § 7001.) . . . Passage of the Act clearly was not motivated by the need to resolve surrogacy disputes, which were virtually unknown in 1975. Yet it facially applies to *any* parentage determination, including the rare case in which a child's maternity is in issue. . . . Not uncommonly, courts must construe statutes in factual settings not contemplated by the enacting legislature . . . We therefore proceed to analyze the parties' contentions within the Act's framework.

These contentions are readily summarized. Anna, of course, predicates her claim of maternity on the fact that she gave birth to the child. The Calverts contend that Crispina's genetic relationship to the child establishes that she is his mother. Counsel for the minor joins in that contention . . . [W]e conclude that presentation of blood test evidence is one means of establishing maternity, as is proof of having given birth . . .

. . . .

... [T]he undisputed evidence [is] that Anna, not Crispina, gave birth to the child and that Crispina, not Anna, is genetically related to him. Both women thus have adduced evidence of a mother and child relationship as contemplated by the Act. (Civ.Code, § § 7003, subd. (1), 7004, subd. (a), 7015; Evid. Code, § § 621, 892.) Yet for any child California law recognizes only one natural mother, despite advances in reproductive technology rendering a different outcome biologically possible.[8]

. . .

Because two women each have presented acceptable proof of maternity, we do not believe this case can be decided without enquiring into the parties' intentions as manifested in the surrogacy agreement. Mark and Crispina are a couple who desired to have a child of their own genetic stock but are physically unable to do so without the help of reproductive technology. They affirmatively intended the birth of the child, and took the steps necessary to effect in vitro fertilization. But for their acted-on intention, the child would not exist. Anna agreed to facilitate the procreation of Mark's and Crispina's child. The parties' aim was to bring Mark's and Crispina's child into the world, not for Mark and Crispina to donate a zygote to Anna. Crispina from the outset intended to be the child's mother. Although the gestative function Anna performed was necessary to bring about the child's birth, it is safe to say that Anna would not have been given the opportunity to gestate or deliver the child had she, prior to implantation of the zygote, manifested her own intent to be the child's mother. No reason appears why Anna's later change of heart should vitiate the determination that Crispina is the child's natural mother.

We conclude that although the Act recognizes both genetic consanguinity and giving birth as means of establishing a mother and child relationship, when the two means do not coincide in one woman, she who intended to procreate the child—that is, she who intended to bring about the birth of a child that she intended to raise as her own—is the natural mother under California law.[10]

. . .

8. We decline to accept the contention of amicus curiae the American Civil Liberties Union (ACLU) that we should find the child has two mothers. Even though rising divorce rates have made multiple parent arrangements common in our society, we see no compelling reason to recognize such a situation here. The Calverts are the genetic and intending parents of their son and have provided him, by all accounts, with a stable, intact, and nurturing home. To recognize parental rights in a third party with whom the Calvert family has had little contact since shortly after the child's birth would diminish Crispina's role as mother.

10. Thus, under our analysis, in a true "egg donation" situation, where a woman gestates and gives birth to a child formed from the egg of another woman with the intent to raise the child as her own, the birth mother is the natural mother under California law. The dissent would decide *parentage* based on the best interests of the child. Such an approach raises the repugnant specter of governmental interference in matters implicating our most fundamental notions of privacy, and confuses concepts of parentage and custody. Logically, the determination of parentage must precede, and should not be dictated by, eventual custody decisions. The implicit assumption of the dissent is that a recognition of the genetic intending mother as the natural mother may sometimes harm the child. This assumption overlooks California's dependency laws, which are designed to protect *all* children irrespective of the man-

The judgment of the Court of Appeal is affirmed.

■ ARABIAN, J., concurring.

I concur in the decision to find under the Uniform Parentage Act that Crispina Calvert is the natural mother of the child she at all times intended to parent and raise as her own with her husband Mark, the child's natural father. That determination answers the question on which this court granted review, and in my view sufficiently resolves the controversy between the parties to warrant no further analysis. I therefore decline to subscribe to the dictum in which the majority find surrogacy contracts "not . . . inconsistent with public policy."

. . .

The multiplicity of considerations at issue in a surrogacy situation plainly transcend traditional principles of contract law and require careful, nonadversarial analysis. For this reason, I do not think it wise for this court to venture unnecessarily into terrain more appropriately cleared by the Legislature in the first instance. . . .

. . .

■ KENNARD, J., dissenting.

When a woman who wants to have a child provides her fertilized ovum to another woman who carries it through pregnancy and gives birth to a child, who is the child's legal mother? Unlike the majority, I do not agree that the determinative consideration should be the intent to have the child that originated with the woman who contributed the ovum. In my view, the woman who provided the fertilized ovum and the woman who gave birth to the child both have substantial claims to legal motherhood. Pregnancy entails a unique commitment, both psychological and emotional, to an unborn child. No less substantial, however, is the contribution of the woman from whose egg the child developed and without whose desire the child would not exist.

For each child, California law accords the legal rights and responsibilities of parenthood to only one "natural mother." When, as here, the female reproductive role is divided between two women, California law requires courts to make a decision as to which woman is the child's natural mother, but provides no standards by which to make that decision. The majority's resort to "intent" to break the "tie" between the genetic and gestational mothers is unsupported by statute, and, in the absence of appropriate protections in the law to guard against abuse of surrogacy arrangements, it is ill-advised. To determine who is the legal mother of a child born of a gestational surrogacy arrangement, I would apply the standard most protective of child welfare—the best interests of the child.

ner of birth or conception. Moreover, the best interests standard poorly serves the child in the present situation: it fosters instability during litigation and, if applied to recognize the gestator as the natural mother, results in a split of custody between the natural father and the gestator, an outcome not likely to benefit the child. Further, it may be argued that, by voluntarily contracting away any rights to the child, the gestator has, in effect, conceded the best interests of the child are not with her.

Buzzanca v. Buzzanca

California Court of Appeals, 1998.
61 Cal.App.4th 1410, 72 Cal.Rptr.2d 280.

■ Sills, J.

INTRODUCTION

Jaycee was born because Luanne and John Buzzanca agreed to have an embryo genetically unrelated to either of them implanted in a woman—a surrogate—who would carry and give birth to the child for them. After the fertilization, implantation and pregnancy, Luanne and John split up, and the question of who are Jaycee's lawful parents came before the trial court.

Luanne claimed that she and her erstwhile husband were the lawful parents, but John disclaimed any responsibility, financial or otherwise. The woman who gave birth also appeared in the case to make it clear that she made no claim to the child.

The trial court then reached an extraordinary conclusion: Jaycee had *no* lawful parents. First, the woman who gave birth to Jaycee was not the mother; the court had—astonishingly—already accepted a stipulation that neither she nor her husband were the "biological" parents. Second, Luanne was not the mother. According to the trial court, she could not be the mother because she had neither contributed the egg nor given birth. And John could not be the father, because, not having contributed the sperm, he had no biological relationship with the child.

We disagree. Let us get right to the point: Jaycee never would have been born had not Luanne and John both agreed to have a fertilized egg implanted in a surrogate.

The trial judge erred because he assumed that legal motherhood, under the relevant California statutes, could *only* be established in one of two ways, either by giving birth or by contributing an egg. He failed to consider the substantial and well-settled body of law holding that there are times when *fatherhood* can be established by conduct apart from giving birth or being genetically related to a child. The typical example is when an infertile husband consents to allowing his wife to be artificially inseminated. As our Supreme Court noted in such a situation over 30 years ago, the husband is the "lawful father" because he *consented* to the procreation of the child. (*See People v. Sorensen*, 437 P.2d 495 (Cal. 1968)).

The same rule which makes a husband the lawful father of a child born because of his consent to artificial insemination should be applied here—by the same parity of reasoning that guided our Supreme Court in the first surrogacy case, *Johnson v. Calvert*, 851 P.2d 776 (Cal. 1993)—to both husband and wife. Just as a husband is deemed to be the lawful father of a child unrelated to him when his wife gives birth after artificial insemination, so should a husband *and* wife be deemed the lawful parents of a child after a surrogate bears a biologically unrelated child on their behalf. In each instance, a child is procreated because a medical procedure was initiated and consented to by intended parents. The only difference is that in this case—unlike artificial insemination—there is no reason to distinguish between husband and wife. We therefore must reverse the trial court's judgment and direct that a new judgment be entered, declaring that both Luanne and John are the lawful parents of Jaycee.

John filed his petition for dissolution of marriage on March 30, 1995, alleging there were no children of the marriage. Luanne filed her response on April 20, alleging that the parties were expecting a child by way of surrogate contract. Jaycee was born six days later. In September 1996 Luanne filed a separate petition to establish herself as Jaycee's mother. Her action was consolidated into the dissolution case. In February 1997, the court accepted a stipulation that the woman who agreed to carry the child, and her husband, were not the "biological parents" of the child. At a hearing held in March, based entirely on oral argument and offers of proof, the trial court determined that Luanne was not the lawful mother of the child and therefore John could not be the lawful father or owe any support.

The trial judge said: "So I think what evidence there is, is stipulated to. And I don't think there would be any more. One, there's no genetic tie between Luanne and the child. Two, she is not the gestational mother. Three, she has not adopted the child. That, folks, to me, respectfully, is clear and convincing evidence that she's not the legal mother."

After another hearing on May 7, regarding attorney fees, a judgment on reserved issues in the dissolution was filed, terminating John's obligation to pay child support, declaring that Luanne was not the legal mother of Jaycee, and declining "to apply any estoppel proposition to the issue of John's responsibility for child support." Luanne then filed a petition for a writ of supersedeas to stay the judgment; she also filed an appeal from it. This court then granted a stay which had the effect of keeping the support order alive for Jaycee. We also consolidated the writ proceeding with the appeal.

In his respondent's brief in this appeal, John tries to intimate—though he stops short of actually saying it—that Jaycee was not born as a result of a surrogacy agreement with his ex-wife. . . .

Concerned with the implication made in John's respondent's brief, members of this court questioned John's attorney at oral argument about it. It turned out that the intimation in John's brief was a red herring, based merely on the fact that John did not sign a *written* contract until after implantation. Jaycee was nonetheless born as a result of a surrogacy agreement on the part of both Luanne *and* John; it was just that the agreement was an *oral* one prior to implantation. The written surrogacy agreement, John's attorney acknowledged in open court, was the written memorialization of that oral contract.

. . .

. . . [E]ven though there was no actual trial in front of the trial court on the matter, this appellate court will assume arguendo that if there had been a trial the judge would have believed John's evidence on the point and concluded that Luanne had indeed promised not to hold John responsible for the child contemplated by their oral surrogacy agreement.

The Statute Governing Artificial Insemination Which Makes a Husband the Lawful Father of a Child Unrelated to Him Applies to Both Intended Parents in This Case

Perhaps recognizing the inherent lack of appeal for any result which makes Jaycee a legal orphan, John now contends that the surrogate is Jaycee's legal mother; and further, by virtue of that fact, the surrogate's husband is the legal father. His reasoning goes like this: Under the Uniform Parentage Act (the Act), and particularly as set forth in section 7610 of Family Code, there are only two ways by which a woman can establish legal motherhood, i.e., giving birth or contributing genetically. Because the genetic contributors are not known to the court, the only candidate left is the surrogate who must therefore be deemed the lawful mother. And, as John's counsel commented at oral argument, if the surrogate and her husband cannot support Jaycee, the burden should fall on the taxpayers.

The law doesn't say what John says it says. It doesn't say: "The legal relationship between mother and child shall be established only by either proof of her giving birth or by genetics." The statute says "may," not "shall," and "under this part," *not* "by genetics." Here is the complete text of Family Code section 7610: "The parent and child relationship may be established as follows: [¶] (a) Between a child and the natural mother, it may be established by proof of her having given birth to the child, or under this part. [¶] (b) Between a child and the natural father, it may be established under this part. [¶] (c) Between a child and an adoptive parent, it may be established by proof of adoption."

The statute thus contains no direct reference to genetics (i.e., blood tests) at all. The *Johnson* decision teaches us that genetics is simply *subsumed* in the words "under this part." In that case, the court held that genetic consanguinity was equally "acceptable" as "proof of maternity" as evidence of giving birth. (*Johnson v. Calvert, supra,* 5 Cal. 4th at 93.)

It is important to realize, however, that in construing the words "under this part" to include genetic testing, the high court in *Johnson* relied on several statutes in the Evidence Code (Evid. Code, former §§ 892, 895, & 895.5) all of which, by their terms, only applied to paternity.... It was only by a "parity of reasoning" that our high court concluded those statutes which, on their face applied only to men, were also "dispositive of the question of maternity." (5 Cal. 4th at 92.)

The point bears reiterating: It was only by a parity of reasoning from statutes which, on their face, referred only to paternity that the court in *Johnson v. Calvert* reached the result it did on the question of maternity. Had the *Johnson* court reasoned as John now urges us to reason—by narrowly confining the means under the Act by which a woman could establish that she was the lawful mother of a child to texts which on their face applied only to motherhood (as distinct from fatherhood)—the court would have reached the opposite result.[5]

. . .

---

5. In *In re Marriage of Moschetta,* 25 Cal. App. 4th 1218, 1224–1226, 30 Cal. Rptr. 2d 893 (1994), the court refused to apply certain presumptions regarding paternity

As noted in *Johnson*, "courts must construe statutes in factual settings not contemplated by the enacting legislature." (*Johnson v. Calvert, supra,* 5 Cal. 4th at 89.) So it is, of course, true that application of the artificial insemination statute to a gestational surrogacy case where the genetic donors are unknown to the court may not have been contemplated by the Legislature. Even so, the two kinds of artificial reproduction are exactly analogous in this crucial respect: Both contemplate the procreation of a child by the consent to a medical procedure of someone who intends to raise the child but who otherwise does not have any biological tie.

If a husband who consents to artificial insemination under Family Code section 7613 is "treated in law" as the father of the child by virtue of his consent, there is no reason the result should be any different in the case of a married couple who consent to in vitro fertilization by unknown donors and subsequent implantation into a woman who is, as a surrogate, willing to carry the embryo to term for them. The statute is, after all, the clearest expression of past legislative intent when the Legislature did contemplate a situation where a person who caused a child to come into being had no biological relationship to the child.

. . .

Sorensen expresses a rule universally in tune with other jurisdictions. . . .

One New York family court even went so far as to hold the lesbian partner of a woman who was artificially inseminated responsible for the support of two children where the partner had dressed as a man and the couple had obtained a marriage license and a wedding ceremony had been performed prior to the inseminations. (*Karin T. v. Michael T.*, 484 N.Y.S.2d 780 (N.Y. Fam. Ct. 1985)).[10] Echoing the themes of causation and estoppel which underlie the cases, the court noted that the lesbian partner had "by her course of conduct in this case . . . brought into the world two innocent

---

found in the Act to overcome the claim of a woman who was both the genetic and birth mother. . . .

It made sense in *Moschetta* not to apply the paternity statutes cited by the father to the biologically unrelated intended mother because those statutes merely embody presumptions. The statutes were: (1) the presumption that a child of a wife cohabiting with her husband at the time of birth is conclusively presumed to be a child of the marriage unless the husband is impotent or sterile (*see* Fam. Code, § 7540), and (2) the presumption that a man is the natural father if he receives the child into his home and openly holds out the child as his own (Fam. Code, § 7611, subd. (d)). We rejected application of these presumptions because, even assuming they could be applied to a woman, they were only presumptions and, just like a paternity case, could be overcome by blood

tests showing an actual genetic relationship. (*In re Marriage of Moschetta, supra,* 25 Cal. App. 4th at 1225–1226.) Most fundamentally, as we pointed out on page 1226 of the opinion, the presumptions were inapposite because they arose out of the "old law of illegitimacy" and were designed as evidentiary devices to make a determination of a child's biological father.

Moschetta thus cannot be read for the proposition that statutes which are part of the Act and refer to an individual of one sex can never be applied to an individual of another. For one reason, *Moschetta* never said that. For another, such a broad proposition would contradict the rationale used by a higher court in *Johnson*.

10. Michael T.'s name was originally Marlene. (*Karin T. v. Michael T., supra,* 484 N.Y.S.2d at 781.)

children" and should not "be allowed to benefit" from her acts to the detriment of the children and public generally. (484 N.Y.S.2d at 784.)[11]

. . .

It must also be noted that in applying the artificial insemination statute to a case where a party has caused a child to be brought into the world, the statutory policy is really echoing a more fundamental idea—a sort of *grundnorm* to borrow Hans Kelsen's famous jurisprudential word—already established in the case law. That idea is often summed up in the legal term "estoppel." Estoppel is an ungainly word from the Middle French (from the word meaning "bung" or "stopper") expressing the law's distaste for inconsistent actions and positions—like consenting to an act which brings a child into existence and then turning around and disclaiming any responsibility.

While the *Johnson v. Calvert* court was able to predicate its decision on the Act rather than making up the result out of whole cloth, it is also true that California courts, prior to the enactment of the Act, had based certain decisions establishing paternity merely on the common law doctrine of estoppel. . . .

There is no need in the present case to predicate our decision on common law estoppel alone, though the doctrine certainly applies. The estoppel concept, after all, is already inherent in the artificial insemination statute. . . .

John argues that the artificial insemination statute should not be applied because, after all, his wife did not give birth. But for purposes of the statute with its core idea of estoppel, the fact that Luanne did not give birth is irrelevant. The statute contemplates the establishment of lawful fatherhood in a situation where an intended father has no biological relationship to a child who is procreated as a result of the father's (as well as the mother's) *consent* to a medical procedure.

Luanne is the Lawful Mother of Jaycee, Not the Surrogate, and Not the Unknown Donor of the Egg

In the present case Luanne is situated like a husband in an artificial insemination case whose consent triggers a medical procedure which results in a pregnancy and eventual birth of a child. Her motherhood may therefore be established "under this part," by virtue of that consent. In light of our conclusion, John's argument that the surrogate should be declared the lawful mother disintegrates. The case is now postured like the

---

11. In Karin T. v. Michael T., the court held in a case involving child support that the lesbian partner was "indeed a 'parent' to whom such responsibility attaches." (484 N.Y.S.2d at 784.) By contrast, *Nancy S. v. Michele G.*, 228 Cal. App. 3d 831, 279 Cal. Rptr. 212 (1991) held that the lesbian partner of a woman who gave birth to two children through artificial insemination was not a parent for purposes of custody and visitation, even though the partner alleged that she "helped facilitate the conception and birth of both children." (Id. at 836.) The parties presented no issue of support obligation in Nancy S., so while the court acknowledged the doctrine of estoppel in that context, it declined to extend the estoppel doctrine "for the purpose of awarding custody and visitation to a nonparent." (Id. at p. 839.)

. . .

Johnson v. Calvert case, where motherhood could have been "established" in either of two women under the Act, and the tie broken by noting the intent to parent as expressed in the surrogacy contract. (*See Johnson v. Calvert, supra*, 5 Cal. 4th at 93.) The only difference is that this case is not even close as between Luanne and the surrogate. Not only was Luanne the clearly intended mother, no bona fide attempt has been made to establish the surrogate as the lawful mother.

We should also add that neither could the woman whose egg was used in the fertilization or implantation make any claim to motherhood, even if she were to come forward at this late date. Again, as between two women who would both be able to establish motherhood under the Act, the *Johnson* decision would mandate that the tie be broken in favor of the intended parent, in this case, Luanne.

. . .

In the case before us, we are not concerned, as John would have us believe, with a question of the enforceability of the oral and written surrogacy contracts into which he entered with Luanne. This case is not about "transferring" parenthood pursuant to those agreements. We are, rather, concerned with the consequences of those agreements as acts which caused the birth of a child.

The legal paradigm adopted by the trial court, and now urged upon us by John, is one where all forms of artificial reproduction in which intended parents have no biological relationship with the child result in legal parentlessness. It means that, absent adoption, such children will be dependents of the state. One might describe this paradigm as the "adoption default" model: The idea is that by not specifically addressing some permutation of artificial reproduction, the Legislature has, in effect, set the default switch on adoption. The underlying theory seems to be that when intended parents resort to artificial reproduction without biological tie the Legislature wanted them to be screened first through the adoption system. (Thus John, in his brief, argues that a surrogacy contract must be "subject to state oversight.")

The "adoption default" model is, however, inconsistent with both statutory law and the Supreme Court's *Johnson* decision. As to the statutory law, the Legislature has already made it perfectly clear that public policy (and, we might add, common sense) favors, whenever possible, the establishment of legal parenthood with the concomitant responsibility....

Very plainly, the Legislature has declared its preference for assigning individual responsibility for the care and maintenance of children; not leaving the task to the taxpayers. That is why it has gone to considerable lengths to ensure that parents will live up to their support obligations.... The adoption default theory flies in the face of that legislative value judgment.

As this court noted in *Jaycee B. v. Superior Court*, 49 Cal. Rptr. 2d 694 (Cal. Ct. App. 1996), the *Johnson* court had occasion, albeit in dicta, to address "pretty much the exact situation before us." The language bears quoting again: "In what we must hope will be the extremely rare situation in which neither the gestator nor the woman who provided the ovum for fertilization is willing to assume custody of the child after birth, a rule recognizing the intending parents as the child's legal, natural parents should best promote certainty and stability...." (*Johnson v. Calvert*, *supra*, 5 Cal. 4th at 94–95.) This language quite literally describes precisely the case before us now: neither the woman whose ovum was used nor the woman who gave birth have come forward to assume custody of the child after birth.

· · ·

Finally, in addition to its contravention of statutorily enunciated public policy and the pronouncement of our high court in *Johnson*, the adoption default model ignores the role of our dependency statutes in protecting children. Parents are not screened for the procreation of their own children; they are screened for the adoption of other people's children. It is the role of the dependency laws to protect children from neglect and abuse from their own parents. The adoption default model is essentially an exercise in circular reasoning, because it assumes the idea that it seeks to prove; namely, that a child who is born as the result of artificial reproduction is somebody else's child from the beginning.

In the case before us, there is absolutely no dispute that Luanne caused Jaycee's conception and birth by initiating the surrogacy arrangement whereby an embryo was implanted into a woman who agreed to carry the baby to term on Luanne's behalf. In applying the artificial insemination statute to a gestational surrogacy case where the genetic donors are unknown, there is, as we have indicated above, no reason to distinguish between husbands and wives. Both are equally situated from the point of view of consenting to an act which brings a child into being. Accordingly, Luanne should have been declared the lawful mother of Jaycee.

John Is the Lawful Father of Jaycee Even If Luanne Did Promise to Assume All Responsibility for Jaycee's Care

The same reasons which impel us to conclude that Luanne is Jaycee's lawful mother also require that John be declared Jaycee's lawful father. Even if the written surrogacy contract had not yet been signed at the time of conception and implantation, those occurrences were nonetheless the direct result of actions taken pursuant to an oral agreement which envisioned that the fertilization, implantation and ensuing pregnancy would go forward. Thus, it is ... accurate to say ... that for all practical purposes John caused Jaycee's conception every bit as much as if things had been done the old-fashioned way.

When pressed at oral argument to make an offer of proof as to the "best facts" which John might be able to show if this case were tried, John's attorney raised the point that Luanne had (allegedly, we must add) promised to assume all responsibility for the child and would not hold him responsible for the child's upbringing. However, even if this case were returned for a trial on this point (we assume that Luanne would dispute the allegation) it could make no difference as to John's lawful paternity. It is well established that parents cannot, by agreement, limit or abrogate a child's right to support.

· · ·

CONCLUSION

Even though neither Luanne nor John are biologically related to Jaycee, they are still her lawful parents given their initiating role as the intended parents in her conception and birth. And, while the absence of a biological connection is what makes this case extraordinary, this court is hardly without statutory basis and legal precedent in so deciding. . . .

Again we must call on the Legislature to sort out the parental rights and responsibilities of those involved in artificial reproduction. No matter what one thinks of artificial insemination, traditional and gestational surrogacy (in all its permutations), and—as now appears in the not-too-distant future, cloning and even gene splicing—courts are still going to be faced with the problem of determining lawful parentage. A child cannot be ignored. Even if all means of artificial reproduction were outlawed with draconian criminal penalties visited on the doctors and parties involved, courts will still be called upon to decide who the lawful parents really are and who—other than the taxpayers—is obligated to provide maintenance and support for the child. These cases will not go away.

That said, we must now conclude the business at hand.

(1) The portion of the judgment which declares that Luanne Buzzanca is not the lawful mother of Jaycee is reversed. The matter is remanded with directions to enter a new judgment declaring her the lawful mother. . . .

(2) The judgment is reversed to the extent that it provides that John Buzzanca is not the lawful father of Jaycee. The matter is remanded with directions to enter a new judgment declaring him the lawful father. Consonant with this determination, today's ruling is without prejudice to John in future proceedings as regards child custody and visitation as his relationship with Jaycee may develop. The judgment shall also reflect that the birth certificate shall be amended to reflect John Buzzanca as the lawful father.

(3) To the degree that the judgment makes no provision for child support it is reversed. The matter is remanded to make an appropriate permanent child support order. . . .

NOTES AND QUESTIONS

1. Are noncommercial, or "altruistic" surrogacy arrangements, especially intra-family arrangements, more acceptable than the arrangements in *Baby M*, *Johnson*, and *Buzzanca*? Consider the arrangement in which a fifty-two year old Texas woman became the gestational surrogate for embryos fertilized in vitro with her son's sperm and daughter-in-law's ova. *See* Associated Press, *Texas Woman Gives Birth to Grandchildren*, Star Ledger, Mar. 4, 2004, at 32. What additional ethical and legal issues arise from such arrangements? Could non-commercial surrogacy potentially exploit women as well, by reinforcing their societally-entrenched roles as altruistic care-givers? *See, e.g.*, Janice G. Raymond, *Reproductive Gifts and Gift-BGiving: The Altruistic Woman*, 20 Hastings Ctr. Rep. 7 (1990).

2. *Buzzanca* describes one type of risk to children resulting from surrogacy arrangements. Are there others? What if the child is born "damaged?" Complications in one surrogate parenting situation served to highlight some of the many legal and ethical uncertainties involved in these arrangements. Judy Stiver, a

Michigan woman, entered into a surrogate parenting contract with Alexander Malahoff, a New York accountant, to have Malahoff's child through artificial insemination. Noel Keane, a Michigan attorney actively involved in arranging surrogate parenting agreements, drafted the contract that the parties signed.

When the child, a boy, was born on January 10, 1983, he suffered from both microcephaly and strep infection. Microcephaly is a congenital disorder that caused the boy's head to be smaller than normal. Usually the disease indicates some degree of mental retardation. Hospital officials were forced to obtain a court order allowing them to treat the strep infection, which the baby's physicians feared threatened his life. The officials claimed that Malahoff ordered the hospital and doctors not to treat the infection or care for the baby, a claim Malahoff later denied. Malahoff based his orders, the hospital officials claimed, on a clause in the surrogate parenting contract giving him custody of the child. *See* WASH. POST, Jan. 21, 1983, at A11, col. 3; N.Y. TIMES, Jan. 23, 1983, § 1 at 19, col. 1.

Sometime later, Malahoff denied paternity of and responsibility for the child. Stiver and her husband Ray disputed these claims. In a unique spectacle, the results of blood tests to determine paternity were announced on an episode of the Phil Donahue television show entitled "The Case of the Layaway Baby." The tests proved that Malahoff could not be the father and that Ray Stiver was the probable father. Later in the episode, Stiver admitted having fathered a child whose head stopped developing in infancy during a previous marriage. That child died a few years after birth. *See*, WASH. POST, Feb. 3, 1983, at A8, col. 1; N.Y. TIMES, Feb. 7, 1983, at A10, col. 1. Stiver later sued Keane and the doctors for negligence, alleging that the birth defects were caused by cytomegalovirus in Malahoff's sperm. Is there more of a risk that children of surrogacy agreements will be treated as "commodities"? Note that both Malahoff and the Stivers initially disclaimed responsibility for the child. *Surrogate Mother's Deformed Baby Rejected*, N.Y. TIMES, Jan. 23, 1983, at 19. Eventually the Stivers accepted responsibility for the child. For objections to surrogacy based on risks to children, see Judith C. Areen, *Baby M. Reconsidered*, 76 GEO. L. J. 1741 (1988), Vicki C. Jackson, *Baby M and the Question of Parenthood*, 76 GEO. L. J. 1811 (1988). Several states have enacted statutes that define the parentage of a child born of a surrogacy agreement. *See* FLA. STAT. ANN. § 742.15 (2004) (commissioner parents will be parents of child unless it is determined that neither is a genetic parent of the child, in which case surrogate will be parent); 750 IL. COMP. STAT. ANN. § 45/6 (2004) (conditions to establishing parentage in surrogacy agreement outlined); VA. CODE ANN. § 20–158 (2004) (intended parents are the parents of child).

3.   Should single men and committed male couples have access to surrogacy? One director of a surrogacy service refuses to accept single men, saying, "If you can't form a long-term relationship, you have no idea what being a parent would be like." Susan Fitzgerald & Mark Bowden, *Baby in Surrogate Case Dies of Beating Injuries*, PHILA. INQ. Jan. 18, 1995, at A1. Do you agree? Is this situation comparable to single women who become parents through artificial insemination? Is it significant that surrogacy is the only method for single men and committed male couples to become "biological" parents? *See* Erica Gesing, *The Fight to be a Parent: How Courts Have Restricted the Constitutionally–Based Challenges Available to Homosexuals*, 38 NEW ENG. L. REV. 841 (2004) (arguing for equal protection of homosexual couples in their right to have children); Catherine DeLair, *Ethical, Moral, Economic, and Legal Barriers to Assisted Reproductive Technologies Employed by Gay Men and Lesbian Women*, 4 DEPAUL J. HEALTH CARE L. 147 (2000) (arguing for legislative reform to provide equal access to ART to gay couples).

4.   In view of the complex legal and ethical issues raised by surrogacy, should surrogacy be regulated? What would be the best legislative approach? A few states have enacted legislation relating to surrogacy. For example, Arkansas has declared that the child of an artificially inseminated surrogate mother is the child of the woman intended to be the mother, and allows for the issuance of a substituted birth certificate to that effect by court order. ARK. CODE ANN. § 9–10–201(c) (Michie 2003). Iowa exempts surrogacy arrangements from its prohibitions on baby selling. IOWA CODE ANN. § 710.11 (West 2003). New Hampshire extensively regulates surrogacy, requiring, inter alia, court approval of the contract, counseling and evaluation of the parties, an opportunity for the surrogate to rescind the contract after birth, and that the surrogate have medical decision-making authority during pregnancy. N.H. REV. STAT. ANN. T. XII, Ch. 168B (2003). In addition, Virginia has adopted the Uniform Status of Children of Assisted Conception Act's Alternative A, VA. CODE. ANN. § 20–159 (Michie 2003) (allowing surrogacy with extensive negotiations), and North Dakota has adopted the Act's Alternative B, N.D. CENT. CODE § 14–18–05 (2003) (declaring surrogacy agreements void).

Most statutes which address surrogacy prohibit commercial surrogacy and/or declare all surrogate contracts, commercial and non-commercial, void and unenforceable. For example, New York declared all surrogate contracts void in commercial surrogacy contracts. N.Y. DOM. REL. LAW §§ 122, 123 (McKinney 2004). Michigan makes it a felony to arrange surrogate contracts for money and declares all surrogate arrangements void and unenforceable. MICH. COMP. LAWS ANN. §§ 722.851–722.863 (West 2004). For a summary of state legislation on surrogacy, see Lori B. Andrews, *Beyond Doctrinal Boundaries: A Legal Framework for Surrogate Motherhood*, 81 VA. L. REV. 2343 (1995); Adam Plant, *With a Little Help from My Friends: The Intersection of the Gestational Carrier Surrogacy Agreement, Legislative Inaction, and Medical Advancement*, 54 ALA. L. REV. 639 (2003).

5. Is there a need for a uniform, comprehensive policy concerning the use of the new reproductive technologies? If so, what should it entail? Consider the view of one author:

> ... [W]e need to move beyond this [permit/prohibit] range of societal responses ... [M]ost Americans would agree that we have a strong tradition ... of regarding questions of reproduction and family life as private matters, into which agents of the government should intervene seldom and only for compelling reasons.... Depending on the biomedical methods in question, prohibition or even regulation may be very difficult, if not impossible, if the state is to avoid becoming involved in the most intimate aspects of its citizen's lives.... If we can anticipate that certain biomedical developments ... may nonetheless undermine basic values or weaken important roles, we ought to make such challenges explicit and then mount the necessary efforts to counter-act their undesirable effects. Such an effort might be termed "creative preservation"— signifying a positive and original effort to enhance important values and relationships ...

Alexander Morgan Capron, The New Reproductive Possibilities: Seeking a Moral Basis for Concerted Action in a Pluralistic Society, 12 L. MED. & HEALTH CARE 192, 193 (1984).

The President's Council on Bioethics declined to recommend general regulation of Assisted Reproductive Technologies. PRESIDENT'S COUNCIL ON BIOETHICS, REPRODUCTION AND RESPONSIBILITY: THE REGULATION OF NEW BIOTECHNOLOGIES 183, 193 (2004). However, the President's Council on Bioethics did believe that regulation was needed: (1) to ensure the safety and well-being of children born using ART by increased oversight and more stringent reporting requirements, (2) to improve and equalize access to ART by requiring insurance coverage of fertility treatment, (3) to regulate and possibly limit genetic screening and selection of embryos for non-disease-related traits, (4) to ban germ-line modification of human embryos or gametes, (5) to ban human cloning and parthenogenesis (activating oocyte so that it starts developing into human without fertilization), and (6) to discourage the commercialization of human reproduction by placing limits on the buying and selling of human gametes and embryos. *See id.* at 194–200.

Britain has passed a comprehensive regulatory statute, the Human Fertilisation and Embryology Act of 1990. The Act, among other things, created a regulatory agency, the Human Fertilisation and Embryology Authority, to oversee the use of ART. It also provides for licensing of fertility and research clinics. The Act prohibits keeping or using any embryo after the emergence of the primitive streak after fourteen days, implanting a human embryo or gamete into any animal, and mixing any animal gametes with human gametes. It also mandates counseling and informed consent for any woman or couple participating in ART and any gamete donor, and it provides that no woman should be treated unless and until account has been taken of the welfare of any child who may be born as a result of the treatment (including the need of that child for a father), and of any other child who may be affected by the birth. *See* Human Fertilisation and Embryology Act 1990 Ch. c. 37.

On April 22, 2004, the Assisted Human Reproduction Act became law in Canada. The purpose of the Act is to protect the health and safety of Canadians who use assisted reproductive technologies. It regulates artificial insemination, *in vitro* fertilization, and preimplantation genetic diagnosis, and it prohibits human cloning. The Act also created the Assisted Human Reproduction Agency of Canada, which enforces the provisions of the Act and provides and renews licenses for assisted human reproductive procedures and research that utilize *in vitro* embryos. *See* Assisted Human Reproduction Act, S.C., ch. 2 (2004) (Can.).

6. In formulating policies on these technologies, what perspective and values should be taken into account? For a review of religious objections to the reproductive technologies generally, and views of other organized religions, see Baruch Brody, *Current Religious Perspectives on the New Reproductive Techniques*, in BEYOND BABY M: ETHICAL ISSUES IN NEW REPRODUCTIVE TECHNOLOGIES (Dianne M. Bartels et al. eds., 1990).

Feminist perspectives on the use of reproductive technologies vary. Some feminists argue that these technologies could promote male domination and control of female reproductive functions and assert that the technologies, especially surrogacy, are exploitative of women's bodies and their role as child-bearers. *See, e.g.,* ROBYN ROWLAND, LIVING LABORATORIES: WOMEN AND REPRODUCTIVE TECHNOLOGIES (1992); CHRISTINE OVERALL, ETHICS AND HUMAN REPRODUCTION: A FEMINIST ANALYSIS (1987). Others respond that this view exhibits a victim mentality and that the technologies can serve to empower women to bear children when they otherwise could not do so. *See, e.g.,* Lori Andrews, ALTERNATIVE MODES OF REPRODUCTION, IN REPRODUCTIVE LAWS FOR THE 1990S (Sherrill Cohen & Nadine Taub eds., 1989). Feminists are also concerned about the use of AI to preselect male offspring.

What account should be taken of our deeply-entrenched desire to have biological offspring? What causes this desire, and what is its significance? *See* Kenneth D. Alpern, *Genetic Puzzles and Stork Stories: On the Meaning and Significance of Having Children*, in THE ETHICS OF REPRODUCTIVE TECHNOLOGY 147 (Kenneth D. Alpern ed., 1992). Should this desire be medically "fixed" regardless of the emotional and social costs? *See, e.g.,* Paul Lauritzen, *What Price Parenthood*, 20 HASTINGS CTR. REP. 38 (1990); *Tales from the Baby Factory*, N.Y. TIMES MAG., Mar. 15, 1992, at 40. What impact could widespread use of these technologies have on adoption? Do these technologies serve to perpetuate an overvaluation of biological ties to offspring at the expense of already existing children who need a home?

A child could conceivably have up to five parents using these technologies: two non-biologically related "social" parents, a semen donor, an ovum donor, and a gestational mother. How could this affect our traditional conceptions of intimacy, sexuality, reproduction, and family? *See, e.g.*, Walter Wadlington, *Artificial Conception: The Challenge for Family Law*, 69 VA. L. REV. 465 (1983).

4.   HUMAN CLONING

THE PRESIDENT'S COUNCIL ON BIOETHICS, HUMAN CLONING AND HUMAN DIGNITY: AN ETHICAL INQUIRY

1, XXVI–XXIX, 60–61 (2002).

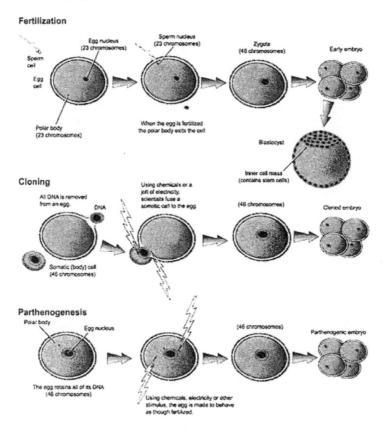

Cloning (Asexual Reproduction) of Mammals

    ... In outline form, the steps used to produce live offspring in the mammalian species that have been cloned so far are:

1.   Obtain an egg cell from a female of a mammalian species.

2.   Remove the nuclear DNA from the egg cell, to produce an enucleated egg.

3.   Insert the nucleus of a donor adult cell into the enucleated egg, to produce a reconstructed egg.

4. Activate the reconstructed egg with chemicals or electric current, to stimulate the reconstructed egg to commence cell division

5. Sustain development of the cloned embryo to a suitable stage in vitro, and then transfer the resulting cloned embryo to the uterus of a female host that has been suitably prepared to receive it.

6. Bring to live birth a cloned animal that is genetically virtually identical (except for the mitochondrial DNA) to the animal that donated the adult cell nucleus.

. . .

Two separate national-level reports on human cloning (NBAC, 1997; NAS, 2002)[2] concluded that attempts to clone a human being would be unethical at this time due to safety concerns and the likelihood of harm to those involved. The Council concurs in this conclusion. But we have extended the work of these distinguished bodies by undertaking a broad ethical examination of the merits of, and difficulties with, cloning-to-produce-children.

Cloning-to-produce-children might serve several purposes. It might allow infertile couples or others to have genetically-related children; permit couples at risk of conceiving a child with a genetic disease to avoid having an afflicted child; allow the bearing of a child who could become an ideal transplant donor for a particular patient in need; enable a parent to keep a living connection with a dead or dying child or spouse; or enable individuals or society to try to "replicate" individuals of great talent or beauty. These purposes have been defended by appeals to the goods of freedom, existence (as opposed to nonexistence), and well-being—all vitally important ideals.

A major weakness in these arguments supporting cloning-to-produce-children is that they overemphasize the freedom, desires, and control of parents, and pay insufficient attention to the well-being of the cloned child-to-be. The Council holds that, once the child-to-be is carefully considered, these arguments are not sufficient to overcome the powerful case against engaging in cloning-to-produce-children.

First, cloning-to-produce-children would violate the principles of the ethics of human research. Given the high rates of morbidity and mortality in the cloning of other mammals, we believe that cloning-to-produce-children would be extremely unsafe, and that attempts to produce a cloned child would be highly unethical. Indeed, our moral analysis of this matter leads us to conclude that this is not, as is sometimes implied, a merely temporary objection, easily removed by the improvement of technique. We offer reasons for believing that the safety risks might be enduring, and offer arguments in support of a strong conclusion: that conducting experiments in an effort to make cloning-to-produce-children less dangerous would itself be an unacceptable violation of the norms of research ethics. *There seems to be no ethical way to try to discover whether cloning-to-produce-children can become safe, now or in the future.*

2. [Eds.—*See* NATIONAL BIOETHICS ADVISORY COMMISSION, CLONING HUMAN BEINGS (1997); NATIONAL ACADEMY OF SCIENCES, HUMAN REPRODUCTIVE CLONING (2002).]

If carefully considered, the concerns about safety also begin to reveal the ethical principles that should guide a broader assessment of cloning-to-produce-children: the principles of freedom, equality, and human dignity. To appreciate the broader human significance of cloning-to-produce-children, one needs first to reflect on the meaning of having children; the meaning of asexual, as opposed to sexual, reproduction; the importance of origins and genetic endowment for identity and sense of self; the meaning of exercising greater human control over the processes and "products" of human reproduction; and the difference between begetting and making. Reflecting on these topics, the Council has identified five categories of concern regarding cloning-to-produce-children. (Different Council Members give varying moral weight to these different concerns.)

- *Problems of identity and individuality.* Cloned children may experience serious problems of identity both because each will be genetically virtually identical to a human being who has already lived and because the expectations for their lives may be shadowed by constant comparisons to the life of the "original."

- *Concerns regarding manufacture.* Cloned children would be the first human beings whose entire genetic makeup is selected in advance. They might come to be considered more like products of a designed manufacturing process than "gifts" whom their parents are prepared to accept as they are. Such an attitude toward children could also contribute to increased commercialization and industrialization of human procreation.

- *The prospect of a new eugenics.* Cloning, if successful, might serve the ends of privately pursued eugenic enhancement, either by avoiding the genetic defects that may arise when human reproduction is left to chance, or by preserving and perpetuating outstanding genetic traits, including the possibility, someday in the future, of using cloning to perpetuate genetically engineered enhancements.

- *Troubled family relations.* By confounding and transgressing the natural boundaries between generations, cloning could strain the social ties between them. Fathers could become "twin brothers" to their "sons"; mothers could give birth to their genetic twins; and grandparents would also be the "genetic parents" of their grandchildren. Genetic relation to only one parent might produce special difficulties for family life.

- *Effects on society.* Cloning-to-produce-children would affect not only the direct participants but also the entire society that allows or supports this activity. Even if practiced on a small scale, it could affect the way society looks at children and set a precedent for future nontherapeutic interventions into the human genetic endowment or novel forms of control by one generation over the next. In the absence of wisdom regarding these matters, prudence dictates caution and restraint.

Conclusion: For some or all of these reasons, the Council is in full agreement that cloning-to-produce-children is not only unsafe but also morally unacceptable, and ought not to be attempted.

NOTES AND QUESTIONS

1. *Cloning to Create Children.* Cloning for reproductive purposes is not a new idea. In 1971, James Watson wrote about the science of cloning and called for open discussions between scientists, politicians, and lay people about the positive and negative consequences of using cloning as a reproductive technology. *See* James D. Watson, *Moving Toward the Clonal Man*, 226 ATLANTIC 50 (1971). As the President's Council on Bioethics notes, a cloned child would be genetically *virtually* (italics added) identical to the donor parent. This is the case because a cloned child would also have a relationship with the egg donor. Once the nucleus from the donor parent is added to the enucleated egg and the egg has been electrically stimulated to reproduce, the resulting embryo will contain both a combination of the donor parent's DNA located in the nucleus and the ovum donor's mitochondrial DNA. PRESIDENT'S COUNCIL ON BIOETHICS, HUMAN CLONING AND HUMAN DIGNITY: AN ETHICAL INQUIRY 58–60 (2002).

In February 2004, scientists in South Korea used somatic cell nuclear transfer to create an embryo with virtually the same genetic composition as the female egg donor. Although the purpose of the study was to create a human embryonic stem cell line, the scientists also succeeded in proving that human cloning is possible. The scientists created the human cloned cell by placing the nucleus of a cumulus cell (a cell that surrounds an egg in the uterus) into an egg that had been enucleated. After stimulation the embryo started to divide and was allowed to develop for one week. At that time, the cells that would have become the placenta were removed, leaving the inner mass of cells that normally develop into the fetus. That inner mass of cells was placed in a culture and left to develop into embryonic stem cell lines. Woo Suk Hwang, *Evidence of a Pluripotent Human Embryonic Stem Cell Line Derived from a Cloned Blastocyst*, 303 SCI. 1669, 1669 (2004); Gretchen Vogel, *Scientists Take Step Towards Therapeutic Cloning*, 303 SCI. 937, 937 (2004).

Another technique of asexual reproduction is parthenogenesis, in which an *unfertilized* egg is stimulated to divide. Research shows that these parthenotes die at a fairly early stage of development; however, they do mimic many of the characteristics of embryos, and therefore have potential for research. NATIONAL INSTITUTES OF HEALTH, REPORT OF THE HUMAN EMBRYO RESEARCH PANEL 49 (1994). However, although plants and some animals can reproduce through parthenogenesis, mammals are unable to do so. *See* David Loebel & Patrick Tam, *Genomic Imprinting: Mice without a Father*, 428 NATURE 809 (2004) (discussing the possibility of altering genetic imprinting in order to make parthenogenesis possible in mammals).

Although scientific technology might one day make it possible to produce children using cloning, the ethical implications of this process need to be considered. The President's Council on Bioethics cites three ethical concerns raised by the prospect of reproductive cloning: effect on childhood identity; effect on parent-child relationships, and the use of manufacture instead of procreation as a means of having children. In contrast to the President's Council on Bioethics, Bonnie Steinbock argues that human cloning creates babies not duplicates of adults, so cloned children should not have identity problems. She notes that identity is influenced by the environment of the mother's uterus, and since the cloned child would be carried in the uterus many years later than the genetically virtually identical parent was carried, the parent and child would be different. Bonnie Steinbock, *Cloning Human Beings: Sorting Through the Ethical Issues, in* HUMAN CLONING: SCIENCE, ETHICS AND PUBLIC POLICY 71 (Barbara Mackinnon ed., 2000).

Furthermore, Bonnie Steinbock argues that cloned children would have a typical parent-child relationship with their parents. For example, in the scenario in which a couple decided to clone the husband because he was infertile, the cloned child's DNA would be identical to that of its father, but it would also share a mitochondrial DNA link with its mother who carried it to term. Steinbock emphasizes that the parental relationship should be based more on whether the adults intend to perform the parental role than on whether there is a genetic link between the adult and child. Steinbock at 71.

Leon Kass, chairman of the President's Council on Bioethics, and James Wilson, chairman of the Council of Academic Advisors for the American Enterprise Institute for Public Policy Research have debated whether human cloning would transform procreation into the manufacturing of children. On the one hand, Kass argues that human cloning is not a form of procreation but instead a form of manufacture because it allows people to create a new person by determining his/her entire genome. Although Kass acknowledges that environmental factors will influence a cloned child's identity, he maintains that forms of assisted reproduction like human cloning that do not involve sexual intercourse should not be allowed because these technologies represent the parents' attempt to control another human being. See Leon Kass & James Wilson, The Ethics of Human Cloning 3–60 (1998).

On the other hand, James Wilson argues that just because a child was created by a method other than sexual intercourse does not mean that the parents manufactured the child. Wilson says that the same emotion that is invested in creating a child through sexual intercourse would be invested in creating a child using cloning. He also notes that children who have been created by the use of other assisted reproductive technologies do not report that they feel like objects that belong to their parents rather than human beings. See Kass & Wilson at 61–76.

Federal and some state regulatory bodies have recommended banning human reproductive cloning. In 1997, the National Bioethics Advisory Commission (NBAC) recommended a five-year moratorium on human cloning research. National Bioethics Advisory Commission, Cloning Human Beings 109 (1997). In July 2002, as that moratorium expired, the President's Council on Bioethics unanimously voted to ban cloning-to-produce-children. President's Council on Bioethics at 205–06. Additionally, the legislatures of Arkansas, California, Iowa, Michigan, Missouri, New Jersey, North Dakota, Rhode Island, South Dakota, and Virginia have passed bills that prohibit reproductive cloning. National Conference of State Legislatures, *State Human Cloning Laws* (2004), *at* http://www.ncsl.org/programs/health/genetics/rt-shcl.htm, last visited July 26, 2004. Virginia has a provision that prevents the implantation of a cloned embryo into a woman's uterus. Arkansas, California, Iowa, New Jersey, North Dakota, and South Dakota also have provisions that prohibit the transfer or receipt of products of human cloning. *Id.*

Susan Wolf has argued that it was a bad decision for NBAC to advocate a moratorium on cloning. She claims that regulation of cloning research is needed rather than a complete ban of the research because a ban will prevent the development of safe procedures for cloning. She also claims that the scope of the ban is too large, that it violates the freedom of scientific inquiry that is protected under the First Amendment to the U.S. Constitution, and that the ban violates the procreative liberty of couples. Wolf further notes that a ban might violate the limits of federal power because health and clinical practice regulation is usually left to the states. Finally, she claims that the ban is bad policy because it halts the opportunity for discussion about the ethics of cloning. She states:

> A federal ban on cloning thus misses the big picture. Cloning is only one of many reproductive technologies that should be safe before application, be it intracytoplasmic sperm injection, cytoplasm transfer, or beyond. The task is to devise a regulatory approach that addresses safety while permitting research and progress in a sphere of immense importance to couples. Cloning should spur us to that delicate balancing act. Simply lowering the boom on cloning does the opposite.

Susan Wolf, *Ban Cloning? Why NBAC is Wrong*, 27 Hastings Ctr. Rep. 12, 12–15 (1997). Is Wolf's argument convincing?

Currently, no countries allow human reproductive cloning. Thus far, thirty countries including Australia, Brazil, Canada, China, France, India, Japan, Mexico, South Africa, and the United Kingdom have adopted legislation prohibiting human reproductive cloning. The international legislation can be divided into three categories: (1) legislation prohibiting the creation of cloned human embryos, (2) legislation prohibiting cloned human embryos from being implanted into a uterus, and (3) legislation prohibiting any attempt to create human beings who are genetically identical to another human being. United Nations Educational, Scientific and Cultural Organization, *National Legislation Concerning Human Reproductive and Therapeutic Cloning* (2004), *at* http://www.unesco.org (last visited July 26, 2004). On March 29, 2004, Canada passed comprehensive legislation which bans the creation of a human clone using any technique. In addition, the legislation bans the creation of *in vitro* embryos for non-reproductive purposes and the payment of money for gametes, embryos, and surrogate mothers. *See* Françoise Baylis, *Canada Bans Human Cloning*, 34 HASTINGS CTR. REP. 5, 5 (2004); Assisted Human Reproduction Act, S.C., ch.2 (2004) (Can.).

The United Nations has also become involved in the reproductive cloning debate. In 2001, France and Germany proposed a convention against reproductive cloning. At the committee meeting in 2002 to plan the convention, a ban on reproductive cloning was proposed but not finalized because the United States and Costa Rica presented a proposal that would ban research cloning as well as reproductive cloning. Since the committee could not decide which proposal to adopt, it deferred consideration of the convention until 2005. However, the committee later decided that the cloning issue would be heard during the May 2004 General Assembly Session with the goal of deciding how to translate anti-cloning principles into policy form. LeRoy Walters, *The United Nations and Human Cloning: A Debate on Hold*, 34 HASTINGS CTR. REP. 5, 5–6 (2004).

Consider John Robertson's opinion that human cloning is a beneficial technology that should be legal:

> ... The use of donor sperm is now widely accepted, as is the right of the couple to have some say in the choice of donor. Indeed, commercial sperm banks in the United States distribute brochures with the height, weight, hair and eye color, ethnic origin, education, and hobbies of donors listed. Embryo donation occurs on a much more limited scale, and so a practice of actual selection of embryos does not now exist, as it does with sperm donation. Yet there is no reason why couples desiring an embryo donation would not want some degree of choice over the embryos that they receive. ... The use of nuclear cell transfer cloning would enable that goal to be achieved more precisely and effectively.

John Robertson, *Reproductive Liberty and the Right to Clone Human Beings*, 913 ANNALS N.Y. ACAD. SCI. 198, 204 (2000). However, Robertson's view of human cloning is not shared by most people in the United States.

In fact, a 2002 study conducted by the Genetics and Public Policy Center found that 82% of Americans disapproved of reproductive cloning. Of the Americans who approved, most were men (26% of men approved while 11% of women approved). Also, most of the people who approved of reproductive cloning were under thirty years of age. Twenty-seven percent of the people who highly approved were eighteen to twenty-nine-years old while only 17% of the high approval group was thirty to forty-nine-years old, and only 14% of the group was fifty years old or more. Another significant difference in beliefs was found between people who thought about the moral and religious implications of technological advances versus those who were more focused on the health and safety implications of human cloning. Forty-nine percent of those people who emphasized the moral and religious consequences were opposed to human cloning whereas only 30% of people who emphasized the health and safety consequences of human cloning were opposed to it. According to the survey, there were no significant differences along racial or ethnic lines in support of general reproductive technology. Twenty-two percent of Hispanics and African–Americans and 16% of Caucasians highly supported genetic technology. Genetics and Public Policy Center, *Attitudes about Genetic Technology* (2002), *at* http://www.dnapolicy.org (last visited July 26, 2004).

2. *Stem Cell Research.* Stem cells are differentiated, specialized body cells that have both the ability to renew themselves indefinitely and to produce differentiated cell types. The controversy over extracting stem cells from embryos is related to cloning for reproductive purposes because the same technique—somatic cell nuclear transfer is one of several ways to create embryos from which stem cells can be extracted. *See Diagram of Early Stages of Human Fertilization, Cloning, and Parthenogenesis*, Sec. II. B. 4, *supra.* Using somatic cell nuclear transplantation in order to extract stem cells is often referred to as therapeutic cloning or cloning-for-biomedical-research. President's Council on Bioethics, Monitoring Stem Cell Research 2–5 (2004).

There are four types of stem cells: embryonic stem cells, embryonic germ cells (embryonic precursors of sperm and ova), adult (non-embryonic) stem cells and cord blood stem cells. Embryonic stem cells come from the inner mass of cells in embryos that is formed five to nine days after fertilization. President's Council on Bioethics at 8–11. In 1998, James A. Thompson, a scientist at the University of Wisconsin, announced that he had isolated human embryonic stem cells derived from donated *in vitro* spare embryos. *See* James Thompson et al., *Embryonic Stem Cells Derived from Human Blastocysts*, 282 Sci. 1145, 1145–47 (1998). As mentioned in the note on cloning to create children, in 2004 a scientist in South Korea used the somatic cell nuclear transfer technique to create embryos from which he could extract embryonic stem cells. Woo Suk Hwang, *Evidence of a Pluripotent Human Embryonic Stem Cell Line Derived from a Cloned Blastocyst*, 303 Sci. 1669, 1669 (2004). The British government announced on August 11, 2004, that it had awarded its first license permitting scientists to create stem cells for research from cloned, unfertilized human embryos. Heather Timmons, *Britain Grants License to Make Human Embryos for Stem Cells*, N.Y. Times, Aug. 12, 2004, at A4, col. 5. Embryonic germ cells are cells that have the potential to develop into sperm and eggs. These cells come from five to nine-week-old aborted fetuses. President's Council on Bioethics at 8–11. In 1998, John Gearhart, a scientist at Johns Hopkins University, announced that he had isolated primordial germ cells from five to nine-week-old aborted fetuses. *See* Michael J. Shamblott et al., *Derivation of Pluripotent Stem Cells from Cultured Human Primordial Germ Cells*, 95 Proceedings Nat'l Acad. Sci. 13726, 13726–31 (1998). Adult (non-embryonic) stem cells are stem cells that are found in children and adults. These cells are partially differentiated and are usually found within the same type of tissue. Finally, cord blood cells are stem cells (also non-embryonic) that are taken from the umbilical cord. The stem cell debate centers around the use of embryonic stem cells because the embryos from which the stem cells are derived have to be destroyed in order for the researchers to obtain the stem cell material. President's Council on Bioethics at 8–11.

Stem cell research has the potential to accomplish several goals. First, information obtained from stem cells might help scientists learn more about various cellular processes and how to prevent those processes from malfunctioning. Second, scientists might eventually be able to develop stem cell lines that could be used as a renewable source for organ donation or regeneration. If embryonic stem cells could be used to produce organs for transplantation, then patients would be able to receive organs that contained their genetic material, thus reducing the possibility that the body would reject the new organ. Furthermore, stem cells might be used to test the effect of certain drugs on the human body. NATIONAL BIOETHICS ADVISORY COMMISSION, ETHICAL ISSUES IN STEM CELL RESEARCH 20–23 (1999).

3. *Efforts to Regulate Embryo and Stem Cell Research.* In 1993, the National Institutes of Health (NIH) created a panel to study the issues related to human embryo research and to create guidelines for funding human embryo research. The committee concluded that some types of human embryo research should be eligible for federal funding and that it was acceptable to create embryos solely for research purposes in certain circumstances. President Clinton accepted some of the recommendations, but he refused to allow federal funds to be used to create embryos for research. In 1995, Congress passed a bill that contained the Dickey Amendment, an act that prohibited the use of federal funds for research that destroyed or endangered human embryos or that created human embryos for research purposes. However, the General Counsel of the Department of Health and Human Services argued that the wording of the law permitted funding of stem cell research if embryos first were destroyed by researchers using private funds. In order to establish guidelines for embryonic stem cell research that would conform to this interpretation of the Dickey Amendment, the National Bioethics Advisory Commission issued a set of recommendations in 1999. *See* NATIONAL BIOETHICS ADVISORY COMMISSION, ETHICAL ISSUES IN HUMAN STEM CELL RESEARCH (1999). NBAC recommended that research using embryonic stem cells from fetal tissue and from embryos that were left after fertility treatments should be eligible for federal funding. They recommended that stem cells from embryos that were created solely for research purposes should not receive federal funds. The Commission also recommended that federal funding should not be provided for research on embryonic stem cells that were created using somatic cell nuclear transfer. Although these guidelines were recommended, President Bush took office before they could be implemented. *See id.*

On August 9, 2001, President George W. Bush announced a federal policy that limits federal funding for embryonic stem cell research. Under the Bush plan, taxpayer money can only be used to fund research on embryonic stem cells derived from embryos created for reproductive purposes only and that existed prior to August 9, 2001. PRESIDENT'S COUNCIL ON BIOETHICS at 28–30.

Opponents of Bush's policy have four major criticisms. First, some scholars claim that the policy creates an atmosphere in which a limited number of private companies have a monopoly over scientists because there is a limited availability of embryonic stem cell lines that are open to federal funding. *See* Eric Passeggio, *Legal Update: Embryonic Stem Cell Research: Shifting Availability of Federal Funds*, 8 B.U.J. SCI. & TECH. L. 347, 351 (2002). Second, critics question whether the existing lines are adequate enough and strong enough to meet research needs. *See* Robin Toner, *The President's Decision: The Reaction; each side finds something to like, and not*, N.Y. TIMES, Aug. 10, 2001, at A17; Elias Zerhouni, *Testimony to the U.S. Senate Appropriations Subcommittee on Labor, HHS, and Education*, (May 22, 2003) (verifying that as of 2003 there were eleven embryonic stem cell lines available for researchers' use). Third, critics claim that federal funding is important because embryonic stem cell research technology is new, so private industries have not had the opportunity to invest large amounts of money to fund research. If researchers had greater access to federal funds, then laboratories could attract the best academic researchers. Correspondingly, critics argue that federal funding would create an open atmosphere in which researchers could collaborate and in which the government could set ethical standards for the research. *See* Sheryl Gay Stolberg, *The President's Decision: A Question of Research, Disappointed by limits, scientists doubt estimate of available cell lines*, N.Y. TIMES, Aug. 10, 2001, at A17. For an additional critique of time-based funding restrictions on embryonic stem cell research, see Andrew W. Seigel, *Temporal Restrictions and the Impasse on Human Embryonic Stem–Cell Research*, 364 LANCET 215 (2004).

Despite the ban on federal funding of embryonic stem cell research, President George W. Bush announced plans in July 2004 for the creation of a federally funded stem cell bank in the United States. The goal of the program would be to ensure that the potential of existing cell lines is exhausted before funding for additional lines is granted. One organization will be picked to run the stem cell bank. The bank will characterize stem cell lines, distribute stem cell lines to researchers at a low cost, and serve as a "help desk" for researchers' questions. Constance Holden, *Advocates Keep Pot Boiling as Bush Plans New Centers*, 305 SCI. 461, 461 (2004).

The ten states—Arkansas, California, Iowa, Michigan, Missouri, New Jersey, North Dakota, Rhode Island, South Dakota, and Virginia—with legislation prohibiting human reproductive cloning also have provisions that deal with embryonic stem cell research. Of those ten states, California, Missouri, New Jersey, and Rhode Island permit somatic cell nuclear transfer to be used to create embryonic stem cells that will be used in biomedical research. *See* National Conference of State Legislatures, *State Human Cloning Laws* (2004), *at* http://www.ncsl.org/programs/health/genetics/rt-shcl.htm (last visited August 13, 2004).

Internationally, countries prohibit either research on embryos and/or the creation of embryos for research, allow some research on embryos that were produced by fertility treatments but prohibit the creation of embryos for research only, or allow embryos to be created for research according to specific guidelines. When the United Nations began debating whether to approve a worldwide ban on embryonic stem cell research in 2002, conflict arose between member states such as the United States who advocated a ban on all types of cloning and those such as China and Japan who only advocated a ban on reproductive cloning and supported efforts to clone embryos for stem cell research. *See* United Nations, *Press Release L/2995* (2003), *at* http://www.un.org (last visited July 26, 2004); Carol A. Tauer, *International Policy Failures: Cloning and Stem–Cell Research*, 364 LANCET 209 (2004) (discussing UN failure to pass treaty on reproductive cloning and connection between reproductive cloning and research cloning). The first stem cell bank has also been created abroad in the United Kingdom. The purpose of the bank is to store, organize, and provide stem cell lines to researchers and eventually to people for treatment. In order for researchers to deposit stem cell lines or access them, they must submit an application, which is reviewed by a steering committee. For more information, see Stephen Pincock, *UK Opens Embryonic Stem Cell Bank*, 363 LANCET 1778 (2004).

Stem cell lines have been created with the use of private funds. For instance, in 2004 Harvard University researchers Douglas Melton and Andrew McMahon created the Harvard Stem Cell Institute (HSCI). The institute is funded by the Howard Hughes Medical Institute, and researchers will be able to obtain stem cell lines at no cost instead of having to pay $5,000 for the stem cell lines that are federally funded. *See* Jonathan Shaw, *Stem-Cell Science: When Medicine Meets Moral Philosophy*, 106 HARVARD MAGAZINE 36 (2004).

4. *Ethical and Policy Issues*. The creation of stem cell banks will raise interesting ethical and policy issues beyond the question of whether stem cell research should be conducted. How should stem cell lines be selected for inclusion in a stem cell bank? Ruth Faden et al. analyze three possible approaches to organizing a stem cell bank. In the straightforward maximizing approach, the stem cell bank would contain the most common cell lines in the United States, which would mainly benefit Caucasians since they comprise the majority of the population. People with less common haplotypes (variant forms of genes that inherited together) would not have their cell lines included and thus will not have the same opportunity to benefit. In the egalitarian approach, stem cell lines would be chosen by lottery, which would increase the access to all people. However, only a small number of people would actually benefit from a lottery-based system because this system would not be designed to address the problem of unequal access for members of different racial or ethnic groups. Furthermore, relatively uncommon haplotypes might be chosen in a lottery, which would limit the number of people who could be helped by the stem cell line. The final approach is the ethnic representation approach in which the stem cell bank would select the most common haplotypes from each of the major ancestral or ethnic groups in the United States and store stem cell lines based on those haplotypes in the bank. This approach would be less efficient than the straightforward maximizing strategy because it would require more stem cell lines to match the same number of people and would require researchers to specifically solicit donations from minority women. However, this approach would provide the greatest access to ethnic groups. *See* Ruth Faden et al., *Public Stem Cell Banks: Considerations of Justice in Stem Cell Research and Therapy*, 33 HASTINGS CTR. REP. 13 (2003); *see also* Hilary Bok et al., *Justice, Ethnicity, and Stem–Cell Banks*, 364 LANCET 118 (2004).

Some researchers have suggested that an effective means of obtaining gametes and embryos is through donation from infertility patients because frozen embryos are often of poor quality and difficult to obtain for research purposes and somatic cell nuclear transfer is a controversial technique. Christopher L.R. Barrat et al., *Clinical Challenges in Providing Embryos for Stem–Cell Initiatives*, 364 LANCET 114 (2004). Should donors be compensated? Faden et al. argue that donations to stem cell banks should be treated like organ donations rather than like donations to infertility programs in which payment is offered. Do you agree?

Should there be limits on who may serve as a donor? If donor gametes and embryos are used in embryonic stem cell research who should be allowed to serve as a donor? After Woo Suk Hwang announced that he had created a human embryo using the somatic cell nuclear transfer technique, other researchers began questioning how Hwang could get sixteen women to volunteer to donate eggs. It has been suggested that two of Hwang's female research assistants donated their eggs. Some ethicists claim that Hwang's use of his research assistants looks like coercion. *See* David Cyranoski, *Korea's Stem–Cell Stars Dogged by Suspicion of Ethical Breach*, 429 NATURE 3 (2004).

C. OBLIGATIONS TO FETUSES AND FUTURE CHILDREN

Bonnie Steinbock & Ron McClamrock, *When Is Birth Unfair to the Child?*

24 HASTINGS CTR. REP. 15 (1994).

Is it wrong to bring children who will have serious diseases and disabilities into the world? In particular, is it unfair to them? . . .

. . . Can we make clear and coherent the prima facie plausible idea that it is unfair for parents to bring children into being without some reasonable prospects at a nonmiserable life?

The very particular and detailed ways such a principle of parental responsibility might be filled out will of course be very different, depending on which ethical theory undergirds it. Whether the theory is utilitarian, virtue-based, deontological, or contractarian, however, it's not hard to see how the parents' special relationship to and control over the life and well-being of the child should be seen as giving them a special responsibility. So rather than spending time trying to fill that out in detail (and by so doing, making the appeal of the idea less rather than more general), we'll content ourselves here with spelling out some of the most general features a principle of parental responsibility might involve, and then in the next section turn to a very general criticism that any such principle must face.

A principle of parental responsibility should require of individuals that they attempt to refrain from having children unless certain minimal conditions can be satisfied. This principle maintains that in deciding whether to have children, people should not be concerned only with their own interests in reproducing. They must think also, and perhaps primarily, of the welfare of the children they will bear. They should ask themselves, "What kind of life is my child likely to have?" Individuals who will make good parents—that is, loving, concerned parents—will want their children to have lives well worth living and will strive to give them such lives. But what if the parents cannot give their children even a decent chance at a good life? The principle of parental responsibility maintains that under such conditions, it is better not to have children, and that it is in fact unfair to children to bring them into the world with "the deck stacked against them."

Although a principle of parental responsibility requires individuals to refrain, when possible, from having children if they cannot give them a decent chance of a happy life, this of course does not imply that responsible parents of born children should be willing to kill them if their lives fall below a certain standard. Given a child with severe handicaps, considerable pain, and a very limited life (but still a life the child finds worth living) parents should choose treatment that will allow their child to go on living as he or she wants, all things being equal—we're not assuming that issues about availability and cost of treatment or the like couldn't bear on the decision as well. Given a preference for life, it is not in general the parents' place to decide that the child would be better off dead.

When the child is too young to have preferences, the parents will have to judge whether continued life is in the child's best interest. Depending on the prognosis, a reasonable judgment might be made either way. A decision to stop life-prolonging treatment could be consistent with, or possibly even required by, the special responsibility the parents have to the child.

But where there is no child at all, the question facing the prospective parents is not, What does my child want? nor, What is best for my child? It's rather a question of whether to create a child who is likely to have a life marked by pain and severe limitations. It seems to us that the answer to this question must be no. What reason could be offered in justification of an affirmative answer? That the child's life, while miserable, is not so awful that he or she will long for death? That is not the kind of answer a loving parent could give. Anyone willing to subject a child to a miserable life when this could be avoided would seem to fail to live up to a minimal ideal of parenting.

We've claimed that a child's being destined to a miserable life may well count strongly against bringing the child into existence. However, the fact that a child would have a happy life if brought into existence does not obligate its putative parents to have the child. If one decides not to have a child, one harms no one. It is not as if there are people in the wings, so to speak, hoping to get the gift of life. No one is injured or made unhappy or deprived by nonbirth. By contrast, if one decides to have a child, then there will exist a real person, with needs and interests that must be considered. Mary Anne Warren expresses the point this way:

> Failing to have a child, even when you could have had a happy one, is neither right nor wrong.... But the same cannot be said of having a child, since in this case the action results in the existence of a new person whose interests must be taken into account. Having a child under conditions which should enable one to predict that it will be very unhappy is morally objectionable, not because it violates the rights of a presently existing potential person, but because it results in the frustration of the interests of an actual person in the future.[6]

. . .

How Bad Is Too Bad?

The principle of parental responsibility maintains that prospective parents are morally obligated to consider the kinds of lives their offspring are likely to have, and to refrain from having children if their lives will be sufficiently awful....

The basic idea is that before embarking on so serious an enterprise as parenthood, people should think about the consequences for their offspring. Some circumstances may be so awful that birth is unfair to the child. However, the principle of parental responsibility says only that it is wrong to bring children into the world when there is good reason to think that their lives will be terrible. It does not suggest that people should not have children unless conditions are ideal, still less that only conventional child-drearing circumstances are morally permissible. Consider, for example, the enormous fuss raised recently by the story of a fifty-nine-year-old British woman who gave birth to twins on Christmas Day 1993. The eggs, donated by a younger woman and fertilized in vitro by the older woman's husband, were implanted into her at a private fertility clinic in Rome. Doctors in London had earlier refused to perform the same procedure because they believed she was too old to face the emotional stress of being a mother. Virginia Bottomley, the British Secretary of Health, told the BBC, "Women do not have the right to have a child. The child has a right to a suitable home." But as the *New York Times* put it in an editorial:

> What makes Ms. Bottomley believe the twins won't have a suitable home? Youth is no guarantee of parenting skills: all too often the contrary is the case. And how would Ms. Bottomley define the homes in which parentless children are raised by grandmothers? Are they, ipso facto, unsuitable?

Undoubtedly, pregnancy poses special risks for many postmenopausal women, but most IVF programs carefully screen out candidates who are not in excellent condition. If society is going to decide which women are physically unsuited for pregnancy, it might start with young teenagers, as pregnancy in children who are not yet full grown is risky for both the

6. Mary Anne Warren, *Do Potential People Have Moral Rights?, in* OBLIGATIONS TO FUTURE GENERATIONS *ed.* R.I. Sikora and Brian Barry (Philadelphia: Temple University Press, 1978), p. 25.

mother and the baby. And young teens are probably less well equipped emotionally to be good parents than women in their fifties or sixties.

Another worry is that postmenopausal women won't live long enough to rear their children. According to Gail Sheehy, author of *Passages* and *The Silent Passage: Menopause,* "It's not a very nice prospect for a child of 10 or 12 to go to sleep every night, praying that his or her mother will live as long as he needs her."[7] However, many women live into their eighties and nineties these days. The Italian doctor who helped the fifty-nine-year-old British woman give birth accepts only patients who have a life expectancy of at least twenty more years, based on their age and family history. They must be non-smokers and pass psychological and physical tests. These are conditions we do not require of any other mothers. Nor are they conditions imposed on fathers. Telly Savalas, the television star of *Kojak* recently died at the age of seventy. The fact that he left behind school-age children was not even a subject of comment, much less outrage. It seems likely that the opposition to older women having babies expresses a prejudice against what is new or unconventional, rather than a position that can be rationally justified. So long as a woman is emotionally and physically equipped to be a reasonably good mother, there is no reason why age should be an absolute barrier for women, any more than it is for men.

Life is always a mixture of good and bad, pleasure and pain. We know that our children will have their share of suffering and adversity; that is the price of the ticket. This fact should stop no one who wants children from having them. At the same time, the judgment that the child you will conceive is likely to have a life that falls below a decent minimum provides a strong reason to avoid procreation. In some cases, all that is necessary is to postpone parenthood, as in the example of the young teenager who wants to have a child. The principle of parental responsibility tells her to wait, because if she does, she will be a much better parent to the child she eventually has. In other cases, where the risk is transmitting a disease, whether a genetic condition, such as sickle-cell anemia or cystic fibrosis, or a viral illness, such as AIDS, postponing pregnancy will not help. Prospective parents will have to base their decision on such factors as the risk of transmission, the nature and seriousness of the disease, the availability of ameliorative therapies, the possibility of a cure, and their ability to provide the child with a good life despite the handicap. The principle of parental responsibility does not provide a formula for deciding such cases. Reasonable people can differ on what a decent chance at a happy life is, and what risks are worth taking.

Throughout this paper we have been assuming that parenthood is deliberately chosen, something that is not always—perhaps not even typically—true. In many parts of the world, fertility is not so easily controlled, and becoming a parent is more a question of what happens to one than a deliberate choice. The principle of parental responsibility is aimed only at those individuals who are capable of controlling their fertility, and of making a conscious decision whether to have children.

7. Quoted in *How Far Should We Push*   p. 56.
Mother Nature?, Newsweek, 17 January 1994,

NOTES AND QUESTIONS

Consider the recommendation of an Institute of Medicine Committee:

Unintended pregnancy is both frequent and widespread in the United States. The most recent estimate is that almost 60 percent of all pregnancies are unintended, either mistimed or unwanted altogether—a percentage higher than that found in several other Western democracies. . . .

The consequences of unintended pregnancy are serious, imposing appreciable burdens on children, women, men, and families. A woman with an unintended pregnancy is less likely to seek early prenatal care and is more likely to expose the fetus to harmful substances. . . . The child of an unwanted conception especially . . . is at greater risk of being born at low birthweight, of dying in its first year of life, of being abused, and of not receiving sufficient resources for healthy development. The mother may be at greater risk of depression and of physical abuse herself, and her relationship with her partner is at greater risk of dissolution. Both mother and father may suffer economic hardship and may fail to achieve their educational and career goals. Such consequences undoubtedly impede the formation and maintenance of strong families. . . .

The committee has concluded that reducing unintended pregnancy will require a new national understanding about this problem and a new consensus that pregnancy should be undertaken only with clear intent. Accordingly, the committee urges, first and foremost, that the nation adopt a new social norm:

All pregnancies should be intended—that is, they should be consciously and clearly desired at the time of conception.

THE BEST INTENTIONS: UNINTENDED PREGNANCY AND THE WELL–BEING OF CHILDREN AND FAMILIES 1–3 (Sarah S. Brown & Leon Eisenberg eds., 1995).

1. PREGNANCY

In re Baby Boy Doe, A Fetus

Appellate Court of Illinois, First District, 1994.
260 Ill.App.3d 392, 198 Ill.Dec. 267, 632 N.E.2d 326.

■ DiVito, J.

This case asks whether an Illinois court can balance whatever rights a fetus may have against the rights of a competent woman to refuse medical advice to obtain a cesarean section for the supposed benefit of her fetus. Following the lead of the Illinois Supreme Court in *Stallman v. Youngquist* (Ill. 1988), 531 N.E.2d 355, we hold that no such balancing should be employed, and that a woman's competent choice to refuse medical treatment as invasive as a cesarean section during pregnancy must be honored, even in circumstances where the choice may be harmful to her fetus.

Both the factual background and the procedural posture of the case are important. "Doe" is a married woman who was expecting her first child. She sought and had been receiving regular prenatal care throughout her pregnancy at St. Joseph's Hospital in Chicago. All parties and the court regarded her as mentally competent.

On November 24, 1993, Dr. James Meserow, a board-certified obstetrician/gynecologist and expert in the field of maternal/fetal medicine who is affiliated with the hospital, examined Doe for the first time. A series of

II. Deciding Whether, When, or How to Reproduce

tests he ordered performed on her suggested to Meserow that something was wrong with the placenta, and that the approximately 35–week, viable fetus was receiving insufficient oxygen. Meserow recommended immediate delivery by cesarean section, in his opinion the safest option for the fetus or, in the alternative, by induced labor. Informed of his recommendation, Doe told Meserow that, because of her personal religious beliefs, she would not consent to either procedure. Instead, given her abiding faith in God's healing powers, she chose to await natural childbirth. Her husband agreed with her decision.

Doe was examined by Dr. Meserow again on December 8, and by a Dr. Gautier from the University of Illinois at Chicago on Thursday, December 9. After consulting with Gautier, Meserow concluded that the condition of the fetus had worsened. Meserow advised Doe and her husband that due to the insufficient oxygen flow to the fetus, failure to provide an immediate delivery by cesarean section (Meserow no longer recommended inducement as an option) could result in the child being born dead or severely retarded. Doe reiterated her opposition to a cesarean section, based on her personal religious beliefs.

On December 8, 1993, Dr. Meserow and St. Joseph's Hospital contacted the office of the Cook County State's Attorney. That office filed a petition for adjudication of wardship of the fetus on December 9, seeking to invoke the jurisdiction of the Juvenile Court Act (705 ILCS 405/1–1 et seq. (West 1992)), and asking that the hospital be appointed custodian of the fetus. . . . The judge, who expressed doubt as to whether the Juvenile Court Act conferred jurisdiction over a fetus in utero, certified the question for immediate appeal to this court, and set the matter for hearing on Friday, December 10.

. . .

. . . [I]n an emergency hearing, the parties' attorneys appeared in chambers before a three-judge panel of this court, along with Doe's husband; Dr. Meserow; John Seibel, attorney for St. Joseph's Hospital; and counsel from the Roger Baldwin Foundation of the ACLU, Inc., seeking leave to appear as amicus curiae. Doe was not present . . .

During the emergency hearing, the assistant state's attorneys asked the court for an order forcing Doe to undergo an immediate cesarean section to deliver the fetus. Following argument, the majority of the panel, one judge dissenting, held that the appellate court lacked jurisdiction to hear the case because no order had yet been entered by the circuit court, and therefore remanded the case to the circuit court. The majority also suggested that jurisdiction would not lie under the Juvenile Court Act, and that an order compelling a pregnant woman to submit to an invasive procedure such as a cesarean section would violate her constitutional rights. The panel further advised the parties that it would remain available that day to hear any appeal that might be taken once the circuit court entered an order.

Later that afternoon, the juvenile court judge commenced the hearing on the issue of the circuit court's jurisdiction, and whether an order compelling Doe to submit to surgery should issue. After oral argument from the parties' attorneys, the court ruled that the Juvenile Court Act does not apply to a fetus. The court held, however, that it had equity jurisdiction over the State's petition as a court of general jurisdiction, and denied the public defender's motion to dismiss the State's petition. The State then sought leave to file an amended petition, which was granted, and filed instanter its amended "Petition for Hearing on Whether a Temporary Custodian Can Be Appointed to Consent to a Medical Procedure: To Wit Cesarean Section."

Counsel for Doe and her husband moved to dismiss the amended petition, and the motion was denied.

.   .   .

The hearing then proceeded on the amended petition. The State called Dr. Meserow as its only witness. Meserow testified that he could not ascertain whether the fetus was already injured, or quantify the degree of risk to the fetus from continuing the pregnancy. He indicated that a fetus has some coping mechanisms to deal with decreased oxygen, and that those mechanisms appeared to be functioning. In his expert opinion, the likelihood of injury to the fetus increased on a daily basis, and the chances that the fetus would survive a natural labor were close to zero. On cross-examination, Meserow further testified about the specific medical procedures involved in a cesarean section, and the serious risks and possible side effects to Doe of such procedures. Although he recommended a cesarean section as the safest mode of delivery for the fetus, Meserow was not advocating that the cesarean section be performed over Doe's objection.

Counsel for Doe and her husband called no witnesses, but entered into a stipulation with the State which was accepted by the court: Doe received the recommendation from the physicians, understood the risks and benefits of the proposed procedures and, in consultation with her husband, decided to await natural childbirth.

On December 11, 1993, the court heard closing arguments and then denied the State's petition. . . .

The court made the following conclusions of law in denying the State's request for an injunction: "1. The Court has jurisdiction of this matter under its grant of general jurisdiction. The Juvenile Court Act is not applicable. A fetus is not a 'minor' within the meaning of the Act. 2. In the circumstances of this case, the state has failed to demonstrate that there is statutory or case law to support justifying the intrusive procedure requested herein by way of a court order against a competent person. 3. The Court denies the State's motion for an injunction. 4. There is no reason to delay an appeal of this matter and this is a final ruling."

. . . This court granted the motion for an expedited hearing on December 14, 1993, heard oral argument from all parties, and in a brief written order affirmed the judgment of the circuit court. In so doing, this court reserved the right to issue an opinion at some future date.

The Public Guardian petitioned the Illinois Supreme Court for leave to appeal. On December 16, 1993, the supreme court denied the petition (No. 76560). The Public Guardian then applied to the United States Supreme

Court for an order remanding the matter to the circuit court of Cook County. That Court, with one justice dissenting, denied the motion on December 18, 1993. (510 U.S. 1032) The Supreme Court subsequently denied certiorari on February 28, 1994 (510 U.S. 1168).

Doe vaginally delivered an apparently normal and healthy, although somewhat underweight, baby boy on December 29, 1993. The ACLU has since petitioned for the issuance of a written opinion, pointing out that the issue involved is serious and that the situation is likely to arise again, with little time for a circuit court to make an informed judgment. Cognizant of the seriousness of the question presented, and believing that the circuit courts of Illinois require some guidance in this area, this court issues the present opinion.

. . .

In its appeal, the Public Guardian requested that this court reverse the order of the circuit court, and enter an order upon Doe directing her to have a cesarean section forthwith so that the baby could be delivered. The Public Guardian strenuously opposed any effort to use force or any other means to compel Doe to have the surgery, but would have reserved the right to file a rule to show cause why she should not be held in contempt if she had refused and the baby had been born either dead or severely retarded.

In its appeal, the State requested this court to reverse the circuit court's denial of its petition to appoint a temporary custodian for Doe, for the sole purpose of consenting to a cesarean section only during the birthing process. It, too, opposed the use of force.

Both the State and the Public Guardian argued that the circuit court should have balanced the rights of the unborn but viable fetus which was nearly at full term and which, if the uncontradicted expert testimony of the physicians had been accurate, would have been born dead or severely retarded if Doe delivered vaginally, against the right of the competent woman to choose the type of medical care she deemed appropriate, based in part on personal religious considerations. We hold today that Illinois courts should not engage in such a balancing, and that a woman's competent choice in refusing medical treatment as invasive as a cesarean section during her pregnancy must be honored, even in circumstances where the choice may be harmful to her fetus.

It cannot be doubted that a competent person has the right to refuse medical treatment. . . .

In Illinois the common law protects the right of a competent individual to refuse medical treatment. . . .

The United States Supreme Court, in *Cruzan v. Director, Missouri Department of Health* (1990), 497 U.S. 261, 277, held that the due process clause of the 14th amendment confers a significant liberty interest in avoiding unwanted medical procedures. Concurring with the majority opinion, Justice O'Connor stated that the liberty guaranteed by the due process clause must protect, if it protects anything, an individual's "deeply personal" decision to reject medical treatment. "Because our notions of liberty are inextricably entwined with our idea of physical freedom and self determination, the Court has often deemed state incursions into the body repugnant to the interests protected by the Due Process Clause." *Cruzan*, 497 U.S. at 287 (O'Connor, J., concurring).

The Illinois Supreme Court has acknowledged that the state right of privacy protects substantive fundamental rights, such as the right to reproductive autonomy. (Family Life League v. Department of Public Aid (Ill. 1986), 493 N.E.2d 1054.) Further, the court has conceptually linked the right to privacy with the right of bodily integrity. In *Stallman v. Youngquist* (Ill. 1988), 531 N.E.2d 355, 360, the supreme court refused to recognize a tort action against a mother for unintentional infliction of prenatal injuries because it would subject the woman's every act while pregnant to state scrutiny, thereby intruding upon her rights to privacy and bodily integrity, and her right to control her own life.

Religious liberty, protected by both federal and Illinois constitutions, similarly requires that a competent adult may refuse medical treatment on religious grounds. In *In re Estate of Brooks* (Ill. 1965), 205 N.E.2d 435, the Illinois Supreme Court held that an adult may refuse medical treatment on religious grounds even under circumstances where treatment is required to save the patient's life. In that case, an adult Jehovah's Witness was rendered temporarily incompetent by a life-threatening medical condition. Despite a previously-expressed wish not to be transfused with blood products, a conservator was appointed to consent to transfusions. The State argued that society's interest in preserving life outweighs a patient's right to the free exercise of religion. The Illinois Supreme Court disagreed, out of a recognition that religious liberty and the right to determine one's own destiny are among the rights "most valued by civilized man." (*Brooks*, 32 Ill.2d at 374, 205 N.E.2d 435.) As such, an individual's free exercise of religion may be limited only "where such exercise endangers, clearly and presently, the public health, welfare or morals." (*Brooks*, 32 Ill.2d at 372, 205 N.E.2d 435.) Recognizing that the decision to refuse medical treatment is a matter of individual conscience and not a question of public welfare, the court concluded: "Even though we may consider appellant's beliefs unwise, foolish or ridiculous, in the absence of an overriding danger to society we may not permit interference therewith . . . for the sole purpose of compelling her to accept medical treatment forbidden by her religious principles and previously refused by her with full knowledge of the probable consequences." *Brooks*, 32 Ill.2d at 373, 205 N.E.2d 435.

The right of a competent adult to refuse medical treatment inconsistent with his or her religious beliefs was reaffirmed in *Baumgartner v. First Church of Christ, Scientist* (Ill. App. Ct. 1986), 490 N.E.2d 1319, *cert. denied* (1986), 479 U.S. 915.

Particularly important to our supreme court's holding in *Stallman* was the recognition that the relationship between a pregnant woman and a fetus is unique, and "unlike the relationship between any other plaintiff and defendant. No other plaintiff depends exclusively on any other defendant for everything necessary for life itself. No other defendant must go through biological changes of the most profound type, possibly at the risk of her own life, in order to bring forth an adversary into the world. It is,

II. Deciding Whether, When, or How to Reproduce

after all, the whole life of the pregnant woman which impacts upon the development of the fetus. . . . [I]t is the mother's every waking and sleeping moment which, for better or worse, shapes the prenatal environment which forms the world for the developing fetus. That this is so is not a pregnant woman's fault; it is a fact of life." *Stallman*, 125 Ill.2d at 278–79, 126 Ill.Dec. 60, 531 N.E.2d 355. Appreciating the fact that "the circumstances in which each individual woman brings forth life are as varied as the circumstances of each woman's life," the court strongly suggested that there can be no consistent and objective legal standard by which to judge a woman's actions during pregnancy. *Stallman*, 125 Ill.2d at 279, 126 Ill.Dec. 60, 531 N.E.2d 355.

Applied in the context of compelled medical treatment of pregnant women, the rationale of *Stallman* directs that a woman's right to refuse invasive medical treatment, derived from her rights to privacy, bodily integrity, and religious liberty, is not diminished during pregnancy. The woman retains the same right to refuse invasive treatment, even of lifesaving or other beneficial nature, that she can exercise when she is not pregnant. The potential impact upon the fetus is not legally relevant; to the contrary, the *Stallman* court explicitly rejected the view that the woman's rights can be subordinated to fetal rights. *Stallman*, 125 Ill.2d at 276, 126 Ill.Dec. 60, 531 N.E.2d 355.

In Illinois a fetus is not treated as only a part of its mother. (*Stallman*, 125 Ill.2d at 276, 126 Ill.Dec. 60, 531 N.E.2d 355.) It has the legal right to begin life with a sound mind and body, assertable against third parties after it has been born alive. (*Stallman*, 125 Ill.2d at 275, 126 Ill.Dec. 60, 531 N.E.2d 355.) This right is not assertable against its mother, however, for the unintentional infliction of prenatal injuries. (*Stallman*, 125 Ill.2d at 280, 126 Ill.Dec. 60, 531 N.E.2d 355.) A woman is under no duty to guarantee the mental and physical health of her child at birth, and thus cannot be compelled to do or not do anything merely for the benefit of her unborn child. The Public Guardian's argument that this case is distinguishable from *Stallman* because Doe's actions amounted to *intentional* infliction of prenatal injuries is not persuasive.

The court of appeals for the District of Columbia has held that a woman's competent choice regarding medical treatment of her pregnancy must be honored, even under circumstances where the choice may be fatal to the fetus. (*In re A.C.* (D.C.App.1990), 573 A.2d 1235.) The appellate court, reviewing the case en banc, vacated the lower court's order, which had required a pregnant, dying woman to undergo a cesarean section because the fetus was potentially viable. The lower court, after first ruling that it could not determine the woman's wishes because it questioned her competency, then reached its decision by balancing the fetus's rights against the woman's rights. The appellate court held that the lower court's approach was erroneous. Instead of balancing, the appellate court instructed, the lower court should have ascertained the woman's wishes by means of the doctrine of substituted judgment. The woman's decision, not the fetus's interest, is the only dispositive factor. If the woman is competent and makes an informed decision, that decision will control "in virtually all cases." (*In re A.C.*, 573 A.2d at 1237, 1249.) While not deciding the question, the court expressed some doubt as to whether there could ever be a situation extraordinary or compelling enough to justify a massive intrusion into a person's body, such as a cesarean section, against that person's will. (*In re A.C.*, 573 A.2d at 1252.) The Public Guardian's argument, that this case represents such a situation, is unpersuasive. The In re A.C. court declined to express an opinion with regard to the circumstances, if any, in which lesser invasions (such as a blood transfusion) might be permitted over the woman's refusal. *In re A.C.*, 573 A.2d at 1246 n. 10.

Two courts have held otherwise, ordering forced cesarean sections against pregnant women. The Supreme Court of Georgia, in *Jefferson v. Griffin Spalding County Hospital Authority* (Ga. 1981), 274 S.E.2d 457, balanced the rights of the viable fetus against the rights of the mother, and determined that an expectant mother in the last weeks of pregnancy lacks the right of other persons to refuse surgery or other medical treatment if the life of the unborn child is at stake. The Superior Court of the District of Columbia followed the same logic and came to the same conclusion in *In re Madyun* (D.C. Super. Ct. July 26, 1986), 114 Daily Wash. L. Rptr. 2233, Appendix to *In re A.C.*, 573 A.2d at 1259.

Those decisions, however, are contrary to the rationale of both *Stallman*, the controlling law in this jurisdiction, and *In re A.C.*, which hold that the rights of the fetus should not be balanced against the rights of the mother. Additionally, neither the *Jefferson* nor the *Madyun* court recognized the constitutional dimension of the woman's right to refuse treatment, or the magnitude of that right. The Supreme Judicial Court of Massachusetts, in *Taft v. Taft* (Mass. 1983), 446 N.E.2d 395, when faced with a similar circumstance, vacated a lower court's order compelling a surgical procedure upon a pregnant woman because the lower court failed to recognize the woman's constitutional right to privacy, and the record did not present circumstances so compelling as to override the right to religious freedom for pregnant Jehovah's Witnesses.

The Public Guardian's reliance on *Raleigh Fitkin–Paul Morgan Memorial Hospital v. Anderson* (N.J. 1964), 201 A.2d 537, *cert. denied* (1964), 377 U.S. 985, is also misplaced. In that case, the Supreme Court of New Jersey held that the unborn child of a woman who did not wish to have blood transfusions because they were against her religious convictions as a Jehovah's Witness was entitled to the law's protection, and an order was entered to ensure a transfusion in the event that the physician in charge determined that one was necessary to save the woman's life or the life of the child. This and other similar blood transfusion cases are inapposite, because they involve a relatively non-invasive and risk-free procedure, as opposed to the massively invasive, risky, and painful cesarean section. Whether such non-invasive procedures are permissible in Illinois, we leave for another case.

Federal constitutional principles prohibiting the balancing of fetal rights against maternal health further bolster a woman's right to refuse a cesarean section. In *Thornburgh v. American College of Obstetricians and Gynecologists* (1986), 476 U.S. 747, the United States Supreme Court struck down a Pennsylvania statute which required that in cases of post-viability abortions, permitted under state law only when necessary to save the woman's life or health, a physician must use the abortion technique providing the best opportunity for the fetus to be aborted alive. The Supreme Court, finding the statute unconstitutional for requiring a "trade-off" between the woman's health and fetal survival, stressed that the woman's health is always the paramount consideration; any degree of increased risk to the woman's health is unacceptable. *Thornburgh*, 476 U.S. at 769.

A cesarean section, by its nature, presents some additional risks to the woman's health. When the procedure is recommended solely for the benefit of the fetus, the additional risk is particularly evident. It is impossible to say that compelling a cesarean section upon a pregnant woman does not subject her to additional risks—even the circuit court's findings of fact in this case indicate increased risk to Doe. Under *Thornburgh*, then, it appears that a forced cesarean section, undertaken for the benefit of the fetus, cannot pass constitutional muster.

Courts in Illinois and elsewhere have consistently refused to force one person to undergo medical procedures for the purpose of benefiting another person—even where the two persons share a blood relationship, and even where the risk to the first person is perceived to be minimal and the benefit to the second person may be great. The Illinois Supreme Court addressed this issue in *Curran v. Bosze* (Ill. 1990), 566 N.E.2d 1319, where it refused to compel twin minors to donate bone marrow to a half-sibling, despite the fact that the procedures involved would pose little risk to the twins, and the sibling's life depended on the transplant. Nor would the court compel the minors to undergo even a blood test for the purpose of determining whether they would be compatible donors. If a sibling cannot be forced to donate bone marrow to save a sibling's life, if an incompetent brother cannot be forced to donate a kidney to save the life of his dying sister (*In re Pescinski* (Wis. 1975), 226 N.W.2d 180), then surely a mother cannot be forced to undergo a cesarean section to benefit her viable fetus.

The Public Guardian argues that *Roe v. Wade* (1973), 410 U.S. 113, 163, seems to imply that a viable fetus does have some rights. *Roe*, however, merely stated that, in the context of abortion, the state's interest in the potential life of the fetus becomes compelling at the point of viability, and therefore the state is permitted to prohibit post-viability abortions, except where necessary to preserve the life or health of the woman. The fact that the state may prohibit post-viability pregnancy terminations does not translate into the proposition that the state may intrude upon the woman's right to remain free from unwanted physical invasion of her person when she chooses to carry her pregnancy to term. *Roe* and its progeny, in particular *Planned Parenthood of Southeastern Pennsylvania v. Casey* (1992), 505 U.S. 833, make it clear that, even in the context of abortion, the state's compelling interest in the potential life of the fetus is insufficient to override the woman's interest in preserving her health.

Courts generally consider four state interests—the preservation of life, the prevention of suicide, the protection of third parties, and the ethical integrity of the medical profession—in considering whether to override competent treatment decisions. None of those state interests justifies overriding Doe's decision here.

The first two interests—the preservation of life and the prevention of suicide—are simply irrelevant here. Although it might be argued that the State has an interest in the preservation of the potential life of the fetus, courts have traditionally examined the refusal of treatment as it impacts upon the preservation of the life of the maker of the decision. The proposed cesarean section was never suggested as necessary, or even useful, to the preservation of Doe's life or health. To the contrary, it would pose greater risk to her. Further, even in cases where the rejected treatment is clearly necessary to sustain life, these factors alone are not sufficiently compelling to outweigh an individual's right to refuse treatment.

Similarly, the third interest—the protection of third parties—is also irrelevant here. The "third parties" referred to in this context are the family members, particularly the children, of the person refusing treatment. Where an individual's decision to refuse treatment will result in orphaning an already-born child, courts have indicated that this is one factor they might consider. At least one court has hinted that, although it would not permit the overriding of a Jehovah's Witness's competent decision to refuse a possibly required blood transfusion subsequent to an accepted cesarean section because the fetus would not be at risk, it might override such a competent decision if it was medically determined that the fetus would be at risk before birth because of the refusal. (*Mercy Hospital, Inc. v. Jackson* (Md. Ct. Spec. App. 1985), 489 A.2d 1130, vacated (Md. 1986), 510 A.2d 562.) . . .

The final factor—the ethical integrity of the medical profession—weighs in Doe's favor, rather than that of the State or the Public Guardian. In the ethical opinions and recommendations it has issued, the medical profession strongly supports upholding the pregnant woman's autonomy in medical decision-making. See, e.g., Legal Interventions During Pregnancy: Court Ordered Medical Treatments and Legal Penalties for Potentially Harmful Behavior by Pregnant Women, 264 J.A.M.A. 2663, 2670 (1990) (cited by Doe, who included a copy in her brief). The American Medical Association's Board of Trustees cautions that the physician's duty is not to dictate the pregnant woman's decision, but to ensure that she is provided with the appropriate information to make an informed decision. If the woman rejects the doctor's recommendation, the appropriate response is not to attempt to force the recommended procedure upon her, but to urge her to seek consultation and counseling from a variety of sources. In this case, then, the actions taken by the medical professionals appear to be inconsistent with the ethical position taken by the profession.

Of not insignificant concern in this case is how a forced cesarean section would be carried out. The Public Guardian specifically opposed any effort to use force or other means to compel Doe to have the surgery; the State also opposed the use of force. Thus, we have been asked to issue an order that no one expects to be carried out. This court, as a simple matter of policy, will not enter an order that is not intended to be enforced.

If such an order were to be carried out, what would be the circumstances? The *In re A.C.* court considered such a question, and concluded that "Enforcement could be accomplished only through physical force or its equivalent. A.C. would have to be fastened with restraints to the operating table, or perhaps rendered unconscious by forcibly injecting her with an anesthetic, and then subjected to unwanted major surgery. Such actions would surely give one pause in a civilized society, especially when A.C. had done no wrong." *In re A.C.*, 573 A.2d at 1244, n. 8. An even more graphic description of what actually happened when a forced cesarean section was carried out may be found in Gallagher, Prenatal Invasions & Interventions: What's Wrong With Fetal Rights, 10 Harvard Women's L.J. 9, 9–10 (1987). We simply cannot envision issuing an order that, if enforced at all, could be enforced only in this fashion.

For all the reasons given above, we affirm the decision of the circuit court.

Affirmed.

NOTES AND QUESTIONS

1.   Do you agree with the Illinois court that a pregnant woman has "no duty to guarantee the mental and physical health of her child at birth"? Since a woman can choose to abort her pregnancy, once she decides to continue, has she committed herself to having a healthy child? At least one author has argued that if a woman chooses not to abort, she has a moral duty to ensure the health of her fetus. John A. Robertson, *Procreative Liberty and the Control of Conception, Pregnancy, and Childbirth*, 69 VA. L. REV. 405 (1983); JOHN A. ROBERTSON, CHILDREN OF CHOICE 179 (1994). Compare Robertson's view with that of Bonnie Steinbock, *Maternal-Fetal Conflict and In Utero Fetal Therapy*, 57 ALB. L. REV. 781 (1994) (arguing that woman has moral but not legal duty to avoid harming future child).

Recall the court's description of the intimacy between mother and fetus from the *Stallman* case, cited supra. Given this close connection, should the woman owe a heightened duty to her fetus based on a "special relationship"? Does the woman owe a greater responsibility to her fetus than a third party? Can you envision situations in which the father has an obligation to the fetus?

Before the D.C. Court of Appeals reversed the trial court's opinion in *In re A.C.*, 573 A.2d 1235 (D.C. App. 1990) (en banc) cited in *Doe*, the cesarean section was performed on Angela Carder. The baby died two hours after delivery; Carder died two days later. Because of the significance of the issue, the Court of Appeals heard the appeal en banc and held that, in the future, decisions regarding the intent of incompetent persons in A.C.'s situation should be made using substituted judgment. *Id.* at 1250–51. For a critique of the case and a response from the attorney appointed by the court to represent the fetus, compare George J. Annas, *She's Going to Die: The Case of Angela C.*, 18 HASTINGS CTR. REP. 23 (1988) with Barbara Mishkin, Letter to the Editor, *But She's Not an "Inanimate Container"* ..., 18 HASTINGS CTR. REP. 40 (1988).

Following A.C.'s death, *supra*, her parents sued the hospital, its administrators and physicians for negligence in placing her fetus's medical needs above A.C.'s and failing to obtain informed consent, false imprisonment, and wrongful death. The civil case settled on the eve of trial resulting in a hospital policy:

> Recognizing the right of a pregnant patient to determine the course of medical treatment on behalf of herself and her fetus and to refuse medical recommendations and emphasizing that it will rarely be appropriate to seek judicial intervention to resolve ethical issues relating to a patient's decision or to assess or override a pregnant patient's decision.

Settlement Agreement between Nettie and Daniel Stoner and George Washington University Hospital, Nov. 21, 1990.

Is it significant that the original decision to perform the cesarean section on A.C. was made by hospital administrators? What role should hospital personnel, including doctors and administrators, play in the decisionmaking process?

2.   In a subsequent decision, an Illinois court answered the question left open in the *Doe* case. *In re Brown*, 294 Ill.App.3d 159, 228 Ill.Dec. 525, 689 N.E.2d 397 (1997) held that a pregnant woman could not be compelled to undergo a blood transfusion for the benefit of her viable fetus. With the development of in utero therapies, should a court order a woman to undergo an invasive procedure including in utero surgery to benefit her fetus? Is the situation different from cesarean sections? Should it matter whether the fetus is viable? *See* Krista Newkirk, Note, *State-Compelled Fetal Surgery: The Viability Test is Not Viable*, 4 WM. & MARY J. WOMEN & L. 467 (1998) (state should not be able to force mother to have invasive medical treatment, whether or not fetus is viable); Rebekah R. Arch, *The Maternal–Fetal Rights Dilemma: Honoring a Woman's Choice of Medical Care During Pregnancy*, 12 J. CONTEMP. HEALTH L. & POL'Y 637 (1996) (it would be unconstitutional to force women to undergo fetal surgery); Alicia Ouellette, *New Medical Technology: A Chance to Reexamine Court–Ordered Medical Procedures During Pregnancy*, 57 Alb. L. Rev. 927 (1994) (women should never be compelled to undergo fetal surgery). Should the father be able to force prenatal surgery on the mother? *See* David C. Blickenstaff, *Defining the Boundaries of Personal Privacy: Is There a Paternal Interest in Compelling Therapeutic Fetal Surgery?*, 88 NW. U. L. REV. 1157 (1994) (although father has interest in fetus's welfare, woman's decision should prevail).

Novel interventions involving maternal-fetal surgery (MFS) raise important ethical, social and legal issues. For example, under what circumstances should these procedures be viewed as innovative therapy? As research subject to human subjects protections? Should such interventions be used only for lethal conditions? Should research on rare conditions be a funding priority or should alternative approaches to preventing the development of conditions be pursued.? For an interesting discussion of these and other issues, see Anne Drapkin Lyerly et al., *Toward the Ethical Evaluation and Use of Maternal–Fetal Surgery*, 98 OBSTETRICS & GYNECOLOGY 689, 689–97 (2001).

3.   As of 2003, thirty-four states had clauses in their advanced directive statutes that prevent pregnant women from being able to execute their wishes as provided for in a living will. Of these thirty-four states, seventeen of them disregarded the living wills of pregnant women throughout their entire pregnancy. *See* Thaddeas A. Hoffmeister, *The Growing Importance of Advanced Directives*, 177 MIL. L. REV. 110 (2003). Are these clauses justified? Do they violate the pregnant woman's rights? For a discussion of this issue, see Katherine A. Taylor, *Compelling Pregnancy at Death's Door*, 7 COLUM. L. REV. 85 (1997); April L. Cherry, *Roe's Legacy: The Nonconsensual Medical Treatment of Pregnant Women and Implications for Female Citizenship* 6 U. PA. J. CONT. L. 723 (2004); Chapter 4, Sec. II. D., *supra*.

State v. McKnight

The Supreme Court of South Carolina, 2003.
352 S.C. 635, 576 S.E.2d 168.

■ WALLER, J.

Appellant, Regina McKnight was convicted of homicide by child abuse; she was sentenced to twenty years, suspended upon service of twelve years. we affirm.

FACTS

On May 15, 1999, McKnight gave birth to a stillborn five-pound baby girl. The baby's gestational age was estimated to be between 34–37 weeks old. An autopsy revealed the presence of benzoylecgonine, a substance which is metabolized by cocaine. The pathologist, Dr. Proctor, testified that the only way for the infant to have the substance present was through cocaine, and that the cocaine had to have come from the mother. Dr. Proctor testified that the baby died one to three days prior to delivery. Dr. Proctor determined the cause of death to be intrauterine fetal demise with mild chorioamnionitis, funisitis and cocaine consumption. He ruled the death a homicide. McKnight was indicted for homicide by child abuse. A first trial held Jan. 8–12, 2002 resulted in a mistrial. At the second trial held May 14–16, 2001, the jury returned a guilty verdict. McKnight was sentenced to twenty years, suspended to service of twelve years.

. . .

1. DIRECTED VERDICT

McKnight asserts the trial court erred in refusing to direct a verdict for her on the grounds that a) there was insufficient evidence of the cause of death, b) there was no evidence of criminal intent, and c) there was no evidence the baby was viable when McKnight ingested the cocaine. We disagree.

. . .

b. Criminal Intent

McKnight next asserts she was entitled to a directed verdict as the state failed to prove she had the requisite criminal intent to commit homicide by child abuse. We disagree.

Under S.C.Code Ann. § 16–3–85(A), a person is guilty of homicide by child abuse if the person causes the death of a child under the age of eleven while committing child abuse or neglect, and the death occurs under circumstances manifesting an extreme indifference to human life. McKnight claims there is no evidence she acted with extreme indifference to human life as there was no evidence of how likely cocaine is to cause stillbirth, or that she knew the risk that her use of cocaine could result in the stillbirth of her child.

Recently, in *State v. Jarrell*, 564 S.E.2d 362, 366 (S.C. Ct. App.2002), the Court of Appeals defined extreme indifference, as used in the homicide by child abuse statute, stating:

> In this state, indifference in the context of criminal statutes has been compared to the conscious act of disregarding a risk which a person's conduct has created, or a failure to exercise ordinary or due care. At least one other jurisdiction with a similar statute has found that "[a] person acts 'under circumstances manifesting extreme indifference to the value of human life' when he engages in deliberate conduct which culminates in the

death of some person." Davis v. State, 925 S.W.2d 768, 773 (Ark. 1996). Therefore, we ... hold that in the context of homicide by abuse statutes, extreme indifference is a mental state akin to intent characterized by a deliberate act culminating in death.

Similarly, in reckless homicide cases, we have held that reckless disregard for the safety of others signifies an indifference to the consequences of one's acts. It denotes a conscious failure to exercise due care or ordinary care or a conscious indifference to the rights and safety of others or a reckless disregard thereof.

In *Whitner v. State*, 492 S.E.2d 777, 782 (S.C. 1997), *cert. denied* 523 U.S. 1145 (1998), this Court noted that although the precise effects of maternal crack use during pregnancy are somewhat unclear, it is well documented and within the realm of public knowledge that such use can cause serious harm to the viable unborn child. Given this common knowledge, Whitner was on notice that her conduct in utilizing cocaine during pregnancy constituted child endangerment....

Here, it is undisputed that McKnight took cocaine on numerous occasions while she was pregnant, that the urine sample taken immediately after she gave birth had very high concentrations of cocaine, and that the baby had benzoylecgonine in its system. The DSS investigator who interviewed McKnight shortly after the birth testified that McKnight admitted she knew she was pregnant and that she had been using cocaine when she could get it, primarily on weekends. Given the fact that it is public knowledge that usage of cocaine is potentially fatal, we find the fact that McKnight took cocaine knowing she was pregnant was sufficient evidence to submit to the jury on whether she acted with extreme indifference to her child's life. Accordingly, the trial court correctly refused a directed verdict.

. . .

2.   DIMISSAL OF HOMICIDE INDICTMENT

McKnight next asserts the trial court erred in refusing to dismiss the homicide by child abuse indictment on the grounds that a) the more specific criminal abortion statute governs, b) the homicide by child abuse statute does not apply to the facts of this case, and c) the legislature did not intend the statute to apply to fetuses. We disagree.

. . .

b.   Application of Homicide by Abuse Statute in This Case

McKnight next asserts the Legislature did not intend the homicide by child abuse statute apply to the stillbirth of a fetus. We disagree.

McKnight asserts the term child, as used in the statute, is most naturally read as including only children already born. In several cases this Court has specifically held that the Legislature's use of the term child includes a viable fetus. State v. Ard, 505 S.E.2d 328 (S.C. 1998); Whitner v. State, 492 S.E.2d 777 (S.C. 1997); State v. Horne, 319 S.E.2d 703 (S.C. 1984).... [G]iven the language of the statute, and this Court's prior opinions defining a child to include a viable fetus, we find the plain language of the statute does not preclude its application to the present case.

c.   Legislative History

McKnight lastly asserts that the legislative history of section 16–3–85 conclusively demonstrates that it does not apply to unborn children. We find this contention unpersuasive.

Section 16–3–85 was amended by 2000 Acts No. 261, § 1....

There is a presumption that the legislature has knowledge of previous legislation as well as of judicial decisions construing that legislation when later statutes are enacted concerning related subjects. The homicide by child abuse statute was amended in May 2000, some three years after this Court, in *Whitner*, had specifically held that the term child includes a viable fetus.[5] The fact that the legislature was well aware of this Court's opinion in *Whitner*, yet failed

to omit viable fetus from the statute's applicability, is persuasive evidence that the legislature did not intend to exempt fetuses from the statute's operation....

. . .

7.   SUPRESSION OF URINE SAMPLE

Finally, McKnight asserts the trial court erred in refusing to suppress the results of a urine sample taken at the hospital after the stillbirth, contending the sample was taken in violation of her fourth amendment rights. We disagree.

5. We granted McKnight's motion to argue against the precedent of *Whitner v. State, supra*. We adhere to our opinion in *Whitner*. As did *Whitner*, McKnight forebodes a parade of horribles and points to commentators who object to the prosecution of pregnant women as being contrary to public policy and deterring women from seeking appropriate medical care and/or creating incentives for women to seek abortions to avoid prosecution. *See e.g.* Tolliver, *Child Abuse Statute Expanded to Protect the Viable Fetus: The Abusive Effects of South Carolina's Interpretation of the Word Child*, 24 S.Ill.U.L.J. 383 (Winter 2000); DeLouth, *Pregnant Drug Addicts As Child Abusers: A South Carolina Ruling*, 14 Berkeley Women's L.J. 96 (1999).

However, not all of the commentaries concerning *Whitner* have been critical. *See* Miller, *Fetal Neglect and State Intervention: Preventing Another Attleboro Cult Baby Death*, 8 Cardozo Women's L.J. 71 (2001)(suggesting that the state's interest in protecting the life of the fetus takes precedence over any rights the mother may have and that the fetus has the right to be protected by the State as soon as the fetus is viable

or when a woman can no longer obtain a legal abortion); Janssen, *Fetal Rights and the Prosecution of Women For Using Drugs During Pregnancy*, 48 Drake L.Rev. 741 (2000); Schueller, *The Use of Cocaine by Pregnant Women: Child Abuse or Choice?* 25 J. Legisl. 163 (1999). As noted by Janssen, although the threat of abortion or lack of prenatal care is real, the burden placed on pregnant substance abusers is not the burden to get an abortion. Rather the burden is on the woman to stop using illegal drugs once she has exercised her constitutional decision not to have an abortion.... Once the mother has made the choice to have a child, she must accept the consequences of that choice. One of the consequences of having children is that it creates certain duties and obligations to that child. If a woman does not fulfill those obligations, then the state must step in to prevent harm to the child. As one judge aptly pointed out, there is simply "no reason to treat a child in utero any differently from a child ex utero where the mother has decided not to destroy the fetus or where the time allowed for such destruction is past." 48 Drake L.Rev. at 762–763 (Internal citation omitted).

Pursuant to a Conway Hospital Protocol for the Management of Drug Abuse during Pregnancy, a medical urine drug screening **may** be ordered at the discretion of the attending physician if an obstetrical patient meets one of several criteria, including lack of prenatal care or unexplained fetal demise. If such a drug screening test turns up positive from the hospital's lab, then hospital personnel are to request consent from the patient for forensic (medical-legal) testing. If consent is obtained, the sample is sent to the hospital's reference lab and the nursery is notified. The Department of Social Services is to be notified of positive medical urine drug screening and the criteria causing the drug screen to be done, and whether forensic testing is being done on the mother or newborn. The protocol states that As mandated by law, it is the obligation of every medical facility, as well as each individual, to report to DSS any suspected abuse or neglect involving an unborn, yet viable, fetus or newborn child. The hospital also has a Chain of Custody form and procedure for handling forensic samples.

Here, an initial drug screen was ordered by the obstetrician, Dr. Niles, due to McKnight's lack of prenatal care. When the initial screen tested positive for cocaine, Mary McBride, a labor and delivery nurse, was instructed to obtain a forensic urine sample from McKnight. Before doing so, McBride read an Informed Consent to Drug Testing form to McKnight. McBride testified she read the form to McKnight, and advised her that it could be used for legal purposes; she did not, however, specifically advise McKnight that police would possibly arrest her. The form states that McKnight acknowledges she has testified positive for cocaine, and is being requested to give consent for a medical-legal (forensic) test which will confirm or deny the initial report. The form further states that "It has been explained to me that I may refuse consent for this test. It has been explained to me that this test may be used for legal purposes." McKnight signed the form indicating her consent. The second sample also tested positive for cocaine.

McKnight asserts the forensic/legal sample was taken in violation of her fourth amendment rights, contrary to the United States Supreme Court's opinion in *Ferguson v. City of Charleston*, 532 U.S. 67 (2001). We disagree. The issue in *Ferguson*, as framed by the Court, was as follows:

> In this case, we must decide whether a state hospital's performance of a diagnostic test to obtain evidence of a patient's criminal conduct for law enforcement purposes is an unreasonable search if the patient has not consented to the procedure. More narrowly, the question is whether the interest in using the threat of criminal sanctions to deter pregnant women from using cocaine can justify a departure from the general rule that an official nonconsensual search is unconstitutional if not authorized by a valid warrant.

532 U.S. at 69–70.

In *Ferguson*, staff members of MUSC developed a written policy, in conjunction with the solicitor and police, for obtaining evidence to prosecute women who bore children who tested positive for drugs at birth. These procedures provided a plan to identify and test pregnant patients suspected of drug use **without their knowledge or consent**. The plan (1) required that a chain of custody be followed when obtaining and testing patients' urine samples, (2) contained police procedures and criteria for arresting patients who tested positive, and (3) encouraged prosecution for drug offenses and child neglect, and specifically set forth the offenses with which the women could be charged, as well as procedures for police to follow upon arresting the women. *Id.* at 70–73.

The Supreme Court held MUSC's performance of diagnostic tests to obtain evidence of the women's criminal conduct for law enforcement purposes was an unreasonable search if the patient had not consented to the procedure. *Id.* at 84–85. The Court held that [g]iven the primary purpose of the Charleston program, which was to use the threat of arrest and prosecution in order to force women into treatment, and given the extensive involvement of law enforcement officials at every stage, the policy did not fit with the closely guarded special needs category which would justify a warrantless, non-consensual search. *Id.*

Ferguson is distinguishable in several respects. First, there is no evidence that Conway Hospital's policy was in any way developed or implemented in conjunction with police, the solicitor, the Attorney General, or any other law enforcement personnel. Second, unlike the policy at issue in *Ferguson,* Conway Hospital's policy did not require hospital staff to turn drug screening results over to law enforcement personnel. On the contrary, the hospital's protocol merely requires that its department of social work services be notified and that a telephone referral be made to DSS when an assessment reveals suspicion of illegal drug use or reason to believe the unborn or newborn child is at risk. A DSS caseworker is not a law enforcement officer.

Third, unlike *Ferguson*, Conway Hospital's testing was not done surreptitiously, but was done with McKnight's knowledge and consent. The labor and delivery nurse specifically testified that she obtained a written consent form from McKnight to perform the second urine specimen; the consent form indicated to McKnight that she had the right to refuse the test, and that it could be used for legal purposes.

. . .

McKnight's conviction and sentence are affirmed.

■ Moore, J., dissenting.

I respectfully dissent. Once again, I must part company with the majority for condoning the prosecution of a pregnant woman under a statute that could not have been intended for such a purpose. Our abortion statute, S.C. Code Ann. § 44–41–80(b) (2002), carries a maximum punishment of two years or a $1,000 fine for the intentional killing of a viable fetus by its mother. In penalizing this conduct, the legislature recognized the unique situation of a feticide by the mother. I do not believe the legislature intended to allow the prosecution of a pregnant woman for homicide by child abuse under S.C. Code Ann. § 16–3–85(A)(1) (Supp.2001) which provides a disproportionately greater punishment of twenty years to life.

As expressed in my dissent in *Whitner v. State*, 492 S.E.2d 777 (S.C. 1997), it is for the legislature to determine whether to penalize a pregnant woman's abuse of her own body because of the potential harm to her fetus. It is not the business of this Court to expand the application of a criminal statute to conduct not clearly within its ambit. To the contrary, we are constrained to strictly construe penal statutes in the defendant's favor.

NOTES AND QUESTIONS

1. Does *McKnight* raise different issues than *Baby Doe*? What is the goal that the state seeks to achieve by prosecuting McKnight? Punishment? Deterrence? Are we trying to protect fetuses in general or to protect individual fetuses? If the state's goal is to protect fetuses, is it more likely to be achieved through the development of programs to assist and support pregnant women? *See* Patricia A. King, *Helping Women Helping Children: Drug Policy and Future Generations, in* CONFRONTING DRUG POLICY: ILLICIT DRUGS IN A FREE SOCIETY 291 (Ronald Bayer & Gerald M. Oppenheimer eds., 1993).

2. Not all women are similarly situated with respect to pregnancy and motherhood. Poverty, abusive relationships, and chemical dependencies all combine to increase the likelihood of maternal behavior that poses risks to fetuses. Moreover, support services are often differentially denied to pregnant women when they need them most. A study of virtually all New York City drug treatment programs in 1990 revealed that only 4% to 6% accepted pregnant women on Medicaid, and only 13% accepted pregnant women on Medcaid who were addicted to crack cocaine. Wendy Chavkin, *Drug Addiction and Pregnancy: Policy Crossroads*, 80 AM. J. PUB. HEALTH 4 (1990); *see Elaine W. v. Joint Diseases N. Gen. Hosp., Inc.*, 81 N.Y.2d 211, 597 N.Y.S.2d 617, 613 N.E.2d 523 (1993) (private hospital must justify blanket exclusion of pregnant women from drug treatment program by demonstrating either that no pregnant woman can be safely treated or that it is impossible to reasonably identify those women who cannot be treated safely). Does the threat of legal prosecution, combined with restricted access to drug treatment programs encourage, or even coerce women to choose abortion to avoid criminal prosecution?

Does legal prosecution disproportionally affect poor and/or minority women? In 1989, the Medical University of South Carolina (MUSC) in conjunction with the Charleston Police Department instituted the Interagency Policy of Management of Substance Abuse During Pregnancy, a policy in which pregnant women were tested for cocaine use without their consent and were arrested and criminally prosecuted if they tested positive. When women sought treatment from an obstetrician at MUSC, they were required to sign a consent form authorizing a urine test. If a patient tested positive for drug use, she was shown a film about the dangers of using cocaine while pregnant and asked to sign a form acknowledging that she had received that information. The hospital also made these women meet with substance abuse counselors, and they were told that if they did not receive substance abuse treatment and prenatal care they would be arrested. If a patient tested positive a second time she was immediately taken into custody or if a patient delivered a baby who tested positive for drugs she was taken into custody immediately and the infant was placed in protective custody. One woman arrested under the policy was handcuffed to the bed during labor while another woman was taken to a holding cell immediately after she gave birth despite the fact that she was still wearing a hospital gown and bleeding heavily. This policy, in place until 1994, only applied to MUSC, a public hospital that primarily served African–American and poor people, and was not instituted at private hospitals in the city. All except one of the women prosecuted under the policy were African–American. *See* Kimani Paul–Emile, *The Charleston Policy: Substance or Abuse?*, 4 MICH. J. RACE & L. 325 (1999).

The Center for Reproductive Law and Policy filed a class action lawsuit on behalf of the patients to enjoin the hospital from continuing the program. Richard

Green, Jr., *Women Challenge Drug–Use Prosecutions*, CHARLESTON POST & COURIER, Oct. 6, 1993. In 2001, the U.S. Supreme Court heard the appeal, *Ferguson v. City of Charleston*, 532 U.S. 67, 121 S.Ct. 1281, 149 L.Ed.2d 205 (2001), in order to determine whether the MUSC policy fit into the "special needs" exception of the Fourth Amendment to the U.S. Constitution. It was held that the urine tests did constitute a search under the Fourth Amendment and that reporting the results of those urine tests to the police constituted an unreasonable search. *See Ferguson*, 532 U.S. at 76–86.

3. It has been estimated that 30–45% of HIV-positive women give birth to HIV-positive babies. Jaspan HB & Garry RF, *Preventing neonatal HIV: A Review*, 1 CURRENT HIV RES. 321 (2003). AZT (zidovudine), an AIDS drug, was commonly used to prevent mother-to-child HIV transmission, because treating pregnant HIV-positive women with AZT reduces transmission risk by over 60%. *Id.* at 323. Later studies indicate that treating HIV-positive pregnant women with NVP (nevirapine), another AIDS drug, reduces transmission risk by 48% more than does AZT. *Id.* at 324. NVP's lower cost in comparison to AZT makes the use of this therapy more feasible for poorer populations. JB Jackson, et al., *Intrapartum and Neonatal Single–Dose Nevirapine Compared with Zidovudine for Prevention of Mother-to-Child Transmission of HIV–1 in Kampala, Uganda: 18–Month Follow–Up of the HIVNET 012 Randomised Trial*, 362 LANCET 859, 866 (2003). In light of this, should all pregnant women be strongly encouraged to be tested for HIV? Centers for Disease Control (CDC) policy recommends that all pregnant women be tested for HIV and that practitioners emphasize HIV testing as a routine part of prenatal care. *See* Centers for Disease Control, *Revised Recommendations for HIV Screening of Pregnant Women*, (2001), *at* http://www.cdc.gov/mmwr/pdf/rr/rr5019.pdf, last visited July 28, 2004. The CDC also recommends making the consent process more flexible and the testing process simpler to facilitate wider testing. *See id.* Should all pregnant women be tested for HIV? Should they have the opportunity to opt out? Should the pregnant woman's informed consent be required? Should a pregnant woman who tests positive for HIV be required to take medication to assist her fetus?

2. THE IMPACT OF GENETIC TECHNOLOGY: AIDING REPRODUCTION, PROVIDING THERAPY, OR PERFECTING PERSONS?

Recent and rapid advances in genetic screening and testing techniques and increased awareness and availability of genetic counseling provide better opportunities for individuals to make informed reproductive decisions. These genetic technologies also raise significant legal, ethical, and social issues for patients, their families, health care providers, and society in general.

Genetic screening, the testing of an asymptomatic population to identify people who may possess a specific genotype, may be undertaken for several purposes. These purposes include, for example, screening to detect worker susceptibility to disease from exposure to substances in the work place, and to assist in the achievement of research-related objectives or screening a population to determine the frequency and distribution of a specified gene. Genetic testing refers to the use of genetic tests in circumstances where individuals are believed to be at risk of having the disease in question based on symptoms expressed or known family history of the disease. This section will focus on the use of genetic screening and testing to provide relevant information for reproductive choices.

In studying the material, consider what role, if any, the government should play in genetic screening programs. If governmental participation in some form is warranted, should such participation be at the federal level, state level, or both? Should involvement of persons be mandatory as opposed to voluntary? Should the nature of the individual's involvement depend on the purpose of the specific genetic screening program? Alternatively consider to what extent parental prerogatives should be recognized and enforced. What information concerning genetic risks is a prospective parent(s) entitled to receive? From whom?

a.   Genetic Screening of Carriers

Linus Pauling, *Reflections on the New Biology*
15 UCLA L. REV. 267, 268–72 (1968).

Molecular medicine may, in one sense, be said to have originated in 1949, when it was shown that patients with the disease sickle-cell anemia have in the red cells of their blood a form of hemoglobin differing in its molecular structure from that present in the red cells of other human beings. It was evident that the molecules of sickle-cell-anemia hemoglobin are manufactured under the guidance of a mutated gene, and that the difference in molecular structure of these molecules from those of normal hemoglobin, a very small difference, is responsible for the manifestations of the disease. Sickle-cell anemia is the first disease to have been called a molecular disease.

The nature of legal problems that arise as a consequence of the development of molecular biology and molecular medicine may be illustrated by reference to sickle-cell anemia. Patients with this disease are homozygotes, persons who possess two sickle-cell genes, one of which has been inherited from the father and one from the mother. They lead a life of suffering and die an early death, almost always without progeny. The parents are heterozygotes, each having one sickle-cell gene and one normal hemoglobin â-chain gene.... The manifestations of the sickle-cell gene in heterozygotes are minor. But there is some evidence that possession of the gene provides protection against malaria, and the gene was valuable for this reason. At the present time in the United States, there are about two million sickle-cell-anemia heterozygotes, and it is estimated that there are about one hundred thousand married couples with both the husband and the wife sickle-cell heterozygotes. In such a marriage, the probability of each child born that the child would be a sickle-cell-anemia homozygote, doomed to a life of suffering and an early death, is twenty-five percent....

　　　　　·　·　·

If all pairs of sickle-cell-anemia heterozygotes were to refrain from having children, there would be no infants born with this disease. This suffering would then be eliminated.

Should not all young people be tested for heterozygosity in this gene, be given the information as to whether or not they possess the gene, and advised about the consequences of marriage of two possessors of the gene?

The test for heterozygosity is an extremely simple one.... I have suggested that there should be tatooed on the forehead of every young person a symbol showing possession of the sickle-cell gene or whatever other similar gene, such as the gene for phenylketonuria, that he has been found to possess in single dose. If this were done, two young people carrying the same seriously defective gene in single dose would recognize this situation at first sight, and would refrain from falling in love with one another. It is my opinion that legislation along this line, compulsory testing for defective genes before marriage, and some form of public or semi-public display of this possession, should be adopted.

. . .

In forming the opinion presented above I have made application of what I consider to be a basic ethical principle, the principle of minimization of human suffering. I believe that we can take actions to decrease the amount of suffering in the world, and that it is our duty to take these actions. I believe that the principle of the minimization of human suffering is a fundamental principle, essentially contained in the teachings of all great religious leaders, but also the consequence of rational consideration of ethical problems. I believe that almost all ethical problems, and legal problems not satisfactorily covered by existing law, can be solved, although often not without effort and difficulty, by the application of this principle.

. . .

... [T]he question of the possibility of legislation about marriages of heterozygotes and about limitation of the number of children arises. I feel that the identification of heterozygotes can be and should be made compulsory, but limiting the number of progeny should be carried out through a process of education and the provision of information. This process of provision of information should, of course, be made compulsory by law.

. . .

NOTES AND QUESTIONS

1. Do you agree with Pauling that carrier screening should be mandatory? Consider the conclusion of the President's Commission, Screening and Counseling for Genetic Conditions 6 (1983):

> Mandatory genetic screening programs are only justified when voluntary testing proves inadequate to prevent serous harm to the defenseless, such as children, that could be avoided were screening performed. The goals of "a healthy gene pool" or a reduction in health costs cannot justify compulsory genetic screening.

Suppose the condition screened for can be successfully treated. Would mandatory screening be warranted? Would it be constitutional? Does your answer depend on whether treatment is invariably successful? Successful less than 50% of the time?

2. Carrier screening began in the United States in the 1970s with the initiation of programs to screen for carriers of sickle cell anemia and Tay–Sachs disease. In contrast to Pauling's views, most programs were voluntary, although a few states passed laws requiring screening of persons with sickle cell anemia and the sickle cell trait. In 1972, Congress enacted the National Sickle Cell Anemia Control Act, which provided funding for research and educational activities of voluntary programs; as a result, many states changed their mandatory laws.

a.   Tay–Sachs disease is caused by improper production of the enzyme hexo-saminidase A, which results in severe neurological problems and death, usually by age four. The autosomal recessive disease occurs rarely in all populations but at relatively high frequency among Jews of eastern European descent. Researchers have developed a fairly simple blood test, thus allowing for mass screening of people in the high risk population. Researchers attribute the success of such programs to the test's ease and accuracy, the careful community-based planning behind the screening program, the affected population's education about the program and their socio-economic status, and the confidential treatment of test results. In addition, prenatal screening was available so that an "at-risk" couple could detect the occurrence of the disease in a fetus and abort the pregnancy, if they so chose.

In 1983, after losing four children to Tay–Sachs disease, a Jewish rabbi created the Chevra Dor Yeshorim genetic screening program in which young Jewish people were tested to determine whether they were carriers of the disease. The results of the tests were catalogued and filed at the screening center under a number that corresponded to each person. Before a Jewish matchmaker officially proposes a match he can call the screening center to determine whether the two people are both Tay–Sachs carriers. If both people are carriers, the family is informed and asked to attend counseling. Within four years of the creation of the program, more than 4,000 people had been tested. *See* Beverly Merz, Matchmaking Scheme Solves Tay–Sachs Problem, 258 JAMA 2636 (1987). In addition, the National Tay–Sachs and Allied Disease Association, Inc. offers carrier screening and prevention services not only for Tay–Sachs but many allied diseases such as Canavan and Gaucher disease. *See* National Tay–Sachs and Allied Diseases Association, *National Tay–Sachs & Allied Diseases Assocation, Inc. Web Site, at* http://www.ntsad.org (2004) (last visited July 30, 2004).

b.   By comparison, carrier screening programs for sickle cell anemia generally have been less successful. Researchers suggest that poor planning, inadequate counseling and education of the affected population about screening, lack of confidential treatment of test results, and dispersion of the Black community all have led to the screening programs' failure. Perhaps most important, no adequate prenatal test was available early in the screening programs' history, so "at-risk" couples either had to "take their chances" of conceiving children with sickle cell anemia or forego normal reproduction and turn instead to sterilization, adoption, or artificial insemination. Moreover, knowledge about sickle cell disease has increased since Professor Pauling wrote the preceding article; the condition has been found to be less severe in many cases than was earlier believed, and better treatment methods have been developed. *See* PRESIDENT'S COMMISSION, SCREENING AND COUNSELING FOR GENETIC CONDITIONS 18–23 (1983); NATIONAL ACADEMY OF SCIENCES, GENETIC SCREENING: PROGRAMS, PRINCIPLES, AND RESEARCH (1975). *See generally*, THOMAS MURRAY, THE ETHICS AND THE LAW (1991); John C. Fletcher & Dorothy C. Wertz, *Ethics, Law, and Medical Genetics: After the Human Genome is Mapped*, 39 EMORY L. J. 747, 790 (1990); March Lappé et al., *Ethical and Social Issues in Screening for Genetic Disease*, 286 NEW ENG. J. MED. 1129 (1972).

In light of the problems with prenatal testing for sickle cell anemia, states began requiring that all newborns be tested for sickle cell anemia. As of 2004 forty-eight states required that all newborns be tested and two states (New Hampshire and South Dakota) require that newborns in specific populations be tested for sickle cell anemia. *See* March of Dimes, *Selected Report Card for March of Dimes Recommended Newborn Screening Conditions* (2004), *at* http://www.marchof-dimes.com/files/NBS_rc_062404.pdf, last visited July 30, 2004.

3.   Genetic diseases occur infrequently in the general population. For instance, among Caucasians one in thirty is a carrier of a cystic fibrosis genetic mutation. Brian Vastag, *Cystic Fibrosis Gene Testing a Challenge: Experts Say Widespread*

Use is Creating Unnecessary Risks, 289 JAMA 2923 (2003). Consequently, there has been a debate about whether to offer genetic screening for diseases such as cystic fibrosis to the general population or whether to restrict it to "high-risk" groups. Advocates of restricting testing argue that testing everybody will yield a high number of false positives and will be too expensive.

In 2001 the American College of Medical Genetics recommended that cystic fibrosis screening should be offered to non-Jewish Caucasians and Askenazi Jews and that the testing should be made available to other ethnic and racial groups provided that they were informed about the prevalence of the disease. *See* American College of Medical Genetics, *Laboratory Standards and Guidelines for Population-based Cystic Fibrosis Carrier Screening*, 3 Genetics in Med. 149 (2001). How should decisions be made about whether to institute such screening programs? Should a cost benefit analysis be used? The President's Commission concluded that "equity is best served" by such an approach. Genetic Screening & Counseling 84 (1983). It recommended the following:

> Access to screening may take account of the incidence of genetic disease in various racial or ethnic groups within the population without violating principles of equity, justice and fairness.

Id. at 8. Do you agree? Is it likely that such a policy would have the effect of stigmatizing persons in "high-risk" groups? Is the burden of having a child with a genetic disease any less for a person who is not a member, or does not know that he or she is a member, of a "high-risk" group? If it is acceptable to take into account the incidence of genetic disease within racial and ethnic groups, should it also be permissible to take into account incidence of disease in different age categories? If data show increasing incidence of a disease with increasing age, can any cutoff point be justified? For many years only women age thirty-five or older have been counseled about amniocentesis in order to detect the presence of chromosomal defects (unless there were other risk factors present). With respect to that practice, the President's Commission recommended:

> First, as limitations on access move from the research context to implicit (or explicit) policies on the availability of a genetic service they should be subjected to review by a broadly based process that will be responsive to the full range of relevant considerations, to changes in the facts over time, and to the needs of the excluded group(s). Second, in light of the facts concerning this particular policy the Commission believes the common medical practice of only informing women age thirty-five or older about amniocentesis should be reevaluated to determine whether fairness and equity would support a more flexible policy that made amniocentesis more generally available to younger women.

Id. at 81. Do you agree? Is it likely that a more flexible policy would overburden available resources? Alternatively, do pregnant women have a moral duty to seek fetal diagnostic services? A legal duty? Should a legal duty to undergo amniocentesis be imposed on all women over thirty-five because of the risk of Down Syndrome? On all Jewish couples to undergo testing for Tay–Sachs disease?

b. Screening Embryos and Fetuses

Laurie Goldberg Strongin, *The Promise of Preimplantation Genetic Diagnosis*

Genetics & Pub. Pol'y Ctr. (2004), *available at* http://www.dnapolicy.org/pdfs/Strongin_PGD_7.03.pdf (last visited July 15, 2004).

On October 25, 1995, I gave birth for the first time, to a boy my husband and I named Henry. Henry was a sweet and precious baby, born with a rare, fatal disease called Fanconi anemia that threatened to take his life before he learned to read, climb a tree or fall in love.

Fanconi anemia (FA) is often accompanied by numerous serious birth defects and always causes bone marrow failure, necessitating a bone marrow transplant. In addition, children with FA are predisposed to cancer. In short, FA is a child killer.

When Henry was born, bone marrow transplants from matched sibling donors had a success rate around 65 percent. In contrast, the success rate for a bone marrow transplant from someone other than a sibling was reported around 18 percent, and it was our understanding that no one with the type of FA that Henry had, had ever survived an unrelated transplant.

Allen and I had planned to have several children, but Fanconi anemia made it about a whole lot more than mere conception. It was about genes and statistical probability, prenatal testing and decisions. It was about hopes, dreams and nightmares. It wasn't just about creating life, but about avoiding certain death. The very best prenatal care might be a good weapon against spina bifida, but is useless against Fanconi anemia.

In retrospect, we had a few options to consider: Hope that lightning doesn't strike twice, cross our fingers and pray for the 75% chance that our second child would be healthy and the 18.75% chance of being both healthy and a bone marrow match for Henry; decide to stop having children; do artificial insemination using donor sperm thereby changing the inherited gene pool; or adopt a child whose genetic makeup didn't foretell premature death. We only considered the first option. The other three didn't even occur to us.

On the day we found out I was pregnant with our second child, Allen and I got a phone call that forever changed our lives. We were informed that there was a fifth option, an experimental procedure that was newly available for FA families–embryo selection using preimplantation genetic diagnosis (PGD). This procedure combines in vitro fertilization (IVF) with genetic testing conducted prior to embryo transfer. Best of all it would allow us to know at the outset of our pregnancy that our baby was healthy and, by using the umbilical cord blood collected at birth, could also be a bone marrow match for Henry. PGD had been used in the past to screen for fatal, childhood diseases like Fanconi anemia, sickle cell anemia and cystic fibrosis, among others, but it had never been used to start a life and save a life at once.

We considered the ethical implications of this procedure, paying close attention to our role and responsibility to protect and advocate for Henry as well as our future children. Allen and I had decided that we couldn't knowingly have another baby with this disease and were therefore very comfortable using PGD to diagnose and transfer only those embryos free of Fanconi anemia. For us, that was the moral thing to do. Not because of what we could or could not endure, but because of what we knew the child must endure throughout his life. I also knew that I couldn't, or at least didn't want to, have an abortion. A significant benefit of PGD for couples facing having a baby with a fatal disease is that the procedure circumvents the psychological pain caused by being in a position of even considering having an abortion. Because there was no evidence anywhere that IVF/ PGD or the collection of umbilical cord blood, posed any risk to the baby, the benefits of the procedure far outweighed the risks as we understood them.

But what about adding matching HLA (human leukocyte antigen), a trait that was critically important to the success of a transplant and thus Henry's survival, but not to the survival of the potential child? Applying PGD in this way was brand new and had not yet gained the status of ethical acceptability. We had heard talk about eugenics and sex selection and designer babies. Did HLA matching fall within the category of disease-related traits or was it non-health related and therefore a genetic enhancement?

We felt strongly that, in our case, testing for HLA fell into the category of testing for disease-related traits as the only reason that HLA is significant to our family is because it is directly connected to Fanconi anemia. We wanted the child to be disease free and Henry needed a sibling with a compatible HLA type because of the disease.

The procedure offered value to every current and future member of our family. We could have a child who would not have Fanconi anemia; secure an HLA-matched sibling donor for Henry thereby significantly increasing the odds of his survival; and prevent our family from the devastating loss of Henry. We believed that Henry's sibling would gain satisfaction from the knowledge that he had saved Henry's life, a status that is revered in our culture.

We attempted PGD nine times between January 1998 and June 2000, suffering numerous public policy-related delays that caused us to run out of time and nearly destroyed the science. Each attempt held the promise of life; each disappointment, the fear of death and then the determination to try again. During the same time period Henry's health rapidly deteriorated. He was hospitalized twice and received four blood transfusions. Henry's transplant progressed from being a distant fear to an emergency.

I had taken 353 injections, produced 198 eggs and had no successful pregnancy. We had spent nearly $135,000, most of which was not covered by insurance, and far too many days apart from one another, our home and our life. Our hopes were raised to the highest heights and crashed to the depths of despair over and over again. There was no medical explanation for our lack of success. Often our best embryos had FA while the poorest quality were FA-free/HLA matches that failed to produce a pregnancy. We would have undergone PGD nine more times if we had the time, but by June 2000, we understood that given Henry's failing health, his chance for survival would be even further jeopardized if we continued to try any longer.

Two weeks after my final PGD attempt, Allen, four-year-old Henry, three-year-old Jack and I left our home in Washington, D.C. and went to the University of Minnesota in Minneapolis where Henry had a transplant with the marrow of the best donor available, a 5/6 antigen mismatched unrelated donor. Henry spent the next two-and-a-half years fighting courageously against a relentless series of life-threatening complications.

On December 11, 2002, Henry died in my arms. His death certificate states the cause of death as aspergillus and pneumonia, but it should have read, "failure of preimplantation genetic diagnosis."

As it turns out, the lives that Allen and I helped save through our experience did not include Henry's. Learning from our case, the doctors were able to improve the technology, and eventually science caught up with our dream. Just as research on others that came before us gave us hope for Henry, in a way we have paid our debt to them by giving others new hope and helping others survive this terrible disease. I am certain that if it had worked for us, I would be cheering Henry on as he scored yet another soccer goal; but instead I can only wonder what he might have been as I visit his grave.

NOTES AND QUESTIONS

Preimplantation Genetic Diagnosis (PGD). PGD is a new technique that combines advances in molecular genetics and assisted reproductive technology. As indicated in the Strongin essay, PGD permits genetic testing of an embryo prior to implantation and before pregnancy begins. It was originally developed to help prospective parents who were at risk of having children with serious and debilitating genetic diseases such as Fanconi Anemia (Henry Strongin's disease), Cystic Fibrosis, and Thalassemia. Couples at risk can insure that their child does not inherit the gene by selecting only unaffected embryos for implantation. PGD spares the couple from testing later in pregnancy with the prospect of clinical abortion. More recently, PGD has also been used to determine whether embryos are not only free of genetic disease, but also tissue matches for a sibling already affected by the disease. Thus, only embryos that are both genetically free of the gene screened for and possessing HLA matched tissue are implanted.

Is the term "preimplantation genetic diagnosis" misleading? Is genetic screening a better phrase? Whose interests should PGD serve the parents or the future child? In what ways, if any, does PGD for genetic disease differ from PGD to produce an HLA-matched donor? What are the arguments for and against use of this technology?

Should the technology be subject to governmental regulation or professional guidelines? Essentially PGD is unregulated in the United States. Although three United States regulatory agencies—the Food and Drug Administration, the National Institutes of Health, and the Centers for Disease Control—each regulate aspects of PGD technology, no one agency exists that can claim complete regulation of Reproductive Technology. The FDA regulates some of the products (drugs and biologics) used in the practice of PGD, but this oversight is limited to insuring the safety and efficacy of a product in its intended use. The CDC collects and publishes some data on the practice of assisted reproduction at clinics in the United States, and the NIH oversees novel protocols.

Is there widespread support for regulation of PGD? In 2002, the Genetics and Public Policy Center at Johns Hopkins University conducted a survey of Americans' views on assisted reproductive technology. Of those polled, 74% of the women and 73% of the men surveyed indicated that they approve of using PGD to avoid serious genetic disease. In addition, slightly fewer Americans (69% overall) approved of using PGD to ensure that a child is a good HLA match for an ill sibling. However, a majority of those surveyed (87% women and 73% men) indicated that they would *not* approve of using PGD to choose desirable benign traits for children, and 78% women and 67% men would *not* approve of using reproductive technology to choose the sex of a child. A second survey conducted by the Genetics and Public Policy Center in 2004 indicates that while slightly fewer Americans (61%) approve of using PGD to produce an HLA-matched donor for an existing child than did in 2002, and fewer Americans (57%) *disapprove* of using PGD to select sex of a child than did in 2002, a majority of 80% surveyed worried that reproductive genetic technologies would "get out of control" if not regulated.

Adrienne Asch, *Reproductive Technology and Disability*
in Reproductive Laws for the 1990's 72, 72–89 (Sherrill Cohen & Nadine Taub eds., 1989).

... [T]he social construction of disability ... demonstrates that it is the attitudes and institutions of the nondisabled, even more than the biological characteristics of the disabled, that turn these characteristics into handicaps....

Implicit in many of the reproductive technologies and explicit in some is the goal of preventing future disability. Sometimes this means men and women are presumed immoral if they choose to create children who themselves will also have the disability....

Although I support both efforts to prevent disability and the right of women to reproductive choice, I believe that genetic screening and prenatal diagnosis followed by abortion differ morally and psychologically from other methods of preventing impairments, and from all other abortions save those for sex selection. What differentiates ending pregnancy after learning of impairment from striving to avoid impairment before life has begun is this: At the point one ends such a pregnancy one is indicating that one cannot accept and welcome the opportunity to nurture a life that will have a potential set of characteristics—impairments perceived as deficits and problems. What differentiates abortion after prenatal diagnosis (and abortion for sex selection) from all other abortions is that the abortion is a response to characteristics of the fetus and would-be child and not to the situation of the woman....

Let us frame our thinking about prenatal diagnosis and selective abortion in a sincere discussion of what we long for in the experience of having children. Let us then ask how a child's disability will compromise that dream. Such discussion will help us to answer the question of whether it is disability inherently that pains or the consequences of disability that might be changed with genuine societal commitment to change them. If we believed that the world was a problem for the child and not the child a problem to the world, we might better be able to imagine how raising a child with a disability could give much the same gratifications as raising another child who did not start life with a disabling condition....

I believe we can and should draw lines concerning the ethical use of selective abortion following prenatal screening. I would urge us to question whether we wish to abort for most disability that will not cause great physical pain or death in early childhood....

NOTES AND QUESTIONS

1. Should individuals be permitted unrestricted access to genetic services? A July 21, 2004 article in the New York Times addressed this issue: "a growing number of patients say the lack of basic information about DNA tests is altering lives in . . . prenatal screening. . . . Even if they decide not to use the new technology because of expense or personal values . . . they should have the choice." Amy Harmon, *As Gene Test Menu Grows, Who Gets to Choose?*, NY Times, July 21, 2004, at A1. Although one can argue that doctors have a duty to offer prenatal genetic services when the patient has a high risk of passing on a serious genetic disease, should doctors have the same duty if the patient expresses an interest in choosing other, benign characteristics for her child? Should a patient be able to select the sex of the future child?

If it were scientifically feasible, should parents be able to screen for other traits, such as sexual orientation? What about race? Consider the views of Adrienne Asch:

> If public health frowns on efforts to select for or against girls or boys and would oppose future efforts to select for or against those who would have a particular sexual orientation, but promotes people's efforts to avoid having children who would have disabilities, it is because medicine and public health view disability as extremely different from and worse than these other forms of human variation. . . .
>
> . . . [M]ost of the problems associated with having a disability stem from discriminatory social arrangements that are changeable. . . .
>
> . . .
>
> [A] just society must appreciate and nurture the lives of all people, whatever the endowments they receive in the natural lottery. . . . [P]eople with disabilities do not merely take from others, they contribute as well. . . . They contribute neither in spite of nor because of their disabilities, but because along with their disabilities come other characteristics of personality, talent, and humanity. . . .

Adrienne Asch, Prenatal Diagnosis and Selective Abortion: A Challenge to Practice and Policy, 89 Am. J. Public Health 1649 (1999).

The President's Council on Bioethics acknowledges that there is no governmental regulation of the technologies, and that regulation is mainly accomplished via professional groups or institutional ethics boards. President's Council on Bioethics, Reproduction and Responsibility 89 (2004). What sort of regulation is necessary?

2. Are parents and doctors seeking perfect babies, or merely disease and disability-free babies? Is there a difference? Where should we draw the line between a disability and a social inconvenience? For example, the availability of genetically engineered human growth hormone has proved useful in treating low growth hormone conditions in children where their adult height would be between four and five feet. What about children who are merely shorter than average? Can below average height be seen as a disability? *See Growth Hormone's Downside*, Wash. Post, May 10, 1995 at A1; Carol A. Tauer, *Human Growth Hormone: A Case Study in Treatment Priorities*, 25 Hastings Ctr. Rep. S18–S20 (Special Supp. 1993).

Do parents practice eugenics when they seek to have the "perfect child"? Consider the following statement:

> The core notion of eugenics, that people's lives will probably go better if they have genes conducive to health and other advantageous traits, has lost little of its appeal. Eugenics, in this very limited sense, shines a beacon even as it casts a shadow. Granted, when our society last undertook to improve our genes, the result was mayhem. The task for humanity now is to accomplish what eluded the eugenicists entirely, to square the pursuit of genetic health and enhancement with the requirements of justice.

Allen Buchanan et al., From Chance to Choice: Genetics & Justice 56–57 (2000).

3. What ethical problems would be posed by gene therapy to alter germs cells—sperm and ova? This technique, while not currently feasible, has the potential to completely change to genetic makeup of future generations. *See* The President's Council on Bioethics, Beyond Therapy: Biotechnology and the Pursuit of Happiness 27 (2003); PG McDonough, *The Ethics of Somatic and Germline Gene Therapy*, 816 Annals of N. Y. Acad. Sciences 378 (1997); EF Cooke, *Germ-line Engineering, Freedom, and Future Generations*, 17 Bioethics 32 (2003).

4. Genetic screening for a specific condition sometimes detects additional information that could be traumatic for the person screened or related individuals. Should genetic counselors always provide such information? The President's Commission made the following recommendation:

> Decisions regarding the release of incidental findings ... or sensitive findings ... should begin with a presumption in favor of disclosure, while still protecting a client's other interests, as determined on an individual basis. In the case of nonpaternity, accurate information about the risk of the mother and putative father bearing an affected child should be provided even when full disclosure is not made.

President's Commission for the Study of Ethical Problems in Medicine and Biomedical and Behavioral Research, Screening and Counseling for Genetic Conditions 7 (1983).

5. The March of Dimes organization recommends that states perform newborn testing for nine metabolic conditions, including phenylketonuria (PKU), galactosemia, congenital hypothyroidism, sickle cell disease, maple syrup urine disease, homocystinuria, biotinidase, congenital adrenal hyperplasia, and medium acyl-CoA dehydrogenase deficiency (MCAD). *See* March of Dimes, *Newborn Screening Tests*, (2004), at http://www.marchofdimes.org/pnhec/298_834.asp (last visited July 28, 2004). Because newborn hearing loss occurs in one to three infants out of every 1000 live births, March of Dimes and CDC also recommend testing newborns for hearing deficiency. *See* id.; Centers for Disease Control, *Infants Tested for Hearing Loss, United States 1999–2001*, 52 Morbidity & Mortality Weekly Rep. 981 (2003).

Screening to detect PKU, a metabolic disorder that can cause brain damage after birth, is the best known example of screening for therapeutic objectives. Brain damage can be prevented if the disease is discovered shortly after birth and the infant is placed on a diet that restricts his or her intake of food containing phenylalanine. *See* Karen Hellerson, *NIH Consensus Statement on Phenylketonuria*, 63 Am. Family Physician 1432 (2001). The National Institute of Health consensus panel recommended that, along with newborn screening for PKU, states should take steps to ensure appropriate treatment for PKU beyond the initial screening. They further noted that a comprehensive, multidisciplinary, integrated system is required for the delivery of care to individuals with PKU, and that consistency and coordination among screening, treatment, data collection, and patient support programs is needed. *Id. at 1434*. Currently, all fifty states administer newborn testing for PKU, along with at least three other diseases, galactosemia, congential hypothyroidism, and sickle cell disorder (forty-eight states screen all newborns, while two screen only a selected population). *See* March of Dimes, *State Report Card on Testing for March of Dimes Recommended Newborn Screening Conditions*, (2004), *at* http://www.modimes.org/files/NBS_rc_062404.pdf (last visited July 27, 2004.)

6. Should genetic information be disclosed to relatives who could benefit from the information?

Greco v. United States

Supreme Court of Nevada, 1995.
111 Nev. 405, 893 P.2d 345.

■ SPRINGER, J.

. . .

On July 20, 1993, the United States District Court for the District of Maryland filed a certification order with this court ... requesting that this court answer certain questions relating to the negligently caused unwanted birth of a child suffering from birth defects.

The Grecos, mother and child, in this case seek to recover damages from the United States arising out of the negligence of physicians who, they claim, negligently failed to make a timely diagnosis of physical defects and anomalies afflicting the child when it was still in the mother's womb. Sundi Greco asserts that the physicians' negligence denied her the opportunity to terminate her pregnancy and thereby caused damages attendant to the avoidable birth of an unwanted and severely deformed child. On Joshua's behalf, Sundi Greco avers that the physicians' negligence and the resultant denial of Joshua's mother's right to terminate her pregnancy caused Joshua to be born into a grossly abnormal life of pain and deprivation.

These kinds of tort claims have been termed "wrongful birth" when brought by a parent and "wrongful life" when brought on behalf of the child for the harm suffered by being born deformed.

THE CHILD'S CAUSE OF ACTION: "WRONGFUL LIFE"

We decline to recognize any action by a child for defects claimed to have been caused to the child by negligent diagnosis or treatment of the child's mother. The Grecos' argument is conditional and narrowly put, so: if this court does not allow Sundi Greco to recover damages for Joshua's care past the age of majority, it should allow Joshua to recover those damages by recognizing claims for "wrongful life." Implicit in this argument is the assumption that the child would be better off had he never been born. These kinds of judgments are very difficult, if not impossible, to make. Indeed, most courts considering the question have denied this cause of action for precisely this reason. Recognizing this kind of claim on behalf of the child would require us to weigh the harms suffered by virtue of the child's having been born with severe handicaps against "the utter void of nonexistence"; this is a calculation the courts are incapable of performing. ... We conclude that Nevada does not recognize a claim by a child for harms the child claims to have suffered by virtue of having been born.

THE MOTHER'S CAUSE OF ACTION

With regard to Sundi Greco's claim against her physician for negligent diagnosis or treatment during pregnancy, we see no reason for compounding or complicating our medical malpractice jurisprudence by according this particular form of professional negligence action some special status apart from presently recognized medical malpractice or by giving it the new name of "wrongful birth."[5] Sundi Greco either does or does not state a claim for medical malpractice; and we conclude that she does.

Medical malpractice, like other forms of negligence, involves a breach of duty which causes injury. To be tortiously liable a physician must have departed from the accepted standard of medical care in a manner that results in injury to a patient. In the case before us, we must accept as fact that Sundi Greco's physicians negligently failed to perform prenatal medical tests or performed or interpreted those tests in a negligent fashion and that they thereby negligently failed to discover and reveal that Sundi Greco was carrying a severely deformed fetus. As a result of such negligence Sundi Greco claims that she was denied the opportunity to terminate her pregnancy and that this denial resulted in her giving birth to a severely deformed child.

It is difficult to formulate any sound reason for denying recovery to Sundi Greco in the case at hand. Sundi Greco is saying, in effect, to her doctors:

> []If you had done what you were supposed to do, I would have known early in my pregnancy that I was carrying a severely deformed baby. I would have then terminated the pregnancy and would not have had to go through the mental and physical agony of delivering this child, nor would I have had to bear the emotional suffering attendant to the birth and nurture of the child, nor the extraordinary expense necessary to care for a child suffering from such extreme deformity and disability.[]

The United States advances two reasons for denying Sundi Greco's claim: first, it argues that she has suffered no injury and that, therefore, the damage element of negligent tort liability is not fulfilled; second, the United States argues that even if Sundi Greco has sustained injury and damages, the damages were not caused by her physicians. To support its first argument, the United States points out that in *Szekeres v. Robinson*, 715 P.2d 1076 (Nev. 1986), this court held that the mother of a normal, healthy child could not recover in tort from a physician who negligently performed her sterilization operation because the birth of a normal, healthy child is not a legally cognizable injury. The United States argues that no distinction can be made between a mother who gives birth to a healthy child and a mother who gives birth to a child with severe deformities and that, therefore, *Szekeres* bars recovery.

Szekeres can be distinguished from the instant case. Unlike the birth of a normal child, the birth of a severely deformed baby of the kind described here is necessarily an unpleasant and aversive event and the cause of inordinate financial burden that would not attend the birth of a normal child. The child in this case will unavoidably and necessarily require the expenditure of extraordinary medical, therapeutic and custodial care expenses by the family, not to mention the additional reserves of physical,

---

5. One commentator observes that the term "wrongful life," "was a play on the statutory tort of 'wrongful death' ". Alexander M. Capron, *Tort Liability in Genetic Counseling*, 79 Col.L.Rev. 618, 634 n. 62 (1979). The related concepts of wrongful birth and wrongful pregnancy or conception were similarly inspired. *Id.* The commentator concludes that the net effect of these terms has been to "spawn confusion" and distort or impair judicial vision. *Id.*

mental and emotional strength that will be required of all concerned. Those who do not wish to undertake the many burdens associated with the birth and continued care of such a child have the legal right, under *Roe v. Wade* and codified by the voters of this state, to terminate their pregnancies. Roe v. Wade, 410 U.S. 113 (1973); NRS 442.250 (codifying by referendum the conditions under which abortion is permitted in this state). Sundi Greco has certainly suffered money damages as a result of her physician's malpractice.

We also reject the United State's second argument that Sundi Greco's physicians did not cause any of the injuries that Sundi Greco might have suffered. We note that the mother is not claiming that her child's defects were *caused* by her physicians' negligence; rather, she claims that her physicians' negligence kept her ignorant of those defects and that it was this negligence which caused her to lose her right to choose whether to carry the child to term. The damage Sundi Greco has sustained is indeed causally related to her physicians' malpractice.

Sundi Greco's claim here can be compared to one in which a physician negligently fails to diagnose cancer in a patient. Even though the physician did not *cause* the cancer, the physician can be held liable for damages resulting from the patient's decreased opportunity to fight the cancer, and for the more extensive pain, suffering and medical treatment the patient must undergo by reason of the negligent diagnosis. *See* Perez v. Las Vegas Medical Center, 805 P.2d 589 (Nev. 1991) (adopting the "loss of chance" doctrine in medical malpractice cases). The "chance" lost here, was Sundi Greco's legally protected right to choose whether to abort a severely deformed fetus. If we were to deny Sundi Greco's claim, we would, in effect, be groundlessly excepting one type of medical malpractice from negligence liability. We see no reason to treat this case any differently from any other medical malpractice case. Sundi Greco has stated a prima facie claim of medical malpractice under Nevada law.

DAMAGE ISSUES

The certified question requires us to decide specifically what types of damages the mother may recover if she succeeds in proving her claim. Courts in these cases have struggled with what items of damages are recoverable because, unlike the typical malpractice claim, claims such as Sundi Greco's do not involve a physical injury to the patient's person. We consider each of Sundi Greco's claimed items of damage separately.

Extraordinary Medical and Custodial Expenses

This claim for damages relates to the medical, therapeutic and custodial costs associated with caring for a severely handicapped child. There is nothing exceptional in allowing this item of damage.... Extraordinary care expenses are a foreseeable result of the negligence alleged in this case, and Sundi Greco should be allowed to recover those expenses if she can prove them. This leads us to the question of how to compensate for these kinds of injuries.

Sundi Greco correctly observes that Nevada law requires the parents of a handicapped child to support that child beyond the age of majority if the child cannot support itself. NRS 125B.110. Nevada recognizes the right of a parent to recover from a tortfeasor any expenses the parent was required to pay because of the injury to his or her minor child. Accordingly, Sundi Greco claims the right to recover damages for these extraordinary costs for a period equal to Joshua's life expectancy. Other states which require parents to care for handicapped children past the age of majority allow plaintiffs to recover these types of damages for the lifetime of the child or until such time as the child is no longer dependent on her or his parents. We agree with these authorities and conclude that Sundi Greco may recover extraordinary medical and custodial expenses associated with caring for Joshua for whatever period of time it is established that Joshua will be dependent upon her to provide such care.

The United States contends that if this court allows the mother to recover such extraordinary medical and custodial expenses, then it should require the district court to offset any such award by the amount it would cost to raise a non-handicapped child. To do otherwise, argues the United States, would be to grant the mother a windfall.

The offset rule has its origins in two doctrines: the "avoidable consequences rule," which requires plaintiffs to mitigate their damages in tort cases, and the expectancy rule of damages employed in contract cases, which seeks to place the plaintiff in the position he or she would have been in had the contract been performed. We conclude that neither of these doctrines is applicable to the case at bar. To enforce the "avoidable consequences" rule in the instant case would impose unreasonable burdens upon the mother such as, perhaps, putting Joshua up for adoption or otherwise seeking to terminate her parental obligations.

With regard to the expectancy rule, it would unnecessarily complicate and limit recovery for patients in other malpractice cases if we were to begin intruding contract damage principles upon our malpractice jurisprudence. The rule for compensatory damages in negligence cases is clear and workable, and we decline to depart from it.

Loss of Services and Companionship

The United States contends that Sundi Greco should not be allowed to recover any damages for the services of her child lost due to the child's handicap, because Sundi Greco claims that but for the negligence of her physician she would never have carried her pregnancy to term. It follows then, that if the child had not been born, Sundi Greco would have had far less in terms of service and companionship than what she can currently expect from her handicapped child.... [H]ere, the crux of Sundi Greco's claim is that she would have aborted the fetus had she been given the opportunity to do so. In that case, she would have had no services or companionship at all. We thus conclude that Sundi Greco may not recover for lost services or companionship.

Damages for Emotional Distress

Sundi Greco asserts that she is suffering and will continue to suffer tremendous mental and emotional pain as a result of the birth of Joshua. Several jurisdictions allow plaintiffs such as Sundi Greco to recover such damages. In line with these cases, we agree that it is reasonably foreseeable that a mother who is denied her right to abort a severely deformed fetus will suffer emotional distress, not just when the child is delivered, but for the rest of the child's life. Consequently, we conclude that the mother in this case should have the opportunity to prove that she suffered and will continue to suffer emotional distress as a result of the birth of her child.

We reject the United States' argument that this court should follow an "offset" rule with regard to damages for emotional distress. Any emotional benefits are simply too speculative to be considered by a jury in awarding emotional distress damages. . . . Moreover, it would unduly complicate the jury's task to require it to weigh one intangible harm against another intangible benefit.

CONCLUSION

We conclude that a mother may maintain a medical malpractice action under Nevada law based on her physicians' failure properly to perform or interpret prenatal examinations when that failure results in the mother losing the opportunity to abort a severely deformed fetus. Sundi Greco should be given the right to prove that she has suffered and will continue to suffer damages in the form of emotional or mental distress and that she has incurred and will continue to incur extraordinary medical and custodial care expenses associated with raising Joshua. We decline to recognize the tort sometimes called "wrongful life."

■ SHEARING, J., with whom ROSE, J. joins, concurring in part and dissenting in part:

I agree with the majority that a mother should have a malpractice claim against professionals who negligently fail to make a timely diagnosis of fetal defects. However, I would also allow the impaired child a cause of action, with the measure of damages being the extraordinary expenses attributable to the child's impairment.

In this case, Joshua was born with congenital defects which result in his suffering paraplegia with no sensation from the hips down and permanent fine and gross motor retardation and mental retardation. It is clear that he will require extraordinary care throughout his life.

This case is not a traditional malpractice claim in which a medical professional directly causes a patient to suffer injuries. In order to find any causation from the medical professional's failure to test for abnormalities, one must accept the proposition that if Joshua's mother had been informed of the condition of the fetus, she would have had a therapeutic abortion and Joshua would never have been born.

Courts have had a great deal of difficulty in dealing with the moral implications of compensating parents or a child for that child's birth, when the plaintiffs' claim is essentially that they would all be better off had the child never been born. One reason the issue of compensation is so knotty is that it runs counter to our conception of the preciousness of human life.

. . .

The majority, along with other courts, rejects the impaired child's cause of action after wrestling with the question of whether damages exist when that determination requires the comparison of the value of an impaired life to the value of no life at all. . . .

However, not all courts have taken the view that these difficulties are so great as to overcome the public policy objectives of tort law—to compensate injured parties and to deter future wrongful conduct. In *Turpin v. Sortini*, 643 P.2d 954 (Cal. 1982), the California Supreme Court quoted with approval a lower court opinion which stated:

> []The reality of the "wrongful life" concept is that such a plaintiff *exists* and *suffers,* due to the negligence of others. It is neither necessary nor just to retreat into meditation on the mysteries of life. We need not be concerned with the fact that had defendants not been negligent, the plaintiff might not have come into existence at all. The certainty of genetic impairment is no longer a mystery. In addition, a reverent appreciation of life compels recognition that plaintiff, however impaired she may be, has come into existence as a living person with certain rights.[]
>
> . . .
>
> Although it is easy to understand and to endorse these decisions' desire to affirm the worth and sanctity of less-than-perfect life, we question whether these considerations alone provide a sound basis for rejecting the child's tort action. To begin with, it is hard to see how an award of damages to a severely handicapped or suffering child would "disavow" the value of life or in any way suggest that the child is not entitled to the full measure of legal and nonlegal rights and privileges accorded to all members of society.

Id. 643 P.2d at 958, 961–62 (*quoting* Curlender v. Bio–Science Laboratories, 165 Cal. Rptr. 477, 488 (Cal. Ct. App. 1980)).

The California Supreme Court went on to hold that both the child and the parents had a cause of action. However, the court rejected the parents' claim for general damages and allowed only the claim for medical expenses and extraordinary expenses for specialized teaching, training and equipment required because of the impairment.

The New Jersey Supreme Court has taken a similar approach . . . in *Procanik by Procanik v. Cillo*, 478 A.2d 755 (N.J. 1984). . . .

The approach of the California and New Jersey courts is sound. These courts refuse to become mired in philosophical discussions of the meaning and value of life, and focus on compensating injured parties and deterring future wrongful conduct.

Our knowledge in the fields of genetics and obstetrics has grown dramatically, with far-reaching consequences for human life. It is clear that responsive treatments and the counseling necessitated by those treatments will develop in accordance with our ever-increasing capability to test and diagnose. It would, therefore, be anomalous for medical practitioners in these fields to be immune from liability for wrongful conduct or for departing from accepted professional standards. Unquestionably the public policy behind tort law supports compensating impaired children and their parents for the special damages resulting from impairment when the negligence of the medical professional results in the birth of the impaired child.

Although this court has stated that the public policy in Nevada is that birth of a normal healthy child is not a legally compensable damage, this court has also recognized that the value of an impaired life is not always greater than the value of non-life. *See* McKay v. Bergstedt, 801 P.2d 617 (Nev. 1990). In addition, the legislature has recognized this fact in setting forth the policy of this state concerning the deprivation of life-sustaining procedures. NRS 449.535–690 ("Withholding or Withdrawal of Life–Sustaining Treatment"). In these statutes, the legislature made clear that a person may choose not to sustain life. The underlying policy recognizes that, in some situations, non-life may be preferable to an impaired life; further, the policy recognizes that each individual has the right to make his or her determination as to the relative value of life and non-life.

Some courts have distinguished, as does the majority, between the wrongful birth action of the parents and the wrongful life action of the child. There is certainly logical justification for this approach under traditional tort concepts. The wrongful life action presents problems regarding duty, causation and damages. However, I agree with the New Jersey court which stated in *Procanik by Procanik*:

> Law is more than an exercise in logic, and logical analysis, although essential to a system of ordered justice, should not become a instrument of injustice. Whatever logic inheres in permitting parents to recover for the cost of extraordinary medical care incurred by a birth-defective child, but in denying the child's own right to recover those expenses, must yield to the injustice of that result. The right to recover the often crushing burden of extraordinary expenses visited by an act of medical malpractice should not depend on the "wholly fortuitous circumstance of whether the parents are available to sue."

478 A.2d 755, 762 (N.J. 1984) (*quoting* Turpin v. Sortini, 643 P.2d 954, 965 (Cal. 1982)). I would allow the child the cost of the extraordinary expenses attributable to the impairment. The claims of the child and the parents are mutually dependent; it would be unfair to deny compensation to the child if the parent or parents are not available to make their claim. While there can be no duplication of recovery, either action should lie.

NOTE AND QUESTION

Why is there such reluctance to recognize the cause of action for wrongful life?

INDEX

References are to Pages.

655

GENETICS AND HUMAN GENOME
—Cont'd

Human Genetic Research Databases (HGRDs), 94–96

Human tissue, market for, 57

In utero gene therapy, 37

Indigenous groups and genetics research, 9–10

Informational privacy, defined, 83

Informed consent for participation in research databases, 96

Intellectual property protections as incentive to future research, 60–61

International guidelines, 66–71

Legal implications, generally, 77–110

Linkable data systems, 96

Mapping
> Generally, 5–10
> HapMap project, 8–11
> Public access to information, 10, 61
> Timeline and accomplishments, 5–8

Mendel and how genetics began, 1–2

Methodological problem of using race in genetic studies, 107

Mining DNA, commercialization, 62–66

Moral principles and ethical theories, 45–56

Patenting problems, DNA, 57–62

Patient's duty, 89–90

Personal feedback, 96

Personal service model and eugenics, 100–101

Pharmacogenomics, this index

Physician's duty to patient and family members, 89, 167–168

Policy and regulation
> Generally, 56–76
> DNA patenting problems, 56–62
> International guidelines, 66–71
> Mining and harvesting, commercialization, 62–66
> Public interest and patenting, 61–62
> Regulatory initiatives in U.S., 71–76
> Secretary's Advisory Committee on Genetic Testing (SACGT), 72–76
> Testing and screening, need for regulation, 23–24

Preimplantation genetic diagnosis (PGD), 641–645

Prenatal diagnosis, 15

Privacy
> Generally, 82–84
> Gene therapy, 38
> Genetic testing and screening, 17–19
> Informational privacy, defined, 83–84
> Linkable data systems, 96
> Public interest exceptions, 90
> Research databases, 94–98

Privately operated biobanks, 96–97

Prophylactic treatment, payment for, 27

Proteomics, 10–13

Psychological impact of testing, 23

Public access to mapping information, 10, 61

Public health model of genetic intervention, 99–102

Public interest
> Patenting and, 61–62

GENETICS AND HUMAN GENOME
—Cont'd

Public interest—Cont'd
> Privacy and exceptionalism, public interest exceptions, 90

Race, genetic stratification based on, 102–107

Regulation. Policy and regulation, above

Reproduction and New Genetics, this index

Research databases, 94–98

Right to know genetic information, 84–94

Scientific discovery and advancement
> Generally, 1–13
> From genomics to proteomics, 10–13
> Mapping, above
> Mendel and how genetics began, 1–2
> Watson and Crick, 50 years after, 2–4

Secretary's Advisory Committee on Genetic Testing (SACGT), 72–75

Sequencing, 5–8

Sickle cell anemia, 640

Social implications, generally, 77–110

Society, genetics and, 77–110

Somatic cells, gene therapy, 37

Stratification, justice, and opportunity
> Generally, 98–110
> Eugenics, historical lessons, 99–102
> Genetic discrimination, 107–110
> Race and ethnicity, genetic stratification based on, 102–107

Structure for DNA, 2–4

Tay-Sachs disease, 639–640

Testing and screening
> Benefits for patients and populations, 19
> Carrier screening, 16, 638–641
> Confidentiality, 17–19
> Cystic fibrosis, 640–641
> Desired traits, selection of, 38–50, 646
> Effective interventions, lack of, 20
> Forensic testing, 16
> Future of, 19
> Impact of genetic technology, 637–654
> Insufficient predictive value, 20
> Newborn screening, 15–16, 647
> Preimplantation genetic diagnosis (PGD), 641–645
> Prenatal diagnosis, 15
> Prophylactic treatment, payment for, 27
> Psychological impact, 23
> Regulation, need for, 23–24
> Reproductive counseling following testing, social acceptability, 20
> Secretary's Advisory Committee on Genetic Testing (SACGT), 72–75
> Sickle cell anemia, 640
> Susceptibility screening, 16
> Tay-Sachs disease, 639–640

Therapy. Gene therapy, above

Tissue donors, 97–98

Trans-national biobanks, promise of, 94–98

Watson and Crick, structure for DNA, 2–4

GEORGIA

Informed consent law, 153–155

GERMLINE GENE THERAPY

Generally, 32–38

†